Managerial Accounting

Managerial Accounting

6th edition

John J. Wild

University of Wisconsin at Madison

Ken W. Shaw

University of Missouri at Columbia

Mc Graw Hill Education

To my students and family, especially **Kimberly, Jonathan, Stephanie,** and **Trevor.**
To my wife **Linda** and children **Erin, Emily,** and **Jacob.**

MANAGERIAL ACCOUNTING, SIXTH EDITION

Published by McGraw-Hill Education, 2 Penn Plaza, New York, NY 10121. Copyright © 2018 by McGraw-Hill Education. All rights reserved. Printed in the United States of America. Previous editions © 2016, 2013, and 2011. No part of this publication may be reproduced or distributed in any form or by any means, or stored in a database or retrieval system, without the prior written consent of McGraw-Hill Education, including, but not limited to, in any network or other electronic storage or transmission, or broadcast for distance learning.

Some ancillaries, including electronic and print components, may not be available to customers outside the United States.

This book is printed on acid-free paper.

1 2 3 4 5 6 7 8 9 LWI 21 20 19 18 17

ISBN 978-1-259-72697-2
MHID 1-259-72697-5

Chief Product Officer, SVP,
    Products & Markets: *G. Scott Virkler*
Vice President, General Manager,
    Products & Markets: *Marty Lange*
Vice President, Content Design &
    Delivery: *Betsy Whalen*
Managing Director: *Tim Vertovec*
Marketing Director: *Natalie King*
Brand Manager: *Steve Schuetz*
Director, Product Development: *Rose Koos*
Associate Director of Digital Content: *Kevin Moran*
Lead Product Developer: *Kris Tibbetts*
Product Developers: *Rebecca Mann, Michael McCormick*
Marketing Manager: *Michelle Williams*

Market Development Manager: *Julie Wolfe*
Digital Product Analyst: *Xin Lin*
Director, Content Design & Delivery: *Linda Avenarius*
Program Manager: *Daryl Horrocks*
Content Project Managers: *Lori Koetters,*
    Brian Nacik
Buyer: *Sandy Ludovissy*
Design: *Debra Kubiak*
Content Licensing Specialists: *Melissa Homer, Melisa*
    Seegmiller, Brianna Kirschbaum
Cover Image: *© Caiaimage/Trevor Adeline/*
    Getty Images
Compositor: *Aptara®, Inc.*
Printer: *LSC Communications*

All credits appearing on page or at the end of the book are considered to be an extension of the copyright page. Icon credits—Background for icons: © *Dizzle52/Getty Images;* Lightbulb: © *Chuhail/Getty Images;* Globe: © *nidwlw/Getty Images;* Chess piece: © *AndSim/Getty Images;* Computer mouse: © *Siede Preis/Getty Images;* Global View globe: © *McGraw-Hill Education.*

Library of Congress Control Number: 2016958449

The Internet addresses listed in the text were accurate at the time of publication. The inclusion of a website does not indicate an endorsement by the authors or McGraw-Hill Education, and McGraw-Hill Education does not guarantee the accuracy of the information presented at these sites.

Adapting to Today's Students

Whether the goal is to become an accountant, a business-person, or simply an informed consumer of accounting information, *Managerial Accounting* has helped generations of students succeed. Its leading-edge accounting content, paired with state-of-the-art technology, supports student learning and elevates understanding of key accounting principles.

This book excels at **engaging students** with content that shows the relevance of accounting. Its chapter-opening vignettes showcase dynamic entrepreneurial companies to highlight the **usefulness of accounting.** This edition's featured companies—**Apple, Google,** and **Samsung**—capture student interest, and their annual reports are a pathway for learning. Need-to-Know demonstrations in each chapter apply key concepts and procedures and include guided video teaching presentations.

This book delivers innovative technology to help student performance. **Connect** provides students a media-rich eBook version of the textbook and offers instant online grading and feedback for assignments. **Connect** takes accounting content to the next level, delivering assessment material in a **more intuitive, less restrictive** format.

Our technology features:

- **A general journal interface** that looks and feels more like that found in practice.
- **An auto-calculation** feature that allows students to focus on concepts rather than rote tasks.
- **A smart (auto-fill) drop-down design.**

The result is content that prepares students for today's world.

Connect also includes digitally based, interactive, adaptive learning tools that engage students more effectively by offering varied instructional methods and more personalized learning paths that build on different learning styles, interests, and abilities.

The revolutionary technology of **SmartBook®** is available only from McGraw-Hill Education. Based on an intelligent learning system, SmartBook uses a series of adaptive questions to pinpoint each student's knowledge gaps and then provides an optimal learning path. Students spend less time in areas they already know and more time in areas they don't. The result: Students study more efficiently, learn faster, and retain more knowledge. Valuable reports provide insights into how students are progressing through textbook content and information useful for shaping in-class time or assessment.

Interactive Presentations teach each chapter's core learning objectives in a rich, multimedia format, bringing the content to life. Your students come to class prepared when you assign Interactive Presentations. Students can also review the Interactive Presentations as they study. **Guided Examples** provide students with narrated, animated, step-by-step walk-throughs of algorithmic versions of assigned exercises. Students appreciate Guided Examples, which help them learn and complete assignments outside of class.

A **General Ledger (GL) application** offers students the ability to see how transactions post from the general journal all the way through the financial statements. It uses an intuitive, less restrictive format, and it adds critical thinking components to each GL question, to ensure understanding of the entire process.

The first and only analytics tool of its kind, **Connect Insight®** is a series of visual data displays—each framed by an intuitive question—to provide information on how your class is doing on five key dimensions.

> "A great enhancement! I love the fact that GL makes the student choose from an entire chart of accounts."
>
> —**TAMMY METZKE, Milwaukee Area Technical College**

About the Authors

Courtesy of John J. Wild

JOHN J. WILD is a distinguished professor of accounting at the University of Wisconsin at Madison. He previously held appointments at Michigan State University and the University of Manchester in England. He received his BBA, MS, and PhD from the University of Wisconsin.

John teaches accounting courses at both the undergraduate and graduate levels. He has received numerous teaching honors, including the Mabel W. Chipman Excellence-in-Teaching Award and the departmental Excellence-in-Teaching Award, and he is a two-time recipient of the Teaching Excellence Award from business graduates at the University of Wisconsin. He also received the Beta Alpha Psi and Roland F. Salmonson Excellence-in-Teaching Award from Michigan State University. John has received several research honors, is a past KPMG Peat Marwick National Fellow, and is a recipient of fellowships from the American Accounting Association and the Ernst and Young Foundation.

John is an active member of the American Accounting Association and its sections. He has served on several committees of these organizations, including the Outstanding Accounting Educator Award, Wildman Award, National Program Advisory, Publications, and Research Committees. John is author of *Fundamental Accounting Principles, Financial Accounting, Financial and Managerial Accounting,* and *College Accounting*, all published by McGraw-Hill Education.

John's research articles on accounting and analysis appear in *The Accounting Review; Journal of Accounting Research; Journal of Accounting and Economics; Contemporary Accounting Research; Journal of Accounting, Auditing and Finance; Journal of Accounting and Public Policy;* and other journals. He is past associate editor of *Contemporary Accounting Research* and has served on several editorial boards including *The Accounting Review*.

In his leisure time, John enjoys hiking, sports, boating, travel, people, and spending time with family and friends.

Courtesy of Ken W. Shaw

KEN W. SHAW is an associate professor of accounting and the KPMG/Joseph A. Silvoso Distinguished Professor of Accounting at the University of Missouri. He previously was on the faculty at the University of Maryland at College Park. He has also taught in international programs at the University of Bergamo (Italy) and the University of Alicante (Spain). He received an accounting degree from Bradley University and an MBA and PhD from the University of Wisconsin. He is a Certified Public Accountant with work experience in public accounting.

Ken teaches accounting at the undergraduate and graduate levels. He has received numerous School of Accountancy, College of Business, and university-level teaching awards. He was voted the "Most Influential Professor" by four School of Accountancy graduating classes and is a two-time recipient of the O'Brien Excellence in Teaching Award. He is the advisor to his school's chapter of the Association of Certified Fraud Examiners.

Ken is an active member of the American Accounting Association and its sections. He has served on many committees of these organizations and presented his research papers at national and regional meetings. Ken's research appears in the *Journal of Accounting Research; The Accounting Review; Contemporary Accounting Research; Journal of Financial and Quantitative Analysis; Journal of the American Taxation Association; Strategic Management Journal; Journal of Accounting, Auditing, and Finance; Journal of Financial Research;* and other journals. He has served on the editorial boards of *Issues in Accounting Education; Journal of Business Research;* and *Research in Accounting Regulation*. Ken is co-author of *Fundamental Accounting Principles, Financial and Managerial Accounting,* and *College Accounting,* all published by McGraw-Hill Education.

In his leisure time, Ken enjoys tennis, cycling, music, and coaching his children's sports teams.

Dear Colleagues and Friends,

As we roll out the new edition of *Managerial Accounting*, we thank each of you who provided suggestions to improve the textbook and its teaching resources. This new edition reflects the advice and wisdom of many dedicated reviewers, symposium and workshop participants, students, and instructors. Throughout the revision process, we steered this textbook and its teaching tools in the manner you directed. As you'll find, the new edition offers a rich set of features—especially digital features—to improve student learning and assist instructor teaching and grading. We believe you and your students will like what you find in this new edition.

Many talented educators and professionals have worked hard to create the materials for this product, and for their efforts, we're grateful. **We extend a special thank-you to our contributing and technology supplement authors,** who have worked so diligently to support this product:

Contributing Author: Kathleen O'Donnell, *Onondaga Community College*

Accuracy Checkers: Dave Krug, *Johnson County Community College;* Mark McCarthy, *East Carolina University;* and Beth Kobylarz

LearnSmart Author: April Mohr, *Jefferson Community and Technical College, SW*

Interactive Presentations: April Mohr, *Jefferson Community and Technical College, SW*

PowerPoint Presentations and **Instructor Resource Manual:** April Mohr, *Jefferson Community and Technical College, SW*

Digital Contributor, Connect Content, General Ledger Problems, Test Bank, and **Exercise PowerPoints:** Kathleen O'Donnell, *Onondaga Community College*

In addition to the invaluable help from the colleagues listed above, we thank the entire team at McGraw-Hill Education: Tim Vertovec, Steve Schuetz, Natalie King, Michelle Williams, Erin Chomat, Kris Tibbetts, Rebecca Mann, Michael McCormick, Lori Koetters, Peggy Hussey, Xin Lin, Kevin Moran, Debra Kubiak, Sarah Evertson, Brian Nacik, and Daryl Horrocks. We could not have published this new edition without your efforts.

John J. Wild   Ken W. Shaw

Innovative Textbook Features . . .

Using Accounting for Decisions

Whether we prepare, analyze, or apply accounting information, one skill remains essential: decision making. To help develop good decision-making habits and to illustrate the relevance of accounting, we use a learning framework to enhance decision making in four ways. (See the four nearby examples for the different types of decision boxes, including those that relate to fraud.) **Decision Insight** provides context for business decisions. **Decision Ethics** and **Decision Maker** are role-playing scenarios that show the relevance of accounting. **Decision Analysis** provides key tools to help assess company performance.

Decision Insight

Make or Buy IT   Companies apply make or buy decisions to their services. Many now outsource their information technology activities. Information technology companies provide infrastructure and services to enable businesses to focus on their key activities. It is argued that outsourcing saves money and streamlines operations, and without the headaches. ∎

Decision Ethics

Production Manager   Three friends go to a restaurant. David, a self-employed entrepreneur, says, "I'll pay and deduct it as a business expense." Denise, a salesperson, takes the check and says, "I'll put this on my company's credit card. It won't cost us anything." Derek, a factory manager, laughs and says, "Neither of you understands. I'll use my company's credit card and call it overhead on a cost-plus contract with a client." (*A cost-plus contract means the company receives its costs plus a percent of those costs.*) Adds Derek, "That way, my company pays for dinner *and* makes a profit." Who should pay the bill? Why? ∎   Answer: All three friends want to pay the bill with someone else's money. David is using money belonging to the tax authorities, Denise is taking money from her company, and Derek is defrauding the client. To prevent such practices, companies have internal controls. Some entertainment expenses are justifiable and even encouraged. For example, the tax law allows certain deductions for entertainment that has a business purpose. Corporate policies sometimes allow and encourage reimbursable spending for social activities, and contracts can include entertainment as an allowable cost. Nevertheless, without further details, this bill should be paid from personal accounts.

Decision Maker

Partner   You are a partner in a small accounting firm that specializes in keeping the books and preparing taxes for clients. A local restaurant is interested in obtaining these services from your firm. Identify factors that are relevant in deciding whether to accept the engagement. ∎   Answer: You should identify the differences between existing clients and this potential client. A key difference is that the restaurant business has additional inventory components (groceries, vegetables, meats) and is likely to have a higher proportion of depreciable assets. These differences imply that the partner must spend more hours auditing the records and understanding the business, regulations, and standards that pertain. Such differences suggest that the partner must use a different "formula" for quoting a price to this potential client vis-à-vis current clients.

Decision Analysis   **Product Pricing**

P1
Determine product selling price using cost data.

Managers use relevant costs in determining prices for special short-term decisions. But longer-run pricing decisions of management need to cover both variable and fixed costs, and yield a profit. There are several methods to help management in setting prices.

Cost-Plus Methods

Cost-plus methods are common, where management adds a **markup** to cost to reach a target price. We will describe the **total cost method**, where management sets price equal to the product's total costs plus a desired profit on the product. This is a three-step process:

1. Determine total cost per unit.

$$\text{Total costs} = \frac{\text{Product (direct materials,}}{\text{direct labor, and overhead) costs}} + \frac{\text{Selling and}}{\text{administrative costs}}$$

> "This textbook does address many learning styles and at the same time allows for many teaching styles . . . our faculty have been very pleased with the continued revisions and supplements. I'm a 'Wild' fan!"
>
> —**RITA HAYS, Southwestern Oklahoma State University**

Chapter Preview

Each chapter opens with a visual chapter preview. Students can begin their reading with a clear understanding of what they will learn and when. Learning objective numbers highlight the location of related content. Each "block" of content concludes with a Need-to-Know (NTK) to aid and reinforce student learning. Organization into "blocks" aids students in quickly searching for answers to homework assignments.

Chapter Preview

IDENTIFYING COST BEHAVIOR	MEASURING COST BEHAVIOR	CONTRIBUTION MARGIN AND BREAK-EVEN	APPLYING COST-VOLUME-PROFIT ANALYSIS
C1 Fixed costs	**P1** Scatter diagrams	**A1** Contribution margin	**C2** Margin of safety
Variable costs	High-low method	**P2** Break-even	Income from sales and costs
Graphing costs	Regression	**P3** Cost-volume-profit chart	Sales for target income
Mixed costs	Comparing cost estimation methods	Impact of estimates on break-even	Strategizing
Step-wise costs			**P4** Sales mix
Curvilinear costs			**A2** Operating leverage
NTK 5-1	**NTK 5-2**	**NTK 5-3**	**NTK 5-4, 5-5**

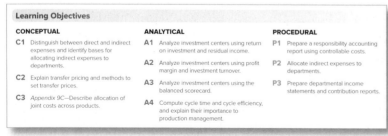

Learning Objectives

CONCEPTUAL

C1 Distinguish between direct and indirect expenses and identify bases for allocating indirect expenses to departments.

C2 Explain transfer pricing and methods to set transfer prices.

C3 *Appendix 9C*—Describe allocation of joint costs across products.

ANALYTICAL

A1 Analyze investment centers using return on investment and residual income.

A2 Analyze investment centers using profit margin and investment turnover.

A3 Analyze investment centers using the balanced scorecard.

A4 Compute cycle time and cycle efficiency, and explain their importance to production management.

PROCEDURAL

P1 Prepare a responsibility accounting report using controllable costs.

P2 Allocate indirect expenses to departments.

P3 Prepare departmental income statements and contribution reports.

CAP Model

The Conceptual/Analytical/Procedural (CAP) model allows courses to be specially designed to meet the teaching needs of a diverse faculty. This model identifies learning objectives, textual materials, assignments, and test items by C, A, or P, allowing different instructors to teach from the same materials, yet easily customize their courses toward a conceptual, analytical, or procedural approach (or a combination thereof) based on personal preferences.

Bring Accounting to Life

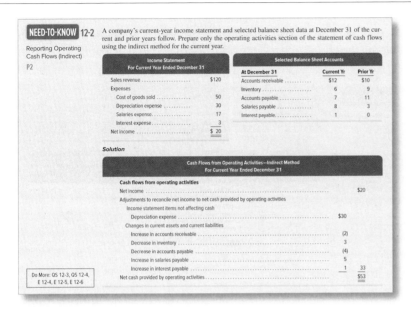

Need-to-Know Demonstrations

Need-to-Know demonstrations are located at key junctures in each chapter. These demonstrations pose questions about the material just presented—content that students "need to know" to successfully learn accounting. Accompanying solutions walk students through key procedures and analysis necessary to be successful with homework and test materials. Need-to-Know demonstrations are supplemented with narrated, animated, step-by-step walk-through videos led by an instructor and available via **Connect**.

Global View

The Global View section explains international accounting practices related to the material covered in that chapter. The aim of this section is to describe accounting practices and to identify the similarities and differences in international accounting practices versus those in the United States. The importance of student familiarity with international accounting continues to grow. This innovative section helps us begin down that path. This section is purposefully located at the very end of each chapter so that each instructor can decide what emphasis, if at all, is to be assigned to it.

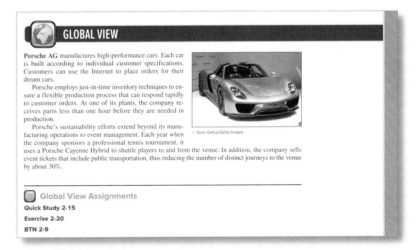

Sustainability and Accounting

This edition has brief sections that highlight the importance of sustainability within the broader context of global accounting (and accountability). Companies increasingly address sustainability in their public reporting and consider the sustainability accounting standards (from the Sustainability Accounting Standards Board) and the expectations of our global society. These sections cover different aspects of sustainability, often within the context of the chapter's featured entrepreneurial company.

Outstanding Assignment Material . . .

Once a student has finished reading the chapter, how well he or she retains the material can depend greatly on the questions, brief exercises, exercises, and problems that reinforce it. This book leads the way in comprehensive, accurate assignments.

Comprehensive Need-to-Know Problems present both a problem and a complete solution, allowing students to review the entire problem-solving process and achieve success. The problems draw on material from the entire chapter.

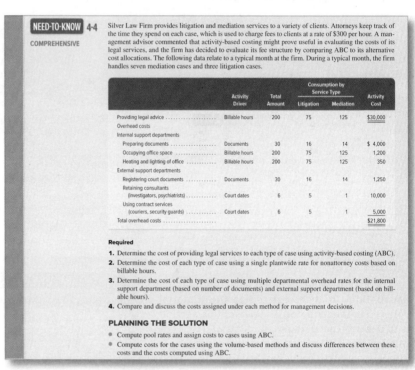

NEED-TO-KNOW 4-4

COMPREHENSIVE

Silver Law Firm provides litigation and mediation services to a variety of clients. Attorneys keep track of the time they spend on each case, which is used to charge fees to clients at a rate of $300 per hour. A management advisor commented that activity-based costing might prove useful in evaluating the costs of its legal services, and the firm has decided to evaluate its fee structure by comparing ABC to its alternative cost allocations. The following data relate to a typical month at the firm. During a typical month, the firm handles seven mediation cases and three litigation cases.

	Activity Driver	Total Amount	Consumption by Service Type		Activity Cost
			Litigation	Mediation	
Providing legal advice	Billable hours	200	75	125	$30,000
Overhead costs					
Internal support departments					
Preparing documents	Documents	30	16	14	$ 4,000
Occupying office space	Billable hours	200	75	125	1,200
Heating and lighting of office	Billable hours	200	75	125	350
External support departments					
Registering court documents	Documents	30	16	14	1,250
Retaining consultants (investigators, psychiatrists)	Court dates	6	5	1	10,000
Using contract services (couriers, security guards)	Court dates	6	5	1	5,000
Total overhead costs					$21,800

Required

1. Determine the cost of providing legal services to each type of case using activity-based costing (ABC).
2. Determine the cost of each type of case using a single plantwide rate for nonattorney costs based on billable hours.
3. Determine the cost of each type of case using multiple departmental overhead rates for the internal support department (based on number of documents) and external support department (based on billable hours).
4. Compare and discuss the costs assigned under each method for management decisions.

PLANNING THE SOLUTION

- Compute pool rates and assign costs to cases using ABC.
- Compute costs for the cases using the volume-based methods and discuss differences between these costs and the costs computed using ABC.

Summary

C1 **Distinguish between direct and indirect expenses and identify bases for allocating indirect expenses to departments.** Direct expenses are traced to a specific department and are incurred for the sole benefit of that department. Indirect expenses benefit more than one department. Indirect expenses are allocated to departments when computing departmental net income. Ideally, we allocate indirect expenses by using a cause-effect relation for the allocation base. When a cause-effect relation is not identifiable, each indirect expense is allocated on a basis reflecting the relative benefit received by each department.

C2 **Explain transfer pricing and methods to set transfer prices.** Transfer prices are used to record transfers of items between divisions of the same company. Transfer prices can be based on costs or market prices, or they can be negotiated by division managers.

C3^C **Describe allocation of joint costs across products.** A joint cost refers to costs incurred to produce or purchase two or more products at the same time. When income statements are prepared, joint costs are usually allocated to the resulting joint products using either a physical or value basis.

A1 **Analyze investment centers using return on investment and residual income.** A financial measure often used to evaluate an investment center manager is the *return on investment*, also called *return on assets*. This measure is computed as the center's income divided by the center's average total assets.

A4 **Compute cycle time and cycle efficiency, and explain their importance to production management.** It is important for companies to reduce the time to produce their products and to improve manufacturing efficiency. One measure of that time is cycle time (CT), defined as Process time + Inspection time + Move time + Wait time. Process time is value-added time; the others are non-value-added time. Cycle efficiency (CE) is the ratio of value-added time to total cycle time. If CE is low, management should evaluate its production process to see if it can reduce non-value-added activities.

P1 **Prepare a responsibility accounting report using controllable costs.** Responsibility accounting systems provide information for evaluating the performance of department managers. A responsibility accounting system's performance reports for evaluating department managers should include only the expenses (and revenues) that each manager controls.

P2 **Allocate indirect expenses to departments.** Indirect expenses include items like depreciation, rent, advertising, and other expenses that cannot be assigned directly to departments. Indirect expenses are recorded in company accounts, an allocation base is identified for each expense, and costs are allocated to departments. Departmental expense allocation spreadsheets are often used in allocating indirect expenses to departments.

Chapter Summaries provide students with a review organized by learning objectives. Chapter Summaries are a component of the CAP model (as discussed in the "Innovative Textbook Features" section), which recaps each conceptual, analytical, and procedural objective.

Key Terms are bolded in the text and repeated at the end of the chapter. A complete glossary of key terms is available online through **Connect**.

Key Terms		
Cost accounting system	Materials ledger card	Services Overhead
Finished Goods Inventory	Materials requisition	Target cost
Job	Overapplied overhead	Time ticket
Job cost sheet	Predetermined overhead rate	Underapplied overhead
Job lot	Process operations	Work in Process Inventory
Job order costing system	Receiving report	
Job order production	Services in Process Inventory	

Helps Students Master Key Concepts

Multiple Choice Quiz questions quickly test chapter knowledge before a student moves on to complete Quick Studies, Exercises, and Problems.

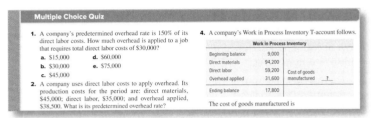

Quick Study assignments are short exercises that often focus on one learning objective. Most are included in **Connect**. There are at least 10–15 Quick Study assignments per chapter.

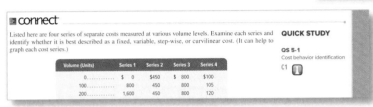

Exercises are one of this book's many strengths and a competitive advantage. There are at least 10–15 per chapter, and most are included in **Connect**.

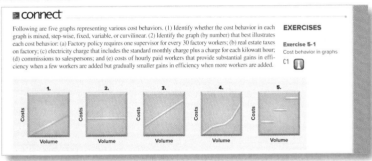

Problem Sets A & B are proven problems that can be assigned as homework or for in-class projects. All problems are coded according to the CAP model (see the "Innovative Textbook Features" section), and Set A is included in **Connect**.

Outstanding Assignment Material . . .

Beyond the Numbers exercises ask students to use accounting figures and understand their meaning. Students also learn how accounting applies to a variety of business situations. These creative and fun exercises are all new or updated and are divided into nine types:

- Reporting in Action
- Comparative Analysis
- Ethics Challenge
- Communicating in Practice
- Taking It to the Net
- Teamwork in Action
- Hitting the Road
- Entrepreneurial Decision
- Global Decision

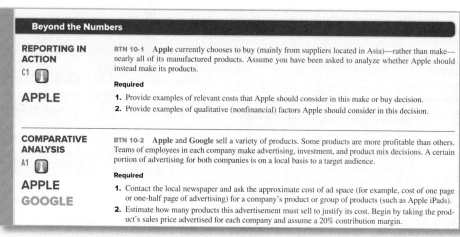

Beyond the Numbers

REPORTING IN ACTION

C1

APPLE

BTN 10-1 **Apple** currently chooses to buy (mainly from suppliers located in Asia)—rather than make—nearly all of its manufactured products. Assume you have been asked to analyze whether Apple should instead make its products.

Required

1. Provide examples of relevant costs that Apple should consider in this make or buy decision.
2. Provide examples of qualitative (nonfinancial) factors Apple should consider in this decision.

COMPARATIVE ANALYSIS

A1

APPLE

GOOGLE

BTN 10-2 **Apple** and **Google** sell a variety of products. Some products are more profitable than others. Teams of employees in each company make advertising, investment, and product mix decisions. A certain portion of advertising for both companies is on a local basis to a target audience.

Required

1. Contact the local newspaper and ask the approximate cost of ad space (for example, cost of one page or one-half page of advertising) for a company's product or group of products (such as Apple iPads).
2. Estimate how many products this advertisement must sell to justify its cost. Begin by taking the product's sales price advertised for each company and assume a 20% contribution margin.

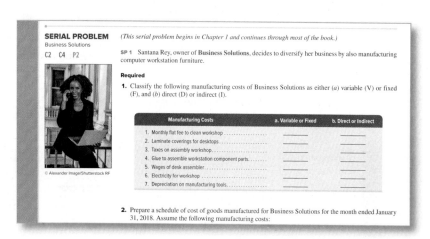

SERIAL PROBLEM
Business Solutions

C2 C4 P2

© Alexander Image/Shutterstock RF

(This serial problem begins in Chapter 1 and continues through most of the book.)

SP 1 Santana Rey, owner of **Business Solutions**, decides to diversify her business by also manufacturing computer workstation furniture.

Required

1. Classify the following manufacturing costs of Business Solutions as either (*a*) variable (V) or fixed (F), and (*b*) direct (D) or indirect (I).

Manufacturing Costs	a. Variable or Fixed	b. Direct or Indirect
1. Monthly flat fee to clean workshop	____	____
2. Laminate coverings for desktops	____	____
3. Taxes on assembly workshop	____	____
4. Glue to assemble workstation component parts	____	____
5. Wages of desk assembler	____	____
6. Electricity for workshop	____	____
7. Depreciation on manufacturing tools	____	____

2. Prepare a schedule of cost of goods manufactured for Business Solutions for the month ended January 31, 2018. Assume the following manufacturing costs:

Serial Problems use a continuous running case study to illustrate chapter concepts in a familiar context. The Serial Problem can be followed continuously from the first chapter or picked up at any later point in the book; enough information is provided to ensure students can get right to work.

"The Serial Problems are excellent. . . . I like the continuation of the same problem to the next chapters if applicable. I use the Quick Studies as practice problems. . . . Students have commented that this really works for them if they work (these questions) before attempting the assigned exercises and problems. I also like the discussion (questions) and make this an assignment. You have done an outstanding job presenting accounting to our students."

—**JERRI TITTLE, Rose State College**

Helps Students Master Key Concepts

General Ledger Problems enable students to see how transactions are entered in the journal, post to the ledger, listed in a trial balance, and reported in financial statements. Students can track an amount in any financial statement all the way back to the original journal entry. Critical thinking components then challenge students to analyze the business activities in the problem.

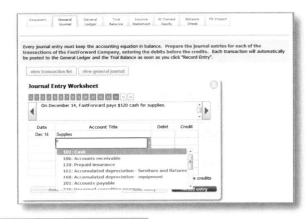

 GENERAL LEDGER PROBLEM

Available only in Connect

connect

The **General Ledger** tool in *Connect* automates several of the procedural steps in accounting so that the financial professional can focus on the impacts of each transaction on various reports and performance measures.

GL 2-1   General Ledger assignment GL 2-1, based on Problem 2-1A, focuses on transactions related to job order costing. Prepare summary journal entries to record the cost of jobs and their flow through the manufacturing environment. Then prepare a schedule of cost of goods manufactured and a partial income statement.

Excel Simulations allow you to practice your Excel skills, such as basic formulas and formatting, within the context of accounting. These questions feature animated, narrated Help and Show Me tutorials (when enabled by your instructor).

The End of the Chapter Is Only the Beginning Our valuable and proven assignments aren't just confined to the book. From problems that require technological solutions to materials found exclusively online, this book's end-of-chapter material is fully integrated with its technology package.

- Quick Studies, Exercises, and Problems available in **Connect** are marked with an icon.

 Assignments that focus on global accounting practices and companies are often identified with an icon.

 Assignments that involve ethical or fraud risk are marked with an icon.

 Assignments that involve decision analysis are identified with an icon.

 Assignments that involve sustainability issues are marked with an icon.

Content Revisions Enhance Learning

This edition's revisions are driven by feedback from instructors and students. They include:

- Many new, revised, and updated assignments throughout, including entrepreneurial and real-world assignments.
- Many Need-to-Know (NTK) demonstrations added to each chapter at key junctures to reinforce learning.
- Updated Sustainability section for each chapter, with examples linked to the new chapter-opening company.
- New annual reports and comparative (BTN) assignments: **Apple**, **Google**, and **Samsung**.

- Revised art program, visual infographics, and text layout.
- Updated ratio/tool analysis using data from well-known firms.
- Revised General Ledger assignments for most chapters.
- New and revised entrepreneurial examples and elements.
- New technology content integrated and referenced throughout.
- Revised Global View section moved to the very end of each chapter following assignments.

Chapter 1

NEW opener—NatureBox and entrepreneurial assignment.
Simplified discussion on purpose of managerial accounting.
Added references to more real-world companies.
Added discussion of enterprise risk management.
Revised Exhibit 1.1 to show common managerial decisions.
Simplified discussion on nature of managerial accounting.
New section on careers in managerial accounting and importance of managerial accounting for nonaccountants.
New exhibit on managerial accounting salaries.
Added example on cost of iPhone.
New section head and revised discussion for nonmanufacturing costs.
Added graphics to cost flow exhibit.
Reduced number of overhead items in exhibit for cost of goods manufactured statement.
Added section on computing cost per unit.
Updated "trends" section to include *gig economy* (**Uber**), triple bottom line, and ISO 9000 standards.
Expanded discussion of sustainability and SASB.
Expanded Sustainability section with Decision Insight chart and **NatureBox** example.
Added Discussion Question on triple bottom line.
Added two Quick Studies on raw materials activity for **3M Co.**
Added Exercises on sustainability reporting for **Starbucks** and **Hyatt**.

Chapter 2

NEW opener—Neha Assar and entrepreneurial assignment.
Simplified discussion of cost accounting systems.
Simplified direct material and direct labor cost flows and entries.
Added time period information to graphic on 4-step overhead process.
Simplified discussion of recording overhead costs.

Added journal entry for depreciation expense on equipment in NTK 2-5.
Revised exhibits for posting of direct materials, direct labor, and overhead to general ledger accounts and job cost sheets.
Added section on using job cost sheet for managerial decisions.
Added entries for transfers of costs to Finished Goods Inventory and to COGS.
Expanded discussion of job order costing for service firms.
New exhibit and cost flows for service firms.
Expanded Sustainability section, including **USPS** and **Neha Assar** examples.
New NTK on using the job cost sheet.
Added new Quick Study and new Exercise on costing for service firms.

Chapter 3

NEW opener—Stance and entrepreneurial assignment.
Revised exhibit on cost flows in job order and process costing systems.
Revised exhibit on production data and physical flow of units.
Added transfer to finished goods and updated ending balance to WIP T-account for second process.
New section on using process cost summary for decisions.
Added discussion of the raw materials yield to "trends" section.
Revised exhibit and discussion of assigning cost using FIFO.
Expanded discussion of hybrid and operation costing.
Expanded Sustainability discussion, including **General Mills** and **Stance** examples.
Added Discussion Question on sustainable raw materials sourcing.

Chapter 4

NEW opener—GrandyOats and entrepreneurial assignment.
Revised discussion of why overhead costs must be assigned.
Revised discussions of plantwide and departmental methods.
New exhibit on overhead allocation using plantwide method.

Revised discussion of applying activity-based costing.
Revised exhibit of overhead allocation using activity-based costing.
Revised discussion of advantages and disadvantages of activity-based costing.
Revised and reorganized discussion of advantages and disadvantages of ABC.
Expanded discussion of lean operations and lean accounting.
Revised Sustainability section on supply chain management.
New NTK on activity levels.
Revised Global View on **Toyota**'s lean manufacturing.

Chapter 5

NEW opener—Sweetgreen and entrepreneurial assignment.
New exhibit on building blocks of CVP analysis.
Revised discussion on uses of CVP analysis.
Revised discussion of fixed and variable costs.
Added data points to margin of fixed and variable cost exhibit.
New graphic on examples of fixed, variable, and mixed costs.
Revised discussion on step-wise and curvilinear costs.
Revised cost data for measuring cost behavior.
Reorganized break-even section into three methods.
Revised discussions of contribution margin income statement and CVP charts.
Moved margin of safety to section on applying CVP.
Added discussion of sales mix and break-even for **Amazon**.
Revised discussion of assumptions in CVP.
Revised Sustainability section with **Nike**, CVP analysis, and **Sweetgreen** example.
Expanded appendix on variable and absorption costing.
Added Discussion Question, four Quick Studies, and 1 Exercise on variable and absorption costing.
Revised Global View on **BMW**'s i3 break-even point.

Chapter 6

NEW opener—Riffraff and entrepreneurial assignment.
Revised discussion of variable and absorption costing.
Revised discussion of income implications of variable and absorption costing.
New graphics on relations between production, sales, and income effects.
Added T-accounts to exhibits of absorption and variable costing income.
Revised discussion and exhibits of product cost assignments to financial statements.
New graphic on relation between changes in inventory and income effects.
Revised discussion of planning production.
Revised discussion of controlling costs.
Added calculation of break-even using variable costing income statement.
Added exhibit on variable costing income statement for service firm.
Added example of special order decision for service firm.
Added NTK problem on pricing and special offer.
Added two new Quick Studies on sustainability.
Revised Sustainability section on **PUMA**'s environmental profit and loss account.

Chapter 7

NEW opener—TaTa Topper and entrepreneurial assignment.
Revised discussion, with new exhibit, of budgeting as a management tool.
Revised discussion on benefits of budgeting.
Added new graphic on benefits of budgeting.
Revised discussion of budgeting and human behavior.
New Decision Insight on zero-based budgeting.
New NTK on the benefits and potential costs of budgeting.
Revised master budget process exhibit to reflect types of activities.
Added graphics showing formulas to compute direct materials requirements and direct labor cost.

Revised discussions of direct materials, direct labor, and factory overhead budgets.
Added discussion and exhibits of estimated cash receipts with alternative collection timing and uncollectible accounts.
Added T-account to cash budget exhibit.
New NTKs on the cash budget.
Added margin point on the impact of credit and debit card fees on cash receipts.
Added section with exhibit on budgeting for service companies.
New Sustainability section with discussion of **Johnson & Johnson** and exhibit and **TaTa Topper** example.
Added Discussion Question and Quick Study on sustainability and budgeting.
Added Exercise on budgeted cash payments on account.

Chapter 8

NEW opener—Riide and entrepreneurial assignment.
New exhibit on fixed versus flexible budgets.
Revised discussion of fixed versus flexible budgets.
New 3-step process to prepare a flexible budget.
Added section on formula for computing total budgeted cost in a flexible budget.
Revised discussion of setting standard costs.
Revised exhibit on cost variance formula.
Added discussion of potential causes of direct labor variances.
New 3-step process for determining standard overhead rate.
New exhibit, formula, and computation of standard overhead applied.
Revised discussion of overhead volume and controllable variances.
Added calculations of controllable variance and budgeted overhead costs.
Added discussion, exhibit, and Discussion Question of the pros and cons of standard costing.
Added discussion of the International Integrated Reporting Council.
New Sustainability section with discussion of **Intel** and executive pay and **Riide** examples.

Added two Quick Studies on sustainability and standard costs.

Chapter 9

NEW opener—Ministry and entrepreneurial assignment.
Reorganized chapter.
Revised discussion of performance evaluation and decentralization.
Revised discussion of **Kraft Heinz** responsibility centers.
Revised exhibit on responsibility accounting.
Revised discussion of responsibility accounting reports.
Added NTKs on responsibility accounting, cost allocations, and balanced scorecard.
Revised discussion of indirect expense allocations.
New exhibit and discussion of general model of expense allocation.
New exhibit on common allocation bases for indirect expenses.
Revised discussion of preparing departmental income.
New exhibit and formula for computing departmental income.
Added short section on transfer pricing.
New Sustainability section with discussion of **General Mills**, **Target** performance reporting, and **Ministry** example.

Chapter 10

NEW opener—Adafruit Industries and entrepreneurial assignment.
Added discussion of outsourcing in make or buy decision.
Revised discussion of relevant costs and benefits.
Revised exhibit on scrap or rework analysis.
Revised Sustainability section on suppliers' labor practices, with **Apple** Code of Conduct and **Adafruit** examples.
Added Appendix and end-of-chapter assignments on product pricing.

Chapter 11

NEW opener—Simply Gum and entrepreneurial assignment.
Added exhibit and discussion of capital budgeting process.

Added exhibit and discussion of cash inflows and outflows in capital budgeting.
Added lists of strengths and weaknesses, with revised discussion, of payback period.
Added list of weaknesses of accounting rate of return method.
New art showing timeline of NPV calculation.
Added discussion of capital rationing.
Added financial calculator and Excel steps for many calculations.
Revised Sustainability section on capital budgeting for solar investments and **Simply Gum** example.
Added two Quick Studies on capital budgeting for solar investments.

Chapter 12

NEW opener—Amazon and entrepreneurial assignment.
Continued infographics on examples of operating, investing, and financing cash flows.
Kept 5-step process for preparing statement of cash flows.
New graphic on use of indirect vs. direct methods.
New presentation to highlight indirect adjustments to income.
Updated box comparing operating cash flows to income for companies.
Kept "Summary T-Account" for learning statement of cash flows.
New Sustainability section on **Amazon**'s initiatives.
Updated cash flow on total assets analysis using **Nike**.

Chapter 13

NEW opener—Morgan Stanley and entrepreneurial assignment.
Streamlined the "Basics of Analysis" section.
Simplified computations for comparative statements.
Updated data for analysis of **Apple** using horizontal, vertical, and ratio analysis.
Updated comparative analysis using **Google** and **Samsung**.
New evidence on accounting ploys by CFOs.

New Sustainability section on **Morgan Stanley**'s initiatives.
Revised "All Else Being Equal" Fraud box using KPMG data.
Revised Appendix 13A to reflect new rules that remove separate disclosure of extraordinary items.
Revised assignments for new standard on extraordinary items.

Appendix A

New financial statements for **Apple**, **Google**, and **Samsung**.

Appendix B

New organization with detailed subheadings.
Added Excel computations for PV and FV of single amounts.
Added Excel computations for PV and FV of annuity.

Appendix C

Simplified discussion on analyzing and recording process.
Streamlined discussion of classified vs. unclassified balance sheet.
Enhanced explanation of computing equity.
Enhanced Exhibit C.4 to identify account categories.
Improved summary of transactions in the ledger.
Streamlined explanation of error correction in entries.
New accounting quality box with reference to KPMG data.
Revised Sustainability section on cost savings for small business.
Updated debt ratio analysis using **Skechers**.
Added two Quick Study assignments.
Updated **Piaggio**'s (IFRS) balance sheet.

Appendix D

Streamlined discussion of partnership characteristics.
New margin T-accounts for Exhibits D.1 and D.2.
Updated Sustainability section describes accounting for nonprofit sales of **Scholly**.
Added two Quick Study assignments, one Exercise, and one Problem.

McGraw-Hill Connect®
Learn Without Limits

Connect is a teaching and learning platform that is proven to deliver better results for students and instructors.

Connect empowers students by continually adapting to deliver precisely what they need, when they need it, and how they need it, so your class time is more engaging and effective.

73% of instructors who use **Connect** require it; instructor satisfaction **increases** by 28% when **Connect** is required.

Connect's Impact on Retention Rates, Pass Rates, and Average Exam Scores

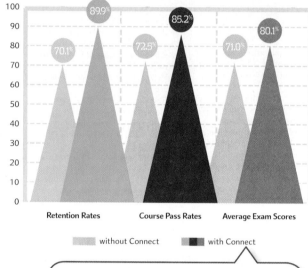

without Connect   with Connect

Using **Connect** improves retention rates by **19.8%**, passing rates by **12.7%**, and exam scores by **9.1%**.

Analytics

Connect Insight®

Connect Insight is Connect's new one-of-a-kind visual analytics dashboard that provides at-a-glance information regarding student performance, which is immediately actionable. By presenting assignment, assessment, and topical performance results together with a time metric that is easily visible for aggregate or individual results, Connect Insight gives the user the ability to take a just-in-time approach to teaching and learning, which was never before available. Connect Insight presents data that helps instructors improve class performance in a way that is efficient and effective.

Impact on Final Course Grade Distribution

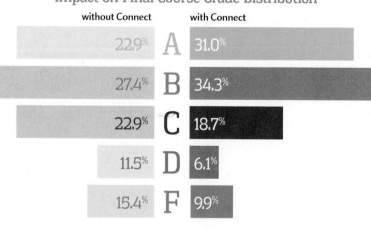

Adaptive

THE **ADAPTIVE** **READING EXPERIENCE**
DESIGNED TO TRANSFORM THE WAY STUDENTS READ

More students earn **A's** and **B's** when they use McGraw-Hill Education **Adaptive** products.

SmartBook®

Proven to help students improve grades and study more efficiently, SmartBook contains the same content within the print book, but actively tailors that content to the needs of the individual. SmartBook's adaptive technology provides precise, personalized instruction on what the student should do next, guiding the student to master and remember key concepts, targeting gaps in knowledge and offering customized feedback, and driving the student toward comprehension and retention of the subject matter. Available on tablets, SmartBook puts learning at the student's fingertips—anywhere, anytime.

Over **8 billion questions** have been answered, making McGraw-Hill Education products more intelligent, reliable, and precise.

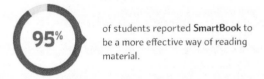
95% of students reported **SmartBook** to be a more effective way of reading material.

100% of students want to use the Practice Quiz feature available within **SmartBook** to help them study.

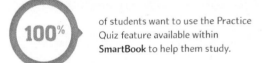
100% of students reported having reliable access to off-campus wifi.

90% of students say they would purchase **SmartBook** over print alone.

95% of students reported that **SmartBook** would impact their study skills in a positive way.

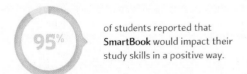

Mc Graw Hill Education

*Findings based on 2015 focus group results administered by McGraw-Hill Education

www.mheducation.com

Acknowledgments

John J. Wild, Ken W. Shaw, and McGraw-Hill Education recognize the following instructors for their valuable feedback and involvement in the development of *Managerial Accounting*, 6e. We are thankful for their suggestions, counsel, and encouragement.

Khaled Abdou, Penn State University–Berks
Anne Marie Anderson, Raritan Valley Community College
Elaine Anes, Heald College–Fresno
Jerome Apple, University of Akron
Jack Aschkenazi, American Intercontinental University
Sidney Askew, Borough of Manhattan Community College
Lawrence Awopetu, University of Arkansas–Pine Bluff
Jon Backman, Spartanburg Community College
Charles Baird, University of Wisconsin–Stout
Michael Barendse, Grossmont College
Richard Barnhart, Grand Rapids Community College
Beverly R. Beatty, Anne Arundel Community College
Anna Beavers, Laney College
Judy Benish, Fox Valley Technical College
Patricia Bentley, Keiser University
Teri Bernstein, Santa Monica College
Jaswinder Bhangal, Chabot College
Sandra Bitenc, University of Texas at Arlington
Susan Blizzard, San Antonio College
Marvin Blye, Wor-Wic Community College
Patrick Borja, Citrus College
Anna Boulware, St. Charles Community College
Gary Bower, Community College of Rhode Island–Flanagan
Leslee Brock, Southwest Mississippi Community College
Gregory Brookins, Santa Monica College
Regina Brown, Eastfield College
Tracy L. Bundy, University of Louisiana at Lafayette
Roy Carson, Anne Arundel Community College
Deborah Carter, Coahoma Community College
Roberto Castaneda, DeVry University Online
Martha Cavalaris, Miami Dade College
Amy Chataginer, Mississippi Gulf Coast Community College
Gerald Childs, Waukesha County Technical College
Colleen Chung, Miami Dade College–Kendall
Shifei Chung, Rowan University
Robert Churchman, Harding University
Marilyn Ciolino, Delgado Community College
Thomas Clement, University of North Dakota
Oyinka Coakley, Broward College
Susan Cockrell, Birmingham-Southern College
Lisa Cole, Johnson County Community College
Robbie R. Coleman, Northeast Mississippi Community College
Christie Comunale, Long Island University–C.W. Post Campus
Jackie Conrecode, Florida Gulf Coast University
Debora Constable, Georgia Perimeter College
Susan Cordes, Johnson County Community College
Anne Cordozo, Broward College
Cheryl Corke, Genesee Community College
James Cosby, John Tyler Community College
Ken Couvillion, Delta College
Loretta Darche, Southwest Florida College
Judy Daulton, Piedmont Technical College
Annette Davis, Glendale Community College
Dorothy Davis, University of Louisiana–Monroe

Walter DeAguero, Saddleback College
Mike Deschamps, MiraCosta College
Pamela Donahue, Northern Essex Community College
Steve Doster, Shawnee State University
Larry Dragosavac, Edison Community College
Samuel Duah, Bowie State University
Robert Dunlevy, Montgomery County Community College
Jerrilyn Eisenhauer, Tulsa Community College–Southeast
Ronald Elders, Virginia College
Terry Elliott, Morehead State University
Patricia Feller, Nashville State Community College
Albert Fisher, College of Southern Nevada
Annette Fisher, Glendale Community College
Ron Fitzgerald, Santa Monica College
David Flannery, Bryant and Stratton College
Hollie Floberg, Tennessee Wesleyan College
Linda Flowers, Houston Community College
Jeannie Folk, College of DuPage
Rebecca Foote, Middle Tennessee State University
Paul Franklin, Kaplan University
Tim Garvey, Westwood College
Barbara Gershman, Northern Virginia Community College–Woodbridge
Barbara Gershowitz, Nashville State Technical Community College
Mike Glasscock, Amarillo College
Diane Glowacki, Tarrant County College
Ernesto Gonzalez, Florida National College
Lori Grady, Bucks County Community College
Gloria Grayless, Sam Houston State University
Ann Gregory, South Plains College
Rameshwar Gupta, Jackson State University
Amy Haas, Kingsborough Community College
Pat Halliday, Santa Monica College
Keith Hallmark, Calhoun Community College
Rebecca Hancock, El Paso Community College–Valley Verde
Mechelle Harris, Bossier Parish Community College
Tracey Hawkins, University of Cincinnati–Clermont College
Thomas Hayes, University of Arkansas–Ft. Smith
Laurie Hays, Western Michigan University
Roger Hehman, University of Cincinnati–Clermont College
Cheri Hernandez, Des Moines Area Community College
Margaret Hicks, Howard University
Melanie Hicks, Liberty University
James Higgins, Holy Family University
Patricia Holmes, Des Moines Area Community College
Barbara Hopkins, Northern Virginia Community College–Manassas
Wade Hopkins, Heald College
Aileen Huang, Santa Monica College
Les Hubbard, Solano College
Deborah Hudson, Gaston College
James Hurst, National College
Constance Hylton, George Mason University
Christine Irujo, Westfield State University
Tamela Jarvis, Prince George's Community College

Fred Jex, Macomb Community College
Gina M. Jones, Aims Community College
Jeff Jones, College of Southern Nevada
Rita Jones, Columbus State University
Odessa Jordan, Calhoun Community College
Dmitriy Kalyagin, Chabot College
Thomas Kam, Hawaii Pacific University
Naomi Karolinski, Monroe Community College
Shirly A. Kleiner, Johnson County Community College
Kenneth A. Koerber, Bucks County Community College
Jill Kolody, Anne Arundel Community College
Tamara Kowalczyk, Appalachian State University
Anita Kroll, University of Wisconsin–Madison
David Krug, Johnson County Community College
Christopher Kwak, DeAnza College
Tara Laken, Joliet Junior College
Jeanette Landin, Empire College
Beth Lasky, Delgado Community College
Neal Leviton, Santa Monica College
Danny Litt, University of California Los Angeles
James L. Lock, Northern Virginia Community College
Steve Ludwig, Northwest Missouri State University
Debra Luna, El Paso Community College
Amado Mabul, Heald College
Lori Major, Luzerne County Community College
Jennifer Malfitano, Delaware County Community College
Maria Mari, Miami Dade College–Kendall
Thomas S. Marsh, Northern Virginia Community College–Annandale
Karen Martinson, University of Wisconsin–Stout
Brenda Mattison, Tri-County Technical College
Stacie Mayes, Rose State College
Mark McCarthy, East Carolina University
Clarice McCoy, Brookhaven College
Tammy Metzke, Milwaukee Area Technical College
Jeanine Metzler, Northampton Community College
Theresa Michalow, Moraine Valley Community College
Julie Miller, Chippewa Valley Tech College
Tim Miller, El Camino College
John Minchin, California Southern University
Edna C. Mitchell, Polk State College
Jill Mitchell, Northern Virginia Community College
April Mohr, Jefferson Community and Technical College, SW
Lynn Moore, Aiken Technical College
Angela Mott, Northeast Mississippi Community College
Andrea Murowski, Brookdale Community College
Timothy Murphy, Diablo Valley College
Kenneth F. O'Brien, Farmingdale State College
Kathleen O'Donnell, Onondaga Community College
Ahmed Omar, Burlington County College
Robert A. Pacheco, Massasoit Community College
Margaret Parilo, Cosumnes River College
Paige Paulsen, Salt Lake Community College
Yvonne Phang, Borough of Manhattan Community College
Gary Pieroni, Diablo Valley College
Debbie Porter, Tidewater Community College, Virginia Beach
Kristen Quinn, Northern Essex Community College
James Racic, Lakeland Community College
David Ravetch, University of California Los Angeles
Ruthie Reynolds, Howard University
Cecile Roberti, Community College of Rhode Island
Morgan Rockett, Moberly Area Community College

Patrick Rogan, Cosumnes River College
Paul Rogers, Community College of Beaver County
Brian Routh, Washington State University–Vancouver
Helen Roybark, Radford University
Alphonse Ruggiero, Suffolk County Community College
Joan Ryan, Clackamas Community College
Martin Sabo, Community College of Denver
Arjan Sadhwani, South University
Gary K. Sanborn, Northwestern Michigan College
Kin Kin Sandhu, Heald College
Marcia Sandvold, Des Moines Area Community College
Gary Schader, Kean University
Barbara Schnathorst, The Write Solution, Inc.
Darlene Schnuck, Waukesha County Technical College
Elizabeth Serapin, Columbia Southern University
Geeta Shankhar, University of Dayton
Regina Shea, Community College of Baltimore County–Essex
James Shelton, Liberty University
Jay Siegel, Union County College
Gerald Singh, New York City College of Technology
Lois Slutsky, Broward College–South
Gerald Smith, University of Northern Iowa
Kathleen Sobieralski, University of Maryland University College
Charles Spector, State University of New York at Oswego
Diane Stark, Phoenix College
Thomas Starks, Heald College
Carolyn L. Strauch, Crowder College
Latazia Stuart, Fortis University Online
Gene Sullivan, Liberty University
David Sulzen, Ferrum College
Dominique Svarc, William Rainey Harper College
Linda Sweeney, Sam Houston State University
Carl Swoboda, Southwest Tennessee Community College, Macon
Margaret Tanner, University of Arkansas–Ft. Smith
Ulysses Taylor, Fayetteville State University
Anthony Teng, Saddleback College
Paula Thomas, Middle Tennessee State University
Teresa Thompson, Chaffey Community College
Leslie Thysell, John Tyler Community College
Melanie Torborg, Globe University
Shafi Ullah, Broward College
Bob Urell, Irvine Valley College
Adam Vitalis, Georgia Tech
Patricia Walczak, Lansing Community College
Terri Walsh, Seminole State College–Oviedo
Shunda Ware, Atlanta Technical College
Janis Weber, University of Louisiana–Monroe
Dave Welch, Franklin University
Jean Wells-Jessup, Howard University
Christopher Widmer, Tidewater Community College
Andrew Williams, Edmonds Community College
Jonathan M. Wild, University of Wisconsin–Madison
Wanda Wong, Chabot College
John Woodward, Polk State College
Patricia Worsham, Norco College, Riverside Community College
Gail E. Wright, Stevenson University
Lynnette Yerbury, Salt Lake Community College
Judy Zander, Grossmont College
Mary Zenner, College of Lake County
Jane Zlojutro, Northwestern Michigan College

Brief Contents

*Appendixes C and D are available in McGraw-Hill Education Connect and as a print copy from a McGraw-Hill Education sales representative.

Contents

8 Flexible Budgets and Standard Costs 308

9 Performance Measurement and Responsibility Accounting 358

10 Relevant Costing for Managerial Decisions 404

11 Capital Budgeting and Investment Analysis 436

*Appendixes C and D are available in McGraw-Hill Education Connect and as a print copy from a McGraw-Hill Education sales representative.

Managerial Accounting

chapter 1

Managerial Accounting Concepts and Principles

Learning Objectives

CONCEPTUAL

C1 Explain the purpose and nature of, and the role of ethics in, managerial accounting.

C2 Describe accounting concepts useful in classifying costs.

C3 Define product and period costs and explain how they impact financial statements.

C4 Explain how balance sheets and income statements for manufacturing, merchandising, and service companies differ.

C5 Explain manufacturing activities and the flow of manufacturing costs.

C6 Describe trends in managerial accounting.

ANALYTICAL

A1 Assess raw materials inventory management using raw materials inventory turnover and days' sales in raw materials inventory.

PROCEDURAL

P1 Compute cost of goods sold for a manufacturer and for a merchandiser.

P2 Prepare a schedule of cost of goods manufactured and explain its purpose and links to financial statements.

Courtesy of NatureBox

Out of the Box

REDWOOD CITY, CA—After losing 70 pounds by learning to eat better, Gautam Gupta developed a keen interest in foods. Gautam's college friend Ken Chen grew up working in his parents' restaurant. Together, they believed they could help people eat healthier snacks. "Everyone snacks," says Gautam, "and they tend to eat what is available." The result was **NatureBox** (**NatureBox.com**), Gautam and Ken's direct-to-consumer business selling healthy snacks. "We thought we could provide value by creating an online experience to personalize a basket of natural food items."

Gautam and Ken found success by creating a niche. "We believe if we know more about you as a customer—what foods you like and don't like," explains Gautam, "we can give you a very unique experience and tailor the products to your needs." NatureBox subscribers indicate how many snacks they wish to receive and how frequently they wish to receive them. Subscribers choose from over 120 snacks.

NatureBox reflects a data-driven relationship: Subscribers identify and adjust their choices based on snacks they like or dislike, and NatureBox's accounting system develops a profile for each customer's preferences. "Think of us as the **Netflix** of food," says Gautam. "We want to understand our customers' needs better than anyone else." The use of accounting analytics is a growing trend.

"We're passionate about using data to change how people eat"
—Gautam Gupta

Gautam and Ken point out that knowing basic managerial principles, cost classifications, and cost flows was crucial to setting up operations. Gautam explains that they use only all-natural ingredients, and offer vegan, gluten-free, nut-free, and non-GMO choices. This wide array of direct materials required that Gautam and Ken set up a managerial accounting system to monitor costs. Their accounting system now captures such information, including data on materials, labor, and overhead costs.

So far, NatureBox's recipes are winning customers. The company is one of the fastest-growing snack food brands, having delivered 50,000 snack boxes in their first year of business. They estimate sales of more than 3 million boxes this year. While expanding sales and profits is crucial, Gautam says he and his co-workers "want to make an impact." Beyond helping snackers eat better, NatureBox donates one meal to end childhood hunger for each box sold.

Gautam offers this advice: "A start-up is a journey. It's a roller-coaster ride. Focus on one thing at a time and do it really well."

Sources: *NatureBox.com website,* January 2017; *CBS MoneyWatch,* August 13, 2014; *USA Today,* April 14, 2014; *FastCompany.com,* June 4, 2014; *TheSurge.com,* December 23, 2014; *Inc.com,* December 11, 2012, and April 25, 2015

MANAGERIAL ACCOUNTING BASICS

Managerial accounting provides financial and nonfinancial information to an organization's managers. Managers include, for example, employees in charge of a company's divisions; the heads of marketing, information technology, and human resources; and top-level managers such as the chief executive officer (CEO) and chief financial officer (CFO). This section explains the purpose of managerial accounting (also called *management accounting*) and compares it with financial accounting.

Purpose of Managerial Accounting

The purpose of managerial accounting is to provide useful information to aid in three key managerial tasks:

C1

Explain the purpose and nature of, and the role of ethics in, managerial accounting.

- Determining the costs of an organization's products and services.
- Planning future activities.
- Comparing actual results to planned results.

For example, managerial accounting information can help the marketing manager decide whether to advertise on social media such as **Twitter**; it also can help **Google**'s information technology manager decide whether to buy new computers.

Point: Costs are important to managers because they impact both the financial position and profitability of a business. Managerial accounting assists in analysis, planning, and control of costs.

Point: Planning involves risk. Enterprise risk management (ERM) includes the systems and processes companies use to minimize risks such as data breaches, fraud, and loss of assets.

The remainder of this book looks carefully at how managerial accounting information is gathered and used. We begin by showing how the managerial accounting system collects cost information and assigns it to an organization's products and services. Cost information is important for many decisions that managers make, such as product pricing, profitability analysis, and whether to make or buy a product or component. More generally, much of managerial accounting involves gathering information about costs for planning and control decisions.

Planning is the process of setting goals and making plans to achieve them. Companies make long-term strategic plans that usually span a 5- to 10-year horizon. Short-term plans then translate the strategic plan into actions, which are more concrete and consist of better-defined goals. A short-term plan often covers a one-year period that, when translated into monetary terms, is known as a budget.

Control is the process of monitoring planning decisions and evaluating an organization's activities and employees. Feedback provided by the control function allows managers to revise their plans. Measurement of actions and processes allows managers to take corrective actions to obtain better outcomes. For example, managers periodically compare actual results with planned results. Exhibit 1.1 portrays the important management functions of planning and control and the types of questions they seek to answer.

EXHIBIT 1.1

Planning and Control (including monitoring and feedback)

Monitoring

Planning
- Build a new factory?
- Develop new products?
- Expand into new markets?

Control
- Are costs too high?
- Are services profitable?
- Are customers satisfied?

Feedback

Nature of Managerial Accounting

Managerial accounting differs from financial accounting. We discuss seven key differences in this section, as summarized in Exhibit 1.2.

	Financial Accounting	**Managerial Accounting**
1. Users and decision makers	External: Investors, creditors, and others outside of the organization's managers	Internal: Managers, employees, and decision makers inside the organization
2. Purpose of information	Help external users make investment, credit, and other decisions	Help managers make planning and control decisions
3. Flexibility of reporting	Structured and often controlled by GAAP	Relatively flexible (no GAAP constraints)
4. Timeliness of information	Often available only after an audit is complete	Available quickly without the need to wait for an audit
5. Time dimension	The past; historical information with some predictions	The future; many projections and estimates, with some historical information
6. Focus of information	The whole organization	An organization's projects, processes, and divisions
7. Nature of information	Monetary information	Mostly monetary; but also nonmonetary information

Users and Decision Makers   Companies report to different groups of decision makers. Financial accounting information is provided primarily to external users including investors, creditors, and regulators. External users do not manage a company's daily activities. Managerial accounting information is provided primarily to internal managers and employees who make and implement decisions about a company's business activities.

Purpose of Information   External users of financial accounting information must often decide whether to invest in or lend to a company. Internal decision makers must plan a company's future to take advantage of opportunities or to overcome obstacles. They also try to control activities.

Flexibility of Reporting   An extensive set of rules, or GAAP, aims to protect external users from false or misleading information in financial reports. Managers are responsible for preventing and detecting fraudulent activities in their companies, including their financial reports. Managerial accounting does not rely on extensive rules. Instead, companies determine what information they need to make planning and control decisions, and then they decide how that information is best collected and reported.

Point: It is desirable to accumulate information for management reports in a database separate from financial accounting records.

Timeliness of Information   Formal financial statements are not immediately available to outside users. Independent certified public accountants often must *audit* a company's financial statements before providing them to external users. As audits often take several weeks to complete, financial reports to outsiders usually are not available until well after the period-end. However, managers can quickly obtain managerial accounting information. External auditors need not review it. Estimates and projections are acceptable. To get information quickly, managers often accept less precision in reports. As an example, an early internal report to management prepared right after the year-end could estimate net income for the year between $4.2 and $4.5 million. An audited income statement could later show net income for the year at $4.4 million. The internal report is not precise, but its information can be more useful because it is available earlier.

Point: *Internal auditing* in managerial accounting evaluates information reliability not only inside but outside the company.

EXHIBIT 1.3

Focus of External and Internal
Reports

Reports to external users focus on
the company as a whole.

Reports to internal users focus on
company units and divisions.

Time Dimension   External financial reports deal primarily with results of past activities and current conditions. While some predictions such as service lives and salvage values of plant assets are necessary, financial accounting avoids predictions whenever possible. In contrast, managerial accounting regularly includes predictions. As an example, one important managerial accounting report is a budget, which predicts revenues, expenses, and other items. Making predictions, and evaluating those predictions, are important skills for managers.

Focus of Information   Companies often organize into divisions and departments, but external investors own shares in or make loans to the entire company. Financial accounting focuses primarily on a company as a whole as depicted in the top part of Exhibit 1.3.

The focus of managerial accounting is different. While the CEO manages the whole company, most other managers are responsible for much smaller sets of activities. These middle-level and lower-level managers need managerial accounting reports dealing with their specific activities. For instance, division sales managers focus on information about results in their division. This information includes the level of success achieved by each individual, product, or department in each division of the whole company as depicted in the bottom part of Exhibit 1.3.

Nature of Information   Both financial and managerial accounting systems report monetary information. Managerial accounting systems also report considerable *nonmonetary* information. Common examples of nonmonetary information include customer and employee satisfaction data, percentage of on-time deliveries, product defect rates, energy from renewable sources, and employee diversity.

Managerial Decision Making

Although financial and managerial accounting differ, the two are not entirely separate. Some information is useful to both external and internal users. For instance, information about costs of manufacturing products is useful to all users in making decisions. Also, both financial and managerial accounting affect people's actions. For example, **Trek**'s sales compensation plan affects the behavior of its sales force when selling its manufactured bikes. Trek also must estimate the effects of promotions on buying patterns of customers. These estimates impact the equipment purchase decisions for manufacturing and can affect the supplier selection criteria established by purchasing. Thus, financial and managerial accounting systems do more than measure; they affect people's decisions and actions.

© James Startt/Agence Zoom/Getty Images

Fraud and Ethics in Managerial Accounting

Fraud, and the role of ethics in reducing fraud, are important factors in running business operations. Fraud involves the use of one's job for personal gain through the deliberate misuse of the employer's assets. Examples include theft of the employer's cash or other assets, overstating reimbursable expenses, payroll schemes, and financial statement fraud. Three factors must exist for a person to commit fraud: opportunity, financial pressure, and rationalization. This is known as the *fraud triangle*. Fraud affects all business and it is costly: The 2016 *Report to the Nations* from the Association of Certified Fraud Examiners (ACFE) estimates the average U.S. business loses 5% of its annual revenues to fraud.

The most common type of fraud, where employees steal or misuse the employer's resources, results in an average loss of $130,000 per occurrence. For example, in a billing fraud, an employee sets up a bogus supplier. The employee then prepares bills from the supplier and pays these bills from the employer's checking account. The employee cashes the checks sent to the bogus supplier and uses them for his or her own personal benefit. An organization's best chance to minimize fraud is through reducing opportunities for employees to commit fraud.

Financial Pressure

Implications of Fraud for Managerial Accounting   Fraud increases a business's costs and hurts information reliability. Left undetected, inaccurate costs can result in poor pricing decisions, an improper product mix, and faulty performance evaluations. All of these can lead to poor results for the company. Managers rely on a reliable **internal control system** to monitor and control business activities. An internal control system is the policies and procedures managers use to:

- Ensure reliable accounting.
- Protect assets.
- Uphold company policies.
- Promote efficient operations.

Point: The IMA issues the Certified Management Accountant (CMA) and the Certified Financial Manager (CFM) certifications.

Combating fraud requires ethics in accounting. **Ethics** are beliefs that distinguish right from wrong. They are accepted standards of good and bad behavior. Identifying the ethical path can be difficult. The **Institute of Management Accountants (IMA),** the professional association for management accountants, has issued a code of ethics to help accountants solve ethical dilemmas. The IMA's Statement of Ethical Professional Practice requires that management accountants be competent, maintain confidentiality, act with integrity, and communicate information in a fair and credible manner.

The IMA provides a "road map" for resolving ethical conflicts. It suggests that an employee follow the company's policies on how to resolve such conflicts. If the conflict remains unresolved, an employee should contact the next level of management (such as the immediate supervisor) who is not involved in the ethical conflict.

Point: The Sarbanes-Oxley Act requires each issuer of securities to disclose whether it has adopted a code of ethics for its senior officers and the content of that code.

■ Decision Ethics

Production Manager   Three friends go to a restaurant. David, a self-employed entrepreneur, says, "I'll pay and deduct it as a business expense." Denise, a salesperson, takes the check and says, "I'll put this on my company's credit card. It won't cost us anything." Derek, a factory manager, laughs and says, "Neither of you understands. I'll use my company's credit card and call it overhead on a cost-plus contract with a client." (*A cost-plus contract means the company receives its costs plus a percent of those costs.*) Adds Derek, "That way, my company pays for dinner *and* makes a profit." Who should pay the bill? Why? ■   *Answer:* All three friends want to pay the bill with someone else's money. David is using money belonging to the tax authorities, Denise is taking money from her company, and Derek is defrauding the client. To prevent such practices, companies have internal controls. Some entertainment expenses are justifiable and even encouraged. For example, the tax law allows certain deductions for entertainment that has a business purpose. Corporate policies sometimes allow and encourage reimbursable spending for social activities, and contracts can include entertainment as an allowable cost. Nevertheless, without further details, this bill should be paid from personal accounts.

Careers in Managerial Accounting

Managerial accountants are highly regarded and in high demand. Managerial accountants must have strong communication skills, understand how businesses work, and be team players. They must be able to analyze information and think critically, and they are often considered to be important business advisors.

Point: Managerial accounting knowledge is useful for all of us. For example, marketers use managerial accounting data to decide which products to promote and to evaluate sales force performance.

Exhibit 1.4 shows estimated annual salaries from recent surveys. Salary variation depends on management level, company size, geographic location, professional designation, experience, and other factors. Employees with the Certified Management Accountant (CMA) or Certified Financial Manager (CFM) certifications typically earn higher salaries than those without.

Management Level	Title	Annual Salary
Top level	Chief financial officer (CFO)	$290,000
	Controller/Treasurer	180,000
Senior management	Division controller	130,000
	General manager	105,000
Middle management	Financial analyst	85,000
	Senior accountant	85,000
Entry level	Staff accountant	60,000

EXHIBIT 1.4

Average Annual Salaries for Selected Management Levels

Sources include: AICPA.org, Kforce.com, Abbott-Langer.com, and IMA Salary Survey.

NEED-TO-KNOW **1-1**

Managerial Accounting
Basics

C1

Following are aspects of accounting information. Classify each as pertaining more to financial accounting or to managerial accounting.

1. Primary users are external
2. Includes more nonmonetary information
3. Focuses more on the future
4. Uses many estimates and projections

5. Controlled by GAAP
6. Used in managers' planning decisions
7. Focuses on the whole organization
8. Not constrained by GAAP

Solution

	Financial	Managerial
1. Primary users are external	X	
2. Includes more nonmonetary information		X
3. Focuses more on the future		X
4. Uses many estimates and projections.		X
5. Controlled by GAAP.	X	
6. Used in managers' planning decisions		X
7. Focuses on the whole organization.	X	
8. Not constrained by GAAP		X

Do More: QS 1-1, E 1-1

MANAGERIAL COST CONCEPTS

C2

Describe accounting
concepts useful in
classifying costs.

Because managers use costs for many different purposes, organizations classify costs in different ways. This section explains three common ways to classify costs and links them to managerial decisions. We illustrate these cost classifications with Rocky Mountain Bikes, a manufacturer of bicycles.

Types of Cost Classifications

Fixed versus Variable   A cost can be classified by how it behaves with changes in the volume of activity.

- **Fixed costs** do not change with changes in the volume of activity (within a range of activity known as an activity's *relevant range*). For example, straight-line depreciation on equipment is a fixed cost.
- **Variable costs** change in proportion to changes in the volume of activity. Sales commissions computed as a percent of sales revenue are variable costs.

Additional examples of fixed and variable costs for a bike manufacturer are provided in Exhibit 1.5. Classifying costs as fixed or variable helps in cost-volume-profit analyses and short-term decision making.

EXHIBIT 1.5

Fixed and Variable Costs

Fixed Cost: Rent for Rocky Mountain Bikes'
building is $22,000, and it doesn't change
with the number of bikes produced.

Variable Cost: Cost of bicycle tires is
variable with the number of bikes
produced—this cost is $15 per pair.

Direct versus Indirect   A cost is often traced to a **cost object,** which is a product, process, department, or customer to which costs are assigned.

- **Direct costs** are traceable to a single cost object.
- **Indirect costs** cannot be easily and cost-beneficially traced to a single cost object.

Assuming the cost object is a bicycle, Rocky Mountain Bikes will identify the costs that can be directly traced to bicycles. The direct costs traceable to a bicycle include direct material and direct labor costs used in its production. Such direct costs include wheels, brakes, chains, and seat, plus the wages and benefits of the employees who work directly on making the bike.

What are indirect costs associated with bicycles? One example is the salary of the supervisor. She monitors the production process and other factory activities, but she does not actually make bikes. Thus, her salary cannot be directly traced to bikes. Likewise, depreciation (other than the units-of-production method) on manufacturing warehouses cannot be traced to individual bikes. Another example is a maintenance department that provides services to two or more departments of a company making bicycles and strollers. If the cost object is the bicycle, the wages of the maintenance department employees who clean the factory area are indirect costs. Exhibit 1.6 identifies examples of direct and indirect costs when the cost object is a bicycle.

EXHIBIT 1.6

Direct and Indirect Costs for a Bicycle

Direct Costs (for bicycle)

- Tires
- Seats
- Handlebars
- Cables
- Bike maker wages
- Frames
- Chains
- Brakes
- Pedals
- Bike maker benefits

Indirect Costs (for bicycle)

- Factory accounting
- Factory administration
- Factory rent
- Factory manager's salary
- Factory light and heat
- Factory intranet
- Insurance on factory
- Factory equipment depreciation*

* For all depreciation methods other than units-of-production.

■ **Decision** Maker ⬤━━━━━━━━━━━━━━━━━━━━━━━━━━━━━━ ♛

Entrepreneur You wish to trace as many of your assembly department's direct costs as possible. You can trace 90% of them in an economical manner. To trace the other 10%, you need sophisticated and costly accounting software. Do you purchase this software? ■ *Answer:* Tracing all costs directly to cost objects is always desirable, but you need to be able to do so in an economically feasible manner. In this case, you are able to trace 90% of the assembly department's direct costs. It may not be economical to spend more money on a new software to trace the final 10% of costs. You need to make a cost-benefit trade-off. If the software offers benefits beyond tracing the remaining 10% of the assembly department's costs, your decision should consider this.

Product versus Period Costs

- **Product costs** are those costs necessary to create a product and consist of: direct materials, direct labor, and factory overhead. Overhead refers to production costs other than direct materials and direct labor. Product costs are capitalized as inventory during and after completion of products; they are recorded as cost of goods sold when those products are sold.
- **Period costs** are nonproduction costs and are usually associated more with activities linked to a time period than with completed products. Common examples of period costs include salaries of the sales staff, wages of maintenance workers, advertising expenses, and depreciation on office furniture and equipment. Period costs are expensed in the period when incurred either as selling expenses or as general and administrative expenses.

Period costs are expensed when incurred and reported on the income statement. Product costs are capitalized as inventory on the balance sheet until that inventory is sold. An ability to understand and identify product costs and period costs is crucial to using and interpreting a *schedule of cost of goods manufactured,* described later in this chapter.

C3

Define product and period costs and explain how they impact financial statements.

EXHIBIT 1.7

Period and Product Costs in Financial Statements

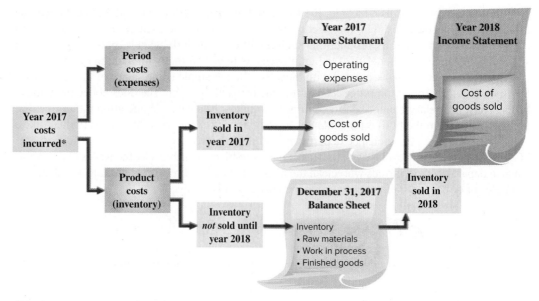

* This diagram excludes costs to acquire assets other than inventory.

Exhibit 1.7 shows the different effects of product and period costs. Period costs flow directly to the current income statement as expenses. They are not reported as assets. Product costs are first assigned to inventory. Their final treatment depends on when inventory is sold or disposed of. Product costs assigned to finished goods that are sold in year 2017 are reported on the 2017 income statement as cost of goods sold. Product costs assigned to unsold inventory are carried forward on the balance sheet at the end of year 2017. If this inventory is sold in year 2018, product costs assigned to it are reported as cost of goods sold in that year's income statement.

Exhibit 1.8 summarizes typical managerial decisions for common cost classifications.

EXHIBIT 1.8

Summary of Cost Classifications and Example Managerial Decisions

Costs Classified As	Example Managerial Decision
Variable or Fixed.............	How many units must we sell to break even?
	What will profit be if we raise selling price?
	Should we add a new line of business?
Direct or Indirect.............	How well did our departments perform?
Product or Period	What is the cost of our inventory?
	Are selling expenses too high?

Identification of Cost Classifications

It is important to understand that a cost can be classified using any one (or combination) of the three different means described here. Understanding how to classify costs in several different ways enables managers to use cost information for a variety of decisions. Factory rent, for instance, is classified as a *product* cost; it is also *fixed* with respect to the number of units produced, and it is *indirect* with respect to the product. Potential multiple classifications are shown in Exhibit 1.9

EXHIBIT 1.9

Examples of Multiple Cost Classifications

Cost Item	Fixed or Variable	Direct or Indirect	Product or Period
Bicycle tires and wheels.....................	Variable	Direct	Product
Wages of assembly worker*	Variable	Direct	Product
Advertising	Fixed	Indirect	Period
Production manager's salary..................	Fixed	Indirect	Product
Office depreciation........................	Fixed	Indirect	Period
Factory depreciation (straight-line)	Fixed	Indirect	Product
Oil and grease applied to gears/chains**	Variable	Indirect	Product
Sales commissions........................	Variable	Indirect	Period

*In some cases wages can be classified as fixed costs. For example, union contracts might limit an employer's ability to adjust its labor force in response to changes in demand. In this book, unless told otherwise, assume that factory wages are variable costs.

**Oil and grease are indirect costs as it is not practical to track how much of each is applied to each bike.

using different cost items incurred in manufacturing mountain bikes. The finished bike is the cost object.

Cost Concepts for Service Companies

The cost concepts described also apply to service organizations. For example, consider **Southwest Airlines**, and assume the cost object is a flight. The airline's cost of beverages for passengers is a variable cost based on number of flights. The monthly cost of leasing an aircraft is fixed with respect to number of flights. We can trace a flight crew's salary to a specific flight, whereas we likely cannot trace wages for the ground crew to a specific flight. Classification as product versus period costs is not relevant to service companies because services are not inventoried. Instead, costs incurred by a service firm are expensed in the reporting period when incurred.

To be effective, managers in service companies must understand and apply cost concepts. For example, an airline manager must often decide between canceling or rerouting flights. The manager must be able to estimate costs saved by canceling a flight versus rerouting. Knowledge of fixed costs is equally important. We explain more about the cost requirements for these and other managerial decisions later in this book.

© Justin Sullivan/Getty Images

Service Costs

- Beverages and snacks
- Cleaning fees
- Pilot and copilot salaries
- Attendant salaries
- Fuel and oil costs
- Travel agent fees
- Ground crew salaries

Following are selected costs of a company that manufactures computer chips. Classify each as either a product cost or a period cost. Then classify each of the product costs as direct material, direct labor, or overhead.

NEED-TO-KNOW 1-2

Cost Classification

C2   C3

1. Plastic boards used to mount chips
2. Advertising costs
3. Factory maintenance workers' salaries
4. Real estate taxes paid on the sales office

5. Real estate taxes paid on the factory
6. Factory supervisor salary
7. Depreciation on factory equipment
8. Assembly worker hourly pay to make chips

Solution

	Product Costs			Period Cost
	Direct Material	Direct Labor	Overhead	
1. Plastic boards used to mount chips	X			
2. Advertising costs........................				X
3. Factory maintenance workers' salaries.......			X	
4. Real estate taxes paid on the sales office.....				X
5. Real estate taxes paid on the factory.........			X	
6. Factory supervisor salary..................			X	
7. Depreciation on factory equipment..........			X	
8. Assembly worker hourly pay to make chips ...		X		

Do More: QS 1-4, QS 1-5, E 1-5

REPORTING OF COSTS

Companies with manufacturing activities differ from both merchandising and service companies. The main difference between merchandising and manufacturing companies is that merchandisers buy goods ready for sale while manufacturers produce goods from materials and labor. **Amazon** is an example of a merchandising company. It buys and sells goods without physically changing them. **Adidas** is primarily a manufacturer of shoes, apparel, and accessories. It purchases materials such as leather, cloth, dye, plastic, rubber, glue, and laces and then uses employees' labor to convert these materials to products. **Southwest Airlines** is a service company that transports people and items. Some companies have several types of activities. For example, **Best Buy** is a merchandiser that also provides services via its Geek Squad.

Manufacturing companies like **Dell**, **PepsiCo**, and **Intel** separate their costs into manufacturing and nonmanufacturing costs. We discuss the reporting of activities for manufacturing, merchandising, and service companies. As these types of organizations have different kinds of costs and they classify costs in different ways, their accounting reports differ in some respects.

Manufacturing Costs

Direct Materials
Direct materials are tangible components of a finished product. **Direct material costs** are the expenditures for direct materials that are separately and readily traced through the manufacturing process to finished goods. Examples of direct materials in manufacturing a mountain bike include its tires, seat, frame, pedals, brakes, cables, gears, and handlebars. The pie chart here shows that direct materials make up about 45% of manufacturing costs in today's products, but this amount varies across products; for example, direct materials are estimated to comprise almost 98% of the cost of an **Apple** iPhone 6S.

Typical Manufacturing Costs in Today's Products

Direct labor
15%

Direct materials
45%

Factory overhead
40%

Direct Labor
Direct labor refers to the efforts of employees who physically convert materials to finished product. **Direct labor costs** are the wages and salaries for direct labor that are separately and readily traced through the manufacturing process to finished goods. Examples of direct labor in manufacturing a mountain bike include operators directly involved in converting raw materials into finished products (welding, painting, forming) and assembly workers who attach materials such as tires, seats, pedals, and brakes.

Factory Overhead
Factory overhead, also called *manufacturing overhead,* consists of all manufacturing costs that are not direct materials or direct labor. **Factory overhead costs** cannot be separately or readily traced to finished goods. Factory overhead costs include maintenance of the mountain bike factory, supervision of its employees, repairing manufacturing equipment, factory utilities (water, gas, electricity), factory manager's salary, factory rent, depreciation on factory buildings and equipment, factory insurance, property taxes on factory buildings and equipment, and factory accounting and legal services. All factory overhead costs are considered indirect costs. These costs include indirect materials, indirect labor, and other costs not directly traceable to the product.

- **Indirect materials** are components used in manufacturing the product, but they are *not* clearly identified with specific product units. Direct materials are often classified as indirect materials when their costs are low. Examples include screws and nuts used in assembling mountain bikes, and staples and glue used in manufacturing shoes. Applying the *materiality principle,* it is not cost-beneficial to trace costs of each of these materials to individual products.

- **Indirect labor** are workers who assist or supervise in manufacturing the product, but they are *not* clearly identified with specific product units. **Indirect labor costs** refer to the costs of workers who assist in or supervise manufacturing. Examples include costs for employees who maintain manufacturing equipment and salaries of production supervisors. Those workers do not assemble products, though they are indirectly related to production. Overtime premiums paid to direct laborers are also included in overhead because overtime is due to delays, interruptions, or constraints not necessarily identifiable to a specific product or batches of product.

Nonmanufacturing Costs

Factory overhead does *not* include selling and administrative expenses because they are not incurred in manufacturing products. These expenses are *period costs,* and they are recorded as expenses on the income statement when incurred. For a manufacturing company, such costs are also called *nonmanufacturing costs.* Examples of nonmanufacturing costs include office worker salaries, depreciation on office equipment, and advertising expenses.

Prime and Conversion Costs

We can classify product costs into prime or conversion costs. Direct materials costs and direct labor costs are **prime costs**—expenditures directly associated with the manufacture of finished goods. Direct labor costs and overhead costs are **conversion costs**—expenditures incurred in the process of converting raw materials to finished goods. Direct labor costs are considered *both* prime costs and conversion costs. Exhibit 1.10 conveys the relation between prime and conversion costs and their components of direct material, direct labor, and factory overhead. Classification into conversion costs is useful for process costing, as we show in a later chapter.

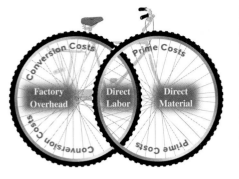

EXHIBIT 1.10

Prime and Conversion Costs and Their Makeup

Prime costs =
Direct materials + Direct labor.

Conversion costs =
Direct labor + Factory overhead.

Costs and the Balance Sheet

Manufacturers have three inventories instead of the single inventory that merchandisers carry. The three inventories are raw materials, work in process, and finished goods.

C4

Explain how balance sheets and income statements for manufacturing, merchandising, and service companies differ.

Raw Materials Inventory   **Raw materials inventory** is the goods a company acquires to use in making products. Companies use raw materials in two ways: directly and indirectly. Raw materials that are possible and practical to trace to a product are called *direct materials;* they are included in raw materials inventory. Raw materials that are either impossible or impractical to trace to a product are classified as indirect materials (such as solder used for welding); they often come from factory supplies or raw materials inventory.

Work in Process Inventory   **Work in process inventory,** also called *goods in process inventory,* consists of products in the process of being manufactured but not yet complete. The amount of work in process inventory depends on the type of production process. For example, work in process inventory is less for a computer maker such as **Dell** than for an airplane maker such as **Boeing**.

© Marco Prosch/Getty Images

Finished Goods Inventory   **Finished goods inventory,** which consists of completed products ready for sale, is similar to merchandise inventory owned by a merchandising company.

Balance Sheets for Manufacturers, Merchandisers, and Servicers   The current assets section of the balance sheet is different for merchandising and service companies as compared to manufacturing companies. A merchandiser reports only merchandise inventory rather than the three types of inventory reported by a manufacturer. A service company's balance sheet does not have any inventory held for sale. Exhibit 1.11 shows the current assets

EXHIBIT 1.11

Balance Sheets for Manufacturer, Merchandiser, and Service Provider

ROCKY MOUNTAIN BIKES Balance Sheet (partial) December 31, 2017	
Assets	
Current assets	
Cash	$11,000
Accounts receivable, net	30,150
Raw materials inventory	9,000
Work in process inventory	7,500
Finished goods inventory	10,300
Factory supplies	350
Prepaid insurance	300
Total current assets	$68,600

TELE-MART (Merchandiser) Balance Sheet (partial) December 31, 2017	
Assets	
Current assets	
Cash	$11,000
Accounts receivable, net	30,150
Merchandise inventory	21,000
Supplies	350
Prepaid insurance	300
Total current assets	$62,800

NORTHEAST AIR (Service Provider) Balance Sheet (partial) December 31, 2017	
Assets	
Current assets	
Cash	$11,000
Accounts receivable, net	30,150
Supplies	350
Prepaid insurance	300
Total current assets	$41,800

section of the balance sheet for a manufacturer, a merchandiser, and a service company. The manufacturer, Rocky Mountain Bikes, shows three different inventories. The merchandiser, Tele-Mart, shows one inventory, and the service provider, Northeast Air, shows no inventory.

Manufacturers often own unique plant assets such as small tools, factory buildings, factory equipment, and patents to manufacture products. Merchandisers and service providers typically own plant assets, including buildings, delivery vehicles, and airplanes.

Costs and the Income Statement

P1

Compute cost of goods sold for a manufacturer and for a merchandiser.

The main difference between the income statement of a manufacturer and that of a merchandiser involves the items making up cost of goods sold. In this section, we look at how manufacturers and merchandisers determine and report cost of goods sold.

Cost of Goods Sold   Exhibit 1.12 compares the components of cost of goods sold for a merchandiser with those for a manufacturer.

- *Merchandisers* add cost of goods purchased to beginning merchandise inventory and then subtract ending merchandise inventory to get cost of goods sold.
- *Manufacturers* add cost of goods manufactured to beginning finished goods inventory and then subtract ending finished goods inventory to get cost of goods sold.

EXHIBIT 1.12

Cost of Goods Sold Computation

In computing cost of goods sold, a merchandiser uses *merchandise* inventory, whereas a manufacturer uses *finished goods* inventory. A manufacturer's inventories of raw materials and work in process are not included in finished goods because they are not available for sale. A manufacturer also shows cost of goods *manufactured* instead of cost of goods *purchased*. This difference occurs because a manufacturer produces its goods instead of purchasing them ready for sale. The Cost of Goods Sold sections for both a merchandiser (Tele-Mart) and a manufacturer (Rocky Mountain Bikes) are shown in Exhibit 1.13 to highlight these differences. The remaining income statement sections are similar for merchandisers and manufacturers.

EXHIBIT 1.13

Cost of Goods Sold for a Merchandiser and Manufacturer

Merchandising Company (Tele-Mart)		Manufacturing Company (Rocky Mtn. Bikes)	
Cost of goods sold		Cost of goods sold	
Beginning *merchandise* inventory	$ 14,200	**Beginning *finished goods* inventory**......	$ 11,200
Cost of merchandise *purchased*	234,150	**Cost of goods *manufactured***	170,500
Goods available for sale	248,350	Goods available for sale	181,700
Less ending *merchandise* inventory	12,100	**Less ending *finished goods* inventory**	10,300
Cost of goods sold	$236,250	Cost of goods sold	$171,400

*Cost of goods manufactured is in the income statement of Exhibit 1.14.

A merchandiser's cost of goods purchased is the cost of buying products to be sold. A manufacturer's cost of goods manufactured is the sum of direct materials, direct labor, and factory overhead costs incurred in making products.

Income Statement for Service Company   Because a service provider does not make or buy inventory to be sold, it does not report cost of goods manufactured or cost of goods sold. Instead, its operating expenses include all of the costs it incurs in providing its service. Southwest Airlines, for example, reports large operating expenses for employee pay and benefits, fuel and oil, and depreciation. Southwest's operating expenses also include selling expenses and general and administrative expenses.

Income Statements for Manufacturers, Merchandisers, and Servicers
Exhibit 1.14 shows the income statement for Rocky Mountain Bikes. Its operating expenses include selling expenses and general and administrative expenses, which include salaries for those business functions as well as depreciation for related equipment. Operating expenses do not include manufacturing costs such as factory workers' wages and depreciation of production equip-

EXHIBIT 1.14

Income Statements for Manufacturer, Merchandiser, and Service Provider

ROCKY MOUNTAIN BIKES (Manufacturer)
Income Statement
For Year Ended December 31, 2017

Sales		$310,000
Cost of goods sold		
Finished goods inventory, Dec. 31, 2016	$ 11,200	
Cost of goods manufactured (from Exhibit 1.13)	170,500	
Goods available for sale	181,700	
Less finished goods inventory, Dec. 31, 2017	10,300	
Cost of goods sold		171,400
Gross profit		138,600
Operating expenses		
Selling expenses	38,150	
General and administrative expenses	21,750	
Total operating expenses		59,900
Income before income taxes		78,700
Income tax expense		32,600
Net income		$ 46,100

TELE-MART (Merchandiser)
Income Statement
For Year Ended December 31, 2017

Sales		$345,000
Cost of goods sold		
Merchandise inventory, Dec. 31, 2016	$ 14,200	
Cost of merchandise purchased	234,150	
Goods available for sale	248,350	
Merchandise inventory, Dec. 31, 2017	12,100	
Cost of goods sold		236,250
Gross profit		108,750
Operating expenses		
Selling expenses	43,150	
General and administrative expenses	26,750	
Total operating expenses		69,900
Income before income taxes		38,850
Income tax expense		16,084
Net income		$ 22,766

NORTHEAST AIR (Service Provider)
Income Statement
For Year Ended December 31, 2017

Service revenue		$425,000
Operating expenses		
Salaries and wages	$127,750	
Fuel and oil	159,375	
Maintenance and repairs	29,750	
Rent	42,500	
Depreciation	14,000	
General and admin. expenses	20,000	
Total operating expenses		393,375
Income before income taxes		31,625
Income tax expense		13,100
Net income		$ 18,525

ment and the factory buildings. These manufacturing costs are reported as part of cost of goods manufactured and included in cost of goods sold. This exhibit also shows the income statement for Tele-Mart (merchandiser) and Northeast Air (service provider). Tele-Mart reports *cost of merchandise purchased* instead of cost of goods manufactured. Tele-Mart reports its operating expenses like those of the manufacturing company. The income statement for Northeast Air shows only operating expenses.

NEED-TO-KNOW **1-3**

Costs and Inventories for Different Businesses

C4

Indicate whether the following financial statement items apply to a manufacturer, a merchandiser, or a service provider. Some items apply to more than one type of organization.

_____ **1.** Merchandise inventory   _____ **5.** Operating expenses
_____ **2.** Finished goods inventory   _____ **6.** Cost of goods manufactured
_____ **3.** Cost of goods sold   _____ **7.** Supplies inventory
_____ **4.** Selling expenses   _____ **8.** Raw materials inventory

Solution

	Manufacturer	Merchandiser	Service Provider
1. Merchandise inventory		✓	
2. Finished goods inventory	✓		
3. Cost of goods sold	✓	✓	
4. Selling expenses	✓	✓	✓
5. Operating expenses	✓	✓	✓
6. Cost of goods manufactured	✓		
7. Supplies inventory	✓	✓	✓
8. Raw materials inventory	✓		

Do More: E 1-7

COST FLOW AND COST OF GOODS MANUFACTURED

Flow of Manufacturing Activities

C5 _____

Explain manufacturing activities and the flow of manufacturing costs.

In addition to income statements and balance sheets, manufacturing companies prepare additional reports for planning and control. To understand these reports, we must know the flow of manufacturing activities and costs. Exhibit 1.15 shows the flow of manufacturing activities and their cost flows. Looking across the top row, the activities flow consists of *materials activity* followed by *production activity* followed by *sales activity*. The boxes below those activities show the costs for each activity and how costs flow across the three activities.

Materials Activity   The left side of Exhibit 1.15 shows the flow of raw materials. Manufacturers usually start a period with some beginning raw materials inventory left over from the previous period. The company then acquires additional raw materials in the current period. Adding these purchases to beginning inventory gives *total raw materials available for use* in production. These raw materials are then either used in production in the current period or remain in raw materials inventory at the end of the period for use in future periods.

Production Activity   The middle section of Exhibit 1.15 describes production activity. Four factors come together in production: beginning work in process inventory, raw materials, direct labor, and overhead. *Beginning work in process inventory* consists of partially complete products from the previous period. To the beginning work in process inventory are added the costs of direct materials, direct labor, and overhead.

The production activity that takes place in the period results in products that are either finished or not finished at the end of the period. The cost of finished products makes up the **cost of goods manufactured** for the current period. The cost of goods manufactured is the total cost of making and finishing products in the period. That amount is included on the income statement in the computation of cost of goods sold, as we showed in Exhibit 1.14. Unfinished products are

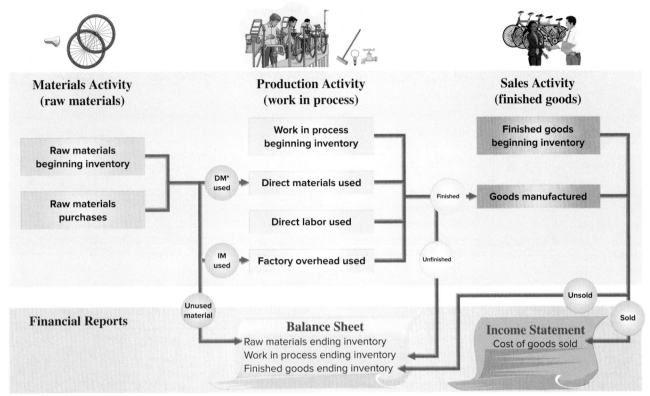

* DM = direct materials, IM = indirect materials.

EXHIBIT 1.15

Activities and Cost Flows in Manufacturing

identified as *ending work in process inventory*. The cost of unfinished products consists of raw materials, direct labor, and factory overhead, and is reported on the current period's balance sheet. The costs of both finished goods manufactured and work in process are *product costs.*

Sales Activity   The far right side of Exhibit 1.15 shows what happens to the finished goods: The company adds the cost of the beginning inventory of finished goods and the cost of the newly completed units (goods manufactured). Together, they make up *total finished goods available for sale* in the current period. As they are sold, the cost of finished products sold is reported on the income statement as cost of goods sold. The cost of any finished products not sold in the period is reported as a current asset, *finished goods inventory,* on the current period's balance sheet.

Schedule of Cost of Goods Manufactured

Managers of manufacturing firms analyze product costs in detail. Those managers aim to make better decisions about materials, labor, and overhead to reduce the cost of goods manufactured and improve income. A company's manufacturing activities are described in a report called a **schedule of cost of goods manufactured** (also called a *manufacturing statement* or a *statement of cost of goods manufactured*). The schedule of cost of goods manufactured summarizes the types and amounts of costs incurred in the manufacturing process. Exhibit 1.16 shows the schedule of cost of goods manufactured for Rocky Mountain Bikes. The schedule is divided into four parts: *direct materials, direct labor, overhead,* and *computation of cost of goods manufactured.*

① **Compute direct materials used.** Add the beginning raw materials inventory of $8,000 to the current period's purchases of $86,500. This yields $94,500 of total raw materials available for use. A physical count of inventory shows $9,000 of ending raw materials inventory. If $94,500 of materials were available for use, and $9,000 of materials remains in inventory, then $85,500 of materials were used in the period.

P2

Prepare a schedule of cost of goods manufactured and explain its purpose and links to financial statements.

Raw Materials Inventory		
Beg. bal.	8,000	
Purch.	86,500	
		Mtls. used 85,500
End. bal.	9,000	

EXHIBIT 1.16

Schedule of Cost of Goods
Manufactured

ROCKY MOUNTAIN BIKES		
Schedule of Cost of Goods Manufactured		
For Year Ended December 31, 2017		

①	**Direct materials**		
	Raw materials inventory, Dec. 31, 2016	$ 8,000	
	Raw materials purchases.	86,500	
	Raw materials available for use	94,500	
	Less raw materials inventory, Dec. 31, 2017	9,000	
	Direct materials used.		$ 85,500
②	**Direct labor**		60,000
③	**Factory overhead**		
	Indirect labor	9,000	
	Factory supervision	6,000	
	Factory utilities.	2,600	
	Repairs—Factory equipment	2,500	
	Property taxes—Factory building	1,900	
	Factory supplies used (indirect materials)	600	
	Factory insurance expired	1,100	
	Depreciation expense—Factory assets	5,500	
	Amortization expense—Patents (on factory equipment)	800	
	Total factory overhead		30,000
④	Total manufacturing costs		$175,500
	Add work in process inventory, Dec. 31, 2016		2,500
	Total cost of work in process.		178,000
	Less work in process inventory, Dec. 31, 2017		7,500
	Cost of goods manufactured.		$170,500

② **Compute direct labor costs used.** Rocky Mountain Bikes had total direct labor costs of $60,000 for the period. This amount includes payroll taxes and fringe benefits.

③ **Compute total factory overhead costs used.** The statement lists each important factory overhead item and its cost. All of these costs are *indirectly* related to manufacturing activities. (Period expenses, such as selling expenses and other costs not related to manufacturing activities, are *not* reported on this statement.) Total factory overhead cost is $30,000. Some companies report only *total* factory overhead on the schedule of cost of goods manufactured and attach a separate schedule listing individual overhead costs.

④ **Compute cost of goods manufactured.** Total manufacturing costs for the period are $175,500 ($85,500 + $60,000 + $30,000), the sum of direct materials, direct labor, and overhead costs incurred. This amount is added to beginning work in process inventory, which gives the total work in process during the period of $178,000 ($175,500 + $2,500). A physical count shows $7,500 of work in process inventory remains at the end of the period. We then compute the current period's cost of goods manufactured of $170,500 by taking the $178,000 total work in process and subtracting the $7,500 cost of ending work in process inventory. The cost of goods manufactured amount is also called *net cost of goods manufactured* or *cost of goods completed.*

Work in Process Inventory			
Beg. bal.	2,500		
Mfg. costs	175,500		
		COG Mfg.	170,500
End. bal.	7,500		

Using the Schedule of Cost of Goods Manufactured   Management uses information in the schedule of cost of goods manufactured to plan and control manufacturing activities. To provide timely information for decision making, the schedule is often prepared monthly, weekly, or even daily. In anticipation of release of its much-hyped tablet, **Microsoft** grew its inventory of critical components and its finished goods inventory. The schedule of cost of goods manufactured contains information useful to external users, but it is rarely published because managers view this information as proprietary and harmful if released to competitors.

© Joe Amon/The Denver Post via
Getty Images

Estimating Cost per Unit Managers use the schedule of cost of goods manufactured to make rough estimates of per unit costs. For example, if Rocky Mountain Bikes makes 1,000 bikes during the year, the average manufacturing cost per unit is $170.50 (computed as $170,500/1,000). Average cost per unit is not always an appropriate cost for managerial decisions. We show in the next two chapters how to compute more reliable unit costs for managerial decisions.

Manufacturing Cost Flows across Accounting Reports Cost information is also used to complete financial statements at the end of an accounting period. Exhibit 1.17 summarizes how product costs flow through the accounting system. Direct materials, direct labor, and overhead costs are summarized in the schedule of cost of goods manufactured; then the amount of cost of goods manufactured from that statement is used to compute cost of goods sold on the income statement. Physical counts determine the dollar amounts of ending raw materials inventory and work in process inventory, and those amounts are included on the end-of-period balance sheet. (*Note:* This exhibit shows only partial reports.)

EXHIBIT 1.17

Manufacturing Cost Flows across Accounting Reports

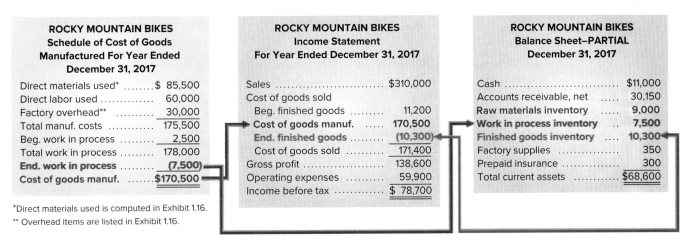

ROCKY MOUNTAIN BIKES Schedule of Cost of Goods Manufactured For Year Ended December 31, 2017	
Direct materials used*	$ 85,500
Direct labor used	60,000
Factory overhead**	30,000
Total manuf. costs	175,500
Beg. work in process	2,500
Total work in process	178,000
End. work in process	(7,500)
Cost of goods manuf.	$170,500

*Direct materials used is computed in Exhibit 1.16.
** Overhead items are listed in Exhibit 1.16.

ROCKY MOUNTAIN BIKES Income Statement For Year Ended December 31, 2017	
Sales	$310,000
Cost of goods sold	
Beg. finished goods	11,200
Cost of goods manuf.	170,500
End. finished goods	(10,300)
Cost of goods sold	171,400
Gross profit	138,600
Operating expenses	59,900
Income before tax	$ 78,700

ROCKY MOUNTAIN BIKES Balance Sheet–PARTIAL December 31, 2017	
Cash	$11,000
Accounts receivable, net	30,150
Raw materials inventory	9,000
Work in process inventory	7,500
Finished goods inventory	10,300
Factory supplies	350
Prepaid insurance	300
Total current assets	$68,600

Part A: Compute the following three cost measures using the information below.

_____ **1.** Cost of materials used
_____ **2.** Cost of goods manufactured
_____ **3.** Cost of goods sold

NEED-TO-KNOW 1-4

Key Cost Measures

P1   P2

Beginning raw materials inventory	$15,500	Ending raw materials inventory	$10,600
Beginning work in process inventory	29,000	Ending work in process inventory	44,000
Beginning finished goods inventory	24,000	Ending finished goods inventory	37,400
Raw materials purchased	66,000	Direct labor used	38,000
Total factory overhead used	80,000		

Solution

1. $70,900   **2.** $173,900   **3.** $160,500

Raw Materials Inventory			
Begin. inv.	15,500		
Purchases	66,000		
Avail. for use	81,500		
		Matls used	70,900
End. inv.	10,600		

Work in Process Inventory			
Begin. inv.	29,000		
Matls used	70,900		
Labor	38,000		
Overhead	80,000		
	217,900		
		Cost of goods mfg	173,900
End. inv.	44,000		

Finished Goods Inventory			
Begin. inv.	24,000		
Cost of goods	173,900		
Avail. for sale	197,900		
		Cost of goods sold	160,500
End. inv.	37,400		

Part B: Refer to the nine cost items listed above with their dollar amounts and indicate in which section of the schedule of cost of goods manufactured it appears as shown in Exhibit 1.16. Section *1* refers to direct materials; *2* refers to direct labor; *3* refers to factory overhead; and *4* refers to computation of cost of goods manufactured. Write *X* for any item that does not appear on the schedule of cost of goods manufactured.

Solution

_1_	Beginning raw materials inventory		_1_	Ending raw materials inventory
_4_	Beginning work in process inventory		_4_	Ending work in process inventory
_X_	Beginning finished goods inventory		_X_	Ending finished goods inventory
_1_	Raw materials purchased		_2_	Direct labor used
_3_	Total factory overhead used			

> Do More: QS 1-8, QS 1-9, QS 1-10, E 1-8, E 1-11

Trends in Managerial Accounting

> **C6**
> Describe trends in managerial accounting.

Tools and techniques of managerial accounting continue to evolve due to changes in the business environment. This section describes some of these changes.

Customer Orientation   There is increased emphasis on *customers* as the most important constituent of a business. Customers expect to derive a certain value for the money they spend to buy products and services. Buyers expect that suppliers provide them the right service (or product) at the right time and the right price. This implies that companies accept the notion of **customer orientation,** which means that managers and employees understand the changing needs and wants of customers and align management and operating practices accordingly.

Global Economy   Our *global economy* expands competitive boundaries and provides customers more choices. The global economy also produces changes in business activities. One notable case that reflects these changes in customer demand and global competition is auto manufacturing. The top three Japanese auto manufacturers (**Honda**, **Nissan**, and **Toyota**) once controlled more than 40% of the U.S. auto market. Customers perceived that Japanese auto

manufacturers provided value not available from other manufacturers. Many European and North American auto manufacturers responded to this challenge and regained much of the lost market share.

E-Commerce   People have become increasingly interconnected via smartphones, text messaging, and other electronic applications. Consumers expect and demand to be able to buy items electronically, whenever and wherever they want. Many businesses allow for online transactions. Online sales make up about 6% of total retail sales. Some companies such as **BucketFeet**, a footwear retailer, only sell online to keep costs lower.

Service Economy   Businesses that provide services, such as telecommunications and health care, constitute an ever-growing part of our economy. Many service companies, such as **Uber**, employ part-time workers. This "gig economy" changes companies' cost structures and the nature of competition. In developed economies, service businesses typically account for over 60% of total economic activity.

Lean Practices   Many companies have adopted the **lean business model,** whose goal is to *eliminate waste* while "satisfying the customer" and "providing a positive return" to the company. This is often paired with continuous improvement. **Continuous improvement** rejects the notions of "good enough" or "acceptable" and challenges employees and managers to continuously experiment with new and improved business practices. This has led companies to adopt

> **Point:** Goals of a TQM process include reduced waste, better inventory control, fewer defects, and continuous improvement. JIT concepts have similar aims.

practices such as total quality management (TQM) and just-in-time (JIT) manufacturing. Continuous improvement underlies both practices; the difference is in the focus.

- **Total quality management** focuses on quality improvement to business activities. Managers and employees seek to uncover waste in business activities, including accounting activities such as payroll and disbursements. To encourage an emphasis on quality, the U.S. Congress established the Malcolm Baldrige National Quality Award (MBNQA). Entrants must conduct a thorough analysis and evaluation of their business using guidelines from the Baldrige committee. **Ritz Carlton Hotel** is a recipient of the Baldrige award in the service category. The company applies a core set of values, collectively called *The Gold Standards,* to improve customer service.

Point: Quality control standards include those developed by the International Organization for Standardization (ISO). To be certified under **ISO 9000 standards,** a company must use a quality control system and document that it achieves the desired quality level.

- **Just-in-time manufacturing** is a system that acquires inventory and produces only when needed. An important aspect of JIT is that companies manufacture products only after they receive an order (a *demand-pull* system) and then deliver the customer's requirements on time. This means that processes must be aligned to eliminate delays and inefficiencies including inferior inputs and outputs. Companies must also establish good communications with their suppliers. On the downside, JIT is more susceptible to disruption than traditional systems. As one example, several **General Motors** plants were temporarily shut down due to a strike at a supplier that provided components *just in time* to the assembly division.

Point: The time between buying raw materials and selling finished goods is called *throughput time.*

Value Chain   The **value chain** refers to the series of activities that add value to a company's products or services. Exhibit 1.18 illustrates a possible value chain for a retail cookie company. Companies can use lean practices across the value chain to increase efficiency and profits.

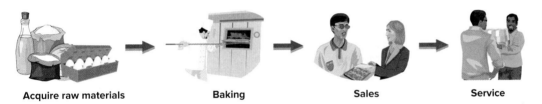

Acquire raw materials   Baking   Sales   Service

EXHIBIT 1.18

Typical Value Chain (cookie retailer)

How Lean Practices Impact the Value Chain   Adopting lean practices can be challenging because systems and procedures that a company follows must be realigned. Managerial accounting has an important role in providing accurate cost and performance information. Developing such a system is important to measuring the "value" provided to customers. The price that customers pay for acquiring goods and services is a key determinant of value. In turn, the costs a company incurs are key determinants of price.

Corporate Social Responsibility   In addition to maximizing shareholder value, corporations must consider the demands of other stakeholders, including employees, suppliers, and society in general. **Corporate social responsibility (CSR)** is a concept that goes beyond following the law. For example, to reduce its impact on the environment, **Three Twins Ice Cream** uses only cups and spoons made from organic ingredients. **United By Blue**, an apparel and jewelry company, removes one pound of trash from waterways for every product sold. Many companies extend the concept of CSR to include sustainability, which considers future generations when making business decisions.

Point: Companies like **Microsoft, Google,** and **Walt Disney,** ranked at the top of large multinational companies in terms of CSR, disclose CSR results on their websites.

Triple Bottom Line   **Triple bottom line** focuses on three measures: financial ("profits"), social ("people"), and environmental ("planet"). Adopting a triple bottom line impacts how businesses report. In response to a growing trend of such reporting, the **Sustainability Accounting Standards Board (SASB)** was established to develop reporting standards for businesses' sustainability activities. Some of the business sectors for which the SASB has developed reporting standards include health care, nonrenewable resources, and renewable resources and alternative energy.

Decision Insight

Balanced Scorecard   The *balanced scorecard* aids continuous improvement by augmenting financial measures with information on the "drivers" (indicators) of future financial performance along four dimensions: **(1)** *financial*—profitability and risk, **(2)** *customer*—value creation and product and service differentiation, **(3)** *internal business processes*—business activities that create customer and owner satisfaction, and **(4)** *learning and growth*—organizational change, innovation, and growth. ∎

SUSTAINABILITY AND ACCOUNTING
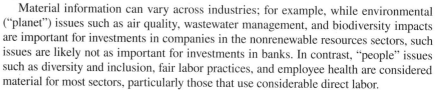

In creating sustainability accounting standards, the Sustainability Accounting Standards Board (SASB) has created reporting guidelines. The SASB considers sustainability information as *material* if its disclosure would affect the views of equity investors on a company's financial condition or operating performance.

Material information can vary across industries; for example, while environmental ("planet") issues such as air quality, wastewater management, and biodiversity impacts are important for investments in companies in the nonrenewable resources sectors, such issues are likely not as important for investments in banks. In contrast, "people" issues such as diversity and inclusion, fair labor practices, and employee health are considered material for most sectors, particularly those that use considerable direct labor.

NatureBox, this chapter's feature company, focuses on sustainability. The company insists on all-natural ingredients in its snack mixes. Founders Gautam Gupta and Ken Chen partner with organizations like **Feeding America** to reduce childhood hunger. Donating one meal for every snack box delivered, the company expects to donate over 1 million meals per year.

"Our company mission is to provide healthier eating choices, and the basic right to have enough food on your plate is fundamental," says NatureBox co-founder and CEO Gautam Gupta. "We're just scratching the surface of what's possible." This is one example of the triple bottom line in action.

Courtesy of NatureBox

Decision Insight

Sustainability Returns   A recent study shows the value of investing in material sustainability issues. Companies with good ratings on material sustainability issues perform better than companies with poor ratings. The chart here shows that high sustainability firms have 4% higher stock returns and almost 7% higher return on sales than low sustainability firms. (Source: hbswk.hbs.edu/item /corporate-sustainability-first-evidence-on-materiality.) ∎

High Sustainability Firms vs. Low Sustainability Firms

Stock return   **+4.05%**

Return on sales   **+6.89%**

0% 2% 4% 6% 8% 10%

  Decision Analysis   **Raw Materials Inventory Turnover and Days' Sales in Raw Materials Inventory**

A1
_____
Assess raw materials inventory management using raw materials inventory turnover and days' sales in raw materials inventory.

Managerial accounting information helps managers perform analyses that are not readily available to external users of accounting information. Inventory management is one example. Using publicly available financial statements, an external user can compute the *inventory turnover* ratio. However, a managerial accountant can go much further.

Raw Materials Inventory Turnover

A manager can assess how effectively a company manages its *raw materials* inventory by computing the **raw materials inventory turnover** ratio as shown in Exhibit 1.19.

EXHIBIT 1.19

Raw Materials Inventory Turnover

> **Raw materials inventory turnover = Raw materials used/Average raw materials inventory**

This ratio reveals how many times a company turns over (uses in production) its raw materials inventory during a period. Generally, a high ratio of raw materials inventory turnover is preferred, as long as raw materials inventory levels are adequate to meet demand. To illustrate, Rocky Mountain Bikes reports direct (raw) materials used of $85,500 for the year, with a beginning raw materials inventory of $8,000 and an ending raw materials inventory of $9,000 (see Exhibit 1.16). Raw materials inventory turnover for Rocky Mountain Bikes for that year is computed as in Exhibit 1.20.

Raw materials inventory turnover = $85,500/[($8,000 + $9,000)/2] = 10.06 (rounded)

EXHIBIT 1.20

Raw Materials Inventory Turnover Computed

Days' Sales in Raw Materials Inventory

To further assess raw materials inventory management, a manager can measure the adequacy of raw materials inventory to meet production demand. **Days' sales in raw materials inventory** reveals how much raw materials inventory is available in terms of the number of days' sales. It is a measure of how long it takes raw materials to be used in production. It is defined and computed for Rocky Mountain Bikes in Exhibit 1.21.

Days' sales in raw materials inventory = (Ending raw materials inventory/Raw materials used) × 365

= ($9,000/$85,500) × 365 = 38.4 days (rounded)

EXHIBIT 1.21

Days' Sales in Raw Materials Inventory Turnover

This computation suggests that it will take 38 days for Rocky Mountain Bikes's raw materials inventory to be used in production. Assuming production needs can be met, companies usually prefer a *lower* number of days' sales in raw materials inventory. Just-in-time manufacturing techniques can be useful in lowering days' sales in raw materials inventory; for example, **Dell** keeps less than seven days of production needs in raw materials inventory for most of its computer components.

"*My boss wants us to appeal to a younger and hipper crowd. So, I'd like to get a tattoo that says-- 'Accounting rules!'*"

Copyright © Jerry King, www.artizans.com

▮ Decision Maker

CFO   Your company regularly reports days' sales in raw materials of 20 days, which is similar to competitors. A manager argues that profit can be increased if the company applies just-in-time principles and cuts it down to 2 days. Do you drop it to 2 days? ▮   *Answer:* Cutting days' sales in raw materials to 2 days *might* increase profits. Having less money tied up in inventory is a positive. However, if the company loses customers over out-of-stock inventory or if production is delayed (with costs), then the increase in profit might be outweighed by the increase in costs.

The following account balances and other information are from SUNN Corporation's accounting records for year-end December 31, 2017. Use this information to prepare (1) a table listing factory overhead costs, (2) a schedule of cost of goods manufactured (show only the total factory overhead cost), and (3) an income statement.

NEED-TO-KNOW 1-5

COMPREHENSIVE

Advertising expense	$ 85,000	Work in process inventory, Dec. 31, 2016	$ 8,000
Amortization expense—Factory patents	16,000	Work in process inventory, Dec. 31, 2017	9,000
Bad debts expense	28,000	Income taxes	53,400
Depreciation expense—Office equipment	37,000	Indirect labor	26,000
Depreciation expense—Factory building	133,000	Interest expense	25,000
Depreciation expense—Factory equipment	78,000	Miscellaneous expense	55,000
Direct labor	250,000	Property taxes on factory equipment	14,000
Factory insurance used up	62,000	Raw materials inventory, Dec. 31, 2016	60,000
Factory supervisor salary	74,000	Raw materials inventory, Dec. 31, 2017	78,000
Factory supplies used	21,000	Raw materials purchases	313,000
Factory utilities	115,000	Repairs expense—Factory equipment	31,000
Finished goods inventory, Dec. 31, 2016	15,000	Salaries expense	150,000
Finished goods inventory, Dec. 31, 2017	12,500	Sales	1,630,000

PLANNING THE SOLUTION

● Analyze the account balances and select those that are part of factory overhead costs.

● Arrange these costs in a table that lists factory overhead costs for the year.

- Analyze the remaining costs and select those related to production activity for the year; selected costs should include the materials and work in process inventories and direct labor.
- Prepare a schedule of cost of goods manufactured for the year showing the calculation of the cost of materials used in production, the cost of direct labor, and the total factory overhead cost. When presenting overhead cost on this statement, report only total overhead cost from the table of overhead costs for the year. Show the costs of beginning and ending work in process inventory to determine cost of goods manufactured.
- Organize the remaining revenue and expense items into the income statement for the year. Combine cost of goods manufactured from the schedule of cost of goods manufactured with the finished goods inventory amounts to compute cost of goods sold for the year.

SOLUTION

SUNN CORPORATION
Factory Overhead Costs
For Year Ended December 31, 2017

Amortization expense—Factory patents	$ 16,000
Depreciation expense—Factory building	133,000
Depreciation expense—Factory equipment	78,000
Factory insurance used up	62,000
Factory supervisor salary	74,000
Factory supplies used	21,000
Factory utilities.................................	115,000
Indirect labor...................................	26,000
Property taxes on factory equipment	14,000
Repairs expense—Factory equipment	31,000
Total factory overhead	$570,000

SUNN CORPORATION
Schedule of Cost of Goods Manufactured
For Year Ended December 31, 2017

Direct materials		
Raw materials inventory, Dec. 31, 2016	$ 60,000	
Raw materials purchase	313,000	
Raw materials available for use	373,000	
Less raw materials inventory, Dec. 31, 2017	78,000	
Direct materials used............................		295,000
Direct labor.....................................		250,000
Factory overhead		570,000
Total manufacturing costs		1,115,000
Add work in process inventory, Dec. 31, 2016		8,000
Total cost of work in process......................		1,123,000
Less work in process inventory, Dec. 31, 2017		9,000
Cost of goods manufactured		$1,114,000

SUNN CORPORATION
Income Statement
For Year Ended December 31, 2017

Sales		$1,630,000
Cost of goods sold		
Finished goods inventory, Dec. 31, 2016..........	$ 15,000	
Cost of goods manufactured	1,114,000	
Goods available for sale	1,129,000	
Less finished goods inventory, Dec. 31, 2017......	12,500	
Cost of goods sold		1,116,500
Gross profit.....................................		513,500
Operating expenses		
Advertising expense	85,000	
Bad debts expense	28,000	
Depreciation expense—Office equipment	37,000	
Interest expense	25,000	
Miscellaneous expense	55,000	
Salaries expense	150,000	
Total operating expenses		380,000
Income before income taxes.....................		133,500
Income taxes....................................		53,400
Net income		$ 80,100

Raw Materials Inventory

12/31/2016	60,000	
Purch.	313,000	
Avail.	373,000	
		Dir. Mtls. Used 295,000
12/31/2017	78,000	

Work in Process Inventory

12/31/2016	8,000	
Dir. Mtls. Used	295,000	
Dir. Labor	250,000	
FOH	570,000	
Avail.	1,123,000	
		COGM 1,114,000
12/31/2017	9,000	

Finished Goods Inventory

12/31/2016	15,000	
COGM	1,114,000	
Avail.	1,129,000	
		COGS 1,116,500
12/31/2017	12,500	

Summary

C1 Explain the purpose and nature of, and the role of ethics in, managerial accounting. The purpose of managerial accounting is to provide useful information to management and other internal decision makers. It does this by collecting, managing, and reporting both monetary and nonmonetary information in a manner useful to internal users. Major characteristics of managerial accounting include (1) focus on internal decision makers, (2) emphasis on planning and control, (3) flexibility, (4) timeliness, (5) reliance on forecasts and estimates, (6) focus on segments and projects, and (7) reporting both monetary and nonmonetary information. Ethics are beliefs that distinguish right from wrong. Ethics can be important in reducing fraud in business operations.

C2 Describe accounting concepts useful in classifying costs. We can classify costs as (1) fixed vs. variable, (2) direct vs. indirect, and (3) product vs. period. A cost can be classified in more than one way, depending on the purpose for which the cost is being determined. These classifications help us understand cost patterns, analyze performance, and plan operations.

C3 Define product and period costs and explain how they impact financial statements. Costs that are capitalized because they are expected to have future value are called *product costs;* costs that are expensed are called *period costs.* This classification is important because it affects the amount of costs expensed in the income statement and the amount of costs assigned to inventory on the balance sheet. Product costs are commonly made up of direct materials, direct labor, and overhead. Period costs include selling and administrative expenses.

C4 Explain how balance sheets and income statements for manufacturing, merchandising, and service companies differ. The main difference is that manufacturers usually carry three inventories on their balance sheets—raw materials, work in process, and finished goods—instead of one inventory that merchandisers carry. Service company balance sheets do not include inventories of items for sale. The main difference between income statements of manufacturers and merchandisers is the items making up cost of goods sold. A merchandiser uses merchandise inventory and the cost of goods purchased to compute cost of goods sold; a manufacturer uses finished goods inventory and the cost of goods manufactured to compute cost of goods sold. A service company's income statement does not include cost of goods sold.

C5 Explain manufacturing activities and the flow of manufacturing costs. Manufacturing activities consist of materials, production, and sales activities. The materials activity consists of the purchase and issuance of materials to production. The production activity consists of converting materials into finished goods. At this stage in the process, the materials, labor, and overhead costs have been incurred and the schedule of cost of goods manufactured is prepared. The sales activity consists of selling some or all of finished goods available for sale. At this stage, the cost of goods sold is determined.

C6 Describe trends in managerial accounting. Important trends in managerial accounting include an increased focus on satisfying customers, the impact of a global economy, and the growing presence of e-commerce and service-based businesses. The lean business model, designed to eliminate waste and satisfy customers, can be useful in responding to recent trends. Concepts such as total quality management, just-in-time production, and the value chain often aid in application of the lean business model. Trends in corporate social responsibility and sustainability activities further change how businesses report information.

A1 Assess raw materials inventory management using raw materials inventory turnover and days' sales in raw materials inventory. A high raw materials inventory turnover suggests a business is more effective in managing its raw materials inventory. We use days' sales in raw materials inventory to assess the likelihood of production being delayed due to inadequate levels of raw materials. We prefer a high raw materials inventory turnover ratio and a small number of days' sales in raw materials inventory, provided that raw materials inventory levels are adequate to keep production steady.

P1 Compute cost of goods sold for a manufacturer and for a merchandiser. A manufacturer adds beginning finished goods inventory to cost of goods manufactured and then subtracts ending finished goods inventory to get cost of goods sold. A merchandiser adds beginning merchandise inventory to cost of goods purchased and then subtracts ending merchandise inventory to get cost of goods sold.

P2 Prepare a schedule of cost of goods manufactured and explain its purpose and links to financial statements. This schedule reports the computation of cost of goods manufactured for the period. It begins by showing the period's costs for direct materials, direct labor, and overhead and then adjusts these numbers for the beginning and ending inventories of the work in process to yield cost of goods manufactured.

Key Terms

Continuous improvement	Customer orientation	Direct materials costs
Control	Days' sales in raw materials inventory	Enterprise risk management (ERM)
Conversion costs	Direct costs	Ethics
Corporate social responsibility (CSR)	Direct labor	Factory overhead
Cost object	Direct labor costs	Factory overhead costs
Cost of goods manufactured	Direct materials	Finished goods inventory

Fixed cost

Indirect costs

Indirect labor

Indirect labor costs

Indirect materials

Institute of Management Accountants (IMA)

Internal control system

ISO 9000 standards

Just-in-time (JIT) manufacturing

Lean business model

Managerial accounting

Period costs

Planning

Prime costs

Product costs

Raw materials inventory

Raw materials inventory turnover

Schedule of cost of goods manufactured

Sustainability Accounting Standards Board (SASB)

Total quality management (TQM)

Triple bottom line

Value chain

Variable cost

Work in process inventory

Multiple Choice Quiz

1. Continuous improvement
   a. Is used to reduce inventory levels.
   b. Is applicable only in service businesses.
   c. Rejects the notion of "good enough."
   d. Is used to reduce ordering costs.
   e. Is applicable only in manufacturing businesses.

2. A direct cost is one that is
   a. Variable with respect to the cost object.
   b. Traceable to the cost object.
   c. Fixed with respect to the cost object.
   d. Allocated to the cost object.
   e. A period cost.

3. Costs that are incurred as part of the manufacturing process, but are not clearly traceable to the specific unit of product or batches of product, are called
   a. Period costs.   **d.** Operating expenses.
   b. Factory overhead.   **e.** Fixed costs.
   c. Variable costs.

4. The three major cost components of manufacturing a product are
   a. Direct materials, direct labor, and factory overhead.
   b. Period costs, product costs, and conversion costs.
   c. Indirect labor, indirect materials, and fixed expenses.
   d. Variable costs, fixed costs, and period costs.
   e. Overhead costs, fixed costs, and direct costs.

5. A company reports the following for the current year.

Finished goods inventory, beginning of year	$6,000
Finished goods inventory, ending of year	3,200
Cost of goods sold	7,500

Its cost of goods manufactured for the current year is
   a. $1,500.   **d.** $2,800.
   b. $1,700.   **e.** $4,700.
   c. $7,500.

ANSWERS TO MULTIPLE CHOICE QUIZ

1. c
2. b
3. b
4. a

5. e; Beginning finished goods + Cost of goods manufactured (COGM) − Ending finished goods = Cost of goods sold
$6,000 + COGM − $3,200 = $7,500
COGM = $4,700

🔲 Icon denotes assignments that involve decision making.

Discussion Questions

1. Describe the managerial accountant's role in business planning, control, and decision making.

2. Distinguish between managerial and financial accounting on
   a. Users and decision makers.   **d.** Time dimension.
   b. Purpose of information.   **e.** Focus of information.
   c. Flexibility of practice.   **f.** Nature of information.

3. 🔲 Identify the usual changes that a company must make when it adopts a customer orientation.

4. Distinguish between direct labor and indirect labor.

5. Distinguish between (a) factory overhead and (b) selling and administrative overhead.

6. Distinguish between direct material and indirect material.

7. What product cost is both a prime cost and a conversion cost?

8. 🕐 Assume that we tour **Apple**'s factory where it makes iPhones. List three direct costs **APPLE** and three indirect costs that we are likely to see.

9. 🕐 Should we evaluate a production manager's performance on the basis of operating expenses? Why?

10. 🕐 Explain why knowledge of cost behavior is useful in product performance evaluation.

11. Explain why product costs are capitalized but period costs are expensed in the current accounting period.

12. 🕐 Explain how business activities and inventories for a manufacturing company, a merchandising company, and a service company differ.

13. 🕐 Why does managerial accounting often involve working with numerous predictions and estimates?

14. How do an income statement and a balance sheet for a manufacturing company and a merchandising company differ?

15. Besides inventories, what other assets often appear on manufacturers' balance sheets but not on merchandisers' balance sheets?

16. Why does a manufacturing company require three different inventory categories?

17. Manufacturing activities of a company are described in the _____. This schedule summarizes the types and amounts of costs incurred in its manufacturing _____.

18. What are the three categories of manufacturing costs?

19. List several examples of factory overhead.

20. 🕐 List the four components of a schedule of cost of goods manufactured and provide specific examples of each for **Apple**. **APPLE**

21. 🕐 Prepare a proper title for the annual schedule of cost of goods manufactured **GOOGLE** of **Google**. Does the date match the balance sheet or income statement? Why?

22. 🕐 Describe the relations among the income statement, the schedule of cost of goods manufactured, and a detailed listing of factory overhead costs.

23. 🕐 Define and describe two measures to assess raw materials inventory management.

24. 🕐 The triple bottom line includes what three main dimensions?

25. Access **3M Co.**'s annual report (10-K) for the fiscal year ended December 31, 2014, at the SEC's EDGAR database (**SEC.gov**) or its website (**3M.com**). From its balance sheet, identify the titles and amounts of its inventory components.

connect

Identify whether each description most likely applies to managerial (M) or financial (F) accounting.

_____ **1.** Its primary users are company managers.
_____ **2.** Its information is often available only after an audit is complete.
_____ **3.** Its primary focus is on the organization as a whole.
_____ **4.** Its principles and practices are very flexible.
_____ **5.** It focuses mainly on past results.

QUICK STUDY

QS 1-1
Managerial accounting versus financial accounting
C1

A cell phone company offers two different plans. Plan A costs $80 per month for unlimited talk and text. Plan B costs $0.20 per minute plus $0.10 per text message sent. You need to purchase a plan for your 14-year-old sister. Your sister currently uses 1,700 minutes and sends 1,600 texts each month.

1. What is your sister's total cost under each of the two plans?

2. Suppose your sister doubles her monthly usage to 3,400 minutes and sends 3,200 texts. What is your sister's total cost under each of the two plans?

QS 1-2
Fixed and variable costs
C2

Listed below are product costs for production of footballs. Classify each cost as either variable (V) or fixed (F).

_____ **1.** Leather covers for footballs
_____ **2.** Machinery depreciation (straight-line)
_____ **3.** Wages of assembly workers
_____ **4.** Lace to hold footballs together
_____ **5.** Insurance premium on building
_____ **6.** Factory supervisor salary

QS 1-3
Fixed and variable costs
C2

Diez Company produces sporting equipment, including leather footballs. Identify each of the following costs as direct (D) or indirect (I). The cost object is a football produced by Diez.

_____ **1.** Electricity used in the production plant
_____ **2.** Labor used on the football production line
_____ **3.** Salary of manager who supervises the entire plant
_____ **4.** Depreciation on equipment used to produce footballs
_____ **5.** Leather used to produce footballs

QS 1-4
Direct and indirect costs
C2

QS 1-5

Classifying product costs

C2

Identify each of the following costs as either direct materials (DM), direct labor (DL), or factory overhead (FO). The company manufactures tennis balls.

_____ **1.** Rubber used to form the cores　　_____ **4.** Glue used in binding rubber cores to felt covers

_____ **2.** Factory maintenance　　_____ **5.** Depreciation—Factory equipment

_____ **3.** Wages paid to assembly workers　　_____ **6.** Cans to package the balls

---

QS 1-6

Product and period costs

C3

Identify each of the following costs as either a product cost (PROD) or a period cost (PER).

_____ **1.** Factory maintenance　　_____ **5.** Rent on factory building

_____ **2.** Sales commissions　　_____ **6.** Interest expense

_____ **3.** Depreciation—Factory equipment　　_____ **7.** Office manager salary

_____ **4.** Depreciation—Office equipment　　_____ **8.** Indirect materials used in making goods

---

QS 1-7

Inventory reporting for manufacturers

C4

Compute ending work in process inventory for a manufacturer with the following information.

Raw materials purchased...............	$124,800	Total factory overhead	$ 95,700
Direct materials used	74,300	Work in process inventory, beginning of year........	26,500
Direct labor used	55,000	Cost of goods manufactured	221,800

QS 1-8

Manufacturing cost flows

C5

Compute the total manufacturing cost for a manufacturer with the following information for the month.

Raw materials purchased..............	$32,400	Salesperson commissions	$6,200
Direct materials used	53,750	Depreciation expense—Factory building...........	3,500
Direct labor used	12,000	Depreciation expense—Delivery equipment.........	2,200
Factory supervisor salary..............	8,000	Indirect materials............................	1,250

QS 1-9

Cost of goods sold

P1

Compute cost of goods sold using the following information:

Finished goods inventory, beginning	$ 500
Cost of goods manufactured	4,000
Finished goods inventory, ending	750

QS 1-10

Cost of goods sold

P1

Compute cost of goods sold for 2017 using the following information.

Finished goods inventory, Dec. 31, 2016	$345,000
Work in process inventory, Dec. 31, 2016	83,500
Work in process inventory, Dec. 31, 2017	72,300
Cost of goods manufactured, 2017	918,700
Finished goods inventory, Dec. 31, 2017	283,600

QS 1-11

Cost of goods manufactured

P2

Prepare the 2017 schedule of cost of goods manufactured for Barton Company using the following information.

Direct materials	$190,500
Direct labor..	63,150
Factory overhead costs	24,000
Work in process, Dec. 31, 2016	157,600
Work in process, Dec. 31, 2017	142,750

Use the following information to compute the cost of direct materials used for the current year.

QS 1-12
Direct materials used
P2

	January 1	December 31
Inventories		
Raw materials inventory	$ 6,000	$7,500
Work in process inventory	12,000	9,000
Finished goods inventory	8,500	5,500
Activity during current year		
Materials purchased		$123,500
Direct labor		94,000
Factory overhead		39,000

Match each concept with its best description by entering its letter *A* through *E* in the blank.

_____ **1.** Just-in-time manufacturing

_____ **2.** Continuous improvement

_____ **3.** Customer orientation

_____ **4.** Total quality management

_____ **5.** Triple bottom line

A. Focuses on quality throughout the production process.

B. Flexible product designs can be modified to accommodate customer choices.

C. Every manager and employee constantly looks for ways to improve company operations.

D. Reports on financial, social, and environmental performance.

E. Inventory is acquired or produced only as needed.

QS 1-13
Trends in managerial accounting

C6

3M Co. reports beginning raw materials inventory of $902 million and ending raw materials inventory of $855 million. If 3M purchased $3,646 million of raw materials during the year, what is the amount of raw materials it used during the year?

QS 1-14
Direct materials used   C5

3M Co. reports beginning raw materials inventory of $902 million and ending raw materials inventory of $855 million. Assume 3M purchased $3,646 million of raw materials and used $3,692 million of raw materials during the year. Compute raw materials inventory turnover and the number of days' sales in raw materials inventory.

QS 1-15
Raw materials inventory management   A1

Nestlé reports beginning raw materials inventory of 3,815 and ending raw materials inventory of 3,499 (both numbers in millions of Swiss francs). If Nestlé purchased 13,860 (in millions of Swiss francs) of raw materials during the year, what is the amount of raw materials it used during the year?

QS 1-16
Direct materials used

C5

Nestlé reports beginning raw materials inventory of 3,815 and ending raw materials inventory of 3,499 (both numbers in millions of Swiss francs). Assume Nestlé purchased 13,860 and used 14,176 (both amounts in millions of Swiss francs) in raw materials during the year. Compute raw materials inventory turnover and the number of days' sales in raw materials inventory.

QS 1-17
Raw materials inventory management

A1

connect

Indicate in the following chart the most likely source of information for each business decision. Use *M* for managerial accounting information and *F* for financial accounting information.

EXERCISES

Exercise 1-1
Sources of accounting information

C1

Business Decision	Primary Information Source
1. Determine whether to lend to a company	_____
2. Evaluate a purchasing department's performance	_____
3. Report financial performance to board of directors	_____
4. Estimate product cost for a new line of shoes	_____
5. Plan the budget for next quarter	_____
6. Measure profitability of an individual store	_____
7. Prepare financial reports according to GAAP	_____
8. Determine location and size for a new plant	_____

Exercise 1-2

Cost classification

C2

Listed here are product costs for the production of soccer balls. Classify each cost (*a*) as either variable (V) or fixed (F) and (*b*) as either direct (D) or indirect (I). What patterns do you see regarding the relation between costs classified in these two ways?

Product Cost	a. Variable or Fixed	b. Direct or Indirect
1. Leather covers for soccer balls	_____	_____
2. Annual flat fee paid for office security	_____	_____
3. Coolants for machinery.	_____	_____
4. Wages of assembly workers.	_____	_____
5. Lace to hold leather together.	_____	_____
6. Taxes on factory.	_____	_____
7. Machinery depreciation (straight-line)	_____	_____

Exercise 1-3

Cost classifications for a service provider

C2

TechPro offers instructional courses in e-commerce website design. The company holds classes in a building that it owns. Classify each of TechPro's costs below as (*a*) variable (V) or fixed (F), and (*b*) direct (D) or indirect (I). Assume the cost object is an individual class.

a. b.

____ ____ **1.** Depreciation on classroom building

____ ____ **2.** Monthly Internet connection cost

____ ____ **3.** Instructional manuals for students

a. b.

____ ____ **4.** Travel expenses for salesperson

____ ____ **5.** Depreciation on computers used for classes

____ ____ **6.** Instructor wage (per class)

Exercise 1-4

Cost classifications for a service company

C2

Listed below are costs of providing an airline service. Classify each cost as (*a*) either variable (V) or fixed (F), and (*b*) either direct (D) or indirect (I). Consider the cost object to be a flight. Flight attendants and pilots are paid based on hours of flight time.

Cost	a. Variable or Fixed	b. Direct or Indirect
1. Advertising.	_____	_____
2. Beverages and snacks	_____	_____
3. Regional vice president salary	_____	_____
4. Depreciation (straight-line) on ground equipment	_____	_____
5. Fuel and oil used in planes.	_____	_____
6. Flight attendant wages.	_____	_____
7. Pilot wages	_____	_____
8. Aircraft maintenance manager salary	_____	_____
9. Customer service salaries.	_____	_____

Exercise 1-5

Classifying manufacturing costs

C3

Selected costs related to **Apple**'s iPad are listed below. Classify each cost as either direct materials (DM), direct labor (DL), factory overhead (FO), selling expenses (S), or general and administrative (GA) expenses.

_____ **1.** Display screen

_____ **2.** Assembly-line supervisor salary

_____ **3.** Wages for assembly workers

_____ **4.** Salary of the chief executive officer

_____ **5.** Glue to hold iPad cases together

_____ **6.** Uniforms provided for each factory worker

_____ **7.** Wages for retail store worker

_____ **8.** Depreciation (straight-line) on robotic equipment used in assembly

Exercise 1-6

Cost classification

C3

Georgia Pacific, a manufacturer, incurs the following costs. (1) Classify each cost as either a product (PROD) or period (PER) cost. If a product cost, identify it as direct materials (DM), direct labor (DL), or factory overhead (FO), and then as a prime (PR) or conversion (CONV) cost. (2) Classify each product cost as either a direct cost (DIR) or an indirect cost (IND) using the product as the cost object.

Cost	Direct or Indirect	Product or Period	If Product Cost, Then: Direct Materials, Direct Labor, or Factory Overhead	If Product Cost, Then: Prime or Conversion
1. Factory utilities				
2. Advertising				
3. Amortization of patents on factory machine				
4. State and federal income taxes				
5. Office supplies used				
6. Insurance on factory building				
7. Wages to assembly workers				

Current assets for two different companies at fiscal year-end 2017 are listed here. One is a manufacturer, Rayzer Skis Mfg., and the other, Sunrise Foods, is a grocery distribution company.

1. Identify which set of numbers relates to the manufacturer and which to the merchandiser.

2. Prepare the current asset section for each company from this information. Discuss why the current asset section for these two companies is different.

Exercise 1-7
Balance sheet identification and preparation
C4

Account	Company 1	Company 2
Cash	$ 7,000	$ 5,000
Raw materials inventory	—	42,000
Merchandise inventory	45,000	—
Work in process inventory	—	30,000
Finished goods inventory	—	50,000
Accounts receivable, net	62,000	75,000
Prepaid expenses	1,500	900

Using the following data from both Garcon Company and Pepper Company for the year ended December 31, 2017, compute (1) the cost of goods manufactured, and (2) the cost of goods sold.

Exercise 1-8
Cost of goods manufactured and cost of goods sold computation
P1   P2

	Garcon Company	Pepper Company
Beginning finished goods inventory	$ 12,000	$ 16,450
Beginning work in process inventory	14,500	19,950
Beginning raw materials inventory	7,250	9,000
Rental cost on factory equipment	27,000	22,750
Direct labor.....................................	19,000	35,000
Ending finished goods inventory	17,650	13,300
Ending work in process inventory	22,000	16,000
Ending raw materials inventory..................	5,300	7,200
Factory utilities...............................	9,000	12,000
Factory supplies used	8,200	3,200
General and administrative expenses	21,000	43,000
Indirect labor.................................	1,250	7,660
Repairs—Factory equipment	4,780	1,500
Raw materials purchases	33,000	52,000
Selling expenses	50,000	46,000
Sales	195,030	290,010
Cash	20,000	15,700
Factory equipment, net	212,500	115,825
Accounts receivable, net	13,200	19,450

Check   Garcon COGS, $91,030

Exercise 1-9
Preparing financial statements for a manufacturer C4 P2

Refer to the data in Exercise 1-8. For each company, prepare (1) an income statement, and (2) the current assets section of the balance sheet. Ignore income taxes.

Exercise 1-10
Cost classification C2

Refer to the data in Exercise 1-8. For each company, compute the total (1) prime costs, and (2) conversion costs.

Exercise 1-11
Cost of goods sold computation
P1

Compute cost of goods sold for each of these two companies for the year ended December 31, 2017.

	A	B	C
1			Precision
2		Unimart	Manufacturing
3	Beginning inventory		
4	Merchandise	$275,000	
5	Finished goods		$450,000
6	Cost of purchases	500,000	
7	Cost of goods manufactured		900,000
8	Ending inventory		
9	Merchandise	115,000	
10	Finished goods		375,000

Check Unimart COGS, $660,000

Exercise 1-12
Components of accounting reports
P2

For each of the following accounts for a manufacturing company, place a ✓ in the appropriate column indicating that it appears on the balance sheet, the income statement, the schedule of cost of goods manufactured, and/or a detailed listing of factory overhead costs. Assume that the income statement shows the calculation of cost of goods sold *and* the schedule of cost of goods manufactured shows only the total amount (not detailed listing) of factory overhead. An account can appear on more than one report.

	A	B	C	D	E
1		Balance	Income	Sched. of Cost	Overhead
2	Account	Sheet	Statement	of Goods Manuf'd.	Report
3	Accounts receivable				
4	Computer supplies used (office)				
5	Beginning finished goods inventory				
6	Beginning work in process inventory				
7	Cash				
8	Depreciation expense—Factory building				
9	Depreciation expense—Office building				
10	Direct labor				
11	Ending work in process inventory				
12	Ending raw materials inventory				
13	Factory maintenance wages				
14	Income taxes				
15	Insurance on factory building				
16	Property taxes on factory building				
17	Raw materials purchases				
18	Sales				

Exercise 1-13
Preparation of schedule of cost of goods manufactured
P2

Given the following selected account balances of Delray Mfg., prepare its schedule of cost of goods manufactured for the year ended December 31, 2017. Include a listing of the individual overhead account balances in this schedule.

Sales	$1,250,000	Repairs—Factory equipment	$ 5,250
Raw materials inventory, Dec. 31, 2016	37,000	Rent cost of factory building	57,000
Work in process inventory, Dec. 31, 2016	53,900	Advertising expense	94,000
Finished goods inventory, Dec. 31, 2016	62,750	General and administrative expenses	129,300
Raw materials purchases	175,600	Raw materials inventory, Dec. 31, 2017	42,700
Direct labor	225,000	Work in process inventory, Dec. 31, 2017	41,500
Factory computer supplies used	17,840	Finished goods inventory, Dec. 31, 2017	67,300
Indirect labor	47,000		

Check Cost of goods manufactured, $534,390

Refer to the information in Exercise 1-13 to prepare an income statement for Delray Mfg. (a manufacturer). Assume that its cost of goods manufactured is $534,390.

Exercise 1-14
Income statement
preparation   P2

Beck Manufacturing reports the account information below for 2017. Using this information:
1. Prepare the schedule of cost of goods manufactured for the year.
2. Compute cost of goods sold for the year.

Exercise 1-15
Schedule of cost of goods
manufactured and cost of
goods sold   P1   P2

Raw Materials Inventory				Work in Process Inventory				Finished Goods Inventory		
Begin. inv.	10,000			Begin. inv.	14,000			Begin. inv.	16,000	
				▶DM used	46,500					
				Direct labor	27,500					
Purchases	45,000			Overhead	55,000			▶Cost of goods mfg.	131,000	
Avail. for use	55,000			Avail. for mfg.	143,000			Avail. for sale	147,000	
		DM used	46,500─			Cost of goods mfg.	131,000─			Cost of goods sold	129,000
End. inv.	8,500			End. inv.	12,000			End. inv.	18,000	

The following chart shows how costs flow through a business as a product is manufactured. Not all boxes in the chart show cost amounts. Compute the cost amounts for the boxes that contain question marks.

Exercise 1-16
Cost flows in manufacturing
C5

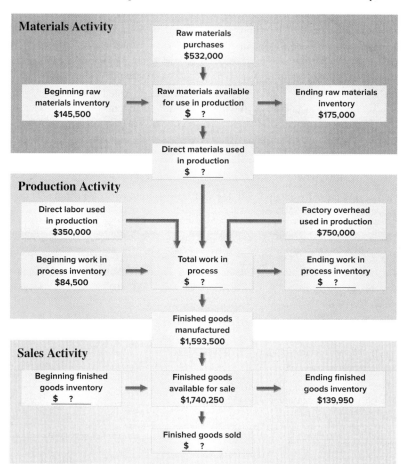

Many fast-food restaurants compete on lean business practices. Match each of the following activities at a fast-food restaurant with one of the three lean business practices *a*, *b*, or *c* that it strives to achieve. Some activities might relate to more than one lean business practice.

Exercise 1-17
Lean business practice
C6

_____ **1.** Courteous employees
_____ **2.** Food produced to order
_____ **3.** Clean tables and floors
_____ **4.** Orders filled within three minutes
_____ **5.** Standardized food-making processes
_____ **6.** New product development

a. Just-in-time (JIT)
b. Continuous improvement (CI)
c. Total quality management (TQM)

Exercise 1-18

Triple bottom line

C6

In its recent annual report and related *Global Responsibility Report*, **Starbucks** provides information on company performance on several dimensions. Indicate whether the following items best fit into the financial (label your answer "Profit"), social (label your answer "People"), or environmental (label your answer "Planet") aspects of triple bottom line reporting.

_____ **1.** Sales revenue totaled $16.5 billion.

_____ **2.** 96% of coffee was purchased from suppliers certified for responsible farming and ethics.

_____ **3.** Reduced water consumption by 4%.

_____ **4.** Reduced energy consumption.

_____ **5.** Operating income totaled $119.2 million.

_____ **6.** Increased purchases of energy from renewable sources.

_____ **7.** All new stores are built using certified green building techniques.

_____ **8.** Decreased amounts of packaging materials.

_____ **9.** Discontinued working with factories that did not meet standards for their working conditions.

Exercise 1-19

Triple bottom line

C6

In its recent annual report and related *Corporate Responsibility Report*, **Hyatt** provides information on company performance on several dimensions. Indicate whether the following items below best fit into the financial (label your answer "Profit"), social (label your answer "People"), or environmental (label your answer "Planet") aspects of triple bottom line reporting.

_____ **1.** Sales revenue totaled $4.4 billion.

_____ **2.** Increased women in management positions by 8%.

_____ **3.** Reduced water consumption at its hotels.

_____ **4.** Invested in career programs in Brazil.

_____ **5.** Operating cash flows totaled $473 million.

_____ **6.** Earned awards for best LGBT workplace.

_____ **7.** 84% of hotels recycle at least one waste stream.

_____ **8.** Invested in reading programs for young students.

_____ **9.** Focused on maximizing long-term shareholder value.

PROBLEM SET A

Problem 1-1A

Cost computation, classification, and analysis

C2 C3

Listed here are the total costs associated with the 2017 production of 1,000 drum sets manufactured by TrueBeat. The drum sets sell for $500 each.

| | Variable or Fixed | | Product or Period | |
Costs	Variable	Fixed	Product	Period
1. Plastic for casing—$17,000	$17,000	_____	$17,000	_____
2. Wages of assembly workers—$82,000..........................	_____	_____	_____	_____
3. Property taxes on factory—$5,000	_____	_____	_____	_____
4. Accounting staff salaries—$35,000.............................	_____	_____	_____	_____
5. Drum stands (1,000 stands purchased)—$26,000................	_____	_____	_____	_____
6. Rent cost of equipment for sales staff—$10,000..................	_____	_____	_____	_____
7. Upper management salaries—$125,000	_____	_____	_____	_____
8. Annual flat fee for factory maintenance service—$10,000	_____	_____	_____	_____
9. Sales commissions—$15 per unit	_____	_____	_____	_____
10. Machinery depreciation, straight-line—$40,000	_____	_____	_____	_____

Required

Check (1) Total variable production cost, $125,000

1. Classify each cost and its amount as (*a*) either variable or fixed and (*b*) either product or period. (The first cost is completed as an example.)

2. Compute the manufacturing cost per drum set.

Analysis Component

3. Assume that 1,200 drum sets are produced in the next year. What do you predict will be the total cost of plastic for the casings and the per unit cost of the plastic for the casings? Explain.

4. Assume that 1,200 drum sets are produced in the next year. What do you predict will be the total cost of property taxes and the per unit cost of the property taxes? Explain.

The following calendar year-end information is taken from the December 31, 2017, adjusted trial balance and other records of Leone Company.

Problem 1-2A
Classifying costs
C2   C3

Advertising expense	$ 28,750	Miscellaneous production costs	$ 8,425
Depreciation expense—Office equipment	7,250	Office salaries expense	63,000
Depreciation expense—Selling equipment	8,600	Raw materials purchases	925,000
Depreciation expense—Factory equipment	33,550	Rent expense—Office space	22,000
Factory supervision	102,600	Rent expense—Selling space	26,100
Factory supplies used	7,350	Rent expense—Factory building	76,800
Factory utilities	33,000	Maintenance expense—Factory equipment	35,400
Direct labor	675,480	Sales	4,462,500
Indirect labor	56,875	Sales salaries expense	392,560

Required

1. Classify each cost as either a product or period cost.
2. Classify each product cost as either direct materials, direct labor, or factory overhead.
3. Classify each period cost as either selling expenses or general and administrative expenses.

Using the data from Problem 1-2A and the following additional inventory information for Leone Company, complete the requirements below. Assume income tax expense is $233,725 for the year.

Problem 1-3A
Schedule of cost of
goods manufactured
and income statement;
inventory analysis
P2   A1

Inventories	
Raw materials, December 31, 2016	$166,850
Raw materials, December 31, 2017	182,000
Work in process, December 31, 2016	15,700
Work in process, December 31, 2017	19,380
Finished goods, December 31, 2016	167,350
Finished goods, December 31, 2017	136,490

Required

1. Prepare the company's 2017 schedule of cost of goods manufactured.
2. Prepare the company's 2017 income statement that reports separate categories for (*a*) selling expenses and (*b*) general and administrative expenses.

Check   (1) Cost of goods
manufactured, $1,935,650

Analysis Component

3. Compute the (*a*) inventory turnover, defined as cost of goods sold divided by average inventory, and (*b*) days' sales in inventory, defined as 365 times ending inventory divided by cost of goods sold, for both its raw materials inventory and its finished goods inventory. (To compute turnover and days' sales in inventory for raw materials, use raw materials used rather than cost of goods sold.) Discuss some possible reasons for differences between these ratios for the two types of inventories. Round answers to one decimal place.

Nazaro's Boot Company makes specialty boots for the rodeo circuit. On December 31, 2016, the company had (*a*) 300 pairs of boots in finished goods inventory and (*b*) 1,200 heels at a cost of $8 each in raw materials inventory. During 2017, the company purchased 35,000 additional heels at $8 each and manufactured 16,600 pairs of boots.

Problem 1-4A
Ending inventory
computation and evaluation
C4

Required

1. Determine the unit and dollar amounts of raw materials inventory in heels at December 31, 2017.

Check   (1) Ending (heel)
inventory, 3,000 units; $24,000

Analysis Component

2. Write a half-page memorandum to the production manager explaining why a just-in-time inventory system for heels should be considered. Include the amount of working capital that can be reduced at December 31, 2017, if the ending heel raw material inventory is cut by half.

Problem 1-5A

Inventory computation and reporting

C4   P1

Shown here are annual financial data at December 31, 2017, taken from two different companies.

	Music World Retail	Wave-Board Manufacturing
Beginning inventory		
Merchandise	$200,000	
Finished goods......................		$500,000
Cost of purchases.....................	300,000	
Cost of goods manufactured		875,000
Ending inventory		
Merchandise	175,000	
Finished goods.....................		225,000

Required

Check (1) Wave-Board's cost of goods sold, $1,150,000

1. Compute the cost of goods sold section of the income statement at December 31, 2017, for each company. Include the proper title and format in the solution.

2. Write a half-page memorandum to your instructor (*a*) identifying the inventory accounts and (*b*) describing where each is reported on the income statement and balance sheet for both companies.

PROBLEM SET B

Problem 1-1B

Cost computation, classification, and analysis

C2   C3

Listed here are the total costs associated with the 2017 production of 15,000 Blu-ray Discs (BDs) manufactured by Maxwell. The BDs sell for $18 each.

		Variable or Fixed		Product or Period	
Costs		Variable	Fixed	Product	Period
1. Plastic for BDs—$1,500		$1,500	____	$1,500	____
2. Wages of assembly workers—$30,000		____	____	____	____
3. Cost of factory rent—$6,750		____	____	____	____
4. Systems staff salaries—$15,000		____	____	____	____
5. Labeling—$0.25 per BD		____	____	____	____
6. Cost of office equipment rent—$1,050......................		____	____	____	____
7. Upper management salaries—$120,000		____	____	____	____
8. Annual fixed fee for cleaning service—$4,520...................		____	____	____	____
9. Sales commissions—$0.50 per BD		____	____	____	____
10. Machinery depreciation, straight-line—$18,000		____	____	____	____

Required

1. Classify each cost and its amount as (*a*) either variable or fixed and (*b*) either product or period. (The first cost is completed as an example.)

Check (2) Total variable production cost, $35,250

2. Compute the manufacturing cost per BD.

Analysis Component

3. Assume that 10,000 BDs are produced in the next year. What do you predict will be the total cost of plastic for the BDs and the per unit cost of the plastic for the BDs? Explain.

4. Assume that 10,000 BDs are produced in the next year. What do you predict will be the total cost of factory rent and the per unit cost of the factory rent? Explain.

Problem 1-2B

Classifying costs

C2   C3

The following calendar year-end information is taken from the December 31, 2017, adjusted trial balance and other records of Best Bikes.

Advertising expense	$ 20,250	Miscellaneous production costs	$ 8,440
Depreciation expense—Office equipment	8,440	Office salaries expense	70,875
Depreciation expense—Selling equipment	10,125	Raw materials purchases.................	894,375
Depreciation expense—Factory equipment	35,400	Rent expense—Office space	23,625
Factory supervision	121,500	Rent expense—Selling space	27,000
Factory supplies used	6,060	Rent expense—Factory building	93,500
Factory utilities...........................	37,500	Maintenance expense—Factory equipment ...	30,375
Direct labor..............................	562,500	Sales	4,942,625
Indirect labor	59,000	Sales salaries expense...................	295,300

Required

1. Classify each cost as either a product or period cost.

2. Classify each product cost as either direct materials, direct labor, or factory overhead.

3. Classify each period cost as either selling expenses or general and administrative expenses.

Using the information from Problem 1-2B and the following additional inventory information for Best Bikes, complete the requirements below. Assume income tax expense is $136,700 for the year.

Problem 1-3B

Schedule of cost of goods manufactured and income statement; analysis of inventories

P2   A1

Inventories	
Raw materials, December 31, 2016..............	$ 40,375
Raw materials, December 31, 2017..............	70,430
Work in process, December 31, 2016	12,500
Work in process, December 31, 2017	14,100
Finished goods, December 31, 2016.............	177,200
Finished goods, December 31, 2017.............	141,750

Required

1. Prepare the company's 2017 schedule of cost of goods manufactured.

2. Prepare the company's 2017 income statement that reports separate categories for (a) selling expenses and (b) general and administrative expenses.

Check   (1) Cost of goods manufactured, $1,816,995

Analysis Component

3. Compute the (a) inventory turnover, defined as cost of goods sold divided by average inventory, and (b) days' sales in inventory, defined as 365 times ending inventory divided by cost of goods sold, for both its raw materials inventory and its finished goods inventory. (To compute turnover and days' sales in inventory for raw materials, use raw materials used rather than cost of goods sold.) Discuss some possible reasons for differences between these ratios for the two types of inventories. Round answers to one decimal place.

Racer's Edge makes specialty skates for the ice skating circuit. On December 31, 2016, the company had (a) 1,500 skates in finished goods inventory and (b) 2,500 blades at a cost of $20 each in raw materials inventory. During 2017, Racer's Edge purchased 45,000 additional blades at $20 each and manufactured 20,750 pairs of skates.

Problem 1-4B

Ending inventory computation and evaluation

C4

Required

1. Determine the unit and dollar amounts of raw materials inventory in blades at December 31, 2017.

Check   (1) Ending (blade) inventory, 6,000 units; $120,000

Analysis Component

2. Write a half-page memorandum to the production manager explaining why a just-in-time inventory system for blades should be considered. Include the amount of working capital that can be reduced at December 31, 2017, if the ending blade raw materials inventory is cut in half.

Problem 1-5B
Inventory computation and reporting

C4   P1

Shown here are annual financial data at December 31, 2017, taken from two different companies.

	TeeMart (Retail)	Aim Labs (Manufacturing)
Beginning inventory		
Merchandise	$100,000	
Finished goods		$300,000
Cost of purchases...................	250,000	
Cost of goods manufactured		586,000
Ending inventory		
Merchandise	150,000	
Finished goods		200,000

Required

Check   (1) TeeMart cost of goods sold, $200,000

1. Compute the cost of goods sold section of the income statement at December 31, 2017, for each company. Include the proper title and format in the solution.
2. Write a half-page memorandum to your instructor (*a*) identifying the inventory accounts and (*b*) identifying where each is reported on the income statement and balance sheet for both companies.

SERIAL PROBLEM
Business Solutions

C2   C4   P2

© Alexander Image/Shutterstock RF

(This serial problem begins in Chapter 1 and continues through most of the book.)

SP 1   Santana Rey, owner of **Business Solutions**, decides to diversify her business by also manufacturing computer workstation furniture.

Required

1. Classify the following manufacturing costs of Business Solutions as either (*a*) variable (V) or fixed (F), and (*b*) direct (D) or indirect (I).

Manufacturing Costs	a. Variable or Fixed	b. Direct or Indirect
1. Monthly flat fee to clean workshop	_____	_____
2. Laminate coverings for desktops....................	_____	_____
3. Taxes on assembly workshop.......................	_____	_____
4. Glue to assemble workstation component parts........	_____	_____
5. Wages of desk assembler..........................	_____	_____
6. Electricity for workshop	_____	_____
7. Depreciation on manufacturing tools.................	_____	_____

2. Prepare a schedule of cost of goods manufactured for Business Solutions for the month ended January 31, 2018. Assume the following manufacturing costs:

Direct materials: $2,200
Factory overhead: $490
Direct labor: $900
Beginning work in process: none (December 31, 2017)
Ending work in process: $540 (January 31, 2018)
Beginning finished goods inventory: none (December 31, 2017)
Ending finished goods inventory: $350 (January 31, 2018)

Check   (3) COGS, $2,700

3. Prepare the cost of goods sold section of a partial income statement for Business Solutions for the month ended January 31, 2018.

Beyond the Numbers

BTN 1-1 Managerial accounting is more than recording, maintaining, and reporting financial results. Managerial accountants must provide managers with both financial and nonfinancial information including estimates, projections, and forecasts. An important estimate for **Apple** is its reserve for warranty claims, and the company must provide shareholders information on these estimates.

REPORTING IN ACTION

C1

APPLE

Required

1. Access Apple's 2015 10-K report, filed with the SEC on October 28, 2015, and find Note 10—*Commitments and Contingencies*. What amount of warranty expense did Apple record for 2015?
2. What amount of warranty claims did Apple pay during 2015?
3. What is Apple's accrued warranty liability at the end of 2015?

Fast Forward

4. Access **Apple**'s annual report for a fiscal year ending after September 26, 2015, from either its website (**Apple.com**) or the SEC's EDGAR database (**SEC.gov**). Answer the questions in parts 1, 2, and 3 after reading the current Note 10. Identify any major changes.

BTN 1-2 Both **Apple** and **Google** (**Alphabet**) have audit committees as part of their boards of directors. Access each company's website (**investor.Apple.com** or **abc.xyz/investor/**) and read about the purpose of the audit committee.

COMPARATIVE ANALYSIS

C2

APPLE

GOOGLE

Required

1. From Apple's website, select Leadership & Governance, Committee Charters, and Audit and Finance Committee. What is the purpose of Apple's audit committee?
2. From Google's website, select Board, then Audit Committee. What is the purpose of its audit committee?
3. Based on your answers to parts 1 and 2, how would management accountants be involved in assisting the audit committee in carrying out its responsibilities?

BTN 1-3 Assume that you are the managerial accountant at Infostore, a manufacturer of hard drives, CDs, and DVDs. Its reporting year-end is December 31. The chief financial officer is concerned about having enough cash to pay the expected income tax bill because of poor cash flow management. On November 15, the purchasing department purchased excess inventory of CD raw materials in anticipation of rapid growth of this product beginning in January. To decrease the company's tax liability, the chief financial officer tells you to record the purchase of this inventory as part of supplies and expense it in the current year; this would decrease the company's tax liability by increasing expenses.

ETHICS CHALLENGE

C1 C3

Required

1. In which account should the purchase of CD raw materials be recorded?
2. How should you respond to this request by the chief financial officer?

BTN 1-4 Write a one-page memorandum to a prospective college student about salary expectations for graduates in business. Compare and contrast the expected salaries for accounting (including different subfields such as public, corporate, tax, audit, and so forth), marketing, management, and finance majors. Prepare a graph showing average starting salaries (and those for experienced professionals in those fields if available). To get this information, stop by your school's career services office; libraries also have this information. The website **JobStar.org** (click on "Salary Info") also can get you started.

COMMUNICATING IN PRACTICE

C6

BTN 1-5 Managerial accounting professionals follow a code of ethics. As a member of the Institute of Management Accountants, the managerial accountant must comply with standards of ethical conduct.

TAKING IT TO THE NET

C1

Required

1. Identify, print, and read the *Statement of Ethical Professional Practice* posted at **IMAnet.org**. (Under "Resources and Publications" select "Ethics Center," and then select "IMA Statement of Ethical Professional Practice.")
2. What four overarching ethical principles underlie the IMA's statement?
3. Describe the courses of action the IMA recommends in resolving ethical conflicts.

TEAMWORK IN ACTION

C5   P2

BTN 1-6   The following calendar-year information is taken from the December 31, 2017, adjusted trial balance and other records of Dahlia Company.

Advertising expense	$ 19,125		Direct labor	$ 650,750
Depreciation expense—Office equipment	8,750		Indirect labor	60,000
Depreciation expense—Selling equipment	10,000		Miscellaneous production costs	8,500
Depreciation expense—Factory equipment	32,500		Office salaries expense	100,875
Factory supervision	122,500		Raw materials purchases	872,500
Factory supplies used	15,750		Rent expense—Office space	21,125
Factory utilities	36,250		Rent expense—Selling space	25,750
Inventories			Rent expense—Factory building	79,750
Raw materials, December 31, 2016	177,500		Maintenance expense—Factory equipment	27,875
Raw materials, December 31, 2017	168,125		Sales	3,275,000
Work in process, December 31, 2016	15,875		Sales discounts	57,500
Work in process, December 31, 2017	14,000		Sales salaries expense	286,250
Finished goods, December 31, 2016	164,375			
Finished goods, December 31, 2017	129,000			

Required

1. *Each* team member is to be responsible for computing **one** of the following amounts. You are not to duplicate your teammates' work. Get any necessary amounts from teammates. Each member is to explain the computation to the team in preparation for reporting to class.

   a. Materials used   **d.** Total cost of work in process
   b. Factory overhead   **e.** Cost of goods manufactured
   c. Total manufacturing costs

2. Check your cost of goods manufactured with the instructor. If it is correct, proceed to part 3.

3. *Each* team member is to be responsible for computing **one** of the following amounts. You are not to duplicate your teammates' work. Get any necessary amounts from teammates. Each member is to explain the computation to the team in preparation for reporting to class.

   a. Net sales   **d.** Total operating expenses
   b. Cost of goods sold **e.** Net income or loss before taxes
   c. Gross profit

ENTREPRENEURIAL DECISION

C1   C2   C6

BTN 1-7   Gautam Gupta and Ken Chen of **NatureBox** must understand manufacturing costs to effectively operate and succeed as a profitable and efficient business.

Required

1. What are the three main categories of manufacturing costs Gautam and Ken must monitor and control? Provide examples of each.

2. What are four goals of a total quality management process? (*Hint:* The goals are listed in a margin "Point.") How can NatureBox use TQM to improve its business activities?

HITTING THE ROAD

C1   C2

BTN 1-8   Visit your favorite fast-food restaurant. Observe its business operations.

Required

1. Describe all business activities from the time a customer arrives to the time that customer departs.

2. List all costs you can identify with the separate activities described in part 1.

3. Classify each cost from part 2 as fixed or variable, and explain your classification.

BTN 1-9   Access **Samsung**'s 2015 annual report from its website (**Samsung.com**). Like **Apple**, Samsung offers warranties on its products.

GLOBAL DECISION

C1

Samsung
APPLE

Required

1. Access and read footnote 18, "Provisions," included in Samsung's 2015 annual report. What amount of warranty expense did Samsung record during 2015? What amount of warranty claims did Samsung pay in 2015?

2. Access and read information on Apple's accrued warranty in footnote 10 of its 2015 annual report. What amount of warranty expense did Apple record during 2015? What amount of warranty claims did Apple pay in 2015?

3. Using your answers from parts 1 and 2, which company was more accurate in estimating warranty claims for 2015?

 ## GLOBAL VIEW

Managerial accounting is more flexible than financial accounting and does not follow a set of strict rules. However, many international businesses use the managerial accounting concepts and principles described in this chapter.

Customer Focus   Nestlé, one of the world's leading nutrition and wellness companies, adopts a customer focus and strives to understand its customers' tastes. For example, Nestlé employees spent three days living with people in Lima, Peru, to understand their motivations, routines, buying habits, and everyday lives. This allowed Nestlé to adjust its products to suit local tastes.

Reporting Manufacturing Activities   Nestlé must classify and report costs. In reporting inventory, Nestlé includes direct production costs, production overhead, and factory depreciation. A recent Nestlé annual report shows the following:

Swiss francs in millions	Ending Inventory	Beginning Inventory
Raw materials, work in progress, and sundry supplies	SFr. 3,499	SFr. 3,815
Finished goods	5,138	5,302

Nestlé managers use this information, along with the more detailed information found in a schedule of cost of goods manufactured, to plan and control manufacturing activities. Nestlé seeks to increase shareholder value by reducing water usage, improving farmers' operations, and enhancing children's nutrition in developing countries.

 Global View Assignments

Discussion Question 2

Quick Study 1-16

Quick Study 1-17

BTN 1-9

chapter 2

Job Order Costing and Analysis

Chapter Preview

JOB ORDER COSTING

Cost accounting system

C1 Job order production

Job order vs. process operations

Production activities

Cost flows

C2 Job cost sheet

NTK 2-1

MATERIALS AND LABOR COSTS

P1 Materials cost flows and documents

P2 Labor cost flows and documents

Linking accounts with job cost sheet

NTK 2-2, 2-3

OVERHEAD COSTS

P3 Predetermined overhead rate

Record applied overhead

Record actual overhead

Summary of cost flows

Job cost sheets for decisions

Schedule of cost of goods manufactured

NTK 2-4, 2-5

ADJUSTING OVERHEAD AND SERVICE USES

Overhead account

P4 Underapplied or overapplied overhead

Job order costing for services

A1 Pricing services

NTK 2-6

Learning Objectives

CONCEPTUAL

C1 Describe important features of job order production.

C2 Explain job cost sheets and how they are used in job order costing.

ANALYTICAL

A1 Apply job order costing in pricing services.

PROCEDURAL

P1 Describe and record the flow of materials costs in job order costing.

P2 Describe and record the flow of labor costs in job order costing.

P3 Describe and record the flow of overhead costs in job order costing.

P4 Determine adjustments for overapplied and underapplied factory overhead.

© Annie Tritt Photography

Drawing Interest

LOS ANGELES—In many cultures, mehndi, temporary "tattoo-like" skin adornment, is part of wedding celebrations. The intricate designs, hand-drawn by mehndi artists with henna paste and often augmented with rhinestones and glitter, are signs of prosperity and happiness. Neha Assar, sole proprietor of **Neha Assar (NehaAssar.com)**, explains that drawing mehndi enables her to use "creativity, experience and passion. My designs are never copied from books, they are never repeated, and they are always exclusive." Accounting for customized services and products, such as Neha's, involves *job order costing.*

Neha uses direct labor (her own). She draws freehand and estimates that each job takes between four and eight hours. Neha's main raw material is henna paste, made from henna leaves and natural oils. Neha's overhead costs are low—all of her materials and tools fit into one cosmetics toolbox.

Neha applies job order costing in pricing her services. "Each bride has her own unique ideas about how extensive and how intricate they want their designs," explains Neha. "These preferences affect how long it will take me."

"Quality is everything"

—Neha Assar

Large mehndi parties require Neha to hire several assistants. Understanding what services her clients want, and the costs required, enables Neha to properly price her services and hire assistants as needed. Job order costing enables Neha to make informed decisions about costs and selling prices.

Job order costing is also important for manufacturers. Custom home builders, for example, track costs to control those costs. Whether for service providers or manufacturers, job order costing enables entrepreneurs to control and monitor the types of costs that are often the downfall of start-ups.

Neha delivers about 100 mehndi events each year. She recently worked Hollywood Oscar parties, L.A. Fashion Week events, and parties for hip-hop artists. "I still get a little starstruck," Neha says. "I'm a 35-year-old mom, and I'm sitting at this rapper's party in Malibu!"

Neha encourages entrepreneurs to be creative. "Avoid formula and routine," she insists. "Believe in yourself."

Sources: *Neha Assar website,* January 2017; *Wall Street Journal,* December 2, 2015; *YouTube.com/watch?v=IMqFRYfwFxk,* May 11, 2015

JOB ORDER COSTING

This section describes a cost accounting system, job order production and costing, and contrasts job order production with process operations.

Cost Accounting System

C1

Describe important features of job order production.

A **cost accounting system** accumulates production costs and then assigns them to products and services. Timely information about inventories and costs is especially helpful in managers' efforts to control costs and determine selling prices.

The two basic types of cost accounting systems are *job order costing* and *process costing*. We describe job order costing in this chapter and process costing in the next.

Job Order Production

Courtesy JJW Images

Many companies produce products individually designed to meet the needs of a specific customer. Each customized product is manufactured separately and its production is called **job order production,** or *job order manufacturing* (also called *customized production,* which is the production of products in response to special orders). Examples of such products or services include special-order machines, a factory building, custom jewelry, wedding invitations, tattoos, and audits by an accounting firm.

The production activities for a customized product represent a **job.** A key feature of job order production is the diversity, often called *heterogeneity,* of the products produced. Each customer order differs from another customer order in some important respect. These differences can be large or small. For example, **Nike** allows custom orders over the Internet, enabling customers to select materials and colors and to personalize their shoes with letters and numbers.

When a job involves producing more than one unit of a custom product, it is often called a **job lot.** Products produced as job lots could include benches for a park, imprinted T-shirts for a 10K race or company picnic, or advertising signs for a chain of stores. Although these orders involve more than one unit, the volume of production is typically low, such as 50 benches, 200 T-shirts, or 100 signs.

Job Order vs. Process Operations

Point: Many professional examinations, including the CPA and CMA exams, require knowledge of job order and process costing.

Process operations, also called *process manufacturing* or *process production,* is the mass production of products in a continuous flow of steps. Unlike job order production, where every product differs depending on customer needs, process operations are designed to mass-produce large quantities of identical products. For example, each year **Penn** makes millions of tennis balls, and **The Hershey Company** produces over a billion pounds of chocolate.

Exhibit 2.1 lists important features of job order and process operations. Movies made by **Walt Disney** and financial audits done by **KPMG** are examples of job order service operations. Order processing in large mail-order firms like **L.L. Bean** is an example of a process service operation.

EXHIBIT 2.1

Comparing Job Order and Process Operations

Job Order Operations	Process Operations
• Custom orders	• Repetitive procedures
• Heterogeneous products and services	• Homogeneous products and services
• Low production volume	• High production volume
• High product flexibility	• Low product flexibility
• Low to medium standardization	• High standardization

Production Activities in Job Order Costing

An overview of job order production activity and cost flows is shown in Exhibit 2.2. This exhibit shows the March production activity of Road Warriors, which installs entertainment systems and security devices in cars and trucks. The company customizes any vehicle by adding speakers, amplifiers, video systems, alarms, and reinforced exteriors.

EXHIBIT 2.2

Job Order Production
Activities and Cost Flows

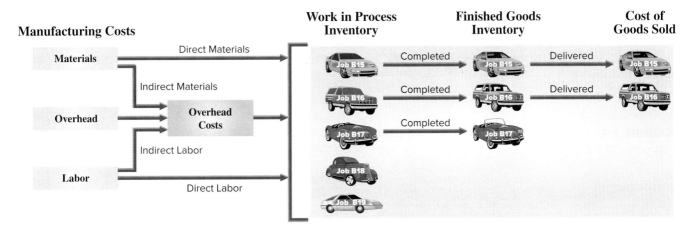

Job order production for Road Warriors requires materials, labor, and overhead costs. Direct materials are used in manufacturing and can be clearly identified with a particular job. Direct labor is effort devoted to a particular job. Overhead costs support production of more than one job. Common overhead items are depreciation on factory buildings and equipment, factory supplies (indirect materials), supervision and maintenance (indirect labor), factory insurance and property taxes, cleaning, and utilities.

Exhibit 2.2 shows that materials, labor, and overhead are added to five jobs started during the month (March). Alarm systems are added to Jobs B15 and B16; Job B17 receives a high-end audio and video entertainment system. Road Warriors completed Jobs B15, B16, and B17 in March and delivered Jobs B15 and B16 to customers. At the end of March, Jobs B18 and B19 remain in work in process inventory and Job B17 is in finished goods inventory.

▓ **Decision** Insight ━━━━━━━━━━━━━━━━━━━━━━━━━━━━━━

Target Costing Many producers determine a **target cost** for their jobs. Target cost is determined as follows: Expected selling price − Desired profit = Target cost. If the projected target cost of the job as determined by job costing is too high, the producer can apply *value engineering,* which is a method of determining ways to reduce job cost until the target cost is met. ▣

Cost Flows

Manufacturing costs flow through inventory accounts (Raw Materials Inventory, Work in Process Inventory, and Finished Goods Inventory) until the related goods are sold. While a job is being produced, its accumulated costs are kept in **Work in Process Inventory.** When a job is finished, its accumulated costs are transferred from Work in Process Inventory to **Finished Goods Inventory.** When a finished job is delivered to a customer, its accumulated costs are transferred from Finished Goods Inventory to Cost of Goods Sold.

Point: Raw Materials Inventory, Work in Process Inventory, Finished Goods Inventory, and Cost of Goods Sold are general ledger accounts.

These general ledger inventory accounts, however, do not provide enough cost detail for managers of job order operations to plan and control production activities. Managers need to know the costs of each individual job (or job lot). Subsidiary records store this information about the costs for each individual job. The next section describes the use of these subsidiary records and how they relate to general ledger accounts.

Job Cost Sheet

A major aim of a **job order costing system** is to determine the cost of producing each job or job lot. In the case of a job lot, the system also computes the cost per unit. The accounting system must include separate records for each job or job lot to accomplish this.

A **job cost sheet** is a cost record maintained for each job. Exhibit 2.3 shows a job cost sheet for Road Warriors. This job cost sheet identifies the customer, the job number, the costs, and key dates. Only product costs are recorded on job cost sheets. Direct materials and direct labor costs incurred on the job are recorded on this sheet. For Job B15, the direct materials and direct labor costs total $600 and $1,000, respectively. *Estimated* overhead costs are included on job cost sheets, through a process we discuss later in the chapter. For Job B15, estimated overhead costs are $1,600, computed as $1,000 of actual direct labor costs × 160%. When each job is complete, the supervisor enters the completion date and signs the sheet. Managers use job cost sheets to monitor costs incurred to date and to predict and control costs for each job.

Point: Documents (electronic and paper) are crucial in a job order system. The job cost sheet is the cornerstone. It aids in grasping concepts of capitalizing product costs and product cost flow.

EXHIBIT 2.3

Job Cost Sheet

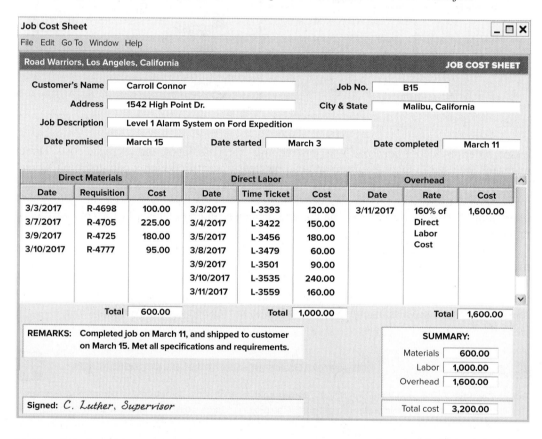

Linking Job Cost Sheets with General Ledger Accounts　The balance in the Work in Process Inventory account at any point in time is the sum of the costs on job cost sheets for all jobs that are not yet complete. The balance in the Finished Goods Inventory account at any point in time is the sum of the costs on job cost sheets for all jobs that *are* complete and awaiting sale. The balance in Cost of Goods Sold is the sum of all costs on job cost sheets for jobs that have been sold and delivered to the customer during that period.

NEED-TO-KNOW 2-1

Job Cost Sheet

C2

A manufacturer's job cost sheet reports direct materials of $1,200 and direct labor of $250 for printing 200 T-shirts for a bikers' reunion. Estimated overhead is computed as 140% of direct labor costs.

1. What is the estimated overhead cost for this job?
2. What is the total cost per T-shirt for this job?
3. What journal entry does the manufacturer make upon completion of this job to transfer costs from work in process to finished goods?

Solution

1. Estimated overhead = $250 \times 140\% = \$350$

2. Cost per T-shirt = Total cost/Total number in job lot = $\$1,800/200 = \$9$ per shirt

3.

Finished Goods Inventory	1,800	
Work in Process Inventory......................		1,800
Transfer cost of completed job.		

Do More: QS 2-7, E 2-2

MATERIALS AND LABOR COST FLOWS

We look at job order costing in more detail, including the source documents for each cost flow.

Materials Cost Flows and Documents

Continuing our example, assume that Road Warriors begins the month (March) with $1,000 in Raw Materials Inventory and $0 balances in the Work in Process Inventory and Finished Goods Inventory accounts. We begin with analysis of the flow of materials costs in Exhibit 2.4. When materials are first received from suppliers, employees count and inspect them and record the items' quantity and cost on a receiving report. The **receiving report** serves as the *source document* for recording materials received in both a materials ledger card and in the general ledger. In nearly all job order cost systems, **materials ledger cards** (or digital files) are perpetual records that are updated each time materials are purchased and each time materials are issued for use in production.

Materials

P1

Describe and record the flow of materials costs in job order costing.

Point: Some companies certify certain suppliers based on the quality of their materials. Goods received from these suppliers are not always inspected by the purchaser to save costs.

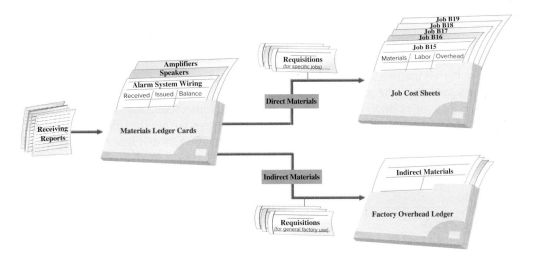

EXHIBIT 2.4

Materials Cost Flows

Materials Purchases   Road Warriors bought $2,750 of materials on credit on March 4, 2017. These include both direct and indirect materials. This purchase is recorded below. Each individual materials ledger card is updated to reflect the added materials.

Mar. 4	Raw Materials Inventory	2,750	
	Accounts Payable................................		2,750
	Record purchase of materials for production.		

Assets = Liabilities + Equity
+2,750   +2,750

Materials Use (Requisitions)   Exhibit 2.4 shows that materials can be requisitioned for use either on a specific job (direct materials) or as overhead (indirect materials). Direct materials include costs, such as alarm system wiring, that are easily traced to individual jobs. Indirect materials include costs, such as those for screws, that are not easily traced to jobs. Direct materials costs flow to job cost sheets. Indirect materials costs flow to the Indirect Materials account in the factory overhead ledger, which is a subsidiary ledger controlled by the Factory Overhead account in the general ledger. The factory overhead ledger includes all of the individual overhead costs.

Exhibit 2.5 shows a materials ledger card for one type of material received and issued by Road Warriors. The card identifies the item as alarm system wiring and shows the item's stock number, its location in the storeroom, information about the maximum and minimum quantities that should be available, and the reorder quantity. For example, two units of alarm system wiring were purchased on March 4, 2017, as evidenced by receiving report C-7117. After this purchase the company has three units of alarm system wiring in inventory.

EXHIBIT 2.5

Materials Ledger Card

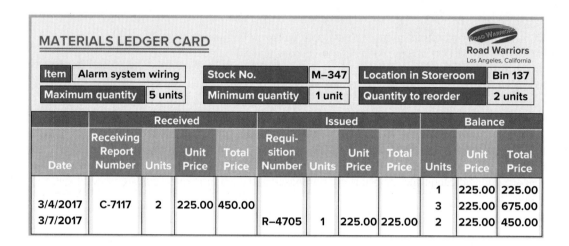

When materials are needed in production, a production manager prepares a **materials requisition** and sends it to the materials manager. For direct materials, the requisition shows the job number, the type of material, the quantity needed, and the production manager's signature. Exhibit 2.6 shows the materials requisition for alarm system wiring for Job B15. For requisitions of indirect materials, the "Job No." line in the requisition form might read "For General Factory Use."

EXHIBIT 2.6

Materials Requisition

Requisitions are often accumulated by job and recorded in one journal entry. The frequency of entries depends on the job, the industry, and management procedures. In this example, Road Warriors records materials requisitions at the end of each week. The total amounts of materials requisitions are shown below.

Direct materials—requisitioned for specific jobs	
Job B15	$ 600
Job B16	300
Job B17	500
Job B18	150
Job B19	250
Total direct materials	**$1,800**
Indirect materials—requisitioned	
for general factory use	550
Total materials requisitions	$ 2,350

The use of direct materials for the week (including alarm system wiring for Job B15) yields the following entry.

Mar. 7	Work in Process Inventory............................	1,800	
	Raw Materials Inventory...........................		1,800
	Record use of direct materials.		

Assets = Liabilities + Equity
+1,800
−1,800

This entry is posted both to general ledger accounts and to subsidiary records. Exhibit 2.7 shows the postings to general ledger accounts (Work in Process Inventory and Raw Materials Inventory) and to the job cost sheets (subsidiary records). The exhibit shows summary job cost sheets for all five jobs, and it shows a detailed partial job cost sheet (excerpted from Exhibit 2.3) for Job B15.

The Raw Materials Inventory account began the month with $1,000 of beginning inventory; it was increased for the March 4 purchase of $2,750. The $1,800 cost of materials used reduces Raw Materials Inventory and increases Work in Process Inventory. The total amount of direct materials used so far ($1,800) is also reflected in the job cost sheets. Later we show the accounting for indirect materials. At this point, it is important to know that requisitions of indirect materials do not directly impact Work in Process Inventory.

EXHIBIT 2.7

Posting Direct Materials Used to the General Ledger and Job Cost Sheets

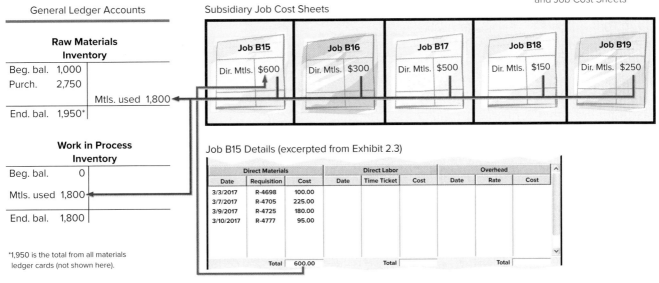

NEED-TO-KNOW 2-2

Recording Direct
Materials

P1

Prepare journal entries to record the following two transactions.
1. A manufacturing company purchased $1,200 of materials (on account) for use in production.
2. The company used $200 of direct materials on Job 1 and $350 of direct materials on Job 2.

Solution

Raw Materials Inventory	1,200	
Accounts Payable		1,200
Record purchase of materials on account.		
Work in Process Inventory	550	
Raw Materials Inventory		550
Record use of direct materials in production.		

Do More: QS 2-4, E 2-8

P2

Describe and record the
flow of labor costs in job
order costing.

Point: Many employee fraud
schemes involve payroll, including
overstated hours on time tickets.

Labor

Labor Cost Flows and Documents

Exhibit 2.8 shows that labor costs are classified as either direct or indirect. Direct labor costs flow to job cost sheets. To assign direct labor costs to individual jobs, companies use **time tickets** to track how each employee's time is used and to record how much time they spent on each job. This process is often automated: Employees swipe electronic identification badges, and a computer system assigns employees' hours worked to individual jobs. An employee who works on several jobs during a day completes separate time tickets for each job. In all cases, supervisors check and approve the accuracy of time tickets.

EXHIBIT 2.8

Labor Cost Flows

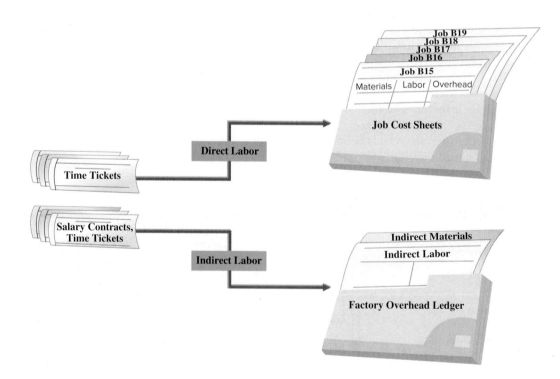

Indirect labor includes factory costs like supervisor salaries and maintenance worker wages. These costs are not assigned directly to individual jobs. Instead, the company determines the amounts of supervisor salaries from their salary contracts and the amounts of maintenance worker wages from time tickets, and classifies those costs as overhead. Indirect labor costs flow to the factory overhead ledger.

Exhibit 2.9 shows a time ticket reporting the time a Road Warrior employee spent working on Job B15. The employee's supervisor signed the ticket to confirm its accuracy. The hourly rate and total labor cost are recorded after the time ticket is turned in.

EXHIBIT 2.9

Time Ticket

No. L–3479

Road Warriors
Los Angeles, California

TIME TICKET   Date March 8 20 17

Employee Name	Employee Number	Job No.
T. Zeller	3969	B15

TIME AND RATE INFORMATION:

Start Time	Finish Time	Elapsed Time	Hourly Rate
9:00	12:00	3.0	$20.00

Remarks

Approved By C. Luther   **Total Cost** $60.00

Time tickets are often accumulated and recorded in one journal entry. The frequency of these entries varies across companies. In this example, Road Warriors journalizes direct labor monthly. During March, Road Warriors's factory payroll costs total $5,300. Of this amount, $4,200 can be traced directly to jobs, and the remaining $1,100 is classified as indirect labor, as shown below.

Direct labor—traceable to specific jobs	
Job B15	$ 1,000
Job B16	800
Job B17	1,100
Job B18	700
Job B19	600
Total direct labor......................	$4,200
Indirect labor—general factory use	1,100
Total labor cost.......................	$ 5,300

The following entry records direct labor based on all the direct labor time tickets for the month.

Mar. 31	Work in Process Inventory............................	4,200	
	Factory Wages Payable		4,200
	Record direct labor used for the month.		

Assets = Liabilities + Equity
+4,200   +4,200

This entry is posted to the general ledger accounts, Work in Process Inventory and Factory Wages Payable (or Cash, if paid), and to individual job cost sheets. Exhibit 2.10 shows these postings. The exhibit shows summary job cost sheets for all five jobs, and it shows a partial job cost sheet (excerpted from Exhibit 2.3) for Job B15.

Time tickets are used to determine how much of the monthly direct labor cost ($4,200) to assign to specific jobs. This total matches the amount of direct labor posted to the Work in Process Inventory general ledger account. After this entry is posted, the balance in Work in Process Inventory is $6,000, consisting of $1,800 of direct materials and $4,200 of direct labor. Later we show the accounting for indirect labor, which does not impact Work in Process Inventory.

EXHIBIT 2.10

Posting Direct Labor to General Ledger and Job Cost Sheets

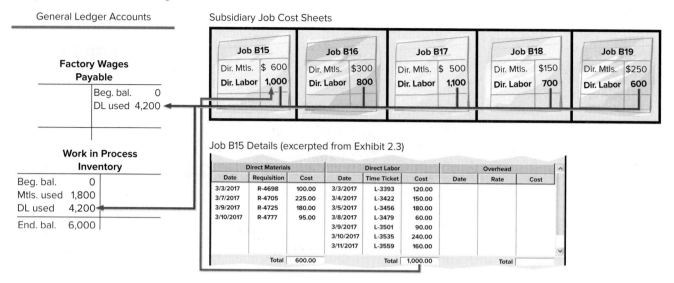

Job B15 Details (excerpted from Exhibit 2.3)

	Direct Materials			Direct Labor			Overhead	
Date	Requisition	Cost	Date	Time Ticket	Cost	Date	Rate	Cost
3/3/2017	R-4698	100.00	3/3/2017	L-3393	120.00			
3/7/2017	R-4705	225.00	3/4/2017	L-3422	150.00			
3/9/2017	R-4725	180.00	3/5/2017	L-3456	180.00			
3/10/2017	R-4777	95.00	3/8/2017	L-3479	60.00			
			3/9/2017	L-3501	90.00			
			3/10/2017	L-3535	240.00			
			3/11/2017	L-3559	160.00			
	Total	600.00		Total	1,000.00		Total	

 **NEED-TO-KNOW** **2-3**

Recording Direct Labor

P2

Do More: QS 2-5, E 2-9

A manufacturing company used $5,400 of direct labor in production activities in May. Of this amount, $3,100 of direct labor was used on Job A1 and $2,300 of direct labor was used on Job A2. Prepare the journal entry to record direct labor used.

Solution

Work in Process Inventory...	5,400	
Factory Wages Payable...		5,400
Record direct labor used in production.		

OVERHEAD COST FLOWS

P3 _____

Describe and record the flow of overhead costs in job order costing.

Overhead

Unlike direct materials and direct labor, overhead costs are not traced directly to individual jobs. Still, each job's total cost must include *estimated* overhead costs.

Overhead Process   The accounting for overhead costs follows the four-step process shown in Exhibit 2.11. Overhead accounting requires managers to first estimate what total overhead costs will be for the coming period. We cannot wait until the end of a period to apply overhead to jobs because managers' decisions require up-to-date costs. Overhead cost, even if it is

EXHIBIT 2.11

Four-Step Process for Overhead

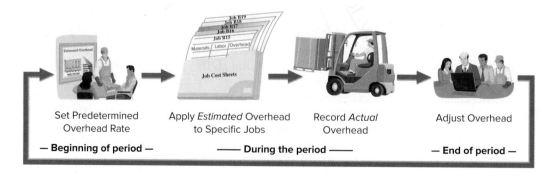

not exactly precise, is needed to estimate a job's total costs before its completion. Such estimated costs are useful in setting prices and identifying costs that are out of control. At the end of the year, the company adjusts its estimated overhead to the actual amount of overhead incurred for that year, and then considers whether to change its predetermined overhead rate for the next year. We discuss each of these steps.

Set Predetermined Overhead Rate

Estimating overhead in advance requires a **predetermined overhead rate,** also called *predetermined overhead allocation* (or *application*) *rate.* This rate requires an estimate of total overhead cost and an activity base such as total direct labor cost *before* the start of the period. Exhibit 2.12 shows the formula for computing a predetermined overhead rate (estimates are commonly based on annual amounts). This rate is used during the period to apply estimated overhead to jobs, based on each job's *actual* usage of the activity. Some companies use multiple predetermined overhead rates for different types of products and services.

Point: Predetermined overhead rates can be estimated using mathematical equations, statistical analysis, or professional experience.

$$\text{Predetermined overhead rate} = \frac{\text{Estimated overhead costs}}{\text{Estimated activity base}}$$

EXHIBIT 2.12

Predetermined Overhead Rate Formula

Overhead Activity Base   We apply overhead by linking it to another factor used in production, such as direct labor or machine hours. The factor to which overhead costs are linked is known as the *activity* (or *allocation*) *base.* There should be a "cause and effect" relation between the base and overhead costs. A manager must think carefully about how many and which activity bases to use. This managerial decision influences the accuracy with which overhead costs are applied to individual jobs, which might impact a manager's decisions for pricing or performance evaluation.

© Royalty-Free/Corbis

Apply Estimated Overhead

Road Warriors applies (also termed *allocates, assigns,* or *charges*) overhead by linking it to direct labor costs. At the start of the current year, management estimates total direct labor costs of $125,000 and total overhead costs of $200,000. Using these estimates, management computes its predetermined overhead rate as 160% of direct labor cost ($200,000 ÷ $125,000). Earlier we showed that Road Warriors used $4,200 of direct labor in March. We now apply the predetermined overhead rate of 160% to get $6,720 (equal to $4,200 × 1.60) of estimated overhead for March. The entry is

Point: Factory Overhead is a temporary account that holds costs. The Factory Overhead account is closed to zero at the end of the year.

Mar. 31	Work in Process Inventory............................	6,720	
	Factory Overhead................................		6,720
	Apply overhead at 160% of direct labor.		

The $6,720 of overhead is then applied to each individual job based on the amount of the activity base that job used (in this example, direct labor). Exhibit 2.13 shows these calculations for March's production activity.

EXHIBIT 2.13

Applying Estimated Overhead to Specific Jobs

Job	Direct Labor Cost	Predetermined Overhead Rate*	Applied Overhead
B15	$1,000	1.6	$1,600
B16	800	1.6	1,280
B17	1,100	1.6	1,760
B18	700	1.6	1,120
B19	600	1.6	960
Total...........	$4,200		$6,720

*160% of direct labor cost

After the applied overhead is recorded and the amounts of overhead applied to each job are determined (Exhibit 2.13), postings to general ledger accounts and to individual job cost sheets follow, as in Exhibit 2.14. For all five jobs, summary job cost sheets are presented first, and then a more detailed partial job cost sheet (excerpted from Exhibit 2.3) is shown for Job B15. (Compare the partial job cost sheet for Job B15 in this exhibit to the complete version in Exhibit 2.3.)

EXHIBIT 2.14

Posting Overhead to General Ledger and Job Cost Sheets

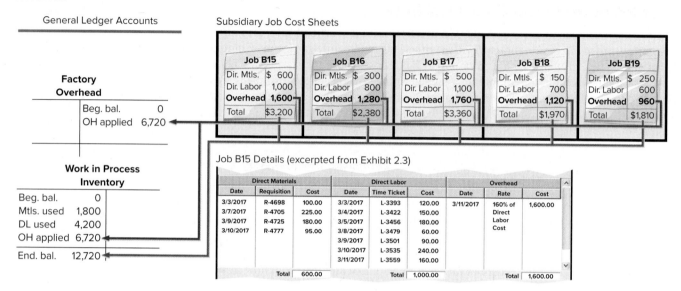

At this point, $6,720 of estimated overhead has been posted to general ledger accounts and to individual job cost sheets. In addition, the ending balance in the Work in Process Inventory account ($12,720) equals the sum of the ending balances in the job cost sheets. In the next section we discuss how to record *actual* overhead.

 **2-4**

Recording Applied Overhead

P3

A manufacturing company estimates it will incur $240,000 of overhead costs in the next year. The company applies overhead using machine hours and estimates it will use 1,600 machine hours in the next year. During the month of June, the company used 80 machine hours on Job 1 and 70 machine hours on Job 2.

1. Compute the predetermined overhead rate to be used to apply overhead during the year.
2. Determine how much overhead should be applied to Job 1 and to Job 2 for June.
3. Prepare the journal entry to record overhead applied for June.

Solution

1. $240,000/1,600 = $150 per machine hour
2. 80 × $150 = $12,000 applied to Job 1; 70 × $150 = $10,500 applied to Job 2
3.

Work in Process Inventory	22,500	
Factory Overhead		22,500
Record applied overhead.		

Do More: QS 2-6, QS 2-7, QS 2-8, E 2-10

Record Actual Overhead

Having shown how estimated overhead costs are accounted for and included in job cost sheets, we now show the accounting for actual overhead costs. Factory overhead includes all factory costs other than direct materials and direct labor. Two major sources of overhead costs are *indirect* materials and *indirect* labor. These costs are recorded from materials requisition forms for indirect materials and from salary contracts or time tickets for indirect labor. Other sources of information on overhead costs include (1) vouchers authorizing payment for factory items such as supplies or utilities and (2) adjusting journal entries for costs such as depreciation on factory assets.

Factory overhead costs are recorded with debits to the Factory Overhead general ledger account and with credits to various accounts. While journal entries for different types of overhead costs might be recorded with varying frequency, in our example we assume these entries are made at the end of the month.

Point: Companies also incur *nonmanufacturing* costs, such as advertising, salespersons' salaries, and depreciation on assets not used in production. These types of costs are not considered overhead, but instead are treated as period costs and charged directly to the income statement.

Record Indirect Materials Used
During March, Road Warriors incurred $550 of actual indirect materials costs, as supported by materials requisitions. The use of these indirect materials yields the following entry.

Mar. 31	Factory Overhead	550	
	Raw Materials Inventory..........................		550
	Record indirect materials used during the month.		

This entry is posted to the general ledger accounts, Factory Overhead and Raw Materials Inventory, and is posted to Indirect Materials in the subsidiary factory overhead ledger. Unlike the recording of *direct* materials, actual *indirect* materials costs incurred are *not* recorded in Work in Process Inventory and are not posted to job cost sheets.

Record Indirect Labor Used
During March, Road Warriors incurred $1,100 of actual indirect labor costs. These costs might be supported by time tickets for maintenance workers or by salary contracts for production supervisors. The use of this indirect labor yields the following entry.

Mar. 31	Factory Overhead	1,100	
	Factory Wages Payable		1,100
	Record indirect labor used during the month.		

This entry is posted to the general ledger accounts, Factory Overhead and Factory Wages Payable, and is posted to Indirect Labor in the subsidiary factory overhead ledger. Unlike the recording of *direct* labor, actual *indirect* labor costs incurred are *not* recorded in Work in Process Inventory and are not posted to job cost sheets.

Record Other Overhead Costs
During March, Road Warriors incurred $5,270 of actual other overhead costs. These costs could include items such as factory building rent, depreciation on the factory building, factory utilities, and other costs indirectly related to production activities. These costs are recorded with debits to Factory Overhead and credits to other accounts such as Cash, Accounts Payable, Utilities Payable, and Accumulated Depreciation—Factory Equipment. The entry to record these other overhead costs for March is as follows.

Mar. 31	Factory Overhead	5,270	
	Accumulated Depreciation—Factory Equipment		2,400
	Rent Payable.....................................		1,620
	Utilities Payable		250
	Prepaid Insurance................................		1,000
	Record actual overhead costs for the month.		

This entry is posted to the general ledger account, Factory Overhead, and is posted to separate accounts for each of the overhead items in the subsidiary factory overhead ledger. These actual overhead costs are *not* recorded in Work in Process Inventory and are not posted to job cost sheets. Only estimated overhead is recorded in Work in Process Inventory and posted to job cost sheets.

NEED-TO-KNOW 2-5

Recording Actual
Overhead

P3

A manufacturing company used $400 of indirect materials and $2,000 of indirect labor during the month. The company also incurred $1,200 for depreciation on general-use factory equipment, $500 for depreciation on office equipment, and $300 for factory utilities. Prepare the necessary journal entries.

Solution

Factory Overhead...	3,900	
Raw Materials Inventory..		400
Factory Wages Payable..		2,000
Accumulated Depreciation—Factory Equipment*............................		1,200
Utilities Payable..		300
Record actual overhead costs used in production.		
Depreciation Expense	500	
Accumulated Depreciation—Office Equipment............................		500
Record depreciation on office equipment.		

Do More: E 2-6, E 2-10

*Depreciation on office equipment is a period cost and is excluded from factory overhead.

Summary of Cost Flows

EXHIBIT 2.15

Cost Flows and Reports

In this section we summarize the flow of costs. Exhibit 2.15 shows how costs for a manufacturing company flow to its financial statements.

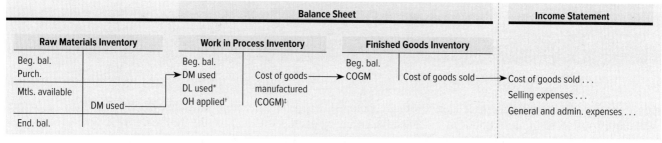

* From time tickets.   † Predetermined overhead rate × Actual amount of activity base used.   ‡ Reported on schedule of cost of goods manufactured.

Exhibit 2.15 shows that direct materials used, direct labor used, and factory overhead applied flow through the Work in Process Inventory and Finished Goods balance sheet accounts. The cost of goods manufactured (COGM) is computed and shown on the schedule of cost of goods manufactured. When goods are sold, their costs are transferred from Finished Goods Inventory to the income statement as cost of goods sold. For Road Warriors, the journal entries to record the flow of costs from Work in Process Inventory to Finished Goods Inventory, and from Finished Goods Inventory to Cost of Goods Sold, are

Point: Sales revenue is also recorded (see Exhibit 2.17).

Mar. 31			
	Finished Goods Inventory...............................	8,940	
	Work in Process Inventory.........................		8,940
	Transfer cost of goods manufactured.		
	Cost of Goods Sold....................................	5,580	
	Finished Goods Inventory		5,580
	Record cost of goods sold.		

Period costs (selling expenses and general and administrative expenses) do not impact inventory accounts. As a result, they do not impact cost of goods sold, and they are not reported on the schedule of cost of goods manufactured. They are reported on the income statement as operating expenses.

Cost Flows—Road Warriors   We next show the flow of costs and their reporting for our Road Warriors example. The upper part of Exhibit 2.16 shows the flow of Road Warriors's product costs through general ledger accounts. Arrow lines are numbered to show the flows of costs for March. Each numbered cost flow reflects journal entries made in March. The lower part of Exhibit 2.16 shows summarized job cost sheets at the end of March. The sum of costs assigned to the two jobs in process ($1,970 + $1,810) equals the $3,780 balance in Work in Process Inventory. Costs assigned to the completed Job B17 equal the $3,360 balance in Finished Goods Inventory. These balances in Work in Process Inventory and Finished Goods Inventory are reported on the end-of-period balance sheet. The sum of costs assigned to the sold Jobs B15 and B16 ($3,200 + $2,380) equals the $5,580 balance in Cost of Goods Sold. This amount is reported on the income statement for the period.

Point: Ending balances on job cost sheets must equal ending balances in general ledger accounts.

EXHIBIT 2.16

Job Order Cost Flows and Ending Job Cost Sheets

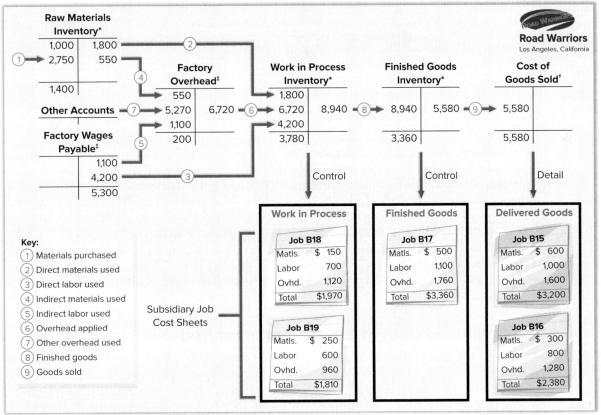

* The ending balances in the inventory accounts are reported on the balance sheet.
† The Cost of Goods Sold balance is reported on the income statement.
‡ Factory Overhead is considered a temporary account; when these costs are applied to jobs, its balance is reduced.

Exhibit 2.17 shows the journal entries made in March. Each entry is numbered to link with the arrow lines in Exhibit 2.16. In addition, Exhibit 2.17 concludes with the summary journal entry to record the sales (on account) of Jobs B15 and B16.

Using Job Cost Sheets for Managerial Decisions

Managers' decisions depend on timely information in job cost sheets. In *controlling* operations, managers must assess the profitability of the company's products or services. Road Warriors completed and sold two jobs (B15 and B16) and earned a total gross profit of $2,280 ($7,780 selling price − $5,580 cost of goods sold). If this gross profit is higher than expected, managers will try to determine if there are production efficiencies that can be applied to future jobs. For example, has the business found a way to reduce the amount of direct labor? If gross profit is less than expected, managers will determine if costs are out of

EXHIBIT 2.17

Entries for Job Order Costing*

①	Raw Materials Inventory	2,750	
	Accounts Payable		2,750
	Acquired raw materials.		
②	Work in Process Inventory	1,800	
	Raw Materials Inventory		1,800
	Assign costs of direct materials used.		
③	Work in Process Inventory	4,200	
	Factory Wages Payable		4,200
	Assign costs of direct labor used.		
④	Factory Overhead	550	
	Raw Materials Inventory		550
	Record use of indirect materials.		
⑤	Factory Overhead	1,100	
	Factory Wages Payable		1,100
	Record indirect labor costs.		

⑥	Work in Process Inventory	6,720	
	Factory Overhead		6,720
	Apply overhead at 160% of direct labor.		
⑦	Factory Overhead	5,270	
	Cash (and other accounts)		5,270
	Record factory overhead costs such as insurance, utilities, rent, and depreciation.		
⑧	Finished Goods Inventory	8,940	
	Work in Process Inventory		8,940
	Record completion of Jobs B15, B16, and B17.		
⑨	Cost of Goods Sold	5,580	
	Finished Goods Inventory		5,580
	Record cost of goods sold for Jobs B15 and B16.		
⑩	Accounts Receivable	7,780	
	Sales		7,780
	Record sale of Jobs B15 and B16.		

* Exhibit 2.17 provides summary journal entries. *Actual* overhead is debited to Factory Overhead. *Applied* overhead is credited to Factory Overhead.

control. In this case, can the company find cheaper raw materials without sacrificing product quality? Is the company using costly overtime to complete jobs? Similarly, managers can evaluate costs to date for the in-process jobs (B18 and B19) to determine whether production processes are going as planned.

In *planning* future production, managers must consider selling prices. Can the company raise selling prices without losing business to competitors? Can the company match competitors' price cuts and earn profit? Managers also can use information in job cost sheets to adjust the company's sales mix toward more profitable types of jobs. The detailed and timely information in job cost sheets helps managers make better decisions for each job and for the business as a whole.

Schedule of Cost of Goods Manufactured

Work in Process Inventory

Beg. bal.	0		
DM. used	1,800		
DL used	4,200		
OH applied	6,720		
Ttl mfg. costs	12,720		
		COGM	8,940
End. bal.	3,780		

We end the Road Warriors example with the schedule of cost of goods manufactured in Exhibit 2.18. This schedule is similar to the one reported in the previous chapter, with one key difference: *Total manufacturing costs include overhead applied rather than actual overhead costs.* In this example, actual overhead costs were $6,920, while applied overhead was $6,720. We discuss how to account for the difference between applied and actual overhead in the next section.

EXHIBIT 2.18

Schedule of Cost of Goods Manufactured

ROAD WARRIORS
Road Warriors
Los Angeles, California
Schedule of Cost of Goods Manufactured
For the Month of March, 2017

Direct materials used	$ 1,800
Direct labor used	4,200
Factory overhead applied*	6,720
Total manufacturing costs	$12,720
Add: Work in process, March 1, 2017	0
Total cost of work in process	12,720
Less: Work in process, March 31, 2017	3,780
Cost of goods manufactured	$ 8,940

Point: Companies sometimes use more detailed schedules of cost of goods manufactured, as seen in the previous chapter.

* Actual overhead = $6,920. Overhead is $200 underapplied.

ADJUSTING OVERHEAD

Refer to the debits in the Factory Overhead account in Exhibit 2.16 (or Exhibit 2.17). The total cost of actual factory overhead incurred during March is $6,920 ($550 + $5,270 + $1,100). The $6,920 of actual overhead costs does not equal the $6,720 of overhead applied to work in process inventory (see ⑥). This leaves a debit balance of $200 in the Factory Overhead account. Because it is hard to precisely forecast future costs, actual overhead rarely equals applied overhead. Companies usually wait until the end of the year to adjust the Factory Overhead account for differences between actual and applied overhead. We show how this is done in the next section.

Factory Overhead Account

Exhibit 2.19 shows a Factory Overhead account. The company applies overhead (credits the Factory Overhead account) using a predetermined rate estimated at the beginning of the year. During the year,

Factory Overhead	
Actual amounts	Applied amounts

EXHIBIT 2.19

Factory Overhead T-account

the company records actual overhead costs with debits to the Factory Overhead account. At year-end we determine whether the applied overhead is more or less than actual overhead:

- When *less* overhead is applied than is actually incurred, the remaining debit balance in the Factory Overhead account is called **underapplied overhead.**
- When *more* overhead is applied than is actually incurred, the resulting credit balance in the Factory Overhead account is called **overapplied overhead.**

When overhead is underapplied, it means that individual jobs have not been charged enough overhead during the year, and cost of goods sold for the year is too low. When overhead is overapplied, it means that jobs have been charged too much overhead during the year, and cost of goods sold is too high. In either case, a journal entry is needed to adjust Factory Overhead and Cost of Goods Sold. Exhibit 2.20 summarizes this entry, assuming the difference between applied and actual overhead is not material.

Example: If we do not adjust for underapplied overhead, will net income be overstated or understated? *Answer:* Overstated.

Overhead Costs	Factory Overhead Balance	Overhead Is	Adjusting Journal Entry Required	
Actual > Applied	Debit	Underapplied	Cost of Goods Sold	#
			Factory Overhead	#
Actual < Applied	Credit	Overapplied	Factory Overhead	#
			Cost of Goods Sold	#

EXHIBIT 2.20

Adjusting Factory Overhead

Adjust Underapplied or Overapplied Overhead

To illustrate, assume that Road Warriors applied $200,000 of overhead to jobs during 2017, which is the amount of overhead estimated in advance for the year. We further assume that Road Warriors incurred a total of $200,480 of actual overhead costs during 2017. This means, at the end of the year, the Factory Overhead account has a debit balance of $480. This amount is the difference between estimated (applied) and actual overhead costs for the year.

The $480 debit balance reflects manufacturing costs not assigned to jobs. This means the balances in Work in Process Inventory, Finished Goods Inventory, and Cost of Goods Sold do not include all production costs incurred. However, the difference between applied and actual overhead in this case is immaterial, and it is closed to Cost of Goods Sold with the following adjusting entry.

P4

Determine adjustments for overapplied and underapplied factory overhead.

Point: When the underapplied or overapplied overhead is material, the amount is normally allocated to the cost of goods sold, finished goods inventory, and work in process inventory accounts. This process is covered in advanced courses.

Dec. 31	Cost of Goods Sold	480	
	Factory Overhead		480
	Adjust for underapplied overhead costs.		

The $480 debit (increase) to Cost of Goods Sold reduces income by $480. After this entry, the Factory Overhead account has a zero balance. Also, Cost of Goods Sold reflects actual overhead costs for the period. If instead we had overapplied overhead at the end of the period, we would debit Factory Overhead and credit Cost of Goods Sold for the amount.

NEED-TO-KNOW 2-6

Adjusting Overhead

P4

A manufacturing company applied $300,000 of overhead to its jobs during the year. For the independent scenarios below, prepare the journal entry to adjust over- or underapplied overhead. Assume the adjustment amounts are not material.

1. Actual overhead costs incurred during the year equal $305,000.
2. Actual overhead costs incurred during the year equal $298,500.

Solution

1.

Cost of Goods Sold...	5,000	
Factory Overhead		5,000
Close underapplied overhead to Cost of Goods Sold.		

2.

Factory Overhead..	1,500	
Cost of Goods Sold		1,500
Close overapplied overhead to Cost of Goods Sold.		

Do More: QS 2-11, QS 2-12, E 2-13, E 2-14

Job Order Costing of Services

Job order costing also applies to service companies. Most service companies meet customers' needs by performing a custom service for a specific customer. Examples include an accountant auditing a client's financial statements, an interior designer remodeling an office, a wedding consultant planning and supervising a reception, and a lawyer defending a client.

Job order costing has some important differences for service firms:

● Most service firms have neither raw materials inventory nor finished goods inventory. They do, however, have inventories of supplies, and they can have work in process inventory. Often these supplies are immaterial and are considered overhead costs.

● Direct labor is often used to apply overhead because service firms do not use direct materials.

● Service firms typically use different account titles, for example **Services in Process Inventory** and **Services Overhead.**

Exhibit 2.21 shows the flow of costs for a service firm called AdWorld, a developer of advertising materials. During the month, AdWorld worked on custom advertising campaigns for clients that wanted ads for three different platforms: mobile devices, television, and radio. In the following Decision Analysis section, we show an example of using job order costing to price advertising services for AdWorld.

EXHIBIT 2.21

Flow of Costs for Service Firms

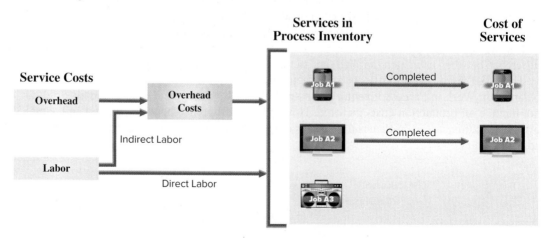

■ Decision Maker

Management Consultant   One of your tasks is to control and manage costs for a consulting company. At the end of a recent month, you find that three consulting jobs were completed and two are 60% complete. Each unfinished job is estimated to cost $10,000 and to earn a revenue of $12,000. You are unsure how to recognize work in process inventory and record costs and revenues. Do you recognize any inventory? If so, how much? How much revenue is recorded for unfinished jobs this month? ■   *Answer:* Service companies (such as this consulting firm) do not recognize work in process inventory or finished goods inventory. For the two jobs that are 60% complete, you could recognize revenues and costs at 60% of the total expected amounts. This means you could recognize revenue of $7,200 (0.60 × $12,000) and costs of $6,000 (0.60 × $10,000), yielding net income of $1,200 from each job.

 # SUSTAINABILITY AND ACCOUNTING

Professional service firms in accounting, consulting, law, and financial services compete for highly talented employees with strong technical skills. In addition, a more diverse workforce is likely to lead to different points of view that can arguably produce even better services and ultimately more profit for the company. Enhancing workforce diversity can also help attract and retain talented people.

Although workforce diversity is typically not recorded on job cost sheets, many companies measure and report it. Along these lines, the Sustainability Accounting Standards Board has developed suggested reporting guidelines for professional service firms. The SASB recommends that companies disclose information on gender and ethnicity for both senior management employees and all other employees.

Consistent with SASB guidelines, the **United States Postal Service (USPS)**, a leading employer of women and minorities, discloses that women comprise roughly 40% and minorities comprise roughly 40% of its overall workforce. Moreover, roughly 21% of USPS's employees are black, 8% Hispanic, and 8% Asian.

Neha Assar, the focus of this chapter's opening feature, focuses her sustainability efforts on raw materials. Neha uses only 100% natural and organic products and does *not* use any chemicals or dyes. This enables her to offer services that are completely nontoxic and safe—a very sustainable combination of raw materials.

Courtesy of Neha Assar

Pricing for Services   **Decision Analysis**

The chapter described job order costing mainly within a manufacturing setting. However, service providers also use job order costing. Consider AdWorld, an advertising agency that develops web-based ads (and ads for other types of media). Each of its customers has unique requirements, so costs for each individual job must be tracked separately.

AdWorld uses two types of labor: web designers ($65 per hour) and computer staff ($50 per hour). It also incurs overhead costs that it assigns using two different predetermined overhead allocation rates: $125 per designer hour and $96 per staff hour. For each job, AdWorld must estimate the number of designer and staff hours needed. Then, total costs of each job are determined using the procedures in the chapter.

To illustrate, a chip manufacturer requested a quote from AdWorld for an advertising engagement. AdWorld estimates that the job will require 43 designer hours and 61 staff hours, with the following total estimated cost for this job.

A1————
Apply job order costing in pricing services.

AdWorld **Estimated Job Cost—Advertising Services**		
Direct Labor		
Designers (43 hours × $65).....................	$2,795	
Staff (61 hours × $50)........................	3,050	
Total direct labor.............................		$ 5,845
Overhead		
Designer related (43 hours × $125)..............	5,375	
Staff related (61 hours × $96)..................	5,856	
Total overhead		11,231
Total estimated job cost........................		$17,076

AdWorld can use this cost information to help determine the price quote for the job (see *Decision Maker*, **Sales Manager,** below).

Another source of information that AdWorld must consider is the market, that is, how much competitors will quote for this job. Competitor information is often unavailable; therefore, AdWorld's managers must use estimates based on their assessment of the competitive environment.

■ Decision Maker

Sales Manager   As AdWorld's sales manager, assume that you estimate costs pertaining to a proposed job as $17,076. Your normal pricing policy is to apply a markup of 18% from total costs. However, you learn that three other agencies are likely to bid for the same job, and that their quotes will range from $16,500 to $22,000. What price should you quote? What factors other than cost must you consider? ■   *Answer:* The price based on AdWorld's normal pricing policy is $20,150 ($17,076 × 1.18), which is within the price range offered by competitors. One option is to apply normal pricing policy and quote a price of $20,150. It is, however, useful to assess competitor pricing, especially in terms of service quality and other benefits. Although price is an input customers use to select suppliers, factors such as quality and timeliness (responsiveness) of suppliers are important. Accordingly, the price can reflect such factors.

NEED-TO-KNOW 2-7

COMPREHENSIVE

The following information reflects Walczak Company's job order production activities for May.

Raw materials purchases..............	$16,000
Factory payroll cost	15,400
Overhead costs incurred	
Indirect materials..................	5,000
Indirect labor	3,500
Other factory overhead	9,500

Walczak's predetermined overhead rate is 150% of direct labor cost. Costs are applied to the three jobs worked on during May as follows.

	Job 401	Job 402	Job 403
Work in process inventory, April 30			
Direct materials	$3,600		
Direct labor..........................	1,700		
Applied overhead	2,550		
Costs during May			
Direct materials	3,550	$3,500	$1,400
Direct labor..........................	5,100	6,000	800
Applied overhead.....................	?	?	?
Status on May 31	**Finished (sold)**	**Finished (unsold)**	**In process**

Required

1. Determine the total cost of:
   a. The April 30 inventory of jobs in process.
   b. Materials (direct and indirect) used during May.
   c. Labor (direct and indirect) used during May.
   d. Factory overhead incurred and applied during May and the amount of any over- or underapplied overhead on May 31.
   e. The total cost of each job as of May 31, the May 31 inventories of both work in process and finished goods, and the cost of goods sold during May.

2. Prepare summarized journal entries for the month to record:
   a. Materials purchases (on credit), direct materials used in production, direct labor used in production, and overhead applied.
   b. Actual overhead costs, including indirect materials, indirect labor, and other overhead costs.
   c. Transfer of each completed job to the Finished Goods Inventory account.
   d. Cost of goods sold.
   e. The sale (on account) of Job 401 for $35,000.
   f. Removal of any underapplied or overapplied overhead from the Factory Overhead account. (Assume the amount is not material.)

3. Prepare a schedule of cost of goods manufactured for May.

PLANNING THE SOLUTION

- Determine the cost of the April 30 work in process inventory by totaling the materials, labor, and applied overhead costs for Job 401.
- Compute the cost of materials used and labor by totaling the amounts assigned to jobs and to overhead.
- Compute the total overhead incurred by summing the amounts for the three components. Compute the amount of applied overhead by multiplying the total direct labor cost by the predetermined overhead rate. Compute the underapplied or overapplied amount as the difference between the actual cost and the applied cost.
- Determine the total cost charged to each job by adding the costs incurred in April (if any) to the cost of materials, labor, and overhead applied during May.
- Group the costs of the jobs according to their completion status.
- Record the direct materials costs assigned to the three jobs.
- Transfer costs of Jobs 401 and 402 from Work in Process Inventory to Finished Goods.
- Record the costs of Job 401 as cost of goods sold.
- Record the sale (on account) of Job 401 for $35,000.
- On the schedule of cost of goods manufactured, remember to include the beginning and ending work in process inventories and to use applied rather than actual overhead.

SOLUTION

1. Total cost of

a. April 30 inventory of jobs in process (Job 401).

Direct materials	$3,600
Direct labor................	1,700
Applied overhead...........	2,550
Total cost..................	$7,850

b. Materials used during May.

Direct materials	
Job 401	$ 3,550
Job 402	3,500
Job 403	1,400
Total direct materials	8,450
Indirect materials	5,000
Total materials used	$13,450

c. Labor used during May.

Direct labor	
Job 401	$ 5,100
Job 402	6,000
Job 403	800
Total direct labor............	11,900
Indirect labor...............	3,500
Total labor used	$15,400

d. Factory overhead incurred in May.

Actual overhead	
Indirect materials...........................	$ 5,000
Indirect labor	3,500
Other factory overhead.....................	9,500
Total actual overhead.......................	18,000
Overhead applied (150% × $11,900)............	17,850
Underapplied overhead......................	$ 150

e. Total cost of each job.

		401	402	403
Work in process, April 30				
	Direct materials	$ 3,600		
	Direct labor.......................	1,700		
	Applied overhead*.................	2,550		
Cost incurred in May				
	Direct materials (from part b)	3,550	$ 3,500	$1,400
	Direct labor.......................	5,100	6,000	800
	Applied overhead*.................	7,650	9,000	1,200
	Total costs........................	$24,150	$18,500	$3,400

* Equals 150% of that job's direct labor cost.

Total cost of the May 31 inventory of work in process (Job 403) = $3,400

Total cost of the May 31 inventory of finished goods (Job 402) = $18,500

Total cost of goods sold during May (Job 401) = $24,150

2. Journal entries.

   a. Record raw materials purchases, direct materials used, direct labor used, and overhead applied.

Raw Materials Inventory	16,000	
Accounts Payable		16,000
Record materials purchases.		
Work in Process Inventory	8,450	
Raw Materials Inventory		8,450
Assign direct materials to jobs.		
Work in Process Inventory	11,900	
Factory Wages Payable		11,900
Assign direct labor to jobs.		
Work in Process Inventory	17,850	
Factory Overhead		17,850
Apply overhead to jobs.		

   b. Record actual overhead costs.

Factory Overhead	5,000	
Raw Materials Inventory		5,000
Record indirect materials.		
Factory Overhead	3,500	
Factory Wages Payable		3,500
Record indirect labor.		
Factory Overhead	9,500	
Cash		9,500
Record other actual factory overhead.		

   c. Transfer cost of completed jobs to Finished Goods Inventory.

Finished Goods Inventory	42,650	
Work in Process Inventory		42,650
Record completion of jobs		
($24,150 for Job 401 + $18,500 for Job 402).		

   d. Record cost of job sold.

Cost of Goods Sold	24,150	
Finished Goods Inventory		24,150
Record costs for sale of Job 401.		

   e. Record sales for job sold.

Accounts Receivable	35,000	
Sales		35,000
Record sale of Job 401.		

   f. Close underapplied overhead to cost of goods sold.

Cost of Goods Sold	150	
Factory Overhead		150
Assign underapplied overhead to Cost of Goods Sold.		

3.

WALCZAK COMPANY
Schedule of Cost of Goods Manufactured
For Month Ended May 31

Direct materials	$ 8,450
Direct labor	11,900
Factory overhead applied*	17,850
Total manufacturing costs	38,200
Add: Work in process, April 30	7,850
Total cost of work in process	46,050
Less: Work in process, May 31	3,400
Cost of goods manufactured	$42,650

* Actual overhead = $18,000. Overhead is $150 underapplied.

Summary

C1 Describe important features of job order production. Certain companies called *job order manufacturers* produce custom-made products for customers. These customized products are produced in response to customers' orders. A job order manufacturer produces products that usually are different and, typically, produced in low volumes. The production systems of job order companies are flexible and are not highly standardized.

C2 Explain job cost sheets and how they are used in job order costing. In a job order costing system, the costs of producing each job are accumulated on a separate job cost sheet. Costs of direct materials, direct labor, and overhead applied are accumulated separately on the job cost sheet and then added to determine the total cost of a job. Job cost sheets for jobs in process, finished jobs, and jobs sold make up subsidiary records controlled by general ledger accounts.

A1 Apply job order costing in pricing services. Job order costing can usefully be applied to a service setting. The resulting job cost estimate can then be used to help determine a price for services.

P1 Describe and record the flow of materials costs in job order costing. Costs of direct materials flow to the Work in Process Inventory account and to job cost sheets. Costs of indirect materials flow to the Factory Overhead account and to the factory overhead subsidiary ledger. Receiving reports evidence the purchase of raw materials, and requisition forms evidence the use of materials in production.

P2 Describe and record the flow of labor costs in job order costing. Costs of direct labor flow to the Work in Process Inventory account and to job cost sheets. Costs of indirect labor flow to the Factory Overhead account and to the factory overhead subsidiary ledger. Time tickets document the use of labor.

P3 Describe and record the flow of overhead costs in job order costing. Overhead costs are charged to jobs using a predetermined overhead rate. Actual overhead costs incurred are accumulated in the Factory Overhead account that controls the subsidiary factory overhead ledger.

P4 Determine adjustments for overapplied and underapplied factory overhead. At the end of each year, the Factory Overhead account usually has a residual debit (underapplied overhead) or credit (overapplied overhead) balance. Assuming the balance is not material, it is transferred to Cost of Goods Sold, and the Factory Overhead account is closed.

Key Terms

Cost accounting system
Finished Goods Inventory
Job
Job cost sheet
Job lot
Job order costing system
Job order production

Materials ledger card
Materials requisition
Overapplied overhead
Predetermined overhead rate
Process operations
Receiving report
Services in Process Inventory

Services Overhead
Target cost
Time ticket
Underapplied overhead
Work in Process Inventory

Multiple Choice Quiz

1. A company's predetermined overhead rate is 150% of its direct labor costs. How much overhead is applied to a job that requires total direct labor costs of $30,000?
   - a. $15,000
   - b. $30,000
   - c. $45,000
   - d. $60,000
   - e. $75,000

2. A company uses direct labor costs to apply overhead. Its production costs for the period are: direct materials, $45,000; direct labor, $35,000; and overhead applied, $38,500. What is its predetermined overhead rate?
   - a. 10%
   - b. 110%
   - c. 86%
   - d. 91%
   - e. 117%

3. A company's ending inventory of finished goods has a total cost of $10,000 and consists of 500 units. If the overhead applied to these goods is $4,000, and the predetermined overhead rate is 80% of direct labor costs, how much direct materials cost was incurred in producing these 500 units?
   - a. $10,000
   - b. $6,000
   - c. $4,000
   - d. $5,000
   - e. $1,000

4. A company's Work in Process Inventory T-account follows.

Work in Process Inventory			
Beginning balance	9,000		
Direct materials	94,200		
Direct labor	59,200	Cost of goods	
Overhead applied	31,600	manufactured	?
Ending balance	17,800		

The cost of goods manufactured is
   - a. $193,000.
   - b. $211,800.
   - c. $185,000.
   - d. $144,600.
   - e. $176,200.

5. At the end of its current year, a company learned that its overhead was underapplied by $1,500 and that this amount is not considered material. Based on this information, the company should
   - a. Credit the $1,500 to Finished Goods Inventory.
   - b. Credit the $1,500 to Cost of Goods Sold.
   - c. Debit the $1,500 to Cost of Goods Sold.
   - d. Do nothing about the $1,500 because it is not material and it is likely that overhead will be overapplied by the same amount next year.
   - e. Include the $1,500 on the income statement as "Other Expense."

ANSWERS TO MULTIPLE CHOICE QUIZ

1. c; $30,000 × 150% = $45,000
2. b; $38,500/$35,000 = 110%
3. e; Direct materials + Direct labor + Overhead = Total cost;
   Direct materials + ($4,000/0.80) + $4,000 = $10,000
   Direct materials = $1,000

4. e; $9,000 + $94,200 + $59,200 + $31,600 − Finished goods = $17,800
   Thus, finished goods = $176,200
5. b

🖫 Icon denotes assignments that involve decision making.

Discussion Questions

1. Why must a company estimate the amount of factory overhead assigned to individual jobs or job lots?

2. 🖫 Some companies use labor cost to apply factory overhead to jobs. Identify another factor (or base) a company might reasonably use to apply overhead costs.

3. 🖫 What information is recorded on a job cost sheet? How do management and employees use job cost sheets?

4. In a job order costing system, what records serve as a subsidiary ledger for Work in Process Inventory? For Finished Goods Inventory?

5. What journal entry is recorded when a materials manager receives a materials requisition and then issues materials (both direct and indirect) for use in the factory?

6. 🖫 How does the materials requisition help safeguard a company's assets?

7. **Google** uses a "time ticket" for some employees. How are time tickets used in job order costing? **GOOGLE**

8. What events cause debits to be recorded in the Factory Overhead account? What events cause credits to be recorded in the Factory Overhead account?

9. **Google** applies overhead to product costs. What account(s) is(are) used to eliminate overapplied or underapplied overhead from the Factory Overhead account, assuming the amount is not material? **GOOGLE**

10. 🖫 Assume that **Apple** produces a batch of 1,000 iPhones. Does it account for this as 1,000 individual jobs or as a job lot? Explain (consider costs and benefits). **APPLE**

11. Why must a company use predetermined overhead rates when using job order costing?

12. 🔲 How would a hospital apply job order costing? Explain.

13. 🔲 **Harley-Davidson** manufactures 30 custom-made, luxury-model motorcycles. Does it account for these motorcycles as 30 individual jobs or as a job lot? Explain.

14. Assume **Sprint** will install and service a server to link all of a customer's employees' smartphones to a centralized company server for an up-front flat price. How can Sprint use a job order costing system?

▦ connect

Determine which of the following are most likely to be considered as a job and which as a job lot.

_____ **1.** Hats imprinted with company logo
_____ **2.** Little League trophies
_____ **3.** A handcrafted table
_____ **4.** A 90-foot motor yacht
_____ **5.** Wedding dresses for a chain of stores
_____ **6.** A custom-designed home

QUICK STUDY

QS 2-1
Jobs and job lots   C1 🔲

Clemens Cars's job cost sheet for Job A40 shows that the cost to add security features to a car was $10,500. The car was delivered to the customer, who paid $14,900 in cash for the added features. What journal entries should Clemens record for the completion and delivery of Job A40?

QS 2-2
Job cost sheets   C2

The left column lists the titles of documents and accounts used in job order costing. The right column presents short descriptions of the purposes of the documents. Match each document in the left column to its numbered description in the right column.

A. Time ticket
B. Materials ledger card
C. Voucher
D. Factory Overhead account
E. Materials requisition

_____ **1.** Shows amount of time an employee works on a job.
_____ **2.** Accumulates the cost of incurred overhead and the overhead cost assigned to specific jobs.
_____ **3.** Perpetual inventory record of raw materials received, used, and available for use.
_____ **4.** Shows amount approved for payment of an overhead or other cost.
_____ **5.** Communicates the need for materials to complete a job.

QS 2-3
Documents in job order costing

P1   P2   P3

During the current month, a company that uses job order costing purchases $50,000 in raw materials for cash. It then uses $12,000 of raw materials indirectly as factory supplies and uses $32,000 of raw materials as direct materials. Prepare journal entries to record these three transactions.

QS 2-4
Raw materials journal entries   P1

During the current month, a company that uses job order costing incurred a monthly factory payroll of $180,000. Of this amount, $40,000 is classified as indirect labor and the remainder as direct. Prepare journal entries to record these transactions.

QS 2-5
Labor journal entries   P2

A company incurred the following manufacturing costs this period: direct labor, $468,000; direct materials, $390,000; and factory overhead, $117,000. Compute its overhead cost as a percent of (1) direct labor and (2) direct materials. Express your answers as percents, rounded to the nearest whole number.

QS 2-6
Factory overhead rates
P3

At the beginning of the year, a company predicts total overhead costs of $560,000. The company applies overhead using machine hours and estimates it will use 1,400 machine hours during the year. What amount of overhead should be applied to Job 65A if that job uses 13 machine hours during January?

QS 2-7
Applying overhead   P3

At the beginning of a year, a company predicts total direct materials costs of $900,000 and total overhead costs of $1,170,000. If the company uses direct materials costs as its activity base to apply overhead, what is the predetermined overhead rate it should use during the year?

QS 2-8
Predetermined overhead rate   P3

QS 2-9

Applying overhead

P3

On March 1 a dressmaker starts work on three custom-designed wedding dresses. The company uses job order costing and applies overhead to each job (dress) at the rate of 40% of direct materials costs. During the month, the jobs used direct materials as shown below. Compute the amount of overhead applied to each of the three jobs.

	Job 1	Job 2	Job 3
Direct materials used	$5,000	$7,000	$1,500

QS 2-10

Manufacturing cost flows

P1   P2   P3

Refer to the information in QS 2-9. During the month, the jobs used direct labor as shown below. Jobs 1 and 3 are not finished by the end of March, and Job 2 is finished but not sold by the end of March. (1) Determine the amounts of direct materials, direct labor, and factory overhead applied that would be reported on job cost sheets for each of the three jobs for March. (2) Determine the total dollar amount of Work in Process Inventory at the end of March. (3) Determine the total dollar amount of Finished Goods Inventory at the end of March. Assume the company has no beginning Work in Process or Finished Goods inventories.

	Job 1	Job 2	Job 3
Direct labor used.	$9,000	$4,000	$3,000

QS 2-11

Entry for over- or underapplied overhead

P4

A company applies overhead at a rate of 150% of direct labor cost. Actual overhead cost for the current period is $950,000, and direct labor cost is $600,000. Prepare the journal entry to close over- or underapplied overhead to Cost of Goods Sold.

QS 2-12

Entry for over- or underapplied overhead

P4

A company's Factory Overhead account shows total debits of $624,000 and total credits of $646,000 at the end of the year. Prepare the journal entry to close the balance in the Factory Overhead account to Cost of Goods Sold.

QS 2-13

Job order costing of services   A1

An advertising agency is estimating costs for advertising a music festival. The job will require 200 direct labor hours at a cost of $50 per hour. Overhead costs are applied at a rate of $65 per direct labor hour. What is the total estimated cost for this job?

QS 2-14

Job order costing of services   A1

An advertising agency used 65 hours of direct labor in creating advertising for a music festival. Direct labor costs $50 per hour. The agency applies overhead at a rate of $40 per direct labor hour. Prepare journal entries to record the agency's direct labor *and* the applied overhead costs for this job.

QS 2-15

Job order production

C1

Refer to this chapter's Global View. **Porsche AG** is the manufacturer of the Porsche automobile line. Does Porsche produce in jobs or in job lots? Explain.

connect

EXERCISES

Exercise 2-1

Job order production

C1

Match each of the terms/phrases numbered 1 through 5 with the best definition *a* through *e*.

_____ 1. Cost accounting system
_____ 2. Target cost
_____ 3. Job lot
_____ 4. Job
_____ 5. Job order production

a. Production of products in response to customer orders.
b. Production activities for a customized product.
c. A system that records manufacturing costs.
d. The expected selling price of a job minus its desired profit.
e. Production of more than one unit of a custom product.

The following information is from the materials requisitions and time tickets for Job 9-1005 completed by Great Bay Boats. The requisitions are identified by code numbers starting with the letter Q, and the time tickets start with W. At the start of the year, management estimated that overhead cost would equal 110% of direct labor cost for each job. Determine the total cost on the job cost sheet for Job 9-1005.

Exercise 2-2
Job cost computation
C2

Date	Document	Amount
7/1/2017.....................	Q-4698	$1,250
7/1/2017.....................	W-3393	600
7/5/2017.....................	Q-4725	1,000
7/5/2017.....................	W-3479	450
7/10/2017....................	W-3559	300

As of the end of June, the job cost sheets at Racing Wheels, Inc., show the following total costs accumulated on three custom jobs.

Exercise 2-3
Analysis of cost flows
C2

	Job 102	Job 103	Job 104
Direct materials	$15,000	$33,000	$27,000
Direct labor..............	8,000	14,200	21,000
Overhead applied.........	4,000	7,100	10,500

Job 102 was started in production in May, and the following costs were assigned to it in May: direct materials, $6,000; direct labor, $1,800; and overhead, $900. Jobs 103 and 104 were started in June. Overhead cost is applied with a predetermined rate based on direct labor cost. Jobs 102 and 103 were finished in June, and Job 104 is expected to be finished in July. No raw materials were used indirectly in June. Using this information, answer the following questions. (Assume this company's predetermined overhead rate did not change across these months.)

1. What was the cost of the raw materials requisitioned in June for each of the three jobs?
2. How much direct labor cost was incurred during June for each of the three jobs?
3. What predetermined overhead rate is used during June?
4. How much total cost is transferred to finished goods during June?

Check   (4) $81,300

Starr Company reports the following information for August.

Exercise 2-4
Recording product costs

P1   P2   P3

Raw materials purchased on account.............	$76,200
Direct materials used in production	$48,000
Factory wages earned (direct labor)..............	$15,350
Overhead rate...............................	120% of direct labor cost

Prepare journal entries to record the following events.

1. Raw materials purchased.
2. Direct materials used in production.
3. Direct labor used in production.
4. Applied overhead.

Custom Cabinetry has one job in process (Job 120) as of June 30; at that time, its job cost sheet reports direct materials of $6,000, direct labor of $2,800, and applied overhead of $2,240. Custom Cabinetry applies overhead at the rate of 80% of direct labor cost. During July, Job 120 is sold (on account) for $22,000, Job 121 is started and completed, and Job 122 is started and still in process at the end of the month. Custom Cabinetry incurs the following costs during July.

Exercise 2-5
Manufacturing cost flows

P1   P2   P3

July Product Costs	Job 120	Job 121	Job 122	Total
Direct materials	$1,000	$6,000	$2,500	$9,500
Direct labor................	2,200	3,700	2,100	8,000
Overhead applied...........	?	?	?	?

1. Prepare journal entries for the following transactions and events *a* through *e* in July.
   a. Direct materials used in production.
   d. The sale of Job 120.
   b. Direct labor used in production.
   e. Cost of goods sold for Job 120.
   c. Overhead applied.

2. Compute the July 31 balances of the Work in Process Inventory and the Finished Goods Inventory accounts. (Assume there are no jobs in Finished Goods Inventory as of June 30.)

Exercise 2-6

Recording events in job order costing

P1   P2   P3   P4

Using Exhibit 2.15 as a guide, prepare summary journal entries to record the following transactions and events *a* through *g* for a company in its first month of operations.

a. Raw materials purchased on account, $90,000.

b. Direct materials used in production, $36,500. Indirect materials used in production, $19,200.

c. Paid cash for factory payroll, $50,000. Of this total, $38,000 is for direct labor and $12,000 is for indirect labor.

d. Paid cash for other actual overhead costs, $11,475.

e. Applied overhead at the rate of 125% of direct labor cost.

f. Transferred cost of jobs completed to finished goods, $56,800.

g. Sold jobs on account for $82,000. The jobs had a cost of $56,800.

Exercise 2-7

Cost flows in a job order costing system

P1   P2   P3   P4

The following information is available for Lock-Tite Company, which produces special-order security products and uses a job order costing system.

	April 30	May 31
Inventories		
Raw materials..	$43,000	$ 52,000
Work in process	10,200	21,300
Finished goods..	63,000	35,600
Activities and information for May		
Raw materials purchases (paid with cash)		210,000
Factory payroll (paid with cash)		345,000
Factory overhead		
Indirect materials...		15,000
Indirect labor...		80,000
Other overhead costs		120,000
Sales (received in cash)...		1,400,000
Predetermined overhead rate based on direct labor cost		70%

Compute the following amounts for the month of May.

1. Cost of direct materials used.
4. Cost of goods sold.*

   *Do not consider any underapplied or overapplied overhead.

2. Cost of direct labor used.
5. Gross profit.

Check   (3) $625,400

3. Cost of goods manufactured.
6. Overapplied or underapplied overhead.

Exercise 2-8

Journal entries for materials

P1

Use information in Exercise 2-7 to prepare journal entries for the following events for the month of May.

1. Raw materials purchases for cash.
3. Indirect materials usage.

2. Direct materials usage.

Exercise 2-9

Journal entries for labor

P2

Use information in Exercise 2-7 to prepare journal entries for the following events for the month of May.

1. Direct labor usage.
3. Total payroll paid in cash.

2. Indirect labor usage.

Exercise 2-10

Journal entries for overhead   P3

Use information in Exercise 2-7 to prepare journal entries for the following events for the month of May.

1. Incurred other overhead costs (record credit to Other Accounts).

2. Applied overhead to work in process.

In December 2016, Shire Computer's management establishes the 2017 predetermined overhead rate based on direct labor cost. The information used in setting this rate includes estimates that the company will incur $747,500 of overhead costs and $575,000 of direct labor cost in year 2017. During March 2017, Shire began and completed Job 13-56.

Exercise 2-11
Overhead rate; costs assigned to jobs
P3

1. What is the predetermined overhead rate for 2017?

2. Use the information on the following job cost sheet to determine the total cost of the job.

Check   (2) $22,710

			JOB COST SHEET				
Customer's Name		Keiser Co.			**Job No.**	13-56	
Job Description		5 plasma monitors—61 inch					

	Direct Materials			**Direct Labor**		**Overhead Costs Applied**	
Date	Requisition No.	Amount	Time-Ticket No.	Amount	Rate	Amount	
Mar. 8	4-129	$5,000	T-306	$ 700			
Mar. 11	4-142	7,020	T-432	1,250			
Mar. 18	4-167	3,330	T-456	1,250			
Totals							

Lorenzo Company uses a job order costing system that charges overhead to jobs on the basis of direct materials cost. At year-end, the Work in Process Inventory account shows the following.

Exercise 2-12
Analysis of costs assigned to work in process
P3

	A	B	C	D	E
1		**Work in Process Inventory**			
2		**Acct. No. 121**			
3	**Date**	**Explanation**	**Debit**	**Credit**	**Balance**
4	2017				
5	Dec. 31	Direct materials cost	1,500,000		1,500,000
6	31	Direct labor cost	300,000		1,800,000
7	31	Overhead applied	600,000		2,400,000
8	31	To finished goods		2,350,000	50,000

1. Determine the predetermined overhead rate used (based on direct materials cost).

2. Only one job remained in work in process inventory at December 31, 2017. Its direct materials cost is $30,000. How much direct labor cost and overhead cost are assigned to this job?

Check   (2) Direct labor cost, $8,000

Refer to information in Exercise 2-7. Prepare the journal entry to close overapplied or underapplied overhead to Cost of Goods Sold.

Exercise 2-13
Adjusting factory overhead   P4

Record the journal entry to close over- or underapplied factory overhead to Cost of Goods Sold for each of the two companies below.

Exercise 2-14
Adjusting factory overhead
P4

	Storm Concert Promotions	**Valle Home Builders**
Actual indirect materials costs.............	$22,000	$ 12,500
Actual indirect labor costs	46,000	46,500
Other overhead costs....................	17,000	47,000
Overhead applied......................	88,200	105,200

Exercise 2-15

Factory overhead computed, applied, and adjusted

P3   P4

In December 2016, Custom Mfg. established its predetermined overhead rate for jobs produced during 2017 by using the following cost predictions: overhead costs, $750,000, and direct materials costs, $625,000. At year-end 2017, the company's records show that actual overhead costs for the year are $830,000. Actual direct materials cost had been assigned to jobs as follows.

Jobs completed and sold....................	$513,750
Jobs in finished goods inventory..............	102,750
Jobs in work in process inventory.............	68,500
Total actual direct materials cost.............	$685,000

1. Determine the predetermined overhead rate, using predicted direct materials costs, for 2017.

2. Set up a T-account for Factory Overhead and enter the overhead costs incurred and the amounts applied to jobs during the year using the predetermined overhead rate.

Check (3) $8,000 underapplied

3. Determine whether overhead is overapplied or underapplied (and the amount) during the year.

4. Prepare the adjusting entry to allocate any over- or underapplied overhead to Cost of Goods Sold.

Exercise 2-16

Factory overhead computed, applied, and adjusted

P3   P4

In December 2016, Infodeo established its predetermined overhead rate for movies produced during 2017 by using the following cost predictions: overhead costs, $1,680,000, and direct labor costs, $480,000. At year-end 2017, the company's records show that actual overhead costs for the year are $1,652,000. Actual direct labor cost had been assigned to jobs as follows.

Movies completed and released...............	$425,000
Movies still in production....................	50,000
Total actual direct labor cost	$475,000

1. Determine the predetermined overhead rate for 2017.

2. Set up a T-account for overhead and enter the overhead costs incurred and the amounts applied to movies during the year using the predetermined overhead rate.

Check (3) $10,500 overapplied

3. Determine whether overhead is overapplied or underapplied (and the amount) during the year.

4. Prepare the adjusting entry to allocate any over- or underapplied overhead to Cost of Goods Sold.

Exercise 2-17

Overhead rate calculation, allocation, and analysis

P3

Moonrise Bakery applies factory overhead based on direct labor costs. The company incurred the following costs during 2017: direct materials costs, $650,000; direct labor costs, $3,000,000; and factory overhead costs applied, $1,800,000.

1. Determine the company's predetermined overhead rate for 2017.

2. Assuming that the company's $71,000 ending Work in Process Inventory account for 2017 had $20,000 of direct labor costs, determine the inventory's direct materials costs.

Check (3) $90,000 overhead costs

3. Assuming that the company's $490,000 ending Finished Goods Inventory account for 2017 had $250,000 of direct materials costs, determine the inventory's direct labor costs and its overhead costs.

Exercise 2-18

Job order costing for services

A1

Hansel Corporation has requested bids from several architects to design its new corporate headquarters. Frey Architects is one of the firms bidding on the job. Frey estimates that the job will require the following direct labor.

	A	B	C
1	**Labor**	**Estimated Hours**	**Hourly Rate**
2	Architects	150	$300
3	Staff	300	75
4	Clerical	500	20

Frey applies overhead to jobs at 175% of direct labor cost. Frey would like to earn at least $80,000 profit on the architectural job. Based on past experience and market research, it estimates that the competition will bid between $285,000 and $350,000 for the job.

Check (1) $213,125

1. What is Frey's estimated cost of the architectural job?

2. What bid would you suggest that Frey submit?

Diaz and Associates incurred the following costs in completing a tax return for a large company. Diaz applies overhead at 50% of direct labor cost.

Exercise 2-19
Job order costing
of services
A1

Labor	Hours Used	Hourly Rate
Partner.....................	5	$500
Senior manager	12	200
Staff accountants	100	50

1. Prepare journal entries to record direct labor *and* the overhead applied.

2. Prepare the journal entry to record the cost of services provided. Assume the beginning Services in Process Inventory account has a zero balance.

A recent balance sheet for **Porsche AG** shows beginning raw materials inventory of €83 million and ending raw materials inventory of €85 million. Assume the company purchased raw materials (on account) for €3,108 million during the year. (1) Prepare journal entries to record (*a*) the purchase of raw materials and (*b*) the use of raw materials in production. (2) What do you notice about the € amounts in your journal entries?

Exercise 2-20
Direct materials journal
entries P1

connect

Marcelino Co.'s March 31 inventory of raw materials is $80,000. Raw materials purchases in April are $500,000, and factory payroll cost in April is $363,000. Overhead costs incurred in April are: indirect materials, $50,000; indirect labor, $23,000; factory rent, $32,000; factory utilities, $19,000; and factory equipment depreciation, $51,000. The predetermined overhead rate is 50% of direct labor cost. Job 306 is sold for $635,000 cash in April. Costs of the three jobs worked on in April follow.

PROBLEM SET A

Problem 2-1A
Production costs
computed and recorded;
reports prepared

C2 P1 P2 P3 P4

	Job 306	Job 307	Job 308
Balances on March 31			
Direct materials	$ 29,000	$ 35,000	
Direct labor.................	20,000	18,000	
Applied overhead............	10,000	9,000	
Costs during April			
Direct materials	135,000	220,000	$100,000
Direct labor.................	85,000	150,000	105,000
Applied overhead............	?	?	?
Status on April 30.............	Finished (sold)	Finished (unsold)	In process

Required

1. Determine the total of each production cost incurred for April (direct labor, direct materials, and applied overhead) and the total cost assigned to each job (including the balances from March 31).

2. Prepare journal entries for the month of April to record the following.

  a. Materials purchases (on credit).

  b. Direct materials used in production.

  c. Direct labor paid and assigned to Work in Process Inventory.

  d. Indirect labor paid and assigned to Factory Overhead.

  e. Overhead costs applied to Work in Process Inventory.

  f. Actual overhead costs incurred, including indirect materials. (Factory rent and utilities are paid in cash.)

  g. Transfer of Jobs 306 and 307 to Finished Goods Inventory.

  h. Cost of goods sold for Job 306.

  i. Revenue from the sale of Job 306.

  j. Assignment of any underapplied or overapplied overhead to the Cost of Goods Sold account. (The amount is not material.)

Check (2*j*) $5,000
underapplied

(3) Cost of goods
manufactured, $828,500

3. Prepare a schedule of cost of goods manufactured.

4. Compute gross profit for April. Show how to present the inventories on the April 30 balance sheet.

Analysis Component

5. The over- or underapplied overhead is closed to Cost of Goods Sold. Discuss how this adjustment impacts business decision making regarding individual jobs or batches of jobs.

Problem 2-2A

Source documents, journal
entries, overhead, and
financial reports

P1   P2   P3   P4

Bergamo Bay's computer system generated the following trial balance on December 31, 2017. The company's manager knows something is wrong with the trial balance because it does not show any balance for Work in Process Inventory but does show a balance for the Factory Overhead account. In addition, the accrued factory payroll (Factory Wages Payable) has not been recorded.

	Debit	Credit
Cash	$170,000	
Accounts receivable	75,000	
Raw materials inventory...............	80,000	
Work in process inventory	0	
Finished goods inventory	15,000	
Prepaid rent	3,000	
Accounts payable		$ 17,000
Notes payable.......................		25,000
Common stock		50,000
Retained earnings		271,000
Sales		373,000
Cost of goods sold	218,000	
Factory overhead....................	115,000	
Operating expenses	60,000	
Totals	$736,000	$736,000

After examining various files, the manager identifies the following six source documents that need to be processed to bring the accounting records up to date.

Materials requisition 21-3010:	$10,200 direct materials to Job 402
Materials requisition 21-3011:	$18,600 direct materials to Job 404
Materials requisition 21-3012:	$5,600 indirect materials
Labor time ticket 6052:	$36,000 direct labor to Job 402
Labor time ticket 6053:	$23,800 direct labor to Job 404
Labor time ticket 6054:	$8,200 indirect labor

Jobs 402 and 404 are the only units in process at year-end. The predetermined overhead rate is 200% of direct labor cost.

Required

1. Use information on the six source documents to prepare journal entries to assign the following costs.
   a. Direct materials costs to Work in Process Inventory.
   b. Direct labor costs to Work in Process Inventory.
   c. Overhead costs to Work in Process Inventory.
   d. Indirect materials costs to the Factory Overhead account.
   e. Indirect labor costs to the Factory Overhead account.

Check   (2) $9,200
underapplied overhead

(3) T. B. totals,
$804,000
(4) Net income,
$85,800

2. Determine the revised balance of the Factory Overhead account after making the entries in part 1. Determine whether there is any under- or overapplied overhead for the year. Prepare the adjusting entry to allocate any over- or underapplied overhead to Cost of Goods Sold, assuming the amount is not material.

3. Prepare a revised trial balance.

4. Prepare an income statement for 2017 and a balance sheet as of December 31, 2017.

Analysis Component

5. Assume that the $5,600 on materials requisition 21-3012 should have been direct materials charged to Job 404. Without providing specific calculations, describe the impact of this error on the income statement for 2017 and the balance sheet at December 31, 2017.

Widmer Watercraft's predetermined overhead rate for 2017 is 200% of direct labor. Information on the company's production activities during May 2017 follows.

a. Purchased raw materials on credit, $200,000.

b. Materials requisitions record use of the following materials for the month.

Job 136.....................................	$ 48,000
Job 137.....................................	32,000
Job 138.....................................	19,200
Job 139.....................................	22,400
Job 140.....................................	6,400
Total direct materials	128,000
Indirect materials	19,500
Total materials used........................	$147,500

c. Paid $15,000 cash to a computer consultant to reprogram factory equipment.

d. Time tickets record use of the following labor for the month. These wages were paid in cash.

Job 136	$ 12,000
Job 137	10,500
Job 138	37,500
Job 139	39,000
Job 140	3,000
Total direct labor	102,000
Indirect labor...............................	24,000
Total	$126,000

e. Applied overhead to Jobs 136, 138, and 139.

f. Transferred Jobs 136, 138, and 139 to Finished Goods.

g. Sold Jobs 136 and 138 on credit at a total price of $525,000.

h. The company incurred the following overhead costs during the month (credit Prepaid Insurance for expired factory insurance).

Depreciation of factory building	$68,000
Depreciation of factory equipment	36,500
Expired factory insurance	10,000
Accrued property taxes payable	35,000

i. Applied overhead at month-end to the Work in Process Inventory account (Jobs 137 and 140) using the predetermined overhead rate of 200% of direct labor cost.

Required

1. Prepare a job cost sheet for each job worked on during the month. Use the following simplified form.

Job No. _____	
Materials...........	$ _____
Labor..............	_____
Overhead	_____
Total cost	$ _____

2. Prepare journal entries to record the events and transactions *a* through *i*.

3. Set up T-accounts for each of the following general ledger accounts, each of which started the month with a zero balance: Raw Materials Inventory; Work in Process Inventory; Finished Goods Inventory; Factory Overhead; Cost of Goods Sold. Then post the journal entries to these T-accounts and determine the balance of each account.

4. Prepare a report showing the total cost of each job in process and prove that the sum of their costs equals the Work in Process Inventory account balance. Prepare similar reports for Finished Goods Inventory and Cost of Goods Sold.

Problem 2-3A

Source documents, journal entries, and accounts in job order costing

P1 P2 P3

Check (2e) Cr. Factory Overhead, $177,000

Check (4) Finished Goods Inventory, $139,400

Problem 2-4A

Overhead allocation and adjustment using a predetermined overhead rate

P3   P4

In December 2016, Learer Company's manager estimated next year's total direct labor cost assuming 50 persons working an average of 2,000 hours each at an average wage rate of $25 per hour. The manager also estimated the following manufacturing overhead costs for 2017.

Indirect labor	$ 319,200
Factory supervision	240,000
Rent on factory building	140,000
Factory utilities	88,000
Factory insurance expired	68,000
Depreciation—Factory equipment	480,000
Repairs expense—Factory equipment	60,000
Factory supplies used	68,800
Miscellaneous production costs	36,000
Total estimated overhead costs	$1,500,000

At the end of 2017, records show the company incurred $1,520,000 of actual overhead costs. It completed and sold five jobs with the following direct labor costs: Job 201, $604,000; Job 202, $563,000; Job 203, $298,000; Job 204, $716,000; and Job 205, $314,000. In addition, Job 206 is in process at the end of 2017 and had been charged $17,000 for direct labor. No jobs were in process at the end of 2016. The company's predetermined overhead rate is based on direct labor cost.

Required

1. Determine the following.

   a. Predetermined overhead rate for 2017.

   b. Total overhead cost applied to each of the six jobs during 2017.

   c. Over- or underapplied overhead at year-end 2017.

Check   (1c) 12,800 underapplied

          (2) Cr. Factory Overhead, $12,800

2. Assuming that any over- or underapplied overhead is not material, prepare the adjusting entry to allocate any over- or underapplied overhead to Cost of Goods Sold at the end of 2017.

Problem 2-5A

Production transactions, subsidiary records, and source documents

P1   P2   P3   P4

Sager Company manufactures variations of its product, a technopress, in response to custom orders from its customers. On May 1, the company had no inventories of work in process or finished goods but held the following raw materials.

Material M	200 units @ $250 =	$50,000
Material R	95 units @ 180 =	17,100
Paint	55 units @ 75 =	4,125
Total cost		$71,225

On May 4, the company began working on two technopresses: Job 102 for Worldwide Company and Job 103 for Reuben Company.

Required

Using Exhibit 2.3 as a guide, prepare job cost sheets for Jobs 102 and 103. Using Exhibit 2.5 as a guide, prepare materials ledger cards for Material M, Material R, and paint. Enter the beginning raw materials inventory dollar amounts for each of these materials on their respective ledger cards. Then, follow the instructions in this list of activities.

a. Purchased raw materials on credit and recorded the following information from receiving reports and invoices.

> Receiving Report No. 426, Material M, 250 units at $250 each.
> Receiving Report No. 427, Material R, 90 units at $180 each.

Instructions: Record these purchases with a single journal entry. Enter the receiving report information on the materials ledger cards.

b. Requisitioned the following raw materials for production.

> Requisition No. 35, for Job 102, 135 units of Material M.
> Requisition No. 36, for Job 102, 72 units of Material R.
> Requisition No. 37, for Job 103, 70 units of Material M.
> Requisition No. 38, for Job 103, 38 units of Material R.
> Requisition No. 39, for 15 units of paint.

Instructions: Enter amounts for direct materials requisitions on the materials ledger cards and the job cost sheets. Enter the indirect materials amount on the materials ledger card. Do not record a journal entry at this time.

c. Received the following employee time tickets for work in May.

> Time tickets Nos. 1 to 10 for direct labor on Job 102, $90,000.
> Time tickets Nos. 11 to 30 for direct labor on Job 103, $65,000.
> Time tickets Nos. 31 to 36 for equipment repairs, $19,250.

Instructions: Record direct labor from the time tickets on the job cost sheets. Do not record a journal entry at this time.

d. Paid cash for the following items during the month: factory payroll, $174,250, and miscellaneous overhead items, $102,000. Use the time tickets to record the total direct and indirect labor costs.

Instructions: Record these payments with journal entries.

e. Finished Job 102 and transferred it to the warehouse. The company assigns overhead to each job with a predetermined overhead rate equal to 80% of direct labor cost.

Instructions: Enter the applied overhead on the cost sheet for Job 102, fill in the cost summary section of the cost sheet, and then mark the cost sheet "Finished." Prepare a journal entry to record the job's completion and its transfer to Finished Goods.

f. Delivered Job 102 and accepted the customer's promise to pay $400,000 within 30 days.

Instructions: Prepare journal entries to record the sale of Job 102 and the cost of goods sold.

g. Applied overhead cost to Job 103 based on the job's direct labor to date.

Instructions: Enter overhead on the job cost sheet but do not make a journal entry at this time.

h. Recorded the total direct and indirect materials costs as reported on all the requisitions for the month.

Instructions: Prepare a journal entry to record these costs.

i. Recorded the total overhead costs applied to jobs.

Instructions: Prepare a journal entry to record the allocation of these overhead costs.

j. Compute the balance in the Factory Overhead account as of the end of May.

Check (*h*) Dr. Work in Process Inventory, $71,050

(*j*) Balance in Factory Overhead, $1,625 Cr., overapplied

Perez Mfg.'s August 31 inventory of raw materials is $150,000. Raw materials purchases in September are $400,000, and factory payroll cost in September is $232,000. Overhead costs incurred in September are: indirect materials, $30,000; indirect labor, $14,000; factory rent, $20,000; factory utilities, $12,000; and factory equipment depreciation, $30,000. The predetermined overhead rate is 50% of direct labor cost. Job 114 is sold for $380,000 cash in September. Costs for the three jobs worked on in September follow.

PROBLEM SET B

Problem 2-1B
Production costs computed and recorded; reports prepared

C2 P1 P2 P3 P4

	Job 114	Job 115	Job 116
Balances on August 31			
Direct materials	$ 14,000	$ 18,000	
Direct labor.....................	18,000	16,000	
Applied overhead...............	9,000	8,000	
Costs during September			
Direct materials	100,000	170,000	$ 80,000
Direct labor.....................	30,000	68,000	120,000
Applied overhead...............	?	?	?
Status on September 30	Finished (sold)	Finished (unsold)	In process

Required

1. Determine the total of each production cost incurred for September (direct labor, direct materials, and applied overhead) and the total cost assigned to each job (including the balances from August 31).
2. Prepare journal entries for the month of September to record the following.
    a. Materials purchases (on credit).
    b. Direct materials used in production.
    c. Direct labor paid and assigned to Work in Process Inventory.
    d. Indirect labor paid and assigned to Factory Overhead.
    e. Overhead costs applied to Work in Process Inventory.
    f. Actual overhead costs incurred, including indirect materials. (Factory rent and utilities are paid in cash.)
    g. Transfer of Jobs 114 and 115 to the Finished Goods Inventory.
    h. Cost of Job 114 in the Cost of Goods Sold account.
    i. Revenue from the sale of Job 114.

Check (2*j*) $3,000
overapplied

   j. Assignment of any underapplied or overapplied overhead to the Cost of Goods Sold account. (The amount is not material.)

     (3) Cost of goods
manufactured, $500,000

3. Prepare a schedule of cost of goods manufactured.
4. Compute gross profit for September. Show how to present the inventories on the September 30 balance sheet.

Analysis Component

5. The over- or underapplied overhead adjustment is closed to Cost of Goods Sold. Discuss how this adjustment impacts business decision making regarding individual jobs or batches of jobs.

Problem 2-2B

Source documents, journal entries, overhead, and financial reports

P1   P2   P3   P4

Cavallo Mfg.'s computer system generated the following trial balance on December 31, 2017. The company's manager knows that the trial balance is wrong because it does not show any balance for Work in Process Inventory but does show a balance for the Factory Overhead account. In addition, the accrued factory payroll (Factory Wages Payable) has not been recorded.

	Debit	Credit
Cash	$ 64,000	
Accounts receivable	42,000	
Raw materials inventory	26,000	
Work in process inventory	0	
Finished goods inventory	9,000	
Prepaid rent	3,000	
Accounts payable		$ 10,500
Notes payable		13,500
Common stock		30,000
Retained earnings		87,000
Sales		180,000
Cost of goods sold	105,000	
Factory overhead	27,000	
Operating expenses	45,000	
Totals	$321,000	$321,000

After examining various files, the manager identifies the following six source documents that need to be processed to bring the accounting records up to date.

Materials requisition 94-231:	$4,600 direct materials to Job 603
Materials requisition 94-232:	$7,600 direct materials to Job 604
Materials requisition 94-233:	$2,100 indirect materials
Labor time ticket 765:	$5,000 direct labor to Job 603
Labor time ticket 766:	$8,000 direct labor to Job 604
Labor time ticket 777:	$3,000 indirect labor

Jobs 603 and 604 are the only units in process at year-end. The predetermined overhead rate is 200% of direct labor cost.

Required

1. Use information on the six source documents to prepare journal entries to assign the following costs.

   a. Direct materials costs to Work in Process Inventory.

   b. Direct labor costs to Work in Process Inventory.

   c. Overhead costs to Work in Process Inventory.

   d. Indirect materials costs to the Factory Overhead account.

   e. Indirect labor costs to the Factory Overhead account.

2. Determine the revised balance of the Factory Overhead account after making the entries in part 1. Determine whether there is under- or overapplied overhead for the year. Prepare the adjusting entry to allocate any over- or underapplied overhead to Cost of Goods Sold, assuming the amount is not material.

3. Prepare a revised trial balance.

4. Prepare an income statement for 2017 and a balance sheet as of December 31, 2017.

Analysis Component

5. Assume that the $2,100 indirect materials on materials requisition 94-233 should have been direct materials charged to Job 604. Without providing specific calculations, describe the impact of this error on the income statement for 2017 and the balance sheet at December 31, 2017.

Check (2) $6,100 underapplied overhead

(3) T. B. totals, $337,000

(4) Net income, $23,900

Starr Mfg.'s predetermined overhead rate is 200% of direct labor. Information on the company's production activities during September 2017 follows.

   a. Purchased raw materials on credit, $125,000.

   b. Materials requisitions record use of the following materials for the month.

Problem 2-3B
Source documents, journal entries, and accounts in job order costing

P1   P2   P3

Job 487	$30,000
Job 488	20,000
Job 489	12,000
Job 490	14,000
Job 491	4,000
Total direct materials	80,000
Indirect materials	12,000
Total materials used	$92,000

   c. Paid $11,000 cash for miscellaneous factory overhead costs.

   d. Time tickets record use of the following labor for the month. These wages are paid in cash.

Job 487	$ 8,000
Job 488	7,000
Job 489	25,000
Job 490	26,000
Job 491	2,000
Total direct labor	68,000
Indirect labor	16,000
Total	$84,000

   e. Applied overhead to Jobs 487, 489, and 490.

   f. Transferred Jobs 487, 489, and 490 to Finished Goods.

g. Sold Jobs 487 and 489 on credit for a total price of $340,000.

h. The company incurred the following overhead costs during the month (credit Prepaid Insurance for expired factory insurance).

Depreciation of factory building...................	$37,000
Depreciation of factory equipment	21,000
Expired factory insurance........................	7,000
Accrued property taxes payable...................	31,000

i. Applied overhead at month-end to the Work in Process Inventory account (Jobs 488 and 491) using the predetermined overhead rate of 200% of direct labor cost.

Required

1. Prepare a job cost sheet for each job worked on in the month. Use the following simplified form.

Job No. _____
Materials........... $ _____
Labor.............. _____
Overhead .... _____
Total cost .... $ _____

Check   (2e) Cr. Factory
Overhead, $118,000
        (3) Finished Goods
Inventory, $92,000 bal.

2. Prepare journal entries to record the events and transactions *a* through *i*.

3. Set up T-accounts for each of the following general ledger accounts, each of which started the month with a zero balance: Raw Materials Inventory, Work in Process Inventory, Finished Goods Inventory, Factory Overhead, Cost of Goods Sold. Then post the journal entries to these T-accounts and determine the balance of each account.

4. Prepare a report showing the total cost of each job in process and prove that the sum of their costs equals the Work in Process Inventory account balance. Prepare similar reports for Finished Goods Inventory and Cost of Goods Sold.

Problem 2-4B

Overhead allocation and adjustment using a predetermined overhead rate

P3   P4

In December 2016, Pavelka Company's manager estimated next year's total direct labor cost assuming 50 persons working an average of 2,000 hours each at an average wage rate of $15 per hour. The manager also estimated the following manufacturing overhead costs for 2017.

Indirect labor	$159,600
Factory supervision.............................	120,000
Rent on factory building	70,000
Factory utilities	44,000
Factory insurance expired	34,000
Depreciation—Factory equipment.................	240,000
Repairs expense—Factory equipment	30,000
Factory supplies used	34,400
Miscellaneous production costs	18,000
Total estimated overhead costs..................	$750,000

At the end of 2017, records show the company incurred $725,000 of actual overhead costs. It completed and sold five jobs with the following direct labor costs: Job 625, $354,000; Job 626, $330,000; Job 627, $175,000; Job 628, $420,000; and Job 629, $184,000. In addition, Job 630 is in process at the end of 2017 and had been charged $10,000 for direct labor. No jobs were in process at the end of 2016. The company's predetermined overhead rate is based on direct labor cost.

Required

1. Determine the following.

   a. Predetermined overhead rate for 2017.

   b. Total overhead cost applied to each of the six jobs during 2017.

   c. Over- or underapplied overhead at year-end 2017.

2. Assuming that any over- or underapplied overhead is not material, prepare the adjusting entry to allocate any over- or underapplied overhead to Cost of Goods Sold at the end of year 2017.

Check (1c) $11,500 overapplied
(2) Dr. Factory Overhead, $11,500

King Company produces variations of its product, a megatron, in response to custom orders from its customers. On June 1, the company had no inventories of work in process or finished goods but held the following raw materials.

Problem 2-5B
Production transactions, subsidiary records, and source documents

P1 P2 P3 P4

Material M......................	120 units @ $200 = $24,000
Material R	80 units @ 160 = 12,800
Paint	44 units @ 72 = 3,168
Total cost......................	$39,968

On June 3, the company began working on two megatrons: Job 450 for Encinita Company and Job 451 for Fargo, Inc.

Required

Using Exhibit 2.3 as a guide, prepare job cost sheets for Jobs 450 and 451. Using Exhibit 2.5 as a guide, prepare materials ledger cards for Material M, Material R, and paint. Enter the beginning raw materials inventory dollar amounts for each of these materials on their respective ledger cards. Then, follow instructions in this list of activities.

a. Purchased raw materials on credit and recorded the following information from receiving reports and invoices.

> Receiving Report No. 20, Material M, 150 units at $200 each.
> Receiving Report No. 21, Material R, 70 units at $160 each.

Instructions: Record these purchases with a single journal entry. Enter the receiving report information on the materials ledger cards.

b. Requisitioned the following raw materials for production.

> Requisition No. 223, for Job 450, 80 units of Material M.
> Requisition No. 224, for Job 450, 60 units of Material R.
> Requisition No. 225, for Job 451, 40 units of Material M.
> Requisition No. 226, for Job 451, 30 units of Material R.
> Requisition No. 227, for 12 units of paint.

Instructions: Enter amounts for direct materials requisitions on the materials ledger cards and the job cost sheets. Enter the indirect materials amount on the materials ledger card. Do not record a journal entry at this time.

c. Received the following employee time tickets for work in June.

> Time tickets Nos. 1 to 10 for direct labor on Job 450, $40,000.
> Time tickets Nos. 11 to 20 for direct labor on Job 451, $32,000.
> Time tickets Nos. 21 to 24 for equipment repairs, $12,000.

Instructions: Record direct labor from the time tickets on the job cost sheets. Do not record a journal entry at this time.

d. Paid cash for the following items during the month: factory payroll, $84,000, and miscellaneous overhead items, $36,800. Use the time tickets to record the total direct and indirect labor costs.

Instructions: Record these payments with journal entries.

e. Finished Job 450 and transferred it to the warehouse. The company assigns overhead to each job with a predetermined overhead rate equal to 70% of direct labor cost.

Instructions: Enter the applied overhead on the cost sheet for Job 450, fill in the cost summary section of the cost sheet, and then mark the cost sheet "Finished." Prepare a journal entry to record the job's completion and its transfer to Finished Goods.

f. Delivered Job 450 and accepted the customer's promise to pay $290,000 within 30 days.

Instructions: Prepare journal entries to record the sale of Job 450 and the cost of goods sold.

g. Applied overhead cost to Job 451 based on the job's direct labor used to date.

Instructions: Enter overhead on the job cost sheet but do not make a journal entry at this time.

Check *(h)* Dr. Work in Process Inventory, $38,400

(j) Balance in Factory Overhead, $736 Cr., overapplied

h. Recorded the total direct and indirect materials costs as reported on all the requisitions for the month.

Instructions: Prepare a journal entry to record these.

i. Recorded the total overhead costs applied to jobs.

Instructions: Prepare a journal entry to record the allocation of these overhead costs.

j. Compute the balance in the Factory Overhead account as of the end of June.

SERIAL PROBLEM
Business Solutions

P1 P2 P3

© Alexander Image/Shutterstock RF

(This serial problem began in Chapter 1 and continues through most of the book. If previous chapter segments were not completed, the serial problem can begin at this point.)

SP 2 The computer workstation furniture manufacturing that Santana Rey started in January is progressing well. As of the end of June, **Business Solutions**'s job cost sheets show the following total costs accumulated on three furniture jobs.

	Job 602	Job 603	Job 604
Direct materials	$1,500	$3,300	$2,700
Direct labor	800	1,420	2,100
Overhead	400	710	1,050

Job 602 was started in production in May, and these costs were assigned to it in May: direct materials, $600; direct labor, $180; and overhead, $90. Jobs 603 and 604 were started in June. Overhead cost is applied with a predetermined rate based on direct labor costs. Jobs 602 and 603 are finished in June, and Job 604 is expected to be finished in July. No raw materials are used indirectly in June. (Assume this company's predetermined overhead rate did not change over these months.)

Required

Check (1) Total materials, $6,900

(3) 50%

1. What is the cost of the raw materials used in June for each of the three jobs and in total?

2. How much total direct labor cost is incurred in June?

3. What predetermined overhead rate is used in June?

4. How much cost is transferred to Finished Goods Inventory in June?

GENERAL LEDGER PROBLEM

GL

Available only in Connect

connect

The **General Ledger** tool in *Connect* automates several of the procedural steps in accounting so that the financial professional can focus on the impacts of each transaction on various reports and performance measures.

GL 2-1 General Ledger assignment GL 2-1, based on Problem 2-1A, focuses on transactions related to job order costing. Prepare summary journal entries to record the cost of jobs and their flow through the manufacturing environment. Then prepare a schedule of cost of goods manufactured and a partial income statement.

Beyond the Numbers

BTN 2-1   Manufacturers and merchandisers can apply just-in-time (JIT) to their inventory management. **Apple** wants to know the impact of a JIT inventory system on operating cash flows. Review Apple's statement of cash flows in Appendix A to answer the following.

REPORTING IN ACTION

P1

APPLE

Required

1. Identify the impact on operating cash flows (increase or decrease) for changes in inventory levels (increase or decrease) for each of the three most recent years.
2. What impact would a JIT inventory system have on Apple's operating income? Link the answer to your response for part 1.
3. Would the move to a JIT system have a one-time or recurring impact on operating cash flow?

BTN 2-2   **Apple**'s and **Google**'s income statements in Appendix A both show increasing sales and cost of sales. The gross margin ratio can be used to analyze how well companies control costs as sales increase.

COMPARATIVE ANALYSIS

P1

APPLE
GOOGLE

Required

1. Compute the gross margin ratio for Apple for each of the three most recent years.
2. Compute the gross margin ratio for Google for each of the three most recent years.
3. Do your computed gross margin ratios indicate good cost control for each company? Explain.

BTN 2-3   Assume that your company sells portable housing to both general contractors and the government. It sells jobs to contractors on a bid basis. A contractor asks for three bids from different manufacturers. The combination of low bid and high quality wins the job. However, jobs sold to the government are bid on a cost-plus basis. This means price is determined by adding all costs plus a profit based on cost at a specified percent, such as 10%. You observe that the amount of overhead applied to government jobs is higher than that applied to contract jobs. These allocations concern you.

ETHICS CHALLENGE

P3

Required

Write a half-page memo to your company's chief financial officer outlining your concerns with overhead allocation.

Point: Students could compare responses and discuss differences in concerns with allocating overhead.

BTN 2-4   Assume that you are preparing for a second interview with a manufacturing company. The company is impressed with your credentials, but it has several qualified applicants. You anticipate that in this second interview, you must show what you offer over other candidates. You learn the company is not satisfied with the timeliness of its information and its inventory management. The company manufactures custom-order holiday decorations and display items. To show your abilities, you plan to recommend that the company use a job order accounting system.

COMMUNICATING IN PRACTICE

C1 C2

Required

In preparation for the interview, prepare notes outlining the following:

1. Your recommendation and why it is suitable for this company.
2. A general description of the documents that the proposed system requires.
3. How the documents in part 2 facilitate the operation of the job order accounting system.

Point: Have students present a mock interview, one assuming the role of the president of the company and the other the applicant.

TAKING IT TO THE NET

C1

BTN 2-5   Many contractors work on custom jobs that require a job order costing system.

Required

Access the website **AMSI.com**; click on "Construction Management Software," and then on "StarBuilder." Prepare a one-page memorandum for the CEO of a construction company providing information about the job order costing software this company offers. Would you recommend that the company purchase this software?

TEAMWORK IN ACTION

C1

BTN 2-6   Consider the activities undertaken by a medical clinic in your area.

Required

1. Is a job order costing system appropriate for the clinic? Explain.
2. Identify as many factors as possible to lead you to conclude that the clinic uses a job order system.

ENTREPRENEURIAL DECISION

C1 C2

BTN 2-7   Refer to the chapter opener regarding Neha Assar and her company, **Neha Assar**. All successful businesses track their costs, and it is especially important for start-up businesses to monitor and control costs.

Required

1. Assume that Neha Assar uses a job order costing system. For the basic cost category of direct materials, explain how Neha's job cost sheet would differ from a job cost sheet for a manufacturing company.
2. For the basic cost categories of direct labor and overhead, provide examples of the types of costs that would fall into each category for Neha Assar.

HITTING THE ROAD

C2 P1 P2 P3

BTN 2-8   Home builders often use job order costing.

Required

1. You (or your team) are to prepare a job cost sheet for a single-family home under construction. List four items of both direct materials and direct labor. Explain how you think overhead should be applied.
2. Contact a builder and compare your job cost sheet to this builder's job cost sheet. If possible, speak to that company's accountant. Write your findings in a short report.

GLOBAL DECISION

P1

APPLE

Samsung

BTN 2-9   **Apple** and **Samsung** are competitors in the global marketplace. Apple's and Samsung's financial statements are in Appendix A.

Required

1. Determine the change in Apple's and Samsung's inventories for the most recent year reported. Then identify the impact on net resources generated by operating activities (increase or decrease) for the change in inventory level (increase or decrease) for Apple and Samsung for that same year.
2. How would the move to a just-in-time (JIT) system likely impact future operating cash flows and operating income?
3. Would a move to a JIT system likely impact Apple more than it would Samsung? Explain.

GLOBAL VIEW

Porsche AG manufactures high-performance cars. Each car is built according to individual customer specifications. Customers can use the Internet to place orders for their dream cars.

Porsche employs just-in-time inventory techniques to ensure a flexible production process that can respond rapidly to customer orders. At one of its plants, the company receives parts less than one hour before they are needed in production.

Porsche's sustainability efforts extend beyond its manufacturing operations to event management. Each year when the company sponsors a professional tennis tournament, it

© Sean Gallup/Getty Images

uses a Porsche Cayenne Hybrid to shuttle players to and from the venue. In addition, the company sells event tickets that include public transportation, thus reducing the number of distinct journeys to the venue by about 30%.

 Global View Assignments

Quick Study 2-15

Exercise 2-20

BTN 2-9

chapter 3

Process Costing and Analysis

Chapter Preview

PROCESS OPERATIONS

C1 Organization of process operations

A1 Process cost vs. job order systems

C2 Equivalent units (EUP)

NTK 3-1

PROCESS COSTING ILLUSTRATION

C3 Overview of GenX

Physical flow of units

Computing EUP

Cost per EUP

Cost reconciliation

Process cost summary

NTK 3-2, 3-3

ACCOUNTING AND REPORTING

P1 Accounting for materials

P2 Accounting for labor

P3 Accounting for overhead

P4 Accounting for transfers

A2 Hybrid costing system

C4 Appendix: FIFO method

NTK 3-4

Learning Objectives

CONCEPTUAL

C1 Explain process operations and the way they differ from job order operations.

C2 Define and compute equivalent units and explain their use in process costing.

C3 Describe accounting for production activity and preparation of a process cost summary using weighted average.

C4 *Appendix 3A*—Describe accounting for production activity and preparation of a process cost summary using FIFO.

ANALYTICAL

A1 Compare process costing and job order costing.

A2 Explain and illustrate a hybrid costing system.

PROCEDURAL

P1 Record the flow of materials costs in process costing.

P2 Record the flow of labor costs in process costing.

P3 Record the flow of factory overhead costs in process costing.

P4 Record the transfer of goods across departments, to Finished Goods Inventory, and to Cost of Goods Sold.

Courtesy of Stance

Uncommon Threads

San Clemente, CA—Strolling the aisles of retailers, serial entrepreneur Jeff Kearl found generic, boring products. "For many products, there's nothing really cool about it, no brand, nothing that sticks out," insists Jeff. Jeff (now CEO), along with co-founders John Wilson (now president), Ryan Kingman, Taylor Shupe, and Aaron Hennings, decided to be different. They came up with socks, but not dull ones. Instead, they imprinted socks with edgy designs, basketball legends, and *Star Wars* characters. The result is **Stance** (**Stance.com**), the official sock provider to the **National Basketball Association** and a favorite of artists and musicians.

"There's always room for innovation"
—Jeff Kearl

Socks are made in process operations and produced in large volumes. This requires production managers to track costs using a *process costing system*. Explains Jeff, "we start with the highest-grade polyester-nylon fabric we can find." Clarke Miyasaki, head of business development, adds, "Quality is critical. We make the best for the best players in the world."

As with many process operations, Stance uses machinery, automation, and continuous improvement of its processes.

Stance's "innovation lab" houses state-of-the-art Italian knitting machines, and a patented process that enables it to print faithful reproductions of NBA stars on its socks. "Not only does our sock-drying process enable us to create better pictures, it also allows us to manufacture socks without seams," says chief product officer Taylor Shupe. In addition to overhead costs of machines, Stance invests in product design and testing. In process costing, overhead costs are allocated to individual processes. The *process cost summary* is a report that managers of process operations use to monitor and control costs.

Stance is profitable and has increased sales by more than 100 percent in each of its first five years. "There's a lot of growth left for socks," insists Jeff. A recent move into women's socks was wildly successful, which now accounts for 20 percent of its sales. Jeff advises aspiring entrepreneurs to "enjoy what you do and work hard."

Sources: *Stance website,* January 2017; *Transworld Business,* July 23, 2012; *Fast Company,* July 9, 2015; *Dick's Sporting Goods* blog, July 3, 2015; Rovell, Darren, "NBA agrees to licensing deal with Stance as league's official sock," *ESPN.com,* April 27, 2015

PROCESS OPERATIONS

C1

Explain process operations and the way they differ from job order operations.

We previously described differences in job order and process operations. Job order operations involve customized jobs. **Process operations** involve the mass production of similar products in a continuous flow of sequential processes. Process operations require a high level of standardization to produce large volumes of products. Thus, process operations use a standardized process to make similar products; job order operations use a customized process to make unique products.

Penn makes tennis balls in a process operation. Tennis players want every tennis ball to be identical in terms of bounce, playability, and durability. This uniformity requires Penn to use a production process that can repeatedly make large volumes of tennis balls to the same specifications. Process operations also extend to services, such as mail sorting in large post offices and order processing in retailers like **Amazon**. Other companies using process operations include:

Company	Product	Company	Product
General Mills	Cereals	Heinz	Ketchup
Pfizer	Pharmaceuticals	Kar's	Trail mix
Procter & Gamble	Household products	Hershey	Chocolate
Coca-Cola	Soft drinks	Suja	Organic juice

Organization of Process Operations

Each of the above products is made in a series of repetitive *processes,* or steps. A production operation that makes tennis balls, for instance, might include the three steps shown in Exhibit 3.1. Understanding such processes is crucial for measuring product costs. Increasingly, process operations use machines and automation to control product quality and reduce manufacturing costs.

EXHIBIT 3.1

Process Operations: Making of Tennis Balls*

* For a virtual tour of a process operation, visit PennRacquet.com/video.html (tennis balls).

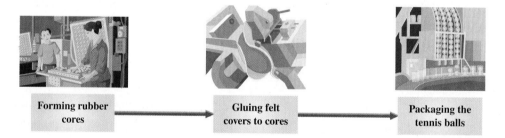

Forming rubber cores   →   Gluing felt covers to cores   →   Packaging the tennis balls

In a process operation, each process is a separate *production department, workstation,* or *work center.* Except for the first process or department, each receives the output from the prior department as a partially processed product. Each process applies direct labor, overhead, and, perhaps, additional direct materials to move the product toward completion. Only the final process or department in the series produces finished goods ready for sale to customers.

In Exhibit 3.1, the first step in tennis ball production involves cutting rubber into pellets and forming the core of each ball. These rubber cores are passed to the second department, where felt is cut into covers and glued to the rubber cores. The completed tennis balls are then passed to the final department for quality checks and packaging.

We must often track costs for several related departments. Because process costing procedures are applied to *the activity of each department or process separately,* we examine only one process at a time. This simplifies procedures. In addition, many of the journal entries in a process costing system are like those in job order costing.

Comparing Process and Job Order Costing Systems

A1

Compare process costing and job order costing.

Both job order costing systems and process costing systems track direct materials, direct labor, and overhead costs. The measurement focus in a job order costing system is on the individual job or batch, whereas in a process costing system it is on the individual process. Regardless of the measurement focus, we aim to compute the cost per unit of product (or service) resulting from either system. While both measure costs per unit, these two accounting systems differ in terms of how they do so.

- A **job order costing system** measures cost per unit upon completion of a job by dividing the total cost for that job by the number of units in that job. Job cost sheets accumulate the costs for each job. In a job order system, the cost object is a job.

- A **process costing system** measures unit costs at the end of a period (for example, a month) by combining the costs per equivalent unit (explained in the next section) from each separate department. In process costing, the cost object is the process.

Differences in the way these two systems apply materials, labor, and overhead costs are highlighted in Exhibit 3.2.

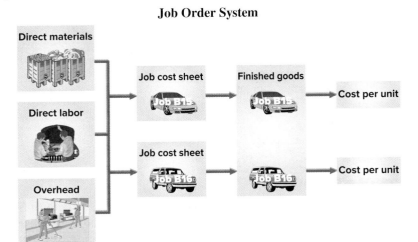

Job Order System

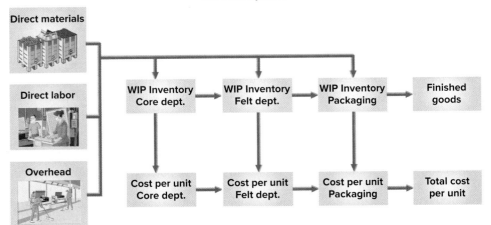

Process System

Transferring Costs across Departments   A key difference between job order and process costing arises with respect to work in process inventory:

- Job order costing often uses *only one* Work in Process Inventory account; the balance in this account agrees with the accumulated balances across all the job cost sheets for the jobs still in process.

- Process costing uses *separate* Work in Process Inventory accounts for each department. After production is complete, the completed goods and their accumulated costs are transferred from the Work in Process Inventory account for the final department in the series of processes to the Finished Goods Inventory account.

Exhibit 3.3 summarizes the journal entries to capture this flow of costs for a tennis ball manufacturer—to Ⓐ, to Ⓑ, to Ⓒ.

EXHIBIT 3.3

Flow of Costs through
Separate Work in
Process Accounts

(A)	Work in Process Inventory—Felt department	#
	Work in Process Inventory—Core department	#
	Transfer costs of partially completed goods to next department.	
(B)	Work in Process Inventory—Packaging department	#
	Work in Process Inventory—Felt department	#
	Transfer costs of partially completed goods to next department.	
(C)	Finished Goods Inventory...	#
	Work in Process Inventory—Packaging department	#
	Transfer costs of completed products to finished goods.	

NEED-TO-KNOW 3-1

Job Order vs. Process
Costing Systems

C1   A1

Complete the following table with either a *yes* or *no* regarding the attributes of job order and process costing systems.

	Job Order	Process
Uses direct materials, direct labor, and overhead costs	a. ____	e. ____
Uses job cost sheets to accumulate costs	b. ____	f. ____
Typically uses several Work in Process Inventory accounts	c. ____	g. ____
Yields a cost per unit of product	d. ____	h. ____

Do More: QS 3-1, QS 3-2,
E 3-1, E 3-2

Solution

a. yes   **b.** yes   **c.** no   **d.** yes   **e.** yes   **f.** no   **g.** yes   **h.** yes

Equivalent Units of Production

C2 _____

Define and compute
equivalent units and explain
their use in process costing.

Companies with process operations typically end each period with inventories of both finished goods and work in process. For example, a maker of tennis balls ends each period with both completed tennis balls and partially completed tennis balls in inventory. How does a process manufacturer measure its production activity when it has some partially completed goods at the end of a period? A key idea in process costing is **equivalent units of production (EUP),** which is the number of units that *could have been* started and completed given the costs incurred during the period.

EUP is explained as follows: 100,000 tennis balls that are 60% through the production process is *equivalent to* 60,000 (100,000 units × 60%) tennis balls that completed the entire production process. This means that the cost to put 100,000 units 60% of the way through the production process is *equivalent to* the cost to put 60,000 units completely through the production process. Knowing the costs of partially completed goods allows us to measure production activity for the period.

EUP for Materials and Conversion Costs   In many processes, the equivalent units of production for direct materials are not the same with respect to direct labor and overhead. For example, direct materials, like rubber for tennis ball cores, might enter production entirely at the beginning of a process. In contrast, direct labor and overhead might be used continuously throughout the process. How does a manufacturer account for these timing differences? The solution is by measuring equivalent units of production. For example, if all of the direct materials to produce 10,000 units have entered the production process, but those units have received only 20% of their direct labor and overhead costs, equivalent units would be computed as:

EUP: Physical unit #s × Complete %	
EUP for direct materials = 10,000 × 100% = 10,000	
EUP for direct labor	= 10,000 × 20% = 2,000
EUP for overhead	= 10,000 × 20% = 2,000

Point: When overhead is applied based on direct labor cost, the percentage of completion for direct labor and overhead will be the same.

Direct labor and factory overhead are often classified as *conversion costs*—that is, as costs of converting direct materials into finished products. Many businesses with process operations compute **conversion cost per equivalent unit,** which is the combined costs of direct labor and factory overhead per equivalent unit. If direct labor and overhead enter the production process at about the same rate, it is convenient to combine them, together, as conversion costs.

Weighted Average versus FIFO   There are different ways to compute the number of equivalent units. These methods make different assumptions about how costs flow. The **weighted-average method** combines units and costs *across two periods* in computing equivalent units. The **FIFO method** computes equivalent units based only on production activity in the *current period*. The objectives, concepts, and journal entries (but not amounts) are the same under the weighted-average and FIFO methods; the computations of equivalent units differ. While the FIFO method is generally more precise than the weighted-average method, it requires more calculations. Often, the differences between the two methods are not large. When using a just-in-time inventory system, these different methods will yield very similar results because inventories are immaterial. **In this chapter we assume the weighted-average method for inventory costs; we illustrate the FIFO method in the appendix.**

PROCESS COSTING ILLUSTRATION

We provide a step-by-step illustration of process costing. Each process (or department) in a process operation follows these steps:

1. Determine the physical flow of units.
2. Compute equivalent units of production.
3. Compute cost per equivalent unit of production.
4. Assign and reconcile costs.

We next show these steps for the first of two sequential processes used by a company to produce one of its products.

C3_____

Describe accounting for production activity and preparation of a process cost summary using weighted average.

Overview of GenX Company's Process Operation

The GenX Company produces an organic trail mix called FitMix. Its target customers are active people who are interested in fitness and the environment. GenX sells FitMix to wholesale distributors, who in turn sell it to retailers. FitMix is manufactured in a continuous, two-process operation (roasting and blending), shown in Exhibit 3.4.

EXHIBIT 3.4

GenX's Process Operation

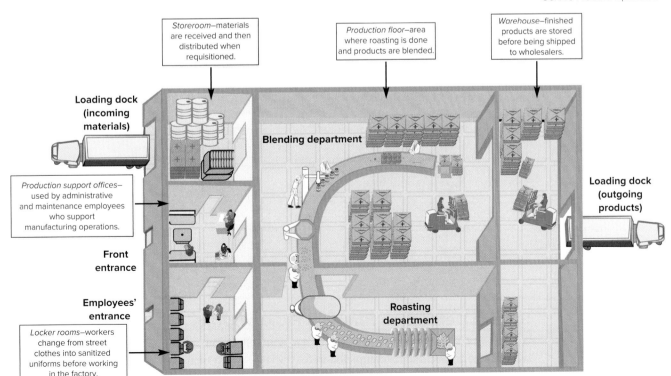

In the first process (roasting department), GenX roasts, oils, and salts organically grown peanuts. These peanuts are then passed to the blending department, the second process. In the blending department, machines blend organic chocolate pieces and organic dried fruits with the peanuts from the first process. The blended mix is then inspected and packaged for delivery. In both departments, direct materials enter production at the beginning of the process, while conversion costs occur continuously throughout each department's processing.

Exhibit 3.5 presents production data (in units) for GenX's roasting department. This exhibit includes the percentage of completion for both materials and conversion; beginning work in process inventory is 100% complete with respect to materials but only 65% complete with respect to conversion. Ending work in process inventory is 100% complete with respect to materials but only 25% complete with respect to conversion. Units completed and transferred to the blending department are 100% complete with respect to both materials and conversion.

EXHIBIT 3.5

Production Data (in units) for Roasting Department

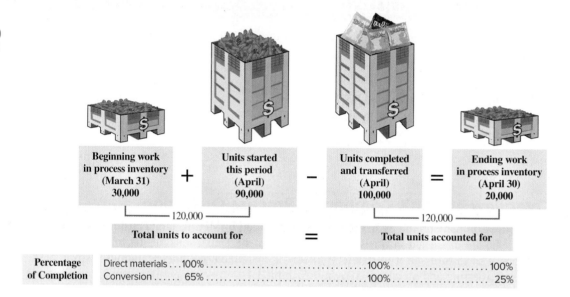

Percentage of Completion				
Direct materials . . . 100%	. . . .	100%	. . . .	100%
Conversion 65%	. . . .	100%	. . . .	25%

Exhibit 3.6 presents production cost data for GenX's roasting department. We use the data in Exhibits 3.5 and 3.6 to illustrate the four-step approach to process costing.

EXHIBIT 3.6

Roasting Department Production Cost Data

GenX—Roasting Department		
Beginning work in process inventory (March 31)		
Direct materials costs	$ 81,000	
Conversion costs	108,900	$ 189,900
Costs during the current period (April)		
Direct materials costs	279,000	
Direct labor costs*	171,000	
Factory overhead costs applied (120% of direct labor)*	205,200	655,200
Total production costs		**$845,100**

*Total conversion costs for the month equal $376,200 ($171,000 + $205,200).

Step 1: Determine Physical Flow of Units

A *physical flow reconciliation* is a report that reconciles (1) the physical units started in a period with (2) the physical units completed in that period. A physical flow reconciliation for GenX's roasting department for April is shown in Exhibit 3.7.

EXHIBIT 3.7

Physical Flow Reconciliation

GenX—Roasting Department			
Units to Account For		**Units Accounted For**	
Beginning work in process inventory............	30,000 units	Units completed and transferred out......................	100,000 units
Units started this period.........	90,000 units	Ending work in process inventory..........	20,000 units
Total units to account for	**120,000 units**	Total units accounted for................	**120,000 units**

reconciled

WIP–Roasting (in units)			
Beg. inv.	30,000		
Started	90,000		
To acct. for	120,000		
		100,000	Tr. out
End. inv.	20,000		

Step 2: Compute Equivalent Units of Production

The second step is to compute *equivalent units of production* for direct materials and conversion costs for April. Because direct materials and conversion costs typically enter a process at different rates, departments must compute equivalent units separately for direct materials and conversion costs. Exhibit 3.8 shows the formula to compute equivalent units under the weighted-average method for both direct materials and conversion costs.

EXHIBIT 3.8

Computing EUP—Weighted-Average Method

$$\text{Equivalent units of production (EUP)} = \frac{\text{Number of whole units}}{\text{completed and transferred out*}} + \frac{\text{Number of equivalent units}}{\text{in ending work in process}}$$

*Transferred to next department or finished goods inventory.

For GenX's roasting department, we convert the 120,000 physical units to *equivalent units* based on how each input has been used. The roasting department fully completed its work on 100,000 units and partially completed its work on 20,000 units (from Exhibit 3.5). Equivalent units are computed by multiplying the number of units accounted for (from step 1) by the percentage of completion for each input—see Exhibit 3.9.

EXHIBIT 3.9

Equivalent Units of Production—Weighted Average

GenX—Roasting Department		
Equivalent Units of Production	**Direct Materials**	**Conversion**
Equivalent units completed and transferred out (100,000 × 100%)	100,000 EUP	100,000 EUP
Equivalent units for ending work in process		
Direct materials (20,000 × 100%)	20,000 EUP	
Conversion (20,000 × 25%)		5,000 EUP
Equivalent units of production.......................................	120,000 EUP	105,000 EUP

The first row of Exhibit 3.9 reflects units transferred out in April. The roasting department entirely completed its work on the 100,000 units transferred out. These units have 100% of the materials and conversion required, or 100,000 equivalent units of each input (100,000 × 100%).

Rows two, three, and four refer to the 20,000 partially completed units. For direct materials, the units in ending work in process inventory include all materials required, so there are 20,000 equivalent units (20,000 × 100%) of materials in the unfinished physical units. For conversion, the units in ending work in process inventory include 25% of the conversion required, which implies 5,000 equivalent units of conversion (20,000 × 25%).

The final row reflects the total equivalent units of production, which is whole units of product that could have been manufactured with the amount of inputs used to create some complete and some incomplete units. The amount of inputs used to produce 100,000 complete units and to start 20,000 additional units is equivalent to the amount of direct materials in 120,000 whole units and the amount of conversion in 105,000 whole units.

© Ken Whitmore/Stone/Getty Images

A department began the month with 8,000 units in work in process inventory. These units were 100% complete with respect to direct materials and 40% complete with respect to conversion.

During the current month, the department started 56,000 units and completed 58,000 units. Ending work in process inventory includes 6,000 units, 80% complete with respect to direct materials and 70% complete with respect to conversion. Use the weighted-average method of process costing to:

1. Compute the department's equivalent units of production for the month for direct materials.
2. Compute the department's equivalent units of production for the month for conversion.

Solution—see supporting account computations to the side

1. EUP for materials = 58,000 + (6,000 × 80%) = 62,800 EUP
2. EUP for conversion = 58,000 + (6,000 × 70%) = 62,200 EUP

WIP (in units)			
Beg. inv.	8,000		
Started	56,000		
To acct. for	64,000		
		58,000	Tr. out
End. inv.	6,000		

Step 3: Compute Cost per Equivalent Unit

Under the weighted-average method, computation of EUP does not separate the units in beginning inventory from those started this period. Similarly, the weighted-average method combines the costs of beginning work in process inventory with the costs incurred in the current period. Total cost is then divided by the equivalent units of production (from step 2) to compute the average **cost per equivalent unit**. This process is illustrated in Exhibit 3.10. For direct materials, the cost averages $3.00 per EUP. For conversion, the cost per equivalent unit averages $4.62 per unit.

Point: Managers can examine changes in monthly costs per equivalent unit to help control production.

EXHIBIT 3.10

Cost per Equivalent Unit of Production—Weighted Average

GenX—Roasting Department		
Cost per Equivalent Unit of Production	Direct Materials	Conversion
Costs of beginning work in process inventory*............	$ 81,000	$108,900
Costs incurred this period*............	279,000	376,200**
Total costs............	$360,000	$485,100
÷ Equivalent units of production (from step 2)............	120,000 EUP	105,000 EUP
= Cost per equivalent unit of production............	$3.00 per EUP†	$4.62 per EUP‡

*From Exhibit 3.6   **$171,000 + $205,200   †$360,000 ÷ 120,000 EUP   ‡$485,100 ÷ 105,000 EUP

Step 4: Assign and Reconcile Costs

The EUP from step 2 and the cost per EUP from step 3 are used in step 4 to assign costs to (a) the 100,000 units that the roasting department completed and transferred to the blending department, and (b) the 20,000 units that remain in process in the roasting department. This is illustrated in Exhibit 3.11.

EXHIBIT 3.11

Report of Costs Accounted For—Weighted Average

GenX—Roasting Department		
Cost of units completed and transferred to Blending dept.		
Direct materials (100,000 EUP × $3.00 per EUP)............	$300,000	
Conversion (100,000 EUP × $4.62 per EUP)............	462,000	
Cost of units completed this period............		$762,000
Cost of ending work in process inventory		
Direct materials (20,000 EUP × $3.00 per EUP)............	60,000	
Conversion (5,000 EUP × $4.62 per EUP)............	23,100	
Cost of ending work in process inventory............		83,100
Total costs accounted for............		**$845,100**

Cost of Units Completed and Transferred   The 100,000 units completed and transferred to the blending department required 100,000 EUP of direct materials and 100,000 EUP of conversion. We assign $300,000 (100,000 EUP × $3.00 per EUP) of direct materials cost to those units. We also assign $462,000 (100,000 EUP × $4.62 per EUP) of conversion cost to those units. Total cost of the 100,000 completed and transferred units is $762,000 ($300,000 + $462,000), and the average cost per unit is $7.62 ($762,000 ÷ 100,000 units).

Cost of Units in Ending Work in Process Inventory   There are 20,000 incomplete units in work in process inventory at period-end. For direct materials, those units have 20,000 EUP of material (from step 2) at a cost of $3.00 per EUP (from step 3), which yields the materials cost of work in process inventory of $60,000 (20,000 EUP × $3.00 per EUP). For conversion, the in-process units reflect 5,000 EUP (from step 2). Using the $4.62 conversion cost per EUP (from step 3), we obtain conversion costs for in-process inventory of $23,100 (5,000 EUP × $4.62 per EUP). Total cost of work in process inventory at period-end is $83,100 ($60,000 + $23,100).

Reconciliation   Management verifies that total costs assigned to units completed and transferred plus the costs of units in process (from Exhibit 3.11) equal the costs incurred by production. Exhibit 3.12 shows the costs incurred by production this period. We then reconcile the *costs accounted for* in Exhibit 3.11 with the *costs to account for* in Exhibit 3.12.

EXHIBIT 3.12

Report of Costs to Account For—Weighted Average

GenX—Roasting Department

Cost of beginning work in process inventory		
Direct materials..	$ 81,000	
Conversion	108,900	$ 189,900
Cost incurred this period		
Direct materials..	279,000	
Conversion	376,200	655,200
Total costs to account for..................................		**$845,100**

The roasting department manager is responsible for $845,100 in costs: $189,000 from beginning work in process plus $655,200 of materials and conversion incurred in the period. At period-end, that manager must show where these costs are assigned. The roasting department manager reports that $83,100 is assigned to units in process and $762,000 is assigned to units completed and transferred out to the blending department (per Exhibit 3.11). The sum of these amounts equals $845,100. Thus, the total *costs to account for* equal the total *costs accounted for* (minor differences sometimes occur from rounding).

A department began the month with conversion costs of $65,000 in its beginning work in process inventory. During the current month, the department incurred $55,000 of conversion costs. Equivalent units of production for conversion for the month was 15,000 units. The department completed and transferred 12,000 units to the next department. The department uses the weighted-average method of process costing.

1. Compute the department's cost per equivalent unit for conversion for the month.

2. Compute the department's conversion cost of units transferred to the next department for the month.

NEED-TO-KNOW 3-3

Cost per EUP—
Conversion, with
Transfer

C3

Solution

1. ($65,000 + $55,000)/15,000 units = $8.00 per EUP for conversion

2. 12,000 units × $8.00 = $96,000 conversion cost transferred to next department

Do More: QS 3-11, QS 3-13, E 3-6

Process Cost Summary

An important managerial accounting report for a process costing system is the **process cost summary** (also called *production report*), which is prepared separately for each process or production department. Three reasons for the summary are to (1) help department managers control and monitor their departments, (2) help factory managers evaluate department managers' performance, and (3) provide cost information for financial statements. A process cost summary achieves these purposes by describing the costs charged to each department, reporting the equivalent units of production achieved by each department, and determining the costs assigned to each department's output. It is prepared using a combination of Exhibits 3.7, 3.9, 3.10, 3.11, and 3.12.

The process cost summary for the roasting department is shown in Exhibit 3.13. The report is divided into three sections.

① This section lists the total costs charged to the department, including direct materials and conversion costs incurred, as well as the cost of the beginning work in process inventory.

② This section describes the equivalent units of production for the department. Equivalent units for materials and conversion are in separate columns. It also reports direct materials and conversion costs per equivalent unit.

③ This section allocates total costs among units worked on in the period. The $762,000 is the total cost of the 100,000 units transferred out of the roasting department to the blending department. The $83,100 is the cost of the 20,000 partially completed units in ending inventory in the

EXHIBIT 3.13

Process Cost Summary
(Weighted Average)

GenX COMPANY—ROASTING DEPARTMENT
Process Cost Summary (Weighted-Average Method)
For Month Ended April 30, 2017

Costs Charged to Production

①	Costs of beginning work in process			
	Direct materials		$ 81,000	
	Conversion		108,900	$ 189,900
	Costs incurred this period			
	Direct materials		279,000	
	Conversion		376,200	655,200
	Total costs to account for			**$845,100**

Unit Information

	Units to account for:		Units accounted for:	
	Beginning work in process	30,000	Completed and transferred out	100,000
	Units started this period	90,000	Ending work in process	20,000
	Total units to account for	120,000	Total units accounted for	120,000

Equivalent Units of Production (EUP)	Direct Materials	Conversion
② Units completed and transferred out (100,000 × 100%)	100,000 EUP	100,000 EUP
Units of ending work in process		
Direct materials (20,000 × 100%)	20,000 EUP	
Conversion (20,000 × 25%)		5,000 EUP
Equivalent units of production	120,000 EUP	105,000 EUP

Cost per EUP	Direct Materials	Conversion
Costs of beginning work in process	$ 81,000	$108,900
Costs incurred this period	279,000	376,200
Total costs	$360,000	$485,100
÷ EUP	120,000 EUP	105,000 EUP
Cost per EUP	$3.00 per EUP	$4.62 per EUP

Cost Assignment and Reconciliation

③	Costs transferred out (cost of goods manufactured)		
	Direct materials (100,000 EUP × $3.00 per EUP)	$300,000	
	Conversion (100,000 EUP × $4.62 per EUP)	462,000	$ 762,000
	Costs of ending work in process		
	Direct materials (20,000 EUP × $3.00 per EUP)	60,000	
	Conversion (5,000 EUP × $4.62 per EUP)	23,100	83,100
	Total costs accounted for		**$845,100**

reconciled

WIP–Roasting (in $)

Beg. inv.	189,900		
Incurred	655,200		
Subtotal	845,100		
		762,000	Tr. out
End. inv.	83,100		

roasting department. The assigned costs are then added to show that the total $845,100 cost charged to the roasting department in section ◇1◇ is now assigned to the units in section ◇3◇.

Using the Process Cost Summary Managers use information in the process cost summary. For example, the roasting department's costs per equivalent unit are $3.00 for direct materials and $4.62 for conversion. Are the unit costs higher or lower than management expected? Are the unit costs higher or lower than prior months' unit costs? Such analyses can help managers find ways to improve production processes and to reduce future costs.

ACCOUNTING AND REPORTING FOR PROCESS COSTING

In this section we illustrate the journal entries to account for a process manufacturer. Exhibit 3.14 illustrates the flow of costs for GenX Company's roasting department. Materials, labor, and overhead costs flow into the manufacturing processes. GenX keeps separate Work in Process Inventory accounts for the roasting and blending departments; when goods are packaged and ready for sale, their costs are transferred to the Finished Goods Inventory account.

As in job order costing, a process costing system uses source documents. For example, *materials requisitions* signal the use of direct and indirect materials. *Time tickets* record the use of direct and indirect labor. While some companies might combine direct labor and overhead into conversion costs when computing costs per equivalent unit (as we showed), labor and overhead costs are accounted for separately within the company's accounts. Also, because overhead costs typically cannot be tied to individual processes, but rather benefit all processes or departments, most companies use a single Factory Overhead account to accumulate actual and applied overhead costs.

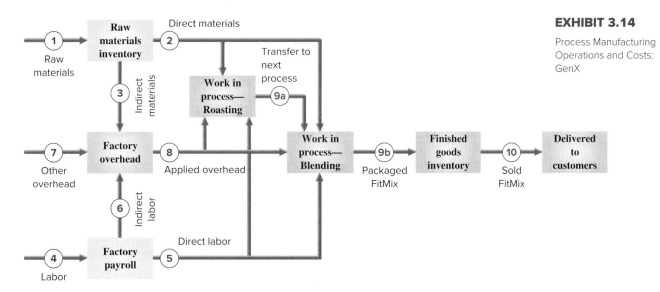

EXHIBIT 3.14

Process Manufacturing Operations and Costs: GenX

As with job order costing, process manufacturers must allocate, or apply, overhead to processes. This requires companies to find good *allocation bases,* such as direct labor hours or machine hours used. With increasing automation, companies with process operations use fewer direct labor hours and thus are more likely to use machine hours to allocate overhead.

Sometimes a single allocation base will not provide good overhead allocations. For example, direct labor cost might be a good allocation base for GenX's roasting department, but not for its blending department. As a result, a process manufacturer can use different overhead allocation rates for different production departments. However, all applied overhead is credited to a single Factory Overhead account.

Exhibit 3.15 presents cost data for GenX. Roasting department costs are from Exhibit 3.6. We use these data to show the journal entries in a process costing system.

Point: Actual overhead is debited to Factory Overhead.

EXHIBIT 3.15

Cost Data—GenX (Weighted Average)

GenX—Cost Data for Month Ending April 30	
Raw materials inventory (March 31)	$100,000
Beginning work in process inventories (March 31)	
Work in process—Roasting	$189,900
Work in process—Blending	151,688
Materials purchased (on account)	$400,000
Materials requisitions during April	
Direct materials—Roasting	$279,000
Direct materials—Blending	102,000
Indirect materials	71,250
Factory payroll for April	
Direct labor—Roasting	$171,000
Direct labor—Blending	183,160
Indirect labor	78,350
Other actual overhead costs during April	
Insurance expense—Factory	$ 11,930
Utilities payable—Factory	7,945
Depreciation expense—Factory equipment	220,650
Other (paid in cash)	21,875

P1

Record the flow of materials costs in process costing.

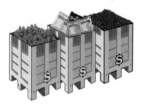

Assets   = Liabilities + Equity
+400,000   +400,000

Accounting for Materials Costs

In Exhibit 3.14, arrow line ① reflects the arrival of materials at GenX's factory. These materials include organic peanuts, chocolate pieces, dried fruits, oil, salt, and packaging. They also include supplies for the production support office. GenX uses a perpetual inventory system and makes all purchases on credit. The summary entry for receipt of raw materials in April follows (dates in journal entries are omitted because they are summary entries, often reflecting two or more transactions or events).

①	Raw Materials Inventory	400,000	
	Accounts Payable		400,000
	Acquired materials on credit for factory use.		

Arrow line ② in Exhibit 3.14 reflects the flow of direct materials to production in the roasting and blending departments. These direct materials are physically combined into the finished product. The manager of a process usually obtains materials by submitting a *materials requisition* to the materials storeroom manager. The entry to record the use of direct materials by GenX's production departments in April follows. These direct materials costs flow into each department's separate Work in Process Inventory account.

Assets   = Liabilities + Equity
+279,000
+102,000
−381,000

②	Work in Process—Roasting	279,000	
	Work in Process—Blending	102,000	
	Raw Materials Inventory		381,000
	Assign costs of direct materials used in production.		

In Exhibit 3.14, arrow line ③ reflects the flow of indirect materials from the storeroom to factory overhead. These materials are not clearly linked with any specific production process or department but are used to support overall production activity. As these costs cannot be linked directly to either the roasting or blending departments, they are recorded in GenX's single Factory Overhead account. The following entry records the cost of indirect materials used by GenX in April.

Example: What types of materials might the flow of arrow line ③ in Exhibit 3.14 reflect? *Answer:* Goggles, gloves, protective clothing, oil, salt, and cleaning supplies.

③	Factory Overhead	71,250	
	Raw Materials Inventory		71,250
	Record indirect materials used in April.		

Accounting for Labor Costs

Exhibit 3.14 shows GenX's factory payroll costs as reflected in arrow line ④. Exhibit 3.15 shows costs of $171,000 for roasting department direct labor, $183,160 for blending department direct labor, and $78,350 for indirect labor. This total payroll of $432,510 is a product cost, and it is allocated to either Work in Process Inventory or Factory Overhead.

Time reports from the production departments and the production support office trigger payroll entries. (For simplicity, we do not separately identify withholdings and additional payroll taxes for employees.) In a process operation, the direct labor of a production department includes all labor used exclusively by that department. This is the case even if labor is not applied to the product itself. If a production department in a process operation, for instance, has a full-time manager and a full-time maintenance worker, their salaries are *direct* labor costs of that process and are not factory overhead.

Arrow line ⑤ in Exhibit 3.14 shows GenX's use of direct labor. The following entry then records direct labor used. These direct labor costs flow into each department's separate Work in Process Inventory account.

P2

Record the flow of labor costs in process costing.

⑤	Work in Process Inventory—Roasting....................	171,000	
	Work in Process Inventory—Blending	183,160	
	Factory Wages Payable		354,160
	Record direct labor used in production.		

Assets = Liabilities + Equity
+171,000   +354,160
+183,160

Arrow line ⑥ in Exhibit 3.14 reflects GenX's indirect labor costs. These employees provide clerical, maintenance, and other services that help production in both the roasting and blending departments. For example, they order materials, deliver them to the factory floor, repair equipment, operate and program computers used in production, keep payroll and other production records, clean up, and move goods across departments. The following entry records these indirect labor costs.

Point: A department's indirect labor cost might include an allocated portion of wages of a manager who supervises two or more departments. Allocation of costs between departments is discussed in a later chapter.

⑥	Factory Overhead	78,350	
	Factory Wages Payable		78,350
	Record indirect labor as overhead.		

After GenX posts these entries for direct and indirect labor, the Factory Wages Payable account has a balance of $432,510 ($354,160 + $78,350). The entry below shows the payment of this total payroll. After this entry, the Factory Wages Payable account has a zero balance.

④	Factory Wages Payable............................	432,510	
	Cash		432,510
	Record factory wages for April.		

Assets = Liabilities + Equity
−432,510   −432,510

Accounting for Factory Overhead

Overhead costs other than indirect materials and indirect labor are reflected by arrow line ⑦ in Exhibit 3.14. These overhead items include the costs of insuring production assets, renting the factory building, using factory utilities, and depreciating factory equipment not directly related to a specific process. The following entry records these other overhead costs for April.

P3

Record the flow of factory overhead costs in process costing.

⑦	Factory Overhead	262,400	
	Prepaid Insurance..............................		11,930
	Utilities Payable		7,945
	Cash		21,875
	Accumulated Depreciation—Factory Equipment		220,650
	Record other overhead costs incurred in April.		

Applying Overhead to Work in Process

Point: The time it takes to process (cycle) products through a process is sometimes used to allocate costs.

Applying Overhead to Work in Process   Companies use *predetermined overhead rates* to apply overhead. These rates are estimated at the beginning of a period and used to apply overhead during the period. This allows managers to obtain up-to-date estimates of the costs of their processes during the period. This is important for process costing, where goods are transferred across departments before the entire production process is complete.

Arrow line ⑧ in Exhibit 3.14 reflects the application of factory overhead to the two production departments. Factory overhead is applied to processes by relating overhead cost to another variable such as direct labor hours or machine hours used. In many situations, a single allocation basis such as direct labor hours (or a single rate for the entire plant) fails to provide useful allocations. As a result, management may use different rates for different production departments. In our example, GenX applies overhead on the basis of direct labor cost as shown in Exhibit 3.16.

EXHIBIT 3.16

Applying Factory Overhead

Production Department	Direct Labor Cost	Predetermined Rate	Overhead Applied
Roasting	$171,000	120%	$205,200
Blending	183,160	120	219,792
Total			$424,992

GenX records its applied overhead with the following entry.

⑧	Work in Process Inventory—Roasting.	205,200	
	Work in Process Inventory—Blending	219,792	
	Factory Overhead.		424,992
	Applied overhead costs to production departments at 120% of direct labor cost.		

Decision Ethics

Budget Officer   You are classifying costs of a new processing department as either direct or indirect. This department's manager instructs you to classify most of the costs as indirect so it will be charged a lower amount of overhead (because this department uses less labor, which is the overhead allocation base). This would penalize other departments with higher allocations and cause the ratings of managers in other departments to suffer. What action do you take? ■   *Answer: By classifing costs as indirect, the manager is passing some of his department's costs to a common overhead pool that other departments will partially absorb. Because overhead costs are allocated on direct labor for this company and the new department has a low direct labor cost, the new department is assigned less overhead. Such action suggests unethical behavior. You must object to such reclassification. If this manager refuses to comply, you must inform someone in a more senior position.*

NEED-TO-KNOW 3-4

Overhead Rate and Costs

P1 P2 P3

Tower Mfg. estimates it will incur $200,000 of total overhead costs during 2017. Tower allocates overhead based on machine hours; it estimates it will use a total of 10,000 machine hours during 2017. During February 2017, the assembly department of Tower Mfg. uses 375 machine hours. In addition, Tower incurred actual overhead costs as follows during February: indirect materials, $1,800; indirect labor, $5,700; depreciation on factory equipment, $8,000; factory utilities, $500.

1. Compute the company's predetermined overhead rate for 2017.

2. Prepare journal entries to record (a) overhead applied for the assembly department for the month and (b) actual overhead costs used during the month.

Solution

1. Predetermined overhead rate = Estimated overhead costs ÷ Estimated activity base
= $200,000/10,000 machine hours = $20 per machine hour

2a.

Work in Process Inventory—Assembly	7,500	
Factory Overhead		7,500
Record applied overhead (375 hours × $20 per hour).		

2b.

Factory Overhead	16,000	
Raw Materials Inventory		1,800
Factory Wages Payable		5,700
Accumulated Depreciation—Factory Equipment		8,000
Utilities Payable		500
Record actual overhead.		

Do More: QS 3-25, E 3-23, E 3-25

Accounting for Transfers

Transfers across Departments   Arrow line ⑨ⓐ in Exhibit 3.14 reflects the transfer of units from the roasting department to the blending department. The process cost summary for the roasting department (Exhibit 3.13) shows that the 100,000 units transferred to the blending department are assigned a cost of $762,000. The entry to record this transfer follows.

P4

Record the transfer of goods across departments, to Finished Goods Inventory, and to Cost of Goods Sold.

⑨ⓐ			
	Work in Process Inventory—Blending	762,000	
	Work in Process Inventory—Roasting		762,000
	Record transfer of 100,000 units from		
	roasting department to blending department.		

Assets = Liabilities + Equity
+762,000
−762,000

Units and costs *transferred out* of the roasting department are *transferred into* the blending department. Exhibit 3.17 shows this transfer using T-accounts for the separate Work in Process Inventory accounts (first in units and then in dollars).

EXHIBIT 3.17

Production and Cost Activity—Transfer to Blending Department

Roasting Department—Units		
Beg. inv. 30,000 units		
Started 90,000 units		
Total 120,000 units		
	100,000 units transferred out	
End. inv. 20,000 units		

Blending Department—Units		
Beg. inv. 12,000 units		
Transferred in 100,000 units		
Total 112,000 units		
		97,000 units transferred to Finished Goods
End. inv. 15,000 units		

WIP Inventory—Roasting Dept.		
Beg. inv.* 189,900		
DM 279,000		
Conv. 376,200		
Total 845,100		
	762,000 Transferred out	
End. inv. 83,100		

WIP Inventory—Blending Dept.		
Beg. inv.† 151,688		
Transferred in 762,000		
DM 102,000		
Conv. 402,952		
Total 1,418,640	1,262,940 Transferred to FG	
End. inv. 155,700		

*$81,000 direct materials + $108,900 conversion

†$91,440 transferred in + $10,000 DM + $50,248 conversion

As Exhibit 3.17 shows, the blending department began the month with 12,000 units in beginning inventory, with a related cost of $151,688. In computing its production activity and costs, the blending department must also consider the units and costs transferred in from the roasting department, as shown in Exhibit 3.17. The 100,000 units transferred in from the roasting department, and their related costs of $762,000, are added to the blending department's number of units and separate Work in Process (WIP) Inventory account.

The blending department adds additional direct materials and conversion costs. The blending department incurred direct materials costs of $102,000 and conversion costs of $402,952 during the month. (Although not illustrated here, the concepts and methods used in this second department would be similar to those we showed in detail for the first department. The units and costs transferred in are considered separately from the materials and conversion added in the second department.)

Accounting for Transfer to Finished Goods   Arrow line ⑨b in Exhibit 3.14 reflects the transfer of units and their related costs from the blending department to finished goods inventory. At the end of the month, the blending department transferred 97,000 completed units, with a related cost of $1,262,940, to finished goods. The entry to record this transfer follows.

Assets = Liabilities + Equity
+1,262,940
−1,262,940

⑨b	Finished Goods Inventory	1,262,940	
	Work in Process Inventory—Blending		1,262,940
	Record transfer of completed goods.		

Accounting for Transfer to Cost of Goods Sold   Arrow line ⑩ reflects the sale of finished goods. Assume that GenX sold 106,000 units of FitMix this period, and that its beginning finished goods inventory was 26,000 units with a cost of $338,520. Also assume that its ending finished goods inventory consists of 20,000 units at a cost of $260,400. Using this information, cost of goods sold is computed as in Exhibit 3.18.

Finished Goods Inventory

Beg. bal.	338,520		
COGM	1,262,940		
Avail.	1,601,460		
		COGS	**1,341,060**
End. bal.	260,400		

EXHIBIT 3.18

Cost of Goods Sold

GenX—Cost of Goods Sold	
Beginning finished goods inventory	$ 338,520
+ Cost of goods manufactured this period	1,262,940 ←
= Cost of goods available for sale	1,601,460
− Ending finished goods inventory	260,400
= Cost of goods sold	$1,341,060

The summary entry to record cost of goods sold for this period follows:

Assets = Liabilities + Equity
−1,341,060   −1,341,060

⑩	Cost of Goods Sold	1,341,060	
	Finished Goods Inventory		1,341,060
	Record cost of goods sold for April.		

Trends in Process Operations

Some recent trends in process operations are discussed next.

Process Design   Management concerns with production efficiency can lead companies to entirely reorganize production processes. For example, instead of producing different types of computers in a series of departments, a separate work center for each computer can be established in one department. The process cost system is then changed to account for each work center's costs.

Just-in-Time Production   Companies are increasingly adopting just-in-time techniques. With a just-in-time inventory system, inventory levels can be minimal. If raw materials are not ordered or received until needed, a Raw Materials Inventory account might be unnecessary. Instead, materials cost is immediately debited to the Work in Process Inventory account. Similarly, a Finished Goods Inventory account may not be needed. Instead, cost of finished goods may be immediately debited to the Cost of Goods Sold account.

Automation Companies are increasingly automating their production processes and using robots. For example, manufacturers use robots on tasks that are hard for humans to perform. This automation results in reduced direct labor costs and a healthier workforce.

Continuous Processing In some companies, like **Pepsi Bottling**, materials move continuously through the manufacturing process. In these cases, a **materials consumption report** summarizes the materials used and replaces materials requisitions.

© Natalia Kolesnikova/AFP/Getty Images

Services Service-based businesses are increasingly prevalent. For routine, standardized services like oil changes and simple tax returns, computing costs based on the process is simpler and more useful than a cost per individual job. More complex service companies use process departments to perform specific tasks for consumers. Hospitals, for example, have radiology and physical therapy facilities, each with special equipment and trained employees. When patients need services, they are processed through departments to receive prescribed care.

Customer Orientation Focus on customer orientation also leads to improved processes. A manufacturer of control devices improved quality and reduced production time by forming teams to study processes and suggest improvements. An ice cream maker studied customer tastes to develop a more pleasing ice cream texture.

Yield Many process operations convert large amounts of raw materials into finished goods. In addition to information in process cost summaries, managers often measure **yield**, which is the amount of material output relative to the amount of material input. For example, assume a maker of trail mix started 10,000 pounds (units) of peanuts into its production process and ended with finished goods of 9,650 pounds. The yield is computed as: 9,650/10,000 = 96.5%. Yield might be less than 100% due to lost or stolen peanuts, roasting issues that burned peanuts, or other production problems. When yields are lower than expected, managers usually ask why and then take corrective action.

 SUSTAINABILITY AND ACCOUNTING

Food processor **General Mills** needs a steady supply of high-quality corn, oats, and sugarcane. These agricultural inputs face risks due to water scarcity and climate change that could disrupt General Mills's process operations and hurt profits.

Buying from suppliers that follow sustainable principles reduces risk of reputational damage. The Sustainability Accounting Standards Board (SASB) recommends that food processors disclose information on *priority food ingredients* (those that are essential to the company's products), including details on the company's strategies to address strategic risks.

Consistent with SASB guidelines, General Mills disclosed the following information in its recent *Global Responsibility Report*.

General Mills Performance Dashboard (partial)			
Ingredient	Primary Challenges	Target*	Progress
Vanilla	Smallholder farmer incomes, quality of ingredients	100%	45%
Oats	Declining supply due to profitability versus other crops	100	35
Sugarcane	Child and forced labor, working conditions	100	42
Palm oil	Deforestation, indigenous peoples' rights	100	83

*Target and progress amounts are the percent of the ingredient sourced sustainably.

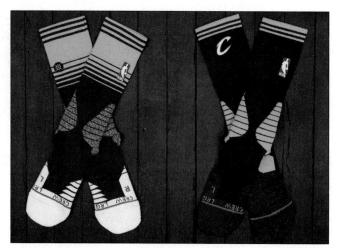

Courtesy of Stance

In addition to making continuous process improvements to reduce materials waste, creative companies such as **Stance** consider the sustainability of their workforce. Stance's headquarters are designed to encourage interaction and teamwork between employees.

Stance's founder, Jeff Kearl, believes that allowing his team to live more balanced lives helps in recruiting and retaining good employees, and helps them be more creative in their work. A basketball court, gym, skate bowl, and volleyball court build fun and teamwork into the workday.

 Decision Analysis **Hybrid Costing System**

A2

Explain and illustrate a hybrid costing system.

Many organizations use a **hybrid costing system** that contains features of both process and job order operations. A recent survey of manufacturers revealed that a majority use hybrid systems (also called **operation costing systems**).

To illustrate, consider a car manufacturer's assembly line. The line resembles a process operation in that the assembly steps for each car are nearly identical. But, the specifications of most cars have several important differences. At the **Ford** Mustang plant, each car assembled can be different from the previous car and the next car. This means that the costs of materials (subassemblies or components) for each car can differ. Accordingly, while the conversion costs (direct labor and overhead) can be accounted for using a process costing system, the component costs (direct materials) are accounted for using a job order system (separately for each car or type of car).

A hybrid system of processes requires a *hybrid costing system* to properly cost products or services. In the Ford plant, the assembly costs per car are readily determined using process costing. The costs of additional components can then be added to the assembly costs to determine each car's total cost (as in job order costing). To illustrate, consider the following information for a daily assembly process at Ford.

Assembly process costs	
Direct materials	$10.6 million
Conversion costs	$12.0 million
Number of cars assembled	1,000
Costs of three different types of wheels	$240, $330, $480
Costs of three different types of sound systems	$620, $840, $1,360

The assembly process costs $22,600 per car. Depending on the type of wheels and sound systems the customer requests, the cost of a car can range from $23,460 to $24,440 (a $980 difference).

Today companies are increasingly trying to standardize processes while attempting to meet individual customer needs. For example, **Lightning Wear** makes custom team uniforms, which are the same except for the team logo and colors added in the final process. The **Planters Company** packages peanuts in different sizes and types of packaging for different retailers. To the extent that differences among individual customers' requests are large, understanding the costs to satisfy those requests is important. Thus, monitoring and controlling both process and job order costs are important.

 **Decision Ethics**

Entrepreneur Your company makes similar products for three different customers. One customer demands 100% quality inspection of products at your location before shipping. The added costs of that inspection are spread across all three customers. If you charge the customer the costs of 100% quality inspection, you could lose that customer and experience a loss. Moreover, your other two customers do not question the amounts they pay. What actions (if any) do you take? ■ *Answer:* By spreading the added quality-related costs across three customers, the price you charge is lower for the customer that demands the 100% quality inspection. You recover much of the added costs from the other two customers. This act likely breaches the trust placed by the other two customers. Your costing system should be changed, and you should consider renegotiating the pricing and/or quality test agreement with this one customer (at the risk of losing this customer).

Pennsylvania Company produces a product that passes through two processes: grinding and mixing. Information related to its grinding department manufacturing activities for July follows. The company uses the weighted-average method of process costing.

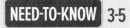

COMPREHENSIVE 1

Weighted-Average Method

Grinding Department			**Grinding Department**	
Raw Materials			Beginning work in process inventory (units)	5,000
Beginning inventory.	$100,000		Percentage completed—Materials.	100%
Raw materials purchased on credit	211,400		Percentage completed—Conversion.	70%
Direct materials used.	(190,000)		Beginning work in process inventory (costs)	
Indirect materials used	(51,400)		Direct materials used	$20,000
Ending inventory	$ 70,000		Direct labor incurred.	9,600
			Overhead applied (200% of direct labor)	19,200
Factory Payroll			Total costs of beginning work in process	$48,800
Direct labor incurred	$ 55,500			
Indirect labor incurred	50,625		Units started this period	20,000
Total payroll	$106,125		Units transferred to mixing this period	17,000
Factory Overhead			Ending work in process inventory (units)	8,000
Indirect materials used	$ 51,400		Percentage completed—Materials.	100%
Indirect labor used.	50,625		Percentage completed—Conversion.	20%
Other overhead costs	71,725			
Total factory overhead incurred	$173,750			
Factory Overhead Applied				
Overhead applied (200% of direct labor)	$111,000			

Required

Complete the requirements below for the grinding department.

1. Prepare a physical flow reconciliation for July.
2. Compute the equivalent units of production in July for direct materials and conversion.
3. Compute the costs per equivalent unit of production in July for direct materials and conversion.
4. Prepare a report of costs accounted for and a report of costs to account for.

PLANNING THE SOLUTION

- Track the physical flow to determine the number of units completed in July.
- Compute the equivalent units of production for direct materials and conversion.
- Compute the costs per equivalent unit of production with respect to direct materials and conversion, and determine the cost per unit for each.
- Compute the total cost of the goods transferred to mixing by using the equivalent units and unit costs. Determine (a) the cost of the beginning work in process inventory, (b) the materials and conversion costs added to the beginning work in process inventory, and (c) the materials and conversion costs added to the units started and completed in the month.

SOLUTION

1. Physical flow reconciliation.

Units to Account For		Units Accounted For	
Beginning work in process inventory.	5,000 units	Units completed and transferred out.	17,000 units
Units started this period.	20,000 units	Ending work in process inventory.	8,000 units
Total units to account for	**25,000 units**	Total units accounted for	**25,000 units**

reconciled

2. Equivalent units of production (weighted average).

Equivalent Units of Production	Direct Materials	Conversion
Equivalent units completed and transferred out	17,000 EUP	17,000 EUP
Equivalent units in ending work in process		
Direct materials (8,000 × 100%)...................	8,000 EUP	
Conversion (8,000 × 20%)		1,600 EUP
Equivalent units of production........................	25,000 EUP	18,600 EUP

3. Costs per equivalent unit of production (weighted average).

Costs per Equivalent Unit of Production	Direct Materials	Conversion
Costs of beginning work in process	$ 20,000	$ 28,800
Costs incurred this period	190,000	166,500*
Total costs	$210,000	$195,300
÷ Equivalent units of production (from part 2)..........	25,000 EUP	18,600 EUP
= Costs per equivalent unit of production	$8.40 per EUP	$10.50 per EUP

*Direct labor of $55,500 + overhead applied of $111,000

4. Reports of costs accounted for and of costs to account for (weighted average).

Report of Costs Accounted For		
Cost of units transferred out (cost of goods manufactured)		
Direct materials ($8.40 per EUP × 17,000 EUP)	$142,800	
Conversion ($10.50 per EUP × 17,000 EUP).................................	178,500	
Cost of units completed this period		$ 321,300
Cost of ending work in process inventory		
Direct materials ($8.40 per EUP × 8,000 EUP)	67,200	
Conversion ($10.50 per EUP × 1,600 EUP).................................	16,800	
Cost of ending work in process inventory		84,000
Total costs accounted for		**$405,300** ◄

Report of Costs to Account For		
Cost of beginning work in process inventory		
Direct materials	$ 20,000	
Conversion	28,800	$ 48,800
Cost incurred this period		
Direct materials	190,000	
Conversion	166,500	356,500
Total costs to account for		**$405,300** ◄

reconciled

Refer to the information in Need-To-Know 3-5. For the grinding department, complete requirements 1 through 4 using the FIFO method. (Round the cost per equivalent unit of conversion to two decimal places.)

SOLUTION

1. Physical flow reconciliation (FIFO).

Units to Account For		Units Accounted For	
Beginning work in process inventory............	5,000 units	Units completed and transferred out.......................	17,000 units
Units started this period.........	20,000 units	Ending work in process inventory..........	8,000 units
Total units to account for	**25,000 units**	Total units accounted for................	**25,000 units**

reconciled

2. Equivalent units of production (FIFO).

Equivalent Units of Production	Direct Materials	Conversion
(a) Equivalent units complete beginning work in process		
Direct materials (5,000 × 0%)	0 EUP	
Conversion (5,000 × 30%)		1,500 EUP
(b) Equivalent units started and completed..........................	12,000 EUP	12,000 EUP
(c) Equivalent units in ending work in process		
Direct materials (8,000 × 100%)	8,000 EUP	
Conversion (8,000 × 20%)		1,600 EUP
Equivalent units of production.....................................	20,000 EUP	15,100 EUP

3. Costs per equivalent unit of production (FIFO).

Costs per Equivalent Unit of Production	Direct Materials	Conversion
Costs incurred this period	$190,000	$ 166,500*
÷ Equivalent units of production (from part 2)...............	20,000 EUP	15,100 EUP
= Costs per equivalent unit of production	$9.50 per EUP	$11.03 per EUP**

*Direct labor of $55,500 plus overhead applied of $111,000   **Rounded

4. Reports of costs accounted for and of costs to account for (FIFO).

Report of Costs Accounted For
Cost of units transferred out (cost of goods manufactured)
Cost of beginning work in process inventory		$ 48,800
Cost to complete beginning work in process		
Direct materials ($9.50 per EUP × 0 EUP)	$ 0	
Conversion ($11.03 per EUP × 1,500 EUP)...................................	16,545	16,545
Cost of units started and completed this period		
Direct materials ($9.50 per EUP × 12,000 EUP)	114,000	
Conversion ($11.03 per EUP × 12,000 EUP).................................	132,360	246,360
Total cost of units finished this period		311,705
Cost of ending work in process inventory		
Direct materials ($9.50 per EUP × 8,000 EUP)	76,000	
Conversion ($11.03 per EUP × 1,600 EUP).................................	17,648	
Total cost of ending work in process inventory		93,648
Total costs accounted for..		**$405,353**
Report of Costs to Account For		
Cost of beginning work in process inventory		
Direct materials	$ 20,000	
Conversion	28,800	$ 48,800
Costs incurred this period		
Direct materials	190,000	
Conversion	166,500	356,500
Total costs to account for...		**$405,300**

reconciled (with $53 rounding difference)

NEED-TO-KNOW **3-7**

COMPREHENSIVE 3

Journal Entries for
Process Costing

Garcia Manufacturing produces a product that passes through a molding process and then through an assembly process. Partial information related to its manufacturing activities for July follows.

Direct materials		Factory Overhead Applied	
Raw materials purchased on credit	$400,000	Molding (150% of direct labor)...............	$ 63,000
Direct materials used—Molding	190,000	Assembly (200% of direct labor)	110,750
Direct materials used—Assembly...........	88,600	Total factory overhead applied	$173,750
Direct Labor		**Cost Transfers**	
Direct labor—Molding	$ 42,000	From molding to assembly..................	$277,200
Direct labor—Assembly...................	55,375	From assembly to finished goods	578,400
Factory Overhead (Actual costs)		From finished goods to cost	
Indirect materials used	$ 51,400	of goods sold	506,100
Indirect labor used	50,625		
Other overhead costs	71,725		
Total factory overhead incurred	$173,750		

Required

Prepare summary journal entries to record the transactions and events of July for: (a) raw materials purchases, (b) direct materials usage, (c) indirect materials usage, (d) direct labor usage, (e) indirect labor usage, (f) other overhead costs (credit Other Accounts), (g) application of overhead to the two departments, (h) transfer of partially completed goods from molding to assembly, (i) transfer of finished goods out of assembly, and (j) the cost of goods sold.

SOLUTION

Summary journal entries for the transactions and events in July.

a.	Raw Materials Inventory.....................	400,000		**f.**	Factory Overhead	71,725	
	Accounts Payable......................		400,000		Other Accounts.......................		71,725
	Record raw materials purchases.				*Record other overhead costs.*		
b.	Work in Process Inventory—Molding	190,000		**g.**	Work in Process Inventory—Molding	63,000	
	Work in Process Inventory—Assembly..........	88,600			Work in Process Inventory—Assembly..........	110,750	
	Raw Materials Inventory		278,600		Factory Overhead		173,750
	Record direct materials usage.				*Record application of overhead.*		
c.	Factory Overhead	51,400		**h.**	Work in Process Inventory—Assembly..........	277,200	
	Raw Materials Inventory		51,400		Work in Process Inventory—Molding		277,200
	Record indirect materials usage.				*Record transfer of partially completed*		
d.	Work in Process Inventory—Molding	42,000			*goods from molding to assembly.*		
	Work in Process Inventory—Assembly..........	55,375		**i.**	Finished Goods Inventory.....................	578,400	
	Factory Wages Payable		97,375		Work in Process Inventory—Assembly		578,400
	Record direct labor usage.				*Record transfer of finished goods*		
e.	Factory Overhead	50,625			*out of assembly.*		
	Factory Wages Payable		50,625	**j.**	Cost of Goods Sold	506,100	
	Record indirect labor usage.				Finished Goods Inventory		506,100
					Record cost of goods sold.		

APPENDIX

3A   FIFO Method of Process Costing

The FIFO method of process costing assigns costs to units assuming a first-in, first-out flow of product. The key difference between the FIFO and weighted-average methods lies in the treatment of beginning work in process inventory. Under the weighted-average method, the number of units and the costs in beginning work in process inventory are combined with production activity in the current period to compute costs per equivalent unit. Thus, the weighted-average method combines production activity across two periods.

The FIFO method, in contrast, focuses on production activity *in the current period only*. The FIFO method assumes that the units that were in process at the beginning of the period are completed during the current period. Thus, under the FIFO method equivalent units of production are computed as shown in Exhibit 3A.1.

C4 _____

Describe accounting for production activity and preparation of a process cost summary using FIFO.

EXHIBIT 3A.1

Computing EUP—FIFO Method

$$\begin{array}{c}\text{Equivalent units of}\\ \text{production (EUP)}\end{array} = \begin{array}{c}\text{Number of equivalent}\\ \text{units needed to complete}\\ \text{beginning work in}\\ \text{process}\end{array} + \begin{array}{c}\text{Number of whole units}\\ \text{started, completed,}\\ \text{and transferred out*}\end{array} + \begin{array}{c}\text{Number of equivalent}\\ \text{units in ending work}\\ \text{in process}\end{array}$$

*Transferred to next department or finished goods inventory.

In computing cost per equivalent unit, the FIFO method ignores the cost of beginning work in process inventory. Instead, FIFO uses *only the costs incurred in the current period*, as shown in Exhibit 3A.2.

EXHIBIT 3A.2

Cost per EUP—FIFO Method

$$\text{Cost per EUP (FIFO)} = \frac{\text{Manufacturing costs added during current period}}{\text{Equivalent units of production during current period}}$$

We use the data in Exhibit 3A.3 to illustrate the FIFO method for GenX's roasting department.

EXHIBIT 3A.3

Production Data—Roasting Department (FIFO method)

GenX—Roasting Department	
Beginning work in process inventory (March 31)	
Units of product	30,000 units
Percentage of completion—Direct materials	100%
Percentage of completion—Conversion costs	65%
Direct materials costs	$ 81,000
Conversion costs	$108,900
Production activity during the current period (April)	
Units started this period	90,000 units
Units transferred out (completed)	100,000 units
Direct materials costs	$279,000
Direct labor costs	$171,000
Factory overhead costs applied (120% of direct labor)	$205,200
Ending work in process inventory (April 30)	
Units of product	20,000 units
Percentage of completion—Direct materials	100%
Percentage of completion—Conversion	25%

Exhibit 3A.3 shows selected information from GenX's roasting department for the month of April. Accounting for a department's activity for a period includes four steps: (1) determine physical flow, (2) compute equivalent units, (3) compute cost per equivalent unit, and (4) determine cost assignment and reconciliation. This appendix describes each of these steps using the FIFO method for process costing.

Step 1: Determine Physical Flow of Units A *physical flow reconciliation* is a report that reconciles (1) the physical units started in a period with (2) the physical units completed in that period. The physical flow reconciliation for GenX's roasting department for April is shown in Exhibit 3A.4.

EXHIBIT 3A.4

Physical Flow Reconciliation

GenX—Roasting Department			
Units to Account For		**Units Accounted For**	
Beginning work in process inventory	30,000 units	Units completed and transferred out	100,000 units
Units started this period	90,000 units	Ending work in process inventory	20,000 units
Total units to account for	**120,000 units**	Total units accounted for	**120,000 units**

reconciled

Point: Step 1 is exactly the same under the weighted-average method.

Step 2: Compute Equivalent Units of Production—FIFO Exhibit 3A.4 shows that the roasting department completed 100,000 units during the month. The FIFO method assumes that the units in beginning inventory were the first units completed during the month. Thus, FIFO assumes that of the 100,000 completed units, 30,000 consist of units in beginning work in process inventory that were completed during the month. This means that 70,000 (100,000 − 30,000) units were both started and completed during the month. This also means that 20,000 units were started but not completed during the month (90,000 units started − 70,000 units started and completed). Exhibit 3A.5 shows how units flowed through the roasting department, assuming FIFO.

EXHIBIT 3A.5

FIFO—Flow of Units

Roasting Department—Units			
Beg. inv.	30,000	30,000 Completed and transferred out	
Started	90,000	70,000 Started and completed	
To account for	**120,000**	**100,000 Transferred out**	
End. inv.	20,000		

In computing equivalent units of production, the roasting department must consider these three distinct groups of units:

- Units in beginning work in process inventory (30,000).
- Units started and completed during the month (70,000).
- Units in ending work in process inventory (20,000).

GenX's roasting department then computes equivalent units of production under FIFO as shown in Exhibit 3A.6. We compute EUP for each of the three distinct groups of units, and sum them to find total EUP.

EXHIBIT 3A.6

Equivalent Units of Production—FIFO

Point: EUP = Number of physical units × Percent of work completed this period.

GenX—Roasting Department		
Equivalent Units of Production	**Direct Materials**	**Conversion**
(a) Equivalent units to complete beginning work in process		
Direct materials (30,000 × 0%)	0 EUP	
Conversion (30,000 × 35%).................................		10,500 EUP
(b) Equivalent units started and completed (70,000 × 100%)*	70,000 EUP	70,000 EUP
(c) Equivalent units in ending work in process		
Direct materials (20,000 × 100%)	20,000 EUP	
Conversion (20,000 × 25%).................................		5,000 EUP
Equivalent units of production	90,000 EUP	85,500 EUP

*Units completed this period...................	100,000 units
Less units in beginning work in process	30,000 units
Units started and completed this period..........	70,000 units

Direct Materials To calculate the equivalent units of production for direct materials, we start with the equivalent units in beginning work in process inventory. We see that beginning work in process inventory was 100% complete with respect to materials; no materials were needed to complete these units. Thus, this group of units required 0 EUP during the month. Next, we consider the units started and completed during the month. In terms of direct materials, the 70,000 units started and completed during the month received 100% of their materials during the month. Thus, EUP for this group is 70,000 units (70,000 × 100%). Finally, we consider the units in ending work in process inventory. The roasting department started but *did not* complete 20,000 units during the month. This group received all of its materials during the month. Thus, EUP for this group is 20,000 units (20,000 × 100%). The sum of the EUP for these three distinct groups of units is 90,000 (computed as 0 + 70,000 + 20,000), which is the total number of equivalent units of production for direct materials during the month.

Conversion To calculate the equivalent units of production for conversion, we start by determining the percentage of conversion costs needed to complete the beginning work in process inventory. As Exhibit 3A.3 shows, the beginning work in process inventory of 30,000 units was 65% complete with respect to conversion. Thus, this group of units required an additional 35% of conversion costs during the period to complete those units (100% − 65%), or 10,500 EUP (30,000 × 35%). Next, we consider the units started and completed during the month. The units started and completed during the month incurred 100% of their conversion costs during the month. Thus, EUP for this group is 70,000 units (70,000 × 100%). Finally, we consider the units in ending work in process inventory. The ending work in process inventory incurred 25% of its conversion costs (see Exhibit 3A.3) during the month. Thus, EUP for this group is 5,000 units (20,000 × 25%). The sum of the EUP for these three distinct groups of units is 85,500 (computed as 10,500 + 70,000 + 5,000). Thus, the roasting department's equivalent units of production for conversion for the month is 85,500 units.

NEED-TO-KNOW 3-8

A department began the month with 50,000 units in work in process inventory. These units were 90% complete with respect to direct materials and 40% complete with respect to conversion. During the month, the department started 286,000 units; 220,000 of these units were completed during the month. The remaining 66,000 units are in ending work in process inventory, 80% complete with respect to direct materials and 30% complete with respect to conversion. Use the FIFO method of process costing to:

1. Compute the department's equivalent units of production for the month for direct materials.
2. Compute the department's equivalent units of production for the month for conversion.

EUP—Direct Materials and Conversion (FIFO)

C4

	Units	Materials Current Month %	Materials EUP	Conversion Current Month %	Conversion EUP
Finish BI	50,000	10%	5,000	60%	30,000
Start & Finish	220,000	100%	220,000	100%	220,000
Start EI	66,000	80%	52,800	30%	19,800
			277,800		269,800

Solution—computations to the side show another way to get solutions

1. EUP for materials = (50,000 × 10%) + (220,000 × 100%) + (66,000 × 80%) = 277,800 EUP
2. EUP for conversion = (50,000 × 60%) + (220,000 × 100%) + (66,000 × 30%) = 269,800 EUP

Do More: QS 3-14, QS 3-15, E 3-5, E 3-10

Step 3: Compute Cost per Equivalent Unit—FIFO   To compute cost per equivalent unit, we take the direct materials and conversion costs added in April and divide by the equivalent units of production from step 2. Exhibit 3A.7 illustrates these computations.

GenX—Roasting Department		
Cost per Equivalent Unit of Production	Direct Materials	Conversion
Costs incurred this period (from Exhibit 3A.3).............	$279,000	$376,200
÷ Equivalent units of production (from step 2)	90,000 EUP	85,500 EUP
Cost per equivalent unit of production....................	$3.10 per EUP	$4.40 per EUP

EXHIBIT 3A.7

Cost per Equivalent Unit of Production—FIFO

It is essential to compute costs per equivalent unit for *each* input because production inputs are added at different times in the process. The FIFO method computes the cost per equivalent unit based solely on this period's EUP and costs (unlike the weighted-average method, which adds in the costs of the beginning work in process inventory).

NEED-TO-KNOW 3-9

A department started the month with beginning work in process inventory of $130,000 ($90,000 for direct materials and $40,000 for conversion). During the month, the department incurred additional direct materials costs of $700,000 and conversion costs of $500,000. Assume that equivalent units for the month were computed as 250,000 for materials and 200,000 for conversion.

1. Compute the department's cost per equivalent unit of production for the month for direct materials.
2. Compute the department's cost per equivalent unit of production for the month for conversion.

Cost per EUP—Direct Materials and Conversion (FIFO)

C4

Solution

1. Cost per EUP of materials = $700,000/250,000 = $2.80
2. Cost per EUP of conversion = $500,000/200,000 = $2.50

Do More: QS 3-15, QS 3-17, E 3-7

Step 4: Assign and Reconcile Costs   The equivalent units determined in step 2 and the cost per equivalent unit computed in step 3 are both used to assign costs (1) to units that the production department completed and transferred to the blending department and (2) to units that remain in process at period-end.

As it did in computing equivalent units in step 2, the roasting department now must compute costs for three distinct groups of units:

● Costs to complete the beginning work in process inventory.
● Costs to complete the units started and completed during the month.
● Costs of ending work in process inventory.

In the first section of Exhibit 3A.8, we see that the cost of units completed in April includes the $189,900 cost carried over from March for work already applied to the 30,000 units that make up beginning work in process inventory, plus the $46,200 incurred in April to complete those units. The next section includes the $525,000 of cost assigned to the 70,000 units started and completed this period. Thus, the total cost of goods manufactured in April is $761,100. The average cost per unit for goods completed in April is $7.611 ($761,100 ÷ 100,000 completed units).

EXHIBIT 3A.8

Report of Costs Accounted For—FIFO

GenX—Roasting Department		
Cost of beginning work in process inventory		$ 189,900
Cost to complete beginning work in process		
Direct materials ($3.10 per EUP × 0 EUP)	$ 0	
Conversion ($4.40 per EUP × 10,500 EUP)	46,200	46,200
Cost of units started and completed this period		
Direct materials ($3.10 per EUP × 70,000 EUP)	217,000	
Conversion ($4.40 per EUP × 70,000 EUP)	308,000	525,000
Total cost of units finished and transferred out this period		761,100
Cost of ending work in process inventory		
Direct materials ($3.10 per EUP × 20,000 EUP)	62,000	
Conversion ($4.40 per EUP × 5,000 EUP)	22,000	
Total cost of ending work in process inventory		84,000
Total costs accounted for		**$845,100**

The computation for cost of ending work in process inventory is in the final section of Exhibit 3A.8. That cost of $84,000 ($62,000 + $22,000) also is the ending balance for the Work in Process Inventory—Roasting account.

The roasting department manager verifies that the total costs assigned to units transferred out and units still in process equal the total costs incurred by production. We reconcile the costs accounted for (in Exhibit 3A.8) to the costs that production was charged for as shown in Exhibit 3A.9.

EXHIBIT 3A.9

Report of Costs to Account For—FIFO

Cost of beginning work in process inventory		
Direct materials	$ 81,000	
Conversion	108,900	$ 189,900
Costs incurred this period		
Direct materials	279,000	
Conversion	376,200	655,200
Total costs to account for		**$845,100**

The roasting department production manager is responsible for $845,100 in costs: $189,900 that had been assigned to the department's work in process inventory as of April 1 plus $655,200 of costs the department incurred in April. At period-end, the manager must identify where those costs were assigned. The production manager can report that $761,100 of cost was assigned to units completed in April and $84,000 was assigned to units still in process at period-end.

Process Cost Summary   The final report is the process cost summary, which summarizes key information from previous exhibits. Reasons for the summary are to (1) help managers control and monitor costs, (2) help upper management assess department manager performance, and (3) provide cost information for financial reporting. The process cost summary, using FIFO, for GenX's roasting department is in Exhibit 3A.10.

①This section lists the total costs charged to the department, including direct materials and conversion costs incurred, as well as the cost of the beginning work in process inventory.

②This section describes the equivalent units of production for the department. Equivalent units for conversion are in separate columns. It also reports direct materials and conversion costs per equivalent unit.

③This section allocates total costs among units worked on in the period.

EXHIBIT 3A.10

Process Cost
Summary (FIFO)

GenX COMPANY— ROASTING DEPARTMENT
Process Cost Summary (FIFO Method)
For Month Ended April 30, 2017

① Costs charged to production

Costs of beginning work in process inventory

Direct materials	$ 81,000	
Conversion	108,900	$ 189,900

Costs incurred this period

Direct materials	279,000	
Conversion	376,200	655,200
Total costs to account for		**$845,100** ◄

Unit information

Units to account for		Units accounted for	
Beginning work in process	30,000	Transferred out	100,000
Units started this period	90,000	Ending work in process	20,000
Total units to account for	120,000	Total units accounted for	120,000

②

Equivalent units of production	Direct Materials	Conversion
Equivalent units to complete beginning work in process		
Direct materials (30,000 × 0%)	0 EUP	
Conversion (30,000 × 35%)		10,500 EUP
Equivalent units started and completed	70,000 EUP	70,000 EUP
Equivalent units in ending work in process		
Direct materials (20,000 × 100%)	20,000 EUP	
Conversion (20,000 × 25%)		5,000 EUP
Equivalent units of production	90,000 EUP	85,500 EUP

Cost per equivalent unit of production	Direct Materials	Conversion
Costs incurred this period	$279,000	$376,200
÷ Equivalent units of production	90,000 EUP	85,500 EUP
Cost per equivalent unit of production	$3.10 per EUP	$4.40 per EUP

reconciled

③ Cost assignment and reconciliation

(cost of units completed and transferred out)

Cost of beginning work in process		$ 189,900
Cost to complete beginning work in process		
Direct materials ($3.10 per EUP × 0 EUP)	$ 0	
Conversion ($4.40 per EUP × 10,500 EUP)	46,200	46,200
Cost of units started and completed this period		
Direct materials ($3.10 per EUP × 70,000 EUP)	217,000	
Conversion ($4.40 per EUP × 70,000 EUP)	308,000	525,000
Total cost of units finished this period		761,100
Cost of ending work in process		
Direct materials ($3.10 per EUP × 20,000 EUP)	62,000	
Conversion ($4.40 per EUP × 5,000 EUP)	22,000	
Total cost of ending work in process		84,000
Total costs accounted for		**$845,100** ◄

Decision Maker

Cost Manager   As cost manager for an electronics manufacturer, you apply a process costing system using FIFO. Your company plans to adopt a just-in-time system and eliminate inventories. What is the impact of the use of FIFO (versus the weighted-average method) given these plans? ■   *Answer:* Differences between the FIFO and weighted-average methods are greatest when large work in process inventories exist and when costs fluctuate. The method used if inventories are eliminated does not matter; both produce identical costs.

Summary

C1 **Explain process operations and the way they differ from job order operations.** Process operations produce large quantities of similar products or services by passing them through a series of processes, or steps, in production. Like job order operations, they combine direct materials, direct labor, and overhead in the operations. Unlike job order operations that assign the responsibility for each *job* to a manager, process operations assign the responsibility for each *process* to a manager.

C2 **Define and compute equivalent units and explain their use in process costing.** Equivalent units of production measure the activity of a process as the number of units that would be completed in a period if all effort had been applied to units that were started and finished. This measure of production activity is used to compute the cost per equivalent unit and to assign costs to finished goods and work in process inventory. To compute equivalent units, determine the number of units that would have been finished if all materials (or conversion) had been used to produce units that were started and completed during the period. The costs incurred by a process are divided by its equivalent units to yield cost per equivalent unit.

C3 **Describe accounting for production activity and preparation of a process cost summary using weighted average.** A process cost summary reports on the activities of a production process or department for a period. It describes the costs charged to the department, the equivalent units of production for the department, and the costs assigned to the output. The report aims to (1) help managers control their departments, (2) help factory managers evaluate department managers' performance, and (3) provide cost information for financial statements. A process cost summary includes the physical flow of units, equivalent units of production, costs per equivalent unit, and a cost reconciliation. It reports the units and costs to account for during the period and how they were accounted for during the period. In terms of units, the summary includes the beginning work in process inventory and the units started during the month. These units are accounted for in terms of the goods completed and transferred out, and the ending work in process inventory. With respect to costs, the summary includes materials and conversion costs assigned to the process during the period. It shows how these costs are assigned to goods completed and transferred out, and to ending work in process inventory.

C4ᴬ **Describe accounting for production activity and preparation of a process cost summary using FIFO.** The FIFO method for process costing is applied and illustrated to (1) report the physical flow of units, (2) compute the equivalent units of production, (3) compute the cost per equivalent unit of production, and (4) assign and reconcile costs.

A1 **Compare process costing and job order costing.** Process and job order manufacturing operations are similar in that both combine materials and conversion to produce products or services. They differ in the way they are organized and managed. In job order operations, the job order costing system assigns product costs to specific jobs. In process operations, the process costing system assigns product costs to specific processes. The total costs associated with each process are then divided by the number of units passing through that process to get cost per equivalent unit. The costs per equivalent unit for all processes are added to determine the total cost per unit of a product or service.

A2 **Explain and illustrate a hybrid costing system.** A hybrid costing system contains features of both job order and process costing systems. Generally, certain direct materials are accounted for by individual products as in job order costing, but direct labor and overhead costs are accounted for similar to process costing.

P1 **Record the flow of materials costs in process costing.** Materials purchased are debited to a Raw Materials Inventory account. As direct materials are issued to processes, they are separately accumulated in a Work in Process Inventory account for that process. As indirect materials are used, their costs are debited to Factory Overhead.

P2 **Record the flow of labor costs in process costing.** Direct labor costs are assigned to the Work in Process Inventory account pertaining to each process. As indirect labor is used, its cost is debited to Factory Overhead.

P3 **Record the flow of factory overhead costs in process costing.** Actual overhead costs are recorded as debits to the Factory Overhead account. Estimated overhead costs are allocated, using a predetermined overhead rate, to the different processes. This allocated amount is credited to the Factory Overhead account and debited to the Work in Process Inventory account for each separate process.

P4 **Record the transfer of goods across departments, to Finished Goods Inventory, and to Cost of Goods Sold.** As units are passed through processes, their accumulated costs are transferred across separate Work in Process Inventory accounts for each process. As units complete the final process and are eventually sold, their accumulated cost is transferred to Finished Goods Inventory and finally to Cost of Goods Sold.

Key Terms

Conversion cost per equivalent unit	Job order costing system	Process costing system
Equivalent units of production (EUP)	Materials consumption report	Process operations
FIFO method	Operation costing system	Process cost summary
Hybrid costing system	Process cost summary	Weighted-average method

Multiple Choice Quiz

1. Equivalent units of production are equal to
   a. Physical units that were completed this period from all effort being applied to them.
   b. The number of units introduced into the process this period.
   c. The number of finished units actually completed this period.
   d. The number of units that could have been started and completed given the cost incurred.
   e. The number of units in the process at the end of the period.

2. Recording the cost of raw materials purchased for use in a process costing system includes a
   a. Credit to Raw Materials Inventory.
   b. Debit to Work in Process Inventory.
   c. Debit to Factory Overhead.
   d. Credit to Factory Overhead.
   e. Debit to Raw Materials Inventory.

3. The production department started the month with a beginning work in process inventory of $20,000. During the month, it was assigned the following costs: direct materials, $152,000; direct labor, $45,000; overhead applied at the rate of 40% of direct labor cost. Inventory with a cost of $218,000 was transferred to finished goods. The ending balance of Work in Process Inventory is

   a. $330,000.   d. $112,000.
   b. $ 17,000.   e. $118,000.
   c. $220,000.

4. A company's beginning work in process inventory consists of 10,000 units that are 20% complete with respect to conversion costs. A total of 40,000 units are completed this period. There are 15,000 units in work in process, one-third complete for conversion, at period-end. The equivalent units of production (EUP) with respect to conversion at period-end, assuming the weighted-average method, are

   a. 45,000 EUP.   d. 37,000 EUP.
   b. 40,000 EUP.   e. 43,000 EUP.
   c. 5,000 EUP.

5. Assume the same information as in question 4. Also assume that beginning work in process had $6,000 in conversion cost and that $84,000 in conversion is added during this period. What is the cost per EUP for conversion?

   a. $0.50 per EUP   d. $2.10 per EUP
   b. $1.87 per EUP   e. $2.25 per EUP
   c. $2.00 per EUP

ANSWERS TO MULTIPLE CHOICE QUIZ

1. d
2. e
3. b; $20,000 + $152,000 + $45,000 + $18,000 − $218,000 = $17,000

4. a; 40,000 + (15,000 × 1/3) = 45,000 EUP
5. c; ($6,000 + $84,000) ÷ 45,000 EUP = $2 per EUP

A *Superscript letter A denotes assignments based on Appendix 3A.*

🔲 Icon denotes assignments that involve decision making.

Discussion Questions

1. 🔲 What is the main factor for a company in choosing between the job order costing and process costing systems? Give two likely applications of each system.

2. The focus in a job order costing system is the job or batch. Identify the main focus in process costing.

3. 🔲 Can services be delivered by means of process operations? Support your answer with an example.

4. Are the journal entries that match cost flows to product flows in process costing primarily the same or much different than those in job order costing? Explain.

5. Identify the control document for materials flow when a materials requisition slip is not used.

6. 🔲 Explain in simple terms the notion of equivalent units of production (EUP). Why is it necessary to use EUP in process costing?

7. 🔲 What are the two main inventory methods used in process costing? What are the differences between these methods?

8. 🔲 Why is it possible for direct labor in process operations to include the labor of employees who do not work directly on products or services?

9. Assume that a company produces a single product by processing it first through a single production department. Direct labor costs flow through what accounts in this company's process cost system?

10. At the end of a period, what balance should remain in the Factory Overhead account?

11. 🔲 Is it possible to have under- or overapplied overhead costs in a process costing system? Explain.

12. Explain why equivalent units of production for both direct labor and overhead can be the same as, and why they can be different from, equivalent units for direct materials.

13. List the four steps in accounting for production activity in a reporting period (for process operations).

14. Companies such as **Apple** commonly prepare a process cost summary. What purposes does a process cost summary serve?   **APPLE**

15. 🔲 Are there situations where **Google** can use process costing? Identify at least one and explain it.   **GOOGLE**

16. 🔲 **Samsung** produces digital televisions with a multiple process production line. Identify and list some of its production processing steps and departments.   **Samsung**

17. 🔲 **General Mills** needs a steady supply of ingredients for processing. What are some risks the company faces regarding its ingredients?

🔲 **connect**

QUICK STUDY

QS 3-1
Process vs. job
order operations   **C1**

For each of the following products and services, indicate whether it is more likely produced in a process operation (P) or in a job order operation (J).

_____ **1.** Tennis courts
_____ **2.** Organic juice
_____ **3.** Audit of financial statements
_____ **4.** Luxury yachts
_____ **5.** Vanilla ice cream
_____ **6.** Tennis balls

QS 3-2
Process vs. job
order costing   **A1**

Label each statement below as either true (T) or false (F).

_____ **1.** The cost per equivalent unit is computed as the total costs of a process divided by the number of equivalent units passing through that process.
_____ **2.** Service companies are not able to use process costing.
_____ **3.** Costs per job are computed in both job order and process costing systems.
_____ **4.** Job order and process operations both combine materials, labor, and overhead in producing products or services.

QS 3-3
Process vs. job
order operations
C1

For each of the following products and services, indicate whether it is more likely produced in a process operation (P) or a job order operation (J).

_____ **1.** Beach toys
_____ **2.** Concrete swimming pool
_____ **3.** iPhones
_____ **4.** Wedding reception
_____ **5.** Custom suits
_____ **6.** Juice
_____ **7.** Tattoos
_____ **8.** Guitar picks

QS 3-4
Physical flow reconciliation
C2

The following refers to units processed in Sunflower Printing's binding department in March. Prepare a physical flow reconciliation.

	Units of Product	Percent of Conversion Added
Beginning work in process............	150,000	80%
Goods started.....................	310,000	100
Goods completed..................	340,000	100
Ending work in process	120,000	25

QS 3-5
Weighted average:
Computing equivalent units of production   **C2**

Refer to QS 3-4. Compute the total equivalent units of production with respect to conversion for March using the weighted-average method.

QS 3-6[A]
FIFO: Computing equivalent units   **C4**

Refer to QS 3-4. Compute the total equivalent units of production with respect to conversion for March using the FIFO method.

A production department's beginning inventory cost includes $394,900 of conversion costs. This department incurs an additional $907,500 in conversion costs in the month of March. Equivalent units of production for conversion total 740,000 for March. Calculate the cost per equivalent unit of conversion using the weighted-average method.

QS 3-7
Weighted average:
Cost per EUP   C3

The following refers to units processed by an ice cream maker in July. Compute the total equivalent units of production with respect to conversion for July using the weighted-average method.

QS 3-8
Weighted average:
Computing equivalent units of production   C2

	Gallons of Product	Percent of Conversion Added
Beginning work in process	320,000	25%
Goods started	620,000	100
Goods completed	680,000	100
Ending work in process	260,000	75

Refer to QS 3-8 and compute the total equivalent units of production with respect to conversion for July using the FIFO method.

QS 3-9ᴬ
FIFO: Computing equivalent units   C4

The following information applies to QS 3-10 through QS 3-17.

The Carlberg Company has two manufacturing departments, assembly and painting. The assembly department started 10,000 units during November. The following production activity unit and cost information refers to the assembly department's November production activities.

QS 3-10
Weighted average:
Equivalent units of production   C2

Assembly Department	Units	Percent of Direct Materials Added	Percent of Conversion Added
Beginning work in process	2,000	60%	40%
Units transferred out	9,000	100	100
Ending work in process	3,000	80	30

Beginning work in process inventory—Assembly dept.	$1,581 (includes $996 for direct materials and $585 for conversion)
Costs added during the month:	
Direct materials	$10,404
Conversion	$12,285

Required

Calculate the assembly department's equivalent units of production for materials and for conversion for November. Use the weighted-average method.

Refer to the information in QS 3-10. Calculate the assembly department's cost per equivalent unit of production for materials and for conversion for November. Use the weighted-average method.

QS 3-11
Weighted average:
Cost per EUP   C2

Refer to the information in QS 3-10. Assign costs to the assembly department's output—specifically, the units transferred out to the painting department and the units that remain in process in the assembly department at month-end. Use the weighted-average method.

QS 3-12
Weighted average:
Assigning costs to output
C3

Refer to the information in QS 3-10. Prepare the November 30 journal entry to record the transfer of units (and costs) from the assembly department to the painting department. Use the weighted-average method.

QS 3-13
Weighted average:
Journal entry to transfer costs   P4

QS 3-14ᴬ
FIFO: Equivalent units
of production   C4

Refer to the information in QS 3-10. Calculate the assembly department's equivalent units of production for materials and for conversion for November. Use the FIFO method.

QS 3-15ᴬ
FIFO: Cost per EUP   C4

Refer to the information in QS 3-10. Calculate the assembly department's cost per equivalent unit of production for materials and for conversion for November. Use the FIFO method.

QS 3-16ᴬ
FIFO: Assigning costs
to output   C4

Refer to the information in QS 3-10. Assign costs to the assembly department's output—specifically, the units transferred out to the painting department and the units that remain in process in the assembly department at month-end. Use the FIFO method.

QS 3-17ᴬ
FIFO: Journal entry to
transfer costs   P4

Refer to the information in QS 3-10. Prepare the November 30 journal entry to record the transfer of units (and costs) from the assembly department to the painting department. Use the FIFO method.

QS 3-18
Weighted average:
Computing equivalent
units and cost per EUP
(direct materials)

C2   C3

The Plastic Flowerpots Company has two manufacturing departments, molding and packaging. At the beginning of the month, the molding department has 2,000 units in inventory, 70% complete as to materials. During the month, the molding department started 18,000 units. At the end of the month, the molding department had 3,000 units in ending inventory, 80% complete as to materials. Units completed in the molding department are transferred into the packaging department.

Cost information for the molding department for the month follows:

Beginning work in process inventory (direct materials)........	$ 1,200
Direct materials added during the month..................	27,900

Using the weighted-average method, compute the molding department's (a) equivalent units of production for materials and (b) cost per equivalent unit of production for materials for the month. (Round to two decimal places.)

QS 3-19
Weighted average:
Assigning costs to output

C3

Refer to information in QS 3-18. Using the weighted-average method, assign direct materials costs to the molding department's output—specifically, the units transferred out to the packaging department and the units that remain in process in the molding department at month-end.

QS 3-20
Transfer of costs; ending
WIP balances

C3

Azule Co. manufactures in two sequential processes, cutting and binding. The two departments report the information below for a recent month. Determine the ending balances in the Work in Process Inventory accounts of each department.

	Cutting	Binding
Beginning work in process		
Transferred in from cutting dept.		$ 1,200
Direct materials	$ 845	1,926
Conversion...........................	2,600	3,300
Costs added during March		
Direct materials	$ 8,240	$ 6,356
Conversion...........................	11,100	18,575
Transferred in from cutting dept.		15,685
Transferred to finished goods.............		30,000

BOGO Inc. has two sequential processing departments, roasting and mixing. At the beginning of the month, the roasting department has 2,000 units in inventory, 70% complete as to materials. During the month, the roasting department started 18,000 units. At the end of the month, the roasting department had 3,000 units in ending inventory, 80% complete as to materials.

Cost information for the roasting department for the month is as follows:

Beginning work in process inventory (direct materials).............	$ 2,170
Direct materials added during the month........................	27,900

Using the FIFO method, compute the roasting department's (a) equivalent units of production for materials and (b) cost per equivalent unit of production for materials for the month.

QS 3-21[A]
FIFO: Computing equivalent units and cost per EUP (direct materials)
C4

Refer to QS 3-21. Using the FIFO method, assign direct materials costs to the roasting department's output—specifically, the units transferred out to the mixing department and the units that remain in process in the roasting department at month-end.

QS 3-22[A]
FIFO: Assigning costs to output   C4

Hotwax makes surfboard wax in a single operation. This period, Hotwax purchased $62,000 in raw materials. Its production department requisitioned $50,000 of those materials for use in production. Prepare journal entries to record its (1) purchase of raw materials and (2) requisition of direct materials.

QS 3-23
Recording costs of materials   P1

Prepare journal entries to record the following production activities for Hotwax.
1. Incurred direct labor of $125,000 (credit Factory Wages Payable).
2. Incurred indirect labor of $10,000 (credit Factory Wages Payable).
3. Total factory payroll of $135,000 was paid in cash.

QS 3-24
Recording costs of labor
P2

Prepare journal entries to record the following production activities for Hotwax.
1. Requisitioned $9,000 of indirect materials for use in production of surfboard wax.
2. Incurred $156,000 overhead costs (credit Other Accounts).
3. Applied overhead at the rate of 140% of direct labor costs. Direct labor costs were $125,000.

QS 3-25
Recording costs of factory overhead
P1   P3

Hotwax completed products costing $275,000 and transferred them to finished goods. Prepare its journal entry to record the transfer of units from production to finished goods inventory.

QS 3-26
Recording transfer of costs to finished goods
P4

Anheuser-Busch InBev is attempting to reduce its water usage. How could a company manager use a process cost summary to determine if the program to reduce water usage is successful?

QS 3-27
Process cost summary
C3

connect

For each of the following products and services, indicate whether it is more likely produced in a process operation (P) or in a job order operation (J).

_____ **1.** Beach towels	_____ **5.** Designed patio	_____ **9.** Concrete swimming pools
_____ **2.** Bolts and nuts	_____ **6.** Door hardware	_____ **10.** Custom tailored dresses
_____ **3.** Lawn chairs	_____ **7.** Cut flower arrangements	_____ **11.** Grand pianos
_____ **4.** Headphones	_____ **8.** House paints	_____ **12.** Table lamps

EXERCISES

Exercise 3-1
Process vs. job order operations

C1

Exercise 3-2

Comparing process and job order operations

C1

Label each item *a* through *h* below as a feature of either a job order (J) or process (P) operation.

_____ **a.** Heterogeneous products and services

_____ **b.** Custom orders

_____ **c.** Low production volume

_____ **d.** Routine, repetitive procedures

_____ **e.** Focus on individual batch

_____ **f.** Low product standardization

_____ **g.** Low product flexibility

_____ **h.** Focus on standardized units

Exercise 3-3

Terminology in process costing

C1   A1

Match each of the following items *A* through *G* with the best numbered description of its purpose.

A. Factory Overhead account

B. Process cost summary

C. Equivalent units of production

D. Work in Process Inventory account

E. Raw Materials Inventory account

F. Materials requisition

G. Finished Goods Inventory account

_____ **1.** Notifies the materials manager to send materials to a production department.

_____ **2.** Holds costs of indirect materials, indirect labor, and similar costs until assigned to production.

_____ **3.** Holds costs of direct materials, direct labor, and applied overhead until products are transferred from production to finished goods (or another department).

_____ **4.** Standardizes partially completed units into equivalent completed units.

_____ **5.** Holds costs of finished products until sold to customers.

_____ **6.** Describes the activity and output of a production department for a period.

_____ **7.** Holds costs of materials until they are used in production or as factory overhead.

Exercise 3-4

Weighted average:

Computing equivalent units

C2

The production department in a process manufacturing system completed 80,000 units of product and transferred them to finished goods during a recent period. Of these units, 24,000 were in process at the beginning of the period. The other 56,000 units were started and completed during the period. At period-end, 16,000 units were in process. Compute the department's equivalent units of production with respect to direct materials under each of three separate assumptions using the weighted-average method:

1. All direct materials are added to products when processing begins.

2. Beginning inventory is 40% complete as to materials and conversion costs. Ending inventory is 75% complete as to materials and conversion costs.

Check   (3) EUP for materials, 84,800

3. Beginning inventory is 60% complete as to materials and 40% complete as to conversion costs. Ending inventory is 30% complete as to materials and 60% complete as to conversion costs.

Exercise 3-5^A

FIFO: Computing equivalent units   C4

Check   (3) EUP for materials, 70,400

Refer to the information in Exercise 3-4 and complete the requirements for each of the three separate assumptions using the FIFO method for process costing.

Exercise 3-6

Weighted average:

Cost per EUP and costs assigned to output

C2

The Fields Company has two manufacturing departments, forming and painting. The company uses the weighted-average method of process costing. At the beginning of the month, the forming department has 25,000 units in inventory, 60% complete as to materials and 40% complete as to conversion costs. The beginning inventory cost of $60,100 consisted of $44,800 of direct materials costs and $15,300 of conversion costs.

During the month, the forming department started 300,000 units. At the end of the month, the forming department had 30,000 units in ending inventory, 80% complete as to materials and 30% complete as to conversion. Units completed in the forming department are transferred to the painting department.

Cost information for the forming department is as follows:

Beginning work in process inventory	$ 60,100
Direct materials added during the month	1,231,200
Conversion added during the month	896,700

1. Calculate the equivalent units of production for the forming department.
2. Calculate the costs per equivalent unit of production for the forming department.
3. Using the weighted-average method, assign costs to the forming department's output—specifically, its units transferred to painting and its ending work in process inventory.

Refer to the information in Exercise 3-6. Assume that Fields uses the FIFO method of process costing.
1. Calculate the equivalent units of production for the forming department.
2. Calculate the costs per equivalent unit of production for the forming department.

Exercise 3-7^A
FIFO: Costs per EUP

C4

During April, the production department of a process manufacturing system completed a number of units of a product and transferred them to finished goods. Of these transferred units, 60,000 were in process in the production department at the beginning of April and 240,000 were started and completed in April. April's beginning inventory units were 60% complete with respect to materials and 40% complete with respect to conversion. At the end of April, 82,000 additional units were in process in the production department and were 80% complete with respect to materials and 30% complete with respect to conversion.
1. Compute the number of units transferred to finished goods.
2. Compute the number of equivalent units with respect to both materials used and conversion used in the production department for April using the weighted-average method.

Exercise 3-8
Weighted average:
Computing equivalent units of production

C2

Check (2) EUP for materials, 365,600

The production department described in Exercise 3-8 had $850,368 of direct materials and $649,296 of conversion costs charged to it during April. Also, its beginning inventory of $167,066 consists of $118,472 of direct materials cost and $48,594 of conversion costs.
1. Compute the direct materials cost and the conversion cost per equivalent unit for the department.
2. Using the weighted-average method, assign April's costs to the department's output—specifically, its units transferred to finished goods and its ending work in process inventory.

Exercise 3-9
Weighted average:
Costs assigned to output and inventories

C2

Check (1) $2.65 per EUP of direct materials

Refer to the information in Exercise 3-8 to compute the number of equivalent units with respect to both materials used and conversion costs in the production department for April using the FIFO method.

Exercise 3-10^A
FIFO: Computing equivalent units of production C4

Refer to the information in Exercise 3-9 and complete its parts 1 and 2 using the FIFO method.

Exercise 3-11^A
FIFO: Costs assigned to output C4 P4

The following partially completed process cost summary describes the July production activities of Ashad Company. Its production output is sent to its warehouse for shipping. All direct materials are added to products when processing begins. Beginning work in process inventory is 20% complete with respect to conversion. Prepare its process cost summary using the weighted-average method.

Exercise 3-12
Weighted average:
Completing a process cost summary C3

Equivalent Units of Production	Direct Materials	Conversion
Units transferred out	32,000 EUP	32,000 EUP
Units of ending work in process	2,500 EUP	1,500 EUP
Equivalent units of production.	34,500 EUP	33,500 EUP

Costs per EUP	Direct Materials	Conversion
Costs of beginning work in process	$ 18,550	$ 2,280
Costs incurred this period	357,500	188,670
Total costs.	$376,050	$190,950
Units in beginning work in process (all completed during July)		2,000
Units started this period.		32,500
Units completed and transferred out		32,000
Units in ending work in process		2,500

Exercise 3-13^A

FIFO: Completing a process cost summary

C3   C4

Refer to the information in Exercise 3-12. Prepare a process cost summary using the FIFO method. (Round cost per equivalent unit calculations to two decimal places.)

Exercise 3-14

Production cost flow and measurement; journal entries

P4

Pro-Weave manufactures stadium blankets by passing the products through a weaving department and a sewing department. The following information is available regarding its June inventories:

	Beginning Inventory	Ending Inventory
Raw materials inventory.	$ 120,000	$ 185,000
Work in process inventory—Weaving	300,000	330,000
Work in process inventory—Sewing	570,000	700,000
Finished goods inventory.	1,266,000	1,206,000

The following additional information describes the company's manufacturing activities for June:

Raw materials purchases (on credit)	$ 500,000
Factory payroll cost (paid in cash)	3,060,000
Other factory overhead cost (Other Accounts credited).	156,000
Materials used	
Direct—Weaving.	$ 240,000
Direct—Sewing.	75,000
Indirect	120,000
Labor used	
Direct—Weaving.	$1,200,000
Direct—Sewing.	360,000
Indirect	1,500,000
Overhead rates as a percent of direct labor	
Weaving	80%
Sewing	150%
Sales (on credit)	$4,000,000

Required

1. Compute the (a) cost of products transferred from weaving to sewing, (b) cost of products transferred from sewing to finished goods, and (c) cost of goods sold.

2. Prepare journal entries dated June 30 to record (a) goods transferred from weaving to sewing, (b) goods transferred from sewing to finished goods, and (c) sale of finished goods.

Check (1c) Cost of goods sold, $3,275,000

Refer to the information in Exercise 3-14. Prepare journal entries dated June 30 to record: (a) raw materials purchases, (b) direct materials usage, (c) indirect materials usage, (d) direct labor usage, (e) indirect labor usage, (f) other overhead costs, (g) overhead applied, and (h) payment of total payroll costs.

Exercise 3-15
Recording product costs
P1   P2   P3

Elliott Company produces large quantities of a standardized product. The following information is available for its production activities for March.

Exercise 3-16
Weighted average:
Process cost summary   C3

Units		Costs		
Beginning work in process inventory	2,000	Beginning work in process inventory		
Started	20,000	Direct materials	$2,500	
Ending work in process inventory	5,000	Conversion	6,360	$ 8,860
		Direct materials added		168,000
		Direct labor added		199,850
Status of ending work in process inventory		Overhead applied (140% of direct labor)		279,790
Materials—Percent complete	100%	Total costs to account for		$656,500
Conversion—Percent complete	35%	Ending work in process inventory		$ 84,110

Prepare a process cost summary report for this company showing costs charged to production, unit cost information, equivalent units of production, cost per EUP, and its cost assignment and reconciliation. Use the weighted-average method.

Check   Cost per equivalent unit: materials, $7.75; conversion, $25.92

Oslo Company produces large quantities of a standardized product. The following information is available for its production activities for May.

Exercise 3-17
Weighted average:
Process cost summary   C3

Units		Costs		
Beginning work in process inventory	4,000	Beginning work in process inventory		
Started	12,000	Direct materials	$2,880	
Ending work in process inventory	3,000	Conversion	5,358	$ 8,238
		Direct materials added		197,120
		Direct labor added		123,680
Status of ending work in process inventory		Overhead applied (90% of direct labor)		111,312
Materials—Percent complete	100%	Total costs to account for		$440,350
Conversion—Percent complete	25%	Ending work in process inventory		$ 50,610

Prepare a process cost summary report for this company showing costs charged to production, unit cost information, equivalent units of production, cost per EUP, and its cost assignment and reconciliation. Use the weighted-average method.

Check   Cost per equivalent unit: materials, $12.50; conversion, $17.48

RSTN Co. produces its product through two sequential processing departments. Direct materials and conversion are added to the product evenly throughout the process. The company uses monthly reporting periods for its process costing system.

During October, the company finished and transferred 150,000 units of its product to Department 2. Of these units, 30,000 were in process at the beginning of the month and 120,000 were started and completed during the month. The beginning work in process inventory was 30% complete. At the end of the month, the work in process inventory consisted of 20,000 units that were 80% complete.

Compute the number of equivalent units of production for October. Use the FIFO method.

Exercise 3-18[A]
FIFO: Equivalent units
C4   P4

Check   157,000 EUP

Exercise 3-19

Production cost flows

P1   P2   P3   P4

The flowchart below shows the August production activity of the punching and bending departments of Wire Box Company. Use the amounts shown on the flowchart to compute the missing numbers identified by question marks.

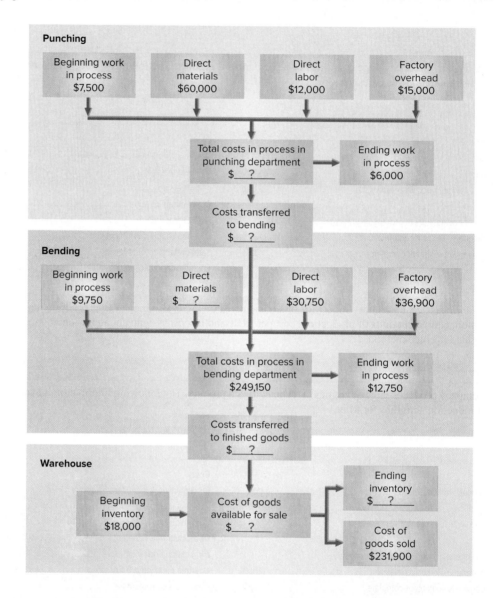

Exercise 3-20

Weighted average:

Process cost summary

C3

Hi-Test Company uses the weighted-average method of process costing to assign production costs to its products. Information for September follows. Assume that all materials are added at the beginning of its production process, and that conversion costs are added uniformly throughout the process.

Work in process inventory, September 1 (2,000 units, 100% complete with respect to direct materials, 80% complete with respect to direct labor and overhead; includes $45,000 of direct materials cost, $25,600 in direct labor cost, $30,720 overhead cost).	$101,320
Units started in September	28,000
Units completed and transferred to finished goods inventory	23,000
Work in process inventory, September 30 (__?__ units, 100% complete with respect to direct materials, 40% complete with respect to direct labor and overhead)	$___?___
Costs incurred in September	
Direct materials	$375,000
Conversion	$341,000

Compute each of the following, assuming Hi-Test uses the weighted-average method of process costing.

1. The number of physical units that were transferred out and the number that are in ending work in process inventory.
2. The number of equivalent units for materials for the month.
3. The number of equivalent units for conversion for the month.
4. The cost per equivalent unit of materials for the month.
5. The cost per equivalent unit for conversion for the month.
6. The total cost of goods transferred out.
7. The total cost of ending work in process inventory.

Prepare journal entries to record the following production activities.

1. Purchased $80,000 of raw materials on credit.
2. Used $42,000 of direct materials in production.
3. Used $22,500 of indirect materials in production.

Exercise 3-21
Recording costs of materials

P1

Prepare journal entries to record the following production activities.

1. Incurred $75,000 of direct labor in production (credit Factory Wages Payable).
2. Incurred $20,000 of indirect labor in production (credit Factory Wages Payable).
3. Paid factory payroll.

Exercise 3-22
Recording costs of labor

P2

Prepare journal entries to record the following production activities.

1. Paid overhead costs (other than indirect materials and indirect labor) of $38,750.
2. Applied overhead at 110% of direct labor costs. Direct labor costs were $75,000.

Exercise 3-23
Recording overhead costs

P3

Prepare journal entries to record the following production activities.

1. Transferred completed goods from the Assembly department to finished goods inventory. The goods cost $135,600.
2. Sold $315,000 of goods on credit. Their cost is $175,000.

Exercise 3-24
Recording cost of completed goods

P4

Laffer Lumber produces bagged bark for use in landscaping. Production involves packaging bark chips in plastic bags in a bagging department. The following information describes production operations for October.

Exercise 3-25
Recording cost flows in a process cost system

P1   P2   P3   P4

	A	B
1		**Bagging**
2		**Department**
3	Direct materials used	$ 522,000
4	Direct labor used	$ 130,000
5	Predetermined overhead rate (based on direct labor)	175%
6	Goods transferred from bagging to finished goods	$(595,000)

The company's revenue for the month totaled $950,000 from credit sales, and its cost of goods sold for the month is $540,000. Prepare summary journal entries dated October 31 to record its October production activities for (1) direct materials usage, (2) direct labor incurred (3) overhead allocation, (4) goods transfer from production to finished goods, and (5) credit sales.

Check   (3) Cr. Factory Overhead, $227,500

Exercise 3-26
Interpretation of journal entries in process costing

P1   P2   P3   P4

The following journal entries are recorded in Kiesha Co.'s process costing system. Kiesha produces apparel and accessories. Overhead is applied to production based on direct labor cost for the period. Prepare a brief explanation (including any overhead rates applied) for each journal entry *a* through *k*.

a.	Raw Materials Inventory	52,000	
	Accounts Payable		52,000
b.	Work in Process Inventory	42,000	
	Raw Materials Inventory		42,000
c.	Work in Process Inventory	32,000	
	Factory Wages Payable		32,000
d.	Factory Overhead	6,000	
	Factory Wages Payable		6,000
e.	Factory Overhead	12,000	
	Cash		12,000
f.	Factory Overhead	10,000	
	Raw Materials Inventory		10,000

g.	Factory Wages Payable	38,000	
	Cash		38,000
h.	Work in Process Inventory	33,600	
	Factory Overhead		33,600
i.	Finished Goods Inventory	88,000	
	Work in Process Inventory		88,000
j.	Accounts Receivable	250,000	
	Sales		250,000
k.	Cost of Goods Sold	100,000	
	Finished Goods Inventory		100,000

Exercise 3-27
Hybrid costing system   A2

Explain a hybrid costing system. Identify a product or service operation that might well fit a hybrid costing system.

📘 **connect**

PROBLEM SET A

Problem 3-1A
Production cost flow and measurement; journal entries

P1   P2   P3   P4

Sierra Company manufactures woven blankets and accounts for product costs using process costing. The company uses a single processing department. The following information is available regarding its May inventories.

	Beginning Inventory	Ending Inventory
Raw materials inventory	$ 60,000	$ 92,500
Work in process inventory	435,000	515,000
Finished goods inventory	633,000	605,000

The following additional information describes the company's production activities for May.

Raw materials purchases (on credit)	$ 250,000
Factory payroll cost (paid in cash)	1,530,000
Other overhead cost (Other Accounts credited)	87,000
Materials used	
Direct	$ 157,500
Indirect	60,000
Labor used	
Direct	$ 780,000
Indirect	750,000
Overhead rate as a percent of direct labor	115%
Sales (on credit)	$2,500,000

Required

Check   (1*b*) Cost of goods sold, $1,782,500

1. Compute the cost of (a) products transferred from production to finished goods and (b) goods sold.
2. Prepare summary journal entries dated May 31 to record the following production activities during May: (a) raw materials purchases, (b) direct materials usage, (c) indirect materials usage, (d) direct labor costs incurred, (e) indirect labor costs incurred, (f) payment of factory payroll, (g) other overhead costs, (h) overhead applied, (i) goods transferred from production to finished goods, and (j) sale of finished goods.

Victory Company uses weighted-average process costing to account for its production costs. Conversion cost is added evenly throughout the process. Direct materials are added at the beginning of the process. During November, the company transferred 700,000 units of product to finished goods. At the end of November, the work in process inventory consists of 180,000 units that are 30% complete with respect to conversion. Beginning inventory had $420,000 of direct materials and $139,000 of conversion cost. The direct material cost added in November is $2,220,000, and the conversion cost added is $3,254,000. Beginning work in process consisted of 60,000 units that were 100% complete with respect to direct materials and 80% complete with respect to conversion. Of the units completed, 60,000 were from beginning work in process and 640,000 units were started and completed during the period.

Required

1. Determine the equivalent units of production with respect to (a) direct materials and (b) conversion.

2. Compute both the direct material cost and the conversion cost per equivalent unit.

3. Compute the direct material cost and the conversion cost assigned to (a) units completed and transferred out and (b) ending work in process inventory.

Analysis Component

4. The company sells and ships all units to customers as soon as they are completed. Assume that an error is made in determining the percentage of completion for units in ending inventory. Instead of being 30% complete with respect to labor, they are actually 60% complete. Write a one-page memo to the plant manager describing how this error affects its November financial statements.

Problem 3-2A
Weighted average:
Cost per equivalent unit; costs assigned to products
C2 C3

Check (2) Conversion cost per equivalent unit, $4.50
(3b) $783,000

Fast Co. produces its product through a single processing department. Direct materials are added at the start of production, and conversion costs are added evenly throughout the process. The company uses monthly reporting periods for its weighted-average process costing system. The Work in Process Inventory account has a balance of $84,300 as of October 1, which consists of $17,100 of direct materials and $67,200 of conversion costs.
During the month, the company incurred the following costs:

Direct materials	$144,400
Conversion	862,400

During October, the company started 140,000 units and transferred 150,000 units to finished goods. At the end of the month, the work in process inventory consisted of 20,000 units that were 80% complete with respect to conversion costs.

Required

1. Prepare the company's process cost summary for October using the weighted-average method.

2. Prepare the journal entry dated October 31 to transfer the cost of the completed units to finished goods inventory.

Problem 3-3A
Weighted average:
Process cost summary; equivalent units
C2 C3 P4

Check (1) Costs transferred out to finished goods, $982,500

Tamar Co. manufactures a single product in one department. All direct materials are added at the beginning of the manufacturing process. Conversion costs are added evenly throughout the process. During May, the company completed and transferred 22,200 units of product to finished goods inventory. Its 3,000 units of beginning work in process consisted of $19,800 of direct materials and $221,940 of conversion costs. It has 2,400 units (100% complete with respect to direct materials and 80% complete with respect to conversion) in process at month-end. During the month, $496,800 of direct material costs and $2,165,940 of conversion costs were charged to production.

Required

1. Prepare the company's process cost summary for May using the weighted-average method.

2. Prepare the journal entry dated May 31 to transfer the cost of completed units to finished goods inventory.

Analysis Component

3. The costing process depends on numerous estimates.

a. Identify two major estimates that determine the cost per equivalent unit.

b. In what direction might you anticipate a bias from management for each estimate in part 3a (assume that management compensation is based on maintaining low inventory amounts)? Explain your answer.

Problem 3-4A
Weighted average:
Process cost summary, equivalent units, cost estimates
C2 C3 P4

Check (1) EUP for conversion, 24,120
(2) Cost transferred out to finished goods, $2,664,000

Problem 3-5A[A]

FIFO: Process cost summary; equivalent units; cost estimates

C3 C4 P4

Refer to the data in Problem 3-4A. Assume that Tamar uses the FIFO method to account for its process costing system. The following additional information is available:

- Beginning work in process consisted of 3,000 units that were 100% complete with respect to direct materials and 40% complete with respect to conversion.
- Of the 22,200 units completed, 3,000 were from beginning work in process. The remaining 19,200 were units started and completed during May.

Check (1) EUP for conversion, 22,920

(2) Cost transferred out to finished goods, $2,667,840

Required

1. Prepare the company's process cost summary for May using FIFO.
2. Prepare the journal entry dated May 31 to transfer the cost of completed units to finished goods inventory.

Problem 3-6A[A]

FIFO: Costs per equivalent unit; costs assigned to products

C2 C4

During May, the production department of a process manufacturing system completed a number of units of a product and transferred them to finished goods. Of these transferred units, 37,500 were in process in the production department at the beginning of May and 150,000 were started and completed in May. May's beginning inventory units were 60% complete with respect to materials and 40% complete with respect to conversion. At the end of May, 51,250 additional units were in process in the production department and were 60% complete with respect to materials and 20% complete with respect to conversion. The production department had $505,035 of direct materials and $396,568 of conversion cost charged to it during May. Its beginning inventory included $74,075 of direct materials cost and $28,493 of conversion cost.

1. Compute the number of units transferred to finished goods.

Check (2) EUP for materials, 195,750

2. Compute the number of equivalent units with respect to both materials used and conversion used in the production department for May using the FIFO method.
3. Compute the direct materials cost and the conversion cost per equivalent unit for the department.
4. Using the FIFO method, assign May's costs to the units transferred to finished goods and assign costs to its ending work in process inventory.

Problem 3-7A[A]

FIFO: Process cost summary, equivalent units, cost estimates

C2 C3 C4 P4

Dengo Co. makes a trail mix in two departments: roasting and blending. Direct materials are added at the beginning of each process, and conversion costs are added evenly throughout each process. The company uses the FIFO method of process costing. During October, the roasting department completed and transferred 22,200 units to the blending department. Of the units completed, 3,000 were from beginning inventory and the remaining 19,200 were started and completed during the month. Beginning work in process was 100% complete with respect to direct materials and 40% complete with respect to conversion. The company has 2,400 units (100% complete with respect to direct materials and 80% complete with respect to conversion) in process at month-end. Information on the roasting department's costs of beginning work in process inventory and costs added during the month follows.

Cost	Direct Materials	Conversion
Of beginning work in process inventory..............	$ 9,900	$ 110,970
Added during the month	248,400	1,082,970

Check (1) EUP for conversion, 22,920

(2) Cost transferred out to blending, $1,333,920

Required

1. Prepare the roasting department's process cost summary for October using the FIFO method.
2. Prepare the journal entry dated October 31 to transfer the cost of completed units to the blending department.

Analysis Component

3. The company provides incentives to department managers by paying monthly bonuses based on their success in controlling costs per equivalent unit of production. Assume that a production department underestimates the percentage of completion for units in ending inventory with the result that its equivalent units of production for October are understated. What impact does this error have on the October bonuses paid to that department's managers? What impact, if any, does this error have on November bonuses?

Dream Toys Company manufactures video game consoles and accounts for product costs using process costing. The company uses a single processing department. The following information is available regarding its June inventories.

PROBLEM SET B

Problem 3-1B
Production cost flow and measurement; journal entries

P1   P2   P3   P4

	Beginning Inventory	Ending Inventory
Raw materials inventory...............	$ 72,000	$110,000
Work in process inventory..............	156,000	250,000
Finished goods inventory...............	160,000	198,000

The following additional information describes the company's production activities for June.

Raw materials purchases (on credit).....................	$ 200,000
Factory payroll cost (paid in cash).......................	400,000
Other overhead cost (Other Accounts credited)............	170,500
Materials used	
Direct	$ 120,000
Indirect	42,000
Labor used	
Direct	$ 350,000
Indirect	50,000
Overhead rate as a percent of direct labor................	75%
Sales (on credit)	$1,000,000

Required

1. Compute the cost of (a) products transferred from production to finished goods and (b) goods sold.
2. Prepare journal entries dated June 30 to record the following production activities during June: (a) raw materials purchases, (b) direct materials usage, (c) indirect materials usage, (d) direct labor costs, (e) indirect labor costs, (f) payment of factory payroll, (g) other overhead costs, (h) overhead applied, (i) goods transferred from production to finished goods, and (j) sale of finished goods.

Check (1*b*) Cost of goods sold, $600,500

Abraham Company uses process costing to account for its production costs. Conversion is added evenly throughout the process. Direct materials are added at the beginning of the process. During September, the production department transferred 80,000 units of product to finished goods. Beginning work in process consisted of 2,000 units that were 100% complete with respect to direct materials and 85% complete with respect to conversion. Of the units completed, 2,000 were from beginning work in process and 78,000 units were started and completed during the period. Beginning work in process had $58,000 of direct materials and $86,400 of conversion cost. At the end of September, the work in process inventory consists of 8,000 units that are 25% complete with respect to conversion. The direct materials cost added in September is $712,000, and conversion cost added is $1,980,000. The company uses the weighted-average method.

Problem 3-2B
Weighted average:
Cost per equivalent unit; costs assigned to products

C2   C3

Required

1. Determine the equivalent units of production with respect to (a) conversion and (b) direct materials.
2. Compute both the conversion cost and the direct materials cost per equivalent unit.
3. Compute both conversion cost and direct materials cost assigned to (a) units completed and transferred out and (b) ending work in process inventory.

Check (2) Conversion cost per equivalent unit, $25.20

(3*b*) $120,400

Analysis Component

4. The company sells and ships all units to customers as soon as they are completed. Assume that an error is made in determining the percentage of completion for units in ending inventory. Instead of being 25% complete with respect to conversion, they are actually 75% complete. Write a one-page memo to the plant manager describing how this error affects its September financial statements.

Problem 3-3B
Weighted average:
Process cost summary;
equivalent units

C2   C3   P4

Braun Company produces its product through a single processing department. Direct materials are added at the beginning of the process. Conversion costs are added to the product evenly throughout the process. The company uses monthly reporting periods for its weighted-average process costing. The Work in Process Inventory account had a balance of $21,300 on November 1, which consisted of $6,800 of direct materials and $14,500 of conversion costs.

During the month, the company incurred the following costs:

Direct materials	$ 116,400
Conversion	1,067,000

During November, the company started 104,500 units and transferred 100,000 units to finished goods. At the end of the month, the work in process inventory consisted of 12,000 units that were 100% complete with respect to direct materials and 25% complete with respect to conversion.

Required

Check   (1) Cost transferred
out to finished goods,
$1,160,000

1. Prepare the company's process cost summary for November using the weighted-average method.

2. Prepare the journal entry dated November 30 to transfer the cost of the completed units to finished goods inventory.

Problem 3-4B
Weighted average:
Process cost summary;
equivalent units;
cost estimates

C2   C3   P4

Switch Co. manufactures a single product in one department. Direct labor and overhead are added evenly throughout the process. Direct materials are added as needed. The company uses monthly reporting periods for its weighted-average process costing. During January, Switch completed and transferred 220,000 units of product to finished goods inventory. Its 10,000 units of beginning work in process consisted of $7,500 of direct materials and $49,850 of conversion. In process at month-end are 40,000 units (50% complete with respect to direct materials and 30% complete with respect to conversion). During the month, the company used direct materials of $112,500 in production and incurred conversion costs of $616,000.

Required

Check   (1) EUP for
conversion, 232,000

       (2) Cost transferred
out to finished goods,
$741,400

1. Prepare the company's process cost summary for January using the weighted-average method.

2. Prepare the journal entry dated January 31 to transfer the cost of completed units to finished goods inventory.

Analysis Component

3. The cost accounting process depends on several estimates.

   a. Identify two major estimates that affect the cost per equivalent unit.

   b. In what direction might you anticipate a bias from management for each estimate in part 3a (assume that management compensation is based on maintaining low inventory amounts)? Explain your answer.

Problem 3-5B^A
FIFO: Process cost
summary; equivalent
units; cost estimates

C3   C4   P4

Refer to the information in Problem 3-4B. Assume that Switch uses the FIFO method to account for its process costing system. The following additional information is available.

• Beginning work in process consists of 10,000 units that were 75% complete with respect to direct materials and 60% complete with respect to conversion.

• Of the 220,000 units completed, 10,000 were from beginning work in process; the remaining 210,000 were units started and completed during January.

Required

Check   (1) Conversion EUP,
226,000

       (2) Cost transferred
out, $743,554

1. Prepare the company's process cost summary for January using FIFO. Round cost per EUP to three decimal places.

2. Prepare the journal entry dated January 31 to transfer the cost of completed units to finished goods inventory.

During May, the production department of a process manufacturing system completed a number of units of a product and transferred them to finished goods. Of these transferred units, 62,500 were in process in the production department at the beginning of May and 175,000 were started and completed in May. May's beginning inventory units were 40% complete with respect to materials and 80% complete with respect to conversion. At the end of May, 76,250 additional units were in process in the production department and were 80% complete with respect to materials and 20% complete with respect to conversion. The production department had $683,750 of direct materials and $446,050 of conversion cost charged to it during May. Its beginning inventory included $99,075 of direct materials cost and $53,493 of conversion cost.

1. Compute the number of units transferred to finished goods.

2. Compute the number of equivalent units with respect to both materials used and conversion used in the production department for May using the FIFO method.

3. Compute the direct materials cost and the conversion cost per equivalent unit for the department.

4. Using the FIFO method, assign May's costs to the units transferred to finished goods and assign costs to its ending work in process inventory.

Problem 3-6B[A]
FIFO: Costs per equivalent unit; costs assigned to products

C2   C4

Check   (2) EUP for materials, 273,500

Belda Co. makes organic juice in two departments: cutting and blending. Direct materials are added at the beginning of each process, and conversion costs are added evenly throughout each process. The company uses the FIFO method of process costing. During March, the cutting department completed and transferred 220,000 units to the blending department. Of the units completed, 10,000 were from beginning inventory and the remaining 210,000 were started and completed during the month. Beginning work in process was 75% complete with respect to direct materials and 60% complete with respect to conversion. The company has 40,000 units (50% complete with respect to direct materials and 30% complete with respect to conversion) in process at month-end. Information on the cutting department's costs of beginning work in process inventory and costs added during the month follows.

Problem 3-7B[A]
FIFO: Process cost summary, equivalent units, cost estimates

C2   C3   C4   P4

Cost	Direct Materials	Conversion
Of beginning work in process inventory	$ 16,800	$ 97,720
Added during the month	223,200	1,233,960

Required

1. Prepare the cutting department's process cost summary for March using the FIFO method.

2. Prepare the journal entry dated March 31 to transfer the cost of completed units to the blending department.

Check   (1) EUP for conversion, 226,000
(2) Cost transferred out, $1,486,960

Analysis Component

3. The company provides incentives to department managers by paying monthly bonuses based on their success in controlling costs per equivalent unit of production. Assume that the production department overestimates the percentage of completion for units in ending inventory with the result that its equivalent units of production for March are overstated. What impact does this error have on bonuses paid to the managers of the production department? What impact, if any, does this error have on these managers' April bonuses?

(This serial problem began in Chapter 1 and continues through most of the book. If previous chapter segments were not completed, the serial problem can begin at this point.)

SERIAL PROBLEM
Business Solutions

C1   A1

SP 3   The computer workstation furniture manufacturing that Santana Rey started for **Business Solutions** is progressing well. Santana uses a job order costing system to account for the production costs of this product line. Santana is wondering whether process costing might be a better method for her to keep track of and monitor her production costs.

Required

1. What are the features that distinguish job order costing from process costing?

2. Should Santana continue to use job order costing or switch to process costing for her workstation furniture manufacturing? Explain.

© Alexander Image/Shutterstock RF

COMPREHENSIVE PROBLEM

Major League Bat Company

Weighted average:
Review of Chapter 1

CP 3 **Major League Bat Company** manufactures baseball bats. In addition to its work in process inventories, the company maintains inventories of raw materials and finished goods. It uses raw materials as direct materials in production and as indirect materials. Its factory payroll costs include direct labor for production and indirect labor. All materials are added at the beginning of the process, and conversion costs are applied uniformly throughout the production process.

Required

You are to maintain records and produce measures of inventories to reflect the July events of this company. Set up the following general ledger accounts and enter the June 30 balances: Raw Materials Inventory, $25,000; Work in Process Inventory, $8,135 ($2,660 of direct materials and $5,475 of conversion); Finished Goods Inventory, $110,000; Sales, $0; Cost of Goods Sold, $0; Factory Wages Payable, $0; and Factory Overhead, $0.

1. Prepare journal entries to record the following July transactions and events.

  a. Purchased raw materials for $125,000 cash (the company uses a perpetual inventory system).

  b. Used raw materials as follows: direct materials, $52,440; and indirect materials, $10,000.

  c. Recorded factory wages payable costs as follows: direct labor, $202,250; and indirect labor, $25,000.

  d. Paid factory payroll cost of $227,250 with cash (ignore taxes).

  e. Incurred additional factory overhead costs of $80,000 paid in cash.

  f. Allocated factory overhead to production at 50% of direct labor costs.

Check (1f) Cr. Factory Overhead, $101,125

Check (2) EUP for conversion, 14,200

2. Information about the July inventories follows. Use this information with that from part 1 to prepare a process cost summary, assuming the weighted-average method is used.

Units	
Beginning inventory	5,000 units
Started	14,000 units
Ending inventory	8,000 units
Beginning inventory	
Materials—Percent complete	100%
Conversion—Percent complete	75%
Ending inventory	
Materials—Percent complete	100%
Conversion—Percent complete	40%

3. Using the results from part 2 and the available information, make computations and prepare journal entries to record the following:

(3g) $271,150

  g. Total costs transferred to finished goods for July (label this entry g).

  h. Sale of finished goods costing $265,700 for $625,000 in cash (label this entry h).

4. Post entries from parts 1 and 3 to the ledger accounts set up at the beginning of the problem.

5. Compute the amount of gross profit from the sales in July. (*Note:* Add any underapplied overhead to, or deduct any overapplied overhead from, the cost of goods sold. Ignore the corresponding journal entry.)

GENERAL LEDGER PROBLEM

Available only in Connect

The **General Ledger** tool in *Connect* automates several of the procedural steps in accounting so that the financial professional can focus on the impacts of each transaction on various reports and performance measures.

GL 3-1 General Ledger assignment GL 3-1, based on Problem 3-1A, focuses on transactions related to process costing. Prepare summary journal entries to record the cost of units manufactured and their flow through the manufacturing environment. Then prepare a schedule of cost of goods manufactured and a partial income statement.

Beyond the Numbers

BTN 3-1 **Apple** reports in notes to its financial statements that, in addition to its products sold, it includes the following costs (among others) in cost of sales: customer shipping and handling expenses and warranty expenses.

REPORTING IN ACTION

C2

APPLE

Required

1. Why do you believe Apple includes these costs in its cost of sales?

2. What effect does this cost accounting policy for its cost of sales have on Apple's financial statements and any analysis of those statements? Explain.

Fast Forward

3. Access Apple's financial statements for the years after September 26, 2015, from its website (**Apple.com**) or the SEC's EDGAR website (**SEC.gov**). Review its footnote relating to Summary of Significant Accounting Policies. Has Apple changed its policy with respect to what costs are included in the cost of sales? Explain.

BTN 3-2 **Apple** and **Google** work to maintain high-quality and low-cost operations. One ratio routinely computed for this assessment is the cost of goods sold divided by total expenses. A decline in this ratio can mean that the company is spending too much on selling and administrative activities. An increase in this ratio beyond a reasonable level can mean that the company is not spending enough on selling activities. (Assume for this analysis that total expenses equal the cost of goods sold plus total operating expenses.)

COMPARATIVE ANALYSIS

C1

APPLE

GOOGLE

Required

1. For Apple and Google, refer to Appendix A and compute the ratios of cost of goods sold to total expenses for their two most recent fiscal years. (Record answers as percents, rounded to one decimal.)

2. Comment on the similarities or differences in the ratio results across both years between the companies.

BTN 3-3 Many accounting and accounting-related professionals are skilled in financial analysis, but most are not skilled in manufacturing. This is especially the case for process manufacturing environments (for example, a bottling plant or chemical factory). To provide professional accounting and financial services, one must understand the industry, product, and processes. We have an ethical responsibility to develop this understanding before offering services to clients in these areas.

ETHICS CHALLENGE

C1

Required

Write a one-page action plan, in memorandum format, discussing how you would obtain an understanding of key business processes of a company that hires you to provide financial services. The memorandum should specify an industry, a product, and one selected process and should draw on at least one reference, such as a professional journal or industry magazine.

BTN 3-4 You hire a new assistant production manager whose prior experience is with a company that produced goods to order. Your company engages in continuous production of homogeneous products that go through various production processes. Your new assistant e-mails you questioning some cost classifications on an internal report—specifically why the costs of some materials that do not actually become part of the finished product, including some labor costs not directly associated with producing the product, are classified as direct costs. Respond to this concern via memorandum.

COMMUNICATING IN PRACTICE

A1 C1 P1 P2

BTN 3-5 Many companies acquire software to help them monitor and control their costs and as an aid to their accounting systems. One company that supplies such software is **proDacapo** (**prodacapo.com**). There are many other such vendors. Access proDacapo's website, click on "Products," then click on "Prodacapo Process Management," and review the information displayed.

TAKING IT TO THE NET

C1

Required

How is process management software helpful to businesses? Explain with reference to costs, efficiency, and examples, if possible.

TEAMWORK IN ACTION

C1   P1   P2   P3   P4

BTN 3-6 The purpose of this team activity is to ensure that each team member understands process operations and the related accounting entries. Find the activities and flows identified in Exhibit 3.14 with numbers ① through ⑩. Pick a member of the team to start by describing activity number ① in this exhibit, then verbalizing the related journal entry, and describing how the amounts in the entry are computed. The other members of the team are to agree or disagree; discussion is to continue until all members express understanding. Rotate to the next numbered activity and next team member until all activities and entries have been discussed. If at any point a team member is uncertain about an answer, the team member may pass and get back in the rotation when he or she can contribute to the team's discussion.

ENTREPRENEURIAL DECISION

C3   A2

BTN 3-7 This chapter's opener featured Jeff Kearl and his company **Stance**.

Required

1. Sock makers like Stance typically use several different processes, including knitting, design imprinting, washing and drying, inspection, and packaging/shipping. What are some benefits of using separate process cost summary reports for each process?

2. Jeff tries to order raw materials just-in-time for their use in production. How does holding raw materials inventories increase costs? If the items are not used in production, how can they impact profits? Explain.

3. How can companies like Stance use *yield* to improve their production processes?

HITTING THE ROAD

C2

BTN 3-8 In process costing, the process is analyzed first, and then a unit measure is computed in the form of equivalent units for direct materials, conversion (direct labor and overhead), and both types of costs combined. The same analysis applies to both manufacturing and service processes.

Required

Point: The class can compare and discuss the different processes studied and the answers provided.

Visit your local **U.S. Postal Service** office. Look into the back room, and you will see several ongoing processes. Select one process, such as sorting, and list the costs associated with this process. Your list should include materials, labor, and overhead; be specific. Classify each cost as fixed or variable. At the bottom of your list, outline how overhead should be assigned to your identified process. The following format (with an example) is suggested.

		Conversion			
Cost Description	Direct Material	Direct Labor	Overhead	Variable Cost	Fixed Cost
Manual sorting		X		X	
⋮					
Overhead allocation suggestions:					

GLOBAL DECISION

C1

Samsung

APPLE

GOOGLE

BTN 3-9 **Samsung**, **Apple**, and **Google** are competitors in the global marketplace. Selected data for Samsung follow.

Korean won in billions	Current Year	Prior Year
Cost of goods sold	₩123,482.1	₩128,278.8
Operating expenses.	50,757.9	52,902.1
Total expenses	₩174,240.0	₩181,180.9

Required

1. Review the discussion of the importance of the cost of goods sold divided by total expenses ratio in BTN 3-2. (Assume for this analysis that total expenses equal cost of goods sold plus operating expenses.) Compute the cost of goods sold to total expenses ratio for Samsung for the two years of data provided. (Record answers as percents, rounded to one decimal.)

2. Comment on the similarities or differences in the ratio results calculated in part 1 and in BTN 3-2 across years and companies. (Record answers as percents, rounded to one decimal.)

GLOBAL VIEW

As part of a series of global environmental goals, **Anheuser-Busch InBev** set targets to reduce its water usage. The company uses massive amounts of water in beer production and in its cleaning and cooling processes.

To meet these goals, the company followed recent trends in process operations. These included extensive redesign of production processes and the use of advanced technology to increase efficiency at wastewater treatment plants.

As a result, water usage decreased by almost 37 percent in its global operations. The effects of such process improvements will also result in lower costs per equivalent unit of materials and increased profits.

 Global View Assignments

Discussion Question 16

Quick Study 3-27

BTN 3-9

4 Activity-Based Costing and Analysis

Chapter Preview

ASSIGNING OVERHEAD COSTS

C1 Alternative methods

P1 Single plantwide overhead rate method

P2 Multiple departmental overhead rate method

A1 Assessing plantwide and departmental rate methods

NTK 4-1

ACTIVITY-BASED COSTING

Steps in activity-based costing

C2 Activity-based costing rates and method

P3 Applying activity-based costing

A2 Assessing activity-based costing

NTK 4-2

ACTIVITY-BASED MANAGEMENT

C3 Types of activities

Costs of quality

Lean manufacturing

NTK 4-3

Learning Objectives

CONCEPTUAL

C1 Distinguish between the plantwide overhead rate method, the departmental overhead rate method, and the activity-based costing method.

C2 Explain cost flows for activity-based costing.

C3 Describe the four types of activities that cause overhead costs.

ANALYTICAL

A1 Identify and assess advantages and disadvantages of the plantwide overhead and departmental overhead rate methods.

A2 Identify and assess advantages and disadvantages of activity-based costing.

PROCEDURAL

P1 Allocate overhead costs to products using the plantwide overhead rate method.

P2 Allocate overhead costs to products using the departmental overhead rate method.

P3 Allocate overhead costs to products using activity-based costing.

Courtesy of GrandyOats

Top of the Food Chain

HIRAM, ME—As the only employee of his granola-making company, Nat Peirce took orders on Monday, baked granola on Tuesday, and delivered to stores on Wednesday. Realizing his limitations, Nat joined forces with Aaron Anker, a college friend. The duo's company, **GrandyOats** (**GrandyOats.com**), now sells a full line of 100% organic granola.

"It's not complicated," explains Aaron. "We make clean, pure food . . . that's our philosophy." The company uses no artificial ingredients or refined sugars, and granola is still hand-mixed in small batches, albeit more of them. Although their production process is simple, making over 1 million pounds of granola each year requires control of costs.

Nat and Aaron know that how they allocate overhead is crucial for product pricing and product mix decisions. Overhead costs such as plant maintenance, supervision, and cleanup must be allocated to products to determine their costs. In small businesses with few product lines, a *single plantwide overhead rate* is often sufficient.

As businesses grow and offer more diverse product lines, more detailed costing techniques are often needed. Beyond the several types of granola GrandyOats sells, it now sells trail mix, roasted nuts, hot cereals, and apparel. The *departmental overhead rate* arguably improves upon the plantwide rate by using multiple overhead rates. *Activity-based costing* is useful when different product lines use different levels of overhead.

GrandyOats's recipe is working. The company has grown from one employee (Nat) and annual sales of less than $100,000 to more than 20 employees and annual sales exceeding $5 million. It is important to Nat and Aaron *how* the company achieves its success—focusing on sustainability, paying employees a good wage, encouraging a work-life balance, recycling and reusing of materials, and moving to a 100% solar-powered facility. "We're authentic," explains Nat, "we follow the most sustainable path, not necessarily the path to the best return on investment." Nat adds, "You can make a difference in the world!"

"Make a difference"
—Nat Peirce

Sources: *GrandyOats website,* January 2017; *Maine Organic Farmers and Gardeners Association,* July 21, 2016; *New Hope Network,* October 1, 2009; *Gourmet News,* February 11, 2016; *Lake Living,* March 21, 2016; *BDN Maine,* July 21, 2016

ASSIGNING OVERHEAD COSTS

C1

Distinguish between the plantwide overhead rate method, the departmental overhead rate method, and the activity-based costing method.

Point: Evidence suggests overhead costs have steadily increased while direct labor costs have steadily decreased as a percentage of total manufacturing costs over recent decades. This puts greater importance on accurate cost allocations.

Product pricing, product mix decisions, and cost control depend on accurate product cost information. Product cost consists of direct materials, direct labor, and overhead (indirect costs). Because direct materials and direct labor can be traced to units of output, assigning these costs to products is usually straightforward. Overhead costs, however, are not directly related to production and cannot be traced to units of product like direct materials and direct labor can. We use an allocation system to assign overhead costs such as utilities and factory maintenance. This chapter shows three methods of overhead allocation: (1) the single plantwide overhead rate method, (2) the departmental overhead rate method, and (3) the activity-based costing method.

Alternative Methods of Overhead Allocation

Exhibit 4.1 summarizes some key features of the three alternative methods.

- The *plantwide overhead rate method* and the *departmental overhead rate method* use volume-based measures such as direct labor hours or machine hours to allocate overhead costs to products. The plantwide method uses a single rate for allocating overhead costs, and the departmental rate method uses at least two rates. The departmental method arguably provides more accurate cost allocations than the plantwide method.
- *Activity-based costing* focuses on activities (not just volume) and their costs. Rates based on these activities are used to assign overhead to products in proportion to the amount of activity required to produce them. Activity-based costing typically uses more overhead allocation rates than the plantwide and departmental methods.

EXHIBIT 4.1

Overhead Cost Allocation Methods

Allocation Method	Overhead Allocations Based on	Overhead Allocation Rates Based on
Plantwide rate..................	One rate	Volume-based measures such as direct labor hours or machine hours
Departmental rate	Two or more rates	Volume-based measures such as direct labor hours or machine hours
Activity-based costing	At least two (but often many) rates	Activities that drive costs, such as number of batches of product produced

Plantwide Overhead Rate Method

P1

Allocate overhead costs to products using the plantwide overhead rate method.

The first method of allocating overhead costs to products is the *single plantwide overhead rate method,* or simply the *plantwide overhead rate method.*

Cost Flows under Plantwide Overhead Rate Method   For the plantwide overhead rate method, the target of the cost assignment, or **cost object,** is the unit of product—see Exhibit 4.2. The overhead rate is determined using a volume-related measure such as direct

EXHIBIT 4.2

Plantwide Overhead Rate Method

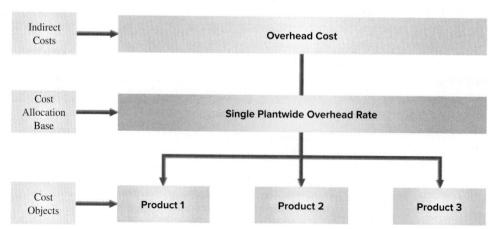

labor hours or machine hours, both of which are readily available in most manufacturing settings. In some industries, overhead costs are closely related to these volume-related measures. If so, it is logical to use this method to assign overhead costs to products.

Applying the Plantwide Overhead Rate Method Under the single plantwide overhead rate method, total budgeted overhead costs are divided by the chosen allocation base, such as total direct labor hours, to arrive at a single plantwide overhead rate. This rate then is applied to assign overhead costs to all products based on their *actual* usage of the allocation base.

To illustrate, consider KartCo, a go-kart manufacturer that produces both standard and custom go-karts for amusement parks. The standard go-kart is a basic model sold mainly to amusement parks that service county and state fairs. Custom go-karts are produced for theme parks that want unique go-karts that coordinate with their respective themes.

Assume that KartCo applies the plantwide overhead rate method and uses direct labor hours (DLH) as its overhead allocation base. KartCo's budgeted DLH information for the coming year is in Exhibit 4.3.

	Number of Units		Direct Labor Hours per Unit		Total Direct Labor Hours
Standard go-kart........	5,000	×	15	=	75,000
Custom go-kart.........	1,000	×	25	=	25,000
Total.................					100,000

EXHIBIT 4.3

KartCo's Budgeted Direct Labor Hours

KartCo's budgeted overhead cost information for the coming year is in Exhibit 4.4. Its overhead cost consists of indirect labor and factory utilities.

Overhead Item	Budgeted Cost
Indirect labor cost	$4,000,000
Factory utilities	800,000
Total budgeted overhead cost	$4,800,000

EXHIBIT 4.4

KartCo's Budgeted Overhead Cost

The single plantwide overhead rate for KartCo is computed as

$$\frac{\text{Plantwide}}{\text{overhead rate}} = \frac{\text{Total budgeted}}{\text{overhead cost}} \div \frac{\text{Total budgeted direct}}{\text{labor hours}}$$
$$= \$4,800,000 \div 100,000 \text{ DLH}$$
$$= \$48 \text{ per DLH}$$

This plantwide overhead rate is then used to allocate overhead cost to products based on the number of direct labor hours required to produce each unit as follows.

Overhead allocated to each product unit = Plantwide overhead rate × DLH per unit

KartCo allocates overhead cost to its two products as follows (on a per unit basis).

Overhead Cost per Unit Using the Plantwide Rate Method	
Standard go-kart	$48 per DLH × 15 DLH per unit = $ 720 per unit
Custom go-kart	$48 per DLH × 25 DLH per unit = $1,200 per unit

Exhibit 4.5 summarizes the plantwide overhead method for KartCo.

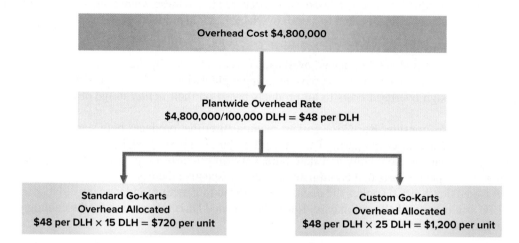

KartCo uses these per unit overhead costs, and per unit direct materials and direct labor costs from other records, to compute product cost per unit as follows.

	Product Cost per Unit Using the Plantwide Rate Method							
	Direct Materials		Direct Labor		Overhead		Product Cost per Unit	
Standard go-kart	$400	+	$350	+	$ 720	=	$1,470	
Custom go-kart.	600	+	500	+	1,200	=	2,300	

© Mark Ralston/AFP/Getty Images

KartCo sells its standard model go-karts for $2,000 and its custom go-karts for $3,500. A recent report from its marketing staff indicates that competitors are selling go-karts like KartCo's standard model for $1,200. KartCo management is concerned that selling at this lower price would result in a loss of $270 ($1,200 − $1,470) on each standard go-kart sold.

Interestingly, KartCo has been swamped with orders for its custom go-kart and cannot meet demand. Accordingly, management is considering dropping the standard model and concentrating on the custom model. Yet management recognizes that its pricing decisions are influenced by its cost allocations. Before making any strategic decisions, management asks its cost analysts to further review KartCo's overhead allocation. The cost analysts first consider the departmental overhead rate method.

Departmental Overhead Rate Method

P2

Allocate overhead costs to products using the departmental overhead rate method.

Many companies have several departments that produce various products using different amounts of overhead. Under such circumstances, a single plantwide overhead rate can produce cost assignments that do not reflect the cost to manufacture products. Multiple overhead rates can result in better overhead cost allocations and improve management decisions.

Cost Flows under Departmental Overhead Rate Method   The *departmental overhead rate method* uses a different overhead rate for each production department. This is usually done through a four-step process (see Exhibit 4.6):

1. Assign overhead costs to departmental *cost pools.*
2. Select an allocation base for each department.
3. Compute overhead allocation rates for each department.
4. Use departmental overhead rates to assign overhead costs to cost objects (products).

The departmental overhead method uses several departments and several overhead rates. This allows each department to have its own overhead rate and its own allocation base. For example, an assembly department may use direct labor hours to allocate its overhead cost, whereas a machining department may use machine hours as its base.

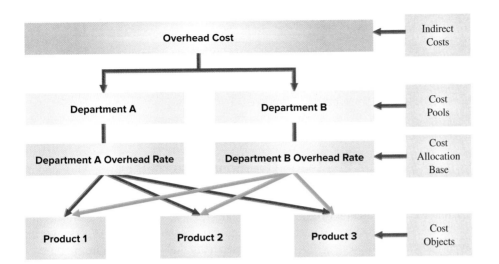

EXHIBIT 4.6

Departmental Overhead
Rate Method

Applying the Departmental Overhead Rate Method   KartCo has two production departments, the machining department and the assembly department.

1 The first step requires that KartCo assign its $4,800,000 overhead cost to its two production departments. KartCo determines that $4,200,000 of overhead costs is traceable to its machining department and the remaining $600,000 is traceable to its assembly department.

2 The second step requires each department to determine an allocation base. For KartCo, the machining department uses machine hours (MH) to allocate its overhead; the assembly department uses direct labor hours (DLH) to allocate its overhead. The budgeted information for KartCo's machining and assembly departments is shown below.

Overhead Cost $4,800,000

Machining $4,200,000   Assembly $600,000

	Number of Units	Machining Department		Assembly Department	
		Hours per Unit	Total Hours	Hours per Unit	Total Hours
Standard go-kart........	5,000	10 MH per unit	50,000 MH	5 DLH per unit	25,000 DLH
Custom go-kart.........	1,000	20 MH per unit	20,000 MH	5 DLH per unit	5,000 DLH
Totals.................			70,000 MH		30,000 DLH

3 In step three, each department computes its own overhead rate using this formula.

$$\text{Departmental overhead rate} = \frac{\text{Total budgeted departmental overhead cost}}{\text{Total amount of departmental allocation base}}$$

KartCo's departmental overhead rates are computed as follows.

$$\text{Machining department overhead rate} = \frac{\$4,200,000}{70,000 \text{ MH}} = \$60 \text{ per MH}$$

$$\text{Assembly department overhead rate} = \frac{\$600,000}{30,000 \text{ DLH}} = \$20 \text{ per DLH}$$

4 Step four applies overhead costs to each product using departmental overhead rates. Because each standard go-kart requires 10 MH from the machining department and five DLH from the assembly department, the overhead cost allocated to each standard go-kart is $600 from the machining department (10 MH × $60 per MH) and $100 from the assembly department (5 DLH × $20 per DLH). The same procedure is applied for its custom go-kart. Exhibit 4.7 summarizes KartCo's overhead allocation per go-kart using the departmental method.

Department	Departmental Overhead Rate	Standard Go-Kart		Custom Go-Kart	
		Hours per Unit	Overhead Allocated	Hours per Unit	Overhead Allocated
Machining.........	$60 per MH	10 MH per unit	$600	20 MH per unit	$1,200
Assembly..........	$20 per DLH	5 DLH per unit	100	5 DLH per unit	100
Totals.............			$700		$1,300

Departmental versus Plantwide Overhead Rate Methods   Allocated overhead costs vary depending upon the allocation methods used. Exhibit 4.8 summarizes and compares the allocated overhead costs for standard and custom go-karts under the single plantwide overhead rate and the departmental overhead rate methods.

The overhead cost allocated to each standard go-kart *decreased* from $720 under the plantwide overhead rate method to $700 under the departmental overhead rate method, whereas overhead cost allocated to each custom go-kart *increased* from $1,200 to $1,300. These differences occur because the custom go-kart requires more hours in the machining department (20 MH) than the standard go-kart requires (10 MH).

Overhead per Unit Using:	Standard Go-Kart	Custom Go-Kart
Plantwide overhead rate method	$720	$1,200
Departmental overhead rate method	700	1,300

For KartCo, using the departmental overhead rate method yields the following total product cost per unit.

	Product Cost per Unit Using Departmental Rate Method							
	Direct Materials		Direct Labor		Overhead		Product Cost per Unit
Standard go-kart	$400	+	$350	+	$ 700	=	$1,450
Custom go-kart	600	+	500	+	1,300	=	2,400

These total product costs per unit under the departmental overhead rate method differ from those under the plantwide overhead rate method. Compared to the plantwide overhead rate method, the departmental overhead rate method usually results in more accurate overhead allocations. When cost analysts are able to logically trace overhead costs to different cost allocation bases, costing accuracy is improved. These cost data imply that KartCo cannot make a profit on its standard go-kart if it meets competitors' $1,200 price, as it would lose $250 (computed as $1,200 − $1,450) per go-kart.

Comparing Plantwide and Departmental Overhead Rate Methods

The plantwide and departmental overhead rate methods have three key advantages: (1) They are based on readily available information, like direct labor hours. (2) They are easy to implement. (3) They are consistent with GAAP and can be used for external reporting. Both suffer from an important disadvantage, in that overhead costs are frequently too complex to be explained by only one factor like direct labor hours or machine hours.

Plantwide Overhead Rate Method   The usefulness of the single plantwide overhead rate depends on two assumptions: (1) overhead costs change with the allocation base (such as direct labor hours) and (2) all products use overhead costs in the same proportions.

For companies with many different products or those with products that use overhead costs in very different ways, the assumptions of the single plantwide rate are not reasonable.

Most of KartCo's overhead is related to machining, and a custom go-kart uses more machine hours than does a standard go-kart. When overhead costs, like machinery depreciation, bear little relation to direct labor hours used, allocating overhead cost using a single plantwide overhead rate based on direct labor hours can distort product cost and lead to poor managerial decisions. Despite such shortcomings, some companies continue to use the plantwide method for its simplicity.

Departmental Overhead Rate Method   The departmental overhead rate method assumes that (1) different products are similar in volume, complexity, and batch size and (2) departmental overhead costs are directly proportional to the department allocation base (such as direct labor hours and machine hours for KartCo).

When products differ in batch size and complexity, they usually consume different amounts of overhead costs. This is likely the case for KartCo with its high-volume standard model and its low-volume custom model built to customer specifications. However, the departmental overhead rate method can distort product costs. Because the departmental overhead rate method still allocates overhead costs based on measures closely related to production volume, it fails to accurately assign many overhead costs, like machine depreciation or utility costs, that are not driven by production volume.

© JoeFox Karting/Alamy

■ **Decision Ethics**

Department Manager   Three department managers hire a consulting firm for advice on increasing departmental effectiveness and efficiency. The consulting firm spends 50% of its efforts on department A and 25% on each of the other two departments. The manager for department A suggests that the three departments equally share the consulting fee. As a manager of one of the other two departments, do you believe equal sharing is fair? ■   *Answer:* When dividing a bill, common sense suggests fairness. That is, if one department consumes more services than another, we attempt to share the bill in proportion to consumption. Equally dividing the bill among the number of departments is fair if each consumed equal services. This same notion applies in assigning costs to products and services. For example, dividing overhead costs by the number of units is fair if all products consumed overhead in equal proportion.

A manufacturer reports the following budgeted data for its two production departments.

NEED-TO-KNOW 4-1

Plantwide and Departmental Rate Methods

P1   P2

	Machining	Assembly
Manufacturing overhead costs	$600,000	$300,000
Machine hours to be used (MH)..............	20,000	0
Direct labor hours to be used (DLH)	20,000	5,000

1. What is the company's single plantwide overhead rate based on direct labor hours?
2. What are the company's departmental overhead rates if the machining department assigns overhead based on machine hours and the assembly department assigns overhead based on direct labor hours?
3. Using the departmental overhead rates from part 2, how much overhead should be assigned to a job that uses 16 machine hours in the machining department and 5 direct labor hours in the assembly department?

Solution

1. Plantwide overhead rate $= \dfrac{\$600,000 + \$300,000}{20,000 \text{ DLH} + 5,000 \text{ DLH}} = \dfrac{\$900,000}{25,000 \text{ DLH}} = \$36$ per direct labor hour

2. Machining department rate $= \dfrac{\$600,000}{20,000 \text{ MH}} = \$30$ per machine hour

Assembly department rate $= \dfrac{\$300,000}{5,000 \text{ DLH}} = \$60$ per direct labor hour

3. Overhead assigned to job $= (16 \text{ MH} \times \$30 \text{ per MH}) + (5 \text{ DLH} \times \$60 \text{ per DLH}) = \$780$

Do More: QS 4-3, QS 4-4, QS 4-5, E 4-1

ACTIVITY-BASED COSTING

C2
Explain cost flows for activity-based costing.

Activity-based costing (ABC) attempts to more accurately assign overhead costs by focusing on *activities*. Unlike the plantwide rate method, ABC uses more than a single rate. Unlike the departmental rate method, ABC focuses on activities rather than departments. We illustrate the activity-based costing method of assigning overhead costs.

Steps in Activity-Based Costing

© Carl Lyttle/ The Image Bank/ Getty Images

The basic principle underlying activity-based costing is that an **activity,** which is a task, operation, or procedure, is what causes costs to be incurred. For example:

● Cutting raw materials consumes labor and machine hours.

● Storing products consumes employee time for driving a forklift, electricity to power the forklift, and wear and tear on the forklift.

● Training employees drives costs such as fees or salaries paid to trainers and the training supplies required.

All activities of an organization can be linked to use of resources. An **activity cost pool** is a collection of costs that are related to the same activity. For example, handling raw materials requires several activities, including wages of receiving department employees, wages of forklift employees who move materials, and depreciation on forklifts. These activities can be grouped into a single cost pool because they are all caused by the amount of materials moved.

There are four basic steps to the ABC method (see Exhibit 4.9):

1. Identify activities and the overhead costs they cause.
2. Trace overhead costs to activity cost pools.
3. Compute overhead allocation rates for each activity.
4. Use the activity overhead rates to assign overhead costs to cost objects (products).

EXHIBIT 4.9

Activity-Based Costing Method

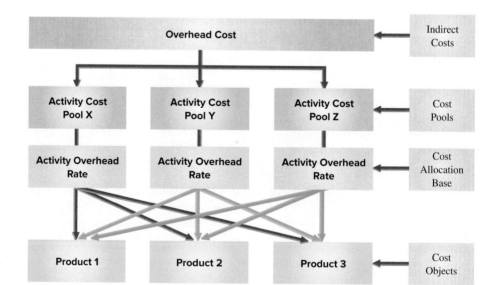

Applying Activity-Based Costing

P3
Allocate overhead costs to products using activity-based costing.

Step 1: Identify Activities and the Overhead Costs They Cause   Step 1 in applying ABC is to identify activities and the costs they cause. KartCo has total overhead costs of $4,800,000, consisting of $4,000,000 in indirect labor costs and $800,000 in factory utilities costs. After reviewing activities with production employees, KartCo identifies the activities and their costs shown in Exhibit 4.10.

Activity	Indirect Labor	Factory Utilities	Total Overhead
Machine setup	$ 700,000	—	$ 700,000
Machine repair.	1,300,000	—	1,300,000
Factory maintenance.	800,000	—	800,000
Engineer salaries	1,200,000	—	1,200,000
Assembly line power.	—	$600,000	600,000
Heating and lighting	—	200,000	200,000
Totals	$4,000,000	$800,000	$4,800,000

EXHIBIT 4.10

KartCo Overhead Cost Details

Step 2: Trace Overhead Costs to Activity Cost Pools   Step 2 in applying ABC is to assign activities and their overhead costs to activity cost pools. KartCo management assigns its overhead costs to four activity cost pools: craftsmanship, setup, design modification, and plant services (see Exhibit 4.11). To assign costs to pools, management looks for costs that are caused by similar activities.

Exhibit 4.11 shows that $600,000 of overhead costs are assigned to the crafts-manship cost pool; $2,000,000 to the setup cost pool; $1,200,000 to the design modification cost pool; and $1,000,000 to the plant services cost pool. The use of cost pools reduces the potential number of overhead rates from six (one for each of its six activities) to four (one for each activity cost pool).

Activity Cost Pools	Activity Cost	Pool Cost
Craftsmanship		
Assembly line power	$ 600,000	$ 600,000
Setup		
Machine setup	700,000	
Machine repair	1,300,000	2,000,000
Design modification		
Engineer salaries	1,200,000	1,200,000
Plant services		
Factory maintenance	800,000	
Heating and lighting	200,000	1,000,000
Total overhead cost		$4,800,000

EXHIBIT 4.11

Assigning Overhead to Activity Cost Pools

Step 3: Compute Overhead Allocation Rates for Each Activity   Step 3 is to compute **activity overhead (cost pool) rates** used to assign overhead costs to final cost objects such as products. Proper determination of activity rates depends on (1) proper identification of the factor that drives the cost in each activity cost pool and (2) proper measures of activities.

The factor that drives cost, or **activity cost driver,** is an activity that causes costs in the pool to be incurred. For KartCo's overhead, craftsmanship costs are mainly driven by the direct labor hours used to assemble products; setup costs are driven by the number of batches produced; design modification costs are driven by the number of new designs; and plant services costs are driven by the square feet of building space occupied. These activity cost drivers serve as the allocation base for each activity cost pool. KartCo then determines an expected activity level for each activity cost pool, as shown below.

© AP Images/Christof Stache

Activity Cost Pools	Activity Driver (# of)	Expected Activity Level
Craftsmanship.	Direct labor hours	30,000 DLH
Setup.	Batches	200 batches
Design modification	Designs	10 design modifications
Plant services	Square feet	20,000 square feet

In general, cost pool activity rates are computed as follows.

> **Cost pool activity rate = Overhead costs assigned to pool ÷ Expected activity level**

For KartCo, the activity rate for the craftsmanship cost pool is computed as follows.

> Craftsmanship cost pool activity rate = $600,000 ÷ 30,000 DLH = $20 per DLH

The activity rate computations for KartCo are summarized in Exhibit 4.12.

EXHIBIT 4.12

Activity Rates for KartCo

Activity Cost Pools	Activity Driver	Overhead Costs Assigned to Pool	÷ Expected Activity Level	= Activity Rate
Craftsmanship	Direct labor hours	$ 600,000	30,000 DLH	$20 per DLH
Setup	Batches	2,000,000	200 batches	$10,000 per batch
Design modification	Number of designs	1,200,000	10 designs	$120,000 per design
Plant services	Square feet	1,000,000	20,000 sq. ft.	$50 per sq. ft.

Step 4: Assign Overhead Costs to Cost Objects   Step 4 is to assign overhead costs in each activity cost pool to cost objects using activity rates. To do this, overhead costs are allocated to products based on the *actual* levels of activities used.

For KartCo, overhead costs in each pool are allocated to the standard go-karts and the custom go-karts using the activity rates from Exhibit 4.12. The actual activities used by each product line and the overhead costs allocated to standard and custom go-karts under ABC for KartCo are summarized in Exhibit 4.13. To illustrate, of the $600,000 of overhead costs in the craftsmanship cost pool, $500,000 is allocated to standard go-karts as follows.

Overhead from craftsmanship pool allocated to standard go-kart	=	**Activities consumed**	×	**Activity rate**
	=	25,000 DLH	×	$20 per DLH
	=	$500,000		

EXHIBIT 4.13

Overhead Allocated to Go-Karts for KartCo

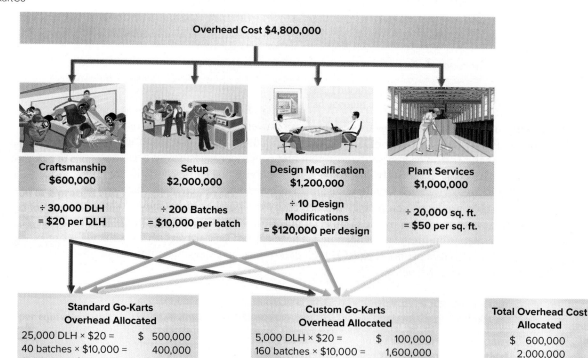

Standard go-karts used 25,000 direct labor hours, and the activity rate for craftsmanship is $20 per direct labor hour. Multiplying the number of direct labor hours by the activity rate yields the craftsmanship costs assigned to standard go-karts ($500,000). Custom go-karts consumed 5,000 direct labor hours, so we assign $100,000 (5,000 DLH × $20 per DLH) of craftsmanship costs to that product line. We similarly allocate overhead costs of setup, design modification, and plant services pools to each type of go-kart.

Point: In ABC, overhead is allocated based on the actual level of activities used, multiplied by a predetermined activity rate for each cost pool.

KartCo assigned no design modification costs to standard go-karts because standard go-karts are sold as "off-the-shelf" items. Using ABC, a total of $1,500,000 of overhead costs is allocated to standard go-karts and a total of $3,300,000 is allocated to custom go-karts. While the $4,800,000 total overhead cost allocated is the same as under the plantwide and departmental rate methods, the amounts allocated to the two product lines differ.

Overhead cost per unit is computed by dividing total overhead cost allocated to each product line by the number of product units. KartCo's overhead cost per unit for its standard and custom go-karts is computed and shown in Exhibit 4.14.

EXHIBIT 4.14

Overhead Cost per Unit for Go-Karts Using ABC

	(A) Total Overhead Cost Allocated	(B) Units Produced	(A ÷ B) Overhead Cost per Unit
Standard go-kart	$1,500,000	5,000 units	$ 300 per unit
Custom go-kart	3,300,000	1,000 units	3,300 per unit

Total product cost per unit for KartCo using ABC for its two products follows.

	Direct Materials		Direct Labor		Overhead		Product Cost per Unit
Standard go-kart	$400	+	$350	+	$ 300	=	$1,050
Custom go-kart	600	+	500	+	3,300	=	4,400

Assuming that ABC more accurately assigns costs, KartCo's management now sees how its competitors can sell their standard models at $1,200 and why KartCo is flooded with orders for custom go-karts. Specifically, if the cost to produce a standard go-kart is $1,050, as shown above (and not $1,470 as computed using the plantwide rate or $1,450 as computed using departmental rates), a profit of $150 ($1,200 − $1,050) occurs on each standard unit sold at the competitive $1,200 market price. Further, selling its custom go-kart at $3,500 is a mistake because KartCo loses $900 ($3,500 − $4,400) on each custom go-kart sold. KartCo has underpriced its custom go-kart relative to its production costs and competitors' prices, which explains why the company has more custom orders than it can supply.

Point: Accurately assigning costs to products is key to setting many product prices. If product costs are inaccurate and result in prices that are too low, the company loses money on each item sold. Likewise, if product prices are improperly set too high, the company loses business to competitors. ABC can be used to more accurately set prices.

Exhibit 4.15 summarizes KartCo's overhead allocation per go-kart under the plantwide rate method, departmental rate method, and ABC. Overhead cost allocated to standard go-karts is much less under ABC than under either of the volume-based costing methods. One reason for this difference is the large design modification costs that were spread over all go-karts under both the plantwide rate and the departmental rate methods even though standard go-karts require no design modification. When ABC is used, overhead costs commonly shift from standardized, high-volume products to low-volume, customized specialty products that consume more resources.

EXHIBIT 4.15

Comparison of Overhead Allocations by Method

Overhead Cost Allocation Method	Overhead Cost per Go-Kart	
	Standard Go-Kart	Custom Go-Kart
Plantwide method............................	$720	$1,200
Departmental method	700	1,300
Activity-based costing	300	3,300

Differences between ABC and Multiple Departmental Rates Using ABC differs from using multiple departmental rates in how overhead cost pools are identified and in how overhead cost in each pool is allocated. When using multiple departmental rates, each *department* is a cost pool, and overhead cost allocated to each department is assigned to products using a volume-based factor (such as direct labor hours or machine hours). This assumes that overhead costs in each department are directly proportional to the volume-based factor.

ABC, on the other hand, recognizes that overhead costs are more complex. For example, purchasing costs might make up one activity cost pool, spanning more than one department and being driven by a single cost driver (number of invoices). ABC emphasizes *activities* and costs of carrying out these activities. Therefore, ABC arguably better reflects the complex nature of overhead costs and how these costs are used in making products.

■ **Decision** Maker

Entrepreneur   You own a start-up pharmaceutical company. You assign overhead to products based on machine hours in the packaging area. Profits are slim due to increased competition. One of your larger overhead costs is $10,000 for cleaning and sterilization that occurs each time the packaging system is converted from one product to another. Can you reduce cleaning and sterilizing costs by reducing the number of units produced? If not, what should you do to control these overhead costs? ■   *Answer:* Cleaning and sterilizing costs are not directly related to the volume of product manufactured. Thus, changing the number of units produced does not necessarily reduce these costs. Costs of cleaning and sterilizing are related to changing from one product line to another. The way to control those costs is to control the number of times the packaging system has to be changed for a different product line. Thus, efficient product scheduling would help reduce those overhead costs and improve profitability.

 **4-2**

Activity-Based Costing

P3

A manufacturer makes two types of snowmobiles, Basic and Deluxe, and reports the following data to be used in applying activity-based costing. The company budgets production of 6,000 Basic snowmobiles and 2,000 Deluxe snowmobiles.

Activity Cost Pool	Activity Cost Driver	Cost Assigned to Pool	Basic	Deluxe
Machine setup	Number of setups	$ 150,000	200 setups	300 setups
Materials handling	Number of parts	250,000	10 parts per unit	20 parts per unit
Machine depreciation	Machine hours (MH)	720,000	1 MH per unit	1.5 MH per unit
Total		$1,120,000		

1. Compute overhead activity rates for each activity cost pool using ABC.

2. Compute the total amount of overhead cost to be allocated to each of the company's product lines using ABC.

3. Compute the overhead cost per unit for each product line using ABC.

Solution

1. Machine setup activity rate $= \dfrac{\$150,000}{200 + 300} = \$300$ per machine setup

Materials handling activity rate $= \dfrac{\$250,000}{60,000 + 40,000*} = \$2.50$ per part

*(6,000 units × 10 parts per unit for Basic, 2,000 units × 20 parts per unit for Deluxe)

Machine depreciation activity rate $= \dfrac{\$720,000}{6,000 + 3,000**} = \$80$ per machine hour

**(6,000 units × 1 MH per unit for Basic, 2,000 units × 1.5 MH per unit for Deluxe)

2.

Activity Cost Pool	Activity Pool Rate	Basic		Deluxe	
Machine setup	$300 per setup	$300 × 200 =	$ 60,000	$300 × 300 =	$ 90,000
Materials handling	$2.50 per part	$2.50 × 6,000 × 10 =	150,000	$2.50 × 2,000 × 20 =	100,000
Machine depreciation...	$80 per MH	$80 × 6,000 × 1 =	480,000	$80 × 2,000 × 1.5 =	240,000
Totals			$690,000		$430,000

3. Basic snowmobile overhead cost per unit $= \dfrac{\$690{,}000}{6{,}000} = \$115$ per unit

Deluxe snowmobile overhead cost per unit $= \dfrac{\$430{,}000}{2{,}000} = \$215$ per unit

Do More: QS 4-8, QS 4-9, QS 4-10, E 4-2, E 4-11, E 4-12

Assessing Activity-Based Costing

While activity-based costing can improve the accuracy of overhead cost allocations to products, it too has limitations. This section describes the major advantages and disadvantages of activity-based costing.

A2

Identify and assess advantages and disadvantages of activity-based costing.

Advantages of Activity-Based Costing

More Effective Overhead Cost Control   KartCo's design modifications were costly. ABC can be used to identify activities that can benefit from process improvement by focusing on activities instead of focusing only on direct labor or machine hours. For KartCo, identification of large design modification costs would allow managers to work on ways to improve this process.

Better Production and Pricing Decisions   As in the KartCo example, ABC can provide more accurate overhead cost allocation. This is because ABC uses more cost pools and activity rates than other methods. More accurate costs allow managers to focus production activities on more profitable products and to set selling prices above product cost.

Additional Uses   ABC has uses beyond determining product costs. For example, ABC can be used to:

- Allocate the selling and administrative costs expensed by GAAP to activities; such costs can include marketing costs, order processing costs, and order return costs. Analyzing these activities and their costs can lead to cost reductions.
- Determine the profitability of various market segments or customers. Accurately assigning the costs of shipping, advertising, and customer service might reveal that some customers or segments should not be pursued. ABC provides better customer profitability information by including all the costs consumed to serve a customer. Many companies use ABC techniques for these analyses, even if they don't use ABC in determining overall product costs.

© Paul Gilham/Getty Images

Disadvantages of Activity-Based Costing

Costs to Implement and Maintain ABC   Designing and implementing an ABC system is costly. For ABC to be effective, a thorough analysis of cost activities must be performed and appropriate cost pools must be determined. Collecting and analyzing cost data is expensive, and so is maintaining an ABC system. While technology, such as bar coding, has made it possible for many companies to use ABC, it is still too costly for some.

Point: ABC is not acceptable under GAAP for external financial reporting.

Some Product Cost Distortion Remains   Even with ABC, product costs can be distorted because:

- Some costs cannot be readily classified into ABC cost pools.
- Some cost drivers may not have a strong cause-effect relation with the costs in some pools.

Uncertainty with Decisions Remains   Managers must interpret ABC data with caution in making decisions. In the KartCo case, given the huge design modification costs for custom go-karts determined under ABC, a manager might be tempted to decline some custom go-kart orders to save overhead costs. However, in the short run, some or all of the design modification costs cannot be saved even if some custom go-kart orders are rejected. Managers must examine carefully the controllability of costs before making decisions.

ACTIVITY-BASED MANAGEMENT

C3

Describe the four types of activities that cause overhead costs.

Activity Levels and Cost Management

Activities causing overhead costs can be separated into four levels: (1) **unit-level activities,** (2) **batch-level activities,** (3) **product-level activities,** and (4) **facility-level activities.** These four activities are described as follows.

Activity Levels

Unit-level activities are performed on each product unit. For example, the machining department needs electricity to power the machinery to produce each unit of product. Unit-level costs tend to change with the number of units produced.

Craftsmanship

Batch-level activities are performed only on each batch or group of units. For example, machine setup is needed only for each batch regardless of the units in that batch, and customer order processing must be performed for each order regardless of the number of units ordered. Batch-level costs do not vary with the number of units, but instead vary with the number of batches.

Setup

Product-level activities are performed on each product line and are not affected by either the numbers of units or batches. For example, product design is needed only for each product line. Product-level costs do not vary with the number of units or batches produced.

Design Modification

Facility-level activities are performed to sustain facility capacity as a whole and are not caused by any specific product. For example, rent and factory maintenance costs are incurred no matter what is being produced. Facility-level costs do not vary with what is manufactured, the number of batches produced, or the output quantity.

Plant Services

In the KartCo example, the craftsmanship pool reflects unit-level costs, the setup pool reflects batch-level costs, the design modification pool reflects product-level costs, and plant services reflect facility-level costs. Exhibit 4.16 shows additional examples of activities commonly found within each of the four activity levels. This list also includes common activity drivers.

EXHIBIT 4.16

Examples of Activities by Activity Level

Activity Level	Examples of Activity	Activity Driver (Measure)
Unit level	Cutting parts	Machine hours
	Assembling components	Direct labor hours
	Printing checks	Number of checks
Batch level	Calibrating machines	Number of batches
	Receiving shipments	Number of orders
	Sampling product quality	Number of lots produced
	Recycling hazardous waste	Tons recycled
Product level	Designing modifications	Change requests
	Organizing production	Engineering hours
	Controlling inventory	Parts per product
Facility level	Cleaning workplace	Square feet of floors*
	Providing electricity	Kilowatt hours*
	Providing personnel support	Number of employees*
	Reducing greenhouse gas emissions	Tons of CO_2

* Facility-level costs are not traceable to individual product lines, batches, or units. They are normally assigned to units using a unit-level driver such as direct labor hours or machine hours even though they are caused by another activity.

Understanding the four levels of overhead costs is a first step toward controlling costs. **Activity-based management (ABM)** is an outgrowth of ABC that uses the link between activities and costs for better management.

Activity-based management can be useful in distinguishing **value-added activities,** which add value to a product, from *non-value-added activities,* which do not. For KartCo, its value-added activities include machining, assembly, and the costs of engineering design changes. Its non-value-added activity is machine repair. ABM aids in cost control by reducing how much of an activity is performed.

Decision Insight

The ABCs of Decisions   Business managers must make long-term strategic decisions, day-to-day operating decisions, and decisions on the type of financing the business needs. Survey evidence suggests that managers find ABC more useful in making strategic, operating, and financing decisions than non-ABC methods. Managers using ABC also felt better able to apply activity-based management. ■

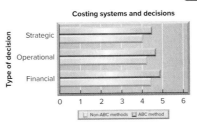

Costing systems and decisions

Average response, 0=Not useful, 6=Extremely useful
Source: Stratton et al., *Management Accounting Quarterly,* 2009.

Costs of Quality

A focus on the costs of activities, via ABC and ABM, lends itself to assessments of the **costs of quality.** These costs refer to costs resulting from manufacturing defective products or providing services that do not meet customer expectations.

Exhibit 4.17 summarizes the typical costs of quality. These costs can be summarized in a **cost of quality report,** which lists the costs of quality activities by category. A focus on activities and quality costs can lead to higher quality and lower costs.

Costs of Good Quality

Prevention costs

Appraisal costs

Costs of Poor Quality

Internal failure costs

External failure costs

Cost of Quality Report	
Quality Activity	Cost
Prevention	
Training.....................	$ 22,000
Appraisal	
Inspecting materials...........	37,500
Testing finished goods.........	14,200
Internal failure	
Rework.....................	8,250
Scrap.......................	11,750
External failure	
Warranty claims..............	45,700
Total cost of quality..............	$139,400

EXHIBIT 4.17

Types and Reporting of Quality Costs

Costs of Good Quality   Prevention and appraisal costs are incurred before a good or service is provided to a customer. The purpose of these costs is to reduce the chance the customer is provided a defective good or service. These are the costs of trying to ensure that only good-quality items are produced.

Point: Prevention and appraisal costs are usually considered value-added costs, while internal and external costs are considered non-value-added costs.

- *Prevention* activities focus on quality training and improvement programs to ensure quality is built into the product or service.
- *Appraisal* activities include the costs of inspections to ensure that materials and supplies meet specifications and inspections of finished goods.

Costs of Poor Quality   Internal and external failure costs are the costs of making poor-quality items.

- *Internal failure costs* are incurred after a company has manufactured a defective product but before that product has been delivered to a customer. Internal failure costs include the costs of reworking products, reinspecting reworked products, and scrap.

- *External failure costs* are incurred after a customer has been provided a defective product or service. Examples of this type of cost include costs of warranty repairs and costs of recalling products. This category also includes lost profits due to dissatisfied customers buying from other companies.

Lean Manufacturing

Focusing on activities is common in *lean manufacturing,* which strives to eliminate waste while satisfying customers. Lean manufacturers produce to customer orders (a "pull" system) rather than to forecasted demand (a "push" system). Common features of lean manufacturing include

- Just-in-time (JIT) inventory systems to reduce the costs of moving and storing inventory. With JIT, raw materials are put into production after a customer order, and the finished goods are delivered soon after completion. This reduces the costs of storing and moving inventory.
- Cellular manufacturing, where products are made by teams of employees in small workstations ("cells"). Producing an entire product in one cell allows manufacturers to reduce machine setup times, produce in smaller batches, and meet customer orders more quickly.
- Building quality into products by focusing on the costs of good quality. Lean manufacturers do not have time to rework defective products and usually are not able to meet customer orders from inventory.

Many lean manufacturers embrace **lean accounting,** which typically includes

- Lean thinking to eliminate waste in the accounting process.
- Alternative performance measures, like the percentage of products made without defects and the percentage of on-time deliveries.
- Simplified product costing. With JIT, most of the product costs during a period will be included in cost of goods sold rather than in inventory. Instead of transferring costs across inventory accounts during a period, a **backflush costing** system measures the costs of inventory only at the end of the period. Costs of unfinished products are "flushed out" of Cost of Goods Sold and transferred to inventory accounts.

ABC for Service Providers

Although we've shown how to use ABC in a manufacturing setting, ABC also applies to service providers. The only requirements for ABC are the existence of costs and demand for reliable cost information. **First Tennessee National Corporation**, a bank, applied ABC and found that 30% of its certificate of deposit (CD) customers provided nearly 90% of its profits from CDs. Further, 30% of the bank's CD customers were actually losing money for the bank. The bank's management used ABC to correct the problem and increase profits.

Laboratories performing medical tests, accounting and law offices, and advertising agencies are other examples of service firms that can benefit from ABC. (Refer to this chapter's Decision Analysis for an example of applying ABC to assess customer profitability and this chapter's Comprehensive Need-To-Know for an example of applying ABC to a law firm.)

NEED-TO-KNOW 4-3

Activities Causing Overhead Costs

C3

Do More: QS 4-13, QS 4-14, E 4-17, E 4-18

Identify the activity levels of each of the following overhead activities as unit level (U), batch level (B), product level (P), or facility level (F).

_____ **1.** Cutting steel for go-kart frames

_____ **2.** Receiving shipments of tires

_____ **3.** Using electricity for equipment

_____ **4.** Modifying custom go-kart design

_____ **5.** Painting go-karts

_____ **6.** Setting up machines for production

_____ **7.** Recycling hazardous waste

_____ **8.** Reducing water usage

Solution

1. U   **2.** B   **3.** F   **4.** P   **5.** U   **6.** B   **7.** B   **8.** F

SUSTAINABILITY AND ACCOUNTING

Analyzing activities leads many companies to study **supply chain management,** which involves the coordination and control of goods, services, and information as they move from suppliers to consumers. A recent study by **Accenture** estimates that supply chains account for 50%–70% of total expenses and greenhouse gas emissions for most manufacturing companies. More effective supply chains can benefit the bottom line and the environment.

© John Patriquin/Portland Press Herald via Getty Images

Walmart, in conjunction with The Sustainability Consortium™, developed an index to assess its suppliers' policies and programs related to sustainability. Companies with high scores on the index are identified as Sustainability Leaders on Walmart's website, enabling customers to readily identify and perhaps buy from companies committed to sustainable practices. Walmart, in conjunction with its suppliers, is meeting its goal of eliminating 20 million metric tons of greenhouse gases from its supply chain.

Nat Peirce and Aaron Anker, owners of **GrandyOats**, this chapter's feature company, try to buy local ingredients whenever possible. According to the company's sustainability statement (located on its **Facebook** page), "sourcing ingredients and services as locally as possible allows [the company] to reduce carbon emissions and keep our local community thriving."

GrandyOats recently converted a former elementary school into a 100% solar-powered plant. This made it the first net-zero food production facility in New England. All of GrandyOats's energy needs for ovens, computers, forklifts, and utilities will be powered by the sun with no carbon fuel used anywhere in the facility. Proclaims Aaron, "Going off the grid has long been one of our goals."

Customer Profitability   **Decision Analysis**

Are all customers equal? To answer this, let's return to KartCo and assume that costs of providing customer support (such as delivery, installation, and warranty work) are related to the distance a technician must travel to provide services. Also assume that, as a result of applying activity-based costing, KartCo plans to sell its standard go-kart for $1,200 per unit. If the annual cost of customer services is expected to be $250,000 and the distance traveled by technicians is 100,000 miles annually, KartCo would want to link the cost of customer services with individual customers to make efficient marketing decisions.

Using these data, an activity rate of $2.50 per mile ($250,000/100,000 miles) is computed for assigning customer service costs to individual customers. For KartCo, it would compute a typical **customer profitability report** for one of its customers, Six Flags, as follows.

Customer Profitability Report—Six Flags		
Sales (10 standard go-karts × $1,200)		$12,000
Less: Product costs		
Direct materials (10 go-karts × $400 per go-kart)	$4,000	
Direct labor (10 go-karts × $350 per go-kart)	3,500	
Overhead (10 go-karts × $300 per go-kart, Exhibit 4.14)	3,000	10,500
Product profit margin		1,500
Less: Customer service costs (200 miles × $2.50 per mile)		500
Customer profit margin		$ 1,000

Analysis indicates that a total profit margin of $1,000 is generated from this customer. The management of KartCo can see that if this customer requires service technicians to travel more than 600 miles ($1,500 ÷ $2.50 per mile), the sale of 10 standard go-karts to this customer would be unprofitable. ABC encourages management to consider all resources consumed to serve a customer, not just manufacturing costs that are the focus of traditional costing methods.

NEED-TO-KNOW **4-4**

COMPREHENSIVE

Silver Law Firm provides litigation and mediation services to a variety of clients. Attorneys keep track of the time they spend on each case, which is used to charge fees to clients at a rate of $300 per hour. A management advisor commented that activity-based costing might prove useful in evaluating the costs of its legal services, and the firm has decided to evaluate its fee structure by comparing ABC to its alternative cost allocations. The following data relate to a typical month at the firm. During a typical month, the firm handles seven mediation cases and three litigation cases.

	Activity Driver	Total Amount	Consumption by Service Type		Activity Cost
			Litigation	Mediation	
Providing legal advice	Billable hours	200	75	125	$30,000
Overhead costs					
Internal support departments					
Preparing documents	Documents	30	16	14	$ 4,000
Occupying office space	Billable hours	200	75	125	1,200
Heating and lighting of office	Billable hours	200	75	125	350
External support departments					
Registering court documents	Documents	30	16	14	1,250
Retaining consultants (investigators, psychiatrists)	Court dates	6	5	1	10,000
Using contract services (couriers, security guards)	Court dates	6	5	1	5,000
Total overhead costs					$21,800

Required

1. Determine the cost of providing legal services to each type of case using activity-based costing (ABC).
2. Determine the cost of each type of case using a single plantwide rate for nonattorney costs based on billable hours.
3. Determine the cost of each type of case using multiple departmental overhead rates for the internal support department (based on number of documents) and external support department (based on billable hours).
4. Compare and discuss the costs assigned under each method for management decisions.

PLANNING THE SOLUTION

- Compute pool rates and assign costs to cases using ABC.
- Compute costs for the cases using the volume-based methods and discuss differences between these costs and the costs computed using ABC.

SOLUTION

1. We need to set up activity pools and compute pool rates for ABC. All activities except "occupying office space" and "heating and lighting" are unit-level activities (meaning they are traceable to the individual cases handled by the law firm). "Preparing documents" and "registering documents" are both driven by the number of documents associated with each case. We can therefore combine these activities and their costs into a single pool, which we call "clerical support." Similarly, "retaining consultants" and "using services" are related to the number of times the attorneys must go to court (court dates). We combine these activities and their costs into another activity cost pool labeled "litigation support." The costs associated with occupying office space and the heating and lighting are

facility-level activities and are not traceable to individual cases, yet they are costs that must be covered by fees charged to clients. We assign these costs using a convenient base—in this example we use the number of billable hours, which attorneys record for each client. Providing legal advice is the direct labor for a law firm.

Activity Cost Pools	Activity Cost	Pool Cost	Activity Driver	Pool Rate (Pool Cost ÷ Activity Driver)
Providing legal advice	$30,000	$30,000	200 billable hours	$150 per billable hour
Clerical support				
Preparing documents	4,000			
Registering documents	1,250	5,250	30 documents	$175 per document
Litigation support				
Retaining consultants	10,000			
Using services	5,000	15,000	6 court dates	$2,500 per court date
Facility costs				
Occupying office space	1,200			
Heating and lighting	350	1,550	200 billable hours	$7.75 per billable hour

We next determine the cost of providing each type of legal service as shown in the following table. Specifically, the pool rates from above are used to assign costs to each type of service provided by the law firm. Because litigation consumed 75 billable hours of attorney time, we assign $11,250 (75 billable hours × $150 per billable hour) of the cost of providing legal advice to this type of case. Mediation required 125 hours of attorney time, so $18,750 (125 billable hours × $150 per billable hour) of the cost to provide legal advice is assigned to mediation cases. Clerical support costs $175 per document, so the costs associated with activities in this cost pool are assigned to litigation cases (16 documents × $175 per document = $2,800) and mediation cases (14 documents × $175 per document = $2,450). The costs of activities in the litigation support and the facility cost pools are similarly assigned to the two case types.

We compute the total cost of litigation ($27,131.25) and mediation ($24,668.75) and divide these totals by the number of cases of each type to determine the average cost of each case type: $9,044 for litigation and $3,524 for mediation. This analysis shows that charging clients $300 per billable hour without regard to the type of case results in litigation clients being charged less than the cost to provide that service ($7,500 versus $9,044).

Activity Cost Pools	Pool Rate	Litigation		Mediation	
Providing legal advice	$150 per billable hour	75 hours	$11,250.00	125 hours	$18,750.00
Clerical support	$175 per document	16 docs	2,800.00	14 docs	2,450.00
Litigation support	$2,500 per court date	5 court dates	12,500.00	1 court date	2,500.00
Facility costs	$7.75 per billable hour	75 hours	581.25	125 hours	968.75
Total cost			$27,131.25		$24,668.75
÷ Number of cases..........			3 cases		7 cases
Average cost per case			**$9,044**		**$3,524**
Average fee per case........			**$7,500***		**$5,357**†

* (75 billable hours × $300 per hour) ÷ 3 cases   † (125 billable hours × $300 per hour) ÷ 7 cases

2. The cost of each type of case using a single plantwide rate for nonattorney costs (that is, all costs except for those related to providing legal advice) based on billable hours is as follows.

Total overhead cost/Total billable hours = $21,800/200 billable hours = $109 per hour

We then determine the cost of providing each type of legal service as follows.

		Litigation		Mediation	
Providing legal advice	$150 per billable hour	75 hours	$11,250	125 hours	$18,750
Overhead (from part 2)............	$109 per billable hour	75 hours	8,175	125 hours	13,625
Total cost......................			$19,425		$32,375
÷ Number of cases...............			3 cases		7 cases
Average cost per case			**$6,475**		**$4,625**
Average fee per case .... (from part 1)			**$7,500**		**$5,357**

3. The cost of each type of case using multiple departmental overhead rates for the internal support department (based on number of documents) and external support department (based on billable hours) is determined as follows.

	Departmental Cost	Base	Departmental Rate (Departmental Cost ÷ Base)
Internal support departments			
Preparing documents	$ 4,000		
Occupying office space	1,200		
Heating and lighting of office	350	$ 5,550	30 documents	$185 per document
External support departments			
Registering documents	1,250		
Retaining consultants	10,000		
Using contract services	5,000	16,250	200 billable hours	$81.25 per hour

The departmental overhead rates computed above are used to assign overhead costs to the two types of legal services. For the internal support department, we use the overhead rate of $185 per document to assign $2,960 ($185 × 16 documents) to litigation and $2,590 ($185 × 14 documents) to mediation. For the external support department, we use the overhead rate of $81.25 per hour to assign $6,093.75 ($81.25 × 75 hours) to litigation and $10,156.25 ($81.25 × 125 hours) to mediation. As shown below, the resulting average costs of litigation cases and mediation cases are $6,768 and $4,499, respectively. Using this method of cost assignment, it *appears* that the fee of $300 per billable hour is adequate to cover costs associated with each case.

		Litigation		Mediation	
Attorney fees	$150 per billable hour	75 hours	$11,250.00	125 hours	$18,750.00
Internal support	$185 per document	16 documents	2,960.00	14 documents	2,590.00
External support..........	$81.25 per hour	75 hours	6,093.75	125 hours	10,156.25
Total cost...............			$20,303.75		$31,496.25
÷ Number of cases........			3 cases		7 cases
Average cost per case			**$6,768**		**$4,499**
Average fee per case...... (from part 1)			**$7,500**		**$5,357**

4. A comparison and discussion of the costs assigned under each method follows.

	Method of Assigning Overhead Costs		
Average Cost per Case	Activity-Based Costing	Plantwide Overhead Rate	Departmental Overhead Rates
Litigation cases....................	$9,044	$6,475	$6,768
Mediation cases	3,524	4,625	4,499

The departmental and plantwide overhead rate methods assign overhead on the basis of volume-related measures (billable hours and document filings). Litigation costs *appear* profitable under these methods because the average costs are below the average revenue of $7,500. ABC, however, focuses attention on activities that drive costs. A large part of overhead costs was for consultants and contract services, which were unrelated to the number of cases but related to the type of cases consuming those resources. Using ABC, the costs shift from the high-volume cases (mediation) to the low-volume cases (litigation). When the firm considers the consumption of resources for these cases using ABC, it finds that the fees charged to litigate cases is insufficient (average revenue of $7,500 versus average cost of $9,044). The law firm is charging too little for the complex cases that require litigation.

Summary

C1 **Distinguish between the plantwide overhead rate method, the departmental overhead rate method, and the activity-based costing method.** Overhead costs can be assigned to cost objects using a plantwide rate that combines all overhead costs into a single rate, usually based on direct labor hours, machine hours, or direct labor cost. Multiple departmental overhead rates that include overhead costs traceable to departments are used to allocate overhead based on departmental functions. ABC links overhead costs to activities and assigns overhead based on how much of each activity is required for a product.

C2 **Explain cost flows for activity-based costing.** With ABC, overhead costs are first traced to the activities that cause them, and then cost pools are formed combining costs caused by the same activity. Overhead rates based on these activities are then used to assign overhead to products in proportion to the amount of activity required to produce them.

C3 **Describe the four types of activities that cause overhead costs.** The four types of activities that cause overhead costs are: (1) unit-level activities, (2) batch-level activities, (3) product-level activities, and (4) facility-level activities. Unit-level activities are performed on each unit, batch-level activities are performed only on each group of units, and product-level activities are performed only on each product line. Facility-level activities are performed to sustain facility capacity and are not caused by any specific product. Understanding these types of activities can help in applying activity-based costing.

A1 **Identify and assess advantages and disadvantages of the plantwide overhead and departmental overhead rate methods.** A single plantwide overhead rate is a simple way to assign overhead cost. A disadvantage is that it can inaccurately assign costs when costs are caused by multiple factors and when different products consume different amounts of inputs. Overhead costing accuracy is improved by use of multiple departmental rates because differences across departmental functions can be linked to costs incurred in departments. Yet, accuracy of cost assignment with departmental rates suffers from the same problems associated with plantwide rates because the activities required for each product are not identified with the costs of providing those activities.

A2 **Identify and assess advantages and disadvantages of activity-based costing.** ABC improves product costing accuracy and draws management attention to relevant factors to control. The cost of constructing and maintaining an ABC system can sometimes outweigh its value.

P1 **Allocate overhead costs to products using the plantwide overhead rate method.** The plantwide overhead rate equals total budgeted overhead divided by budgeted plant volume, the latter often measured in direct labor hours or machine hours. This rate multiplied by the number of direct labor hours (or machine hours) required for each product provides the overhead assigned to each product.

P2 **Allocate overhead costs to products using the departmental overhead rate method.** When using multiple departmental rates, overhead costs must first be traced to each department and then divided by the measure of output for that department to yield the departmental overhead rate. Overhead is applied to products using this rate as products pass through each department.

P3 **Allocate overhead costs to products using activity-based costing.** With ABC, overhead costs are matched to the activities that cause them. If there is more than one cost with the same activity, these costs are combined into pools. An overhead rate for each pool is determined by dividing total cost for that pool by its activity measure. Overhead costs are assigned to products by multiplying the ABC pool rate by the amount of the activity required for each product.

Key Terms

Activity	Backflush costing	Lean accounting
Activity-based costing (ABC)	Batch-level activities	Product-level activities
Activity-based management (ABM)	Cost object	Supply chain management
Activity cost driver	Cost of quality report	Unit-level activities
Activity cost pool	Costs of quality	Value-added activities
Activity overhead (cost pool) rate	Facility-level activities	

Multiple Choice Quiz

1. In comparison to a traditional cost system, and when there are batch-level or product-level costs, an activity-based costing system usually shifts costs from
   a. low-volume to high-volume products.
   b. high-volume to low-volume products.
   c. standardized to specialized products.
   d. specialized to standardized products.

2. Which of the following statements is true?
   a. An activity-based costing system is generally easier to implement and maintain than a traditional costing system.
   b. Activity-based management eliminates waste by allocating costs to products that waste resources.
   c. Activity-based costing uses a single rate to allocate overhead.
   d. Activity rates in activity-based costing are computed by dividing costs from the first-stage allocations by the activity measure for each activity cost pool.

3. All of the following are examples of batch-level activities except
   a. purchase order processing.
   b. setting up equipment.
   c. clerical activity associated with processing purchase orders to produce an order for a standard product.
   d. employee recreational facilities.

4. A company has two products: A and B. It uses activity-based costing and prepares the following analysis showing budgeted cost and activity for each of its three activity cost pools.

Activity Cost Pool	Budgeted Overhead Cost	Budgeted Activity		
		Product A	Product B	Total
Activity 1	$ 80,000	200	800	1,000
Activity 2	58,400	1,000	500	1,500
Activity 3	360,000	600	5,400	6,000

The annual production and sales level of Product A is 18,188 units, and the annual production and sales level of Product B is 31,652 units. The approximate overhead cost per unit of Product B under activity-based costing is
   a. $2.02.   c. $12.87.
   b. $5.00.   d. $22.40.

5. A company uses activity-based costing to determine the costs of its two products: A and B. The budgeted cost and activity for each of the company's three activity cost pools follow.

Activity Cost Pool	Budgeted Cost	Budgeted Activity		
		Product A	Product B	Total
Activity 1	$19,800	800	300	1,100
Activity 2	16,000	2,200	1,800	4,000
Activity 3	14,000	400	300	700

The activity rate under the activity-based costing method for Activity 3 is
   a. $4.00.   c. $18.00.
   b. $8.59.   d. $20.00.

ANSWERS TO MULTIPLE CHOICE QUIZ

1. b; Under traditional costing methods, overhead costs are allocated to products on the basis of some measure of volume such as direct labor hours or machine hours. This results in much of the overhead cost being allocated to high-volume products. In contrast, under activity-based costing, some overhead costs are allocated on the basis of batch-level or product-level activities. This change in allocation bases results in shifting overhead costs from high-volume products to low-volume products.

2. d; Generally, an activity-based costing system is more difficult to implement and maintain than a traditional costing system (thus answer **a** is false). Instead of eliminating waste by allocating costs to products that waste resources, activity-based management is a management approach that focuses on managing activities as a means of eliminating waste and reducing delays and defects (thus answer **b** is false). Instead of using a single allocation base (such as direct labor hours), activity-based costing uses a number of allocation bases for assigning costs to products (thus answer **c** is false). Answer **d** is true.

3. d; Batch-level activities are activities that are performed each time a batch of goods is handled or processed, regardless of how many units are in a batch. Further, the amount of resources consumed depends on the number of batches rather than on the number of units in the batch. Worker recreational facilities relate to the organization as a whole rather than to specific batches and, as such, are not considered to be batch level. On the other hand,

purchase order processing, setting up equipment, and the clerical activities described are activities that are performed each time a batch of goods is handled or processed, and, as such, are batch-level activities.

4. c;

Activity Cost Pools	(A) Activity Rate (Budgeted overhead cost ÷ Budgeted activity)	(B) Actual Activity	(A × B) Overhead Cost Applied to Production
Activity 1.....	($80,000 ÷ 1,000) = $80.00	800	$ 64,000
Activity 2.....	($58,400 ÷ 1,500) = $38.93*	500	19,465
Activity 3.....	($360,000 ÷ 6,000) = $60.00	5,400	324,000
Total overhead cost for Product B			$407,465
Number of units produced			÷ 31,652
Overhead cost per unit of Product B			$ 12.87*

*Rounded

5. d; The activity rate for Activity 3 is determined as follows:

Budgeted cost ÷ Budgeted activity = Activity rate

$14,000   ÷   700   = $20

Icon denotes assignments that involve decision making.

Discussion Questions

1. Why are overhead costs allocated to products and not traced to products as direct materials and direct labor are?
2. What are three common methods of assigning overhead costs to a product?
3. Why are direct labor hours and machine hours commonly used as the bases for overhead allocation?
4. What are the advantages of using a single plantwide overhead rate?
5. The usefulness of a single plantwide overhead rate is based on two assumptions. What are those assumptions?
6. What is a cost object?
7. Explain why a single plantwide overhead rate can distort the cost of a particular product.
8. Why are multiple departmental overhead rates more accurate for product costing than a single plantwide overhead rate?
9. In what way are departmental overhead rates similar to a single plantwide overhead rate? How are they different?
10. Why is overhead allocation under ABC usually more accurate than either the plantwide overhead allocation method or the departmental overhead allocation method?

11. **Google** reports costs in financial statements. If plantwide overhead rates **GOOGLE** are allowed for reporting costs to external users, why might a company choose to use a more complicated and more expensive method for assigning overhead costs to products?
12. What is the first step in applying activity-based costing?
13. What is an activity cost driver?
14. **Apple**'s production requires activities. What **APPLE** are value-added activities?
15. What are the four activity levels associated with activity-based costing? Define each.
16. **Samsung** is a manufacturer. "Activity-based costing is only useful **Samsung** for manufacturing companies." Is this a true statement? Explain.
17. **Apple** must assign overhead costs to its products. Activity-based costing is generally **APPLE** considered more accurate than other methods of assigning overhead. If this is so, why don't all manufacturing companies use it?

connect

In the blank next to each of the following terms, place the letter A through D that corresponds to the description of that term. Some letters are used more than once.

_____ 1. Activity-based costing
_____ 2. Plantwide overhead rate method
_____ 3. Departmental overhead rate method

A. Uses more than one rate to allocate overhead costs to products.
B. Uses only volume-based measures such as direct labor hours to allocate overhead costs to products.
C. Typically uses the most overhead allocation rates.
D. Focuses on the costs of carrying out activities.

QUICK STUDY

QS 4-1
Overhead cost allocation methods
C1

---

1. Which costing method assumes all products use overhead costs in the same proportions?
   a. Activity-based costing
   b. Plantwide overhead rate method
   c. Departmental overhead rate method
   d. All cost allocation methods
2. Which of the following would usually *not* be used in computing plantwide overhead rates?
   a. Direct labor hours
   b. Number of quality inspections
   c. Direct labor dollars
   d. Machine hours
3. With ABC, overhead costs should be traced to which cost object first?
   a. Units of product
   b. Departments
   c. Activities
   d. Product batches

QS 4-2
Cost allocation methods
C1

A manufacturer uses machine hours to assign overhead costs to products. Budgeted information for the next year follows. Compute the plantwide overhead rate for the next year based on machine hours.

QS 4-3
Plantwide rate method
P1

Budgeted factory overhead costs..........................	$544,000
Budgeted machine hours.................................	6,400

QS 4-4

Computing plantwide
overhead rates

P1

Rafner Manufacturing identified the following budgeted data in its two production departments.

	Assembly	Finishing
Manufacturing overhead costs	$1,200,000	$600,000
Direct labor hours.	12,000 DLH	20,000 DLH
Machine hours	6,000 MH	16,000 MH

1. What is the company's single plantwide overhead rate based on direct labor hours?

2. What is the company's single plantwide overhead rate based on machine hours? (Round your answer to two decimal places.)

QS 4-5

Computing departmental
overhead rates   P2

Refer to the information in QS 4-4. What are the company's departmental overhead rates if the assembly department assigns overhead based on direct labor hours and the finishing department assigns overhead based on machine hours?

QS 4-6

Advantages of plantwide
and departmental rate
methods   A1

List the three main advantages of the plantwide and departmental overhead rate methods.

QS 4-7

Costing terminology

C2

In the blank next to the following terms, place the letter A through D that corresponds to the best description of that term.

_____ **1.** Activity

_____ **2.** Activity driver

_____ **3.** Cost object

_____ **4.** Cost pool

A. Measurement associated with an activity.

B. A group of costs that have the same activity drivers.

C. Anything to which costs will be assigned.

D. A task that causes a cost to be incurred.

QS 4-8

Computing activity rates

P3

A manufacturer uses activity-based costing to assign overhead costs to products. Budgeted cost information for selected activities for next year follows. Form two cost pools and compute activity rates for each of the cost pools.

Activity	Expected Cost	Cost Driver	Expected Usage of Cost Driver
Purchasing	$135,000	Purchase orders	4,500 purchase orders
Cleaning factory	32,000	Square feet	5,000 square feet
Providing utilities	65,000	Square feet	5,000 square feet

QS 4-9

Assigning service costs
using ABC

P3

Aziz Company sells two types of products, basic and deluxe. The company provides technical support for users of its products at an expected cost of $250,000 per year. The company expects to process 10,000 customer service calls per year.

1. Determine the company's cost of technical support per customer service call.

2. During the month of January, Aziz received 550 calls for customer service on its deluxe model and 250 calls for customer service on its basic model. Assign technical support costs to each model using activity-based costing (ABC).

QS 4-10

Computing activity rates

P3

A company uses activity-based costing to determine the costs of its three products: A, B, and C. The budgeted cost and cost driver activity for each of the company's three activity cost pools follow. Compute the activity rates for each of the company's three activities.

Activity Cost Pools	Budgeted Cost	Budgeted Activity of Cost Driver		
		Product A	Product B	Product C
Activity 1	$140,000	20,000	9,000	6,000
Activity 2	$ 90,000	8,000	15,000	7,000
Activity 3	$ 82,000	1,625	1,000	2,500

1. If management wants the most accurate product cost, which of the following costing methods should be used?

  a. Volume-based costing using departmental overhead rates

  b. Volume-based costing using a plantwide overhead rate

  c. Normal costing using a plantwide overhead rate

  d. Activity-based costing

2. Which costing method tends to overstate the cost of high-volume products?

  a. Traditional volume-based costing

  b. Activity-based costing

  c. Job order costing

  d. Differential costing

3. Disadvantages of activity-based costing include

  a. It is not acceptable under GAAP for external reporting.

  b. It can be costly to implement.

  c. It can be used in activity-based management.

  d. Both a. and b.

QS 4-11
Multiple choice overhead questions
A2

A list of activities that generate quality costs is provided below. For each activity, indicate whether it relates to a prevention (P), appraisal (A), internal failure (I), or external failure (E) activity.

_____ **1.** Inspecting raw materials

_____ **2.** Training workers in quality techniques

_____ **3.** Collecting data on a manufacturing process

_____ **4.** Overtime labor to rework products

_____ **5.** Cost of additional materials to rework a product

_____ **6.** Inspecting finished goods inventory

_____ **7.** Scrapping defective goods

_____ **8.** Lost sales due to customer dissatisfaction

QS 4-12
Costs of quality
A2

Classify each of the following activities as unit level (U), batch level (B), product level (P), or facility level (F) for a manufacturer of organic juices.

_____ **1.** Cutting fruit

_____ **2.** Developing new types of juice

_____ **3.** Blending fruit into juice

_____ **4.** Receiving fruit shipments

_____ **5.** Cleaning blending machines

_____ **6.** Reducing water usage

QS 4-13
Identifying activity levels
C3

Classify each of the following activities as unit level (U), batch level (B), product level (P), or facility level (F) for a manufacturer of trail mix.

_____ **1.** Roasting peanuts

_____ **2.** Cleaning roasting machines

_____ **3.** Sampling product quality

_____ **4.** Providing utilities for factory

_____ **5.** Calibrating mixing machines

_____ **6.** Reducing electricity usage

QS 4-14
Identifying activity levels
C3

Toyota embraces lean techniques, including lean accounting. What are the key components of lean accounting?

QS 4-15
Lean accounting and ABC
C3

A manufacturer uses activity-based costing to assign overhead costs to products. In the coming year it expects to incur $825,000 of costs to dispose of 3,300 tons of hazardous waste.

1. Compute the company's cost of hazardous waste disposal per ton.

2. During the year the company disposes of 5 tons of hazardous waste in the completion of Job #125. Assign hazardous waste disposal cost to Job #125 using activity-based costing.

QS 4-16
Activity-based costing
P3

---

connect

Xie Company identified the following activities, costs, and activity drivers for 2017. The company manufactures two types of go-karts: deluxe and basic.

Activity	Expected Costs	Expected Activity
Handling materials	$625,000	100,000 parts
Inspecting product	900,000	1,500 batches
Processing purchase orders	105,000	700 orders
Paying suppliers	175,000	500 invoices
Insuring the factory	300,000	40,000 square feet
Designing packaging	75,000	2 models

EXERCISES

Exercise 4-1
Computing plantwide overhead rates
P1

Required

1. Compute a single plantwide overhead rate, assuming that the company assigns overhead based on 125,000 budgeted direct labor hours.

2. In January 2017, the deluxe model required 2,500 direct labor hours and the basic model required 6,000 direct labor hours. Assign overhead costs to each model using the single plantwide overhead rate.

Exercise 4-2

Computing overhead rates under ABC **P3**

Refer to the information in Exercise 4-1. Compute the activity rate for each activity, assuming the company uses activity-based costing.

Exercise 4-3

Assigning costs using ABC

P3

Refer to the information in Exercise 4-1. Assume that the following information is available for the company's two products for the first quarter of 2017.

	Deluxe Model	Basic Model
Production volume	10,000 units	30,000 units
Parts required	20,000 parts	30,000 parts
Batches made	250 batches	100 batches
Purchase orders	50 orders	20 orders
Invoices	50 invoices	10 invoices
Space occupied	10,000 square feet	7,000 square feet
Models	1 model	1 model

Required

Compute activity rates for each activity and assign overhead costs to each product model using activity-based costing (ABC). What is the overhead cost per unit of each model?

Exercise 4-4

Plantwide overhead rate

P1

Textra Plastics produces parts for a variety of small machine manufacturers. Most products go through two operations, molding and trimming, before they are ready for packaging. Expected costs and activities for the molding department and for the trimming department for 2017 follow.

	Molding	Trimming
Direct labor hours	52,000 DLH	48,000 DLH
Machine hours	30,500 MH	3,600 MH
Overhead costs	$730,000	$590,000

Data for two special order parts to be manufactured by the company in 2017 follow.

	Part A27C	Part X82B
Number of units	9,800 units	54,500 units
Machine hours		
Molding	5,100 MH	1,020 MH
Trimming	2,600 MH	650 MH
Direct labor hours		
Molding	5,500 DLH	2,150 DLH
Trimming	700 DLH	3,500 DLH

Required

1. Compute the plantwide overhead rate using direct labor hours as the base.

2. Determine the overhead cost assigned to each product line using the plantwide rate computed in requirement 1.

Exercise 4-5

Departmental overhead rates

P2

Refer to the information in Exercise 4-4.

Required

1. Compute a departmental overhead rate for the molding department based on machine hours and a department overhead rate for the trimming department based on direct labor hours.

2. Determine the total overhead cost assigned to each product line using the departmental overhead rates from requirement 2.

3. Determine the overhead cost per unit for each product line using the departmental rate.

Laval produces lamps and home lighting fixtures. Its most popular product is a brushed aluminum desk lamp. This lamp is made from components shaped in the fabricating department and assembled in the assembly department. Information related to the 35,000 desk lamps produced annually follows.

Exercise 4-6
Assigning overhead costs
using the plantwide rate
and departmental rate
methods

P1   P2

Direct materials	$280,000
Direct labor	
Fabricating department (7,000 DLH × $20 per DLH)	$140,000
Assembly department (16,000 DLH × $29 per DLH)	$464,000
Machine hours	
Fabricating department.	15,040 MH
Assembly department	21,000 MH

Expected overhead cost and related data for the two production departments follow.

	Fabricating	Assembly
Direct labor hours.	75,000 DLH	125,000 DLH
Machine hours	80,000 MH	62,500 MH
Overhead cost	$300,000	$200,000

Required

1. Determine the plantwide overhead rate for Laval using direct labor hours as a base.

2. Determine the total manufacturing cost per unit for the aluminum desk lamp using the plantwide overhead rate.

Check   (2) $26.90 per unit

3. Compute departmental overhead rates based on machine hours in the fabricating department and direct labor hours in the assembly department.

4. Use departmental overhead rates from requirement 3 to determine the total manufacturing cost per unit for the aluminum desk lamps.

(4) $27.60 per unit

Way Cool produces two different models of air conditioners. The company produces the mechanical systems in their components department. The mechanical systems are combined with the housing assembly in its finishing department. The activities, costs, and drivers associated with these two manufacturing processes and the production support process follow.

Exercise 4-7
Using the plantwide
overhead rate to assess
prices

P1

Process	Activity	Overhead Cost	Driver	Quantity
Components	Changeover	$ 500,000	Number of batches	800
	Machining	279,000	Machine hours	6,000
	Setups	· 225,000	Number of setups	120
		$1,004,000		
Finishing	Welding	$ 180,300	Welding hours	3,000
	Inspecting	210,000	Number of inspections	700
	Rework	75,000	Rework orders	300
		$ 465,300		
Support	Purchasing	$ 135,000	Purchase orders	450
	Providing space	32,000	Number of units	5,000
	Providing utilities	65,000	Number of units	5,000
		$ 232,000		

Additional production information concerning its two product lines follows.

	Model 145	Model 212
Units produced.	1,500	3,500
Welding hours.	800	2,200
Batches	400	400
Number of inspections.	400	300
Machine hours	1,800	4,200
Setups	60	60
Rework orders	160	140
Purchase orders	300	150

Required

1. Using a plantwide overhead rate based on machine hours, compute the overhead cost per unit for each product line.

2. Determine the total cost per unit for each product line if the direct labor and direct materials costs per unit are $250 for Model 145 and $180 for Model 212.

Check (3) Model 212, $(40.26) per unit loss

3. If the market price for Model 145 is $820 and the market price for Model 212 is $480, determine the profit or loss per unit for each model. Comment on the results.

Exercise 4-8
Using departmental overhead rates to assess prices

P2

Refer to the information in Exercise 4-7 to answer the following requirements.

Required

1. Determine departmental overhead rates and compute the overhead cost per unit for each product line. Base your overhead assignment for the components department on machine hours. Use welding hours to assign overhead costs to the finishing department. Assign costs to the support department based on number of purchase orders.

2. Determine the total cost per unit for each product line if the direct labor and direct materials costs per unit are $250 for Model 145 and $180 for Model 212.

Check (3) Model 212, $(20.38) per unit loss

3. If the market price for Model 145 is $820 and the market price for Model 212 is $480, determine the profit or loss per unit for each model. Comment on the results.

Exercise 4-9
Using ABC to assess prices

P3

Refer to the information in Exercise 4-7 to answer the following requirements.

Required

1. Using ABC, compute the overhead cost per unit for each product line.

2. Determine the total cost per unit for each product line if the direct labor and direct materials costs per unit are $250 for Model 145 and $180 for Model 212.

Check (3) Model 212, $34.88 per unit profit

3. If the market price for Model 145 is $820 and the market price for Model 212 is $480, determine the profit or loss per unit for each model. Comment on the results.

Exercise 4-10
Using ABC for strategic decisions

P1   P3

Consider the following data for two products of Gitano Manufacturing.

	Overhead Cost	Product A	Product B
Number of units produced.		10,000 units	2,000 units
Direct labor cost (@ $24 per DLH).		0.20 DLH per unit	0.25 DLH per unit
Direct materials cost		$2 per unit	$3 per unit
Activity			
Machine setup	$121,000		
Materials handling	48,000		
Quality control inspections	80,000		
	$249,000		

Required

1. Using direct labor hours as the basis for assigning overhead costs, determine the total production cost per unit for each product line.
2. If the market price for Product A is $20 and the market price for Product B is $60, determine the profit or loss per unit for each product. Comment on the results.
3. Consider the following additional information about these two product lines. If ABC is used for assigning overhead costs to products, what is the cost per unit for Product A and for Product B?

Check   (2) Product B, $26.10 per unit profit

	Product A	Product B
Number of setups required for production...............	10 setups	12 setups
Number of parts required...........................	1 part/unit	3 parts/unit
Inspection hours required	40 hours	210 hours

4. Determine the profit or loss per unit for each product. Should this information influence company strategy? Explain.

(4) Product B, $(24.60) per unit loss

The following is taken from Ronda Co.'s internal records of its factory with two production departments. The cost driver for indirect labor and supplies is direct labor costs, and the cost driver for the remaining overhead items is number of hours of machine use. Compute the total amount of overhead cost allocated to Department 1 using activity-based costing.

Exercise 4-11
Activity-based costing and overhead cost allocation
P3

	Direct Labor	Machine Use Hours
Department 1	$18,800	2,000
Department 2	13,200	1,200
Totals...............................	$32,000	3,200
Factory overhead costs		
Rent and utilities		$12,200
Indirect labor		5,400
General office expense		4,000
Depreciation—Equipment.............................		3,000
Supplies		2,600
Total factory overhead................................		$27,200

Check   Dept. 1 allocation, $16,700

A company has two products: standard and deluxe. The company expects to produce 36,375 standard units and 62,240 deluxe units. It uses activity-based costing and has prepared the following analysis showing budgeted cost and cost driver activity for each of its three activity cost pools.

Exercise 4-12
Activity-based costing rates and allocations
P3

Activity Cost Pool	Budgeted Cost	Budgeted Activity of Cost Driver	
		Standard	Deluxe
Activity 1	$93,000	2,500	5,250
Activity 2	$92,000	4,500	5,500
Activity 3	$87,000	3,000	2,800

Required

1. Compute overhead rates for each of the three activities.
2. What is the expected overhead cost per unit for the standard units?
3. What is the expected overhead cost per unit for the deluxe units?

Exercise 4-13
Using ABC in a service company
P3

Cardiff and Delp is an architectural firm that provides services for residential construction projects. The following data pertain to a recent reporting period.

	Activities	Costs
Design department		
Client consultation	1,500 contact hours	$270,000
Drawings	2,000 design hours	115,000
Modeling	40,000 square feet	30,000
Project management department		
Supervision	600 days	$120,000
Billing	8 jobs	10,000
Collections	8 jobs	12,000

Required

1. Using ABC, compute the firm's activity overhead rates. Form activity cost pools where appropriate.

Check (2) $150,200

2. Assign costs to a 9,200-square-foot job that requires 450 contact hours, 340 design hours, and 200 days to complete.

Exercise 4-14
Activity-based costing
P3   A2

Glassworks Inc. produces two types of glass shelving, rounded edge and squared edge, on the same production line. For the current period, the company reports the following data.

	Rounded Edge	Squared Edge	Total
Direct materials	$19,000	$ 43,200	$ 62,200
Direct labor	12,200	23,800	36,000
Overhead (300% of direct labor cost)	36,600	71,400	108,000
Total cost	$67,800	$138,400	$206,200
Quantity produced	10,500 ft.	14,100 ft.	
Average cost per ft. (rounded)	$ 6.46	$ 9.82	

Glassworks's controller wishes to apply activity-based costing (ABC) to allocate the $108,000 of overhead costs incurred by the two product lines to see whether cost per foot would change markedly from that reported above. She has collected the following information.

Overhead Cost Category (Activity Cost Pool)	Cost
Supervision	$ 5,400
Depreciation of machinery	56,600
Assembly line preparation	46,000
Total overhead	$108,000

She has also collected the following information about the cost drivers for each category (cost pool) and the amount of each driver used by the two product lines.

Overhead Cost Category (Activity Cost Pool)	Driver	Usage		
		Rounded Edge	Squared Edge	Total
Supervision	Direct labor cost ($)	$12,200	$23,800	$36,000
Depreciation of machinery	Machine hours	500 hours	1,500 hours	2,000 hours
Assembly line preparation	Setups (number)	40 times	210 times	250 times

Required

1. Assign these three overhead cost pools to each of the two products using ABC.

Check (2) Rounded edge, $5.19; Squared edge, $10.76

2. Determine average cost per foot for each of the two products using ABC.

3. Compare the average cost per foot under ABC with the average cost per foot under the current method for each product. Explain why a difference between the two cost allocation methods exists.

Surgery Center is an outpatient surgical clinic that was profitable for many years, but Medicare has cut its reimbursements by as much as 40%. As a result, the clinic wants to better understand its costs. It decides to prepare an activity-based cost analysis, including an estimate of the average cost of both general surgery and orthopedic surgery. The clinic's three activity cost pools and their cost drivers follow.

Exercise 4-15
Activity-based costing
P3

Activity Cost Pool	Cost	Cost Driver	Driver Quantity
Professional salaries	$1,600,000	Professional hours	10,000
Patient services and supplies	27,000	Number of patients	600
Building cost	150,000	Square feet	1,500

The two main surgical units and their related data follow.

Service	Hours	Square Feet*	Patients
General surgery	2,500	600	400
Orthopedic surgery......................	7,500	900	200

* Orthopedic surgery requires more space for patients, supplies, and equipment.

Required

1. Compute the cost per cost driver for each of the three activity cost pools.
2. Use the results from part 1 to allocate costs to both the general surgery and the orthopedic surgery units. Compute total cost and average cost per patient for both the general surgery and the orthopedic surgery units.

Check (2) Average cost of general (orthopedic) surgery, $1,195 ($6,495) per patient

---

Smythe Co. makes furniture. The following data are taken from its production plans for the year.

Exercise 4-16
Comparing costs under ABC to traditional plantwide overhead rate

P1   P3   A1   A2

Direct labor costs	$5,870,000
Hazardous waste disposal costs	630,000

	Chairs	Tables
Expected production	211,000 units	17,000 units
Direct labor hours required	254,000 DLH	16,400 DLH
Hazardous waste disposed	200 pounds	800 pounds

Required

1. Determine the hazardous waste disposal cost per unit for chairs and for tables if costs are assigned using a single plantwide overhead rate based on direct labor hours.
2. Determine hazardous waste disposal costs per unit for chairs and for tables if costs are assigned based on the number of pounds disposed of.
3. Which method is better for assigning costs to each product? Explain.

Check (2) Tables, $29.65 per unit

Identify each of the following activities as unit level (U), batch level (B), product level (P), or facility level (F) to indicate the way each is incurred with respect to production.

Exercise 4-17
Identifying activity levels

C3

_____ **1.** Paying real estate taxes on the factory building
_____ **2.** Attaching labels to collars of shirts
_____ **3.** Redesigning a bicycle seat in response to customer feedback
_____ **4.** Cleaning the assembly department
_____ **5.** Polishing gold wedding rings
_____ **6.** Mixing bread dough in a commercial bakery
_____ **7.** Sampling cookies to determine quality
_____ **8.** Recycling hazardous waste
_____ **9.** Reducing greenhouse gas emissions

Exercise 4-18

Activity classification

C3

Following are activities in providing medical services at Healthsmart Clinic.

A. Registering patients
B. Cleaning beds
C. Stocking examination rooms
D. Washing linens

E. Ordering medical equipment
F. Heating the clinic
G. Providing security services
H. Filling prescriptions

Required

1. Classify each activity as unit level (U), batch level (B), product level (P), or facility level (F).
2. Identify an activity driver that might be used to measure these activities at the clinic.

PROBLEM SET A

Problem 4-1A

Comparing costs using ABC with the plantwide overhead rate

P1   P3   A1   A2

The following data are for the two products produced by Tadros Company.

	Product A	Product B
Direct materials	$15 per unit	$24 per unit
Direct labor hours.	0.3 DLH per unit	1.6 DLH per unit
Machine hours	0.1 MH per unit	1.2 MH per unit
Batches.	125 batches	225 batches
Volume	10,000 units	2,000 units
Engineering modifications	12 modifications	58 modifications
Number of customers.	500 customers	400 customers
Market price	$30 per unit	$120 per unit

The company's direct labor rate is $20 per direct labor hour (DLH). Additional information follows.

	Costs	Driver
Indirect manufacturing		
Engineering support	$24,500	Engineering modifications
Electricity	34,000	Machine hours
Setup costs	52,500	Batches
Nonmanufacturing		
Customer service.	81,000	Number of customers

Required

Check   (1) Product A, $26.37 per unit cost

1. Compute the manufacturing cost per unit using the plantwide overhead rate based on direct labor hours. What is the gross profit per unit?

2. How much gross profit is generated by each customer of Product A using the plantwide overhead rate? How much gross profit is generated by each customer of Product B using the plantwide overhead rate? What is the cost of providing customer service to each customer? What information is provided by this comparison?

(3) Product A, $24.30 per unit cost

3. Determine the manufacturing cost per unit of each product line using ABC. What is the gross profit per unit?

4. How much gross profit is generated by each customer of Product A using ABC? How much gross profit is generated by each customer of Product B using ABC? Is the gross profit per customer adequate?

5. Which method of product costing gives better information to managers of this company? Explain why.

Problem 4-2A

Assessing impacts of using a plantwide overhead rate versus ABC

A1   A2

Xylon Company manufactures custom-made furniture for its local market and produces a line of home furnishings sold in retail stores across the country. The company uses traditional volume-based methods of assigning direct materials and direct labor to its product lines. Overhead has always been assigned by using a plantwide overhead rate based on direct labor hours. In the past few years, management has seen its line of retail products continue to sell at high volumes, but competition has forced it to lower prices on these items. The prices are declining to a level close to its cost of production.

Meanwhile, its custom-made furniture is in high demand, and customers have commented on its favorable (lower) prices compared to its competitors. Management is considering dropping its line of retail products and devoting all of its resources to custom-made furniture.

Required

1. What reasons could explain why competitors are forcing the company to lower prices on its high-volume retail products?
2. Why do you believe the company charges less for custom-order products than its competitors?
3. Does a company's costing method have any effect on its pricing decisions? Explain.
4. Aside from the differences in volume of output, what production differences do you believe exist between making custom-order furniture and mass-market furnishings?
5. What information might the company obtain from using ABC that it might not obtain using volume-based costing methods?

Craft Pro Machining produces machine tools for the construction industry. The following details about overhead costs were taken from its company records.

Problem 4-3A
Applying activity-based costing

P1   P3   A1   A2   C3

Production Activity	Indirect Labor	Indirect Materials	Other Overhead
Grinding...................	$320,000		
Polishing................		$135,000	
Product modification	600,000		
Providing power..............			$255,000
System calibration	500,000		

Additional information on the drivers for its production activities follows.

Grinding...	13,000 machine hours
Polishing..	13,000 machine hours
Product modification	1,500 engineering hours
Providing power...	17,000 direct labor hours
System calibration	400 batches

Required

1. Classify each activity as unit level, batch level, product level, or facility level.
2. Compute the activity overhead rates using ABC. Combine the grinding and polishing activities into a single cost pool.
3. Determine overhead costs to assign to the following jobs using ABC.

	Job 3175	Job 4286
Number of units	200 units	2,500 units
Machine hours	550 MH	5,500 MH
Engineering hours	26 eng. hours	32 eng. hours
Batches	30 batches	90 batches
Direct labor hours	500 DLH	4,375 DLH

4. What is the overhead cost per unit for Job 3175? What is the overhead cost per unit for Job 4286?
5. If the company uses a plantwide overhead rate based on direct labor hours, what is the overhead cost for each unit of Job 3175? Of Job 4286?
6. Compare the overhead costs per unit computed in requirements 4 and 5 for each job. Which method more accurately assigns overhead costs?

Check   (4) Job 3175, $373.25 per unit

Problem 4-4A

Evaluating product line costs and prices using ABC

P3

Bright Day Company produces two beverages, Hi-Voltage and EasySlim. Data about these products follow.

	Hi-Voltage	EasySlim
Production volume	12,500 bottles	180,000 bottles
Liquid materials	1,400 gallons	37,000 gallons
Dry materials	620 pounds	12,000 pounds
Bottles...	12,500 bottles	180,000 bottles
Labels	3 labels per bottle	1 label per bottle
Machine setups	500 setups	300 setups
Machine hours	200 MH	3,750 MH

Additional data from its two production departments follow.

Department	Driver	Cost
Mixing department		
Liquid materials	Gallons	$ 2,304
Dry materials	Pounds	6,941
Utilities	Machine hours	1,422
Bottling department		
Bottles...	Units	$77,000
Labeling	Labels per bottle	6,525
Machine setup	Setups	20,000

Required

1. Determine the cost of each product line using ABC.
2. What is the cost per bottle of Hi-Voltage? What is the cost per bottle of EasySlim? (*Hint:* Your answer should draw on the total cost for each product line computed in requirement 1.)

Check   (3) $2.22 profit per bottle

3. If Hi-Voltage sells for $3.75 per bottle, how much profit does the company earn per bottle of Hi-Voltage that it sells?
4. What is the minimum price that the company should set per bottle of EasySlim? Explain.

Problem 4-5A

Pricing analysis with ABC and a plantwide overhead rate

A1   A2   P1   P3

Sara's Salsa Company produces its condiments in two types: Extra Fine for restaurant customers and Family Style for home use. Salsa is prepared in department 1 and packaged in department 2. The activities, overhead costs, and drivers associated with these two manufacturing processes and the company's production support activities follow.

Process	Activity	Overhead Cost	Driver	Quantity
Department 1	Mixing	$ 4,500	Machine hours	1,500
	Cooking	11,250	Machine hours	1,500
	Product testing	112,500	Batches	600
		$128,250		
Department 2	Machine calibration	$250,000	Production runs	400
	Labeling	12,000	Cases of output	120,000
	Defects	6,000	Cases of output	120,000
		$268,000		
Support	Recipe formulation	$ 90,000	Focus groups	45
	Heat, lights, and water	27,000	Machine hours	1,500
	Materials handling	65,000	Container types	8
		$182,000		

Additional production information about its two product lines follows.

	Extra Fine	Family Style
Units produced......................	20,000 cases	100,000 cases
Batches............................	200 batches	400 batches
Machine hours	500 MH	1,000 MH
Focus groups	30 groups	15 groups
Container types	5 containers	3 containers
Production runs	200 runs	200 runs

Required

1. Using a plantwide overhead rate based on cases, compute the overhead cost that is assigned to each case of Extra Fine Salsa and each case of Family Style Salsa.

2. Using the plantwide overhead rate, determine the total cost per case for the two products if the direct materials and direct labor cost is $6 per case of Extra Fine and $5 per case of Family Style.

3. If the market price of Extra Fine Salsa is $18 per case and the market price of Family Style Salsa is $9 per case, determine the gross profit per case for each product. What might management conclude about each product line?

4. Using ABC, compute the total cost per case for each product type if the direct labor and direct materials cost is $6 per case of Extra Fine and $5 per case of Family Style.

5. If the market price is $18 per case of Extra Fine and $9 per case of Family Style, determine the gross profit per case for each product. How should management interpret the market prices given your computations?

6. Would your pricing analysis be improved if the company used departmental rates based on machine hours in department 1 and number of cases in department 2 instead of ABC? Explain.

Check (2) Cost per case: Extra Fine, $10.82; Family Style, $9.82

(4) Cost per case: Extra Fine, $20.02; Family Style, $7.98

Wade Company makes two distinct products, with the following information available for each.

PROBLEM SET B

Problem 4-1B
Comparing costs using ABC with the plantwide overhead rate

A1 A2 P1 P3

	Standard	Deluxe
Direct materials	$4 per unit	$8 per unit
Direct labor hours	4 DLH per unit	5 DLH per unit
Machine hours	3 MH per unit	3 MH per unit
Batches	175 batches	75 batches
Volume	40,000 units	10,000 units
Engineering modifications...........	50 modifications	25 modifications
Number of customers...............	1,000 customers	1,000 customers
Market price	$92 per unit	$125 per unit

The company's direct labor rate is $20 per direct labor hour (DLH). Additional information follows.

	Costs	Driver
Indirect manufacturing		
Engineering support	$ 56,250	Engineering modifications
Electricity	112,500	Machine hours
Setup costs....................	41,250	Batches
Nonmanufacturing		
Customer service...............	250,000	Number of customers

Required

1. Compute the manufacturing cost per unit using the plantwide overhead rate based on machine hours. What is the gross profit per unit?

2. How much gross profit is generated by each customer of the standard product using the plantwide overhead rate? How much gross profit is generated by each customer of the deluxe product using the plantwide overhead rate? What is the cost of providing customer service to each customer? What information is provided by this comparison?

3. Determine the manufacturing cost per unit of each product line using ABC. What is the gross profit per unit?

4. How much gross profit is generated by each customer of the standard product using ABC? How much gross profit is generated by each customer of the deluxe product using ABC? Is the gross profit per customer adequate?

5. Which method of product costing gives better information to managers of this company? Explain.

Problem 4-2B

Assessing impacts of using a plantwide overhead rate versus ABC

A1   A2

Midwest Paper produces cardboard boxes. The boxes require designing, cutting, and printing. (The boxes are shipped flat, and customers fold them as necessary.) Midwest has a reputation for providing high-quality products and excellent service to customers, who are major U.S. manufacturers. Costs are assigned to products based on the number of machine hours required to produce them.

Three years ago, a new marketing executive was hired. She suggested the company offer custom design and manufacturing services to small specialty manufacturers. These customers required boxes for their products and were eager to have Midwest as a supplier. Within one year, Midwest found that it was so busy with orders from small customers, it had trouble supplying boxes to all its customers on a timely basis. Large, long-time customers began to complain about slow service, and several took their business elsewhere. Within another 18 months, Midwest was in financial distress with a backlog of orders to be filled.

Required

1. What do you believe are the major costs of making boxes? How are those costs related to the volume of boxes produced?

2. How did Midwest's new customers differ from its previous customers?

3. Would the unit cost to produce a box for new customers be different from the unit cost to produce a box for its previous customers? Explain.

4. Could Midwest's fate have been different if it had used ABC for determining the cost of its boxes?

5. What information would have been available with ABC that might have been overlooked using a traditional volume-based costing method?

Problem 4-3B

Applying activity-based costing

P1 P3 A1 A2 C3

Ryan Foods produces gourmet gift baskets that it distributes online as well as from its small retail store. The following details about overhead costs are taken from its records.

Production Activity	Indirect Labor	Indirect Materials	Other Overhead
Wrapping........................	$300,000	$200,000	
Assembling	400,000		
Product design	180,000		
Quality inspection	100,000		
Cooking..........................	150,000	120,000	

Additional information on the drivers for its production activities follows.

Wrapping...	100,000 units
Assembling	20,000 direct labor hours
Product design	3,000 design hours
Quality inspection	20,000 direct labor hours
Cooking..	1,000 batches

Required

1. Classify each activity as unit level, batch level, product level, or facility level.
2. Compute the activity overhead rates using ABC. Combine the assembling and quality inspection activities into a single cost pool.
3. Determine the overhead costs to assign to the following jobs using ABC.

	Holiday Basket	Executive Basket
Number of units	8,000 units	1,000 units
Direct labor hours	2,000 DLH	500 DLH
Design hours	40 design hours	40 design hours
Batches	80 batches	200 batches

4. What is the overhead cost per unit for the Holiday Basket? What is the overhead cost per unit for the Executive Basket?
5. If the company used a plantwide overhead rate based on direct labor hours, what is the overhead cost for each Holiday Basket unit? What would be the overhead cost for each Executive Basket unit if a single plantwide overhead rate were used?
6. Compare the costs per unit computed in requirements 4 and 5 for each job. Which cost assignment method provides the most accurate cost? Explain.

Check (4) Holiday Basket, $14.25 per unit

(5) Holiday Basket, $18.13 per unit

Mathwerks produces two electronic, handheld educational games: *Fun with Fractions* and *Count Calculus*. Data on these products follow.

Problem 4-4B
Evaluating product line costs and prices using ABC

P3

	Fun with Fractions	*Count Calculus*
Production volume	150,000 units	10,000 units
Components	450,000 parts	100,000 parts
Direct labor hours	15,000 DLH	2,000 DLH
Packaging materials	150,000 boxes	10,000 boxes
Shipping cartons	100 units per carton	25 units per carton
Machine setups	52 setups	52 setups
Machine hours	5,000 MH	2,000 MH

Additional data from its two production departments follow.

Department	Driver	Cost
Assembly department		
Component cost	Parts	$495,000
Assembly labor	Direct labor hours	244,800
Maintenance	Machine hours	100,800
Wrapping department		
Packaging materials	Boxes	$460,800
Shipping	Cartons	27,360
Machine setup	Setups	187,200

Required

1. Using ABC, determine the cost of each product line.
2. What is the cost per unit of *Fun with Fractions*? What is the cost per unit of *Count Calculus*?
3. If *Count Calculus* sells for $59.95 per unit, how much profit does the company earn per unit of *Count Calculus* sold?
4. What is the minimum price that the company should set per unit of *Fun with Fractions*? Explain.

Check (3) $32.37 profit per unit

Problem 4-5B
Pricing analysis with ABC and a plantwide overhead rate

A1   A2   P1   P3

Tent Pro produces two lines of tents sold to outdoor enthusiasts. The tents are cut to specifications in department A. In department B, the tents are sewn and folded. The activities, costs, and drivers associated with these two manufacturing processes and the company's production support activities follow.

Process	Activity	Overhead Cost	Driver	Quantity
Department A	Pattern alignment	$ 64,400	Batches	560
	Cutting	50,430	Machine hours	12,300
	Moving product	100,800	Moves	2,400
		$215,630		
Department B	Sewing	$327,600	Direct labor hours	4,200
	Inspecting	24,000	Inspections	600
	Folding	47,880	Units	22,800
		$399,480		
Support	Design	$280,000	Modification orders	280
	Providing space	51,600	Square feet	8,600
	Materials handling	184,000	Square yards	920,000
		$515,600		

Additional production information on the two lines of tents follows.

	Pup Tent	Pop-up Tent
Units produced..................	15,200 units	7,600 units
Moves........................	800 moves	1,600 moves
Batches.......................	140 batches	420 batches
Number of inspections...........	240 inspections	360 inspections
Machine hours	7,000 MH	5,300 MH
Direct labor hours...............	2,600 DLH	1,600 DLH
Modification orders	70 modification orders	210 modification orders
Space occupied	4,300 square feet	4,300 square feet
Material required	450,000 square yards	470,000 square yards

Required

1. Using a plantwide overhead rate based on direct labor hours, compute the overhead cost that is assigned to each pup tent and each pop-up tent.

2. Using the plantwide overhead rate, determine the total cost per unit for the two products if the direct materials and direct labor cost is $25 per pup tent and $32 per pop-up tent.

3. If the market price of the pup tent is $65 and the market price of the pop-up tent is $200, determine the gross profit per unit for each tent. What might management conclude about the pup tent?

Check   (4) Pup tent, $58.46 per unit cost

4. Using ABC, compute the total cost per unit for each tent if the direct labor and direct materials cost is $25 per pup tent and $32 per pop-up tent.

5. If the market price is $65 per pup tent and $200 per pop-up tent, determine the gross profit per unit for each tent. Comment on the results.

6. Would your pricing analysis be improved if the company used, instead of ABC, departmental rates determined using machine hours in department A and direct labor hours in department B? Explain.

SERIAL PROBLEM
Business Solutions

P3

(This serial problem began in Chapter 1 and continues through most of the book. If previous chapter segments were not completed, the serial problem can begin at this point.)

SP 4   After reading an article about activity-based costing in a trade journal for the furniture industry, Santana Rey wondered if it was time to critically analyze overhead costs at **Business Solutions.** In a recent month, Santana found that setup costs, inspection costs, and utility costs made up most of its overhead. Additional information about overhead follows.

Activity	Cost	Driver
Setting up machines.............	$20,000	25 batches
Inspecting components	$ 7,500	5,000 parts
Providing utilities	$10,000	5,000 machine hours

Overhead has been applied to output at a rate of 50% of direct labor costs. The following data pertain to Job 615.

Direct materials	$2,500
Direct labor....................................	$3,500
Batches..	2 batches
Number of parts	400 parts
Machine hours	600 machine hours

© Alexander Image/Shutterstock RF

Required

1. Classify each of its three overhead activities as unit level, batch level, product level, or facility level.
2. What is the total cost of Job 615 if Business Solutions applies overhead at 50% of direct labor cost?
3. What is the total cost of Job 615 if Business Solutions uses activity-based costing?
4. Which approach to assigning overhead gives a better representation of the costs incurred to produce Job 615? Explain.

Beyond the Numbers

BTN 4-1   Refer to the financial statements of **Apple** (**Apple.com**) and **Google** (**Google.com**) to answer the following.

Required

1. Identify at least two activities at Apple and at Google that cause costs to be incurred. Do you believe these companies should be concerned about controlling costs of the activities you identified? Explain.
2. Would you classify Apple and Google as service, merchandising, or manufacturing companies? Explain.
3. Is activity-based costing useful for companies such as Apple and Google? Explain.

REPORTING IN ACTION

C3   A2

APPLE
GOOGLE

BTN 4-2   Compare **Apple**'s and **Google**'s income statements and answer the following.

Required

1. Which company has a higher ratio of costs, defined as cost of goods sold plus total operating expenses, to revenues? Use the two most recent years' income statements from Appendix A. Show your analysis.
2. How might the use of activity-based costing help the less competitive company become *more* competitive?
3. Assume Apple is considering opening a new retail store. What are the activities associated with opening a new retail store?

COMPARATIVE ANALYSIS

C2   A2

APPLE
GOOGLE

BTN 4-3   In conducting interviews and observing factory operations to implement an activity-based costing system, you determine that several activities are unnecessary or redundant. For example, warehouse personnel were inspecting purchased components as they were received at the loading dock. Later that day, the components were inspected again on the shop floor before being installed in the final product. Both of these activities caused costs to be incurred but were not adding value to the product. If you include this observation in your report, one or more employees who perform inspections will likely lose their jobs.

ETHICS CHALLENGE

A2   C3

Required

1. As a plant employee, what is your responsibility to report your findings to superiors?
2. Should you attempt to determine if the redundancy is justified? Explain.
3. What is your responsibility to the employees whose jobs will likely be lost because of your report?
4. What facts should you consider before making your decision to report or not?

COMMUNICATING IN PRACTICE
A2

BTN 4-4   The chief executive officer (CEO) of your company recently returned from a luncheon meeting where activity-based costing was presented and discussed. Though her background is not in accounting, she has worked for the company for 15 years and is thoroughly familiar with its operations. Her impression of the presentation about ABC was that it was just another way of dividing up total overhead cost and that the total would still be the same "no matter how you sliced it."

Required

Write a memorandum to the CEO, no more than one page, explaining how ABC is different from traditional volume-based costing methods. Also, identify its advantages and disadvantages vis-à-vis traditional methods. Be sure it is written to be understandable to someone who is not an accountant.

TAKING IT TO THE NET
A2

BTN 4-5   Accounting professionals who work for private companies often obtain the Certified Management Accountant (CMA) designation to indicate their proficiency in several business areas in addition to managerial accounting. The CMA examination is administered by the Institute of Management Accountants (IMA).

Required

Go to the IMA website (**IMAnet.org**) and determine which parts of the CMA exam likely cover activity-based costing. A person planning to become a CMA should take what college coursework?

TEAMWORK IN ACTION
C2   C3

BTN 4-6   Observe the operations at your favorite fast-food restaurant.

Required

1. How many people does it take to fill a typical order of a sandwich, beverage, and one side order?
2. Describe the activities involved in its food service process.
3. What costs are related to each activity identified in requirement 2?

ENTREPRENEURIAL DECISION
C3

BTN 4-7   **GrandyOats** has expanded its product offerings to include many varieties of organic granola. Company founders Nat Peirce and Aaron Anker know that financial success depends on cost control as well as revenue generation.

Required

1. If GrandyOats wanted to expand its product line to include organic energy bars, what activities would it need to perform that are not required for its current product lines?
2. Related to part 1, should the additional overhead costs related to new product lines be shared by existing product lines? Explain your reasoning.

HITTING THE ROAD
C2   C3

BTN 4-8   Visit and observe the processes of three different fast-food restaurants—these visits can be done as individuals or as teams. The objective of activity-based costing is to accurately assign costs to products and to improve operational efficiency.

Required

1. Individuals (or teams) can be assigned to each of three different fast-food establishments. Make a list of the activities required to process an order of a sandwich, beverage, and one side order at each restaurant. Record the time required for each process, from placing the order to receiving the completed order.

2. What activities do the three establishments have in common? What activities are different across the establishments?

3. Is the number of activities related to the time required to process an order? Is the number of activities related to the price charged to customers? Explain both.

4. Make recommendations for improving the processes you observe. Would your recommendations increase or decrease the cost of operations?

BTN 4-9   Visit the websites and review the financial statements for **Apple** (**Apple.com**) and **Samsung** (**Samsung.com**). Each of these companies sells electronic devices like smartphones in global markets.

GLOBAL DECISION

C3

APPLE
Samsung

Required

1. For Apple in 2015, what are the largest three geographic markets in which it sells products? What is the amount (in millions of dollars) of sales in each market?

2. For Samsung in 2015, what are the largest three geographic markets in which it sells products? What is the amount (in millions of Korean won) of sales in each market? (Use "revenue from external customers.")

3. How would customer service activities differ across different geographic markets?

 # GLOBAL VIEW

Toyota Motor Corporation pioneered lean manufacturing, making cars in response to customer orders. The Toyota Production System focuses on the elimination of waste. The company uses just-in-time processing and "automation with a human touch," or *jidoka,* to ensure that high-quality products are produced. When problems occur, production is stopped immediately and not restarted until the problem is resolved.

The figure below shows how this approach builds quality and continuous process improvement.

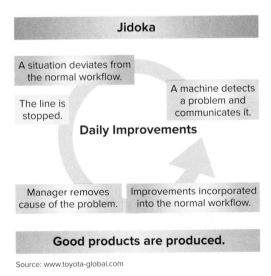

Source: www.toyota-global.com

 Global View Assignments

Discussion Question 16

Quick Study 4-15

BTN 4-9

chapter 5

Cost Behavior and Cost-Volume-Profit Analysis

Chapter Preview

IDENTIFYING COST BEHAVIOR

C1 Fixed costs

Variable costs

Graphing costs

Mixed costs

Step-wise costs

Curvilinear costs

NTK 5-1

MEASURING COST BEHAVIOR

P1 Scatter diagrams

High-low method

Regression

Comparing cost estimation methods

NTK 5-2

CONTRIBUTION MARGIN AND BREAK-EVEN

A1 Contribution margin

P2 Break-even

P3 Cost-volume-profit chart

Impact of estimates on break-even

NTK 5-3

APPLYING COST-VOLUME-PROFIT ANALYSIS

C2 Margin of safety

Income from sales and costs

Sales for target income

Strategizing

P4 Sales mix

A2 Operating leverage

NTK 5-4, 5-5

Learning Objectives

CONCEPTUAL

C1 Describe different types of cost behavior in relation to production and sales volume.

C2 Describe several applications of cost-volume-profit analysis.

ANALYTICAL

A1 Compute the contribution margin and describe what it reveals about a company's cost structure.

A2 Analyze changes in sales using the degree of operating leverage.

PROCEDURAL

P1 Determine cost estimates using the scatter diagram, high-low, and regression methods of estimating costs.

P2 Compute the break-even point for a single product company.

P3 Graph costs and sales for a single product company.

P4 Compute the break-even point for a multiproduct company.

P5 *Appendix 5B*—Compute unit cost and income under both absorption and variable costing.

© Joshua Bright/The New York Times/Redux

Sweet Green

WASHINGTON, DC—Nearing graduation, Nicolas (Nic) Jammet, Jonathan (Jon) Neman, and Nathaniel (Nate) Ru knew they wanted to start their own business. Explains Nic, "standard job choices didn't appeal to us." And they were "sick of the food options in the area," recalls Jon. The trio's idea—to open a salad shop that sourced local, organic ingredients—evolved into a national company, **Sweetgreen** (**Sweetgreen.com**). Sweetgreen posted revenues of $50 million in 2014. "We want to feed people better food," insists Nate, "it's a lifestyle choice for better living."

"We're making healthy eating cool"
—Nathaniel Ru

The owners must understand and control costs. They say accounting is the key. "I met Nate the first day of Accounting 101," proclaims Jon. All three explain that they apply concepts of fixed and variable costs and how to control costs to break even and make profits.

Sweetgreen relies on small, local suppliers, which increases variable costs. The result is a better salad that customers will pay more for. Using cost-volume-profit analysis enables the owners to see how changes in selling prices, variable costs, and fixed costs impact profits.

As Sweetgreen grows, the owners face new decisions, such as where to open new stores. "It's complicated," insists Jon, as costs vary by location. The trio uses contribution margin income statements, including forecasted costs for potential new locations.

The owners have expanded beyond salad into Sweetgreen clothing. With diverse products, sales mix and multiproduct break-even points are important—which they analyze using accounting data.

The owners are building a national brand that follows sustainable practices. "One of our five core values is to think sustainably," insists Nic, "and make decisions that will last longer." By understanding costs and using cost-volume-profit analysis, the trio pursue sustainability initiatives.

Jon recalls that they started by "trying to solve a problem [and] . . . to change the way people live, starting with how they think about food." He advises entrepreneurs to pursue their dreams and "make it happen!"

Sources: *Sweetgreen website,* January 2017; *Business Insider,* June 6, 2014; *CBS This Morning* video, July 7, 2015; *Huffington Post,* May 2, 2013; *Bloomberg,* October 12, 2015; *The New Potato,* January 7, 2015; *Fortune,* February 18, 2016

IDENTIFYING COST BEHAVIOR

Planning a company's future activities is crucial to successful management. Managers use **cost-volume-profit (CVP) analysis** to predict how changes in costs and sales levels affect profit. CVP analysis requires four inputs, as shown in Exhibit 5.1.

EXHIBIT 5.1

Inputs for CVP analysis

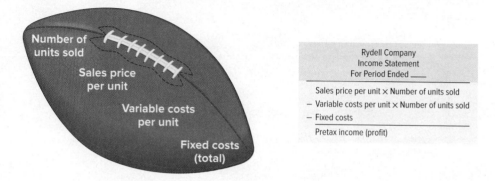

Using these four inputs, managers apply CVP analysis to answer questions such as:

- How many units must we sell to break even?
- How much will income increase if we install a new machine to reduce labor costs?
- What is the change in income if selling prices decline and sales volume increases?
- How will income change if we change the sales mix of our products or services?
- What sales volume is needed to earn a target income?

This chapter uses Rydell, a football manufacturer, to explain CVP analysis. We first review cost classifications like fixed and variable costs, and then we show methods for measuring these costs.

The concept of *relevant range* is important to classifying costs for CVP analysis. The **relevant range of operations** is the normal operating range for a business. Except for unusually good or bad times, management plans for operations within a range of volume neither close to zero nor at maximum capacity. The relevant range excludes extremely high or low operating levels that are unlikely to occur. CVP analysis requires management to classify costs as either *fixed* or *variable* with respect to production or sales volume, within the relevant range of operations. The remainder of this section discusses concepts of cost behavior.

Fixed Costs

C1

Describe different types of cost behavior in relation to production and sales volume.

Fixed costs do not change when the volume of activity changes (within a relevant range). For example, $32,000 in monthly rent paid for a factory building remains the same whether the factory operates with a single eight-hour shift or around the clock with three shifts. This means that rent cost is the same each month at any level of output from zero to the plant's full productive capacity.

Though the *total* amount of fixed cost does not change as volume changes, fixed cost *per unit* of output decreases as volume increases. For instance, if 200 units are produced when monthly rent is $32,000, the average rent cost per unit is $160 (computed as $32,000/200 units). When production increases to 1,000 units per month, the average rent cost per unit decreases to $32 (computed as $32,000/1,000 units).

Variable Costs

Variable costs change in proportion to changes in volume of activity. Direct materials cost is one example of a variable cost. If one unit of product requires materials costing

$20, total materials costs are $200 when 10 units are manufactured, $400 for 20 units, and so on. While the *total* amount of variable cost changes with the level of production, variable cost *per unit* remains constant as volume changes.

Graph of Costs to Volume

When production volume and costs are graphed, units of product are usually plotted on the *horizontal axis* and dollars of cost are plotted on the *vertical axis*. The upper graph in Exhibit 5.2 shows the relation between total fixed costs and volume, and the relation between total variable costs and volume. Total fixed costs of $32,000 remain the same at all production levels up to the company's monthly capacity of 2,000 units. Total variable costs increase by $20 per unit for each additional unit produced. When variable costs are plotted on a graph of cost and volume, they appear as an upward-sloping straight line starting at the zero cost level.

The lower graph in Exhibit 5.2 shows that fixed costs *per unit* decrease as production increases. This drop in per unit costs as production increases is known as *economies of scale*. This lower graph also shows that variable costs per unit remain constant as production levels change.

© gerenme/Vetta/Getty Images

Point: Fixed costs stay constant in total but decrease per unit as more units are produced. Variable costs vary in total but are fixed per unit as production changes.

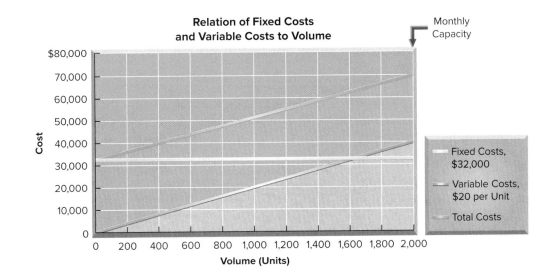

EXHIBIT 5.2

Relations of Total and Per Unit Costs to Volume

Units Produced	Total Fixed Costs	Total Variable Costs
0	$32,000	$ 0
200	32,000	4,000
400	32,000	8,000
⋮	⋮	⋮
1,800	32,000	36,000
2,000	32,000	40,000

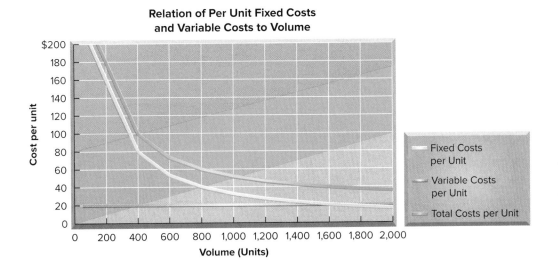

Units Produced	Per Unit Fixed Costs	Per Unit Variable Costs
1	$32,000	$20
200	160	20
400	80	20
⋮	⋮	⋮
2,000	16	20

Mixed Costs

Are all costs either fixed or variable? No. **Mixed costs** include both fixed and variable cost components. For example, compensation for sales representatives often includes a fixed monthly salary and a variable commission based on sales. Utilities can also be considered a mixed cost; even if no units are produced, it is not likely a manufacturing plant will use no electricity or water. Like a fixed cost, a mixed cost is greater than zero when volume is zero; but unlike a fixed cost, it increases steadily in proportion to increases in volume.

The total cost line in the top graph in Exhibit 5.2 starts on the vertical axis at the $32,000 fixed cost point. At the zero volume level, total cost equals the fixed costs. As the volume of activity increases, the total cost line increases at an amount equal to the variable cost per unit. This total cost line is a "mixed cost"—and it is highest when the volume of activity is at 2,000 units (the end point of the relevant range). In CVP analysis, mixed costs should be separated into fixed and variable components. The fixed component is added to other fixed costs, and the variable component is added to other variable costs. We show how to separate costs later in this chapter.

Shown below are examples of fixed, variable, and mixed costs for a manufacturer of footballs.

Fixed Costs	Variable Costs	Mixed Costs
• Rent	• Direct materials	• Electricity
• Depreciation*	• Direct labor	• Water
• Property taxes	• Shipping	• Sales rep (salary plus commission)
• Supervisor salaries	• Packaging	• Natural gas
• Office salaries	• Indirect materials	• Maintenance

*Computed using a method other than the units-of-production.

Step-wise Costs

A **step-wise cost** (or *stair-step cost*) reflects a step pattern in costs. Salaries of production supervisors are fixed within a *relevant range* of the current production volume. However, if production volume expands greatly (for example, with the addition of another shift), more supervisors must be hired. This means that the total cost for supervisory salaries steps up by a lump-sum amount. Similarly, if production volume takes another large step up, supervisory salaries will increase by another lump sum. This behavior is graphed in Exhibit 5.3. See how the step-wise cost line is flat within ranges, called the *relevant range*.

EXHIBIT 5.3

Step-wise and Curvilinear Costs

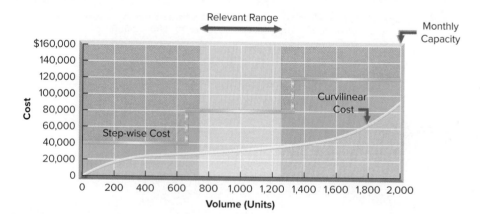

Curvilinear Costs

Curvilinear costs increase as volume increases, but at a nonconstant rate. The curved line in Exhibit 5.3 shows a curvilinear cost beginning at zero (when production is zero) and increasing at different rates as volume increases.

One example of a curvilinear cost is total direct labor cost. At low levels of production, employees can specialize in certain tasks. This efficiency results in a flatter slope in the curvilinear cost graph at lower levels of production in Exhibit 5.3. At some point, adding more employees creates inefficiencies (they get in each other's way or do not have special skills). This inefficiency is reflected in a steeper slope at higher levels of production in the curvilinear cost graph in Exhibit 5.3.

In CVP analysis, step-wise costs are usually treated as either fixed or variable costs. Likewise, curvilinear costs are typically treated as variable costs, and thus remain constant per unit. These treatments involve manager judgment and depend on the width of the relevant range and the expected volume.

Determine whether each of the following is best described as a fixed, variable, mixed, step-wise, or curvilinear cost as the number of product units changes.

NEED-TO-KNOW **5-1**

Classifying Costs

C1

	Type of Cost
Rubber used to manufacture tennis balls	a. _____
Depreciation (straight-line method).	b. _____
Electricity usage	c. _____
Supervisory salaries	d. _____
A salesperson's commission is 7% for sales of up to $100,000, and 10% of sales for sales above $100,000	e. _____

Solution

a. variable **b.** fixed **c.** mixed **d.** fixed* **e.** curvilinear

_____
*If more shifts are added, then supervisory salaries behave like a step-wise cost with respect to the number of shifts.

Do More: QS 5-1, QS 5-2, E 5-1, E 5-2, E 5-3

MEASURING COST BEHAVIOR

Identifying and measuring cost behavior requires analysis and judgment. A key part of this process is to classify costs as either fixed or variable, which often requires analysis of past cost behavior. A goal of classifying costs is to develop a *cost equation*. The cost equation expresses total costs as a function of total fixed costs plus variable cost per unit. Three methods are commonly used:

- Scatter diagram
- High-low method
- Regression

P1_____

Determine cost estimates using the scatter diagram, high-low, and regression methods of estimating costs.

Each method is explained using the unit and cost data shown in Exhibit 5.4, which are from a start-up company that uses units produced as the activity base in estimating cost behavior.

EXHIBIT 5.4

Data for Estimating Cost Behavior

Month	Units Produced	Total Cost
January	27,500	$21,500
February	22,500	20,500
March	25,000	25,000
April.	35,000	21,500
May	47,500	25,500
June.	17,500	18,500
July	30,000	23,500
August.	52,500	28,500
September	37,500	26,000
October.	62,500	29,000
November.	67,500	31,000
December	57,500	26,000

Scatter Diagram

A **scatter diagram** is a graph of unit volume and cost data. Units are plotted on the horizontal axis and costs are plotted on the vertical axis. Each point on a scatter diagram reflects the cost and number of units for a prior period. In Exhibit 5.5a, the prior 12 months' costs and units are graphed. Each point reflects total costs incurred and units produced in that month. For instance, the point labeled March had units produced of 25,000 and costs of $25,000.

EXHIBIT 5.5a

Scatter Diagram

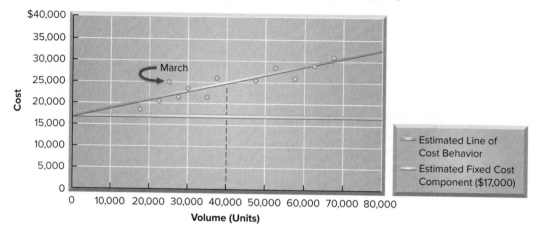

The **estimated line of cost behavior** is drawn on a scatter diagram to reflect the relation between cost and unit volume. This line best visually "fits" the points in a scatter diagram. Fitting this line demands judgment, or can be done with spreadsheet software, as we illustrate in Appendix 5A. The line drawn in Exhibit 5.5a intersects the vertical axis at approximately $17,000, which reflects fixed cost. To compute variable cost per unit, follow three steps:

Step 1: Select any two levels of units produced, say 0 and 25,000.

Step 2: Identify total costs at those production levels (at zero units of output, total costs equal fixed costs of $17,000; at 25,000 units of output, total costs equal $25,000).

Step 3: Compute the *slope* of the line, which is the change in cost divided by the change in units. This is the estimated variable cost per unit.

This computation is shown in Exhibit 5.5b.

EXHIBIT 5.5b

Variable Cost per Unit—
Scatter Diagram

Example: If units are projected at 30,000, what is the predicted cost? *Answer:* Approximately $26,600.

$$\frac{\text{Change in cost}}{\text{Change in units}} = \frac{\$25,000 - \$17,000}{25,000 - 0} = \frac{\$8,000}{25,000} = \$0.32 \text{ per unit}$$

Variable cost is $0.32 per unit. Thus, the cost equation that management will use to estimate costs for different unit levels is **$17,000 plus $0.32 per unit produced.**

High-Low Method

The **high-low method** is a way to estimate the cost equation using just two points: the highest and lowest *volume* levels. The high-low method follows three steps:

Step 1: Identify the highest and lowest volume levels. These might not be the highest or lowest levels of *costs*.

Step 2: Compute the slope (variable cost per unit) using the high and low volume levels.

Step 3: Compute the total fixed costs by computing the total variable cost at either the high or low volume level, and then subtracting that amount from the total cost at that volume level.

We illustrate the high-low method next.

Step 1: In our case, the lowest number of units is 17,500 and the highest is 67,500. The costs corresponding to these unit volumes are $18,500 and $31,000, respectively (see the data in Exhibit 5.4).

Step 2: The variable cost per unit is calculated using a simple formula: change in cost divided by the change in units. Using the data from the high and low unit volumes, this results in a slope, or variable cost per unit, of $0.25 as computed in Exhibit 5.6.

$$\frac{\text{Change in cost}}{\text{Change in units}} = \frac{\$31,000 - \$18,500}{67,500 - 17,500} = \frac{\$12,500}{50,000} = \$0.25 \text{ per unit}$$

EXHIBIT 5.6

Variable Cost per Unit—
High-Low Method

Step 3: To estimate the fixed cost for the high-low method, we use the knowledge that total cost equals fixed cost plus variable cost per unit times the number of units. Then we pick either the high or low point (based on volume) to determine the fixed cost. This computation is shown in Exhibit 5.7—where we use the high point (67,500 units) in determining the fixed cost of $14,125. (Use of the low point yields the same fixed cost estimate.)

Total cost = Fixed cost + (Variable cost per unit × Units)

$31,000 = Fixed cost + ($0.25 per unit × 67,500 units)

$31,000 = Fixed cost + $16,875

$14,125 = Fixed cost

EXHIBIT 5.7

Determining Fixed Costs—
High-Low Method

Thus, the cost equation from the high-low method is **$14,125 plus $0.25 per unit produced**. This cost equation differs from that determined from the scatter diagram method. A weakness of the high-low method is that it ignores all data points except the highest and lowest volume levels.

Example: Using information from Exhibit 5.7, what is the amount of fixed cost at the low level of volume? *Answer:* $14,125, computed as $18,500 − ($0.25 × 17,500 units).

Regression

Least-squares regression, or simply *regression*, is a statistical method for identifying cost behavior. We use the cost equation estimated from this method but leave the computational details for advanced courses. Computations for least-squares regression are readily done using most spreadsheet programs or calculators. We illustrate this using Excel in Appendix A of this chapter. Using least-squares regression, the cost equation for the data presented in Exhibit 5.4 is **$16,688 plus $0.20 per unit produced**; that is, the fixed cost is estimated as $16,688 and the variable cost at $0.20 per unit.

Comparing Cost Estimation Methods

The three cost estimation methods result in different estimates of fixed and variable costs, as summarized in Exhibit 5.8. Estimates from the scatter diagram, unless done with spreadsheet software, are based on a visual fit of the cost line and are subject to interpretation. Estimates from the high-low method use only two sets of values corresponding to the lowest and highest unit volumes. Sometimes these two extreme activity levels do not reflect the more usual conditions likely to recur. Estimates from least-squares regression use a statistical technique and all available data points.

Estimation Method	Fixed Cost	Variable Cost
Scatter diagram	$17,000	$0.32 per unit
High-low method	14,125	0.25 per unit
Regression	16,688	0.20 per unit

EXHIBIT 5.8

Comparison of Cost
Estimation Methods

All three methods use *past data.* Thus, cost estimates resulting from these methods are only as good as the data used. Managers must establish that the data are reliable. If the data are reliable, the use of more data points, as in the regression or scatter diagram methods, should yield more accurate estimates than the high-low method. However, the high-low method is easier to apply and thus might be useful for obtaining a quick cost equation estimate.

 **5-2**

High-Low Method

P1

Using the information below, apply the high-low method to determine the *cost equation* (total fixed costs plus variable costs per unit).

Volume	Units Produced	Total Cost
Lowest.............	1,600	$ 9,800
Highest	4,000	17,000

Solution

The variable cost per unit is computed as: [$17,000 − $9,800]/[4,000 units − 1,600 units] = $3 per unit. Total fixed costs using the lowest activity level are computed from the following equation: $9,800 = Fixed costs + ($3 × 1,600 units); thus, fixed costs = $5,000. This implies the cost equation is **$5,000 plus $3 per unit produced.** We can prove the accuracy of this cost equation at either the highest or lowest point shown here.

Highest point:
Total cost = $5,000 + ($3 per unit × 4,000 units)
          = $5,000 + $12,000
          = $17,000

Lowest point:
Total cost = $5,000 + ($3 per unit × 1,600 units)
          = $5,000 + $4,800
          = $9,800

Do More: QS 5-3, E 5-6

CONTRIBUTION MARGIN AND BREAK-EVEN ANALYSIS

This section explains *contribution margin,* a key measure in CVP analysis. We also discuss break-even analysis, an important special case of CVP analysis.

Contribution Margin and Its Measures

A1

Compute the contribution margin and describe what it reveals about a company's cost structure.

After classifying costs as fixed or variable, we can compute **contribution margin,** which equals total sales minus total variable costs. Contribution margin contributes to covering fixed costs and generating profits. **Contribution margin per unit,** or *unit contribution margin,* is the amount by which a product's unit selling price exceeds its variable cost per unit. Exhibit 5.9 shows the formula for contribution margin per unit.

EXHIBIT 5.9

Contribution Margin per Unit

$$\text{Contribution margin per unit} = \text{Selling price per unit} - \text{Total variable cost per unit}$$

Contribution margin ratio is the percent of a unit's selling price that exceeds total unit variable cost. It is interpreted as the percent of each sales dollar that remains after deducting the unit variable cost. Exhibit 5.10 shows the formula for contribution margin ratio.

EXHIBIT 5.10

Contribution Margin Ratio

$$\text{Contribution margin ratio} = \frac{\text{Contribution margin per unit}}{\text{Selling price per unit}}$$

To illustrate contribution margin, consider Rydell, which sells footballs for $100 each and incurs variable costs of $70 per football sold. Its fixed costs are $24,000 per month with monthly capacity of 1,800 units (footballs). Rydell's contribution margin per unit is $30, which is computed as follows.

AP Images/Skip Peterson

Selling price per unit	$100
Variable cost per unit...................	70
Contribution margin per unit	$ 30

This means at a selling price of $100 per football, Rydell covers its per unit variable costs and makes $30 per unit to contribute to fixed costs and profit. Rydell's contribution margin ratio is 30%, computed as $30/$100. A contribution margin ratio of 30% implies that for each $1 in sales, Rydell has $0.30 that contributes to fixed cost and profit. Next we show how to use these contribution margin measures in break-even analysis.

Decision Maker

Sales Manager   You can accept only one of two customer orders due to limited capacity. The first order is for 100 units with a contribution margin ratio of 60% and a selling price of $1,000 per unit. The second order is for 500 units with a contribution margin ratio of 20% and a selling price of $800 per unit. Incremental fixed costs are the same for both orders. Which order do you accept? ■   *Answer:* The contribution margin per unit for the first order is $600 (60% of $1,000); the contribution margin per unit for the second order is $160 (20% of $800). You are likely tempted to accept the first order based on its higher contribution margin per unit, but you must compute the *total* contribution margin for each order. Total contribution margin is $60,000 ($600 per unit × 100 units) and $80,000 ($160 per unit × 500 units) for the two orders, respectively. The second order provides the largest return in absolute dollars and is the order you would accept. Another factor to consider in your selection is the potential for a long-term relationship with these customers including repeat sales and growth.

Break-Even Point

The **break-even point** is the sales level at which total sales equal total costs and a company neither earns a profit nor incurs a loss. Break-even applies to nearly all organizations, activities, and events. A key concern when launching a project is whether it will break even—that is, whether sales will at least cover total costs. The break-even point can be expressed in either units or dollars of sales. To illustrate break-even analysis, let's again look at Rydell, which sells footballs for $100 per unit and incurs $70 of variable costs per unit sold. Its fixed costs are $24,000 per month. Three different methods are used to find the break-even point.

- Formula method
- Contribution margin income statement
- Cost-volume-profit chart

Formula Method   We compute the break-even point using the formula in Exhibit 5.11. This formula uses the contribution margin per unit (calculated above), which for Rydell is $30 ($100 − $70). The break-even sales volume in units is:

$$\text{Break-even point in units} = \frac{\text{Fixed costs}}{\text{Contribution margin per unit}}$$
$$= \$24{,}000/\$30$$
$$= 800 \text{ units per month}$$

If Rydell sells 800 units, its profit will be zero. Profit increases or decreases by $30 for every unit sold above or below that break-even point; if Rydell sells 801 units, profit will equal $30. We also can calculate the break-even point in dollars. Also called *break-even sales dollars,* it uses the contribution margin ratio to determine the required sales dollars needed for the company to break even. Exhibit 5.12 shows the formula and Rydell's break-even point in dollars:

$$\text{Break-even point in dollars} = \frac{\text{Fixed costs}}{\text{Contribution margin ratio}}$$
$$= \$24{,}000/30\%$$
$$= \$24{,}000/0.30$$
$$= \$80{,}000 \text{ of monthly sales}$$

P2

Compute the break-even point for a single product company.

Point: Selling prices and variable costs are usually expressed in per unit amounts. Fixed costs are usually expressed in total amounts.

EXHIBIT 5.11

Formula for Computing Break-Even Sales (in Units)

Point: Even if a company operates at a level above its break-even point, management may decide to stop operating because it is not earning a reasonable return on investment.

EXHIBIT 5.12

Formula for Computing Break-Even Sales (in Dollars)

EXHIBIT 5.13

Contribution Margin Income Statement for Break-Even Sales

Income Statement (Traditional)

Sales.	$#
Cost of sales	#
Gross profit	#
Selling and admin.	#
Income (pretax).	$#

COMPANY
Contribution Margin Income Statement Format

Sales
− Variable costs
Contribution margin
− Fixed costs
Income (pretax)

RYDELL COMPANY
Contribution Margin Income Statement (at Break-Even)
For Month Ended January 31, 2017

Sales (800 units at $100 each)	$80,000
Variable costs (800 units at $70 each)	56,000
Contribution margin (800 units at $30 each) . . .	24,000
Fixed costs	24,000
Income (pretax).	$ 0

Contribution Margin Income Statement Method   The left side of Exhibit 5.13 shows the general format of a *contribution margin income statement*. It differs in format from a traditional income statement in two ways. First, it separately classifies costs and expenses as variable or fixed. Second, it reports contribution margin (sales − variable costs).

The right side of Exhibit 5.13 uses this format to find the break-even point for Rydell. To use this method, set income equal to zero and work up the income statement to find sales. Rydell's contribution margin must exactly equal its fixed costs of $24,000. For Rydell's contribution margin to equal $24,000, it must sell 800 units ($24,000/$30). The resulting contribution margin income statement shows that the $80,000 revenue from sales of 800 units exactly equals the sum of variable and fixed costs.

NEED-TO-KNOW 5-3

Contribution Margin and Break-Even Point

A1   P2

Hudson Co. predicts fixed costs of $400,000 for 2017. Its one product sells for $170 per unit, and it incurs variable costs of $150 per unit. The company predicts total sales of 25,000 units for the next year.

1. Compute the contribution margin per unit.
2. Compute the break-even point (in units) using the formula method.
3. Prepare a contribution margin income statement at the break-even point.

Solution

1. Contribution margin per unit = $170 − $150 = $20
2. Break-even point = $400,000/$20 = 20,000 units
3.

HUDSON CO.
Contribution Margin Income Statement (at Break-Even)
For Year Ended December 31, 2017

Sales (20,000 units at $170 each).	$3,400,000
Variable costs (20,000 units at $150 each)	3,000,000
Contribution margin (20,000 units at $20 each) . . .	400,000
Fixed costs	400,000
Income (pretax).	$ 0

Do More: QS 5-5, QS 5-6, QS 5-10, E 5-8, E 5-9, E 5-16

P3

Graph costs and sales for a single product company.

Point: CVP charts can also be drawn with computer programs.

Cost-Volume-Profit Chart

A third way to find the break-even point is to make a **cost-volume-profit (CVP) chart** (*break-even chart*). Exhibit 5.14 shows Rydell's CVP chart. In a CVP chart, the horizontal axis is the number of units produced and sold, and the vertical axis is dollars of sales and costs. The lines in the chart show both sales and costs at different output levels.

We follow three steps to prepare a CVP chart:

◇ **Plot fixed costs on the vertical axis** ($24,000 for Rydell). Draw a horizontal line at this level to show that fixed costs remain unchanged regardless of output volume (drawing this fixed cost line is not essential to the chart).

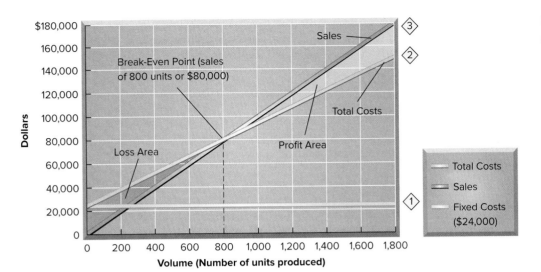

EXHIBIT 5.14

Cost-Volume-Profit Chart

⟨2⟩ **Draw the total (variable plus fixed) cost line for a relevant range of volume levels.** This line starts at the fixed costs level on the vertical axis because total costs equal fixed costs at zero volume. The slope of the total cost line equals the variable cost per unit ($70). To draw the line, compute the total costs for any volume level and connect this point with the vertical axis intercept ($24,000). For example, if 1,800 units are produced and sold, then total costs are $150,000. Do not draw this line beyond the productive capacity for the planning period (1,800 units for Rydell).

⟨3⟩ **Draw the sales line.** Start at the origin (zero units and zero dollars of sales) and make the slope of this line equal to the selling price per unit ($100). To draw the line, compute dollar sales for any volume level and connect this point with the origin. For example, if 1,800 units are sold, then total sales are $180,000. Do not extend this line beyond the productive capacity. Total sales will be highest at maximum capacity.

The total cost line and the sales line intersect at 800 units in Exhibit 5.14, which is the break-even point—the point where total dollar sales of $80,000 equals the sum of both fixed and variable costs ($80,000). (The 800 units is the same result from the formula in Exhibit 5.11 and from the contribution margin income statement in Exhibit 5.13.)

On either side of the break-even point, the vertical distance between the sales line and the total cost line at any specific volume is the profit or loss expected at that point. At volume levels to the left of the break-even point, this vertical distance is the amount of the expected loss because the total costs line is above the total sales line. At volume levels to the right of the break-even point, this vertical distance is the expected profit because the total sales line is above the total cost line.

Changes in Estimates   CVP analysis uses estimates, and knowing how changes in those estimates impact break-even is useful. For example, a manager might form three estimates for each of the inputs of break-even: optimistic, most likely, and pessimistic. Then ranges of break-even points in units can be computed, using any of the three methods shown above. To illustrate, assume Rydell's managers provide the estimates in Exhibit 5.15.

Point: CVP analysis is often based on *sales volume*, using either units sold or dollar sales. Other output measures, such as the number of units produced, can also be used.

Example: In Exhibit 5.14, the sales line intersects the total cost line at 800 units. At what point would the two lines intersect if selling price is increased by 20% to $120 per unit? *Answer:* $24,000/($120 − $70) = 480 units

EXHIBIT 5.15

Alternative Estimates for Break-Even Analysis

	Selling Price per Unit	Variable Cost per Unit	Total Fixed Costs
Optimistic...........	$105	$68	$21,000
Most likely...........	100	70	24,000
Pessimistic..........	95	72	27,000

If, for example, Rydell's managers believe they can raise the selling price of a football to $105, without any change in unit variable or total fixed costs, then the revised contribution margin per football is $35 ($105 − $70), and the revised break-even in units follows in Exhibit 5.16.

EXHIBIT 5.16

Revised Break-Even in Units

$$\text{Revised break-even point in units} = \frac{\$24,000}{\$35} = 686 \text{ units (rounded)}$$

EXHIBIT 5.17

Break-Even Points for Alternative Estimates

Repeating this calculation using each of the other eight separate estimates above (keeping other estimates unchanged from their original amounts), and graphing the results, yields the three graphs in Exhibit 5.17.

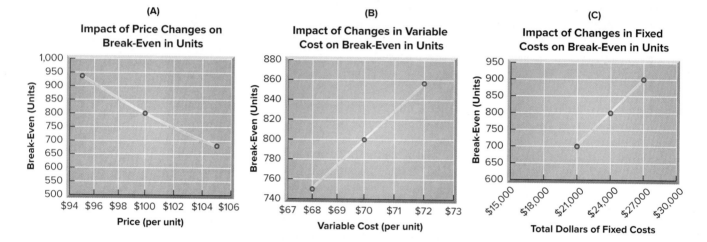

These graphs show how changes in selling prices, variable costs, and fixed costs impact break-even. When selling prices can be increased without impacting unit variable costs or total fixed costs, break-even decreases (graph A). When competition reduces selling prices, and the company cannot reduce costs, break-even increases (graph A). Increases in either variable (graph B) or fixed costs (graph C), if they cannot be passed on to customers via higher selling prices, will increase break-even. If costs can be reduced and selling prices held constant, the break-even point decreases.

Point: This analysis changed only one estimate at a time; managers can examine how combinations of changes in estimates impact break-even.

■ **Decision Ethics**

Supervisor   Your team is conducting a CVP analysis for a new product. Different sales projections have different incomes. One member suggests picking numbers yielding favorable income because any estimate is "as good as any other." Another member suggests dropping unfavorable data points for cost estimation. What do you do? ■   *Answer:* Your dilemma is whether to go along with the suggestions to "manage" the numbers to make the project look like it will achieve sufficient profits. You should not succumb to these suggestions. Many people will likely be affected negatively if you manage the predicted numbers and the project eventually is unprofitable. Moreover, if it does fail, an investigation would likely reveal that data in the proposal were "fixed" to make the proposal look good. One way to deal with this dilemma is to prepare several analyses showing results under different assumptions and then let senior management make the decision.

APPLYING COST-VOLUME-PROFIT ANALYSIS

Managers consider a variety of strategies in planning business operations. Cost-volume-profit analysis is useful in helping managers evaluate the likely effects of these strategies.

C2

Describe several applications of cost-volume-profit analysis.

Margin of Safety

All companies wish to do more than break even. The excess of expected sales over the break-even sales level is called **margin of safety,** the amount that sales can drop before the company incurs a loss. It is often expressed in dollars or as a percent of the expected sales level.

To illustrate, Rydell's break-even point in dollars is $80,000. If its expected sales are $100,000, the margin of safety is $20,000 ($100,000 − $80,000). As a percent, the margin of safety is 20% of expected sales, as shown in Exhibit 5.18.

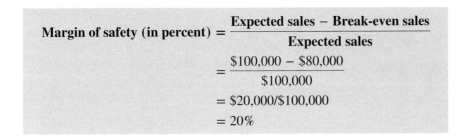

$$\text{Margin of safety (in percent)} = \frac{\text{Expected sales} - \text{Break-even sales}}{\text{Expected sales}}$$

$$= \frac{\$100,000 - \$80,000}{\$100,000}$$

$$= \$20,000 / \$100,000$$

$$= 20\%$$

EXHIBIT 5.18

Computing Margin of Safety (in Percent)

Management must assess whether the margin of safety is adequate in light of factors such as sales variability, competition, consumer tastes, and economic conditions.

Computing Income from Sales and Costs

Managers often use contribution margin income statements to forecast future sales or income. Exhibit 5.19 shows the key variables in CVP analysis—sales, variable costs, contribution margin, and fixed costs, and their relations to income (pretax). To answer the question "What is the predicted income from a predicted level of sales?" we work our way down this income statement to compute income.

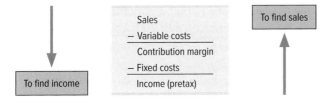

EXHIBIT 5.19

Income Relations in CVP Analysis

To illustrate, assume Rydell's management expects to sell 1,500 units in January 2017. What is the amount of income if this sales level is achieved? We first compute dollar sales, and then use the format in Exhibit 5.19 to compute Rydell's expected income in Exhibit 5.20. This $21,000 income amount can also be computed as (units sold × contribution margin per unit) − fixed costs, or (1,500 × $30) − $24,000. The $21,000 income is pretax.

Point: 1,500 units of sales is 700 units above Rydell's break-even point. Income can also be computed as 700 units × $30 contribution margin per unit.

EXHIBIT 5.20

Computing Expected Pretax Income from Expected Sales

RYDELL COMPANY	
Contribution Margin Income Statement (Pretax)	
For Month Ended January 31, 2017	
Sales (1,500 units at $100 each)	$150,000
Variable costs (1,500 units at $70 each)	105,000
Contribution margin (1,500 units at $30 each)	45,000
Fixed costs	24,000
Income (pretax)	$ 21,000

Computing After-Tax Income   To find the amount of *after-tax* income from selling 1,500 units, management uses the tax rate. Assume that the tax rate is 25%. Then we can prepare a projected after-tax income statement, shown in Exhibit 5.21. After-tax income can also be computed as: pretax income × (1 − tax rate).

EXHIBIT 5.21

Computing Expected
After-Tax Income from
Expected Sales

RYDELL COMPANY	
Contribution Margin Income Statement (After-Tax)	
For Month Ended January 31, 2017	
Sales (1,500 units at $100 each)	$150,000
Variable costs (1,500 units at $70 each)	105,000
Contribution margin (1,500 units at $30 each)	45,000
Fixed costs	24,000
Pretax income	21,000
Income taxes ($21,000 × 25%)	5,250
Net income (after tax)	$ 15,750

Point: Pretax income
= $15,750/(1 − 0.25), or $21,000.

"How many units must we sell to earn $50,000?"

Management then assesses whether this income is an adequate return on assets invested. Management will also consider whether sales and income can be increased by raising or lowering prices. CVP analysis is good for addressing these kinds of "what-if" questions.

Computing Sales for a Target Income

Many companies' annual plans are based on income targets (sometimes called *budgets*). Rydell's goal for this year is to increase income by 10% over the prior year. CVP analysis helps to determine the sales level needed to achieve the target income. Planning for the year is then based on this level.

We use the formula in Exhibit 5.22 to compute sales for a target income (pretax). To illustrate, Rydell has monthly fixed costs of $24,000 and a 30% contribution margin ratio. Assume that it sets a target monthly income of $12,000. Using the formula in Exhibit 5.22, we find that Rydell needs $120,000 of sales to produce a $12,000 pretax target income.

EXHIBIT 5.22

Computing Sales (Dollars)
for a Target Income

$$\text{Dollar sales at target income} = \frac{\text{Fixed costs} + \text{Target income (pretax)}}{\text{Contribution margin ratio}}$$

$$= \frac{\$24,000 + \$12,000}{30\%} = \$120,000$$

Point: Break-even is a special case of the formulas in Exhibits 5.22 and 5.23; simply set target income to $0, and the formulas reduce to those in Exhibits 5.11 and 5.12.

Alternatively, we can compute *unit sales* instead of dollar sales. To do this, use *contribution margin per unit*. Exhibit 5.23 illustrates this for Rydell. The two computations in Exhibits 5.22 and 5.23 are equivalent because sales of 1,200 units at $100 per unit equal $120,000 of sales.

EXHIBIT 5.23

Computing Sales (Units) for
a Target Income

$$\text{Unit sales at target income} = \frac{\text{Fixed costs} + \text{Target income (pretax)}}{\text{Contribution margin per unit}}$$

$$= \frac{\$24,000 + \$12,000}{\$30} = 1,200 \text{ units}$$

We can also use the contribution margin income statement approach to compute sales for a target income in two steps.

Step 1: Insert the fixed costs ($24,000) and the target profit level ($12,000) into a contribution margin income statement, as shown in Exhibit 5.24. To cover its fixed costs of $24,000 and yield target income of $12,000, Rydell must generate a contribution margin of $36,000 (computed as $24,000 plus $12,000).

Step 2: Enter $36,000 in the contribution margin row as step 2. With a contribution margin ratio of 30%, sales must be $120,000, computed as $36,000/0.30, to yield a contribution margin of $36,000. We enter $120,000 in the sales row of the contribution margin income statement and solve for variable costs of $84,000 (computed as $120,000 − $36,000). At a selling price of $100 per unit, Rydell must sell 1,200 units ($120,000/$100) to earn a target income of $12,000.

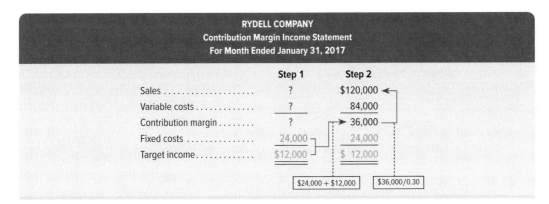

EXHIBIT 5.24

Using the Contribution Margin Income Statement to Find Target Sales

---

A manufacturer predicts fixed costs of $502,000 for the next year. Its one product sells for $180 per unit, and it incurs variable costs of $126 per unit. Its target (pretax) income is $200,000.

1. Compute the contribution margin ratio.
2. Compute the dollar sales needed to yield the target income.
3. Compute the unit sales needed to yield the target income.
4. Assume break-even sales of 9,296 units. Compute the margin of safety (in dollars) if the company expects to sell 10,000 units.

NEED-TO-KNOW 5-4

Contribution Margin, Target Income, and Margin of Safety

A1   C2

Solution

1. Contribution margin ratio = [$180 − $126]/$180 = 30%
2. Dollar sales at target income = [$502,000 + $200,000]/0.30 = $2,340,000
3. Unit sales at target income = [$502,000 + $200,000]/[$180 − $126] = 13,000 units
4. Margin of safety = (10,000 × $180) − (9,296 × $180) = $126,720

Do More: QS 5-9, QS 5-11, QS 5-13, E 5-12, E 5-17

Evaluating Strategies

Earlier we showed how changing one of the estimates in a CVP analysis impacts break-even. We can examine strategies that impact several estimates in the CVP analysis. For instance, we might want to know what happens to income if we automate a currently manual process. We can use *sensitivity analysis* to predict income if we can describe how these changes affect a company's fixed costs, variable costs, selling price, and volume. CVP analyses based on different estimates can be useful to management in planning business strategy. We provide some examples.

Buy a Productive Asset   Assume Rydell is considering buying a new machine that would increase monthly fixed costs from $24,000 to $30,000 and would decrease variable costs by $10 per unit (from $70 per unit to $60 per unit). Rydell's break-even point in dollars is currently $80,000. How would the new machine affect Rydell's break-even point in dollars? If Rydell maintains its selling price of $100 per unit, its contribution margin per unit will increase to $40—computed as the sales price of $100 per unit minus the (new) variable costs of $60 per unit. With this new machine, the revised contribution margin ratio per unit is 40% (computed as $40/$100). Rydell's revised break-even point in dollars would be $75,000, as computed in Exhibit 5.25. The new machine would lower Rydell's break-even point by $5,000, or 50 units, per month. The revised margin of safety increases to 25%, computed as ($100,000 − $75,000)/$100,000.

EXHIBIT 5.25

Revised Break-Even

$$\text{Revised break-even point in dollars} = \frac{\text{Revised fixed costs}}{\text{Revised contribution margin ratio}} = \frac{\$30,000}{40\%} = \$75,000$$

Increase Operating Expense   Instead of buying a new machine, Rydell's advertising manager suggests increasing advertising instead. She believes that an increase of $3,000 in the monthly advertising budget will increase sales by $25,000 per month (at a selling price of $100 per unit). The contribution margin will continue to be $30 per unit. Exhibit 5.8 showed the company's margin of safety was 20% when Rydell's expected sales level was $100,000. With the advertising campaign, Rydell's revised break-even point in dollars is $90,000, as computed in Exhibit 5.26.

EXHIBIT 5.26

Revised Break-Even (in Dollars)

$$\text{Revised break-even point in dollars} = \frac{\text{Revised fixed costs}}{\text{Revised contribution margin ratio}} = \frac{\$27,000}{30\%} = \$90,000$$

The revised margin of safety is computed in Exhibit 5.27. Without considering other factors, the advertising campaign would increase Rydell's margin of safety from 20% to 28%.

EXHIBIT 5.27

Revised Margin of Safety (in Percent)

$$\text{Revised margin of safety (in percent)} = \frac{\text{Expected sales} - \text{Break-even sales}}{\text{Expected sales}}$$
$$= \frac{\$125,000 - \$90,000}{\$125,000} = 28\%$$

Sales Mix and Break-Even

P4

Compute the break-even point for a multiproduct company.

© Kali9/E+/Getty Images

So far we have looked only at cases where the company sells a single product or service. However, many companies sell multiple products or services, and we can modify the CVP analysis for these cases. An important assumption in a multiproduct setting is that the sales mix of different products is known and remains constant during the planning period. **Sales mix** is the ratio (proportion) of the sales volumes for the various products. For instance, if a company normally sells 10,000 footballs, 5,000 softballs, and 4,000 basketballs per month, its sales mix can be expressed as 10:5:4 for footballs, softballs, and basketballs.

When companies sell more than one product or service, we estimate the break-even point by using a **composite unit,** which summarizes the sales mix and contribution margins of each product. Multiproduct CVP analysis treats this composite unit as a single product. To illustrate, let's look at Hair-Today, a styling salon that offers three cuts: basic, ultra, and budget in the ratio of 4 basic cuts to 2 ultra cuts to 1 budget cut (expressed as 4:2:1). Management wants to estimate its break-even point for next year. Unit selling prices for these three cuts are basic, $20; ultra, $32; and budget, $16. Unit variable costs for these three cuts are basic, $13; ultra, $18; and budget, $8. Using the 4:2:1 sales mix, the selling price and variable costs of a composite unit of the three products are computed as follows.

Selling price per composite unit	
4 units of basic @ $20 per unit	$ 80
2 units of ultra @ $32 per unit	64
1 unit of budget @ $16 per unit.	16
Selling price of a composite unit.	**$160**

Variable costs per composite unit	
4 units of basic @ $13 per unit	$52
2 units of ultra @ $18 per unit	36
1 unit of budget @ $8 per unit.	8
Variable costs of a composite unit.	**$96**

We compute the contribution margin for a *composite unit* using essentially the same formula used earlier (see Exhibit 5.9), as shown in Exhibit 5.28:

Contribution margin per composite unit	=	Selling price per composite unit	−	Variable cost per composite unit
$64	=	$160	−	$96

EXHIBIT 5.28

Contribution Margin per Composite Unit

Assuming Hair-Today's fixed costs are $192,000 per year, we compute its break-even point in composite units in Exhibit 5.29.

$$\text{Break-even point in composite units} = \frac{\text{Fixed costs}}{\text{Contribution margin per composite unit}}$$

$$= \frac{\$192,000}{\$64} = 3,000 \text{ composite units}$$

EXHIBIT 5.29

Break-Even Point in Composite Units

This computation implies that Hair-Today breaks even when it sells 3,000 *composite* units. Each composite unit represents seven haircuts. To determine how many units of each product it must sell to break even, we use the expected sales mix of 4:2:1 and multiply the number of units of each product in the composite by 3,000, as follows.

Point: The break-even point in dollars for Exhibit 5.29 is $192,000/($64/$160) = $480,000.

Basic:	4 × 3,000	12,000 units
Ultra:	2 × 3,000	6,000 units
Budget:	1 × 3,000	3,000 units
	7 × 3,000	21,000 units

Exhibit 5.30 verifies that with this sales mix and unit sales computed above, Hair-Today would break even.

	Basic	Ultra	Budget	Total
Contribution margin				
Basic (12,000 @ $7).	$84,000			
Ultra (6,000 @ $14)		$84,000		
Budget (3,000 @ $8)			$24,000	
Total contribution margin				$192,000
Fixed costs				192,000
Net income				$ 0

EXHIBIT 5.30

Multiproduct Break-Even Income

If the sales mix changes, the break-even point will likely change. For example, if Hair-Today sells more ultra cuts and fewer basic cuts, its break-even point will decrease. We can vary the sales mix to see what happens under alternative strategies.

For companies that sell many different products, multiproduct break-even computations can become hard. **Amazon**, for example, sells over 200 million different products. In such cases, managers can group these products into departments (such as clothing, sporting goods, music) and compute department contribution margins. The department contribution margins and the sales mix can be used as we illustrate in this section.

Point: Enterprise resource planning (ERP) systems can quickly generate multiproduct break-even analyses.

Decision Maker

Entrepreneur CVP analysis indicates that your start-up will break even with the current sales mix and price levels. You have a target income in mind. What analysis might you perform to assess the likelihood of achieving this income?

■ *Answer:* First compute the level of sales to achieve the desired net income. Then conduct sensitivity analysis by varying the price, sales mix, and cost estimates to assess the possibility of reaching the target sales level. For instance, you might have to pursue aggressive marketing strategies to push the high-margin products, you might have to cut prices to increase sales and profits, or another strategy might emerge.

NEED-TO-KNOW 5-5

Contribution Margin and
Break-Even Point,
Composite Units

P4

The sales mix of a company's two products, X and Y, is 2:1. Unit variable costs for both products are $2, and unit selling prices are $5 for X and $4 for Y. The company has $640,000 of fixed costs.

1. What is the contribution margin per composite unit?
2. What is the break-even point in composite units?
3. How many units of X and how many units of Y will be sold at the break-even point?

Solution

1.

Selling price of a composite unit		Variable costs of a composite unit	
2 units of X @ $5 per unit..................	$10	2 units of X @ $2 per unit...................	$4
1 unit of Y @ $4 per unit...................	4	1 unit of Y @ $2 per unit...................	2
Selling price of a composite unit.............	$14	Variable costs of a composite unit	$6

Do More: QS 5-14,
E 5-22, E 5-23

Therefore, the contribution margin per composite unit is $8.

2. The break-even point in composite units = $640,000/$8 = 80,000 units.
3. At break-even, the company will sell 160,000 units (80,000 × 2) of X and 80,000 units of Y (80,000 × 1).

Assumptions in Cost-Volume-Profit Analysis

CVP analysis relies on several assumptions:

- Costs can be classified as variable or fixed.
- Costs are linear within the relevant range.
- All units produced are sold (inventory levels do not change).
- Sales mix is constant.

If costs and sales differ from these assumptions, the results of CVP analysis can be less useful. Managers understand that CVP analysis gives approximate answers to questions and enables them to make rough estimates about the future.

SUSTAINABILITY AND ACCOUNTING

Manufacturers try to increase the sustainability of their materials and packaging. **Nike** recently reengineered its shoeboxes to use 30% less material. These lighter shoeboxes can be shipped in cartons that are 20% lighter.

Nike also now uses recycled polyester in much of its clothing. The company estimates it has reused the equivalent of 2 billion plastic bottles since 2010.

These and other sustainability initiatives impact both variable and fixed costs, and CVP analysis. Consider Rydell, the football manufacturer illustrated in this chapter. Rydell expects to sell 1,500 footballs per month, at a price of $100 per unit. Variable costs are $70 per unit and monthly fixed costs are $24,000. Rydell is considering using some recycled materials. This would add $1,160 in fixed costs per month and reduce variable costs by $4 per unit. Management wants to know how this initiative would impact the company's break-even point, margin of safety, and forecasted income. Relevant calculations follow.

$$\text{Revised break-even point in units} = \frac{\text{Revised fixed costs}}{\text{Revised contribution margin}} = \frac{\$25,160}{\$34} = 740 \text{ units}$$

$$\text{Revised margin of safety} = \frac{\text{Expected sales} - \text{Break-even sales}}{\text{Expected sales}} = \frac{\$150,000 - \$74,000}{\$150,000} = 50.7\%$$

$$\text{Revised forecasted income} = (\text{Units sold} \times \text{Contribution margin per unit}) - \text{Fixed costs}$$

$$= (1,500 \times \$34) - \$25,160 = \$25,840$$

Sweetgreen, this chapter's opening company, is devoted to sustainability. In addition to sourcing organic ingredients from local farmers, the tables in the company's restaurants (see photo here) are made from reclaimed wood and old bowling lanes.

Once a customer orders $100 of food through the company's app, Sweetgreen donates a percentage of future purchases to **FoodCorps**, a nonprofit organization devoted to providing healthy food for underprivileged students. "It takes a little more work and a little more money," explains Jon Neman, one of the company's founders, "but it's worth it!"

© Joshua Bright/The New York Times/Redux

Degree of Operating Leverage **Decision Analysis**

CVP analysis is especially useful when management begins the planning process and wishes to predict outcomes of alternative strategies. These strategies can involve changes in selling prices, fixed costs, variable costs, sales volume, and product mix. Managers are interested in seeing the effects of changes in some or all of these factors.

One goal of all managers is to get maximum benefits from their fixed costs. Managers would like to use 100% of their output capacity so that fixed costs are spread over the largest number of units. This would decrease fixed cost per unit and increase income. The extent, or relative size, of fixed costs in the total cost structure is known as **operating leverage.** Companies having a higher proportion of fixed costs in their total cost structure are said to have higher operating leverage. An example of this is a company that chooses to automate its processes instead of using direct labor, increasing its fixed costs and lowering its variable costs.

A useful managerial measure to help assess the effect of changes in the level of sales on income is the **degree of operating leverage (DOL),** calculated as shown in Exhibit 5.31.

A2

Analyze changes in sales using the degree of operating leverage.

$$\text{DOL} = \text{Total contribution margin (in dollars)}/\text{Pretax income}$$

EXHIBIT 5.31

Degree of Operating Leverage

To illustrate, assume Rydell Company sells 1,200 footballs. At this sales level, its contribution margin (in dollars) and pretax income are computed as:

Rydell Company	
Sales (1,200 × $100)	$120,000
Variable costs (1,200 × $70)	84,000
Contribution margin	36,000
Fixed costs	24,000
Income (pretax)	$ 12,000

Rydell's degree of operating leverage (DOL) is then computed as shown in Exhibit 5.32.

$$\text{DOL} = \text{Total contribution margin (in dollars)}/\text{Pretax income}$$
$$\text{DOL} = \$36,000/\$12,000 = 3.0$$

EXHIBIT 5.32

Rydell's Degree of Operating Leverage

We then can use DOL to measure the effect of changes in the level of sales on pretax income. For example, if Rydell expects sales can either increase or decrease by 10%, and these changes would be within Rydell's relevant range, we can compute the change in pretax income using DOL, as shown in Exhibit 5.33.

$$\text{Change in income (\%)} = \text{DOL} \times \text{Change in sales (\%)}$$
$$= 3.0 \times 10\%$$
$$= 30\%$$

EXHIBIT 5.33

Impact of Change in Sales on Income

Thus, if Rydell's sales *increase* by 10%, its income will increase by $3,600 (computed as $12,000 × 30%), to $15,600. If, instead, Rydell's sales decrease by 10%, its net income will decrease by $3,600, to $8,400. We can prove these results with contribution margin income statements, as shown below.

	Current	Sales Increase by 10%	Sales Decrease by 10%
Sales..........................	$120,000	$132,000	$108,000
Variable costs	84,000	92,400	75,600
Contribution margin	$ 36,000	$ 39,600	$ 32,400
Fixed costs.....................	24,000	24,000	24,000
Target (pretax) income	$ 12,000	$ 15,600	$ 8,400

COMPREHENSIVE

Sport Caps Co. manufactures and sells caps for different sporting events. The fixed costs of operating the company are $150,000 per month, and variable costs are $5 per cap. The caps are sold for $8 per unit. The production capacity is 100,000 caps per month.

Required

1. Use the formulas in the chapter to compute the following:
   a. Contribution margin per cap.
   b. Break-even point in terms of the number of caps produced and sold.
   c. Amount of income at 30,000 caps sold per month (ignore taxes).
   d. Amount of income at 85,000 caps sold per month (ignore taxes).
   e. Number of caps to be produced and sold to provide $60,000 of income (pretax).
2. Draw a CVP chart for the company, showing cap output on the horizontal axis. Identify (*a*) the break-even point and (*b*) the amount of pretax income when the level of cap production is 70,000. (Omit the fixed cost line.)
3. Use the formulas in the chapter to compute the
   a. Contribution margin ratio.
   b. Break-even point in terms of sales dollars.
   c. Amount of income at $250,000 of sales per month (ignore taxes).
   d. Amount of income at $600,000 of sales per month (ignore taxes).
   e. Dollars of sales needed to provide $60,000 of pretax income.

PLANNING THE SOLUTION

- Identify the formulas in the chapter for the required items expressed in units and solve them using the data given in the problem.
- Draw a CVP chart that reflects the facts in the problem. The horizontal axis should plot the volume in units up to 100,000, and the vertical axis should plot the total dollars up to $800,000. Plot the total cost line as upward sloping, starting at the fixed cost level ($150,000) on the vertical axis and increasing until it reaches $650,000 at the maximum volume of 100,000 units. Verify that the break-even point (where the two lines cross) equals the amount you computed in part 1.
- Identify the formulas in the chapter for the required items expressed in dollars and solve them using the data given in the problem.

SOLUTION

1. a. Contribution margin per cap $= \text{Selling price per unit} - \text{Variable cost per unit}$
$$= \$8 - \$5 = \$3$$

b. Break-even point in caps $= \dfrac{\text{Fixed costs}}{\text{Contribution margin per cap}} = \dfrac{\$150,000}{\$3} = 50,000 \text{ caps}$

c. Income at 30,000 caps sold

= (Units × Contribution margin per unit) − Fixed costs
= (30,000 × $3) − $150,000 = $(60,000) loss

d. Income at 85,000 caps sold

= (Units × Contribution margin per unit) − Fixed costs
= (85,000 × $3) − $150,000 = $105,000 profit

e. Units needed for $60,000 income $= \dfrac{\text{Fixed costs} + \text{Target income}}{\text{Contribution margin per cap}}$

$= \dfrac{\$150,000 + \$60,000}{\$3} = \underline{\underline{70,000 \text{ caps}}}$

2. CVP chart.

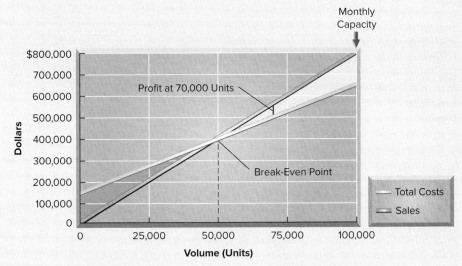

3. a. Contribution margin ratio $= \dfrac{\text{Contribution margin per unit}}{\text{Selling price per unit}} = \dfrac{\$3}{\$8} = \underline{0.375} \text{ or } \underline{37.5\%}$

b. Break-even point in dollars $= \dfrac{\text{Fixed costs}}{\text{Contribution margin ratio}} = \dfrac{\$150,000}{37.5\%} = \underline{\underline{\$400,000}}$

c. Income at sales of $250,000

= (Sales × Contribution margin ratio) − Fixed costs
= ($250,000 × 37.5%) − $150,000 = $(56,250) loss

d. Income at sales of $600,000

= (Sales × Contribution margin ratio) − Fixed costs
= ($600,000 × 37.5%) − $150,000 = $75,000 income

e. Dollars of sales to yield $60,000 pretax income $= \dfrac{\text{Fixed costs} + \text{Target pretax income}}{\text{Contribution margin ratio}}$

$= \dfrac{\$150,000 + \$60,000}{37.5\%} = \underline{\underline{\$560,000}}$

APPENDIX

Using Excel to Estimate Least-Squares Regression

5A

Microsoft Excel® and other spreadsheet software can be used to perform least-squares regressions to identify cost behavior. In Excel, the INTERCEPT and SLOPE functions are used. The following screen shot reports the data from Exhibit 5.4 in cells Al through C13 and shows the cell contents to find the intercept (cell B15) and slope (cell B16). Cell B15 uses Excel to find the intercept from a least-squares regression of total cost (shown as C2:C13 in cell B15) on units produced (shown as B2:B13 in cell B15). Spreadsheet software is useful in understanding cost behavior when many data points (such as monthly total costs and units produced) are available.

	A	B	C
1	**Month**	**Units Produced**	**Total Cost**
2	January	27,500	$21,500
3	February	22,500	20,500
4	March	25,000	25,000
5	April	35,000	21,500
6	May	47,500	25,500
7	June	17,500	18,500
8	July	30,000	23,500
9	August	52,500	28,500
10	September	37,500	26,000
11	October	62,500	29,000
12	November	67,500	31,000
13	December	57,500	26,000
14			**Result**
15	**Intercept**	=INTERCEPT(C2:C13, B2:B13)	$16,688.24
16	**Slope**	=SLOPE(C2:C13, B2:B13)	$ 0.1995

Point: The intercept function solves for total fixed costs. The slope function solves for the variable cost per unit.

Excel can also be used to create scatter diagrams such as that in Exhibit 5.5a. In contrast to visually drawing a line that "fits" the data, Excel more precisely fits the regression line. To draw a scatter diagram with a line of fit, follow these steps:

1. Highlight the data cells you wish to diagram; in this example, start from cell C13 and highlight through cell B2.
2. Then select "Insert" and "Scatter" from the drop-down menus. Selecting the chart type in the upper left corner of the choices under "Scatter" will produce a diagram that looks like that in Exhibit 5.5a, without a line of fit.
3. To add a line of fit (also called a trend line), select "Design," "Add Chart Element," "Trendline," and "Linear" from the drop-down menus. This will produce a diagram that looks like that in Exhibit 5.5a, including the line of fit.

APPENDIX

5B

Variable Costing and Performance Reporting

P5

Compute unit cost and income under both absorption and variable costing.

This chapter showed the usefulness of *contribution margin,* or selling price minus variable costs, in CVP analysis. The contribution margin income statement introduced in this chapter is also known as a **variable costing income statement.** In **variable costing,** only costs that change in total with changes in production levels are included in product costs. These costs include direct materials, direct labor, and *variable* overhead costs. Thus, under variable costing, *fixed* overhead costs are excluded from product costs and instead are expensed in the period incurred. As we showed in this chapter, a variable costing approach can be useful in many managerial analyses and decisions.

The variable costing method is not allowed, however, for external financial reporting. Instead, GAAP requires **absorption costing.** Under absorption costing, product costs include direct materials, direct labor, *and all overhead,* both variable and fixed. Thus, under absorption costing, fixed overhead costs are expensed when the goods are sold. Managers can use variable costing information for internal decision making, but they must use absorption costing for external reporting purposes.

Computing Unit Cost   To illustrate the difference between absorption costing and variable costing, let's consider the product cost data in Exhibit 5B.1 from IceAge, a skate manufacturer.

Direct materials cost	$4 per unit
Direct labor cost	$8 per unit
Overhead cost	
Variable overhead cost.	$180,000
Fixed overhead cost.	600,000
Total overhead cost	$780,000
Expected units produced	60,000 units

Using the product cost data, Exhibit 5B.2 shows the product cost per unit computations for both absorption and variable costing. These computations are shown both in a tabular format (left side of exhibit) and a visual format (right side of exhibit). For absorption costing, the product cost per unit is $25, which consists of $4 in direct materials, $8 in direct labor, $3 in variable overhead ($180,000/60,000 units), and $10 in fixed overhead ($600,000/60,000 units).

For variable costing, the product cost per unit is $15, which consists of $4 in direct materials, $8 in direct labor, and $3 in variable overhead. Fixed overhead costs of $600,000 are treated as a period cost and are recorded as expense in the period incurred. *The difference between the two costing methods is the exclusion of fixed overhead from product costs for variable costing.*

	Product Cost per Unit	
	Absorption Costing	**Variable Costing**
Direct materials	$ 4	$ 4
Direct labor	8	8
Overhead costs		
Variable overhead	3	3
Fixed overhead	**10**	—
Total product cost per unit . . .	$25	$15

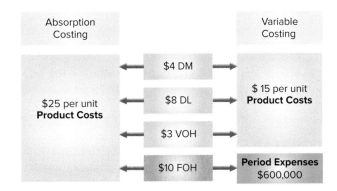

A manufacturer reports the following data.

Direct materials cost.	$6 per unit	Variable overhead	$220,000 per year
Direct labor cost	$14 per unit	Fixed overhead.	$680,000 per year
Expected units produced	20,000 units		

1. Compute the total product cost per unit under absorption costing.
2. Compute the total product cost per unit under variable costing.

Solution

Per Unit Costs	(1) Absorption Costing	(2) Variable Costing
Direct materials	$ 6	$ 6
Direct labor	14	14
Variable overhead ($220,000/20,000)	11	11
Fixed overhead ($680,000/20,000)*	34	—
Total product cost per unit.	$65	$31

*Not included in product costs under variable costing.

Do More: QS 5-17, QS 5-18, QS 5-19, QS 5-20, E 5-26

Income Reporting   The prior section showed how the different treatment of fixed overhead costs leads to different product costs per unit under absorption and variable costing. This section shows the implications of this difference for income reporting.

To illustrate the income reporting implications, we return to IceAge Company. Below are the manufacturing cost data for IceAge as well as additional data on selling and administrative expenses. Assume that IceAge began year 2017 with no units in inventory. During 2017, IceAge produced 60,000 units and sold 40,000 units at $40 each, leaving 20,000 units in ending inventory.

Using the information above, we next prepare income statements for IceAge both under absorption costing and under variable costing. Under variable costing, expenses are grouped according to cost behavior—variable or fixed, and production or nonproduction. Under the traditional format of absorption costing, expenses are grouped by function but not separated into variable and fixed components.

Units Produced Exceed Units Sold   Exhibit 5B.3 shows absorption costing and variable costing income statements for 2017. In 2017, 60,000 units were produced, but only 40,000 units were sold, which means 20,000 units remain in ending inventory.

EXHIBIT 5B.3

Income under Absorption or Variable Costing

ICEAGE COMPANY Income Statement (Absorption Costing) For Year Ended December 31, 2017		
Sales* (40,000 × $40)		$1,600,000
Cost of goods sold (40,000 × $25**)		1,000,000
Gross margin		600,000
Selling and administrative expenses		
[$200,000 + (40,000 × $2)]		280,000
Net income		$ 320,000

* Units produced equal 60,000; units sold equal 40,000.
** $4 DM + $8 DL + $3 VOH + $10 FOH.
† $4 DM + $8 DL + $3 VOH.

ICEAGE COMPANY Income Statement (Variable Costing) For Year Ended December 31, 2017		
Sales* (40,000 × $40)		$1,600,000
Variable expenses		
Variable production costs		
(40,000 × $15†)	$600,000	
Variable selling and administrative		
expenses (40,000 × $2)	80,000	680,000
Contribution margin		920,000
Fixed expenses		
Fixed overhead	600,000	
Fixed selling and		
administrative expense	200,000	800,000
Net income		$ 120,000

The income statements reveal that for 2017, income is $320,000 under absorption costing. Under variable costing, income is $120,000, which is $200,000 less than under absorption costing. This $200,000 difference is due to the different treatment of fixed overhead under the two costing methods. Because variable costing expenses fixed manufacturing overhead (FOH) based on the number of units produced (60,000 × $10), and absorption costing expenses FOH based on the number of units sold (40,000 × $10), net income is lower under variable costing by $200,000 (20,000 units × $10).

Under variable costing, the entire $600,000 fixed overhead cost is treated as an expense in computing 2017 income. Under absorption costing, the fixed overhead cost is allocated to each unit of product at the rate of $10 per unit (from Exhibit 5B.2). When production exceeds sales by 20,000 units (60,000 versus 40,000), the $200,000 ($10 × 20,000 units) of fixed overhead cost allocated to these 20,000 units is included in the cost of ending inventory. This means that $200,000 of fixed overhead cost incurred in 2017 is not expensed until future years under absorption costing, when it is reported in cost of goods sold as those products are sold. Consequently, income for 2017 under absorption costing is $200,000 higher than income under variable costing. Even though sales (of 40,000 units) and the number of units produced (totaling 60,000) are the same under both costing methods, net income differs greatly due to the treatment of fixed overhead.

©TOSHIFUMI KITAMURA/AFP/ Getty Images

Converting Income under Variable Costing to Income under Absorption Costing   In 2017, IceAge produced 20,000 more units than it sold. Those 20,000 units remaining in ending inventory will be sold in future years. When those units are sold, the $200,000 of fixed overhead costs attached to them will be expensed, resulting in lower income under the absorption costing method. This leads to a simple way to convert income under variable costing to income under absorption costing:

$$\text{Income under absorption costing} = \text{Income under variable costing} + \text{Fixed overhead cost in ending inventory} - \text{Fixed overhead cost in beginning inventory}$$

For example, assume IceAge produces 60,000 units and sells 80,000 units in 2018, and reports income under variable costing of $1,040,000. Income under absorption costing is then computed as:

$$\text{Income under absorption costing} = \$1,040,000 + \$0 - \$200,000 = \$840,000$$

Summary

C1 **Describe different types of cost behavior in relation to production and sales volume.** Cost behavior is described in terms of how its amount changes in relation to changes in volume of activity within a relevant range. Fixed costs remain constant to changes in volume. Total variable costs change in direct proportion to volume changes. Mixed costs display the effects of both fixed and variable components. Step-wise costs remain constant over a small volume range, then change by a lump sum and remain constant over another volume range, and so on. Curvilinear costs change in a nonlinear relation to volume changes.

C2 **Describe several applications of cost-volume-profit analysis.** Cost-volume-profit analysis can be used to predict what can happen under alternative strategies concerning sales volume, selling prices, variable costs, or fixed costs. Applications include "what-if" analysis, computing sales for a target income, and break-even analysis.

A1 **Compute the contribution margin and describe what it reveals about a company's cost structure.** Contribution margin per unit is a product's selling price less its total variable costs. Contribution margin ratio is a product's contribution margin per unit divided by its selling price. Unit contribution margin is the amount received from each sale that contributes to fixed costs and income. The contribution margin ratio reveals what portion of each sales dollar is available as contribution to fixed costs and income.

A2 **Analyze changes in sales using the degree of operating leverage.** The extent, or relative size, of fixed costs in a company's total cost structure is known as *operating leverage.* One tool useful in assessing the effect of changes in sales on income is the degree of operating leverage, or DOL. DOL is the ratio of the contribution margin divided by pretax income. This ratio can be used to determine the expected percent change in income given a percent change in sales.

P1 **Determine cost estimates using the scatter diagram, high-low, and regression methods of estimating costs.** Three different methods used to estimate costs are the scatter diagram, the high-low method, and least-squares regression. All three methods use past data to estimate costs. Cost estimates from a scatter diagram are based on a visual fit of the cost line. Estimates from the high-low method are based only on costs corresponding to the lowest and highest sales. The least-squares regression method is a statistical technique and uses all data points.

P2 **Compute the break-even point for a single product company.** A company's break-even point for a period is the sales volume at which total revenues equal total costs. To compute a break-even point in terms of sales units, we divide total fixed costs by the contribution margin per unit. To compute a break-even point in terms of sales dollars, divide total fixed costs by the contribution margin ratio.

P3 **Graph costs and sales for a single product company.** The costs and sales for a company can be graphically illustrated using a CVP chart. In this chart, the horizontal axis represents the number of units sold and the vertical axis represents dollars of sales or costs. Straight lines are used to depict both costs and sales on the CVP chart.

P4 **Compute the break-even point for a multiproduct company.** CVP analysis can be applied to a multiproduct company by expressing sales volume in terms of composite units. A composite unit consists of a specific number of units of each product in proportion to their expected sales mix. Multiproduct CVP analysis treats this composite unit as a single product.

P5ᴮ **Compute unit cost and income under both absorption and variable costing.** Absorption cost per unit includes direct materials, direct labor, and *all* overhead, whereas variable cost per unit includes direct materials, direct labor, and only *variable* overhead. Absorption costing income is equal to variable costing income plus the fixed overhead cost in ending inventory minus the fixed overhead cost in beginning inventory.

Key Terms

Absorption costing	Curvilinear cost	Relevant range of operations
Break-even point	Degree of operating leverage (DOL)	Sales mix
Composite unit	Estimated line of cost behavior	Scatter diagram
Contribution margin	High-low method	Step-wise cost
Contribution margin per unit	Least-squares regression	Variable costing
Contribution margin ratio	Margin of safety	Variable costing income statement
Cost-volume-profit (CVP) analysis	Mixed cost	
Cost-volume-profit (CVP) chart	Operating leverage	

Multiple Choice Quiz

1. A company's only product sells for $150 per unit. Its variable costs per unit are $100, and its fixed costs total $75,000. What is its contribution margin per unit?
   a. $50
   b. $250
   c. $100
   d. $150
   e. $25

2. Using information from question 1, what is the company's contribution margin ratio?
   a. 66⅔%
   b. 100%
   c. 50%
   d. 0%
   e. 33⅓%

3. Using information from question 1, what is the company's break-even point in units?
   a. 500 units
   b. 750 units
   c. 1,500 units
   d. 3,000 units
   e. 1,000 units

4. A company's forecasted sales are $300,000 and its sales at break-even are $180,000. Its margin of safety in dollars is
   a. $180,000.
   b. $120,000.
   c. $480,000.
   d. $60,000.
   e. $300,000.

5. A product sells for $400 per unit and its variable costs per unit are $260. The company's fixed costs are $840,000. If the company desires $70,000 pretax income, what is the required dollar sales?
   a. $2,400,000
   b. $200,000
   c. $2,600,000
   d. $2,275,000
   e. $1,400,000

ANSWERS TO MULTIPLE CHOICE QUIZ

1. a; $150 − $100 = $50
2. e; ($150 − $100)/$150 = 33⅓%
3. c; $75,000/$50 CM per unit = 1,500 units
4. b; $300,000 − $180,000 = $120,000
5. c; Contribution margin ratio = ($400 − $260)/$400 = 0.35
   Targeted sales = ($840,000 + $70,000)/0.35 = $2,600,000

A,B Superscript letter A(B) denotes assignments based on Appendix 5A (5B).

🎲 Icon denotes assignments that involve decision making.

Discussion Questions

1. What is a variable cost? Identify two variable costs.
2. 🎲 When output volume increases, do variable costs per unit increase, decrease, or stay the same within the relevant range of activity? Explain.
3. 🎲 When output volume increases, do fixed costs per unit increase, decrease, or stay the same within the relevant range of activity? Explain.
4. 🎲 How is cost-volume-profit analysis useful?
5. How do step-wise costs and curvilinear costs differ?
6. Describe the contribution margin ratio in layperson's terms.
7. Define and explain the *contribution margin ratio*.
8. Define and describe *contribution margin per unit*.
9. In performing CVP analysis for a manufacturing company, what simplifying assumption is usually made about the volume of production and the volume of sales?
10. What two arguments tend to justify classifying all costs as either fixed or variable even though individual costs might not behave exactly as classified?
11. 🎲 How does assuming that operating activity occurs within a relevant range affect cost-volume-profit analysis?
12. List three methods to measure cost behavior.
13. How is a scatter diagram used to identify and measure the behavior of a company's costs?
14. In cost-volume-profit analysis, what is the estimated profit at the break-even point?
15. 🎲 Assume that a straight line on a CVP chart intersects the vertical axis at the level of fixed costs and has a positive slope that rises with each additional unit of volume by the amount of the variable costs per unit. What does this line represent?
16. **Google** has both fixed and variable costs. Why are fixed costs depicted as a horizontal line on a CVP chart? **GOOGLE**
17. 🎲 Each of two similar companies has sales of $20,000 and total costs of $15,000 for a month. Company A's total costs include $10,000 of variable costs and $5,000 of fixed costs. If Company B's total costs include $4,000 of variable costs and $11,000 of fixed costs, which company will enjoy more profit if sales double?
18. _____ of _____ reflects expected sales in excess of the level of break-even sales.
19. 🎲 **Apple** produces tablet computers for sale. Identify some of the variable and fixed product costs associated with that production. (*Hint:* Limit costs to product costs.) **APPLE**
20. 🎲 Should **Apple** use single product or multiproduct break-even analysis? Explain. **APPLE**
21. 🎲 **Samsung** is thinking of expanding sales of its most popular smartphone model by 65%. Should we expect its variable and fixed costs for this model to stay within the relevant range? Explain. **Samsung**
22.B **Google** uses variable costing for several business decisions. How can variable costing income be converted to absorption costing income? **GOOGLE**

connect

Listed here are four series of separate costs measured at various volume levels. Examine each series and identify whether it is best described as a fixed, variable, step-wise, or curvilinear cost. (It can help to graph each cost series.)

QUICK STUDY

QS 5-1
Cost behavior identification

C1

Volume (Units)	Series 1	Series 2	Series 3	Series 4
0	$ 0	$450	$ 800	$100
100	800	450	800	105
200	1,600	450	800	120
300	2,400	450	1,600	145
400	3,200	450	1,600	190
500	4,000	450	2,400	250
600	4,800	450	2,400	320

Determine whether each of the following is best described as a fixed, variable, or mixed cost with respect to product units.

QS 5-2
Cost behavior identification

C1

_____ **1.** Rubber used to manufacture athletic shoes.

_____ **2.** Maintenance of factory machinery.

_____ **3.** Packaging expense.

_____ **4.** Wages of an assembly-line worker paid on the basis of acceptable units produced.

_____ **5.** Factory supervisor's salary.

_____ **6.** Taxes on factory building.

_____ **7.** Depreciation expense of warehouse.

The following information is available for a company's maintenance cost over the last seven months. Using the high-low method, estimate both the fixed and variable components of its maintenance cost.

QS 5-3
Cost behavior estimation—
high-low method

P1

Month	Maintenance Hours	Maintenance Cost
June.	9	$5,450
July	18	6,900
August	12	5,100
September	15	6,000
October	21	6,900
November	24	8,100
December	6	3,600

This scatter diagram reflects past maintenance hours and their corresponding maintenance costs.

QS 5-4
Cost behavior estimation—
scatter diagram

P1

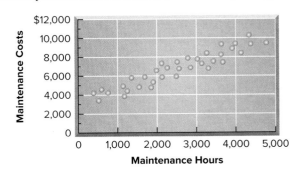

1. Draw an estimated line of cost behavior.

2. Estimate the fixed and variable components of maintenance costs.

Compute and interpret the contribution margin ratio using the following data: sales, $5,000; total variable cost, $3,000.

QS 5-5
Contribution margin
ratio   A1

QS 5-6 Contribution margin per unit and break-even units P2	SBD Phone Company sells its waterproof phone case for $90 per unit. Fixed costs total $162,000, and variable costs are $36 per unit. Determine the (1) contribution margin per unit and (2) break-even point in units.
QS 5-7 Assumptions in CVP analysis C2	SBD Phone Company sells its waterproof phone case for $90 per unit. Fixed costs total $162,000, and variable costs are $36 per unit. How will the break-even point in units change in response to each of the following independent changes in selling price per unit, variable cost per unit, or total fixed costs? Use I for increase and D for decrease. (It is not necessary to compute new break-even points.)

Change	Break-Even in Units will _____
1. Total fixed costs to $190,000	_____
2. Variable costs to $34 per unit	_____
3. Selling price per unit to $80	_____
4. Variable costs to $67 per unit	_____
5. Total fixed costs to $150,000	_____
6. Selling price per unit to $120	_____

QS 5-8 Contribution margin ratio and break-even dollars P2	SBD Phone Company sells its waterproof phone case for $90 per unit. Fixed costs total $162,000, and variable costs are $36 per unit. Determine the (1) contribution margin ratio and (2) break-even point in dollars.
QS 5-9 CVP analysis and target income P2	SBD Phone Company sells its waterproof phone case for $90 per unit. Fixed costs total $162,000, and variable costs are $36 per unit. Compute the units of product that must be sold to earn pretax income of $200,000. (Round to the nearest whole unit.)
QS 5-10 Computing break-even P2	Zhao Co. has fixed costs of $354,000. Its single product sells for $175 per unit, and variable costs are $116 per unit. Determine the break-even point in units.
QS 5-11 Margin of safety C2	Zhao Co. has fixed costs of $354,000. Its single product sells for $175 per unit, and variable costs are $116 per unit. If the company expects sales of 10,000 units, compute its margin of safety (a) in dollars and (b) as a percent of expected sales.
QS 5-12 Contribution margin income statement P2	Zhao Co. has fixed costs of $354,000. Its single product sells for $175 per unit, and variable costs are $116 per unit. The company expects sales of 10,000 units. Prepare a contribution margin income statement for the year ended December 31, 2017.
QS 5-13 Target income C2	Zhao Co. has fixed costs of $354,000. Its single product sells for $175 per unit, and variable costs are $116 per unit. Compute the level of sales in units needed to produce a target (pretax) income of $118,000.
QS 5-14 Sales mix and break-even P4	US-Mobile manufactures and sells two products, tablet computers and smartphones, in the ratio of 5:3. Fixed costs are $105,000, and the contribution margin per composite unit is $125. What number of each type of product is sold at the break-even point?
QS 5-15 CVP chart P3	Corme Company expects sales of $34 million (400,000 units). The company's total fixed costs are $17.5 million and its variable costs are $35 per unit. Prepare a CVP chart from this information.
QS 5-16 Operating leverage analysis A2	Singh Co. reports a contribution margin of $960,000 and fixed costs of $720,000. (1) Compute the company's degree of operating leverage. (2) If sales increase by 15%, what amount of income will Singh Co. report?
QS 5-17[B] Computing unit cost under absorption costing P5	Vijay Company reports the following information regarding its production costs. Compute its product cost per unit under absorption costing.

Direct materials	$10 per unit
Direct labor	$20 per unit
Overhead costs for the year	
Variable overhead	$10 per unit
Fixed overhead	$160,000
Units produced	20,000 units

Refer to Vijay Company's data in QS 5-17. Compute its product cost per unit under variable costing.

QS 5-18^B
Computing unit cost under variable costing   P5

Aces Inc., a manufacturer of tennis rackets, began operations this year. The company produced 6,000 rackets and sold 4,900. Each racket was sold at a price of $90. Fixed overhead costs are $78,000, and fixed selling and administrative costs are $65,200. The company also reports the following per unit costs for the year. Prepare an income statement under variable costing.

QS 5-19^B
Variable costing income statement   P5

Variable production costs	$25
Variable selling and administrative expenses	2

Aces Inc., a manufacturer of tennis rackets, began operations this year. The company produced 6,000 rackets and sold 4,900. Each racket was sold at a price of $90. Fixed overhead costs are $78,000, and fixed selling and administrative costs are $65,200. The company also reports the following per unit costs for the year. Prepare an income statement under absorption costing.

QS 5-20^B
Absorption costing income statement

P5

Variable production costs	$25
Variable selling and administrative expenses	2

A recent income statement for **BMW** reports the following (in € millions). Assume 75 percent of the cost of sales and 75 percent of the selling and administrative costs are variable costs, and the remaining 25 percent of each is fixed. Compute the contribution margin (in € millions). (Round computations using percentages to the nearest whole euro.)

QS 5-21
Contribution margin

A1

BMW Automotive Group	
Sales	€92,175
Cost of sales	74,043
Selling and administrative expenses	8,633

▣ connect

Following are five graphs representing various cost behaviors. (1) Identify whether the cost behavior in each graph is mixed, step-wise, fixed, variable, or curvilinear. (2) Identify the graph (by number) that best illustrates each cost behavior: (a) Factory policy requires one supervisor for every 30 factory workers; (b) real estate taxes on factory; (c) electricity charge that includes the standard monthly charge plus a charge for each kilowatt hour; (d) commissions to salespersons; and (e) costs of hourly paid workers that provide substantial gains in efficiency when a few workers are added but gradually smaller gains in efficiency when more workers are added.

EXERCISES

Exercise 5-1
Cost behavior in graphs

C1

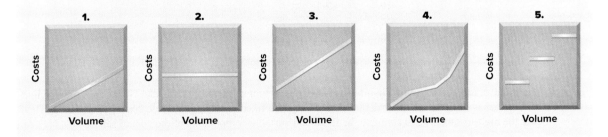

Exercise 5-2

Cost behavior defined

C1

The left column lists several cost classifications. The right column presents short definitions of those costs. In the blank space beside each of the numbers in the right column, write the letter of the cost best described by the definition.

A. Total cost

B. Mixed cost

C. Variable cost

D. Curvilinear cost

E. Step-wise cost

F. Fixed cost

———— **1.** This cost is the combined amount of all the other costs.

———— **2.** This cost remains constant over a limited range of volume; when it reaches the end of its limited range, it changes by a lump sum and remains at that level until it exceeds another limited range.

———— **3.** This cost has a component that remains the same over all volume levels and another component that increases in direct proportion to increases in volume.

———— **4.** This cost increases when volume increases, but the increase is not constant for each unit produced.

———— **5.** This cost remains constant over all volume levels within the productive capacity for the planning period.

———— **6.** This cost increases in direct proportion to increases in volume; its amount is constant for each unit produced.

Exercise 5-3

Cost behavior identification

C1

Following are five series of costs A through E measured at various volume levels. Identify each series as either fixed, variable, mixed, step-wise, or curvilinear.

	A	B	C	D	E	F
	Volume (Units)	Series A	Series B	Series C	Series D	Series E
1	0	$ 0	$2,500	$ 0	$1,000	$5,000
2	400	3,600	3,100	6,000	1,000	5,000
3	800	7,200	3,700	6,600	2,000	5,000
4	1,200	10,800	4,300	7,200	2,000	5,000
5	1,600	14,400	4,900	8,200	3,000	5,000
6	2,000	18,000	5,500	9,600	3,000	5,000
7	2,400	21,600	6,100	13,500	4,000	5,000

Exercise 5-4

Measurement of cost behavior using a scatter diagram

P1

A company reports the following information about its unit sales and its cost of sales. Each unit sells for $500. Use these data to prepare a scatter diagram. Draw an estimated line of cost behavior and determine whether the cost appears to be variable, fixed, or mixed.

Period	Unit Sales	Cost of Sales	Period	Unit Sales	Cost of Sales
1	22,500	$15,150	4	11,250	$ 8,250
2	17,250	11,250	5	13,500	9,000
3	15,750	10,500	6	18,750	14,250

Exercise 5-5

Scatter diagram and measurement of cost behavior

P1

Use the following information about unit sales and total cost of sales to prepare a scatter diagram. Draw a cost line that reflects the behavior displayed by this cost. Determine whether the cost is variable, step-wise, fixed, mixed, or curvilinear.

Period	Unit Sales	Cost of Sales	Period	Unit Sales	Cost of Sales
1	760	$590	9	580	$390
2	800	560	10	320	240
3	200	230	11	240	230
4	400	400	12	720	550
5	480	390	13	280	260
6	620	550	14	440	410
7	680	590	15	380	260
8	540	430			

Exercise 5-6

Cost behavior estimation— scatter diagram and high-low   P1

Felix & Co. reports the following information about its unit sales and cost of sales. Draw an estimated line of cost behavior using a scatter diagram, and compute fixed costs and variable costs per unit sold. Then use the high-low method to estimate the fixed and variable components of the cost of sales.

Period	Unit Sales	Cost of Sales	Period	Unit Sales	Cost of Sales
1	0	$2,500	6	2,000	$5,500
2	400	3,100	7	2,400	6,100
3	800	3,700	8	2,800	6,700
4	1,200	4,300	9	3,200	7,300
5	1,600	4,900	10	3,600	7,900

Refer to the information from Exercise 5-6. Use spreadsheet software to use ordinary least-squares regression to estimate the cost equation, including fixed and variable cost amounts.

Exercise 5-7[A]
Measurement of cost behavior using regression   P1

A jeans maker is designing a new line of jeans called Slims. The jeans will sell for $205 per pair and cost $164 per pair in variable costs to make.

1. Compute the contribution margin per pair.
2. Compute the contribution margin ratio.
3. Describe what the contribution margin ratio reveals about this new jeans line.

Exercise 5-8
Contribution margin

A1

Blanchard Company manufactures a single product that sells for $180 per unit and whose total variable costs are $135 per unit. The company's annual fixed costs are $562,500. Use this information to compute the company's (a) contribution margin, (b) contribution margin ratio, (c) break-even point in units, and (d) break-even point in dollars of sales.

Exercise 5-9
Contribution margin and break-even   P2

Blanchard Company manufactures a single product that sells for $180 per unit and whose total variable costs are $135 per unit. The company's annual fixed costs are $562,500. Prepare a CVP chart for the company.

Exercise 5-10
CVP chart   P3

Blanchard Company manufactures a single product that sells for $180 per unit and whose total variable costs are $135 per unit. The company's annual fixed costs are $562,500.

1. Prepare a contribution margin income statement for Blanchard Company showing sales, variable costs, and fixed costs at the break-even point.
2. If the company's fixed costs increase by $135,000, what amount of sales (in dollars) is needed to break even? Explain.

Exercise 5-11
Income reporting and break-even analysis
P2

Blanchard Company manufactures a single product that sells for $180 per unit and whose total variable costs are $135 per unit. The company's annual fixed costs are $562,500. Management targets an annual pretax income of $1,012,500. Assume that fixed costs remain at $562,500. Compute the (1) unit sales to earn the target income and (2) dollar sales to earn the target income.

Exercise 5-12
Computing sales to achieve target income   C2

Blanchard Company manufactures a single product that sells for $180 per unit and whose total variable costs are $135 per unit. The company's annual fixed costs are $562,500. The sales manager predicts that annual sales of the company's product will soon reach 40,000 units and its price will increase to $200 per unit. According to the production manager, variable costs are expected to increase to $140 per unit, but fixed costs will remain at $562,500. The income tax rate is 20%. What amounts of pretax and after-tax income can the company expect to earn from these predicted changes? (*Hint:* Prepare a forecasted contribution margin income statement as in Exhibit 5.21.)

Exercise 5-13
Forecasted income statement   C2

Check   Forecasted after-tax income, $1,470,000

Bloom Company management predicts that it will incur fixed costs of $160,000 and earn pretax income of $164,000 in the next period. Its expected contribution margin ratio is 25%. Use this information to compute the amounts of (1) total dollar sales and (2) total variable costs.

Exercise 5-14
Predicting sales and variable costs using contribution margin   C2

Harrison Co. expects to sell 200,000 units of its product next year, which would generate total sales of $17 million. Management predicts that pretax net income for next year will be $1,250,000 and that the contribution margin per unit will be $25. Use this information to compute next year's total expected (a) variable costs and (b) fixed costs.

Exercise 5-15
Computing variable and fixed costs   C2

Exercise 5-16

Break-even

P2

Hudson Co. reports the contribution margin income statement for 2017 below. Using this information, compute Hudson Co.'s (1) break-even point in units and (2) break-even point in sales dollars.

HUDSON CO.
Contribution Margin Income Statement
For Year Ended December 31, 2017

Sales (9,600 units at $225 each).................	$2,160,000
Variable costs (9,600 units at $180 each)	1,728,000
Contribution margin............................	432,000
Fixed costs	324,000
Pretax income.................................	$ 108,000

Exercise 5-17

Target income and margin of safety (in dollars)

C2

Refer to the information in Exercise 5-16.

1. Assume Hudson Co. has a target pretax income of $162,000 for 2018. What amount of sales (in dollars) is needed to produce this target income?
2. If Hudson achieves its target pretax income for 2018, what is its margin of safety (in percent)? (Round to one decimal place.)

Exercise 5-18

Evaluating strategies

C2

Refer to the information in Exercise 5-16. Assume the company is considering investing in a new machine that will increase its fixed costs by $40,500 per year and decrease its variable costs by $9 per unit. Prepare a forecasted contribution margin income statement for 2018 assuming the company purchases this machine.

Exercise 5-19

Evaluating strategies   C2

Refer to the information in Exercise 5-16. If the company raises its selling price to $240 per unit, compute its (1) contribution margin per unit, (2) contribution margin ratio, (3) break-even point in units, and (4) break-even point in sales dollars.

Exercise 5-20

Evaluating strategies   C2

Refer to the information in Exercise 5-16. The marketing manager believes that increasing advertising costs by $81,000 in 2018 will increase the company's sales volume to 11,000 units. Prepare a forecasted contribution margin income statement for 2018 assuming the company incurs the additional advertising costs.

Exercise 5-21

Predicting unit and dollar sales   C2

Nombre Company management predicts $390,000 of variable costs, $430,000 of fixed costs, and a pretax income of $155,000 in the next period. Management also predicts that the contribution margin per unit will be $9. Use this information to compute the (1) total expected dollar sales for next period and (2) number of units expected to be sold next period.

Exercise 5-22

CVP analysis using composite units   P4

Check   (3) 1,000 composite units

Handy Home sells windows and doors in the ratio of 8:2 (windows:doors). The selling price of each window is $200 and of each door is $500. The variable cost of a window is $125 and of a door is $350. Fixed costs are $900,000. Use this information to determine the (1) selling price per composite unit, (2) variable costs per composite unit, (3) break-even point in composite units, and (4) number of units of each product that will be sold at the break-even point.

Exercise 5-23

CVP analysis using composite units

P4

R&R Tax Service offers tax and consulting services to individuals and small businesses. Data for fees and costs of three types of tax returns follow. R&R provides services in the ratio of 5:3:2 (easy, moderate, business). Fixed costs total $18,000 for the tax season. Use this information to determine the (1) selling price per composite unit, (2) variable costs per composite unit, (3) break-even point in composite units, and (4) number of units of each product that will be sold at the break-even point.

Type of Return	Fee Charged	Variable Cost per Return
Easy (Form 1040EZ)	$ 50	$ 30
Moderate (Form 1040)	125	75
Business	275	100

Exercise 5-24

Operating leverage computed and applied

A2

Company A is a manufacturer with current sales of $6,000,000 and a 60% contribution margin. Its fixed costs equal $2,600,000. Company B is a consulting firm with current service revenues of $4,500,000 and a 25% contribution margin. Its fixed costs equal $375,000. Compute the degree of operating leverage (DOL) for each company. Identify which company benefits more from a 20% increase in sales and explain why.

Refer to the information in Exercise 5-16.
1. Compute the company's degree of operating leverage for 2017.
2. If sales decrease by 5% in 2018, what will be the company's pretax income?
3. Assume sales for 2018 decrease by 5%. Prepare a contribution margin income statement for 2018.

Exercise 5-25
Degree of operating leverage
A2

A manufacturer reports the information below for three recent years. Compute income for each of the three years using absorption costing.

Exercise 5-26ᴮ
Computing absorption costing income
P5

	Year 1	Year 2	Year 3
Variable costing income	$110,000	$114,400	$118,950
Beginning finished goods inventory (units)	0	1,200	700
Ending finished goods inventory (units)	1,200	700	800
Fixed manufacturing overhead per unit	$2.50	$2.50	$2.50

Use the amounts shown on the contribution margin income statement below to compute the missing amounts denoted by letters *a* through *n*.

Exercise 5-27
Contribution margin income statement
A1

	Company A Total	Company A Per unit	Company B Total	Company B Per unit
Number of units sold	*a*		1,975	
Sales	$208,000	$65	*h*	*i*
Variable costs	150,400	*b*	$39,500	*j*
Contribution margin	*c*	*d*	43,450	*k*
Fixed costs	*e*	*f*	19,750	*l*
Net income	$ 46,400	*g*	*m*	*n*

connect

The following costs result from the production and sale of 1,000 drum sets manufactured by Tight Drums Company for the year ended December 31, 2017. The drum sets sell for $500 each. The company has a 25% income tax rate.

PROBLEM SET A

Problem 5-1A
Contribution margin income statement and contribution margin ratio
A1

Variable production costs		Fixed manufacturing costs	
Plastic for casing	$ 17,000	Taxes on factory	$ 5,000
Wages of assembly workers	82,000	Factory maintenance	10,000
Drum stands	26,000	Factory machinery depreciation	40,000
Variable selling costs		Fixed selling and administrative costs	
Sales commissions	15,000	Lease of equipment for sales staff	10,000
		Accounting staff salaries	35,000
		Administrative management salaries	125,000

Required
1. Prepare a contribution margin income statement for the company.
2. Compute its contribution margin per unit and its contribution margin ratio.

Check (1) Net income, $101,250

Analysis Component
3. Interpret the contribution margin and contribution margin ratio from part 2.

Alden Co.'s monthly unit sales and total cost data for its operating activities of the past year follow. Management wants to use these data to predict future fixed and variable costs.

Problem 5-2A
Scatter diagram and cost behavior estimation
P1

Month	Units Sold	Total Cost	Month	Units Sold	Total Cost
1	320,000	$160,000	7	340,000	$220,000
2	160,000	100,000	8	280,000	160,000
3	280,000	220,000	9	80,000	64,000
4	200,000	100,000	10	160,000	140,000
5	300,000	230,000	11	100,000	100,000
6	200,000	120,000	12	110,000	80,000

Required

1. Prepare a scatter diagram for these data with sales volume (in units) plotted on the horizontal axis and total cost plotted on the vertical axis.

2. Estimate both the variable costs per unit and the total monthly fixed costs using the high-low method. Draw the total costs line on the scatter diagram in part 1.

3. Use the estimated line of cost behavior and results from part 2 to predict future total costs when sales volume is (a) 200,000 units and (b) 300,000 units.

Problem 5-3A

CVP analysis and charting

P2   P3

Praveen Co. manufactures and markets a number of rope products. Management is considering the future of Product XT, a special rope for hang gliding, that has not been as profitable as planned. Since Product XT is manufactured and marketed independently of the other products, its total costs can be precisely measured. Next year's plans call for a $200 selling price per 100 yards of XT rope. Its fixed costs for the year are expected to be $270,000, up to a maximum capacity of 700,000 yards of rope. Forecasted variable costs are $140 per 100 yards of XT rope.

Required

1. Estimate Product XT's break-even point in terms of (a) sales units and (b) sales dollars.

2. Prepare a CVP chart for Product XT like that in Exhibit 5.14. Use 7,000 units (700,000 yards/100 yards) as the maximum number of sales units on the horizontal axis of the graph, and $1,400,000 as the maximum dollar amount on the vertical axis.

3. Prepare a contribution margin income statement showing sales, variable costs, and fixed costs for Product XT at the break-even point.

Problem 5-4A

Break-even analysis; income targeting and forecasting

C2   P2   A1

Astro Co. sold 20,000 units of its only product and incurred a $50,000 loss (ignoring taxes) for the current year, as shown here. During a planning session for year 2018's activities, the production manager notes that variable costs can be reduced 50% by installing a machine that automates several operations. To obtain these savings, the company must increase its annual fixed costs by $200,000. The maximum output capacity of the company is 40,000 units per year.

ASTRO COMPANY Contribution Margin Income Statement For Year Ended December 31, 2017	
Sales	$1,000,000
Variable costs	800,000
Contribution margin	200,000
Fixed costs	250,000
Net loss	$ (50,000)

Required

1. Compute the break-even point in dollar sales for year 2017.

2. Compute the predicted break-even point in dollar sales for year 2018 assuming the machine is installed and there is no change in the unit selling price.

3. Prepare a forecasted contribution margin income statement for 2018 that shows the expected results with the machine installed. Assume that the unit selling price and the number of units sold will not change, and no income taxes will be due.

4. Compute the sales level required in both dollars and units to earn $200,000 of target pretax income in 2018 with the machine installed and no change in unit sales price. Round answers to whole dollars and whole units.

5. Prepare a forecasted contribution margin income statement that shows the results at the sales level computed in part 4. Assume no income taxes will be due.

Problem 5-5A

Break-even analysis, different cost structures, and income calculations

C2   A1   P4

Henna Co. produces and sells two products, T and O. It manufactures these products in separate factories and markets them through different channels. They have no shared costs. This year, the company sold 50,000 units of each product. Sales and costs for each product follow.

	Product T	Product O
Sales	$2,000,000	$2,000,000
Variable costs..................	1,600,000	250,000
Contribution margin	400,000	1,750,000
Fixed costs	125,000	1,475,000
Income before taxes.............	275,000	275,000
Income taxes (32% rate)...........	88,000	88,000
Net income	$ 187,000	$ 187,000

Required

1. Compute the break-even point in dollar sales for each product. (Round the answer to whole dollars.)

2. Assume that the company expects sales of each product to decline to 30,000 units next year with no change in unit selling price. Prepare forecasted financial results for next year following the format of the contribution margin income statement as just shown with columns for each of the two products (assume a 32% tax rate). Also, assume that any loss before taxes yields a 32% tax benefit.

3. Assume that the company expects sales of each product to increase to 60,000 units next year with no change in unit selling price. Prepare forecasted financial results for next year following the format of the contribution margin income statement shown with columns for each of the two products (assume a 32% tax rate).

Analysis Component

4. If sales greatly decrease, which product would experience a greater loss? Explain.

5. Describe some factors that might have created the different cost structures for these two products.

Check (2) After-tax income: T, $78,200; O, $(289,000)

(3) After-tax income: T, $241,400; O, $425,000

This year Burchard Company sold 40,000 units of its only product for $25 per unit. Manufacturing and selling the product required $200,000 of fixed manufacturing costs and $325,000 of fixed selling and administrative costs. Its per unit variable costs follow.

Problem 5-6A
Analysis of price, cost, and volume changes for contribution margin and net income

P2 A1

Material..	$8.00
Direct labor (paid on the basis of completed units)	5.00
Variable overhead costs.......................................	1.00
Variable selling and administrative costs	0.50

Next year the company will use new material, which will reduce material costs by 50% and direct labor costs by 60% and will not affect product quality or marketability. Management is considering an increase in the unit selling price to reduce the number of units sold because the factory's output is nearing its annual output capacity of 45,000 units. Two plans are being considered. Under plan 1, the company will keep the selling price at the current level and sell the same volume as last year. This plan will increase income because of the reduced costs from using the new material. Under plan 2, the company will increase the selling price by 20%. This plan will decrease unit sales volume by 10%. Under both plans 1 and 2, the total fixed costs and the variable costs per unit for overhead and for selling and administrative costs will remain the same.

Required

1. Compute the break-even point in dollar sales for both (a) plan 1 and (b) plan 2.

2. Prepare a forecasted contribution margin income statement with two columns showing the expected results of plan 1 and plan 2. The statements should report sales, total variable costs, contribution margin, total fixed costs, income before taxes, income taxes (30% rate), and net income.

Check (1) Break-even: Plan 1, $750,000; Plan 2, $700,000

(2) Net income: Plan 1, $122,500; Plan 2, $199,500

Patriot Co. manufactures and sells three products: red, white, and blue. Their unit selling prices are red, $20; white, $35; and blue, $65. The per unit variable costs to manufacture and sell these products are red, $12; white, $22; and blue, $50. Their sales mix is reflected in a ratio of 5:4:2 (red:white:blue). Annual fixed costs shared by all three products are $250,000. One type of raw material has been used to manufacture all three products. The company has developed a new material of equal quality for less cost. The new material would reduce variable costs per unit as follows: red, by $6; white, by $12; and blue, by $10. However, the new material requires new equipment, which will increase annual fixed costs by $50,000. (Round answers to whole composite units.)

Problem 5-7A
Break-even analysis with composite units

P4

Required

1. If the company continues to use the old material, determine its break-even point in both sales units and sales dollars of each individual product.

2. If the company uses the new material, determine its new break-even point in both sales units and sales dollars of each individual product.

Analysis Component

3. What insight does this analysis offer management for long-term planning?

PROBLEM SET B

Problem 5-1B

Contribution margin income statement and contribution margin ratio

A1

The following costs result from the production and sale of 12,000 CD sets manufactured by Gilmore Company for the year ended December 31, 2017. The CD sets sell for $18 each. The company has a 25% income tax rate.

Variable manufacturing costs	
Plastic for CD sets	$ 1,500
Wages of assembly workers	30,000
Labeling	3,000
Variable selling costs	
Sales commissions.	6,000
Fixed manufacturing costs	
Rent on factory.	6,750
Factory cleaning service	4,520
Factory machinery depreciation	20,000
Fixed selling and administrative costs	
Lease of office equipment.	1,050
Systems staff salaries	15,000
Administrative management salaries	120,000

Required

1. Prepare a contribution margin income statement for the company.

2. Compute its contribution margin per unit and its contribution margin ratio.

Analysis Component

3. Interpret the contribution margin and contribution margin ratio from part 2.

Problem 5-2B

Scatter diagram and cost behavior estimation

P1

Sun Co.'s monthly unit sales and total cost data for its operating activities of the past year follow. Management wants to use these data to predict future fixed and variable costs. (Dollar and unit amounts are in thousands.)

Month	Units Sold	Total Cost	Month	Units Sold	Total Cost
1	195	$ 97	7	145	$ 93
2	125	87	8	185	105
3	105	73	9	135	85
4	155	89	10	85	58
5	95	81	11	175	95
6	215	110	12	115	79

Required

1. Prepare a scatter diagram for these data with sales volume (in units) plotted on the horizontal axis and total costs plotted on the vertical axis.

2. Estimate both the variable costs per unit and the total monthly fixed costs using the high-low method. Draw the total costs line on the scatter diagram in part 1.

3. Use the estimated line of cost behavior and results from part 2 to predict future total costs when sales volume is (a) 100 units and (b) 170 units.

Hip-Hop Co. manufactures and markets several products. Management is considering the future of one product, electronic keyboards, that has not been as profitable as planned. Since this product is manufactured and marketed independently of the other products, its total costs can be precisely measured. Next year's plans call for a $350 selling price per unit. The fixed costs for the year are expected to be $42,000, up to a maximum capacity of 700 units. Forecasted variable costs are $210 per unit.

Problem 5-3B
CVP analysis and charting
P2   P3

Required

1. Estimate the keyboards' break-even point in terms of (a) sales units and (b) sales dollars.
2. Prepare a CVP chart for keyboards like that in Exhibit 5.14. Use 700 keyboards as the maximum number of sales units on the horizontal axis of the graph, and $250,000 as the maximum dollar amount on the vertical axis.
3. Prepare a contribution margin income statement showing sales, variable costs, and fixed costs for keyboards at the break-even point.

Check (1) Break-even sales, 300 units

Rivera Co. sold 20,000 units of its only product and incurred a $50,000 loss (ignoring taxes) for the current year, as shown here. During a planning session for year 2018's activities, the production manager notes that variable costs can be reduced 50% by installing a machine that automates several operations. To obtain these savings, the company must increase its annual fixed costs by $150,000. The maximum output capacity of the company is 40,000 units per year.

Problem 5-4B
Break-even analysis; income targeting and forecasting
C2   P2   A1

RIVERA COMPANY	
Contribution Margin Income Statement	
For Year Ended December 31, 2017	
Sales	$750,000
Variable costs	600,000
Contribution margin	150,000
Fixed costs	200,000
Net loss	$ (50,000)

Required

1. Compute the break-even point in dollar sales for year 2017.
2. Compute the predicted break-even point in dollar sales for year 2018 assuming the machine is installed and no change occurs in the unit selling price. (Round the change in variable costs to a whole number.)
3. Prepare a forecasted contribution margin income statement for 2018 that shows the expected results with the machine installed. Assume that the unit selling price and the number of units sold will not change, and no income taxes will be due.
4. Compute the sales level required in both dollars and units to earn $200,000 of target pretax income in 2018 with the machine installed and no change in unit sales price. (Round answers to whole dollars and whole units.)
5. Prepare a forecasted contribution margin income statement that shows the results at the sales level computed in part 4. Assume no income taxes will be due.

Check (3) Net income, $100,000

(4) Required sales, $916,667 or 24,445 units (both rounded)

Stam Co. produces and sells two products, BB and TT. It manufactures these products in separate factories and markets them through different channels. They have no shared costs. This year, the company sold 50,000 units of each product. Sales and costs for each product follow.

Problem 5-5B
Break-even analysis, different cost structures, and income calculations
C2   P4   A1

	Product BB	Product TT
Sales	$800,000	$800,000
Variable costs	560,000	100,000
Contribution margin	240,000	700,000
Fixed costs	100,000	560,000
Income before taxes...............	140,000	140,000
Income taxes (32% rate)............	44,800	44,800
Net income	$ 95,200	$ 95,200

Required

1. Compute the break-even point in dollar sales for each product. (Round the answer to the next whole dollar.)

Check   (2) After-tax income: BB, $39,712; TT, $(66,640)

2. Assume that the company expects sales of each product to decline to 33,000 units next year with no change in the unit selling price. Prepare forecasted financial results for next year following the format of the contribution margin income statement as shown here with columns for each of the two products (assume a 32% tax rate, and that any loss before taxes yields a 32% tax benefit).

(3) After-tax income: BB, $140,896; TT, $228,480

3. Assume that the company expects sales of each product to increase to 64,000 units next year with no change in the unit selling prices. Prepare forecasted financial results for next year following the format of the contribution margin income statement as shown here with columns for each of the two products (assume a 32% tax rate).

Analysis Component

4. If sales greatly increase, which product would experience a greater increase in profit? Explain.

5. Describe some factors that might have created the different cost structures for these two products.

Problem 5-6B

Analysis of price, cost, and volume changes for contribution margin and net income

A1   P2

This year Best Company earned a disappointing 5.6% after-tax return on sales (net income/sales) from marketing 100,000 units of its only product. The company buys its product in bulk and repackages it for resale at the price of $20 per unit. Best incurred the following costs this year.

Total variable unit costs	$800,000
Total variable packaging costs.	$100,000
Fixed costs	$950,000
Income tax rate.	25%

The marketing manager claims that next year's results will be the same as this year's unless some changes are made. The manager predicts the company can increase the number of units sold by 80% if it reduces the selling price by 20% and upgrades the packaging. This change would increase variable packaging costs by 20%. Increased sales would allow the company to take advantage of a 25% quantity purchase discount on the cost of the bulk product. Neither the packaging change nor the volume discount would affect fixed costs, which provide an annual output capacity of 200,000 units.

Required

Check   (1b) Break-even sales for new strategy, $1,727,273 (rounded)
(2) Net income: Existing strategy, $112,500; new strategy, $475,500

1. Compute the break-even point in dollar sales under the (a) existing business strategy and (b) new strategy that alters both unit selling price and variable costs. (Round answers to the next whole dollar.)

2. Prepare a forecasted contribution margin income statement with two columns showing the expected results of (a) the existing strategy and (b) changing to the new strategy. The statements should report sales, total variable costs (unit and packaging), contribution margin, fixed costs, income before taxes, income taxes, and net income. Also determine the after-tax return on sales for these two strategies.

Problem 5-7B

Break-even analysis with composite units

P4

Milano Co. manufactures and sells three products: product 1, product 2, and product 3. Their unit selling prices are product 1, $40; product 2, $30; and product 3, $20. The per unit variable costs to manufacture and sell these products are product 1, $30; product 2, $15; and product 3, $8. Their sales mix is reflected in a ratio of 6:4:2. Annual fixed costs shared by all three products are $270,000. One type of raw material has been used to manufacture products 1 and 2. The company has developed a new material of equal quality for less cost. The new material would reduce variable costs per unit as follows: product 1 by $10 and product 2 by $5. However, the new material requires new equipment, which will increase annual fixed costs by $50,000.

Required

Check   (1) Old plan break-even, 1,875 composite units
(2) New plan break-even, 1,429 composite units (rounded)

1. If the company continues to use the old material, determine its break-even point in both sales units and sales dollars of each individual product.

2. If the company uses the new material, determine its new break-even point in both sales units and sales dollars of each individual product. (Round to the next whole unit.)

Analysis Component

3. What insight does this analysis offer management for long-term planning?

(This serial problem began in Chapter 1 and continues through most of the book. If previous chapter segments were not completed, the serial problem can begin at this point.)

SP 5   **Business Solutions** sells upscale modular desk units and office chairs in the ratio of 3:2 (desk unit:chair). The selling prices are $1,250 per desk unit and $500 per chair. The variable costs are $750 per desk unit and $250 per chair. Fixed costs are $120,000.

Required

1. Compute the selling price per composite unit.
2. Compute the variable costs per composite unit.
3. Compute the break-even point in composite units.
4. Compute the number of units of each product that would be sold at the break-even point.

Check   (3) 60 composite units

© Alexander Image/Shutterstock RF

Beyond the Numbers

BTN 5-1   **Apple** offers extended service contracts that provide repair coverage for its products. As you complete the following requirements, assume that Apple's repair services department uses many of the company's existing resources such as its facilities, repair machinery, and computer systems.

Required

1. Identify several of the variable, mixed, and fixed costs that Apple's repair services department is likely to incur in carrying out its services.
2. Assume that Apple's repair service revenues are expected to grow by 25% in the next year. How would we expect the costs identified in part 1 to change, if at all?
3. Based on the answer to part 2, can Apple use the contribution margin ratio to predict how income will change in response to increases in Apple's repair service revenues?

BTN 5-2   Both **Apple** and **Google** sell electronic devices, and each of these companies has a different product mix.

Required

1. Assume the following data are available for both companies. Compute each company's break-even point in unit sales. (Each company sells many devices at many different selling prices, and each has its own variable costs. This assignment assumes an *average* selling price per unit and an *average* cost per item.)

	Apple	Google
Average selling price per unit sold	$550 per unit	$470 per unit
Average variable cost per unit sold.	$250 per unit	$270 per unit
Total fixed costs ($ in millions).	$36,000	$10,000

2. If unit sales were to decline, which company would experience the larger decline in operating profit? Explain.

BTN 5-3   Labor costs of an auto repair mechanic are seldom based on actual hours worked. Instead, this labor cost is based on an industry average of time estimated to complete a repair job. This means a customer can pay, for example, $120 for two hours of work on a car when the actual time worked was only one hour. Many experienced mechanics can complete repair jobs faster than the industry average. Assume that you are asked to complete such a survey for a repair center. The survey calls for objective input, and many questions require detailed cost data and analysis. The mechanics and owners know you have the survey and encourage you to complete it in a way that increases the average billable hours for repair work.

Required

Write a one-page memorandum to the mechanics and owners that describes the direct labor analysis you will undertake in completing this survey.

COMMUNICATING IN PRACTICE

C2

BTN 5-4 Several important assumptions underlie CVP analysis. Assumptions often help simplify and focus our analysis of sales and costs. A common application of CVP analysis is as a tool to forecast sales, costs, and income.

Required

Assume that you are actively searching for a job. Prepare a half-page report identifying (1) three assumptions relating to your expected revenue (salary) and (2) three assumptions relating to your expected costs for the first year of your new job. Be prepared to discuss your assumptions in class.

TAKING IT TO THE NET

C1

BTN 5-5 Access and review the entrepreneurial information at **Business Owner's Toolkit** (**Toolkit.com**). Access and review its *New Business Cash Needs Checklist* (or similar worksheets related to controls of cash and costs) under the "Starting Up" link. (Look under the heading "Free Startup Downloads.")

Required

Write a half-page report that describes the information and resources available at the Business Owner's Toolkit to help the owner of a start-up business control and monitor its cash flows and costs.

TEAMWORK IN ACTION

C2

BTN 5-6 A local movie theater owner explains to you that ticket sales on weekends and evenings are strong, but attendance during the weekdays, Monday through Thursday, is poor. The owner proposes to offer a contract to the local grade school to show educational materials at the theater for a set charge per student during school hours. The owner asks your help to prepare a CVP analysis listing the cost and sales projections for the proposal. The owner must propose to the school's administration a charge per child. At a minimum, the charge per child needs to be sufficient for the theater to break even.

Required

Your team is to prepare two separate lists of questions that enable you to complete a reliable CVP analysis of this situation. One list is to be answered by the school's administration, the other by the owner of the movie theater.

ENTREPRENEURIAL DECISION

C1   A1

BTN 5-7 **Sweetgreen**, launched by entrepreneurs Nic Jammet, Jon Neman, and Nate Ru, is a fast-casual restaurant brand devoted to healthy salad choices. The company also sells T-shirts, hats, and other apparel.

Required

1. Identify at least two fixed costs that will not change regardless of how much salad Sweetgreen sells.
2. Sweetgreen is expanding. How could overly optimistic sales estimates potentially hurt its business?
3. Explain how cost-volume-profit analysis can help Nic, Jon, and Nate manage Sweetgreen.

HITTING THE ROAD

P4

BTN 5-8 Multiproduct break-even analysis is often viewed differently when actually applied in practice. You are to visit a local fast-food restaurant and count the number of items on the menu. To apply multiproduct break-even analysis to the restaurant, similar menu items must often be fit into groups. A reasonable approach is to classify menu items into approximately five groups. We then estimate average selling price and average variable cost to compute average contribution margin. (*Hint:* For fast-food restaurants, the highest contribution margin is with its beverages, at about 90%.)

Required

1. Prepare a one-year multiproduct break-even analysis for the restaurant you visit. Begin by establishing groups. Next, estimate each group's volume and contribution margin. These estimates are necessary to compute each group's contribution margin. Assume that annual fixed costs in total are $500,000 per year. (*Hint:* You must develop your own estimates on volume and contribution margin for each group to obtain the break-even point and sales.)

2. Prepare a one-page report on the results of your analysis. Comment on the volume of sales necessary to break even at a fast-food restaurant.

BTN 5-9   Access and review **Samsung**'s website (Samsung.com) to answer the following questions.

GLOBAL DECISION

P4

Samsung

Required

1. Do you believe that Samsung's managers use single product CVP analysis or multiproduct break-even analysis? Explain.

2. How does the addition of a new product line affect Samsung's CVP analysis?

 GLOBAL VIEW

Survey evidence shows that many German companies have elaborate and detailed cost accounting systems. Over 90 percent of companies surveyed report their systems focus on *contribution margin*. This focus helps German companies like **BMW** control costs and plan production levels.

Recently, an auto analyst took apart a BMW i3 to determine its cost. With that cost estimate, and an estimated selling price of $50,000 per i3, the analyst estimates BMW can break even by selling 20,000 i3s per year. (Source: *Forbes.com,* "Unlocking the Secrets of BMW's Remarkable Car of the Future.")

 Global View Assignments

Discussion Question 21

Quick Study 5-21

BTN 5-9

6

chapter

Variable Costing and Analysis

Learning Objectives

CONCEPTUAL

C1 Describe how absorption costing can result in overproduction.

ANALYTICAL

A1 Use variable costing in pricing special orders.

PROCEDURAL

P1 Compute unit cost under both absorption and variable costing.

P2 Prepare and analyze an income statement using absorption costing and using variable costing.

P3 Convert income under variable costing to the absorption cost basis.

P4 Determine product selling price based on absorption costing.

© Cindy Ord/Getty Images for NRF Foundation

Value of Riffraff

FAYETTEVILLE, AR—In her senior year of college, Kirsten Blowers Stuckey took $100 earned from her internship and bought as much used furniture as she could. After refurbishing and repainting, she then sold her inventory to her Facebook friends. With that success, Kirsten promptly quit her internship to start **Riffraff** (**ShopRiffraff.com**), a start-up retail store selling refurbished furniture. "After class I'd head straight to my store to open it," laughs Kirsten. Today, Riffraff sells clothing, shoes, and accessories.

"It was terrifying," Kirsten says of launching her business. She had to set up an accounting system to measure, track, and report on her operations, and she relied heavily on social media advertising. Kristen recalls measuring variable costs and contribution margins. Riffraff's sales were just over $100,000 in its first year, but they more than tripled in the next year. Kirsten keeps fixed costs low by selling many of her products online. She also uses her employees as advertising models.

Kirsten credits Riffraff's ability to evolve as key to its success. When Kirsten noticed a trend in potential custom-

"When things slow down . . . evolve!"

—Kirsten Blowers Stuckey

ers refurbishing furniture themselves, she moved into selling small complementary items. After moving to a new location, Kirsten found clothing racks left behind by the previous owner. "I didn't have any money to take them out," admits Kirsten, "so the only alternative was to start selling clothes!" On its reopening day, Riffraff sold out all of its clothing inventory.

The need to evolve continues as the tastes of her target customers—millennial women—change rapidly. "Not everyone likes what I like!" laughs Kirsten. She also regularly monitors contribution margins by product line to decide where to expand or reduce her product offerings.

Kirsten advises entrepreneurs to know what their customers like and to have the courage to evolve. "Work hard every day," advises Kirsten. "Owning a business is not always glamorous."

Sources: *Riffraff website,* January 2017; *Fayetteville Business Owners* blog, November 5, 2014; *Inc.com,* "30 Under 30," 2015; National Retail Federation, "25 People Shaping Retail's Future," 2015

INTRODUCING VARIABLE COSTING AND ABSORPTION COSTING

This chapter illustrates and compares two costing methods.

- **Variable costing,** where direct materials, direct labor, and *variable* overhead costs are included in product costs. This method is useful for many managerial decisions, but it cannot be used for external financial reporting.
- **Absorption costing,** where direct materials, direct labor, and both *variable* and *fixed* overhead costs are included in product costs. This method is required for external financial reporting under U.S. GAAP, but it can result in misleading product cost information and poor managerial decisions.

Exhibit 6.1 compares the absorption and variable costing methods. Both methods include direct materials, direct labor, and variable overhead in product costs. The key difference between the methods lies in their treatment of *fixed* overhead costs—such costs are included in product costs under absorption costing but included in period expenses under variable costing. Product costs are included in inventory until the goods are sold, at which time they are included in cost of goods sold. Period expenses are reported as expenses immediately in the period in which they are incurred.

Point: Under variable costing, fixed overhead is expensed at the time the units are produced. Under absorption costing, fixed overhead is expensed at the time the units are sold (as a component of cost of goods sold).

EXHIBIT 6.1

Absorption Costing versus Variable Costing

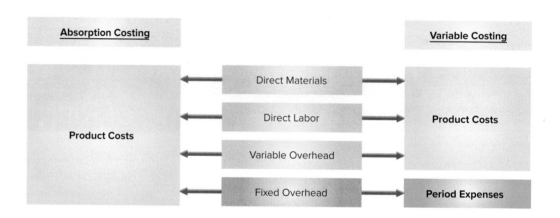

Exhibit 6.1 helps us understand when the absorption and variable costing methods will yield different income amounts. Differences in income resulting from the alternative costing methods will be *small* when:

- Fixed overhead is a small percentage of total manufacturing costs.
- Inventory levels are low. As more companies adopt lean techniques, including just-in-time manufacturing, inventory levels fall. Lower inventory levels reduce income differences between absorption and variable costing.
- Inventory turnover is rapid. The more quickly inventory turns over, the more product costs are included in cost of goods sold, relative to the product costs that remain in inventory.
- The period of analysis is long. Different costing methods might yield very different income numbers over a quarter or year, but these differences will decrease as income is compared over longer periods.

P1

Compute unit cost under both absorption and variable costing.

Computing Unit Product Cost

To illustrate the difference between absorption costing and variable costing, consider the product cost data in Exhibit 6.2 from IceAge, a skate manufacturer.

EXHIBIT 6.2

Summary Product Cost Data

Direct materials	$4 per unit
Direct labor	$8 per unit
Overhead (per year)	
Variable overhead	$ 180,000
Fixed overhead	600,000
Total overhead	$ 780,000
Expected units produced (per year)..............	60,000 units

Using this product cost data, Exhibit 6.3 shows the product cost per unit computations for both absorption and variable costing. These computations are shown both in a tabular format (left side of exhibit) and a visual format (right side of exhibit).

- For absorption costing, the product cost per unit is $25, which consists of $4 in direct materials, $8 in direct labor, $3 in variable overhead ($180,000/60,000 units), and $10 in fixed overhead ($600,000/60,000 units).
- For variable costing, the product cost per unit is $15, which consists of $4 in direct materials, $8 in direct labor, and $3 in variable overhead. Fixed overhead costs of $600,000 are treated as a period cost and are recorded as expense in the period incurred. **The difference between the two costing methods is the exclusion of fixed overhead from product costs for variable costing.**

EXHIBIT 6.3

Unit Cost Computation

	Product Cost per Unit	
	Absorption Costing	Variable Costing
Direct materials	$ 4	$ 4
Direct labor.........................	8	8
Overhead costs		
Variable overhead	3	3
Fixed overhead...................	10	—
Total product cost per unit.............	$25	$15

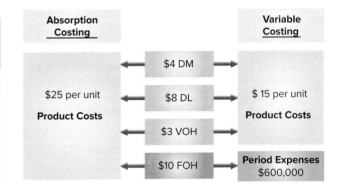

A manufacturer reports the following data.

Direct materials cost	$6 per unit	Variable overhead	$220,000 per year
Direct labor cost...................	$14 per unit	Fixed overhead	$680,000 per year
Expected units produced	20,000 units		

1. Compute the total product cost per unit under absorption costing.
2. Compute the total product cost per unit under variable costing.

Solution

Per Unit Costs	(1) Absorption Costing	(2) Variable Costing
Direct materials	$ 6	$ 6
Direct labor	14	14
Variable overhead ($220,000/20,000)	11	11
Fixed overhead ($680,000/20,000)*	34	—
Total product cost per unit	$65	$31

*Not included in product costs under variable costing.

NEED-TO-KNOW 6-1

Computing Product Cost per Unit

P1

Do More: QS 6-1, QS 6-2, E 6-1, E 6-2

INCOME REPORTING IMPLICATIONS

The different treatment of fixed overhead costs leads to different product costs per unit under absorption and variable costing. This section shows how this impacts income reporting.

Below are data for IceAge Company. Assume IceAge's variable costs per unit are constant and its annual fixed costs do not change during the three-year period 2015 through 2017.

Manufacturing Costs		Selling and Administrative Expenses	
Direct materials	$4 per unit	Variable.	$2 per unit
Direct labor	$8 per unit	Fixed	$200,000 per year
Variable overhead	$3 per unit		
Fixed overhead.	$600,000 per year		

Sales and production information for IceAge follows. Its sales price was a constant $40 per unit over this time period. Units produced equal those sold for 2015, exceed those sold for 2016, and are less than those sold for 2017. IceAge began 2015 with no units in beginning inventory.

	Units Produced	Units Sold	Units in Ending Inventory
2015	60,000	60,000	0
2016	60,000	40,000	20,000
2017	60,000	80,000	0

We prepare income statements for IceAge under absorption costing and under variable costing. We consider three different cases: when units produced are equal to, exceed, or are less than units sold. **In general, income differs between the costing methods when inventory levels change.** Inventory levels change when units produced do not equal units sold.

Units Produced Equal Units Sold

Exhibit 6.4 presents the 2015 income statement for both costing methods (2016 and 2017 statements will follow). The income statement under variable costing (on the right) is a **contribution margin income statement.** Contribution margin is the excess of sales over variable costs. This margin contributes to covering all fixed costs and earning income. In the absorption costing income statement, expenses are not separated into variable and fixed components.

Production	=	Sales
60,000 pairs	=	60,000 pairs

Income under
Absorption costing = Variable costing
$580,000 = $580,000

EXHIBIT 6.4

Income for 2015—Quantity Produced Equals Quantity Sold*

ICEAGE COMPANY
Income Statement (Absorption Costing)
For Year Ended December 31, 2015

Sales* (60,000 × $40)	$2,400,000
Cost of goods sold (60,000 × $25**)	1,500,000
Gross margin	900,000
Selling and administrative expenses	
[$200,000 + (60,000 × $2)].	320,000
Net income	**$ 580,000**

* Units produced equal 60,000; units sold equal 60,000.
** ($4 DM + $8 DL + $3 VOH + $10 FOH)
† ($4 DM + $8 DL + $3 VOH)

A performance report that excludes fixed expenses and net income is a *contribution margin report.* Its bottom line is contribution margin.

ICEAGE COMPANY
Income Statement (Variable Costing)
For Year Ended December 31, 2015

Sales* (60,000 × $40)		$2,400,000
Variable expenses		
Variable production costs		
(60,000 × $15†)	$900,000	
Variable selling and administrative		
expenses (60,000 × $2).	120,000	1,020,000
Contribution margin.		1,380,000
Fixed expenses		
Fixed overhead	600,000	
Fixed selling and		
administrative expenses	200,000	800,000
Net income		**$ 580,000**

Exhibit 6.4 reveals that **reported income is identical under absorption costing and variable costing when the number of units produced equals the number of units sold.** Because variable costing expenses the same amount of fixed overhead cost ($600,000) as the period cost that absorption costing includes in cost of goods sold ($600,000 = 60,000 units × $10 fixed overhead per unit), net income is the same under either method when units produced equal units sold.

Exhibit 6.5 reorganizes the information from Exhibit 6.4 to show the assignment of costs to different expenses and assets under both absorption costing and variable costing. In this year, there are no units in ending inventory, so the finished goods inventory is $0 under both methods. When units produced equal units sold, there is no difference in *total* expenses reported on the income statement. Yet, there is a difference in what categories receive those costs. Absorption costing assigns $1,500,000 to cost of goods sold compared to $900,000 for variable costing. The $600,000 difference is a period cost for variable costing.

Point: Contribution margin income statements prepared under variable costing are useful in performing cost-volume-profit analyses.

EXHIBIT 6.5

Production Cost
Assignment for 2015

Absorption Costing		For Year 2015
Beginning finished goods inventory		$ 0
Cost of goods manufactured		
Direct materials	$240,000	
Direct labor.	480,000	
Variable manufacturing overhead.	180,000	
Fixed manufacturing overhead	600,000	1,500,000
Cost of goods available for sale		1,500,000
Less: Ending finished goods inventory		0
Cost of goods sold		$1,500,000

Income statement

Balance sheet

(Absorption) FG Inventory		
Beg.	0	
COGM	1,500,000	
		1,500,000 COGS
End.	0	

Variable Costing		For Year 2015
Beginning finished goods inventory		$ 0
Cost of goods manufactured		
Direct materials	$240,000	
Direct labor.	480,000	
Variable manufacturing overhead.	180,000	
Fixed manufacturing overhead	0	900,000
Cost of goods available for sale		900,000
Less: Ending finished goods inventory		0
Cost of goods sold.		900,000
Period costs		
Fixed manufacturing overhead		600,000
Total expenses		$1,500,000

Balance sheet   Income statement

(Variable) FG Inventory		
Beg.	0	
COGM	900,000	
		900,000 COGS
End.	0	

■ **Decision** Insight

Manufacturing Margin   Some managers compute **manufacturing margin** (also called *production margin*), which is sales less variable production costs. Some managers also require that internal income statements show this amount to highlight the impact of variable product costs on income. The contribution margin section of IceAge's variable costing income statement would appear as follows (compare this to Exhibit 6.4).

Sales	$2,400,000
Variable production costs	900,000
Manufacturing margin.	1,500,000
Variable selling & admin. exp.	120,000
Contribution margin	$1,380,000

© Steve Mason/Getty Images

Units Produced Exceed Units Sold

Exhibit 6.6 shows absorption costing and variable costing income statements for 2016. In 2016, 60,000 units were produced, which is the same as in 2015. However, only 40,000 units were sold, which means 20,000 units remain in ending inventory.

For 2016, income is $320,000 under absorption costing. Under variable costing income is $120,000. The cause of this $200,000 income difference is the different treatment of fixed overhead. Because

Production	>	**Sales**
60,000 pairs	>	40,000 pairs

Income under

Absorption costing > Variable costing
$320,000 > $120,000

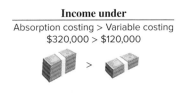

EXHIBIT 6.6

Income for 2016—Quantity Produced Exceeds Quantity Sold

ICEAGE COMPANY
Income Statement (Absorption Costing)
For Year Ended December 31, 2016

Sales* (40,000 × $40).	$1,600,000
Cost of goods sold (40,000 × $25**)	1,000,000
Gross margin	600,000
Selling and administrative expenses	
[$200,000 + (40,000 × $2)].	280,000
Net income	**$ 320,000**

* Units produced equal 60,000; units sold equal 40,000.
** ($4 DM + $8 DL + $3 VOH + $10 FOH)
† ($4 DM + $8 DL + $3 VOH)

ICEAGE COMPANY
Income Statement (Variable Costing)
For Year Ended December 31, 2016

Sales* (40,000 × $40).		$1,600,000
Variable expenses		
Variable production costs		
(40,000 × $15†)	$600,000	
Variable selling and administrative		
expenses (40,000 × $2)	80,000	680,000
Contribution margin.		920,000
Fixed expenses		
Fixed overhead	600,000	
Fixed selling and		
administrative expense	200,000	800,000
Net income		**$ 120,000**

variable costing expenses the $600,000 of fixed manufacturing overhead (FOH) as a period cost, and absorption costing expenses FOH based on the number of units sold (40,000 × $10), net income is lower under variable costing by $200,000 (20,000 units × $10).

Exhibit 6.7 reorganizes the information from Exhibit 6.6 to show the assignment of costs to different expenses and assets under both absorption costing and variable costing. When units produced exceed units sold, there is a difference in total expenses. Under absorption costing, cost of goods sold of $1,000,000 is $200,000 lower than the total expenses ($1,200,000) under variable costing. As a result, income (and ending finished goods inventory) under absorption costing is $200,000 greater than under variable costing because of the fixed overhead cost included in ending inventory (asset) under absorption costing. This $200,000 of fixed overhead cost will be reported in cost of goods sold in future years (under absorption costing) as those products are sold.

EXHIBIT 6.7

Production Cost Assignment for 2016

Absorption Costing		For Year 2016
Beginning finished goods inventory		$ 0
Cost of goods manufactured		
Direct materials	$240,000	
Direct labor.	480,000	
Variable manufacturing overhead.	180,000	
Fixed manufacturing overhead	600,000	1,500,000
Cost of goods available for sale		1,500,000
Less: Ending finished goods inventory		500,000*
Cost of goods sold		$1,000,000

* 20,000 units × $25 per unit
** 20,000 units × $15 per unit

(Absorption) FG Inventory			
Beg.	0		
COGM	1,500,000		
		1,000,000	COGS
End.	500,000		

Variable Costing		For Year 2016
Beginning finished goods inventory		$ 0
Cost of goods manufactured		
Direct materials	$240,000	
Direct labor.	480,000	
Variable manufacturing overhead.	180,000	
Fixed manufacturing overhead	0	900,000
Cost of goods available for sale		900,000
Less: Ending finished goods inventory		300,000**
Cost of goods sold		600,000
Period costs		
Fixed manufacturing overhead		600,000
Total expenses		$1,200,000

(Variable) FG Inventory			
Beg.	0		
COGM	900,000		
		600,000	COGS
End.	300,000		

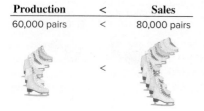

Production	<	Sales
60,000 pairs	<	80,000 pairs

Income under
Absorption costing < Variable costing
$840,000 < $1,040,000

Units Produced Are Less Than Units Sold

Exhibit 6.8 shows absorption costing and variable costing income statements for 2017. In 2017, IceAge produced 60,000 units and sold 80,000 units. Thus, IceAge produced

20,000 units fewer than it sold. This means IceAge sold all that it produced during the period, and it sold all of its beginning finished goods inventory. IceAge's income is $840,000 under absorption costing, but it is $1,040,000 under variable costing.

Point: IceAge can sell more units than it produced in 2017 because of inventory carried over from 2016.

EXHIBIT 6.8

Income for 2017—Quantity Produced Is Less Than Quantity Sold

ICEAGE COMPANY Income Statement (Absorption Costing) For Year Ended December 31, 2017		
Sales* (80,000 × $40).		$3,200,000
Cost of goods sold (80,000 × $25**).		2,000,000
Gross margin		1,200,000
Selling and administrative expenses [$200,000 + (80,000 × $2)].		360,000
Net income		**$ 840,000**

* Units produced equal 60,000; units sold equal 80,000.
** ($4 DM + $8 DL + $3 VOH)
† ($4 DM + $8 DL + $3 VOH + $10 FOH)

ICEAGE COMPANY Income Statement (Variable Costing) For Year Ended December 31, 2017		
Sales* (80,000 × $40).		$ 3,200,000
Variable expenses		
Variable production costs (80,000 × $15†)	$1,200,000	
Variable selling and administrative expenses (80,000 × $2)	160,000	1,360,000
Contribution margin.		1,840,000
Fixed expenses		
Fixed overhead	600,000	
Fixed selling and administrative expense.	200,000	800,000
Net income		**$1,040,000**

This $200,000 income difference is due to the treatment of fixed overhead (FOH). Beginning inventory in 2017 under absorption costing included $200,000 of fixed overhead cost incurred in 2016, which is assigned to cost of goods sold in 2017 under absorption costing. Because absorption costing expenses FOH based on the number of units sold (80,000), net income is higher under variable costing by $200,000 (20,000 units × $10).

Exhibit 6.9 reorganizes the information from Exhibit 6.8 to show the assignment of costs to different expenses and assets under both absorption costing and variable costing. When quantity produced is less than quantity sold, there is a difference in total costs assigned.

EXHIBIT 6.9

Production Cost Assignment for 2017

Absorption Costing		For Year 2017
Beginning finished goods inventory		$ 500,000*
Cost of goods manufactured		
Direct materials	$240,000	
Direct labor.	480,000	
Variable manufacturing overhead.	180,000	
Fixed manufacturing overhead	600,000	1,500,000
Cost of goods available for sale		2,000,000
Less: Ending finished goods inventory		0
Cost of goods sold.		$2,000,000

* 20,000 units × $25 per unit
** 20,000 units × $15 per unit

Income statement

Balance sheet

(Absorption) FG Inventory			
Beg.	500,000		
COGM	1,500,000		
		2,000,000	COGS
End.	0		

Variable Costing		For Year 2017
Beginning finished goods inventory		$ 300,000**
Cost of goods manufactured		
Direct materials	$240,000	
Direct labor.	480,000	
Variable manufacturing overhead.	180,000	
Fixed manufacturing overhead	0	900,000
Cost of goods available for sale		1,200,000
Less: Ending finished goods inventory		0
Cost of goods sold.		1,200,000
Period costs		
Fixed manufacturing overhead		600,000
Total expenses		$1,800,000

Income statement

Balance sheet

(Variable) FG Inventory			
Beg.	300,000		
COGM	900,000		
		1,200,000	COGS
End.	0		

Specifically, beginning inventory in 2017 under absorption costing was $500,000 (20,000 units × $25), whereas it was only $300,000 (20,000 units × $15) under variable costing. Consequently, when that inventory is sold in 2017, that $200,000 difference in inventory is included in cost of goods sold under absorption costing. Thus, the 2017 income under absorption costing is $200,000 less than the income under variable costing.

Summarizing Income Reporting

Income reported under both variable costing and absorption costing for the years 2015 through 2017 for IceAge is summarized in Exhibit 6.10. Total income is $1,740,000 for this time period for *both* methods. Further, **income under absorption costing and that under variable costing differ whenever the quantity produced and the quantity sold differ.** These differences in income are due to the different timing with which fixed overhead costs are reported in income under the two methods. Specifically, *income under absorption costing is higher when more units are produced than are sold and is lower when fewer units are produced than are sold.*

FG Inventory	Income Effect
No change	No difference
Increases	Absorption > Variable
Decreases	Variable > Absorption

EXHIBIT 6.10

Summary of Income
Reporting

	Units Produced	Units Sold	Income under Absorption Costing	Income under Variable Costing	Income Differences
2015	60,000	60,000	$ 580,000	$ 580,000	$ 0
2016	60,000	40,000	320,000	120,000	200,000
2017	60,000	80,000	840,000	1,040,000	(200,000)
Totals	180,000	180,000	$1,740,000	$1,740,000	$ 0

Point: In our illustration the company produces the same number of units (60,000) each year. We provide an example with varying yearly production levels in Need-To-Know 6-4 at the end of the chapter.

For IceAge, the total number of units produced over 2015–2017 exactly equals the number of units sold over that period. This meant that the difference between absorption costing income and variable costing income for the *total* three-year period is zero. In reality, it is unusual for production and sales quantities to exactly equal each other over such a short period of time. We normally see differences in income for these two methods extending over several years.

NEED-TO-KNOW 6-2

Computing Income under Absorption and Variable Costing

P2

ZBest Mfg. reports the following data for 2017.

Direct materials cost........	$6 per unit	Units produced	20,000 units
Direct labor cost...........	$11 per unit	Units sold	14,000 units
Variable overhead cost	$3 per unit	Variable selling and administrative expenses	$2 per unit
Fixed overhead	$680,000 per year	Fixed selling and administrative expenses.......	$112,000 per year
Sales price...............	$80 per unit		

1. Prepare an income statement for 2017 under absorption costing.
2. Prepare an income statement for 2017 under variable costing.

Solution

ZBEST MFG. Income Statement (Absorption Costing) For Year Ended December 31, 2017	
Sales (14,000 × $80)...................	$1,120,000
Cost of goods sold (14,000 × $54)*.......	756,000
Gross margin	364,000
Selling and admin. expenses [$112,000 + (14,000 × $2)]..........	140,000
Net income.........................	$ 224,000

* $6 DM + $11 DL + $3 VOH + $20 FOH ($680,000/20,000)
  = $54 per unit
** $6 DM + $11 DL + $3 VOH = $20 per unit
† 14,000 × $2 per unit.

ZBEST MFG. Income Statement (Variable Costing) For Year Ended December 31, 2017		
Sales (14,000 × $80).............		$1,120,000
Variable expenses		
Variable production costs (14,000 × $20)**	$280,000	
Variable selling and admin. expenses†	28,000	308,000
Contribution margin.............		812,000
Fixed expenses		
Fixed overhead	680,000	
Fixed selling and admin. expenses	112,000	792,000
Net income....................		$ 20,000

Do More: QS 6-3, QS 6-4,
E 6-3, E 6-4, E 6-5.

The difference in income between the two methods ($204,000) can be computed as the 6,000 units added to ending inventory × $34 FOH per unit.

Converting Income under Variable Costing to Absorption Costing

Companies can use variable costing for *internal* reporting and business decisions, but they must use absorption costing for *external* reporting and tax reporting. For companies concerned about maintaining two costing systems, we can readily convert reports under variable costing to those using absorption costing.

Income under variable costing is restated to that under absorption costing by adding the fixed overhead cost in ending inventory and subtracting the fixed overhead cost in beginning inventory. Exhibit 6.11 shows the formula for this calculation.

P3

Convert income under variable costing to the absorption cost basis.

$$\begin{array}{c}\text{Income under}\\\text{absorption costing}\end{array} = \begin{array}{c}\text{Income under}\\\text{variable costing}\end{array} + \begin{array}{c}\text{Fixed overhead cost}\\\text{in ending inventory*}\end{array} - \begin{array}{c}\text{Fixed overhead cost}\\\text{in beginning inventory*}\end{array}$$

*Under absorption costing.

EXHIBIT 6.11

Formula to Convert Variable Costing Income to Absorption Costing

Exhibit 6.12 shows the computations of absorption costing income. To restate variable costing income to absorption costing income for 2016, add back the **fixed overhead cost deferred in** (ending) **inventory.** To restate variable costing income to absorption costing income for 2017, deduct the **fixed overhead cost recognized from** (beginning) **inventory,** which was incurred in 2016, but expensed in the 2017 cost of goods sold when the inventory was sold.

	2015	2016	2017
Variable costing income (Exhibit 6.10)	$580,000	$120,000	$1,040,000
Add: Fixed overhead cost deferred in ending inventory			
(20,000 × $10).	0	200,000	0
Less: Fixed overhead cost recognized from beginning inventory			
(20,000 × $10).	0	0	(200,000)
Absorption costing income	$580,000	$320,000	$ 840,000

EXHIBIT 6.12

Converting Variable Costing Income to Absorption Costing Income

COMPARING VARIABLE COSTING AND ABSORPTION COSTING

This section compares the roles of absorption and variable costing in the following decisions.

- Planning production
- Setting prices
- Controlling costs
- Cost-volume-profit analysis

Planning Production

Many companies link manager bonuses to income computed under absorption costing because this is how income is reported to shareholders (per GAAP). This can lead such managers to produce excess inventory, as we show next.

C1

Describe how absorption costing can result in overproduction.

To illustrate how a reward system can lead to overproduction under absorption costing, let's use IceAge's 2015 data with one change: its manager decides to produce 100,000 units instead of 60,000. Because only 60,000 units are sold, the 40,000 units of excess production will be stored in ending finished goods inventory.

The left side of Exhibit 6.13 shows the product cost per unit under absorption costing when 60,000 units are produced (same as Exhibit 6.3). The right side shows unit cost when 100,000 units are produced.

Total product cost *per unit* is $4 less when 100,000 units are produced. This is because the company is spreading the $600,000 fixed overhead cost over 40,000 more units when 100,000 units are produced than when 60,000 units are produced.

EXHIBIT 6.13

Unit Cost under Absorption Costing for Different Production Levels

Absorption Costing When 60,000 Units Are Produced		Absorption Costing When 100,000 Units Are Produced	
	Per Unit		**Per Unit**
Direct materials	$ 4	Direct materials............................	$ 4
Direct labor	8	Direct labor	8
Variable overhead	3	Variable overhead.........................	3
Total variable	15	Total variable	15
Fixed overhead.........................		Fixed overhead	
($600,000/60,000 units)	10	($600,000/100,000 units)	6
Total product cost	**$25**	**Total product cost**	**$21**

The $4 per unit difference in product cost per unit impacts income reporting. Exhibit 6.14 presents the 2015 income statement under absorption costing for the two alternative production levels.

EXHIBIT 6.14

Income under Absorption Costing for Different Production Levels

ICEAGE COMPANY Income Statement (Absorption Costing) For Year Ended December 31, 2015 [60,000 Units Produced; 60,000 Units Sold]			ICEAGE COMPANY Income Statement (Absorption Costing) For Year Ended December 31, 2015 [100,000 Units Produced; 60,000 Units Sold]		
Sales (60,000 × $40)		$2,400,000	Sales (60,000 × $40)		$2,400,000
Cost of goods sold (60,000 × $25)		1,500,000	Cost of goods sold (60,000 × $21)		1,260,000
Gross margin		900,000	Gross margin		1,140,000
Selling and administrative expenses			Selling and administrative expenses		
Variable (60,000 × $2)......	$120,000		Variable (60,000 × $2)	$120,000	
Fixed...................	200,000	320,000	Fixed..................	200,000	320,000
Net income		**$ 580,000**	**Net income**		**$ 820,000**

Common sense suggests that because the company's variable cost per unit, total fixed costs, and sales are identical in both cases, merely producing more units and creating excess ending inventory should not increase income. Yet, income under absorption costing is $240,000 greater if IceAge produces 40,000 more units than necessary and builds up ending inventory. The reason is that $240,000 of fixed overhead (40,000 units × $6) is assigned to ending inventory instead of being expensed as cost of goods sold in 2015. This shows that under absorption costing, a manager can increase income just by producing more and disregarding whether the excess units can be sold or not. This incentive problem encourages inventory buildup, which leads to increased costs in storage, financing, and obsolescence. If the excess inventory is never sold, it will be disposed of at a loss.

The manager incentive problem is avoided when income is measured using variable costing. To illustrate, Exhibit 6.15 reports income under variable costing for the same production levels used in Exhibit 6.14. This demonstrates that managers cannot increase income under variable costing by merely increasing production without increasing sales.

Reported income under variable costing is not affected by production level changes because *all* fixed production costs are expensed in the year when incurred. Under variable costing, companies increase income by selling more units, not by producing excess inventory.

■ **Decision** Ethics

Production Manager   Your company produces and sells MP3 players. Due to competition, your company projects sales to be 35% less than last year. The CEO is concerned that top executives won't receive bonuses because of the expected sales decrease. The controller suggests that if the company produces as many units as last year, reported income might achieve the level for bonuses to be paid. Should your company produce excess inventory to maintain income? What ethical issues arise? ■   *Answer:* Under absorption costing, fixed overhead costs are spread over all units produced. Thus, fixed cost for each unit will be lower if more units are produced. This means the company can increase income by producing excess units even if sales remain constant. But excess inventory leads to increased financing cost and obsolescence. Also, producing excess inventory to meet income levels for bonuses harms company owners and is unethical. You must discuss this with the appropriate managers.

ICEAGE COMPANY Income Statement (Variable Costing) For Year Ended December 31, 2015 [60,000 Units Produced; 60,000 Units Sold]		
Sales (60,000 × $40)		$2,400,000
Variable expenses		
Variable production costs (60,000 × $15)..........	$900,000	
Variable selling and administrative expenses (60,000 × $2)..........	120,000	1,020,000
Contribution margin...........		1,380,000
Fixed expenses		
Fixed overhead	600,000	
Fixed selling and administrative expense...............	200,000	800,000
Net income		**$ 580,000**

ICEAGE COMPANY Income Statement (Variable Costing) For Year Ended December 31, 2015 [100,000 Units Produced; 60,000 Units Sold]		
Sales (60,000 × $40).........		$2,400,000
Variable expenses		
Variable production costs (60,000 × $15)..........	$900,000	
Variable selling and administrative expenses (60,000 × $2)..........	120,000	1,020,000
Contribution margin...........		1,380,000
Fixed expenses		
Fixed overhead	600,000	
Fixed selling and administrative expenses...............	200,000	800,000
Net income		**$ 580,000**

EXHIBIT 6.15

Income under Variable Costing for Different Production Levels

Setting Prices

Over the long run, prices must be high enough to cover all costs, including variable costs and fixed costs, and still provide an acceptable return to owners. For this purpose, *absorption* cost information is useful because it reflects the full costs that sales must exceed for the company to be profitable. We can use a three-step process to determine product selling prices:

P4

Determine product selling price based on absorption costing.

Step 1: Determine the product cost per unit using absorption costing.

Step 2: Determine the target *markup* on product cost per unit.

Step 3: Add the target markup to the product cost to find the target selling price.

To illustrate, consider IceAge. Under absorption costing, its product cost is $25 per unit (from Exhibit 6.3). IceAge's management must then determine a target markup on this product cost. This target markup could be based on industry averages, prices that have been charged in the past, or other information. In addition, this markup must be set high enough to cover selling and administrative expenses (both variable and fixed) that are excluded from product costs. Assume IceAge targets a markup of 60% of absorption cost. With that information, the company computes a target selling price as in Exhibit 6.16.

Step 1	Absorption cost per unit (from Exhibit 6.3)	$25
Step 2	Target markup per unit ($25 × 60%)	15
Step 3	Target selling price per unit	$40

EXHIBIT 6.16

Determining Selling Price with Absorption Costing

IceAge can use this target selling price as a starting point in setting prices. Management must also consider the level of competition in its industry and customer preferences. If customers are not willing to pay $40 per unit, IceAge must either lower its target markup or find ways to reduce its costs.

While absorption cost information is useful in setting long-run prices, it can lead to misleading decisions in analyzing special orders. We show how variable cost information can be used to analyze special order decisions in the Decision Analysis at the end of the chapter.

Controlling Costs

An effective management practice is to hold managers responsible only for their **controllable costs.** A cost is controllable if a manager can determine or greatly affect the amount incurred.

Uncontrollable costs are not within the manager's influence. In general, variable production costs and fixed production costs are controlled at different levels of management.

- Variable production costs, like direct materials and direct labor, are controlled by the production supervisor.
- Fixed costs related to production capacity, like depreciation, are controlled by higher-level managers that make decisions to change factory size or add new machines.

Income statements that separately report variable and fixed costs, as is done in the **contribution format** used in variable costing, are more useful for controlling costs. Because absorption costing does not separate variable from fixed costs, it is less useful in evaluating the effectiveness of cost control by different levels of managers.

▇ Decision Maker

Internal Auditor   Your company uses absorption costing. Management is disappointed because its external auditors are requiring it to write off an inventory amount because it exceeds what the company could reasonably sell in the foreseeable future. Why would management produce more than it sells? Why would management be disappointed about the write-off? ■   *Answer:* If bonuses are tied to income, managers have incentives to increase income for personal gain. If absorption costing is used to determine income, management can reduce current period expenses (and raise income) with overproduction, which shifts fixed production costs to future periods. This decision fails to consider whether there is a viable market for all units that are produced. If there is not, an auditor can conclude that the inventory does not have "future economic value" and pressure management to write it off. Such a write-off reduces income by the cost of the excess inventory.

CVP Analysis

The previous chapter discussed cost-volume-profit (CVP) analysis for making managerial decisions. If the income statement is prepared under variable costing and presented in the contribution format, the data for CVP analysis are readily available.

Using the variable costing income statement from the left side of Exhibit 6.15, IceAge computes its break-even point as follows.

$$\frac{\text{Break-even}}{\text{(in units)}} = \frac{\text{Fixed costs}}{\text{Contribution margin per unit}} = \frac{\$800,000}{\$23^*} = 34,783 \text{ (rounded)}$$

* Total contribution margin/Units produced = \$1,380,000/60,000

If the income statement is prepared under absorption costing, the data needed for CVP analysis are not readily available. Thus, we must reclassify cost data in order to conduct CVP analysis if absorption costing is used.

Variable Costing for Service Firms

Variable costing also applies to service companies. Because service companies do not produce inventory, the differences in income from absorption and variable costing shown for a manufacturer do not apply. Still, a focus on variable costs can be useful in managerial decisions for service firms. One example is a hotel receiving an offer to reserve a large block of rooms at a discounted price. Another example is "special order" pricing for airlines when they sell tickets shortly before a flight at deeply discounted prices. If the discounted price exceeds variable costs, such sales increase contribution margin and net income.

For example, BlueSky provides charter airline services. Its variable costing income for 2017 is shown in Exhibit 6.17. Based on an activity level of 120 flights (60% of its capacity), BlueSky's variable cost per flight is \$30,000, computed as \$3,600,000/120. BlueSky's normal price is \$50,000 per flight. A community group has offered BlueSky \$35,000 to fly its

EXHIBIT 6.17

Variable Costing Income Statement for Service Provider

BLUESKY Income Statement (Variable Costing) For Year Ended December 31, 2017		
Revenue (120 flights)...................		$6,000,000
Variable expenses		
Wages, salaries, and benefits..........	$1,920,000	
Fuel and oil.........................	1,080,000	
Food and beverages	600,000	3,600,000
Contribution margin		2,400,000
Fixed expenses		
Depreciation........................	300,000	
Rentals	420,000	720,000
Operating income.....................		$1,680,000

members to Washington, D.C. In making its decision, BlueSky should *ignore allocated fixed costs*. If fixed costs will not increase from accepting this charter flight, the company's expected contribution margin from the special offer is

Revenue from charter flight	$35,000
Variable costs of charter flight	30,000
Contribution margin of charter flight	$ 5,000

BlueSky should accept the charter-flight offer, as it provides a contribution margin of $5,000. An incorrect analysis based on absorption costing might lead management to reject the offer.

Part 1. A manufacturer's absorption cost per unit is $60. Compute the target selling price per unit if a 30% markup is targeted.

Solution

Absorption cost per unit	$60
Target markup per unit ($60 × 30%)	18
Target selling price per unit	$78

Part 2. A hotel rents its 200 luxury suites at a rate of $500 per night per suite. The hotel's cost per night is $400, consisting of:

Variable costs	$160
Fixed costs (allocated)	240
Total cost per night per room	$400

The hotel's manager has received an offer to reserve a block of 40 suites for $250 per suite per night during the hotel's off-season, when it has many available suites. Determine whether the offer should be accepted or rejected.

Solution

The allocated fixed costs should be ignored. Because the offer price of $250 per suite is greater than the variable costs of $160 per suite, the offer should be accepted.

NEED-TO-KNOW 6-3

Setting Prices

P4

Do More: QS 6-17, E 6-11

Considering Special Offers

A1

Do More: QS 6-18, E 6-13, E 6-14, E 6-15

SUSTAINABILITY AND ACCOUNTING

EP&L

EXHIBIT 6.18

Environmental Profit and
Loss Reporting

This chapter showed alternative ways to compute income. When businesses consider the effects of their operations on the environment, more ways to measure income emerge.

For example, **Puma,** a maker of athletic shoes and apparel, developed an **environmental profit and loss (EP&L) account,** also called EP&L report, which is a listing in monetary terms of the impact on human welfare from PUMA's business activities. In this report, profit is the monetary value of activities that benefit the environment and loss is the monetary value of activities that harm the environment. While many companies measure and attempt to reduce their water usage, carbon emissions, and waste, PUMA takes the next step by putting environmental impacts into monetary terms.

Exhibit 6.18 shows one form of an EP&L report for PUMA. In this year, PUMA reported no profits from activities that benefited the environment, but did report losses (costs) of several activities that harmed the environment.

Environmental Profit and Loss		
Environmental profits		€ 0
Environmental losses		
Water use.	€47	
Carbon emissions	47	
Land use	37	
Air pollution.	11	
Waste.	3	145
Net environmental loss		€145

Putting environmental impacts into monetary terms enables companies to better grasp the effects of their activities. PUMA's €145 net environmental loss from Exhibit 6.18, although not included in computing GAAP net income, was over 70% of net income for that year. In addition, over 85% of the company's environmental costs are from suppliers and processors at early stages of the company's supply chain, and roughly 66% of its environmental costs are from its footwear division. The EP&L report enables managers to develop strategies that are likely to have the greatest impact in reducing environmental costs.

Riffraff, this chapter's opening company, advocates the importance of small, local businesses for sustainable communities and jobs. "Small businesses are the largest employer nationally," explains Kirsten, "and local businesses have less environmental impact. We buy locally and are located in the city center, reducing transportation costs, habitat loss, and pollution."

© Kevin Dodge/Corbis/Getty Images

 Decision Analysis **Pricing Special Orders**

A1_____

Use variable costing in
pricing special orders.

Point: Total cost per unit is computed under absorption costing.

Point: Use of relevant costs in special order and other managerial decisions is covered more extensively in a later chapter.

Point: Fixed overhead costs won't increase when these additional units are sold because the company already has the capacity.

Over the long run, prices must cover all fixed and variable costs. Over the short run, however, fixed production costs such as the cost to maintain plant capacity do not change with changes in production levels. With excess capacity, increases in production levels would increase variable production costs, but not fixed costs. This implies that while managers try to maintain the long-run price on existing orders, which covers all production costs, managers should accept special orders *provided the special order price exceeds variable cost.*

To illustrate, let's return to the data of IceAge Company. Recall that its variable production cost per unit is $15 and its total production cost per unit is $25 (at a production level of 60,000 units). Assume that it receives a special order for 1,000 pairs of skates at an offer price of $22 per pair from a foreign skating school. This special order will not affect IceAge's regular sales, and its plant has excess capacity to fill the order.

Using absorption costing information, cost is $25 per unit and the special order price is $22 per unit. These data might suggest that management reject the order as it would lose $3,000, computed as 1,000 units at $3 loss per pair ($22 − $25).

However, closer analysis suggests that this order should be accepted. The $22 order price exceeds the $15 variable cost of the product. Specifically, Exhibit 6.19 reveals that the incremental revenue from accepting the order is $22,000 (1,000 units at $22 per unit), whereas the incremental production cost of the order is $15,000 (1,000 units at $15 per unit) and the incremental variable selling and administrative cost is $2,000 (1,000 units at $2 per unit). Thus, both contribution margin and net income would increase by $5,000 from accepting the order. Variable costing reveals this profitable opportunity while absorption costing hides it.

The reason for increased income from accepting the special order lies in the different behavior of variable and fixed production costs. If the order is rejected, only variable costs are saved. Fixed costs, however, do not change in the short run regardless of rejecting or accepting this order. Because incremental

EXHIBIT 6.19

Computing Incremental
Income for a Special Order

Reject Special Order		Accept Special Order	
Incremental sales	$0	Incremental sales (1,000 × $22)	$22,000
Incremental costs	0	Incremental costs	
		Variable production cost (1,000 × $15)	15,000
		Variable selling and admin. expense (1,000 × $2)	2,000
Incremental income	$0	Incremental income	$ 5,000

revenue from the order exceeds incremental costs (only variable costs in this case), accepting the special
order increases company income.

Navaroli Company began operations on January 5, 2016. Cost and sales information for its first two calendar years of operations are summarized below.

NEED-TO-KNOW 6-4

COMPREHENSIVE

Manufacturing costs		Production and sales data	
Direct materials	$80 per unit	Units produced, 2016	200,000 units
Direct labor.	$120 per unit	Units sold, 2016.	140,000 units
Factory overhead costs for the year		Units in ending inventory, 2016	60,000 units
Variable overhead	$30 per unit	Units produced, 2017	80,000 units
Fixed overhead	$14,000,000	Units sold, 2017.	140,000 units
Nonmanufacturing costs		Units in ending inventory, 2017	0 units
Variable selling and administrative.	$10 per unit	Sales price per unit	$600 per unit
Fixed selling and administrative	$ 8,000,000		

Required

1. Prepare an income statement for the company for 2016 under absorption costing.
2. Prepare an income statement for the company for 2016 under variable costing.
3. Explain the source(s) of the difference in reported income for 2016 under the two costing methods.
4. Prepare an income statement for the company for 2017 under absorption costing.
5. Prepare an income statement for the company for 2017 under variable costing.
6. Prepare a schedule to convert variable costing income to absorption costing income for each of the
   years 2016 and 2017. Use the format in Exhibit 6.12.

PLANNING THE SOLUTION

- Set up a table to compute the product cost per unit under the two costing methods (refer to Exhibit 6.3).
- Prepare income statements under the two costing methods (refer to Exhibit 6.6).
- Consider differences in the treatment of fixed overhead costs for the income statement to answer re-
  quirements 3 and 6.

SOLUTION

Before the income statement for 2016 is prepared, unit costs for 2016 are computed under the two costing
methods as follows.

	Product Cost per Unit	
	Absorption Costing	**Variable Costing**
Direct materials	$ 80	$ 80
Direct labor	120	120
Overhead		
Variable overhead.	30	30
Fixed overhead*	70	—
Total product cost per unit	$300	$230

*Fixed overhead per unit = $14,000,000 ÷ 200,000 units = $70 per unit.

1. Absorption costing income statement for 2016.

NAVAROLI COMPANY Income Statement (Absorption Costing) For Year Ended December 31, 2016	
Sales (140,000 × $600)	$84,000,000
Cost of goods sold (140,000 × $300)	42,000,000
Gross margin	42,000,000
Selling and administrative expenses ($1,400,000 + $8,000,000)	9,400,000
Net income	$32,600,000

2. Variable costing income statement for 2016.

NAVAROLI COMPANY Income Statement (Variable Costing) For Year Ended December 31, 2016		
Sales (140,000 × $600)		$84,000,000
Variable expenses		
Variable production costs (140,000 × $230)	$32,200,000	
Variable selling and administrative costs	1,400,000	33,600,000
Contribution margin		50,400,000
Fixed expenses		
Fixed overhead	14,000,000	
Fixed selling and administrative	8,000,000	22,000,000
Net income		$28,400,000

3. Income under absorption costing is $4,200,000 more than that under variable costing even though sales are identical for each. This difference is due to the different treatment of fixed overhead cost. Under variable costing, the entire $14,000,000 of fixed overhead is expensed on the 2016 income statement. However, under absorption costing, $70 of fixed overhead cost is allocated to each of the 200,000 units produced. Because there were 60,000 units unsold at year-end, $4,200,000 (60,000 units × $70 per unit) of fixed overhead cost allocated to these units will be carried on its balance sheet in ending inventory. Consequently, reported income under absorption costing is $4,200,000 higher than variable costing income for the current period.

Before the income statement for 2017 is prepared, product cost per unit in 2017 is computed under the two costing methods as follows.

	Product Cost per Unit	
	Absorption Costing	Variable Costing
Direct materials	$ 80	$ 80
Direct labor	120	120
Overhead		
Variable overhead	30	30
Fixed overhead*	175	
Total product cost	$405	$230

*Fixed overhead per unit = $14,000,000/80,000 units = $175 per unit.

4. Absorption costing income statement for 2017.

NAVAROLI COMPANY Income Statement (Absorption Costing) For Year Ended December 31, 2017		
Sales (140,000 × $600).....................................		$84,000,000
Cost of goods sold		
From beginning inventory (60,000 × $300)	$18,000,000	
Produced during the year (80,000 × $405)	32,400,000	50,400,000
Gross margin.....................................		33,600,000
Selling and administrative expenses ($1,400,000 + $8,000,000)...........		9,400,000
Net income.....................................		$24,200,000

5. Variable costing income statement for 2017.

NAVAROLI COMPANY Income Statement (Variable Costing) For Year Ended December 31, 2017		
Sales (140,000 × $600)		$84,000,000
Variable expenses		
Variable product costs (140,000 × $230)................	$32,200,000	
Variable selling and administrative costs	1,400,000	33,600,000
Contribution margin		50,400,000
Fixed expenses		
Fixed overhead.....................................	14,000,000	
Fixed selling and administrative	8,000,000	22,000,000
Net income		$28,400,000

6. Conversion of variable costing income to absorption costing income.

	2016	2017
Variable costing income..................................	$28,400,000	$28,400,000
Add: Fixed overhead cost deferred in ending inventory (60,000 × $70)................	4,200,000	0
Less: Fixed overhead cost recognized from beginning inventory (60,000 × $70).............	0	(4,200,000)
Absorption costing income	$32,600,000	$24,200,000

Point: Total income over the two years equals $56,800,000 under both costing methods. This is because the total number of units produced over these two years equals the total number of units sold over these two years.

Summary

C1 Describe how absorption costing can result in overproduction. Under absorption costing, fixed overhead costs are allocated to all units including both units sold and units in ending inventory. Consequently, expenses associated with the fixed overhead allocated to ending inventory are deferred to a future period. As a result, the larger ending inventory is, the more overhead cost is deferred to the future, and the greater current period income is.

A1 Use variable costing in pricing special orders. Over the short run, fixed production costs such as cost of maintaining plant capacity do not change with changes in production levels. When there is excess capacity, increases in production levels would only increase variable costs. Thus, managers should accept special orders as long as the order price is greater than the variable cost. This is because accepting the special order would increase only variable costs.

P1 Compute unit cost under both absorption and variable costing. Absorption cost per unit includes direct materials, direct labor, and *all* overhead, whereas variable cost per unit includes direct materials, direct labor, and only *variable* overhead.

P2 Prepare and analyze an income statement using absorption costing and using variable costing. The variable costing income statement differs from the absorption costing income statement in that it classifies expenses based on cost behavior rather than function. Instead of gross margin, the variable costing income statement shows contribution margin. This contribution margin format focuses attention on the relation between costs and sales that is not evident from the absorption costing format. Under absorption costing, some fixed overhead cost is allocated to ending inventory and is carried on the balance sheet to the next period. However, all fixed costs are expensed in the period incurred under variable costing. Consequently, absorption costing income is generally greater than variable costing income if units produced exceed units sold, and conversely.

P3 **Convert income under variable costing to the absorption cost basis.** Variable costing income can be adjusted to absorption costing income by adding the fixed cost allocated to ending inventory and subtracting the fixed cost previously allocated to beginning inventory.

P4 **Determine product selling price based on absorption costing.** Target selling prices can be determined by adding a markup to the total product cost under absorption costing. The markup should be enough to cover selling and administrative expenses, provide for a target profit, and yield a competitive price.

Key Terms

Absorption costing (also called **full costing**)

Contribution format

Contribution margin income statement

Controllable costs

Environmental profit and loss (EP&L) account

Fixed overhead cost deferred in inventory

Fixed overhead cost recognized from inventory

Manufacturing margin

Uncontrollable costs

Variable costing (also called **direct** or **marginal costing**)

Multiple Choice Quiz

Answer questions 1 and 2 using the following data.

Units produced	1,000
Variable costs	
Direct materials	$3 per unit
Direct labor.	$5 per unit
Variable overhead	$3 per unit
Variable selling and administrative.	$1 per unit
Fixed overhead	$3,000 total
Fixed selling and administrative	$1,000 total

1. Product cost per unit under absorption costing is:
   a. $11.   **c.** $14.   **e.** $16.
   b. $12.   **d.** $15.

2. Product cost per unit under variable costing is:
   a. $11.   **c.** $14.   **e.** $16.
   b. $12.   **d.** $15.

3. Under variable costing, which costs are included in product cost?
   a. All variable product costs, including direct materials, direct labor, and variable overhead.

   b. All variable and fixed allocations of product costs, including direct materials, direct labor, and both variable and fixed overhead.
   c. All variable product costs except for variable overhead.
   d. All variable and fixed allocations of product costs, except for both variable and fixed overhead.

4. The difference between product cost per unit under absorption costing as compared to that under variable costing is:
   a. Direct materials and direct labor.
   b. Fixed and variable portions of overhead.
   c. Fixed overhead only.
   d. Variable overhead only.

5. When production exceeds sales, which of the following is true?
   a. No change occurs to inventories for either absorption costing or variable costing methods.
   b. Use of absorption costing produces a higher net income than the use of variable costing.
   c. Use of absorption costing produces a lower net income than the use of variable costing.
   d. Use of absorption costing causes inventory value to decrease more than it would through the use of variable costing.

ANSWERS TO MULTIPLE CHOICE QUIZ

1. c; $14, computed as $3 + $5 + $3 + ($3,000/1,000 units).

2. a; $11, computed as $3 + $5 + $3 (consisting of all variable product costs).

3. a

4. c

5. b

Icon denotes assignments that involve decision making.

Discussion Questions

1. What costs are normally included in product costs under variable costing?

2. What costs are normally included in product costs under absorption costing?

3. When units produced exceed units sold for a reporting period, would income under variable costing be greater than, equal to, or less than income under absorption costing? Explain.

4. Describe how the following items are computed: *a.* Gross margin and *b.* Contribution margin.

5. How can absorption costing lead to incorrect short-run pricing decisions?

6. What conditions must exist to achieve accurate short-run pricing decisions using variable costing?

7. Describe the usefulness of variable costing for controlling company costs.

8. Describe how use of absorption costing in determining income can lead to overproduction and a buildup of inventory. Explain how variable costing can avoid this same problem.

9. What are the major limitations of variable costing?

10. **Google** uses variable costing for several business decisions. How can variable **GOOGLE** costing income statements be converted to absorption costing?

11. Explain how contribution margin analysis is useful for managerial decisions and performance evaluations.

12. **Samsung**'s managers rely on reports of variable costs. How can variable costing reports prepared using the contribution margin format help managers in computing break-even volume in units? **Samsung**

13. Assume that **Apple** has received a special order from a retailer for 1,000 specially outfitted iPads. This is a one-time order, which will not require any additional capacity or fixed costs. What should Apple consider when determining a selling price for these iPads? **APPLE**

14. How can **Samsung** use variable costing to help better understand its operations and to make better pricing decisions? **Samsung**

connect

Vijay Company reports the following information regarding its production costs. Compute its product cost per unit under absorption costing.

Direct materials	$10 per unit
Direct labor	$20 per unit
Overhead costs for the year	
Variable overhead	$10 per unit
Fixed overhead	$160,000
Units produced	20,000 units

QUICK STUDY

QS 6-1
Computing unit cost under absorption costing
P1

Refer to Vijay Company's data in QS 6-1. Compute its product cost per unit under variable costing.

QS 6-2
Computing unit cost under variable costing   P1

Aces Inc., a manufacturer of tennis rackets, began operations this year. The company produced 6,000 rackets and sold 4,900. Each racket was sold at a price of $90. Fixed overhead costs are $78,000, and fixed selling and administrative costs are $65,200. The company also reports the following per unit variable costs for the year. Prepare an income statement under variable costing.

Variable product costs	$25.00
Variable selling and administrative expenses	2.00

QS 6-3
Variable costing income statement
P2

Aces Inc., a manufacturer of tennis rackets, began operations this year. The company produced 6,000 rackets and sold 4,900. Each racket was sold at a price of $90. Fixed overhead costs are $78,000, and fixed selling and administrative costs are $65,200. The company also reports the following per unit variable costs for the year. Prepare an income statement under absorption costing.

Variable product costs	$25.00
Variable selling and administrative expenses	2.00

QS 6-4
Absorption costing income statement
P2

QS 6-5

Absorption costing and gross margin

P2

Ramort Company reports the following cost data for its single product. The company regularly sells 20,000 units of its product at a price of $60 per unit. Compute gross margin under absorption costing.

Direct materials	$10 per unit
Direct labor	$12 per unit
Overhead costs for the year	
Variable overhead	$3 per unit
Fixed overhead per year	$40,000
Selling and administrative costs for the year	
Variable	$2 per unit
Fixed	$65,200
Normal production level (in units)	20,000 units

QS 6-6

Absorption costing and gross margin **P2**

Refer to the information about Ramort Company in QS 6-5. If Ramort doubles its production to 40,000 units while sales remain at the current 20,000-unit level, by how much would the company's gross margin increase or decrease under absorption costing?

QS 6-7

Variable costing and contribution margin **P2**

Refer to the information about Ramort Company in QS 6-5. Compute contribution margin under variable costing.

QS 6-8

Variable costing and contribution margin **P2**

Refer to the information about Ramort Company in QS 6-5. If Ramort doubles its production to 40,000 units while sales remain at the current 20,000-unit level, by how much would the company's contribution margin increase or decrease under variable costing?

QS 6-9

Computing manufacturing margin **P2**

D'Souza Company sold 10,000 units of its product at a price of $80 per unit. Total variable cost is $50 per unit, consisting of $40 in variable production cost and $10 in variable selling and administrative cost. Compute the manufacturing (production) margin for the company under variable costing.

QS 6-10

Computing contribution margin **P2**

D'Souza Company sold 10,000 units of its product at a price of $80 per unit. Total variable cost is $50 per unit, consisting of $40 in variable production cost and $10 in variable selling and administrative cost. Compute the contribution margin.

QS 6-11

Converting variable costing income to absorption costing

P3

Diaz Company reports the following variable costing income statement for its single product. This company's sales totaled 50,000 units, but its production was 80,000 units. It had no beginning finished goods inventory for the current period.

DIAZ COMPANY
Income Statement (Variable Costing)

Sales (50,000 units × $60 per unit)	$3,000,000
Variable expenses	
Variable manufacturing expense (50,000 units × $28 per unit)	1,400,000
Variable selling and admin. expense (50,000 units × $5 per unit)	250,000
Total variable expenses.	1,650,000
Contribution margin	1,350,000
Fixed expenses	
Fixed overhead	320,000
Fixed selling and administrative expense	160,000
Total fixed expenses	480,000
Net income	$ 870,000

1. Convert this company's variable costing income statement to an absorption costing income statement.
2. Explain the difference in income between the variable costing and absorption costing income statement.

Ming Company had net income of $772,200 based on variable costing. Beginning and ending inventories were 7,800 units and 5,200 units, respectively. Assume the fixed overhead per unit was $3.00 for both the beginning and ending inventory. What is net income under absorption costing?

QS 6-12
Converting variable costing income to absorption costing income   P3

Mortech had net income of $250,000 based on variable costing. Beginning and ending inventories were 50,000 units and 48,000 units, respectively. Assume the fixed overhead per unit was $0.75 for both the beginning and ending inventory. What is net income under absorption costing?

QS 6-13
Converting variable costing income to absorption costing income   P3

Hong Co. had net income of $386,100 under variable costing. Beginning and ending inventories were 2,600 units and 3,900 units, respectively. Fixed overhead cost was $4.00 per unit for both the beginning and ending inventory. What is net income under absorption costing?

QS 6-14
Converting variable costing income to absorption costing income   P3

E-Com had net income of $130,000 under variable costing. Beginning and ending inventories were 1,200 units and 4,900 units, respectively. Fixed overhead cost was $2.50 per unit for both the beginning and ending inventory. What is net income under absorption costing?

QS 6-15
Converting variable costing income to absorption costing income   P3

Under absorption costing a company had the following per unit costs when 10,000 units were produced.

QS 6-16
Absorption costing and overproduction

C1

Direct labor...	$ 2
Direct material	3
Variable overhead	4
Total variable cost..	9
Fixed overhead ($50,000/10,000 units)	5
Total product cost per unit	$14

1. Compute the company's total product cost per unit if 12,500 units had been produced.
2. Why might a manager of a company using absorption costing produce more units than can currently be sold?

A manufacturer reports the following information on its product. Compute the target selling price per unit under absorption costing.

QS 6-17
Absorption costing and product pricing

P4

Direct materials cost	$50 per unit
Direct labor cost	$12 per unit
Variable overhead cost	$6 per unit
Fixed overhead cost.....................................	$2 per unit
Target markup	40%

Li Company produces a product that sells for $84 per unit. A customer contacts Li and offers to purchase 2,000 units of its product at a price of $68 per unit. Variable production costs with this order would be $30 per unit, and variable selling expenses would be $18 per unit. Assuming that this special order would not require any additional fixed costs, and that Li has sufficient capacity to produce the product without affecting regular sales, explain to Li's management why it might be a good decision to accept this special order.

QS 6-18
Special order pricing

A1

Refer to the information in QS 6-16. The company sells its product for $50 per unit. Due to new regulations, the company must now incur $2 per unit of hazardous waste disposal costs and $8,500 per year of fixed hazardous waste disposal costs. Compute the contribution margin per unit, including hazardous waste disposal costs.

QS 6-19
Sustainability and product costing   P1

Refer to the information in QS 6-16. The company sells its product for $50 per unit. Due to new regulations, the company must now incur $2 per unit of hazardous waste disposal costs and $8,500 per year of fixed hazardous waste disposal costs. Compute the company's break-even point (in units), including hazardous waste disposal costs.

QS 6-20
Sustainability and product costing   P1

EXERCISES

Trio Company reports the following information for the current year, which is its first year of operations.

Exercise 6-1

Computing unit and inventory costs under absorption costing

P1

Direct materials	$15 per unit
Direct labor..	$16 per unit
Overhead costs for the year	
Variable overhead	$ 80,000 per year
Fixed overhead	$160,000 per year
Units produced this year	20,000 units
Units sold this year	14,000 units
Ending finished goods inventory in units	6,000 units

Check (1) Absorption cost per unit, $43

1. Compute the product cost per unit using absorption costing.
2. Determine the cost of ending finished goods inventory using absorption costing.
3. Determine the cost of goods sold using absorption costing.

Exercise 6-2

Computing unit and inventory costs under variable costing   P1

Check (1) Variable cost per unit, $35

Refer to the information in Exercise 6-1. Assume instead that Trio Company uses variable costing.
1. Compute the product cost per unit using variable costing.
2. Determine the cost of ending finished goods inventory using variable costing.
3. Determine the cost of goods sold using variable costing.

Exercise 6-3

Income reporting under absorption costing and variable costing

P2

Sims Company, a manufacturer of tablet computers, began operations on January 1, 2017. Its cost and sales information for this year follows.

Manufacturing costs	
Direct materials	$40 per unit
Direct labor...	$60 per unit
Overhead costs for the year	
Variable overhead.............................	$3,000,000
Fixed overhead	$7,000,000
Selling and administrative costs for the year	
Variable...	$770,000
Fixed	$4,250,000
Production and sales for the year	
Units produced......................................	100,000 units
Units sold	70,000 units
Sales price per unit	$350 per unit

Check (1) Variable costing income, $3,380,000

1. Prepare an income statement for the year using variable costing.
2. Prepare an income statement for the year using absorption costing.
3. Under what circumstance(s) is reported income identical under both absorption costing and variable costing?

Exercise 6-4

Variable costing income statement

P2

Kenzi Kayaking, a manufacturer of kayaks, began operations this year. During this first year, the company produced 1,050 kayaks and sold 800 at a price of $1,050 each. At this first year-end, the company reported the following income statement information using absorption costing.

Sales (800 × $1,050)	$840,000
Cost of goods sold (800 × $500)	400,000
Gross margin...	440,000
Selling and administrative expenses	230,000
Net income	$210,000

Additional Information

a. Product cost per kayak totals $500, which consists of $400 in variable production cost and $100 in fixed production cost—the latter amount is based on $105,000 of fixed production costs allocated to the 1,050 kayaks produced.

b. The $230,000 in selling and administrative expense consists of $75,000 that is variable and $155,000 that is fixed.

1. Prepare an income statement for the current year under variable costing.

2. Explain the difference in income between the variable costing and absorption costing income statement.

Rey Company's single product sells at a price of $216 per unit. Data for its single product for its first year of operations follow. Prepare an income statement for the year assuming (*a*) absorption costing and (*b*) variable costing.

Exercise 6-5
Absorption costing and variable costing income statements

P2

Direct materials	$20 per unit
Direct labor	$28 per unit
Overhead costs	
Variable overhead	$6 per unit
Fixed overhead per year	$160,000 per year
Selling and administrative expenses	
Variable	$18 per unit
Fixed	$200,000 per year
Units produced (and sold)	20,000 units

Hayek Bikes prepares the income statement under variable costing for its managerial reports, and it prepares the income statement under absorption costing for external reporting. For its first month of operations, 375 bikes were produced and 225 were sold; this left 150 bikes in ending inventory. The income statement information under variable costing follows.

Exercise 6-6
Absorption costing income statement

P2

Sales (225 × $1,600)	$360,000
Variable product cost (225 × $625)	140,625
Variable selling and administrative expenses (225 × $65)	14,625
Contribution margin	204,750
Fixed overhead cost	56,250
Fixed selling and administrative expense	75,000
Net income	$ 73,500

1. Prepare this company's income statement for its first month of operations under absorption costing.

2. Explain the difference in income between the variable costing and absorption costing income statements.

Oak Mart, a producer of solid oak tables, reports the following data from its second year of business.

Exercise 6-7
Income reporting under absorption costing and variable costing

P2

Sales price per unit	$320 per unit	Manufacturing costs this year		
Units produced this year	115,000 units	Direct materials	$40 per unit	
Units sold this year	118,000 units	Direct labor	$62 per unit	
Units in beginning-year inventory	3,000 units	Overhead costs this year		
Beginning inventory costs		Variable overhead	$3,220,000	
Variable (3,000 units × $135)	$405,000	Fixed overhead	$7,400,000	
Fixed (3,000 units × $80)	240,000	Selling and administrative costs this year		
Total	$645,000	Variable	$1,416,000	
		Fixed	4,600,000	

1. Prepare the current-year income statement for the company using variable costing.

2. Prepare the current-year income statement for the company using absorption costing.

3. Explain any difference between the two income numbers under the two costing methods in parts 1 and 2.

Check   (2) Absorption costing income, $8,749,000

Exercise 6-8

Contribution margin format income statement

P2

Polarix is a retailer of ATVs (all-terrain vehicles) and accessories. An income statement for its Consumer ATV Department for the current year follows. ATVs sell for $3,800 each. Variable selling expenses are $270 per ATV. The remaining selling expenses are fixed. Administrative expenses are 40% variable and 60% fixed. The company does not manufacture its own ATVs; it purchases them from a supplier for $1,830 each.

POLARIX Income Statement—Consumer ATV Department For Year Ended December 31, 2017		
Sales		$646,000
Cost of goods sold		311,100
Gross margin...		334,900
Operating expenses		
Selling expenses	$135,000	
Administrative expenses	59,500	194,500
Net income		$140,400

Check (2) $1,560

1. Prepare an income statement for this current year using the contribution margin format.

2. For each ATV sold during this year, what is the contribution toward covering fixed expenses and earning income?

Exercise 6-9

Income statement under absorption costing and variable costing

P1   P2

Cool Sky reports the following costing data on its product for its first year of operations. During this first year, the company produced 44,000 units and sold 36,000 units at a price of $140 per unit.

Manufacturing costs	
Direct materials per unit	$60
Direct labor per unit	$22
Variable overhead per unit	$8
Fixed overhead for the year	$528,000
Selling and administrative costs	
Variable selling and administrative cost per unit	$11
Fixed selling and administrative cost per year	$105,000

Check (1a) Absorption cost per unit, $102

(2a) Variable cost per unit, $90

1. Assume the company uses absorption costing.

   a. Determine its product cost per unit.

   b. Prepare its income statement for the year under absorption costing.

2. Assume the company uses variable costing.

   a. Determine its product cost per unit.

   b. Prepare its income statement for the year under variable costing.

Exercise 6-10

Computing absorption costing income

P3

A manufacturer reports the information below for three recent years. Compute income for each of the three years using absorption costing.

	Year 1	Year 2	Year 3
Variable costing income........................	$110,000	$114,400	$118,950
Beginning finished goods inventory (units).........	0	1,200	700
Ending finished goods inventory (units)	1,200	700	800
Fixed manufacturing overhead per unit	$ 2.50	$ 2.50	$ 2.50

Exercise 6-11

Absorption costing and product pricing   P4

Sirhuds Inc., a maker of smartwatches, reports the information below on its product. The company uses absorption costing and has a target markup of 40% of absorption cost per unit. Compute the target selling price per unit under absorption costing.

Direct materials cost	$100 per unit
Direct labor cost	$30 per unit
Variable overhead cost	$8 per unit
Fixed overhead cost...	$600,000 per year
Variable selling and administrative expenses.......................	$3 per unit
Fixed selling and administrative expenses	$120,000 per year
Expected production (and sales)...................................	50,000 units per year

Jacquie Inc. reports the following annual cost data for its single product.

Exercise 6-12
Absorption costing and overproduction

C1

Normal production and sales level	60,000 units
Sales price...	$56.00 per unit
Direct materials	$9.00 per unit
Direct labor..	$6.50 per unit
Variable overhead	$11.00 per unit
Fixed overhead	$720,000 in total

If Jacquie increases its production to 80,000 units, while sales remain at the current 60,000-unit level, by how much would the company's gross margin increase or decrease under absorption costing? Assume the company has idle capacity to double current production.

Grand Garden is a luxury hotel with 150 suites. Its regular suite rate is $250 per night per suite. The hotel's cost per night is $140 per suite and consists of the following.

Exercise 6-13
Variable cost analysis for a special order

A1

Variable direct labor and materials cost	$ 30
Fixed cost	110
Total cost per night per suite.....................................	$140

The hotel manager received an offer to hold the local Bikers' Club annual meeting at the hotel in March, which is the hotel's low season with an occupancy rate of under 50%. The Bikers' Club would reserve 50 suites for three nights if the hotel could offer a 50% discount, or a rate of $125 per night. The hotel manager is inclined to reject the offer because the cost per suite per night is $140. Prepare an analysis of this offer for the hotel manager. Explain (with supporting computations) whether the offer from the Bikers' Club should be accepted or rejected.

Empire Plaza Hotel is a luxury hotel with 400 rooms. Its regular room rate is $300 per night per room. The hotel's cost is $165 per night per room and consists of the following.

Exercise 6-14
Variable cost analysis for a special order

A1

Variable direct labor and materials cost	$ 40
Fixed cost	125
Total cost per night per room.....................................	$165

The hotel manager received an offer to hold the Junior States of America (JSA) convention at the hotel in February, which is the hotel's low season with an occupancy rate of under 45%. JSA would reserve 100 rooms for four nights if the hotel could offer a 50% discount, or a rate of $150 per night. The hotel manager is inclined to reject the offer because the cost per room per night is $165. Prepare an analysis of this offer for the hotel manager. Explain (with supporting computations) whether the offer from JSA should be accepted or rejected.

MidCoast Airlines provides charter airplane services. In October of this year, the company is operating at 60% of its capacity when it receives a bid from the local community college. The college is organizing a Washington, D.C., trip for its international student group. The college budgeted only $30,000 for round-trip airfare. MidCoast Airlines normally charges between $50,000 and $60,000 for such service. MidCoast determines its cost for the round-trip flight to Washington to be $44,000, which consists of the following:

Exercise 6-15
Variable cost analysis for a special order

A1

Variable cost..	$15,000
Fixed cost (allocated)	29,000
Total cost..	$44,000

Although the manager at MidCoast supports the college's educational efforts, she cannot justify accepting the $30,000 bid for the trip given the projected $14,000 loss. Still, she decides to consult with you, an independent financial consultant. Do you believe the airline should accept the bid from the college? Prepare a memorandum, with supporting computations, explaining why or why not.

Exercise 6-16

Analyzing income growth

P2

A recent annual report for **Nike** reports the following operating income for its United States and China geographic segments:

$ millions	2016	2015
United States	$3,763	$3,645
China..	1,372	993

Required

1. Is operating income growing faster in the United States or in the China segment? Explain.

2. Is the difference in operating income growth due to the use of different costing methods (absorption or variable costing) in the two geographic segments? Explain.

PROBLEM SET A

Problem 6-1A

Variable costing income statement and conversion to absorption costing income (two consecutive years)

P2   P3

Dowell Company produces a single product. Its income statements under absorption costing for its first two years of operation follow.

	2016	2017
Sales ($46 per unit)	$920,000	$1,840,000
Cost of goods sold ($31 per unit)	620,000	1,240,000
Gross margin	300,000	600,000
Selling and administrative expenses	290,000	340,000
Net income..	$ 10,000	$ 260,000

Additional Information

a. Sales and production data for these first two years follow.

	2016	2017
Units produced...	30,000	30,000
Units sold..	20,000	40,000

b. Variable cost per unit and total fixed costs are unchanged during 2016 and 2017. The company's $31 per unit product cost consists of the following.

Direct materials	$ 5
Direct labor...	9
Variable overhead	7
Fixed overhead ($300,000/30,000 units)	10
Total product cost per unit...	$31

c. Selling and administrative expenses consist of the following.

	2016	2017
Variable selling and administrative expenses ($2.50 per unit)	$ 50,000	$100,000
Fixed selling and administrative expenses..	240,000	240,000
Total selling and administrative expenses	$290,000	$340,000

Required

Check   (1) 2016 net loss, $(90,000)

1. Prepare income statements for the company for each of its first two years under variable costing.

2. Explain any difference between the absorption costing income and the variable costing income for these two years.

Trez Company began operations this year. During this first year, the company produced 100,000 units and sold 80,000 units. The absorption costing income statement for this year follows.

Sales (80,000 units × $50 per unit)		$4,000,000
Cost of goods sold		
Beginning inventory	$ 0	
Cost of goods manufactured (100,000 units × $30 per unit)	3,000,000	
Cost of goods available for sale	3,000,000	
Ending inventory (20,000 × $30)	600,000	
Cost of goods sold		2,400,000
Gross margin		1,600,000
Selling and administrative expenses		530,000
Net income		$1,070,000

Additional Information

a. Selling and administrative expenses consist of $350,000 in annual fixed expenses and $2.25 per unit in variable selling and administrative expenses.

b. The company's product cost of $30 per unit is computed as follows.

Direct materials	$5 per unit
Direct labor	$14 per unit
Variable overhead	$2 per unit
Fixed overhead ($900,000/100,000 units)	$9 per unit

Required

1. Prepare an income statement for the company under variable costing.

2. Explain any difference between the income under variable costing (from part 1) and the income reported above.

Blazer Chemical produces and sells an ice-melting granular used on roadways and sidewalks in winter. It annually produces and sells about 100 tons of its granular. In its nine-year history, the company has never reported a net loss. However, because of this year's unusually mild winter, projected demand for its product is only 60 tons. Based on its predicted production and sales of 60 tons, the company projects the following income statement (under absorption costing).

Sales (60 tons at $21,000 per ton)	$1,260,000
Cost of goods sold (60 tons at $16,000 per ton)	960,000
Gross margin	300,000
Selling and administrative expenses	318,600
Net loss	$ (18,600)

Its product cost information follows and consists mainly of fixed cost because of its automated production process requiring expensive equipment.

Variable direct labor and material costs per ton	$ 3,500
Fixed cost per ton ($750,000 ÷ 60 tons)	12,500
Total product cost per ton	$16,000

Selling and administrative expenses consist of variable selling and administrative expenses of $310 per ton and fixed selling and administrative expenses of $300,000 per year. The company's president is concerned about the adverse reaction from its creditors and shareholders if the projected net loss is reported.

The operations manager mentions that since the company has large storage capacity, it can report a net income by keeping its production at the usual 100-ton level even though it expects to sell only 60 tons. The president was puzzled by the suggestion that the company can report income by producing more without increasing sales.

Required

1. Can the company report a net income by increasing production to 100 tons and storing the excess production in inventory? Your explanation should include an income statement (using absorption costing) based on production of 100 tons and sales of 60 tons.

2. Should the company produce 100 tons given that projected demand is 60 tons? Explain, and also refer to any ethical implications of such a managerial decision.

PROBLEM SET B

Problem 6-1B

Variable costing income statement and conversion to absorption costing income (two consecutive years)

P2   P3

Azule Company produces a single product. Its income statements under absorption costing for its first two years of operation follow.

	2016	2017
Sales ($35 per unit)	$1,925,000	$2,275,000
Cost of goods sold ($26 per unit)	1,430,000	1,690,000
Gross margin..	495,000	585,000
Selling and administrative expenses	465,000	495,000
Net income	$ 30,000	$ 90,000

Additional Information

a. Sales and production data for these first two years follow:

	2016	2017
Units produced..	60,000	60,000
Units sold	55,000	65,000

b. Its variable cost per unit and total fixed costs are unchanged during 2016 and 2017. Its $26 per unit product cost consists of the following.

Direct materials	$ 4
Direct labor..	6
Variable overhead	8
Fixed overhead ($480,000/60,000 units)	8
Total product cost per unit	$26

c. Its selling and administrative expenses consist of the following.

	2016	2017
Variable selling and administrative expenses ($3 per unit)......	$165,000	$195,000
Fixed selling and administrative expenses.......................	300,000	300,000
Total selling and administrative expenses	$465,000	$495,000

Required

Check   (1) 2016 net loss, $(10,000)

1. Prepare this company's income statements under variable costing for each of its first two years.

2. Explain any difference between the absorption costing income and the variable costing income for these two years.

E'Lonte Company began operations this year. During this first year, the company produced 300,000 units and sold 250,000 units. Its income statement under absorption costing for this year follows.

Problem 6-2B

Variable costing income statement and conversion to absorption costing income

P2   P3

Sales (250,000 units × $18 per unit)...............................		$4,500,000
Cost of goods sold		
Beginning inventory	$ 0	
Cost of goods manufactured (300,000 units × $7.50 per unit).............	2,250,000	
Cost of goods available for sale........................	2,250,000	
Ending inventory (50,000 × $7.50).......................	375,000	
Cost of goods sold		1,875,000
Gross margin...		2,625,000
Selling and administrative expenses		2,200,000
Net income..		$ 425,000

Additional Information

a. Selling and administrative expenses consist of $1,200,000 in annual fixed expenses and $4 per unit in variable selling and administrative expenses.

b. The company's product cost of $7.50 per unit is computed as follows.

Direct materials	$2.00 per unit
Direct labor..	$2.40 per unit
Variable overhead	$1.60 per unit
Fixed overhead ($450,000/300,000 units)	$1.50 per unit

Required

1. Prepare the company's income statement under variable costing.

2. Explain any difference between the company's income under variable costing (from part 1) and the income reported above.

Check   (1) Variable costing income, $350,000

Chem-Melt produces and sells an ice-melting granular used on roadways and sidewalks in winter. The company annually produces and sells about 300,000 pounds of its granular. In its 10-year history, the company has never reported a net loss. Because of this year's unusually mild winter, projected demand for its product is only 250,000 pounds. Based on its predicted production and sales of 250,000 pounds, the company projects the following income statement under absorption costing.

Problem 6-3B

Income reporting, absorption costing, and managerial ethics

P2   C1

Sales (250,000 lbs. at $8 per lb.)......................................	$2,000,000
Cost of goods sold (250,000 lbs. at $6.80 per lb.)	1,700,000
Gross margin..	300,000
Selling and administrative expenses	450,000
Net loss	$ (150,000)

Its product cost information follows and consists mainly of fixed production cost because of its automated production process requiring expensive equipment.

Variable direct labor and materials costs per pound.......................	$2.00
Fixed production cost per pound ($1,200,000/250,000 lbs.)	4.80
Total product cost per pound	$6.80

The company's selling and administrative expenses are all fixed. The president is concerned about the adverse reaction from its creditors and shareholders if the projected net loss is reported. The controller suggests that since the company has large storage capacity, it can report a net income by keeping its production at the usual 300,000-pound level even though it expects to sell only 250,000 pounds. The president was puzzled by the suggestion that the company can report a profit by producing more without increasing sales.

Required

1. Can the company report a net income by increasing production to 300,000 pounds and storing the excess production in inventory? Your explanation should include an income statement (using absorption costing) based on production of 300,000 pounds and sales of 250,000 pounds.

2. Should the company produce 300,000 pounds given that projected demand is 250,000 pounds? Explain, and also refer to any ethical implications of such a managerial decision.

SERIAL PROBLEM
Business Solutions

P2   P3

© Alexander Image/Shutterstock RF

(This serial problem began in Chapter 1 and continues through most of the book. If previous chapter segments were not completed, the serial problem can begin at this point.)

SP 6   Santana Rey expects sales of **Business Solutions**'s line of computer workstation furniture to equal 300 workstations (at a sales price of $3,000 each) for 2018. The workstations' manufacturing costs include the following.

Direct materials	$800 per unit
Direct labor	$400 per unit
Variable overhead	$100 per unit
Fixed overhead	$24,000 per year

The selling expenses related to these workstations follow.

Variable selling expenses	$50 per unit
Fixed selling expenses	$4,000 per year

Santana is considering how many workstations to produce in 2018. She is confident that she will be able to sell any workstations in her 2018 ending inventory during 2019. However, Santana does not want to overproduce as she does not have sufficient storage space for many more workstations.

Required

1. Compute Business Solutions's absorption costing income assuming
    a. 300 workstations are produced.
    b. 320 workstations are produced.
2. Compute Business Solutions's variable costing income assuming
    a. 300 workstations are produced.
    b. 320 workstations are produced.
3. Explain to Santana any differences in the income figures determined in parts 1 and 2. How should Santana use the information from parts 1 and 2 to make production decisions?

Beyond the Numbers

REPORTING IN ACTION

P2

APPLE

BTN 6-1   Apple's ending inventory amounts (in $ millions) are shown below:

	2015	2014	2013
Ending inventory	$2,349	$2,111	$1,764

Required

1. Assume Apple uses variable costing for some of its internal reports. For each of the years 2015 and 2014, would net income based on variable costing be higher, lower, or no different from net income based on absorption costing? Explain.

2. Assume Apple is considering implementing a just-in-time (JIT) inventory system. Would a JIT system increase, decrease, or have no effect on differences in net income between absorption costing and variable costing? Explain.

BTN 6-2 **Apple** offers repair service on its products. Assume that **Google** wants to offer in-home and online services for computer repair and support.

COMPARATIVE ANALYSIS

P2

APPLE

GOOGLE

Required

1. What are some of the costs that Google must consider when deciding to offer these additional computer services? Are these costs different from what Apple must consider when offering additional new types of repair and support services?

2. Would variable or absorption costing be more useful to Google in analyzing whether repair and support services are profitable?

BTN 6-3 FDP Company produces a variety of home security products. Gary Price, the company's president, is concerned with the fourth-quarter market demand for the company's products. Unless something is done in the last two months of the year, the company is likely to miss its earnings expectation of Wall Street analysts. Price still remembers when FDP's earnings were below analysts' expectation by two cents a share three years ago, and the company's share price fell 19% the day earnings were announced. In a recent meeting, Price told his top management that something must be done quickly. One proposal by the marketing vice president was to give a deep discount to the company's major customers to increase the company's sales in the fourth quarter. The company controller pointed out that while the discount could increase sales, it may not help the bottom line; to the contrary, it could lower income. The controller said, "Since we have enough storage capacity, we might simply increase our production in the fourth quarter to increase our reported profit."

ETHICS CHALLENGE

C1

Required

1. Gary Price is not sure how the increase in production without a corresponding increase in sales could help boost the company's income. Explain to Price how reported income varies with respect to production level.

2. Is there an ethical concern in this situation? If so, which parties are affected? Explain.

BTN 6-4 Mertz Chemical has three divisions. Its consumer product division faces strong competition from companies overseas. During its recent teleconference, Ryan Peterson, the consumer product division manager, reported that his division's sales for the current year were below its break-even point. However, when the division's annual reports were received, Billie Mertz, the company president, was surprised that the consumer product division actually reported a profit of $264,000. How could this be possible?

COMMUNICATING IN PRACTICE

P3

Required

Assume that you work in the corporate controller's office. Write a half-page memorandum to the president explaining how the division can report income even if its sales are below the break-even point.

TAKING IT TO THE NET
P2

BTN 6-5   This chapter discussed the variable costing method and how to use variable costing information to make various business decisions. We also can find several websites on variable costing and its business applications.

Required

1. Review the website of **Value Based Management** at **ValueBasedManagement.net**. Identify and read the page on the topic of variable costing (**valuebasedmanagement.net/methods_variable_costing.html**).
2. What other phrases are used in practice for *variable costing*?
3. According to this website, what are the consequences of variable costing for profit calculation?

TEAMWORK IN ACTION
P4

BTN 6-6   This chapter identified several decision contexts in which managers use product cost information.

Required

Break into teams and identify at least one specific decision context in which absorption costing information is more relevant than variable costing information and at least one decision context in which variable costing information is more relevant than absorption costing. Be prepared to discuss your answers in class.

ENTREPRENEURIAL DECISION
P3

BTN 6-7   **Riffraff**, launched by entrepreneur Kirsten Blowers Stuckey, sells clothing, jewelry, and gifts.

Required

Kirsten uses variable costing in her business decisions. If Riffraff used absorption costing, would you expect the company's income to be more than, less than, or about the same as its income measured under variable costing? Explain.

HITTING THE ROAD
A1

BTN 6-8   Visit a local hotel and observe its daily operating activities. The costs associated with some of its activities are variable while others are fixed with respect to occupancy levels.

Required

1. List costs that are likely variable for the hotel.
2. List costs that are likely fixed for the hotel.
3. Using your lists from parts 1 and 2, which type of costs (fixed or variable) is likely to be larger (in dollars)?
4. Based on your observations and the answers to parts 1 through 3, explain why many hotels offer discounts as high as 50% or more during their low occupancy season.

GLOBAL DECISION
P2

Samsung
APPLE

BTN 6-9   Assume that **Samsung** (**Samsung.com**) is considering offering a service similar to **Apple**'s iTunes music download store. However, instead of developing the division internally, Samsung is considering buying a company that already offers such services.

Required

Would absorption or variable costing be most useful to Samsung in evaluating whether to acquire an existing business that provides services similar to iTunes? Explain.

GLOBAL VIEW

U.S. multinational companies must change their business processes when moving their operations to international locations. These changes can impact a company's cost structure.

For example, both **McDonald's** and **Yum! Brands** offer delivery services in major international cities like Beijing (China) and Seoul (South Korea). Cities like these are heavily populated, and real estate costs are high. These factors discourage the building of drive-through facilities, which would increase fixed overhead costs. Fixed overhead costs also fall as these companies process more orders over the Internet and thus build fewer call centers. As fixed overhead costs decrease, the difference in net income that would result from applying variable costing versus absorption costing also decreases.

©Krzystztof Dydynski/Lonely Planet Images/Getty Images

 Global View Assignments

Discussion Question 14

Exercise 6-16

BTN 6-9

Master Budgets and Performance Planning

Chapter Preview

BUDGET PROCESS AND ADMINISTRATION

C1 Budgeting process

Benefits of budgeting

Human behavior

Reporting and timing

NTK 7-1

THE MASTER BUDGET AND ITS PREPARATION

C2 Master budget components

P1 Operating budgets

Capital expenditures budget

Investing budgets

Financing budgets

P2 Cash budget

NTK 7-2, 7-3, 7-4, 7-5

BUDGETED FINANCIAL STATEMENTS

P3 Budgeted income statement

Budgeted balance sheet

Using the master budget

Service companies

A1 Activity-based budgeting

P4 Merchandiser budgeting

NTK 7-8

Learning Objectives

CONCEPTUAL

C1 Describe the benefits of budgeting.

C2 Describe a master budget and the process of preparing it.

ANALYTICAL

A1 Analyze expense planning using activity-based budgeting.

PROCEDURAL

P1 Prepare each component of a master budget—for a manufacturing company.

P2 Prepare a cash budget.

P3 Prepare budgeted financial statements.

P4 *Appendix 7A*—Prepare each component of a master budget—for a merchandising company.

Courtesy of TaTa Topper

Top This!

RICHMOND, VA—Breast Cancer Awareness Month, Coaches vs. Cancer basketball games, and student fund-raisers increase awareness and money to help cure cancer. Meanwhile, survivors struggle with basics such as being able to sleep comfortably. After a double mastectomy, Michelle Logan told her friend Marilyn Collins, a breast cancer survivor, that she could no longer sleep on her side or stomach. "I get it," insisted Marilyn, "I was you four years ago." Marilyn devised a solution. "I had a problem," recalls Michelle, "and Marilyn had a great idea!"

Marilyn's idea led to the **TaTa Topper** (**MarilynAndMichelle. com**), a 4-inch-thick mattress cover with cutouts in the breast area. The design allowed the women to sleep comfortably. Although Marilyn and Michelle did not set out to start a business, they realized their product's potential. "Knowing that I can help other women, it's meaningful," explains Marilyn.

Michelle had worked in banking and had started and sold a successful business, but she and Marilyn had much to learn about making their venture viable. They began by attending a six-week class on starting a business. "I had no idea what a 'pitch' was," laughs Marilyn. They learned quickly and soon had

"Fix a problem"
—Marilyn Collins

developed product prototypes, designed packaging, and determined a price. They also found local businesses to make the foam toppers and fitted sheets.

The two learned to budget their cost of merchandise purchases, shipping, and other costs. "The manufacturer stores our inventory," explains Marilyn, "so we have very little overhead cost." Marilyn and Michelle are now developing more formal budget procedures. "If we don't plan for and make profits," admits Marilyn, "we can't help any women."

Michelle stresses that "sales forecasts are challenging because there are so many variables and unknowns." But a good sales forecast is the cornerstone of a good budget. All companies budget—manufacturers budget costs of materials, labor, and overhead, whereas service providers focus on labor budgets.

Both Marilyn and Michelle stress the importance of good mentors. Marilyn insists that "if you fix a problem and make people's lives better, you make a difference."

Sources: *Marilyn and Michelle website*, January 2017; *Richmond Times-Dispatch*, February 15, 2015; *WRIC News* interview, March 25, 2016; Author phone interview, April 9, 2016

BUDGET PROCESS AND ADMINISTRATION

Budgeting Process

Managers must ensure that activities of employees and departments contribute to meeting the company's overall goals. This requires coordination and budgeting. **Budgeting,** the process of planning future business actions and expressing them as formal plans, helps to achieve this coordination.

A **budget** is a formal statement of a company's plans, expressed in monetary terms. Unlike long-term *strategic plans,* budgets typically cover shorter periods such as a month, quarter, or year. Budgets are useful in controlling operations. The **budgetary control** process, shown in Exhibit 7.1, refers to management's use of budgets to see that planned objectives are met.

EXHIBIT 7.1

Process of Budgetary Control

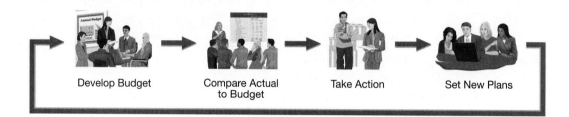

Develop Budget   Compare Actual to Budget   Take Action   Set New Plans

The budgetary control process involves at least four steps: (1) develop the budget from planned objectives, (2) compare actual results to budgeted amounts and analyze any differences, (3) take corrective and strategic actions, and (4) establish new planned objectives and prepare a new budget.

In this chapter we focus on the first step in the budgetary control process, developing a budget. In the next chapter we show how managers compare budgeted and actual amounts to guide corrective actions and make new plans.

Benefits of Budgeting

Budgets help fulfill the key managerial functions of planning and controlling. Benefits of written budgets include:

- **Planning** A budget focuses on the future opportunities and threats to the organization. This focus on the future is important because the daily pressures of operating an organization can divert management's attention from planning. Budgeting makes managers devote time to *plan* for the future.

- **Control** The *control* function requires management to evaluate (benchmark) operations against some norm. Because budgeted performance considers important company, industry, and economic factors, a comparison of actual to budgeted performance provides an effective monitoring and control system. This comparison assists management in identifying problems and taking corrective actions if necessary.

- **Coordination** Budgeting helps to *coordinate* activities so that all employees and departments understand and work toward the company's overall goals.

- **Communication** Written budgets effectively *communicate* management's specific action plans to all employees. When plans are not written down, conversations can lead to uncertainty and confusion among employees.

- **Motivation** Budgets can be used to *motivate* employees. Budgeted performance levels can provide goals for employees to attain or even exceed. Many companies provide incentives, like cash bonuses, for employee performance that meets or exceeds budget goals.

Decision Insight

Incentive Pay   Budgets are important in determining managers' pay. A recent survey shows that 82% of large companies tie managers' bonus payments to beating budget goals. For these companies, bonus payments are frequently more than 20% of total manager pay. ■

Budgeting and Human Behavior

Budgets provide standards for evaluating performance and can affect the attitudes of employees evaluated by them. Budgeted levels of performance must be realistic to avoid discouraging employees. Employees who will be evaluated should help prepare the budget to increase their commitment to it. For example, the sales department should be involved in developing sales estimates, while the production department should prepare its initial expense budget. This *bottom-up* process is usually more useful than a *top-down* approach in which top management passes down the budget without input. Performance evaluations must allow the affected employees to explain the reasons for apparent performance deficiencies, rather than assigning blame.

Budgeting has three important guidelines:

1. Employees affected by a budget should help prepare it (*participatory budgeting*).
2. Goals reflected in a budget should be challenging but attainable.
3. Evaluations offer opportunities to explain differences between actual and budgeted amounts.

Budgeting can be a positive motivating force when the guidelines are followed.

Potential Negative Outcomes of Budgeting   Managers must be aware of potential negative outcomes of budgeting. Under participatory budgeting, some employees might understate sales budgets and overstate expense budgets to allow themselves a cushion, or *budgetary slack,* to aid in meeting targets. Sometimes, pressure to meet budgeted results leads employees to engage in unethical behavior or commit fraud. Finally, some employees might always spend their budgeted amounts, even on unnecessary items, to ensure their budgets aren't reduced for the next period.

Example: Assume a company's sales force receives a bonus when sales exceed the budgeted amount. How would this arrangement affect the participatory sales forecasts? *Answer:* Sales reps may understate their budgeted sales.

Decision Insight

Planning   Most companies allocate dollars based on budgets submitted by department managers. These managers verify the numbers and monitor the budget. Managers must remember, however, that a budget is judged by its success in helping achieve the company's mission. One analogy is that a hiker must know the route to properly plan a hike and monitor hiking progress. ■

© Pixland/AGE fotostock

Budget Reporting and Timing

The budget period usually coincides with the company's fiscal year. To provide specific guidance to help control operations, the annual budget usually is separated into quarterly or monthly budgets. These short-term budgets allow management to periodically evaluate performance and take corrective action.

The time required to prepare a budget can vary a lot. Large, complex organizations usually take longer to prepare their budgets than do smaller ones. This is because considerable effort is required to coordinate the different units (departments) within large organizations.

Companies Using Rolling Budgets

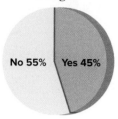

No 55%   Yes 45%

Many companies apply **continuous budgeting** by preparing **rolling budgets.** In continuous budgeting, a company continually revises its budgets as time passes. In a rolling budget, a company revises its entire set of budgets by adding a new quarterly budget to replace the quarter that just elapsed. Thus, at any point in time, monthly or quarterly budgets are available for the next 12 months or four quarters. The rolling budget below shows rolling budgets prepared at the end of five consecutive periods. The first set (at top) is prepared in December 2016 and covers the four calendar quarters of 2017. In March 2017, the company prepares another rolling budget for the next four quarters through March 2018. This same process is repeated every three months. As a result, management is continuously planning ahead.

The rolling budget below reflects an annual budget composed of four quarters, prepared four times per year using the most recent information available. When continuous budgeting is not used, the fourth-quarter budget is nine months old and perhaps out of date when applied.

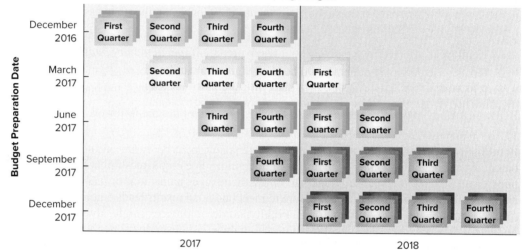

Rolling Budgets

Decision Insight

From Scratch Many companies use **zero-based budgeting,** an approach that requires all expenses to be justified for each new budget. Rather than using last period's budgeted or actual amounts to determine this period's budgets, managers instead analyze each activity in the organization to see if it is necessary. Managers then build budgets around only those necessary activities. Made-from-scratch budgets can be useful in identifying waste and reducing costs. ∎

NEED-TO-KNOW 7-1

Budgeting Benefits

C1

Label each item below with *yes* if it describes a benefit of budgeting or *no* if it describes a potential negative outcome of budgeting.

_____ **1.** Budgets provide goals for employees to work toward.

_____ **2.** Written budgets help communicate plans to all employees.

_____ **3.** Some employees might understate sales targets in budgets.

_____ **4.** A budget forces managers to spend time planning for the future.

_____ **5.** Some employees might always spend budgeted amounts.

_____ **6.** With rolling budgets, managers can continuously plan ahead.

Do More: QS 7-1, QS 7-2, E 7-1

Solution

1. Yes   **2.** Yes   **3.** No   **4.** Yes   **5.** No   **6.** Yes

THE MASTER BUDGET

A **master budget** is a formal, comprehensive plan for a company's future. It contains several individual budgets that are linked with each other to form a coordinated plan.

C2

Describe a master budget and the process of preparing it.

Master Budget Components

Exhibit 7.2 summarizes the master budgeting process. The master budgeting process typically begins with the sales budget and ends with a cash budget and budgeted financial statements. The master budget includes individual budgets for sales, production (or purchases), various expenses, capital expenditures, and cash.

EXHIBIT 7.2

Master Budget Process for a Manufacturer

```
                        ┌─────────────┐
                        │    Sales    │
                        └──────┬──────┘
                               ↓
                        ┌─────────────┐
                        │ Production  │
                        └──────┬──────┘
              ┌────────────────┼────────────────┐
              ↓                ↓                 ↓
      ┌──────────────┐  ┌─────────────┐  ┌──────────────────┐
      │Direct materials│ │Direct labor │  │ Factory overhead │
      └──────┬───────┘  └──────┬──────┘  └────────┬─────────┘
             └────────────────┐│┌────────────────┘
                              ↓↓↓
 ┌──────────────────┐  ┌─────────────┐  ┌──────────────────────┐
 │Capital expenditures│→│    Cash     │←─│  Selling expenses    │
 └──────────────────┘  └─────────────┘  │ General & admin expenses│
                                         └──────────────────────┘
           └──────────────────┬──────────────────┘
              Budgeted financial statements
```

☐ Operating budgets
☐ Investing budgets
☐ Financing budgets

The number and types of budgets included in a master budget depend on the company's size and complexity. A manufacturer's master budget should include, at a minimum, several *operating* budgets (shown in yellow in Exhibit 7.2), a capital expenditures budget, and a cash budget. The capital expenditures budget summarizes the effects of *investing* activities on cash. The cash budget helps determine the company's need for *financing*.

Managers often express the expected financial results of these planned activities with a budgeted balance sheet and a budgeted income statement. Some budgets require the input of other budgets. For example, direct materials and direct labor budgets cannot be prepared until a production budget is prepared. A company cannot plan its production until it prepares a sales budget.

The rest of this chapter explains how Toronto Sticks Company (TSC), a manufacturer of youth hockey sticks, prepares its budgets. Its master budget includes operating, capital expenditures, and cash budgets for each month in each quarter. It also includes a budgeted income statement for each quarter and a budgeted balance sheet as of the last day of each quarter. We show how TSC prepares budgets for October, November, and December 2017. Exhibit 7.3 presents TSC's balance sheet at the start of this budgeting period, which we often refer to as we prepare the component budgets.

Point: Merchandisers prepare *merchandise purchase* budgets instead of the production and manufacturing budgets in Exhibit 7.2.

Courtesy JJW Images

Operating Budgets

This section explains TSC's preparation of operating budgets. Its operating budgets consist of the sales budget, production and manufacturing budgets, selling expense budget, and general and administrative expense budget. (The preparation of merchandising budgets is described in this chapter's appendix.)

P1

Prepare each component of a master budget—for a manufacturing company.

Sales Budget   The first step in preparing the master budget is the **sales budget,** which shows the planned sales units and the expected dollars from these sales. The sales budget is

EXHIBIT 7.3

Balance Sheet prior to the Budgeting Periods

TORONTO STICKS COMPANY
Balance Sheet
September 30, 2017

Assets

Cash		$ 20,000
Accounts receivable		25,200
Raw materials inventory (178 pounds @ $20)		3,560
Finished goods inventory (1,010 units @ $17)		17,170
Equipment*	$200,000	
Less: Accumulated depreciation	36,000	164,000
Total assets		$229,930

Liabilities and Equity

Liabilities		
Accounts payable	$ 7,060	
Income taxes payable (due 10/31/2017)	20,000	
Note payable	10,000	$ 37,060
Stockholders' equity		
Common stock	150,000	
Retained earnings	42,870	192,870
Total liabilities and equity		$229,930

* Equipment is depreciated on a straight-line basis over 10 years (salvage value is $20,000).

the starting point in the budgeting process because plans for most departments are linked to sales.

Operating Budgets

Sales
Production
Direct labor
Direct materials
Factory overhead
Selling expenses
General & administrative

The sales budget comes from a careful analysis of forecasted economic and market conditions, business capacity, and advertising plans. To illustrate, in September 2017, TSC sold 700 hockey sticks at $60 per unit. After considering sales predictions and market conditions, TSC prepares its sales budget for the next three months (see Exhibit 7.4). The sales budget in Exhibit 7.4 includes forecasts of both unit sales and unit prices. Some sales budgets are expressed only in total sales dollars, but most are more detailed and can include budgets for many different products, regions, departments, and sales representatives.

EXHIBIT 7.4

Sales Budget

	A	B	C	D	E
1		TORONTO STICKS COMPANY			
2		Sales Budget			
3		October 2017–December 2017			
4		October	November	December	Totals
5	Budgeted sales (units)	1,000	800	1,400	3,200
6	Selling price per unit	× $ 60	× $ 60	× $ 60	× $ 60
7	Total budgeted sales (dollars)	$60,000	$48,000	$84,000	$192,000

 **Decision** Maker

Entrepreneur You run a start-up that manufactures designer clothes. Business is seasonal, and fashions and designs quickly change. How do you prepare reliable annual sales budgets? ■   *Answer:* You must deal with two issues. First, because fashions and designs frequently change, you cannot heavily rely on previous budgets. As a result, you must carefully analyze the market to understand what designs are in vogue. This will help you plan the product mix and estimate demand. The second issue is the budgeting period. An annual sales budget may be unreliable because tastes can quickly change. Your best bet might be to prepare monthly and quarterly sales budgets that you continuously monitor and revise.

Production Budget   A manufacturer prepares a **production budget,** which shows the number of units to be produced in a period. The production budget is based on the budgeted unit sales from the sales budget, along with inventory considerations. Manufacturers often determine a certain amount of **safety stock,** a quantity of inventory that provides protection against lost sales caused by unfulfilled demands from customers or delays in shipments from suppliers. Exhibit 7.5 shows how to compute the production required for a period. *A production budget does not show costs; it is always expressed in units of product.*

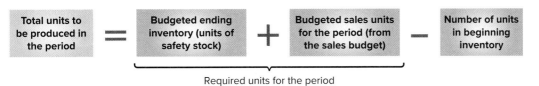

EXHIBIT 7.5

Computing Production Requirements

After assessing the cost of keeping inventory along with the risk and cost of inventory shortages, TSC decided that the number of units in its finished goods inventory at each month-end should equal 90% of next month's predicted sales. For example, inventory at the end of October should equal 90% of budgeted November sales, and so on. This information, along with knowledge of 1,010 units in inventory at September 30 (see Exhibit 7.3), allows the company to prepare the production budget shown in Exhibit 7.6. The actual number of units of ending inventory at September 30 is not consistent with TSC's policy. This is common, as sales forecasts are uncertain and production can sometimes be disrupted.

Example: Under a JIT system, how will sales in units differ from the number of units to produce? *Answer:* The two amounts are similar because future inventory should be near zero.

	A	B	C	D
1	**TORONTO STICKS COMPANY**			
2	**Production Budget**			
3	**October 2017–December 2017**			
4		**October**	**November**	**December**
5	Next month's budgeted sales (units) from sales budget*	800	1,400	900
6	Ratio of inventory to future sales	× 90%	× 90%	× 90%
7	Budgeted ending inventory (units)	720	1,260	810
8	Add: Budgeted sales (units)	1,000	800	1,400
9	Required units of available production	1,720	2,060	2,210
10	Deduct: Beginning inventory (units)	1,010**	720	1,260
11	Units to be produced	710	1,340	950

EXHIBIT 7.6

Production Budget

Budgeted ending inventory
+ Budgeted sales
– Beginning inventory
= Units to produce

*From sales budget (Exhibit 7.4); January budgeted sales of 900 units from next quarter's sales budget.
**October's beginning inventory (1,010 units) is inconsistent with company policy.

Use three steps to complete the production budget:

1. Compute budgeted ending inventory based on the company's inventory policy.
2. Add budgeted sales (from the sales budget).
3. Subtract beginning inventory.

The result is the required units to be produced for the period. The number of units to be produced provides the basis for *manufacturing budgets* for the production costs of those units—direct materials, direct labor, and overhead.

Courtesy JJW Images

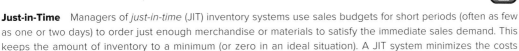

Decision Insight

Just-in-Time   Managers of *just-in-time* (JIT) inventory systems use sales budgets for short periods (often as few as one or two days) to order just enough merchandise or materials to satisfy the immediate sales demand. This keeps the amount of inventory to a minimum (or zero in an ideal situation). A JIT system minimizes the costs of maintaining inventory, but it is practical only if customers are content to order in advance or if managers can accurately determine short-term sales demand. Suppliers also must be able and willing to ship small quantities regularly and promptly. ■

Point: Accurate estimates of future sales are crucial in a JIT system.

A manufacturing company predicts sales of 220 units for May and 250 units for June. The company wants each month's ending inventory to equal 30% of next month's predicted unit sales. Beginning inventory for May is 66 units. Compute the company's budgeted production in units for May.

Solution

	Units
Budgeted ending inventory for May (250 × 30%)	75
Plus: Budgeted sales for May	220
Required units of available production	295
Less: Beginning inventory	(66)
Total units to be produced during May	229

Direct Materials Budget   The **direct materials budget** shows the budgeted costs for the direct materials that must be purchased to satisfy the budgeted production for the period. Whereas the production budget shows *units* to be produced, the direct materials budget translates the units to be produced into budgeted *costs*. (The same is true for the other two manufacturing budgets that we will discuss below—the direct labor budget and the factory overhead budget).

A direct materials budget requires the following inputs:

1. Number of units to produce (from the production budget).
2. Materials requirements per unit—How many units (pounds, gallons, etc.) of direct materials go into each unit of finished product?
3. Budgeted ending inventory (in units) of direct materials—As with finished goods, most companies maintain a safety stock of materials to ensure that production can continue.
4. Beginning inventory (in units) of direct materials.
5. Cost per unit of direct materials.

Materials (in pounds) to purchase are computed as:

$$\text{Materials to be purchased (pounds)} = \text{Budgeted production (units)} \times \text{Materials required for each unit (pounds)} + \text{Budgeted ending materials inventory (pounds)} - \text{Beginning materials inventory (pounds)}$$

Exhibit 7.7 shows the direct materials budget for TSC.
1. This budget begins with the budgeted production from the production budget.
2. Next, TSC needs to know the amount of direct materials needed for each of the units to be produced—in this case, half a pound (0.5) of wood. With these two inputs we can compute the amount of direct materials needed for production. For example, to produce 710 hockey sticks in October, TSC will need 355 pounds of wood (710 units × 0.5 lbs. = 355 lbs.).
3. TSC wants a safety stock of direct materials in inventory at the end of each month to complete 50% of the budgeted units to be produced in the next month. Because TSC expects to produce 1,340 units in November, requiring 670 pounds of materials, it needs ending inventory of direct materials of 335 pounds (50% × 670) in inventory at the end of October. TSC's total direct materials requirement for October is therefore 690 pounds (355 + 335).
4. TSC already has 178 pounds of direct materials in its beginning inventory (refer to Exhibit 7.3). TSC deducts this amount from the total materials requirements for the month. For October, the calculation is 690 pounds – 178 pounds = 512 pounds of direct materials to be purchased in October.

EXHIBIT 7.7

Direct Materials Budget

A	B	C	D
TORONTO STICKS COMPANY Direct Materials Budget October 2017–December 2017			
	October	**November**	**December**
5 Budgeted production units*	710	1,340	950
6 Materials requirements per unit	× 0.5	× 0.5	× 0.5
7 Materials needed for production (pounds)	355	×50% 670	×50% 475
8 Add: Budgeted ending inventory (pounds)	335	237.5	247.5**
9 Total materials requirements (pounds)	690	907.5	722.5
10 Deduct: Beginning inventory (pounds)	(178)	(335)	(237.5)
11 Materials to be purchased (pounds)	512	572.5	485.0
12			
13 Material price per pound	$ 20	$ 20	$ 20
14 Total cost of direct materials purchases	$10,240	$11,450	$9,700

Materials needed for production
+ Budgeted ending mtls. inventory
− Beginning mtls. inventory
= Materials to be purchased

*From production budget (Exhibit 7.6).

**Computed from January 2018 production requirements, assumed to be 990 units. 990 units × 0.5 lbs. per unit × 50% safety stock = 247.5 lbs.

5 The direct materials budget next translates the *pounds* of direct materials to be purchased into budgeted *costs*. TSC estimates that the cost of direct materials will be $20 per pound over the quarter. At $20 per pound, purchasing 512 pounds of direct materials for October production will cost $10,240 (computed as $20 × 512). Similar calculations yield the cost of direct materials purchases for November ($11,450) and December ($9,700). (For December, assume the budgeted ending inventory of direct materials, based on January's production requirements, is 247.5 pounds).

If the company expects direct materials costs to change in the future, it can easily include changes in the direct materials budget. For example, if the price of wood jumps to $25 per pound in December—say, because a long-term contract with the supplier is about to expire—TSC could simply change December's material price per pound in the direct materials budget.

Direct Labor Budget   The **direct labor budget** shows the budgeted costs for the direct labor that will be needed to satisfy the budgeted production for the period. Because there is no "inventory" of labor, the direct labor budget is easier to prepare than the direct materials budget.

A direct labor budget requires the following inputs:

1 Number of units to produce (from the production budget).

2 Labor requirements per unit—direct labor hours for each unit of finished product.

3 Cost per direct labor hour.

Budgeted amount of direct labor cost is computed as:

TSC's direct labor budget is shown in Exhibit 7.8.

1 The budgeted production line is taken from the production budget.

2 Fifteen minutes of labor time (a quarter of an hour) are required to produce one unit. Compute budgeted direct labor hours by multiplying the budgeted production for each month by one-quarter (0.25) of an hour.

3 Labor is paid $12 per hour. Compute the total cost of direct labor by multiplying budgeted labor hours by the labor rate of $12 per hour.

Estimated changes in direct labor costs can be easily included in the budgeting process. Companies thus can ensure the right amount of direct labor for periods in which production is expected to change or to take into account expected changes in direct labor rates.

Point: A quarter of an hour can be expressed as 0.25 hours (15 minutes/60 minutes = 0.25 hours).

EXHIBIT 7.8

Direct Labor Budget

	A	B	C	D
1	**TORONTO STICKS COMPANY**			
2	**Direct Labor Budget**			
3	**October 2017–December 2017**			
4		**October**	**November**	**December**
5	Budgeted production (units)*	710	1,340	950
6	Direct labor requirements per unit (hours)	× 0.25	× 0.25	× 0.25
7	Total direct labor hours needed	177.5	335	237.5
8				
9	Direct labor rate (per hour)	$ 12	$ 12	$ 12
10	Total cost of direct labor	$2,130	$4,020	$2,850

*From production budget (Exhibit 7.6).

Example: If TSC can reduce its direct labor requirements to 0.20 hours per unit by paying $14 per hour for more skilled workers, what is the total direct labor cost for December? *Answer:* $2,660.

NEED-TO-KNOW 7-3

Direct Materials and Direct Labor Budgets

P1

A manufacturing company budgets production of 800 units during June and 900 units during July. Each unit of finished goods requires 2 pounds of direct materials, at a cost of $8 per pound. The company maintains an inventory of direct materials equal to 10% of next month's budgeted production. Beginning direct materials inventory for June is 160 pounds. Each finished unit requires 1 hour of direct labor at the rate of $14 per hour. Compute the budgeted (a) cost of direct materials purchases for June and (b) direct labor cost for June.

Solution

a.

Direct Materials Budget (June)

Budgeted production (units)	800
Materials requirements per unit (lbs.)	× 2
Materials needed for production (lbs.)	1,600
Add: Budgeted ending inventory (lbs.)	180*
Total materials requirements (lbs.)	1,780
Less: Beginning inventory (lbs.)	(160)
Materials to be purchased (lbs.)	1,620
Material price per pound	$ 8
Total cost of direct materials purchases	$12,960

*900 units × 2 lbs. per unit × 10% = 180 lbs.

b.

Direct Labor Budget (June)

Budgeted production (units)	800
Labor requirements per unit (hours)	× 1
Total direct labor hours needed.	800
Labor rate (per hour)	$ 14
Direct labor cost (June)	$11,200

> Do More: QS 7-7, QS 7-8, QS 7-13, QS 7-14, E 7-4, E 7-5, E 7-8

Factory Overhead Budget   The **factory overhead budget** shows the budgeted costs for factory overhead that will be needed to complete the budgeted production for the period. TSC's factory overhead budget is shown in Exhibit 7.9. TSC separates variable and fixed overhead costs in its overhead budget, as do many companies.

Separating variable and fixed overhead costs enables companies to more closely estimate changes in overhead costs as production volume varies. TSC assigns the variable portion of overhead using a predetermined overhead rate of $2.50 per unit of production. This rate might

Point: Companies can use scatter diagrams, the high-low method, or regression analysis to classify overhead costs as fixed or variable.

EXHIBIT 7.9

Factory Overhead Budget

	A	B	C	D
1	**TORONTO STICKS COMPANY**			
2	**Factory Overhead Budget**			
3	**October 2017–December 2017**			
4		**October**	**November**	**December**
5	Budgeted production (units)*	710	1,340	950
6	Variable factory overhead rate	× $ 2.50	× $ 2.50	× $ 2.50
7	Budgeted variable overhead	1,775	3,350	2,375
8	Budgeted fixed overhead	1,500	1,500	1,500
9	Budgeted total overhead	$3,275	$4,850	$3,875

*From production budget (Exhibit 7.6).

be based on inputs such as direct materials costs, machine hours, direct labor hours, or other activity measures.

TSC's fixed overhead consists entirely of depreciation on manufacturing equipment. From Exhibit 7.3, this is computed as $18,000 per year [($200,000 – $20,000)/10 years], or $1,500 per month ($18,000/12 months). This fixed overhead cost stays constant at $1,500 per month.

The budget in Exhibit 7.9 is in condensed form; most overhead budgets are more detailed, listing each overhead cost item. Overhead budgets also commonly include supervisor salaries, indirect materials, indirect labor, utilities, and maintenance of manufacturing equipment. We explain these more detailed overhead budgets in the next chapter.

Product Cost per Unit   With the information from the three manufacturing budgets (direct materials, direct labor, and factory overhead), we can compute TSC's product cost per unit. This amount is useful in computing cost of goods sold and preparing a budgeted income statement, as we show later. For budgeting purposes, TSC assumes it will normally produce 3,000 units of product each quarter, yielding fixed overhead of $1.50 per unit (computed as $4,500/3,000). TSC's other product costs are all variable. Exhibit 7.10 summarizes the product cost per unit calculation.

Product Cost	Per Unit
Direct materials (½ pound of materials × $20 per pound of materials)	$10.00
Direct labor (0.25 hours of direct labor × $12 per hour of direct labor)	3.00
Variable overhead (from predetermined overhead rate)	2.50
Fixed overhead ($4,500 total fixed overhead per quarter/3,000 units of expected production per quarter)	1.50
Total product cost per unit*	$17.00

*At the normal production level of 3,000 units per quarter.

EXHIBIT 7.10

Product Cost per Unit

Selling Expense Budget   The **selling expense budget** is an estimate of the types and amounts of selling expenses expected during the budget period. It is usually prepared by the vice president of marketing or a sales manager. Budgeted selling expenses are based on the sales budget, plus a fixed amount of sales manager salaries.

TSC's selling expense budget is in Exhibit 7.11. The firm's selling expenses consist of commissions paid to sales personnel and a $2,000 monthly salary paid to the sales manager. Sales commissions equal 10% of total sales and are paid in the month sales occur. Sales commissions vary with sales volume, but the sales manager's salary is fixed. Other common selling expenses include advertising, delivery expenses, and marketing expenses.

	A	B	C	D	E
1		TORONTO STICKS COMPANY			
2		Selling Expense Budget			
3		October 2017–December 2017			
4		October	November	December	Totals
5	Budgeted sales*	$60,000	$48,000	$ 84,000	$192,000
6	Sales commission %	× 10%	× 10%	× 10%	× 10%
7	Sales commissions	6,000	4,800	8,400	19,200
8	Salary for sales manager	2,000	2,000	2,000	6,000
9	Total selling expenses	$ 8,000	$ 6,800	$ 10,400	$ 25,200

*From sales budget (Exhibit 7.4).

EXHIBIT 7.11

Selling Expense Budget

Example: If TSC expects a 12% sales commission will result in budgeted sales of $220,000 for the quarter, what is the total amount of selling expenses for the quarter? Answer: $32,400.

General and Administrative Expense Budget   The **general and administrative expense budget** plans the predicted operating expenses not included in the selling expenses or manufacturing budgets. The office manager responsible for general administration often is responsible for preparing the general and administrative expense budget.

Exhibit 7.12 shows TSC's general and administrative expense budget. It includes salaries of $54,000 per year, or $4,500 per month (paid each month when they are earned). Insurance, taxes, and depreciation on nonmanufacturing assets are other common examples of general and administrative expenses.

EXHIBIT 7.12

General and Administrative Expense Budget

	A	B	C	D	E
1	TORONTO STICKS COMPANY				
2	General and Administrative Expense Budget				
3	October 2017–December 2017				
4		October	November	December	Totals
5	Administrative salaries	$4,500	$4,500	$4,500	$13,500
6	Total general and administrative expenses	$4,500	$4,500	$4,500	$13,500

Example: In Exhibit 7.12, how would a rental agreement of $5,000 per month plus 1% of sales affect the general and administrative expense budget? (Budgeted sales are in Exhibit 7.4.) *Answer: Rent expense:* Oct. = $5,600; Nov. = $5,480; Dec. = $5,840; Total = $16,920; *Revised total general and administrative expenses:* Oct. = $10,100; Nov. = $9,980; Dec. = $10,340; Total = $30,420.

Decision Insight

No Biz Like Snow Biz   Ski resorts' costs of making snow are in the millions of dollars for equipment alone. Snowmaking involves spraying droplets of water into the air, causing them to freeze and come down as snow. Making snow can cost more than $2,000 an hour. Snowmaking accounts for 40 to 50 percent of the budgeted costs for many ski resorts. ■

© Gail Shotlander/Getty Images

NEED-TO-KNOW 7-4

Selling and General and Administrative Expense Budgets

P1

Do More: QS 7-5, QS 7-11

A manufacturing company budgets sales of $70,000 during July. It pays sales commissions of 5% of sales and also pays a sales manager a salary of $3,000 per month. Other monthly costs include depreciation on office equipment ($500), insurance expense ($200), advertising ($1,000), and an office manager salary of $2,500 per month. For the month of July, compute the total (a) budgeted selling expense and (b) budgeted general and administrative expense.

Solution

a. Total budgeted selling expense = ($70,000 × 5%) + $3,000 + $1,000 = $7,500

b. Total budgeted general and administrative expense = $500 + $200 + $2,500 = $3,200

Investing Budgets

Information from operating budgets in the prior section is useful in preparing the capital expenditures budget—a key part of investing budgets.

Investing Budgets

Capital expenditures

Capital Expenditures Budget   The **capital expenditures budget** shows dollar amounts estimated to be spent to purchase additional plant assets and any cash expected to be received from plant asset disposals. This means the capital expenditures budget shows the company's expected investing activities in plant assets. It is usually prepared after the operating budgets. Because a company's plant assets determine its productive capacity, this budget is usually affected by long-range plans for the business. The process of preparing other budgets can reveal that the company requires more (or less) plant assets.

TSC does not anticipate disposal of any plant assets through December 2017, but it does plan to buy additional equipment for $25,000 cash near the end of December 2017. This is the only budgeted capital expenditure from October 2017 through December 2017. Thus, no separate budget is shown. TSC's cash budget will reflect this $25,000 planned expenditure.

Financing Budgets

Once we prepare operating and investing budgets, we normally proceed to financing budgets such as the cash budget, which is the focus of this section.

Cash Budget   A **cash budget** shows expected cash inflows and outflows during the budget period. Managing cash flows is vital for a firm's success. Most companies set an amount of cash they require. The cash budget is important because it helps the company meet this cash balance goal. If the cash budget indicates a potential cash shortfall, the company can prearrange loans to meet its obligations. If the cash budget indicates a potential cash windfall, the company can plan to pay off prior loans or make other investments. Exhibit 7.13 shows the general formula for the cash budget.

P2_____

Prepare a cash budget.

Financing Budgets
Cash budgets

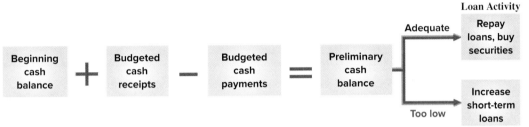

EXHIBIT 7.13

General Formula for Cash Budget

When preparing a cash budget, add budgeted cash receipts to the beginning cash balance and subtract budgeted cash payments. If the preliminary cash balance is too low, additional cash requirements appear in the budget as planned increases from short-term loans. If the preliminary cash balance exceeds the balance the company wants to maintain, the excess is used to repay loans (if any) or to acquire short-term investments.

Information for preparing the cash budget is mainly taken from the operating and capital expenditures budgets. Preparing the cash budget typically requires the preparation of other supporting schedules; we show the first of these, a schedule of cash receipts from sales, next.

Cash Receipts from Sales   Managers use the sales budget and knowledge about how frequently customers pay on credit sales to budget monthly cash receipts. To illustrate, Exhibit 7.14 presents TSC's schedule of budgeted cash receipts.

	A	B	C	D	E
1	**TORONTO STICKS COMPANY**				
2	**Schedule of Cash Receipts from Sales**				
3	**October 2017–December 2017**				
4		**September**	**October**	**November**	**December**
5	Sales*	$42,000	$60,000	$48,000	$84,000
6	**Less:** Ending accounts receivable (60%)	25,200**	36,000	28,800	50,400
7	Cash receipts from				
8	Cash sales (40% of sales)		24,000	19,200	33,600
9	Collections of prior month's receivables		25,200	36,000	28,800
10	Total cash receipts		$49,200	$55,200	$62,400

EXHIBIT 7.14

Computing Budgeted Cash Receipts from Sales

*From sales budget (Exhibit 7.4).
**Accounts receivable balance from September 30 balance sheet (Exhibit 7.3).

We begin with TSC's budgeted sales (Exhibit 7.4). Analysis of past sales indicates that 40% of the firm's sales are for cash. The remaining 60% are credit sales; these customers are expected to pay in full in the month following the sales. We now can compute the budgeted cash receipts from customers, as shown in Exhibit 7.14. October's budgeted cash receipts consist of $24,000 from expected October cash sales ($60,000 × 40%) plus the anticipated collection of $25,200 of accounts receivable from the end of September.

Alternative Collection Timing   The schedule above can be modified for alternative collection timing and/or uncollectible accounts. For example, if TSC collects 80% of credit sales in the first month after sale, 20% of credit sales in the second month after sale, and all other assumptions are unchanged, budgeted cash receipts for December are:

December budgeted cash receipts with alternative collection timing	
Cash receipts from December cash sales..	$ 33,600
Collections of November's receivables ($48,000 × 60% × 80%)...................	23,040
Collections of October's receivables ($60,000 × 60% × 20%)...................	7,200
Total cash receipts	**$63,840**

Uncollectible Accounts   Some companies consider uncollectible accounts in their cash budgets. To do so, multiply credit sales by (1 − % of uncollectible receivables). For example, if in addition to the alternative collection timing above TSC estimates that 5% of all credit sales will not be collected, it computes its December cash receipts as:

December budgeted cash receipts with alternative collection timing and uncollectible accounts	
Cash receipts from December cash sales..	$ 33,600
Collections of November's receivables ($48,000 × 95% × 60% × 80%).............	21,888
Collections of October's receivables ($60,000 × 95% × 60% × 20%)...............	6,840
Total cash receipts	**$62,328**

Cash Payments for Materials   Managers use the beginning balance sheet (Exhibit 7.3) and the direct materials budget (Exhibit 7.7) to help prepare a schedule of cash payments for materials. Managers must also know *how* TSC purchases direct materials (pay cash or on account), and for credit purchases, how quickly TSC pays. TSC's materials purchases are entirely on account. It makes full payment during the month following its purchases. Using this information, the schedule of cash payments for materials is shown in Exhibit 7.15.

EXHIBIT 7.15

Computing Cash Payments for Materials Purchases

	A	B	C	D
1	TORONTO STICKS COMPANY			
2	Schedule of Cash Payments for Direct Materials			
3	October 2017–December 2017			
4		October	November	December
5	Materials purchases*	$10,240	$11,450	$ 9,700
6	Cash payments for			
7	Current month purchases (0%)	0	0	0
8	Prior month purchases (100%)	7,060**	10,240	11,450
9	Total cash payments for direct materials	$ 7,060	$10,240	$11,450

*From direct materials budget (Exhibit 7.7).
**Accounts Payable balance from September 30 balance sheet (Exhibit 7.3).

The schedule above can be modified for alternative payment timing. For example, if TSC paid for 20% of its purchases in the month of purchase and paid the remaining 80% of a month's purchases in the following month, its cash payments in December would equal $11,100, computed as (20% × $9,700) plus (80% × $11,450).

Preparing the Cash Budget   The cash budget summarizes many other budgets in terms of their effects on cash. To prepare the cash budget, TSC's managers use the budgets and other schedules listed below.

1. Cash receipts from sales (Exhibit 7.14).
2. Cash payments for direct materials (Exhibit 7.15).
3. Cash payments for direct labor (Exhibit 7.8).

4. Cash payments for overhead (Exhibit 7.9).
5. Cash payments for selling expenses (Exhibit 7.11).
6. Cash payments for general and administrative expenses (Exhibit 7.12).

The *fixed overhead* assigned to depreciation in the factory overhead budget (Exhibit 7.9) does not require a cash payment. Therefore, it is not included in the cash budget. Other types of fixed overhead—such as payments for property taxes and insurance—*are* included if they require cash payments.

Additional information is typically needed to prepare the cash budget. For TSC, this additional information includes:

1. Income taxes payable (from the beginning balance sheet, Exhibit 7.3).
2. Expected dividend payments: TSC plans to pay $3,000 of cash dividends in the second month of each quarter.
3. Loan activity: TSC wants to maintain a minimum cash balance of $20,000 at each month-end. This is important, as it helps ensure TSC maintains enough cash to pay its bills as they come due. If TSC borrows cash, it must pay interest at the rate of 1% per month.

Exhibit 7.16 shows the full cash budget for TSC. The company begins October with $20,000 in cash. To this is added $49,200 in expected cash receipts from customers (from Exhibit 7.14). We next subtract expected cash payments for direct materials, direct labor, overhead, selling expenses, and general and administrative expenses. Income taxes of $20,000 were due as of the end of September 30, 2017, and payable in October. We next discuss TSC's loan activity, including any interest payments.

Courtesy JJW Images

EXHIBIT 7.16

Cash Budget

	A	B	C	D
1	TORONTO STICKS COMPANY			
2	Cash Budget			
3	October 2017–December 2017			
4		October	November	December
5	Beginning cash balance	$20,000	$20,000	$ 38,881
6	Add: Cash receipts from customers (Exhibit 7.14)	49,200	55,200	62,400
7	Total cash available	69,200	75,200	101,281
8	Less: Cash payments for			
9	Direct materials (Exhibit 7.15)	7,060	10,240	11,450
10	Direct labor (Exhibit 7.8)	2,130	4,020	2,850
11	Variable overhead (Exhibit 7.9)	1,775	3,350	2,375
12	Sales commissions (Exhibit 7.11)	6,000	4,800	8,400
13	Sales salaries (Exhibit 7.11)	2,000	2,000	2,000
14	General and administrative expenses (Exhibit 7.12)	4,500	4,500	4,500
15	Income taxes payable (Exhibit 7.3)	20,000		
16	Dividends		3,000	
17	Interest on bank loan			
18	October ($10,000 × 1%)*	100		
19	November ($4,365 × 1%)**		44	
20	Purchase of equipment			25,000
21	Total cash payments	43,565	31,954	56,575
22	Preliminary cash balance	$25,635	$43,246	$ 44,706
23	**Loan activity**			
24	Additional loan from bank			
25	Repayment of loan to bank	5,635	4,365	
26	Ending cash balance	$20,000	$38,881	$ 44,706
27	Loan balance, end of month†	$ 4,365	$ 0	$ 0

Cash	
Oct. 1 20,000	
Receipts 49,200	
	43,565 Payments
Prelim. bal. 25,635	
	5,635 Repay loan
Oct. 31 20,000	

* Beginning loan balance (note payable) from Exhibit 7.3.   ** Rounded to the nearest dollar.
† Beginning loan balance + New loans – Loan repayments. For October: $10,000 – $5,635 = $4,365.

Loan Activity   TSC has an agreement with its bank that promises additional loans at each month-end, if necessary, so that the company keeps a minimum cash balance of $20,000. If the cash balance exceeds $20,000 at month-end, TSC uses the excess to repay loans (if any) or buy short-term investments. If the cash balance is less than $20,000 at month-end, the bank loans TSC the difference.

At the end of each month, TSC pays the bank interest on any outstanding loan amount, at the monthly rate of 1% of the beginning balance of these loans. For October, this payment of $100 is 1% of the $10,000 note payable amount reported in the September 30 balance sheet of Exhibit 7.3. For November, TSC expects to pay interest of $44, computed as 1% of the $4,365 expected loan balance at October 31. No interest is budgeted for December because the company expects to repay the loans in full at the end of November. Exhibit 7.16 shows that the October 31 cash balance increases to $25,635 (before any loan-related activity). This amount is more than the $20,000 minimum. Thus, TSC will use the excess cash of $5,635 (computed as $25,635 – $20,000) to pay off a portion of its loan. At the end of November, TSC's preliminary cash balance is sufficient to pay off its remaining loan balance.

Had TSC's preliminary cash balance been below the $20,000 minimum in any month, TSC would have increased its loan from the bank so that the ending cash balance was $20,000. We show an example of this situation in **Need-To-Know 7-7** at the end of this chapter.

Decision Insight

Cash Cushion   Why do some companies maintain a minimum cash balance even when the budget shows extra cash is not needed? For example, **Apple's** cash and short-term investments balance is over $40 billion. According to Apple's CEO, Tim Cook, the cushion provides "flexibility and security," important in navigating uncertain economic times. A cash cushion enables companies to jump on new ventures or acquisitions that may present themselves. The **Boston Red Sox** keep a cash cushion for its trades involving players with "cash considerations." ∎

© Adam Glanzman/Getty Images

NEED-TO-KNOW 7-5

Cash Budget

P2

Part 1

Diaz Co. predicts sales of $80,000 for January and $90,000 for February. Seventy percent of Diaz's sales are for cash, and the remaining 30% are credit sales. All credit sales are collected in the month after sale. January's beginning accounts receivable balance is $20,000. Compute budgeted cash receipts for January and February.

Solution

Budgeted Cash Receipts	January	February
Sales	$80,000	$90,000
Less: Ending accounts receivable (30%)	24,000	27,000
Cash receipts from		
Cash sales (70% of sales)	56,000	63,000
Collections of prior month's receivables	20,000	24,000
Total cash receipts	$76,000	$87,000

Do More: QS 7-6, QS 7-10, QS 7-19, E 7-18

Part 2

Use the following information to prepare a cash budget for the month ended January 31 for Garcia Company. The company requires a minimum $30,000 cash balance at the end of each month. Any preliminary cash balance above $30,000 is used to repay loans (if any). Garcia has a $2,000 loan outstanding at the beginning of January.

a. January 1 cash balance, $30,000
b. Cash receipts from sales, $132,000
c. Budgeted cash payments for materials, $63,500

d. Budgeted cash payments for labor, $33,400
e. Other budgeted cash expenses,* $8,200
f. Cash repayment of bank loan, $2,000

*Including loan interest for January.

Solution

GARCIA COMPANY Cash Budget For Month Ended January 31		
Beginning cash balance	$ 30,000	
Add: Cash receipts from sales	132,000	
Total cash available		$162,000
Less: Cash payments for		
Direct materials	63,500	
Direct labor	33,400	
Other cash expenses.....................	8,200	
Total cash payments		105,100
Preliminary cash balance..................		$ 56,900
Loan activity:		
Repayment of loan to bank		2,000
Ending cash balance		$ 54,900
Loan balance, end of month		$ 0

> Do More: QS 7-24, E 7-17, E 7-21, E 7-22

BUDGETED FINANCIAL STATEMENTS

One of the final steps in the budgeting process is summarizing the financial statement effects. We next illustrate TSC's budgeted income statement and budgeted balance sheet.

Budgeted Income Statement

The **budgeted income statement** is a managerial accounting report showing predicted amounts of sales and expenses for the budget period. It summarizes the predicted income effects of the budgeted activities. Information needed to prepare a budgeted income statement is primarily taken from already-prepared budgets. The volume of information summarized in the budgeted income statement is so large for some companies that they often use spreadsheets to accumulate the budgeted transactions and classify them by their effects on income.

We condense TSC's budgeted income statement and show it in Exhibit 7.17. All information in this exhibit is taken from the component budgets we've examined in this chapter. Also, we now can predict the amount of income tax expense for the quarter, computed as 40% of the budgeted pretax income. For TSC, these taxes are not payable until January 31, 2018. Thus, these taxes are not shown on the October–December 2017 cash budget in Exhibit 7.16, but they are included on the December 31, 2017, balance sheet (shown next).

P3

Prepare budgeted financial statements.

> **Budgeted Financial Statements**
> Income statement
> Balance sheet

Point: Lenders often require potential borrowers to provide cash budgets, budgeted income statements, and budgeted balance sheets, as well as data on past performance.

TORONTO STICKS COMPANY Budgeted Income Statement For Three Months Ended December 31, 2017		
Sales (Exhibit 7.4, 3,200 units @ $60)		$192,000
Cost of goods sold (3,200 units @ $17)*		54,400
Gross profit		137,600
Operating expenses		
Sales commissions (Exhibit 7.11)	$19,200	
Sales salaries (Exhibit 7.11)	6,000	
Administrative salaries (Exhibit 7.12)	13,500	
Interest expense (Exhibit 7.16)	144	38,844
Income before income taxes		98,756
Income tax expense ($98,756 × 40%)**		39,502
Net income		$ 59,254

*$17 product cost per unit from Exhibit 7.10.   **Rounded to the nearest dollar.

EXHIBIT 7.17

Budgeted Income Statement

Budgeted Balance Sheet

The final step in preparing the master budget is summarizing the company's predicted financial position. The **budgeted balance sheet** shows predicted amounts for the company's assets, liabilities, and equity as of the end of the budget period. TSC's budgeted balance sheet in Exhibit 7.18 is prepared using information from the other budgets. The sources of amounts are reported in the notes to the budgeted balance sheet.

EXHIBIT 7.18

Budgeted Balance Sheet

TORONTO STICKS COMPANY
Budgeted Balance Sheet
December 31, 2017

Assets

Cash[a]		$ 44,706
Accounts receivable[b]		50,400
Raw materials inventory[c]		4,950
Finished goods inventory[d]		13,770
Equipment[e]	$225,000	
Less: Accumulated depreciation[f]	40,500	184,500
Total assets		$298,326

Liabilities and Equity

Liabilities		
Accounts payable[g]	$ 9,700	
Income taxes payable[h]	39,502	$ 49,202
Stockholders' equity		
Common stock[i]	150,000	
Retained earnings[j]	99,124	249,124
Total liabilities and equity		$298,326

Retained Earnings	
	42,870 Sep. 30
	59,254 Net income
Dividends 3,000	
	99,124 Oct. 31

[a] Ending balance for December from the cash budget (in Exhibit 7.16).
[b] 60% of $84,000 sales budgeted for December from the sales budget (in Exhibit 7.4).
[c] 247.5 pounds of raw materials in budgeted ending inventory at the budgeted cost of $20 per pound (direct materials budget, Exhibit 7.7).
[d] 810 units in budgeted finished goods inventory (Exhibit 7.6) at the budgeted cost of $17 per unit (Exhibit 7.10).
[e] September 30 balance of $200,000 from the beginning balance sheet in Exhibit 7.3 plus $25,000 cost of new equipment from the cash budget in Exhibit 7.16.
[f] September 30 balance of $36,000 from the beginning balance sheet in Exhibit 7.3 plus $4,500 depreciation expense from the factory overhead budget in Exhibit 7.9.
[g] Budgeted cost of materials purchases for December from Exhibit 7.7, to be paid in January.
[h] Income tax expense from the budgeted income statement for the fourth quarter in Exhibit 7.17, to be paid in January.
[i] Unchanged from the beginning balance sheet in Exhibit 7.3.
[j] September 30 balance of $42,870 from the beginning balance sheet in Exhibit 7.3 plus budgeted net income of $59,254 from the budgeted income statement in Exhibit 7.17 minus budgeted cash dividends of $3,000 from the cash budget in Exhibit 7.16.

Using the Master Budget

For a master budget to be cost-beneficial, managers must use it to plan and control activities. The master budget is clearly a plan for future activities. In addition, any stage in the master budgeting process might reveal undesirable outcomes. The new information can cause management to change its decisions. For example, an early version of the cash budget could show an insufficient amount of cash unless cash outlays are reduced. This information could yield a reduction in planned equipment purchases. Likewise, a budgeted balance sheet might reveal too much debt from too many planned equipment purchases; the company could reduce its planned equipment purchases and thus reduce its need for borrowing.

In *controlling* operations, managers typically compare actual results to budgeted results. Differences between actual and budgeted results are called *variances*. Management examines variances, particularly large ones, to identify areas for improvement and take corrective action. We discuss variances in more detail in the next chapter.

Budgeting for Service Companies

Service providers also use master budgets. Because service providers do not manufacture goods and hold no inventory, they typically need fewer operating budgets than manufacturers do. Exhibit 7.19 shows the master budget process for a service provider.

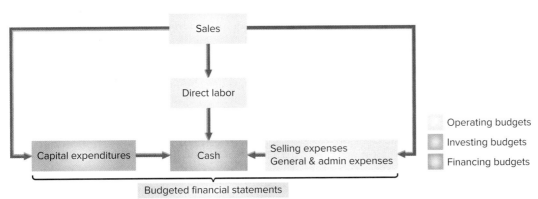

EXHIBIT 7.19

Master Budget Process for a Service Company

Exhibit 7.19 shows that service providers *do not prepare production, direct materials, or factory overhead budgets.* In addition, because many services such as accounting, banking, and landscaping are labor-intensive, the direct labor budget is important. If an accounting firm greatly underestimates the hours needed to complete an audit, it might charge too low a price. If the accounting firm greatly overestimates the hours needed, it might bid too high a price (and lose jobs) or incur excessive labor costs. Either way, the firm's profits can suffer if its direct labor budget is unrealistic.

SUSTAINABILITY AND ACCOUNTING

Budgets translate an organization's strategic goals into dollar terms. When deciding on strategic goals, managers must consider their effects on budgets. **Johnson & Johnson**, a large manufacturer of pharmaceuticals, medical devices, and consumer health products, sets goals for both profits and sustainable practices. A recent company sustainability report discusses several sustainability goals and strategies, including some shown in Exhibit 7.20.

Sustainability Goal	Strategy to Achieve Goal
Reduce waste by 10%.	Purchase pulping machine to grind and recycle packaging.
Reduce CO_2 emissions by 20%.	Purchase hybrid vehicles.
Reduce water usage by 10%.	Update plumbing, install water recovery systems, employee training.

EXHIBIT 7.20

Sustainability Goals and Strategies

Several of the company's strategies involve asset purchases that will impact the capital expenditures budget. Additional employee training will impact the overhead budget. By reducing waste, increasing recycling, and reducing water usage, the company hopes to reduce some of the costs reflected in the direct materials and overhead budgets. Company managers periodically evaluate performance with respect to these goals and make any necessary adjustments to budgets.

TaTa Topper, this chapter's feature company, incorporates sustainability into its packaging. "We make our packaging as small as possible," says co-founder Marilyn Collins. "It reduces shelf space, which means our product is more likely to appear in stores, and it's good for the environment."

The owners discovered that by having the manufacturer hand roll rather than vacuum seal the toppers, they could use smaller boxes and avoid shipping problems due to their product bulging out of the boxes. These types of continuous improvements help companies both profit and reduce their environmental impact.

Courtesy of TaTa Topper

Decision Analysis   Activity-Based Budgeting

A1
_____

Analyze expense planning using activity-based budgeting.

Activity-based budgeting (ABB) is a budget system based on expected *activities*. Knowledge of expected activities and their levels for the budget period enables management to plan for resources required to perform the activities.

Exhibit 7.21 contrasts a traditional budget with an activity-based budget for a company's accounting department. With a traditional budget, management often makes across-the-board budget cuts or increases. For example, management might decide that each of the line items in the traditional budget must be cut by 5%. This might not be a good strategic decision.

ABB requires management to list activities performed by, say, the accounting department such as auditing, tax reporting, financial reporting, and cost accounting. By focusing on the relation between activities and costs, management can attempt to reduce costs by eliminating nonvalue-added activities.

EXHIBIT 7.21

Activity-Based Budgeting versus Traditional Budgeting (for an accounting department)

Traditional Budget		Activity-Based Budget	
Salaries	$152,000	Auditing	$ 58,000
Supplies....................	22,000	Tax reporting	71,000
Depreciation.................	36,000	Financial reporting	63,000
Utilities	14,000	Cost accounting	32,000
Total.......................	$224,000	Total	$224,000

 Decision Maker

Environmental Manager   You hold the new position of environmental control manager for a chemical company. You are asked to develop a budget for your job and identify job responsibilities. How do you proceed? ■   *Answer:* You are unlikely to have data on this new position to use in preparing your budget. In this situation, you can use activity-based budgeting. This requires developing a list of activities to conduct, the resources required to perform these activities, and the expenses associated with these resources. You should challenge yourself to be absolutely certain that the listed activities are necessary and that the listed resources are required.

NEED-TO-KNOW **7-6**

COMPREHENSIVE 1

Master Budget—
Manufacturer

Payne Company's management asks you to prepare its master budget using the following information. The budget is to cover the months of April, May, and June of 2017.

PAYNE COMPANY
Balance Sheet
March 31, 2017

Assets			Liabilities and Equity		
Cash	$ 50,000		Accounts payable	$ 63,818	
Accounts receivable	175,000		Short-term notes payable	12,000	
Raw materials inventory	30,798*		Total current liabilities		$ 75,818
Finished goods inventory	96,600**		Long-term note payable		200,000
Total current assets		$352,398	Total liabilities		275,818
Equipment	480,000		Common stock	435,000	
Less: Accumulated depreciation	(90,000)		Retained earnings	31,580	
Equipment, net		390,000	Total stockholders' equity		466,580
Total assets		$742,398	Total liabilities and equity		$742,398

*2,425 pounds @$12.70, rounded to nearest whole dollar   **8,400 units @ $11.50 per unit

Additional Information

a. Sales for March total 10,000 units. Expected sales (in units) are: 10,500 (April), 9,500 (May), 10,000 (June), and 10,500 (July). The product's selling price is $25 per unit.

b. Company policy calls for a given month's ending finished goods inventory to equal 80% of the next month's expected unit sales. The March 31 finished goods inventory is 8,400 units, which complies with the policy. The product's manufacturing cost is $11.50 per unit, including per unit costs of $6.35 for materials (0.5 lbs. at $12.70 per lb.), $3.75 for direct labor (0.25 hour × $15 direct labor rate per hour), $0.90 for variable overhead, and $0.50 for fixed overhead. Fixed overhead consists entirely of $5,000 of monthly depreciation expense. Company policy also calls for a given month's ending raw materials inventory to equal 50% of next month's expected materials needed for production. The March 31 inventory is 2,425 units of materials, which complies with the policy. The company expects to have 2,100 units of materials inventory on June 30.

c. Sales representatives' commissions are 12% of sales and are paid in the month of the sales. The sales manager's monthly salary will be $3,500 in April and $4,000 per month thereafter.

d. Monthly general and administrative expenses include $8,000 administrative salaries and 0.9% monthly interest on the long-term note payable.

e. The company expects 30% of sales to be for cash and the remaining 70% on credit. Receivables are collected in full in the month following the sale (none is collected in the month of the sale).

f. All direct materials purchases are on credit, and no payables arise from any other transactions. One month's purchases are fully paid in the next month. Materials cost $12.70 per pound.

g. The minimum ending cash balance for all months is $50,000. If necessary, the company borrows enough cash using a short-term note to reach the minimum. Short-term notes require an interest payment of 1% at each month-end (before any repayment). If the ending cash balance exceeds the minimum, the excess will be applied to repaying the short-term notes payable balance.

h. Dividends of $100,000 are to be declared and paid in May.

i. No cash payments for income taxes are to be made during the second calendar quarter. Income taxes will be assessed at 35% in the quarter.

j. Equipment purchases of $55,000 are scheduled for June.

Required

Prepare the following budgets and other financial information as required:

1. Sales budget, including budgeted sales for July.
2. Production budget.
3. Direct materials budget. Round costs of materials purchases to the nearest dollar.
4. Direct labor budget.
5. Factory overhead budget.
6. Selling expense budget.
7. General and administrative expense budget.
8. Expected cash receipts from customers and the expected June 30 balance of accounts receivable.
9. Expected cash payments for purchases and the expected June 30 balance of accounts payable.
10. Cash budget.
11. Budgeted income statement, budgeted statement of retained earnings, and budgeted balance sheet.

SOLUTION

1.

	A	B	C	D	E
1	**Sales Budget**	**April**	**May**	**June**	**Quarter**
2	Projected unit sales	10,500	9,500	10,000	
3	Selling price per unit	× $ 25	× $ 25	× $ 25	
4	Projected sales	$262,500	$237,500	$250,000	$750,000

2.

	A	B	C	D	E
1	**Production Budget**	**April**	**May**	**June**	**Quarter**
2	Next period's unit sales (part I)	9,500	10,000	10,500	
3	Ending inventory percent	× 80%	× 80%	× 80%	
4	Desired ending inventory	7,600	8,000	8,400	
5	Current period's unit sales (part I)	10,500	9,500	10,000	
6	Required units of available production	18,100	17,500	18,400	
7	Less: Beginning inventory	8,400	7,600	8,000	
8	Total units to be produced	9,700	9,900	10,400	

3.

	A	B	C	D
1	**Direct Materials Budget**	April	May	June
2	Budgeted production (units) (part 2)	9,700	9,900	10,400
3	Materials requirements per unit (pounds)	× 0.5	× 0.5	× 0.5
4	Materials needed for production (pounds)	4,850	4,950	5,200
5	Add: Budgeted ending inventory (pounds)	2,475	2,600	2,100
6	Total material requirements (pounds)	7,325	7,550	7,300
7	Deduct: Beginning inventory (pounds)	2,425	2,475	2,600
8	Materials to be purchased (pounds)	4,900	5,075	4,700
9				
10	Materials price per pound	$ 12.70	$ 12.70	$ 12.70
11	Total cost of direct materials purchases	$62,230	$64,453*	$59,690

*Rounded to nearest dollar.

4.

	A	B	C	D
1	**Direct Labor Budget**	April	May	June
2	Budgeted production (units) (part 2)	9,700	9,900	10,400
3	Labor requirements per unit (hours)	× 0.25	× 0.25	× 0.25
4	Total labor hours needed	2,425	2,475	2,600
5				
6	Labor rate (per hour)	$ 15	$ 15	$ 15
7	Total direct labor cost	$36,375	$37,125	$39,000

5.

	A	B	C	D
1	**Factory Overhead Budget**	April	May	June
2	Budgeted production (units) (part 2)	9,700	9,900	10,400
3	Variable factory overhead rate	× $ 0.90	× $ 0.90	× $ 0.90
4	Budgeted variable overhead	8,730	8,910	9,360
5	Budgeted fixed overhead	5,000	5,000	5,000
6	Budgeted total overhead	$13,730	$13,910	$14,360

6.

	A	B	C	D	E
1	**Selling Expense Budget**	April	May	June	Quarter
2	Budgeted sales (part 1)	$262,500	$237,500	$250,000	$750,000
3	Commission %	× 12%	× 12%	× 12%	× 12%
4	Sales commissions	31,500	28,500	30,000	90,000
5	Manager's salary	3,500	4,000	4,000	11,500
6	Budgeted selling expenses	$ 35,000	$ 32,500	$ 34,000	$101,500

7.

	A	B	C	D	E
1	**General and Administrative Expense Budget**	April	May	June	Quarter
2	Administrative salaries	$8,000	$8,000	$8,000	$24,000
3	Interest on long-term note				
4	payable (0.9% × $200,000)	1,800	1,800	1,800	5,400
5	Budgeted general and administrative expenses	$9,800	$9,800	$9,800	$29,400

8.

	A	B	C	D	E
1	**Schedule of Cash Receipts**	April	May	June	Quarter
2	Budgeted sales (part 1)	$262,500	$237,500	$250,000	
3	Ending accounts receivable (70%)	$183,750	$166,250	$175,000	
4	Cash receipts				
5	Cash sales (30% of budgeted sales)	$ 78,750	$ 71,250	$ 75,000	$225,000
6	Collections of prior month's receivables	175,000*	183,750	166,250	525,000
7	Total cash to be collected	$253,750	$255,000	$ 241,250	$750,000

*Accounts receivable balance from March 31 balance sheet.

9.

	A	B	C	D	E
1	**Schedule of Cash Payments for Materials**	April	May	June	Quarter
2	Cash payments (equal to prior month's				
3	materials purchases)	$63,818*	$62,230	$64,453	$190,501
4	Expected June 30 balance of accounts				
5	payable (June purchases)			$59,690	

*Accounts payable balance from March 31 balance sheet.

10.

	A	B	C	D
1	**Cash Budget**	**April**	**May**	**June**
2	Beginning cash balance	$ 50,000	$137,907	$142,342
3	Add: Cash receipts from customers (part 8)	253,750	255,000	241,250
4	Total cash available	303,750	392,907	383,592
5	Less: Cash payments for			
6	Direct materials (part 9)	63,818	62,230	64,453
7	Direct labor (part 4)	36,375	37,125	39,000
8	Variable overhead (part 5)	8,730	8,910	9,360
9	Sales commissions (part 6)	31,500	28,500	30,000
10	Salaries			
11	Sales (part 6)	3,500	4,000	4,000
12	Administrative (part 7)	8,000	8,000	8,000
13	Dividends		100,000	
14	Interest on long-term note (part 7)	1,800	1,800	1,800
15	Interest on bank loan			
16	October ($12,000 × 1%)	120		
17	Purchase of equipment			55,000
18	Total cash payments	153,843	250,565	211,613
19	**Loan activity:** Preliminary cash balance	$149,907	$142,342	$171,979
20	Additional loan from bank			
21	Repayment of loan to bank	12,000	0	0
22	Ending cash balance	$137,907	$142,342	$171,979
23	Loan balance, end of month	$ 0	$ 0	$ 0

11.

PAYNE COMPANY
Budgeted Income Statement
For Quarter Ended June 30, 2017

Sales (part 1)		$750,000
Cost of goods sold (30,000 units @ $11.50)		345,000
Gross profit		405,000
Operating expenses		
Sales commissions (part 6)	$90,000	
Sales salaries (part 6)	11,500	
Administrative salaries (part 7)	24,000	
Interest on long-term note (part 7)	5,400	
Interest on short-term notes (part 10)	120	
Total operating expenses		131,020
Income before income taxes		273,980
Income taxes ($273,980 × 35%)		95,893
Net income		$178,087

PAYNE COMPANY
Budgeted Statement of Retained Earnings
For Quarter Ended June 30, 2017

Retained earnings, March 31, 2017	$ 31,580
Net income	178,087
	209,667
Less: Cash dividends (part 10)	100,000
Retained earnings, June 30, 2017	$109,667

PAYNE COMPANY
Budgeted Balance Sheet
June 30, 2017

Assets			Liabilities and Equity		
Cash (part 10)	$171,979		Accounts payable (part 9)	$ 59,690	
Accounts receivable (part 8)	175,000		Income taxes payable	95,893	
Raw materials inventory (2,100 pounds @ $12.70)*	26,671		Total current liabilities		$155,583
Finished goods inventory (8,400 units @ $11.50)	96,600		Long-term note payable (Mar. 31 bal.)		200,000
Total current assets		$470,250	Total liabilities		355,583
Equipment (Mar. 31 bal. plus purchase)	535,000		Common stock (Mar. 31 bal.)	435,000	
Less: Accumulated depreciation			Retained earnings	109,667	
(Mar. 31 bal. plus depreciation expense)	105,000	430,000	Total stockholders' equity		544,667
Total assets		$900,250	Total liabilities and equity		$900,250

*Plus $1 rounding difference.

NEED-TO-KNOW 7-7

COMPREHENSIVE 2

Master Budget—
Merchandiser

Wild Wood Company's management asks you to prepare its master budget using the following information. The budget is to cover the months of April, May, and June of 2017. Wild Wood is a merchandiser.

WILD WOOD COMPANY			
Balance Sheet			
March 31, 2017			
Assets		**Liabilities and Equity**	
Cash	$ 50,000	Accounts payable	$156,000
Accounts receivable	175,000	Short-term notes payable	12,000
Merchandise inventory (8,400 units × $15)......	126,000	Total current liabilities	168,000
Total current assets	351,000	Long-term note payable	200,000
Equipment	480,000	Total liabilities	368,000
Less: Accumulated depreciation	(90,000)	Common stock	235,000
Equipment, net	390,000	Retained earnings	138,000
		Total stockholders' equity	373,000
Total assets	$741,000	Total liabilities and equity	$741,000

Additional Information

a. Sales for March total 10,000 units. Each month's sales are expected to exceed the prior month's results by 5%. The product's selling price is $25 per unit.

b. Company policy calls for a given month's ending inventory to equal 80% of the next month's expected unit sales. The March 31 inventory is 8,400 units, which complies with the policy. The purchase price is $15 per unit.

c. Sales representatives' commissions are 12.5% of sales and are paid in the month of the sales. The sales manager's monthly salary will be $3,500 in April and $4,000 per month thereafter.

d. Monthly general and administrative expenses include $8,000 administrative salaries, $5,000 depreciation, and 0.9% monthly interest on the long-term note payable.

e. The company expects 30% of sales to be for cash and the remaining 70% on credit. Receivables are collected in full in the month following the sale (none is collected in the month of the sale).

f. All merchandise purchases are on credit, and no payables arise from any other transactions. One month's purchases are fully paid in the next month.

g. The minimum ending cash balance for all months is $50,000. If necessary, the company borrows enough cash using a short-term note to reach the minimum. Short-term notes require an interest payment of 1% at each month-end (before any repayment). If the ending cash balance exceeds the minimum, the excess will be applied to repaying the short-term notes payable balance.

h. Dividends of $100,000 are to be declared and paid in May.

i. No cash payments for income taxes are to be made during the second calendar quarter. Income taxes will be assessed at 35% in the quarter.

j. Equipment purchases of $55,000 are scheduled for June.

Required

Prepare the following budgets and other financial information as required:

1. Sales budget, including budgeted sales for July.
2. Purchases budget.
3. Selling expense budget.
4. General and administrative expense budget.
5. Expected cash receipts from customers and the expected June 30 balance of accounts receivable.
6. Expected cash payments for purchases and the expected June 30 balance of accounts payable.
7. Cash budget.
8. Budgeted income statement, budgeted statement of retained earnings, and budgeted balance sheet.

PLANNING THE SOLUTION

- The sales budget shows expected sales for each month in the quarter. Start by multiplying March sales by 105% and then do the same for the remaining months. July's sales are needed for the purchases budget. To complete the budget, multiply the expected unit sales by the selling price of $25 per unit.

- Use these results and the 80% inventory policy to budget the size of ending inventory for April, May, and June. Add the budgeted sales to these numbers and subtract the actual or expected beginning inventory for each month. The result is the number of units to be purchased each month. Multiply these numbers by the per unit cost of $15. Find the budgeted cost of goods sold by multiplying the unit sales in each month by the $15 cost per unit. Compute the cost of the June 30 ending inventory by multiplying the expected units available at that date by the $15 cost per unit.

- The selling expense budget has only two items. Find the amount of the sales representatives' commissions by multiplying the expected dollar sales in each month by the 12.5% commission rate. Then include the sales manager's salary of $3,500 in April and $4,000 in May and June.

- The general and administrative expense budget should show three items. Administrative salaries are fixed at $8,000 per month, and depreciation is $5,000 per month. Budget the monthly interest expense on the long-term note by multiplying its $200,000 balance by the 0.9% monthly interest rate.

- Determine the amounts of cash sales in each month by multiplying the budgeted sales by 30%. Add to this amount the credit sales of the prior month (computed as 70% of prior month's sales). April's cash receipts from collecting receivables equals the March 31 balance of $175,000. The expected June 30 accounts receivable balance equals 70% of June's total budgeted sales.

- Determine expected cash payments on accounts payable for each month by making them equal to the merchandise purchases in the prior month. The payments for April equal the March 31 balance of accounts payable shown on the beginning balance sheet. The June 30 balance of accounts payable equals merchandise purchases for June.

- Prepare the cash budget by combining the given information and the amounts of cash receipts and cash payments on account that you computed. Complete the cash budget for each month by either borrowing enough to raise the preliminary balance to the minimum or paying off short-term debt as much as the balance allows without falling below the minimum. Show the ending balance of the short-term note in the budget.

- Prepare the budgeted income statement by combining the budgeted items for all three months. Determine the income before income taxes and multiply it by the 35% rate to find the quarter's income tax expense.

- The budgeted statement of retained earnings should show the March 31 balance plus the quarter's net income minus the quarter's dividends.

- The budgeted balance sheet includes updated balances for all items that appear in the beginning balance sheet and an additional liability for unpaid income taxes. Amounts for all asset, liability, and equity accounts can be found either in the budgets, in other calculations, or by adding amounts found there to the beginning balances.

SOLUTION

1.

	A	B	C	D	E
1	**Calculation of Unit Sales**	**April**	**May**	**June**	**July**
2	Prior period's unit sales	10,000	10,500	11,025	11,576
3	Plus 5% growth*	500	525	551	579
4	Projected unit sales	10,500	11,025	11,576	12,155

*Rounded to nearest whole unit.

	A	B	C	D	E
1	**Sales Budget**	**April**	**May**	**June**	**Quarter**
2	Projected unit sales	10,500	11,025	11,576	
3	Selling price per unit	× $ 25	× $ 25	× $ 25	
4	Projected sales	$262,500	$275,625	$289,400	$827,525

2.

	A	B	C	D	E
1	**Purchases Budget**	**April**	**May**	**June**	**Quarter**
2	Next period's unit sales (part 1)	11,025	11,576	12,155	
3	Ending inventory percent	× 80%	× 80%	× 80%	
4	Desired ending inventory (units)	8,820	9,261	9,724	
5	Add: Current period's unit sales (part 1)	10,500	11,025	11,576	
6	Units to be available	19,320	20,286	21,300	
7	Less: Beginning inventory (units)	8,400	8,820	9,261	
8	Units to be purchased	10,920	11,466	12,039	
9	Budgeted cost per unit	× $ 15	× $ 15	× $ 15	
10	Budgeted purchases	$163,800	$171,990	$180,585	$516,375

3.

	A	B	C	D	E
1	**Selling Expense Budget**	**April**	**May**	**June**	**Quarter**
2	Budgeted sales (part 1)	$262,500	$275,625	$289,400	$827,525
3	Commission %	× 12.5%	× 12.5%	× 12.5%	× 12.5%
4	Sales commissions*	32,813	34,453	36,175	103,441
5	Manager's salary	3,500	4,000	4,000	11,500
6	Budgeted selling expenses*	$ 36,313	$ 38,453	$ 40,175	$114,941

*Rounded to the nearest dollar.

4.

	A	B	C	D	E
1	**General and Administrative Expense Budget**	**April**	**May**	**June**	**Quarter**
2	Administrative salaries	$ 8,000	$ 8,000	$ 8,000	$24,000
3	Depreciation	5,000	5,000	5,000	15,000
4	Interest on long-term note payable (0.9% × $200,000)	1,800	1,800	1,800	5,400
5	Budgeted expenses	$14,800	$14,800	$14,800	$44,400

5.

	A	B	C	D	E
1	**Schedule of Cash Receipts from Sales**	**April**	**May**	**June**	**Quarter**
2	Budgeted sales (part 1)	$262,500	$275,625	$289,400	
3	Ending accounts receivable (70% of sales)	$183,750	$192,938	$202,580	
4	Cash receipts				
5	Cash sales (30% of budgeted sales)	$ 78,750	$ 82,687	$ 86,820	$248,257
6	Collections of prior month's receivables	175,000*	183,750	192,938	551,688
7	Total cash to be collected	$253,750	$266,437	$ 279,758	$799,945

*March 31 Accounts Receivable balance (from balance sheet).

6.

	A	B	C	D	E
1	**Schedule of Cash Payments to Suppliers**	**April**	**May**	**June**	**Quarter**
2	Cash payments (equal to prior month's				
3	purchases)	$156,000*	$163,800	$171,990	$491,790
4	Expected June 30 balance of accounts				
5	payable (part 2, June purchases)			$180,585	

*March 31 Accounts Payable balance (from balance sheet).

7.

	A	B	C	D
1	**Cash Budget**	**April**	**May**	**June**
2	Beginning cash balance	$ 50,000	$ 89,517	$ 50,000
3	Add: Cash receipts (part 5)	253,750	266,437	279,758
4	Total cash available	303,750	355,954	329,758
5	Less: Cash payments for			
6	Merchandise (part 6)	156,000	163,800	171,990
7	Sales commissions (part 3)	32,813	34,453	36,175
8	Salaries			
9	Sales (part 3)	3,500	4,000	4,000
10	Administrative (part 4)	8,000	8,000	8,000
11	Interest on long-term note (part 4)	1,800	1,800	1,800
12	Dividends		100,000	
13	Equipment purchase			55,000
14	Interest on short-term notes			
15	April ($12,000 × 1%)	120		
16	June ($6,099 × 1%)			61
17	Total cash payments	202,233	312,053	277,026
18	Preliminary balance	101,517	43,901	52,732
19	Loan activity			
20	Additional loan		6,099	
21	Loan repayment	(12,000)		(2,732)
22	Ending cash balance	$ 89,517	$ 50,000	$ 50,000
23	Ending short-term notes payable balance	$ 0	$ 6,099	$ 3,367

8.

WILD WOOD COMPANY
Budgeted Income Statement
For Quarter Ended June 30, 2017

Sales (part 1)		$827,525
Cost of goods sold*		496,515
Gross profit		331,010
Operating expenses		
Sales commissions (part 3)	$103,441	
Sales salaries (part 3)	11,500	
Administrative salaries (part 4)	24,000	
Depreciation (part 4)	15,000	
Interest on long-term note (part 4)	5,400	
Interest on short-term note (part 7)	181	
Total operating expenses		159,522
Income before income taxes		171,488
Income taxes (35%)		60,021
Net income		$111,467

*33,101 units sold @ $15 per unit

WILD WOOD COMPANY
Budgeted Statement of Retained Earnings
For Quarter Ended June 30, 2017

Beginning retained earnings (Mar. 31 bal.)	$138,000
Net income	111,467
	249,467
Less: Cash dividends (part 7)	100,000
Ending retained earnings	$149,467

WILD WOOD COMPANY
Budgeted Balance Sheet
June 30, 2017

Assets

Cash (part 7)	$ 50,000	
Accounts receivable (part 5)	202,580	
Inventory (9,724 units @ $15 each)	145,860	
Total current assets		$398,440
Equipment (Mar. 31 bal. plus purchase)	535,000	
Less: Accumulated depreciation		
(Mar. 31 bal. plus depreciation expense)	105,000	430,000
Total assets		$828,440

Liabilities and Equity

Accounts payable (part 6)	$180,585	
Short-term notes payable (part 7)	3,367	
Income taxes payable	60,021	
Total current liabilities		$243,973
Long-term note payable (Mar. 31 bal.)		200,000
Total liabilities		443,973
Common stock (Mar. 31 bal.)	235,000	
Retained earnings	149,467	
Total stockholders' equity		384,467
Total liabilities and equity		$828,440

APPENDIX

Merchandise Purchases Budget

7A

P4

Prepare each component of a master budget—for a merchandising company.

Exhibit 7A.1 shows the master budget sequence for a merchandiser. Unlike a manufacturing company, a merchandiser must prepare a merchandise purchases budget rather than a production budget. In addition, a merchandiser does not prepare direct materials, direct labor, or factory overhead budgets. In this appendix we show the merchandise purchases budget for Hockey Den (HD), a retailer of hockey sticks.

EXHIBIT 7A.1

Master Budget
Sequence—Merchandiser

Preparing the Merchandise Purchases Budget   A merchandiser usually expresses a **merchandise purchases budget** in both units and dollars. Exhibit 7A.2 shows the general layout for this budget in equation form. If this formula is expressed in units and only one product is involved, we can compute the number of dollars of inventory to be purchased for the budget by multiplying the units to be purchased by the cost per unit.

EXHIBIT 7A.2

General Formula
for Merchandise
Purchases Budget

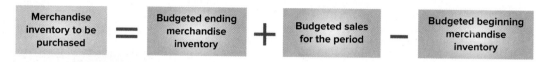

A merchandise purchases budget requires the following inputs:

1 Sales budget (in units).

2 Budgeted ending inventory (in units).

3 Cost per unit.

1 Toronto Sticks Company is an exclusive supplier of hockey sticks to HD, meaning that the companies use the same budgeted sales figures in preparing budgets. Thus, HD predicts unit sales as follows: October, 1,000; November, 800; December, 1,400; and January, 900.

2 After considering the costs of keeping inventory and inventory shortages, HD set a policy that ending inventory (in units) should equal 90% of next month's predicted sales. For example, inventory at the end of October should equal 90% of November's budgeted sales.

3 Finally, HD expects the per unit purchase cost of $60 to remain unchanged through the budgeting period. This information, along with knowledge of 1,010 units in inventory at September 30 (given), allows the company to prepare the merchandise purchases budget shown in Exhibit 7A.3.

EXHIBIT 7A.3

Merchandise
Purchases Budget

Units to Purchase

   Budgeted ending inventory
+ Budgeted sales
− Beginning inventory

= Units to be purchased

	A	B	C	D
1	**HOCKEY DEN**			
2	**Merchandise Purchases Budget**			
3	**October 2017–December 2017**			
4		**October**	**November**	**December**
5	Next month's budgeted sales (units)	800	1,400	900
6	Ratio of inventory to future sales	× 90%	× 90%	× 90%
7	Budgeted ending inventory (units)	720	1,260	810
8	**Add:** Budgeted sales (units)	1,000	800	1,400
9	Required units of available merchandise	1,720	2,060	2,210
10	**Deduct:** Beginning inventory (units)	1,010*	720	1,260
11	Total units to be purchased	710	1,340	950
12				
13	Budgeted cost per unit	$ 60	$ 60	$ 60
14	Budgeted cost of merchandise purchases	$42,600	$80,400	$57,000

*Does not comply with company policy.

The first three lines of HD's merchandise purchases budget determine the required ending inventories (in units). Budgeted unit sales are then added to the desired ending inventory to give the required units of available merchandise. We then subtract beginning inventory to determine the budgeted number of units to be purchased. The last line is the budgeted cost of the purchases, computed by multiplying the number of units to be purchased by the predicted cost per unit.

Other Master Budget Differences—Merchandiser vs. Manufacturer   In addition to preparing a purchases budget instead of production, direct materials, direct labor, and overhead budgets, other key differences in master budgets for merchandisers include:

● Depreciation expense is included in the general and administrative expense budget of the merchandiser. For the manufacturer, depreciation on manufacturing assets is included in the factory overhead budget and treated as a product cost.

● The budgeted balance sheet for the merchandiser will report only one asset for inventory. The balance sheet for the manufacturer will typically report three inventory assets: raw materials, work in process, and finished goods.

See Need-To-Know 7-7 for illustration of a complete master budget, including budgeted financial statements, for a merchandising company.

In preparing monthly budgets for the third quarter, a company budgeted sales of 120 units for July and 140 units for August. Management wants each month's ending inventory to be 60% of next month's sales. The June 30 inventory consists of 72 units. How many units should be purchased in July?

NEED-TO-KNOW 7-8

Merchandise Purchases Budget

P4

Solution

Merchandise Purchases Budget	July
Next month's budgeted sales (units)...............	140
Ratio of inventory to future sales..................	× 60%
Budgeted ending inventory (units)	84
Add: Budgeted sales (units)......................	+120
Required units of available merchandise	204
Deduct: Beginning inventory (units)...............	− 72
Units to be purchased	132

Do More: QS 7-28, QS 7-29, QS 7-30, E 7-24

Summary

C1 Describe the benefits of budgeting. Planning is a management responsibility of critical importance to business success. Budgeting is the process management uses to formalize its plans. Budgeting promotes management analysis and focuses its attention on the future. Budgeting also provides a basis for evaluating performance, serves as a source of motivation, is a means of coordinating activities, and communicates management's plans and instructions to employees.

C2 Describe a master budget and the process of preparing it. A master budget is a formal overall plan for a company. It consists of plans for business operations and capital expenditures, plus the financial results of those activities. The budgeting process begins with a sales budget. Based on expected sales volume, companies can budget production and manufacturing costs, selling expenses, and administrative expenses. Next, the capital expenditures budget is prepared, followed by the cash budget and budgeted financial statements.

A1 Analyze expense planning using activity-based budgeting. Activity-based budgeting requires management to identify activities performed by departments, plan necessary activity levels, identify resources required to perform these activities, and budget the resources.

P1 Prepare each component of a master budget—for a manufacturing company. A *master budget* is a collection of component budgets. From budgeted sales a manufacturer

prepares a *production budget.* A *manufacturing budget* shows the budgeted production costs for direct materials, direct labor, and overhead. *Selling* and *general and administrative expense* budgets complete the operating budgets of the master budget. The *capital expenditures budget* reflects expected and asset purchases and disposals. The *cash budget* shows the impact of budgeted activities on cash.

P2 Prepare a cash budget. The cash budget shows expected cash inflows and outflows during a budgeting period. This budget helps management maintain the company's desired cash balance.

P3 Prepare budgeted financial statements. The operating budgets, capital expenditures budget, and cash budget contain much of the information to prepare a budgeted income statement for the budget period and a budgeted balance sheet at the end of the budget period. Budgeted financial statements show the expected financial consequences of the planned activities described in the budgets.

P4A Prepare each component of a master budget—for a merchandising company. Merchandisers budget merchandise purchases instead of manufacturing costs. Merchandisers also prepare capital expenditure, selling expense, general and administrative expense, and cash budgets.

Key Terms

Activity-based budgeting (ABB)
Budget
Budgetary control
Budgeted balance sheet

Budgeted income statement
Budgeting
Capital expenditures budget
Cash budget

Continuous budgeting
Direct labor budget
Direct materials budget
Factory overhead budget

General and administrative expense budget	Production budget	Sales budget
Master budget	Rolling budget	Selling expense budget
Merchandise purchases budget	Safety stock	Zero-based budgeting

Multiple Choice Quiz

1. A plan that reports the units of merchandise to be produced by a manufacturing company during the budget period is called a
   a. Capital expenditures budget.
   b. Cash budget.
   c. Production budget.
   d. Manufacturing budget.
   e. Sales budget.

2.ᴬ A hardware store has budgeted sales of $36,000 for its power tool department in July. Management wants to have $7,000 in power tool inventory at the end of July. Its beginning inventory of power tools is expected to be $6,000. What is the budgeted dollar amount of merchandise purchases?
   a. $36,000
   c. $42,000
   e. $37,000
   b. $43,000
   d. $35,000

3. A store has the following budgeted sales for the next five months.

May	$210,000
June	186,000
July	180,000
August	220,000
September	240,000

Cash sales are 25% of total sales and all credit sales are expected to be collected in the month following the sale. The total amount of cash expected to be received from customers in September is
   a. $240,000.
   c. $60,000.
   e. $220,000.
   b. $225,000.
   d. $165,000.

4. A plan that shows the expected cash inflows and cash outflows during the budget period, including receipts from loans needed to maintain a minimum cash balance and repayments of such loans, is called
   a. A rolling budget.
   d. A cash budget.
   b. An income statement.
   e. An operating budget.
   c. A balance sheet.

5. The following sales are predicted for a company's next four months.

	April	May	June	July
Unit sales	480	560	600	480

Each month's ending inventory of finished goods should be 30% of the next month's sales. At April 1, the finished goods inventory is 140 units. The budgeted production of units for May is
   a. 572 units.
   c. 548 units.
   e. 180 units.
   b. 560 units.
   d. 600 units.

ANSWERS TO MULTIPLE CHOICE QUIZ

1. c
2. e; Budgeted purchases = $36,000 + $7,000 − $6,000 = $37,000
3. b; Cash collected = 25% of September sales + 75% of August sales = (0.25 × $240,000) + (0.75 × $220,000) = $225,000

4. d
5. a; 560 units + (0.30 × 600 units) − (0.30 × 560 units) = 572 units

---

ᴬ Superscript letter A denotes assignments based on Appendix 7A, which relates to budgets for merchandising companies.

🔲 Icon denotes assignments that involve decision making.

Discussion Questions

1. 🔲 Identify at least three benefits of budgeting in helping managers plan and control a business.
2. How does a budget benefit management in its control function?
3. 🔲 What is the benefit of continuous budgeting?
4. Identify three usual time horizons for short-term planning and budgets.

5. 🔲 Why should each department participate in preparing its own budget?
6. 🔲 How does budgeting help management coordinate and plan business activities?
7. 🔲 Why is the sales budget so important to the budgeting process?
8. What is a selling expense budget? What is a capital expenditures budget?

9. Identify at least two potential negative outcomes of budgeting.

10. Google prepares a cash budget. What is a cash budget? Why must operating budgets and the capital expenditures budget be prepared before the cash budget?   **GOOGLE**

11. Apple regularly uses budgets. What is the difference between a production budget and a manufacturing budget?   **APPLE**

12. 🔼 Would a manager of an **Apple** retail store participate more in budgeting than a manager at the corporate offices? Explain.   **APPLE**

13. 🔼 Does the manager of a **Samsung** distribution center participate in long-term budgeting? Explain.   **Samsung**

14. 🔼 Assume that **Samsung**'s consumer electronics division is charged with preparing a master budget. Identify the participants—for example, the sales manager for the sales budget—and describe the information each person provides in preparing the master budget.   **Samsung**

15. 🔼 **Coca-Cola** recently redesigned its bottle to reduce its use of glass, thus lowering its bottle's weight and CO_2 emissions. Which budgets in the company's master budget will this redesign impact?

■ connect

For each of the following items 1 through 5, indicate *yes* if the item is an important budgeting guideline or *no* if it is not.

_____ **1.** Employees should have the opportunity to explain differences from budgeted amounts.

_____ **2.** Budgets should include budgetary slack.

_____ **3.** Employees impacted by a budget should be consulted when it is prepared.

_____ **4.** Goals in a budget should be set low so targets can be reached.

_____ **5.** Budgetary goals should be attainable.

QUICK STUDY

QS 7-1
Budget motivation
C1

For each of the following items 1 through 6, indicate *yes* if it describes a potential benefit of budgeting or *no* if it describes a potential negative outcome of budgeting.

_____ **1.** Budgets help coordinate activities across departments.

_____ **2.** Budgets are useful in assigning blame for unexpected results.

_____ **3.** A budget forces managers to spend time planning for the future.

_____ **4.** Some employees might overstate expenses in budgets.

_____ **5.** Budgets can lead to excessive pressure to meet budgeted results.

_____ **6.** Budgets can provide incentives for good performance.

QS 7-2
Budgeting benefits
C1 🔼

Identify which of the following sets of items are necessary components of the master budget.

_____ **1.** Operating budgets, historical income statement, and budgeted balance sheet.

_____ **2.** Prior sales reports, capital expenditures budget, and financial budgets.

_____ **3.** Sales budget, operating budgets, and historical financial budgets.

_____ **4.** Operating budgets, financial budgets, and capital expenditures budget.

QS 7-3
Components of a master budget
C2

Grace manufactures and sells miniature digital cameras for $250 each. 1,000 units were sold in May, and management forecasts 4% growth in unit sales each month. Determine (a) the number of units of camera sales and (b) the dollar amount of camera sales for the month of June.

QS 7-4
Sales budget P1

Zilly Co. predicts sales of $400,000 for June. Zilly pays a sales manager a monthly salary of $6,000 and a commission of 8% of that month's sales dollars. Prepare a selling expense budget for the month of June.

QS 7-5
Selling expense budget P1

Liza's predicts sales of $40,000 for May and $52,000 for June. Assume 60% of Liza's sales are for cash. The remaining 40% are credit sales; credit customers pay in the month following the sale. Compute the budgeted cash receipts for June.

QS 7-6
Cash budget P2

QS 7-7
Manufacturing: Direct
materials budget   P1

Zortek Corp. budgets production of 400 units in January and 200 units in February. Each finished unit requires five pounds of raw material Z, which costs $2 per pound. Each month's ending inventory of raw materials should be 40% of the following month's budgeted production. The January 1 raw materials inventory has 130 pounds of Z. Prepare a direct materials budget for January.

QS 7-8
Manufacturing: Direct
labor budget   P1

Tora Co. plans to produce 1,020 units in July. Each unit requires two hours of direct labor. The direct labor rate is $20 per hour. Prepare a direct labor budget for July.

QS 7-9
Sales budget

P1

Scora, Inc., is preparing its master budget for the quarter ending March 31. It sells a single product for $50 per unit. Budgeted sales for the next three months follow. Prepare a sales budget for the months of January, February, and March.

	January	February	March
Sales in units	1,200	2,000	1,600

QS 7-10
Cash receipts budget   P2

X-Tel budgets sales of $60,000 for April, $100,000 for May, and $80,000 for June. In addition, sales are 40% cash and 60% on credit. All credit sales are collected in the month following the sale. The April 1 balance in accounts receivable is $15,000. Prepare a schedule of budgeted cash receipts for April, May, and June.

QS 7-11
Selling expense budget

P1

X-Tel budgets sales of $60,000 for April, $100,000 for May, and $80,000 for June. In addition, sales commissions are 10% of sales dollars and the company pays a sales manager a salary of $6,000 per month. Sales commissions and salaries are paid in the month incurred. Prepare a selling expense budget for April, May, and June.

QS 7-12
Manufacturing:
Production budget

P1

Champ, Inc., predicts the following sales in units for the coming two months:

	May	June
Sales in units	180	200

Each month's ending inventory of finished units should be 60% of the next month's sales. The April 30 finished goods inventory is 108 units. Compute budgeted production (in units) for May.

QS 7-13
Manufacturing: Direct
materials budget

P1

Miami Solar manufactures solar panels for industrial use. The company budgets production of 5,000 units (solar panels) in July and 5,300 units in August. Each unit requires 3 pounds of direct materials, which cost $6 per pound. The company's policy is to maintain direct materials inventory equal to 30% of the next month's direct materials requirement. As of June 30, the company has 4,500 pounds of direct materials in inventory, which complies with the policy. Prepare a direct materials budget for July.

QS 7-14
Manufacturing: Direct
labor budget   P1

Miami Solar budgets production of 5,000 solar panels in July. Each unit requires 4 hours of direct labor at a rate of $16 per hour. Prepare a direct labor budget for July.

QS 7-15
Manufacturing: Factory
overhead budget   P1

Miami Solar budgets production of 5,300 solar panels for August. Each unit requires 4 hours of direct labor at a rate of $16 per hour. Variable factory overhead is budgeted to be 70% of direct labor cost, and fixed factory overhead is $180,000 per month. Prepare a factory overhead budget for August.

QS 7-16
Manufacturing:
Production budget

P1

Atlantic Surf manufactures surfboards. The company's sales budget for the next three months is shown below. In addition, company policy is to maintain finished goods inventory equal (in units) to 40% of the next month's unit sales. As of June 30, the company has 1,600 finished surfboards in inventory, which complies with the policy. Prepare a production budget for the months of July and August.

	July	August	September
Sales (in units).........	4,000	6,500	3,500

Forrest Company manufactures phone chargers and has a JIT policy that ending inventory must equal 10% of the next month's sales. It estimates that October's actual ending inventory will consist of 40,000 units. November and December sales are estimated to be 400,000 and 350,000 units, respectively. Compute the number of units to be produced for the month of November.

QS 7-17
Manufacturing:
Production budget
P1

Hockey Pro budgets production of 3,900 hockey pucks during May. The company assigns variable overhead at the rate of $1.50 per unit. Fixed overhead equals $46,000 per month. Prepare a factory overhead budget for May.

QS 7-18
Manufacturing: Factory overhead budget   P1

Music World reports the following sales forecast: August, $150,000; and September, $170,000. Cash sales are normally 40% of total sales and all credit sales are expected to be collected in the month following the date of sale. Prepare a schedule of cash receipts for September.

QS 7-19
Cash receipts   P2

The Guitar Shoppe reports the following sales forecast: August, $150,000; September, $170,000. Cash sales are normally 40% of total sales, 55% of credit sales are collected in the month following sale, and the remaining 5% of credit sales are written off as uncollectible. Prepare a schedule of cash receipts for September.

QS 7-20
Cash receipts, with uncollectible accounts
P2

Wells Company reports the following sales forecast: September, $55,000; October, $66,000; and November, $80,000. All sales are on account. Collections of credit sales are received as follows: 25% in the month of sale, 60% in the first month after sale, and 10% in the second month after sale. 5% of all credit sales are written off as uncollectible. Prepare a schedule of cash receipts for November.

QS 7-21
Cash receipts, with uncollectible accounts   P2

Kingston anticipates total sales for June and July of $420,000 and $398,000, respectively. Cash sales are normally 60% of total sales. Of the credit sales, 20% are collected in the same month as the sale, 70% are collected during the first month after the sale, and the remaining 10% are collected in the second month after the sale. Determine the amount of accounts receivable reported on the company's budgeted balance sheet as of July 31.

QS 7-22
Computing budgeted accounts receivable
P2

Santos Co. is preparing a cash budget for February. The company has $20,000 cash at the beginning of February and anticipates $75,000 in cash receipts and $100,250 in cash payments during February. What amount, if any, must the company borrow during February to maintain a $5,000 cash balance? The company has no loans outstanding on February 1.

QS 7-23
Budgeted loan activity
P2

Use the following information to prepare a cash budget for the month ended on March 31 for Gado Company. The budget should show expected cash receipts and cash payments for the month of March and the balance expected on March 31.

a. Beginning cash balance on March 1, $72,000.
b. Cash receipts from sales, $300,000.
c. Budgeted cash payments for direct materials, $140,000.
d. Budgeted cash payments for direct labor, $80,000.
e. Other budgeted cash expenses, $45,000.
f. Cash repayment of bank loan, $20,000.

QS 7-24
Manufacturing:
Cash budget
P2

Following are selected accounts for a company. For each account, indicate whether it will appear on a budgeted income statement (BIS) or a budgeted balance sheet (BBS). If an item will not appear on either budgeted financial statement, label it NA.

QS 7-25
Budgeted financial statements
P3

Sales	_____	Interest expense on loan payable	_____
Office salaries expense	_____	Cash dividends paid	_____
Accumulated depreciation	_____	Bank loan owed	_____
Amortization expense	_____	Cost of goods sold	_____

QS 7-26ᴬ
Merchandising:
Cash payments for
merchandise P4

Garda purchased $600,000 of merchandise in August and expects to purchase $720,000 in September. Merchandise purchases are paid as follows: 25% in the month of purchase and 75% in the following month. Compute cash payments for merchandise for September.

QS 7-27ᴬ
Merchandising:
Cash payments for
merchandise P4

Torres Co. forecasts merchandise purchases of $15,800 in January, $18,600 in February, and $20,200 in March; 40% of purchases are paid in the month of purchase and 60% are paid in the following month. At December 31 of the prior year, the balance of accounts payable (for December purchases) is $22,000. Prepare a schedule of cash payments for merchandise for each of the months of January, February, and March.

QS 7-28ᴬ
Merchandising:
Computing purchases P4

Raider-X Company forecasts sales of 18,000 units for April. Beginning inventory is 3,000 units. The desired ending inventory is 30% higher than the beginning inventory. How many units should Raider-X purchase in April?

QS 7-29ᴬ
Merchandising:
Computing purchases P4

Lexi Company forecasts unit sales of 1,040,000 in April, 1,220,000 in May, 980,000 in June, and 1,020,000 in July. Beginning inventory on April 1 is 280,000 units, and the company wants to have 30% of next month's sales in inventory at the end of each month. Prepare a merchandise purchases budget for the months of April, May, and June.

QS 7-30ᴬ
Merchandising:
Purchases budget P4

Montel Company's July sales budget calls for sales of $600,000. The store expects to begin July with $50,000 of inventory and to end the month with $40,000 of inventory. Gross margin is typically 40% of sales. Determine the budgeted cost of merchandise purchases for July.

QS 7-31
Activity-based budgeting

A1

Activity-based budgeting is a budget system based on *expected activities*. (1) Describe activity-based budgeting, and explain its preparation of budgets. (2) How does activity-based budgeting differ from traditional budgeting?

QS 7-32
Operating budgets

P1

Royal Philips Electronics of the Netherlands reports sales of €24,244 million for a recent year. Assume that the company expects sales growth of 3% for the next year. Also assume that selling expenses are typically 20% of sales, while general and administrative expenses are 4% of sales.

1. Compute budgeted sales for the next year.

2. Assume budgeted sales for next year is €25,000 million, and then compute budgeted selling expenses and budgeted general and administrative expenses for the next year.

QS 7-33
Sustainability and selling
expense budget

P1

MM Co. predicts sales of $30,000 for May. MM Co. pays a sales manager a monthly salary of $3,000 plus a commission of 6% of sales dollars. MM's production manager recently found a way to reduce the amount of packaging MM uses. As a result, MM's product will receive better placement on store shelves and thus May sales are predicted to increase by 8%. In addition, MM's shipping costs are predicted to decrease from 4% of sales to 3% of sales. Compute budgeted sales and budgeted selling expenses for May assuming MM switches to this more sustainable packaging.

---

connect

EXERCISES

Exercise 7-1
Budget consequences

C1

Participatory budgeting can sometimes lead to negative consequences. From the following list of outcomes that can arise from participatory budgeting, identify those with potentially *negative* consequences.

_____ **a.** Budgetary slack will not be available to meet budgeted results.

_____ **b.** Employees might understate expense budgets.

_____ **c.** Employees might commit unethical or fraudulent acts to meet budgeted results.

_____ **d.** Employees set sales targets too high.

_____ **e.** Employees always spend budgeted amounts, even if on unnecessary items.

_____ **f.** Employees might understate sales budgets and overstate expense budgets.

Match the definitions 1 through 9 with the term or phrase *a* through *i*.

a. Budget
d. Safety stock
g. Sales budget

b. Cash budget
e. Budgeted income statement
h. Master budget

c. Merchandise purchases budget
f. General and administrative expense budget
i. Budgeted balance sheet

_____ **1.** A comprehensive business plan that includes specific plans for expected sales, the units of product to be produced, the merchandise or materials to be purchased, the expenses to be incurred, the long-term assets to be purchased, and the amounts of cash to be borrowed or loans to be repaid, as well as a budgeted income statement and balance sheet.

_____ **2.** A quantity of inventory or materials over the minimum to reduce the risk of running short.

_____ **3.** A plan showing the units of goods to be sold and the sales to be derived; the usual starting point in the budgeting process.

_____ **4.** An accounting report that presents predicted amounts of the company's revenues and expenses for the budgeting period.

_____ **5.** An accounting report that presents predicted amounts of the company's assets, liabilities, and equity balances at the end of the budget period.

_____ **6.** A plan that shows the units or costs of merchandise to be purchased by a merchandising company during the budget period.

_____ **7.** A formal statement of a company's future plans, usually expressed in monetary terms.

_____ **8.** A plan that shows predicted operating expenses not included in the selling expenses budget.

_____ **9.** A plan that shows the expected cash inflows and cash outflows during the budget period, including receipts from any loans needed to maintain a minimum cash balance and repayments of such loans.

Exercise 7-2
Master budget definitions
C2

Ruiz Co. provides the following sales forecast for the next four months:

	April	May	June	July
Sales (units)..........	500	580	540	620

The company wants to end each month with ending finished goods inventory equal to 25% of next month's forecasted sales. Finished goods inventory on April 1 is 190 units. Assume July's budgeted production is 540 units. Prepare a production budget for the months of April, May, and June.

Exercise 7-3
Manufacturing:
Production budget
P1

Refer to the information in Exercise 7-3. In addition, each finished unit requires five pounds of raw materials and the company wants to end each month with raw materials inventory equal to 30% of next month's production needs. Beginning raw materials inventory for April was 663 pounds. Assume direct materials cost $4 per pound. Prepare a direct materials budget for April, May, and June.

Exercise 7-4
Manufacturing: Direct
materials budget P1

The production budget for Manner Company shows units to be produced as follows: July, 620; August, 680; and September, 540. Each unit produced requires two hours of direct labor. The direct labor rate is currently $20 per hour but is predicted to be $21 per hour in September. Prepare a direct labor budget for the months July, August, and September.

Exercise 7-5
Manufacturing: Direct
labor budget P1

Rida, Inc., a manufacturer in a seasonal industry, is preparing its direct materials budget for the second quarter. It plans production of 240,000 units in the second quarter and 52,500 units in the third quarter. Raw material inventory is 43,200 pounds at the beginning of the second quarter. Other information follows. Prepare a direct materials budget for the second quarter.

Exercise 7-6
Manufacturing: Direct
materials budget
P1

Direct materials	Each unit requires 0.60 pounds of a key raw material, priced at $175 per pound. The company plans to end each quarter with an ending inventory of materials equal to 30% of next quarter's budgeted materials requirements.

Exercise 7-7
Manufacturing: Direct labor and factory overhead budgets P1

Addison Co. budgets production of 2,400 units during the second quarter. In addition, information on its direct labor and its variable and fixed overhead is shown below. For the second quarter, prepare (1) a direct labor budget and (2) a factory overhead budget.

Direct labor.................	Each finished unit requires 4 direct labor hours, at a cost of $20 per hour.
Variable overhead	Applied at the rate of $11 per direct labor hour.
Fixed overhead.............	Budgeted at $450,000 per quarter.

Exercise 7-8
Manufacturing: Direct materials budget
P1

Ramos Co. provides the following sales forecast and production budget for the next four months:

	April	May	June	July
Sales (units).........................	500	580	530	600
Budgeted production (units)	442	570	544	540

The company plans for finished goods inventory of 120 units at the end of June. In addition, each finished unit requires 5 pounds of direct materials and the company wants to end each month with direct materials inventory equal to 30% of next month's production needs. Beginning direct materials inventory for April was 663 pounds. Direct materials cost $2 per pound. Each finished unit requires 0.50 hours of direct labor at the rate of $16 per hour. The company budgets variable overhead at the rate of $20 per direct labor hour and budgets fixed overhead of $8,000 per month. Prepare a direct materials budget for April, May, and June.

Exercise 7-9
Manufacturing: Direct labor and factory overhead budgets P1

Refer to Exercise 7-8. Prepare (1) a direct labor budget and (2) a factory overhead budget for April, May, and June.

Exercise 7-10
Manufacturing:
Production budget   P1

Blue Wave Co. predicts the following unit sales for the coming four months: September, 4,000 units; October, 5,000 units; November, 7,000 units; and December, 7,600 units. The company's policy is to maintain finished goods inventory equal to 60% of the next month's sales. At the end of August, the company had 2,400 finished units on hand. Prepare a production budget for each of the months of September, October, and November.

Exercise 7-11
Manufacturing:
Production budget
P1

Tyler Co. predicts the following unit sales for the next four months: April, 3,000 units; May, 4,000 units; June, 6,000 units; and July, 2,000 units. The company's policy is to maintain finished goods inventory equal to 30% of the next month's sales. At the end of March, the company had 900 finished units on hand. Prepare a production budget for each of the months of April, May, and June.

Exercise 7-12
Manufacturing: Preparing production budgets (for two periods) P1

Check   Second-quarter production, 465,000 units

Electro Company manufactures an innovative automobile transmission for electric cars. Management predicts that ending finished goods inventory for the first quarter will be 90,000 units. The following unit sales of the transmissions are expected during the rest of the year: second quarter, 450,000 units; third quarter, 525,000 units; and fourth quarter, 475,000 units. Company policy calls for the ending finished goods inventory of a quarter to equal 20% of the next quarter's budgeted sales. Prepare a production budget for both the second and third quarters that shows the number of transmissions to manufacture.

Exercise 7-13
Manufacturing: Direct materials budget P1

Electro Company budgets production of 450,000 transmissions in the second quarter and 520,000 transmissions in the third quarter. Each transmission requires 0.80 pounds of a key raw material. The company aims to end each quarter with an ending inventory of direct materials equal to 20% of next quarter's budgeted materials requirements. Beginning inventory of this raw material is 72,000 pounds. Direct materials cost $1.70 per pound. Prepare a direct materials budget for the second quarter.

Exercise 7-14
Manufacturing: Direct labor budget P1

Branson Belts makes handcrafted belts. The company budgets production of 4,500 belts during the second quarter. Each belt requires 4 direct labor hours, at a cost of $17 per hour. Prepare a direct labor budget for the second quarter.

MCO Leather Goods manufactures leather purses. Each purse requires 2 pounds of direct materials at a cost of $4 per pound and 0.8 direct labor hours at a rate of $16 per hour. Variable manufacturing overhead is charged at a rate of $2 per direct labor hour. Fixed manufacturing overhead is $10,000 per month. The company's policy is to end each month with direct materials inventory equal to 40% of the next month's materials requirement. At the end of August the company had 3,680 pounds of direct materials in inventory. The company's production budget reports the following. Prepare budgets for September and October for (1) direct materials, (2) direct labor, and (3) factory overhead.

Production Budget	September	October	November
Units to be produced	4,600	6,200	5,800

Ornamental Sculptures Mfg. manufactures garden sculptures. Each sculpture requires 8 pounds of direct materials at a cost of $3 per pound and 0.5 direct labor hours at a rate of $18 per hour. Variable manufacturing overhead is charged at a rate of $3 per direct labor hour. Fixed manufacturing overhead is $4,000 per month. The company's policy is to maintain direct materials inventory equal to 20% of the next month's materials requirement. At the end of March the company had 5,280 pounds of direct materials in inventory. The company's production budget reports the following. Prepare budgets for March and April for (1) direct materials, (2) direct labor, and (3) factory overhead.

Production Budget	March	April	May
Units to be produced	3,300	4,600	4,800

Kayak Co. budgeted the following cash receipts (excluding cash receipts from loans received) and cash payments (excluding cash payments for loan principal and interest payments) for the first three months of next year.

	Cash Receipts	Cash Payments
January	$525,000	$475,000
February	400,000	350,000
March	450,000	525,000

According to a credit agreement with the company's bank, Kayak promises to have a minimum cash balance of $30,000 at each month-end. In return, the bank has agreed that the company can borrow up to $150,000 at a monthly interest rate of 1%, paid on the last day of each month. The interest is computed based on the beginning balance of the loan for the month. The company repays loan principal with any cash in excess of $30,000 on the last day of each month. The company has a cash balance of $30,000 and a loan balance of $60,000 at January 1. Prepare monthly cash budgets for January, February, and March.

Jasper Company has sales on account and for cash. Specifically, 70% of its sales are on account and 30% are for cash. Credit sales are collected in full in the month following the sale. The company forecasts sales of $525,000 for April, $535,000 for May, and $560,000 for June. The beginning balance of accounts receivable is $400,000 on April 1. Prepare a schedule of budgeted cash receipts for April, May, and June.

Zisk Co. purchases raw materials on account. Budgeted purchase amounts are: April, $80,000; May, $110,000; and June, $120,000. Payments are made as follows: 70% in the month of purchase and 30% in the month after purchase. The March 31 balance of accounts payable is $22,000. Prepare a schedule of budgeted cash payments for April, May, and June.

Karim Corp. requires a minimum $8,000 cash balance. If necessary, loans are taken to meet this requirement at a cost of 1% interest per month (paid monthly). Any excess cash is used to repay loans at month-end. The cash balance on July 1 is $8,400, and the company has no outstanding loans. Forecasted cash receipts (other than for loans received) and forecasted cash payments (other than for loan or interest payments) follow. Prepare a cash budget for July, August, and September. (Round interest payments to the nearest whole dollar.)

	July	August	September
Cash receipts	$20,000	$26,000	$40,000
Cash payments.	28,000	30,000	22,000

Exercise 7-21

Cash budget

P2

Foyert Corp. requires a minimum $30,000 cash balance. If necessary, loans are taken to meet this requirement at a cost of 1% interest per month (paid monthly). Any excess cash is used to repay loans at month-end. The cash balance on October 1 is $30,000, and the company has an outstanding loan of $10,000. Forecasted cash receipts (other than for loans received) and forecasted cash payments (other than for loan or interest payments) follow. Prepare a cash budget for October, November, and December. (Round interest payments to the nearest whole dollar.)

	October	November	December
Cash receipts	$110,000	$80,000	$100,000
Cash payments..............	120,000	75,000	80,000

Exercise 7-22

Manufacturing: Cash budget

P2

Use the following information to prepare the September cash budget for PTO Manufacturing Co. The following information relates to expected cash receipts and cash payments for the month ended September 30.

a. Beginning cash balance, September 1, $40,000.

b. Budgeted cash receipts from sales in September, $255,000.

c. Raw materials are purchased on account. Purchase amounts are: August (actual), $80,000; and September (budgeted), $110,000. Payments for direct materials are made as follows: 65% in the month of purchase and 35% in the month following purchase.

d. Budgeted cash payments for direct labor in September, $40,000.

e. Budgeted depreciation expense for September, $4,000.

f. Other cash expenses budgeted for September, $60,000.

g. Accrued income taxes payable in September, $10,000.

h. Bank loan interest payable in September, $1,000.

Exercise 7-23

Manufacturing: Cash budget

P2

Mike's Motors Corp. manufactures motors for dirt bikes. The company requires a minimum $30,000 cash balance at each month-end. If necessary, the company borrows to meet this requirement, at a cost of 2% interest per month (paid at the end of each month). Any cash balance above $30,000 at month-end is used to repay loans. The cash balance on July 1 is $34,000, and the company has no outstanding loans at that time. Forecasted cash receipts and forecasted cash payments (other than for loan activity) are as follows. Prepare a cash budget for July, August, and September.

	Cash Receipts	Cash Payments
July	$ 85,000	$113,000
August.....................	111,000	99,900
September	150,000	127,400

Exercise 7-24ᴬ

Merchandising:
Preparation of purchases budgets (for three periods)

P4

Walker Company prepares monthly budgets. The current budget plans for a September ending merchandise inventory of 30,000 units. Company policy is to end each month with merchandise inventory equal to 15% of budgeted sales for the following month. Budgeted sales and merchandise purchases for the next three months follow. The company budgets sales of 200,000 units in October.

Prepare the merchandise purchases budgets for the months of July, August, and September.

	Sales (Units)	Purchases (Units)
July	180,000	200,250
August.............	315,000	308,250
September	270,000	259,500

Exercise 7-25ᴬ

Merchandising:
Preparing a cash budget

P4

Use the following information to prepare the July cash budget for Acco Co. It should show expected cash receipts and cash payments for the month and the cash balance expected on July 31.

a. Beginning cash balance on July 1: $50,000.

b. Cash receipts from sales: 30% is collected in the month of sale, 50% in the next month, and 20% in the second month after sale (uncollectible accounts are negligible and can be ignored). Sales amounts are: May (actual), $1,720,000; June (actual), $1,200,000; and July (budgeted), $1,400,000.

c. Payments on merchandise purchases: 60% in the month of purchase and 40% in the month following purchase. Purchases amounts are: June (actual), $700,000; and July (budgeted), $750,000.

d. Budgeted cash payments for salaries in July: $275,000.

e. Budgeted depreciation expense for July: $36,000.

f. Other cash expenses budgeted for July: $200,000.

g. Accrued income taxes due in July: $80,000.

h. Bank loan interest paid in July: $6,600.

Check Ending cash balance, $122,400

Use the information in Exercise 7-25 and the following additional information to prepare a budgeted income statement for the month of July and a budgeted balance sheet for July 31.

a. Cost of goods sold is 55% of sales.

b. Inventory at the end of June is $80,000 and at the end of July is $60,000.

c. Salaries payable on June 30 are $50,000 and are expected to be $60,000 on July 31.

d. The equipment account balance is $1,600,000 on July 31. On June 30, the accumulated depreciation on equipment is $280,000.

e. The $6,600 cash payment of interest represents the 1% monthly expense on a bank loan of $660,000.

f. Income taxes payable on July 31 are $30,720, and the income tax rate is 30%.

g. The only other balance sheet accounts are: Common Stock, with a balance of $600,000 on June 30; and Retained Earnings, with a balance of $964,000 on June 30.

Exercise 7-26ᴬ
Merchandising: Preparing a budgeted income statement and balance sheet
P4

Check Net income, $71,680; Total assets, $2,686,400

Hardy Company's cost of goods sold is consistently 60% of sales. The company plans ending merchandise inventory for each month equal to 20% of the next month's budgeted cost of goods sold. All merchandise is purchased on credit, and 50% of the purchases made during a month is paid for in that month. Another 35% is paid for during the first month after purchase, and the remaining 15% is paid for during the second month after purchase. Expected sales are: August (actual), $325,000; September (actual), $320,000; October (estimated), $250,000; and November (estimated), $310,000. Use this information to determine October's expected cash payments for purchases.

Exercise 7-27ᴬ
Merchandising: Computing budgeted cash payments for purchases P4

Check Budgeted purchases: August, $194,400; October, $157,200

Ahmed Company purchases all merchandise on credit. It recently budgeted the following month-end accounts payable balances and merchandise inventory balances. Cash payments on accounts payable during each month are expected to be: May, $1,600,000; June, $1,490,000; July, $1,425,000; and August, $1,495,000. Use the available information to compute the budgeted amounts of (1) merchandise purchases for June, July, and August and (2) cost of goods sold for June, July, and August.

Exercise 7-28ᴬ
Merchandising: Computing budgeted purchases and cost of goods sold
P4

	Accounts Payable	Merchandise Inventory
May 31	$150,000	$250,000
June 30	200,000	400,000
July 31	235,000	300,000
August 31	195,000	330,000

Check June purchases, $1,540,000; June cost of goods sold, $1,390,000

Big Sound, a merchandising company specializing in home computer speakers, budgets its monthly cost of goods sold to equal 70% of sales. Its inventory policy calls for ending inventory at the end of each month to equal 20% of the next month's budgeted cost of goods sold. All purchases are on credit, and 25% of the purchases in a month is paid for in the same month. Another 60% is paid for during the first month after purchase, and the remaining 15% is paid for in the second month after purchase. The following sales budgets are set: July, $350,000; August, $290,000; September, $320,000; October, $275,000; and November, $265,000.

Compute the following: (1) budgeted merchandise purchases for July, August, September, and October; (2) budgeted payments on accounts payable for September and October; and (3) budgeted ending balances of accounts payable for September and October. (*Hint:* For part 1, refer to Exhibits 7A.2 and 7A.3 for guidance, but note that budgeted sales are in dollars for this assignment.)

Exercise 7-29ᴬ
Merchandising: Computing budgeted accounts payable and purchases—sales forecast in dollars
P4

Check July purchases, $236,600; Sep. payments on accts. pay., $214,235

Exercise 7-30ᴬ
Merchandising: Budgeted cash payments

P4

Hector Company reports the following sales and purchases data. Payments for purchases are made in the month after purchase. Selling expenses are 10% of sales, administrative expenses are 8% of sales, and both are paid in the month of sale. Rent expense of $7,400 is paid monthly. Depreciation expense is $2,300 per month. Prepare a schedule of budgeted cash payments for August and September.

	July	August	September
Sales	$50,000	$72,000	$66,000
Purchases	14,400	19,200	21,600

Exercise 7-31ᴬ
Merchandising: Cash budget

P4

Castor, Inc., is preparing its master budget for the quarter ended June 30. Budgeted sales and cash payments for merchandise for the next three months follow:

Budgeted	April	May	June
Sales	$32,000	$40,000	$24,000
Cash payments for merchandise	20,200	16,800	17,200

Sales are 50% cash and 50% on credit. All credit sales are collected in the month following the sale. The March 31 balance sheet includes balances of $12,000 in cash, $12,000 in accounts receivable, $11,000 in accounts payable, and a $2,000 balance in loans payable. A minimum cash balance of $12,000 is required. Loans are obtained at the end of any month when a cash shortage occurs. Interest is 1% per month based on the beginning of the month loan balance and is paid at each month-end. If an excess balance of cash exists, loans are repaid at the end of the month. Operating expenses are paid in the month incurred and include sales commissions (10% of sales), shipping (2% of sales), office salaries ($5,000 per month), and rent ($3,000 per month). Prepare a cash budget for each of the months of April, May, and June (round all dollar amounts to the nearest whole dollar).

Exercise 7-32ᴬ
Merchandising: Cash budget

P4

Kelsey is preparing its master budget for the quarter ended September 30. Budgeted sales and cash payments for merchandise for the next three months follow:

Budgeted	July	August	September
Sales	$64,000	$80,000	$48,000
Cash payments for merchandise	40,400	33,600	34,400

Sales are 20% cash and 80% on credit. All credit sales are collected in the month following the sale. The June 30 balance sheet includes balances of $15,000 in cash; $45,000 in accounts receivable; $4,500 in accounts payable; and a $5,000 balance in loans payable. A minimum cash balance of $15,000 is required. Loans are obtained at the end of any month when a cash shortage occurs. Interest is 1% per month based on the beginning-of-the-month loan balance and is paid at each month-end. If an excess balance of cash exists, loans are repaid at the end of the month. Operating expenses are paid in the month incurred and consist of sales commissions (10% of sales), office salaries ($4,000 per month), and rent ($6,500 per month). (1) Prepare a cash receipts budget for July, August, and September. (2) Prepare a cash budget for each of the months of July, August, and September. (Round all dollar amounts to the nearest whole dollar.)

Exercise 7-33ᴬ
Merchandising: Budgeted balance sheet

P3

The following information is available for Zetrov Company:

a. The cash budget for March shows an ending bank loan of $10,000 and an ending cash balance of $50,000.

b. The sales budget for March indicates sales of $140,000. Accounts receivable are expected to be 70% of the current-month sales.

c. The merchandise purchases budget indicates that $89,000 in merchandise will be purchased on account in March. Purchases on account are paid 100% in the month following the purchase. Ending inventory for March is predicted to be 600 units at a cost of $35 each.

d. The budgeted income statement for March shows net income of $48,000. Depreciation expense of $1,000 and $26,000 in income tax expense were used in computing net income for March. Accrued taxes will be paid in April.

e. The balance sheet for February shows equipment of $84,000 with accumulated depreciation of $46,000, common stock of $25,000, and ending retained earnings of $8,000. There are no changes budgeted in the Equipment or Common Stock accounts.

Prepare a budgeted balance sheet at the end of March.

Fortune, Inc., is preparing its master budget for the first quarter. The company sells a single product at a price of $25 per unit. Sales (in units) are forecasted at 45,000 for January, 55,000 for February, and 50,000 for March. Cost of goods sold is $14 per unit. Other expense information for the first quarter follows. Prepare a budgeted income statement for this first quarter. (Round expense amounts to the nearest dollar.)

Exercise 7-34
Budgeted income statement
P3

Commissions	8% of sales dollars
Rent	$14,000 per month
Advertising	15% of sales dollars
Office salaries	$75,000 per month
Depreciation	$40,000 per month
Interest	5% annually on a $250,000 note payable
Tax rate	30%

Render Co. CPA is preparing activity-based budgets for 2017. The partners expect the firm to generate billable hours for the year as follows:

Exercise 7-35
Activity-based budgeting
A1

Data entry	2,200 hours
Auditing	4,800 hours
Tax	4,300 hours
Consulting	750 hours

The company pays $10 per hour to data-entry clerks, $40 per hour to audit personnel, $50 per hour to tax personnel, and $50 per hour to consulting personnel. Prepare a schedule of budgeted labor costs for 2017 using activity-based budgeting.

connect

Black Diamond Company produces snow skis. Each ski requires 2 pounds of carbon fiber. The company's management predicts that 5,000 skis and 6,000 pounds of carbon fiber will be in inventory on June 30 of the current year and that 150,000 skis will be sold during the next (third) quarter. A set of two skis sells for $300. Management wants to end the third quarter with 3,500 skis and 4,000 pounds of carbon fiber in inventory. Carbon fiber can be purchased for $15 per pound. Each ski requires 0.5 hours of direct labor at $20 per hour. Variable overhead is applied at the rate of $8 per direct labor hour. The company budgets fixed overhead of $1,782,000 for the quarter.

PROBLEM SET A

Problem 7-1A
Manufacturing: Preparing production and manufacturing budgets
C2 P1

Required

1. Prepare the third-quarter production budget for skis.
2. Prepare the third-quarter direct materials (carbon fiber) budget; include the dollar cost of purchases.
3. Prepare the direct labor budget for the third quarter.
4. Prepare the factory overhead budget for the third quarter.

Check (1) Units manuf., 148,500

(2) Cost of carbon fiber purchases, $4,425,000

Built-Tight is preparing its master budget for the quarter ended September 30, 2017. Budgeted sales and cash payments for product costs for the quarter follow:

Problem 7-2A
Manufacturing: Cash budget
P2

	A	B	C	D
1		**July**	**August**	**September**
2	Budgeted sales	$64,000	$80,000	$48,000
3	Budgeted cash payments for			
4	Direct materials	16,160	13,440	13,760
5	Direct labor	4,040	3,360	3,440
6	Factory overhead	20,200	16,800	17,200

Sales are 20% cash and 80% on credit. All credit sales are collected in the month following the sale. The June 30 balance sheet includes balances of $15,000 in cash; $45,000 in accounts receivable; $4,500 in accounts payable; and a $5,000 balance in loans payable. A minimum cash balance of $15,000 is required. Loans are obtained at the end of any month when a cash shortage occurs. Interest is 1% per month based on the beginning-of-the-month loan balance and is paid at each month-end. If an excess balance of cash exists, loans are repaid at the end of the month. Operating expenses are paid in the month incurred and consist of sales commissions (10% of sales), office salaries ($4,000 per month), and rent ($6,500 per month).

1. Prepare a cash receipts budget for July, August, and September.
2. Prepare a cash budget for each of the months of July, August, and September. (Round amounts to the dollar.)

Problem 7-3A

Manufacturing:

Preparation and analysis of budgeted income statements

P3

Merline Manufacturing makes its product for $75 per unit and sells it for $150 per unit. The sales staff receives a 10% commission on the sale of each unit. Its December income statement follows.

MERLINE MANUFACTURING Income Statement For Month Ended December 31, 2017	
Sales	$2,250,000
Cost of goods sold	1,125,000
Gross profit	1,125,000
Operating expenses	
Sales commissions (10%)	225,000
Advertising	250,000
Store rent	30,000
Administrative salaries	45,000
Depreciation—Office equipment	50,000
Other expenses	10,000
Total expenses	610,000
Net income	$ 515,000

Management expects December's results to be repeated in January, February, and March of 2018 without any changes in strategy. Management, however, has an alternative plan. It believes that unit sales will increase at a rate of 10% *each* month for the next three months (beginning with January) if the item's selling price is reduced to $125 per unit and advertising expenses are increased by 15% and remain at that level for all three months. The cost of its product will remain at $75 per unit, the sales staff will continue to earn a 10% commission, and the remaining expenses will stay the same.

Required

Check   (1) Budgeted net income: January, $196,250; February, $258,125; March, $326,187

1. Prepare budgeted income statements for each of the months of January, February, and March that show the expected results from implementing the proposed changes. Use a three-column format, with one column for each month.

Analysis Component

2. Use the budgeted income statements from part 1 to recommend whether management should implement the proposed changes. Explain.

Problem 7-4A

Manufacturing:

Preparation of a complete master budget

P1   P2   P3

The management of Zigby Manufacturing prepared the following estimated balance sheet for March 2017:

ZIGBY MANUFACTURING Estimated Balance Sheet March 31, 2017			
Assets		**Liabilities and Equity**	
Cash	$ 40,000	Accounts payable	$ 200,500
Accounts receivable	342,248	Short-term notes payable	12,000
Raw materials inventory	98,500	Total current liabilities	212,500
Finished goods inventory	325,540	Long-term note payable.............	500,000
Total current assets	806,288	Total liabilities	712,500
Equipment	600,000	Common stock	335,000
Accumulated depreciation	(150,000)	Retained earnings	208,788
Equipment, net.....................	450,000	Total stockholders' equity	543,788
Total assets.......................	$1,256,288	Total liabilities and equity	$1,256,288

To prepare a master budget for April, May, and June of 2017, management gathers the following information:

a. Sales for March total 20,500 units. Forecasted sales in units are as follows: April, 20,500; May, 19,500; June, 20,000; and July, 20,500. Sales of 240,000 units are forecasted for the entire year. The product's selling price is $23.85 per unit and its total product cost is $19.85 per unit.

b. Company policy calls for a given month's ending raw materials inventory to equal 50% of the next month's materials requirements. The March 31 raw materials inventory is 4,925 units, which complies with the policy. The expected June 30 ending raw materials inventory is 4,000 units. Raw materials cost $20 per unit. Each finished unit requires 0.50 units of raw materials.

c. Company policy calls for a given month's ending finished goods inventory to equal 80% of the next month's expected unit sales. The March 31 finished goods inventory is 16,400 units, which complies with the policy.

d. Each finished unit requires 0.50 hours of direct labor at a rate of $15 per hour.

e. Overhead is allocated based on direct labor hours. The predetermined variable overhead rate is $2.70 per direct labor hour. Depreciation of $20,000 per month is treated as fixed factory overhead.

f. Sales representatives' commissions are 8% of sales and are paid in the month of the sales. The sales manager's monthly salary is $3,000.

g. Monthly general and administrative expenses include $12,000 administrative salaries and 0.9% monthly interest on the long-term note payable.

h. The company expects 30% of sales to be for cash and the remaining 70% on credit. Receivables are collected in full in the month following the sale (none are collected in the month of the sale).

i. All raw materials purchases are on credit, and no payables arise from any other transactions. One month's raw materials purchases are fully paid in the next month.

j. The minimum ending cash balance for all months is $40,000. If necessary, the company borrows enough cash using a short-term note to reach the minimum. Short-term notes require an interest payment of 1% at each month-end (before any repayment). If the ending cash balance exceeds the minimum, the excess will be applied to repaying the short-term notes payable balance.

k. Dividends of $10,000 are to be declared and paid in May.

l. No cash payments for income taxes are to be made during the second calendar quarter. Income tax will be assessed at 35% in the quarter and paid in the third calendar quarter.

m. Equipment purchases of $130,000 are budgeted for the last day of June.

Required

Prepare the following budgets and other financial information as required. All budgets and other financial information should be prepared for the second calendar quarter, except as otherwise noted below. Round calculations up to the nearest whole dollar, except for the amount of cash sales, which should be rounded down to the nearest whole dollar.

1. Sales budget.

2. Production budget.

3. Raw materials budget.

4. Direct labor budget.

5. Factory overhead budget.

6. Selling expense budget.

7. General and administrative expense budget.

8. Cash budget.

9. Budgeted income statement for the entire second quarter (not for each month separately).

10. Budgeted balance sheet as of the end of the second calendar quarter.

Check   (2) Units to produce: April, 19,700; May, 19,900
(3) Cost of raw materials purchases: April, $198,000
(5) Total overhead cost: May, $46,865
(8) Ending cash balance: April, $83,346; May, $124,295
(10) Budgeted total assets: June 30, $1,299,440

Keggler's Supply is a merchandiser of three different products. The company's February 28 inventories are footwear, 20,000 units; sports equipment, 80,000 units; and apparel, 50,000 units. Management believes each of these inventories is too high. As a result, a new policy dictates that ending inventory in any month should equal 30% of the expected unit sales for the following month. Expected sales in units for March, April, May, and June follow.

Problem 7-5A[A]
Merchandising:
Preparation and analysis of purchases budgets

P4

	Budgeted Sales in Units			
	March	April	May	June
Footwear.................	15,000	25,000	32,000	35,000
Sports equipment	70,000	90,000	95,000	90,000
Apparel	40,000	38,000	37,000	25,000

Required

1. Prepare a merchandise purchases budget (in units) for each product for each of the months of March, April, and May.

Analysis Component

2. What business conditions might lead to inventory levels becoming too high?

Problem 7-6A[A]

Merchandising:

Preparation of cash
budgets (for three periods)

P4

During the last week of August, Oneida Company's owner approaches the bank for a $100,000 loan to be made on September 2 and repaid on November 30 with annual interest of 12%, for an interest cost of $3,000. The owner plans to increase the store's inventory by $80,000 during September and needs the loan to pay for inventory acquisitions. The bank's loan officer needs more information about Oneida's ability to repay the loan and asks the owner to forecast the store's November 30 cash position. On September 1, Oneida is expected to have a $5,000 cash balance, $159,100 of net accounts receivable, and $125,000 of accounts payable. Its budgeted sales, merchandise purchases, and various cash payments for the next three months follow.

	A	B	C	D
1	**Budgeted Figures***	**September**	**October**	**November**
2	Sales	$250,000	$375,000	$400,000
3	Merchandise purchases	240,000	225,000	200,000
4	Cash payments			
5	Payroll	20,000	22,000	24,000
6	Rent	10,000	10,000	10,000
7	Other cash expenses	35,000	30,000	20,000
8	Repayment of bank loan			100,000
9	Interest on the bank loan			3,000

*Operations began in August; August sales were $215,000 and purchases were $125,000.

The budgeted September merchandise purchases include the inventory increase. All sales are on account. The company predicts that 25% of credit sales is collected in the month of the sale, 45% in the month following the sale, 20% in the second month, 9% in the third, and the remainder is uncollectible. Applying these percents to the August credit sales, for example, shows that $96,750 of the $215,000 will be collected in September, $43,000 in October, and $19,350 in November. All merchandise is purchased on credit; 80% of the balance is paid in the month following a purchase, and the remaining 20% is paid in the second month. For example, of the $125,000 August purchases, $100,000 will be paid in September and $25,000 in October.

Required

Prepare a cash budget for September, October, and November. Show supporting calculations as needed.

Problem 7-7A[A]

Merchandising:

Preparation and analysis
of cash budgets with
supporting inventory and
purchases budgets

P4

Aztec Company sells its product for $180 per unit. Its actual and budgeted sales follow.

	Units	Dollars
April (actual)	4,000	$ 720,000
May (actual).	2,000	360,000
June (budgeted)	6,000	1,080,000
July (budgeted).	5,000	900,000
August (budgeted)	3,800	684,000

All sales are on credit. Recent experience shows that 20% of credit sales is collected in the month of the sale, 50% in the month after the sale, 28% in the second month after the sale, and 2% proves to be uncollectible. The product's purchase price is $110 per unit. 60% of purchases made in a month is paid in that month and the other 40% is paid in the next month. The company has a policy to maintain an ending monthly inventory of 20% of the next month's unit sales plus a safety stock of 100 units. The April 30 and May 31 actual inventory levels are consistent with this policy. Selling and administrative expenses for the year are $1,320,000 and are paid evenly throughout the year in cash. The company's minimum cash balance at month-end is $100,000. This minimum is maintained, if necessary, by borrowing cash from the bank. If the balance exceeds $100,000, the company repays as much of the loan as it can without going below the minimum. This type of loan carries an annual 12% interest rate. On May 31, the loan balance is $25,000, and the company's cash balance is $100,000. (Round amounts to the nearest dollar.)

Required

1. Prepare a schedule that shows the computation of cash collections of its credit sales (accounts receivable) in each of the months of June and July.

2. Prepare a schedule that shows the computation of budgeted ending inventories (in units) for April, May, June, and July.

3. Prepare the merchandise purchases budget for May, June, and July. Report calculations in units and then show the dollar amount of purchases for each month.

4. Prepare a schedule showing the computation of cash payments for product purchases for June and July.

5. Prepare a cash budget for June and July, including any loan activity and interest expense. Compute the loan balance at the end of each month.

Check   (1) Cash collections: June, $597,600; July, $820,800

(3) Budgeted purchases: May, $308,000; June, $638,000

(5) Budgeted ending loan balance: June, $43,650; July, $0

Analysis Component

6. Refer to your answer to part 5. The cash budget indicates the company will need to borrow more than $18,000 in June. Suggest some reasons that knowing this information in May would be helpful to management.

Near the end of 2017, the management of Dimsdale Sports Co., a merchandising company, prepared the following estimated balance sheet for December 31, 2017.

Problem 7-8A[A]
Merchandising: Preparation of a complete master budget   P4

DIMSDALE SPORTS COMPANY
Estimated Balance Sheet
December 31, 2017

Assets			Liabilities and Equity		
Cash	$ 36,000		Accounts payable	$360,000	
Accounts receivable	525,000		Bank loan payable	15,000	
Inventory	150,000		Taxes payable (due 3/15/2018)	90,000	
Total current assets		$ 711,000	Total liabilities		$ 465,000
Equipment	540,000		Common stock	472,500	
Less: Accumulated depreciation	67,500		Retained earnings	246,000	
Equipment, net		472,500	Total stockholders' equity		718,500
Total assets		$1,183,500	Total liabilities and equity		$1,183,500

To prepare a master budget for January, February, and March of 2018, management gathers the following information.

a. The company's single product is purchased for $30 per unit and resold for $55 per unit. The expected inventory level of 5,000 units on December 31, 2017, is more than management's desired level, which is 20% of the next month's expected sales (in units). Expected sales are: January, 7,000 units; February, 9,000 units; March, 11,000 units; and April, 10,000 units.

b. Cash sales and credit sales represent 25% and 75%, respectively, of total sales. Of the credit sales, 60% is collected in the first month after the month of sale and 40% in the second month after the month of sale. For the December 31, 2017, accounts receivable balance, $125,000 is collected in January and the remaining $400,000 is collected in February.

c. Merchandise purchases are paid for as follows: 20% in the first month after the month of purchase and 80% in the second month after the month of purchase. For the December 31, 2017, accounts payable balance, $80,000 is paid in January 2018 and the remaining $280,000 is paid in February 2018.

d. Sales commissions equal to 20% of sales are paid each month. Sales salaries (excluding commissions) are $60,000 per year.

e. General and administrative salaries are $144,000 per year. Maintenance expense equals $2,000 per month and is paid in cash.

f. Equipment reported in the December 31, 2017, balance sheet was purchased in January 2017. It is being depreciated over eight years under the straight-line method with no salvage value. The following amounts for new equipment purchases are planned in the coming quarter: January, $36,000; February, $96,000; and March, $28,800. This equipment will be depreciated under the straight-line method over eight years with no salvage value. A full month's depreciation is taken for the month in which equipment is purchased.

g. The company plans to buy land at the end of March at a cost of $150,000, which will be paid with cash on the last day of the month.

h. The company has a working arrangement with its bank to obtain additional loans as needed. The interest rate is 12% per year, and interest is paid at each month-end based on the beginning balance. Partial or full payments on these loans can be made on the last day of the month. The company has agreed to maintain a minimum ending cash balance of $25,000 at the end of each month.

i. The income tax rate for the company is 40%. Income taxes on the first quarter's income will not be paid until April 15.

Required

Prepare a master budget for each of the first three months of 2018; include the following component budgets (show supporting calculations as needed, and round amounts to the nearest dollar):

1. Monthly sales budgets (showing both budgeted unit sales and dollar sales).
2. Monthly merchandise purchases budgets.
3. Monthly selling expense budgets.
4. Monthly general and administrative expense budgets.
5. Monthly capital expenditures budgets.
6. Monthly cash budgets.
7. Budgeted income statement for the entire first quarter (not for each month).
8. Budgeted balance sheet as of March 31, 2018.

PROBLEM SET B

Problem 7-1B

Manufacturing:

Preparing production and manufacturing budgets

C2   P1

NSA Company produces baseball bats. Each bat requires 3 pounds of aluminum alloy. Management predicts that 8,000 bats and 15,000 pounds of aluminum alloy will be in inventory on March 31 of the current year and that 250,000 bats will be sold during this year's second quarter. Bats sell for $80 each. Management wants to end the second quarter with 6,000 finished bats and 12,000 pounds of aluminum alloy in inventory. Aluminum alloy can be purchased for $4 per pound. Each bat requires 0.5 hours of direct labor at $18 per hour. Variable overhead is applied at the rate of $12 per direct labor hour. The company budgets fixed overhead of $1,776,000 for the quarter.

Required

1. Prepare the second-quarter production budget for bats.
2. Prepare the second-quarter direct materials (aluminum alloy) budget; include the dollar cost of purchases.
3. Prepare the direct labor budget for the second quarter.
4. Prepare the factory overhead budget for the second quarter.

Problem 7-2B

Manufacturing:

Cash budget

P2

A1 Manufacturing is preparing its master budget for the quarter ended September 30, 2017. Budgeted sales and cash payments for product costs for the quarter follow.

	A	B	C	D
1		July	August	September
2	Budgeted sales	$63,400	$80,600	$48,600
3	Budgeted cash payments for			
4	Direct materials	12,480	9,900	10,140
5	Direct labor	10,400	8,250	8,450
6	Factory overhead	18,720	14,850	15,210

Sales are 20% cash and 80% on credit. All credit sales are collected in the month following the sale. The June 30 balance sheet includes balances of $12,900 in cash; $47,000 in accounts receivable; $5,100 in accounts payable; and a $2,600 balance in loans payable. A minimum cash balance of $12,600 is required. Loans are obtained at the end of any month when a cash shortage occurs. Interest is 1% per month based on the beginning-of-the-month loan balance and is paid at each month-end. If an excess balance of cash exists, loans are repaid at the end of the month. Operating expenses are paid in the month incurred and consist of sales commissions (10% of sales), office salaries ($4,600 per month), and rent ($7,100 per month).

1. Prepare a cash receipts budget for July, August, and September.
2. Prepare a cash budget for each of the months of July, August, and September. (Round amounts to the dollar.)

HCS MFG. makes its product for $60 per unit and sells it for $130 per unit. The sales staff receives a commission of 10% of dollar sales. Its June income statement follows.

Problem 7-3B
Manufacturing:
Preparation and analysis of budgeted income statements   **P3**

HCS MFG. Income Statement For Month Ended June 30, 2017	
Sales	$1,300,000
Cost of goods sold	600,000
Gross profit	700,000
Operating expenses	
Sales commissions (10%)	130,000
Advertising................................	200,000
Store rent	24,000
Administrative salaries	40,000
Depreciation—Office equipment	50,000
Other expenses	12,000
Total expenses	456,000
Net income	$ 244,000

Management expects June's results to be repeated in July, August, and September without any changes in strategy. Management, however, has another plan. It believes that unit sales will increase at a rate of 10% *each* month for the next three months (beginning with July) if the item's selling price is reduced to $115 per unit and advertising expenses are increased by 25% and remain at that level for all three months. The cost of its product will remain at $60 per unit, the sales staff will continue to earn a 10% commission, and the remaining expenses will stay the same.

Required

1. Prepare budgeted income statements for each of the months of July, August, and September that show the expected results from implementing the proposed changes. Use a three-column format, with one column for each month.

Check   Budgeted net income: July, $102,500; August, $150,350; September, $202,985

Analysis Component

2. Use the budgeted income statements from part 1 to recommend whether management should implement the proposed plan. Explain.

The management of Nabar Manufacturing prepared the following estimated balance sheet for June 2017:

Problem 7-4B
Manufacturing:
Preparation of a complete master budget

P1   P2   P3

NABAR MANUFACTURING
Estimated Balance Sheet
June 30, 2017

Assets		Liabilities and Equity	
Cash	$ 40,000	Accounts payable	$ 51,400
Accounts receivable	249,900	Income taxes payable...............	10,000
Raw materials inventory	35,000	Short-term notes payable	24,000
Finished goods inventory	241,080	Total current liabilities	85,400
Total current assets	565,980	Long-term note payable.............	300,000
Equipment	720,000	Total liabilities	385,400
Accumulated depreciation	(240,000)	Common stock	600,000
Equipment, net.....................	480,000	Retained earnings	60,580
		Total stockholders' equity	660,580
Total assets.......................	$1,045,980	Total liabilities and equity	$1,045,980

To prepare a master budget for July, August, and September of 2017, management gathers the following information:

a. Sales were 20,000 units in June. Forecasted sales in units are as follows: July, 21,000; August, 19,000; September, 20,000; and October, 24,000. The product's selling price is $17 per unit and its total product cost is $14.35 per unit.

b. Company policy calls for a given month's ending finished goods inventory to equal 70% of the next month's expected unit sales. The June 30 finished goods inventory is 16,800 units, which does not comply with the policy.

c. Company policy calls for a given month's ending raw materials inventory to equal 20% of the next month's materials requirements. The June 30 raw materials inventory is 4,375 units (which also fails to meet the policy). The budgeted September 30 raw materials inventory is 1,980 units. Raw materials cost $8 per unit. Each finished unit requires 0.50 units of raw materials.

d. Each finished unit requires 0.50 hours of direct labor at a rate of $16 per hour.

e. Overhead is allocated based on direct labor hours. The predetermined variable overhead rate is $2.70 per direct labor hour. Depreciation of $20,000 per month is treated as fixed factory overhead.

f. Monthly general and administrative expenses include $9,000 administrative salaries and 0.9% monthly interest on the long-term note payable.

g. Sales representatives' commissions are 10% of sales and are paid in the month of the sales. The sales manager's monthly salary is $3,500.

h. The company expects 30% of sales to be for cash and the remaining 70% on credit. Receivables are collected in full in the month following the sale (none are collected in the month of the sale).

i. All raw materials purchases are on credit, and no payables arise from any other transactions. One month's raw materials purchases are fully paid in the next month.

j. Dividends of $20,000 are to be declared and paid in August.

k. Income taxes payable at June 30 will be paid in July. Income tax expense will be assessed at 35% in the quarter and paid in October.

l. Equipment purchases of $100,000 are budgeted for the last day of September.

m. The minimum ending cash balance for all months is $40,000. If necessary, the company borrows enough cash using a short-term note to reach the minimum. Short-term notes require an interest payment of 1% at each month-end (before any repayment). If the ending cash balance exceeds the minimum, the excess will be applied to repaying the short-term notes payable balance.

Check   (2) Units to produce:
July, 17,500; August, 19,700
         (3) Cost of raw
materials purchases: July,
$50,760
         (5) Total overhead
cost: August, $46,595
         (8) Ending cash
balance: July, $96,835;
August, $141,180
         (10) Budgeted total
assets: Sep. 30, $1,054,920

Required

Prepare the following budgets and other financial information as required. All budgets and other financial information should be prepared for the third calendar quarter, except as otherwise noted below. Round calculations to the nearest whole dollar.

1. Sales budget.
2. Production budget.
3. Raw materials budget.
4. Direct labor budget.
5. Factory overhead budget.
6. Selling expense budget.
7. General and administrative expense budget.
8. Cash budget.
9. Budgeted income statement for the entire quarter (not for each month separately).
10. Budgeted balance sheet as of September 30, 2017.

Problem 7-5B[A]

Merchandising:

Preparation and analysis of purchases budgets

P4

H20 Sports is a merchandiser of three different products. The company's March 31 inventories are water skis, 40,000 units; tow ropes, 90,000 units; and life jackets, 150,000 units. Management believes inventory levels are too high for all three products. As a result, a new policy dictates that ending inventory in any month should equal 10% of the expected unit sales for the following month. Expected sales in units for April, May, June, and July follow.

	Budgeted Sales in Units			
	April	May	June	July
Water skis	70,000	90,000	130,000	100,000
Tow ropes	100,000	90,000	110,000	100,000
Life jackets	160,000	190,000	200,000	120,000

Required

Check   (1) April budgeted
purchases: Water skis,
39,000; Tow ropes, 19,000;
Life jackets, 29,000

1. Prepare a merchandise purchases budget (in units) for each product for each of the months of April, May, and June.

Analysis Component

2. What business conditions might lead to inventory levels becoming too high?

Problem 7-6B[A]

Merchandising:

Preparation of cash budgets (for three periods)   **P4**

During the last week of March, Sony Stereo's owner approaches the bank for an $80,000 loan to be made on April 1 and repaid on June 30 with annual interest of 12%, for an interest cost of $2,400. The owner plans to increase the store's inventory by $60,000 in April and needs the loan to pay for inventory acquisitions. The bank's loan officer needs more information about Sony Stereo's ability to repay the loan and asks the owner to forecast the store's June 30 cash position. On April 1, Sony Stereo is expected to have a $3,000 cash balance, $135,000 of accounts receivable, and $100,000 of accounts payable. Its budgeted sales, merchandise purchases, and various cash payments for the next three months follow.

	A	B	C	D
1	**Budgeted Figures***	**April**	**May**	**June**
2	Sales	$220,000	$300,000	$380,000
3	Merchandise purchases	210,000	180,000	220,000
4	Cash payments			
5	Payroll	16,000	17,000	18,000
6	Rent	6,000	6,000	6,000
7	Other cash expenses	64,000	8,000	7,000
8	Repayment of bank loan			80,000
9	Interest on bank loan			2,400

*Operations began in March; March sales were $180,000 and purchases were $100,000.

The budgeted April merchandise purchases include the inventory increase. All sales are on account. The company predicts that 25% of credit sales is collected in the month of the sale, 45% in the month following the sale, 20% in the second month, 9% in the third, and the remainder is uncollectible. Applying these percents to the March credit sales, for example, shows that $81,000 of the $180,000 will be collected in April, $36,000 in May, and $16,200 in June. All merchandise is purchased on credit; 80% of the balance is paid in the month following a purchase and the remaining 20% is paid in the second month. For example, of the $100,000 March purchases, $80,000 will be paid in April and $20,000 in May.

Required

Prepare a cash budget for April, May, and June. Show supporting calculations as needed.

Check Budgeted cash balance: April, $53,000; May, $44,000; June, $34,800

Connick Company sells its product for $22 per unit. Its actual and budgeted sales follow.

	Units	Dollars
January (actual)	18,000	$396,000
February (actual)	22,500	495,000
March (budgeted)	19,000	418,000
April (budgeted)	18,750	412,500
May (budgeted)	21,000	462,000

Problem 7-7B[A]
Merchandising:
Preparation and analysis of cash budgets with supporting inventory and purchases budgets

P4

All sales are on credit. Recent experience shows that 40% of credit sales is collected in the month of the sale, 35% in the month after the sale, 23% in the second month after the sale, and 2% proves to be uncollectible. The product's purchase price is $12 per unit. Of purchases made in a month, 30% is paid in that month and the other 70% is paid in the next month. The company has a policy to maintain an ending monthly inventory of 20% of the next month's unit sales plus a safety stock of 100 units. The January 31 and February 28 actual inventory levels are consistent with this policy. Selling and administrative expenses for the year are $1,920,000 and are paid evenly throughout the year in cash. The company's minimum cash balance for month-end is $50,000. This minimum is maintained, if necessary, by borrowing cash from the bank. If the balance exceeds $50,000, the company repays as much of the loan as it can without going below the minimum. This type of loan carries an annual 12% interest rate. At February 28, the loan balance is $12,000, and the company's cash balance is $50,000.

Required

1. Prepare a schedule that shows the computation of cash collections of its credit sales (accounts receivable) in each of the months of March and April.

2. Prepare a schedule showing the computations of budgeted ending inventories (units) for January, February, March, and April.

3. Prepare the merchandise purchases budget for February, March, and April. Report calculations in units and then show the dollar amount of purchases for each month.

4. Prepare a schedule showing the computation of cash payments on product purchases for March and April.

5. Prepare a cash budget for March and April, including any loan activity and interest expense. Compute the loan balance at the end of each month.

Check (1) Cash collections: March, $431,530; April, $425,150

(3) Budgeted purchases: February, $261,600; March, $227,400

(5) Ending cash balance: March, $58,070; April, $94,920

Analysis Component

6. Refer to your answer to part 5. The cash budget indicates whether the company must borrow additional funds at the end of March. Suggest some reasons that knowing the loan needs in advance would be helpful to management.

Problem 7-8B^A

Merchandising: Preparation of a complete master budget

P4

Near the end of 2017, the management of Isle Corp., a merchandising company, prepared the following estimated balance sheet for December 31, 2017.

ISLE CORPORATION					
Estimated Balance Sheet					
December 31, 2017					
Assets			**Liabilities and Equity**		
Cash	$ 36,000		Accounts payable	$360,000	
Accounts receivable	525,000		Bank loan payable	15,000	
Inventory	150,000		Taxes payable (due 3/15/2018)	90,000	
Total current assets		$ 711,000	Total liabilities		$ 465,000
Equipment	540,000		Common stock	472,500	
Less: Accumulated depreciation	67,500		Retained earnings	246,000	
Equipment, net................		472,500	Total stockholders' equity		718,500
Total assets		$1,183,500	Total liabilities and equity		$1,183,500

To prepare a master budget for January, February, and March of 2018, management gathers the following information.

a. The company's single product is purchased for $30 per unit and resold for $45 per unit. The expected inventory level of 5,000 units on December 31, 2017, is more than management's desired level for 2018, which is 25% of the next month's expected sales (in units). Expected sales are: January, 6,000 units; February, 8,000 units; March, 10,000 units; and April, 9,000 units.

b. Cash sales and credit sales represent 25% and 75%, respectively, of total sales. Of the credit sales, 60% is collected in the first month after the month of sale and 40% in the second month after the month of sale. For the $525,000 accounts receivable balance at December 31, 2017, $315,000 is collected in January 2018 and the remaining $210,000 is collected in February 2018.

c. Merchandise purchases are paid for as follows: 20% in the first month after the month of purchase and 80% in the second month after the month of purchase. For the $360,000 accounts payable balance at December 31, 2017, $72,000 is paid in January 2018 and the remaining $288,000 is paid in February 2018.

d. Sales commissions equal to 20% of sales dollars are paid each month. Sales salaries (excluding commissions) are $90,000 per year.

e. General and administrative salaries are $144,000 per year. Maintenance expense equals $3,000 per month and is paid in cash.

f. Equipment reported in the December 31, 2017, balance sheet was purchased in January 2017. It is being depreciated over eight years under the straight-line method with no salvage value. The following amounts for new equipment purchases are planned in the coming quarter: January, $72,000; February, $96,000; and March, $28,800. This equipment will be depreciated using the straight-line method over eight years with no salvage value. A full month's depreciation is taken for the month in which equipment is purchased.

g. The company plans to buy land at the end of March at a cost of $150,000, which will be paid with cash on the last day of the month.

h. The company has a contract with its bank to obtain additional loans as needed. The interest rate is 12% per year, and interest is paid at each month-end based on the beginning balance. Partial or full payments on these loans are made on the last day of the month. The company has agreed to maintain a minimum ending cash balance of $36,000 at the end of each month.

i. The income tax rate for the company is 40%. Income taxes on the first quarter's income will not be paid until April 15.

Required

Check (2) Budgeted purchases: January, $90,000; February, $255,000

(3) Budgeted selling expenses: January, $61,500; February, $79,500

Prepare a master budget for each of the first three months of 2018; include the following component budgets (show supporting calculations as needed, and round amounts to the nearest dollar):

1. Monthly sales budgets (showing both budgeted unit sales and dollar sales).

2. Monthly merchandise purchases budgets.

3. Monthly selling expense budgets.

4. Monthly general and administrative expense budgets.

5. Monthly capital expenditures budgets.

6. Monthly cash budgets.

7. Budgeted income statement for the entire first quarter (not for each month).

8. Budgeted balance sheet as of March 31, 2018.

(6) Ending cash bal.:
January, $182,850; February,
$107,850

(8) Budgeted total
assets at March 31,
$1,346,875

(This serial problem began in Chapter 1 and continues through most of the book. If previous chapter segments were not completed, the serial problem can begin at this point.)

SERIAL PROBLEM
Business Solutions

P3

SP 7   Santana Rey expects second-quarter 2018 sales of **Business Solutions**'s line of computer furniture to be the same as the first quarter's sales (reported below) without any changes in strategy. Monthly sales averaged 40 desk units (sales price of $1,250) and 20 chairs (sales price of $500).

BUSINESS SOLUTIONS—Computer Furniture Segment Segment Income Statement* For Quarter Ended March 31, 2018	
Sales†.................................	$180,000
Cost of goods sold‡....................	115,000
Gross profit..........................	65,000
Expenses	
Sales commissions (10%)...............	18,000
Advertising expenses..................	9,000
Other fixed expenses..................	18,000
Total expenses.......................	45,000
Net income...........................	$ 20,000

© Alexander Image/Shutterstock RF

* Reflects revenue and expense activity only related to the computer furniture segment.
† Revenue: (120 desks × $1,250) + (60 chairs × $500) = $150,000 + $30,000 = $180,000
‡ Cost of goods sold: (120 desks × $750) + (60 chairs × $250) + $10,000 = $115,000

Santana Rey believes that sales will increase each month for the next three months (April, 48 desks, 32 chairs; May, 52 desks, 35 chairs; June, 56 desks, 38 chairs) *if* selling prices are reduced to $1,150 for desks and $450 for chairs, and advertising expenses are increased by 10% and remain at that level for all three months. The products' variable cost will remain at $750 for desks and $250 for chairs. The sales staff will continue to earn a 10% commission, the fixed manufacturing costs per month will remain at $10,000, and other fixed expenses will remain at $6,000 per month.

Required

1. Prepare budgeted income statements for the computer furniture segment for each of the months of April, May, and June that show the expected results from implementing the proposed changes. Use a three-column format, with one column for each month.

Check (1) Budgeted income
(loss): April, $(660); May, $945

2. Use the budgeted income statements from part 1 to recommend whether Santana Rey should implement the proposed changes. Explain.

Beyond the Numbers

BTN 7-1   Financial statements often serve as a starting point in formulating budgets. Review **Apple**'s financial statements in Appendix A to determine its cash paid for acquisitions of property, plant, and equipment in the current year and the budgeted cash needed for such acquisitions in the next year.

**REPORTING IN
ACTION**

P3

APPLE

Required

1. Which financial statement reports the amount of cash paid for acquisitions of property, plant, and equipment? Explain where on the statement this information is reported.

2. Indicate the amount of cash (a) paid for acquisitions of property and equipment in the year ended September 26, 2015, and (b) to be paid (budgeted for) next year under the assumption that annual acquisitions of property and equipment equal 20% of the prior year's net income.

Fast Forward

3. Access Apple's financial statements for a year ending after September 26, 2015, from either its website [**Apple.com**] or the SEC's EDGAR database [**SEC.gov**]. Compare your answer for part 2 with actual cash paid for acquisitions of property and equipment for that fiscal year. Compute the error, if any, in your estimate. Speculate as to why cash paid for acquisitions of property and equipment was higher or lower than your estimate.

COMPARATIVE ANALYSIS

P2

APPLE
GOOGLE

BTN 7-2   Companies often budget selling expenses and general and administrative expenses (SGA) as a percentage of expected sales.

Required

1. For both **Apple** and **Google**, list the prior three years' sales (in dollars) and *total* selling expenses and general and administrative expenses (in dollars). Use the financial statements in Appendix A.

2. Compute the ratio of *total* selling expenses and general and administrative expenses to sales for each of the three years.

3. Using the data from part *2*, predict both companies' *total* selling expenses and general and administrative expenses (in dollars) for the next two years. (If possible, compare your predictions to actual amounts for those years.)

ETHICS CHALLENGE

C1

BTN 7-3   Both the budget process and budgets themselves can impact management actions, both positively and negatively. For instance, a common practice among not-for-profit organizations and government agencies is for management to spend any amounts remaining in a budget at the end of the budget period, a practice often called "use it or lose it." The view is that if a department manager does not spend the budgeted amount, top management will reduce next year's budget by the amount not spent. To avoid losing budget dollars, department managers often spend all budgeted amounts regardless of the value added to products or services. All of us pay for the costs associated with this budget system.

Required

Write a half-page report to a local not-for-profit organization or government agency offering a solution to the "use it or lose it" budgeting problem.

COMMUNICATING IN PRACTICE

C2

BTN 7-4   The sales budget is usually the first and most crucial of the component budgets in a master budget because all other budgets usually rely on it for planning purposes.

Required

Assume that your company's sales staff provides information on expected sales and selling prices for items making up the sales budget. Prepare a one-page memorandum to your supervisor outlining concerns with the sales staff's input in the sales budget when its compensation is at least partly tied to these budgets. More generally, explain the importance of assessing any potential bias in information provided to the budget process.

TAKING IT TO THE NET

C1

BTN 7-5   Access information on e-budgets through **TheManageMentor** website (**https://web.archive.org/web/20091031091622/http://www.themanagementor.com/ICASL/frame.asp?page=../kuniverse/index.htm**). Select: Finance, then Corporate Finance and Accounting, and then Turn budgeting into a management tool. Read the information.

Required

1. Assume the role of a senior manager in a large, multidivision company. What are the benefits of using e-budgets?

2. As a senior manager, what concerns do you have with the concept and application of e-budgets?

TEAMWORK IN ACTION

A1

BTN 7-6   Your team is to prepare a budget report outlining the costs of attending college (full-time) for the next two semesters (30 hours) or three quarters (45 hours). This budget's focus is solely on attending college; do not include personal items in the team's budget. Your budget must include tuition, books, supplies, club fees, food, housing, and all costs associated with travel to and from college. This budgeting exercise is similar to the initial phase in activity-based budgeting. Include a list of any assumptions you use in completing the budget. Be prepared to present your budget in class.

ENTREPRENEURIAL DECISION

C1

BTN 7-7 **Marilyn and Michelle** sells a foam mattress cover that allows patients to sleep better after surgery. Co-founders Marilyn Collins and Michelle Logan stress the importance of planning and budgeting for business success.

Required

1. How can budgeting help Marilyn and Michelle efficiently develop and operate their business?
2. Marilyn and Michelle hope to expand their business. How can a budget be useful in expanding a business's operations?

HITTING THE ROAD

C2   P1

BTN 7-8 To help understand the factors impacting a sales budget, you are to visit three businesses with the same ownership or franchise membership. Record the selling prices of two identical products at each location, such as regular and premium gas sold at **Chevron** stations. You are likely to find a difference in prices for at least one of the three locations you visit.

Required

1. Identify at least three external factors that must be considered when setting the sales budget. (*Note:* There is a difference between internal and external factors that impact the sales budget.)
2. What factors might explain any differences identified in the prices of the businesses you visited?

GLOBAL DECISION

P1

Samsung

BTN 7-9 Access **Samsung**'s income statement (in Appendix A) for the business year 2015.

Required

1. Is Samsung's selling and administrative expenses budget likely to be an important budget in its master budgeting process? Explain.
2. Identify three examples of expenses that would be reported as selling and administrative expenses on Samsung's income statement.
3. Who likely has the initial responsibility for Samsung's selling and administrative expense budget? Explain.

GLOBAL VIEW

Royal Philips Electronics of the Netherlands is a diversified company. Preparing budgets and evaluating progress help the company achieve its goals. In a recent annual report, the company reports that it budgets sales to grow at a faster pace than overall economic growth. Based on this sales target, company managers prepare detailed operating, capital expenditure, and financial budgets.

Budgeted and actual results of companies that do global business are impacted by changes in foreign currency exchange rates. While most of Royal Philips's cash payments are in euros, the company's sales are in euros, U.S. dollars, Chinese yuan, Brazilian real, and other currencies.

Forecasting future exchange rates and their impact on sales budgets is difficult. In addition, global economic and political uncertainties add to budgeting challenges.

 Global View Assignments

Discussion Question 13

Discussion Question 14

Quick Study 7-32

BTN 7-9

Flexible Budgets and Standard Costs

Learning Objectives

CONCEPTUAL

C1 Define *standard costs* and explain how standard cost information is useful for management by exception.

C2 Describe cost variances and what they reveal about performance.

ANALYTICAL

A1 Analyze changes in sales from expected amounts.

PROCEDURAL

P1 Prepare a flexible budget and interpret a flexible budget performance report.

P2 Compute materials and labor variances.

P3 Compute overhead controllable and volume variances.

P4 *Appendix 8A*—Compute overhead spending and efficiency variances.

P5 *Appendix 8A*—Prepare journal entries for standard costs and account for price and quantity variances.

E-Z Riider

WASHINGTON, DC—Avid bikers Amber Wason and Jeff Stefanis believe electric bicycles are the solution to urban congestion and global energy needs. However, "we didn't see anything at an affordable price that people would want to ride," recalls Jeff. Amber adds, "no one in the U.S. had done it, so we decided to design and build our own."

Amber and Jeff spent a year and their own money to design and develop **Riide** (**Riide.com**), a lighter and cheaper e-bike. The duo set out to make their e-bike maintenance-free. "We obsessed over every detail," explains Jeff, "and we developed precise standards." They set standards for materials and labor. "We use only the highest quality components," says Amber, "and we reject any material that does not meet our requirements."

Amber and Jeff focus on *variances* between actual and expected costs. Materials price and quantity variances are used to control the costs of expensive raw materials. Unfavorable materials price variances can result from rising materials prices, which can lead them to consider alternative suppliers or to raise selling price.

Each Riide bike is assembled by hand, so the company knows precisely how long each bike should take to assemble. If assembly takes longer than expected, Amber and Jeff investigate why and take corrective action.

Riide has sold out all of its production for many months in advance. "Our biggest challenge is keeping up with demand!" explains Amber. "We want to accelerate production."

When production accelerates, budgets quickly can become outdated. *Flexible budgets,* which reflect budgeted costs at different production levels, are useful in analyzing performance and controlling costs.

While attention to budgeting, standard costs, and variances is important, Amber and Jeff encourage others to have passion and give back. "We have a grand vision," claims Amber. "We have to."

"Have a vision"
—**Amber Wason**

Sources: *Riide website,* January 2017; *Pando,* January 9, 2014; *Urbanful,* January 13, 2015; *DCInno,* February 8, 2016; *Washington Post,* August 4, 2014

Section 1—Fixed and Flexible Budgets

Point: Budget reports are often used to determine bonuses of managers.

Managers use budgets to control operations and see that planned objectives are met. **Budget reports** compare budgeted results to actual results. Budget reports are progress reports, or *report cards,* on management's performance in achieving planned objectives. These reports can be prepared at any time and for any period. Three common periods for a budget report are a month, quarter, and year.

As we showed in the previous chapter, a *master budget* is based on a predicted level of activity, such as sales volume, for the budget period. In preparing a master budget, two alternative approaches can be used: *fixed budgeting* or *flexible budgeting.*

- A **fixed budget,** also called a *static budget,* is based on a single predicted amount of sales or other activity measure.
- A **flexible budget,** also called a *variable budget,* is based on several different amounts of sales or other activity measure.

Exhibit 8.1 shows the fixed and flexible budgets for a guitar manufacturer.

EXHIBIT 8.1

Fixed versus Flexible Budgets (condensed)

Fixed Budget (One activity level)		Flexible Budget (Several activity levels)			
Sales (in units)............	100	Sales (in units)	100	120	140
Sales (in dollars)	$80,000	Sales (in dollars)...........	$80,000	$96,000	$112,000
Costs..................	56,000	Costs...................	56,000	67,200	78,400
Net income	$24,000	Net income	$24,000	$28,800	$ 33,600

Exhibit 8.1 shows that the guitar maker forecasts $24,000 of net income if it sells 100 guitars. Only if the guitar maker sells exactly 100 guitars will the fixed budget be useful in evaluating how well the company controlled costs. A flexible budget can be prepared for any sales level (three are shown in Exhibit 8.1). It is more useful when the actual number of units sold differs from the expected level of unit sales predicted.

We next look at fixed budget reports. Knowing the limitations of such reports helps us see the benefits of flexible budgets.

FIXED BUDGET REPORTS

Fixed Budget Performance Report

One use of a budget is to compare actual results with planned activities. Information for this analysis is often presented in a *performance report* that shows budgeted amounts, actual amounts, and **variances** (differences between budgeted and actual amounts). In a fixed budget, the master budget is based on a *single prediction* for sales volume, and the budgeted amount for each cost essentially assumes this specific (or *fixed*) amount of sales will occur.

We illustrate fixed budget performance reports with SolCel, which manufactures portable solar cell phone chargers and related supplies. For January 2017, SolCel based its fixed budget on a prediction of 10,000 (composite) units of sales; costs also were budgeted based on 10,000 composite units of sales.

Exhibit 8.2 shows a **fixed budget performance report,** a report that compares actual results with the results expected under a fixed budget. SolCel's actual sales for the period were 12,000 composite units. In addition, SolCel produced 12,000 composite units during the period (meaning its inventory level did not change). The final column in the performance report shows the differences (variances) between the budgeted and actual dollar amounts for each budget item.

EXHIBIT 8.2

Fixed Budget Performance
Report

SOLCEL Fixed Budget Performance Report For Month Ended January 31, 2017	Fixed Budget	Actual Results	Variances*
Sales (in units).	**10,000**	**12,000**	
Sales (in dollars)	$100,000	$125,000	$25,000 F
Cost of goods sold			
Direct materials	10,000	13,000	3,000 U
Direct labor.	15,000	20,000	5,000 U
Overhead			
Factory supplies	2,000	2,100	100 U
Utilities.	3,000	4,000	1,000 U
Depreciation—Machinery	8,000	8,000	0
Supervisory salaries	11,000	11,000	0
Selling expenses			
Sales commissions.	9,000	10,800	1,800 U
Shipping expenses.	4,000	4,300	300 U
General and administrative expenses			
Office supplies	5,000	5,200	200 U
Insurance expenses.	1,000	1,200	200 U
Depreciation—Office equipment.	7,000	7,000	0
Administrative salaries.	13,000	13,000	0
Total expenses	88,000	99,600	11,600 U
Income from operations.	$ 12,000	$ 25,400	$13,400 F

* F = Favorable variance; U = Unfavorable variance.

This type of performance report designates differences between budgeted and actual results as *variances*. We use the letters *F* and *U* to describe variances, with meanings as follows:

F = **Favorable variance**   When compared to budget, the actual cost or revenue contributes to a *higher* income. That is, actual revenue is higher than budgeted revenue, or actual cost is lower than budgeted cost.

U = **Unfavorable variance**   When compared to budget, the actual cost or revenue contributes to a *lower* income; actual revenue is lower than budgeted revenue, or actual cost is higher than budgeted cost.

Example: How is it that the favorable sales variance in Exhibit 8.2 is linked with so many unfavorable cost and expense variances? *Answer:* Costs have increased with the increase in sales.

Budget Reports for Evaluation

A primary use of budget reports is as a tool for management to monitor and control operations. From the fixed budget performance report in Exhibit 8.2, SolCel's management might raise questions such as:

- Why is actual income from operations $13,400 higher than budgeted?
- Is manufacturing using too much direct material?
- Is manufacturing using too much direct labor?
- Why are sales commissions higher than budgeted?
- Why are so many of the variances unfavorable?

The performance report in Exhibit 8.2 will not be very useful in answering these types of questions because it is not based on an "apples to apples" comparison. That is, the budgeted dollar amounts are based on 10,000 units of sales, but the actual dollar amounts are based on 12,000 units of sales. Clearly, the costs to make

12,000 units will be greater than the costs to make 10,000 units, so it is no surprise that SolCel's total expense variance is unfavorable. In addition, the costs in Exhibit 8.2 with the highest unfavorable variances (direct materials, direct labor, and sales commissions) are typically considered *variable* costs, which increase directly with sales activity. In general, the *fixed* budget performance report is not as useful in analyzing performance when actual sales differ from predicted sales. In the next section, we show how a *flexible* budget can be more useful in analyzing performance.

■ **Decision** Insight

Cruise Control Budget reporting and evaluation are used at service providers such as **Royal Caribbean Cruises**, **Carnival Cruise Line**, and **Norwegian Cruise Line**. These service providers regularly prepare performance plans and budget requests for their fleets of cruise ships, which describe performance goals, measure outcomes, and analyze variances. ■

© Melanie Stetson Freeman/The Christian Science Monitor/Getty Images

FLEXIBLE BUDGET REPORTS

Purpose of Flexible Budgets

To address limitations with the fixed budget performance report due to its lack of adjustment to changes in sales volume, management can use a flexible budget. A flexible budget is useful both before and after the period's activities are complete.

- A flexible budget prepared **before** the period is often based on several levels of activity. Budgets for those different levels can provide a "what-if" look at operations. The different levels often include both a best-case and worst-case scenario. This allows management to make adjustments to avoid or lessen the effects of the worst-case scenario.

- A flexible budget prepared **after** the period helps management evaluate past performance. It is especially useful for such an evaluation because it reflects budgeted revenues and costs based on the actual level of activity. The flexible budget gives an "apples to apples" comparison because the budgeted activity level is the same as the actual activity level. With a flexible budget, comparisons of actual results with budgeted performance are likely to reveal the real causes of any differences. Such information can help managers focus attention on real problem areas and implement corrective actions.

Preparation of Flexible Budgets

P1

Prepare a flexible budget and interpret a flexible budget performance report.

To prepare a flexible budget, follow these steps:

1 Identify the activity level, such as units produced or sold.

2 Identify costs and classify them as fixed or variable within the relevant range of activity.

3 Compute budgeted *sales* (sales price per unit × number of units of activity). Then subtract the sum of budgeted *variable costs* (variable cost per unit × number of units of activity) plus budgeted *fixed* costs.

In a flexible budget, we express each variable cost in one of two ways: either as (1) a constant dollar amount per unit of sales or as (2) a constant percentage of a sales dollar. In the case of a fixed cost, we express its budgeted amount as the total amount expected to occur at any sales volume within the relevant range.

Exhibit 8.3 shows a set of flexible budgets for SolCel for January 2017.

1 SolCel's management decides that the number of units sold is the relevant activity level. (For SolCel, the number of units sold equals the number of units produced.) For purposes of preparing the flexible budget, management decides it wants budgets at three different activity levels: 10,000 units, 12,000 units, and 14,000 units.

EXHIBIT 8.3

Flexible Budgets (prepared before the period)

SOLCEL
Flexible Budgets
For Month Ended January 31, 2017

| | Flexible Budget | | Flexible Budget for Unit Sales of | | |
	Variable Amount per Unit	Total Fixed Cost	10,000	12,000	14,000
Sales	$10.00		$100,000	$120,000	$140,000
Variable costs					
Direct materials	1.00		10,000	12,000	14,000
Direct labor.	1.50		15,000	18,000	21,000
Factory supplies	0.20		2,000	2,400	2,800
Utilities	0.30		3,000	3,600	4,200
Sales commissions.	0.90		9,000	10,800	12,600
Shipping expenses.	0.40		4,000	4,800	5,600
Office supplies	0.50		5,000	6,000	7,000
Total variable costs	4.80		48,000	57,600	67,200
Contribution margin	$ 5.20		$ 52,000	$ 62,400	$ 72,800
Fixed costs					
Depreciation—Machinery		$ 8,000	8,000	8,000	8,000
Supervisory salaries.		11,000	11,000	11,000	11,000
Insurance expense.		1,000	1,000	1,000	1,000
Depreciation—Office equipment.		7,000	7,000	7,000	7,000
Administrative salaries.		13,000	13,000	13,000	13,000
Total fixed costs		$40,000	40,000	40,000	40,000
Income from operations.			$ 12,000	$ 22,400	$ 32,800

2 SolCel's management classifies its costs as variable (seven items listed under the "Variable costs" heading) or fixed (five costs listed under the "Fixed costs" heading). These classifications result from management's investigation of each expense using techniques such as the high-low or regression methods we showed in a previous chapter. Variable and fixed expense categories are *not* the same for every company, and we must avoid drawing conclusions from specific cases.

3 SolCel uses the sales price per unit, the variable cost per unit for each variable cost, and the three activity levels to compute sales and variable costs. For example, at the three different activity levels, sales are budgeted to equal $100,000 (computed as $10 × 10,000), $120,000 (computed as $10 × 12,000), and $140,000 (computed as $10 × 14,000), respectively. Likewise, budgeted direct labor equals $15,000 (computed as $1.50 × 10,000) if 10,000 units are sold and $21,000 (computed as $1.50 × 14,000) if 14,000 units are sold. SolCel then lists each of the fixed costs in total.

The flexible budgets in Exhibit 8.3 follow a *contribution margin format*—beginning with sales followed by variable costs and then fixed costs. The first column of numbers in Exhibit 8.3 shows the variable costs per unit for each of SolCel's variable costs. The second column of numbers shows SolCel's fixed costs, which won't change in total as sales volume changes. The third, fourth, and fifth number columns show the flexible budget amounts computed for three different sales volumes. For instance, the third number column's flexible budget is based on 10,000 units. In this column, total variable costs for each of SolCel's seven variable costs are computed as the variable cost per unit (from column 1) multiplied by 10,000 units. The fixed cost amounts in this column are the same as those in the second number column. Overall, the fixed cost amounts in the third number column of Exhibit 8.3 are the same as those in the fixed budget of Exhibit 8.2 because the expected sales volume (10,000 units) is the same for both budgets.

Point: The usefulness of a flexible budget depends on valid classification of variable and fixed costs. Some costs are mixed and must be analyzed to determine their variable and fixed portions.

Example: Using Exhibit 8.3, what is the budgeted income from operations for unit sales of (a) 11,000 and (b) 13,000? *Answers:* $17,200 for unit sales of 11,000; $27,600 for unit sales of 13,000.

Point: Flexible budgeting allows a budget to be prepared at any *actual* output level. Performance reports are then prepared comparing the flexible budget to actual revenues and costs.

The flexible budget in Exhibit 8.3 also reports budgeted costs for activity levels of 12,000 and 14,000 units. The total variable costs increase as the activity levels increase, but the total fixed costs stay unchanged as activity increases. A flexible budget like that in Exhibit 8.3 can be useful to management in planning operations. In addition, as we will show in the next section, a flexible budget prepared after period-end is particularly useful in analyzing performance when actual sales volume differs from that predicted by a fixed budget.

Formula for Total Budgeted Costs   For approximate "what-if" analyses, management can compute total budgeted costs at any activity level with this flexible budget formula.

> **Total budgeted costs = Total fixed costs + (Total variable cost per unit × Units of activity level)**

Using this formula, management can compute total budgeted costs for any number of activity levels, and then, at the end of the period, compare actual costs to budgeted costs at any activity level. For example, if 11,250 units are actually sold, total budgeted costs are computed as:

$$\$94{,}000 = \$40{,}000 + (\$4.80 \times 11{,}250)$$

Flexible Budget Performance Report

SolCel's actual sales volume for January was 12,000 units. This sales volume is 2,000 units more than the 10,000 units originally predicted in the fixed budget. So, when management evaluates SolCel's performance, it needs a flexible budget showing actual and budgeted dollar amounts at 12,000 units.

A **flexible budget performance report** compares actual performance and budgeted performance based on actual sales volume (or other activity level). This report directs management's attention to those costs or revenues that differ substantially from budgeted amounts. In SolCel's

EXHIBIT 8.4

Flexible Budget Performance Report (prepared after the period)

SOLCEL Flexible Budget Performance Report For Month Ended January 31, 2017	Flexible Budget (12,000 units)	Actual Results (12,000 units)	Variances*
Sales..	$120,000	$125,000	$5,000 F
Variable costs			
Direct materials..........................	12,000	13,000	1,000 U
Direct labor.............................	18,000	20,000	2,000 U
Factory supplies.........................	2,400	2,100	300 F
Utilities................................	3,600	4,000	400 U
Sales commissions.......................	10,800	10,800	0
Shipping expenses.......................	4,800	4,300	500 F
Office supplies..........................	6,000	5,200	800 F
Total variable costs......................	57,600	59,400	1,800 U
Contribution margin......................	62,400	65,600	3,200 F
Fixed costs			
Depreciation—Machinery....................	8,000	8,000	0
Supervisory salaries......................	11,000	11,000	0
Insurance expense.......................	1,000	1,200	200 U
Depreciation—Office equipment.............	7,000	7,000	0
Administrative salaries....................	13,000	13,000	0
Total fixed costs........................	40,000	40,200	200 U
Income from operations...................	$ 22,400	$ 25,400	$3,000 F

Point: Total budgeted costs = $97,600, computed as $40,000 + ($4.80 × 12,000).

* F = Favorable variance; U = Unfavorable variance.

case, we prepare this report after January's sales volume is known to be 12,000 units. Exhibit 8.4 shows SolCel's flexible budget performance report for January.

The flexible budget report shows a favorable income variance of $3,000. Management uses this report to investigate variances and evaluate SolCel's performance. Quite often management will focus on large variances. This report shows a $5,000 favorable variance in total dollar sales. Because actual and budgeted volumes are both 12,000 units, the $5,000 favorable sales variance must have resulted from a higher-than-expected selling price. Management would like to determine if the conditions that resulted in higher selling prices are likely to continue.

The other variances in Exhibit 8.4 also direct management's attention to areas where corrective actions can help control SolCel's operations. For example, both the direct materials and direct labor variances are relatively large and unfavorable. On the other hand, relatively large favorable variances are observed for shipping expenses and office supplies. Management will try to determine the causes for these variances, both favorable and unfavorable, and make changes to SolCel's operations if needed.

In addition to analyzing variances using a flexible budget performance report, management can also take a more detailed approach based on a *standard cost* system. We illustrate this analysis next in the Standard Costs section.

Decision Maker

Entrepreneur The head of the strategic consulting division of your financial services firm complains to you about the unfavorable variances on the division's performance reports. "We worked on more consulting assignments than planned. It's not surprising our costs are higher than expected. To top it off, this report characterizes our work as *poor*!" How do you respond? ■ *Answer:* From the complaints, this performance report appears to compare actual results with a fixed budget. This comparison is useful in determining whether the amount of work actually performed was more or less than planned, but it is not useful in determining whether the division was more or less efficient than planned. If the division worked on more assignments than expected, some costs will certainly increase. Therefore, you should prepare a flexible budget using the actual number of consulting assignments and then compare actual performance to the flexible budget.

A manufacturing company reports the following fixed budget and actual results for the past year. The fixed budget assumes a selling price of $40 per unit. The fixed budget is based on 20,000 units of sales, and the actual results are based on 24,000 units of sales. Prepare a flexible budget performance report for the past year. Label variances as favorable (F) or unfavorable (U).

NEED-TO-KNOW 8-1

Flexible Budget

P1

	Fixed Budget (20,000 units)	Actual Results (24,000 units)
Sales	$800,000	$972,000
Variable costs*	160,000	240,000
Fixed costs	500,000	490,000

*Budgeted variable cost per unit = $160,000/20,000 = $8.00

Solution

Flexible Budget Performance Report			
	Flexible Budget (24,000 units)	Actual Results (24,000 units)	Variances
Sales	$960,000*	$972,000	$12,000 F
Variable costs	192,000**	240,000	48,000 U
Contribution margin	768,000	732,000	36,000 U
Fixed costs	500,000	490,000	10,000 F
Income from operations...........	$268,000	$242,000	$26,000 U

*24,000 × $40   **24,000 × $8

Do More: QS 8-1, QS 8-2, QS 8-3, QS 8-4, E 8-3, E 8-4

Section 2—Standard Costs

C1
_____

Define *standard costs* and explain how standard cost information is useful for management by exception.

We show how *standard costs* can be used in a flexible budgeting system to enable management to better understand the reasons for variances. **Standard costs** are preset costs for delivering a product or service under normal conditions. These costs are established by personnel, engineering, and accounting studies using past experiences. Standard costs vary across companies, though manufacturing companies usually use standard costing for direct materials, direct labor, and overhead costs.

Management can use standard costs to assess the reasonableness of actual costs incurred for producing the product or providing the service. When actual costs vary from standard costs, management follows up to identify potential problems and take corrective actions. **Management by exception** means that managers focus attention on the most significant differences between actual costs and standard costs and give less attention to areas where performance is reasonably close to standard. Management by exception is especially useful when directed at controllable items, enabling top management to affect the actions of lower-level managers responsible for the company's revenues and costs.

Standard costs are often used in preparing budgets because they are the anticipated costs incurred under normal conditions. Terms such as *standard materials cost, standard labor cost,* and *standard overhead cost* are often used to refer to amounts budgeted for direct materials, direct labor, and overhead.

While many managers use standard costs to investigate manufacturing costs, standard costs can also help control *nonmanufacturing* costs. Companies providing services instead of products can also benefit from the use of standard costs. For example, while quality medical service is paramount, efficiency in providing that service is also important in controlling medical costs. The use of budgeting and standard costing is touted as an effective means to control and monitor medical costs, especially overhead.

MATERIALS AND LABOR STANDARDS

This section explains how to set direct materials and direct labor standards and how to prepare a standard cost card. Managerial accountants, engineers, personnel administrators, and other managers work together to set standard costs. To identify standards for direct labor costs, we can conduct time and motion studies for each labor operation in the process of providing a product or service. From these studies, management can learn the best way to perform the operation and then set the standard labor time required for the operation under normal conditions. Similarly, standards for direct materials are set by studying the quantity, grade, and cost of each material used. Standards should be challenging but attainable and should acknowledge machine breakdowns, material waste, and idle time.

Example: What factors might be considered when deciding whether to revise standard costs? *Answer:* Changes in the processes and/or resources needed to carry out the processes.

Regardless of the care used in setting standard costs and in revising them as conditions change, actual costs frequently differ from standard costs. For instance, the actual quantity of material or hours of direct labor used can differ from the standard, or the price paid per unit of material or hours of direct labor can differ from the standard.

Decision Insight

Cruis'n Standards   The **Tesla** Model S consists of hundreds of parts for which engineers set standards. Various types of labor are also involved in its production, including machining, assembly, painting, and welding, and standards are set for each. Actual results are periodically compared with standards to assess performance. ∎

© Jasper Juinen/Bloomberg via Getty Images

Setting Standard Costs

To illustrate the setting of standard costs, we consider wooden baseball bats manufactured by ProBat. Its engineers have determined that manufacturing one bat requires 0.90 kilograms (kg) of high-grade wood. They also expect some loss of material as part of the process because of inefficiencies and waste. This results in adding an *allowance* of 0.10 kg, making the standard requirement 1.0 kg of wood for each bat.

The 0.90 kg portion is called an *ideal standard;* it is the quantity of material required if the process is 100% efficient without any loss or waste. Reality suggests that some loss of material usually occurs with any process. The standard of 1.0 kg is known as the *practical standard,* the quantity of material required under normal application of the process. The standard direct labor rate should include allowances for employee breaks, cleanup, and machine downtime. Most companies use practical rather than ideal standards.

Point: Companies promoting continuous improvement strive to achieve ideal standards by eliminating inefficiencies and waste.

ProBat needs to develop standard costs for direct materials, direct labor, and overhead. For direct materials and direct labor, ProBat must develop standard quantities and standard prices. For overhead, ProBat must consider the activities that drive overhead costs. ProBat's standard costs are:

Direct materials High-grade wood is purchased at a standard price of $25 per kg. The purchasing department sets this price as the expected price for the budget period. To determine this price, the purchasing department considers factors such as the quality of materials, economic conditions, supply factors (shortages and excesses), and available discounts.

Direct labor Two hours of labor time are required to manufacture a bat. The direct labor rate is $20 per hour (better-than-average skilled labor is required). This rate includes wages, taxes, and fringe benefits. When wage rates differ across employees due to seniority or skill level, the standard direct labor rate is based on the expected mix of workers.

Overhead ProBat assigns overhead at the rate of $10 per direct labor hour.

The standard costs of direct materials, direct labor, and overhead for one bat are shown in Exhibit 8.5 in a *standard cost card.* These standard cost amounts are then used to prepare manufacturing budgets for a budgeted level of production.

EXHIBIT 8.5

Standard Cost Card

STANDARD COST CARD			
Production Factor	**Standard Quantity**	**Standard Cost per Unit**	**Total Standard Cost**
Direct materials (wood)	**1 kg**	**$25 per kg**	**$25**
Direct labor	**2 hours**	**$20 per hour**	40
Overhead	**2 labor hours**	**$10 per hour**	20
		Total	**$85**

Cost Variance Analysis

Companies analyze differences between actual costs and standard costs to assess performance. A **cost variance,** also simply called a *variance,* is the difference between actual and standard costs. Cost variances can be favorable (F) or unfavorable (U).

  C2

Describe cost variances and what they reveal about performance.

- If actual cost is less than standard cost, the variance is considered favorable (F).
- If actual costs are greater than standard costs, the variance is unfavorable (U).[1]

This section discusses cost variance analysis. (In the Decision Analysis section of this chapter, we discuss sales variances.)

---

[1] Short-term favorable variances can sometimes lead to long-term unfavorable variances. For instance, if management spends less than the budgeted amount on maintenance or insurance, the performance report would show a favorable variance. Cutting these expenses can lead to major losses in the long run if machinery wears out prematurely or insurance coverage proves inadequate.

Exhibit 8.6 shows the flow of events in **variance analysis:** (1) preparing a standard cost performance report, (2) computing and analyzing variances, (3) identifying questions and their explanations, and (4) taking corrective and strategic actions (if needed). These variance analysis steps are interrelated and are frequently applied in good organizations.

EXHIBIT 8.6

Variance Analysis

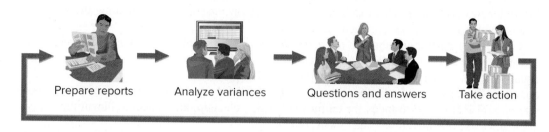

Prepare reports → Analyze variances → Questions and answers → Take action

Cost Variance Computation   Exhibit 8.7 shows a general formula for computing any cost variance (CV).

EXHIBIT 8.7

Cost Variance Formulas*

$$\underset{AQ \times AP}{\text{Actual Cost (AC)}} \quad - \quad \underset{SQ \times SP}{\text{Standard Cost (SC)}}$$

Cost Variance (CV)

*AQ is actual quantity; AP is actual price; SP is standard price; SQ is standard quantity allowed for actual output.

Actual quantity (AQ) is the actual amount of material or labor used to manufacture the actual quantity of output for the period. Standard quantity (SQ) is the standard amount of input for the actual quantity of output for the period. For example, if ProBat's actual output is 500 bats, its standard quantity of direct labor is 1,000 hours (500 bats × 2 hours per bat). Actual price (AP) is the actual amount paid to acquire the actual direct material or direct labor used for the period. SP is the standard price.

Model of Price and Quantity Variances   Two main factors cause a cost variance:

1. A difference between actual price per unit of input and standard price per unit of input results in a **price** (or rate) **variance.**
2. A difference between actual quantity of input used and standard quantity of input used results in a **quantity** (or usage or efficiency) **variance.**

Isolating these price and quantity factors in a cost variance leads to the formulas in Exhibit 8.8.

EXHIBIT 8.8

Price Variance and Quantity Variance Formulas

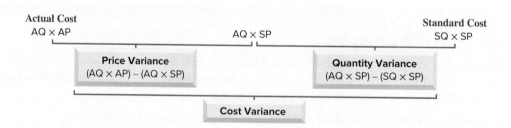

Actual Cost		Standard Cost
AQ × AP	AQ × SP	SQ × SP

Price Variance
(AQ × AP) − (AQ × SP)

Quantity Variance
(AQ × SP) − (SQ × SP)

Cost Variance

The model in Exhibit 8.8 separates total cost variance into separate price and quantity variances, which is useful in analyzing performance. Exhibit 8.8 illustrates three important rules in computing variances:

1. In computing a price variance, the quantity (actual) is held constant.
2. In computing a quantity variance, the price (standard) is held constant.
3. Cost variance, or total variance, is the sum of price and quantity variances.

Managers sometimes find it useful to use an alternative (but equivalent) computation for the price and quantity variances, as shown in Exhibit 8.9.

> Price Variance (PV) = [**Actual Price** (AP) − **Standard Price** (SP)] × **Actual Quantity** (AQ)
>
> Quantity Variance (QV) = [**Actual Quantity** (AQ) − **Standard Quantity** (SQ)] × **Standard Price** (SP)

The results from applying the formulas in Exhibits 8.8 and 8.9 are identical.

Computing Materials and Labor Variances

We show how to compute the direct materials and direct labor cost variances using data from G-Max, a manufacturer of specialty golf equipment and accessories. G-Max set the following standard quantities and costs for direct materials and direct labor per unit for one of its hand-crafted golf clubheads:

Standard Quantities and Costs	
Direct materials (0.5 lb. per unit at $20 per lb.)	$10.00
Direct labor (1 hr. per unit at $16 per hr.)	16.00
Total standard direct cost per unit.	$26.00

Materials Cost Variances During May 2017, G-Max budgeted to produce 4,000 club-heads (units). It actually produced only 3,500 units. It used 1,800 pounds of direct materials (ti-tanium) costing $21 per pound, meaning its total direct materials cost was $37,800. To produce 3,500 units, G-Max should have used 1,750 pounds of direct materials (3,500 × 0.5 lb. per unit). This amount of 1,750 pounds is the standard quantity of direct materials that should have been used to produce 3,500 units. This information allows us to compute both actual and standard direct materials costs for G-Max's 3,500 units and its total direct materials cost variance as follows:

Direct Materials	Quantity		Price per Unit		Cost
Actual cost	1,800 lbs.	×	$21 per lb.	=	$37,800
Standard cost	1,750 lbs.*	×	$20 per lb.	=	35,000
Direct materials cost variance				=	**$ 2,800** U

© Kristjan Maack/Getty Images/ Nordic Photos

*Standard quantity = 3,500 units × 0.5 lb. per unit

Management wishes to determine if this unfavorable cost variance is due to unfavorable quantity or price variances, or both. To better isolate the causes of this $2,800 unfavorable total direct materials cost variance, the materials price and quantity variances are computed and shown in Exhibit 8.10.

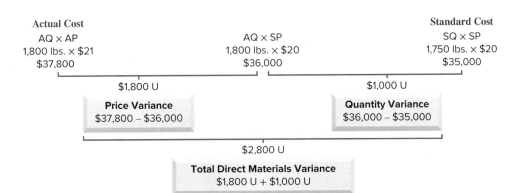

*AQ is actual quantity; AP is actual price; SP is standard price; SQ is standard quantity allowed for actual output.

We now can see the two components of the $2,800 unfavorable direct materials cost variance: The $1,800 unfavorable price variance results from paying $1 more per pound than the standard price, computed as 1,800 lbs. × $1. G-Max also used 50 pounds more of materials than the standard quantity (1,800 actual pounds −1,750 standard pounds). The $1,000 unfavorable quantity variance is computed as [(1,800 actual lbs. − 1,750 standard lbs.) × $20 standard price per lb.]. Detailed price and quantity variances allow management to ask the responsible individuals for explanations and corrective actions.

Evaluating Materials Variances   The purchasing department is usually responsible for the price paid for materials. Responsibility for explaining the price variance in this case rests with the purchasing manager as a price higher than standard caused the variance. The production department is usually responsible for the amount of material used. In this case, the production manager is responsible for explaining why the process used more than the standard amount of materials.

Variance analysis presents challenges. For instance, the production department could have used more than the standard amount of material because the materials' quality did not meet specifications and led to excessive waste. In this case, the purchasing manager is responsible for explaining why inferior materials were acquired. However, if analysis shows that waste was due to inefficiencies, not poor-quality material, the production manager is responsible for explaining what happened.

In evaluating price variances, managers must recognize that a favorable price variance can indicate a problem with poor product quality. **Redhook Ale**, a microbrewery in the Pacific Northwest, can probably save 10% to 15% in material prices by buying six-row barley malt instead of the better two-row from Washington's Yakima Valley. Attention to quality, however, has helped Redhook Ale increase its sales. Purchasing activities are judged on both the quality of the materials and the purchase price variance.

© ClarkandCompany/Getty Images

NEED-TO-KNOW 8-2

Direct Materials Price and Quantity Variances

P2

Do More: QS 8-8, E 8-9, E 8-11, E 8-12, E 8-13

A manufacturing company reports the following for one of its products. Compute the direct materials (*a*) price variance and (*b*) quantity variance and classify each as favorable or unfavorable.

Direct materials standard.................	8 pounds @ $6 per pound
Actual direct materials used	83,000 pounds @ $5.80 per pound
Actual finished units produced	10,000

Solution

a. Price variance   = (Actual quantity × Actual price) − (Actual quantity × Standard price)
  = (83,000 × $5.80) − (83,000 × $6) = $16,600 Favorable

b. Quantity variance = (Actual quantity × Standard price) − (Standard quantity* × Standard price)
  = (83,000 × $6) − (80,000 × $6) = $18,000 Unfavorable

*Standard quantity = 10,000 units × 8 standard pounds per unit = 80,000 pounds

Labor Cost Variances   Labor cost for a product or service depends on the number of hours worked (quantity) and the wage rate paid to employees (price). To illustrate, G-Max's direct labor standard for 3,500 units of its handcrafted clubheads is one direct labor hour per unit, or 3,500 hours at $16 per hour. But because only 3,400 hours at $16.50 per hour were actually used to complete the units, the actual and standard direct labor costs are:

Direct Labor	Quantity	Rate per Hour	Cost
Actual cost	3,400 hrs.	× $16.50 per hr.	= $56,100
Standard cost	3,500 hrs.*	× $16.00 per hr.	= 56,000
Direct labor cost variance			= $ 100 U

*Standard quantity = 3,500 units × 1 standard direct labor hour per unit

Actual direct labor cost is merely $100 over the standard; that small difference might suggest no immediate concern. A closer look, however, might suggest problems. The direct labor cost variance can be divided into price and quantity variances, which are usually called *rate* and *efficiency* variances. Computing both the labor rate and efficiency variances reveals a more precise picture, as shown in Exhibit 8.11.

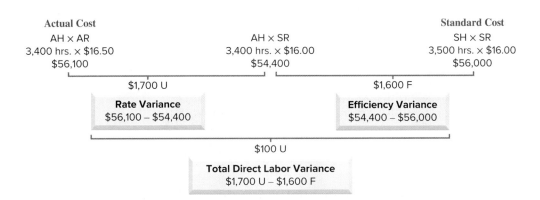

EXHIBIT 8.11

Labor Rate and Efficiency Variances*

* Here, we employ hours (H) for quantity (Q), and the wage rate (R) for price (P). Thus: AH is actual direct labor hours; AR is actual wage rate; SH is standard direct labor hours allowed for actual output; SR is standard wage rate.

Point: The direct labor efficiency variance can also be computed as $(3,400 - 3,500) \times \$16 = \$1,600$. The direct labor rate variance can also be computed as $(\$16.50 - \$16) \times 3,400 = \$1,700$.

Evaluating Labor Variances   Exhibit 8.11 shows that the $100 total unfavorable labor cost variance results from a $1,600 favorable efficiency variance and a $1,700 unfavorable rate variance. To produce 3,500 units, G-Max should use 3,500 direct labor hours (3,500 units × 1 direct labor hour per unit). The favorable efficiency variance results from using 100 fewer direct labor hours (3,400 actual DLH − 3,500 standard DLH) than standard for the units produced. The unfavorable rate variance results from paying a wage rate that is $0.50 per hour higher ($16.50 actual rate − $16.00 standard rate) than standard. The personnel administrator or the production manager needs to explain why the wage rate is higher than expected. The production manager should explain how the labor hours were reduced. If this experience can be repeated and transferred to other departments, more savings are possible.

One possible explanation of these labor rate and efficiency variances is the use of workers with different skill levels. If so, management must discuss the implications with the production manager who assigns workers to tasks. In this case, an investigation might show that higher-skilled workers were used to produce 3,500 units of handcrafted clubheads. As a result, fewer labor hours might be required for the work, but the wage rate paid these workers is higher than standard because of their greater skills. The effect of this strategy is a higher-than-standard total cost, which would require actions to remedy the situation or adjust the standard.

Other explanations for direct labor variances are possible. Lower-quality materials, poor employee training or supervision, equipment breakdowns, and idle workers due to reduced demand for the company's products could lead to unfavorable direct labor efficiency variances.

Example: Compute the rate variance and the efficiency variance for Exhibit 8.11 if 3,700 actual hours are used at an actual price of $15.50 per hour. *Answer:* $1,700 favorable labor rate variance and $3,200 unfavorable labor efficiency variance.

 **Decision** Maker

Production Manager   You receive the manufacturing variance report for June and discover a large unfavorable labor efficiency (quantity) variance. What factors do you investigate to identify its possible causes? ■   *Answer:* An unfavorable labor efficiency variance occurs because more labor hours than standard were used during the period. Possible reasons for this include: (1) materials quality could be poor, resulting in more labor consumption due to rework; (2) unplanned interruptions (strike, breakdowns, accidents) could have occurred during the period; and (3) a different labor mix might have occurred for a strategic reason such as to expedite orders. This new labor mix could have consisted of a larger proportion of untrained labor, which resulted in more labor hours.

NEED-TO-KNOW 8-3

Direct Labor Rate and
Efficiency Variances

P2

The following information is available for a manufacturer. Compute the direct labor rate and efficiency variances and label them as favorable (F) or unfavorable (U).

Actual direct labor cost (6,250 hours @ $13.10 per hour)...............	$81,875
Standard direct labor hours per unit.................................	2.0 hours
Standard direct labor rate per hour.................................	$13.00
Actual production (units)...	2,500 units
Budgeted production (units)..	3,000 units

Solution

Do More: QS 8-11, E 8-10,
E 8-11, E 8-12, E 8-16

Total standard hours = 2,500 × 2.0 = 5,000
Rate variance   = ($13.10 − $13.00) × 6,250 = $625 U
Efficiency variance   = (6,250 − 5,000) × $13.00 = $16,250 U

OVERHEAD STANDARDS AND VARIANCES

In previous chapters we showed how companies can use *predetermined overhead rates* to allocate overhead costs to products or services. In a standard costing system, this allocation is done using the *standard* amount of the overhead allocation base, such as standard labor hours or standard machine hours. We now show how to use standard costs to develop flexible overhead budgets.

Flexible Overhead Budgets

Standard overhead costs are the overhead amounts expected to occur at a certain activity level. Overhead includes fixed costs and variable costs. This requires management to classify overhead costs as fixed or variable (within a relevant range), and to develop a flexible budget for overhead costs.

To illustrate, the first two number columns of Exhibit 8.12 show the overhead cost structure to develop G-Max's flexible overhead budgets for May 2017. At the beginning of the year, G-Max predicted variable overhead costs of $1.00 per unit (clubhead), comprised of $0.40 per unit for indirect labor, $0.30 per unit for indirect materials, $0.20 per unit for power and lights, and $0.10 per unit for factory maintenance. In addition, G-Max predicts monthly fixed overhead of $4,000.

With these variable and fixed overhead cost amounts, G-Max can prepare flexible overhead budgets at various capacity levels (four rightmost number columns in Exhibit 8.12). At its maximum capacity (100% column), G-Max could produce 5,000 clubheads. At 70% of maximum capacity, G-Max could produce 3,500 (computed as 5,000 × 70%) clubheads. Recall that total variable costs will increase as production activity increases, but total fixed costs will not change as production activity changes. At 70% capacity, variable overhead costs are budgeted at $3,500 (3,500 × $1.00), while at 100% capacity variable costs are budgeted at $5,000 (5,000 × $1.00). At all capacity levels within the relevant range, fixed overhead costs are budgeted at $4,000 per month.

Point: With increased automation, machine hours are frequently used in applying overhead instead of labor hours.

Standard Overhead Rate

To apply overhead costs to products or services, management establishes the standard overhead cost rate using the three-step process below.

Step 1: Determine an Allocation Base   The allocation base is a measure of input that management believes is related to overhead costs. Examples can include direct labor hours or machine hours. In this section, we assume that G-Max uses direct labor hours as an allocation base, and it has a standard of one direct labor hour per finished unit.

© Halfdark/Getty Images

G-MAX Flexible Overhead Budgets For Month Ended May 31, 2017 Flexible Budget	Variable Amount per Unit	Total Fixed Cost	Flexible Budget at Capacity Level of			
			70%	80%	90%	100%
Production (in units)	1 unit		3,500	4,000	4,500	5,000
Factory overhead						
Variable costs						
Indirect labor	$0.40/unit		$1,400	$1,600	$1,800	$2,000
Indirect materials.	0.30/unit		1,050	1,200	1,350	1,500
Power and lights	0.20/unit		700	800	900	1,000
Maintenance	0.10/unit		350	400	450	500
Total variable overhead costs.	$1.00/unit		3,500	4,000	4,500	5,000
Fixed costs (per month)						
Building rent		$1,000	1,000	1,000	1,000	1,000
Depreciation—Machinery		1,200	1,200	1,200	1,200	1,200
Supervisory salaries		1,800	1,800	1,800	1,800	1,800
Total fixed overhead costs		$4,000	4,000	4,000	4,000	4,000
Total factory overhead.			$7,500	$8,000	$8,500	$9,000
Standard direct labor hours (1 DL hr./unit). . . .			3,500 hrs.	4,000 hrs.	4,500 hrs.	5,000 hrs.
Predetermined overhead rate per standard direct labor hour.				$ 2.00		

EXHIBIT 8.12

Flexible Overhead Budgets

Step 2: Choose a Predicted Activity Level
When choosing the predicted activity level, management considers many factors. The level is rarely set at 100% of capacity. Difficulties in scheduling work, equipment breakdowns, and insufficient product demand typically cause the activity level to be less than full capacity. Also, good long-run management practices usually call for some excess plant capacity, to allow for special opportunities and demand changes. G-Max managers predicted an 80% activity level for May, or a production volume of 4,000 clubheads.

Point: According to the U.S. Federal Reserve Board, U.S. businesses operated at an average capacity level of 80.1% between 1972 and 2013. Average capacity usage levels ranged from 78.7% for manufacturing businesses to 87.4% for mining companies.

Step 3: Compute the Standard Overhead Rate
At the predicted activity level of 4,000 units, the flexible budget in Exhibit 8.12 predicts total overhead of $8,000. At this activity level of 4,000 units, G-Max's standard direct labor hours are 4,000 hours (4,000 units × 1 direct labor hour per unit). G-Max's standard overhead rate is then computed as:

$$\text{Standard overhead rate} = \frac{\text{Total overhead cost at predicted activity level}}{\text{Total direct labor hours at predicted activity level}}$$

$$= \frac{\$8,000}{4,000} = \$2 \text{ per direct labor hour}$$

This standard overhead rate is used in computing overhead cost variances, as we show next, and in recording journal entries in a standard cost system, which we show in the appendix to this chapter.

Example: What would G-Max's standard overhead rate per unit be if management expected to operate at 70% capacity? At 100% capacity? *Answer:* At 70% capacity, the standard overhead rate is $2.14 per unit (rounded), computed as $7,500/3,500 direct labor hours. At 100% capacity, the standard overhead rate per unit is $1.80 ($9,000/5,000).

Decision Insight

Measuring Up In the spirit of continuous improvement, competitors compare their processes and performance standards against benchmarks established by industry leaders. Companies that use **benchmarking** include **Jiffy Lube**, **All Tune and Lube**, and **SpeeDee Oil Change and Auto Service**. ∎

P3_____

Compute overhead controllable and volume variances.

EXHIBIT 8.13

Applying Standard Overhead Cost

Computing Overhead Cost Variances

In a standard costing system, overhead is applied with the formula in Exhibit 8.13.

$$\begin{array}{c} \text{Standard overhead} \\ \text{applied} \end{array} = \begin{array}{c} \text{Actual} \\ \text{production} \end{array} \times \begin{array}{c} \text{Standard amount of} \\ \text{allocation base} \end{array} \times \begin{array}{c} \text{Standard overhead rate} \\ \text{(at predicted activity level)} \end{array}$$

The standard overhead applied is based on the standard amount of the allocation base that *should have been used,* based on the actual production. This standard activity amount is then multiplied by the predetermined standard overhead rate (at the predicted activity level). For G-Max, standard overhead applied is computed as:

$$3,500 \text{ units} \times 1 \text{ DLH per unit} \times \$2.00 \text{ per DLH} = \$7,000$$

G-Max produced 3,500 units during the month, which should have used 3,500 direct labor hours. At G-Max's predicted capacity level of 80%, the standard overhead rate was $2.00 per direct labor hour. The standard overhead applied is $7,000, as computed above.

Actual overhead incurred might differ from the standard overhead applied for the period, and management again will use *variance analysis*. The difference between the standard amount of overhead cost applied and the total actual overhead incurred is the **overhead cost variance** (total overhead variance), shown in Exhibit 8.14.

EXHIBIT 8.14

Overhead Cost Variance

$$\begin{array}{c} \text{Overhead cost} \\ \text{variance (OCV)} \end{array} = \begin{array}{c} \text{Actual overhead} \\ \text{incurred (AOI)} \end{array} - \begin{array}{c} \text{Standard overhead} \\ \text{applied (SOA)} \end{array}$$

To illustrate, G-Max's actual overhead cost incurred in the month (found in other cost reports) is $7,650. Using the formula in Exhibit 8.14, G-Max's total overhead variance is $650, computed as:

Total Overhead Variance	
Actual total overhead (given)	$7,650
Standard overhead applied (3,500 units × 1 DLH per unit × $2.00 per DLH)	7,000
Total overhead variance	$ 650 U

This variance is unfavorable: G-Max's actual overhead was higher than the standard amount.

Overhead Controllable and Volume Variances   To help identify factors causing the total overhead cost variance, managers compute *overhead volume* and *overhead controllable variances,* as illustrated in Exhibit 8.15. The results are useful for taking strategic actions to improve company performance.

EXHIBIT 8.15

Framework for Understanding Total Overhead Variance

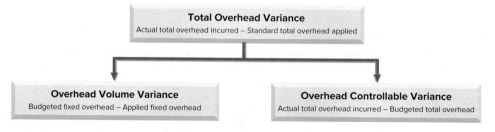

A **volume variance** occurs when the company operates at a different capacity level than was predicted. G-Max predicted it would manufacture 4,000 units, but it only manufactured

3,500 units. The volume variance is usually considered outside the control of the production manager, as it depends mainly on customer demand for the company's products.

The volume variance is based solely on *fixed* overhead. Recall that G-Max's standard *fixed* overhead rate at the predicted capacity level of 4,000 units was $1 per direct labor hour. The overhead volume variance is computed as:

Overhead Volume Variance	
Budgeted fixed overhead (at predicted capacity)	$4,000
Applied fixed overhead (3,500 units × 1 DLH per unit × $1.00 per DLH)	3,500
Volume variance	$ 500 U

The volume variance is unfavorable because G-Max made 500 fewer units than it expected. With a total overhead variance of $650 (unfavorable) and a volume variance of $500 (unfavorable), the controllable overhead variance is computed as:

Controllable variance = Total overhead variance − Overhead volume variance
$$\$150 \text{ U} = \$650 - \$500$$

More formally, the **controllable variance** is the difference between the actual overhead costs incurred and the budgeted overhead costs for the standard hours that should have been used for actual production. Controllable variance is the portion of total overhead variance that is considered to be under management's control. Since G-Max only produced 3,500 units during the month, we need to compare *actual* overhead costs to make 3,500 units to the *budgeted* cost to make 3,500 units. Budgeted total overhead cost to make 3,500 units is computed as:

Budgeted Total Overhead Cost	
Budgeted variable overhead cost	
(3,500 units × 1 DLH per unit × $1 VOH* rate per DLH)	$3,500
Budgeted fixed overhead cost	4,000
Budgeted total overhead cost	$7,500

*VOH is variable overhead

Controllable variance is then computed as:

Overhead Controllable Variance	
Actual total overhead (given)	$7,650
Budgeted total overhead (from above)	7,500
Controllable variance	$ 150 U

Analyzing Overhead Controllable and Volume Variances How should management of G-Max interpret the unfavorable overhead controllable and volume variances? An unfavorable volume variance means that the company did not reach its predicted operating level. In this case, 80% of manufacturing capacity was budgeted, but only 70% was used. Management needs to know why the actual level of production differs from the expected level. The main purpose of the volume variance is to identify what portion of total overhead variance is caused by failing to meet the expected production level. Often the reasons for failing to meet this expected production level are due to factors, such as customer demand, that are beyond employees' control. This information permits management to focus on explanations for the controllable variance, as we discuss next.

Overhead Variance Reports

To help management isolate the reasons for the $150 unfavorable overhead controllable variance, an *overhead variance report* can be prepared. A complete overhead variance report provides managers information about specific overhead costs and how they differ from budgeted amounts. Exhibit 8.16 shows G-Max's overhead variance report for May. The overhead variance report shows the total overhead volume variance of $500 unfavorable (shown near the top of the report) and the $150 unfavorable overhead controllable variance (shown at the bottom right of the report). The detailed listing of individual overhead costs reveals the following: (1) Fixed overhead costs and variable factory maintenance costs were incurred as expected. (2) Costs for indirect labor and power and lights were higher than expected. (3) Indirect materials cost was less than expected. Management can use the variance overhead report to identify the individual overhead costs it wants to investigate.

Appendix 8A describes an expanded analysis of overhead variances.

EXHIBIT 8.16

Overhead Variance Report

G-MAX Overhead Variance Report For Month Ended May 31, 2017			
Overhead Volume Variance			
Expected production level..........................	80% of capacity (4,000 units)		
Production level achieved	70% of capacity (3,500 units)		
Budgeted fixed overhead (4,000 DLH × $1.00).........	$4,000		
Fixed overhead applied (3,500 DLH × $1.00)	$3,500		
Volume variance..................................	$ 500 U ◄		

Overhead Controllable Variance	Flexible Budget	Actual Results	Variances*
Variable overhead costs			
Indirect labor	$1,400	$1,525	$125 U
Indirect materials...............................	1,050	1,025	25 F
Power and lights	700	750	50 U
Maintenance.....................................	350	350	0
Total variable overhead costs.....................	3,500	3,650	150 U
Fixed overhead costs			
Building rent....................................	1,000	1,000	0
Depreciation—Machinery	1,200	1,200	0
Supervisory salaries.............................	1,800	1,800	0
Total fixed overhead costs........................	4,000	4,000	0
Total overhead costs	$7,500	$7,650	$150 U ◄

Total overhead variance = $650 unfavorable

Point: Both the flexible budget and actual results are based on 3,500 units produced.

* F = Favorable variance; U = Unfavorable variance.

NEED-TO-KNOW 8-4

Overhead Variances

P3

A manufacturing company uses standard costs and reports the information below for January. The company uses machine hours to apply overhead, and the standard is two machine hours per finished unit. Compute the total overhead cost variance, overhead controllable variance, and overhead volume variance for January. Indicate whether each variance is favorable or unfavorable.

Predicted activity level.........................	1,500 units
Variable overhead rate budgeted	$2.50 per machine hour
Fixed overhead budgeted	$6,000 per month ($2.00 per machine hour at predicted activity level)
Actual activity level...........................	1,800 units
Actual overhead costs	$15,800

Solution

Total overhead cost variance

Actual total overhead cost (given)...	$15,800
Standard overhead applied (1,800 × 2 × $4.50)...........................	16,200
Total overhead variance...	$ 400 F

> Do More: QS 8-13, QS 8-14, QS 8-15, E 8-17, E 8-19, E 8-20

Overhead controllable variance

Actual total overhead cost (given)......................................	$15,800
Budgeted total overhead (1,800 × 2 × $2.50) + $6,000................	15,000
Overhead controllable variance	$ 800 U

Overhead volume variance

Budgeted fixed overhead........................	$ 6,000
Applied fixed overhead (1,800 × 2 × $2)	7,200
Overhead volume variance	$1,200 F

Standard Costing—Management Considerations

Companies must consider many factors, both positive and negative, in deciding whether and how to use standard costing systems. Exhibit 8.17 summarizes some of these factors.

EXHIBIT 8.17

Standard Costing Pros and Cons

Standard Costing Considerations	
Positives	**Negatives**
Provides benchmarks for management by exception.	Standards are costly to develop and keep up to date.
Motivates employees to work toward goals.	Variances are not timely for adapting to rapidly changing business conditions.
Useful in the budgeting process.	
Isolates reasons for good or bad performance.	Employees might not try for continuous improvement.

 SUSTAINABILITY AND ACCOUNTING

As more companies report on their sustainability efforts, organizations provide structure for these reports. One group, the **International Integrated Reporting Council** (IIRC), is a global group of regulators, investors, and accountants that develops methods for integrated reporting. **Integrated reporting** is designed to concisely report how an organization's strategy, performance, sustainability efforts, and governance lead to value creation.

Intel, a maker of computer chips, follows many of the IIRC's recommendations. In its integrated report, Intel notes it links executive pay, in part, to corporate responsibility metrics. For example, 50% of top management's annual cash bonus is based on meeting operating performance targets, including those for corporate responsibility and environmental sustainability. For 2015, Intel's top five managers were paid nearly $10 million for meeting performance targets. By linking executive pay to sustainability targets, Intel motivates managers to integrate sustainability initiatives with their efforts to make financial profits and increase firm value.

Riide, this chapter's feature company, is built around environmental sustainability. Amber "hates traffic" and is focused on alternative energy solutions. At age three, Jeff ditched the training wheels on his Batman bike and never stopped riding.

The duo combined their passion for biking and energy conservation to design an e-bike that is environmentally friendly. They also give back to their community by working with the robotics club at a local high school. "We coach them on what it's like to bring a product to market," says Amber.

Kate Warren/Courtesy of Riide

Decision Analysis **Sales Variances**

A1

Analyze changes in sales from expected amounts.

This chapter explained the computation and analysis of cost variances. A similar variance analysis can be applied to sales. For this analysis, the budgeted amount of unit sales is the predicted activity level, and the budgeted selling price can be treated as a "standard" price. To illustrate, consider the following sales data from G-Max for two of its golf products, Excel golf balls and Big Bert drivers.

	Budgeted	Actual
Sales of Excel golf balls (units).	1,000 units	1,100 units
Sales price per Excel golf ball	$10	$10.50
Sales of Big Bert drivers (units)	150 units	140 units
Sales price per Big Bert driver.	$200	$190

Using this information, we compute both the *sales price variance* and the *sales volume variance*, as shown in Exhibit 8.18. The sales price variance measures the impact of the actual sales price differing from the expected price. The sales volume variance measures the impact of operating at a different capacity level than predicted by the fixed budget. The total sales price variance is $850 unfavorable, and the total sales volume variance is $1,000 unfavorable. However, further analysis of these total sales variances reveals that both the sales price and sales volume variances for Excel golf balls are favorable, while both variances are unfavorable for the Big Bert driver.

EXHIBIT 8.18

Computing Sales Variances*

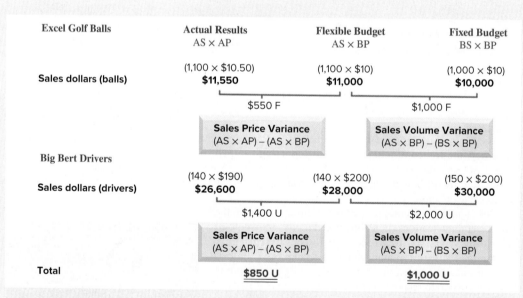

* AS = actual sales units; AP = actual sales price; BP = budgeted sales price; BS = budgeted sales units (fixed budget).

Managers use sales variances for planning and control purposes. G-Max sold 90 combined total units (both balls and drivers) more than budgeted, yet its total sales price and sales volume variances are unfavorable. The unfavorable sales price variance is due mainly to a decrease in the selling price of Big Bert drivers by $10 per unit. Management must assess whether this price decrease will continue. Likewise, the unfavorable sales volume variance is due to G-Max selling fewer Big Bert drivers (140) than were budgeted (150). Management must assess whether this decreased demand for Big Bert drivers will persist.

Overall, management can use the detailed sales variances to examine what caused the company to sell more golf balls and fewer drivers. Managers can also use this information to evaluate and even reward salespeople. Extra compensation is paid to salespeople who contribute to a higher profit margin.

Decision Maker

Sales Manager   The current performance report reveals a large favorable sales volume variance but an unfavorable sales price variance. You did not expect a large increase in sales volume. What steps do you take to analyze this situation? ■   *Answer:* The unfavorable sales price variance suggests that actual prices were lower than budgeted prices. As the sales manager, you want to know the reasons for a lower-than-expected price. Perhaps your salespeople lowered the price of certain products by offering quantity discounts. You then might want to know what prompted them to offer the quantity discounts (perhaps competitors were offering discounts). You want to determine if the increased sales volume is due mainly to discounted prices or other factors (such as advertising).

Pacific Company provides the following information about its budgeted and actual results for June 2017. Although the expected June volume was 25,000 units produced and sold, the company actually produced and sold 27,000 units, as detailed here:

NEED-TO-KNOW 8-5

COMPREHENSIVE

	Budget (25,000 units)	Actual (27,000 units)
Selling price	$5.00 per unit	$141,210
Variable costs (per unit)		
Direct materials	1.24 per unit	$30,800
Direct labor	1.50 per unit	37,800
Factory supplies*	0.25 per unit	9,990
Utilities*	0.50 per unit	16,200
Selling costs	0.40 per unit	9,180
Fixed costs (per month)		
Depreciation—Machinery*	$3,750	$3,710
Depreciation—Factory building*	2,500	2,500
General liability insurance	1,200	1,250
Property taxes on office equipment	500	485
Other administrative expense	750	900

* Indicates factory overhead item; $0.75 per unit or $3 per direct labor hour for variable overhead, and $0.25 per unit or $1 per direct labor hour for fixed overhead.

Standard costs based on expected output of 25,000 units:

	Standard Quantity	Total Cost
Direct materials, 4 oz. per unit @ $0.31 per oz.	100,000 oz.	$31,000
Direct labor, 0.25 hrs. per unit @ $6.00 per hr.	6,250 hrs.	37,500
Overhead, 6,250 standard hours × $4.00 per DLH		25,000

Actual costs incurred to produce 27,000 units:

	Actual Quantity	Total Cost
Direct materials, 110,000 oz. @ $0.28 per oz.	110,000 oz.	$30,800
Direct labor, 5,400 hrs. @ $7.00 per hr.	5,400 hrs.	37,800
Overhead ($9,990 + $16,200 + $3,710 + $2,500)		32,400

Required

1. Prepare June flexible budgets showing expected sales, costs, and net income assuming 20,000, 25,000, and 30,000 units of output produced and sold.
2. Prepare a flexible budget performance report that compares actual results with the amounts budgeted if the actual volume of 27,000 units had been expected.
3. Apply variance analysis for direct materials and direct labor.
4. Compute the total overhead variance and the overhead controllable and overhead volume variances.
5. Compute spending and efficiency variances for overhead. (Refer to Appendix 8A.)
6. Prepare journal entries to record standard costs, and price and quantity variances, for direct materials, direct labor, and factory overhead. (Refer to Appendix 8A.)

PLANNING THE SOLUTION

- Prepare a table showing the expected results at the three specified levels of output. Compute the variable costs by multiplying the per unit variable costs by the expected volumes. Include fixed costs at the given amounts. Combine the amounts in the table to show total variable costs, contribution margin, total fixed costs, and income from operations.

- Prepare a table showing the actual results and the amounts that should be incurred at 27,000 units. Show any differences in the third column and label them with an *F* for favorable if they increase income or a *U* for unfavorable if they decrease income.

- Using the chapter's format, compute these total variances and the individual variances requested:
  - Total materials variance (including the direct materials quantity variance and the direct materials price variance).
  - Total direct labor variance (including the direct labor efficiency variance and rate variance).
  - Total overhead variance (including both controllable and volume overhead variances and their component variances). Variable overhead is applied at the rate of $3.00 per direct labor hour. Fixed overhead is applied at the rate of $1.00 per direct labor hour.

SOLUTION

1.

PACIFIC COMPANY
Flexible Budgets
For Month Ended June 30, 2017

	Flexible Budget		Flexible Budget for Unit Sales of		
	Variable Amount per Unit	Total Fixed Cost	20,000	25,000	30,000
Sales	$5.00		$100,000	$125,000	$150,000
Variable costs					
Direct materials	1.24		24,800	31,000	37,200
Direct labor.	1.50		30,000	37,500	45,000
Factory supplies.	0.25		5,000	6,250	7,500
Utilities	0.50		10,000	12,500	15,000
Selling costs	0.40		8,000	10,000	12,000
Total variable costs	3.89		77,800	97,250	116,700
Contribution margin	$1.11		22,200	27,750	33,300
Fixed costs					
Depreciation—Machinery		$3,750	3,750	3,750	3,750
Depreciation—Factory building.		2,500	2,500	2,500	2,500
General liability insurance.		1,200	1,200	1,200	1,200
Property taxes on office equipment		500	500	500	500
Other administrative expense.		750	750	750	750
Total fixed costs		$8,700	8,700	8,700	8,700
Income from operations.			$ 13,500	$ 19,050	$ 24,600

2.

PACIFIC COMPANY Flexible Budget Performance Report For Month Ended June 30, 2017	Flexible Budget	Actual Results	Variance**
Sales (27,000 units)	$135,000	$141,210	$6,210 F
Variable costs			
Direct materials	33,480	30,800	2,680 F
Direct labor	40,500	37,800	2,700 F
Factory supplies*	6,750	9,990	3,240 U
Utilities*	13,500	16,200	2,700 U
Selling costs	10,800	9,180	1,620 F
Total variable costs	105,030	103,970	1,060 F
Contribution margin	29,970	37,240	7,270 F
Fixed costs			
Depreciation—Machinery*	3,750	3,710	40 F
Depreciation—Factory building*	2,500	2,500	0
General liability insurance	1,200	1,250	50 U
Property taxes on office equipment	500	485	15 F
Other administrative expense	750	900	150 U
Total fixed costs	8,700	8,845	145 U
Income from operations	$ 21,270	$ 28,395	$7,125 F

* Indicates factory overhead item.   ** Abbreviations: F = Favorable variance; U = Unfavorable variance.

3. Variance analysis of materials and labor costs.

Direct materials cost variances

Actual cost	110,000 oz. @ $0.28	$30,800
Standard cost	108,000 oz. @ $0.31	33,480
Direct materials cost variance		$ 2,680 F

Price and quantity variances (based on formulas in Exhibit 8.10):

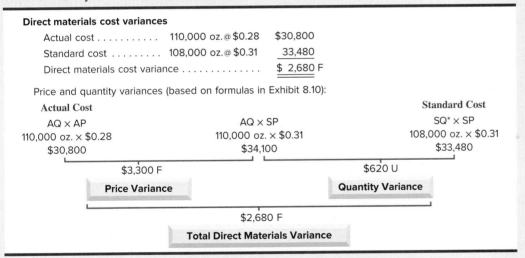

*SQ = 27,000 actual units of output × 4 oz. standard quantity per unit

Direct labor cost variances

Actual cost	5,400 hrs. @ $7.00	$37,800
Standard cost	6,750 hrs. @ $6.00	40,500
Direct labor cost variance		$ 2,700 F

Rate and efficiency variances (based on formulas in Exhibit 8.11):

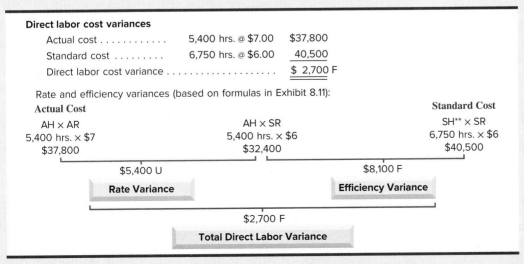

**SH = 27,000 actual units of output × 0.25 standard DLH per unit

4. Total, controllable, and volume variances for overhead.

Total overhead cost variance		
Total overhead cost incurred . . . . (given)		$32,400
Total overhead applied . . . . (27,000 units × 0.25 DLH per unit × $4 per DLH)		27,000
Overhead cost variance		$ 5,400 U
Controllable variance		
Total overhead cost incurred (given)		$32,400
Budgeted overhead (from flexible budget for 27,000 units)		26,500
Controllable variance		$ 5,900 U
Volume variance		
Budgeted fixed overhead (at predicted capacity)		$ 6,250
Applied fixed overhead (6,750 standard DLH × $1.00 fixed overhead rate per DLH)		6,750
Volume variance		$ 500 F

5. Variable overhead spending variance, variable overhead efficiency variance, fixed overhead spending variance, and fixed overhead volume variance. (See Appendix 8A.)

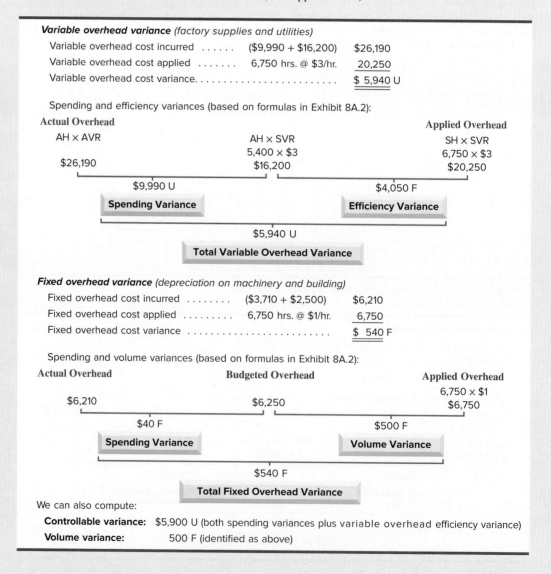

Variable overhead variance (factory supplies and utilities)		
Variable overhead cost incurred	($9,990 + $16,200)	$26,190
Variable overhead cost applied	6,750 hrs. @ $3/hr.	20,250
Variable overhead cost variance.		$ 5,940 U

Spending and efficiency variances (based on formulas in Exhibit 8A.2):

Actual Overhead		**Applied Overhead**
AH × AVR	AH × SVR	SH × SVR
	5,400 × $3	6,750 × $3
$26,190	$16,200	$20,250

$9,990 U — **Spending Variance**

$4,050 F — **Efficiency Variance**

$5,940 U
Total Variable Overhead Variance

Fixed overhead variance (depreciation on machinery and building)		
Fixed overhead cost incurred	($3,710 + $2,500)	$6,210
Fixed overhead cost applied	6,750 hrs. @ $1/hr.	6,750
Fixed overhead cost variance		$ 540 F

Spending and volume variances (based on formulas in Exhibit 8A.2):

Actual Overhead	**Budgeted Overhead**	**Applied Overhead**
		6,750 × $1
$6,210	$6,250	$6,750

$40 F — **Spending Variance**

$500 F — **Volume Variance**

$540 F
Total Fixed Overhead Variance

We can also compute:

Controllable variance: $5,900 U (both spending variances plus variable overhead efficiency variance)

Volume variance: 500 F (identified as above)

6. Journal entries under a standard cost system. (Refer to Appendix 8A.)

Work in Process Inventory	33,480	
Direct Materials Quantity Variance	620	
Direct Materials Price Variance		3,300
Raw Materials Inventory		30,800
Work in Process Inventory	40,500	
Direct Labor Rate Variance	5,400	
Direct Labor Efficiency Variance		8,100
Factory Wages Payable		37,800
Work in Process Inventory*	27,000	
Variable Overhead Spending Variance	9,990	
Variable Overhead Efficiency Variance		4,050
Fixed Overhead Spending Variance		40
Fixed Overhead Volume Variance		500
Factory Overhead**		32,400

   * Overhead applied = 6,750 standard DLH × $4 per DLH
** Overhead incurred = $9,990 + $16,200 + $3,710 + $2,500

Expanded Overhead Variances and Standard Cost Accounting System

8A

EXPANDED OVERHEAD VARIANCES

Similar to analysis of direct materials and direct labor, overhead variances can be analyzed further. Exhibit 8A.1 shows an expanded framework for understanding these overhead variances.

This framework uses classifications of overhead costs as either variable or fixed. Within those two classifications are further types of variances—spending, efficiency, and volume variances. Volume variances were explained in the body of the chapter.

A **spending variance** occurs when management pays an amount different from the standard price to acquire an item. For instance, the actual wage rate paid to indirect labor might be higher than the standard rate. Similarly, actual supervisory salaries might be different than expected. Spending variances such as these cause management to investigate the reasons why the amount paid differs from the standard. Both variable and fixed overhead costs can yield their own spending variances.

Analyzing variable overhead includes computing an **efficiency variance,** which occurs when standard direct labor hours (the allocation base) expected for actual production differ from the actual direct labor hours used. This efficiency variance reflects on the cost-effectiveness in using the overhead allocation base (such as direct labor).

Exhibit 8A.1 shows that we can combine the variable overhead spending variance, the fixed overhead spending variance, and the variable overhead efficiency variance to get the controllable variance.

P4

Compute overhead spending and efficiency variances.

EXHIBIT 8A.1

Expanded Framework for Total Overhead Variance

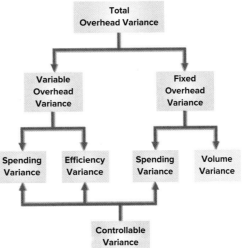

Computing Variable and Fixed Overhead Cost Variances To illustrate the computation of more detailed overhead cost variances, we return to G-Max. G-Max produced 3,500 units when 4,000 units were budgeted. Additional data from cost reports (from Exhibit 8.16) show that the actual overhead cost incurred is $7,650 (the variable portion of $3,650 and the fixed portion of $4,000). From Exhibit 8.12, each unit requires one hour of direct labor, variable overhead is applied at a rate of $1.00 per direct labor hour, and the predetermined fixed overhead rate is $1.00 per direct labor hour. With this information, we compute overhead variances for both variable and fixed overhead as follows:

Variable Overhead Variance	
Actual variable overhead (given)	$3,650
Applied variable overhead (3,500 units × 1 standard DLH × $1.00 VOH rate per DLH)	3,500
Variable overhead variance	$ 150 U

Fixed Overhead Variance	
Actual fixed overhead (given)	$4,000
Applied fixed overhead (3,500 units × 1 standard DLH × $1.00 FOH rate per DLH)	3,500
Fixed overhead variance	$ 500 U

Management should seek to determine the causes of these unfavorable variances and take corrective action. To help better isolate the causes of these variances, more detailed overhead variances can be used, as we show next.

Expanded Overhead Variance Formulas   Exhibit 8A.2 shows formulas to use in computing detailed overhead variances.

EXHIBIT 8A.2

Variable and Fixed
Overhead Variances

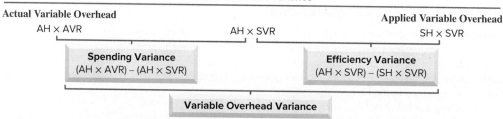

* AH = actual direct labor hours; AVR = actual variable overhead rate; SH = standard direct labor hours; SVR = standard variable overhead rate.

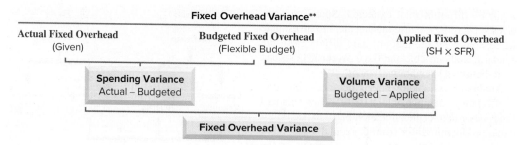

**SH = standard direct labor hours; SFR = standard fixed overhead rate.

Variable Overhead Cost Variances   Using these formulas, Exhibit 8A.3 offers insight into the causes of G-Max's $150 unfavorable variable overhead cost variance. G-Max applies overhead based on direct labor hours. It used 3,400 direct labor hours to produce 3,500 units. This compares favorably to the standard requirement of 3,500 direct labor hours at one labor hour per unit. At a standard variable overhead rate of $1.00 per direct labor hour, this should have resulted in variable overhead costs of $3,400 (middle column of Exhibit 8A.3).

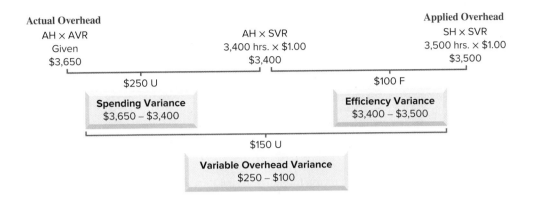

EXHIBIT 8A.3

Computing Variable
Overhead Cost Variances

G-Max's cost records, however, report actual variable overhead of $3,650, or $250 higher than expected. This means G-Max has an unfavorable variable overhead spending variance of $250 ($3,650 − $3,400). On the other hand, G-Max used 100 fewer labor hours than expected to make 3,500 units, and its actual variable overhead is lower than its applied variable overhead. Thus, G-Max has a favorable variable overhead efficiency variance of $100 ($3,400 − $3,500).

Fixed Overhead Cost Variances   Exhibit 8A.4 provides insight into the causes of G-Max's $500 unfavorable fixed overhead variance. G-Max reports that it incurred $4,000 in actual fixed overhead; this amount equals the budgeted fixed overhead for May at the expected production level of 4,000 units (see Exhibit 8.12). Thus, the fixed overhead spending variance is zero, suggesting good control of fixed overhead costs. G-Max's budgeted fixed overhead application rate is $1 per hour ($4,000/4,000 direct labor hours), but the actual production level is only 3,500 units.

With this information, we compute the fixed overhead volume variance shown in Exhibit 8A.4. The applied fixed overhead is computed by multiplying 3,500 standard hours allowed for the actual production by the $1 fixed overhead allocation rate. The volume variance of $500 occurs because 500 fewer units are produced than budgeted; namely, 80% of the manufacturing capacity is budgeted, but only 70% is used. Management needs to know why the actual level of production differs from the expected level.

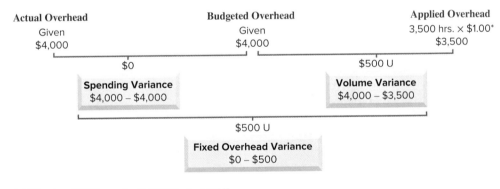

EXHIBIT 8A.4

Computing Fixed Overhead
Cost Variances

* 3,500 units × 1 DLH per unit × $1.00 FOH rate per DLH

STANDARD COST ACCOUNTING SYSTEM

We have shown how companies use standard costs in management reports. Most standard cost systems also record these costs and variances in accounts. This practice simplifies recordkeeping and helps in preparing reports. Although we do not need knowledge of standard cost accounting practices to understand standard costs and their use, we must know how to interpret the accounts in which standard costs and variances are recorded. The entries in this section briefly illustrate the important aspects of this process for G-Max's standard costs and variances for May.

The first of these entries records standard materials cost incurred in May in the Work in Process Inventory account. This part of the entry is similar to the usual accounting entry, but the amount of the debit equals the standard cost ($35,000) instead of the actual cost ($37,800). This entry credits Raw Materials Inventory for actual cost. The difference between standard and actual direct materials costs is recorded with debits to two separate materials variance accounts (recall Exhibit 8.10). Both the materials price and quantity variances are recorded as debits because they reflect additional costs higher than the standard cost (if actual costs were less than the standard, they are recorded as credits). This treatment (debit) reflects their unfavorable effect because they represent higher costs and lower income.

P5

Prepare journal entries
for standard costs and
account for price and
quantity variances.

May 31	Work in Process Inventory............................	35,000	
	Direct Materials Price Variance*	**1,800**	
	Direct Materials Quantity Variance...................	**1,000**	
	Raw Materials Inventory..........................		37,800
	Charge production for standard quantity of materials used (1,750 lbs.) at the standard price ($20 per lb.), and record material price and material quantity variances.		

* Many companies record the materials price variance when materials are purchased. For simplicity, we record both the materials price and quantity variances when materials are issued to production.

The second entry debits Work in Process Inventory for the standard labor cost of the goods manufactured during May ($56,000). Actual labor cost ($56,100) is recorded with a credit to the Factory Wages Payable account. The difference between standard and actual labor costs is explained by two variances (see Exhibit 8.11). The direct labor rate variance is unfavorable and is debited to that account. The direct labor efficiency variance is favorable and that account is credited. The direct labor efficiency variance is favorable because it represents a lower cost and a higher net income.

May 31	Work in Process Inventory............................	56,000	
	Direct Labor Rate Variance...........................	**1,700**	
	Direct Labor Efficiency Variance.................		**1,600**
	Factory Wages Payable		56,100
	Charge production with 3,500 standard hours of direct labor at the standard $16 per hour rate, and record the labor rate and efficiency variances.		

The entry to assign standard predetermined overhead to the cost of goods manufactured must debit the $7,000 predetermined amount to the Work in Process Inventory account. Actual overhead costs of $7,650 were debited to Factory Overhead during the period (entries not shown here). Thus, when Factory Overhead is applied to Work in Process Inventory, the actual amount is credited to the Factory Overhead account. To account for the difference between actual and standard overhead costs, the entry includes a $250 debit to the Variable Overhead Spending Variance, a $100 credit to the Variable Overhead Efficiency Variance, and a $500 debit to the Volume Variance (recall Exhibits 8A.3 and 8A.4). (An alternative [simpler] approach is to record the difference with a $150 debit to the Controllable Variance account and a $500 debit to the Volume Variance account.)

May 31	Work in Process Inventory............................	7,000	
	Volume Variance	**500**	
	Variable Overhead Spending Variance.................	**250**	
	Variable Overhead Efficiency Variance		**100**
	Factory Overhead..............................		7,650
	Apply overhead at the standard rate of $2 per standard direct labor hour (3,500 hours), and record overhead variances.		

Point: If variances are material, they can be allocated between Work in Process Inventory, Finished Goods Inventory, and Cost of Goods Sold. This closing process is explained in advanced courses.

The balances of these different variance accounts accumulate until the end of the accounting period. As a result, the unfavorable variances of some months can offset the favorable variances of other months.

These ending variance account balances, which reflect results of the period's various transactions and events, are closed at period-end. If the amounts are *immaterial,* they are added to or subtracted from the balance of the Cost of Goods Sold account. This process is similar to that shown in the job order costing chapter for eliminating an underapplied or overapplied balance in the Factory Overhead account. (*Note:* These variance balances, which represent differences between actual and standard costs, must be added to or subtracted from the materials, labor, and overhead costs recorded. In this way, the recorded costs equal the actual costs incurred in the period; a company must use actual costs in external financial statements prepared in accordance with generally accepted accounting principles.)

Standard Costing Income Statement In addition to the reports discussed in this chapter, management can use a **standard costing income statement** to summarize company performance for a period. This income statement reports sales and cost of goods sold at their *standard* amounts, and then lists the individual sales and cost variances to compute gross profit at actual cost. Exhibit 8A.5 provides an example. Unfavorable variances are *added* to cost of goods sold at standard cost; favorable variances are *subtracted* from cost of goods sold at standard cost.

G-MAX
Standard Costing Income Statement
For Year Ended December 31, 2017

Sales revenue (at standard)		•••••
Sales price variance	•••	
Sales volume variance	••• •••	
Sales revenue (actual)		•••••
Cost of goods sold (at standard)		•••••
Manufacturing cost variances		
Direct materials price variance	•••	
Direct materials quantity variance	•••	
Direct labor rate variance	•••	
Direct labor efficiency variance	•••	
Variable overhead spending variance	•••	
Variable overhead efficiency variance	•••	
Fixed overhead spending variance	•••	
Fixed overhead volume variance	•••	
Total manufacturing cost variances	•••	
Cost of goods sold (actual)		••••••
Gross profit		••••
Selling expenses		•••
General and administrative expenses		•••
Income from operations		•••••

Add unfavorable variances; subtract favorable variances.

EXHIBIT 8A.5

Standard Costing Income Statement

Prepare the journal entry to record these direct materials variances:

Direct materials cost actually incurred	$73,200
Direct materials quantity variance	3,800 F
Direct materials price variance	1,300 U

NEED-TO-KNOW 8-6

Recording Variances

P4

Solution

Work in Process Inventory	75,700	
Direct Materials Price Variance	1,300	
Direct Materials Quantity Variance		3,800
Raw Materials Inventory		73,200

Do More: QS 8-17, E 8-14

Summary

C1 **Define *standard costs* and explain how standard cost information is useful for management by exception.** Standard costs are the normal costs that should be incurred to produce a product or perform a service. They should be based on a careful examination of the processes used to produce a product or perform a service as well as the quantities and prices that should be incurred in carrying out those processes. On a performance report, standard costs (which are flexible budget amounts) are compared to actual costs, and the differences are presented as variances. Standard cost accounting provides management information about costs that differ from budgeted (expected) amounts. Performance reports disclose the costs or areas of operations that have significant variances from budgeted amounts. This allows managers to focus more attention on the exceptions and less attention on areas proceeding normally.

C2 **Describe cost variances and what they reveal about performance.** Management can use variances to monitor and control activities. Total cost variances can be broken into price and quantity variances to direct management's attention to those responsible for quantities used and prices paid.

A1 **Analyze changes in sales from expected amounts.** Actual sales can differ from budgeted sales, and managers can investigate this difference by computing both the sales price and sales volume variances. The *sales price variance* refers to that portion of total variance resulting from a difference between actual and budgeted selling prices. The *sales volume variance* refers to that portion of total variance resulting from a difference between actual and budgeted sales quantities.

P1 **Prepare a flexible budget and interpret a flexible budget performance report.** A flexible budget expresses variable costs in per unit terms so that it can be used to develop budgeted amounts for any volume level within the relevant range. Thus, managers compute budgeted amounts for evaluation after a period for the volume that actually occurred. To prepare a flexible budget, we express each variable cost as a constant amount per unit of sales (or as a percent of sales dollars). In contrast, the budgeted amount of each fixed cost is expressed as a total amount expected to occur at any sales volume within the relevant range. The flexible budget is then determined using these computations and amounts for fixed and variable costs at the expected sales volume.

P2 **Compute materials and labor variances.** Materials and labor variances are due to differences between the actual costs incurred and the budgeted costs. The price (or rate) variance is computed by comparing the actual cost with

the flexible budget amount that should have been incurred to acquire the actual quantity of resources. The quantity (or efficiency) variance is computed by comparing the flexible budget amount that should have been incurred to acquire the actual quantity of resources with the flexible budget amount that should have been incurred to acquire the standard quantity of resources.

P3 **Compute overhead controllable and volume variances.** Overhead variances are due to differences between the actual overhead costs incurred and the overhead applied to production. The overhead controllable variance equals the actual overhead minus the budgeted overhead. The volume variance equals the budgeted fixed overhead minus the applied fixed overhead.

P4ᴬ **Compute overhead spending and efficiency variances.** An overhead spending variance occurs when management pays an amount different from the standard price to acquire an item. An overhead efficiency variance occurs when the standard amount of the allocation base to assign overhead differs from the actual amount of the allocation base used.

P5ᴬ **Prepare journal entries for standard costs and account for price and quantity variances.** When a company records standard costs in its accounts, the standard costs of direct materials, direct labor, and overhead are debited to the Work in Process Inventory account. Based on an analysis of the material, labor, and overhead costs, each quantity variance, price variance, volume variance, and controllable variance is recorded in a separate account. At period-end, if the variances are not material, they are debited (if unfavorable) or credited (if favorable) to the Cost of Goods Sold account.

Key Terms

Benchmarking	Flexible budget	Quantity variance
Budget report	Flexible budget performance report	Spending variance
Controllable variance	Integrated reporting	Standard costing income statement
Cost variance	International Integrated Reporting	Standard costs
Efficiency variance	Council	Unfavorable variance
Favorable variance	Management by exception	Variance
Fixed budget	Overhead cost variance	Variance analysis
Fixed budget performance report	Price variance	Volume variance

Multiple Choice Quiz

1. A company predicts its production and sales will be 24,000 units. At that level of activity, its fixed costs are budgeted at $300,000, and its variable costs are budgeted at $246,000. If its activity level declines to 20,000 units, what will be its budgeted fixed costs and its variable costs?

 a. Fixed, $300,000; variable, $246,000
 b. Fixed, $250,000; variable, $205,000
 c. Fixed, $300,000; variable, $205,000
 d. Fixed, $250,000; variable, $246,000
 e. Fixed, $300,000; variable, $300,000

2. Using the following information about a single product company, compute its total actual cost of direct materials used.
- Direct materials standard cost: 5 lbs. × $2 per lb. = $10.
- Total direct materials cost variance: $15,000 unfavorable.
- Actual direct materials used: 300,000 lbs.
- Actual units produced: 60,000 units.
 a. $585,000   **c.** $300,000   **e.** $615,000
 b. $600,000   **d.** $315,000

3. A company uses four hours of direct labor to produce a product unit. The standard direct labor cost is $20 per hour. This period the company produced 20,000 units and used 84,160 hours of direct labor at a total cost of $1,599,040. What is its labor rate variance for the period?
 a. $83,200 F   **c.** $84,160 F   **e.** $960 F
 b. $84,160 U   **d.** $83,200 U

ANSWERS TO MULTIPLE CHOICE QUIZ

1. c; Fixed costs remain at $300,000; Variable costs = ($246,000/24,000 units) × 20,000 units = $205,000

2. e; Budgeted direct materials + Unfavorable variance = Actual cost of direct materials used; or 60,000 units × $10 per unit = $600,000 + $15,000 U = $615,000

3. c; (AH × AR) − (AH × SR) = $1,599,040 − (84,160 hours × $20 per hour) = $84,160 F

4. A company's standard for a unit of its single product is $6 per unit in variable overhead (4 hours × $1.50 per hour). Actual data for the period show variable overhead costs of $150,000 and production of 24,000 units. Its total variable overhead cost variance is
 a. $6,000 F.   **c.** $114,000 U.   **e.** $0.
 b. $6,000 U.   **d.** $114,000 F.

5. A company's standard for a unit of its single product is $4 per unit in fixed overhead ($24,000 total/6,000 units budgeted). Actual data for the period show total actual fixed overhead of $24,100 and production of 4,800 units. Its volume variance is
 a. $4,800 U.   **c.** $100 U.   **e.** $4,900 U.
 b. $4,800 F.   **d.** $100 F.

4. b; Actual variable overhead − Variable overhead applied to production = Variable overhead cost variance; or $150,000 − (96,000 hours × $1.50 per hour) = $6,000 U

5. a; Budgeted fixed overhead − Fixed overhead applied to production = Volume variance; or $24,000 − (4,800 units × $4 per unit) = $4,800 U

A Superscript letter A denotes assignments based on Appendix 8A.

Icon denotes assignments that involve decision making.

Discussion Questions

1. What limits the usefulness to managers of fixed budget performance reports?

2. Identify the main purpose of a flexible budget for managers.

3. Prepare a flexible budget performance report title (in proper form) for Spalding Company for the calendar year 2017. Why is a proper title important for this or any report?

4. What type of analysis does a flexible budget performance report help management perform?

5. In what sense can a variable cost be considered constant?

6. What department is usually responsible for a direct labor rate variance? What department is usually responsible for a direct labor efficiency variance? Explain.

7. What is a price variance? What is a quantity variance?

8. What is the purpose of using standard costs?

9. **Google** monitors its fixed overhead. In an analysis of fixed overhead cost variances, what is the volume variance? GOOGLE

10. What is the predetermined standard overhead rate? How is it computed?

11. In general, variance analysis is said to provide information about _____ and _____ variances.

12. **Samsung** monitors its overhead. In an analysis of overhead cost variances, what is the controllable variance and what causes it? **Samsung**

13. What are the relations among standard costs, flexible budgets, variance analysis, and management by exception?

14. How can the manager of advertising sales at **Google** use flexible budgets to enhance performance? GOOGLE

15. Is it possible for a retail store such as **Apple** to use variances in analyzing its operating performance? Explain. **APPLE**

16. Assume that **Samsung** is budgeted to operate at 80% of capacity but actually operates at 75% of capacity. What effect will the 5% deviation have on its controllable variance? Its volume variance? **Samsung**

17. List at least two positive and two negative features of standard costing systems.

18. Describe the concept of *management by exception* and explain how standard costs help managers apply this concept to control costs.

connect

QUICK STUDY

QS 8-1
Flexible budget
performance report
P1

Beech Company produced and sold 105,000 units of its product in May. For the level of production achieved in May, the budgeted amounts were: sales, $1,300,000; variable costs, $750,000; and fixed costs, $300,000. The following actual financial results are available for May. Prepare a flexible budget performance report for May.

	Actual
Sales (105,000 units)	$1,275,000
Variable costs	712,500
Fixed costs	300,000

QS 8-2
Flexible budget   P1

Based on predicted production of 24,000 units, a company anticipates $300,000 of fixed costs and $246,000 of variable costs. If the company actually produces 20,000 units, what are the flexible budget amounts of fixed and variable costs?

QS 8-3
Flexible budget
P1

Brodrick Company expects to produce 20,000 units for the year ending December 31. A flexible budget for 20,000 units of production reflects sales of $400,000; variable costs of $80,000; and fixed costs of $150,000. If the company instead expects to produce and sell 26,000 units for the year, calculate the expected level of income from operations.

QS 8-4
Flexible budget
performance report   P1

Refer to information in QS 8-3. Assume that actual sales for the year are $480,000 (26,000 units), actual variable costs for the year are $112,000, and actual fixed costs for the year are $145,000. Prepare a flexible budget performance report for the year.

QS 8-5
Standard cost card   C1

BatCo makes metal baseball bats. Each bat requires 1 kg of aluminum at $18 per kg and 0.25 direct labor hours at $20 per hour. Overhead is assigned at the rate of $40 per direct labor hour. What amounts would appear on a standard cost card for BatCo?

QS 8-6
Cost variances   C2

Refer to information in QS 8-5. Assume the actual cost to manufacture one metal bat is $40. Compute the cost variance and classify it as favorable or unfavorable.

QS 8-7
Materials variances
P2

Tercer reports the following for one of its products. Compute the total direct materials cost variance and classify it as favorable or unfavorable.

Direct materials standard (4 lbs. @ $2 per lb.)	$8 per finished unit
Actual finished units produced	60,000 units
Actual cost of direct materials used	$535,000

QS 8-8
Materials variances
P2

Tercer reports the following for one of its products. Compute the direct materials price and quantity variances and classify each as favorable or unfavorable.

Direct materials standard (4 lbs. @ $2 per lb.)	$8 per finished unit
Actual direct materials used	300,000 lbs.
Actual finished units produced	60,000 units
Actual cost of direct materials used	$535,000

QS 8-9
Materials cost variances   P2

For the current period, Kayenta Company's manufacturing operations yield a $4,000 unfavorable direct materials price variance. The actual price per pound of material is $78; the standard price is $77.50 per pound. How many pounds of material were used in the current period?

QS 8-10
Materials cost variances   P2

Juan Company's output for the current period was assigned a $150,000 standard direct materials cost. The direct materials variances included a $12,000 favorable price variance and a $2,000 favorable quantity variance. What is the actual total direct materials cost for the current period?

The following information describes a company's direct labor usage in a recent period. Compute the direct labor rate and efficiency variances for the period and classify each as favorable or unfavorable.

QS 8-11
Direct labor variances
P2

Actual direct labor hours used...	65,000
Actual direct labor rate per hour...	$15
Standard direct labor rate per hour...	$14
Standard direct labor hours for units produced	67,000

Frontera Company's output for the current period results in a $20,000 unfavorable direct labor rate variance and a $10,000 unfavorable direct labor efficiency variance. Production for the current period was assigned a $400,000 standard direct labor cost. What is the actual total direct labor cost for the current period?

QS 8-12
Labor cost variances   P2

Fogel Co. expects to produce 116,000 units for the year. The company's flexible budget for 116,000 units of production shows variable overhead costs of $162,400 and fixed overhead costs of $124,000. For the year, the company incurred actual overhead costs of $262,800 while producing 110,000 units. Compute the controllable overhead variance and classify it as favorable or unfavorable.

QS 8-13
Controllable overhead
variance   P3

AirPro Corp. reports the following for November. Compute the total overhead variance and controllable overhead variance for November and classify each as favorable or unfavorable.

QS 8-14
Controllable overhead
variance
P3

Actual total factory overhead incurred	$28,175
Standard factory overhead:	
Variable overhead	$3.10 per unit produced
Fixed overhead	
($12,000/12,000 predicted units to be produced)	$1 per unit
Predicted units to produce......................................	12,000 units
Actual units produced	9,800 units

Refer to information in QS 8-14. Compute the overhead volume variance for November and classify it as favorable or unfavorable.

QS 8-15
Volume variance   P3

Alvarez Company's output for the current period yields a $20,000 favorable overhead volume variance and a $60,400 unfavorable overhead controllable variance. Standard overhead applied to production for the period is $225,000. What is the actual total overhead cost incurred for the period?

QS 8-16
Overhead cost variances
P3

Refer to the information in QS 8-16. Alvarez records standard costs in its accounts. Prepare the journal entry to charge overhead costs to the Work in Process Inventory account and to record any variances.

QS 8-17^A
Preparing overhead entries
P5

Mosaic Company applies overhead using machine hours and reports the following information. Compute the total variable overhead cost variance and classify it as favorable or unfavorable.

QS 8-18^A
Total variable overhead
cost variance
P4

Actual machine hours used	4,700 hours
Standard machine hours (for actual production)	5,000 hours
Actual variable overhead rate per hour	$4.15
Standard variable overhead rate per hour	$4.00

Refer to the information from QS 8-18. Compute the variable overhead spending variance and the variable overhead efficiency variance and classify each as favorable or unfavorable.

QS 8-19^A
Overhead spending and
efficiency variances   P4

Farad, Inc., specializes in selling used trucks. During the month, Farad sold 50 trucks at an average price of $9,000 each. The budget for the month was to sell 45 trucks at an average price of $9,500 each. Compute the dealership's sales price variance and sales volume variance for the month and classify each as favorable or unfavorable.

QS 8-20
Computing sales price and
volume variances   A1

In a recent year, **BMW** sold 182,158 of its 1 Series cars. Assume the company expected to sell 191,158 of these cars during the year. Also assume the budgeted sales price for each car was $30,000 and the actual sales price for each car was $30,200. Compute the sales price variance and the sales volume variance.

QS 8-21
Sales variances   A1

QS 8-22

Sustainability and standard costs

P1

MM Co. uses corrugated cardboard to ship its product to customers. Management believes it has found a more efficient way to package its products and use less cardboard. This new approach will reduce shipping costs from $10.00 per shipment to $9.25 per shipment. If the company forecasts 1,200 shipments this year, what amount of total direct materials costs would appear on the shipping department's flexible budget? How much is this sustainability improvement predicted to save in direct materials costs for this coming year?

QS 8-23

Sustainability and standard overhead rate

P3

HH Co. uses corrugated cardboard to ship its product to customers. Currently, the company's returns department incurs annual overhead costs of $72,000 and forecasts 2,000 returns per year. Management believes it has a found a better way to package its products. As a result, the company expects to reduce the number of shipments that are returned due to damage by 5%. In addition, the initiative is expected to reduce the department's annual overhead by $12,000. Compute the returns department's standard overhead rate per return (a) before the sustainability improvement and (b) after the sustainability improvement. (Round to the nearest cent.)

---

connect

EXERCISES

Exercise 8-1

Classification of costs as fixed or variable

P1

JPAK Company manufactures and sells mountain bikes. It normally operates eight hours a day, five days a week. Using this information, classify each of the following costs as fixed or variable with respect to the number of bikes made.

_____ **a.** Bike frames
_____ **b.** Screws for assembly
_____ **c.** Direct labor

_____ **d.** Taxes on property
_____ **e.** Bike tires
_____ **f.** Gas used for heating

_____ **g.** Office supplies
_____ **h.** Depreciation on tools
_____ **i.** Management salaries

Exercise 8-2

Preparing flexible budgets

P1

Tempo Company's fixed budget (based on sales of 7,000 units) for the first quarter of calendar year 2017 reveals the following. Prepare flexible budgets following the format of Exhibit 8.3 that show variable costs per unit, fixed costs, and three different flexible budgets for sales volumes of 6,000, 7,000, and 8,000 units.

		Fixed Budget
Sales (7,000 units)		$2,800,000
Cost of goods sold		
Direct materials	$280,000	
Direct labor	490,000	
Production supplies	175,000	
Plant manager salary	65,000	1,010,000
Gross profit		1,790,000
Selling expenses		
Sales commissions	140,000	
Packaging	154,000	
Advertising	125,000	419,000
Administrative expenses		
Administrative salaries	85,000	
Depreciation—Office equip.	35,000	
Insurance	20,000	
Office rent	36,000	176,000
Income from operations		$1,195,000

Check Income (at 6,000 units), $972,000

Exercise 8-3

Preparing a flexible budget performance report

P1

Solitaire Company's fixed budget performance report for June follows. The $315,000 budgeted expenses include $294,000 variable expenses and $21,000 fixed expenses. Actual expenses include $27,000 fixed expenses. Prepare a flexible budget performance report showing any variances between budgeted and actual results. List fixed and variable expenses separately.

	Fixed Budget	Actual Results	Variances
Sales (in units)	8,400	10,800	
Sales (in dollars)	$420,000	$540,000	$120,000 F
Total expenses	315,000	378,000	63,000 U
Income from operations	$105,000	$162,000	$ 57,000 F

Check Income variance, $21,000 F

Bay City Company's fixed budget performance report for July follows. The $647,500 budgeted total expenses include $487,500 variable expenses and $160,000 fixed expenses. Actual expenses include $158,000 fixed expenses. Prepare a flexible budget performance report that shows any variances between budgeted results and actual results. List fixed and variable expenses separately.

Exercise 8-4
Preparing a flexible budget performance report
P1

	Fixed Budget	Actual Results	Variances
Sales (in units)	7,500	7,200	
Sales (in dollars)	$750,000	$737,000	$13,000 U
Total expenses	647,500	641,000	6,500 F
Income from operations	$102,500	$ 96,000	$ 6,500 U

Check Income variance, $4,000 F

Match the terms *a* through *e* with their correct definition 1 through 5.

Exercise 8-5
Standard costs
C1

a. Standard cost card
b. Management by exception
c. Standard cost
d. Ideal standard
e. Practical standard

____ **1.** Quantity of input required under normal conditions.
____ **2.** Quantity of input required if a production process is 100% efficient.
____ **3.** Managing by focusing on large differences from standard costs.
____ **4.** Record that accumulates standard cost information.
____ **5.** Preset cost for delivering a product or service under normal conditions.

Resset Co. provides the following results of April's operations: *F* indicates favorable and *U* indicates unfavorable. Applying the management by exception approach, which variances are of greatest concern? Why?

Exercise 8-6
Management by exception
C1

Direct materials price variance	$ 300 F
Direct materials quantity variance	3,000 U
Direct labor rate variance	100 U
Direct labor efficiency variance	2,200 F
Controllable overhead variance	400 U
Fixed overhead volume variance	500 F

Presented below are terms preceded by letters *a* through *j* and a list of definitions 1 through 10. Enter the letter of the term with the definition, using the space preceding the definition.

Exercise 8-7
Cost variances
C2

a. Fixed budget
b. Standard costs
c. Price variance
d. Quantity variance
e. Volume variance
f. Controllable variance
g. Cost variance
h. Flexible budget
i. Variance analysis
j. Management by exception

____ **1.** The difference between actual and budgeted sales or cost caused by the difference between the actual price per unit and the budgeted price per unit.
____ **2.** A planning budget based on a single predicted amount of sales or production volume; unsuitable for evaluations if the actual volume differs from the predicted volume.
____ **3.** Preset costs for delivering a product, component, or service under normal conditions.
____ **4.** A process of examining the differences between actual and budgeted sales or costs and describing them in terms of the amounts that resulted from price and quantity differences.
____ **5.** The difference between the total budgeted overhead cost and the overhead cost that was allocated to products using the predetermined fixed overhead rate.
____ **6.** A budget prepared based on predicted amounts of revenues and expenses corresponding to the actual level of output.
____ **7.** The difference between actual and budgeted cost caused by the difference between the actual quantity and the budgeted quantity.
____ **8.** The combination of both overhead spending variances (variable and fixed) and the variable overhead efficiency variance.
____ **9.** A management process to focus on significant variances and give less attention to areas where performance is close to the standard.
____ **10.** The difference between actual cost and standard cost, made up of a price variance and a quantity variance.

Exercise 8-8

Standard unit cost; total cost variance

C2

A manufactured product has the following information for June.

	Standard	Actual
Direct materials	6 lbs. @ $8 per lb.	48,500 lbs. @ $8.10 per lb.
Direct labor	2 hrs. @ $16 per hr.	15,700 hrs. @ $16.50 per hr.
Overhead	2 hrs. @ $12 per hr.	$198,000
Units manufactured		8,000

Compute the (1) standard cost per unit and (2) total cost variance for June. Indicate whether the cost variance is favorable or unfavorable.

Exercise 8-9

Direct materials variances P2

Refer to the information in Exercise 8-8 and compute the (1) direct materials price and (2) direct materials quantity variances. Indicate whether each variance is favorable or unfavorable.

Exercise 8-10

Direct labor variances

P2

Refer to the information in Exercise 8-8 and compute the (1) direct labor rate and (2) direct labor efficiency variances. Indicate whether each variance is favorable or unfavorable.

Exercise 8-11

Direct materials and direct labor variances

P2

Hutto Corp. has set the following standard direct materials and direct labor costs per unit for the product it manufactures.

Direct materials (15 lbs. @ $4 per lb.)	$60
Direct labor (3 hrs. @ $15 per hr.)	45

During May the company incurred the following actual costs to produce 9,000 units.

Direct materials (138,000 lbs. @ $3.75 per lb.)	$517,500
Direct labor (31,000 hrs. @ $15.10 per hr.)	468,100

Compute the (1) direct materials price and quantity variances and (2) direct labor rate and efficiency variances. Indicate whether each variance is favorable or unfavorable.

Exercise 8-12

Direct materials and direct labor variances

P2

Reed Corp. has set the following standard direct materials and direct labor costs per unit for the product it manufactures.

Direct materials (10 lbs. @ $3 per lb.)	$30
Direct labor (2 hrs. @ $12 per hr.)	24

During June the company incurred the following actual costs to produce 9,000 units.

Direct materials (92,000 lbs. @ $2.95 per lb.)	$271,400
Direct labor (18,800 hrs. @ $12.05 per hr.)	226,540

Compute the (1) direct materials price and quantity variances and (2) direct labor rate and efficiency variances. Indicate whether each variance is favorable or unfavorable.

Exercise 8-13

Computation and interpretation of materials variances P2

Check Price variance, $2,200 U

Hart Company made 3,000 bookshelves using 22,000 board feet of wood costing $266,200. The company's direct materials standards for one bookshelf are 8 board feet of wood at $12 per board foot.

1. Compute the direct materials price and quantity variances and classify each as favorable or unfavorable.

2. Interpret the direct materials variances.

Refer to Exercise 8-13. Hart Company records standard costs in its accounts and its materials variances in separate accounts when it assigns materials costs to the Work in Process Inventory account.

1. Show the journal entry that both charges the direct materials costs to the Work in Process Inventory account and records the materials variances in their proper accounts.

2. Assume that Hart's materials variances are the only variances accumulated in the accounting period and that they are immaterial. Prepare the adjusting journal entry to close the variance accounts at period-end.

3. Identify the variance that should be investigated according to the management by exception concept. Explain.

Exercise 8-14^A

Materials variances recorded and closed

P5

Check   (2) Cr. to Cost of Goods Sold, $21,800

The following information describes production activities of Mercer Manufacturing for the year.

Actual direct materials used	16,000 lbs. at $4.05 per lb.
Actual direct labor used..................	5,545 hours for a total of $105,355
Actual units produced	30,000

Budgeted standards for each unit produced are 0.50 pounds of direct material at $4.00 per pound and 10 minutes of direct labor at $20 per hour.

1. Compute the direct materials price and quantity variances and classify each as favorable or unfavorable.

2. Compute the direct labor rate and efficiency variances and classify each as favorable or unfavorable.

Exercise 8-15

Direct materials and direct labor variances

P2

After evaluating Null Company's manufacturing process, management decides to establish standards of 3 hours of direct labor per unit of product and $15 per hour for the labor rate. During October, the company uses 16,250 hours of direct labor at a $247,000 total cost to produce 5,600 units of product. In November, the company uses 22,000 hours of direct labor at a $335,500 total cost to produce 6,000 units of product.

1. Compute the direct labor rate variance, the direct labor efficiency variance, and the total direct labor cost variance for each of these two months. Classify each variance as favorable or unfavorable.

2. Interpret the October direct labor variances.

Exercise 8-16

Computation and interpretation of labor variances   P2

Check   (1) October rate variance, $3,250 U

Sedona Company set the following standard costs for one unit of its product for 2017.

Direct material (20 lbs. @ $2.50 per lb.)	$ 50
Direct labor (10 hrs. @ $22.00 per hr.)	220
Factory variable overhead (10 hrs. @ $4.00 per hr.)	40
Factory fixed overhead (10 hrs. @ $1.60 per hr.)	16
Standard cost	$326

Exercise 8-17

Computation of total variable and fixed overhead variances

P3

The $5.60 ($4.00 + $1.60) total overhead rate per direct labor hour is based on an expected operating level equal to 75% of the factory's capacity of 50,000 units per month. The following monthly flexible budget information is also available.

A	B	C	D
1		Operating Levels (% of capacity)	
2	**Flexible Budget**	**70%**	**75%**	**80%**
3	Budgeted output (units)	35,000	37,500	40,000
4	Budgeted labor (standard hours)	350,000	375,000	400,000
5	Budgeted overhead (dollars)			
6	Variable overhead	$1,400,000	$1,500,000	$1,600,000
7	Fixed overhead	600,000	600,000	600,000
8	Total overhead	$2,000,000	$2,100,000	$2,200,000

During the current month, the company operated at 70% of capacity, employees worked 340,000 hours, and the following actual overhead costs were incurred.

Variable overhead costs	$1,375,000
Fixed overhead costs	628,600
Total overhead costs	$2,003,600

Check   (2) Variable overhead cost variance, $25,000 F

1. Show how the company computed its predetermined overhead application rate per hour for total overhead, variable overhead, and fixed overhead.

2. Compute the total variable and total fixed overhead variances and classify each as favorable or unfavorable.

Exercise 8-18ᴬ

Computation and interpretation of overhead spending, efficiency, and volume variances   P4

Check   (1) Variable overhead: Spending, $15,000 U; Efficiency, $40,000 F

Refer to the information from Exercise 8-17. Compute and interpret the following.

1. Variable overhead spending and efficiency variances.

2. Fixed overhead spending and volume variances.

3. Controllable variance.

Exercise 8-19

Computation of total overhead rate and total overhead variance

P3

Check   (1) Overhead rate, $13.00 per hour

World Company expects to operate at 80% of its productive capacity of 50,000 units per month. At this planned level, the company expects to use 25,000 standard hours of direct labor. Overhead is allocated to products using a predetermined standard rate of 0.625 direct labor hours per unit. At the 80% capacity level, the total budgeted cost includes $50,000 fixed overhead cost and $275,000 variable overhead cost. In the current month, the company incurred $305,000 actual overhead and 22,000 actual labor hours while producing 35,000 units.

1. Compute the predetermined standard overhead rate for total overhead.

2. Compute and interpret the total overhead variance.

Exercise 8-20

Computation of volume and controllable overhead variances   P3

Check   (2) $14,375 U

Refer to the information from Exercise 8-19. Compute the (1) overhead volume variance and (2) overhead controllable variance and classify each as favorable or unfavorable.

Exercise 8-21

Overhead controllable and volume variances; overhead variance report

P3

James Corp. applies overhead on the basis of direct labor hours. For the month of May, the company planned production of 8,000 units (80% of its production capacity of 10,000 units) and prepared the following overhead budget.

	Operating Level
Overhead Budget	**80%**
Production in units	8,000
Standard direct labor hours	24,000
Budgeted overhead	
Variable overhead costs	
Indirect materials...................	$15,000
Indirect labor.....................	24,000
Power...........................	6,000
Maintenance	3,000
Total variable costs	48,000
Fixed overhead costs	
Rent of factory building	15,000
Depreciation—Machinery............	10,000
Supervisory salaries	19,400
Total fixed costs	44,400
Total overhead costs	$92,400

During May, the company operated at 90% capacity (9,000 units) and incurred the following actual overhead costs.

Overhead costs (actual)	
Indirect materials	$15,000
Indirect labor	26,500
Power	6,750
Maintenance	4,000
Rent of factory building	15,000
Depreciation—Machinery	10,000
Supervisory salaries	22,000
Total actual overhead costs	$99,250

1. Compute the overhead controllable variance and classify it as favorable or unfavorable.
2. Compute the overhead volume variance and classify it as favorable or unfavorable.
3. Prepare an overhead variance report at the actual activity level of 9,000 units.

Blaze Corp. applies overhead on the basis of direct labor hours. For the month of March, the company planned production of 8,000 units (80% of its production capacity of 10,000 units) and prepared the following budget.

Exercise 8-22
Overhead controllable and volume variances; overhead variance report

P3

	Operating Level
Overhead Budget	**80%**
Production in units	8,000
Standard direct labor hours	32,000
Budgeted overhead	
Variable overhead costs	
Indirect materials	$10,000
Indirect labor	16,000
Power	4,000
Maintenance	2,000
Total variable costs	32,000
Fixed overhead costs	
Rent of factory building	12,000
Depreciation—Machinery	20,000
Taxes and insurance	2,400
Supervisory salaries	13,600
Total fixed costs	48,000
Total overhead costs	$80,000

During March, the company operated at 90% capacity (9,000 units), and it incurred the following actual overhead costs.

Overhead costs (actual)	
Indirect materials	$10,000
Indirect labor	16,000
Power	4,500
Maintenance	3,000
Rent of factory building	12,000
Depreciation—Machinery	19,200
Taxes and insurance	3,000
Supervisory salaries	14,000
Total actual overhead costs	$81,700

1. Compute the overhead controllable variance.
2. Compute the overhead volume variance.
3. Prepare an overhead variance report at the actual activity level of 9,000 units.

Comp Wiz sells computers. During May 2017, it sold 350 computers at a $1,200 average price each. The May 2017 fixed budget included sales of 365 computers at an average price of $1,100 each.

Exercise 8-23
Computing and interpreting sales variances   A1

1. Compute the sales price variance and the sales volume variance for May 2017.
2. Interpret the findings.

PROBLEM SET A

Problem 8-1A
Preparation and analysis of a flexible budget

P1

Phoenix Company's 2017 master budget included the following fixed budget report. It is based on an expected production and sales volume of 15,000 units.

PHOENIX COMPANY
Fixed Budget Report
For Year Ended December 31, 2017

Sales		$3,000,000
Cost of goods sold		
Direct materials	$975,000	
Direct labor.	225,000	
Machinery repairs (variable cost)	60,000	
Depreciation—Plant equipment (straight-line)	300,000	
Utilities ($45,000 is variable)	195,000	
Plant management salaries	200,000	1,955,000
Gross profit		1,045,000
Selling expenses		
Packaging.	75,000	
Shipping	105,000	
Sales salary (fixed annual amount)	250,000	430,000
General and administrative expenses		
Advertising expense	125,000	
Salaries.	241,000	
Entertainment expense	90,000	456,000
Income from operations		$ 159,000

Required

1. Classify all items listed in the fixed budget as variable or fixed. Also determine their amounts per unit or their amounts for the year, as appropriate.

Check (2) Budgeted income at 16,000 units, $260,000

2. Prepare flexible budgets (see Exhibit 8.3) for the company at sales volumes of 14,000 and 16,000 units.

3. The company's business conditions are improving. One possible result is a sales volume of 18,000 units. The company president is confident that this volume is within the relevant range of existing capacity. How much would operating income increase over the 2017 budgeted amount of $159,000 if this level is reached without increasing capacity?

(4) Potential operating loss, $(144,000)

4. An unfavorable change in business is remotely possible; in this case, production and sales volume for 2017 could fall to 12,000 units. How much income (or loss) from operations would occur if sales volume falls to this level?

Problem 8-2A
Preparation and analysis of a flexible budget performance report

P1   P2   A1

Refer to the information in Problem 8-1A. Phoenix Company's actual income statement for 2017 follows.

PHOENIX COMPANY
Statement of Income from Operations
For Year Ended December 31, 2017

Sales (18,000 units)		$3,648,000
Cost of goods sold		
Direct materials	$1,185,000	
Direct labor.	278,000	
Machinery repairs (variable cost)	63,000	
Depreciation—Plant equipment	300,000	
Utilities (fixed cost is $147,500)	200,500	
Plant management salaries.	210,000	2,236,500
Gross profit		1,411,500
Selling expenses		
Packaging.	87,500	
Shipping	118,500	
Sales salary (annual)	268,000	474,000
General and administrative expenses		
Advertising expense	132,000	
Salaries.	241,000	
Entertainment expense	93,500	466,500
Income from operations		$ 471,000

Required

1. Prepare a flexible budget performance report for 2017.

Analysis Component

2. Analyze and interpret both the (a) sales variance and (b) direct materials cost variance.

Check   (1) Variances: Fixed costs, $36,000 U; Income, $9,000 F

Antuan Company set the following standard costs for one unit of its product.

Direct materials (6 lbs. @ $5 per lb.)	$ 30
Direct labor (2 hrs. @ $17 per hr.)	34
Overhead (2 hrs. @ $18.50 per hr.)	37
Total standard cost	$101

Problem 8-3A
Flexible budget preparation; computation of materials, labor, and overhead variances; and overhead variance report

P1   P2   P3

The predetermined overhead rate ($18.50 per direct labor hour) is based on an expected volume of 75% of the factory's capacity of 20,000 units per month. Following are the company's budgeted overhead costs per month at the 75% capacity level.

Overhead Budget (75% Capacity)		
Variable overhead costs		
Indirect materials	$ 45,000	
Indirect labor	180,000	
Power	45,000	
Repairs and maintenance	90,000	
Total variable overhead costs		$360,000
Fixed overhead costs		
Depreciation—Building	24,000	
Depreciation—Machinery	80,000	
Taxes and insurance	12,000	
Supervision	79,000	
Total fixed overhead costs		195,000
Total overhead costs		$555,000

The company incurred the following actual costs when it operated at 75% of capacity in October.

Direct materials (91,000 lbs. @ $5.10 per lb.)		$ 464,100
Direct labor (30,500 hrs. @ $17.25 per hr.)		526,125
Overhead costs		
Indirect materials	$ 44,250	
Indirect labor	177,750	
Power	43,000	
Repairs and maintenance	96,000	
Depreciation—Building	24,000	
Depreciation—Machinery	75,000	
Taxes and insurance	11,500	
Supervision	89,000	560,500
Total costs		$1,550,725

Required

1. Examine the monthly overhead budget to (a) determine the costs per unit for each variable overhead item and its total per unit costs and (b) identify the total fixed costs per month.

2. Prepare flexible overhead budgets (as in Exhibit 8.12) for October showing the amounts of each variable and fixed cost at the 65%, 75%, and 85% capacity levels.

3. Compute the direct materials cost variance, including its price and quantity variances.

Check   (2) Budgeted total overhead at 13,000 units, $507,000

(3) Materials variances: Price, $9,100 U; Quantity, $5,000 U

(4) Labor variances:
Rate, $7,625 U; Efficiency,
$8,500 U

4. Compute the direct labor cost variance, including its rate and efficiency variances.
5. Prepare a detailed overhead variance report (as in Exhibit 8.16) that shows the variances for individual items of overhead.

Problem 8-4A
Computation of materials, labor, and overhead variances

P2   P3

Trico Company set the following standard unit costs for its single product.

Direct materials (30 lbs. @ $4 per lb.)	$120
Direct labor (5 hrs. @ $14 per hr.)	70
Factory overhead—variable (5 hrs. @ $8 per hr.)	40
Factory overhead—fixed (5 hrs. @ $10 per hr.)	50
Total standard cost	$280

The predetermined overhead rate is based on a planned operating volume of 80% of the productive capacity of 60,000 units per quarter. The following flexible budget information is available.

	Operating Levels		
	70%	80%	90%
Production in units	42,000	48,000	54,000
Standard direct labor hours	210,000	240,000	270,000
Budgeted overhead			
Fixed factory overhead	$2,400,000	$2,400,000	$2,400,000
Variable factory overhead	$1,680,000	$1,920,000	$2,160,000

During the current quarter, the company operated at 90% of capacity and produced 54,000 units of product; actual direct labor totaled 265,000 hours. Units produced were assigned the following standard costs.

Direct materials (1,620,000 lbs. @ $4 per lb.)	$ 6,480,000
Direct labor (270,000 hrs. @ $14 per hr.)	3,780,000
Factory overhead (270,000 hrs. @ $18 per hr.)	4,860,000
Total standard cost	$15,120,000

Actual costs incurred during the current quarter follow.

Direct materials (1,615,000 lbs. @ $4.10 per lb.)	$ 6,621,500
Direct labor (265,000 hrs. @ $13.75 per hr.)	3,643,750
Fixed factory overhead costs	2,350,000
Variable factory overhead costs	2,200,000
Total actual costs	$14,815,250

Check   (1) Materials
variances: Price, $161,500 U;
Quantity, $20,000 F
          (2) Labor variances:
Rate, $66,250 F; Efficiency,
$70,000 F

Required

1. Compute the direct materials cost variance, including its price and quantity variances.
2. Compute the direct labor cost variance, including its rate and efficiency variances.
3. Compute the overhead controllable and volume variances.

Problem 8-5A^A
Expanded overhead variances

P4

Refer to the information in Problem 8-4A.

Required

Compute these variances: (a) variable overhead spending and efficiency, (b) fixed overhead spending and volume, and (c) total overhead controllable.

Boss Company's standard cost accounting system recorded this information from its December operations.

Standard direct materials cost...	$100,000
Direct materials quantity variance (unfavorable)	3,000
Direct materials price variance (favorable)............................	500
Actual direct labor cost	90,000
Direct labor efficiency variance (favorable)	7,000
Direct labor rate variance (unfavorable)...............................	1,200
Actual overhead cost	375,000
Volume variance (unfavorable)	12,000
Controllable variance (unfavorable)	9,000

Problem 8-6A[A]

Materials, labor, and overhead variances recorded and analyzed

C1   P5

Required

1. Prepare December 31 journal entries to record the company's costs and variances for the month. (Do not prepare the journal entry to close the variances.)

Analysis Component

2. Identify the variances that would attract the attention of a manager who uses management by exception. Explain what action(s) the manager should consider.

Check   (1) Dr. Work in Process Inventory (for overhead), $354,000

Tohono Company's 2017 master budget included the following fixed budget report. It is based on an expected production and sales volume of 20,000 units.

PROBLEM SET B

Problem 8-1B
Preparation and analysis of a flexible budget

P1   A1

TOHONO COMPANY Fixed Budget Report For Year Ended December 31, 2017		
Sales		$3,000,000
Cost of goods sold		
Direct materials	$1,200,000	
Direct labor...	260,000	
Machinery repairs (variable cost)	57,000	
Depreciation—Machinery (straight-line).................	250,000	
Utilities (25% is variable cost)	200,000	
Plant manager salaries	140,000	2,107,000
Gross profit...		893,000
Selling expenses		
Packaging..	80,000	
Shipping	116,000	
Sales salary (fixed annual amount)......................	160,000	356,000
General and administrative expenses		
Advertising..	81,000	
Salaries..	241,000	
Entertainment expense...............................	90,000	412,000
Income from operations.................................		$ 125,000

Required

1. Classify all items listed in the fixed budget as variable or fixed. Also determine their amounts per unit or their amounts for the year, as appropriate.

2. Prepare flexible budgets (see Exhibit 8.3) for the company at sales volumes of 18,000 and 24,000 units.

3. The company's business conditions are improving. One possible result is a sales volume of 28,000 units. The company president is confident that this volume is within the relevant range of existing capacity. How much would operating income increase over the 2017 budgeted amount of $125,000 if this level is reached without increasing capacity?

4. An unfavorable change in business is remotely possible; in this case, production and sales volume for 2017 could fall to 14,000 units. How much income (or loss) from operations would occur if sales volume falls to this level?

Check   (2) Budgeted income at 24,000 units, $372,400

(4) Potential operating loss, $(246,100)

Problem 8-2B

Preparation and analysis of a flexible budget performance report

P1   A1

Refer to the information in Problem 8-1B. Tohono Company's actual income statement for 2017 follows.

TOHONO COMPANY		
Statement of Income from Operations		
For Year Ended December 31, 2017		
Sales (24,000 units)		$3,648,000
Cost of goods sold		
Direct materials	$1,400,000	
Direct labor.	360,000	
Machinery repairs (variable cost)	60,000	
Depreciation—Machinery	250,000	
Utilities (variable cost, $64,000).	218,000	
Plant manager salaries	155,000	2,443,000
Gross profit.		1,205,000
Selling expenses		
Packaging.	90,000	
Shipping	124,000	
Sales salary (annual)	162,000	376,000
General and administrative expenses		
Advertising expense	104,000	
Salaries	232,000	
Entertainment expense	100,000	436,000
Income from operations		$ 393,000

Required

1. Prepare a flexible budget performance report for 2017.

Analysis Component

2. Analyze and interpret both the (a) sales variance and (b) direct materials cost variance.

Problem 8-3B

Flexible budget preparation; computation of materials, labor, and overhead variances; and overhead variance report

P1   P2   P3

Suncoast Company set the following standard costs for one unit of its product.

Direct materials (4.5 lbs. @ $6 per lb.)	$27
Direct labor (1.5 hrs. @ $12 per hr.)	18
Overhead (1.5 hrs. @ $16 per hr.)	24
Total standard cost.	$69

The predetermined overhead rate ($16.00 per direct labor hour) is based on an expected volume of 75% of the factory's capacity of 20,000 units per month. Following are the company's budgeted overhead costs per month at the 75% capacity level.

Overhead Budget (75% Capacity)		
Variable overhead costs		
Indirect materials	$22,500	
Indirect labor	90,000	
Power	22,500	
Repairs and maintenance	45,000	
Total variable overhead costs		$180,000
Fixed overhead costs		
Depreciation—Building	24,000	
Depreciation—Machinery	72,000	
Taxes and insurance	18,000	
Supervision	66,000	
Total fixed overhead costs.		180,000
Total overhead costs		$360,000

The company incurred the following actual costs when it operated at 75% of capacity in December.

Direct materials (69,000 lbs. @ $6.10 per lb.)		$ 420,900
Direct labor (22,800 hrs. @ $12.30 per hr.)		280,440
Overhead costs		
Indirect materials	$21,600	
Indirect labor	82,260	
Power	23,100	
Repairs and maintenance	46,800	
Depreciation—Building	24,000	
Depreciation—Machinery	75,000	
Taxes and insurance	16,500	
Supervision	66,000	355,260
Total costs		$1,056,600

Required

1. Examine the monthly overhead budget to (a) determine the costs per unit for each variable overhead item and its total per unit costs and (b) identify the total fixed costs per month.
2. Prepare flexible overhead budgets (as in Exhibit 8.12) for December showing the amounts of each variable and fixed cost at the 65%, 75%, and 85% capacity levels.
3. Compute the direct materials cost variance, including its price and quantity variances.
4. Compute the direct labor cost variance, including its rate and efficiency variances.
5. Prepare a detailed overhead variance report (as in Exhibit 8.16) that shows the variances for individual items of overhead.

Check   (2) Budgeted total overhead at 17,000 units, $384,000

(3) Materials variances: Price, $6,900 U; Quantity, $9,000 U

(4) Labor variances: Rate, $6,840 U; Efficiency, $3,600 U

Kryll Company set the following standard unit costs for its single product.

Problem 8-4B
Computation of materials, labor, and overhead variances

P2   P3

Direct materials (25 lbs. @ $4 per lb.).	$100
Direct labor (6 hrs. @ $8 per hr.)	48
Factory overhead—Variable (6 hrs. @ $5 per hr.)	30
Factory overhead—Fixed (6 hrs. @ $7 per hr.)	42
Total standard cost	$220

The predetermined overhead rate is based on a planned operating volume of 80% of the productive capacity of 60,000 units per quarter. The following flexible budget information is available.

	Operating Levels		
	70%	**80%**	**90%**
Production in units	42,000	48,000	54,000
Standard direct labor hours	252,000	288,000	324,000
Budgeted overhead			
Fixed factory overhead	$2,016,000	$2,016,000	$2,016,000
Variable factory overhead	1,260,000	1,440,000	1,620,000

During the current quarter, the company operated at 70% of capacity and produced 42,000 units of product; direct labor hours worked were 250,000. Units produced were assigned the following standard costs:

Direct materials (1,050,000 lbs. @ $4 per lb.)	$4,200,000
Direct labor (252,000 hrs. @ $8 per hr.)	2,016,000
Factory overhead (252,000 hrs. @ $12 per hr.)	3,024,000
Total standard cost	$9,240,000

354   Chapter 8   Flexible Budgets and Standard Costs

Actual costs incurred during the current quarter follow.

Direct materials (1,000,000 lbs. @ $4.25 per lb.)	$4,250,000
Direct labor (250,000 hrs. @ $7.75 per hr.)	1,937,500
Fixed factory overhead costs.......................................	1,960,000
Variable factory overhead costs....................................	1,200,000
Total actual costs	$9,347,500

Check (1) Materials variances: Price, $250,000 U; Quantity, $200,000 F; (2) Labor variances: Rate, $62,500 F; Efficiency, $16,000 F

Required

1. Compute the direct materials cost variance, including its price and quantity variances.
2. Compute the direct labor cost variance, including its rate and efficiency variances.
3. Compute the total overhead controllable and volume variances.

Problem 8-5B^A
Expanded overhead variances

P4

Refer to the information in Problem 8-4B.

Required

Compute these variances: (a) variable overhead spending and efficiency, (b) fixed overhead spending and volume, and (c) total overhead controllable.

Problem 8-6B^A
Materials, labor, and overhead variances recorded and analyzed

C1   P5

Kenya Company's standard cost accounting system recorded this information from its June operations.

Standard direct materials cost..	$130,000
Direct materials quantity variance (favorable)	5,000
Direct materials price variance (favorable)...............................	1,500
Actual direct labor cost	65,000
Direct labor efficiency variance (favorable)	3,000
Direct labor rate variance (unfavorable).................................	500
Actual overhead cost	250,000
Volume variance (unfavorable)...	12,000
Controllable variance (unfavorable)	8,000

Required

1. Prepare journal entries dated June 30 to record the company's costs and variances for the month. (Do not prepare the journal entry to close the variances.)

Analysis Component

2. Identify the variances that would attract the attention of a manager who uses management by exception. Describe what action(s) the manager should consider.

SERIAL PROBLEM
Business Solutions

P1

© Alexander Image/Shutterstock RF

(This serial problem began in Chapter 1 and continues through most of the book. If previous chapter segments were not completed, the serial problem can begin at this point.)

SP 8 Business Solutions's second-quarter 2018 fixed budget performance report for its computer furniture operations follows. The $156,000 budgeted expenses include $108,000 in variable expenses for desks and $18,000 in variable expenses for chairs, as well as $30,000 fixed expenses. The actual expenses include $31,000 fixed expenses. Prepare a flexible budget performance report that shows any variances between budgeted results and actual results. List fixed and variable expenses separately.

	Fixed Budget	Actual Results	Variances
Desk sales (in units)	144	150	
Chair sales (in units)................	72	80	
Desk sales......................	$180,000	$186,000	$6,000 F
Chair sales	36,000	41,200	5,200 F
Total expenses	156,000	163,880	7,880 U
Income from operations...........	$ 60,000	$ 63,320	$3,320 F

Beyond the Numbers

BTN 8-1   Analysis of flexible budgets and standard costs emphasizes the importance of a similar unit of measure for meaningful comparisons and evaluations. When **Apple** compiles its financial reports in compliance with GAAP, it applies the same unit of measurement, U.S. dollars, for most measures of business operations. One issue for Apple is how best to adjust account values for its subsidiaries that compile financial reports in currencies other than the U.S. dollar.

REPORTING IN ACTION

C1

APPLE

Required

1. Read Apple's Note 1 in Appendix A and identify the financial statement where it reports the annual adjustment for foreign currency translation for subsidiaries that do not use the U.S. dollar as their functional currency.
2. Translating financial statements requires the use of a currency exchange rate. For each of the following financial statement items, explain the exchange rate the company would apply to translate into U.S. dollars.
   a. Cash
   b. Sales revenue
   c. Property, plant and equipment

BTN 8-2   The usefulness of budgets, variances, and related analyses often depends on the accuracy of management's estimates of future sales activity.

COMPARATIVE ANALYSIS

A1

APPLE
GOOGLE

Required

1. Identify and record the prior three years' sales (in dollars) for **Apple** and **Google** using their financial statements in Appendix A.
2. Using the data in part 1, predict both companies' sales activity for the next two to three years. (If possible, compare your predictions to actual sales figures for those years.)

BTN 8-3   Setting materials, labor, and overhead standards is challenging. If standards are set too low, companies might purchase inferior products and employees might not work to their full potential. If standards are set too high, companies could be unable to offer a quality product at a profitable price and employees could be overworked. The ethical challenge is to set a high but reasonable standard. Assume that as a manager you are asked to set the standard materials price and quantity for the new 1,000 CKB Mega-Max chip, a technically advanced product. To properly set the price and quantity standards, you assemble a team of specialists to provide input.

ETHICS CHALLENGE

C1

Required

Identify four types of specialists that you would assemble to provide information to help set the materials price and quantity standards. Briefly explain why you chose each individual.

BTN 8-4   The reason we use the words *favorable* and *unfavorable* when evaluating variances is made clear when we look at the closing of accounts. To see this, consider that (1) all variance accounts are closed at the end of each period (temporary accounts), (2) a favorable variance is always a credit balance, and (3) an unfavorable variance is always a debit balance. Write a half-page memorandum to your instructor with three parts that answer the three following requirements. (Assume that variance accounts are closed to Cost of Goods Sold.)

COMMUNICATING IN PRACTICE

P5   C2

Required

1. Does Cost of Goods Sold increase or decrease when closing a favorable variance? Does gross margin increase or decrease when a favorable variance is closed to Cost of Goods Sold? Explain.
2. Does Cost of Goods Sold increase or decrease when closing an unfavorable variance? Does gross margin increase or decrease when an unfavorable variance is closed to Cost of Goods Sold? Explain.
3. Explain the meaning of a favorable variance and an unfavorable variance.

TAKING IT TO THE NET

C1

BTN 8-5 Access **iSixSigma**'s website (**iSixSigma.com**) to search for and read information about the purpose and use of *benchmarking* to complete the following requirements. (*Hint:* Look in the "Methodology" link.)

Required

1. Write a one-paragraph explanation (in layperson's terms) of benchmarking.
2. How does standard costing relate to benchmarking?

TEAMWORK IN ACTION

C2

BTN 8-6 Many service industries link labor rate and time (quantity) standards with their processes. One example is the standard time to board an aircraft. The reason time plays such an important role in the service industry is that it is viewed as a competitive advantage: best service in the shortest amount of time. Although the labor rate component is difficult to observe, the time component of a service delivery standard is often readily apparent—for example, "Lunch will be served in less than five minutes, or it is free."

Required

Break into teams and select two service industries for your analysis. Identify and describe all the time elements each industry uses to create a competitive advantage.

ENTREPRENEURIAL DECISION

C1 C2

BTN 8-7   Riide, as discussed in the chapter opener, uses a costing system with standard costs for direct materials, direct labor, and overhead costs. Two comments frequently are mentioned in relation to standard costing and variance analysis: "Variances are not explanations" and "Management's goal is not to minimize variances."

Required

Write a short memo (no more than one page) to Amber Wason and Jeff Stefanis, Riide's co-founders, interpreting these two comments in the context of their electric bike business.

HITTING THE ROAD

C1

BTN 8-8 Training employees to use standard amounts of materials in production is common. Typically, large companies invest in this training but small organizations do not. One can observe these different practices in a trip to two different pizza businesses. Visit both a local pizza business and a national pizza chain business and then complete the following.

Required

1. Observe and record the number of raw material items used to make a typical cheese pizza. Also observe how the person making the pizza applies each item when preparing the pizza.
2. Record any differences in how items are applied between the two businesses.
3. Estimate which business is more profitable from your observations. Explain.

GLOBAL DECISION

A1

Samsung

BTN 8-9 Access the annual report of **Samsung** (at **samsung.com**) for the year ended December 31, 2015. The usefulness of its budgets, variances, and related analyses depends on the accuracy of management's estimates of future sales activity.

Required

1. Identify and record the prior two years' sales (in ₩ millions) for Samsung from its income statement.
2. Using the data in part 1, predict sales activity for Samsung for the next two years. Explain your prediction process.

GLOBAL VIEW

BMW, a German automobile manufacturer, uses standard costing and variance analysis. Production begins with huge rolls of steel and aluminum, which are then cut and pressed by large machines. Material must meet high quality standards, and the company sets standards for each of its machine operations.

In the assembly department, highly trained employees complete the assembly of the painted car chassis, often to customer specifications. BMW sets standards for how much labor should be used and monitors its employee performance. The company then computes and analyzes materials price and quantity variances and labor rate and efficiency variances and takes action as needed.

Like most manufacturers, BMW uses *practical standards* and thus must address waste of raw materials in its production process. In a recent year, BMW used over 3 million tons of steel, plastic, and aluminum to make over 1.8 million cars. Of the 665,000 tons of these raw materials wasted in production, over 98% are recyclable.

 Global View Assignments

Discussion Question 12

Discussion Question 16

Quick Study 8-21

BTN 8-9

Performance Measurement and Responsibility Accounting

Chapter Preview

RESPONSIBILITY ACCOUNTING

Performance evaluatioin

Controllable versus uncontrollable costs

P1 Responsibility accounting for cost centers

NTK 9-1

PROFIT CENTERS

C1 Direct and indirect expenses

P2 Allocation of expenses

P3 Departmental income statements

Departmental contribution to overhead

NTK 9-2

INVESTMENT CENTERS

A1 ROI and residual income

A2 Margin and turnover

A3 Nonfinancial measures

C2 Transfer pricing

A4 Cycle time

C3 Joint costs

NTK 9-3, 9-4, 9-5

Learning Objectives

CONCEPTUAL

C1 Distinguish between direct and indirect expenses and identify bases for allocating indirect expenses to departments.

C2 Explain transfer pricing and methods to set transfer prices.

C3 *Appendix 9C—*Describe allocation of joint costs across products.

ANALYTICAL

A1 Analyze investment centers using return on investment and residual income.

A2 Analyze investment centers using profit margin and investment turnover.

A3 Analyze investment centers using the balanced scorecard.

A4 Compute cycle time and cycle efficiency, and explain their importance to production management.

PROCEDURAL

P1 Prepare a responsibility accounting report using controllable costs.

P2 Allocate indirect expenses to departments.

P3 Prepare departmental income statements and contribution reports.

© Bryce Vickmark/
The New York Times/Redux

Sew Cool

BOSTON—Aman Advani, Gihan Amarasiriwardena, and Kit Hickey wanted to design everyday clothes with performance features like those in athletic gear. Kit's work suits were stiff compared to her rock-climbing gear. Gihan couldn't find dress shirts to keep up with his bicycle commuting.

"Lines between work, play, and downtime are blurred," insists Aman. "We need clothes to keep up with our entire day." In response, the trio launched **Ministry (Ministry.co)**.

"We design our products around real customers' daily activities," explains Aman. The company uses new materials, 3D printing, and thermal analysis to design better-fitting menswear that combats heat, moisture, and odor.

Their "frankensock" is a dress sock with an athletic sock sewn inside. The Mercury sweater has carbonized coffee in the fabric to absorb odors. One line of dress shirts uses a material engineered by NASA to adjust to changing temperatures. Gihan exclaims, "this is the next generation of clothing manufacturing and design."

The company carefully monitors its costs, including design, materials, labor, and overhead. The company is organized around product lines—shirts, pants, blazers, sweaters, and accessories—and the founders study income by product line to monitor performance and control costs. They apply cost concepts such as direct and indirect expenses and how to allocate expenses to product lines.

In addition to financial measures such as return on investment (ROI), residual income, and departmental income, the owners use nonfinancial information to guide their efforts. "We use customer feedback to continually improve our products," explains Kit, noting "we tried more than 20 iterations of our dress shirt."

"Invent something new"
—Kit Hickey

Gihan, who ran a marathon in one of his company's suits, believes the "future of apparel will involve taking customer measurements by a scan and printing a garment for their unique body shape."

Ministry's high-tech approach has raised over $6 million in financing. Aman adds that "we work to triple total sales each year." Although accounting goals are important, the founders donate a portion of all sales to educational programs to fit their philosophy to *make a difference in the world.*

Sources: *Ministry website,* January 2017; *Mashable.com,* April 14, 2016; *Esquire.com,* April 14, 2016; *Businessnewsdaily.com,* November 19, 2014; *New York Times,* May 19, 2013

RESPONSIBILITY ACCOUNTING

Callaway Golf

Golf Clubs   Golf Balls

Point: Responsibility accounting does not place blame. Instead, it is used to identify opportunities for improving performance.

Performance Evaluation

Many large companies are easier to manage if they are divided into smaller units, called *divisions, segments,* or *departments.* For example, **LinkedIn** organizes its operations around three geographic segments: North America, Europe, and Asia-Pacific. **Callaway Golf** organizes its operations around two product lines, golf balls and golf clubs, while **Kraft Heinz** organizes its operations both geographically and around several product lines. In these **decentralized organizations,** decisions are made by unit managers rather than by top management. Top management then evaluates the performance of unit managers.

In **responsibility accounting,** unit managers are evaluated only on things they have control over. Methods of performance evaluation vary for cost centers, profit centers, and investment centers.

- A **cost center** incurs costs without directly generating revenues. The manufacturing departments of a manufacturer are cost centers. Also, its service departments, such as accounting, advertising, and purchasing, are cost centers. Kraft Heinz's Dover, Delaware, manufacturing plant is a cost center. *Cost center managers are evaluated on their success in controlling actual costs* compared to budgeted costs.

- A **profit center** generates revenues and incurs costs. Product lines are often evaluated as profit centers. Kraft Heinz's beverage and condiments product lines are profit centers. *Profit center managers are evaluated on their success in generating income.* A profit center manager would not have the authority to make major investing decisions, such as the decision to build a new manufacturing plant.

- An **investment center** generates revenues and incurs costs, and its manager is also responsible for the investments made in its operating assets. Kraft Heinz's chief operating officer for U.S. operations has the authority to make decisions such as building a new manufacturing plant. *Investment center managers are evaluated on their use of investment center assets to generate income.*

This chapter describes ways to measure performance for these three types of responsibility centers.

P1

Prepare a responsibility accounting report using controllable costs.

Controllable versus Uncontrollable Costs

We often evaluate a manager's performance using responsibility accounting reports that describe a department's activities in terms of whether a cost is controllable.

- **Controllable costs** are those for which a manager has the power to determine or at least significantly affect the amount incurred.
- **Uncontrollable costs** are not within the manager's control or influence.

Point: *Cost* refers to a monetary outlay to acquire some resource that has a future benefit. *Expense* usually refers to an expired cost.

For example, department managers often have little or no control over depreciation expense because they cannot affect the amount of equipment assigned to their departments. Also, department managers rarely control their own salaries. However, they can control or influence items such as the cost of supplies used in their department. When evaluating managers' performance, we should use data reflecting their departments' outputs along with their controllable costs and expenses.

A responsibility accounting system recognizes that control over costs and expenses belongs to several levels of management. We illustrate this in the partial organization chart in Exhibit 9.1. The lines in this chart connecting the managerial positions reflect channels of authority. For example, the three department managers (beverage, food, and service) in this company are responsible for controllable costs incurred in their departments. These department managers report to the vice president (VP) of the West region, who has overall control of the department costs. Similarly, the costs of the West region are reported to and controlled

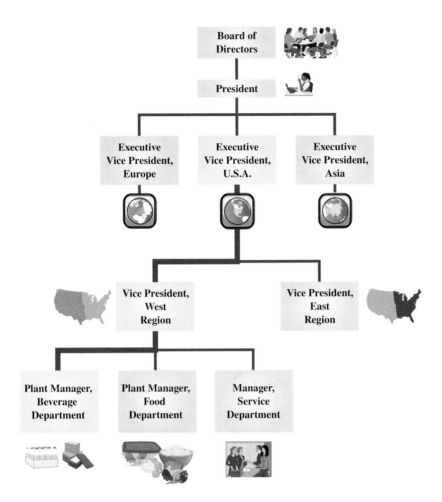

EXHIBIT 9.1

Responsibility Accounting
Chart (partial)

by the executive vice president (EVP) of U.S. operations, who in turn reports to the president, and, ultimately, the board of directors.

Responsibility Accounting for Cost Centers

A **responsibility accounting performance report** lists actual expenses that a manager is responsible for and their budgeted amounts. Management's analysis of differences between budgeted and actual amounts often results in corrective or strategic managerial actions. Upper-level management uses performance reports to evaluate the effectiveness of lower-level managers in keeping costs within budgeted amounts.

Exhibit 9.2 shows summarized performance reports for the three management levels identified in Exhibit 9.1. The beverage department is a *cost center*, and its manager is responsible for controlling costs. Costs under the control of the beverage department plant manager are totaled and included among the controllable costs of the VP of the West region. Costs under the control of this VP are totaled and included among the controllable costs of the EVP of U.S. operations. In this way, responsibility accounting reports provide relevant information for each management level. (If the VP and EVP are responsible for more than just costs, the responsibility accounting system is expanded, as we show later in this chapter.)

The number of controllable costs reported varies across management levels. At lower levels, managers have limited responsibility and fewer controllable costs. Responsibility and control broaden for higher-level managers; their reports span a wider range of costs. However, reports to higher-level managers usually are summarized because: (1) lower-level managers are often responsible for detailed costs, and (2) detailed reports can obscure the broader issues facing top managers of an organization.

Point: Responsibility accounting typically uses *flexible* budgets.

Point: Responsibility accounting divides a company into subunits, or *responsibility centers.*

EXHIBIT 9.2

Responsibility Accounting
Performance Reports

Executive Vice President, U.S. Operations

	For July		
Controllable Costs	**Budgeted Amount**	**Actual Amount**	**Over (Under) Budget**
Salaries, VPs..............................	$ 80,000	$ 80,000	$ 0
Quality control costs........................	21,000	22,400	1,400
Office costs	29,500	28,800	(700)
West region.............................	**276,700**	**279,500**	**2,800**
East region	390,000	380,600	(9,400)
Totals.....................................	$797,200	$ 791,300	$(5,900)

Vice President, West Region

	For July		
Controllable Costs	**Budgeted Amount**	**Actual Amount**	**Over (Under) Budget**
Salaries, department managers	$ 75,000	$ 76,500	$ 1,500
Depreciation	10,600	10,600	0
Insurance	6,800	6,300	(500)
Beverage department......................	**79,600**	**79,900**	**300**
Food department..........................	61,500	64,200	2,700
Service department........................	43,200	42,000	(1,200)
Totals.....................................	**$276,700**	**$279,500**	**$ 2,800**

Plant Manager, Beverage Department

	For July		
Controllable Costs	**Budgeted Amount**	**Actual Amount**	**Over (Under) Budget**
Direct materials	$ 51,600	$ 52,500	$ 900
Direct labor	20,000	19,600	(400)
Overhead	8,000	7,800	(200)
Totals.....................................	**$ 79,600**	**$ 79,900**	**$ 300**

NEED-TO-KNOW 9-1

Responsibility
Accounting

P1

Below are the annual budgeted and actual costs for the Western region's manufacturing plant of Rios Co. The plant has two operating departments: motorcycle and ATV. The plant manager is responsible for all of the plant's costs (other than her own salary). Each operating department has a manager who is responsible for that department's direct materials, direct labor, and overhead costs. Prepare responsibility accounting reports like those in Exhibit 9.2 for (1) the plant manager and (2) each operating department manager.

	Budgeted Amount		Actual Amount	
	Motorcycle	**ATV**	**Motorcycle**	**ATV**
Direct materials	$ 97,000	$138,000	$ 98,500	$133,800
Direct labor...............	52,000	105,000	56,100	101,300
Dept. mgr. salary..........	60,000	56,000	60,000	56,000
Rent and utilities...........	9,000	12,000	8,400	10,900
Overhead	45,000	81,000	47,000	78,000
Totals....................	$263,000	$392,000	$270,000	$380,000

Solution 1.

Responsibility Accounting Performance Report
Plant Manager, Western Region

	Budgeted	Actual	Over (Under) Budget
Dept. mgr. salaries	$116,000	$116,000	$ 0
Rent and utilities...........	21,000	19,300	(1,700)
Motorcycle dept.*	194,000	201,600	7,600
ATV dept.**	324,000	313,100	(10,900)
Totals....................	$655,000	$650,000	$ (5,000)

* Costs are from Motorcycle responsibility report, solution *2a*.
**Costs are from ATV responsibility report, solution *2b*.

2a.

Responsibility Accounting Performance Report
Department Manager, Motorcycle Department

	Budgeted	Actual	Over (Under) Budget
Direct materials	$ 97,000	$ 98,500	$1,500
Direct labor	52,000	56,100	4,100
Overhead	45,000	47,000	2,000
Totals	$194,000	$201,600	$7,600

2b.

Responsibility Accounting Performance Report
Department Manager, ATV Department

	Budgeted	Actual	Over (Under) Budget
Direct materials	$138,000	$133,800	$ (4,200)
Direct labor	105,000	101,300	(3,700)
Overhead	81,000	78,000	(3,000)
Totals	$324,000	$313,100	$(10,900)

> Do More: QS 9-4, E 9-1, E 9-2, P 9-1

PROFIT CENTERS

When departments are organized as profit centers, responsibility accounting focuses on how well each department controlled costs *and* generated revenues. This leads to **departmental income statements** as a common way to report profit center performance. When computing departmental profits, we confront two accounting challenges that involve allocating expenses:

1. How to allocate *indirect expenses* such as rent and utilities, which benefit several departments.
2. How to allocate *service department expenses* such as payroll or purchasing, which perform services that benefit several departments.

We next explain these allocations and profit center income reporting.

Direct and Indirect Expenses

Direct expenses are costs readily traced to a department because they are incurred for that department's sole benefit. They are not allocated across departments. For example, the salary of an employee who works in only one department is a direct expense of that one department. Direct expenses are often, but not always, controllable costs.

  Indirect expenses are costs incurred for the joint benefit of more than one department; they cannot be readily traced to only one department. For example, if two or more departments share a single building, all enjoy the benefits of the expenses for rent, heat, and light. Likewise, the *operating departments* that perform an organization's main functions, for example, manufacturing and selling, benefit from the work of *service departments*. Service departments, like payroll and human resource management, do not generate revenues, but their support is crucial for the operating departments' success.

C1
Distinguish between direct and indirect expenses and identify bases for allocating indirect expenses to departments.

Point: Service department expenses can be viewed as a special case of indirect expenses.

Expense Allocations

General Model Indirect and service department expenses are allocated across departments that benefit from them. Ideally, we allocate these expenses by using a cause-effect relation. Often such cause-effect relations are hard to identify. When we cannot identify cause-effect relations, we allocate each indirect or service department expense based on *approximating* the relative benefit each department receives. Exhibit 9.3 summarizes the general model for cost allocation.

> **Allocated cost = Total cost to allocate × Percentage of allocation base used**

EXHIBIT 9.3
General Model for Cost Allocation

Allocating Indirect Expenses   Allocation bases vary across departments and organizations. No standard rule for the "best" allocation bases exists. Managers must use judgment in developing allocation bases because employee morale can suffer if allocations are perceived as unfair. Exhibit 9.4 shows some commonly used bases for allocating indirect expenses.

EXHIBIT 9.4

Bases for Allocating
Indirect Expenses

Indirect Expense	Common Allocation Bases
Wages and salaries	Relative amount of hours worked in each department
Rent	Square feet of space occupied
Utilities	Square feet of space occupied
Advertising	Percentage of total sales
Depreciation	Hours of depreciable asset used

© Purestock/SuperStock

Point: Some companies ask supervisors to estimate time spent supervising specific departments for purposes of expense allocation.

More complicated allocation schemes are possible. For example, some locations in a retail store (ground floor near the entrance, for example) are more valuable than others. Departments with better locations can be allocated more cost. Advertising campaigns can be analyzed to see the amount of advertising devoted to each department, or utilities costs can be allocated based on machine hours used in each department. Management must determine whether these more accurate cost allocations justify the effort and expense to compute them.

Allocating Service Department Expenses   To generate revenues, operating departments require services provided by departments such as personnel, payroll, and purchasing. Such service departments are typically evaluated as *cost centers* because they do not produce revenues. A departmental accounting system can accumulate and report costs incurred by each service department for this purpose. The system then allocates a service department's expenses to operating departments that benefit from them. Exhibit 9.5 shows some commonly used bases for allocating service department expenses to operating departments.

EXHIBIT 9.5

Bases for Allocating Service
Department Expenses

Service Department	Common Allocation Bases
Office expenses	Number of employees or sales in each department
Personnel expenses	Number of employees in each department
Payroll expenses	Number of employees in each department
Purchasing costs	Dollar amounts of purchases or number of purchase orders processed
Maintenance expenses	Square feet of floor space occupied

Illustration of Cost Allocation   We illustrate the general approach to allocating costs by looking at cleaning services for a retail store (an indirect cost). An outside company cleans the retail store for a total cost of $800 per month. Management allocates this cost across the store's three departments based on floor space (in square feet) that each department occupies. Exhibit 9.6 shows this allocation.

EXHIBIT 9.6

Cost Allocation

Department	Department Square Feet	Percent of Total Square Feet	Cost Allocated to Department
Jewelry	2,400	60% (2,400 sq ft/ 4,000 sq ft)	$480
Watch repair	600	15 (600 sq ft/ 4,000 sq ft)	120
China and silver	1,000	25 (1,000 sq ft/ 4,000 sq ft)	200
Totals	4,000	100%	$800

The total cost to allocate is $800. Because the jewelry department occupies 60% of the store's total floor space (2,400 square feet/4,000 square feet), it is allocated 60% of the total cleaning cost. This allocated cost of $480 is computed as $800 × 60%. When the allocation process is complete, these and other allocated costs are deducted in computing the net income for each department. The calculations are similar for other allocation bases and for service department costs.

Allocate a retailer's purchasing department's costs of $20,000 to its operating departments using each department's percentage of total purchase orders.

Department	Number of Purchase Orders
Clothing...............	250
Health care.............	450
Sporting goods..........	300
Total.................	1,000

Solution

Department		
Clothing...............	$20,000 × 25% =	$ 5,000
Health care.............	20,000 × 45% =	9,000
Sporting goods..........	20,000 × 30% =	6,000
Total.................		$20,000

Do More: QS 9-5, QS 9-6, QS 9-7, E 9-3, E 9-4, E 9-5

Departmental Income Statements

Departmental income is computed using the formula in Exhibit 9.7.

EXHIBIT 9.7

Departmental Income

$$\text{Departmental income} = \text{Department sales} - \text{Department direct expenses} - \text{Allocated indirect expenses} - \text{Allocated service department expenses}$$

P3 _____

Prepare departmental income statements and contribution reports.

We prepare departmental income statements using **A-1 Hardware** and its five departments. Two of them (general office and purchasing) are service departments, and the other three (hardware, housewares, and appliances) are operating departments. Since the service departments do not generate sales, we do not prepare departmental income statements for them. Instead, we allocate their expenses to operating departments.

Preparing departmental income statements involves four steps.

Step ①: Accumulating revenues, direct expenses, and indirect expenses by department.

Step ②: Allocating indirect expenses across both service and operating departments.

Step ③: Allocating service department expenses to operating departments.

Step ④: Preparing departmental income statements.

Exhibit 9.8 summarizes these steps in preparing departmental performance reports for cost centers and profit centers (links to the steps are coded with circled numbers *1* through *4*). A-1 Hardware's service departments (general office and purchasing) are cost centers, so their

Point: Operating departments generate revenues. Service departments do not.

EXHIBIT 9.8

Departmental Performance Reporting

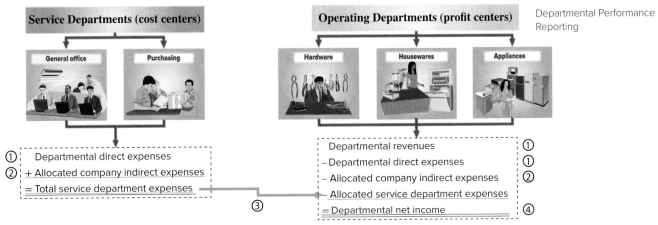

performance is based on how well they control their direct department expenses. The company's operating departments (hardware, housewares, and appliances) are **profit centers**, and their performance is based on how well they generate departmental net income.

Apply Step 1:   We first collect the necessary data from general company and departmental accounts. Exhibit 9.9 shows these data.

EXHIBIT 9.9

Cost Data

	A	B	C	D	E	F	G
			A-1 HARDWARE				
			Revenues and Expenses				
			For Year Ended December 31, 2017				
			Service Departments		**Operating Departments**		
		Expense Account Balance	**General Office**	**Purchasing**	**Hardware**	**Housewares**	**Appliances**
8	Sales............................		$ 0	$ 0	$119,500	$71,700	$47,800
9	**Direct expenses**						
10	Cost of goods sold...........	$ 147,800	0	0	73,800	43,800	30,200
11	Salaries............................	51,900	13,300	8,200	15,600	7,000	7,800
12	Depreciation—Equip.......	1,500	500	300	400	100	200
13	Supplies............................	900	200	100	300	200	100
14	**Indirect expenses**						
15	Rent	12,000					
16	Utilities............................	2,400					
17	Advertising......................	1,000					
18	Insurance.........................	2,500					
19	**Total expenses.............**	**$220,000**					

Exhibit 9.9 shows the direct and indirect expenses by department. Each department uses payroll records, fixed asset and depreciation records, and supplies requisitions to determine the amounts of its expenses for salaries, depreciation, and supplies. The total amount for each of these direct expenses is entered in the Expense Account Balance column. That column also lists the amount of each indirect expense.

EXHIBIT 9.10

Departmental Expense Allocation Spreadsheet

Apply Step 2:   Using the general model, A-1 Hardware allocates indirect costs. We show this with the *departmental expense allocation spreadsheet* in Exhibit 9.10. After selecting allocation

	A	B	C	D	E	F	G
			A-1 HARDWARE				
			Departmental Expense Allocations				
			For Year Ended December 31, 2017				
				Allocation of Expenses to Departments			
	Allocation Base	**Expense Account Balance**	**General Office Dept.**	**Purchasing Dept.**	**Hardware Dept.**	**Housewares Dept.**	**Appliances Dept.**
8	**Direct expenses**						
9	Salaries expense............ (see note *a* below)	$ 51,900	$13,300	$8,200	$ 15,600	$ 7,000	$ 7,800
10	Depreciation—Equipment........ (see note *a* below)	1,500	500	300	400	100	200
11	Supplies expense............ (see note *a* below)	900	200	100	300	200	100
12	**Indirect expenses**						
13	Rent expense................ Amount and value of space....	12,000	600	600	4,860	3,240	2,700
14	Utilities expense............ Floor space.......................	2,400	300	300	810	540	450
15	Advertising expense.......... Sales................................	1,000			500	300	200
16	Insurance expense.......... Value of insured assets............	2,500	400	200	900	600	400
17	**Total department expenses.......**	72,200	15,300	9,700	23,370	11,980	11,850
18	**Service department expenses**						
19	General office department..... Sales................................		(15,300)		7,650	4,590	3,060
20	Purchasing department............ Purchasing orders................			(9,700)	3,880	2,630	3,190
21	**Total expenses allocated to operating departments.........**	**$72,200**	**$ 0**	**$ 0**	**$34,900**	**$19,200**	**$18,100**

^a The allocation base is not relevant as direct expenses are *not* allocated.

bases, indirect expenses are recorded in company accounts and allocated to both operating and service departments. **Detailed calculations for indirect expense allocations, which follow the general model of cost allocation, are in Appendix 9A** (see Exhibits 9A.1 through 9A.6).

Apply Step 3: We then allocate service department expenses to operating departments. Service department expenses typically are not allocated to other service departments. After service department costs are allocated, no expenses remain in the service departments, as shown in row 21 of Exhibit 9.10. **Detailed calculations for service department expense allocations, which follow the general model of cost allocation, are in Appendix 9A** (see Exhibits 9A.7 and 9A.8).

Apply Step 4: The departmental expense allocation spreadsheet is now used to prepare departmental performance reports. The general office and purchasing departments are cost centers, and their managers are evaluated on their control of costs.

Exhibit 9.11 shows income statements for the three operating departments. This exhibit uses the spreadsheet (in Exhibit 9.10) for its operating expenses; information on sales and cost of goods sold comes from departmental records.

EXHIBIT 9.11

Departmental Income Statements (operating departments)

A-1 HARDWARE Departmental Income Statements For Year Ended December 31, 2017	Hardware Department	Housewares Department	Appliances Department	Combined	
Sales	$119,500	$71,700	$47,800	$239,000	
Cost of goods sold	73,800	43,800	30,200	147,800	
Gross profit	45,700	27,900	17,600	91,200	
Operating expenses					
Salaries expense	15,600	7,000	7,800	30,400	⎤
Depreciation expense—Equipment	400	100	200	700	Direct expenses
Supplies expense.	300	200	100	600	⎦
Rent expense	4,860	3,240	2,700	10,800	⎤
Utilities expense.	810	540	450	1,800	Allocated indirect
Advertising expense	500	300	200	1,000	expenses
Insurance expense.	900	600	400	1,900	⎦
Share of general office expenses	7,650	4,590	3,060	15,300	⎤ Allocated service
Share of purchasing expenses	3,880	2,630	3,190	9,700	⎦ department expenses
Total operating expenses	34,900	19,200	18,100	72,200	
Operating income (loss).	$ 10,800	$ 8,700	$ (500)	$ 19,000	

Higher-level managers use departmental income statements to determine which of a company's departments are most profitable. After considering all costs, the hardware department is most profitable. The company might attempt to expand its hardware department.

Departmental Contribution to Overhead

Exhibit 9.11 shows that the appliances department reported an operating loss of $(500). Should this department be eliminated? We must be careful when indirect expenses are a large portion of total expenses and when weaknesses in assumptions and decisions in allocating indirect expenses can greatly affect income. Also, operating department managers might have no control over the level of service department services they use. In these and other cases, we might better evaluate profit center performance using the **departmental contribution to overhead,** a measure of the amount of sales less *direct* expenses. A department's contribution is said to be "to overhead" because of the practice of considering all indirect expenses as overhead. Thus, the excess of a department's sales over direct expenses is a contribution toward at least a portion of total overhead.

The upper half of Exhibit 9.12 shows a departmental contribution to overhead as part of an expanded income statement. Departmental contribution to overhead, because it focuses on the direct expenses that are under the profit center manager's control, is often a better way to assess that manager's performance.

EXHIBIT 9.12

Departmental Contribution to Overhead

A-1 HARDWARE Income Statement Showing Departmental Contribution to Overhead For Year Ended December 31, 2017				
	Hardware Department	Housewares Department	Appliances Department	Combined
Sales	$119,500	$ 71,700	$47,800	$239,000
Cost of goods sold	73,800	43,800	30,200	147,800
Gross profit	45,700	27,900	17,600	91,200
Direct expenses				
Salaries expense	15,600	7,000	7,800	30,400
Depreciation expense—Equipment	400	100	200	700
Supplies expense	300	200	100	600
Total direct expenses	16,300	7,300	8,100	31,700
Departmental contributions				
to overhead	**$ 29,400**	**$20,600**	**$ 9,500**	**$ 59,500**
Indirect expenses				
Rent expense				10,800
Utilities expense				1,800
Advertising expense				1,000
Insurance expense				1,900
General office department expense				15,300
Purchasing department expense				9,700
Total indirect expenses				40,500
Operating income				**$ 19,000**

Point: Operating income is the same in Exhibits 9.11 and 9.12. The method of reporting indirect expenses in Exhibit 9.12 does not change total income but does identify each operating department's contribution to overhead.

Exhibit 9.12 shows a $9,500 positive contribution to overhead for the appliances department. If this department were eliminated, the company would be worse off. Further, the appliance department's manager is better evaluated using this $9,500 than on the department's operating loss of $(500). The company also compares each department's contribution to overhead to budgeted amounts to assess each department's performance.

Behavioral Aspects of Departmental Performance Reports An organization must consider potential effects on employee behavior from departmental income statements and contribution to overhead reports. These include:

- Indirect expenses are typically uncontrollable costs for department managers. Thus, departmental contribution to overhead might be a better way to evaluate department manager performance. Including uncontrollable costs in performance evaluation is inconsistent with responsibility accounting and can reduce manager morale.

- Alternatively, including indirect expenses in the department manager's performance evaluation can lead the manager to be more careful in using service departments, which can reduce the organization's costs.

- Some companies allocate *budgeted* service department costs rather than actual service costs. In this way, operating departments are not held responsible for excessive costs from service departments, and service departments are more likely to control their costs.

INVESTMENT CENTERS

We describe both financial and nonfinancial measures of investment center performance.

Financial Performance Evaluation Measures

Investment center managers are typically evaluated using performance measures that combine income and assets. These measures include:

- return on investment
- profit margin
- residual income
- investment turnover

A1

Analyze investment centers using return on investment and residual income.

To illustrate, let's consider ZTel Company, which operates two divisions as **investment centers:** LCD and S-Phone. The LCD division manufactures liquid crystal display (LCD) touch-screen monitors and sells them for use in computers, cellular phones, and other products. The S-Phone division sells smartphones. Exhibit 9.13 shows current-year income and assets for the divisions.

	LCD Division	S-Phone Division
Investment center income	$ 526,500	$ 417,600
Investment center average invested assets	2,500,000	1,850,000

EXHIBIT 9.13

Investment Center Income and Assets

Investment Center Return on Investment One measure to evaluate division performance is the investment center **return on investment (ROI),** also called *return on assets* (ROA). This measure is computed as follows:

$$\text{Return on investment} = \frac{\textbf{Investment center income}}{\textbf{Investment center average invested assets}}$$

The return on investment for the LCD division is 21% (rounded), computed as $526,500/$2,500,000. The S-Phone division's return on investment is 23% (rounded), computed as $417,600/$1,850,000. ZTel's management can use ROI as part of its performance evaluation for its investment center managers. For example, actual ROI can be compared to targeted ROI or to the ROI for similar departments at competing businesses.

Investment Center Residual Income Another way to evaluate division performance is to compute investment center **residual income,** which is computed as follows:

$$\text{Residual income} = \frac{\textbf{Investment center}}{\textbf{income}} - \frac{\textbf{Target investment center}}{\textbf{income}}$$

© princigalli/iStock/360/Getty Images

Assume ZTel's top management sets target income at 8% of investment center assets. For an investment center, this target percentage is typically the cost of obtaining financing. Applying this formula using data from Exhibit 9.13 yields the residual income for ZTel's divisions in Exhibit 9.14.

	LCD Division	S-Phone Division
Investment center income	$526,500	$417,600
Less: Target investment center income		
$2,500,000 × 8%	200,000	
$1,850,000 × 8%		148,000
Investment center residual income	$326,500	$269,600

EXHIBIT 9.14

Investment Center Residual Income

Residual income is usually expressed in dollars. The LCD division produced more dollars of residual income than the S-Phone division. ZTel's management can use residual income, along with ROI, to evaluate investment center manager performance.

Using residual income to evaluate division performance encourages division managers to accept all opportunities that return more than the target income, thus increasing company value. For example, the S-Phone division might (mistakenly) not want to accept a new customer that will provide a 15% return on investment because that will reduce the S-Phone division's overall return on investment (23%, as shown above). However, the S-Phone division *should* accept this opportunity because the new customer would increase residual income by providing income above the target income of 8% of invested assets.

NEED-TO-KNOW **9-3**

Return on Investment and Residual income

A1

Do More: QS 9-9, QS 9-10, E 9-9, E 9-10

The media division of a company reports income of $600,000, average invested assets of $7,500,000, and a target income of 6% of average invested assets. Compute the division's (a) return on investment and (b) residual income.

Solution

a. $600,000/$7,500,000 = 8%

b. $600,000 − ($7,500,000 × 6%) = $150,000

Issues in Computing Return on Investment and Residual Income   Evaluations of investment center performance using return on investment and residual income can be affected by how a company answers these questions:

1. How do you compute *average* invested assets? It is common to compute the average by adding the year's beginning amount of invested assets to the year's ending amount of invested assets, and dividing that sum by 2. Averages based on monthly or quarterly asset amounts are also acceptable. Seasonal variations in invested assets, if any, impact this average.

2. How do you measure invested assets? It is common to measure invested assets using their *net* book values. For example, depreciable assets would be measured at their cost minus accumulated depreciation. As net book value declines over a depreciable asset's useful life, the result is that return on investment and residual income would increase over that asset's life. This might cause managers not to invest in new assets. In addition, in measuring invested assets, companies commonly exclude assets that are not used in generating investment center income, such as land held for resale.

3. How do you measure investment center income? It is common to exclude both interest expense and tax expense from investment center income. Interest expense reflects a company's financing decisions, and tax expense is typically considered outside the control of an investment center manager. Excluding interest and taxes in these calculations enables more meaningful comparisons of return on investment and residual income across investment centers and companies.

Point: *Economic Value Added* (EVA®), developed and trade-marked by Stern, Stewart, and Co., is an approach to address issues in computing residual income. This method uses a variety of adjustments to compute income, assets, and the target rate.

■ **Decision** Insight

In the Money   Executive pay is often linked to performance measures. Bonus payments are often based on exceeding a target return on investment or certain balanced scorecard indicators. Stock awards, such as stock options and restricted stock, reward executives when their company's stock price rises. The goal of bonus plans and stock awards is to encourage executives to make decisions that increase company performance and value. ■

A2

Analyze investment centers using profit margin and investment turnover.

Investment Center Profit Margin and Investment Turnover   We can further examine investment center (division) performance by splitting return on investment into two measures—profit margin and investment turnover—as follows.

| Return on investment | = | Profit margin | × | Investment turnover |

$$\text{Return on investment} = \frac{\text{Investment center income}}{\text{Investment center sales}} \times \frac{\text{Investment center sales}}{\text{Investment center average assets}}$$

- **Profit margin** measures the income earned per dollar of sales. It equals investment center income divided by investment center sales. In analyzing investment center performance, we typically use a measure of income *before* tax.
- **Investment turnover** measures how efficiently an investment center generates sales from its invested assets. It equals investment center sales divided by investment center average assets.

Profit margin is expressed as a percent, while investment turnover is interpreted as the number of times assets were converted into sales. Higher profit margin and higher investment turnover indicate better performance.

Point: This partitioning of return on investment is sometimes called DuPont analysis.

To illustrate, consider **Walt Disney Co.**, which reports in Exhibit 9.15 results for two of its operating divisions: Media Networks and Parks and Resorts.

$ millions	Media Networks	Parks and Resorts
Sales	$23,264	$16,162
Income.........................	7,793	3,031
Average invested assets	30,262	23,335

EXHIBIT 9.15

Walt Disney Division Sales, Income, and Assets

Profit margin and investment turnover for these two divisions are computed and shown in Exhibit 9.16.

$ millions	Media Networks	Parks and Resorts
Profit margin		
$7,793/$23,264	33.50%	
$3,031/$16,162		18.75%
Investment turnover		
$23,264/$30,262	0.77	
$16,162/$23,335		0.69
Return on investment		
33.50% × 0.77...............	25.80%	
18.75% × 0.69...............		12.94

EXHIBIT 9.16

Walt Disney Division Profit Margin and Investment Turnover

Disney's Media Networks division makes 33.50 cents of profit for every dollar of sales, while its Parks and Resorts division makes 18.75 cents of profit per dollar of sales. The Media Networks division (0.77 investment turnover) is slightly more efficient than the Parks and Resorts division (0.69 investment turnover) in using assets. Top management can use profit margin and investment turnover to evaluate the performance of division managers. The measures can also aid management when considering further investment in its divisions. Because of both a much higher profit margin and higher investment turnover, the Media Networks division's return on investment (25.80%) is much greater than that of the Parks and Resorts division (12.94%).

■ **Decision** Maker ══════════════════════════════════

Division Manager   You manage a division in a highly competitive industry. You will receive a cash bonus if your division achieves an ROI above 12%. Your division's profit margin is 7%, equal to the industry average, and your division's investment turnover is 1.5. How can you increase your chance of receiving the bonus? ■   *Answer:* Your division's ROI is 10.5% (7% × 1.5). In a competitive industry, it is difficult to increase profit margins by raising prices. Your division might be better able to control costs than increase profit margin. You might increase advertising to increase sales without increasing invested assets. Investment turnover and ROI increase if the advertising attracts customers.

A division reports sales of $50,000, income of $2,000, and average invested assets of $10,000. Compute the division's (a) profit margin, (b) investment turnover, and (c) return on investment.

Solution

a. $2,000/$50,000 = 4%
b. $50,000/$10,000 = 5.0
c. $2,000/$10,000 = 20%

NEED-TO-KNOW 9-4

Margin, Turnover, and Return

A2

Do More: QS 9-12, E 9-10, E 9-11, E 9-12

Nonfinancial Performance Evaluation Measures

A3

Analyze investment centers using the balanced scorecard.

Evaluating performance solely on financial measures has limitations. For example, some investment center managers might forgo profitable opportunities to keep their return on investment high. Also, residual income is less useful when comparing investment centers of different size. And, both return on investment and residual income can encourage managers to focus too heavily on short-term financial goals.

In response to these limitations, companies consider *nonfinancial* measures. A delivery company such as **FedEx** might track the percentage of on-time deliveries. The percentage of defective tennis balls manufactured can be used to assess performance of **Penn**'s production managers. **Walmart**'s credit card screens commonly ask customers at checkout whether the cashier was friendly or the store was clean. **Coca-Cola** measures its water usage as part of an effort to enhance the sustainability of its production process. This kind of information can help division managers run their divisions and help top management evaluate division manager performance. A popular measure that includes nonfinancial indicators is the balanced scorecard.

Balanced Scorecard   The **balanced scorecard** is a system of performance measures, including nonfinancial measures, used to assess company and division manager performance. The balanced scorecard requires managers to think of their company from four perspectives:

1. **Customer:** What do customers think of us?
2. **Internal processes:** Which of our operations are critical to meeting customer needs?
3. **Innovation and learning:** How can we improve?
4. **Financial:** What do our owners think of us?

Point: One survey indicates that nearly 60% of global companies use some form of balanced scorecard.

The balanced scorecard collects information on several *key performance indicators* (KPIs) within each of the four perspectives. These key indicators vary across companies. Exhibit 9.17 lists common performance indicators used in the balanced scorecard.

EXHIBIT 9.17

Balanced Scorecard Performance Indicators

Customer	Internal Processes	Innovation/Learning	Financial
• Customer satisfaction rating	• Defect rates	• Employee satisfaction	• Net income
• # of new customers acquired	• Cycle time	• Employee turnover	• ROI
• % of on-time deliveries	• Product costs	• $ spent on training	• Sales growth
• % of sales from new products	• Labor hours per order	• # of new products	• Cash flow
• Time to fill orders	• Production days without an accident	• # of patents	• Residual income
• % of sales returned		• $ spent on research	• Stock price

After selecting key performance indicators, companies collect data on each indicator and compare actual amounts to target (goal) amounts to assess performance. For example, a company might have a goal of filling 98% of customer orders within two hours. Balanced scorecard reports are often presented in graphs or tables that can be updated frequently. Such timely information aids division managers in their decisions and can be used by top management to evaluate division manager performance.

Exhibit 9.18 is an example of balanced scorecard reporting on the customer perspective for an Internet retailer. This scorecard reports that the retailer is getting 62% of its potential customers successfully through the purchasing process, and that 2.2% of all orders are returned. The *color* of the circles in the Trend column reveals whether the company is exceeding its goal (green), roughly meeting the goal (gray), or not meeting the goal (red). The *direction* of the arrows reveals any trend in performance: an upward arrow indicates improvement, a downward arrow indicates declining performance, and an arrow pointing sideways indicates no change.

A review of this balanced scorecard suggests the retailer is meeting or exceeding its goals on orders returned and customer satisfaction. Further, purchasing success and customer satisfaction are improving. The company has received more customer complaints than was hoped for; *however,*

EXHIBIT 9.18

Balanced Scorecard
Reporting: Internet Retailer

KPI: Customer Perspective	Actual	Goal	Trend
Potential customers purchasing	62%	80%	
Orders returned	2.2%	2%	
Customer satisfaction rating	9.5 of 10.0	9.5	
Number of customer complaints	142	100	

the number of customer complaints is declining. A manager would combine this information with similar information from the other three performance indicators (internal processes, innovation and learning, and financial perspectives) to get an overall view of division performance.

NEED-TO-KNOW 9-5

Classify each of the performance measures below into the most likely balanced scorecard perspective to which it relates: customer (C), internal processes (P), innovation and growth (I), or financial (F).

1. On-time delivery rate
2. Accident-free days
3. Sustainability training workshops held
4. Defective products made

5. Residual income
6. Patents applied for
7. Sales returns
8. Customer complaints

Balanced Scorecard

A3

Solution

1. C **2.** P **3.** I **4.** P **5.** F **6.** I **7.** C **8.** C

Do More: QS 9-14,
E 9-16, E 9-17

 **Decision** Maker

Center Manager   Your center's usual return on investment is 19%. You are considering two new investments. The first requires a $250,000 average investment and is expected to yield annual net income of $50,000. The second requires a $1 million average investment with an expected annual net income of $175,000. Do you pursue either? ■   *Answer:* The two investments are not comparable on the absolute dollars of income or on assets. For instance, the second provides a higher income in absolute dollars but requires a higher investment. We need return on investment for each: (1) $50,000 ÷ $250,000 = 20% and (2) $175,000 ÷ $1 million = 17.5%. Do you pursue one, both, or neither? Because alternative 1's return is higher than the center's usual return of 19%, it should be pursued, assuming its risks are acceptable. Alternative 2's return is lower than the usual 19% and is likely not acceptable.

Transfer Pricing

Divisions in decentralized companies sometimes do business with one another. For example, a separate division of **Harley-Davidson** manufactures its plastic and fiberglass parts used in the company's motorcycles. **Anheuser-Busch InBev**'s metal container division makes cans used in its brewing operations, and also sells cans to soft-drink companies. A division of **Prince** produces strings used in tennis rackets made by Prince and other manufacturers.

The price used to record transfers of goods across divisions of the same company is called the **transfer price.** Transfer prices can be used in cost, profit, and investment centers.

In decentralized organizations, division managers have input on or decide transfer prices. Since these transfers are not with customers outside the company, the transfer price has no direct impact on the *company's* overall profits. However, transfer prices can impact *division* performance evaluations and, if set incorrectly, lead to bad decisions.

Transfer prices are set using one of three approaches:

1. Cost (for example, variable manufacturing cost per unit)
2. Market price
3. Negotiated price

To illustrate the impact of alternative transfer prices on divisional profits, consider ZTel, a smartphone manufacturer. ZTel's LCD division makes touch-screen monitors that are used in ZTel's smartphone division or sold to outside customers. LCD's variable manufacturing cost is

C2 _____

Explain transfer pricing and methods to set transfer prices.

Point: Transfer pricing can impact company profits when divisions are located in countries with different tax rates; this is covered in advanced courses.

$40 per monitor, and the market price is $80 per monitor. There are two extreme positions one can take for the transfer price.

- **Low Transfer Price** The *smartphone division manager* wants to pay a *low* transfer price. The transfer price cannot be less than $40 per monitor, as any lower price would cause the LCD manager to lose money on each monitor sold.
- **High Transfer Price** The *LCD division manager* wants to receive a *high* transfer price. The transfer price cannot be more than $80 per monitor, as the smartphone division manager will not pay more than the market price.

This means the transfer price must be between $40 and $80 per monitor, and a negotiated price somewhere between these two extremes is reasonable. Appendix 9B expands on transfer pricing and details on the three approaches.

SUSTAINABILITY AND ACCOUNTING

This chapter focused on performance measurement and reporting. Companies report on their sustainability performance in a variety of ways. One approach integrates sustainability metrics in the four balanced scorecard perspectives (customer, internal process, innovation and learning, and financial). Many key performance indicators address the internal process and innovation and learning perspectives. For example, **General Mills** reports on its environmental targets and progress in its annual corporate sustainability report. Exhibit 9.19 captures how this information might appear as part of a balanced scorecard report.

EXHIBIT 9.19

Balanced Scorecard—
Sustainability

KPI: Internal Process Perspective	Actual Reduction	Target Reduction	Trend
Emissions	23%	20%	⬆
Energy usage	10	20	⬆
Solid waste	38	50	⬆
Fuel	25	35	⬆

Courtesy of Ministry of Supply

Some companies can report the direct effects on profits from a focus on sustainability. For example, **Target** recently started a *Made to Matter* department. To be sold in this department, brands must focus on consumer wellness and be committed to social responsibility. Target's *Made to Matter* department reported sales of over $1 billion in a recent year.

Ministry, this chapter's feature company, weaves sustainability into its production process. Instead of the traditional "cut-and-sew" approach, the company uses a "3D Robotic Knitting" process to make seamless garments with 3D printers. Not only do such seamless garments fit better, production is more sustainable as it wastes less fabric. According to Gihan Amarasiriwardena, one of the company's founders, "the traditional process wastes up to 30% of fabric. With our method, there is zero waste."

 Decision Analysis **Cycle Time and Cycle Efficiency**

A4
Compute cycle time and cycle efficiency, and explain their importance to production management.

Manufacturing companies commonly use nonfinancial measures to evaluate the performance of their production processes. For example, as lean manufacturing practices help companies move toward just-in-time manufacturing, it is important for these companies to reduce the time to manufacture their products and to improve manufacturing efficiency. One metric that measures that time element is **cycle time (CT)**, which describes the time it takes to produce a product or service. It is defined in Exhibit 9.20.

EXHIBIT 9.20

Cycle Time

Cycle time = Process time + Inspection time + Move time + Wait time

Process time is the time spent producing the product. *Inspection time* is the time spent inspecting (1) raw materials when received, (2) work in process while in production, and (3) finished goods prior to shipment. *Move time* is the time spent moving (1) raw materials from storage to production and (2) work in process from one factory location to another factory location. *Wait time* is the time that an order or job sits with no production applied to it. Wait time can be due to order delays, bottlenecks in production, or poor scheduling.

Process time is considered **value-added time:** it is the only activity in cycle time that adds value to the product from the customer's perspective. The other three activities are considered **non-value-added time:** they add no value to the customer.

Companies strive to reduce non-value-added time to improve **cycle efficiency (CE),** which is a measure of production efficiency. Cycle efficiency is the ratio of value-added time to total cycle time, as shown in Exhibit 9.21.

$$\text{Cycle efficiency} = \frac{\text{Value-added time}}{\text{Cycle time}}$$

EXHIBIT 9.21

Cycle Efficiency

To illustrate, assume that Rocky Mountain Bikes receives and produces an order for 500 Tracker mountain bikes. Assume that it took the following times to produce this order.

Process time... 1.8 days

Inspection time... 0.5 days

Move time... 0.7 days

Wait time... 3.0 days

In this case, cycle time is 6.0 days (1.8 + 0.5 + 0.7 + 3.0 days). Cycle efficiency is 0.3, or 30%, computed as 1.8 days divided by 6.0 days. This means that Rocky Mountain Bikes's value-added time (its process time, or time spent working on the product) is 30%. The other 70% is spent on non-value-added activities.

If a company has a CE of 1, it means that its time is spent entirely on value-added activities. If the CE is low, the company should evaluate its production process to see if it can identify ways to reduce non-value-added activities. The 30% CE for Rocky Mountain Bikes is low, and its management should try to reduce non-value-added activities.

NEED-TO-KNOW 9-6

COMPREHENSIVE

Management requests departmental income statements for Gamer's Haven, a computer store that has five departments. Three are operating departments (hardware, software, and repairs) and two are service departments (general office and purchasing).

	General Office	Purchasing	Hardware	Software	Repairs
Sales	—	—	$960,000	$600,000	$840,000
Cost of goods sold	—	—	500,000	300,000	200,000
Direct expenses					
Payroll	$60,000	$45,000	80,000	25,000	325,000
Depreciation	6,000	7,200	33,000	4,200	9,600
Supplies	15,000	10,000	10,000	2,000	25,000

The departments incur several indirect expenses. To prepare departmental income statements, the indirect expenses must be allocated across the five departments. Then the expenses of the two service departments must be allocated to the three operating departments. Total cost amounts and the allocation bases for each indirect expense follow.

Indirect Expense	Total Cost	Allocation Basis
Rent..	$150,000	Square footage occupied
Utilities	50,000	Square footage occupied
Advertising	125,000	Dollars of sales
Insurance	30,000	Value of assets insured
Service departments		
General office...	?	Number of employees
Purchasing	?	Dollars of cost of goods sold

The following additional information is needed for indirect expense allocations.

Department	Square Feet	Sales	Insured Assets	Employees	Cost of Goods Sold
General office	500		$ 60,000		
Purchasing	500		72,000		
Hardware	4,000	$ 960,000	330,000	5	$ 500,000
Software	3,000	600,000	42,000	5	300,000
Repairs	2,000	840,000	96,000	10	200,000
Totals.	10,000	$2,400,000	$600,000	20	$1,000,000

Required

1. Prepare a departmental expense allocation spreadsheet for Gamer's Haven.
2. Prepare a departmental income statement reporting net income for each operating department and for all operating departments combined.

PLANNING THE SOLUTION

- Set up and complete four tables to allocate the indirect expenses—one each for rent, utilities, advertising, and insurance.
- Allocate the departments' indirect expenses using a spreadsheet like the one in Exhibit 9.10. Enter the given amounts of the direct expenses for each department. Then enter the allocated amounts of the indirect expenses that you computed.
- Complete two tables for allocating the general office and purchasing department costs to the three operating departments. Enter these amounts on the spreadsheet and determine the total expenses allocated to the three operating departments.
- Prepare departmental income statements like the one in Exhibit 9.11. Show sales, cost of goods sold, gross profit, individual expenses, and net income for each of the three operating departments and for the combined company.

SOLUTION

Allocations of the four indirect expenses across the five departments.

Rent	Square Feet	Percent of Total	Allocated Cost
General office	500	5.0%	$ 7,500
Purchasing	500	5.0	7,500
Hardware	4,000	40.0	60,000
Software	3,000	30.0	45,000
Repairs	2,000	20.0	30,000
Totals.	10,000	100.0%	$150,000

Utilities	Square Feet	Percent of Total	Allocated Cost
General office	500	5.0%	$ 2,500
Purchasing	500	5.0	2,500
Hardware	4,000	40.0	20,000
Software	3,000	30.0	15,000
Repairs	2,000	20.0	10,000
Totals.	10,000	100.0%	$50,000

Advertising	Sales Dollars	Percent of Total	Allocated Cost
Hardware	$ 960,000	40.0%	$ 50,000
Software	600,000	25.0	31,250
Repairs	840,000	35.0	43,750
Totals.	$2,400,000	100.0%	$125,000

Insurance	Assets Insured	Percent of Total	Allocated Cost
General office	$ 60,000	10.0%	$ 3,000
Purchasing	72,000	12.0	3,600
Hardware	330,000	55.0	16,500
Software	42,000	7.0	2,100
Repairs	96,000	16.0	4,800
Totals.	$600,000	100.0%	$30,000

1. Allocations of service department expenses to the three operating departments.

General Office Allocations to	Employees	Percent of Total	Allocated Cost
Hardware	5	25.0%	$23,500
Software	5	25.0	23,500
Repairs	10	50.0	47,000
Totals	20	100.0%	$94,000

Purchasing Allocations to	Cost of Goods Sold	Percent of Total	Allocated Cost
Hardware	$ 500,000	50.0%	$37,900
Software	300,000	30.0	22,740
Repairs	200,000	20.0	15,160
Totals	$1,000,000	100.0%	$75,800

GAMER'S HAVEN
Departmental Expense Allocations
For Year Ended December 31, 2017

	Allocation Base	Expense Account Balance	General Office Dept.	Purchasing Dept.	Hardware Dept.	Software Dept.	Repairs Dept.
Direct Expenses							
Payroll		$ 535,000	$ 60,000	$ 45,000	$ 80,000	$ 25,000	$ 325,000
Depreciation		60,000	6,000	7,200	33,000	4,200	9,600
Supplies		62,000	15,000	10,000	10,000	2,000	25,000
Indirect Expenses							
Rent	Square ft.	150,000	7,500	7,500	60,000	45,000	30,000
Utilities	Square ft.	50,000	2,500	2,500	20,000	15,000	10,000
Advertising	Sales	125,000	—	—	50,000	31,250	43,750
Insurance	Assets	30,000	3,000	3,600	16,500	2,100	4,800
Total expenses		1,012,000	94,000	75,800	269,500	124,550	448,150
Service Department Expenses							
General office	Employees		(94,000)		23,500	23,500	47,000
Purchasing	Goods sold			(75,800)	37,900	22,740	15,160
Total expenses allocated to operating departments		$1,012,000	$ 0	$ 0	$330,900	$170,790	$510,310

2. Departmental income statements.

GAMER'S HAVEN
Departmental Income Statements
For Year Ended December 31, 2017

	Hardware	Software	Repairs	Combined
Sales	$ 960,000	$ 600,000	$ 840,000	$2,400,000
Cost of goods sold	500,000	300,000	200,000	1,000,000
Gross profit	460,000	300,000	640,000	1,400,000
Expenses				
Payroll	80,000	25,000	325,000	430,000
Depreciation	33,000	4,200	9,600	46,800
Supplies	10,000	2,000	25,000	37,000
Rent	60,000	45,000	30,000	135,000
Utilities	20,000	15,000	10,000	45,000
Advertising	50,000	31,250	43,750	125,000
Insurance	16,500	2,100	4,800	23,400
Share of general office	23,500	23,500	47,000	94,000
Share of purchasing	37,900	22,740	15,160	75,800
Total expenses	330,900	170,790	510,310	1,012,000
Operating income	$129,100	$129,210	$129,690	$ 388,000

9A

Cost Allocations

In this appendix we use our general model of cost allocation (see Exhibit 9.3) to show how the cost allocations in Exhibits 9.10 and 9.11 are computed. A-1 Hardware's departments use the allocation bases in Exhibit 9A.1: square feet of floor space, dollar value of insured assets, sales dollars, and number of purchase orders.

EXHIBIT 9A.1

Departments' Allocation Bases

Department	Floor Space (square feet)	Value of Insured Assets ($)	Sales ($)	Number of Purchase Orders*
General office	1,500	$ 38,000		—
Purchasing.............	1,500	19,000		—
Hardware.............	4,050	85,500	$119,500	394
Housewares	2,700	57,000	71,700	267
Appliances............	2,250	38,000	47,800	324
Total.................	12,000	$237,500	$239,000	985

*Purchasing department tracks purchase orders by department.

For each cost allocation that follows, we use the general formula here from Exhibit 9.3 to allocate indirect and service department costs.

> **Allocated cost = Total cost to allocate × Percentage of allocation base used**

From Exhibit 9.9, the company has these four indirect costs to allocate:

Rent expense.............	$12,000	Advertising expense	$1,000
Utilities expense	2,400	Insurance expense	2,500

Allocation of Rent　The two service departments (general office and purchasing) occupy 25% of the total space (3,000 sq. feet/12,000 sq. feet). However, they are located near the back of the building, which is of lower value than space near the front that is occupied by operating departments. Management estimates that space near the back accounts for $1,200 (10%) of the total rent expense of $12,000. Exhibit 9A.2 shows how we allocate the $1,200 rent expense between these two service departments in proportion to their square footage.

EXHIBIT 9A.2

Allocating Indirect (Rent) Expense to Service Departments

Department	Square Feet	Percent of Total	Allocated Cost*
General office	1,500	50.0%	$ 600
Purchasing.............	1,500	50.0	600
Totals	3,000	100.0%	$1,200

*See row 13 of departmental expense allocation spreadsheet (Exhibit 9.10).

We then have the remaining amount of $10,800 ($12,000 − $1,200) of rent expense to allocate to the three operating departments, as shown in Exhibit 9A.3.

EXHIBIT 9A.3

Allocating Indirect (Rent) Expense to Operating Departments

Department	Square Feet	Percent of Total	Allocated Cost*
Hardware	4,050	45.0%	$ 4,860
Housewares.............	2,700	30.0	3,240
Appliances	2,250	25.0	2,700
Totals	9,000	100.0%	$10,800

*See row 13 of departmental expense allocation spreadsheet (Exhibit 9.10).

Allocation of Utilities   We next allocate the $2,400 of utilities expense to all departments based on square footage occupied, as shown in Exhibit 9A.4.

Department	Square Feet	Percent of Total	Allocated Cost*
General office	1,500	12.50%	$ 300
Purchasing	1,500	12.50	300
Hardware	4,050	33.75	810
Housewares	2,700	22.50	540
Appliances	2,250	18.75	450
Totals...................	12,000	100.00%	$2,400

EXHIBIT 9A.4

Allocating Indirect (Utilities) Expense to All Departments

*See row 14 of departmental expense allocation spreadsheet (Exhibit 9.10).

Allocation of Advertising   Exhibit 9A.5 shows the allocation of $1,000 of advertising expense to the three operating departments on the basis of sales dollars. We exclude the service departments from this allocation because they do not generate sales.

Department	Sales	Percent of Total	Allocated Cost*
Hardware	$119,500	50.0%	$ 500
Housewares	71,700	30.0	300
Appliances	47,800	20.0	200
Totals..................	$239,000	100.0%	$1,000

EXHIBIT 9A.5

Allocating Indirect (Advertising) Expense to Operating Departments

*See row 15 of departmental expense allocation spreadsheet (Exhibit 9.10).

Allocation of Insurance   We allocate the $2,500 of insurance expense to each service and operating department, as shown in Exhibit 9A.6.

Department	Value of Insured Assets	Percent of Total	Allocated Cost*
General office............	$ 38,000	16.0%	$ 400
Purchasing	19,000	8.0	200
Hardware	85,500	36.0	900
Housewares	57,000	24.0	600
Appliances	38,000	16.0	400
Total....................	$237,500	100.0%	$2,500

EXHIBIT 9A.6

Allocating Indirect (Insurance) Expense to All Departments

*See row 16 of departmental expense allocation spreadsheet (Exhibit 9.10).

Allocation of Service Department Expenses   Next we allocate the total expenses of the two service departments to the three operating departments. Exhibit 9A.7 shows the allocation of total general office expenses ($15,300) to operating departments. This amount of $15,300 includes the $14,000 of direct service department expenses, plus $1,300 of indirect expenses that were allocated to the general office department.

Department	Sales	Percent of Total	Allocated Cost*
Hardware	$119,500	50.0%	$ 7,650
Housewares	71,700	30.0	4,590
Appliances	47,800	20.0	3,060
Total....................	$239,000	100.0%	$15,300

EXHIBIT 9A.7

Allocating Service Department (General Office) Expenses to Operating Departments

*See row 19 of departmental expense allocation spreadsheet (Exhibit 9.10).

Exhibit 9A.8 shows the allocation of total purchasing department expenses ($9,700) to operating departments. This amount of $9,700 includes $8,600 of direct expenses plus $1,100 of indirect expenses that were allocated to the purchasing department.

EXHIBIT 9A.8

Allocating Service Department (Purchasing) Expenses to Operating Departments

Department	Number of Purchase Orders	Percent of Total	Allocated Cost*
Hardware	394	40.00%	$3,880
Housewares	267	27.11	2,630
Appliances	324	32.89	3,190
Total...................	985	100.00%	$9,700

*See row 20 of departmental expense allocation spreadsheet (Exhibit 9.10).

APPENDIX

9B
Transfer Pricing

In this appendix we show how to determine transfer prices and discuss issues in transfer pricing.

Alternative Transfer Prices The top portion of Exhibit 9B.1 reports data on the LCD division of ZTel. That division manufactures liquid crystal display (LCD) touch-screen monitors for use in ZTel's S-Phone division's smartphones. The monitors can also be used in other products. The LCD division can sell its monitors to the S-Phone division as well as to buyers other than S-Phone. Likewise, the S-Phone division can purchase monitors from suppliers other than LCD.

EXHIBIT 9B.1

LCD Division Manufacturing Information—Monitors

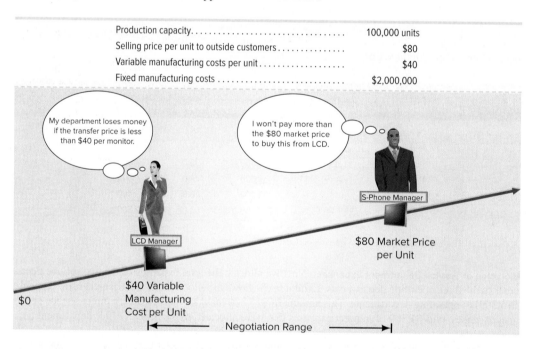

Production capacity................................	100,000 units
Selling price per unit to outside customers...............	$80
Variable manufacturing costs per unit...................	$40
Fixed manufacturing costs	$2,000,000

The bottom portion of Exhibit 9B.1 reveals the range of transfer prices for transfers of monitors from LCD to S-Phone. The transfer price can reasonably range from $40 (the variable manufacturing cost per unit) to $80 (the cost of buying the monitor from an outside supplier).

- The manager of LCD wants to report a divisional profit. Thus, this manager will not accept a transfer price less than $40; a price less than $40 would cause the division to lose money on each monitor transferred. The LCD manager will consider transfer prices of only $40 or more.

- The S-Phone division manager also wants to report a divisional profit. Thus, this manager will not pay more than $80 per monitor because similar monitors can be bought from outside suppliers at that price. The S-Phone manager will consider transfer prices of only $80 or less.

As any transfer price between $40 and $80 per monitor is possible, how does ZTel determine the transfer price? The answer depends in part on whether the LCD division has excess capacity to manufacture monitors.

No Excess Capacity If the LCD division can sell every monitor it produces (100,000 units) at a market price of $80 per monitor, LCD managers would not accept any transfer price less than $80 per monitor. This is a **market-based transfer price**—one based on the market price of the good or service being transferred. Any transfer price less than $80 would cause the LCD division managers to incur an unnecessary *opportunity cost* that would lower the division's income and hurt its managers' performance evaluation.

Typically, a division operating at full capacity will sell to external customers rather than sell internally. Still, the market-based transfer price of $80 can be considered the maximum possible transfer price when there is excess capacity, which is the case we consider next.

Excess Capacity Assume the LCD division is producing only 80,000 units. Because LCD has $2,000,000 of fixed manufacturing costs, both the LCD division and the top management of ZTel prefer that the S-Phone division purchases its monitors from LCD. For example, if S-Phone purchases its monitors from an outside supplier at the market price of $80 each, LCD manufactures no units. Then, LCD reports a division loss equal to its fixed costs, and ZTel overall reports a lower net income. With excess capacity, LCD should accept any transfer price of $40 per unit or greater, and S-Phone should purchase monitors from LCD. This will allow LCD to recover some (or all) of its fixed costs and increase ZTel's overall profits.

For example, if a transfer price of $50 per monitor is used, the S-Phone manager is pleased to buy from LCD since that price is below the market price of $80. For each monitor transferred from LCD to S-Phone at $50, the LCD division receives a *contribution margin* of $10 (computed as $50 transfer price less $40 variable cost) to contribute toward recovering its fixed costs. This form of transfer pricing is called **cost-based transfer pricing.** Under this approach the transfer price might be based on variable costs, total costs, or variable costs plus a markup.

With excess capacity, division managers will often negotiate a transfer price that lies between the variable cost per unit and the market price per unit. In this case, the **negotiated transfer price** and resulting departmental performance reports reflect, in part, the negotiating skills of the respective division managers. This might not be best for overall company performance. Determining the transfer price under excess capacity is complex and is covered in advanced courses.

Additional Issues in Transfer Pricing Several additional issues arise in determining transfer prices that include the following:

- **No market price exists.** Sometimes there is no market price for the product being transferred. The product might be a key component that requires additional conversion costs at the next stage and is not easily replicated by an outside company. For example, there is no market for a console for a **Nissan** Maxima and there is no substitute console Nissan can use in assembling a Maxima. In this case, a market-based transfer price cannot be used.

- **Cost control.** To provide incentives for cost control, transfer prices might be based on standard, rather than actual, costs. For example, if a transfer price of actual variable costs plus a markup of $20 per unit is used in the case above, LCD has no incentive to control its costs.

- **Nonfinancial factors.** Factors such as quality control, reduced lead times, and impact on employee morale can be important factors in determining transfer prices.

Transfer Pricing Approaches Used by Companies

Cost 46%
Market 37%
Negotiated 17%

Joint Costs and Their Allocation

9C

C3

Describe allocation of joint costs across products.

Most manufacturing processes involve **joint costs,** which refer to costs incurred to produce or purchase two or more products at the same time. For example, a sawmill company incurs joint costs when it buys logs that it cuts into lumber, as shown in Exhibit 9C.1. The joint costs include the logs (raw material) and their being cut (conversion) into boards classified as Clear, Select, No. 1 Common, No. 2 Common, No. 3 Common, and other types of lumber and by-products. After the logs are cut into boards, any further processing costs on the boards are not joint costs.

When a joint cost is incurred, a question arises as to whether to allocate it to different products resulting from it. The answer is that when management wishes to estimate the costs of individual products, joint costs are included and must be allocated to these joint products. However, when management needs information to help decide whether to sell a product at a certain point in the production process or to process it further,

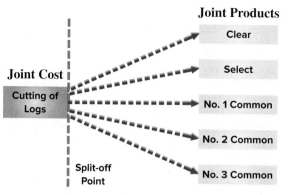

the joint costs are ignored. (We study this sell-or-process-further decision in a later chapter.)

Financial statements prepared according to GAAP must assign joint costs to products. To do this, management must decide how to allocate joint costs across products benefiting from these costs. If some products are sold and others remain in inventory, allocating joint costs involves assigning costs to both cost of goods sold and ending inventory.

The two usual methods to allocate joint costs are the (1) *physical basis* and (2) *value basis*. The physical basis typically involves allocating a joint cost using physical characteristics such as the ratio of pounds, cubic feet, or gallons of each joint product to the total pounds, cubic feet, or gallons of all joint products flowing from the cost. This method is not preferred because the resulting cost allocations do not reflect the relative market values the joint cost generates. The preferred approach is the value basis, which allocates a joint cost in proportion to the sales value of the output produced by the process at the "split-off point"; see Exhibit 9C.1. The split-off point is the point at which separate products can be identified.

Physical Basis Allocation of Joint Costs   To illustrate the physical basis of allocating a joint cost, we consider a sawmill that bought logs for $30,000. When cut, these logs produce 100,000 board feet of lumber in the grades and amounts shown in Exhibit 9C.2. The logs produce 20,000 board feet of No. 3 Common lumber, which is 20% of the total. With physical allocation, the No. 3 Common lumber is assigned 20% of the $30,000 cost of the logs, or $6,000 ($30,000 × 20%). Because this low-grade lumber sells for $4,000, this allocation gives a $2,000 loss from its production and sale. The physical basis for allocating joint costs does not reflect the extra value flowing into some products or the inferior value flowing into others. That is, the portion of a log that produces Clear and Select grade lumber is worth more than the portion used to produce the three grades of common lumber, but the physical basis fails to reflect this.

Grade of Lumber	Board Feet Produced	Percent of Total	Allocated Cost	Sales Value	Gross Profit
Clear and Select	10,000	10.0%	$ 3,000	$12,000	$ 9,000
No. 1 Common	30,000	30.0	9,000	18,000	9,000
No. 2 Common	40,000	40.0	12,000	16,000	4,000
No. 3 Common	20,000	20.0	6,000	4,000	(2,000)
Totals	100,000	100.0%	$30,000	$50,000	$20,000

Value Basis Allocation of Joint Costs   Exhibit 9C.3 illustrates the value basis method of allocation. It determines the percents of the total costs allocated to each grade by the ratio of each grade's sales value at the split-off point to the total sales value of $50,000 (sales value is the unit selling price multiplied by the number of units produced). The Clear and Select lumber grades receive 24% of the total cost ($12,000/$50,000) instead of the 10% portion using a physical basis. The No. 3 Common lumber receives only 8% of the total cost, or $2,400, which is much less than the $6,000 assigned to it using the physical basis.

Grade of Lumber	Sales Value	Percent of Total	Allocated Cost	Gross Profit
Clear and Select	$12,000	24.0%	$ 7,200	$ 4,800
No. 1 Common	18,000	36.0	10,800	7,200
No. 2 Common	16,000	32.0	9,600	6,400
No. 3 Common	4,000	8.0	2,400	1,600
Totals	$50,000	100.0%	$30,000	$20,000

An outcome of value basis allocation is that *each* grade produces exactly the same 40% gross profit at the split-off point. This 40% rate equals the gross profit rate from selling all the lumber made from the $30,000 logs for a combined price of $50,000. It is this closer matching of cost and revenues that makes the value basis allocation of joint costs the preferred method.

Summary

C1 **Distinguish between direct and indirect expenses and identify bases for allocating indirect expenses to departments.** Direct expenses are traced to a specific department and are incurred for the sole benefit of that department. Indirect expenses benefit more than one department. Indirect expenses are allocated to departments when computing departmental net income. Ideally, we allocate indirect expenses by using a cause-effect relation for the allocation base. When a cause-effect relation is not identifiable, each indirect expense is allocated on a basis reflecting the relative benefit received by each department.

C2 **Explain transfer pricing and methods to set transfer prices.** Transfer prices are used to record transfers of items between divisions of the same company. Transfer prices can be based on costs or market prices, or they can be negotiated by division managers.

C3ᶜ **Describe allocation of joint costs across products.** A joint cost refers to costs incurred to produce or purchase two or more products at the same time. When income statements are prepared, joint costs are usually allocated to the resulting joint products using either a physical or value basis.

A1 **Analyze investment centers using return on investment and residual income.** A financial measure often used to evaluate an investment center manager is the *return on investment,* also called *return on assets.* This measure is computed as the center's income divided by the center's average total assets. Residual income, computed as investment center income minus a target income, is an alternative financial measure of investment center performance.

A2 **Analyze investment centers using profit margin and investment turnover.** Return on investment can also be computed as profit margin times investment turnover. Profit margin (equal to income/sales) measures the income earned per dollar of sales, and investment turnover (equal to sales/assets) measures how efficiently a division uses its assets.

A3 **Analyze investment centers using the balanced scorecard.** A balanced scorecard uses a combination of financial and nonfinancial measures to evaluate performance. Customer, internal process, and innovation and learning are the three primary perspectives of nonfinancial measures used in balanced scorecards.

A4 **Compute cycle time and cycle efficiency, and explain their importance to production management.** It is important for companies to reduce the time to produce their products and to improve manufacturing efficiency. One measure of that time is cycle time (CT), defined as Process time + Inspection time + Move time + Wait time. Process time is value-added time; the others are non-value-added time. Cycle efficiency (CE) is the ratio of value-added time to total cycle time. If CE is low, management should evaluate its production process to see if it can reduce non-value-added activities.

P1 **Prepare a responsibility accounting report using controllable costs.** Responsibility accounting systems provide information for evaluating the performance of department managers. A responsibility accounting system's performance reports for evaluating department managers should include only the expenses (and revenues) that each manager controls.

P2 **Allocate indirect expenses to departments.** Indirect expenses include items like depreciation, rent, advertising, and other expenses that cannot be assigned directly to departments. Indirect expenses are recorded in company accounts, an allocation base is identified for each expense, and costs are allocated to departments. Departmental expense allocation spreadsheets are often used in allocating indirect expenses to departments.

P3 **Prepare departmental income statements and contribution reports.** Each profit center (department) is assigned its expenses to yield its own income statement. These costs include its direct expenses and its share of indirect expenses. The departmental income statement lists its revenues and costs of goods sold to determine gross profit. Its operating expenses (direct expenses and its indirect expenses allocated to the department) are deducted from gross profit to yield departmental net income. The departmental contribution report is similar to the departmental income statement in terms of computing the gross profit for each department. Then the direct operating expenses for each department are deducted from gross profit to determine the contribution generated by each department. Indirect operating expenses are deducted *in total* from the company's combined contribution.

Key Terms

Balanced scorecard	Direct expenses	Profit margin
Controllable costs	Indirect expenses	Residual income
Cost-based transfer pricing	Investment center	Responsibility accounting
Cost center	Investment turnover	Responsibility accounting performance report
Cycle efficiency (CE)	Joint cost	Return on investment
Cycle time (CT)	Market-based transfer price	Transfer price
Decentralized organization	Negotiated transfer price	Uncontrollable costs
Departmental contribution to overhead	Non-value-added time	Value-added time
Departmental income statements	Profit center	

Multiple Choice Quiz

1. A retailer has three departments—housewares, appliances, and clothing—and buys advertising that benefits all departments. Advertising expense is $150,000 for the year, and departmental sales for the year follow: housewares, $356,250; appliances, $641,250; and clothing, $427,500. How much advertising expense is allocated to appliances if allocation is based on departmental sales?

    a. $37,500   c. $45,000   e. $641,250

    b. $67,500   d. $150,000

2. Indirect expenses

    a. Cannot be readily traced to one department.

    b. Are allocated to departments based on the relative benefit each department receives.

    c. Are the same as uncontrollable expenses.

    d. *a*, *b*, and *c* above are all true.

    e. *a* and *b* above are true.

3. A division reports the information below. What is the division's investment turnover?

Sales	$500,000
Income	75,000
Average assets	200,000

    a. 37.5%   c. 2.5   e. 4

    b. 15   d. 2.67

4. A company operates three retail departments X, Y, and Z as profit centers. Which department has the largest dollar amount of departmental contribution to overhead, and what is the dollar amount contributed?

Department	Sales	Cost of Goods Sold	Direct Expenses	Allocated Indirect Expenses
X	$500,000	$350,000	$50,000	$40,000
Y	200,000	75,000	20,000	50,000
Z	350,000	150,000	75,000	10,000

    a. Department Y, $55,000   d. Department Z, $200,000

    b. Department Z, $125,000   e. Department X, $60,000

    c. Department X, $500,000

5. Using the data in question 4, Department X's contribution to overhead as a percentage of sales is

    a. 20%.   c. 12%.   e. 32%.

    b. 30%.   d. 48%.

ANSWERS TO MULTIPLE CHOICE QUIZ

1. b; [$641,250/($356,250 + $641,250 + $427,500)] × $150,000 = $67,500

2. d

3. c; $500,000/200,000 = 2.5

4. b;

	Department X	Department Y	Department Z
Sales.	$500,000	$200,000	$350,000
Cost of goods sold.	350,000	75,000	150,000
Gross profit.	150,000	125,000	200,000
Direct expenses	50,000	20,000	75,000
Departmental contribution to overhead . . .	$100,000	$105,000	$125,000

5. a; $100,000/$500,000 = 20%

---

^{A,B,C} *Superscript letter A, B, or C denotes assignments based on Appendixes 9A, 9B, or 9C.*

Ⓘ Icon denotes assignments that involve decision making.

Discussion Questions

1. Why are many companies divided into departments?

2. What is the difference between operating departments and service departments?

3. Ⓘ What are controllable costs?

4. _____ costs are not within the manager's control or influence.

5. Ⓘ In responsibility accounting, why are reports to higher-level managers usually summarized?

6. Ⓘ How are decisions made in decentralized organizations?

7. Ⓘ Is it possible to evaluate a cost center's profitability? Explain.

8. What is the difference between direct and indirect expenses?

9. Ⓘ Suggest a reasonable basis for allocating each of the following indirect expenses to departments: (a) salary of a supervisor who manages several departments, (b) rent, (c) heat, (d) electricity for lighting, (e) janitorial services,

(f) advertising, (g) expired insurance on equipment, and (h) property taxes on equipment.

10. **Samsung** has many departments. How is a department's contribution to overhead measured? **Samsung**

11. [ ] **Google** aims to give its managers timely cost reports. In responsibility accounting, who receives timely cost reports and specific cost information? Explain. **GOOGLE**

12. What is a transfer price? What are the three main approaches to setting transfer prices?

13.ᴮ Under what conditions is a market-based transfer price most likely to be used?

14.ᶜ What is a joint cost? How are joint costs usually allocated among the products produced from them?

15. [ ] Each **Apple** retail store has several departments. Why is it useful for its management **APPLE**

to (a) collect accounting information about each department and (b) treat each department as a profit center?

16. [ ] **Apple** delivers its products to locations around the world. List three controllable and three uncontrollable costs for its delivery department. **APPLE**

17. [ ] Define and describe *cycle time* and identify the components of cycle time.

18. [ ] Explain the difference between value-added time and non-value-added time.

19. Define and describe *cycle efficiency*.

20. [ ] Can management of a company such as **Samsung** use cycle time and cycle efficiency as useful measures of performance? Explain. **Samsung**

connect

In each blank next to the following terms, place the identifying letter of its best description.

_____ **1.** Cost center
_____ **2.** Investment center
_____ **3.** Departmental accounting system
_____ **4.** Operating department
_____ **5.** Profit center
_____ **6.** Responsibility accounting system
_____ **7.** Service department

A. Incurs costs without directly yielding revenues.
B. Provides information used to evaluate the performance of a department.
C. Holds manager responsible for revenues, costs, and investments.
D. Engages directly in manufacturing or in making sales directly to customers.
E. Does not directly manufacture products but contributes to profitability of the entire company.
F. Incurs costs and also generates revenues.
G. Provides information used to evaluate the performance of a department manager.

QS 9-1
Allocation and measurement terms
C1

For each of the following types of indirect expenses and service department expenses, identify one allocation basis that could be used to distribute it to the departments indicated.
_____ **1.** Computer service expenses of production scheduling for operating departments.
_____ **2.** General office department expenses of the operating departments.
_____ **3.** Maintenance department expenses of the operating departments.
_____ **4.** Electric utility expenses of all departments.

QS 9-2
Basis for cost allocation
C1 [ ]

In each blank next to the following terms, place the identifying letter of its best description.
_____ **1.** Indirect expenses
_____ **2.** Controllable costs
_____ **3.** Direct expenses
_____ **4.** Uncontrollable costs

A. Costs not within a manager's control or influence.
B. Costs that can be readily traced to a department.
C. Costs that a manager has the ability to affect.
D. Costs incurred for the joint benefit of more than one department.

QS 9-3
Responsibility accounting terms
C1

Jose Ruiz manages a car dealer's service department. His department is organized as a cost center. Costs for a recent quarter are shown below. List the costs that would appear on a responsibility accounting report for the service department.

QS 9-4
Responsibility accounting report
P1

Cost of parts	$22,400	Shop supplies	$1,200
Mechanics' wages	14,300	Utilities (allocated)	800
Manager's salary	8,000	Administrative costs (allocated)	2,200
Building depreciation (allocated)	4,500		

QS 9-5
Allocating costs
to departments
P2

Macee Department Store has three departments, and it conducts advertising campaigns that benefit all departments. Advertising costs are $100,000 this year, and departmental sales for this year follow. How much advertising cost is allocated to each department if the allocation is based on departmental sales?

Department	Sales
1	$220,000
2	400,000
3	180,000

QS 9-6
Allocating costs
to departments   P2

Mervon Company has two operating departments: mixing and bottling. Mixing has 300 employees and bottling has 200 employees. Indirect factory costs include administrative costs of $160,000. Administrative costs are allocated to operating departments based on the number of workers. Determine the administrative costs allocated to each operating department.

QS 9-7
Allocating costs
to departments   P2

Mervon Company has two operating departments: mixing and bottling. Mixing occupies 22,000 square feet. Bottling occupies 18,000 square feet. Indirect factory costs include maintenance costs of $200,000. If maintenance costs are allocated to operating departments based on square footage occupied, determine the amount of maintenance costs allocated to each operating department.

QS 9-8
Rent expense allocated
to departments

P2

A retailer pays $130,000 rent each year for its two-story building. The space in this building is occupied by five departments as specified here.

Department	Square feet occupied
Jewelry	1,440 (first-floor)
Cosmetics	3,360 (first-floor)
Housewares	2,016 (second-floor)
Tools	960 (second-floor)
Shoes	1,824 (second-floor)

Check Allocated to jewelry
dept., $25,350

The company allocates 65% of total rent expense to the first floor and 35% to the second floor, and then allocates rent expense for each floor to the departments occupying that floor on the basis of space occupied. Determine the rent expense to be allocated to each department. (Round percents to the nearest one-tenth and dollar amounts to the nearest whole dollar.)

QS 9-9
Departmental contribution
to overhead

P3

Use the information in the following table to compute each department's contribution to overhead (both in dollars and as a percent). Which department contributes the largest dollar amount to total overhead? Which contributes the highest percent (as a percent of sales)? Round percents to one decimal.

	Dept. A	Dept. B	Dept. C
Sales	$53,000	$180,000	$84,000
Cost of goods sold	34,185	103,700	49,560
Gross profit	18,815	76,300	34,440
Total direct expenses	3,660	37,060	7,386
Contribution to overhead	$	$	$
Contribution percent (of sales)	%	%	%

QS 9-10
Computing return
on investment

A1

Compute return on investment for each of the divisions below (each is an investment center). Comment on the relative performance of each investment center.

Investment Center	Net Income	Average Assets	Return on Investment
Cameras and camcorders	$4,500,000	$20,000,000	%
Phones and communications	1,500,000	12,500,000	
Computers and accessories	800,000	10,000,000	

Refer to the information in QS 9-10. Assume a target income of 12% of average invested assets. Compute residual income for each division.

QS 9-11
Computing residual
income   A1

Fill in the blanks in the schedule below for two separate investment centers A and B. Round answers to the nearest whole percent.

QS 9-12
Performance measures

A1   A2

	Investment Center	
	A	**B**
Sales	$_____	$10,400,000
Net income	$ 352,000	$ _____
Average invested assets	$1,400,000	$ _____
Profit margin.....................	8.0%	_____%
Investment turnover...............	_____	1.5
Return on investment..............	_____%	12.0%

A company's shipping division (an investment center) has sales of $2,420,000, net income of $516,000, and average invested assets of $2,250,000. Compute the division's profit margin and investment turnover.

QS 9-13
Computing profit margin and
investment turnover   A2

Classify each of the performance measures below into the most likely balanced scorecard perspective it relates to. Label your answers using C (customer), P (internal process), I (innovation and growth), or F (financial).

QS 9-14
Performance measures—
balanced scorecard

A3

_____ **1.** Customer wait time

_____ **2.** Number of days of employee absences

_____ **3.** Profit margin

_____ **4.** Number of new products introduced

_____ **5.** Change in market share

_____ **6.** Employee sustainability training sessions attended

_____ **7.** Length of time raw materials are in inventory

_____ **8.** Customer satisfaction index

_____ **9.** Gallons of water reused

_____ **10.** CO_2 emissions

Walt Disney reports the following information for its two Parks and Resorts divisions.

QS 9-15
Performance measures—
balanced scorecard

A3

	U.S.		International	
	Current Year	**Prior Year**	**Current Year**	**Prior Year**
Hotel occupancy rates	87%	83%	79%	78%

Assume Walt Disney uses a balanced scorecard and sets a target of 85% occupancy in its resorts. Using Exhibit 9.18 as a guide, show how the company's performance on hotel occupancy would appear on a balanced scorecard report.

Compute and interpret (*a*) manufacturing cycle time and (*b*) manufacturing cycle efficiency using the following information from a manufacturing company.

QS 9-16
Manufacturing cycle time
and efficiency

A4

Process time............	15.0 minutes
Inspection time...........	2.0 minutes
Move time..............	6.4 minutes
Wait time...............	36.6 minutes

The windshield division of Fast Car Co. makes windshields for use in Fast Car's assembly division. The windshield division incurs variable costs of $200 per windshield and has capacity to make 500,000 windshields per year. The market price is $450 per windshield. The windshield division incurs total fixed costs of $3,000,000 per year. If the windshield division is operating at full capacity, what transfer price should be used on transfers between the windshield and assembly divisions? Explain.

QS 9-17[B]
Determining transfer prices
without excess capacity

C2

QS 9-18^B

QS 9-18ᴮ

Determining transfer prices
with excess capacity   **C2**

The windshield division of Fast Car Co. makes windshields for use in Fast Car's assembly division. The windshield division incurs variable costs of $200 per windshield and has capacity to make 500,000 windshields per year. The market price is $450 per windshield. The windshield division incurs total fixed costs of $3,000,000 per year. If the windshield division has excess capacity, what is the range of possible transfer prices that could be used on transfers between the windshield and assembly divisions? Explain.

QS 9-19ᶜ

Joint cost allocation

C3

A company purchases a 10,020-square-foot commercial building for $325,000 and spends an additional $50,000 to divide the space into two separate rental units and prepare it for rent. Unit A, which has the desirable location on the corner and contains 3,340 square feet, will be rented for $1.00 per square foot. Unit B contains 6,680 square feet and will be rented for $0.75 per square foot. How much of the joint cost should be assigned to Unit B using the value basis of allocation?

QS 9-20

Return on investment

A1

For a recent year **L'Oréal** reported operating profit of €3,385 (in millions) for its cosmetics division. Total assets were €12,888 (in millions) at the beginning of the year and €13,099 (in millions) at the end of the year. Compute return on investment for the year. State your answer as a percent, rounded to one decimal.

EXERCISES

Exercise 9-1

Responsibility accounting
report—cost center

P1

Arctica manufactures snowmobiles and ATVs. These products are made in different departments, and each department has its own manager. Each responsibility performance report only includes those costs that the particular department manager can control: raw materials, wages, supplies used, and equipment depreciation. Using the data below, prepare a responsibility accounting report for the snowmobile department.

	A	B	C	D	E	F	G
1			Budget			Actual	
2							
3		Snowmobile	ATV	Combined	Snowmobile	ATV	Combined
4	Raw materials	$ 19,500	$27,500	$ 47,000	$ 19,420	$28,820	$ 48,240
5	Employee wages	10,400	20,500	30,900	10,660	21,240	31,900
6	Dept. manager salary	4,300	5,200	9,500	4,400	4,400	8,800
7	Supplies used	3,300	900	4,200	3,170	920	4,090
8	Depreciation—Equip.	6,000	12,500	18,500	6,000	12,500	18,500
9	Utilities	360	540	900	330	500	830
10	Rent	5,700	6,300	12,000	5,300	6,300	11,600
11	**Totals**	$49,560	$73,440	$123,000	$49,280	$74,680	$123,960

Exercise 9-2

Responsibility accounting
report—cost center   **P1**

Refer to the information in Exercise 9-1 and prepare a responsibility accounting report for the ATV department.

Exercise 9-3

Service department
expenses allocated to
operating departments   **P2**

The following is a partially completed lower section of a departmental expense allocation spreadsheet for Cozy Bookstore. It reports the total amounts of direct and indirect expenses allocated to its five departments. Complete the spreadsheet by allocating the expenses of the two service departments (advertising and purchasing) to the three operating departments.

	A	B	C	D	E	F	G
1				Allocation of Expenses to Departments			
2			Expense				
3		Allocation	Account	Advertising	Purchasing	Books	Magazines	Newspapers
4		Base	Balance	Dept.	Dept.	Dept.	Dept.	Dept.
5	Total department expenses..........		$698,000	$24,000	$34,000	$425,000	$90,000	$125,000
6	**Service department expenses**							
7	Advertising department............. Sales			?		?	?	?
8	Purchasing department............. Purch. orders				?	?	?	?
9	Total expenses allocated to operating departments.............		?	$ 0	$ 0	?	?	?

Continued on next page . . .

Advertising and purchasing department expenses are allocated to operating departments on the basis of dollar sales and purchase orders, respectively. Information about the allocation bases for the three operating departments follows.

Department	Sales	Purchase Orders
Books	$495,000	516
Magazines	198,000	360
Newspapers	207,000	324
Total	$900,000	1,200

Check Total expenses allocated to books dept., $452,820

Jessica Porter works in both the jewelry department and the cosmetics department of a retail store. She assists customers in both departments and arranges and stocks merchandise in both departments. The store allocates her $30,000 annual wages between the two departments based on the time worked in the two departments. Jessica reported the following hours and activities spent in the two departments. Allocate Jessica's annual wages between the two departments.

Exercise 9-4
Indirect payroll expense allocated to departments
P2

Activities	Hours
Selling in jewelry department	51
Arranging and stocking merchandise in jewelry department	6
Selling in cosmetics department	12
Arranging and stocking merchandise in cosmetics department	7
Idle time spent waiting for a customer to enter one of the departments	4

Check Assign $7,500 to cosmetics

Woh Che Co. has four departments: materials, personnel, manufacturing, and packaging. In a recent month, the four departments incurred three shared indirect expenses. The amounts of these indirect expenses and the bases used to allocate them follow.

Exercise 9-5
Departmental expense allocations
P2

Indirect Expense	Cost	Allocation Base
Supervision	$ 82,500	Number of employees
Utilities	50,000	Square feet occupied
Insurance	22,500	Value of assets in use
Total	$155,000	

Departmental data for the company's recent reporting period follow.

Department	Employees	Square Feet	Asset Values
Materials	27	25,000	$ 6,000
Personnel	9	5,000	1,200
Manufacturing	63	55,000	37,800
Packaging	51	15,000	15,000
Total	150	100,000	$60,000

1. Use this information to allocate each of the three indirect expenses across the four departments.
2. Prepare a summary table that reports the indirect expenses assigned to each of the four departments.

Check (2) Total of $29,600 assigned to materials dept.

Marathon Running Shop has two service departments (advertising and administrative) and two operating departments (shoes and clothing). The table that follows shows the direct expenses incurred and square footage occupied by all four departments, as well as total sales for the two operating departments for the year 2017.

Exercise 9-6
Departmental expense allocation spreadsheet
P2

Department	Direct Expenses	Square Feet	Sales
Advertising	$ 18,000	1,120	—
Administrative	25,000	1,400	—
Shoes	103,000	7,140	$273,000
Clothing	15,000	4,340	77,000

The advertising department developed and distributed 120 advertisements during the year. Of these, 90 promoted shoes and 30 promoted clothing. Utilities expense of $64,000 is an indirect expense to all departments. Prepare a departmental expense allocation spreadsheet for Marathon Running Shop. The spreadsheet should assign (1) direct expenses to each of the four departments, (2) the $64,000 of utilities expense to the four departments on the basis of floor space occupied, (3) the advertising department's expenses to the two operating departments on the basis of the number of ads placed that promoted a department's products, and (4) the administrative department's expenses to the two operating departments based on the amount of sales. Provide supporting computations for the expense allocations.

Check   Total expenses allocated to shoes dept., $177,472

Exercise 9-7
Departmental
contribution report

P3

Below are departmental income statements for a guitar manufacturer. The manufacturer is considering eliminating its electric guitar department since it has a net loss. The company classifies advertising, rent, and utilities expenses as indirect.

WHOLESALE GUITARS Departmental Income Statements For Year Ended December 31, 2017		
	Acoustic	**Electric**
Sales.	$112,500	$105,500
Cost of goods sold.	55,675	66,750
Gross profit	56,825	38,750
Operating expenses		
Advertising expense	8,075	6,250
Depreciation expense—Equipment	10,150	9,000
Salaries expense.	17,300	13,500
Supplies expense	2,030	1,700
Rent expense.	6,105	5,950
Utilities expense	3,045	2,550
Total operating expenses	46,705	38,950
Net income (loss)	**$ 10,120**	**$ (200)**

1. Prepare a departmental contribution report that shows each department's contribution to overhead.

2. Based on contribution to overhead, should the electric guitar department be eliminated?

Exercise 9-8
Departmental income
statement and contribution
to overhead

P3

Jansen Company reports the following for its ski department for the year 2017. All of its costs are direct, except as noted.

Sales	$605,000
Cost of goods sold	425,000
Salaries	112,000 ($15,000 is indirect)
Utilities	14,000 ($3,000 is indirect)
Depreciation	42,000 ($10,000 is indirect)
Office expenses	20,000 (all indirect)

Prepare a (1) departmental income statement for 2017 and (2) departmental contribution to overhead report for 2017. (3) Based on these two performance reports, should Jansen eliminate the ski department?

Exercise 9-9
Investment center analysis

A1

You must prepare a return on investment analysis for the regional manager of Fast & Great Burgers. This growing chain is trying to decide which outlet of two alternatives to open. The first location (A) requires a $1,000,000 investment and is expected to yield annual net income of $160,000. The second location (B) requires a $600,000 investment and is expected to yield annual net income of $108,000. Compute the return on investment for each Fast & Great Burgers alternative and then make your recommendation in a half-page memorandum to the regional manager. (The chain currently generates an 18% return on total assets.)

Megamart, a retailer of consumer goods, provides the following information on two of its departments (each considered an investment center).

Investment Center	Sales	Income	Average Invested Assets
Electronics....................	$40,000,000	$2,880,000	$16,000,000
Sporting goods................	20,000,000	2,040,000	12,000,000

Exercise 9-10
Computing return on investment and residual income; investing decision

A1

1. Compute return on investment for each department. Using return on investment, which department is most efficient at using assets to generate returns for the company?

2. Assume a target income level of 12% of average invested assets. Compute residual income for each department. Which department generated the most residual income for the company?

3. Assume the electronics department is presented with a new investment opportunity that will yield a 15% return on investment. Should the new investment opportunity be accepted? Explain.

Refer to information in Exercise 9-10. Compute profit margin and investment turnover for each department. Which department generates the most net income per dollar of sales? Which department is most efficient at generating sales from average invested assets?

Exercise 9-11
Computing margin and turnover; department efficiency   A2

A food manufacturer reports the following for two of its divisions for a recent year.

$ millions	Beverage Division	Cheese Division
Invested assets, beginning	$2,662	$4,455
Invested assets, ending..............	2,593	4,400
Sales	2,681	3,925
Operating income...................	349	634

Exercise 9-12
Return on investment

A1   A2

For each division, compute (1) return on investment, (2) profit margin, and (3) investment turnover for the year. Round answers to two decimal places.

Refer to the information in Exercise 9-12. Assume that each of the company's divisions has a required rate of return of 7%. Compute residual income for each division.

Exercise 9-13
Residual income   A1

Apple Inc. reports the following for three of its geographic segments for a recent year.

$ millions	Americas	Europe	China
Operating income....................	$31,186	$16,527	$23,002
Sales	93,864	50,337	58,715

Exercise 9-14
Profit margin   A2

Compute profit margin for each division. Express answers as percentages, rounded to one decimal place.

ZNet Co. is a web-based retail company. The company reports the following for 2017.

Sales	$ 5,000,000
Operating income...	1,000,000
Average invested assets	12,500,000

Exercise 9-15
Return on investment

A1   A2

The company's CEO believes that sales for 2018 will increase by 20% and both profit margin (%) and the level of average invested assets will be the same as for 2017.

1. Compute return on investment for 2017.

2. Compute profit margin for 2017.

3. If the CEO's forecast is correct, what will return on investment equal for 2018?

4. If the CEO's forecast is correct, what will investment turnover equal for 2018?

Exercise 9-16
Performance measures—balanced scorecard
A3

USA Airlines uses the following performance measures. Classify each of the performance measures below into the most likely balanced scorecard perspective it relates to. Label your answers using C (customer), P (internal process), I (innovation and growth), or F (financial).

_____ **1.** Cash flow from operations
_____ **2.** Number of reports of mishandled or lost baggage
_____ **3.** Percentage of on-time departures
_____ **4.** On-time flight percentage
_____ **5.** Percentage of ground crew trained
_____ **6.** Return on investment
_____ **7.** Market value
_____ **8.** Accidents or safety incidents per mile flown
_____ **9.** Customer complaints
_____ **10.** Flight attendant training sessions attended
_____ **11.** Time airplane is on ground between flights
_____ **12.** Airplane miles per gallon of fuel
_____ **13.** Revenue per seat
_____ **14.** Cost of leasing airplanes

Exercise 9-17
Sustainability and the balanced scorecard
A3

Midwest Mfg. uses a balanced scorecard as part of its performance evaluation. The company wants to include information on its sustainability efforts in its balanced scorecard. For each of the sustainability items below, indicate the most likely balanced scorecard perspective it relates to. Label your answers using C (customer), P (internal process), I (innovation and learning), or F (financial).

_____ **1.** CO_2 emissions
_____ **2.** Number of solar panels installed
_____ **3.** Gallons of water used
_____ **4.** Customer surveys of company's sustainability reputation
_____ **5.** Pounds of recyclable packaging used
_____ **6.** Pounds of trash diverted from landfill
_____ **7.** Dollar sales of green products
_____ **8.** Number of sustainability training workshops held
_____ **9.** Cubic feet of natural gas used
_____ **10.** Patents for green products applied for

Exercise 9-18
Manufacturing cycle time and efficiency
A4

Oakwood Company produces maple bookcases. The following information is available for the production of a recent order of 500 bookcases.

Process time	6.0 days	Move time	3.2 days
Inspection time	0.8 days	Wait time	5.0 days

Check (2) Manufacturing cycle efficiency, 0.40

1. Compute the company's manufacturing cycle time.
2. Compute the company's manufacturing cycle efficiency. Interpret your answer.
3. Management believes it can reduce move time by 1.2 days and wait time by 2.8 days by adopting lean manufacturing techniques. Compute the company's manufacturing cycle efficiency assuming the company's predictions are correct.

Exercise 9-19
Manufacturing cycle time and efficiency
A4

Best Ink produces printers for personal computers. The following information is available for production of a recent order of 500 printers.

Process time	16.0 hours	Move time	9.0 hours
Inspection time	3.5 hours	Wait time	21.5 hours

1. Compute the company's manufacturing cycle time.
2. Compute the company's manufacturing cycle efficiency. Interpret your answer.
3. Assume the company wishes to increase its manufacturing cycle efficiency to 0.80. What are some ways to accomplish this?

Exercise 9-20^B
Determining transfer prices
C2

The trailer division of Baxter Bicycles makes bike trailers that attach to bicycles and can carry children or cargo. The trailers have a retail price of $200 each. Each trailer incurs $80 of variable manufacturing costs. The trailer division has capacity for 40,000 trailers per year and incurs fixed costs of $1,000,000 per year.

1. Assume the assembly division of Baxter Bicycles wants to buy 15,000 trailers per year from the trailer division. If the trailer division can sell all of the trailers it manufactures to outside customers, what price should be used on transfers between Baxter Bicycles's divisions? Explain.

Continued on next page . . .

2. Assume the trailer division currently only sells 20,000 trailers to outside customers, and the assembly division wants to buy 15,000 trailers per year from the trailer division. What is the range of acceptable prices that could be used on transfers between Baxter Bicycles's divisions? Explain.

3. Assume transfer prices of either $80 per trailer or $140 per trailer are being considered. Comment on the preferred transfer prices from the perspectives of the trailer division manager, the assembly division manager, and the top management of Baxter Bicycles.

Heart & Home Properties is developing a subdivision that includes 600 home lots. The 450 lots in the Canyon section are below a ridge and do not have views of the neighboring canyons and hills; the 150 lots in the Hilltop section offer unobstructed views. The expected selling price for each Canyon lot is $55,000 and for each Hilltop lot is $110,000. The developer acquired the land for $4,000,000 and spent another $3,500,000 on street and utilities improvements. Assign the joint land and improvement costs to the lots using the value basis of allocation and determine the average cost per lot.

Exercise 9-21[C]
Assigning joint real estate costs **C3**

Check Total Hilltop cost, $3,000,000

Pirate Seafood Company purchases lobsters and processes them into tails and flakes. It sells the lobster tails for $21 per pound and the flakes for $14 per pound. On average, 100 pounds of lobster are processed into 52 pounds of tails and 22 pounds of flakes, with 26 pounds of waste. Assume that the company purchased 2,400 pounds of lobster for $4.50 per pound and processed the lobsters with an additional labor cost of $1,800. No materials or labor costs are assigned to the waste. If 1,096 pounds of tails and 324 pounds of flakes are sold, what is (1) the allocated cost of the sold items and (2) the allocated cost of the ending inventory? The company allocates joint costs on a value basis. (Round the dollar cost per pound to the nearest thousandth.)

Exercise 9-22[C]
Assigning joint product costs

C3

Check (2) Inventory cost, $2,268

L'Oréal reports the following for a recent year for the major divisions in its cosmetics branch.

Exercise 9-23
Profit margin and investment turnover

A2

€ millions	Sales	Income	Total Assets End of Year	Total Assets Beginning of Year
Professional products............	€ 2,717	€ 552	€ 2,624	€ 2,516
Consumer products	9,530	1,765	5,994	5,496
Luxury products	4,507	791	3,651	4,059
Active cosmetics................	1,386	278	830	817
Total.........................	€18,140	€3,386	€13,099	€12,888

1. Compute profit margin for each division. State your answers as percents, rounded to two decimal places. Which L'Oréal division has the highest profit margin?

2. Compute investment turnover for each division. Round your answers to two decimal places. Which L'Oréal division has the best investment turnover?

▇ connect

Billie Whitehorse, the plant manager of Travel Free's Indiana plant, is responsible for all of that plant's costs other than her own salary. The plant has two operating departments and one service department. The camper and trailer operating departments manufacture different products and have their own managers. The office department, which Whitehorse also manages, provides services equally to the two operating departments. A budget is prepared for each operating department and the office department. The company's responsibility accounting system must assemble information to present budgeted and actual costs in performance reports for each operating department manager and the plant manager. Each performance report includes only those costs that a particular operating department manager can control: raw materials, wages, supplies used, and equipment depreciation. The plant manager is responsible for the department managers' salaries, utilities, building rent, office salaries other than her own, and other office costs plus all costs controlled by the two operating department managers. The annual departmental budgets and actual costs for the two operating departments follow.

PROBLEM SET A

Problem 9-1A
Responsibility accounting performance reports; controllable and budgeted costs

P1

	Budget			Actual		
	Campers	Trailers	Combined	Campers	Trailers	Combined
Raw materials.................	$195,000	$275,000	$ 470,000	$194,200	$273,200	$ 467,400
Employee wages	104,000	205,000	309,000	106,600	206,400	313,000
Dept. manager salary...........	43,000	52,000	95,000	44,000	53,500	97,500
Supplies used	33,000	90,000	123,000	31,700	91,600	123,300
Depreciation—Equip.	60,000	125,000	185,000	60,000	125,000	185,000
Utilities	3,600	5,400	9,000	3,300	5,000	8,300
Building rent	5,700	9,300	15,000	5,300	8,700	14,000
Office department costs.........	68,750	68,750	137,500	67,550	67,550	135,100
Totals.......................	$513,050	$830,450	$1,343,500	$512,650	$830,950	$1,343,600

The office department's annual budget and its actual costs follow.

	Budget	Actual
Plant manager salary	$ 80,000	$ 82,000
Other office salaries	32,500	30,100
Other office costs	25,000	23,000
Totals.......................	$137,500	$135,100

Required

1. Prepare responsibility accounting performance reports like those in Exhibit 9.2 that list costs controlled by the following:

Check   (1a) $500 total over budget

(1c) Indiana plant controllable costs, $1,900 total under budget

a. Manager of the camper department.
b. Manager of the trailer department.
c. Manager of the Indiana plant.

In each report, include the budgeted and actual costs and show the amount that each actual cost is over or under the budgeted amount.

Analysis Component

2. Did the plant manager or the operating department managers better manage costs? Explain.

Problem 9-2A
Allocation of building occupancy costs to departments

P2

National Bank has several departments that occupy both floors of a two-story building. The departmental accounting system has a single account, Building Occupancy Cost, in its ledger. The types and amounts of occupancy costs recorded in this account for the current period follow.

Depreciation—Building	$18,000
Interest—Building mortgage	27,000
Taxes—Building and land..............	9,000
Gas (heating) expense	3,000
Lighting expense	3,000
Maintenance expense	6,000
Total occupancy cost	$66,000

The building has 4,000 square feet on each floor. In prior periods, the accounting manager merely divided the $66,000 occupancy cost by 8,000 square feet to find an average cost of $8.25 per square foot and then charged each department a building occupancy cost equal to this rate times the number of square feet that it occupied.

Diane Linder manages a first-floor department that occupies 1,000 square feet, and Juan Chiro manages a second-floor department that occupies 1,800 square feet of floor space. In discussing the departmental reports, the second-floor manager questions whether using the same rate per square foot for all departments makes sense because the first-floor space is more valuable. This manager also references a recent real estate study of average local rental costs for similar space that shows first-floor space worth $30 per square foot and second-floor space worth $20 per square foot (excluding costs for heating, lighting, and maintenance).

Required

1. Allocate occupancy costs to the Linder and Chiro departments using the current allocation method.

2. Allocate the depreciation, interest, and taxes occupancy costs to the Linder and Chiro departments in proportion to the relative market values of the floor space. Allocate the heating, lighting, and maintenance costs to the Linder and Chiro departments in proportion to the square feet occupied (ignoring floor space market values).

Analysis Component

3. Which allocation method would you prefer if you were a manager of a second-floor department? Explain.

Check   (1) Total allocated to Linder and Chiro, $23,100
(2) Total occupancy cost to Linder, $9,600

Williams Company began operations in January 2017 with two operating (selling) departments and one service (office) department. Its departmental income statements follow.

Problem 9-3A
Departmental income statements; forecasts

P3

WILLIAMS COMPANY Departmental Income Statements For Year Ended December 31, 2017			
	Clock	**Mirror**	**Combined**
Sales	$130,000	$55,000	$185,000
Cost of goods sold	63,700	34,100	97,800
Gross profit	66,300	20,900	87,200
Direct expenses			
Sales salaries	20,000	7,000	27,000
Advertising	1,200	500	1,700
Store supplies used	900	400	1,300
Depreciation—Equipment	1,500	300	1,800
Total direct expenses	23,600	8,200	31,800
Allocated expenses			
Rent expense	7,020	3,780	10,800
Utilities expense	2,600	1,400	4,000
Share of office department expenses	10,500	4,500	15,000
Total allocated expenses	20,120	9,680	29,800
Total expenses	43,720	17,880	61,600
Net income	$ 22,580	$ 3,020	$ 25,600

Williams plans to open a third department in January 2018 that will sell paintings. Management predicts that the new department will generate $50,000 in sales with a 55% gross profit margin and will require the following direct expenses: sales salaries, $8,000; advertising, $800; store supplies, $500; and equipment depreciation, $200. It will fit the new department into the current rented space by taking some square footage from the other two departments. When opened, the new painting department will fill one-fifth of the space presently used by the clock department and one-fourth used by the mirror department. Management does not predict any increase in utilities costs, which are allocated to the departments in proportion to occupied space (or rent expense). The company allocates office department expenses to the operating departments in proportion to their sales. It expects the painting department to increase total office department expenses by $7,000. Since the painting department will bring new customers into the store, management expects sales in both the clock and mirror departments to increase by 8%. No changes for those departments' gross profit percents or their direct expenses are expected except for store supplies used, which will increase in proportion to sales.

Required

Prepare departmental income statements that show the company's predicted results of operations for calendar-year 2018 for the three operating (selling) departments and their combined totals. (Round percents to the nearest one-tenth and dollar amounts to the nearest whole dollar.)

Check   2018 forecasted combined net income (sales), $43,472 ($249,800)

Problem 9-4A

Departmental contribution
to income

P3

Vortex Company operates a retail store with two departments. Information about those departments follows.

	Department A	Department B
Sales	$800,000	$450,000
Cost of goods sold	497,000	291,000
Direct expenses		
Salaries......................	125,000	88,000
Insurance	20,000	10,000
Utilities	24,000	14,000
Depreciation..................	21,000	12,000
Maintenance..................	7,000	5,000

The company also incurred the following indirect costs.

Salaries	$36,000
Insurance	6,000
Depreciation.............	15,000
Office expenses	50,000

Indirect costs are allocated as follows: salaries on the basis of sales; insurance and depreciation on the basis of square footage; and office expenses on the basis of number of employees. Additional information about the departments follows.

Department	Square Footage	Number of Employees
A	28,000	75
B	12,000	50

Required

Check   (1) Dept. A net
income, $38,260

1. For each department, determine the departmental contribution to overhead and the departmental net income.

2. Should Department B be eliminated? Explain.

Problem 9-5A[C]

Allocation of joint costs

C3

Georgia Orchards produced a good crop of peaches this year. After preparing the following income statement, the company is concerned about the net loss on its No. 3 peaches.

GEORGIA ORCHARDS Income Statement For Year Ended December 31, 2017				
	No. 1	No. 2	No. 3	Combined
Sales (by grade)				
No. 1: 300,000 lbs. @ $1.50/lb....................	$450,000			
No. 2: 300,000 lbs. @ $1.00/lb....................		$300,000		
No. 3: 750,000 lbs. @ $0.25/lb....................			$ 187,500	
Total sales..				$937,500
Costs				
Tree pruning and care @ $0.30/lb	90,000	90,000	225,000	405,000
Picking, sorting, and grading @ $0.15/lb.............	45,000	45,000	112,500	202,500
Delivery costs.....................................	15,000	15,000	37,500	67,500
Total costs..	150,000	150,000	375,000	675,000
Net income (loss)	$300,000	$150,000	$(187,500)	$262,500

In preparing this statement, the company allocated joint costs among the grades on a physical basis as an equal amount per pound. The company's delivery cost records show that $30,000 of the $67,500 relates to crating the No. 1 and No. 2 peaches and hauling them to the buyer. The remaining $37,500 of delivery costs is for crating the No. 3 peaches and hauling them to the cannery.

Required

1. Prepare reports showing cost allocations on a sales value basis to the three grades of peaches. Separate the delivery costs into the amounts directly identifiable with each grade. Then allocate any shared delivery costs on the basis of the relative sales value of each grade. (Round percents to the nearest one-tenth and dollar amounts to the nearest whole dollar.)

2. Using your answers to part 1, prepare an income statement using the joint costs allocated on a sales value basis.

Analysis Component

3. Do you think delivery costs fit the definition of a joint cost? Explain.

Check (1) $129,600 tree pruning and care costs allocated to No. 2

(2) Net income from No. 1 & No. 2 peaches, $140,400 & $93,600

Britney Brown, the plant manager of LMN Co.'s Chicago plant, is responsible for all of that plant's costs other than her own salary. The plant has two operating departments and one service department. The refrigerator and dishwasher operating departments manufacture different products and have their own managers. The office department, which Brown also manages, provides services equally to the two operating departments. A monthly budget is prepared for each operating department and the office department. The company's responsibility accounting system must assemble information to present budgeted and actual costs in performance reports for each operating department manager and the plant manager. Each performance report includes only those costs that a particular operating department manager can control: raw materials, wages, supplies used, and equipment depreciation. The plant manager is responsible for the department managers' salaries, utilities, building rent, office salaries other than her own, and other office costs plus all costs controlled by the two operating department managers. The April departmental budgets and actual costs for the two operating departments follow.

PROBLEM SET B

Problem 9-1B
Responsibility accounting performance reports; controllable and budgeted costs

P1

	Budget			Actual		
	Refrigerators	Dishwashers	Combined	Refrigerators	Dishwashers	Combined
Raw materials..............	$400,000	$200,000	$ 600,000	$385,000	$202,000	$ 587,000
Employee wages	170,000	80,000	250,000	174,700	81,500	256,200
Dept. manager salary.........	55,000	49,000	104,000	55,000	46,500	101,500
Supplies used	15,000	9,000	24,000	14,000	9,700	23,700
Depreciation—Equip..........	53,000	37,000	90,000	53,000	37,000	90,000
Utilities	30,000	18,000	48,000	34,500	20,700	55,200
Building rent...............	63,000	17,000	80,000	65,800	16,500	82,300
Office department costs.......	70,500	70,500	141,000	75,000	75,000	150,000
Totals.....................	$856,500	$480,500	$1,337,000	$857,000	$488,900	$1,345,900

The office department's budget and its actual costs for April follow.

	Budget	Actual
Plant manager salary...........	$ 80,000	$ 85,000
Other office salaries............	40,000	35,200
Other office costs	21,000	29,800
Totals.......................	$141,000	$150,000

Required

1. Prepare responsibility accounting performance reports like those in Exhibit 9.2 that list costs controlled by the following:
  a. Manager of the refrigerator department.
  b. Manager of the dishwasher department.
  c. Manager of the Chicago plant.
  In each report, include the budgeted and actual costs for the month and show the amount by which each actual cost is over or under the budgeted amount.

Check (1a) $11,300 total under budget

(1c) Chicago plant controllable costs, $3,900 total over budget

Analysis Component

2. Did the plant manager or the operating department managers better manage costs? Explain.

Problem 9-2B

Allocation of building
occupancy costs to
departments

P2

Harmon's has several departments that occupy all floors of a two-story building that includes a basement floor. Harmon rented this building under a long-term lease negotiated when rental rates were low. The departmental accounting system has a single account, Building Occupancy Cost, in its ledger. The types and amounts of occupancy costs recorded in this account for the current period follow.

Building rent	$400,000
Lighting expense	25,000
Cleaning expense.	40,000
Total occupancy cost	$465,000

The building has 7,500 square feet on each of the upper two floors but only 5,000 square feet in the basement. In prior periods, the accounting manager merely divided the $465,000 occupancy cost by 20,000 square feet to find an average cost of $23.25 per square foot and then charged each department a building occupancy cost equal to this rate times the number of square feet that it occupies.

Jordan Style manages a department that occupies 2,000 square feet of basement floor space. In discussing the departmental reports with other managers, she questions whether using the same rate per square foot for all departments makes sense because different floor space has different values. Style checked a recent real estate report of average local rental costs for similar space that shows first-floor space worth $40 per square foot, second-floor space worth $20 per square foot, and basement space worth $10 per square foot (excluding costs for lighting and cleaning).

Required

Check   (1) Total costs
allocated to Style's dept.,
$46,500
        (2) Total occupancy
cost to Style, $22,500

1. Allocate occupancy costs to Style's department using the current allocation method.
2. Allocate the building rent cost to Style's department in proportion to the relative market value of the floor space. Allocate to Style's department the lighting and cleaning costs in proportion to the square feet occupied (ignoring floor space market values). Then, compute the total occupancy cost allocated to Style's department.

Analysis Component

3. Which allocation method would you prefer if you were a manager of a basement department?

Problem 9-3B

Departmental income
statements; forecasts

P3

Bonanza Entertainment began operations in January 2017 with two operating (selling) departments and one service (office) department. Its departmental income statements follow.

BONANZA ENTERTAINMENT			
Departmental Income Statements			
For Year Ended December 31, 2017			
	Movies	**Video Games**	**Combined**
Sales	$600,000	$200,000	$800,000
Cost of goods sold	420,000	154,000	574,000
Gross profit	180,000	46,000	226,000
Direct expenses			
Sales salaries	37,000	15,000	52,000
Advertising	12,500	6,000	18,500
Store supplies used	4,000	1,000	5,000
Depreciation—Equipment	4,500	3,000	7,500
Total direct expenses.	58,000	25,000	83,000
Allocated expenses			
Rent expense	41,000	9,000	50,000
Utilities expense.	7,380	1,620	9,000
Share of office department expenses.	56,250	18,750	75,000
Total allocated expenses.	104,630	29,370	134,000
Total expenses	162,630	54,370	217,000
Net income (loss)	$ 17,370	$ (8,370)	$ 9,000

The company plans to open a third department in January 2018 that will sell compact discs. Management predicts that the new department will generate $300,000 in sales with a 35% gross profit margin and will require the following direct expenses: sales salaries, $18,000; advertising, $10,000; store supplies, $2,000; and equipment depreciation, $1,200. The company will fit the new department into the current rented space by taking some square footage from the other two departments. When opened, the new compact disc department will fill one-fourth of the space presently used by the movie department and one-third of the space used by the video game department. Management does not predict any increase in utilities costs, which are allocated to the departments in proportion to occupied space (or rent expense). The company allocates office department expenses to the operating departments in proportion to their sales. It expects the compact disc department to increase total office department expenses by $10,000. Since the compact disc department will bring new customers into the store, management expects sales in both the movie and video game departments to increase by 8%. No changes for those departments' gross profit percents or for their direct expenses are expected except for store supplies used, which will increase in proportion to sales.

Required

Prepare departmental income statements that show the company's predicted results of operations for calendar-year 2018 for the three operating (selling) departments and their combined totals. (Round percents to the nearest one-tenth and dollar amounts to the nearest whole dollar.)

Check   2018 forecasted Movies net income (sales), $52,450 ($648,000)

Sadar Company operates a store with two departments: guitar and piano. Information about those departments follows.

Problem 9-4B
Departmental contribution to income

P3

	Guitar Department	Piano Department
Sales	$370,500	$279,500
Cost of goods sold	320,000	175,000
Direct expenses		
Salaries....................	35,000	25,000
Maintenance...............	12,000	10,000
Utilities	5,000	4,500
Insurance	4,200	3,700

The company also incurred the following indirect costs.

Advertising...............	$15,000
Salaries..................	27,000
Office expenses...........	3,200

Indirect costs are allocated as follows: advertising on the basis of sales; salaries on the basis of number of employees; and office expenses on the basis of square footage. Additional information about the departments follows.

Department	Square Footage	Number of Employees
Guitar...........	5,000	3
Piano...........	3,000	2

Required

1. For each department, determine the departmental contribution to overhead and the departmental net income.

2. Should the guitar department be eliminated? Explain.

Check   (1) Piano dept. net income, $42,850

Problem 9-5B^C

Allocation of joint costs

C3

Rita and Rick Redding own and operate a tomato grove. After preparing the following income statement, Rita and Rick are concerned about the loss on the No. 3 tomatoes.

RITA AND RICK REDDING Income Statement For Year Ended December 31, 2017				
	No. 1	No. 2	No. 3	Combined
Sales (by grade)				
No. 1: 500,000 lbs. @ $1.80/lb.	$900,000			
No. 2: 400,000 lbs. @ $1.25/lb.		$500,000		
No. 3: 100,000 lbs. @ $0.40/lb.			$ 40,000	
Total sales.				$1,440,000
Costs				
Land preparation, seeding, and cultivating @ $0.70/lb.	350,000	280,000	70,000	700,000
Harvesting, sorting, and grading @ $0.04/lb.	20,000	16,000	4,000	40,000
Delivery costs.	10,000	7,000	3,000	20,000
Total costs.	380,000	303,000	77,000	760,000
Net income (loss)	$520,000	$197,000	$(37,000)	$ 680,000

In preparing this statement, Rita and Rick allocated joint costs among the grades on a physical basis as an equal amount per pound. Also, their delivery cost records show that $17,000 of the $20,000 relates to crating the No. 1 and No. 2 tomatoes and hauling them to the buyer. The remaining $3,000 of delivery costs is for crating the No. 3 tomatoes and hauling them to the cannery.

Required

Check   (1) $1,120 harvesting, sorting, and grading costs allocated to No. 3

1. Prepare reports showing cost allocations on a sales value basis to the three grades of tomatoes. Separate the delivery costs into the amounts directly identifiable with each grade. Then allocate any shared delivery costs on the basis of the relative sales value of each grade. (Round percents to the nearest one-tenth and dollar amounts to the nearest whole dollar.)

(2) Net income from No. 1 & No. 2 tomatoes, $426,569 & $237,151

2. Using your answers to part 1, prepare an income statement using the joint costs allocated on a sales value basis.

Analysis Component

3. Do you think delivery costs fit the definition of a joint cost? Explain.

SERIAL PROBLEM

Business Solutions   A3

© Alexander Image/Shutterstock RF

(This serial problem began in Chapter 1 and continues through most of the book. If previous chapter segments were not completed, the serial problem can begin at this point.)

SP 9   Santana Rey's two departments, computer consulting services and computer workstation furniture manufacturing, have each been profitable for **Business Solutions**. Santana has heard of the balanced scorecard and wants you to provide details on how it could be used to measure performance of her departments.

Required

1. Explain the four performance perspectives included in a balanced scorecard.
2. For each of the four performance perspectives included in a balanced scorecard, provide examples of measures Santana could use to measure performance of her departments.

Beyond the Numbers

REPORTING IN ACTION

C1

BTN 9-1   Review **Apple**'s income statement in Appendix A and identify its revenues for the year ended September 26, 2015, and each of the prior two years. For the year ended September 26, 2015, Apple reports the following product revenue mix. (Assume that its product revenue mix is the same for each of the three years reported when answering the requirements.)

iPhone	iPad	Mac	Services	Other
66%	10%	11%	9%	4%

Required

1. Compute the amount of revenue from each of its product lines for each of the three years reported.
2. If Apple wishes to evaluate each of its product lines, how can it allocate its operating expenses to each of them to determine each product line's profitability?

Fast Forward

3. Access Apple's annual report for a fiscal year ending after September 26, 2015, from its website (**Apple.com**) or the SEC's EDGAR database (**SEC.gov**). Locate its table of "Net Sales by Product" in the footnotes. How has its product mix changed from 2015?

BTN 9-2   **Apple** and **Google** compete in several product categories. Sales, income, and asset information are provided for fiscal year 2015 for each company below.

$ millions	Apple	Google
Sales	$233,715	$ 74,989
Net income	53,394	16,348
Invested assets, beginning of year	231,839	129,187
Invested assets, end of year	290,479	147,461

COMPARATIVE ANALYSIS

A2

APPLE

GOOGLE

Required

1. Compute profit margin for each company.
2. Compute investment turnover for each company.

Analysis Component

3. Using your answers to the questions above, compare the companies' performance for the year.

BTN 9-3   Super Security Co. offers a range of security services for athletes and entertainers. Each type of service is considered within a separate department. Marc Pincus, the overall manager, is compensated partly on the basis of departmental performance by staying within the quarterly cost budget. He often revises operations to make sure departments stay within budget. Says Pincus, "I will not go over budget even if it means slightly compromising the level and quality of service. These are minor compromises that don't significantly affect my clients, at least in the short term."

ETHICS CHALLENGE

P3

Required

1. Is there an ethical concern in this situation? If so, which parties are affected? Explain.
2. Can Pincus take action to eliminate or reduce any ethical concerns? Explain.
3. What is Super Security's ethical responsibility in offering professional services?

BTN 9-4   Improvement Station is a national home improvement chain with more than 100 stores throughout the country. The manager of each store receives a salary plus a bonus equal to a percent of the store's net income for the reporting period. The following net income calculation is on the Denver store manager's performance report for the recent monthly period.

COMMUNICATING IN PRACTICE

P2

Sales	$2,500,000
Cost of goods sold	800,000
Wages expense	500,000
Utilities expense	200,000
Home office expense	75,000
Net income	$ 925,000
Manager's bonus (0.5%)	$ 4,625

In previous periods, the bonus had also been 0.5%, but the performance report had not included any charges for the home office expense, which is now assigned to each store as a percent of its sales.

Required

Assume that you are the national office manager. Write a half-page memorandum to your store managers explaining why home office expense is in the new performance report.

TAKING IT TO THE NET

P2

BTN 9-5   This chapter described and used spreadsheets to prepare various managerial reports (see Exhibit 9.10). You can download from websites various tutorials showing how spreadsheets are used in managerial accounting and other business applications.

Required

1. Link to the website **Lacher.com**. Select "Table of Contents" under "Microsoft Excel Examples." Identify and list three tutorials for review.
2. Describe in a half-page memorandum to your instructor how the applications described in each tutorial are helpful in business and managerial decision making.

TEAMWORK IN ACTION

P1

APPLE

Samsung

BTN 9-6   **Apple** and **Samsung** compete across the world in several markets.

Required

1. Design a three-tier responsibility accounting organizational chart assuming that you have available internal information for both companies. Use Exhibit 9.1 as an example. The goal of this assignment is to design a reporting framework for the companies; numbers are not required. Limit your reporting framework to sales activity only.
2. Explain why it is important to have similar performance reports when comparing performance within a company (and across different companies). Be specific in your response.

ENTREPRENEURIAL DECISION

P3

BTN 9-7   Aman Advani, Gihan Amarasiriwardena, and Kit Hickey's company **Ministry** sells men's clothes and is organized by different product lines (departments).

Required

1. How can Ministry use departmental income statements to assist in understanding and controlling operations?
2. Are departmental income statements always the best measure of a department's performance? Explain.
3. Provide examples of nonfinancial performance indicators Ministry might use as part of a balanced scorecard system of performance evaluation.

HITTING THE ROAD

C1 P1

BTN 9-8   Visit a local movie theater and check out both its concession area and its viewing areas. The manager of a theater must confront questions such as:

- How much return do we earn on concessions?
- What types of movies generate the greatest sales?
- What types of movies generate the greatest net income?

Required

Assume that you are the new accounting manager for a 16-screen movie theater. You are to set up a responsibility accounting reporting framework for the theater.

1. Recommend how to segment the different departments of a movie theater for responsibility reporting.
2. Propose an expense allocation system for heat, rent, insurance, and maintenance costs of the theater.

GLOBAL DECISION

P3

Samsung

BTN 9-9   Selected product data from **Samsung** (www.samsung.com) follow.

Product Segment for Year Ended (billions of Korean won)	Net Sales		Operating Income	
	Dec. 31, 2015	Dec. 31, 2014	Dec. 31, 2015	Dec. 31, 2014
Consumer electronics................	₩ 46,895	₩ 50,183	₩ 1,254	₩ 1,184
IT and mobile communications	103,554	111,765	10,142	14,563

Required

1. Compute the percentage growth (or decline) in net sales for each product line from fiscal year 2014 to 2015. Round percents to one decimal.
2. Which product line's net sales grew (or declined) the most?
3. Which segment was the most profitable?
4. How can Samsung's managers use this information?

 GLOBAL VIEW

L'Oréal is an international cosmetics company incorporated in France. With multiple brands and operations in over 100 countries, the company uses concepts of departmental accounting and controllable costs to evaluate performance. For example, for 2015 the company reports the following for the major divisions in its cosmetics branch:

Division (€ millions)	Operating Profit	
Consumer products	€2,386	
Professional products.................	679	
Luxury products	1,498	
Active cosmetics.....................	415	€4,978
Nonallocated costs...................		(644)
Cosmetics branch total...............		€4,334

Similar to "Departmental contributions to overhead" in Exhibit 9.12

Similar to "Operating income" in Exhibit 9.12

For L'Oréal, nonallocated costs include costs that are not controllable by division managers, including fundamental research and development and costs of service operations like insurance and banking. Excluding noncontrollable costs enables L'Oréal to prepare more meaningful division performance evaluations.

 Global View Assignments

Discussion Question 10

Discussion Question 20

Quick Study 9-20

Exercise 9-14

Exercise 9-23

BTN 9-9

10

chapter

Relevant Costing for Managerial Decisions

Chapter Preview

DECISIONS AND INFORMATION

Managerial decisions

C1 Costs vs. benefits

Incremental costs

Relevant benefits

NTK 10-1

DECISION SCENARIOS

A1 Additional business

Make or buy

Scrap or rework

Sell or process

Sales mix

Segment elimination

Keep or replace

P1 Product pricing

NTK 10-2, 3, 4, 5, 6

Learning Objectives

CONCEPTUAL

C1 Describe the importance of relevant costs for short-term decisions.

ANALYTICAL

A1 Evaluate short-term managerial decisions using relevant costs.

PROCEDURAL

P1 Determine product selling price using cost data.

Courtesy of Adafruit (adafruit.com)

High Energy

NEW YORK—Studying computer science and electrical engineering, Limor Fried used the skills she learned in class to make electrical devices like MP3 players, synthesizers, and toys. Inundated with requests to sell her designs as project kits, Limor invested her tuition money in a large quantity of parts and began designing. The result is her company **Adafruit Industries** (**Adafruit.com**), a 100% woman-owned company, which now boasts sales of over $33 million per year and over 700% growth over the past few years.

Adafruit started with Limor working from her dorm room. "The company took off," says Limor, "because we sold learning projects that you would actually use." Projects like MintyBoost (a mobile-device charger assembled from an Altoids tin and electronic components), a set of bicycle lights that spell out words and draw symbols as you ride, and a mini-electric guitar are both fun to make and fun to use. "People learn about electronics by assembling the kits and end with a useful handmade good."

Limor uses accounting information to make business decisions. Her kits yield about a $10 contribution margin each.

"We put our heart and soul into it . . . every day"

—Limor Fried

Focusing on contribution margins enables Adafruit to add more-profitable products and eliminate less-profitable ones. In addition to profits, Limor focuses on customer satisfaction. "Everything is designed to be painless," says Limor. "I spend a lot of time thinking about how customers will interact with products, and we always give good documentation."

For Limor, though, business is not just about making more profit. She is passionate about education, and in particular about encouraging young women to pursue engineering and related technical fields. "It is possible to help people while running a business," she says. "Entrepreneurship is cool," says Limor. "It's about freedom, the ability to do great work with great people for great customers. It's hard to do this if you are working for someone else."

Sources: *Adafruit Industries website,* January 2017; *Entrepreneur.com,* December 18, 2012; *New York Times,* November 15, 2007; *Inc.com,* 2015 Inc. 500 rankings

This chapter focuses on the use of accounting information to make several important managerial decisions. Most of these involve short-term decisions. This differs from methods used for longer-term managerial decisions described in the next chapter and in several other chapters of this book.

DECISIONS AND INFORMATION

This section explains how managers make decisions and the information relevant to those decisions.

Decision Making

Managerial decision making involves five steps: (1) define the decision task, (2) identify alternative courses of action, (3) collect relevant information and evaluate each alternative, (4) select the preferred course of action, and (5) analyze and assess decisions made. These five steps are illustrated in Exhibit 10.1.

EXHIBIT 10.1

Managerial Decision Making

| Define task and goal | Identify alternative actions | Collect relevant information | Select course of action | Analyze and assess decision |

Both managerial and financial accounting information play important roles in most management decisions. The accounting system is expected to provide primarily *financial* information such as performance reports and budget analyses for decision making. *Nonfinancial* information is also relevant, however; it includes information on environmental effects, political sensitivities, and social responsibility.

Relevant Costs and Benefits

C1
_____
Describe the importance of relevant costs for short-term decisions.

In making short-term decisions, managers should focus on the relevant benefits and the relevant costs.

- **Incremental costs,** also called differential costs, are the relevant costs in making decisions. These are the additional costs incurred if a company pursues a certain course of action.
- **Relevant benefits,** the additional or *incremental* revenue generated by selecting a certain course of action over another, are the key rewards from that action.

Three types of costs are pertinent to our discussion of relevant costs: sunk costs, out-of-pocket costs, and opportunity costs.

- A *sunk cost* arises from a past decision and cannot be avoided or changed; it is irrelevant to future decisions. An example is the cost of computer equipment previously purchased by a company. This cost is not relevant to the decision of whether to replace the computer equipment. Likewise, depreciation of the original cost of plant (and intangible) assets is a sunk cost. Most of a company's allocated costs, including fixed overhead items such as depreciation and administrative expenses, are sunk costs.

"Sunk costs are not relevant to my decision." "I must consider out-of-pocket and opportunity costs."

- An *out-of-pocket cost* requires a future outlay of cash and is relevant for current and future decisions. These costs are usually the direct result of management's decisions. For instance, future purchases of computer equipment involve out-of-pocket costs. The cost of future computer purchases is relevant to the decision of whether to replace the computer equipment.
- An *opportunity cost* is the potential benefit lost by taking a specific action when two or more alternative choices are available. An example is a student giving up wages

from a job to attend summer school. The forgone wages should be considered as part of the total cost of attending summer school. Companies continually must choose from alternative courses of action. For instance, a company making standardized products might be approached by a customer to supply a special (nonstandard) product. A decision to accept or reject the special order must consider not only the profit to be made from the special order but also the profit given up by devoting time and resources to this order instead of pursuing an alternative project. The profit given up is an opportunity cost. Consideration of opportunity costs is important. Although opportunity costs are not entered in accounting records, they are relevant to many managerial decisions.

We show how to apply relevant costs and benefits to analyze common managerial decisions. We also discuss some qualitative factors, not easily expressed in terms of costs and benefits, that managers must consider.

Match each of the terms below with its definition.

NEED-TO-KNOW 10-1

Relevant Costs

C1

_____ **1.** Sunk cost
_____ **2.** Out-of-pocket cost
_____ **3.** Opportunity cost
_____ **4.** Incremental cost
_____ **5.** Relevant benefit

a. Additional costs incurred from a course of action
b. Incremental revenue from a course of action
c. A future outlay of cash
d. Potential benefit lost from taking a course of action
e. A cost that arises from a past decision and cannot be changed

Solution

1. e **2.** c **3.** d **4.** a **5.** b

Do More: QS 10-5, E 10-1

MANAGERIAL DECISION SCENARIOS

Managers experience many different scenarios that require analyzing alternative actions and making decisions. We describe several different decision scenarios in this section. We set these tasks in the context of FasTrac, an exercise supplies and equipment manufacturer. *We treat each of these decision tasks as separate from each other.*

A1
Evaluate short-term managerial decisions using relevant costs.

Additional Business

FasTrac is operating at its normal level of 80% of full capacity. At this level, it produces and sells approximately 100,000 units of product annually. Its per unit and annual total sales and costs are shown in the contribution margin income statement in Exhibit 10.2. Its normal selling price is $10.00 per unit, and each unit sold generates $1.00 per unit of operating income.

EXHIBIT 10.2

Selected Operating Income Data

FasTrac Contribution Margin Income Statement For Year Ended December 31, 2017	Per Unit	Annual Total
Sales (100,000 units)	$10.00	$1,000,000
Variable costs		
Direct materials	(3.50)	(350,000)
Direct labor	(2.20)	(220,000)
Variable overhead	(0.50)	(50,000)
Selling expenses	(1.40)	(140,000)
Contribution margin	2.40	240,000
Fixed costs		
Fixed overhead	0.60	(60,000)
Administrative expenses	0.80	(80,000)
Operating income	$ 1.00	$ 100,000

A current buyer of FasTrac's products wants to purchase additional units of its product and export them to another country. This buyer offers to buy 10,000 units of the product at $8.50 per unit, or $1.50 less than the current price. The offer price is low, but FasTrac is considering the proposal because this sale would be several times larger than any single previous sale and it would use idle capacity. Also, the units will be exported, so this new business will not affect current domestic sales.

To determine whether to accept or reject this order, management needs to know whether accepting the offer will increase net income. If management relies incorrectly on per unit historical costs, it would mistakenly reject the sale because the selling price ($8.50) per unit is less than the total historical costs per unit ($9.00).

To correctly make its decision, FasTrac must analyze the costs of this potential new business differently. The $9.00 historical cost per unit is not necessarily the incremental cost of this special order. The following information regarding the order is available:

- The variable manufacturing costs to produce this order will be the same as for FasTrac's normal business—$3.50 per unit for direct materials, $2.20 per unit for direct labor, and $0.50 per unit for variable overhead.

- Selling expenses for this order will be $0.20 per unit, which is less than the selling expenses of FasTrac's normal business.

- Fixed overhead expenses will not change regardless of whether this order is accepted. They are not relevant to the decision.

- This order will incur *incremental* administrative expenses of $1,000 for clerical work. These are additional fixed costs due to this order.

We use this incremental cost information to determine whether FasTrac should accept this new business. The analysis of relevant benefits and costs in Exhibit 10.3 suggests that the additional business should be accepted. **The incremental revenue ($8.50 per unit) exceeds the incremental cost ($6.50 per unit), and the order would yield $20,000 of additional pretax income.** More generally, FasTrac would increase its income with any price that exceeds $6.50 per unit ($65,000 incremental cost/10,000 additional units). The key point is that *management must not blindly use historical costs, especially allocated overhead costs.* Instead, management must focus on the incremental costs to be incurred if the additional business is accepted.

EXHIBIT 10.3

Analysis of Additional
Business Using
Relevant Costs

FasTrac Contribution Margin Income Statement (for special order) For Year Ended December 31, 2017		
	Per Unit*	**Annual Total**
Sales (10,000 units)......................	$ 8.50	$ 85,000
Variable costs		
Direct materials.......................	(3.50)	(35,000)
Direct labor	(2.20)	(22,000)
Variable overhead....................	(0.50)	(5,000)
Selling expenses......................	(0.20)	(2,000)
Contribution margin	2.10	21,000
Fixed costs		
Fixed overhead	—	—
Administrative expenses	(0.10)	(1,000)
Operating income (incremental)...........	$ 2.00	$ 20,000

*Total cost per unit = $3.50 + $2.20 + $0.50 + $0.20 + $0.10 = $6.50

Point: Ignore allocated overhead costs. The analysis in Exhibit 10.3 uses only *incremental* fixed overhead costs.

Example: Exhibit 10.3 uses quantitative information. Suggest some qualitative factors to be considered when deciding whether to accept this project. *Answer:* (1) Impact on relationships with other customers and (2) improved relationship with customer buying additional units.

Additional Factors   An analysis of the incremental costs pertaining to the additional volume is always relevant for this type of decision. We must be careful when the additional volume approaches or exceeds the factory's existing available capacity. If the additional volume requires the company to expand its capacity by obtaining more equipment, more space, or more personnel, the incremental costs could quickly exceed the incremental revenue.

Another cautionary note is the effect on existing sales. All new units of the extra business will be sold outside FasTrac's normal domestic sales channels. If accepting additional business would cause existing sales to decline, this information must be included in our analysis. The contribution margin lost from a decline in sales is an opportunity cost. The company must also consider whether this customer is really a one-time customer. If not, can the company continue to offer this low price in the long run?

■ **Decision** Maker

Partner   You are a partner in a small accounting firm that specializes in keeping the books and preparing taxes for clients. A local restaurant is interested in obtaining these services from your firm. Identify factors that are relevant in deciding whether to accept the engagement. ■ *Answer:* You should identify the differences between existing clients and this potential client. A key difference is that the restaurant business has additional inventory components (groceries, vegetables, meats) and is likely to have a higher proportion of depreciable assets. These differences imply that the partner must spend more hours auditing the records and understanding the business, regulations, and standards that pertain. Such differences suggest that the partner must use a different "formula" for quoting a price to this potential client vis-à-vis current clients.

> **NEED-TO-KNOW 10-2**
>
> Special Order
>
> A1

A company receives a special order for 200 units that requires stamping the buyer's name on each unit, yielding an additional fixed cost of $400. Without the order, the company is operating at 75% of capacity and produces 7,500 units of product at the costs below. The company's normal selling price is $22 per unit.

Direct materials	$37,500
Direct labor	60,000
Overhead (30% variable)	20,000
Selling expenses (60% variable)	25,000

The sales price for the special order is $18 per unit. The special order will not affect normal unit sales and will not increase fixed overhead or fixed selling expenses. Variable selling expenses on the special order are reduced to one-half the normal amount. Should the company accept the special order?

Solution

Incremental variable costs per unit for this order of 200 units are computed as follows:

Direct materials ($37,500/7,500)	$ 5.00
Direct labor ($60,000/7,500)	8.00
Variable overhead [(0.30 × $20,000)/7,500]	0.80
Variable selling expenses [(0.60 × $25,000 × 0.5)/7,500]	1.00
Total incremental variable costs per unit	$14.80

The contribution margin from the special order is $640, computed as [($18.00 − $14.80) × 200]. This will cover the incremental fixed costs of $400 and yield incremental income of $240. **The offer should be accepted.**

> Do More: QS 10-6, E 10-2, E 10-3

Make or Buy

The managerial decision to make or buy a component is common. For example, **Apple** buys the component parts for its electronic products, but it could consider making these components in its own manufacturing facilities. The process of buying goods or services from an external supplier is called **outsourcing.** This decision depends on incremental costs. We return to FasTrac to illustrate.

FasTrac currently buys part 417, a component of the main product it sells, for $1.20 per unit. FasTrac has excess productive capacity, and management is considering making part 417 instead of buying it. FasTrac estimates that making part 417 would incur variable costs of $0.45 for direct materials and $0.50 for direct labor. FasTrac's normal predetermined overhead rate is 100% of direct labor cost. If management *incorrectly* relies on this historical overhead rate, it would mistakenly believe that the cost to make the component part is $1.45 per unit ($0.45 + $0.50 + $0.50) and conclude the company is better off buying the part at $1.20 per unit. This analysis is flawed, however, because it uses the historical predetermined overhead rate.

Only *incremental* overhead costs are relevant to this decision. Incremental overhead costs of making the part might include, for example, additional power for operating machines, extra supplies, added cleanup costs, materials handling, and quality control. Assume that management computes an *incremental overhead rate* of $0.20 per unit if it makes the part. We can then prepare a per unit analysis, using relevant costs, as shown in Exhibit 10.4.

EXHIBIT 10.4

Make or Buy Analysis Using
Relevant Costs

$s per unit	Make	Buy
Direct materials	$0.45	—
Direct labor	0.50	—
Overhead costs (using incremental rate)	**0.20**	—
Purchase price	—	$1.20
Total cost per unit	$1.15	$1.20

Exhibit 10.4 shows that the relevant cost to make part 417 is $1.15. This shows it is cheaper to make the part than to buy it. We can see that if incremental overhead costs are less than $0.25 per unit, the total cost of making the part will be less than the purchase price of $1.20 per unit.

Additional Factors   While our analysis suggests it is cheaper to make part 417, FasTrac must consider several nonfinancial factors in the make or buy decision. These factors might include product quality, timeliness of delivery (especially in a just-in-time setting), reactions of customers and suppliers, and other intangibles like employee morale and workload. It must also consider whether making the part requires incremental fixed costs to expand plant capacity. When these additional factors are considered, small cost differences might not matter.

■ **Decision** Insight

Make or Buy IT   Companies apply make or buy decisions to their services. Many now outsource their information technology activities. Information technology companies provide infrastructure and services to enable businesses to focus on their key activities. It is argued that outsourcing saves money and streamlines operations, and without the headaches. ■

NEED-TO-KNOW 10-3

Make or Buy

A1

A company currently pays $5 per unit to buy a key part for a product it manufactures. The company believes it can make the part for $1.50 per unit for direct materials and $2.50 per unit for direct labor. The company allocates overhead costs at the rate of 50% of direct labor. Incremental overhead costs to make this part are $0.75 per unit. Should the company make or buy the part?

Solution

$s per unit	Make	Buy
Direct materials	$1.50	—
Direct labor	2.50	—
Overhead (incremental)	0.75	—
Cost to buy the part	—	$5.00
Total cost per unit	$4.75	$5.00

Do More: QS 10-7, QS 10-8,
E 10-4, E 10-5

The company should **make the part** because the cost to make it is less than the cost to buy it.

Scrap or Rework

Manufacturing processes sometimes yield defective products. In such cases, managers must make a decision on whether to scrap or rework products in process. Two points are important here. First, costs already incurred in manufacturing the defective units are sunk and not relevant. Second, we must consider opportunity costs—reworking the defective products uses productive capacity that could be devoted to normal operations.

To illustrate, assume that FasTrac has 10,000 defective units of a product that have already cost $1 per unit to manufacture. These units can be sold as is (as scrap) for $0.40 each, or they can be reworked for $0.80 per unit and then sold for their full price of $1.50 each. Should Fas-Trac sell the units as scrap or rework them?

The $1 per unit manufacturing cost already incurred is a sunk cost and irrelevant. Further, if FasTrac is operating near its maximum capacity, reworking the defects means that FasTrac is unable to manufacture 10,000 *new* units with an incremental cost of $1 per unit and a selling price of $1.50 per unit, meaning it incurs an *opportunity cost* of $0.50 per unit ($1.50 selling price − $1.00 incremental cost). Our analysis is reflected in Exhibit 10.5.

$s per unit	Scrap	Rework
Sale of scrapped/reworked units	$0.40	$ 1.50
Less out-of-pocket costs to rework defects		(0.80)
Less opportunity cost of not making new units		**(0.50)**
Incremental net income (per unit)	$0.40	$ 0.20

EXHIBIT 10.5

Scrap or Rework Analysis

Scrapping the 10,000 units would yield incremental income of $4,000, computed as 10,000 × $0.40; reworking the units would yield only $2,000 of income. Based on this analysis, the defective units should be scrapped and sold as is for $0.40 each. If we had failed to include the opportunity costs of $0.50 per unit, the rework option would mistakenly have seemed more favorable than scrapping.

Sell or Process Further

Some companies must decide whether to sell partially completed products as is or to process them further for sale as other products. For example, a peanut grower could sell its peanut harvest as is, or it could process peanuts into other products such as peanut butter, trail mix, and candy. The decision depends on the incremental costs and benefits of further processing.

To illustrate, suppose that FasTrac has 40,000 units of partially finished Product Q. It has already spent $30,000 to manufacture these 40,000 units. FasTrac can sell the 40,000 units to another manufacturer as raw material for $50,000. Alternatively, it can process them further and produce finished Products X, Y, and Z. Processing the units further will cost an additional $80,000 and will yield total revenues of $150,000. FasTrac must decide whether the added revenues from selling finished Products X, Y, and Z exceed the costs of finishing them.

Point: This $30,000 is a sunk cost. It won't change whether FasTrac sells now or processes further.

Exhibit 10.6 presents the analysis.

	Sell as Product Q	Process Further into Products X, Y, and Z
Incremental revenue	$50,000	$150,000
Incremental cost	—	(80,000)
Incremental income	$50,000	$ 70,000

EXHIBIT 10.6

Sell or Process Further Analysis

The analysis shows that the incremental income from processing further ($70,000) is greater than the incremental income ($50,000) from selling Product Q as is. Therefore, FasTrac should process further and earn an additional $20,000 of income ($70,000 − $50,000). The $30,000 of previously incurred manufacturing costs are *excluded* from the analysis. These costs are sunk, and they are not relevant to the decision. The incremental revenue from selling Product Q as is ($50,000) is properly included. It is the opportunity cost associated with processing further. The net benefit to processing further is $20,000.

 **10-4**

Sell or Process Further

A1

For each of the two independent scenarios below, determine whether the company should sell the partially completed product as is or process it further into other saleable products.

1. $10,000 of manufacturing costs have been incurred to produce Product Alpha. Alpha can be sold as is for $30,000 or processed further into two separate products. The further processing will cost $15,000, and the resulting products can be sold for total revenues of $60,000.

2. $5,000 of manufacturing costs have been incurred to produce Product Delta. Delta can be sold as is for $150,000 or processed further into two separate products. The further processing will cost $75,000, and the resulting products can be sold for total revenues of $200,000.

Solution

1.

Alpha	Sell As Is	Process Further
Incremental revenue	$30,000	$ 60,000
Incremental cost..............	—	(15,000)
Incremental income	$30,000	$ 45,000

Alpha should be **processed further**; doing so will yield an extra $15,000 ($45,000 − $30,000) of income.

2.

Delta	Sell As Is	Process Further
Incremental revenue	$150,000	$200,000
Incremental cost	—	(75,000)
Incremental income	$150,000	$125,000

Do More: QS 10-10, QS 10-11, E 10-8

Delta should be **sold as is**; doing so will yield an extra $25,000 ($150,000 − $125,000) of income.

Sales Mix Selection When Resources Are Constrained

Point: A method called *linear programming* is useful for finding the optimal sales mix for several products subject to many market and production constraints. This method is described in advanced courses.

When a company sells a mix of products, some are more profitable than others. Management concentrates sales efforts on more profitable products. If production facilities or other factors are limited, producing more of one product usually requires producing less of others. In this case, management must identify the most profitable combination, or *sales mix,* of products. To identify the best sales mix, management focuses on the *contribution margin per unit of scarce resource.*

To illustrate, assume that FasTrac makes and sells two products, A and B. The same machines are used to produce both products. A and B have the following selling prices and variable costs per unit:

$s per unit	Product A	Product B
Selling price	$5.00	$7.50
Variable costs	3.50	5.50

FasTrac has an existing capacity of 100,000 machine hours per year. In addition, Product A uses 1 machine hour per unit while Product B uses 2 machine hours per unit. With limited resources, FasTrac should focus its productive capacity on the product that yields the highest contribution margin *per machine hour,* until market demand for that product is satisfied. Exhibit 10.7 shows the relevant analysis.

EXHIBIT 10.7

Sales Mix Analysis

	Product A	Product B
Selling price per unit...	$5.00	$7.50
Variable costs per unit	3.50	5.50
Contribution margin per unit (a).....................................	$1.50	$2.00
Machine hours per unit (b)	1 hr.	2 hr.
Contribution margin per machine hour (a) ÷ (b)...................	$1.50	$1.00

Exhibit 10.7 shows that although Product B has a higher contribution margin per *unit,* Product A has a higher contribution margin per *machine hour*. In this case, FasTrac should produce as much of Product A as possible, up to the market demand. For example, if the market will buy all of Product A that FasTrac can produce, FasTrac should produce 100,000 units of Product A and none of Product B. This sales mix would yield a contribution margin of $150,000 per year, the maximum the company could make subject to its resource constraint.

Point: With such high demand, management should consider expanding its productive capacity.

If demand for Product A is limited—say, to 80,000 units—FasTrac will begin by producing those 80,000 units. This production level would leave 20,000 machine hours to devote to production of Product B. FasTrac would use these remaining machine hours to produce 10,000 units (20,000 machine hours/2 machine hours per unit) of Product B. This sales mix would yield the contribution margin shown in Exhibit 10.8.

Sales Mix	Contribution Margin	Machine Hours Used
Product A (80,000 × $1.50 per unit).............	$120,000	80,000
Product B (10,000 × $2.00 per unit).............	20,000	20,000
Total.......................................	$140,000	100,000

EXHIBIT 10.8

Contribution Margin from Sales Mix, with Resource Constraint

With limited demand for Product A, the optimal sales mix yields a contribution margin of $140,000, the best the company can do subject to its resource constraint and market demand. In general, if demand for products is limited, management should produce its most profitable product (per unit of scarce resource) up to the point of total demand (or its capacity constraint). It then uses remaining capacity to produce its next most profitable product.

Point: FasTrac might consider buying more machines to reduce the constraint on production. A strategy designed to reduce the impact of constraints or bottlenecks on production is called the *theory of constraints.*

Decision Insight

Fashion Mix Companies such as **Gap**, **TJX Companies**, **Urban Outfitters**, and **American Eagle** must continuously monitor and manage the sales mix of their product lists. Selling their products worldwide further complicates their decision process. The contribution margin of each product is crucial to their product mix strategies. ■

© BananaStock/Punchstock

A company produces two products, Gamma and Omega. Gamma sells for $10 per unit and Omega sells for $12.50 per unit. Variable costs are $7 per unit of Gamma and $8 per unit of Omega. The company has a capacity of 5,000 machine hours per month. Gamma uses 1 machine hour per unit and Omega uses 3 machine hours per unit.

1. Compute the contribution margin per machine hour for each product.

2. Assume demand for Gamma is limited to 3,800 units per month. How many units of Gamma and Omega should the company produce, and what will be the total contribution margin from this sales mix?

NEED-TO-KNOW 10-5

Sales Mix with Constrained Resources

A1

Solution

1.

	Gamma	Omega
Selling price per unit	$10.00	$12.50
Variable costs per unit	7.00	8.00
Contribution margin per unit (a)........................	$ 3.00	$ 4.50
Machine hours per unit (b)...........................	1 hr.	3 hr.
Contribution margin per machine hour [(a) ÷ (b)]	**$ 3.00**	**$ 1.50**

2. The company will begin by producing Gamma to meet the market demand of 3,800 units. This production level will consume 3,800 machine hours, leaving 1,200 machine hours to produce Omega. With 1,200 machine hours, the company can produce 400 units (1,200 machine hours/3 machine hours per unit) of Omega. The total contribution margin from this sales mix is:

Gamma	3,800 units × $3.00 per unit =	$ 11,400
Omega	400 units × $4.50 per unit =	1,800
Total contribution margin		**$13,200**

Do More: QS 10-12, E 10-9, E 10-11

Segment Elimination

When a segment, division, or store is performing poorly, management must consider eliminating it. As we showed in a previous chapter, determining a segment's *contribution to overhead* is an important first step in this analysis. Segments with revenues less than direct costs are candidates for elimination. However, contribution to overhead is not sufficient for this decision. Instead, we must further classify the segment's expenses as avoidable or unavoidable.

- **Avoidable expenses** are amounts the company would not incur if it eliminated the segment.
- **Unavoidable expenses** are amounts that would continue even if the segment was eliminated.

Example: How can insurance be classified as either avoidable or unavoidable? *Answer:* It depends on whether the assets insured can be removed and the premiums canceled.

To illustrate, FasTrac is considering eliminating its treadmill division, which reported a $500 operating loss for the recent year, as shown in Exhibit 10.9. Exhibit 10.9 shows the treadmill division contributes $9,700 to recovery of overhead costs. The next step is to classify the division's costs as either avoidable or unavoidable. Variable costs, such as cost of goods sold and wages expense, are avoidable. In addition, some of the division's indirect expenses are avoidable; for example, if the treadmill division were eliminated, FasTrac could reduce its overall advertising expense by $400 and its overall insurance expense by $300. In addition, FasTrac could avoid office department expenses of $2,200 and purchasing expenses of $1,000 if the treadmill division were eliminated. These *avoidable* expenses would not be allocated to other divisions of the company; rather, these expenses would be eliminated. *Unavoidable* expenses, however, will be reallocated to other divisions if the treadmill division is eliminated.

EXHIBIT 10.9

Classification of Segment Operating Expenses for Analysis

Treadmill Division	Total	Avoidable Expenses	Unavoidable Expenses
Sales	$47,800		
Cost of goods sold	30,000	$30,000	
Gross profit	17,800		
Direct expenses			
Wages expense	7,900	7,900	
Depreciation expense—Equipment	200		$ 200
Total direct expenses	8,100		
Departmental contribution to overhead	$ 9,700		
Indirect expenses			
Rent and utilities expense	3,150		3,150
Advertising expense	400	400	
Insurance expense	400	300	100
Share of office department expenses	3,060	2,200	860
Share of purchasing department expenses	3,190	1,000	2,190
Total indirect expenses	10,200		
Operating income (loss)	$ (500)		
Total avoidable expenses		$41,800	
Total unavoidable expenses			$6,500

Point: Analysis is summarized as:
Sales $ 47,800
Avoidable expenses   (41,800)
Reduction in income $ 6,000
Because sales > avoidable expenses, do *not* eliminate division.

FasTrac can avoid a total of $41,800 of expenses if it eliminates the treadmill division. However, because this division's sales are $47,800, eliminating the division would reduce FasTrac's income by $6,000 ($47,800 − $41,800). Based on this analysis, FasTrac should not eliminate its treadmill division. *Our decision rule is that a segment is a candidate for elimination if its revenues are less than its avoidable expenses.* Avoidable expenses can be viewed as the costs to generate this segment's revenues.

Additional Factors When considering elimination of a segment, we must assess its impact on other segments. A segment could be unprofitable on its own, but it might still contribute to other segments' revenues and profits. It is possible then to continue a segment even when its revenues are less than its avoidable expenses. Similarly, a profitable segment might be discontinued if its space, assets, or staff can be more profitably used by expanding existing segments or by creating new ones. Our decision to keep or eliminate a segment requires a more complex analysis than simply looking at a segment's performance report.

A bike maker is considering eliminating its tandem bike division because it operates at a loss of $6,000 per year. Division sales for the year total $40,000, and the company reports the costs for this division as shown below. Should the tandem bike division be eliminated?

NEED-TO-KNOW 10-6

Segment Elimination

A1

	Avoidable Expenses	Unavoidable Expenses
Cost of goods sold	$30,000	$ —
Direct expenses	8,000	—
Indirect expenses	2,500	3,000
Service department costs	250	2,250
Total	$40,750	$5,250

Solution

Total avoidable costs of $40,750 are greater than the division's sales of $40,000, suggesting the division **should be eliminated**. Other factors might be relevant since the shortfall in sales ($750) is low. For example, are tandem bike sales expected to increase in the future? Does the sale of tandem bikes generate sales of other types of products?

Do More: QS 10-13, QS 10-14, E 10-13

Keep or Replace Equipment

Businesses periodically must decide whether to keep using equipment or replace it. Advances in technology typically mean newer equipment can operate more efficiently and at lower cost than older equipment. If the reduction in *variable* manufacturing costs with the new equipment is greater than its net purchase price, the equipment should be replaced. In this setting, the net purchase price of the equipment is its total cost minus any trade-in allowance or cash receipt for the old equipment.

For example, FasTrac has a piece of manufacturing equipment with a book value (cost minus accumulated depreciation) of $20,000 and a remaining useful life of four years. At the end of four years the equipment will have a salvage value of zero. The market value of the equipment is currently $25,000.

FasTrac can purchase a new machine for $100,000 and receive $25,000 in return for trading in its old machine. The new machine will reduce FasTrac's variable manufacturing costs by $18,000 per year over the four-year life of the new machine. FasTrac's incremental analysis is shown in Exhibit 10.10.

Point: The book value of the old equipment is a sunk cost. It won't change regardless of FasTrac's decision.

EXHIBIT 10.10

Keep or Replace Analysis

	Increase or (Decrease) in Net Income
Cost to buy new machine	$(100,000)
Cash received to trade in old machine	25,000
Reduction in variable manufacturing costs	72,000*
Total increase (decrease) in net income	$ (3,000)

*18,000 × 4 years

Exhibit 10.10 shows that FasTrac should not replace the old equipment with this newer version as it will decrease income by $3,000. The book value of the old equipment ($20,000) is not relevant to this analysis. Book value is a sunk cost, and it cannot be changed regardless of whether FasTrac keeps or replaces this equipment.

SUSTAINABILITY AND ACCOUNTING

Courtesy of Adafruit (adafruit.com)

Managers consider sustainability issues in many of the decisions discussed in this chapter. Companies that buy rather than make components must consider the labor and safety practices of their suppliers. **Apple** requires its suppliers to comply with its *Supplier Code of Conduct* (**apple.com/supplier-responsibility/ accountability/**). This code details Apple's requirements with respect to anti-discrimination, anti-harassment, prevention of involuntary labor and human trafficking, and other issues.

For example, workers are allowed to work no more than 60 hours per week, with a required day of rest every seven days. A real-time work-hour tracking system and frequent reporting enable Apple to assess compliance with the code. In a recent report, Apple noted 97% compliance with its workweek requirement.

In addition to her current labor force, **Adafruit**'s founder Limor Fried invests in programs to educate future engineers and entrepreneurs. In this way, Limor helps to develop and sustain the human capital that will benefit her company and, more generally, society in the future.

Decision Analysis **Product Pricing**

P1

Determine product selling price using cost data.

Managers use relevant costs in determining prices for special short-term decisions. But longer-run pricing decisions of management need to cover both variable and fixed costs, and yield a profit. There are several methods to help management in setting prices.

Cost-Plus Methods

Cost-plus methods are common, where management adds a **markup** to cost to reach a target price. We will describe the **total cost method,** where management sets price equal to the product's total costs plus a desired profit on the product. This is a three-step process:

1. Determine total cost per unit.

$$\text{Total costs} = \frac{\text{Product (direct materials,}}{\text{direct labor, and overhead) costs}} + \frac{\text{Selling and}}{\text{administrative costs}}$$

$$\text{Total cost per unit} = \text{Total costs} \div \text{Total units expected to be produced and sold}$$

2. Determine the dollar markup per unit.

$$\text{Markup per unit} = \text{Total cost per unit} \times \text{Markup percentage}$$

3. Determine selling price per unit.

$$\text{Selling price per unit} = \text{Total cost per unit} + \text{Markup per unit}$$

To illustrate, consider MpPro, a company that produces MP3 players. The company desires a 20% markup on the total cost of this product. It expects to produce and sell 10,000 players. The following additional information is available:

Variable costs (per unit)		Fixed costs (in dollars)	
Product costs	$44	Overhead	$140,000
Selling and administrative costs	6	Selling and administrative costs	60,000

We apply the three-step total cost method to determine price.

1. Total costs = Product costs + Selling and administrative costs
   = [($44 × 10,000 units) + $140,000] + [($6 × 10,000 units) + $60,000]
   = $700,000

   Total cost per unit = Total costs/Total units expected to be produced and sold
   = $700,000/10,000
   = $70

2. Markup per unit = Total cost per unit × Markup percentage
   = $70 × 20%
   = $14

3. Selling price per unit = Total cost per unit + Markup per unit
   = $70 + $14
   = $84

Companies often use cost-plus pricing as a starting point in determining selling prices. Many factors determine price, including consumer preferences and competition.

Target Costing   When competition is high, companies might be "price takers," and have little control in setting prices. In such cases *target costing* can be useful. Target cost is defined as:

$$\text{Target cost} = \text{Expected selling price} - \text{Desired profit}$$

If the target cost is too high, lean techniques can be used to determine whether the cost can be reduced enough that the desired profit can be made. For example, if the market price for MP3 players is $80 each and MpPro still wants to make a profit of $14 per unit, it must find a way to reduce its total cost per unit to $66 (computed as $80 price − $14 desired profit).

Sometimes companies compute the desired markup percentage using a target return on investment. For example, if MpPro targets a 14% return on invested assets of $1,000,000, its target profit is $140,000. This equals $14 per unit if 10,000 units are sold, as in this example. The markup percentage is then $14/$70 = 20%.

Variable Cost Method

In addition to the total cost approach of the cost-plus methods, one alternative is to base price on variable cost. Because variable cost is less than total cost, companies that use this method must increase the markup percentage to ensure that the selling price covers all costs. For the **variable cost method**, the markup percentage to variable cost is determined as:

$$\text{Markup percentage to variable cost} = \frac{\text{Target profit} + \text{Fixed overhead costs} + \text{Fixed selling and administrative costs}}{\text{Total variable cost}}$$

For MpPro, the markup percentage, using the variable cost approach, is computed as:

$$\text{Markup percentage to variable cost} = \frac{\$140,000 + \$140,000 + \$60,000}{[(\$44 + \$6) \times 10,000]} = 68\%$$

With this markup percentage and total variable cost per unit of $50 (from $44 + $6), the selling price is computed as:

$$\text{Selling price} = \$50 + (\$50 \times 68\%) = \$84$$

Determine the appropriate action in each of the following managerial decision situations.

1. Packer Company is operating at 80% of its manufacturing capacity of 100,000 product units per year. A chain store has offered to buy an additional 10,000 units at $22 each and sell them to customers so as not to compete with Packer Company. The following data are available.

Costs at 80% Capacity	Per Unit	Total
Direct materials	$ 8.00	$ 640,000
Direct labor	7.00	560,000
Overhead (fixed and variable)	12.50	1,000,000
Totals	$27.50	$2,200,000

In producing 10,000 additional units, fixed overhead costs would remain at their current level, but incremental variable overhead costs of $3 per unit would be incurred. Should the company accept or reject this order?

2. Green Company uses Part JR3 in manufacturing its products. It has always purchased this part from a supplier for $40 each. It recently upgraded its own manufacturing capabilities and has enough excess capacity (including trained workers) to begin manufacturing Part JR3 instead of buying it. The company prepares the following cost projections of making the part, assuming that overhead is allocated to the part at the normal predetermined rate of 200% of direct labor cost.

Direct materials	$11
Direct labor	15
Overhead (fixed and variable) (200% of direct labor)	30
Total	$56

The required volume of output to produce the part will not require any incremental fixed overhead. Incremental variable overhead cost will be $17 per unit. Should the company make or buy this part?

3. Gold Company's manufacturing process causes a relatively large number of defective parts to be produced. The defective parts can be (a) sold for scrap, (b) melted to recover the recycled metal for reuse, or (c) reworked to be good units. Reworking defective parts reduces the output of other good units because no excess capacity exists. Each unit reworked means that one new unit cannot be produced. The following information reflects 500 defective parts currently available.

Proceeds of selling as scrap	$2,500
Additional cost of melting down defective parts	400
Cost of purchases avoided by using recycled metal from defects	4,800
Cost to rework 500 defective parts	
Direct materials	0
Direct labor	1,500
Incremental overhead	1,750
Cost to produce 500 new parts	
Direct materials	6,000
Direct labor	5,000
Incremental overhead	3,200
Selling price per good unit	40

Should the company melt the parts, sell them as scrap, or rework them?

PLANNING THE SOLUTION

- Determine whether Packer Company should accept the additional business by finding the incremental costs of materials, labor, and overhead that will be incurred if the order is accepted. Omit fixed costs that the order will not increase. If the incremental revenue exceeds the incremental cost, accept the order.

- Determine whether Green Company should make or buy the component by finding the incremental cost of making each unit. If the incremental cost exceeds the purchase price, the component should be purchased. If the incremental cost is less than the purchase price, make the component.
- Determine whether Gold Company should sell the defective parts, melt them down and recycle the metal, or rework them. To compare the three choices, examine all costs incurred and benefits received from the alternatives in working with the 500 defective units versus the production of 500 new units. For the scrapping alternative, include the costs of producing 500 new units and subtract the $2,500 proceeds from selling the old ones. For the melting alternative, include the costs of melting the defective units, add the net cost of new materials in excess over those obtained from recycling, and add the direct labor and overhead costs. For the reworking alternative, add the costs of direct labor and incremental overhead. Select the alternative that has the lowest cost. The cost assigned to the 500 defective units is sunk and not relevant in choosing among the three alternatives.

SOLUTION

1. This decision involves accepting additional business. Since current unit costs are $27.50, it appears initially as if the offer to sell for $22 should be rejected, but the $27.50 cost includes fixed costs. When the analysis includes only *incremental* costs, the per unit cost is as shown in the following table. The offer should be accepted because it will produce $4 of additional profit per unit (computed as $22 price less $18 incremental cost), which yields a total profit of $40,000 for the 10,000 additional units.

Direct materials	$ 8.00
Direct labor......................	7.00
Variable overhead (given)	3.00
Total incremental cost	$18.00

2. For this make or buy decision, the analysis must include only incremental overhead per unit ($30 − $17). When only the $17 incremental overhead is included, the relevant unit cost of manufacturing the part is shown in the following table. It would be better to continue buying the part for $40 instead of making it for $43.

Direct materials	$11.00
Direct labor......................	15.00
Variable overhead	17.00
Total incremental cost	$43.00

3. The goal of this scrap or rework decision is to identify the alternative that produces the greatest net benefit to the company. To compare the alternatives, we determine the net cost of obtaining 500 marketable units as follows:

Incremental Cost to Produce 500 Marketable Units	Sell As Is	Melt and Recycle	Rework Units
Direct materials			
New materials	$ 6,000	$6,000	
Recycled metal materials....................................		(4,800)	
Net materials cost		1,200	
Melting costs		400	
Total direct materials cost	6,000	1,600	
Direct labor...	5,000	5,000	$1,500
Incremental overhead	3,200	3,200	1,750
Cost to produce 500 marketable units	14,200	9,800	3,250
Less proceeds of selling defects as scrap....................	(2,500)		
Opportunity costs*			5,800
Incremental cost...	$11,700	$9,800	$9,050

* The $5,800 opportunity cost is the lost contribution margin from not being able to produce and sell 500 units because of reworking, computed as ($40 − [$14,200/500 units]) × 500 units.

The incremental cost of 500 marketable parts is smallest if the defects are reworked.

Summary

C1 **Describe the importance of relevant costs for short-term decisions.** A company must rely on relevant costs pertaining to alternative courses of action rather than historical costs. Out-of-pocket expenses and opportunity costs are relevant because these are avoidable; sunk costs are irrelevant because they result from past decisions and are therefore unavoidable. Managers must also consider the relevant benefits associated with alternative decisions.

A1 **Evaluate short-term managerial decisions using relevant costs.** Relevant costs are useful in making decisions such as to accept additional business, make or buy, and sell as is or process further. For example, the relevant factors in deciding whether to produce and sell additional units of product are incremental costs and incremental revenues from the additional volume.

P1 **Determine product selling price using cost data.** Product selling price can be estimated using total costs, plus a markup. Total costs include both product costs and selling and administrative expenses. A markup is added to yield management's desired profit.

Key Terms

Avoidable expense

Incremental cost

Markup

Outsourcing

Relevant benefits

Total cost method

Unavoidable expense

Multiple Choice Quiz

1. A company inadvertently produced 3,000 defective MP3 players. The players cost $12 each to produce. A recycler offers to purchase the defective players as they are for $8 each. The production manager reports that the defects can be corrected for $10 each, enabling them to be sold at their regular market price of $19 each. The company should:

   a. Correct the defect and sell them at the regular price.

   b. Sell the players to the recycler for $8 each.

   c. Sell 2,000 to the recycler and repair the rest.

   d. Sell 1,000 to the recycler and repair the rest.

   e. Throw the players away.

2. A company's productive capacity is limited to 480,000 machine hours. Product X requires 10 machine hours to produce; Product Y requires 2 machine hours to produce. Product X sells for $32 per unit and has variable costs of $12 per unit; Product Y sells for $24 per unit and has variable costs of $10 per unit. Assuming that the company can sell as many of either product as it produces, it should:

   a. Produce X and Y in the ratio of 57% X and 43% Y.

   b. Produce X and Y in the ratio of 83% X and 17% Y.

   c. Produce equal amounts of Product X and Product Y.

   d. Produce only Product X.

   e. Produce only Product Y.

3. A company receives a special one-time order for 3,000 units of its product at $15 per unit. The company has excess capacity and it currently produces and sells the units at $20 each to its regular customers. Production costs are $13.50 per unit, which includes $9 of variable costs. To produce the special order, the company must incur additional fixed costs of $5,000. Should the company accept the special order?

   a. Yes, because incremental revenue exceeds incremental costs.

   b. No, because incremental costs exceed incremental revenue.

   c. No, because the units are being sold for $5 less than the regular price.

   d. Yes, because incremental costs exceed incremental revenue.

   e. No, because incremental costs exceed $15 per unit when total costs are considered.

4. A cost that cannot be changed because it arises from a past decision and is irrelevant to future decisions is

   a. An uncontrollable cost.   d. An opportunity cost.

   b. An out-of-pocket cost.   e. An incremental cost.

   c. A sunk cost.

5. The potential benefit of one alternative that is lost by choosing another is known as

   a. An alternative cost.   d. An opportunity cost.

   b. A sunk cost.   e. An out-of-pocket cost.

   c. A differential cost.

ANSWERS TO MULTIPLE CHOICE QUIZ

1. a; Reworking provides incremental revenue of $11 per unit ($19 − $8); it costs $10 to rework them. The company is better off by $1 per unit when it reworks these products and sells them at the regular price.

2. e; Product X has a $2 contribution margin per machine hour [($32 − $12)/10 MH]; Product Y has a $7 contribution margin per machine hour [($24 − $10)/2 MH]. It should produce as much of Product Y as possible.

3. a; Total revenue from the special order = 3,000 units × $15 per unit = $45,000; and Total costs for the special order = (3,000 units × $9 per unit) + $5,000 = $32,000. Net income from the special order = $45,000 − $32,000 = $13,000. Thus, yes, it should accept the order.

4. c

5. d

🔲 Icon denotes assignments that involve decision making.

Discussion Questions

1. 🔲 Identify the five steps involved in the managerial decision-making process.

2. Is nonfinancial information ever useful in managerial decision making?

3. What is a relevant cost? Identify the two types of relevant costs.

4. 🔲 Why are sunk costs irrelevant in deciding whether to sell a product in its present condition or to make it into a new product through additional processing?

5. 🔲 Identify some qualitative factors that should be considered when making managerial decisions.

6. **Google** has many types of costs. What is an out-of-pocket cost? What is an opportunity cost? Are opportunity costs recorded in the accounting records?   GOOGLE

7. 🔲 **Samsung** must confront sunk costs. Why are sunk costs irrelevant in **Samsung**

deciding whether to sell a product in its present condition or to make it into a new product through additional processing?

8. 🔲 Identify the incremental costs incurred by **Apple** for shipping one additional iPod from a warehouse to a retail store along with the store's normal order of 75 iPods.   **APPLE**

9. 🔲 **Apple** is considering eliminating one of its stores in a large U.S. city. What are some factors that it should consider in making this decision?   **APPLE**

10. 🔲 Assume that **Samsung** manufactures and sells 60,000 units of a product at $11,000 per unit in domestic markets. It costs $6,000 per unit to manufacture ($4,000 variable cost per unit, $2,000 fixed cost per unit). Can you describe a situation under which the company is willing to sell an additional 8,000 units of the product in an international market at $5,000 per unit?   **Samsung**

📖 connect

Helix Company has been approached by a new customer to provide 2,000 units of its regular product at a special price of $6 per unit. The regular selling price of the product is $8 per unit. Helix is operating at 75% of its capacity of 10,000 units. Identify whether the following costs are relevant to Helix's decision as to whether to accept the order at the special selling price. No additional fixed manufacturing overhead will be incurred because of this order. The only additional selling expense on this order will be a $0.50 per unit shipping cost. There will be no additional administrative expenses because of this order. Place an X in the appropriate column to identify whether the cost is relevant or irrelevant to accepting this order.

QUICK STUDY

QS 10-1
Identification of relevant costs

C1

Item	Relevant	Not Relevant
a. Selling price of $6.00 per unit	_____	_____
b. Direct materials cost of $1.00 per unit	_____	_____
c. Direct labor of $2.00 per unit	_____	_____
d. Variable manufacturing overhead of $1.50 per unit	_____	_____
e. Fixed manufacturing overhead of $0.75 per unit	_____	_____
f. Regular selling expenses of $1.25 per unit	_____	_____
g. Additional selling expenses of $0.50 per unit	_____	_____
h. Administrative expenses of $0.60 per unit	_____	_____

Refer to the data in QS 10-1. Based on financial considerations alone, should Helix accept this order at the special price? Explain.

QS 10-2
Analysis of relevant costs   A1

QS 10-3

Identification of relevant nonfinancial factors   **C1**

Refer to QS 10-1 and QS 10-2. What nonfinancial factors should Helix consider before accepting this order? Explain.

QS 10-4

Sell or process

A1

Garcia Company has 10,000 units of its product that were produced last year at a total cost of $150,000. The units were damaged in a rainstorm because the warehouse where they were stored developed a leak in the roof. Garcia can sell the units as is for $2 each or it can repair the units at a total cost of $18,000 and then sell them for $5 each. Should Garcia sell the units as is or repair them and then sell them? Explain.

QS 10-5

Relevant costs

C1

Label each of the following statements as either true ("T") or false ("F").

_____ **1.** Relevant costs are also known as unavoidable costs.

_____ **2.** Incremental costs are also known as differential costs.

_____ **3.** An out-of-pocket cost requires a current and/or future outlay of cash.

_____ **4.** An opportunity cost is the potential benefit that is lost by taking a specific action when two or more alternative choices are available.

_____ **5.** A sunk cost will change with a future course of action.

QS 10-6

Additional business

A1

Radar Company sells bikes for $300 each. The company currently sells 3,750 bikes per year and could make as many as 5,000 bikes per year. The bikes cost $225 each to make: $150 in variable costs per bike and $75 of fixed costs per bike. Radar received an offer from a potential customer who wants to buy 750 bikes for $250 each. Incremental fixed costs to make this order are $50,000. No other costs will change if this order is accepted. Compute Radar's additional income (ignore taxes) if it accepts this order.

QS 10-7

Make or buy

A1

Kando Company incurs a $9 per unit cost for Product A, which it currently manufactures and sells for $13.50 per unit. Instead of manufacturing and selling this product, the company can purchase it for $5 per unit and sell it for $12 per unit. If it does so, unit sales would remain unchanged and $5 of the $9 per unit costs of Product A would be eliminated. Should the company continue to manufacture Product A or purchase it for resale?

QS 10-8

Make or buy

A1

Xia Co. currently buys a component part for $5 per unit. Xia believes that making the part would require $2.25 per unit of direct materials and $1.00 per unit of direct labor. Xia allocates overhead using a predetermined overhead rate of 200% of direct labor cost. Xia estimates an incremental overhead rate of $0.75 per unit to make the part. Should Xia make or buy the part?

QS 10-9

Scrap or rework

A1

Signal mistakenly produced 1,000 defective cell phones. The phones cost $60 each to produce. A salvage company will buy the defective phones as they are for $30 each. It would cost Signal $80 per phone to rework the phones. If the phones are reworked, Signal could sell them for $120 each. Assume there is no opportunity cost associated with reworking the phones. Compute the incremental net income from reworking the phones.

QS 10-10

Sell or process further

A1

Holmes Company produces a product that can be either sold as is or processed further. Holmes has already spent $50,000 to produce 1,250 units that can be sold now for $67,500 to another manufacturer. Alternatively, Holmes can process the units further at an incremental cost of $250 per unit. If Holmes processes further, the units can be sold for $375 each. Compute the incremental income if Holmes processes further.

QS 10-11

Sell or process further   **A1**

A company has already incurred $5,000 of costs in producing 6,000 units of Product XY. Product XY can be sold as is for $15 per unit. Instead, the company could incur further processing costs of $8 per unit and sell the resulting product for $21 per unit. Should the company sell Product XY as is or process it further?

QS 10-12

Selection of sales mix

A1

Excel Memory Company can sell all units of computer memory X and Y that it can produce, but it has limited production capacity. It can produce two units of X per hour *or* three units of Y per hour, and it has 4,000 production hours available. Contribution margin is $5 for Product X and $4 for Product Y. What is the most profitable sales mix for this company?

A guitar manufacturer is considering eliminating its electric guitar division because its $76,000 expenses are higher than its $72,000 sales. The company reports the following expenses for this division. Should the division be eliminated?

QS 10-13
Segment elimination
A1

	Avoidable Expenses	Unavoidable Expenses
Cost of goods sold	$56,000	
Direct expenses	9,250	$1,250
Indirect expenses	470	1,600
Service department costs	6,000	1,430

A division of a large company reports the information shown below for a recent year. Variable costs and direct fixed costs are avoidable, and 40% of the indirect fixed costs are avoidable. Based on this information, should the division be eliminated?

QS 10-14
Segment elimination
A1

	Total
Sales	$200,000
Variable costs	145,000
Fixed costs	
Direct	30,000
Indirect	50,000
Operating loss.	$ (25,000)

Rory Company has a machine with a book value of $75,000 and a remaining five-year useful life. A new machine is available at a cost of $112,500, and Rory can also receive $60,000 for trading in its old machine. The new machine will reduce variable manufacturing costs by $13,000 per year over its five-year useful life. Should the machine be replaced?

QS 10-15
Keep or replace
A1

Garcia Co. sells snowboards. Each snowboard requires direct materials of $100, direct labor of $30, and variable overhead of $45. The company expects fixed overhead costs of $635,000 and fixed selling and administrative costs of $115,000 for the next year. It expects to produce and sell 10,000 snowboards in the next year. What will be the selling price per unit if Garcia uses a markup of 15% of total cost?

QS 10-16
Product pricing
P1

José Ruiz wants to start a company that makes snowboards. Competitors sell a similar snowboard for $240 each. José believes he can produce a snowboard for a total cost of $200 per unit, and he plans a 25% markup on his total cost. Compute José's planned selling price. Can José compete with his planned selling price?

QS 10-17
Product pricing
P1

GoSnow sells snowboards. Each snowboard requires direct materials of $110, direct labor of $35, and variable overhead of $45. The company expects fixed overhead costs of $265,000 and fixed selling and administrative costs of $211,000 for the next year. The company has a target profit of $200,000. It expects to produce and sell 10,000 snowboards in the next year. Compute the selling price using the variable cost method.

QS 10-18
Product pricing using
variable costs P1

connect

Complete the following descriptions using terms *a* through *e*.

a. Opportunity cost **b.** Avoidable costs **c.** Sunk cost **d.** Relevant benefits **e.** Out-of-pocket cost

1. A _____ arises from a past decision and cannot be avoided or changed; it is irrelevant to future decisions.

2. _____ refer to the incremental revenue generated from taking one particular action over another.

3. Relevant costs are also known as _____.

4. An _____ requires a future outlay of cash and is relevant for current and future decision making.

5. An _____ is the potential benefit lost by taking a specific action when two or more alternative choices are available.

EXERCISES

Exercise 10-1
Relevant costs

C1

Exercise 10-2

Accept new business or not

A1

Farrow Co. expects to sell 150,000 units of its product in the next period with the following results.

Sales (150,000 units)	$2,250,000
Costs and expenses	
Direct materials	300,000
Direct labor	600,000
Overhead	150,000
Selling expenses	225,000
Administrative expenses	385,500
Total costs and expenses	1,660,500
Net income	$ 589,500

Check Income increase, $3,000

The company has an opportunity to sell 15,000 additional units at $12 per unit. The additional sales would not affect its current expected sales. Direct materials and labor costs per unit would be the same for the additional units as they are for the regular units. However, the additional volume would create the following incremental costs: (1) total overhead would increase by 15% and (2) administrative expenses would increase by $64,500. Prepare an analysis to determine whether the company should accept or reject the offer to sell additional units at the reduced price of $12 per unit.

Exercise 10-3

Accept new business or not

A1

Goshford Company produces a single product and has capacity to produce 100,000 units per month. Costs to produce its current sales of 80,000 units follow. The regular selling price of the product is $100 per unit. Management is approached by a new customer who wants to purchase 20,000 units of the product for $75 per unit. If the order is accepted, there will be no additional fixed manufacturing overhead and no additional fixed selling and administrative expenses. The customer is not in the company's regular selling territory, so there will be a $5 per unit shipping expense in addition to the regular variable selling and administrative expenses.

	Per Unit	Costs at 80,000 Units
Direct materials	$12.50	$1,000,000
Direct labor	15.00	1,200,000
Variable manufacturing overhead	10.00	800,000
Fixed manufacturing overhead	17.50	1,400,000
Variable selling and administrative expenses	14.00	1,120,000
Fixed selling and administrative expenses	13.00	1,040,000
Totals	$82.00	$6,560,000

Check (1) Additional volume effect on net income, $370,000

1. Determine whether management should accept or reject the new business.
2. What nonfinancial factors should management consider when deciding whether to take this order?

Exercise 10-4

Make or buy decision

A1

Check $9,500 increased costs to buy

Gilberto Company currently manufactures 65,000 units per year of one of its crucial parts. Variable costs are $1.95 per unit, fixed costs related to making this part are $75,000 per year, and allocated fixed costs are $62,000 per year. Allocated fixed costs are unavoidable whether the company makes or buys the part. Gilberto is considering buying the part from a supplier for a quoted price of $3.25 per unit guaranteed for a three-year period. Should the company continue to manufacture the part, or should it buy the part from the outside supplier? Support your answer with analyses.

Exercise 10-5

Make or buy

A1

Check Increased cost to make, $3,000

Gelb Company currently manufactures 40,000 units per year of a key component for its manufacturing process. Variable costs are $1.95 per unit, fixed costs related to making this component are $65,000 per year, and allocated fixed costs are $58,500 per year. The allocated fixed costs are unavoidable whether the company makes or buys this component. The company is considering buying this component from a supplier for $3.50 per unit. Should it continue to manufacture the component, or should it buy this component from the outside supplier? Support your decision with analysis of the data provided.

A company must decide between scrapping or reworking units that do not pass inspection. The company has 22,000 defective units that cost $6 per unit to manufacture. The units can be sold as is for $2.00 each, or they can be reworked for $4.50 each and then sold for the full price of $8.50 each. If the units are sold as is, the company will be able to build 22,000 replacement units at a cost of $6 each, and sell them at the full price of $8.50 each. (1) What is the incremental income from selling the units as scrap? (2) What is the incremental income from reworking and selling the units? (3) Should the company sell the units as scrap or rework them?

Exercise 10-6
Scrap or rework
A1

Varto Company has 7,000 units of its sole product in inventory that it produced last year at a cost of $22 each. This year's model is superior to last year's, and the 7,000 units cannot be sold at last year's regular selling price of $35 each. Varto has two alternatives for these items: (1) they can be sold to a wholesaler for $8 each or (2) they can be reworked at a cost of $125,000 and then sold for $25 each. Prepare an analysis to determine whether Varto should sell the products as is or rework them and then sell them.

Exercise 10-7
Scrap or rework   A1

Check   Incremental net income of reworking, $(6,000)

Cobe Company has already manufactured 28,000 units of Product A at a cost of $28 per unit. The 28,000 units can be sold at this stage for $700,000. Alternatively, the units can be further processed at a $420,000 total additional cost and be converted into 5,600 units of Product B and 11,200 units of Product C. Per unit selling price for Product B is $105 and for Product C is $70. Prepare an analysis that shows whether the 28,000 units of Product A should be processed further or not.

Exercise 10-8
Sell or process further
A1

Colt Company owns a machine that can produce two specialized products. Production time for Product TLX is two units per hour and for Product MTV is five units per hour. The machine's capacity is 2,750 hours per year. Both products are sold to a single customer who has agreed to buy all of the company's output up to a maximum of 4,700 units of Product TLX and 2,500 units of Product MTV. Selling prices and variable costs per unit to produce the products follow. Determine (1) the company's most profitable sales mix and (2) the contribution margin that results from that sales mix.

Exercise 10-9
Sales mix determination and analysis
A1

$s per unit	Product TLX	Product MTV
Selling price per unit	$15.00	$9.50
Variable costs per unit.	4.80	5.50

Check   (2) $55,940

Suresh Co. expects its five departments to yield the following income for next year.

Exercise 10-10
Analysis of income effects from eliminating departments
A1

	A	B	C	D	E	F	G
1		**Dept. M**	**Dept. N**	**Dept. O**	**Dept. P**	**Dept. T**	**Total**
2	Sales	$63,000	$ 35,000	$56,000	$42,000	$28,000	$224,000
3	Expenses						
4	Avoidable	9,800	36,400	22,400	14,000	37,800	120,400
5	Unavoidable	51,800	12,600	4,200	29,400	9,800	107,800
6	Total expenses	61,600	49,000	26,600	43,400	47,600	228,200
7	Net income (loss)	$ 1,400	$(14,000)	$29,400	$ (1,400)	$(19,600)	$ (4,200)

Recompute and prepare the departmental income statements (including a combined total column) for the company under each of the following separate scenarios: Management (1) eliminates departments with expected net losses and (2) eliminates departments with sales dollars that are less than avoidable expenses. Explain your answers to parts 1 and 2.

Check   Total income (loss) (1) $(21,000), (2) $7,000

Childress Company produces three products, K1, S5, and G9. Each product uses the same type of direct material. K1 uses 4 pounds of the material, S5 uses 3 pounds of the material, and G9 uses 6 pounds of the material. Demand for all products is strong, but only 50,000 pounds of material are available. Information about the selling price per unit and variable cost per unit of each product follows. Orders for which product should be produced and filled first, then second, and then third? Support your answer.

Exercise 10-11
Sales mix
A1

	K1	S5	G9
Selling price	$160	$112	$210
Variable costs	96	85	144

Check   K1 contribution margin per pound, $16

Exercise 10-12
Keep or replace
A1

Xinhong Company is considering replacing one of its manufacturing machines. The machine has a book value of $45,000 and a remaining useful life of five years, at which time its salvage value will be zero. It has a current market value of $52,000. Variable manufacturing costs are $36,000 per year for this machine. Information on two alternative replacement machines follows. Should Xinhong keep or replace its manufacturing machine? If the machine should be replaced, which alternative new machine should Xinhong purchase?

	Alternative A	Alternative B
Cost....................................	$115,000	$125,000
Variable manufacturing costs per year	19,000	15,000

Exercise 10-13
Income analysis of
eliminating departments
A1

Marinette Company makes several products, including canoes. The company has been experiencing losses from its canoe segment and is considering dropping that product line. The following information is available regarding its canoe segment. Should management discontinue the manufacturing of canoes? Support your decision.

MARINETTE COMPANY		
Income Statement—Canoe Segment		
Sales		$2,000,000
Variable costs		
Direct materials	$450,000	
Direct labor.................................	500,000	
Variable overhead	300,000	
Variable selling and administrative...............	200,000	
Total variable costs...........................		1,450,000
Contribution margin		550,000
Fixed costs		
Direct	375,000	
Indirect	300,000	
Total fixed costs		675,000
Net income		$ (125,000)

Check   Income impact if
canoe segment dropped,
$(175,000)

Exercise 10-14
Product pricing using
total costs
P1

Steeze Co. makes snowboards and uses the total cost approach in setting product prices. Its costs for producing 10,000 units follow. The company targets a profit of $300,000 on this product.

Variable Costs per Unit		Fixed Costs (in total)	
Direct materials.............................	$100	Overhead.............................	$470,000
Direct labor	25	Selling	105,000
Overhead..................................	20	Administrative	325,000
Selling	5		

1. Compute the total cost per unit.
2. Compute the markup percentage on total cost.
3. Compute the product's selling price using the total cost method.

Exercise 10-15
Product pricing using
variable costs
P1

Rios Co. makes drones and uses the variable cost approach in setting product prices. Its costs for producing 20,000 units follow. The company targets a profit of $300,000 on this product.

Variable Costs per Unit		Fixed Costs (in total)	
Direct materials.............................	$70	Overhead.............................	$670,000
Direct labor	40	Selling	305,000
Overhead..................................	25	Administrative	285,000
Selling	15		

1. Compute the variable cost per unit.
2. Compute the markup percentage on variable cost.
3. Compute the product's selling price using the variable cost method.

■ connect

Jones Products manufactures and sells to wholesalers approximately 400,000 packages per year of underwater markers at $6 per package. Annual costs for the production and sale of this quantity are shown in the table.

Direct materials	$ 576,000
Direct labor.	144,000
Overhead	320,000
Selling expenses.	150,000
Administrative expenses	100,000
Total costs and expenses.	$1,290,000

PROBLEM SET A

Problem 10-1A
Analysis of income effects of additional business

A1

A new wholesaler has offered to buy 50,000 packages for $5.20 each. These markers would be marketed under the wholesaler's name and would not affect Jones Products's sales through its normal channels. A study of the costs of this additional business reveals the following:

● Direct materials costs are 100% variable.
● Per unit direct labor costs for the additional units would be 50% higher than normal because their production would require overtime pay at 1½ times the usual labor rate.
● Twenty-five percent of the normal annual overhead costs are fixed at any production level from 350,000 to 500,000 units. The remaining 75% of the annual overhead cost is variable with volume.
● Accepting the new business would involve no additional selling expenses.
● Accepting the new business would increase administrative expenses by a $5,000 fixed amount.

Required

Prepare a three-column comparative income statement that shows the following:

1. Annual operating income without the special order (column 1).
2. Annual operating income received from the new business only (column 2).
3. Combined annual operating income from normal business and the new business (column 3).

Check Operating income:
(1) $1,110,000
(2) $126,000

Calla Company produces skateboards that sell for $50 per unit. The company currently has the capacity to produce 90,000 skateboards per year, but is selling 80,000 skateboards per year. Annual costs for 80,000 skateboards follow.

Problem 10-2A
Analysis of income effects of additional business

A1

Direct materials	$ 800,000
Direct labor.	640,000
Overhead	960,000
Selling expenses.	560,000
Administrative expenses	480,000
Total costs and expenses.	$3,440,000

A new retail store has offered to buy 10,000 of its skateboards for $45 per unit. The store is in a different market from Calla's regular customers and would not affect regular sales. A study of its costs in anticipation of this additional business reveals the following:

● Direct materials and direct labor are 100% variable.
● Thirty percent of overhead is fixed at any production level from 80,000 units to 90,000 units; the remaining 70% of annual overhead costs are variable with respect to volume.
● Selling expenses are 60% variable with respect to number of units sold, and the other 40% of selling expenses are fixed.
● There will be an additional $2 per unit selling expense for this order.
● Administrative expenses would increase by a $1,000 fixed amount.

Required

1. Prepare a three-column comparative income statement that reports the following:
   a. Annual income without the special order.
   b. Annual income from the special order.
   c. Combined annual income from normal business and the new business.

2. Should Calla accept this order? What nonfinancial factors should Calla consider? Explain.

Analysis Component

3. Assume that the new customer wants to buy 15,000 units instead of 10,000 units—it will only buy 15,000 units or none and will not take a partial order. Without any computations, how does this change your answer for part 2?

Problem 10-3A
Make or buy
A1

Haver Company currently produces component RX5 for its sole product. The current cost per unit to manufacture the required 50,000 units of RX5 follows.

Direct materials	$ 5.00
Direct labor	8.00
Overhead	9.00
Total cost per unit	$22.00

Direct materials and direct labor are 100% variable. Overhead is 80% fixed. An outside supplier has offered to supply the 50,000 units of RX5 for $18.00 per unit.

Required

1. Determine whether the company should make or buy the RX5.
2. What factors besides cost must management consider when deciding whether to make or buy RX5?

Problem 10-4A
Sell or process
A1

Harold Manufacturing produces denim clothing. This year, it produced 5,000 denim jackets at a manufacturing cost of $45 each. These jackets were damaged in the warehouse during storage. Management investigated the matter and identified three alternatives for these jackets.

1. Jackets can be sold to a secondhand clothing shop for $6 each.
2. Jackets can be disassembled at a cost of $32,000 and sold to a recycler for $12 each.
3. Jackets can be reworked and turned into good jackets. However, with the damage, management estimates it will be able to assemble the good parts of the 5,000 jackets into only 3,000 jackets. The remaining pieces of fabric will be discarded. The cost of reworking the jackets will be $102,000, but the jackets can then be sold for their regular price of $45 each.

Required

Which alternative should Harold choose? Show analysis for each alternative.

Problem 10-5A
Analysis of sales mix strategies
A1

Edgerron Company is able to produce two products, G and B, with the same machine in its factory. The following information is available.

	Product G	Product B
Selling price per unit	$120	$160
Variable costs per unit	40	90
Contribution margin per unit	$ 80	$ 70
Machine hours to produce 1 unit	0.4 hours	1.0 hours
Maximum unit sales per month	600 units	200 units

The company presently operates the machine for a single eight-hour shift for 22 working days each month. Management is thinking about operating the machine for two shifts, which will increase its productivity by another eight hours per day for 22 days per month. This change would require $15,000 additional fixed costs per month.

Required

1. Determine the contribution margin per machine hour that each product generates.

2. How many units of Product G and Product B should the company produce if it continues to operate with only one shift? How much total contribution margin does this mix produce each month?

3. If the company adds another shift, how many units of Product G and Product B should it produce? How much total contribution margin would this mix produce each month? Should the company add the new shift? Explain.

4. Suppose that the company determines that it can increase Product G's maximum sales to 700 units per month by spending $12,000 per month in marketing efforts. Should the company pursue this strategy and the double shift? Explain.

Check Units of Product G:
(2) 440

(3) 600

Elegant Decor Company's management is trying to decide whether to eliminate Department 200, which has produced losses or low profits for several years. The company's 2017 departmental income statements show the following.

Problem 10-6A
Analysis of possible elimination of a department

A1

ELEGANT DECOR COMPANY Departmental Income Statements For Year Ended December 31, 2017	Dept. 100	Dept. 200	Combined
Sales	$436,000	$290,000	$726,000
Cost of goods sold	262,000	207,000	469,000
Gross profit	174,000	83,000	257,000
Operating expenses			
Direct expenses			
Advertising	17,000	12,000	29,000
Store supplies used	4,000	3,800	7,800
Depreciation—Store equipment	5,000	3,300	8,300
Total direct expenses	26,000	19,100	45,100
Allocated expenses			
Sales salaries	65,000	39,000	104,000
Rent expense	9,440	4,720	14,160
Bad debts expense	9,900	8,100	18,000
Office salary	18,720	12,480	31,200
Insurance expense	2,000	1,100	3,100
Miscellaneous office expenses	2,400	1,600	4,000
Total allocated expenses	107,460	67,000	174,460
Total expenses	133,460	86,100	219,560
Net income (loss)	$ 40,540	$ (3,100)	$ 37,440

In analyzing whether to eliminate Department 200, management considers the following:

a. The company has one office worker who earns $600 per week, or $31,200 per year, and four sales-clerks who each earns $500 per week, or $26,000 per year for each salesclerk.

b. The full salaries of two salesclerks are charged to Department 100. The full salary of one salesclerk is charged to Department 200. The salary of the fourth clerk, who works half-time in both departments, is divided evenly between the two departments.

c. Eliminating Department 200 would avoid the sales salaries and the office salary currently allocated to it. However, management prefers another plan. Two salesclerks have indicated that they will be quit-ting soon. Management believes that their work can be done by the other two clerks if the one office worker works in sales half-time. Eliminating Department 200 will allow this shift of duties. If this change is implemented, half the office worker's salary would be reported as sales salaries and half would be reported as office salary.

d. The store building is rented under a long-term lease that cannot be changed. Therefore, Department 100 will use the space and equipment currently used by Department 200.

e. Closing Department 200 will eliminate its expenses for advertising, bad debts, and store supplies; 70% of the insurance expense allocated to it to cover its merchandise inventory; and 25% of the miscella-neous office expenses presently allocated to it.

Required

1. Prepare a three-column report that lists items and amounts for (a) the company's total expenses (including cost of goods sold)—in column 1, (b) the expenses that would be eliminated by closing Department 200—in column 2, and (c) the expenses that will continue—in column 3.

2. Prepare a forecasted annual income statement for the company reflecting the elimination of Department 200 assuming that it will not affect Department 100's sales and gross profit. The statement should reflect the reassignment of the office worker to one-half time as a salesclerk.

Analysis Component

3. Reconcile the company's combined net income with the forecasted net income assuming that Department 200 is eliminated (list both items and amounts). Analyze the reconciliation and explain why you think the department should or should not be eliminated.

PROBLEM SET B

Problem 10-1B
Analysis of income effects of additional business

A1

Windmire Company manufactures and sells to local wholesalers approximately 300,000 units per month at a sales price of $4 per unit. Monthly costs for the production and sale of this quantity follow.

Direct materials	$384,000
Direct labor.......................	96,000
Overhead	288,000
Selling expenses..................	120,000
Administrative expenses	80,000
Total costs and expenses...........	$968,000

A new out-of-state distributor has offered to buy 50,000 units next month for $3.44 each. These units would be marketed in other states and would not affect Windmire's sales through its normal channels. A study of the costs of this new business reveals the following:

- Direct materials costs are 100% variable.
- Per unit direct labor costs for the additional units would be 50% higher than normal because their production would require overtime pay at 1½ times their normal rate to meet the distributor's deadline.
- Twenty-five percent of the normal annual overhead costs are fixed at any production level from 250,000 to 400,000 units. The remaining 75% is variable with volume.
- Accepting the new business would involve no additional selling expenses.
- Accepting the new business would increase administrative expenses by a $4,000 fixed amount.

Required

Prepare a three-column comparative income statement that shows the following:

1. Monthly operating income without the special order (column 1).

2. Monthly operating income received from the new business only (column 2).

3. Combined monthly operating income from normal business and the new business (column 3).

Problem 10-2B
Analysis of income effects of additional business

A1

Mervin Company produces circuit boards that sell for $8 per unit. It currently has capacity to produce 600,000 circuit boards per year, but is selling 550,000 boards per year. Annual costs for the 550,000 circuit boards follow.

Direct materials	$ 825,000
Direct labor.......................	1,100,000
Overhead	1,375,000
Selling expenses..................	275,000
Administrative expenses	550,000
Total costs and expenses...........	$4,125,000

An overseas customer has offered to buy 50,000 circuit boards for $6 per unit. The customer is in a different market from Mervin's regular customers and would not affect regular sales. A study of its costs in anticipation of this additional business reveals the following:

- Direct materials and direct labor are 100% variable.
- Twenty percent of overhead is fixed at any production level from 550,000 units to 600,000 units; the remaining 80% of annual overhead costs are variable with respect to volume.
- Selling expenses are 40% variable with respect to number of units sold, and the other 60% of selling expenses are fixed.
- There will be an additional $0.20 per unit selling expense for this order.
- Administrative expenses would increase by a $700 fixed amount.

Required

1. Prepare a three-column comparative income statement that reports the following:
   a. Annual income without the special order.
   b. Annual income from the special order.
   c. Combined annual income from normal business and the new business.

2. Should management accept the order? What nonfinancial factors should Mervin consider? Explain.

Check (1*b*) Additional income from order, $4,300

Analysis Component

3. Assume that the new customer wants to buy 100,000 units instead of 50,000 units—it will only buy 100,000 units or none and will not take a partial order. Without any computations, how does this change your answer in part 2?

Alto Company currently produces component TH1 for its sole product. The current cost per unit to manufacture its required 400,000 units of TH1 follows.

Problem 10-3B
Make or buy

A1

Direct materials	$1.20
Direct labor	1.50
Overhead	6.00
Total cost per unit	$8.70

Direct materials and direct labor are 100% variable. Overhead is 75% fixed. An outside supplier has offered to supply the 400,000 units of TH1 for $4 per unit.

Required

1. Determine whether management should make or buy the TH1.
2. What factors besides cost must management consider when deciding whether to make or buy TH1?

Check (1) Incremental cost to make TH1, $1,680,000

Micron Manufacturing produces electronic equipment. This year, it produced 7,500 oscilloscopes at a manufacturing cost of $300 each. These oscilloscopes were damaged in the warehouse during storage and, while usable, cannot be sold at their regular selling price of $500 each. Management has investigated the matter and has identified three alternatives for these oscilloscopes.

Problem 10-4B
Sell or process

A1

1. They can be sold to a wholesaler for $75 each.
2. They can be disassembled at a cost of $400,000 and the parts sold to a recycler for $130 each.
3. They can be reworked and turned into good units. The cost of reworking the units will be $3,200,000, after which the units can be sold at their regular price of $500 each.

Required

Which alternative should management pursue? Show analysis for each alternative.

Check Incremental income for alternative 2, $575,000

Problem 10-5B

Analysis of sales mix strategies

A1

Sung Company is able to produce two products, R and T, with the same machine in its factory. The following information is available.

	Product R	Product T
Selling price per unit	$60	$80
Variable costs per unit	20	45
Contribution margin per unit	$40	$35
Machine hours to produce 1 unit	0.4 hours	1.0 hours
Maximum unit sales per month	550 units	175 units

The company presently operates the machine for a single eight-hour shift for 22 working days each month. Management is thinking about operating the machine for two shifts, which will increase its productivity by another eight hours per day for 22 days per month. This change would require $3,250 additional fixed costs per month.

Required

Check Units of Product R: (2) 440 (3) 550

1. Determine the contribution margin per machine hour that each product generates.

2. How many units of Product R and Product T should the company produce if it continues to operate with only one shift? How much total contribution margin does this mix produce each month?

3. If the company adds another shift, how many units of Product R and Product T should it produce? How much total contribution margin would this mix produce each month? Should the company add the new shift? Explain.

4. Suppose that the company determines that it can increase Product R's maximum sales to 675 units per month by spending $4,500 per month in marketing efforts. Should the company pursue this strategy and the double shift? Explain.

Problem 10-6B

Analysis of possible elimination of a department

A1

Esme Company's management is trying to decide whether to eliminate Department Z, which has produced low profits or losses for several years. The company's 2017 departmental income statements show the following.

ESME COMPANY
Departmental Income Statements
For Year Ended December 31, 2017

	Dept. A	Dept. Z	Combined
Sales	$700,000	$175,000	$875,000
Cost of goods sold	461,300	125,100	586,400
Gross profit	238,700	49,900	288,600
Operating expenses			
Direct expenses			
Advertising	27,000	3,000	30,000
Store supplies used	5,600	1,400	7,000
Depreciation—Store equipment	14,000	7,000	21,000
Total direct expenses	46,600	11,400	58,000
Allocated expenses			
Sales salaries	70,200	23,400	93,600
Rent expense	22,080	5,520	27,600
Bad debts expense	21,000	4,000	25,000
Office salary	20,800	5,200	26,000
Insurance expense	4,200	1,400	5,600
Miscellaneous office expenses	1,700	2,500	4,200
Total allocated expenses	139,980	42,020	182,000
Total expenses	186,580	53,420	240,000
Net income (loss)	$ 52,120	$ (3,520)	$ 48,600

In analyzing whether to eliminate Department Z, management considers the following items:

a. The company has one office worker who earns $500 per week or $26,000 per year and four salesclerks who each earns $450 per week, or $23,400 per year for each salesclerk.

b. The full salaries of three salesclerks are charged to Department A. The full salary of one salesclerk is charged to Department Z.

c. Eliminating Department Z would avoid the sales salaries and the office salary currently allocated to it. However, management prefers another plan. Two salesclerks have indicated that they will be quitting soon. Management believes that their work can be done by the two remaining clerks if the one office worker works in sales half-time. Eliminating Department Z will allow this shift of duties. If this change is implemented, half the office worker's salary would be reported as sales salaries and half would be reported as office salary.

d. The store building is rented under a long-term lease that cannot be changed. Therefore, Department A will use the space and equipment currently used by Department Z.

e. Closing Department Z will eliminate its expenses for advertising, bad debts, and store supplies; 65% of the insurance expense allocated to it to cover its merchandise inventory; and 30% of the miscellaneous office expenses presently allocated to it.

Required

1. Prepare a three-column report that lists items and amounts for (a) the company's total expenses (including cost of goods sold)—in column 1, (b) the expenses that would be eliminated by closing Department Z—in column 2, and (c) the expenses that will continue—in column 3.

2. Prepare a forecasted annual income statement for the company reflecting the elimination of Department Z assuming that it will not affect Department A's sales and gross profit. The statement should reflect the reassignment of the office worker to one-half time as a salesclerk.

Check (1) Total expenses: (a) $826,400, (b) $181,960

(2) Forecasted net income without Department Z, $55,560

Analysis Component

3. Reconcile the company's combined net income with the forecasted net income assuming that Department Z is eliminated (list both items and amounts). Analyze the reconciliation and explain why you think the department should or should not be eliminated.

(This serial problem began in Chapter 1 and continues through most of the book. If previous chapter segments were not completed, the serial problem can begin at this point.)

SP 10 Santana Rey has found that **Business Solutions**'s line of computer desks and chairs has become very popular, and she is finding it hard to keep up with demand. She knows that she cannot fill all of her orders for both items, so she decides she must determine the optimal sales mix given the resources she has available. Information about the desks and chairs follows.

SERIAL PROBLEM
Business Solutions

A1

© Alexander Image/Shutterstock RF

	Desks	Chairs
Selling price per unit	$1,125	$375
Variable costs per unit	500	200
Contribution margin per unit	$ 625	$175
Direct labor hours per unit	5 hours	4 hours
Expected demand for next quarter	175 desks	50 chairs

Santana has determined that she only has 1,015 direct labor hours available for the next quarter and wants to optimize her contribution margin given the limited number of direct labor hours available.

Required

Determine the optimal sales mix and the contribution margin the business will earn at that sales mix.

Beyond the Numbers

REPORTING IN ACTION

C1

APPLE

BTN 10-1 **Apple** currently chooses to buy (mainly from suppliers located in Asia)—rather than make—nearly all of its manufactured products. Assume you have been asked to analyze whether Apple should instead make its products.

Required

1. Provide examples of relevant costs that Apple should consider in this make or buy decision.
2. Provide examples of qualitative (nonfinancial) factors Apple should consider in this decision.

COMPARATIVE ANALYSIS

A1

APPLE
GOOGLE

BTN 10-2 **Apple** and **Google** sell a variety of products. Some products are more profitable than others. Teams of employees in each company make advertising, investment, and product mix decisions. A certain portion of advertising for both companies is on a local basis to a target audience.

Required

1. Contact the local newspaper and ask the approximate cost of ad space (for example, cost of one page or one-half page of advertising) for a company's product or group of products (such as Apple iPads).
2. Estimate how many products this advertisement must sell to justify its cost. Begin by taking the product's sales price advertised for each company and assume a 20% contribution margin.
3. Prepare a half-page memorandum explaining the importance of effective advertising when making a product mix decision. Be prepared to present your ideas in class.

ETHICS CHALLENGE

A1

BTN 10-3 Bert Asiago, a salesperson for Convertco, received an order from a potential new customer for 50,000 units of Convertco's single product at a price $25 below its regular selling price of $65. Asiago knows that Convertco has the capacity to produce this order without affecting regular sales. He has spoken to Convertco's controller, Bia Morgan, who has informed Asiago that at the $40 selling price, Convertco will not be covering its variable costs of $42 for the product, and she recommends the order not be accepted. Asiago knows that variable costs include his sales commission of $4 per unit. If he accepts a $2 per unit commission, the sale will produce a contribution margin of zero. Asiago is eager to get the new customer because he believes that this could lead to the new customer becoming a regular customer.

Required

1. Determine the contribution margin per unit on the order as determined by the controller.
2. Determine the contribution margin per unit on the order as determined by Asiago if he takes the lower commission.
3. Do you recommend Convertco accept the special order? What factors must management consider?

COMMUNICATING IN PRACTICE

C1

BTN 10-4 Assume that you work for Greeble's Department Store, and your manager requests that you outline the pros and cons of discontinuing its hardware department. That department appears to be generating losses, and your manager believes that discontinuing it will increase overall store profits.

Required

Prepare a memorandum to your manager outlining what Greeble's management should consider when trying to decide whether to discontinue its hardware department.

TAKING IT TO THE NET

A1

BTN 10-5 Many companies must determine whether to internally produce their component parts or to outsource them. Further, some companies now outsource key components or business processes to international providers. Access the website **SourcingMag.com** and review the available information on business process outsourcing (click on "What is BPO?").

Required

1. According to this website, what is business process outsourcing?
2. What types of processes are commonly outsourced, according to this website?
3. What are some of the benefits of business process outsourcing?

BTN 10-6 Break into teams and identify costs that an airline such as **Delta Airlines** would incur on a flight from Green Bay to Minneapolis. (1) Identify the individual costs as variable or fixed. (2) Assume that Delta is trying to decide whether to drop this flight because it seems to be unprofitable. Determine which costs are likely to be saved if the flight is dropped. Set up your answer in the following format.

TEAMWORK IN ACTION

C1

Cost	Variable or Fixed	Cost Saved If Flight Is Dropped	Rationale

BTN 10-7 Suppose Limor Fried expands her business, **Adafruit Industries**, to make electric scooters. Limor must decide on the best sales mix. Assume the company has a capacity of 400 hours of processing time available each month and it makes two types of scooters, Deluxe and Premium. Information on these products follows.

ENTREPRENEURIAL DECISION

A1

	Deluxe	Premium
Selling price per unit	$70	$90
Variable costs per unit	$40	$50
Processing minutes per unit	60 minutes	120 minutes

Required

1. Assume the markets for both types of scooters are unlimited. How many Deluxe scooters and how many Premium scooters should the company make each month? Explain. How much total contribution margin does this mix produce each month?

2. Assume the market for the Deluxe model is limited to 60 per month, with no market limit for the Premium model. How many Deluxe scooters and how many Premium scooters should the company make each month? Explain. How much total contribution margin does this mix produce each month?

BTN 10-8 Restaurants often add and remove menu items. Visit a restaurant and identify a new food item. Make a list of costs that the restaurant must consider when deciding whether to add that new item. Also, make a list of nonfinancial factors that the restaurant must consider when adding that item.

HITTING THE ROAD

C1

BTN 10-9 **Samsung**'s 2016 Corporate Sustainability Report notes that the company spent 523 billion Korean won in 2015 for programs devoted to better health and education for children.

GLOBAL DECISION

C1

Samsung

Required

Explain why a company like Samsung would pursue such a costly program.

 GLOBAL VIEW

Heinz India Private Limited, headquartered in India, is a maker of ketchup, energy drinks, and other products. The company recently decided to eliminate several unprofitable segments, including those that made biscuits and ready-to-eat packaged foods, in order to focus on more profitable segments. Analyses of avoidable and unavoidable expenses, along with consideration of these segments' potential impact on other segments, support such decisions.

🌐 **Global View Assignments**

Discussion Question 7

Discussion Question 10

BTN 10-9

11 Capital Budgeting and Investment Analysis

chapter

Learning Objectives

ANALYTICAL

A1 Analyze a capital investment project using break-even time.

PROCEDURAL

P1 Compute payback period and describe its use.

P2 Compute accounting rate of return and explain its use.

P3 Compute net present value and describe its use.

P4 Compute internal rate of return and explain its use.

Courtesy of Simply Gum

Chew On This

NEW YORK—Caron Proschan finished lunch and reached for a piece of chewing gum. In contrast to the organic juice and salad she just finished, the gum was a mix of "alien" colors and chemicals. "I thought . . . there must be a natural gum," insists Caron. "After researching it, I found out there wasn't one." So, Caron launched her company, **Simply Gum** (**SimplyGum.com**).

Simply Gum is made using natural flavors, a natural chicle base, organic ingredients, and no synthetics. "We experimented with a lot of ingredients and flavors," explains Caron. Compared with its two main competitors, which have 95% of U.S. gum sales, Simply Gum can quickly change its manufacturing process, flavors, and distribution. "Our recipe is never done," exclaims Adeena Cohen, senior marketing manager. "We're constantly perfecting flavor and texture."

Caron uses contribution margins to decide whether adding new flavors would increase profits and whether to eliminate less profitable flavors. Unlike some companies that can rework substandard materials, Caron explains that "raw materials that don't meet our standards never enter our production process."

"We want our gum to be everywhere"
—Caron Proschan

In addition to profits, Caron considers qualitative factors, including customer satisfaction. "We found out that people really want a better-for-you gum option," insists Caron.

In addition to short-term decisions involving sales mix, Simply Gum confronts long-run decisions on capital investments. "I assumed we'd find a contract manufacturer to make our gum, and we would figure out packaging, marketing, and sales," recalls Caron. "It turns out there was no manufacturer to make it, so we make it." This required Caron to consider the size of her manufacturing plant and the number and types of machines to use. Capital budgeting techniques—like payback period, net present value, and internal rate of return—help guide her.

Simply Gum now is sold in over 1,200 stores in the U.S. "We believe we've found a niche," proclaims Caron. She insists others can do the same if they "stay focused, work hard, and seek guidance."

Sources: *Simply Gum website,* January 2017; *The Wall Street Journal,* May 1, 2016; *Brandettes.com,* October 27, 2015; *Foodbusinessnews.net,* December 10, 2015; *Forbes.com,* January 11, 2016

Capital budgeting is the process of analyzing alternative long-term investments and deciding which assets to acquire or sell. Common examples of capital budgeting decisions include buying a machine or a building or acquiring an entire company. An objective for these decisions is to earn a satisfactory return on investment.

Exhibit 11.1 summarizes the capital budgeting process.

EXHIBIT 11.1

Capital Budgeting Process

The process begins when department or plant managers submit proposals for new investments in property, plant, and equipment. A capital budget committee, usually consists of members with accounting and finance expertise, evaluates the proposals and forms recommendations for approval or rejection. Finally, the board of directors approves the capital expenditures for the year.

Capital budgeting decisions require careful analysis because they are usually the most difficult and risky decisions that managers make. These decisions are difficult because they require predicting events that will not occur until well into the future. A capital budgeting decision is risky because (1) the outcome is uncertain, (2) large amounts of money are usually involved, (3) the investment involves a long-term commitment, and (4) the decision could be difficult or impossible to reverse, no matter how poor it turns out to be. Risk is especially high for investments in technology due to innovations and uncertainty.

Managers use several methods to evaluate capital budgeting decisions. Nearly all of these methods involve predicting future cash inflows and cash outflows of proposed investments, assessing the risk of and returns on those cash flows, and then choosing which investments to make. Exhibit 11.2 summarizes cash outflows (−) and cash inflows (+) over the life of a typical capital expenditure for a depreciable asset.

EXHIBIT 11.2

Capital Investment
Cash Flows

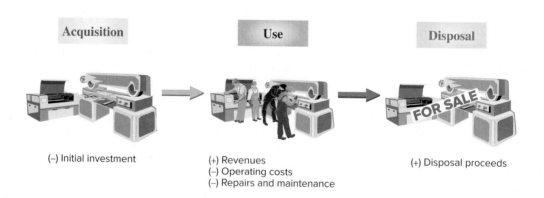

The investment begins with an initial cash outflow to acquire the depreciable asset. Over the asset's life it generates cash inflows from revenues. The asset also creates cash outflows for operating costs, repairs, and maintenance. Finally, the asset is disposed of, and its salvage value can provide another cash inflow.

Management often restates future cash flows in terms of their present value. This approach applies the time value of money: *A dollar today is worth more than a dollar tomorrow.* Similarly, a dollar tomorrow is worth less than a dollar today. Restating future cash flows in terms of their present value is called *discounting*. The time value of money is important when evaluating capital investments, but managers sometimes use methods that ignore it.

METHODS NOT USING TIME VALUE OF MONEY

All investments, whether they involve the purchase of a machine or another long-term asset, are expected to produce net cash flows. *Net cash flow* is cash inflows minus cash outflows. Sometimes managers perform simple analyses of the financial feasibility of an investment's net cash flow without using the time value of money. This section explains two common methods in this category: (1) payback period and (2) accounting rate of return.

Payback Period

An investment's **payback period (PBP)** is the expected amount of time to recover the initial investment amount. Managers prefer investing in assets with shorter payback periods to reduce the risk of an unprofitable investment over the long run. Acquiring assets with short payback periods reduces a company's risk from potentially inaccurate long-term predictions of future cash flows.

P1_____

Compute payback period and describe its use.

Payback Period with Even Cash Flows   To illustrate payback period for an investment with even cash flows, we look at data from FasTrac, a manufacturer of exercise equipment and supplies. (*Even cash flows* are cash flows that are the same amount each year; *uneven cash flows* are cash flows that are not all equal in amount.) FasTrac is considering several different capital investments, one of which is to purchase a machine to use in manufacturing a new product. The machine has these features:

Cost...	$16,000
Useful life	8 years
Salvage value	$0
Expected production per year..................	1,000 units
Product selling price per unit................	$30

Exhibit 11.3 shows the expected annual net income and expected annual net cash flows for this asset over its life.

EXHIBIT 11.3

Cash Flow Analysis

FASTRAC Cash Flow Analysis—Machinery Investment	Expected Net Income	Expected Net Cash Flow
Annual sales of new product	$30,000	$30,000
Less annual expenses		
Materials, labor, and overhead (except depreciation)	15,500	15,500
Depreciation—Machinery.......................................	2,000	
Additional selling and administrative expenses	9,500	9,500
Annual pretax income.......................................	3,000	
Income taxes (30% of pretax income)	900	900
Annual net income	$ 2,100	
Annual net cash flow...		$ 4,100

Point: The payback method uses cash flows, not net income.

The amount of net cash flow from the machinery is computed by subtracting expected cash outflows from expected cash inflows. The Expected Net Cash Flow column of Exhibit 11.3 excludes all noncash revenues and expenses. Because depreciation does not impact cash flows, it is excluded. Alternatively, managers can adjust the projected net income for revenue and expense items that do not affect cash flows. For FasTrac, this means taking the $2,100 net income and adding back the $2,000 depreciation, to yield $4,100 of net cash flow.

The formula for computing the payback period of an investment that produces even net cash flows is in Exhibit 11.4.

EXHIBIT 11.4

Payback Period Formula with Even Cash Flows

$$\text{Payback period} = \frac{\text{Cost of investment}}{\text{Annual net cash flow}}$$

The payback period reflects the amount of time for the investment to generate enough net cash flow to return (or pay back) the cash initially invested to purchase it. FasTrac's payback period for this machine is just under four years.

$$\text{Payback period} = \frac{\$16,000}{\$4,100} = 3.9 \text{ years}$$

Point: Excel for payback.

	A	B
1	Investment	$16,000
2	Cash flow	$4,100
3	Payback period	◄

=B1/B2 = 3.9

The initial investment is fully recovered in 3.9 years, or just before reaching the halfway point of this machine's useful life of eight years.

Companies prefer short payback periods to increase return and reduce risk. The more quickly a company receives cash, the sooner it is available for other uses and the less time it is at risk of loss. A shorter payback period also improves the company's ability to respond to unanticipated changes and lowers its risk of having to keep an unprofitable investment.

■ Decision Insight

e-Payback   Health care providers are increasingly using electronic systems to improve their operations. With *e-charting,* doctors' orders and notes are saved electronically. Such systems allow for more personalized care plans, more efficient staffing, and reduced costs. Investments in such systems are evaluated on the basis of payback periods and other financial measures. ■

© Tetra Images/Getty Images

Payback Period with Uneven Cash Flows

What happens if the net cash flows are uneven? In this case, the payback period is computed using the *cumulative total of net cash flows.* The word *cumulative* refers to the addition of each period's net cash flows as we progress through time. To illustrate, consider data for another investment that FasTrac is considering. This machine is predicted to generate uneven net cash flows over the next eight years. The relevant data and payback period computation are shown in Exhibit 11.5.

Year 0 refers to the date of initial investment at which the $16,000 cash outflow occurs to acquire the machinery. By the end of year 1, the cumulative net cash flow is reduced to $(13,000), computed as the $(16,000) initial cash outflow plus year 1's $3,000 cash inflow. This process continues throughout the asset's life. The cumulative net cash flow amount changes from negative to positive in year 5. Specifically, at the end of year 4, the cumulative net cash flow is $(1,000). As soon as FasTrac receives net cash inflow of $1,000 during the fifth year, it has fully recovered the $16,000 initial investment. If we assume that cash flows are received uniformly *within* each year, receipt of the $1,000 occurs about one-fifth (0.20) of the way through the fifth year. This is computed as $1,000 divided by year 5's total net cash flow of $5,000, or 0.20. This yields a payback period of 4.2 years, computed as 4 years plus 0.20 of year 5.

EXHIBIT 11.5

Payback Period Calculation
with Uneven Cash Flows

Period*	Expected Net Cash Flows	Cumulative Net Cash Flows
Year 0	$(16,000)	$(16,000)
Year 1	3,000	(13,000)
Year 2	4,000	(9,000)
Year 3	4,000	(5,000)
Year 4	4,000	**(1,000)**
Year 5	**5,000**	**4,000**
Year 6	3,000	7,000
Year 7	2,000	9,000
Year 8	2,000	11,000
Payback period = 4 years + $1,000/$5,000 of year 5 = 4.2 years		

Payback occurs between years 4 and 5.

Example: Find the payback period in Exhibit 11.5 if net cash flows for the first 4 years are: Year 1 = $6,000; Year 2 = $5,000; Year 3 = $4,000; Year 4 = $3,000. *Answer:* 3.33 years

* All cash inflows and outflows occur uniformly within each year 1 through 8.

Evaluating Payback Period   Payback period has two strengths.

- It uses cash flows, not income.
- It is easy to use.

Payback period has three main weaknesses.

- It does not reflect differences in the *timing* of net cash flows within the payback period.
- It ignores *all* cash flows after the point where an investment's costs are fully recovered.
- It ignores the time value of money.

To illustrate, if FasTrac had another investment with predicted cash inflows of $9,000, $3,000, $2,000, $1,800, and $1,000 in its first 5 years, its payback period would be 4.2 years. However, this alternative is more desirable because it returns cash more quickly. In addition, an investment with a 3-year payback period that stops producing cash after 4 years is likely not as good as an alternative with a 5-year payback period that generates net cash flows for 15 years. Because of these limitations, payback period should never be the only consideration in capital budgeting decisions.

A company is considering purchasing equipment costing $75,000. Future annual net cash flows from this equipment are $30,000, $25,000, $15,000, $10,000, and $5,000. Cash flows occur uniformly within each year. What is this investment's payback period?

NEED-TO-KNOW 11-1

Payback Period

P1

Solution

Period	Expected Net Cash Flows	Cumulative Net Cash Flows
Year 0	$(75,000)	$(75,000)
Year 1	30,000	(45,000)
Year 2	25,000	(20,000)
Year 3	15,000	(5,000)
Year 4	10,000	5,000
Year 5	5,000	10,000
Payback period = 3.5 years, computed as 3 + $5,000/$10,000		

Payback occurs between years 3 and 4.

Do More: QS 11-1, QS 11-5, E 11-1, E 11-3, E 11-5

Accounting Rate of Return

The **accounting rate of return (ARR)** is the percentage accounting return on annual average investment. It is called an "accounting" return because it is based on net income, rather than on cash flows. It is computed by dividing a project's after-tax net income by the average amount invested in it. To illustrate, we return to FasTrac's $16,000 machinery investment described in

P2

Compute accounting rate of return and explain its use.

Exhibit 11.3. We first compute (1) the after-tax net income and (2) the average amount invested. The $2,100 after-tax net income is from Exhibit 11.3.

If a company uses straight-line depreciation, we find the average amount invested by using the formula in Exhibit 11.6. Because FasTrac uses straight-line depreciation, its average amount invested for the eight years equals the sum of the book value at the beginning of the asset's investment period and the book value at the end of its investment period, divided by 2, as shown in Exhibit 11.6.

EXHIBIT 11.6

Computing Average Amount Invested under Straight-Line Depreciation

$$\text{Annual average investment} = \frac{\text{Beginning book value} + \text{Ending book value}}{2}$$
$$\text{(straight-line case only)}$$
$$= \frac{\$16,000 + \$0}{2} = \$8,000$$

If an investment has a salvage value, the average amount invested when using straight-line depreciation is computed as (Beginning book value + Salvage value)/2.

If a company uses a depreciation method other than straight-line, for example, MACRS for tax purposes, the calculation of average book value is more complicated. In this case, the book value of the asset is computed for *each year* of its life. The general formula for the annual average investment is shown in Exhibit 11.7.

EXHIBIT 11.7

General Formula for Average Amount Invested

$$\text{Annual average investment} = \frac{\text{Sum of individual years' average book values}}{\text{Number of years of the planned investment}}$$
$$\text{(general case)}$$

Once we determine the annual after-tax net income and the annual average amount invested, the accounting rate of return is computed as shown in Exhibit 11.8. The numbers used are from FasTrac.

EXHIBIT 11.8

Accounting Rate of Return Formula

$$\text{Accounting rate of return} = \frac{\text{Annual after-tax net income}}{\text{Annual average investment}}$$
$$= \frac{\$2,100}{\$8,000} = 26.25\%$$

	A	B
1	Beg. book value	$16,000
2	End. book value	$0
3	Net income	$2,100
4	Acctg rate of return	

=B3/((B1+B2)/2) = 26.25%

FasTrac management must decide whether a 26.25% accounting rate of return is satisfactory. To make this decision, we must consider the investment's risk. We cannot say an investment with a 26.25% return is preferred over one with a lower return unless we consider any differences in risk. When comparing investments with similar lives and risk, a company will prefer the investment with the higher accounting rate of return.

Evaluating Accounting Rate of Return   The accounting rate of return has three weaknesses.

- It ignores the time value of money.
- It focuses on income, not cash flows.
- If income (and thus the accounting rate of return) varies from year to year, the project might appear desirable in some years and not in others.

Because of these limitations, the accounting rate of return should never be the only consideration in capital budgeting decisions.

The following data relate to a company's decision on whether to purchase a machine:

Cost	$180,000
Salvage value	15,000
Annual after-tax net income	40,000

Assume the company uses straight-line depreciation. What is the machine's accounting rate of return?

Solution

Annual average investment = ($180,000 + $15,000)/2 = $97,500
Accounting rate of return = $40,000/$97,500 = 41% (rounded)

NEED-TO-KNOW 11-2

Accounting Rate of Return

P2

Do More: QS 11-6, QS 11-7, E 11-7, E 11-8

METHODS USING TIME VALUE OF MONEY

This section describes two capital budgeting methods that use the time value of money: (1) net present value and (2) internal rate of return. *(To apply these methods, you need a basic understanding of the concept of present value. An expanded explanation of present value concepts is in Appendix B near the end of the book. You can use the present value tables at the end of Appendix B to solve many of this chapter's assignments that use time value of money. Spreadsheet software like Excel and financial calculators can also be used.)*

Net Present Value

Net present value analysis applies the time value of money to future cash inflows and cash outflows so management can evaluate a project's benefits and costs at one point in time. Specifically, **net present value (NPV)** is computed by discounting the future net cash flows from the investment at the project's required rate of return and then subtracting the initial amount invested. A company's required return, often called its *hurdle rate,* is typically its **cost of capital,** which is an average of the rate the company must pay to its lenders.

To illustrate, let's return to FasTrac's proposed machinery purchase described in Exhibit 11.3. Does this machine provide a satisfactory return while recovering the amount invested? Recall that the machine requires a $16,000 investment and is expected to provide $4,100 annual net cash inflows for the next eight years. If we assume that net cash inflows from this machine are received at each year-end and that FasTrac requires a 12% annual return, net present value can be computed as in Exhibit 11.9.

Methods Using Time Value of Money

P3

Compute net present value and describe its use.

Point: The assumption of end-of-year cash flows simplifies computations and is common in practice.

EXHIBIT 11.9

Net Present Value Calculation with Equal Cash Flows

	Net Cash Flows*	Present Value of 1 at 12%**	Present Value of Net Cash Flows
Year 1	$ 4,100	0.8929	$ 3,661
Year 2	4,100	0.7972	3,269
Year 3	4,100	0.7118	2,918
Year 4	4,100	0.6355	2,606
Year 5	4,100	0.5674	2,326
Year 6	4,100	0.5066	2,077
Year 7	4,100	0.4523	1,854
Year 8	4,100	0.4039	1,656
Totals	$32,800		20,367
Initial investment			(16,000)
Net present value			$ 4,367

* Cash flows occur at the end of each year.
** Present value of 1 factors are taken from Table B.1 in Appendix B.

Example: What is the net present value in Exhibit 11.9 if a 10% return is applied? *Answer:* $5,873

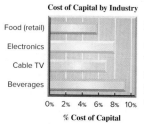

Cost of Capital by Industry

Food (retail)

Electronics

Cable TV

Beverages

0% 2% 4% 6% 8% 10%

% Cost of Capital

Source: pages.stern.nyu.edu/
~adamodar/

Point: Cost of capital computation is covered in advanced courses.

The first number column of Exhibit 11.9 shows annual net cash flows. Present value of 1 factors, also called *discount factors,* are shown in the second column. Taken from Table B.1 in Appendix B, they assume that net cash flows are received at each year-end. *(To simplify present value computations and for assignment material at the end of this chapter, we assume that net cash flows are received at year-end.)* Annual net cash flows from Exhibit 11.9 are multiplied by the discount factors to give present values of annual net cash flows in the far-right column. These annual amounts are summed to yield total present value of net cash flows of $20,367.

The last three lines of Exhibit 11.9 show the NPV computations. The asset's $16,000 initial cost is deducted from the $20,367 total present value of all future net cash flows to give this asset's NPV of $4,367. This means the present value of this machine's future net cash flows exceeds the initial $16,000 investment by $4,367. FasTrac should invest in this machine. **Rule: If NPV > 0, invest.**

Net Present Value Decision Rule

The decision rule in applying NPV is as follows: When an asset's expected future cash flows yield a *positive* net present value when discounted at the required rate of return, the asset should be acquired. This decision rule is reflected in the graphic below. When comparing several investment opportunities of similar cost and risk, we prefer the one with the highest positive net present value.

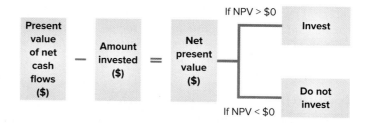

Simplifying Computations—Annuity

The computations in Exhibit 11.9 use separate present value of 1 factors for each of the eight years. Each year's net cash flow is multiplied by its present value of 1 factor to determine its present value; these are then added to give the asset's total present value. This computation can be simplified if annual net cash flows are equal in amount. A series of cash flows of equal dollar amount is called an **annuity.** In this case we use Table B.3, which gives the present value of 1 to be received periodically for a number of periods. To determine the present value of these eight annual receipts discounted at 12%, go down the 12% column of Table B.3 to the factor on the eighth line. This cumulative discount factor, also known as an *annuity* factor, is 4.9676. We then compute the $20,367 present value for these eight annual $4,100 receipts, computed as 4.9676 × $4,100. These calculations are summarized below.

Example: Why does the net present value of an investment increase when a lower discount rate is used? *Answer:* The present value of net cash flows increases.

Point: Excel for NPV.

	A	B
1	Investment	$16,000
2	Cash flow	$4,100
3	Periods	8
4	Interest rate	12%
5	Net present value	◄

=PV(B4,B3,−B2)−B1 = $4,367

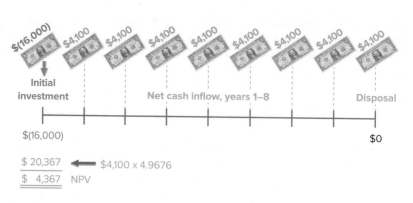

$ 20,367 ◄ $4,100 x 4.9676

$ 4,367   NPV

With a financial calculator:

N   8
I/Y   12
PMT   4100
CPT   PV
Multiply answer ($−20,367) by −1 since the company is receiving cash, and subtract initial investment ($16,000) to yield NPV of $4,367.

Simplifying Computations—Calculator or Excel

Another way to simplify present value calculations, whether net cash flows are equal in amount or not, is to use a calculator with compound interest functions or a spreadsheet program. Whatever procedure you use, it is important to understand the concepts behind these computations.

Decision Ethics

Systems Manager Management adopts a policy requiring purchases above $5,000 to be submitted with cash flow projections for capital budget approval. As systems manager, you want to upgrade your computers at a $25,000 cost. You consider submitting several orders each under $5,000 to avoid the approval process. You believe the computers will increase profits and wish to avoid a delay. What do you do? ■ *Answer: Your dilemma is whether to abide by rules designed to prevent abuse or to bend them to acquire an investment that you believe will benefit the firm. You should not pursue the latter action because breaking up the order into small components is dishonest and there are consequences. Develop a proposal for the entire package and then do all you can to expedite its processing, particularly by pointing out its benefits.*

Net Present Value Complications

The following factors can complicate NPV analysis. We discuss each of them.

- Unequal cash flows
- Salvage value
- Accelerated depreciation
- Comparing positive NPV projects
- Capital rationing
- Inflation

Uneven Cash Flows   Net present value analysis can also be used when net cash flows are uneven (unequal). To illustrate, assume that FasTrac can choose only one capital investment from among Projects A, B, and C. Each project requires the same $12,000 initial investment. Future net cash flows for each project are shown in the first three number columns of Exhibit 11.10.

EXHIBIT 11.10

Net Present Value Calculation with Uneven Cash Flows

	Net Cash Flows			Present Value of 1 at 10%	Present Value of Net Cash Flows		
	A	B	C		A	B	C
Year 1	$ 5,000	$ 8,000	$ 1,000	0.9091	$ 4,546	$ 7,273	$ 909
Year 2	5,000	5,000	5,000	0.8264	4,132	4,132	4,132
Year 3	5,000	2,000	9,000	0.7513	3,757	1,503	6,762
Totals	$15,000	$15,000	$15,000		12,435	12,908	11,803
Initial investment					(12,000)	(12,000)	(12,000)
Net present value					$ 435	$ 908	$ (197)

The three projects in Exhibit 11.10 have the same expected total net cash flows of $15,000. Project A is expected to produce equal amounts of $5,000 each year. Project B is expected to produce a larger amount in the first year. Project C is expected to produce a larger amount in the third year. The fourth column of Exhibit 11.10 shows the present value of 1 factors from Table B.1 assuming 10% required return.

Computations in the three rightmost columns show that Project A has a $435 positive NPV. Project B has the largest NPV of $908 because it brings in cash more quickly. Project C has a $(197) *negative* NPV because its larger cash inflows are delayed. Projects with higher cash flows in earlier years generally yield higher net present values. If FasTrac requires a 10% return, it should reject Project C because its NPV implies a return *under* 10%. If only one project can be accepted, Project B appears best because it yields the highest NPV.

Salvage Value   FasTrac predicted the $16,000 machine to have zero salvage value at the end of its useful life. In many cases, assets are expected to have salvage values. If so, this amount is an additional net cash inflow expected to be received at the end of the final year of the asset's life. All other computations remain the same. For example, the net present value of the $16,000 investment that yields $4,100 of net cash flows for eight years is $4,367, as shown in Exhibit 11.9. If that machine is expected to have a $1,500 salvage value at the end of its eight-year life, the present value of this salvage amount is $606 (computed as $1,500 × 0.4039). The net present value of the machine, including the present value of its expected salvage amount, is $4,973 (computed as $4,367 + $606).

Example: If 12% is the required return in Exhibit 11.10, which project is preferred? Answer: Project B. Net present values are: A = $10; B = $553; C = $(715).

Example: Will the rankings of Projects A, B, and C change with the use of different discount rates, assuming the same rate is used for all projects? Answer: No; only the NPV amounts will change.

Point: Excel for PV of salvage value.

	A	B
1	Salvage value	$1,500
2	Useful life	8
3	Interest rate	12%
4	Present value	

=PV(B3,B2,0,−B1) = $606

Accelerated Depreciation   Depreciation methods can affect net present value analysis. FasTrac computes depreciation using the straight-line method. Accelerated depreciation is commonly used for income tax purposes. Accelerated depreciation produces larger depreciation deductions in the early years of an asset's life and smaller deductions in later years. This pattern results in smaller income tax payments in early years and larger tax payments in later years. Accelerated depreciation does not change the basics of a present value analysis, but it can change the result. Using accelerated depreciation for tax reporting increases the NPV of an asset's cash flows because it produces larger net cash inflows in the early years of the asset's life. Using accelerated depreciation for tax reporting always makes an investment more desirable because early cash flows are more valuable than later ones.

Comparing Positive NPV Projects   When considering several projects of similar investment amounts and risk levels, we can compare the different projects' NPVs and rank them on the dollar amounts of their NPVs. However, if the amount invested differs substantially across projects, this is of limited value for comparison purposes. One way to compare projects, especially when a company cannot fund all positive net present value projects, is to use the **profitability index,** which is computed as

$$\text{Profitability index} = \frac{\textbf{Present value of net cash flows}}{\textbf{Initial investment}}$$

Exhibit 11.11 illustrates computation of the profitability index for three potential investments. A profitability index less than 1 indicates an investment with a *negative* net present value. Investment 3 shows an index of 0.9, meaning a negative NPV. This means we can drop #3 from consideration. Both Investments 1 and 2 have profitability indexes greater than 1, thus they have positive net present values. Investment 1's NPV equals $150,000 (computed as $900,000 − $750,000); Investment 2's NPV equals $125,000 (computed as $375,000 − $250,000). Ideally, the company would accept all positive NPV projects, but if forced to choose, it should select the project with the higher profitability index. Thus, Investment 2 is ranked ahead of Investment 1 based on its higher profitability index. **Rule:** Invest in the project with the highest profitability index.

EXHIBIT 11.11

Profitability Index

	Investment		
	1	**2**	**3**
Present value of net cash flows (a)	$900,000	$375,000	$270,000
Amount invested (b)	750,000	250,000	300,000
Profitability index (a)/(b)	**1.2**	**1.5**	**0.9**

Capital Rationing   Some firms face **capital rationing,** or financing constraints that limit them from accepting all positive NPV projects. This can be in two forms, hard rationing and soft rationing. *Hard rationing* is imposed by external forces, such as debt covenants that restrict the firm's ability to borrow more money. *Soft rationing* is internally imposed by management and the board of directors. For example, management might place spending limits on certain employees until they show they can make good decisions. Whether due to hard or soft capital rationing, the profitability index can be used to select the best of several competing projects.

Inflation   Large price-level increases should be considered in NPV analyses. Discount rates should already include inflation forecasts. Net cash flows can be adjusted for inflation by using *future value* computations. For example, if the expected net cash inflow in year 1 is $4,100 and 5% inflation is expected, then the expected net cash inflow in year 2 is $4,305, computed as $4,100 × 1.05 (1.05 is the future value of $1 [Table B.2] for 1 period with a 5% rate).

A company is considering two potential projects. Each project requires a $20,000 initial investment and is expected to generate end-of-year annual cash flows as shown below. Assuming a discount rate of 10%, compute the net present value of each project.

NEED-TO-KNOW 11-3

Net Present Value

P3

	Net Cash Inflows			
	Year 1	**Year 2**	**Year 3**	**Total**
Project A	$12,000	$8,500	$ 4,000	$24,500
Project B	4,500	8,500	13,000	26,000

Solution

Net present values are computed as follows.

			Project A		**Project B**	
Year	Present Value of 1 at 10%	Net Cash Flows	Present Value of Net Cash Flows	Net Cash Flows	Present Value of Net Cash Flows
1	0.9091	$12,000	$ 10,909	$ 4,500	$ 4,091
2	0.8264	8,500	7,024	8,500	7,024
3	0.7513	4,000	3,005	13,000	9,767
Totals		$24,500	$ 20,938	$26,000	$ 20,882
Initial investment			(20,000)		(20,000)
Net present value			$ 938		$ 882

Do More: QS 11-2, QS 11-8, QS 11-9, QS 11-11, E 11-2, E 11-6, E 11-9

Internal Rate of Return

Another means to evaluate capital investments is to use the **internal rate of return (IRR)**, which equals the discount rate that yields an NPV of zero for an investment. This means that if we compute the total present value of a project's net cash flows using the IRR as the discount rate and then subtract the initial investment from this total present value, we get a zero NPV.

P4

Compute internal rate of return and explain its use.

To illustrate, we use the data for FasTrac's Project A from Exhibit 11.10 to compute its IRR. Below is the two-step process for computing IRR with even cash flows.

Step 1: Compute the present value factor for the investment project.

$$\text{Present value factor} = \frac{\text{Amount invested}}{\text{Annual net cash flows}} = \frac{\$12,000}{\$5,000} = 2.4000$$

Step 2: Identify the discount rate (IRR) yielding the present value factor.

Search Table B.3 for a present value factor of 2.4000 in the 3-year row (equaling the 3-year project duration). The 12% discount rate yields a present value factor of 2.4018. This implies that the IRR is approximately 12%.

When cash flows are equal, as with Project A, we compute the present value factor by dividing the initial investment by its annual net cash flows. We then use an annuity table to determine the discount rate equal to this present value factor. For FasTrac's Project A, we look across the 3-period row of Table B.3 and find that the discount rate corresponding to the present value

Net Cash Flows Project A

Investment . . . . $(12,000)
Year 1 5,000
Year 2 5,000
Year 3 5,000
Hurdle rate = 10%

Point: Excel for IRR.

	A	B
1	Investment	–$12,000
2	Cash flow year 1	5,000
3	Cash flow year 2	5,000
4	Cash flow year 3	5,000
5	Internal rate of return	

=IRR(B1:B4) = 12.04%

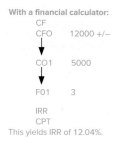

factor of 2.4000 roughly equals the 2.4018 value for the 12% rate. This row of Table B.3 is reproduced here:

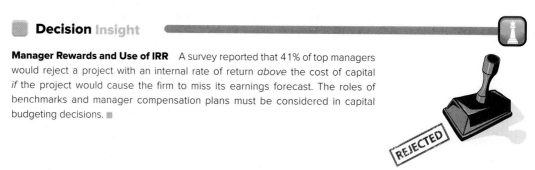

Present Value of an Annuity of 1 for Three Periods					
			Discount Rate		
Periods	1%	5%	10%	12%	15%
3	2.9410	2.7232	2.4869	**2.4018**	2.2832

The 12% rate is the project's IRR. Because this project's IRR is greater than the hurdle rate of 10%, it should be accepted. **Rule:** If IRR > hurdle rate, invest.

Uneven Cash Flows   If net cash flows are uneven, it is best to use either a calculator or spreadsheet software to compute IRR. We can also use trial and error to compute IRR. We do this by selecting any reasonable discount rate and computing the NPV. If the amount is positive (negative), we recompute the NPV using a higher (lower) discount rate. We continue these steps until we reach a point where two consecutive computations result in NPVs having different signs (positive and negative). Because the NPV is zero using IRR, we know that the IRR lies between these two discount rates. We can then estimate its value.

▣ **Decision** Insight ━━━━━━━━━━━━━━━━━━━━━━━━━━━━━━━

Manager Rewards and Use of IRR   A survey reported that 41% of top managers would reject a project with an internal rate of return *above* the cost of capital *if* the project would cause the firm to miss its earnings forecast. The roles of benchmarks and manager compensation plans must be considered in capital budgeting decisions. ▦

Use of Internal Rate of Return   To use the IRR to evaluate a project, compare it to a predetermined **hurdle rate,** which is a minimum acceptable rate of return. The decision rule using IRR is applied as follows:

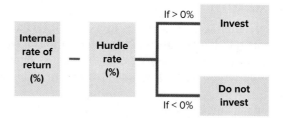

Management selects the hurdle rate to use in evaluating capital investments. If the IRR is higher than the hurdle rate, the investment should be made.

Comparing Projects Using IRR   Multiple projects are often ranked by the extent to which their IRR exceeds the hurdle rate. IRR can be used to compare projects with different amounts invested because the IRR is expressed as a percent rather than as a dollar value in NPV. The NPV approach is preferred to the IRR method when considering projects where the net annual cash flows change sign more than once over the project. This complication is explained in advanced courses.

▣ **Decision** Maker ━━━━━━━━━━━━━━━━━━━━━━━━━━━━━━━

Entrepreneur   You are developing a new product and you use a 12% discount rate to compute its NPV. Your banker, from whom you hope to obtain a loan, expresses concern that your discount rate is too low. How do you respond? ▦   *Answer:* The banker is probably concerned because new products are risky and should therefore be evaluated using a higher rate of return. You should conduct a thorough technical analysis and obtain detailed market data and information about any similar products. These factors might support the use of a lower return. You must convince yourself that the risk level is consistent with the discount rate used. You should also be confident that your company has the capacity and the resources to handle the new product.

A machine costing $58,880 is expected to generate net cash flows of $8,000 per year for each of the next 10 years.

1. Compute the machine's internal rate of return (IRR).

2. If a company's hurdle rate is 6.5%, use IRR to determine whether the company should purchase this machine.

Solution

1. PV factor = Amount invested/Net cash flows = $58,880/$8,000 = 7.36. Scanning the "Periods equal 10" row in Table B.3 for a present value factor near 7.36 indicates the IRR is <u>6%</u>.

2. The machine should <u>not</u> be purchased because its IRR (6%) is less than the company's hurdle rate (6.5%).

Comparison of Capital Budgeting Methods

We explained four methods that managers use to evaluate capital investment projects. How do these methods compare with each other? Exhibit 11.12 addresses that question. Neither the payback period nor the accounting rate of return considers the time value of money. Both the net present value and the internal rate of return do.

EXHIBIT 11.12

Comparing Capital Budgeting Methods

	Payback Period	Accounting Rate of Return	Net Present Value	Internal Rate of Return
Measurement basis	• Cash flows	• Accrual income	• Cash flows	• Cash flows
Measurement unit	• Years	• Percent	• Dollars	• Percent
Strengths	• Easy to understand • Allows comparison of projects	• Easy to understand • Allows comparison of projects	• Reflects time value of money • Reflects varying risks over project's life	• Reflects time value of money • Allows comparisons of dissimilar projects
Limitations	• Ignores time value of money • Ignores cash flows after payback period	• Ignores time value of money • Ignores annual rates over life of project	• Difficult to compare dissimilar projects	• Ignores varying risks over life of project

● Payback period is probably the simplest method. It gives managers an estimate of how soon they will recover their initial investment. Managers sometimes use this method when they have limited cash to invest and a number of projects to choose from.

● Accounting rate of return yields a percent measure computed using accrual income instead of cash flows. The accounting rate of return is an average rate for the entire investment period.

● Net present value considers all estimated net cash flows for the project's expected life. It can be applied to even and uneven cash flows and can reflect changes in the level of risk over a project's life. Because NPV yields a dollar measure, comparing projects of unequal sizes is more difficult. The profitability index, based on each project's net present value, can be used in this case.

● Internal rate of return considers all cash flows from a project. It is readily computed when the cash flows are even but requires some trial and error or use of a financial calculator or computer when cash flows are uneven. Because the IRR is a percent measure, it is readily used to compare projects with different investment amounts. However, IRR does not reflect changes in risk over a project's life.

Decision Insight

And the Winner Is . . .   How do we choose among the methods for evaluating capital investments? Management surveys consistently show the internal rate of return (IRR) as the most popular method, followed by the payback period and net present value (NPV). Few companies use the accounting rate of return (ARR), but nearly all use more than one method. ■

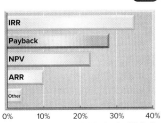
Company Usage of Capital Budgeting Methods

SUSTAINABILITY AND ACCOUNTING

Net present value calculations extend to investments in sustainable energy sources like solar power. To illustrate, consider a potential investment of $11,000 in a solar panel system in Phoenix. The system is expected to last for 30 years and require $100 of maintenance costs per year. The typical home uses 14,000 kilowatt hours (kWh) of electricity per year, at a cost of $0.12 per kilowatt hour. According to the **National Renewable Energy Laboratory** (**pvwatts.nrel.gov**), a typical solar panel system in Phoenix could supply 8,642 kilowatts of electricity per year. The net present value of a potential investment in a solar panel system, using a 6% discount rate, is computed in Exhibit 11.13. The NPV is $1,898, indicating the investment should be accepted.

EXHIBIT 11.13

NPV of Solar Investment

Electricity cost savings (8,642 × $0.12)	$ 1,037
Annual maintenance costs.	(100)
Net annual cash inflows.	$ 937
Present value of net cash inflows ($937 × 13.7648*)	$12,898
Initial investment	(11,000)
Net present value	**$ 1,898**

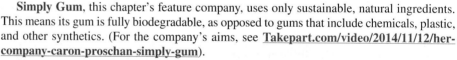

*From Table B.3: 30 periods, 6%

Predicting the future benefits of solar panel installations in terms of reduced energy costs, however, is challenging for several reasons. First, the amount of solar energy that can be produced depends on geographic location, with locations nearer the equator typically better. Second, south-facing roofs are better able to capture solar energy than other orientations. Third, cost savings from solar energy require predictions of the future costs of other sources of power, which can be volatile. These factors must be considered when performing a net present value calculation on a potential investment in solar power.

© Mike Coppola/Getty Images

Simply Gum, this chapter's feature company, uses only sustainable, natural ingredients. This means its gum is fully biodegradable, as opposed to gums that include chemicals, plastic, and other synthetics. (For the company's aims, see **Takepart.com/video/2014/11/12/her-company-caron-proschan-simply-gum**).

Simply Gum also uses recyclable materials for its packaging. Each piece of its gum includes a "post-chew" wrapper for convenient and clean disposal.

Decision Analysis   Break-Even Time

A1 _____

Analyze a capital investment project using break-even time.

The first section of this chapter explained several methods to evaluate capital investments. Break-even time of an investment project is a variation of the payback period method that overcomes the limitation of not using the time value of money. **Break-even time (BET)** is a time-based measure used to evaluate a capital investment's acceptability. Its computation yields a measure of expected time, reflecting the time period until the *present value* of the net cash flows from an investment equals the initial cost of the investment. In basic terms, break-even time is computed by restating future cash flows in terms of present values and then determining the payback period using these present values.

To illustrate, we return to the FasTrac case involving a $16,000 investment in machinery. The annual net cash flows from this investment are projected at $4,100 for eight years. Exhibit 11.14 shows the computation of break-even time for this investment decision.

The rightmost column of this exhibit shows that break-even time is between 5 and 6 years, or about 5.2 years—also see margin graph (where the line crosses the zero point). This is the time the project takes to break even after considering the time value of money (recall that the payback period computed without considering the time value of money was 3.9 years). We interpret this as cash flows earned after 5.2 years contribute to a positive net present value that, in this case, eventually amounts to $5,872.

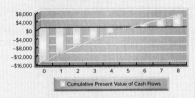

EXHIBIT 11.14

Break-Even Time Analysis*

Year	Cash Flows	Present Value of 1 at 10%	Present Value of Cash Flows	Cumulative Present Value of Cash Flows
0	$(16,000)	1.0000	$(16,000)	$(16,000)
1	4,100	0.9091	3,727	(12,273)
2	4,100	0.8264	3,388	(8,885)
3	4,100	0.7513	3,080	(5,805)
4	4,100	0.6830	2,800	(3,005)
5	4,100	0.6209	2,546	(459)
6	4,100	0.5645	2,314	1,855
7	4,100	0.5132	2,104	3,959
8	4,100	0.4665	1,913	5,872

Break-even time

* The time of analysis is the start of year 1 (same as end of year 0). All cash flows occur at the end of each year.

Break-even time is a useful measure for managers because it identifies the point in time when they can expect the cash flows to begin to yield net positive returns. Managers expect a positive net present value from an investment if break-even time is less than the investment's estimated life. The method allows managers to compare and rank alternative investments, giving the project with the shortest break-even time the highest rank.

Cumulative Present Value of Cash Flows

■ Decision Maker

Investment Manager Management asks you, the investment manager, to evaluate three alternative investments. Investment recovery time is crucial because cash is scarce. The time value of money is also important. Which capital budgeting method(s) do you use to assess the investments? ■ *Answer: You should probably focus on either the payback period or break-even time because both the time value of money and recovery time are important. The break-even time method is superior because it accounts for the time value of money, which is an important consideration in this decision.*

White Company can invest in one of two projects, TD1 or TD2. Each project requires an initial investment of $101,250 and produces the year-end cash inflows shown in the following table.

NEED-TO-KNOW 11-5

COMPREHENSIVE

	Net Cash Flows	
	TD1	**TD2**
Year 1	$ 20,000	$ 40,000
Year 2	30,000	40,000
Year 3	70,000	40,000
Totals	$120,000	$120,000

Required

1. Compute the payback period for both projects. Which project has the shortest payback period?

2. Assume that the company requires a 10% return from its investments. Compute the net present value of each project.

3. Drawing on your answers to parts 1 and 2, determine which project, if any, should be chosen.

4. Compute the internal rate of return for Project TD2. Based on its internal rate of return, should Project TD2 be chosen?

PLANNING THE SOLUTION

● Compute the payback period for the series of unequal cash flows (Project TD1) and for the series of equal cash flows (Project TD2).

● Compute White Company's net present value of each investment using a 10% discount rate.

● Use the payback and net present value rules to determine which project, if any, should be selected.

● Compute the internal rate of return for the series of equal cash flows (Project TD2) and determine whether that internal rate of return is greater than the company's 10% discount rate.

SOLUTION

1. The payback period for a project with a series of equal cash flows is computed as follows:

$$\text{Payback period} = \frac{\text{Cost of investment}}{\text{Annual net cash flow}}$$

For Project TD2, the payback period equals 2.53 (rounded), computed as $101,250/$40,000. This means that the company expects to recover its investment in Project TD2 after approximately two and one-half years of its three-year life.

Next, determining the payback period for a series of unequal cash flows (as in Project TD1) requires us to compute the cumulative net cash flows from the project at the end of each year. Assuming the cash outflow for Project TD1 occurs at the end of year 0, and cash inflows occur continuously over years 1, 2, and 3, the payback period calculation follows.

TD1:

Period	Expected Net Cash Flows	Cumulative Net Cash Flows
0	$(101,250)	$(101,250)
1	20,000	(81,250)
2	30,000	(51,250)
3	70,000	18,750

The cumulative net cash flow for Project TD1 changes from negative to positive in year 3. As cash flows are received continuously, the point at which the company has recovered its investment into year 3 is 0.73 (rounded), computed as $51,250/$70,000. This means that the payback period for TD1 is 2.73 years, computed as 2 years plus 0.73 of year 3.

2. TD1:

	Net Cash Flows	Present Value of 1 at 10%	Present Value of Net Cash Flows
Year 1	$ 20,000	0.9091	$ 18,182
Year 2	30,000	0.8264	24,792
Year 3	70,000	0.7513	52,591
Totals.......................	$120,000		95,565
Amount invested..............			(101,250)
Net present value			**$ (5,685)**

TD2:

	Net Cash Flows	Present Value of 1 at 10%	Present Value of Net Cash Flows
Year 1	$ 40,000	0.9091	$ 36,364
Year 2	40,000	0.8264	33,056
Year 3	40,000	0.7513	30,052
Totals.......................	$120,000		99,472
Amount invested..............			(101,250)
Net present value			**$ (1,778)**

3. White Company should not invest in either project. Both are expected to yield a negative net present value, and it should invest only in positive net present value projects. Although the company expects to recover its investment from both projects before the end of these projects' useful lives, the projects are not acceptable after considering the time value of money.

4. To compute Project TD2's internal rate of return, we first compute a present value factor as follows:

$$\text{Present value factor} = \frac{\text{Amount invested}}{\text{Net cash flow}} = \$101,250/\$40,000 = 2.5313 \text{ (rounded)}$$

Then, we search Table B.3 for the discount rate that corresponds to the present value factor of 2.5313 for three periods. From Table B.3, this discount rate is 9%. Project TD2's internal rate of return of 9% is below this company's hurdle rate of 10%. Thus, Project TD2 should *not* be chosen.

Using Excel to Compute Net Present Value and Internal Rate of Return

11A

Computing present values and internal rates of return for projects with uneven cash flows is tedious and error prone. These calculations can be performed simply and accurately by using functions built into Excel. Many calculators and other types of spreadsheet software can perform them too. To illustrate, consider FasTrac, a company that is considering investing in a new machine with the expected cash flows shown in the following spreadsheet. Cash outflows are entered as negative numbers, and cash inflows are entered as positive numbers. Assume FasTrac requires a 12% annual return, entered as 0.12 in cell C1.

	A	B	C
1	Annual discount rate		0.12
2	Initial investment, made at beginning of period 1		−16000
3	Annual cash flows received at end of period:		
4		1	3000
5		2	4000
6		3	4000
7		4	4000
8		5	5000
9		6	3000
10		7	2000
11		8	2000
12			
13			=NPV(C1,C4:C11)+C2
14			
15			=IRR(C2:C11)

To compute the net present value of this project, the following is entered into cell C13:

$$=NPV(C1,C4:C11)+C2$$

This instructs Excel to use its NPV function to compute the present value of the cash flows in cells C4 through C11, using the discount rate in cell C1, and then add the amount of the (negative) initial investment. For this stream of cash flows and a discount rate of 12%, the net present value is $1,326.03.

To compute the internal rate of return for this project, the following is entered into cell C15:

$$=IRR(C2:C11)$$

This instructs Excel to use its IRR function to compute the internal rate of return of the cash flows in cells C2 through C11. By default, Excel starts with a guess of 10%, and then uses trial and error to find the IRR. The IRR equals 14% for this project.

Summary

A1 **Analyze a capital investment project using break-even time.** Break-even time (BET) is a method for evaluating capital investments by restating future cash flows in terms of their present values (discounting the cash flows) and then calculating the payback period using these present values of cash flows.

P1 **Compute payback period and describe its use.** One way to compare potential investments is to compute and compare their payback periods. The payback period is an estimate of the expected time before the cumulative net cash inflow from the investment equals its initial cost. A payback period analysis fails to reflect risk of the cash flows, differences in the timing of cash flows within the payback period, and cash flows that occur after the payback period.

P2 **Compute accounting rate of return and explain its use.** A project's accounting rate of return is computed by dividing the expected annual after-tax net income by the average amount of investment in the project. When the net cash flows are received evenly throughout each period and straight-line depreciation is used, the average investment is computed as the average of the investment's initial book value and its salvage value.

P3   Compute net present value and describe its use. An investment's net present value is determined by predicting the future cash flows it is expected to generate, discounting them at a rate that represents an acceptable return, and then subtracting the investment's initial cost from the sum of the present values. This technique can deal with any pattern of expected cash flows and applies a superior concept of return on investment.

P4   Compute internal rate of return and explain its use. The internal rate of return (IRR) is the discount rate that results in a zero net present value. When the cash flows are equal, we can compute the present value factor corresponding to the IRR by dividing the initial investment by the annual cash flows. We then use the annuity tables to determine the discount rate corresponding to this present value factor.

Key Terms

Accounting rate of return (ARR)
Annuity
Break-even time (BET)
Capital budgeting

Capital rationing
Cost of capital
Hurdle rate
Internal rate of return (IRR)

Net present value (NPV)
Payback period (PBP)
Profitability index

Multiple Choice Quiz

1. The minimum acceptable rate of return for an investment decision is called the

  a. Hurdle rate of return.   **d.** Average rate of return.

  b. Payback rate of return.   **e.** Maximum rate of return.

  c. Internal rate of return.

2. A corporation is considering the purchase of new equipment costing $90,000. The projected after-tax annual net income from the equipment is $3,600, after deducting $30,000 depreciation. Assume that revenue is to be received at each year-end, and the machine has a useful life of three years with zero salvage value. Management requires a 12% return on its investments. What is the net present value of this machine?

  a. $ 60,444   **c.** $(88,560)   **e.** $ (9,300)

  b. $ 80,700   **d.** $ 90,000

3. A disadvantage of using the payback period to compare investment alternatives is that it

  a. Ignores cash flows beyond the payback period.

  b. Cannot be used to compare alternatives with different initial investments.

  c. Cannot be used when cash flows are not uniform.

  d. Involves the time value of money.

  e. Cannot be used if a company records depreciation.

4. A company is considering the purchase of equipment for $270,000. Projected annual cash inflow from this equipment is $61,200 per year. The payback period is:

  a. 0.2 years.   **c.** 4.4 years.   **e.** 3.9 years.

  b. 5.0 years.   **d.** 2.3 years.

5. A company buys a machine for $180,000 that has an expected life of nine years and no salvage value. The company expects an annual net income (after taxes of 30%) of $8,550. What is the accounting rate of return?

  a. 4.75%   **c.** 2.85%   **e.** 6.65%

  b. 42.75%   **d.** 9.50%

ANSWERS TO MULTIPLE CHOICE QUIZ

1. a

2. e;

	Net Cash Flow	Present Value of an Annuity of 1 at 12%	Present Value of Cash Flows
Years 1–3	$3,600 + $30,000	2.4018	$ 80,700
Amount invested			(90,000)
Net present value			$ (9,300)

3. a

4. c; Payback = $270,000/$61,200 per year = 4.4 years

5. d; Accounting rate of return = $8,550/[($180,000 + $0)/2] = 9.5%

A *Superscript letter A denotes assignments based on Appendix 11A.*

🔲 Icon denotes assignments that involve decision making.

Discussion Questions

1. Capital budgeting decisions require careful analysis because they are generally the most _____ and _____ decisions that management faces.

2. What is capital budgeting?

3. 🔲 Identify four reasons that capital budgeting decisions are risky.

4. Identify two disadvantages of using the payback period for comparing investments.

5. 🔲 Why is an investment more attractive to management if it has a shorter payback period?

6. What is the average amount invested in a machine during its predicted five-year life if it costs $200,000 and has a $20,000 salvage value? Assume that net income is received evenly throughout each year and straight-line depreciation is used.

7. If the present value of the expected net cash flows from a machine, discounted at 10%, exceeds the amount to be invested, what can you say about the investment's expected rate of return? What can you say about the expected rate of return if the present value of the net cash flows, discounted at 10%, is less than the investment amount?

8. Why is the present value of $100 that you expect to receive one year from today worth less than $100 received today?

What is the present value of $100 that you expect to receive one year from today, discounted at 12%?

9. 🔲 If a potential investment's internal rate of return is above the company's hurdle rate, should the investment be made?

10. 🔲 **Google** managers must select depreciation methods. Why does the use of the accelerated depreciation method (instead of straight-line) for income tax reporting increase an investment's value?   **GOOGLE**

11. The management of **Samsung** is planning to invest in a new companywide computerized inventory tracking system. What makes this potential investment risky?   **Samsung**

12. The management of **Google** is planning to acquire new equipment to manufacture tablet computers. What are some of the costs and benefits that would be included in Google's analysis?   **GOOGLE**

13. 🔲 **Apple** is considering expanding a store. Identify three methods management can use to evaluate whether to expand.   **APPLE**

connect

Park Co. is considering an investment that requires immediate payment of $27,000 and provides expected cash inflows of $9,000 annually for four years. What is the investment's payback period?

QUICK STUDY

QS 11-1
Payback period   P1

Park Co. is considering an investment that requires immediate payment of $27,000 and provides expected cash inflows of $9,000 annually for four years. If Park Co. requires a 10% return on its investments, what is the net present value of this investment? (Round your calculations to the nearest dollar.)

QS 11-2
Net present value   P3

Park Co. is considering an investment that requires immediate payment of $27,000 and provides expected cash inflows of $9,000 annually for four years. Assume Park Co. requires a 10% return on its investments. Based on its internal rate of return, should Park Co. make the investment?

QS 11-3
Internal rate of return   P4

Howard Co. is considering two alternative investments. The payback period is 3.5 years for Investment A and 4 years for Investment B.
1. If management relies on the payback period, which investment is preferred?
2. Why might Howard's analysis of these two alternatives lead to the selection of B over A?

QS 11-4
Analyzing payback periods   P1

Project A requires a $280,000 initial investment for new machinery with a five-year life and a salvage value of $30,000. The company uses straight-line depreciation. Project A is expected to yield annual net income of $20,000 per year for the next five years. Compute Project A's payback period.

QS 11-5
Payback period   P1

Project A requires a $280,000 initial investment for new machinery with a five-year life and a salvage value of $30,000. The company uses straight-line depreciation. Project A is expected to yield annual net income of $20,000 per year for the next five years. Compute Project A's accounting rate of return. Express your answer as a percentage, rounded to two decimal places.

QS 11-6
Accounting rate of return
P2

QS 11-7

Computation of accounting rate of return   P2

Peng Company is considering an investment expected to generate an average net income after taxes of $1,950 for three years. The investment costs $45,000 and has an estimated $6,000 salvage value. Compute the accounting rate of return for this investment; assume the company uses straight-line depreciation. Express your answer as a percentage, rounded to two decimal places.

QS 11-8

Net present value   P3

Peng Company is considering an investment expected to generate an average net income after taxes of $1,950 for three years. The investment costs $45,000 and has an estimated $6,000 salvage value. Assume Peng requires a 15% return on its investments. Compute the net present value of this investment. (Round each present value calculation to the nearest dollar.)

QS 11-9

Compute net present value   P3

If Quail Company invests $50,000 today, it can expect to receive $10,000 at the end of each year for the next seven years, plus an extra $6,000 at the end of the seventh year. What is the net present value of this investment assuming a required 10% return on investments? (Round present value calculations to the nearest dollar.)

QS 11-10

Profitability index   P3

Yokam Company is considering two alternative projects. Project 1 requires an initial investment of $400,000 and has a present value of cash flows of $1,100,000. Project 2 requires an initial investment of $4 million and has a present value of cash flows of $6 million. Compute the profitability index for each project. Based on the profitability index, which project should the company prefer? Explain.

QS 11-11

Net present value   P3

Following is information on an investment considered by Hudson Co. The investment has zero salvage value. The company requires a 12% return from its investments. Compute this investment's net present value.

	Investment A1
Initial investment	$(200,000)
Expected net cash flows in year:	
1	100,000
2	90,000
3	75,000

QS 11-12

Net present value, with salvage value   P3

Refer to the information in QS 11-11 and instead assume the investment has a salvage value of $20,000. Compute the investment's net present value.

QS 11-13

Internal rate of return   P4

A company is considering investing in a new machine that requires a cash payment of $47,947 today. The machine will generate annual cash flows of $21,000 for the next three years. What is the internal rate of return if the company buys this machine?

QS 11-14

Net present value   P3

A company is considering investing in a new machine that requires a cash payment of $47,947 today. The machine will generate annual cash flows of $21,000 for the next three years. Assume the company uses an 8% discount rate. Compute the net present value of this investment. (Round your answer to the nearest dollar.)

QS 11-15

Net present value

P3

A company is investing in a solar panel system to reduce its electricity costs. The system requires a cash payment of $125,374.60 today. The system is expected to generate net cash flows of $13,000 per year for the next 35 years. The investment has zero salvage value. The company requires an 8% return on its investments. Compute the net present value of this investment.

QS 11-16

Internal rate of return

P4

A company is investing in a solar panel system to reduce its electricity costs. The system requires a cash payment of $125,374.60 today. The system is expected to generate net cash flows of $13,000 per year for the next 35 years. The investment has zero salvage value. Compute the internal rate of return on this investment.

Heels, a shoe manufacturer, is evaluating the costs and benefits of new equipment that would custom fit each pair of athletic shoes. The customer would have his or her foot scanned by digital computer equipment; this information would be used to cut the raw materials to provide the customer a perfect fit. The new equipment costs $90,000 and is expected to generate an additional $35,000 in cash flows for five years. A bank will make a $90,000 loan to the company at a 10% interest rate for this equipment's purchase. Use the following table to determine the break-even time for this equipment. (Round the present value of cash flows to the nearest dollar.)

QS 11-17
Computation of break-even time
A1

Year	Cash Flows*	Present Value of 1 at 10%	Present Value of Cash Flows	Cumulative Present Value of Cash Flows
0	$(90,000)	1.0000	_____	_____
1	35,000	0.9091	_____	_____
2	35,000	0.8264	_____	_____
3	35,000	0.7513	_____	_____
4	35,000	0.6830	_____	_____
5	35,000	0.6209	_____	_____

* All cash flows occur at year-end.

Siemens AG invests €80 million to build a manufacturing plant to build wind turbines. The company predicts net cash flows of €16 million per year for the next eight years. Assume the company requires an 8% rate of return from its investments.

QS 11-18
Capital budgeting methods
P1   P3

1. What is the payback period of this investment?

2. What is the net present value of this investment?

connect

Beyer Company is considering the purchase of an asset for $180,000. It is expected to produce the following net cash flows. The cash flows occur evenly within each year. Compute the payback period for this investment (round years to two decimals).

EXERCISES

Exercise 11-1
Payback period computation; uneven cash flows   P1
Check   3.08 years

	Year 1	Year 2	Year 3	Year 4	Year 5	Total
Net cash flows	$60,000	$40,000	$70,000	$125,000	$35,000	$330,000

Refer to the information in Exercise 11-1 and assume that Beyer requires a 10% return on its investments. Compute the net present value of this investment. (Round to the nearest dollar.) Should Beyer accept the investment?

Exercise 11-2
Net present value   P3

A machine can be purchased for $150,000 and used for five years, yielding the following net incomes. In projecting net incomes, straight-line depreciation is applied, using a five-year life and a zero salvage value. Compute the machine's payback period (ignore taxes). (Round the payback period to three decimals.)

Exercise 11-3
Payback period computation; straight-line depreciation
P1

	Year 1	Year 2	Year 3	Year 4	Year 5
Net income	$10,000	$25,000	$50,000	$37,500	$100,000

Refer to the information in Exercise 11-3 and assume instead that double-declining depreciation is applied. Compute the machine's payback period (ignore taxes). (Round the payback period to three decimals.)

Exercise 11-4
Payback period; accelerated depreciation   P1
Check   2.265 years

Exercise 11-5
Payback period
computation; even
cash flows
P1

Compute the payback period for each of these two separate investments (round the payback period to two decimals):

a. A new operating system for an existing machine is expected to cost $520,000 and have a useful life of six years. The system yields an incremental after-tax income of $150,000 each year after deducting its straight-line depreciation. The predicted salvage value of the system is $10,000.

b. A machine costs $380,000, has a $20,000 salvage value, is expected to last eight years, and will generate an after-tax income of $60,000 per year after straight-line depreciation.

Exercise 11-6
Net present value   P3

Refer to the information in Exercise 11-5. Assume the company requires a 10% rate of return on its investments. Compute the net present value of each potential investment. (Round to the nearest dollar.)

Exercise 11-7
Accounting rate of return
P2

A machine costs $700,000 and is expected to yield an after-tax net income of $52,000 each year. Management predicts this machine has a 10-year service life and a $100,000 salvage value, and it uses straight-line depreciation. Compute this machine's accounting rate of return.

Exercise 11-8
Payback period and
accounting rate of return
on investment
P1   P2

B2B Co. is considering the purchase of equipment that would allow the company to add a new product to its line. The equipment is expected to cost $360,000 with a 12-year life and no salvage value. It will be depreciated on a straight-line basis. The company expects to sell 144,000 units of the equipment's product each year. The expected annual income related to this equipment follows. Compute the (1) payback period and (2) accounting rate of return for this equipment.

Sales	$225,000
Costs	
Materials, labor, and overhead (except depreciation on new equipment)	120,000
Depreciation on new equipment	30,000
Selling and administrative expenses	22,500
Total costs and expenses	172,500
Pretax income	52,500
Income taxes (30%)	15,750
Net income	$ 36,750

Check (1) 5.39 years,
(2) 20.42%

Exercise 11-9
Computing net
present value   P3

After evaluating the risk of the investment described in Exercise 11-8, B2B Co. concludes that it must earn at least an 8% return on this investment. Compute the net present value of this investment. (Round the net present value to the nearest dollar.)

Exercise 11-10
NPV and profitability index
P3

Following is information on two alternative investments being considered by Jolee Company. The company requires a 10% return from its investments.

	Project A	Project B
Initial investment	$(160,000)	$(105,000)
Expected net cash flows in year:		
1	40,000	32,000
2	56,000	50,000
3	80,295	66,000
4	90,400	72,000
5	65,000	24,000

For each alternative project, compute the (a) net present value and (b) profitability index. (Round your answers in part *b* to two decimal places.) If the company can only select one project, which should it choose? Explain.

Following is information on two alternative investments being considered by Tiger Co. The company requires a 4% return from its investments.

	Project X1	Project X2
Initial investment	$(80,000)	$(120,000)
Expected net cash flows in year:		
1	25,000	60,000
2	35,500	50,000
3	60,500	40,000

Compute each project's (a) net present value and (b) profitability index. (Round present value calculations to the nearest dollar and round the profitability index to two decimal places.) If the company can choose only one project, which should it choose? Explain.

Exercise 11-11
Net present value, profitability index
P3

Refer to the information in Exercise 11-11 and instead assume the company requires a 12% return on its investments. Compute each project's (a) net present value and (b) profitability index. (Round present value calculations to the nearest dollar.) Express the profitability index as a percentage (rounded to two decimal places). If the company can choose only one project, which should it choose? Explain.

Exercise 11-12
Net present value, profitability index   P3

Refer to the information in Exercise 11-11. Create an Excel spreadsheet to compute the internal rate of return for each of the projects. Based on internal rate of return, determine whether the company should accept either of the two projects.

Exercise 11-13^A
Internal rate of return   P4

Phoenix Company can invest in each of three cheese-making projects: C1, C2, and C3. Each project requires an initial investment of $228,000 and would yield the following annual cash flows.

	C1	C2	C3
Year 1	$ 12,000	$ 96,000	$180,000
Year 2	108,000	96,000	60,000
Year 3	168,000	96,000	48,000
Totals.	$288,000	$288,000	$288,000

Exercise 11-14
Computation and interpretation of net present value and internal rate of return

P3   P4

1. Assuming that the company requires a 12% return from its investments, use net present value to determine which projects, if any, should be acquired.
2. Using the answer from part 1, explain whether the internal rate of return is higher or lower than 12% for Project C2.

Refer to the information in Exercise 11-10. Create an Excel spreadsheet to compute the internal rate of return for each of the projects. Round the percentage return to two decimals.

Exercise 11-15^A
Using Excel to compute IRR   P4

This chapter explained two methods to evaluate investments using recovery time, the payback period and break-even time (BET). Refer to QS 11-17 and (1) compute the recovery time for both the payback period and break-even time, (2) discuss the advantage(s) of break-even time over the payback period, and (3) list two conditions under which payback period and break-even time are similar.

Exercise 11-16
Comparison of payback and BET   P1   A1

■ connect

PROBLEM SET A

Problem 11-1A
Computation of payback period, accounting rate of return, and net present value

P1 P2 P3

Factor Company is planning to add a new product to its line. To manufacture this product, the company needs to buy a new machine at a $480,000 cost with an expected four-year life and a $20,000 salvage value. All sales are for cash, and all costs are out-of-pocket, except for depreciation on the new machine. Additional information includes the following.

Expected annual sales of new product.......................................	$1,840,000
Expected annual costs of new product	
Direct materials	480,000
Direct labor..	672,000
Overhead (excluding straight-line depreciation on new machine).............	336,000
Selling and administrative expenses	160,000
Income taxes	30%

Required

1. Compute straight-line depreciation for each year of this new machine's life. (Round depreciation amounts to the nearest dollar.)

2. Determine expected net income and net cash flow for each year of this machine's life. (Round answers to the nearest dollar.)

3. Compute this machine's payback period, assuming that cash flows occur evenly throughout each year. (Round the payback period to two decimals.)

Check (4) 21.56%

4. Compute this machine's accounting rate of return, assuming that income is earned evenly throughout each year. (Round the percentage return to two decimals.)

(5) $107,356

5. Compute the net present value for this machine using a discount rate of 7% and assuming that cash flows occur at each year-end. (*Hint:* Salvage value is a cash inflow at the end of the asset's life. Round the net present value to the nearest dollar.)

Problem 11-2A
Analysis and computation of payback period, accounting rate of return, and net present value

P1 P2 P3

Most Company has an opportunity to invest in one of two new projects. Project Y requires a $350,000 investment for new machinery with a four-year life and no salvage value. Project Z requires a $350,000 investment for new machinery with a three-year life and no salvage value. The two projects yield the following predicted annual results. The company uses straight-line depreciation, and cash flows occur evenly throughout each year.

	Project Y	Project Z
Sales	$350,000	$280,000
Expenses		
Direct materials	49,000	35,000
Direct labor................................	70,000	42,000
Overhead including depreciation	126,000	126,000
Selling and administrative expenses	25,000	25,000
Total expenses	270,000	228,000
Pretax income..............................	80,000	52,000
Income taxes (30%)	24,000	15,600
Net income	$ 56,000	$ 36,400

Required

1. Compute each project's annual expected net cash flows. (Round the net cash flows to the nearest dollar.)

Check For Project Y:
(2) 2.44 years, (3) 32%

2. Determine each project's payback period. (Round the payback period to two decimals.)

3. Compute each project's accounting rate of return. (Round the percentage return to one decimal.)

(4) $125,286

4. Determine each project's net present value using 8% as the discount rate. For part 4 only, assume that cash flows occur at each year-end. (Round the net present value to the nearest dollar.)

Analysis Component

5. Identify the project you would recommend to management and explain your choice.

Manning Corporation is considering a new project requiring a $90,000 investment in test equipment with no salvage value. The project would produce $66,000 of pretax income before depreciation at the end of each of the next six years. The company's income tax rate is 40%. In compiling its tax return and computing its income tax payments, the company can choose between the two alternative depreciation schedules shown in the table.

	Straight-Line Depreciation	MACRS Depreciation*
Year 1	$ 9,000	$18,000
Year 2	18,000	28,800
Year 3	18,000	17,280
Year 4	18,000	10,368
Year 5	18,000	10,368
Year 6	9,000	5,184
Totals	$90,000	$90,000

* The modified accelerated cost recovery system (MACRS) for depreciation is discussed in financial accounting courses.

Required

1. Prepare a five-column table that reports amounts (assuming use of straight-line depreciation) for each of the following for each of the six years: (a) pretax income before depreciation, (b) straight-line depreciation expense, (c) taxable income, (d) income taxes, and (e) net cash flow. Net cash flow equals the amount of income before depreciation minus the income taxes. (Round answers to the nearest dollar.)

2. Prepare a five-column table that reports amounts (assuming use of MACRS depreciation) for each of the following for each of the six years: (a) pretax income before depreciation, (b) MACRS depreciation expense, (c) taxable income, (d) income taxes, and (e) net cash flow. Net cash flow equals the income amount before depreciation minus the income taxes. (Round answers to the nearest dollar.)

3. Compute the net present value of the investment if straight-line depreciation is used. Use 10% as the discount rate. (Round the net present value to the nearest dollar.)

4. Compute the net present value of the investment if MACRS depreciation is used. Use 10% as the discount rate. (Round the net present value to the nearest dollar.)

Analysis Component

5. Explain why the MACRS depreciation method increases this project's net present value.

Interstate Manufacturing is considering either replacing one of its old machines with a new machine or having the old machine overhauled. Information about the two alternatives follows. Management requires a 10% rate of return on its investments.

Alternative 1: Keep the old machine and have it overhauled. If the old machine is overhauled, it will be kept for another five years and then sold for its salvage value.

Cost of old machine	$112,000
Cost of overhaul	150,000
Annual expected revenues generated	95,000
Annual cash operating costs after overhaul	42,000
Salvage value of old machine in 5 years	15,000

Alternative 2: Sell the old machine and buy a new one. The new machine is more efficient and will yield substantial operating cost savings with more product being produced and sold.

Cost of new machine	$300,000
Salvage value of old machine now	29,000
Annual expected revenues generated	100,000
Annual cash operating costs	32,000
Salvage value of new machine in 5 years	20,000

Required

Check   (1) Net present value of alternative 1, $60,226

1. Determine the net present value of alternative 1.

2. Determine the net present value of alternative 2.

3. Which alternative do you recommend that management select? Explain.

Problem 11-5A

Payback period, break-even time, and net present value

P1 A1

Sentinel Company is considering an investment in technology to improve its operations. The investment will require an initial outlay of $250,000 and will yield the following expected cash flows. Management requires investments to have a payback period of three years, and it requires a 10% return on investments.

Period	Cash Flow
1	$ 47,000
2	52,000
3	75,000
4	94,000
5	125,000

Required

Check   (1) Payback period, 3.8 years

1. Determine the payback period for this investment. (Round the answer to one decimal.)

2. Determine the break-even time for this investment. (Round the answer to one decimal.)

3. Determine the net present value for this investment.

Analysis Component

4. Should management invest in this project? Explain.

Problem 11-6A

Payback period, break-even time, and net present value

P1 A1

Lenitnes Company is considering an investment in technology to improve its operations. The investment will require an initial outlay of $250,000 and will yield the following expected cash flows. Management requires investments to have a payback period of three years, and it requires a 10% return on its investments.

Period	Cash Flow
1	$125,000
2	94,000
3	75,000
4	52,000
5	47,000

Required

Check   (1) Payback period, 2.4 years

1. Determine the payback period for this investment. (Round the answer to one decimal.)

2. Determine the break-even time for this investment. (Round the answer to one decimal.)

3. Determine the net present value for this investment.

Analysis Component

4. Should management invest in this project? Explain.

5. Compare your answers for parts 1 through 4 with those for Problem 11-5A. What are the causes of the differences in results and your conclusions?

PROBLEM SET B

Problem 11-1B

Computation of payback period, accounting rate of return, and net present value

P1 P2 P3

Cortino Company is planning to add a new product to its line. To manufacture this product, the company needs to buy a new machine at a $300,000 cost with an expected four-year life and a $20,000 salvage value. All sales are for cash and all costs are out-of-pocket, except for depreciation on the new machine. Additional information includes the following.

Expected annual sales of new product......................................	$1,150,000
Expected annual costs of new product	
Direct materials	300,000
Direct labor..	420,000
Overhead (excluding straight-line depreciation on new machine)...............	210,000
Selling and administrative expenses	100,000
Income taxes	30%

Required

1. Compute straight-line depreciation for each year of this new machine's life. (Round depreciation amounts to the nearest dollar.)

2. Determine expected net income and net cash flow for each year of this machine's life. (Round answers to the nearest dollar.)

3. Compute this machine's payback period, assuming that cash flows occur evenly throughout each year. (Round the payback period to two decimals.)

4. Compute this machine's accounting rate of return, assuming that income is earned evenly throughout each year. (Round the percentage return to two decimals.)

5. Compute the net present value for this machine using a discount rate of 7% and assuming that cash flows occur at each year-end. (*Hint:* Salvage value is a cash inflow at the end of the asset's life.)

Check (4) 21.88%

(5) $70,915

Aikman Company has an opportunity to invest in one of two projects. Project A requires a $240,000 investment for new machinery with a four-year life and no salvage value. Project B also requires a $240,000 investment for new machinery with a three-year life and no salvage value. The two projects yield the following predicted annual results. The company uses straight-line depreciation, and cash flows occur evenly throughout each year.

Problem 11-2B

Analysis and computation of payback period, accounting rate of return, and net present value

P1   P2   P3

	Project A	Project B
Sales	$250,000	$200,000
Expenses		
Direct materials	35,000	25,000
Direct labor	50,000	30,000
Overhead including depreciation	90,000	90,000
Selling and administrative expenses	18,000	18,000
Total expenses	193,000	163,000
Pretax income	57,000	37,000
Income taxes (30%)	17,100	11,100
Net income	$ 39,900	$ 25,900

Required

1. Compute each project's annual expected net cash flows. (Round net cash flows to the nearest dollar.)

2. Determine each project's payback period. (Round the payback period to two decimals.)

3. Compute each project's accounting rate of return. (Round the percentage return to one decimal.)

4. Determine each project's net present value using 8% as the discount rate. For part 4 only, assume that cash flows occur at each year-end. (Round net present values to the nearest dollar.)

Check For Project A:

(2) 2.4 years

(3) 33.3%

(4) $90,879

Analysis Component

5. Identify the project you would recommend to management and explain your choice.

Grossman Corporation is considering a new project requiring a $30,000 investment in an asset having no salvage value. The project would produce $12,000 of pretax income before depreciation at the end of each of the next six years. The company's income tax rate is 40%. In compiling its tax return and computing its income tax payments, the company can choose between two alternative depreciation schedules as shown in the table.

Problem 11-3B

Computation of cash flows and net present values with alternative depreciation methods

P3

	Straight-Line Depreciation	MACRS Depreciation*
Year 1	$ 3,000	$ 6,000
Year 2	6,000	9,600
Year 3	6,000	5,760
Year 4	6,000	3,456
Year 5	6,000	3,456
Year 6	3,000	1,728
Totals	$30,000	$30,000

* The modified accelerated cost recovery system (MACRS) for depreciation is discussed in financial accounting courses.

Required

1. Prepare a five-column table that reports amounts (assuming use of straight-line depreciation) for each of the following items for each of the six years: (a) pretax income before depreciation, (b) straight-line depreciation expense, (c) taxable income, (d) income taxes, and (e) net cash flow. Net cash flow equals the amount of income before depreciation minus the income taxes. (Round answers to the nearest dollar.)

2. Prepare a five-column table that reports amounts (assuming use of MACRS depreciation) for each of the following items for each of the six years: (a) pretax income before depreciation, (b) MACRS depreciation expense, (c) taxable income, (d) income taxes, and (e) net cash flow. Net cash flow equals the amount of income before depreciation minus the income taxes. (Round answers to the nearest dollar.)

Check   Net present value:
(3) $10,041

(4) $10,635

3. Compute the net present value of the investment if straight-line depreciation is used. Use 10% as the discount rate. (Round the net present value to the nearest dollar.)

4. Compute the net present value of the investment if MACRS depreciation is used. Use 10% as the discount rate. (Round the net present value to the nearest dollar.)

Analysis Component

5. Explain why the MACRS depreciation method increases the net present value of this project.

Problem 11-4B
Computing net present value of alternate investments

P3

Archer Foods has a freezer that is in need of repair and is considering whether to replace the old freezer with a new freezer or have the old freezer extensively repaired. Information about the two alternatives follows. Management requires a 10% rate of return on its investments.

Alternative 1: Keep the old freezer and have it repaired. If the old freezer is repaired, it will be kept for another eight years and then sold for its salvage value.

Cost of old freezer	$75,000
Cost of repair	50,000
Annual expected revenues generated	63,000
Annual cash operating costs after repair	55,000
Salvage value of old freezer in 8 years	3,000

Alternative 2: Sell the old freezer and buy a new one. The new freezer is larger than the old one and will allow the company to expand its product offerings, thereby generating more revenues. Also, it is more energy efficient and will yield substantial operating cost savings.

Cost of new freezer	$150,000
Salvage value of old freezer now	5,000
Annual expected revenues generated	68,000
Annual cash operating costs	30,000
Salvage value of new freezer in 8 years	8,000

Required

Check   (1) Net present value
of alternative 1, $(5,921)

1. Determine the net present value of alternative 1.
2. Determine the net present value of alternative 2.
3. Which alternative do you recommend that management select? Explain.

Problem 11-5B
Payback period, break-even time, and net present value

P1   A1

Aster Company is considering an investment in technology to improve its operations. The investment will require an initial outlay of $800,000 and yield the following expected cash flows. Management requires investments to have a payback period of two years, and it requires a 10% return on its investments.

Period	Cash Flow
1	$300,000
2	350,000
3	400,000
4	450,000

Required

1. Determine the payback period for this investment.
2. Determine the break-even time for this investment.
3. Determine the net present value for this investment.

Analysis Component

4. Should management invest in this project? Explain.

Retsa Company is considering an investment in technology to improve its operations. The investment will require an initial outlay of $800,000 and will yield the following expected cash flows. Management requires investments to have a payback period of two years, and it requires a 10% return on its investments.

Problem 11-6B
Payback period, break-even time, and net present value

P1 A1

Period	Cash Flow
1	$450,000
2	400,000
3	350,000
4	300,000

Required

1. Determine the payback period for this investment. (Round the answer to one decimal.)
2. Determine the break-even time for this investment. (Round the answer to one decimal.)
3. Determine the net present value for this investment.

Analysis Component

4. Should management invest in this project? Explain.
5. Compare your answers for parts 1 through 4 with those for Problem 11-5B. What are the causes of the differences in results and your conclusions?

(This serial problem began in Chapter 1 and continues through most of the book. If previous chapter segments were not completed, the serial problem can begin at this point.)

SP 11 Santana Rey is considering the purchase of equipment for **Business Solutions** that would allow the company to add a new product to its computer furniture line. The equipment is expected to cost $300,000 and to have a six-year life and no salvage value. It will be depreciated on a straight-line basis. Business Solutions expects to sell 100 units of the equipment's product each year. The expected annual income related to this equipment follows.

SERIAL PROBLEM
Business Solutions

P1 P2

Sales	$375,000
Costs	
Materials, labor, and overhead (except depreciation)	200,000
Depreciation on new equipment	50,000
Selling and administrative expenses	37,500
Total costs and expenses	287,500
Pretax income	87,500
Income taxes (30%)	26,250
Net income	$ 61,250

© Alexander Image/Shutterstock RF

Required

Compute the (1) payback period and (2) accounting rate of return for this equipment. (Record ARR answers as percents, rounded to one decimal.)

Beyond the Numbers

REPORTING IN ACTION

P3

APPLE

BTN 11-1   Assume **Apple** invested $2.12 billion to expand its manufacturing capacity. Assume that these assets have a 10-year life and that Apple requires a 10% internal rate of return on these assets.

Required

1. What is the amount of annual cash flows that Apple must earn from these projects to have a 10% internal rate of return? (*Hint:* Identify the 10-period, 10% factor from the present value of an annuity table, and then divide $2.12 billion by this factor to get the annual cash flows necessary.)

Fast Forward

2. Access Apple's financial statements for fiscal years ended after September 26, 2015, from its website (**Apple.com**) or the SEC's website (**SEC.gov**).
    a. Determine the amount that Apple invested in capital assets for the most recent year. (*Hint:* Refer to the statement of cash flows.)
    b. Assume a 10-year life and a 10% internal rate of return. What is the amount of cash flows that Apple must earn on these new projects?

COMPARATIVE ANALYSIS

P3 P4

GOOGLE APPLE

BTN 11-2   Assume that **Google** invests $2.42 billion in capital expenditures, including $1.08 billion related to manufacturing capacity. Assume that these projects have a seven-year life and that management requires a 15% internal rate of return on those projects.

Required

1. What is the amount of annual cash flows that Google must earn from those expenditures to achieve a 15% internal rate of return? (*Hint:* Identify the seven-period, 15% factor from the present value of an annuity table and then divide $1.08 billion by the factor to get the annual cash flows required.)
2. BTN 11-1 must be completed to answer part 2. How does your answer to part 1 compare to **Apple**'s required cash flows determined in BTN 11-1? What does this imply about each company's cash flow requirements for these types of projects?

ETHICS CHALLENGE

P3

BTN 11-3   A consultant commented that "too often the numbers look good but feel bad." This comment often stems from *estimation error* common to capital budgeting proposals that relate to future cash flows. Three reasons for this error often exist. First, reliably predicting cash flows several years into the future is very difficult. Second, the present value of cash flows many years into the future (say, beyond 10 years) is often very small. Third, personal biases and expectations can influence present value computations.

Required

1. Compute the present value of $100 to be received in 10 years assuming a 12% discount rate.
2. Why is understanding the three reasons mentioned for estimation error important when evaluating investment projects? Link this response to your answer for part 1.

COMMUNICATING IN PRACTICE

P1 P2 P3 P4

BTN 11-4   Payback period, accounting rate of return, net present value, and internal rate of return are common methods to evaluate capital investment opportunities. Assume that your manager asks you to identify the measurement basis and unit that each method offers and to list the advantages and disadvantages of each method. Present your response in memorandum format of less than one page.

BTN 11-5   Capital budgeting is an important topic, and there are websites designed to help people understand the methods available. Access **TeachMeFinance.com**'s capital budgeting web page (**teachmefinance.com/capitalbudgeting.html**). This web page contains an example of a capital budgeting case involving a $15,000 initial cash outflow.

Required

Compute the payback period and the net present value (assuming a 10% required rate of return) of the following investment—assume that its cash flows occur at year-end. Compared to the example case at the website, the larger cash inflows in the example below occur in the later years of the project's life. Is this investment acceptable based on the application of these two capital budgeting methods? Explain.

Year	Cash Flow
0...........	$(15,000)
1...........	1,000
2...........	2,000
3...........	3,000
4...........	6,000
5...........	7,000

BTN 11-6   Break into teams and identify four reasons that an international airline such as **Southwest** or **Delta** would invest in a project when an analysis using both payback period and net present value indicates it to be a poor investment. (*Hint:* Think about qualitative factors.) Provide an example of an investment project that supports your answer.

BTN 11-7   Read the chapter opener about Caron Proschan and her company, **Simply Gum**. Suppose Caron's business continues to grow, and she builds a massive new manufacturing facility and warehousing center to make her business more efficient and reduce costs.

Required

1. What are some of the management tools that Caron can use to evaluate whether the new manufacturing facility and warehousing center will be a good investment?
2. What information does Caron need to use the tools that you identified in your answer to part 1?
3. What are some of the advantages and disadvantages of each tool identified in your answer to part 1?

BTN 11-8   Visit or call a local auto dealership and inquire about leasing a car. Ask about the down payment and the required monthly payments. You will likely find the salesperson does not discuss the cost to purchase this car but focuses on the affordability of the monthly payments. This chapter gives you the tools to compute the cost of this car using the lease payment schedule in present dollars and to estimate the profit from leasing for an auto dealership.

Required

1. Compare the cost of leasing the car to buying it in present dollars using the information from the dealership you contact. (Assume you will make a final payment at the end of the lease and then own the car.)
2. Is it more costly to lease or buy the car? Support your answer with computations.

Chapter 11 Capital Budgeting and Investment Analysis — page 468

GLOBAL DECISION P3 P4

Samsung

BTN 11-9 Samsung's annual report includes information about its debt and interest rates. Its annual report reveals that Samsung recently issued bonds with an interest rate of 4.1%.

Required

Explain how Samsung would use that 4.1% rate to evaluate its investments in capital projects.

 GLOBAL VIEW

Siemens AG is a global electrical engineering and electronics company headquartered in Germany. Recently, the company invested £160 million to build a wind turbine plant in the United Kingdom. Net present value analyses support such decisions. In this case, Siemens foresees strong future cash flows based on increased demand for clean sources of energy, such as wind power.

 Global View Assignments

Discussion Question 11

Quick Study 11-18

BTN 11-9

12 chapter

Reporting Cash Flows

Learning Objectives

CONCEPTUAL

C1 Distinguish between operating, investing, and financing activities, and describe how noncash investing and financing activities are disclosed.

ANALYTICAL

A1 Analyze the statement of cash flows and apply the cash flow on total assets ratio.

PROCEDURAL

P1 Prepare a statement of cash flows.

P2 Compute cash flows from operating activities using the indirect method.

P3 Determine cash flows from both investing and financing activities.

P4 *Appendix 12A*—Illustrate use of a spreadsheet to prepare a statement of cash flows.

P5 *Appendix 12B*—Compute cash flows from operating activities using the direct method.

© Manjunath Kiran/AFP/Getty Images

Keeping Amazon above Water

SEATTLE—Market gurus warn us of companies with losses and rising debt. One of those companies, however, is **Amazon.com** (**Amazon.com**), the largest U.S. Internet retailer. Jeff Bezos, founder and CEO of Amazon, started the company in his garage. "The first initial start-up capital for Amazon.com came primarily from my parents, and they invested a large fraction of their life savings," recalls Jeff. "My dad's first question was, 'What's the Internet?' . . . He wasn't making a bet on this company or this concept. He was making a bet on his son."

Jeff has grown Amazon from an online bookstore into one of the world's largest online retail stores to compete with the likes of Walmart and Target. Interestingly, although Amazon reports negative income and rising debt, the market sees the company in a positive light.

Forbes named Amazon the sixth "Most Innovative Company in the World" and ranked it as the thirteenth "World's Most Valuable Brand." Given Amazon's losses and debt levels, is the market failing to fully reflect the accounting information? Is there something else that the market is focusing on?

"Your margin is my opportunity"
—Jeff Bezos

Let's dig a bit deeper. Amazon's financial statements reveal rising sales, nearly doubling over the past four years. Although costs exceeded sales in two of the recent four years, the growth in revenues foretells a positive future.

Amazon's cash flows are equally revealing. The key here is its operating cash flows, which have increased 185% over the past four years . . . an impressive result! In addition, its large investing cash outflows are what we expect from a growth company. Its relatively small financing cash inflows reveal that much of its expansion is self-funded—a good situation.

Analysis of Amazon requires examination of its cash flows. While only the future can reveal if the positive cash flow trend will lead to positive income, it is clear the market uses cash flow numbers in predicting Amazon's future. "We earn trust with customers over time," insists Jeff. "And that actually does maximize free cash flow over the long term."

Sources: *Amazon website,* January 2017; *Biography.com,* January 2016; *GreenBiz,* August 2014; *Fundable,* June 2015; *Inc.com,* May 2014; *Bloomberg,* January 2013; *Wall Street Journal,* October 2011

BASICS OF CASH FLOW REPORTING

This section describes the basics of cash flow reporting, including its purpose, measurement, classification, format, and preparation.

Purpose of the Statement of Cash Flows

The purpose of the **statement of cash flows** is to report cash receipts (inflows) and cash payments (outflows) during a period. This includes separately identifying the cash flows related to operating, investing, and financing activities. It is the detailed disclosure of individual sources and uses of cash that makes this statement useful. The statement of cash flows helps users answer questions such as:

Point: Internal users use the statement of cash flows to make investing and financing decisions. External users use this statement to assess the amount and timing of a company's cash flows.

- What explains the change in the cash balance?
- Where does a company spend its cash?
- How does a company receive its cash?

- Why do income and cash flows differ?
- How much is paid in dividends?
- Is there a cash shortage?

Importance of Cash Flows

Information about cash flows influences decisions. For instance, we prefer a company to pay expenses with cash from operations rather than by selling assets. Information about cash flows helps users decide whether a company has enough cash to pay its debts. It also helps evaluate a company's ability to pay unexpected obligations and pursue unexpected opportunities. Managers use cash flow information to plan day-to-day operations and make long-term investment decisions.

The case of **W. T. Grant Co.** is a classic example of the importance of cash flows. Grant reported net income of more than $40 million per year for three consecutive years. At that same time, it was experiencing an alarming decrease in cash from its operations. For instance, net cash outflow was more than $90 million by the end of that three-year period. Grant soon went bankrupt. Users who relied solely on Grant's income numbers were unpleasantly surprised. This reminds us that cash flows as well as income statement and balance sheet information are crucial in business decisions.

Source: Boston Public Library

Decision Insight

Know Cash Flows   "A lender must have a complete understanding of a borrower's cash flows to assess both the borrowing needs and repayment sources. This requires information about the major types of cash inflows and outflows. I have seen many companies, whose financial statements indicate good profitability, experience severe financial problems because the owners or managers lacked a good understanding of cash flows."—Mary E. Garza, **Bank of America** ■

Measurement of Cash Flows

Cash flows include both *cash* and *cash equivalents*. The statement of cash flows explains the difference between the beginning and ending balances of cash and cash equivalents. We continue to use the phrases *cash flows* and the *statement of cash flows,* but remember that both phrases refer to cash *and* cash equivalents.

A cash equivalent has two criteria: (1) be readily convertible to a known amount of cash and (2) be sufficiently close to its maturity so its market value is unaffected by interest rate changes. **American Express** defines its cash equivalents as including "highly liquid investments with original maturities of 90 days or less."

Classification of Cash Flows

Because cash and cash equivalents are combined, the statement of cash flows does not report transactions *between* cash and cash equivalents, such as cash paid to purchase cash equivalents

Cash Equivalents

and cash received from selling cash equivalents. However, all other cash receipts and cash payments are classified on the statement in one of three categories—operating, investing, or financing activities. Individual cash receipts and payments for each of these three categories are labeled to identify their originating transactions or events. A net cash inflow (source) occurs when the receipts in a category exceed the payments. A net cash outflow (use) occurs when the payments in a category exceed the receipts.

C1_____

Distinguish between operating, investing, and financing activities, and describe how noncash investing and financing activities are disclosed.

Operating Activities   **Operating activities** include those transactions and events that determine net income. Examples are the production and purchase of inventory, the sale of goods and services to customers, and the expenditures to operate the business. Not all items in income, such as unusual gains and losses, are operating activities (we discuss these exceptions later). Exhibit 12.1 lists common cash inflows and outflows from operating activities.

EXHIBIT 12.1

Cash Flows from Operating Activities

Point: *Cash dividends received* and *cash interest received* are reported as operating activities.

Investing Activities   **Investing activities** generally include those transactions and events that affect long-term assets—namely, the purchase and sale of long-term assets. They also include (1) the purchase and sale of short-term investments, *except* trading securities, and (2) lending and collecting money for notes receivable. Exhibit 12.2 lists examples of cash flows from investing activities. Cash from collecting the principal amounts of notes is classified as investing. However, the collection of interest on notes is reported as an operating activity; also, if a note results from sales to customers, it is classified as operating.

EXHIBIT 12.2

Cash Flows from Investing Activities

Financing Activities   **Financing activities** include those transactions and events that affect long-term liabilities and equity. Examples are (1) obtaining cash from issuing debt and repaying the amounts borrowed and (2) receiving cash from or distributing cash to owners. These activities involve transactions with a company's owners and creditors. Borrowing and repaying principal amounts relating to both short- and long-term debt are financing activities. However, payments of interest expense are classified as operating activities. Exhibit 12.3 lists examples of cash flows from financing activities.

EXHIBIT 12.3

Cash Flows from
Financing Activities

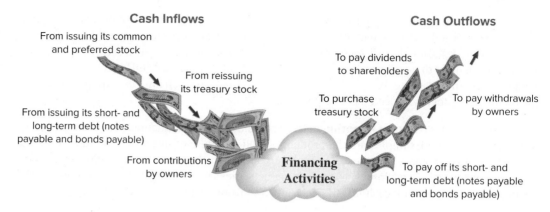

Link between Classification of Cash Flows and the Balance Sheet   Operating, investing, and financing activities are loosely linked to different parts of the balance sheet. Operating activities are affected by changes in current assets and current liabilities (and the income statement). Investing activities are affected by changes in long-term assets. Financing activities are affected by changes in long-term liabilities and equity. These links are shown in Exhibit 12.4. Exceptions to these links include (1) current assets *unrelated* to operations—such as short-term notes receivable from noncustomers and marketable (not trading) securities, which are considered investing activities, and (2) current liabilities *unrelated* to operations—such as short-term notes payable and dividends payable, which are considered financing activities.

EXHIBIT 12.4

Linkage of Cash Flow
Classifications to the
Balance Sheet

 Decision Insight

Where in the Statement Are Cash Flows?   Cash flows can be delayed or accelerated at the end of a period to improve or reduce current period cash flows. Also, cash flows can be misclassified. Cash outflows reported under operating activities are interpreted as expense payments. However, cash outflows reported under investing activities are interpreted as a positive sign of growth potential. Thus, managers face incentives to misclassify cash flows. For these reasons, cash flow reporting requires scrutiny. ▪

Noncash Investing and Financing

Some important investing and financing activities do not affect cash receipts or payments. One example is the purchase of long-term assets using a long-term note payable (loan). This transaction involves both investing and financing activities but does not affect any immediate cash inflow or outflow, so it is not reported in any of the three sections of the statement of cash flows. Such transactions are reported at the bottom of the statement of cash flows or in a note to the statement—common examples are in Exhibit 12.5.

EXHIBIT 12.5

Examples of Noncash
Investing and Financing
Activities

- Retirement of debt by issuing equity stock.
- Conversion of preferred stock to common stock.
- Lease of assets in a capital lease transaction.
- Purchase of long-term assets by issuing a note or bond.
- Exchange of noncash assets for other noncash assets.
- Purchase of noncash assets by issuing equity or debt.

Format of the Statement of Cash Flows

P1_____

Prepare a statement of
cash flows.

A statement of cash flows reports information about a company's cash receipts and cash payments during the period. Exhibit 12.6 shows the usual format. A company reports cash flows from three activities: operating, investing, and financing. The statement then shows

EXHIBIT 12.6

Format of the Statement of Cash Flows

COMPANY NAME
Statement of Cash Flows
For *period* Ended *date*

Cash flows from operating activities

[Compute operating cash flows using indirect or direct method]

Net cash provided (used) by operating activities .... $ #

Cash flows from investing activities

[List of individual inflows and outflows]

Net cash provided (used) by investing activities............................. #

Cash flows from financing activities

[List of individual inflows and outflows]

Net cash provided (used) by financing activities............................. #

Net increase (decrease) in cash. .... $ #

Cash (and equivalents) balance at prior period-end .... #

Cash (and equivalents) balance at current period-end .... $ #

Separate schedule or note disclosure of any noncash investing and financing transactions is required.

Point: Positive cash flows for a section are titled net cash "provided by" or "from." Negative cash flows are labeled as net cash "used by" or "for."

the net increase or decrease from those activities. Finally, it explains how transactions and events impact the prior period-end cash balance to produce its current period-end balance. Any noncash investing and financing transactions are disclosed in a note disclosure or separate schedule.

 **Decision** Maker

Entrepreneur   You are considering purchasing a start-up business that recently reported a $110,000 annual net loss and a $225,000 annual net cash inflow. How are these results possible? ■   *Answer:* Several factors can explain an increase in net cash flows when a net loss is reported, including (1) early recognition of expenses relative to revenues generated (such as research and development), (2) cash advances on long-term sales contracts not yet recognized in income, (3) issuances of debt or equity for cash to finance expansion, (4) cash sale of assets, (5) delay of cash payments, and (6) cash prepayment on sales.

Preparing the Statement of Cash Flows

Preparing a statement of cash flows involves five steps shown in Exhibit 12.7.

Step 1 Compute net increase or decrease in cash.

Step 2 Compute net cash from or for operating activities.

Step 3 Compute net cash from or for investing activities.

EXHIBIT 12.7

Five Steps in Preparing the Statement of Cash Flows

Step 4 Compute net cash from or for financing activities.

Step 5 Compute net cash from all sources; then *prove* it by adding it to beginning cash to get ending cash.

Computing the net increase or net decrease in cash is a simple but crucial computation. It equals the current period's cash balance minus the prior period's cash balance. This is the *bottom-line* figure for the statement of cash flows and is a check on accuracy.

Point: View the change in cash as a *target* number (or check figure) that we will fully explain and prove in the statement of cash flows.

Analyzing the Cash Account   A company's cash receipts and cash payments are recorded in the Cash account in its general ledger. The Cash account is therefore a place to look for information about cash flows. To illustrate, see the summarized Cash T-account of Genesis, Inc., in Exhibit 12.8.

EXHIBIT 12.8

Summarized Cash Account

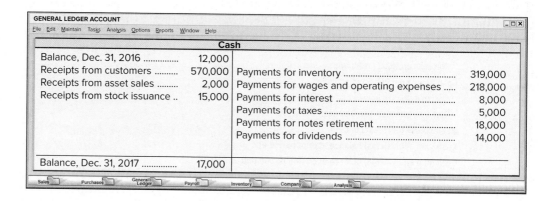

The statement of cash flows summarizes and classifies the transactions that led to the $5,000 increase in the Cash account. Preparing a statement of cash flows from Exhibit 12.8 requires determining whether an individual cash inflow or outflow is an operating, investing, or financing activity, and then listing each by activity. (We return to this approach in Exhibit 12.14.)

Analyzing Noncash Accounts   A second approach to preparing the statement of cash flows is analyzing noncash accounts. This approach uses the fact that when a company records cash inflows and outflows with debits and credits to the Cash account (see Exhibit 12.8), it also records credits and debits in noncash accounts (reflecting double-entry accounting). Many of these noncash accounts are balance sheet accounts—for instance, from the sale of land for cash. Others are revenue and expense accounts that are closed to equity. For instance, the sale of services for cash yields a credit to Services Revenue that is closed to Retained Earnings for a corporation. *All cash transactions eventually affect noncash balance sheet accounts.* Thus, we can determine cash inflows and outflows by analyzing changes in noncash balance sheet accounts.

Exhibit 12.9 uses the accounting equation to show the relation between the Cash account and the noncash balance sheet accounts. This exhibit starts with the accounting equation (at the top). It is then expanded in line (2) to separate cash from noncash asset accounts. To isolate cash on one side of the equation, line (3) shows noncash asset accounts being subtracted from both sides of the equation. Cash now equals the sum of the liability and equity accounts *minus* the noncash asset accounts. Line (4) points out that *changes* on one side of the accounting equation equal *changes* on the other side. It shows that we can explain changes in cash by

EXHIBIT 12.9

Relation between Cash
and Noncash Accounts

Information on changes in cash
is from analyzing *either* the
Cash account *or* the noncash
accounts.

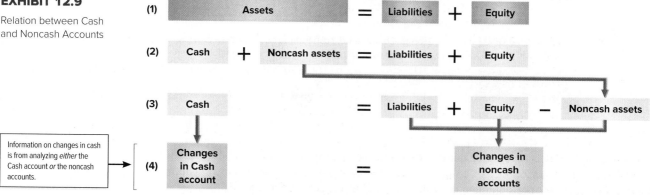

analyzing changes in the noncash accounts consisting of liability accounts, equity accounts, and noncash asset accounts. By analyzing noncash balance sheet accounts and any related income statement accounts, we can prepare a statement of cash flows.

Information to Prepare the Statement   Information to prepare the statement of cash flows usually comes from three sources: (1) comparative balance sheets, (2) the current income statement, and (3) additional information. Comparative balance sheets are used to compute changes in noncash accounts from the beginning to the end of the period. The current income statement is used to help compute cash flows from operating activities. Additional information often includes details on transactions and events that help explain both the cash flows and non-cash investing and financing activities.

Classify each of the following cash flows as operating, investing, or financing activities.

____ **a.** Purchase equipment for cash

____ **b.** Cash payment of wages

____ **c.** Issuance of stock for cash

____ **d.** Receipt of cash dividends from investments

____ **e.** Cash collections from customers

____ **f.** Note payable issued for cash

____ **g.** Cash paid for utilities

____ **h.** Cash paid to acquire investments

____ **i.** Cash paid to retire debt

____ **j.** Cash received as interest on investments

____ **k.** Cash received from selling investments

____ **l.** Cash received from a bank loan

NEED-TO-KNOW 12-1

Classifying Cash Flows

C1

Solution

a. Investing	**c.** Financing	**e.** Operating	**g.** Operating	**i.** Financing	**k.** Investing
b. Operating	**d.** Operating	**f.** Financing	**h.** Investing	**j.** Operating	**l.** Financing

Do More: QS 12-1, QS 12-2, E 12-1

CASH FLOWS FROM OPERATING

Indirect and Direct Methods of Reporting

Cash flows provided (used) by operating activities are reported in one of two ways: the *direct method* or the *indirect method.* **These two different methods apply only to the operating activities section.**

- The **direct method** separately lists each major item of operating cash receipts (such as cash received from customers) and each major item of operating cash payments (such as cash paid for inventory). The cash payments are subtracted from cash receipts to determine the net cash provided (used) by operating activities.

- The **indirect method** reports net income and then adjusts it to obtain net cash provided or used by operating activities. It does *not* report individual items of cash inflows and cash outflows from operating activities. Instead, the indirect method reports the necessary adjustments to reconcile net income to net cash provided or used by operating activities.

Firms Using Indirect vs. Direct

Indirect 99%   Direct 1%

The net cash amount provided by operating activities is *identical* **under both the direct and indirect methods.** The difference in these methods is with the computation and presentation. The indirect method is arguably easier to compute. Nearly all companies report operating cash flows using the indirect method (see margin graphic from recent survey), including **Apple, Google,** and **Samsung** in Appendix A.

To illustrate, we prepare the operating activities section of the statement of cash flows for Genesis. Exhibit 12.10 shows the December 31, 2016 and 2017, balance sheets of

Genesis along with its 2017 income statement. We use this information to prepare a statement of cash flows that explains the $5,000 increase in cash for 2017 as highlighted in its balance sheets. This $5,000 is computed as Cash of $17,000 at the end of 2017 minus Cash of $12,000 at the end of 2016.

EXHIBIT 12.10

Financial Statements

GENESIS
Income Statement
For Year Ended December 31, 2017

Sales		$590,000
Cost of goods sold	$300,000	
Wages and other operating expenses	216,000	
Interest expense	7,000	
Depreciation expense	24,000	(547,000)
		43,000
Other gains (losses)		
Loss on sale of plant assets	(6,000)	
Gain on retirement of notes	16,000	10,000
Income before taxes		53,000
Income taxes expense		(15,000)
Net income		$ 38,000

Additional information for 2017

a. The accounts payable balances result from inventory purchases.

b. Purchased $60,000 in plant assets by issuing $60,000 of notes payable.

c. Sold plant assets with a book value of $8,000 (original cost of $20,000 and accumulated depreciation of $12,000) for $2,000 cash, yielding a $6,000 loss.

d. Received $15,000 cash from issuing 3,000 shares of common stock.

e. Paid $18,000 cash to retire notes with a $34,000 book value, yielding a $16,000 gain.

f. Declared and paid cash dividends of $14,000.

GENESIS
Balance Sheets
December 31, 2017 and 2016

	2017	2016	Change
Assets			
Current assets			
Cash	$ 17,000	$ 12,000	$ 5,000 Increase
Accounts receivable	60,000	40,000	20,000 Increase
Inventory	84,000	70,000	14,000 Increase
Prepaid expenses	6,000	4,000	2,000 Increase
Total current assets	167,000	126,000	
Long-term assets			
Plant assets	250,000	210,000	40,000 Increase
Accumulated depreciation	(60,000)	(48,000)	12,000 Increase
Total assets	$357,000	$288,000	
Liabilities			
Current liabilities			
Accounts payable	$ 35,000	$ 40,000	$ 5,000 Decrease
Interest payable	3,000	4,000	1,000 Decrease
Income taxes payable	22,000	12,000	10,000 Increase
Total current liabilities	60,000	56,000	
Long-term notes payable	90,000	64,000	26,000 Increase
Total liabilities	150,000	120,000	
Equity			
Common stock, $5 par	95,000	80,000	15,000 Increase
Retained earnings	112,000	88,000	24,000 Increase
Total equity	207,000	168,000	
Total liabilities and equity	$357,000	$288,000	

> The next section describes the indirect method. Appendix 12B describes the direct method. An instructor can choose to cover either one or both methods. Neither section depends on the other. If the indirect method is skipped, then read Appendix 12B and return to the section titled "Cash Flows from Investing."

Applying the Indirect Method

P2

Compute cash flows from operating activities using the indirect method.

Net income is computed using accrual accounting. Revenues and expenses do not necessarily reflect the receipt and payment of cash. The indirect method adjusts the net income figure to obtain the net cash provided or used by operating activities. This includes subtracting noncash increases from net income and adding noncash charges back to net income.

To illustrate, the indirect method begins with Genesis's net income of $38,000 and adjusts it to obtain net cash provided by operating activities of $20,000—see Exhibit 12.11. There are two types of adjustments. There are ① adjustments to income statement items that neither provide nor use cash and ② adjustments to reflect changes in balance sheet current assets and current liabilities (linked to operating activities). Nearly all companies group adjustments into these two types, including Apple, Google, and Samsung in Appendix A. This section describes these two adjustments.

EXHIBIT 12.11

Operating Activities
Section—Indirect Method

GENESIS
Statement of Cash Flows—Operating Section under Indirect Method
For Year Ended December 31, 2017

Cash flows from operating activities	
Net income	$ 38,000
Adjustments to reconcile net income to net cash provided by operating activities	
Income statement items not affecting cash	
① Depreciation expense	24,000
Loss on sale of plant assets	6,000
Gain on retirement of notes	(16,000)
Changes in current assets and liabilities	
Increase in accounts receivable	(20,000)
Increase in inventory	(14,000)
② Increase in prepaid expenses	(2,000)
Decrease in accounts payable	(5,000)
Decrease in interest payable	(1,000)
Increase in income taxes payable	10,000
Net cash provided by operating activities	**$20,000**

① Adjustments for Income Statement Items Not Affecting Cash   The income statement usually includes some expenses and losses that do not reflect cash outflows. Examples are depreciation, amortization, depletion, bad debts expense, loss from an asset sale, and loss from retirement of notes payable. When there are expenses and losses that do not reflect cash outflows, the indirect method for reporting operating cash flows requires the following adjustment:

Expenses and losses with no cash outflows are added back to net income.

To see the logic of this adjustment, recall that expenses such as depreciation, amortization, and depletion have *no* cash effect, and adding them back cancels their deductions. To see the logic for losses, consider that items such as a plant asset sale and a notes retirement are usually recorded by recognizing the cash, removing all plant asset or notes accounts, and recording any loss or gain. The cash received or paid is part of either investing or financing cash flows; but because *no* operating cash flow effect occurs, we add the loss back to income to reverse the deduction.

Similarly, when net income includes revenues and gains that do not reflect cash inflows, the indirect method for reporting operating cash flows requires the following adjustment:

Revenues and gains with no cash inflows are subtracted from net income.

We apply these adjustments to the income statement items in Exhibit 12.10 that do not affect cash.

Point: An income statement reports revenues, gains, expenses, and losses on an accrual basis. The statement of cash flows reports cash received and cash paid for operating, financing, and investing activities.

Depreciation   Depreciation expense is Genesis's only operating item that has no effect on cash flows. We must add back the $24,000 depreciation expense to net income when computing cash provided by operating activities because depreciation is not a cash outflow.

Loss on Sale of Plant Assets   Genesis reports a $6,000 loss on sale of plant assets that reduces income but has no effect on cash flows. This $6,000 loss is added back to net income because it is not a cash outflow.

Gain on Retirement of Debt   A $16,000 gain on retirement of debt increases income but has no effect on cash flows. This means the $16,000 gain is subtracted from income because it is not a cash inflow.

These three adjustments to net income for "items not affecting cash" are shown as follows:

Net income		$ 38,000
Adjustments to reconcile net income to net cash provided by operating activities		
	Income statement items not affecting cash	
①	Depreciation expense	24,000
	Loss on sale of plant assets	6,000
	Gain on retirement of notes	(16,000)

② Adjustments for Changes in Current Assets and Current Liabilities This section describes adjustments for changes in current assets and current liabilities.

Adjustments for Changes in Current Assets Decreases in current assets require the following adjustment:

> **Decreases in current assets are added to net income.**

Increases in current assets require the following adjustment:

> **Increases in current assets are subtracted from net income.**

Adjustments for Changes in Current Liabilities Increases in current liabilities require the following adjustment:

> **Increases in current liabilities are added to net income.**

Decreases in current liabilities require the following adjustment:

> **Decreases in current liabilities are subtracted from net income.**

To illustrate, we apply these adjustment rules to the three noncash current assets and three current liabilities in Exhibit 12.10, which are then reported as follows.

Net income		$ 38,000
Adjustments to reconcile net income to net cash provided by operating activities		
	Increase in accounts receivable	(20,000)
	Increase in inventory	(14,000)
	Increase in prepaid expenses	(2,000)
②	Decrease in accounts payable	(5,000)
	Decrease in interest payable	(1,000)
	Increase in income taxes payable	10,000

Following is an explanation, including T-account analysis, for how these adjustments result in cash receipts and cash payments.

Accounts Receivable Following the rule above, the $20,000 increase in the current asset of accounts receivable is subtracted from income. This increase implies that Genesis collects less cash than is reported in sales. To see this, it is helpful to use *account analysis*. This involves setting up a T-account and reconstructing its major entries to compute cash receipts or payments as follows. We see that sales are $20,000 greater than cash receipts. This $20,000—reflected in the increase in Accounts Receivable—is subtracted from net income when computing cash provided by operating activities.

	Accounts Receivable		
Numbers in black are taken from Exhibit 12.10. The red number is the computed (plug) figure. →			
Bal., Dec. 31, 2016	40,000		
Sales	590,000	Cash receipts =	570,000
Bal., Dec. 31, 2017	60,000		

Inventory   The $14,000 increase in inventory is subtracted from income. This increase implies that Genesis had greater cash purchases than cost of goods sold, as shown here:

Inventory			
Bal., Dec. 31, 2016	70,000		
Purchases =	**314,000**	Cost of goods sold	300,000
Bal., Dec. 31, 2017	84,000		

Prepaid Expenses   The $2,000 increase in prepaid expenses is subtracted from income, implying that Genesis's cash payments exceed its recorded prepaid expenses, as shown here:

Prepaid Expenses			
Bal., Dec. 31, 2016	4,000		
Cash payments =	**218,000**	Wages and other operating exp.	216,000
Bal., Dec. 31, 2017	6,000		

Accounts Payable   The $5,000 decrease in the current liability for accounts payable is subtracted from income. This decrease implies that cash payments to suppliers exceed purchases, which is shown here:

Accounts Payable			
		Bal., Dec. 31, 2016	40,000
Cash payments =	**319,000**	Purchases	314,000
		Bal., Dec. 31, 2017	35,000

Interest Payable   The $1,000 decrease in interest payable is subtracted from income. This decrease indicates that cash paid for interest exceeds interest expense, which is shown here:

Interest Payable			
		Bal., Dec. 31, 2016	4,000
Cash paid for interest =	**8,000**	Interest expense	7,000
		Bal., Dec. 31, 2017	3,000

Income Taxes Payable   The $10,000 increase in income taxes payable is added to income. This increase implies that reported income taxes exceed the cash paid for taxes, which is shown here:

Income Taxes Payable			
		Bal., Dec. 31, 2016	12,000
Cash paid for taxes =	**5,000**	Income taxes expense	15,000
		Bal., Dec. 31, 2017	22,000

Summary Adjustments for Indirect Method

Exhibit 12.12 summarizes the adjustments to net income when computing net cash provided or used by operating activities under the indirect method.

EXHIBIT 12.12

Summary of Adjustments
for Operating Activities—
Indirect Method

Net Income (or Loss)

① Adjustments for operating items not providing or using cash

  + Noncash expenses and losses

   Examples: Expenses for depreciation, depletion, and amortization; losses from disposal of long-term assets and from retirement of debt

  − Noncash revenues and gains

   Examples: Gains from disposal of long-term assets and from retirement of debt

② Adjustments for changes in current assets and current liabilities

  + Decrease in noncash current operating asset

  − Increase in noncash current operating asset

  + Increase in current operating liability

  − Decrease in current operating liability

Net cash provided (used) by operating activities

■ **Decision** Insight

How Much Cash in Income?   The difference between net income and operating cash flows can be large and sometimes reflects on the quality of earnings. This bar chart shows the net income and operating cash flows of three companies. Operating cash flows can be either higher or lower than net income. ■

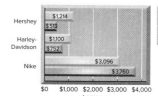

NEED-TO-KNOW 12-2

Reporting Operating
Cash Flows (Indirect)

P2

A company's current-year income statement and selected balance sheet data at December 31 of the current and prior years follow. Prepare only the operating activities section of the statement of cash flows using the indirect method for the current year.

Income Statement For Current Year Ended December 31	
Sales revenue	$120
Expenses	
Cost of goods sold	50
Depreciation expense	30
Salaries expense................	17
Interest expense................	3
Net income	$ 20

Selected Balance Sheet Accounts		
At December 31	**Current Yr**	**Prior Yr**
Accounts receivable	$12	$10
Inventory	6	9
Accounts payable	7	11
Salaries payable	8	3
Interest payable...............	1	0

Solution

Cash Flows from Operating Activities—Indirect Method For Current Year Ended December 31		
Cash flows from operating activities		
Net income		$20
Adjustments to reconcile net income to net cash provided by operating activities		
Income statement items not affecting cash		
Depreciation expense	$30	
Changes in current assets and current liabilities		
Increase in accounts receivable	(2)	
Decrease in inventory	3	
Decrease in accounts payable	(4)	
Increase in salaries payable	5	
Increase in interest payable	1	33
Net cash provided by operating activities................................		$53

Do More: QS 12-3, QS 12-4,
E 12-4, E 12-5, E 12-6

CASH FLOWS FROM INVESTING

The third step in preparing the statement of cash flows is to compute and report cash flows from investing activities. We do this by identifying changes in (1) all noncurrent asset accounts and (2) the current accounts for both notes receivable and investments in securities (excluding trading securities). We then analyze changes in these accounts to determine their effect, if any, on cash and report the cash flow effects in the investing activities section of the statement of cash flows. **Reporting of investing activities is identical under the direct method and indirect method.**

Three-Stage Process of Analysis

Information to compute cash flows from investing activities is usually taken from beginning and ending balance sheets and the income statement. We use a three-stage process to determine cash provided or used by investing activities: (1) identify changes in investing-related accounts, (2) explain these changes using reconstruction analysis, and (3) report their cash flow effects.

P3 _____

Determine cash flows from both investing and financing activities.

Analyzing Noncurrent Assets

Genesis both purchased and sold plant assets during the period. Both transactions are investing activities and are analyzed for their cash flow effects in this section.

Plant Asset Transactions   The *first stage* in analyzing the Plant Assets account and its related Accumulated Depreciation account is to identify any changes in these accounts from comparative balance sheets in Exhibit 12.10. This analysis reveals a $40,000 increase in plant assets from $210,000 to $250,000 and a $12,000 increase in accumulated depreciation from $48,000 to $60,000.

Point: Investing activities include (1) purchasing and selling long-term assets, (2) lending and collecting on notes receivable, and (3) purchasing and selling short-term investments other than cash equivalents and trading securities.

The *second stage* is to explain these changes. Items *b* and *c* of the additional information in Exhibit 12.10 affect plant assets. Recall that the Plant Assets account is affected by both asset purchases and sales; its Accumulated Depreciation account is normally increased from depreciation and decreased from the removal of accumulated depreciation in asset sales. To explain changes in these accounts and to identify their cash flow effects, we prepare *reconstructed entries* from prior transactions; *they are not the actual entries by the preparer.*

To illustrate, item *b* reports that Genesis purchased plant assets of $60,000 by issuing $60,000 in notes payable to the seller. The reconstructed entry for analysis of item *b* follows.

Reconstruction	Plant Assets	60,000	
	Notes Payable.		60,000

Next, item *c* reports that Genesis sold plant assets costing $20,000 (with $12,000 of accumulated depreciation) for $2,000 cash, resulting in a $6,000 loss. The reconstructed entry for analysis of item *c* follows.

Reconstruction	Cash.	2,000	
	Accumulated Depreciation	12,000	
	Loss on Sale of Plant Assets	6,000	
	Plant Assets.		20,000

We also reconstruct the entry for Depreciation Expense from the income statement. Depreciation expense results in no cash flow effect.

Reconstruction	Depreciation Expense	24,000	
	Accumulated Depreciation.		24,000

These three reconstructed entries are reflected in the following plant asset and related T-accounts.

Plant Assets				
Bal., Dec. 31, 2016	210,000			
Purchase	**60,000**	**Sale**	**20,000**	
Bal., Dec. 31, 2017	250,000			

Accumulated Depreciation—Plant Assets				
		Bal., Dec. 31, 2016	48,000	
Sale	**12,000**	**Depr. expense**	**24,000**	
		Bal., Dec. 31, 2017	60,000	

This reconstruction analysis is complete in that the change in plant assets from $210,000 to $250,000 is fully explained by the $60,000 purchase and the $20,000 sale. Also, the change in accumulated depreciation from $48,000 to $60,000 is fully explained by depreciation expense of $24,000 and the removal of $12,000 in accumulated depreciation from the asset sale.

The *third stage* in analyzing the Plant Assets account looks back at the reconstructed entries to identify any cash flows. The identified cash flow effect is reported in the investing section of the statement as follows:

Cash flows from investing activities	
Cash received from sale of plant assets	$2,000

Example: If a plant asset costing $40,000 with $37,000 of accumulated depreciation is sold at a $1,000 loss, what is the cash flow? What is the cash flow if this asset is sold at a gain of $3,000?
Answers: +$2,000; +$6,000

The $60,000 purchase described in item *b* and financed by issuing notes is a noncash investing and financing activity. It is reported in a note or in a separate schedule to the statement as follows:

Noncash investing and financing activity	
Purchased plant assets with issuance of notes	$60,000

Analyzing Additional Assets

Genesis did not have any additional noncurrent assets (or nonoperating current assets) and, therefore, we have no additional investing transactions to analyze. If other investing assets did exist, we would identify and report the investing cash flows using the same three-stage process illustrated for plant assets.

NEED-TO-KNOW 12-3

Reporting Investing
Cash Flows

P3

Use the following information to determine this company's cash flows from investing activities.
a. A factory with a book value of $100 and an original cost of $800 was sold at a loss of $10.
b. Paid $70 cash for new equipment.
c. Long-term stock investments were sold for $20 cash, yielding a loss of $4.
d. Sold land costing $175 for $160 cash, yielding a loss of $15.

Solution

Cash flows from investing activities	
Cash received from sale of factory (from *a**)	$ 90
Cash paid for new equipment (from *b*)	(70)
Cash received from sale of long-term investments (from *c*)	20
Cash received from sale of land (from *d*)	160
Net cash provided by investing activities	$200

Do More: QS 12-5, QS 12-6, QS 12-8, E 12-7

* Cash received from sale of factory = Book value − Loss = $100 − $10 = $90

CASH FLOWS FROM FINANCING

The fourth step in preparing the statement of cash flows is to compute and report cash flows from financing activities. We do this by identifying changes in all noncurrent liability accounts (including the current portion of any notes and bonds) and the equity accounts. These accounts include long-term debt, notes payable, bonds payable, common stock, and retained earnings. Changes in these accounts are then analyzed to determine their effect, if any, on cash. Results are reported in the financing activities section of the statement. **Reporting of financing activities is identical under the direct method and indirect method.**

Three-Stage Process of Analysis

We use a three-stage process to determine cash provided or used by financing activities: (1) identify changes in financing-related accounts, (2) explain these changes using reconstruction analysis, and (3) report their cash flow effects.

Analyzing Noncurrent Liabilities

Genesis had two transactions involving noncurrent liabilities. We analyzed one of those, the $60,000 issuance of notes payable to purchase plant assets. This transaction is reported as a significant noncash investing and financing activity in a footnote or a separate schedule to the statement of cash flows. The other remaining transaction involving noncurrent liabilities is the cash settlement of notes payable.

Point: Examples of financing activities are (1) receiving cash from issuing debt or repaying amounts borrowed and (2) receiving cash from or distributing cash to owners.

Notes Payable Transactions   The *first stage* in analysis of notes is to review the comparative balance sheets from Exhibit 12.10. This analysis reveals an increase in notes payable from $64,000 to $90,000.

The *second stage* explains this change. Item *e* of the additional information in Exhibit 12.10 reports that notes with a carrying value of $34,000 are retired for $18,000 cash, resulting in a $16,000 gain. The reconstructed entry for analysis of item *e* follows:

Reconstruction	Notes Payable	34,000	
	Gain on retirement of debt.......................		16,000
	Cash		**18,000**

This entry reveals an $18,000 cash outflow for retirement of notes and a $16,000 gain from comparing the notes payable carrying value to the cash received. This gain does not reflect any cash inflow or outflow. Also, item *b* of the additional information reports that Genesis purchased plant assets costing $60,000 by issuing $60,000 in notes payable to the seller. We reconstructed this entry when analyzing investing activities: It showed a $60,000 increase to notes payable that is reported as a noncash investing and financing transaction. The Notes Payable account is explained by these reconstructed entries as follows:

		Notes Payable	
		Bal., Dec. 31, 2016	64,000
Retired notes	34,000	Issued notes	**60,000**
		Bal., Dec. 31, 2017	90,000

The *third stage* is to report the cash flow effect of the notes retirement in the financing section of the statement as follows:

Cash flows from financing activities	
Cash paid to retire notes........................	$(18,000)

Analyzing Equity

Genesis had two transactions involving equity accounts. The first is the issuance of common stock for cash. The second is the declaration and payment of cash dividends. We analyze both.

Common Stock Transactions   The *first stage* in analyzing common stock is to review the comparative balance sheets from Exhibit 12.10, which reveal an increase in common stock from $80,000 to $95,000.

The *second stage* explains this change. Item *d* of the additional information in Exhibit 12.10 reports that 3,000 shares of common stock are issued at par for $5 per share. The reconstructed entry for analysis of item *d* follows:

Reconstruction	Cash..	15,000	
	Common Stock		15,000

This entry reveals a $15,000 cash inflow from stock issuance and is reflected in (and explains) the Common Stock account as follows:

Common Stock		
	Bal., Dec. 31, 2016	80,000
	Issued stock	**15,000**
	Bal., Dec. 31, 2017	95,000

The *third stage* reports the cash flow effect from stock issuance in the financing section of the statement as follows:

Cash flows from financing activities	
Cash received from issuing stock	$15,000

Retained Earnings Transactions   The *first stage* in analyzing the Retained Earnings account is to review the comparative balance sheets from Exhibit 12.10. This reveals an increase in retained earnings from $88,000 to $112,000.

The *second stage* explains this change. Item *f* of the additional information in Exhibit 12.10 reports that cash dividends of $14,000 are paid. The reconstructed entry follows:

Reconstruction	Retained Earnings	14,000	
	Cash		**14,000**

This entry reveals a $14,000 cash outflow for cash dividends. Also see that the Retained Earnings account is impacted by net income of $38,000. (Net income was analyzed under the operating section of the statement of cash flows.) The reconstructed Retained Earnings account follows:

Retained Earnings			
		Bal., Dec. 31, 2016	88,000
Cash dividend	**14,000**	**Net income**	**38,000**
		Bal., Dec. 31, 2017	112,000

Point: Financing activities not affecting cash flow include *declaration* of a cash dividend, *declaration* of a stock dividend, issuance of a stock dividend, and a stock split.

The *third stage* reports the cash flow effect from the cash dividend in the financing section of the statement as follows:

Cash flows from financing activities	
Cash paid for dividends	$(14,000)

We now have identified and explained all of the Genesis cash inflows and cash outflows and one noncash investing and financing transaction.

Proving Cash Balances

The final step in preparing the statement is to report the beginning and ending cash balances and prove that the *net change in cash* is explained by operating, investing, and financing cash flows. This step is shown here for Genesis.

Net cash provided by operating activities	$ 20,000
Net cash provided by investing activities	2,000
Net cash used in financing activities	(17,000)
Net increase in cash	**$ 5,000**
Cash balance at 2016 year-end	12,000
Cash balance at 2017 year-end	$ 17,000

The preceding table shows that the $5,000 net increase in cash, from $12,000 at the beginning of the period to $17,000 at the end, is reconciled by net cash flows from operating ($20,000 inflow), investing ($2,000 inflow), and financing ($17,000 outflow) activities. This is reported at the bottom of the statement of cash flows as shown in Exhibit 12.13.

EXHIBIT 12.13

Complete Statement of Cash Flows—Indirect Method

GENESIS Statement of Cash Flows (Indirect Method) For Year Ended December 31, 2017		
Cash flows from operating activities		
Net income	$ 38,000	
Adjustments to reconcile net income to net cash provided by operating activities		
Income statement items not affecting cash		
Depreciation expense	24,000	
Loss on sale of plant assets	6,000	
Gain on retirement of notes	(16,000)	
Changes in current assets and liabilities		
Increase in accounts receivable	(20,000)	
Increase in inventory.	(14,000)	
Increase in prepaid expenses.	(2,000)	
Decrease in accounts payable	(5,000)	
Decrease in interest payable	(1,000)	
Increase in income taxes payable.	10,000	
Net cash provided by operating activities.		$20,000
Cash flows from investing activities		
Cash received from sale of plant assets	2,000	
Net cash provided by investing activities		2,000
Cash flows from financing activities		
Cash received from issuing stock	15,000	
Cash paid to retire notes	(18,000)	
Cash paid for dividends	(14,000)	
Net cash used in financing activities		(17,000)
Net increase in cash		$ 5,000
Cash balance at prior year-end		12,000
Cash balance at current year-end		$17,000

Point: Refer to Exhibit 12.10 and identify the $5,000 change in cash. This change is what the statement of cash flows explains; it serves as a check.

Point: The statement of cash flows is usually the last of the four financial statements to be prepared.

Decision Maker

Reporter Management is in labor contract negotiations and grants you an interview. It highlights a recent $600,000 net loss that involves a $930,000 unusual loss and a total net cash outflow of $550,000 (which includes net cash outflows of $850,000 for investing activities and $350,000 for financing activities). What is your assessment of this company? ■ *Answer: An initial reaction from the $600,000 loss and a $550,000 decrease in net cash is not positive. However, closer scrutiny reveals a more positive picture. Cash flow from operations is $650,000, computed as [?] − $850,000 − $350,000 = $(550,000). We also see that net income before the unusual loss is $330,000, computed as [?] − $930,000 = $(600,000).*

Use the following information to determine this company's cash flows from financing activities.
a. Issued common stock for $40 cash.
b. Paid $70 cash to retire a note payable at its $70 maturity value.
c. Paid cash dividend of $15.
d. Paid $5 cash to acquire its treasury stock.

NEED-TO-KNOW 12-4

Reporting Financing Cash Flows

P3

Solution

Cash flows from financing activities	
Cash received from issuance of common stock (from *a*)	$ 40
Cash paid to settle note payable (from *b*).	(70)
Cash paid for dividend (from *c*)	(15)
Cash paid to acquire treasury stock (from *d*)	(5)
Net cash used by financing activities	$(50)

Do More: QS 12-9, QS 12-10, QS 12-13, E 12-8

SUMMARY USING T-ACCOUNTS

Exhibit 12.14 uses T-accounts to summarize how changes in Genesis's noncash balance sheet accounts affect its cash inflows and outflows (dollar amounts in thousands). The top of the exhibit shows the company's Cash T-account, and the lower part shows T-accounts for its remaining balance sheet accounts. We see that the $20,000 net cash provided by operating activities and the $5,000 net increase in cash shown in the Cash T-account agree with the same figures in the statement of cash flows in Exhibit 12.13. We explain Exhibit 12.14 in five parts:

a. Entry (1) records $38 net income on the credit side of the Retained Earnings account and the debit side of the Cash account. This $38 net income in the Cash T-account is adjusted until it reflects the $5 net increase in cash.

b. Entries (2) through (4) add the $24 depreciation and $6 loss on asset sale to net income and subtract the $16 gain on retirement of notes.

c. Entries (5) through (10) adjust net income for changes in current asset and current liability accounts.

d. Entry (11) records the noncash investing and financing transaction involving a $60 purchase of assets by issuing $60 of notes.

e. Entries (12) and (13) record the $15 stock issuance and the $14 dividend.

EXHIBIT 12.14

Balance Sheet T-Accounts to Explain the Change in Cash ($ thousands)

Cash

(1) Net income	38		
(2) Depreciation	24	(4) Gain on retirement of notes	16
(3) Loss on sale of plant assets	6		
(10) Increase in income taxes payable	10	(5) Increase in accounts receivable	20
		(6) Increase in inventory	14
		(7) Increase in prepaid expense	2
		(8) Decrease in accounts payable	5
		(9) Decrease in interest payable	1
Net cash provided by operating activities	20		
(3) Cash received from sale of plant assets	2	(4) Cash paid to retire notes	18
(12) Cash received from issuing stock	15	(13) Cash paid for dividends	14
Net increase in cash	5		

Info to prepare statement of cash flows

Accounts Receivable

Beg. 40	
(5) 20	
End. 60	

Inventory

Beg. 70	
(6) 14	
End. 84	

Prepaid Expenses

Beg. 4	
(7) 2	
End. 6	

Plant Assets

Beg. 210	(3) 20
(11) 60	
End. 250	

Accumulated Depreciation

	Beg. 48
(3) 12	(2) 24
	End. 60

Accounts Payable

	Beg. 40
(8) 5	
	End. 35

Interest Payable

	Beg. 4
(9) 1	
	End. 3

Income Taxes Payable

	Beg. 12
	(10) 10
	End. 22

Long-Term Notes Payable

	Beg. 64
(4) 34	
	(11) 60
	End. 90

Common Stock

	Beg. 80
	(12) 15
	End. 95

Retained Earnings

	Beg. 88
	(1) 38
(13) 14	
	End. 112

SUSTAINABILITY AND ACCOUNTING

Amazon.com seeks to reduce its environmental impact through a number of sustainability initiatives. One is frustration-free packaging. This multiyear initiative is "designed to make it easier for customers to liberate products from their packages."

Not only does this initiative lead to higher customer satisfaction, it also reduces waste and the use of plastic. According to Amazon's website, the frustration-free packaging is "100% recyclable" and eliminates "hard plastic clamshell cases and plastic-coated ties." Moreover, Amazon's packaging is made up of 50% recycled content.

Amazon supports charitable and nonprofit organizations through a program called *AmazonSmile*. According to its website, "AmazonSmile is a simple and automatic way for you to support your favorite charitable organization every time you shop, at no cost to you." AmazonSmile donates 0.5% of the purchase price of certain products to the charity or non-profit organization of your choice.

To ensure AmazonSmile sales are correctly tracked, Amazon relies on its accounting system to record separately its eligible and ineligible sales. The accounting system both records AmazonSmile sales and computes the amount to be donated.

Amazon sets up an accounts payable account for each charity that will receive a donation. At a future date, Amazon donates the cash to the charity and settles the accounts payable. Because of Amazon's charitable program and effective accounting system, programs such as the **American Red Cross** and **Doctors Without Borders** receive thousands in additional donations each year.

© Hardy Mueller/laif/Redux

Cash Flow Analysis **Decision Analysis**

Analyzing Cash Sources and Uses

Most managers stress the importance of understanding and predicting cash flows for business decisions. Creditors evaluate a company's ability to generate cash before deciding whether to lend money. Investors also assess cash inflows and outflows before buying and selling stock. Information in the statement of cash flows helps address questions such as (1) How much cash is generated from or used in operations? (2) What expenditures are made with cash from operations? (3) What is the source of cash for debt payments? (4) What is the source of cash for distributions to owners? (5) How is the increase in investing activities financed? (6) What is the source of cash for new plant assets? (7) Why is cash flow from operations different from income? (8) How is cash from financing used?

To effectively answer these questions, it is important to separately analyze investing, financing, and operating activities. To illustrate, consider data from three different companies in Exhibit 12.15. These companies operate in the same industry and have been in business for several years.

A1

Analyze the statement of cash flows and apply the cash flow on total assets ratio.

$ thousands	BMX	ATV	Trex
Cash provided (used) by operating activities	$90,000	$40,000	$(24,000)
Cash provided (used) by investing activities			
Proceeds from sale of plant assets.			26,000
Purchase of plant assets	(48,000)	(25,000)	
Cash provided (used) by financing activities			
Proceeds from issuance of debt			13,000
Repayment of debt	(27,000)		
Net increase (decrease) in cash	$15,000	$15,000	$ 15,000

EXHIBIT 12.15

Cash Flows of Competing Companies

Each company generates an identical $15,000 net increase in cash, but its sources and uses of cash flows are very different. BMX's operating activities provide net cash flows of $90,000, allowing it to purchase plant assets of $48,000 and repay $27,000 of its debt. ATV's operating activities provide $40,000 of cash flows, limiting its purchase of plant assets to $25,000. Trex's $15,000 net cash increase is due to selling plant assets and incurring additional debt. Its operating activities yield a net cash outflow of $24,000. Overall, analysis of these cash flows reveals that BMX is more capable of generating future cash flows than is ATV or Trex.

■ **Decision** Insight

Free Cash Flows   Many investors use cash flows to value company stock. However, cash-based valuation models often yield different stock values due to differences in measurement of cash flows. Most models require cash flows that are "free" for distribution to shareholders. These *free cash flows* are defined as cash flows available to shareholders after operating asset reinvestments and debt payments. Knowledge of the statement of cash flows is key to proper computation of free cash flows. A company's growth and financial flexibility depend on adequate free cash flows. ■

Cash Flow on Total Assets

Cash flow information has limitations, but it can help measure a company's ability to meet its obligations, pay dividends, expand operations, and obtain financing. Users often compute and analyze a cash-based ratio similar to return on total assets except that its numerator is net cash flow from operating activities. The **cash flow on total assets** ratio is shown in Exhibit 12.16.

Point: CFO (cash flow from operations)
Less: Capital expenditures
Less: Debt repayments
= FCF (free cash flows)

EXHIBIT 12.16

Cash Flow on Total Assets

$$\text{Cash flow on total assets} = \frac{\text{Cash flow from operations}}{\text{Average total assets}}$$

This ratio reflects actual cash flows and is not affected by accounting income recognition and measurement. It can help business decision makers estimate the amount and timing of cash flows when planning and analyzing operating activities.

To illustrate, the 2015 cash flow on total assets ratio for **Nike** is 23.3%—see Exhibit 12.17. Is a 23.3% ratio good or bad? To answer this question, we compare this ratio with the ratios of prior years (we could also compare its ratio with those of its competitors and the market). Nike's cash flow on total assets ratio for several prior years is in the second (middle) column of Exhibit 12.17. Results show that its 23.3% return is its highest return over the past five years.

EXHIBIT 12.17

Nike's Cash Flow on Total Assets

Year	Cash Flow on Total Assets	Return on Total Assets
2015	23.3%	16.3%
2014	16.6	14.9
2013	18.3	15.0
2012	12.5	14.6
2011	12.3	14.5

As an indicator of *earnings quality,* some analysts compare the cash flow on total assets ratio to the return on total assets ratio. Nike's return on total assets is provided in the third column of Exhibit 12.17. Nike's cash flow on total assets ratio exceeds its return on total assets in three of the past five years, leading some analysts to infer that Nike's earnings quality is not as good for that period because much of its earnings are not being realized in the form of cash.

■ **Decision** Insight

Cash Flow Ratios   Analysts use various other cash-based ratios, including the following two:

Point: The following ratio helps assess whether operating cash flow is adequate to meet long-term obligations:

Cash coverage of debt = Cash flow from operations ÷ Noncurrent liabilities.

A low ratio suggests a higher risk of insolvency; a high ratio suggests a greater ability to meet long-term obligations.

(1) $$\text{Cash coverage of growth} = \frac{\text{Operating cash flow}}{\text{Cash outflow for plant assets}}$$

where a low ratio (less than 1) implies cash inadequacy to meet asset growth, whereas a high ratio implies cash adequacy for asset growth.

(2) $$\text{Operating cash flow to sales} = \frac{\text{Operating cash flow}}{\text{Net sales}}$$

When this ratio substantially and consistently differs from the operating income to net sales ratio, the risk of accounting improprieties increases. ■

Comparative balance sheets, income statement, and additional information follow.

UMA COMPANY
Balance Sheets
December 31, 2017 and 2016

	2017	2016
Assets		
Cash	$ 43,050	$ 23,925
Accounts receivable	34,125	39,825
Inventory	156,000	146,475
Prepaid expenses	3,600	1,650
Total current assets	236,775	211,875
Equipment	135,825	146,700
Accum. depreciation—Equipment	(61,950)	(47,550)
Total assets	$310,650	$311,025
Liabilities		
Accounts payable	$ 28,800	$ 33,750
Income taxes payable	5,100	4,425
Dividends payable	0	4,500
Total current liabilities	33,900	42,675
Bonds payable	0	37,500
Total liabilities	33,900	80,175
Equity		
Common stock, $10 par	168,750	168,750
Retained earnings	108,000	62,100
Total liabilities and equity	$310,650	$311,025

UMA COMPANY
Income Statement
For Year Ended December 31, 2017

Sales		$446,100
Cost of goods sold	$222,300	
Other operating expenses	120,300	
Depreciation expense	25,500	(368,100)
		78,000
Other gains (losses)		
Loss on sale of equipment	3,300	
Loss on retirement of bonds	825	(4,125)
Income before taxes		73,875
Income taxes expense		(13,725)
Net income		$ 60,150

Additional Information

a. Equipment costing $21,375 with accumulated depreciation of $11,100 is sold for cash.
b. Equipment purchases are for cash.
c. Accumulated Depreciation is affected by depreciation expense and the sale of equipment.
d. The balance of Retained Earnings is affected by dividend declarations and net income.
e. All sales are made on credit.
f. All inventory purchases are on credit.
g. Accounts Payable balances result from inventory purchases.
h. Prepaid expenses relate to "other operating expenses."

Required

1. Prepare a statement of cash flows using the indirect method for year 2017.
2.ᴮ Prepare a statement of cash flows using the direct method for year 2017.

PLANNING THE SOLUTION

- Prepare two blank statements of cash flows with sections for operating, investing, and financing activities using the (1) indirect method format and (2) direct method format.
- Compute the cash paid for equipment and the cash received from the sale of equipment using the additional information provided along with the amount for depreciation expense and the change in the balances of Equipment and Accumulated Depreciation. Use T-accounts to help chart the effects of the sale and purchase of equipment on the balances of the Equipment account and the Accumulated Depreciation account.

- Compute the effect of net income on the change in the Retained Earnings account balance. Assign the difference between the change in retained earnings and the amount of net income to dividends declared. Adjust the dividends declared amount for the change in the Dividends Payable balance.
- Compute cash received from customers, cash paid for inventory, cash paid for other operating expenses, and cash paid for taxes as illustrated in the chapter.
- Enter the cash effects of reconstruction entries to the appropriate section(s) of the statement.
- Total each section of the statement, determine the total net change in cash, and add it to the beginning balance to get the ending balance of cash.

SOLUTION

Supporting computations for cash receipts and cash payments.

(1) *Cost of equipment sold		$ 21,375
	Accumulated depreciation of equipment sold	(11,100)
	Book value of equipment sold	10,275
	Loss on sale of equipment	(3,300)
	Cash received from sale of equipment	$ 6,975
	Cost of equipment sold	$ 21,375
	Less decrease in the Equipment account balance	(10,875)
	Cash paid for new equipment	$ 10,500
(2)	Loss on retirement of bonds	$ 825
	Carrying value of bonds retired	37,500
	Cash paid to retire bonds	$ 38,325
(3)	Net income	$ 60,150
	Less increase in retained earnings	45,900
	Dividends declared	14,250
	Plus decrease in dividends payable	4,500
	Cash paid for dividends	$ 18,750
(4)B	Sales	$ 446,100
	Add decrease in accounts receivable	5,700
	Cash received from customers	$451,800
(5)B	Cost of goods sold	$ 222,300
	Plus increase in inventory	9,525
	Purchases	231,825
	Plus decrease in accounts payable	4,950
	Cash paid for inventory	$236,775
(6)B	Other operating expenses	$ 120,300
	Plus increase in prepaid expenses	1,950
	Cash paid for other operating expenses	$122,250
(7)B	Income taxes expense	$ 13,725
	Less increase in income taxes payable	(675)
	Cash paid for income taxes	$ 13,050

* Supporting T-account analysis for part 1 follows.

Equipment					Accumulated Depreciation—Equipment		
Bal., Dec. 31, 2016	146,700					Bal., Dec. 31, 2016	47,550
Cash purchase	10,500	Sale	21,375	Sale 11,100	Depr. expense	25,500
Bal., Dec. 31, 2017	135,825					Bal., Dec. 31, 2017	61,950

1. Indirect method:

UMA COMPANY
Statement of Cash Flows (Indirect Method)
For Year Ended December 31, 2017

Cash flows from operating activities		
Net income		$ 60,150
Adjustments to reconcile net income to net cash provided by operating activities		
Income statement items not affecting cash		
Depreciation expense	25,500	
Loss on sale of plant assets	3,300	
Loss on retirement of bonds	825	
Changes in current assets and current liabilities		
Decrease in accounts receivable	5,700	
Increase in inventory	(9,525)	
Increase in prepaid expenses	(1,950)	
Decrease in accounts payable	(4,950)	
Increase in income taxes payable	675	
Net cash provided by operating activities		$79,725
Cash flows from investing activities		
Cash received from sale of equipment	6,975	
Cash paid for equipment	(10,500)	
Net cash used in investing activities		(3,525)
Cash flows from financing activities		
Cash paid to retire bonds payable	(38,325)	
Cash paid for dividends	(18,750)	
Net cash used in financing activities		(57,075)
Net increase in cash		$19,125
Cash balance at prior year-end		23,925
Cash balance at current year-end		$43,050

2.[B] Direct method (Appendix 12B):

UMA COMPANY
Statement of Cash Flows (Direct Method)
For Year Ended December 31, 2017

Cash flows from operating activities		
Cash received from customers	$ 451,800	
Cash paid for inventory	(236,775)	
Cash paid for other operating expenses	(122,250)	
Cash paid for income taxes	(13,050)	
Net cash provided by operating activities		$ 79,725
Cash flows from investing activities		
Cash received from sale of equipment	6,975	
Cash paid for equipment	(10,500)	
Net cash used in investing activities		(3,525)
Cash flows from financing activities		
Cash paid to retire bonds payable	(38,325)	
Cash paid for dividends	(18,750)	
Net cash used in financing activities		(57,075)
Net increase in cash		$ 19,125
Cash balance at prior year-end		23,925
Cash balance at current year-end		$ 43,050

12A

Spreadsheet Preparation of the Statement of Cash Flows

This appendix explains how to use a spreadsheet (work sheet) to prepare the statement of cash flows under the indirect method.

P4
___

Illustrate use of a spreadsheet to prepare a statement of cash flows.

Preparing the Indirect Method Spreadsheet   Analyzing noncash accounts can be challenging when a company has a large number of accounts and many operating, investing, and financing transactions. A *spreadsheet,* also called *work sheet* or *working paper,* can help us organize the information needed to prepare a statement of cash flows. A spreadsheet also makes it easier to check the accuracy of our work. To illustrate, we return to the comparative balance sheets and income statement shown in Exhibit 12.10. We use the following identifying letters *a* through *g* to code changes in accounts, and letters *h* through *m* for additional information, to prepare the statement of cash flows:

  a. Net income is $38,000.
  b. Accounts receivable increase by $20,000.
  c. Inventory increases by $14,000.
  d. Prepaid expenses increase by $2,000.
  e. Accounts payable decrease by $5,000.
  f. Interest payable decreases by $1,000.
  g. Income taxes payable increase by $10,000.
  h. Depreciation expense is $24,000.
  i. Plant assets costing $20,000 with accumulated depreciation of $12,000 are sold for $2,000 cash. This yields a loss on sale of assets of $6,000.
  j. Notes with a book value of $34,000 are retired with a cash payment of $18,000, yielding a $16,000 gain on retirement.
  k. Plant assets costing $60,000 are purchased with an issuance of notes payable for $60,000.
  l. Issued 3,000 shares of common stock for $15,000 cash.
  m. Paid cash dividends of $14,000.

Exhibit 12A.1 shows the indirect method spreadsheet for Genesis. We enter both beginning and ending balance sheet amounts on the spreadsheet. We also enter information in the Analysis of Changes columns (keyed to the additional information items *a* through *m*) to explain changes in the accounts and determine the cash flows for operating, investing, and financing activities. Information about noncash investing and financing activities is reported near the bottom.

Entering the Analysis of Changes on the Spreadsheet   The following sequence of procedures is used to complete the spreadsheet after the beginning and ending balances of the balance sheet accounts are entered:

Point: Analysis of the changes on the spreadsheet are summarized here:

1. Cash flows from operating activities generally affect net income, current assets, and current liabilities.

2. Cash flows from investing activities generally affect noncurrent asset accounts.

3. Cash flows from financing activities generally affect noncurrent liability and equity accounts.

① Enter net income as the first item in the statement of cash flows section for computing operating cash inflow (debit) and as a credit to Retained Earnings.

② In the statement of cash flows section, adjustments to net income are entered as debits if they increase cash flows and as credits if they decrease cash flows. Applying this same rule, adjust net income for the change in each noncash current asset and current liability account related to operating activities. For each adjustment to net income, the offsetting debit or credit must help reconcile the beginning and ending balances of a current asset or current liability account.

③ Enter adjustments to net income for income statement items not providing or using cash in the period. For each adjustment, the offsetting debit or credit must help reconcile a noncash balance sheet account.

④ Adjust net income to eliminate any gains or losses from investing and financing activities. Because the cash from a gain must be excluded from operating activities, the gain is entered as a credit in the operating activities section. Losses are entered as debits. For each adjustment, the related debit and/or credit must help reconcile balance sheet accounts and involve reconstructed entries to show the cash flow from investing or financing activities.

EXHIBIT 12A.1

Spreadsheet for Preparing
Statement of Cash Flows—
Indirect Method

	A	B	C	D	E	F	G
1				GENESIS			
2				Spreadsheet for Statement of Cash Flows—Indirect Method			
3				For Year Ended December 31, 2017			
4			Dec. 31,	Analysis of Changes			Dec. 31,
5			2016	Debit		Credit	2017
6	**Balance Sheet—Debit Bal. Accounts**						
7	Cash		$ 12,000				$ 17,000
8	Accounts receivable		40,000	(b) $ 20,000			60,000
9	Inventory		70,000	(c) 14,000			84,000
10	Prepaid expenses		4,000	(d) 2,000			6,000
11	Plant assets		210,000	(k1) 60,000	(i) $ 20,000		250,000
12			$336,000				$417,000
13	**Balance Sheet—Credit Bal. Accounts**						
14	Accumulated depreciation		$ 48,000	(i) 12,000	(h)	24,000	$ 60,000
15	Accounts payable		40,000	(e) 5,000			35,000
16	Interest payable		4,000	(f) 1,000			3,000
17	Income taxes payable		12,000		(g)	10,000	22,000
18	Notes payable		64,000	(j) 34,000	(k2)	60,000	90,000
19	Common stock, $5 par value		80,000		(l)	15,000	95,000
20	Retained earnings		88,000	(m) 14,000	(a)	38,000	112,000
21			$336,000				$417,000
22	**Statement of Cash Flows**						
23	Operating activities						
24	Net income			(a) 38,000			
25	Increase in accounts receivable				(b)	20,000	
26	Increase in inventory				(c)	14,000	
27	Increase in prepaid expenses				(d)	2,000	
28	Decrease in accounts payable				(e)	5,000	
29	Decrease in interest payable				(f)	1,000	
30	Increase in income taxes payable			(g) 10,000			
31	Depreciation expense			(h) 24,000			
32	Loss on sale of plant assets			(i) 6,000			
33	Gain on retirement of notes				(j)	16,000	
34	Investing activities						
35	Receipts from sale of plant assets			(i) 2,000			
36	Financing activities						
37	Payment to retire notes				(j)	18,000	
38	Receipts from issuing stock			(l) 15,000			
39	Payment of cash dividends				(m)	14,000	
40							
41	**Noncash Investing and Financing Activities**						
42	Purchase of plant assets with notes			(k2) 60,000	(k1)	60,000	
				$317,000		$317,000	

⑤ After reviewing any unreconciled balance sheet accounts and related information, enter the remaining reconciling entries for investing and financing activities. Examples are purchases of plant assets, issuances of long-term debt, stock issuances, and dividend payments. Some of these may require entries in the noncash investing and financing section of the spreadsheet (reconciled).

⑥ Check accuracy by totaling the Analysis of Changes columns and by determining that the change in each balance sheet account has been explained (reconciled).

We illustrate these steps in Exhibit 12A.1 for Genesis:

Step	Entries
①	(a)
②	(b) through (g)
③	(h)
④	(i) through (j)
⑤	(k) through (m)

Because adjustments *i, j,* and *k* are more challenging, we show them in the following debit and credit format. These entries are for purposes of our understanding; they are *not* the entries actually made in the journals. Changes in the Cash account are identified as sources or uses of cash.

i.	Cash—Receipt from sale of plant assets **(source of cash)**	2,000	
	Loss from sale of plant assets	6,000	
	Accumulated depreciation.	12,000	
	Plant assets		20,000
	Describe sale of plant assets.		
j.	Notes payable	34,000	
	Cash—Payments to retire notes **(use of cash)**		18,000
	Gain on retirement of notes		16,000
	Describe retirement of notes.		
k1.	Plant assets	60,000	
	Cash—Purchase of plant assets financed by notes.		60,000
	Describe purchase of plant assets.		
k2.	Cash—Purchase of plant assets financed by notes	60,000	
	Notes payable		60,000
	Issue notes for purchase of assets.		

12B

Direct Method of Reporting Operating Cash Flows

P5

Compute cash flows from operating activities using the direct method.

We compute cash flows from operating activities under the direct method by adjusting accrual-based income statement items to the cash basis. The usual approach is to adjust income statement accounts related to operating activities for changes in their related balance sheet accounts as follows:

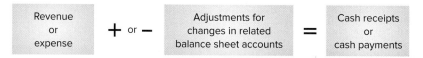

The framework for reporting cash receipts and cash payments for the operating section of the cash flow statement under the direct method is presented in Exhibit 12B.1. We consider cash receipts first and then cash payments.

EXHIBIT 12B.1

Major Classes of Operating Cash Flows

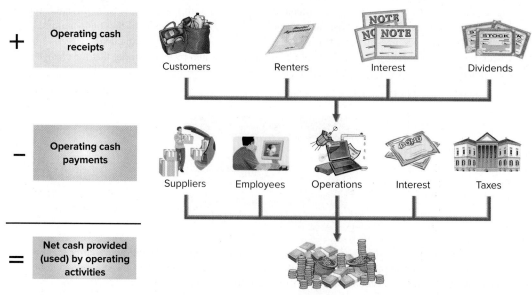

Operating Cash Receipts   A review of Exhibit 12.10 and the additional information reported by Genesis suggests only one potential cash receipt: sales to customers. This section, therefore, starts with sales to customers as reported on the income statement and then adjusts it as necessary to obtain cash received from customers to report on the statement of cash flows.

Cash Received from Customers   If all sales are for cash, the amount received from customers equals the sales reported on the income statement. When some or all sales are on account, however, we must adjust the amount of sales for the change in Accounts Receivable. It is often helpful to use *account analysis* to do this. This usually involves setting up a T-account and reconstructing its major entries, with emphasis on cash receipts and payments.

To illustrate, we use a T-account that includes accounts receivable balances for Genesis on December 31, 2016 and 2017. The beginning balance is $40,000 and the ending balance is $60,000. Next, the income statement shows sales of $590,000, which we enter on the debit side of this account. We now can reconstruct the Accounts Receivable account to determine the amount of cash received from customers as follows:

Point: An accounts receivable increase implies that cash received from customers is less than sales (the converse is also true).

Accounts Receivable			
Bal., Dec. 31, 2016	40,000		
Sales	590,000	Cash receipts =	**570,000**
Bal., Dec. 31, 2017	60,000		

Reconstructed Entry

Cash	570,000	
Accts Recble	20,000	
Sales		590,000

This T-account shows that the Accounts Receivable balance begins at $40,000 and increases to $630,000 from sales of $590,000, yet its ending balance is only $60,000. This implies that cash receipts from customers are $570,000, computed as $40,000 + $590,000 − [?] = $60,000. This computation can be rearranged to express cash received as equal to sales of $590,000 minus a $20,000 increase in accounts receivable. This computation is summarized as a general rule in Exhibit 12B.2. Genesis reports the $570,000 cash received from customers as a cash inflow from operating activities.

Example: If the ending balance of Accounts Receivable is $20,000 (instead of $60,000), what is cash received from customers? *Answer:* $610,000

$$\text{Cash received from customers} = \text{Sales}\quad\begin{array}{l}+ \textbf{ Decrease} \text{ in accounts receivable}\\ \textbf{or}\\ - \textbf{ Increase} \text{ in accounts receivable}\end{array}$$

EXHIBIT 12B.2

Formula to Compute Cash Received from Customers— Direct Method

Other Cash Receipts   While Genesis's cash receipts are limited to collections from customers, we often see other types of cash receipts, most commonly cash receipts involving rent, interest, and dividends. We compute cash received from these items by subtracting an increase in their respective receivable or adding a decrease. For instance, if rent receivable increases in the period, cash received from renters is less than rent revenue reported on the income statement. If rent receivable decreases, cash received is more than reported rent revenue. The same logic applies to interest and dividends. The formulas for these computations are summarized later in this appendix.

Point: Net income is measured using accrual accounting. Cash flows from operations are measured using cash basis accounting.

Operating Cash Payments   A review of Exhibit 12.10 and the additional Genesis information shows four operating expenses: cost of goods sold; wages and other operating expenses; interest expense; and taxes expense. We analyze each expense to compute its cash amounts for the statement of cash flows. (We then examine depreciation and the other losses and gains.)

Cash Paid for Inventory   We compute cash paid for inventory by analyzing both cost of goods sold and inventory. If all inventory purchases are for cash and the ending balance of Inventory is unchanged from the beginning balance, the amount of cash paid for inventory equals cost of goods sold—an uncommon situation. Instead, there normally is some change in the Inventory balance. Also, some or all purchases are often made on credit, and this yields changes in the Accounts Payable balance. When the balances of both Inventory and Accounts Payable change, we must adjust the cost of goods sold for changes in both accounts to compute cash paid for inventory. This is a two-step adjustment.

First, we use the change in the account balance of Inventory, along with the cost of goods sold amount, to compute cost of purchases for the period. An increase in inventory implies that we bought more than we sold, and we add this inventory increase to cost of goods sold to compute cost of purchases. A decrease in inventory implies that we bought less than we sold, and we subtract the inventory decrease from cost of goods sold to compute purchases. We illustrate the *first step* by reconstructing the Inventory account.

Inventory			
Bal., Dec. 31, 2016	70,000		
Purchases =	**314,000**	Cost of goods sold	300,000
Bal., Dec. 31, 2017	84,000		

The beginning balance is $70,000, and the ending balance is $84,000. The income statement shows that cost of goods sold is $300,000, which we enter on the credit side of this account. With this information, we determine the amount for cost of purchases to be $314,000. This computation can be rearranged to express cost of purchases as equal to cost of goods sold of $300,000 plus the $14,000 increase in inventory.

The second step uses the change in the balance of Accounts Payable, and the amount of cost of purchases, to compute cash paid for inventory. A decrease in accounts payable implies that we paid for more goods than we acquired this period, and we would then add the accounts payable decrease to cost of purchases to compute cash paid for inventory. An increase in accounts payable implies that we paid for less than the amount of goods acquired, and we would subtract the accounts payable increase from purchases to compute cash paid for inventory. The *second step* is applied to Genesis by reconstructing its Accounts Payable account.

Reconstructed Entry

COGS 300,000
Inventory 14,000
Accounts Payable . . 5,000
   Cash.   319,000

Accounts Payable			
		Bal., Dec. 31, 2016	40,000
Cash payments =	**319,000**	Purchases	314,000
		Bal., Dec. 31, 2017	35,000

Its beginning balance of $40,000 plus purchases of $314,000 minus an ending balance of $35,000 yields cash paid of $319,000 (or $40,000 + $314,000 − [?] = $35,000). Alternatively, we can express cash paid for inventory as equal to purchases of $314,000 plus the $5,000 decrease in accounts payable. The $319,000 cash paid for inventory is reported on the statement of cash flows as a cash outflow under operating activities.

Example: If the ending balances of Inventory and Accounts Payable are $60,000 and $50,000, respectively (instead of $84,000 and $35,000), what is cash paid for inventory? *Answer:* $280,000

We summarize this two-step adjustment to cost of goods sold to compute cash paid for inventory in Exhibit 12B.3.

EXHIBIT 12B.3

Two Steps to Compute Cash Paid for Inventory—Direct Method

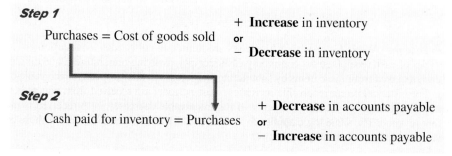

Cash Paid for Wages and Operating Expenses (Excluding Depreciation)   The income statement of Genesis shows wages and other operating expenses of $216,000 (see Exhibit 12.10). To compute cash paid for wages and other operating expenses, we adjust this amount for any changes in their related balance sheet accounts. We begin by looking for any prepaid expenses and accrued liabilities related to wages and other operating expenses in the balance sheets of Genesis in Exhibit 12.10. The balance sheets show prepaid expenses but no accrued liabilities. Thus, the adjustment is limited to the change in prepaid expenses. The amount of adjustment is computed by assuming that all cash paid for wages and other operating expenses is initially debited to Prepaid Expenses. This assumption allows us to reconstruct the Prepaid Expenses account as follows:

Reconstructed Entry

Wages and Other
   Expenses. 216,000
Prepaid Expenses . .   2,000
   Cash.   218,000

Prepaid Expenses			
Bal., Dec. 31, 2016	4,000		
Cash payments =	**218,000**	Wages and other operating exp.	216,000
Bal., Dec. 31, 2017	6,000		

Prepaid expenses increase by $2,000 in the period, meaning that cash paid for wages and other operating expenses exceeds the reported expense by $2,000. Alternatively, we can express cash paid for wages and other operating expenses as equal to its reported expenses of $216,000 plus the $2,000 increase in prepaid expenses.[1]

Exhibit 12B.4 summarizes the adjustments to wages (including salaries) and other operating expenses. The Genesis balance sheet did not report accrued liabilities, but we include them in the formula to explain the adjustment to cash when they do exist. A decrease in accrued liabilities implies that we paid cash for more goods or services than received this period, so we add the decrease in accrued liabilities to the expense amount to obtain cash paid for these goods or services. An increase in accrued liabilities implies that we paid cash for less than what was acquired, so we subtract this increase in accrued liabilities from the expense amount to get cash paid.

Point: A decrease in prepaid expenses implies that reported expenses include an amount(s) that did not require a cash outflow in the period.

EXHIBIT 12B.4

Formula to Compute Cash Paid for Wages and Operating Expenses—Direct Method

$$\begin{array}{c} \text{Cash paid for} \\ \text{wages and other} \\ \text{operating expenses} \end{array} = \begin{array}{c} \text{Wages and} \\ \text{other} \\ \text{operating} \\ \text{expenses} \end{array} \quad \begin{array}{c} + \textbf{ Increase} \text{ in prepaid} \\ \text{expenses} \\ \textit{or} \\ - \textbf{ Decrease} \text{ in prepaid} \\ \text{expenses} \end{array} \quad \begin{array}{c} + \textbf{ Decrease} \text{ in accrued} \\ \text{liabilities} \\ \textit{or} \\ - \textbf{ Increase} \text{ in accrued} \\ \text{liabilities} \end{array}$$

Cash Paid for Interest and Income Taxes   Computing operating cash flows for interest and taxes is similar to that for operating expenses. Both require adjustments to their amounts reported on the income statement for changes in their related balance sheet accounts. We begin with the Genesis income statement showing interest expense of $7,000 and income taxes expense of $15,000. To compute the cash paid, we adjust interest expense for the change in interest payable and then the income taxes expense for the change in income taxes payable. These computations involve reconstructing both liability accounts.

Interest Payable			
		Bal., Dec. 31, 2016	4,000
Cash paid for interest =	8,000	Interest expense	7,000
		Bal., Dec. 31, 2017	3,000

Reconstructed Entry
Int. Expense.........	7,000	
Int. Payable	1,000	
Cash.............		8,000

Income Taxes Payable			
		Bal., Dec. 31, 2016	12,000
Cash paid for taxes =	5,000	Income taxes expense	15,000
		Bal., Dec. 31, 2017	22,000

Reconstructed Entry
Inc. Tax Exp..........	15,000	
Inc. Tax Pay........		10,000
Cash.............		5,000

These T-accounts reveal cash paid for interest of $8,000 and cash paid for income taxes of $5,000. The formulas to compute these amounts are in Exhibit 12B.5. Both of these cash payments are reported as operating cash outflows on the statement of cash flows.

EXHIBIT 12B.5

Formulas to Compute Cash Paid for Both Interest and Taxes—Direct Method

$$\begin{array}{c} \text{Cash paid} \\ \text{for interest} \end{array} = \text{Interest expense} \quad \begin{array}{c} + \textbf{ Decrease} \text{ in interest payable} \\ \textit{or} \\ - \textbf{ Increase} \text{ in interest payable} \end{array}$$

$$\begin{array}{c} \text{Cash paid} \\ \text{for taxes} \end{array} = \text{Income taxes expense} \quad \begin{array}{c} + \textbf{ Decrease} \text{ in income taxes payable} \\ \textit{or} \\ - \textbf{ Increase} \text{ in income taxes payable} \end{array}$$

---

[1] The assumption that all cash payments for wages and operating expenses are initially debited to Prepaid Expenses is not necessary for our analysis to hold. If cash payments are debited directly to the expense account, the total amount of cash paid for wages and other operating expenses still equals the $216,000 expense plus the $2,000 increase in prepaid expenses (which arise from end-of-period adjusting entries).

Analyzing Additional Expenses, Gains, and Losses Genesis has three additional items reported on its income statement: depreciation, loss on sale of assets, and gain on retirement of debt. We must consider each for its potential cash effects.

Depreciation Expense Depreciation expense is $24,000. It is often called a *noncash expense* because depreciation has no cash flows. Depreciation expense is an allocation of an asset's depreciable cost. The cash outflow with a plant asset is reported as part of investing activities when it is paid for. Thus, depreciation expense is *never* reported on a statement of cash flows using the direct method; nor is depletion or amortization expense.

Loss on Sale of Assets Sales of assets frequently result in gains and losses reported as part of net income, but the amount of recorded gain or loss does *not* reflect any cash flows in these transactions. Asset sales result in cash inflow equal to the cash amount received, regardless of whether the asset was sold at a gain or a loss. This cash inflow is reported under investing activities. Thus, the loss or gain on a sale of assets is *never* reported on a statement of cash flows using the direct method.

Point: The direct method is usually viewed as *user friendly* because less accounting knowledge is required to understand and use it.

Gain on Retirement of Debt Retirement of debt usually yields a gain or loss reported as part of net income, but that gain or loss does *not* reflect cash flow in this transaction. Debt retirement results in cash outflow equal to the cash paid to settle the debt, regardless of whether the debt is retired at a gain or loss. This cash outflow is reported under financing activities; the loss or gain from retirement of debt is *never* reported on a statement of cash flows using the direct method.

Summary of Adjustments for Direct Method Exhibit 12B.6 summarizes common adjustments for net income to yield net cash provided (used) by operating activities under the direct method.

EXHIBIT 12B.6

Summary of Selected Adjustments for Direct Method

Item	From Income Statement	Adjustments to Obtain Cash Flow Numbers	
Receipts			
From sales	Sales Revenue	+ Decrease in Accounts Receivable − Increase in Accounts Receivable	
From rent	Rent Revenue	+ Decrease in Rent Receivable − Increase in Rent Receivable	
From interest	Interest Revenue	+ Decrease in Interest Receivable − Increase in Interest Receivable	
From dividends	Dividend Revenue	+ Decrease in Dividends Receivable − Increase in Dividends Receivable	
Payments			
To suppliers	Cost of Goods Sold	+ Increase in Inventory − Decrease in Inventory	+ Decrease in Accounts Payable − Increase in Accounts Payable
For operations	Operating Expense	+ Increase in Prepaids − Decrease in Prepaids	+ Decrease in Accrued Liabilities − Increase in Accrued Liabilities
To employees	Wages (Salaries) Expense	+ Decrease in Wages (Salaries) Payable − Increase in Wages (Salaries) Payable	
For interest	Interest Expense	+ Decrease in Interest Payable − Increase in Interest Payable	
For taxes	Income Tax Expense	+ Decrease in Income Tax Payable − Increase in Income Tax Payable	

Direct Method Format of Operating Activities Section Exhibit 12B.7 shows the Genesis statement of cash flows using the direct method. Major items of cash inflows and cash outflows are listed separately in the operating activities section. The format requires that operating cash outflows be subtracted from operating cash inflows to get net cash provided (used) by operating activities.

The FASB recommends that the operating activities section of the statement of cash flows be reported using the direct method. *However, the FASB requires a reconciliation of net income to net cash provided (used) by operating activities when the direct method is used* (which can be reported in the notes). This reconciliation follows the preparation of the operating activities section of the statement of cash flows using the indirect method.

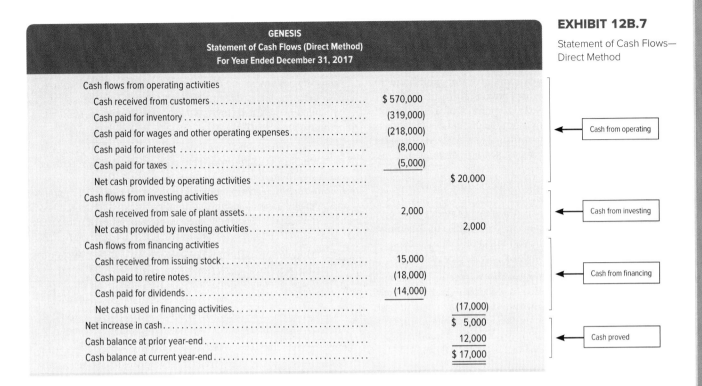

EXHIBIT 12B.7

Statement of Cash Flows—
Direct Method

A company's current-year income statement and selected balance sheet data at December 31 of the current and prior years follow. Prepare only the operating activities section of the statement of cash flows using the direct method for the current year.

NEED-TO-KNOW 12-6

Reporting Operating
Cash Flows (Direct)

P5

Income Statement For Current Year Ended December 31	
Sales revenue	$120
Expenses	
Cost of goods sold	50
Depreciation expense	30
Salaries expense....................	17
Interest expense....................	3
Net income	$ 20

Selected Balance Sheet Accounts		
At December 31	Current Yr	Prior Yr
Accounts receivable	$12	$10
Inventory	6	9
Accounts payable	7	11
Salaries payable	8	3
Interest payable..............	1	0

Solution

Cash Flows from Operating Activities—Direct Method For Current Year Ended December 31	
Cash flows from operating activities*	
Cash received from customers	$118
Cash paid for inventory	(51)
Cash paid for salaries	(12)
Cash paid for interest	(2)
Net cash provided by operating activities...............	$53

* Supporting computations:
 Cash received from customers = Sales of $120 − Accounts Receivable increase of $2.
 Cash paid for inventory = COGS of $50 − Inventory decrease of $3 + Accounts Payable decrease of $4.
 Cash paid for salaries = Salaries Expense of $17 − Salaries Payable increase of $5.
 Cash paid for interest = Interest Expense of $3 − Interest Payable increase of $1.

Do More: QS 12-14, QS 12-15,
QS 12-16, E 12-12, E 12-14,
E 12-15, E 12-16

Summary

C1 **Distinguish between operating, investing, and financing activities, and describe how noncash investing and financing activities are disclosed.** The purpose of the statement of cash flows is to report major cash receipts and cash payments related to operating, investing, or financing activities. Operating activities include transactions and events that determine net income. Investing activities include transactions and events that mainly affect long-term assets. Financing activities include transactions and events that mainly affect long-term liabilities and equity. Noncash investing and financing activities must be disclosed in either a note or a separate schedule to the statement of cash flows. Examples are the retirement of debt by issuing equity and the exchange of a note payable for plant assets.

A1 **Analyze the statement of cash flows and apply the cash flow on total assets ratio.** To understand and predict cash flows, users stress identification of the sources and uses of cash flows by operating, investing, and financing activities. Emphasis is on operating cash flows since they derive from continuing operations. The cash flow on total assets ratio is defined as operating cash flows divided by average total assets. Analysis of current and past values for this ratio can reflect a company's ability to yield regular and positive cash flows. It is also viewed as a measure of earnings quality.

P1 **Prepare a statement of cash flows.** Preparation of a statement of cash flows involves five steps: (1) Compute the net increase or decrease in cash; (2) compute net cash provided or used by operating activities (*using either the direct or indirect method*); (3) compute net cash provided or used by investing activities; (4) compute net cash provided or used by

financing activities; and (5) report the beginning and ending cash balances and prove that the ending cash balance is explained by net cash flows. Noncash investing and financing activities are also disclosed.

P2 **Compute cash flows from operating activities using the indirect method.** The indirect method for reporting net cash provided or used by operating activities starts with net income and then adjusts it for three items: (1) changes in non-cash current assets and current liabilities related to operating activities, (2) revenues and expenses not providing or using cash, and (3) gains and losses from investing and financing activities.

P3 **Determine cash flows from both investing and financing activities.** Cash flows from both investing and financing activities are determined by identifying the cash flow effects of transactions and events affecting each balance sheet account related to these activities. All cash flows from these activities are identified when we can explain changes in these accounts from the beginning to the end of the period.

P4ᴬ **Illustrate use of a spreadsheet to prepare a statement of cash flows.** A spreadsheet is a useful tool in preparing a statement of cash flows. Six key steps (see Appendix 12A) are applied when using the spreadsheet to prepare the statement.

P5ᴮ **Compute cash flows from operating activities using the direct method.** The direct method for reporting net cash provided or used by operating activities lists major operating cash inflows less cash outflows to yield net cash inflow or outflow from operations.

Key Terms

Cash flow on total assets	Indirect method	Operating activities
Direct method	Investing activities	Statement of cash flows
Financing activities		

Multiple Choice Quiz

1. A company uses the indirect method to determine its cash flows from operating activities. Use the following information to determine its net cash provided or used by operating activities.

Net income	$15,200
Depreciation expense	10,000
Cash payment on note payable	8,000
Gain on sale of land	3,000
Increase in inventory	1,500
Increase in accounts payable	2,850

   a. $23,550 used by operating activities
   b. $23,550 provided by operating activities
   c. $15,550 provided by operating activities

   d. $42,400 provided by operating activities
   e. $20,850 provided by operating activities

2. A machine with a cost of $175,000 and accumulated depreciation of $94,000 is sold for $87,000 cash. The amount reported as a source of cash under cash flows from investing activities is
   a. $81,000.
   b. $6,000.
   c. $87,000.
   d. Zero; this is a financing activity.
   e. Zero; this is an operating activity.

3. A company settles a long-term note payable plus interest by paying $68,000 cash toward the principal amount and

$5,440 cash for interest. The amount reported as a use of cash under cash flows from financing activities is

a. Zero; this is an investing activity.

b. Zero; this is an operating activity.

c. $73,440.

d. $68,000.

e. $5,440.

4. The following information is available regarding a company's annual salaries and wages. What amount of cash is paid for salaries and wages?

Salaries and wages expense	$255,000
Salaries and wages payable, prior year-end	8,200
Salaries and wages payable, current year-end	10,900

ANSWERS TO MULTIPLE CHOICE QUIZ

1. b;

Net income	$15,200
Depreciation expense	10,000
Gain on sale of land	(3,000)
Increase in inventory	(1,500)
Increase in accounts payable	2,850
Net cash provided by operations.	$23,550

a. $252,300   **c.** $255,000   **e.** $235,900

b. $257,700   **d.** $274,100

5. The following information is available for a company. What amount of cash is paid for inventory for the current year?

Cost of goods sold	$545,000
Inventory, prior year-end	105,000
Inventory, current year-end	112,000
Accounts payable, prior year-end	98,500
Accounts payable, current year-end	101,300

a. $545,000   **c.** $540,800   **e.** $549,200

b. $554,800   **d.** $535,200

2. c; Cash received from sale of machine is reported as an investing activity.

3. d; FASB requires cash interest paid to be reported under operating.

4. a; Cash paid for salaries and wages = $255,000 + $8,200 − $10,900 = $252,300

5. e; Increase in inventory = $112,000 − $105,000 = $7,000

Increase in accounts payable = $101,300 − $98,500 = $2,800

Cash paid for inventory = $545,000 + $7,000 − $2,800 = $549,200

A(B) *Superscript letter A (B) denotes assignments based on Appendix 12A (12B).*

🔓 Icon denotes assignments that involve decision making.

Discussion Questions

1. What is the reporting purpose of the statement of cash flows? Identify at least two questions that this statement can answer.

2. What are some investing activities reported on the statement of cash flows?

3. What are some financing activities reported on the statement of cash flows?

4.ᴮ Describe the direct method of reporting cash flows from operating activities.

5. When a statement of cash flows is prepared using the direct method, what are some of the operating cash flows?

6. Describe the indirect method of reporting cash flows from operating activities.

7. Where on the statement of cash flows is the payment of cash dividends reported?

8. 🔓 Assume that a company purchases land for $1,000,000, paying $400,000 cash and borrowing the remainder with a long-term note payable. How should this transaction be reported on a statement of cash flows?

9. 🔓 On June 3, a company borrows $200,000 cash by giving its bank a 90-day, interest-bearing note. On the statement of cash flows, where should this be reported?

10. 🔓 If a company reports positive net income for the year, can it also show a net cash outflow from operating activities? Explain.

11. 🔓 Is depreciation a source of cash flow?

12. 🔓 Refer to **Apple**'s statement of cash flows in Appendix A. (*a*) Which method is used to **APPLE** compute its net cash provided by operating activities? (*b*) Its balance sheet shows a decrease in accounts receivable from September 27, 2014, to September 26, 2015; why is this decrease in accounts receivable added when computing net cash provided by operating activities for the fiscal year ended September 26, 2015?

13. 🔓 Refer to **Google**'s statement of cash flows in Appendix A. What are its cash **GOOGLE** flows from financing activities for the year ended December 31, 2015? List the items and amounts.

14. 🔓 Refer to **Samsung**'s 2015 statement of cash flows in Appendix A. List **Samsung** its cash flows from operating activities, investing activities, and financing activities.

15. 🔓 Refer to **Samsung**'s statement of cash flows in Appendix A. What in- **Samsung** vesting activities result in cash outflows for the year ended December 31, 2015? List items and amounts.

QUICK STUDY

QS 12-1

Transaction classification by activity

C1

Classify the following cash flows as either operating (O), investing (I), or financing (F) activities.

_____ **1.** Sold long-term investments for cash.

_____ **2.** Received cash payments from customers.

_____ **3.** Paid cash for wages and salaries.

_____ **4.** Purchased inventories for cash.

_____ **5.** Paid cash dividends.

_____ **6.** Issued common stock for cash.

_____ **7.** Received cash interest on a note.

_____ **8.** Paid cash interest on outstanding notes.

_____ **9.** Received cash from sale of land at a loss.

_____ **10.** Paid cash for property taxes on building.

QS 12-2

Statement of cash flows

P1

Label the following headings, line items, and notes with the numbers _1_ through _13_ according to their sequential order (from top to bottom) for presentation of the statement of cash flows.

_____ **a.** "Cash flows from investing activities" title

_____ **b.** "For _period_ Ended _date_" heading

_____ **c.** "Cash flows from operating activities" title

_____ **d.** Company name

_____ **e.** Schedule or note disclosure of noncash investing and financing transactions

_____ **f.** "Statement of Cash Flows" heading

_____ **g.** Net increase (decrease) in cash . . . . $ #

_____ **h.** Net cash provided (used) by operating activities . . . . $ #

_____ **i.** Cash (and equivalents) balance at prior period-end . . . . $ #

_____ **j.** Net cash provided (used) by financing activities . . . . $ #

_____ **k.** "Cash flows from financing activities" title

_____ **l.** Net cash provided (used) by investing activities. . . . . $ #

_____ **m.** Cash (and equivalents) balance at current period-end . . . . $ #

QS 12-3

Indirect: Computing cash flows from operations

P2

For each of the following three separate cases X, Y, and Z, compute cash flows from operations using the _indirect method._ The list includes all balance sheet accounts related to cash from operating activities.

	Case X	Case Y	Case Z
Net income	$ 4,000	$100,000	$72,000
Depreciation expense	30,000	8,000	24,000
Accounts receivable increase (decrease)	40,000	20,000	(4,000)
Inventory increase (decrease)	(20,000)	(10,000)	10,000
Accounts payable increase (decrease)	24,000	(22,000)	14,000
Accrued liabilities increase (decrease)	(44,000)	12,000	(8,000)

QS 12-4

Indirect: Computing cash from operations   P2

Use the following information to determine this company's cash flows from operating activities using the _indirect method._

MOSS COMPANY
Selected Balance Sheet Information
December 31, 2017 and 2016

	2017	2016
Current assets		
Cash	$84,650	$26,800
Accounts receivable.	25,000	32,000
Inventory.	60,000	54,100
Current liabilities		
Accounts payable.	30,400	25,700
Income taxes payable	2,050	2,200

MOSS COMPANY
Income Statement
For Year Ended December 31, 2017

Sales		$515,000
Cost of goods sold		331,600
Gross profit		183,400
Operating expenses		
Depreciation expense	$ 36,000	
Other expenses	121,500	157,500
Income before taxes.		25,900
Income taxes expense		7,700
Net income		$ 18,200

The plant assets section of the comparative balance sheets of Anders Company is reported below.

QS 12-5
Indirect: Computing
investing cash flows
P2

ANDERS COMPANY Comparative Balance Sheets		
	2017	**2016**
Plant assets		
Equipment	$ 180,000	$270,000
Accum. depr.—Equipment	(100,000)	(210,000)
Equipment, net.....................	$ 80,000	$ 60,000
Buildings..........................	$ 380,000	$400,000
Accum. depr.—Buildings	(100,000)	(285,000)
Buildings, net	$ 280,000	$115,000

Refer to the balance sheet data above from Anders Company. During 2017, equipment with a book value of $40,000 and an original cost of $210,000 was sold at a loss of $3,000.

1. How much cash did Anders receive from the sale of equipment?
2. How much depreciation expense was recorded on equipment during 2017?
3. What was the cost of new equipment purchased by Anders during 2017?

Refer to the balance sheet data in QS 12-5 from Anders Company. During 2017, a building with a book value of $70,000 and an original cost of $300,000 was sold at a gain of $60,000.

QS 12-6
Indirect: Computing
investing cash flows
P2

1. How much cash did Anders receive from the sale of the building?
2. How much depreciation expense was recorded on buildings during 2017?
3. What was the cost of buildings purchased by Anders during 2017?

The following selected information is from Ellerby Company's comparative balance sheets.

QS 12-7
Computing cash from
asset sales
P3

At December 31	2017	2016
Furniture	$132,000	$ 184,500
Accumulated depreciation—Furniture......	(88,700)	(110,700)

The income statement reports depreciation expense for the year of $18,000. Also, furniture costing $52,500 was sold for its book value. Compute the cash received from the sale of furniture.

Compute cash flows from investing activities using the following company information.

QS 12-8
Computing cash flows
from investing
P3

Sale of short-term investments	$ 6,000
Cash collections from customers........................	16,000
Purchase of used equipment...........................	5,000
Depreciation expense	2,000

The following selected information is from Princeton Company's comparative balance sheets.

QS 12-9
Computing financing
cash flows
P3

At December 31	2017	2016
Common stock, $10 par value...........	$105,000	$100,000
Paid-in capital in excess of par	567,000	342,000
Retained earnings	313,500	287,500

The company's net income for the year ended December 31, 2017, was $48,000.
1. Compute the cash received from the sale of its common stock during 2017.
2. Compute the cash paid for dividends during 2017.

QS 12-10

Computing cash flows
from financing

P3

Compute cash flows from financing activities using the following company information.

Additional short-term borrowings	$20,000
Purchase of short-term investments	5,000
Cash dividends paid	16,000
Interest paid	8,000

QS 12-11

Indirect: Computing cash
from operations   P2

CRUZ, INC.
Comparative Balance Sheets
December 31, 2017

	2017	2016
Assets		
Cash	$ 94,800	$ 24,000
Accounts receivable, net	41,000	51,000
Inventory	85,800	95,800
Prepaid expenses	5,400	4,200
Total current assets	227,000	175,000
Furniture	109,000	119,000
Accum. depreciation—Furniture	(17,000)	(9,000)
Total assets	$319,000	$285,000
Liabilities and Equity		
Accounts payable	$ 15,000	$ 21,000
Wages payable	9,000	5,000
Income taxes payable	1,400	2,600
Total current liabilities	25,400	28,600
Notes payable (long-term)	29,000	69,000
Total liabilities	54,400	97,600
Equity		
Common stock, $5 par value	229,000	179,000
Retained earnings	35,600	8,400
Total liabilities and equity	$319,000	$285,000

CRUZ, INC.
Income Statement
For Year Ended December 31, 2017

Sales		$488,000
Cost of goods sold		314,000
Gross profit		174,000
Operating expenses		
Depreciation expense	$37,600	
Other expenses	89,100	126,700
Income before taxes		47,300
Income taxes expense		17,300
Net income		$ 30,000

Required

Use the *indirect method* to prepare the cash provided or used from operating activities section only of the statement of cash flows for this company.

QS 12-12

Computing cash from
asset sales   P3

Refer to the data in QS 12-11.
Furniture costing $55,000 is sold at its book value in 2017. Acquisitions of furniture total $45,000 cash, on which no depreciation is necessary because it is acquired at year-end. What is the cash inflow related to the sale of furniture?

QS 12-13

Computing financing
cash outflows   P3

Refer to the data in QS 12-11.
1. Assume that all common stock is issued for cash. What amount of cash dividends is paid during 2017?
2. Assume that no additional notes payable are issued in 2017. What cash amount is paid to reduce the notes payable balance in 2017?

QS 12-14ᴮ

Direct: Computing cash
received from customers

P5

Refer to the data in QS 12-11.
1. How much cash is received from sales to customers for year 2017?
2. What is the net increase or decrease in cash for year 2017?

QS 12-15ᴮ

Direct: Computing operating
cash outflows   P5

Refer to the data in QS 12-11.
1. How much cash is paid to acquire inventory during year 2017?
2. How much cash is paid for "other expenses" during year 2017? (*Hint:* Examine prepaid expenses and wages payable.)

Refer to the data in QS 12-11.
Use the *direct method* to prepare the cash provided or used from operating activities section only of the statement of cash flows for this company.

QS 12-16ᴮ
Direct: Computing cash
from operations   **P5**

Financial data from three competitors in the same industry follow.
1. Which of the three competitors is in the strongest position as shown by its statement of cash flows?
2. Analyze and compare the strength of Moore's cash flow on total assets ratio to that of Sykes.

QS 12-17
Analyzing sources and
uses of cash

A1

	A	B	C	D
1	**$ thousands**	**Moore**	**Sykes**	**Kritch**
2	Cash provided (used) by operating activities	$ 70,000	$ 60,000	$ (24,000)
3	Cash provided (used) by investing activities			
4	Proceeds from sale of operating assets			26,000
5	Purchase of operating assets	(28,000)	(34,000)	
6	Cash provided (used) by financing activities			
7	Proceeds from issuance of debt			23,000
8	Repayment of debt	(6,000)		
9	Net increase (decrease) in cash	$ 36,000	$ 26,000	$ 25,000
10				
11	Average total assets	$790,000	$625,000	$300,000

When a spreadsheet for a statement of cash flows is prepared, all changes in noncash balance sheet accounts are fully explained on the spreadsheet. Explain how these noncash balance sheet accounts are used to fully account for cash flows on a spreadsheet.

QS 12-18ᴬ
Noncash accounts
on a spreadsheet   **P4**

Use the following financial statements and additional information to (1) prepare a statement of cash flows for the year ended December 31, 2018, using the *indirect method,* and (2) analyze and briefly discuss the statement prepared in part 1 with special attention to operating activities and to the company's cash level.

QS 12-19
Indirect: Preparing
statement of cash flows

P1   P2   P3

MONTGOMERY INC.
Comparative Balance Sheets
December 31, 2018 and 2017

	2018	2017
Assets		
Cash	$ 30,400	$ 30,550
Accounts receivable, net	10,050	12,150
Inventory	90,100	70,150
Total current assets	130,550	112,850
Equipment	49,900	41,500
Accum. depreciation—Equipment	(22,500)	(15,300)
Total assets	$157,950	$139,050
Liabilities and Equity		
Accounts payable	$ 23,900	$ 25,400
Salaries payable	500	600
Total current liabilities	24,400	26,000
Equity		
Common stock, no par value	110,000	100,000
Retained earnings	23,550	13,050
Total liabilities and equity	$157,950	$139,050

MONTGOMERY INC.
Income Statement
For Year Ended December 31, 2018

Sales		$45,575
Cost of goods sold		(18,950)
Gross profit		26,625
Operating expenses		
Depreciation expense	$7,200	
Other expenses	5,550	
Total operating expense		12,750
Income before taxes		13,875
Income tax expense		3,375
Net income		$10,500

Additional Information
a. No dividends are declared or paid in 2018.
b. Issued additional stock for $10,000 cash in 2018.
c. Purchased equipment for cash in 2018; no equipment was sold in 2018.

QS 12-20
International cash
flow disclosures

C1

Answer each of the following questions related to international accounting standards.

1. Which method, indirect or direct, is acceptable for reporting operating cash flows under IFRS?
2. For each of the following four cash flows, identify whether it is reported under the operating, investing, or financing section (or some combination) within the indirect format of the statement of cash flows reported under IFRS and under U.S. GAAP.

Cash Flow Source	US GAAP Reporting	IFRS Reporting
a. Interest paid		
b. Dividends paid		
c. Interest received		
d. Dividends received		

Mc Graw Hill Education connect

EXERCISES

Exercise 12-1
Indirect: Cash flow classification   C1

The following transactions and events occurred during the year. Assuming that this company uses the *indirect method* to report cash provided by operating activities, indicate where each item would appear on its statement of cash flows by placing an *x* in the appropriate column.

	Statement of Cash Flows			Noncash Investing and Financing Activities	Not Reported on Statement or in Notes
	Operating Activities	Investing Activities	Financing Activities		
a. Declared and paid a cash dividend	___	___	___	___	___
b. Recorded depreciation expense	___	___	___	___	___
c. Paid cash to settle long-term note payable.............	___	___	___	___	___
d. Prepaid expenses increased in the year	___	___	___	___	___
e. Accounts receivable decreased in the year	___	___	___	___	___
f. Purchased land by issuing common stock	___	___	___	___	___
g. Inventory increased in the year	___	___	___	___	___
h. Sold equipment for cash, yielding a loss	___	___	___	___	___
i. Accounts payable decreased in the year	___	___	___	___	___
j. Income taxes payable increased in the year	___	___	___	___	___

Exercise 12-2
Indirect: Reporting cash flows from operations

P2

Hampton Company reports the following information for its recent calendar year. Prepare the operating activities section of the statement of cash flows for Hampton Company using the *indirect method*.

Income Statement Data			Selected Year-End Balance Sheet Data	
Sales..........................	$160,000		Accounts receivable increase.............	$10,000
Expenses			Inventory decrease......................	16,000
Cost of goods sold	100,000		Salaries payable increase.................	1,000
Salaries expense....................	24,000			
Depreciation expense	12,000			
Net income	$ 24,000			

Exercise 12-3
Indirect: Reporting and interpreting cash flows from operations

P2

Arundel Company disclosed the following information for its recent calendar year.

Income Statement Data			Selected Year-End Balance Sheet Data	
Revenues............................	$100,000		Accounts receivable decrease	$24,000
Expenses			Purchased a machine for cash	10,000
Salaries expense.....................	84,000		Salaries payable increase.................	18,000
Utilities expense.....................	14,000		Other accrued liabilities decrease	8,000
Depreciation expense	14,600			
Other expenses......................	3,400			
Net loss	$ (16,000)			

Required

1. Prepare the operating activities section of the statement of cash flows using the *indirect method*.
2. What were the major reasons that this company was able to report a net loss but positive cash flow from operations?
3. Of the potential causes of differences between cash flow from operations and net income, which are the most important to investors?

The following income statement and information about changes in noncash current assets and current liabilities are reported.

Exercise 12-4
Indirect: Cash flows from operating activities

P2

SONAD COMPANY Income Statement For Year Ended December 31, 2017		
Sales		$1,828,000
Cost of goods sold		991,000
Gross profit		837,000
Operating expenses		
Salaries expense	$245,535	
Depreciation expense	44,200	
Rent expense	49,600	
Amortization expense—Patents	4,200	
Utilities expense	18,125	361,660
		475,340
Gain on sale of equipment		6,200
Net income		$ 481,540

Changes in current asset and current liability accounts for the year that relate to operations follow.

Accounts receivable	$30,500 increase	Accounts payable	$12,500 decrease
Inventory	25,000 increase	Salaries payable	3,500 decrease

Required

Prepare only the cash flows from operating activities section of the statement of cash flows using the *indirect method*.

Fitz Company reports the following information. Use the *indirect method* to prepare only the operating activities section of its statement of cash flows for the year ended December 31, 2017.

Exercise 12-5
Indirect: Cash flows from operating activities

P2

Selected 2017 Income Statement Data		Selected Year-End 2017 Balance Sheet Data	
Net income	$374,000	Accounts receivable decrease	$17,100
Depreciation expense	44,000	Inventory decrease	42,000
Amortization expense	7,200	Prepaid expenses increase	4,700
Gain on sale of plant assets	6,000	Accounts payable decrease	8,200
		Salaries payable increase	1,200

Salud Company reports the following information. Use the *indirect method* to prepare only the operating activities section of its statement of cash flows for the year ended December 31, 2017.

Exercise 12-6
Indirect: Cash flow from operations

P2

Selected 2017 Income Statement Data		Selected Year-End 2017 Balance Sheet Data	
Net income	$400,000	Accounts receivable increase	$40,000
Depreciation expense	80,000	Prepaid expenses decrease	12,000
Gain on sale of machinery	20,000	Accounts payable increase	6,000
		Wages payable decrease	2,000

Use the following information to determine this company's cash flows from investing activities.

Exercise 12-7
Cash flows from investing activities

P3

a. Equipment with a book value of $65,300 and an original cost of $133,000 was sold at a loss of $14,000.
b. Paid $89,000 cash for a new truck.
c. Sold land costing $154,000 for $198,000 cash, yielding a gain of $44,000.
d. Long-term investments in stock were sold for $60,800 cash, yielding a gain of $4,150.

Exercise 12-8

Cash flows from financing activities

P3

Use the following information to determine this company's cash flows from financing activities.

a. Net income was $35,000.

b. Issued common stock for $64,000 cash.

c. Paid cash dividend of $14,600.

d. Paid $50,000 cash to settle a note payable at its $50,000 maturity value.

e. Paid $12,000 cash to acquire its treasury stock.

f. Purchased equipment for $39,000 cash.

Exercise 12-9

Indirect: Statement of cash flows under IFRS

P1

Peugeot S.A. reports the following financial information for the year ended December 31, 2014 (euros in millions). Prepare its statement of cash flows under the *indirect method*. (*Hint:* Each line item below is titled, and any necessary parentheses added, as it is reported in the statement of cash flows.)

Net income (loss)............................	€ (822)	Cash from issuances of shares...................	€ 2,961
Depreciation, amortization, and impairment....	2,530	Cash paid for other financing activities............	(1,891)
Losses on disposals and other................	42	Cash from disposal of plant assets &	
Net decrease in current operating		intangibles.....................................	206
assets & other............................	2,314	Cash paid for plant assets, intangibles & other......	(2,542)
Cash paid for dividends	(58)	Cash and cash equivalents, December 31, 2013....	8,162

Exercise 12-10

Analyzing cash flow on total assets

A1

A company reported average total assets of $1,240,000 in 2016 and $1,510,000 in 2017. Its net operating cash flow was $102,920 in 2016 and $138,920 in 2017. Calculate its cash flow on total assets ratio for both years. Comment on the results and any change in performance.

Exercise 12-11

Indirect: Preparing statement of cash flows

P1   P2   P3   A1

The following financial statements and additional information are reported.

IKIBAN INC. Income Statement For Year Ended June 30, 2017		
Sales		$678,000
Cost of goods sold		411,000
Gross profit............................		267,000
Operating expenses		
Depreciation expense	$58,600	
Other expenses	67,000	
Total operating expenses................		125,600
		141,400
Other gains (losses)		
Gain on sale of equipment		2,000
Income before taxes....................		143,400
Income taxes expense		43,890
Net income		$ 99,510

IKIBAN INC. Comparative Balance Sheets June 30, 2017 and 2016		
	2017	2016
Assets		
Cash	$ 87,500	$ 44,000
Accounts receivable, net	65,000	51,000
Inventory......................................	63,800	86,500
Prepaid expenses............................	4,400	5,400
Total current assets	220,700	186,900
Equipment...................................	124,000	115,000
Accum. depreciation—Equipment.............	(27,000)	(9,000)
Total assets................................	$317,700	$292,900
Liabilities and Equity		
Accounts payable...........................	$ 25,000	$ 30,000
Wages payable.............................	6,000	15,000
Income taxes payable	3,400	3,800
Total current liabilities	34,400	48,800
Notes payable (long term)	30,000	60,000
Total liabilities..............................	64,400	108,800
Equity		
Common stock, $5 par value.................	220,000	160,000
Retained earnings	33,300	24,100
Total liabilities and equity...................	$317,700	$292,900

Additional Information

a. A $30,000 note payable is retired at its $30,000 carrying (book) value in exchange for cash.

b. The only changes affecting retained earnings are net income and cash dividends paid.

c. New equipment is acquired for $57,600 cash.

d. Received cash for the sale of equipment that had cost $48,600, yielding a $2,000 gain.

e. Prepaid Expenses and Wages Payable relate to Other Expenses on the income statement.

f. All purchases and sales of inventory are on credit.

Check (1*b*) Cash paid for dividends, $90,310

(1*d*) Cash received from equip. sale, $10,000

Required

1. Prepare a statement of cash flows for the year ended June 30, 2017, using the *indirect method.*

2. Compute the company's cash flow on total assets ratio for its fiscal year 2017.

Refer to the information in Exercise 12-11. Using the *direct method,* prepare the statement of cash flows for the year ended June 30, 2017.

Exercise 12-12ᴮ
Direct: Preparing statement of cash flows

P1 P3 P5

Complete the following spreadsheet in preparation of the statement of cash flows. (The statement of cash flows is not required.) Prepare the spreadsheet as in Exhibit 12A.1; report operating activities under the *indirect method.* Identify the debits and credits in the Analysis of Changes columns with letters that correspond to the following transactions and events *a* through *h.*

Exercise 12-13
Indirect: Cash flows spreadsheet

P4

a. Net income for the year was $100,000.

b. Dividends of $80,000 cash were declared and paid.

c. Scoreteck's only noncash expense was $70,000 of depreciation.

d. The company purchased plant assets for $70,000 cash.

e. Notes payable of $20,000 were issued for $20,000 cash.

f. Change in accounts receivable.

g. Change in inventory.

h. Change in accounts payable.

	A	B	C	D	E	F	G
1	SCORETECK CORPORATION						
2	Spreadsheet for Statement of Cash Flows—Indirect Method						
3	For Year Ended December 31, 2017						
4				Analysis of Changes			
5		Dec. 31, 2016		Debit		Credit	Dec. 31, 2017
6	**Balance Sheet—Debit Bal. Accounts**						
7	Cash	$ 80,000					$ 60,000
8	Accounts receivable	120,000					190,000
9	Inventory	250,000					230,000
10	Plant assets	600,000					670,000
11		$1,050,000					$1,150,000
12	**Balance Sheet—Credit Bal. Accounts**						
13	Accumulated depreciation	$ 100,000					$ 170,000
14	Accounts payable	150,000					140,000
15	Notes payable	370,000					390,000
16	Common stock	200,000					200,000
17	Retained earnings	230,000					250,000
18		$1,050,000					$1,150,000
19	**Statement of Cash Flows**						
20	Operating activities						
21	Net income						
22	Increase in accounts receivable						
23	Decrease in inventory						
24	Decrease in accounts payable						
25	Depreciation expense						
26	Investing activities						
27	Cash paid to purchase plant assets						
28	Financing activities						
29	Cash paid for dividends						
30	Cash from issuance of notes						

Exercise 12-14[B]
Direct: Cash flow classification

C1   P5

The following transactions and events occurred during the year. Assuming that this company uses the *direct method* to report cash provided by operating activities, indicate where each item would appear on the statement of cash flows by placing an *x* in the appropriate column.

	Statement of Cash Flows			Noncash Investing and Financing Activities	Not Reported on Statement or in Notes
	Operating Activities	Investing Activities	Financing Activities		
a. Retired long-term notes payable by issuing common stock	_____	_____	_____	_____	_____
b. Paid cash toward accounts payable	_____	_____	_____	_____	_____
c. Sold inventory for cash	_____	_____	_____	_____	_____
d. Paid cash dividend that was declared in a prior period	_____	_____	_____	_____	_____
e. Accepted six-month note receivable in exchange for plant assets	_____	_____	_____	_____	_____
f. Recorded depreciation expense	_____	_____	_____	_____	_____
g. Paid cash to acquire treasury stock	_____	_____	_____	_____	_____
h. Collected cash from sales	_____	_____	_____	_____	_____
i. Borrowed cash from bank by signing a nine-month note payable	_____	_____	_____	_____	_____
j. Paid cash to purchase a patent	_____	_____	_____	_____	_____

Exercise 12-15[B]
Direct: Computing cash flows

P5

For each of the following three separate cases, use the information provided about the calendar-year 2018 operations of Sahim Company to compute the required cash flow information.

Case X: Compute cash received from customers:

Sales	$515,000
Accounts receivable, December 31, 2017	27,200
Accounts receivable, December 31, 2018	33,600

Case Y: Compute cash paid for rent:

Rent expense	$139,800
Rent payable, December 31, 2017	7,800
Rent payable, December 31, 2018	6,200

Case Z: Compute cash paid for inventory:

Cost of goods sold	$525,000
Inventory, December 31, 2017	158,600
Accounts payable, December 31, 2017	66,700
Inventory, December 31, 2018	130,400
Accounts payable, December 31, 2018	82,000

Exercise 12-16[B]
Direct: Cash flows from operating activities   P5

Refer to the information about Sonad Company in Exercise 12-4. Use the *direct method* to prepare only the cash provided or used by operating activities section of the statement of cash flows for this company.

Exercise 12-17[B]
Direct: Preparing statement of cash flows and supporting note

P1   P3   P5

Use the following information about the cash flows of Ferron Company to prepare a complete statement of cash flows (*direct method*) for the year ended December 31, 2017. Use a note disclosure for any non-cash investing and financing activities.

Cash and cash equivalents balance, December 31, 2016	$ 40,000
Cash and cash equivalents balance, December 31, 2017	148,000
Cash received as interest	3,500
Cash paid for salaries	76,500

[continued on next page]

[continued from previous page]

Bonds payable retired by issuing common stock (no gain or loss on retirement).................	$185,500
Cash paid to retire long-term notes payable...	100,000
Cash received from sale of equipment	60,250
Cash received in exchange for six-month note payable...................................	35,000
Land purchased by issuing long-term note payable.....................................	105,250
Cash paid for store equipment...	24,750
Cash dividends paid	10,000
Cash paid for other expenses...	20,000
Cash received from customers...	495,000
Cash paid for inventory...	254,500

The following summarized Cash T-account reflects the total debits and total credits to the Cash account of Thomas Corporation for calendar-year 2017.

1. Use this information to prepare a complete statement of cash flows for year 2017. The cash provided or used by operating activities should be reported using the *direct method.*

2. Refer to the statement of cash flows prepared for part 1 to answer the following questions *a* through *d:* (*a*) Which section—operating, investing, or financing—shows the largest cash (i) inflow and (ii) outflow? (*b*) What is the largest individual item among the investing cash outflows? (*c*) Are the cash proceeds larger from issuing notes or issuing stock? (*d*) Does the company have a net cash inflow or outflow from borrowing activities?

Exercise 12-18[B]
Direct: Preparing statement of cash flows from Cash T-account

P1 P3 P5

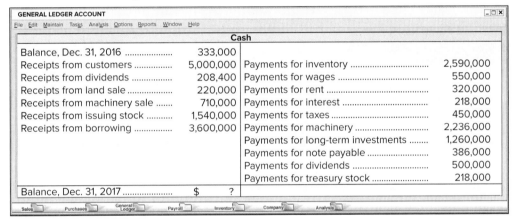

GENERAL LEDGER ACCOUNT

File Edit Maintain Tasks Analysis Options Reports Window Help

Cash			
Balance, Dec. 31, 2016	333,000		
Receipts from customers	5,000,000	Payments for inventory	2,590,000
Receipts from dividends	208,400	Payments for wages	550,000
Receipts from land sale	220,000	Payments for rent	320,000
Receipts from machinery sale	710,000	Payments for interest	218,000
Receipts from issuing stock	1,540,000	Payments for taxes	450,000
Receipts from borrowing	3,600,000	Payments for machinery	2,236,000
		Payments for long-term investments	1,260,000
		Payments for note payable	386,000
		Payments for dividends	500,000
		Payments for treasury stock	218,000
Balance, Dec. 31, 2017	$?		

Sales   Purchases   General Ledger   Payroll   Inventory   Company   Analysis

connect

Lansing Company's 2017 income statement and selected balance sheet data (for current assets and current liabilities) at December 31, 2016 and 2017, follow.

PROBLEM SET A

Problem 12-1A
Indirect: Computing cash flows from operations

P2

LANSING COMPANY		
Income Statement		
For Year Ended December 31, 2017		
Sales revenue		$97,200
Expenses		
Cost of goods sold	42,000	
Depreciation expense	12,000	
Salaries expense................	18,000	
Rent expense	9,000	
Insurance expense	3,800	
Interest expense................	3,600	
Utilities expense...............	2,800	
Net income		$ 6,000

LANSING COMPANY		
Selected Balance Sheet Accounts		
At December 31	2017	2016
Accounts receivable........	$5,600	$5,800
Inventory.................	1,980	1,540
Accounts payable..........	4,400	4,600
Salaries payable...........	880	700
Utilities payable	220	160
Prepaid insurance..........	260	280
Prepaid rent	220	180

Required

Prepare the cash flows from operating activities section only of the company's 2017 statement of cash flows using the *indirect method.*

Check Cash from operating activities, $17,780

Problem 12-2A^B

Direct: Computing cash flows from operations

P5

Refer to the information in Problem 12-1A.

Required

Prepare the cash flows from operating activities section only of the company's 2017 statement of cash flows using the *direct method*.

Problem 12-3A

Indirect: Statement of cash flows

A1   P1   P2   P3

Forten Company, a merchandiser, recently completed its calendar-year 2017 operations. For the year, (1) all sales are credit sales, (2) all credits to Accounts Receivable reflect cash receipts from customers, (3) all purchases of inventory are on credit, (4) all debits to Accounts Payable reflect cash payments for inventory, and (5) Other Expenses are paid in advance and are initially debited to Prepaid Expenses. The company's income statement and balance sheets follow.

FORTEN COMPANY
Comparative Balance Sheets
December 31, 2017 and 2016

	2017	2016
Assets		
Cash.....................................	$ 49,800	$ 73,500
Accounts receivable	65,810	50,625
Inventory	275,656	251,800
Prepaid expenses	1,250	1,875
Total current assets.......................	392,516	377,800
Equipment	157,500	108,000
Accum. depreciation—Equipment	(36,625)	(46,000)
Total assets	$513,391	$439,800
Liabilities and Equity		
Accounts payable	$ 53,141	$114,675
Short-term notes payable..................	10,000	6,000
Total current liabilities....................	63,141	120,675
Long-term notes payable	65,000	48,750
Total liabilities	128,141	169,425
Equity		
Common stock, $5 par value	162,750	150,250
Paid-in capital in excess of par,		
common stock.........................	37,500	0
Retained earnings........................	185,000	120,125
Total liabilities and equity..................	$513,391	$439,800

FORTEN COMPANY
Income Statement
For Year Ended December 31, 2017

Sales		$582,500
Cost of goods sold		285,000
Gross profit.............................		297,500
Operating expenses		
Depreciation expense	$ 20,750	
Other expenses	132,400	153,150
Other gains (losses)		
Loss on sale of equipment.............		(5,125)
Income before taxes....................		139,225
Income taxes expense		24,250
Net income		$114,975

Additional Information on Year 2017 Transactions

a. The loss on the cash sale of equipment was $5,125 (details in *b*).

b. Sold equipment costing $46,875, with accumulated depreciation of $30,125, for $11,625 cash.

c. Purchased equipment costing $96,375 by paying $30,000 cash and signing a long-term note payable for the balance.

d. Borrowed $4,000 cash by signing a short-term note payable.

e. Paid $50,125 cash to reduce the long-term notes payable.

f. Issued 2,500 shares of common stock for $20 cash per share.

g. Declared and paid cash dividends of $50,100.

Required

Check Cash from operating activities, $40,900

1. Prepare a complete statement of cash flows; report its operating activities using the *indirect method*. Disclose any noncash investing and financing activities in a note.

Analysis Component

2. Analyze and discuss the statement of cash flows prepared in part 1, giving special attention to the wisdom of the cash dividend payment.

Refer to the information reported about Forten Company in Problem 12-3A.

Problem 12-4A^A

Indirect: Cash flows
spreadsheet

Required

Prepare a complete statement of cash flows using a spreadsheet as in Exhibit 12A.1; report its operating
activities using the *indirect method*. Identify the debits and credits in the Analysis of Changes columns
with letters that correspond to the following list of transactions and events.

P1   P2   P3   P4

a. Net income was $114,975.

b. Accounts receivable increased.

c. Inventory increased.

d. Prepaid expenses decreased.

e. Accounts payable decreased.

f. Depreciation expense was $20,750.

g. Sold equipment costing $46,875, with accumulated depreciation of $30,125, for $11,625 cash. This
yielded a loss of $5,125.

h. Purchased equipment costing $96,375 by paying $30,000 cash and **(i.)** by signing a long-term note
payable for the balance.

j. Borrowed $4,000 cash by signing a short-term note payable.

k. Paid $50,125 cash to reduce the long-term notes payable.

l. Issued 2,500 shares of common stock for $20 cash per share.

Check Analysis of Changes
column totals, $600,775

m. Declared and paid cash dividends of $50,100.

Refer to Forten Company's financial statements and related information in Problem 12-3A.

Problem 12-5A^B

Direct: Statement of
cash flows   P1   P3   P5

Required

Prepare a complete statement of cash flows; report its operating activities according to the *direct method*.
Disclose any noncash investing and financing activities in a note.

Check Cash used in
financing activities, $(46,225)

Golden Corp., a merchandiser, recently completed its 2017 operations. For the year, (1) all sales are credit
sales, (2) all credits to Accounts Receivable reflect cash receipts from customers, (3) all purchases of inventory are on credit, (4) all debits to Accounts Payable reflect cash payments for inventory, (5) Other
Expenses are all cash expenses, and (6) any change in Income Taxes Payable reflects the accrual and cash
payment of taxes. The company's balance sheets and income statement follow.

Problem 12-6A

Indirect: Statement
of cash flows

P1   P2   P3

GOLDEN CORPORATION
Comparative Balance Sheets
December 31, 2017 and 2016

	2017	2016
Assets		
Cash......................................	$ 164,000	$107,000
Accounts receivable	83,000	71,000
Inventory	601,000	526,000
Total current assets......................	848,000	704,000
Equipment	335,000	299,000
Accum. depreciation—Equipment	(158,000)	(104,000)
Total assets	$1,025,000	$899,000
Liabilities and Equity		
Accounts payable	$ 87,000	$ 71,000
Income taxes payable......................	28,000	25,000
Total current liabilities.................	115,000	96,000
Equity		
Common stock, $2 par value	592,000	568,000
Paid-in capital in excess		
of par value, common stock................	196,000	160,000
Retained earnings.........................	122,000	75,000
Total liabilities and equity..............	$1,025,000	$899,000

GOLDEN CORPORATION
Income Statement
For Year Ended December 31, 2017

Sales		$1,792,000
Cost of goods sold		1,086,000
Gross profit		706,000
Operating expenses		
Depreciation expense	$ 54,000	
Other expenses	494,000	548,000
Income before taxes..............		158,000
Income taxes expense		22,000
Net income		$ 136,000

Additional Information on Year 2017 Transactions

a. Purchased equipment for $36,000 cash.

b. Issued 12,000 shares of common stock for $5 cash per share.

c. Declared and paid $89,000 in cash dividends.

Required

Check   Cash from operating activities, $122,000

Prepare a complete statement of cash flows; report its cash inflows and cash outflows from operating activities according to the *indirect method*.

Problem 12-7A[A]

Indirect: Cash flows spreadsheet

P1   P2   P3   P4

Refer to the information reported about Golden Corporation in Problem 12-6A.

Required

Prepare a complete statement of cash flows using a spreadsheet as in Exhibit 12A.1; report operating activities under the *indirect method*. Identify the debits and credits in the Analysis of Changes columns with letters that correspond to the following list of transactions and events.

a. Net income was $136,000.

b. Accounts receivable increased.

c. Inventory increased.

d. Accounts payable increased.

e. Income taxes payable increased.

f. Depreciation expense was $54,000.

g. Purchased equipment for $36,000 cash.

Check   Analysis of Changes column totals, $481,000

h. Issued 12,000 shares at $5 cash per share.

i. Declared and paid $89,000 of cash dividends.

Problem 12-8A[B]

Direct: Statement of cash flows

P1   P3   P5

Check   Cash used in financing activities, $(29,000)

Refer to Golden Corporation's financial statements and related information in Problem 12-6A.

Required

Prepare a complete statement of cash flows; report its cash flows from operating activities according to the *direct method*.

PROBLEM SET B

Problem 12-1B

Indirect: Computing cash flows from operations

P2

Salt Lake Company's 2017 income statement and selected balance sheet data (for current assets and current liabilities) at December 31, 2016 and 2017, follow.

SALT LAKE COMPANY Income Statement For Year Ended December 31, 2017	
Sales revenue	$156,000
Expenses	
Cost of goods sold	72,000
Depreciation expense	32,000
Salaries expense................	20,000
Rent expense	5,000
Insurance expense..............	2,600
Interest expense................	2,400
Utilities expense................	2,000
Net income	$ 20,000

SALT LAKE COMPANY Selected Balance Sheet Accounts		
At December 31	2017	2016
Accounts receivable	$3,600	$3,000
Inventory	860	980
Accounts payable	2,400	2,600
Salaries payable	900	600
Utilities payable...............	200	0
Prepaid insurance............	140	180
Prepaid rent.................	100	200

Required

Prepare the cash flows from operating activities section only of the company's 2017 statement of cash flows using the *indirect method*.

Check Cash from operating activities, $51,960

Refer to the information in Problem 12-1B.

Problem 12-2B^B

Direct: Computing cash flows from operations

Required

Prepare the cash flows from operating activities section only of the company's 2017 statement of cash flows using the *direct method*.

P5

Gazelle Corporation, a merchandiser, recently completed its calendar-year 2017 operations. For the year, (1) all sales are credit sales, (2) all credits to Accounts Receivable reflect cash receipts from customers, (3) all purchases of inventory are on credit, (4) all debits to Accounts Payable reflect cash payments for inventory, and (5) Other Expenses are paid in advance and are initially debited to Prepaid Expenses. The company's balance sheets and income statement follow.

Problem 12-3B

Indirect: Statement of cash flows

A1   P1   P2   P3

GAZELLE CORPORATION
Comparative Balance Sheets
December 31, 2017 and 2016

	2017	2016
Assets		
Cash.	$123,450	$ 61,550
Accounts receivable	77,100	80,750
Inventory	240,600	250,700
Prepaid expenses	15,100	17,000
Total current assets.	456,250	410,000
Equipment	262,250	200,000
Accum. depreciation—Equipment	(110,750)	(95,000)
Total assets	$607,750	$515,000
Liabilities and Equity		
Accounts payable	$ 17,750	$102,000
Short-term notes payable.	15,000	10,000
Total current liabilities.	32,750	112,000
Long-term notes payable	100,000	77,500
Total liabilities	132,750	189,500
Equity		
Common stock, $5 par	215,000	200,000
Paid-in capital in excess		
of par, common stock.	30,000	0
Retained earnings.	230,000	125,500
Total liabilities and equity.	$607,750	$515,000

GAZELLE CORPORATION
Income Statement
For Year Ended December 31, 2017

Sales		$1,185,000
Cost of goods sold		595,000
Gross profit		590,000
Operating expenses		
Depreciation expense	$ 38,600	
Other expenses	362,850	
Total operating expenses.		401,450
		188,550
Other gains (losses)		
Loss on sale of equipment.		(2,100)
Income before taxes.		186,450
Income taxes expense		28,350
Net income		$ 158,100

Additional Information on Year 2017 Transactions

a. The loss on the cash sale of equipment was $2,100 (details in *b*).

b. Sold equipment costing $51,000, with accumulated depreciation of $22,850, for $26,050 cash.

c. Purchased equipment costing $113,250 by paying $43,250 cash and signing a long-term note payable for the balance.

d. Borrowed $5,000 cash by signing a short-term note payable.

e. Paid $47,500 cash to reduce the long-term notes payable.

f. Issued 3,000 shares of common stock for $15 cash per share.

g. Declared and paid cash dividends of $53,600.

Required

1. Prepare a complete statement of cash flows; report its operating activities using the *indirect method.*
Disclose any noncash investing and financing activities in a note.

Analysis Component

2. Analyze and discuss the statement of cash flows prepared in part 1, giving special attention to the
wisdom of the cash dividend payment.

Problem 12-4B[A]
Indirect: Cash flows
spreadsheet
P1   P2   P3   P4

Refer to the information reported about Gazelle Corporation in Problem 12-3B.

Required

Prepare a complete statement of cash flows using a spreadsheet as in Exhibit 12A.1; report its operating
activities using the *indirect method.* Identify the debits and credits in the Analysis of Changes columns
with letters that correspond to the following list of transactions and events.

a. Net income was $158,100.
b. Accounts receivable decreased.
c. Inventory decreased.
d. Prepaid expenses decreased.
e. Accounts payable decreased.
f. Depreciation expense was $38,600.
g. Sold equipment costing $51,000, with accumulated depreciation of $22,850, for $26,050 cash. This
yielded a loss of $2,100.
h. Purchased equipment costing $113,250 by paying $43,250 cash and **(i.)** by signing a long-term note
payable for the balance.
j. Borrowed $5,000 cash by signing a short-term note payable.
k. Paid $47,500 cash to reduce the long-term notes payable.

l. Issued 3,000 shares of common stock for $15 cash per share.
m. Declared and paid cash dividends of $53,600.

Problem 12-5B[B]
Direct: Statement of
cash flows
P1   P3   P5

Refer to Gazelle Corporation's financial statements and related information in Problem 12-3B.

Required

Prepare a complete statement of cash flows; report its operating activities according to the *direct method.*
Disclose any noncash investing and financing activities in a note.

Problem 12-6B
Indirect: Statement of
cash flows
P1   P2   P3

Satu Company, a merchandiser, recently completed its 2017 operations. For the year, (1) all sales are
credit sales, (2) all credits to Accounts Receivable reflect cash receipts from customers, (3) all purchases
of inventory are on credit, (4) all debits to Accounts Payable reflect cash payments for inventory, (5) Other
Expenses are cash expenses, and (6) any change in Income Taxes Payable reflects the accrual and cash
payment of taxes. The company's balance sheets and income statement follow.

SATU COMPANY
Comparative Balance Sheets
December 31, 2017 and 2016

	2017	2016
Assets		
Cash..................................	$ 58,750	$ 28,400
Accounts receivable	20,222	25,860
Total current assets......................	78,972	54,260
Inventory	165,667	140,320
Equipment..............................	107,750	77,500
Accum. depreciation—Equipment	(46,700)	(31,000)
Total assets	$305,689	$241,080
Liabilities and Equity		
Accounts payable	$ 20,372	$157,530
Income taxes payable....................	2,100	6,100
Total current liabilities....................	22,472	163,630
Equity		
Common stock, $5 par value	40,000	25,000
Paid-in capital in excess		
of par, common stock...................	68,000	20,000
Retained earnings.......................	175,217	32,450
Total liabilities and equity.................	$305,689	$241,080

SATU COMPANY
Income Statement
For Year Ended December 31, 2017

Sales		$750,800
Cost of goods sold		269,200
Gross profit.......................		481,600
Operating expenses		
Depreciation expense	$ 15,700	
Other expenses	173,933	189,633
Income before taxes...............		291,967
Income taxes expense		89,200
Net income		$202,767

Additional Information on Year 2017 Transactions

a. Purchased equipment for $30,250 cash.

b. Issued 3,000 shares of common stock for $21 cash per share.

c. Declared and paid $60,000 of cash dividends.

Required

Prepare a complete statement of cash flows; report its cash inflows and cash outflows from operating activities according to the *indirect method.*

Check Cash from operating activities, $57,600

Refer to the information reported about Satu Company in Problem 12-6B.

Problem 12-7B^A
Indirect: Cash flows spreadsheet

P1 P2 P3 P4

Required

Prepare a complete statement of cash flows using a spreadsheet as in Exhibit 12A.1; report operating activities under the *indirect method.* Identify the debits and credits in the Analysis of Changes columns with letters that correspond to the following list of transactions and events.

a. Net income was $202,767.

b. Accounts receivable decreased.

c. Inventory increased.

d. Accounts payable decreased.

e. Income taxes payable decreased.

f. Depreciation expense was $15,700.

g. Purchased equipment for $30,250 cash.

h. Issued 3,000 shares at $21 cash per share.

i. Declared and paid $60,000 of cash dividends.

Check Analysis of Changes column totals, $543,860

Refer to Satu Company's financial statements and related information in Problem 12-6B.

Problem 12-8B^B
Direct: Statement of cash flows

P1 P3 P5

Required

Prepare a complete statement of cash flows; report its cash flows from operating activities according to the *direct method.*

Check Cash provided by financing activities, $3,000

SERIAL PROBLEM
Business Solutions **(Indirect)**

P1 P2 P3

© Alexander Image/Shutterstock RF

(This serial problem began in Chapter 1 and continues through most of the book. If previous chapter segments were not completed, the serial problem can begin at this point.)

SP 12   Santana Rey, owner of **Business Solutions**, decides to prepare a statement of cash flows for her business. (Although the serial problem allowed for various ownership changes in earlier chapters, we will prepare the statement of cash flows using the following financial data.)

BUSINESS SOLUTIONS Income Statement For Three Months Ended March 31, 2018		
Computer services revenue............		$25,307
Net sales........................		18,693
Total revenue		44,000
Cost of goods sold	$14,052	
Depreciation expense— Office equipment................	400	
Depreciation expense— Computer equipment.............	1,250	
Wages expense	3,250	
Insurance expense...............	555	
Rent expense	2,475	
Computer supplies expense	1,305	
Advertising expense..............	600	
Mileage expense	320	
Repairs expense—Computer..........	960	
Total expenses		25,167
Net income....................		$18,833

BUSINESS SOLUTIONS Comparative Balance Sheets December 31, 2017, and March 31, 2018		
	Mar. 31, 2018	**Dec. 31, 2017**
Assets		
Cash	$ 68,057	$48,372
Accounts receivable.....................	22,867	5,668
Inventory............................	704	0
Computer supplies	2,005	580
Prepaid insurance.......................	1,110	1,665
Prepaid rent	825	825
Total current assets	95,568	57,110
Office equipment	8,000	8,000
Accumulated depreciation—Office equipment	(800)	(400)
Computer equipment....................	20,000	20,000
Accumulated depreciation— Computer equipment..................	(2,500)	(1,250)
Total assets...........................	$120,268	$83,460
Liabilities and Equity		
Accounts payable......................	$ 0	$ 1,100
Wages payable........................	875	500
Unearned computer service revenue	0	1,500
Total current liabilities	875	3,100
Equity		
Common stock	98,000	73,000
Retained earnings	21,393	7,360
Total liabilities and equity..............	$120,268	$83,460

Required

Check   Cash flows used by operations: $(515)

Prepare a statement of cash flows for Business Solutions using the *indirect method* for the three months ended March 31, 2018. Recall that owner Santana Rey contributed $25,000 to the business in exchange for additional stock in the first quarter of 2018 and has received $4,800 in cash dividends.

 GENERAL LEDGER PROBLEM

Available only in Connect

The following **General Ledger** assignments highlight the impact, or lack thereof, on the statement of cash flows from summary journal entries derived from consecutive trial balances. Prepare summary journal entries reflecting changes in consecutive trial balances. Then prepare the statement of cash flows (direct method) from those entries. Finally, prepare the reconciliation to the indirect method for net cash provided (used) by operating activities.

GL 12-1   General Ledger assignment based on Exercise 12-11

GL 12-2   General Ledger assignment based on Problem 12-1

GL 12-3   General Ledger assignment based on Problem 12-6

Beyond the Numbers

BTN 12-1   Refer to **Apple**'s financial statements in Appendix A to answer the following.

1. Is Apple's statement of cash flows prepared under the direct method or the indirect method? How do you know?
2. For each fiscal year 2015, 2014, and 2013, is the amount of cash provided by operating activities more or less than the cash paid for dividends?
3. What is the largest amount in reconciling the difference between net income and cash flow from operating activities in fiscal 2015? In fiscal 2014? In fiscal 2013?
4. Identify the largest cash inflow and cash outflow for investing *and* for financing activities in fiscal 2015 and in fiscal 2014.

Fast Forward

5. Obtain Apple's financial statements for a fiscal year ending after September 27, 2015, from either its website (**Apple.com**) or the SEC's database (**SEC.gov**). Since September 27, 2015, what are Apple's largest cash outflows and cash inflows in the investing and in the financing sections of its statement of cash flows?

REPORTING IN ACTION

A1

APPLE

BTN 12-2   Key figures for **Apple** and **Google** follow.

$ millions	Apple			Google		
	Current Year	1 Year Prior	2 Years Prior	Current Year	1 Year Prior	2 Years Prior
Operating cash flows	$ 81,266	$ 59,713	$ 53,666	$ 26,024	$ 22,376	$ 18,659
Total assets	290,479	231,839	207,000	147,461	129,187	109,050

COMPARATIVE ANALYSIS

A1

APPLE
GOOGLE

Required

1. Compute the recent two years' cash flow on total assets ratios for Apple and Google.
2. What does the cash flow on total assets ratio measure?
3. Which company has the highest cash flow on total assets ratio for the periods shown?
4. Does the cash flow on total assets ratio reflect on the quality of earnings? Explain.

BTN 12-3   Katie Murphy is preparing for a meeting with her banker. Her business is finishing its fourth year of operations. In the first year, it had negative cash flows from operations. In the second and third years, cash flows from operations were positive. However, inventory costs rose significantly in year 4, and cash flows from operations will probably be down 25%. Murphy wants to secure a line of credit from her banker as a financing buffer. From experience, she knows the banker will scrutinize operating cash flows for years 1 through 4 and will want a projected number for year 5. Murphy knows that a steady progression upward in operating cash flows for years 1 through 4 will help her case. She decides to use her discretion as owner and considers several business actions that will turn her operating cash flow in year 4 from a decrease to an increase.

ETHICS CHALLENGE

C1   A1

Required

1. Identify two business actions Murphy might take to improve cash flows from operations.
2. Comment on the ethics and possible consequences of Murphy's decision to pursue these actions.

BTN 12-4   Your friend, Diana Wood, recently completed the second year of her business and just received annual financial statements from her accountant. Wood finds the income statement and balance sheet informative but does not understand the statement of cash flows. She says the first section is especially confusing because it contains a lot of additions and subtractions that do not make sense to her. Wood adds, "The income statement tells me the business is more profitable than last year and that's most important. If I want to know how cash changes, I can look at comparative balance sheets."

COMMUNICATING IN PRACTICE

C1

Required

Write a half-page memorandum to your friend explaining the purpose of the statement of cash flows. Speculate as to why the first section is so confusing and how it might be rectified.

TAKING IT TO THE NET

A1

BTN 12-5   Access the April 14, 2016, filing of the 10-K report (for year ending December 31, 2015) of **Mendocino Brewing Company, Inc.** (ticker: MENB) at **SEC.gov**.

Required

1. Does Mendocino Brewing use the direct or indirect method to construct its consolidated statement of cash flows?

2. For the year ended December 31, 2015, what is the largest item in reconciling the net income (or loss) to net cash provided by operating activities?

3. In the recent two years, has the company been more successful in generating operating cash flows or in generating net income? Identify the figures to support the answer.

4. In the year ended December 31, 2015, what was the largest cash outflow for investing activities *and* for financing activities?

5. What item(s) does the company report as supplemental cash flow information?

6. Does the company report any noncash financing activities for 2015? Identify them, if any.

TEAMWORK IN ACTION

C1   A1   P2   P5

BTN 12-6   Team members are to coordinate and independently answer one question within each of the following three sections. Team members should then report to the team and confirm or correct teammates' answers.

1. Answer *one* of the following questions about the statement of cash flows.
   a. What are this statement's reporting objectives?
   b. What two methods are used to prepare it? Identify similarities and differences between them.
   c. What steps are followed to prepare the statement?
   d. What types of analyses are often made from this statement's information?

2. Identify and explain the adjustment from net income to obtain cash flows from operating activities using the indirect method for *one* of the following items.
   a. Noncash operating revenues and expenses.
   b. Nonoperating gains and losses.
   c. Increases and decreases in noncash current assets.
   d. Increases and decreases in current liabilities.

3.ᴮ Identify and explain the formula for computing cash flows from operating activities using the direct method for *one* of the following items.
   a. Cash receipts from sales to customers.
   b. Cash paid for inventory.
   c. Cash paid for wages and operating expenses.
   d. Cash paid for interest and taxes.

Note: For teams of more than four, some pairing within teams is necessary. Use as an in-class activity or as an assignment. If used in class, specify a time limit on each part. Conclude with reports to the entire class, using team rotation. Each team can prepare responses on a transparency.

ENTREPRENEURIAL DECISION

C1   A1

BTN 12-7   Review the chapter's opener involving **Amazon.com** and its founder, Jeff Bezos.

Required

1. In a business such as Amazon, monitoring cash flow is always a priority. Even though Amazon now has billions in annual sales and sometimes earns a positive net income, explain how cash flow can lag behind net income.

2. Amazon is a publicly traded corporation. What are potential sources of financing for its future expansion?

ENTREPRENEURIAL DECISION

C1   A1

BTN 12-8   Jenna and Matt Wilder are completing their second year operating Mountain High, a downhill ski area and resort. Mountain High reports a net loss of $(10,000) for its second year, which includes an $85,000 unusual loss from fire. This past year also involved major purchases of plant assets for renovation and expansion, yielding a year-end total asset amount of $800,000. Mountain High's net cash outflow for its second year is $(5,000); a summarized version of its statement of cash flows follows.

Net cash flow provided by operating activities	$ 295,000
Net cash flow used by investing activities	(310,000)
Net cash flow provided by financing activities	10,000

Required

Write a one-page memorandum to the Wilders evaluating Mountain High's current performance and assessing its future. Give special emphasis to cash flow data and their interpretation.

HITTING THE ROAD

C1

BTN 12-9   Visit **The Motley Fool**'s website (<u>Fool.com</u>). Enter the *Fool's School* (at *Fool.com/School*). Identify and select the link "How to Value Stocks." (This site might ask you to register with your e-mail address; registration had been free and did grant access to articles.)

Required

1. Click on "Introduction to Valuation Methods," and then "Cash-Flow Based Valuations." How does the Fool's School define cash flow? What is the school's reasoning for this definition?

2. Per the school's instruction, why do analysts focus on earnings before interest and taxes (EBIT)?

3. Visit other links at this website that interest you such as "How to Read a Balance Sheet," or find out what the "Fool's Ratio" is. Write a half-page report on what you find.

GLOBAL DECISION

C1

Samsung
APPLE
GOOGLE

BTN 12-10   Key comparative information for **Samsung** (<u>Samsung.com</u>), a leading manufacturer of electronic consumer products, follows.

₩ in millions	Current Year	1 Year Prior	2 Years Prior
Operating cash flows	₩ 40,061,761	₩ 36,975,389	₩ 46,707,440
Total assets	242,179,521	230,422,958	214,075,018

Required

1. Compute the recent two years' cash flow on total assets ratio for Samsung.

2. How does Samsung's ratio compare to **Apple**'s and **Google**'s ratios from BTN 12-2?

 # GLOBAL VIEW

The statement of cash flows, which explains changes in cash (including cash equivalents) from period to period, is required under both U.S. GAAP and IFRS. This section discusses similarities and differences between U.S. GAAP and IFRS in reporting that statement.

Reporting Cash Flows from Operating   Both U.S. GAAP and IFRS permit the reporting of cash flows from operating activities using either the direct or indirect method. Basic requirements underlying the application of both methods are fairly consistent across U.S. GAAP and IFRS. Appendix A shows that **Samsung** reports its cash flows from operating activities using the indirect method, and in a manner similar to that explained in this chapter. Further, the definition of cash and cash equivalents is roughly similar for U.S. GAAP and IFRS.

There are some differences between U.S. GAAP and IFRS in reporting operating cash flows. We mention two of the more notable. First, U.S. GAAP requires that cash inflows from interest revenue and dividend revenue be classified as operating, whereas IFRS permits classification under operating or investing provided that this classification is consistently applied. Samsung reports its cash from interest received under operating, consistent with U.S. GAAP. Second, U.S. GAAP requires cash outflows for interest expense be classified as operating, whereas IFRS again permits classification under operating or financing provided that it is consistently applied. (Some believe that interest payments, like dividend payments, are better classified as financing because they represent payments to financiers.) Samsung reports cash outflows for interest under operating, which is consistent with U.S. GAAP and acceptable under IFRS.

Samsung

Global: There are no requirements to separate domestic and international cash flows, leading some users to ask, "Where in the world is cash flow?"

Reporting Cash Flows from Investing and Financing   U.S. GAAP and IFRS are broadly similar in computing and classifying cash flows from investing and financing activities. A quick review of these two sections for **Samsung**'s statement of cash flows shows a structure similar to that explained in this chapter. One notable exception is that U.S. GAAP requires that cash outflows for income tax be classified as operating, whereas IFRS permits the splitting of those cash flows among operating, investing, and financing depending on the sources of that tax. Samsung reports its cash outflows for income tax under operating, which is similar to U.S. GAAP.

 Global View Assignments

Discussion Questions 14 and 15

Quick Study 12-20

Exercise 12-9

BTN 12-10

13 chapter

Analysis of Financial Statements

Chapter Preview

BASICS OF ANALYSIS

C1 Analysis purpose

Building blocks

C2 Standards for comparisons

Analysis tools

HORIZONTAL ANALYSIS

P1 Application of:

Comparative balance sheets

Comparative income statements

Trend analysis

NTK 13-1

VERTICAL ANALYSIS

P2 Application of:

Common-size balance sheet

Common-size income statement

Common-size graphics

NTK 13-2

RATIO ANALYSIS AND REPORTING

P3 Liquidity and efficiency

Solvency

Profitability

Market prospects

A1 Analysis reports

NTK 13-3

Learning Objectives

CONCEPTUAL

C1 Explain the purpose and identify the building blocks of analysis.

C2 Describe standards for comparisons in analysis.

ANALYTICAL

A1 Summarize and report results of analysis.

A2 *Appendix 13A*—Explain the form and assess the content of a complete income statement.

PROCEDURAL

P1 Explain and apply methods of horizontal analysis.

P2 Describe and apply methods of vertical analysis.

P3 Define and apply ratio analysis.

CARLA HARRIS
MORGAN STANLEY, VICE CHAIRMAN, WEALTH MANAGEMENT, MANAGING DIRECTOR & SENIOR CLIENT ADVISOR

© Alberto E. Rodriguez/Getty Images

Numbers Rule

NEW YORK—"I grew up as an only child in a no-nonsense, no-excuses household," recalls Carla Harris. "My parents gave me the sense that I was supposed to do well." Fast-forward and Carla is now vice chairman of **Morgan Stanley**'s (**MorganStanley.com**) prized global wealth-management division and past-chair of the Morgan Stanley Foundation.

Carla Harris and her colleagues at Morgan Stanley analyze financial statements for profit. Their success in analyzing financial statements is well documented.

One of Morgan Stanley's key tools for analysis is *ModelWare*. ModelWare is a framework to analyze the nuts and bolts of companies' financial statements, and then to compare those companies head-to-head. One of its key aims is to provide comparable information that focuses on sustainable performance. To do this, it works with the underlying accounting numbers and footnotes.

Morgan Stanley uses the accounting numbers in financial statements to produce comparable metrics using techniques such as horizontal and vertical analysis. It also computes financial ratios for

"Expect to win!"
—**Carla Harris**

analysis and interpretation. Those ratios include return on equity, return on assets, asset turnover, profit margin, price-to-earnings, and many other accounting measures. The focus is to uncover the drivers of profitability and to predict future levels of those drivers.

Carla has experienced much success through analyzing financial statements. As Carla likes to say, "I'm tough and analytical!" She says that people do not take full advantage of information available in financial statements. Accordingly, those with accounting know-how continue to earn profits from financial statement analysis and interpretation.

Carla and Morgan Stanley are proud to play by the rules. *Fortune* writes, "Morgan Stanley has earned some bragging rights. It's the only major bank that hasn't paid a federal fine related to the financial crisis. [It] hasn't even been accused of breaking the law." Carla is proud of such praise and adds: "always start from a place of doing the right thing."

Sources: *Morgan Stanley website*, January 2017; *MorganStanleyIQ*, November 2007; *Alumni.HBS.edu/Stories*, September 2006; *Fortune*, August 2013 and March 2016

BASICS OF ANALYSIS

C1
Explain the purpose and identify the building blocks of analysis.

Financial statement analysis applies analytical tools to financial statements and related data for making business decisions. This section describes the purpose of financial statement analysis, its information sources, the use of comparisons, and issues in computation.

Purpose of Analysis

Internal users of accounting information manage and operate the company. They include managers, officers, and internal auditors. The purpose of financial statement analysis for internal users is to provide strategic information to improve company efficiency and effectiveness.

External users of accounting information are *not* directly involved in running the company. External users rely on financial statement analysis in pursuing their own goals. Shareholders and creditors assess company prospects to make investing and lending decisions. A board of directors analyzes financial statements in monitoring management's decisions. Suppliers use financial statement information in establishing credit terms. Auditors use financial statements in assessing the "fair presentation" of financial results. Analyst services such as **Moody's** and **Standard & Poor's** use financial statements in making buy-sell recommendations and in setting credit ratings.

Point: Financial statement analysis is a topic on the CPA, CMA, CIA, and CFA exams.

The common goal of these users is to evaluate company performance and financial condition. This includes evaluating (1) past and current performance, (2) current financial position, and (3) future performance and risk.

Building Blocks of Analysis

Financial statement analysis focuses on one or more elements of a company's financial condition or performance. We emphasize four *building blocks* of financial statement analysis:

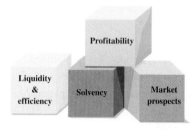

- **Liquidity** and **efficiency**—ability to meet short-term obligations and to efficiently generate revenues.
- **Solvency**—ability to generate future revenues and meet long-term obligations.
- **Profitability**—ability to provide financial rewards to attract and retain financing.
- **Market prospects**—ability to generate positive market expectations.

The four building blocks highlight different aspects of financial condition or performance, yet they are interrelated.

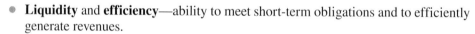

■ **Decision** Insight

Chips and Brokers   The phrase *blue chips* refers to stock of big, profitable companies. The phrase comes from poker, where the most valuable chips are blue. The term *brokers* refers to those who execute orders to buy or sell stock. The term comes from wine retailers—individuals who broach (break) wine casks. ■

Information for Analysis

Financial analysis uses **general-purpose financial statements** that include the (1) income statement, (2) balance sheet, (3) statement of stockholders' equity (or statement of retained earnings), (4) statement of cash flows, and (5) notes to these statements.

Financial reporting is the communication of financial information useful for making investment, credit, and other business decisions. Financial reporting includes general-purpose financial statements, information from SEC 10-K and other filings, press releases, shareholders' meetings, forecasts, management letters, and auditors' reports.

Management's Discussion and Analysis (MD&A) is one example of useful information outside usual financial statements. **Apple**'s MD&A (available at <u>**Investor.Apple.com**</u> and "Item 7" in the annual report) begins with an overview, followed by critical accounting policies and estimates. It then discusses operating results followed by financial condition (liquidity, capital resources, and cash flows). The final few parts discuss legal proceedings, market risk of financial instruments, and risks from interest rate and foreign currency fluctuations. The MD&A is an excellent starting point in understanding a company's business.

Standards for Comparisons

When interpreting financial statements, we use standards (benchmarks) for comparisons that include:

C2 _____
Describe standards for comparisons in analysis.

- *Intracompany*—The company's current performance is compared to its prior performance and its relations between financial items. **Apple**'s current net income, for instance, can be compared with its prior years' net income and in relation to its revenues or total assets.
- *Competitor*—Competitors provide standards for comparisons. **Coca-Cola**'s profit margin, for instance, can be compared with **PepsiCo**'s profit margin.
- *Industry*—Industry statistics provide standards of comparisons. **Intel**'s profit margin can be compared with the industry's profit margin.
- *Guidelines (rules of thumb)*—Standards of comparisons can develop from experience. Examples are the 2:1 level for the current ratio or 1:1 level for the acid-test ratio.

Point: Each chapter's *Reporting in Action* problems engage students in *intracompany* analysis, whereas *Comparative Analysis* problems require competitor analysis (**Apple** vs. **Google** vs. **Samsung**).

Benchmarks from a selected competitor or group of competitors are often best. Intracompany and industry measures are also good. Guidelines can be applied, but only if they seem reasonable given recent experience.

Tools of Analysis

Three tools of financial statement analysis are

1. **Horizontal analysis**—comparison of a company's financial condition and performance across time.
2. **Vertical analysis**—comparison of a company's financial condition and performance to a base amount.
3. **Ratio analysis**—measurement of key relations between financial statement items.

The remainder of this chapter describes these analysis tools and how to apply them.

▣ Decision Insight ▲

Busting Frauds Horizontal, vertical, and ratio analysis tools can uncover fraud by identifying amounts out of line with expectations. One can then follow up and ask questions that can either identify a logical reason for such results or confirm/raise suspicions of fraud. Many past fraud schemes could have been identified much earlier had people applied these tools and pressured management for explanations. ▪

HORIZONTAL ANALYSIS

Horizontal analysis refers to examination of financial statement data *across time*. (The term *horizontal analysis* comes from the left-to-right [or right-to-left] movement of our eyes as we review comparative financial statements across time.)

P1 _____
Explain and apply methods of horizontal analysis.

Comparative Statements

Comparative financial statements show financial amounts in side-by-side columns on a single statement, called a *comparative format*. Using **Apple**'s financial statements, this section explains how to compute dollar changes and percent changes for comparative statements.

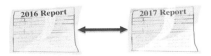

Dollar Changes and Percent Changes   Comparing financial statements over short time periods—two to three years—is often done by analyzing changes in line items. A change analysis includes analyzing dollar amount changes and percent changes. Both analyses are relevant because small dollar changes can yield large percent changes inconsistent with their importance. For instance, a 50% change from a base figure of $100 is less important than a 50% change from a base amount of $100,000. Reference to dollar amounts helps keep a perspective on the importance of changes. We compute the *dollar change* for a financial statement item as follows:

Dollar change = Analysis period amount − Base period amount

Analysis period is the point or period of time for the financial statements under analysis, and *base period* is the point or period of time for the financial statements used for comparison purposes. The prior year is commonly used as a base period. We compute the *percent change* by dividing the dollar change by the base period amount and then multiplying this quantity by 100 as follows:

$$\text{Percent change (\%)} = \frac{\text{Analysis period amount} - \text{Base period amount}}{\text{Base period amount}} \times 100$$

Point: Percents and ratios are usually rounded to one or two decimals, depending on how key they are to the decision.

We must know a few rules in working with percent changes. To illustrate, look at four separate cases in this chart:

Case	Analysis Period	Base Period	Change Analysis Dollar	Change Analysis Percent
A	$ 1,500	$(4,500)	$ 6,000	—
B	(1,000)	2,000	(3,000)	—
C	8,000	—	8,000	—
D	0	10,000	(10,000)	(100%)

- **Cases A and B:** When a negative amount is in the base period and a positive amount in the analysis period (or vice versa), we cannot compute a meaningful percent change.
- **Case C:** When no amount is in the base period, no percent change is computable.
- **Case D:** When an item has an amount in the base period and zero in the analysis period, the decrease is 100 percent.

Example: When there is a value in the base period and zero in the analysis period, the decrease is 100%. Why isn't the reverse situation an increase of 100%? *Answer:* A 100% increase of zero is still zero.

Comparative Balance Sheets   Comparative balance sheets consist of amounts from two or more dates arranged side by side. This method of analysis is improved by showing each item's dollar change and percent change to highlight large changes.

Analysis of comparative financial statements begins by focusing on large dollar and percent changes. We then identify the reasons for these changes and determine whether they are favorable or unfavorable. We also follow up on items with small changes when we expected the changes to be large.

APPLE

Exhibit 13.1 shows comparative balance sheets for **Apple Inc.** (ticker: AAPL). A few items stand out on the asset side. Apple's cash and cash equivalents increased by 52.6%, and short-term marketable securities increased by 82.3%. This is a substantial increase in liquid assets. In response, Apple raised its 2016 dividend 9.6% and increased its share repurchase plan by 25%. Dividends and share repurchase plans are likely to slow Apple's growth of cash and short-term securities. Other notable increases occur with (1) other noncurrent assets, partially related to derivatives; (2) vendor nontrade receivables; and (3) especially long-term marketable securities. Interestingly, accounts receivable decreased by 3.5% while sales increased by 27.9%. This suggests Apple is improving its collection of receivables, a positive trend.

On Apple's financing side, we see its overall 25.3% increase is driven by a 42.3% increase in liabilities; equity increased only 7.0%. The largest increase is due to long-term debt, which increased by $24,476 million, or 84.4%. Much of this increase results from bond offerings by

Example: Which is a more significant change, a 70% increase on a $1,000 expense or a 30% increase on a $400,000 expense? *Answer:* The 30% increase.

EXHIBIT 13.1

Comparative Balance Sheets

APPLE

APPLE INC.
Comparative Balance Sheets
September 26, 2015, and September 27, 2014

$ millions	2015	2014	Dollar Change	Percent Change
Assets				
Cash and cash equivalents	$ 21,120	$ 13,844	$ 7,276	52.6%
Short-term marketable securities	20,481	11,233	9,248	82.3
Accounts receivable, net	16,849	17,460	(611)	(3.5)
Inventories	2,349	2,111	238	11.3
Deferred tax assets	5,546	4,318	1,228	28.4
Vendor non-trade receivables	13,494	9,759	3,735	38.3
Other current assets	9,539	9,806	(267)	(2.7)
Total current assets	89,378	68,531	20,847	30.4
Long-term marketable securities	164,065	130,162	33,903	26.0
Property, plant and equipment, net	22,471	20,624	1,847	9.0
Goodwill	5,116	4,616	500	10.8
Acquired intangible assets, net	3,893	4,142	(249)	(6.0)
Other assets	5,556	3,764	1,792	47.6
Total assets	$290,479	$231,839	$ 58,640	25.3
Liabilities				
Accounts payable	$ 35,490	$ 30,196	$ 5,294	17.5%
Accrued expenses	25,181	18,453	6,728	36.5
Deferred revenue	8,940	8,491	449	5.3
Commercial paper	8,499	6,308	2,191	34.7
Current portion of long-term debt	2,500	0	2,500	—
Total current liabilities	80,610	63,448	17,162	27.0
Deferred revenue—noncurrent	3,624	3,031	593	19.6
Long-term debt	53,463	28,987	24,476	84.4
Other noncurrent liabilities	33,427	24,826	8,601	34.6
Total liabilities	171,124	120,292	50,832	42.3
Stockholders' Equity				
Common stock	27,416	23,313	4,103	17.6
Retained earnings	92,284	87,152	5,132	5.9
Accumulated other comprehensive income	(345)	1,082	(1,427)	—
Total stockholders' equity	119,355	111,547	7,808	7.0
Total liabilities and stockholders' equity	$290,479	$231,839	$ 58,640	25.3

Apple to take advantage of low interest rates. We also see a modest increase of 5.9% ($5,132) in retained earnings, which consists of a strong income of $53,394 that is reduced by cash dividends and stock repurchases.

Comparative Income Statements   Exhibit 13.2 shows Apple's comparative income statements prepared similarly to comparative balance sheets. Amounts for two periods are placed side by side, with additional columns for dollar and percent changes.

Apple reports substantial sales growth of 27.9% in 2015. This finding helps support management's 25.3% growth in assets as reflected in comparative balance sheets. The 24.8% growth in cost of sales is less that its 27.9% sales increase, which suggests good control over its main costs. Additionally, the 24.2% increase in operating expenses is less than the 27.9% sales growth, which again is good news. Much of the 24.2% increase in operating expenses is driven by greater research and development costs, from which management/investors hope to reap future income. Apple currently reports an increase of 35.1% in income, which is mainly driven by its $23,089 million growth in gross margin.

EXHIBIT 13.2

Comparative Income
Statements

APPLE

	APPLE INC. Comparative Income Statements For Years Ended September 26, 2015, and September 27, 2014			
$ millions, except per share	**2015**	**2014**	**Dollar Change**	**Percent Change**
Net sales	$233,715	$182,795	$50,920	27.9%
Cost of sales	140,089	112,258	27,831	24.8
Gross margin.	93,626	70,537	23,089	32.7
Research and development.	8,067	6,041	2,026	33.5
Selling, general and administrative.	14,329	11,993	2,336	19.5
Total operating expenses.	22,396	18,034	4,362	24.2
Operating income.	71,230	52,503	18,727	35.7
Other income, net.	1,285	980	305	31.1
Income before provision for income taxes	72,515	53,483	19,032	35.6
Provision for income taxes.	19,121	13,973	5,148	36.8
Net income	$ 53,394	$ 39,510	13,884	35.1
Basic earnings per share	$ 9.28	$ 6.49	$ 2.79	43.0
Diluted earnings per share.	$ 9.22	$ 6.45	$ 2.77	42.9

Point: Percent change can also be computed by dividing the current period by the prior period and subtracting 1.0. For example, the 27.9% sales increase in Exhibit 13.2 is computed as: ($233,715/$182,795) − 1.

Trend Analysis

Point: *Index* refers to the comparison of the analysis period to the base period. Percents determined for each period are called *index numbers*.

Trend analysis, also called *trend percent analysis* or *index number trend analysis,* is a form of horizontal analysis that can reveal patterns in data across successive periods. It involves computing trend percents for a series of financial numbers and is a variation on the use of percent changes. The difference is that trend analysis does not subtract the base period amount in the numerator. To compute trend percents, we do the following:

1. Select a *base period* and assign each item in the base period a weight of 100%.
2. Express financial numbers as a percent of their base period number.

Specifically, a *trend percent,* also called an *index number,* is computed as follows:

$$\text{Trend percent (\%)} = \frac{\text{Analysis period amount}}{\text{Base period amount}} \times 100$$

To illustrate trend analysis, we use the Apple data shown in Exhibit 13.3. These data are from Apple's current and prior financial statements.

EXHIBIT 13.3

Sales and Expenses

$ millions	**2015**	**2014**	**2013**	**2012**	**2011**
Net sales.	$233,715	$182,795	$170,910	$156,508	$108,249
Cost of sales.	140,089	112,258	106,606	87,846	64,431
Operating expenses.	22,396	18,034	15,305	13,421	10,028

The trend percents—using the data from Exhibit 13.3—are shown in Exhibit 13.4. The base period is 2011, and the trend percent is computed in each subsequent year by dividing that year's amount by its 2011 amount. For instance, the revenue trend percent for 2015 is 215.9%, computed as $233,715/$108,249.

Point: Trend analysis expresses a percent of base, not a percent of change.

EXHIBIT 13.4

Trend Percents for Sales and Expenses

In trend percent	**2015**	**2014**	**2013**	**2012**	**2011**
Net sales.	215.9%	168.9%	157.9%	144.6%	100.0%
Cost of sales.	217.4	174.2	165.5	136.3	100.0
Operating expenses.	223.3	179.8	152.6	133.8	100.0

Graphical depictions often aid analysis of trend percents. Exhibit 13.5 shows the trend percents from Exhibit 13.4 in a *line graph,* which helps us identify trends and detect changes in direction or magnitude. It reveals that the trend line for net sales has been exceeded by both cost of sales and operating expenses in 2014 and 2015. In years prior to 2013,

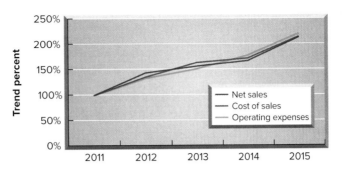

EXHIBIT 13.5

Trend Percent Lines for Sales and Expenses of Apple

the net sales trend line exceeded both cost of sales and operating expenses. The marked increase for cost of sales in 2013 is concerning, with a reduction in the difference in trend lines for 2014 and 2015. Long-run profitability will suffer if those costs are not controlled. By 2015, the difference in trend lines is reduced and net sales is nearly on par with cost of sales.

Exhibit 13.6 compares Apple's revenue trend line to those of **Google** and **Samsung**. Apple and Google were both able to grow revenue in each year relative to the base year. In this respect, Apple and Google have outperformed their competitor Samsung. We can say from these data that Apple and Google products and services have been met with consumer acceptance.

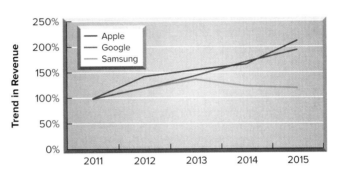

EXHIBIT 13.6

Revenue Trend Percent Lines—Apple, Google, and Samsung

APPLE
GOOGLE
Samsung

Trend analysis of financial statement items can include comparisons of relations between items on different financial statements. For instance, Exhibit 13.7 compares Apple's revenue and total assets. The increase in total assets (149.6%) exceeds the increase in net sales (115.9%) since 2011. Is this result favorable or not? One interpretation is that Apple was *less* efficient in using its assets in 2015 versus 2011. This means that management has not generated net sales sufficient to compensate for the asset growth.

EXHIBIT 13.7

Sales and Asset Data for Apple

$ millions	2015	2011	Change (2015 vs. 2011)
Net sales...............	$233,715	$108,249	115.9%
Total assets............	290,479	116,371	149.6%

■ **Decision** Maker

Auditor Your tests reveal a 3% increase in sales from $200,000 to $206,000 and a 4% decrease in expenses from $190,000 to $182,400. Both changes are within your "reasonableness" criterion of ±5%, and thus you don't pursue additional tests. The audit partner in charge questions your lack of follow-up and mentions the *joint relation* between sales and expenses. To what is the partner referring? ■ *Answer:* Both *individual* accounts (sales and expenses) yield percent changes within the ±5% acceptable range. However, a *joint analysis* reveals an increase in sales and a decrease in expenses producing a more than 5% increase in income. This client's profit margin is 11.46% ([$206,000 − $182,400]/$206,000) for the current year compared with 5.0% ([$200,000 − $190,000]/$200,000) for the prior year—a 129% increase! This is what concerns the partner, and it suggests expanding audit tests of the client's numbers.

Compute trend percents for the following accounts, using 2014 as the base year (round percents to whole numbers). State whether the situation as revealed by the trends appears to be favorable or unfavorable for each account.

NEED-TO-KNOW 13-1

Horizontal Analysis

P1

$ millions	2017	2016	2015	2014
Sales.....................	$500	$350	$250	$200
Cost of goods sold..........	400	175	100	50

Solution

$ millions	2017	2016	2015	2014
Sales	250%	175%	125%	100%
	($500/$200)	($350/$200)	($250/$200)	($200/$200)
Cost of goods sold	800%	350%	200%	100%
	($400/$50)	($175/$50)	($100/$50)	($50/$50)

Analysis: The trend in sales is favorable; however, we need more information about economic conditions such as inflation rates and competitors' performances to better assess it. Cost of sales is also rising (as expected with increasing sales); however, cost of sales is rising faster than the increase in sales, which is unfavorable and bad news. A quick analysis of the gross margin percentage would highlight this concern.

Do More: QS 13-3, QS 13-4, E 13-3

VERTICAL ANALYSIS

P2

Describe and apply methods of vertical analysis.

Vertical analysis is a tool to evaluate individual financial statement items or a group of items in terms of a specific base amount. We usually define a key aggregate figure as the base, which for an income statement is usually revenue and for a balance sheet is usually total assets. This section explains vertical analysis and applies it to **Apple**. (The term *vertical analysis* comes from the up-down [or down-up] movement of our eyes as we review common-size financial statements. Vertical analysis is also called *common-size analysis*.)

Common-Size Statements

Income Statement	
Sales	10,000
Expenses	6,000
Income	4,000

The comparative statements in Exhibits 13.1 and 13.2 show the change in each item over time, but they do not show the relative importance of each item. We use **common-size financial statements** to show changes in the relative importance of each financial statement item. All individual amounts in common-size statements are redefined in terms of common-size percents. A *common-size percent* is measured by dividing each individual financial statement amount under analysis by its base amount:

$$\text{Common-size percent (\%)} = \frac{\text{Analysis amount}}{\text{Base amount}} \times 100$$

Point: The *base* amount in common-size analysis is an *aggregate* amount from that period's financial statement.

Point: Common-size statements often are used to compare two or more companies in the same industry.

Point: Common-size statements are also useful in comparing firms that report in different currencies.

Common-Size Balance Sheets   Common-size statements show each item as a percent of a *base amount,* which for a common-size balance sheet is usually total assets. The base amount is assigned a value of 100%. (This implies that the total amount of liabilities plus equity equals 100% since this amount equals total assets.) We then compute a common-size percent for each asset, liability, and equity item using total assets as the base amount. When we present a company's successive balance sheets in this way, changes in the mixture of assets, liabilities, and equity are highlighted.

Exhibit 13.8 shows common-size comparative balance sheets for Apple. Two results that stand out on both a magnitude and percentage basis include (1) issuance of long-term debt—a 5.9% increase from 12.5% to 18.4%, the largest of any liability, and (2) a 5.8% decrease from 37.6% to 31.8% in retained earnings—likely the result of dividends and share repurchases. The absence of other substantial changes in Apple's balance sheet suggests a mature company, but with some lack of focus as evidenced by the large and increasing amounts for short-term and especially long-term securities. This buildup in securities is a concern as the return on securities is historically smaller than the return on operating assets. Time will tell whether Apple can continue to generate sufficient revenue and income from its expanding asset base.

Common-Size Income Statements   Analysis also involves the use of a common-size income statement. Revenue is usually the base amount, which is assigned a value of 100%. Each common-size income statement item is shown as a percent of revenue. If we think of the 100%

EXHIBIT 13.8

Common-Size Comparative
Balance Sheets

APPLE

APPLE INC.
Common-Size Comparative Balance Sheets
September 26, 2015, and September 27, 2014

$ millions	2015	2014	Common-Size Percents* 2015	Common-Size Percents* 2014
Assets				
Cash and cash equivalents	$ 21,120	$ 13,844	7.3%	6.0%
Short-term marketable securities	20,481	11,233	7.1	4.8
Accounts receivable, net.	16,849	17,460	5.8	7.5
Inventories	2,349	2,111	0.8	0.9
Deferred tax assets	5,546	4,318	1.9	1.9
Vendor non-trade receivables.	13,494	9,759	4.6	4.2
Other current assets	9,539	9,806	3.3	4.2
Total current assets	89,378	68,531	30.8	29.6
Long-term marketable securities	164,065	130,162	56.5	56.1
Property, plant and equipment, net	22,471	20,624	7.7	8.9
Goodwill	5,116	4,616	1.8	2.0
Acquired intangible assets, net.	3,893	4,142	1.3	1.8
Other assets	5,556	3,764	1.9	1.6
Total assets.	$290,479	$231,839	100.0%	100.0%
Liabilities				
Accounts payable.	$ 35,490	$ 30,196	12.2%	13.0%
Accrued expenses	25,181	18,453	8.7	8.0
Deferred revenue.	8,940	8,491	3.1	3.7
Commercial paper	8,499	6,308	2.9	2.7
Current portion of long-term debt.	2,500	0	0.9	0.0
Total current liabilities.	80,610	63,448	27.8	27.4
Deferred revenue—noncurrent.	3,624	3,031	1.2	1.3
Long-term debt.	53,463	28,987	18.4	12.5
Other noncurrent liabilities	33,427	24,826	11.5	10.7
Total liabilities.	171,124	120,292	58.9	51.9
Stockholders' Equity				
Common stock	27,416	23,313	9.4	10.1
Retained earnings	92,284	87,152	31.8	37.6
Accumulated other comprehensive income.	(345)	1,082	(0.1)	0.5
Total stockholders' equity	119,355	111,547	41.1	48.1
Total liabilities and stockholders' equity.	$290,479	$231,839	100.0%	100.0%

* Percents are rounded to tenths and thus may not exactly sum to totals and subtotals.

revenue amount as representing one sales dollar, the remaining items show how each revenue dollar is distributed among costs, expenses, and income.

Exhibit 13.9 shows common-size comparative income statements for each dollar of Apple's net sales. The past two years' common-size numbers are similar with two exceptions. One is the decrease of 1.5 cents in the cost of sales, which is a positive development. Another is the decrease of 0.3 cent in total operating expenses. This was achieved in spite of an increase of 0.2 cent in research and development costs (an operating expense). In sum, analysis of common-size percents for successive income statements uncovered key changes in cost management.

Common-Size Graphics

Two tools of common-size analysis are trend analysis of common-size statements and graphical analysis. The trend analysis of common-size statements is similar to that of comparative

EXHIBIT 13.9

Common-Size Comparative
Income Statements

APPLE

APPLE INC. Common-Size Comparative Income Statements For Years Ended September 26, 2015, and September 27, 2014				
			Common-Size Percents*	
$ millions	2015	2014	2015	2014
Net sales	$233,715	$182,795	100.0%	100.0%
Cost of sales	140,089	112,258	59.9	61.4
Gross margin	93,626	70,537	40.1	38.6
Research and development	8,067	6,041	3.5	3.3
Selling, general and administrative	14,329	11,993	6.1	6.6
Total operating expenses	22,396	18,034	9.6	9.9
Operating income	71,230	52,503	30.5	28.7
Other income, net	1,285	980	0.5	0.5
Income before provision for income taxes	72,515	53,483	31.0	29.3
Provision for income taxes	19,121	13,973	8.2	7.6
Net income	$ 53,394	$ 39,510	22.8%	21.6%

* Percents are rounded to tenths and thus may not exactly sum to totals and subtotals.

EXHIBIT 13.10

Common-Size Graphic of
Income Statement

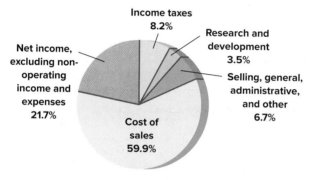

statements discussed under vertical analysis. It is not illustrated here because the only difference is the substitution of common-size percents for trend percents. Instead, this section discusses graphical analysis of common-size statements.

Exhibit 13.10 shows Apple's 2015 common-size income statement in graphical form. This pie chart highlights the contribution of each cost component of net sales for net income (for this graph, "other income, net" is included in selling, general, and administrative costs).

Exhibit 13.11 previews more complex graphical analyses and the insights provided. The data for this exhibit are taken from Apple's *Segments* footnote. Apple reports five operating segments for 2015: (1) Americas, (2) Europe, (3) China, (4) Japan, and (5) Asia Pacific.

EXHIBIT 13.11

Sales and Operating
Income Margin Breakdown
by Segment

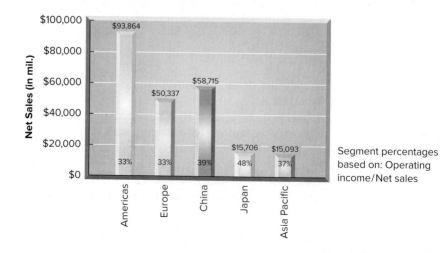

The bars in Exhibit 13.11 show the level of net sales for each of Apple's five operating segments. Its Americas segment generates $93,864 million net sales, which is roughly 40% of its

total sales. The four other bars show sales generated from each of the other international segments.
Within each bar is that segment's operating income
margin, defined as segment operating income divided by segment net sales. The Americas segment
has a 33% operating income margin. This type of
graphic can raise questions about the profitability
of each segment and discussion of further expan-
sions into more lucrative segments. For example,
the Japan segment has an operating margin of 48%.
A natural question for management is what potential is there to further expand sales into the Japan
segment and maintain a similar operating margin?
This type of analysis can help in determining strategic plans and actions.

   Graphical analysis is also used to identify
(1) sources of financing, including the distribution
among current liabilities, noncurrent liabilities, and
equity capital, and (2) focuses of investing activities, including the distribution among current and
noncurrent assets. To illustrate, Exhibit 13.12
shows a common-size graphical display of Apple's
assets. Common-size balance sheet analysis can be
extended to examine the composition of these subgroups. For instance, in assessing liquidity of
current assets, knowing what proportion of *current* assets consists of inventories is usually important, and not simply what proportion inventories are of *total* assets.

   Common-size financial statements are also useful in comparing companies. Exhibit 13.13
shows common-size graphics of Apple, Google, and Samsung on financing sources. This
graphic highlights the larger percent of equity financing for Google versus Apple and Samsung.
It also highlights the larger noncurrent (debt) financing of Apple versus Google and Samsung.
Comparison of a company's common-size statements with competitors' or industry common-
size statistics alerts us to differences in the structure or distribution of its financial statements
but not to their dollar magnitude.

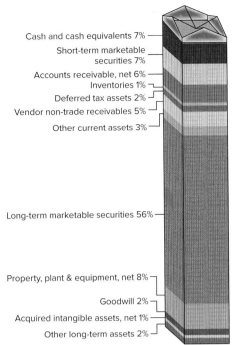

EXHIBIT 13.12

Common-Size Graphic of Asset Components

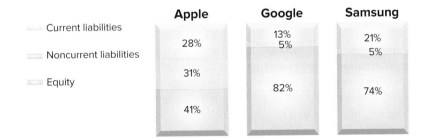

EXHIBIT 13.13

Common-Size Graphic of Financing Sources—Competitor Analysis

APPLE
GOOGLE
Samsung

Decision Insight

Seeing Truth In a survey of nearly 200
CFOs of large companies, roughly 20% say
that firms, based on their experience, use
accounting ploys to report earnings that do
not fully reflect the firms' underlying operations. One goal of financial analysis is to see
through such ploys. The top five reasons
CFOs gave for this behavior are shown here
(*Wall Street Journal,* October 2012). ▨

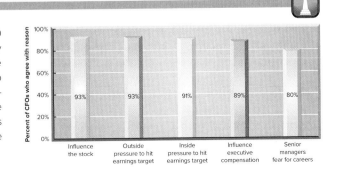

NEED-TO-KNOW 13-2

Vertical Analysis

P2

Express the following comparative income statements in common-size percents and assess whether or not this company's situation has improved in the most recent year (round percents to whole numbers).

Comparative Income Statements For Years Ended December 31, 2017 and 2016		
	2017	**2016**
Sales	$800	$500
Total expenses	560	400
Net income	$240	$100

Solution

	2017	**2016**
Sales	100%	100%
	($800/$800)	($500/$500)
Total expenses	70%	80%
	($560/$800)	($400/$500)
Net income	30%	20%

Do More: QS 13-5, E 13-4, E 13-6

Analysis: This company's situation has improved. This is evident from its substantial increase in net income as a percent of sales for 2017 (30%) relative to 2016 (20%). Further, the company's sales increased from $500 in 2016 to $800 in 2017 (while expenses declined as a percent of sales from 80% to 70%).

RATIO ANALYSIS

P3

Define and apply ratio analysis.

Ratios are widely used in financial analysis because they help us uncover conditions and trends difficult to detect by looking at individual amounts.

A ratio expresses a relation between two quantities. It can be expressed as a percent, rate, or proportion. For instance, a change in an account balance from $100 to $250 can be expressed as (1) 150% increase, (2) 2.5 times, or (3) 2.5 to 1 (or 2.5:1). To be meaningful, a ratio must refer to an economically important relation. For example, a ratio of cost of goods sold to sales is meaningful, but a ratio of freight costs to patents is not.

This section describes important financial ratios and their application. The ratios are organized into the four building blocks of financial statement analysis: (1) liquidity and efficiency, (2) solvency, (3) profitability, and (4) market prospects. The purpose here is to organize and apply them under a summary framework. We use four standards for comparison: intracompany, competitor, industry, and guidelines.

Liquidity and Efficiency

Liquidity refers to the availability of resources to meet short-term cash requirements. It is affected by the timing of cash inflows and outflows along with prospects for future performance.

Efficiency refers to how productive a company is in using its assets. Efficiency is usually measured relative to how much revenue is generated from assets. A lack of liquidity is often linked to lower profitability. To creditors, lack of liquidity can yield delays in collecting payments. Moreover, inefficient use of assets can cause liquidity problems. This section covers key ratios used to assess liquidity and efficiency.

Working Capital and Current Ratio   The amount of current assets minus current liabilities is called **working capital,** or *net working capital.* A company needs enough working capital to meet current debts, to carry sufficient inventories, and to take advantage of cash discounts. A company that runs low on working capital is less likely to meet current obligations or to continue operating. When evaluating a company's working capital, we must look at the dollar amount of current assets minus current liabilities *and* at their ratio. The *current ratio* is defined as follows.

$$\text{Current ratio} = \frac{\text{Current assets}}{\text{Current liabilities}}$$

Using information in Exhibit 13.1, **Apple**'s working capital and current ratio for both 2015 and 2014 are shown in Exhibit 13.14. Also, **Google** (4.67), **Samsung** (2.47), and the industry's current ratio (2.5) are shown in the margin. Apple's 2015 ratio (1.11) is lower than competitors' ratios, but it is not in danger of defaulting on loan payments. A high current ratio suggests a strong liquidity position and an ability to meet current obligations. An excessively high current ratio means that the company has invested too much in current assets compared to its current obligations. An excessive investment in current assets is not an efficient use of funds because current assets normally generate a low return on investment (compared with long-term assets).

EXHIBIT 13.14

Apple's Working Capital and Current Ratio

$ millions	2015	2014
Current assets..............	$89,378	$68,531
Current liabilities...........	80,610	63,448
Working capital............	$ 8,768	$ 5,083
Current ratio		
$89,378/$80,610 =	1.11 to 1	
$68,531/$63,448 =		1.08 to 1

Current ratio
Google = 4.67
Samsung = 2.47
Industry = 2.5

Many users apply a guideline of 2:1 (or 1.5:1) for the current ratio. A 2:1 or higher ratio is judged a good credit risk in the short run. Any analysis of the current ratio must recognize at least three additional factors: (1) type of business, (2) composition of current assets, and (3) turnover rate of current asset components.

Type of Business A service company that grants little or no credit and carries few inventories can probably operate on a current ratio of less than 1:1 if its revenues generate enough cash to pay its current liabilities. On the other hand, a company selling high-priced clothing or furniture requires a higher ratio because of difficulties in judging customer demand and cash receipts. For instance, if demand falls, inventory may not generate as much cash as expected. Accordingly, analysis of the current ratio should include a comparison with competitors.

Composition of Current Assets The composition of a company's current assets is important to an evaluation of short-term liquidity. For instance, cash, cash equivalents, and short-term investments are more liquid than accounts and notes receivable. An excessive amount of receivables and inventory weakens a company's ability to pay current liabilities. The acid-test ratio (covered next) can help with this assessment.

Global: Ratio analysis helps overcome currency translation problems, but it does *not* overcome differences in accounting principles.

Turnover Rate of Assets Asset turnover measures a company's efficiency in using its assets. One relevant measure of asset efficiency is the revenue generated. A measure of total asset turnover is revenues divided by total assets, but evaluation of turnover for individual assets is also useful. We discuss both receivables turnover and inventory turnover next.

■ Decision Maker

Banker A company requests a one-year, $200,000 loan for expansion. This company's current ratio is 4:1, with current assets of $160,000. Key competitors carry a current ratio of about 1.9:1. Using this information, do you approve the loan? Does your decision change if the application is for a 10-year loan? ■ *Answer:* The loan application is likely approved for at least two reasons. First, the current ratio suggests an ability to meet short-term obligations. Second, current assets of $160,000 and a current ratio of 4:1 imply current liabilities of $40,000 (one-fourth of current assets) and a working capital excess of $120,000. The working capital excess is 60% of the loan. Finally, if the application is for a 10-year loan, a decision is less clear as the high current ratio and working capital suggest some inefficiency—for example, a 4:1 current ratio is more than double that of its peers.

Acid-Test Ratio

Quick assets are cash, short-term investments, and current receivables. These are the most liquid types of current assets. The *acid-test ratio,* also called *quick ratio,* reflects a company's short-term liquidity.

$$\text{Acid-test ratio} = \frac{\text{Cash + Short-term investments + Current receivables}}{\text{Current liabilities}}$$

Apple's acid-test ratio is computed in Exhibit 13.15. Apple's 2015 acid-test ratio (0.73) is lower than those for Google (4.41) and Samsung (1.98), as well as lower than the 1:1 common guideline for an acceptable acid-test ratio. The ratio for Apple is also less than the 0.9 industry norm; thus, it raises some concern. As with analysis of the current ratio, we need to consider other factors. For instance, the frequency with which a company converts its current assets into cash affects its working capital requirements. This implies that analysis of short-term liquidity should also include an analysis of receivables and inventories, which we consider next.

EXHIBIT 13.15

Acid-Test Ratio

Acid-test ratio
Google = 4.41
Samsung = 1.98
Industry = 0.9

$ millions	2015	2014
Cash and equivalents	$21,120	$13,844
Short-term securities	20,481	11,233
Current receivables	16,849	17,460
Total quick assets	$58,450	$42,537
Current liabilities	$80,610	$63,448
Acid-test ratio		
$58,450/$80,610	0.73 to 1	
$42,537/$63,448		0.67 to 1

Accounts Receivable Turnover

We can measure how frequently a company converts its receivables into cash by computing the *accounts receivable turnover.* This ratio is defined as follows.

$$\text{Accounts receivable turnover} = \frac{\text{Net sales}}{\text{Average accounts receivable, net}}$$

Point: Some users prefer using gross accounts receivable (before subtracting the allowance for doubtful accounts) to avoid the influence of a manager's bad debts estimate.

Accounts receivable turnover
Google = 7.2
Samsung = 7.1
Industry = 5.0

Short-term receivables from customers are often included in the denominator along with accounts receivable. Also, accounts receivable turnover is more precise if credit sales are used for the numerator, but external users generally use net sales (or net revenues) because information about credit sales is typically not reported. Apple's 2015 accounts receivable turnover is computed as follows ($ millions).

$$\frac{\$233,715}{(\$17,460 + \$16,849)/2} = 13.6 \text{ times}$$

Apple's turnover of 13.6 exceeds Google's 7.2 and Samsung's 7.1 turnover. Accounts receivable turnover is high when accounts receivable are quickly collected. A high turnover is favorable because it means the company need not commit large amounts of funds to accounts receivable. However, an accounts receivable turnover can be too high; this can occur when credit terms are so restrictive that they decrease sales.

Inventory Turnover

How long a company holds inventory before selling it will affect working capital. One measure of this effect is *inventory turnover,* also called *merchandise turnover* or *merchandise inventory turnover,* which is defined as follows.

$$\text{Inventory turnover} = \frac{\text{Cost of goods sold}}{\text{Average inventory}}$$

Using Apple's cost of goods sold and inventories information, we compute its inventory turnover for 2015 as follows.

$$\frac{\$140,089}{(\$2,111 + \$2,349)/2} = 62.82 \text{ times}$$

Apple's inventory turnover of 62.82 is higher than Samsung's 6.84 and the industry's 7.0. A company with a high turnover requires a smaller investment in inventory than one producing the same sales with a lower turnover. Inventory turnover can be too high, however, if inventory is so small and sales decrease due to stock-outs.

Days' Sales Uncollected   Accounts receivable turnover expresses how frequently a company collects its accounts. Days' sales uncollected is one measure of this activity, which is defined as follows.

$$\text{Days' sales uncollected} = \frac{\text{Accounts receivable, net}}{\text{Net sales}} \times 365$$

ChinaFotoPress/ChinaFotoPress via Getty Images

Any short-term notes receivable from customers are normally included in the numerator. Apple's 2015 days' sales uncollected follows.

$$\frac{\$16,849}{\$233,715} \times 365 = 26.3 \text{ days}$$

Both Google's days' sales uncollected of 56.2 days and Samsung's 51.9 days are more than the 26.3 days for Apple. Days' sales uncollected is more meaningful if we know company credit terms. A rough guideline states that days' sales uncollected should not exceed 1⅓ times the days in its (1) credit period, *if* discounts are not offered, or (2) discount period, *if* favorable discounts are offered.

Days' Sales in Inventory   *Days' sales in inventory* is a useful measure in evaluating inventory liquidity. We compute days' sales in inventory as follows.

$$\text{Days' sales in inventory} = \frac{\text{Ending inventory}}{\text{Cost of goods sold}} \times 365$$

Apple's days' sales in inventory for 2015 follows.

$$\frac{\$2,349}{\$140,089} \times 365 = 6.1 \text{ days}$$

If the products in Apple's inventory are in demand by customers, this formula estimates that its inventory will be converted into receivables (or cash) in 6.1 days. If all of Apple's sales were credit sales, the conversion of inventory to receivables in 6.1 days *plus* the conversion of receivables to cash in 26.3 days implies that inventory will be converted to cash in about 32.4 days (6.1 + 26.3).

Total Asset Turnover   *Total asset turnover* reflects a company's ability to use its assets to generate sales and is an important measure of operating efficiency. The definition of this ratio follows.

$$\text{Total asset turnover} = \frac{\text{Net sales}}{\text{Average total assets}}$$

Apple's total asset turnover of 0.89 for 2015 follows, which is greater than that for Google (0.54) and Samsung (0.85).

$$\frac{\$233,715}{(\$290,479 + \$231,839)/2} = 0.89 \text{ times}$$

Solvency

Solvency refers to a company's long-run financial viability and its ability to meet long-term obligations. Analysis of solvency is long term and uses broader measures than liquidity. An important component of solvency analysis is a company's capital structure. *Capital structure* refers to a company's makeup of equity and debt financing. Our analysis here focuses on a company's ability to both meet its obligations and provide security to its creditors *over the long run*.

Debt and Equity Ratios   One part of solvency analysis is to assess the portion of a company's assets contributed by its owners and the portion contributed by creditors. This relation is reflected in the debt ratio (also described in Appendix C). The *debt ratio* expresses total liabilities as a percent of total assets. The **equity ratio** expresses total equity as a percent of total assets. **Apple**'s debt and equity ratios follow.

$ millions	2015	Ratios	
Total liabilities....................	$171,124	58.9%	[Debt ratio]
Total equity.....................	119,355	41.1	[Equity ratio]
Total liabilities and equity............	$290,479	100.0%	

Apple's financial statements reveal slightly more debt than equity. A company is considered less risky if its capital structure (equity plus long-term debt) contains more equity. One risk factor is the required payment for interest and principal when debt is outstanding. Stockholders cannot require payment from the company. From the stockholders' point of view, if a company earns a return on borrowed capital that is higher than the cost of borrowing, the difference represents increased income to stockholders. The inclusion of debt is described as *financial leverage* because debt can have the effect of increasing the return to stockholders.

Debt-to-Equity Ratio   The ratio of total liabilities to equity is another measure of solvency. We compute the ratio as follows.

$$\text{Debt-to-equity ratio} = \frac{\textbf{Total liabilities}}{\textbf{Total equity}}$$

Apple's debt-to-equity ratio for 2015 is

$$\$171,124/\$119,355 = 1.43$$

Apple's 1.43 debt-to-equity ratio is higher than those of Samsung (0.35) and Google (0.23), and greater than the industry ratio of 0.6. Consistent with our inferences from the debt ratio, Apple's capital structure has more debt than equity. Recall that debt must be repaid with interest, while equity does not. Debt requirements can be burdensome when the industry and/or the economy experience a downturn. A larger debt-to-equity ratio also implies less opportunity to expand through use of additional debt financing.

Times Interest Earned

The amount of income before deductions for interest expense and income taxes is the amount available to pay interest expense. The following *times interest earned* ratio reflects the creditors' risk of loan repayments with interest.

Point: The times interest earned ratio and the debt and equity ratios are of special interest to bank lending officers.

$$\text{Times interest earned} = \frac{\text{Income before interest expense and income taxes}}{\text{Interest expense}}$$

The larger this ratio, the less risky is the company for creditors. One guideline says that creditors are reasonably safe if the company earns its fixed interest expense two or more times each year. Apple's times interest earned ratio follows. Apple's 99.9 result suggests that its creditors have little risk of nonrepayment.

$$\frac{\$53,394 + \$733 + \$19,121}{\$733} = 99.9 \text{ times}$$

Times interest earned
Google = 190.0
Samsung = 34.4

Decision Insight

Bears and Bulls A *bear market* is a declining market. The phrase comes from bear-skin jobbers who often sold the skins before the bears were caught. The term *bear* was then used to describe investors who sold shares they did not own in anticipation of a price decline. A *bull market* is a rising market. This phrase comes from the once popular sport of bear and bull baiting. The term *bull* came to mean the opposite of *bear*. ■

Profitability

Profitability refers to a company's ability to earn an adequate return on invested capital. Return is judged by assessing earnings relative to the level and sources of financing. This section covers key profitability measures.

Profit Margin

A company's operating efficiency and profitability can be expressed by two measures. The first is *profit margin,* which reflects a company's ability to earn net income from sales. It is measured by expressing net income as a percent of sales (*sales* and *revenues* are similar terms). Apple's profit margin follows.

$$\text{Profit margin} = \frac{\text{Net income}}{\text{Net sales}} = \frac{\$53,394}{\$233,715} = 22.8\%$$

Profit margin
Google = 21.8%
Samsung = 9.5%
Industry = 11%

To evaluate profit margin, we must consider the industry. For instance, an appliance company might require a profit margin between 10% and 15%, whereas a retail supermarket might require a profit margin of 1% or 2%. Apple's 22.8% profit margin is better than Google's 21.8%, Samsung's 9.5%, and the industry's 11% margin.

Return on Total Assets

Return on total assets is defined as follows.

$$\text{Return on total assets} = \frac{\text{Net income}}{\text{Average total assets}}$$

Apple's 2015 return on total assets is

$$\frac{\$53,394}{(\$290,479 + \$231,839)/2} = 20.4\%$$

Return on total assets
Google = 11.8%
Samsung = 8.1%
Industry = 9%

Apple's 20.4% return on total assets is higher than that for many businesses and is higher than Google's 11.8%, Samsung's 8.1%, and the industry's 9% returns. We also should evaluate any trend in the rate of return.

The following equation shows the important relation between profit margin, total asset turnover, and return on total assets.

$$\textbf{Profit margin} \times \textbf{Total asset turnover} = \textbf{Return on total assets}$$

or

$$\frac{\textbf{Net income}}{\textbf{Net sales}} \times \frac{\textbf{Net sales}}{\textbf{Average total assets}} = \frac{\textbf{Net income}}{\textbf{Average total assets}}$$

Both profit margin and total asset turnover contribute to overall operating efficiency, as measured by return on total assets. If we apply this formula to Apple, we get

Google: 21.8% × 0.54 ≈ 11.8%
Samsung: 9.5% × 0.85 ≈ 8.1%
(with rounding)

$$22.8\% \times 0.89 = 20.3\% \text{ (with rounding)}$$

This analysis shows that Apple's superior return on assets versus that of both Google and Samsung is driven by its higher profit margin and better asset turnover.

Return on Common Stockholders' Equity   The most important goal in operating a company is to earn income for its owner(s). *Return on common stockholders' equity* measures a company's success in reaching this goal and is defined as follows.

$$\textbf{Return on common stockholders' equity} = \frac{\textbf{Net income} - \textbf{Preferred dividends}}{\textbf{Average common stockholders' equity}}$$

Apple's 2015 return on common stockholders' equity is computed as follows.

Return on common equity
Google = 14.6%
Samsung = 10.8%
Industry = 15%

$$\frac{\$53,394 - \$0}{(\$111,547 + \$119,355)/2} = 46.2\%$$

The denominator in this computation is the book value of common equity (noncontrolling interest is often included in common equity for this ratio). To compute common stockholders' equity, the dividends on cumulative preferred stock are subtracted whether they are declared or are in arrears. If preferred stock is noncumulative, its dividends are subtracted only if declared. Apple's 46.2% return on common stockholders' equity is superior to Google's 14.6% and Samsung's 10.8%.

 **Decision** Insight

Wall Street   *Wall Street* is synonymous with financial markets, but its name comes from the street location of the original New York Stock Exchange. The street's name derives from stockades built by early settlers to protect New York from pirate attacks. ■

Market Prospects

Market measures are useful for analyzing corporations with publicly traded stock. These market measures use stock price, which reflects the market's (public's) expectations for the company. This includes market expectations of both company return and risk.

Price-Earnings Ratio   Computation of the *price-earnings ratio* follows.

$$\text{Price-earnings ratio} = \frac{\text{Market price per common share}}{\text{Earnings per share}}$$

Predicted earnings per share for the next period is often used in the denominator of this computation. Reported earnings per share for the most recent period is also commonly used. In both cases, the ratio is used as an indicator of market's expectations for future growth and risk of a company's earnings.

   The market price of Apple's common stock at the start of fiscal year 2016 was $116.44. Using Apple's $9.28 basic earnings per share, we compute its price-earnings ratio as follows.

$$\frac{\$116.44}{\$9.28} = 12.5$$

Point: High expected risk suggests a lower PE ratio. High expected growth suggests a higher PE ratio.

PE (year-end)
Google = 33.7
Samsung = 10.0
Industry = 11

Apple's price-earnings ratio is less than that for Google, but it is higher than that for Samsung and near the industry norm for this period.

Point: Some investors avoid stocks with high PE ratios, believing they are "overpriced."

Dividend Yield   *Dividend yield* is used to compare the dividend-paying performance of different companies. We compute dividend yield as follows.

$$\text{Dividend yield} = \frac{\text{Annual cash dividends per share}}{\text{Market price per share}}$$

Apple's dividend yield, based on its fiscal year-end market price per share of $116.44 and its $1.98 cash dividends per share, is computed as follows.

$$\frac{\$1.98}{\$116.44} = 1.7\%$$

Dividend yield
Google = 0.0%
Samsung = 1.6%

Some companies, such as Google, do not pay dividends because they reinvest the cash to grow their businesses in the hope of generating greater future earnings and dividends.

Summary of Ratios

Exhibit 13.16 summarizes the ratios illustrated in this chapter.

Decision Insight

Ticker Prices   *Ticker prices* refer to a band of moving data on a monitor carrying up-to-the-minute stock prices. The phrase comes from *ticker tape,* a 1-inch-wide strip of paper spewing stock prices from a printer that ticked as it ran. Most of today's investors have never seen actual ticker tape, but the phrase survives. ▦

© Comstock Images/Jupiter Images

EXHIBIT 13.16

Financial Statement Analysis Ratios*

Ratio	Formula	Measure of
Liquidity and Efficiency		
Current ratio	$= \dfrac{\text{Current assets}}{\text{Current liabilities}}$	Short-term debt-paying ability
Acid-test ratio	$= \dfrac{\text{Cash + Short-term investments + Current receivables}}{\text{Current liabilities}}$	Immediate short-term debt-paying ability
Accounts receivable turnover	$= \dfrac{\text{Net sales}}{\text{Average accounts receivable, net}}$	Efficiency of collection
Inventory turnover	$= \dfrac{\text{Cost of goods sold}}{\text{Average inventory}}$	Efficiency of inventory management
Days' sales uncollected	$= \dfrac{\text{Accounts receivable, net}}{\text{Net sales}} \times 365$	Liquidity of receivables
Days' sales in inventory	$= \dfrac{\text{Ending inventory}}{\text{Cost of goods sold}} \times 365$	Liquidity of inventory
Total asset turnover	$= \dfrac{\text{Net sales}}{\text{Average total assets}}$	Efficiency of assets in producing sales
Solvency		
Debt ratio	$= \dfrac{\text{Total liabilities}}{\text{Total assets}}$	Creditor financing and leverage
Equity ratio	$= \dfrac{\text{Total equity}}{\text{Total assets}}$	Owner financing
Debt-to-equity ratio	$= \dfrac{\text{Total liabilities}}{\text{Total equity}}$	Debt versus equity financing
Times interest earned	$= \dfrac{\text{Income before interest expense and income taxes}}{\text{Interest expense}}$	Protection in meeting interest payments
Profitability		
Profit margin ratio	$= \dfrac{\text{Net income}}{\text{Net sales}}$	Net income in each sales dollar
Gross margin ratio	$= \dfrac{\text{Net sales} - \text{Cost of goods sold}}{\text{Net sales}}$	Gross margin in each sales dollar
Return on total assets	$= \dfrac{\text{Net income}}{\text{Average total assets}}$	Overall profitability of assets
Return on common stockholders' equity	$= \dfrac{\text{Net income} - \text{Preferred dividends}}{\text{Average common stockholders' equity}}$	Profitability of owner investment
Book value per common share	$= \dfrac{\text{Shareholders' equity applicable to common shares}}{\text{Number of common shares outstanding}}$	Liquidation at reported amounts
Basic earnings per share	$= \dfrac{\text{Net income} - \text{Preferred dividends}}{\text{Weighted-average common shares outstanding}}$	Net income per common share
Market Prospects		
Price-earnings ratio	$= \dfrac{\text{Market price per common share}}{\text{Earnings per share}}$	Market value relative to earnings
Dividend yield	$= \dfrac{\text{Annual cash dividends per share}}{\text{Market price per share}}$	Cash return per common share

* Additional ratios examined in previous chapters included credit risk ratio; plant asset useful life; plant asset age; days' cash expense coverage; cash coverage of growth; cash coverage of debt; free cash flow; cash flow on total assets; and payout ratio.

For each ratio listed, identify whether the change in ratio value from 2016 to 2017 is regarded as favorable or unfavorable.

NEED-TO-KNOW 13-3

Ratio Analysis

P3

Ratio	2017	2016
1. Profit margin	6%	8%
2. Debt ratio	50%	70%
3. Gross margin	40%	36%
4. Accounts receivable turnover	8.8	9.4
5. Basic earnings per share	$2.10	$2.00
6. Inventory turnover	3.6	4.0

Solution

Ratio	2017	2016	Change
1. Profit margin ratio	6%	8%	Unfavorable
2. Debt ratio	50%	70%	Favorable
3. Gross margin ratio	40%	36%	Favorable
4. Accounts receivable turnover	8.8	9.4	Unfavorable
5. Basic earnings per share	$2.10	$2.00	Favorable
6. Inventory turnover	3.6	4.0	Unfavorable

Do More: QS 13-6, E 13-7, E 13-8, E 13-9, E 13-10, E 13-11, P 13-4

SUSTAINABILITY AND ACCOUNTING

Morgan Stanley's sustainability initiative is focused on reducing its environmental impact and investing in sustainable projects. Carla Harris, of Morgan Stanley, explains that reducing the company's carbon footprint is a priority. She points out that Morgan Stanley has set a goal of cutting the greenhouse gas intensity of its building operations by 15%.

Morgan Stanley's sustainability report says the company has earned several awards for its work on sustainability. This includes being one of three finalists for Sustainable Global Bank of the Year, S&P 500 Carbon Performance Leadership, and Global 500 Carbon Performance Leadership.

Morgan Stanley is also a leader in sustainable investments. It launched the *Morgan Stanley Institute for Sustainable Investing*. Morgan Stanley's Sustainability Report outlines three core initiatives for the Institute:

- Setting a $10 billion goal for client assets in the Investing with Impact Platform, to consist of investments that deliver positive environmental or social impact.

- Investing $1 billion in a sustainable communities initiative to provide rapid access to capital for low- and moderate-income households.

- Establishing a Sustainable Investing Fellowship with Columbia Business School to develop a cadre of emerging leaders in sustainable finance.

Carla proudly believes that Morgan Stanley safeguards scarce resources and invests wisely for the future.

© Andrew Harrer/Bloomberg via Getty Images

Decision Insight

All Else Being Equal   Financial regulation has several goals. Two of them are to ensure adequate accounting disclosure and to strengthen corporate governance. For disclosure purposes, companies must now provide details of related-party transactions and material off-balance-sheet agreements. This is motivated by several major frauds. For corporate governance, the CEO and CFO must now certify the fairness of financial statements and the effectiveness of internal controls. Yet, concerns remain. A study reports that 30% of management and administrative employees observed activities that posed a conflict of interest in the past year (KPMG 2013). Another 24% witnessed the falsifying or manipulating of accounting information. The bottom line: All financial statements are *not* of equal quality. ■

 Decision Analysis   **Analysis Reporting**

A1
Summarize and report
results of analysis.

Understanding the purpose of financial statement analysis is crucial to the usefulness of any analysis. This understanding leads to efficiency of effort, effectiveness in application, and relevance in focus. The purpose of most financial statement analyses is to reduce uncertainty in business decisions through a rigorous and sound evaluation. A *financial statement analysis report* helps by directly addressing the building blocks of analysis and by identifying weaknesses in inference by requiring explanation: It forces us to organize our reasoning and to verify its flow and logic. A report also serves as a communication link with readers, and the writing process reinforces our judgments and vice versa. Finally, the report helps us (re)evaluate evidence and refine conclusions on key building blocks. A good analysis report usually consists of six sections:

1. **Executive summary**—brief focus on important analysis results and conclusions.
2. **Analysis overview**—background on the company, its industry, and its economic setting.
3. **Evidential matter**—financial statements and information used in the analysis, including ratios, trends, comparisons, statistics, and all analytical measures assembled; often organized under the building blocks of analysis.
4. **Assumptions**—identification of important assumptions regarding a company's industry and economic environment, and other important assumptions for estimates.
5. **Key factors**—list of important favorable and unfavorable factors, both quantitative and qualitative, for company performance; usually organized by areas of analysis.
6. **Inferences**—forecasts, estimates, interpretations, and conclusions drawing on all sections of the report.

Point: WikiLeaks includes thousands of analysis reports and valuation reports on its website.

We must remember that the user dictates relevance, meaning that the analysis report should include a brief table of contents to help readers focus on those areas most relevant to their decisions. All irrelevant matter must be eliminated. For example, decades-old details of obscure transactions and detailed miscues of the analysis are irrelevant. Ambiguities and qualifications to avoid responsibility or hedging inferences must be eliminated. Finally, writing is important. Mistakes in grammar and errors of fact compromise the report's credibility.

Decision Insight

Short Selling   *Short selling* refers to selling stock before you buy it. Here's an example: You borrow 100 shares of **Nike** stock, sell them at $40 each, and receive money from their sale. You then wait. You hope that Nike's stock price falls to, say, $35 each and you can replace the borrowed stock for less than you sold it, reaping a profit of $5 each less any transaction costs. ■

NEED-TO-KNOW 13-4

COMPREHENSIVE

Use the following financial statements of Precision Co. to complete these requirements.

1. Prepare comparative income statements showing the percent increase or decrease for year 2017 in comparison to year 2016.

2. Prepare common-size comparative balance sheets for years 2017 and 2016.

3. Compute the following ratios as of December 31, 2017, or for the year ended December 31, 2017, and identify its building block category for financial statement analysis.

a. Current ratio

b. Acid-test ratio

c. Accounts receivable turnover

d. Days' sales uncollected

e. Inventory turnover

f. Debt ratio

g. Debt-to-equity ratio

h. Times interest earned

i. Profit margin ratio

j. Total asset turnover

k. Return on total assets

l. Return on common stockholders' equity

PRECISION COMPANY
Comparative Income Statements
For Years Ended December 31, 2017 and 2016

	2017	2016
Sales	$2,486,000	$2,075,000
Cost of goods sold	1,523,000	1,222,000
Gross profit........................	963,000	853,000
Operating expenses		
Advertising expense	145,000	100,000
Sales salaries expense	240,000	280,000
Office salaries expense.............	165,000	200,000
Insurance expense.................	100,000	45,000
Supplies expense..................	26,000	35,000
Depreciation expense	85,000	75,000
Miscellaneous expenses	17,000	15,000
Total operating expenses	778,000	750,000
Operating income....................	185,000	103,000
Interest expense.....................	44,000	46,000
Income before taxes.................	141,000	57,000
Income taxes........................	47,000	19,000
Net income	$ 94,000	$ 38,000
Earnings per share	$ 0.99	$ 0.40

PRECISION COMPANY
Comparative Balance Sheets
December 31, 2017 and 2016

	2017	2016
Assets		
Current assets		
Cash	$ 79,000	$ 42,000
Short-term investments	65,000	96,000
Accounts receivable, net...............	120,000	100,000
Merchandise inventory	250,000	265,000
Total current assets	514,000	503,000
Plant assets		
Store equipment, net..................	400,000	350,000
Office equipment, net	45,000	50,000
Buildings, net	625,000	675,000
Land	100,000	100,000
Total plant assets	1,170,000	1,175,000
Total assets...........................	$1,684,000	$1,678,000
Liabilities		
Current liabilities		
Accounts payable.....................	$ 164,000	$ 190,000
Short-term notes payable	75,000	90,000
Taxes payable........................	26,000	12,000
Total current liabilities	265,000	292,000
Long-term liabilities		
Notes payable (secured by mortgage on buildings)..............	400,000	420,000
Total liabilities.......................	665,000	712,000
Stockholders' Equity		
Common stock, $5 par value.............	475,000	475,000
Retained earnings	544,000	491,000
Total stockholders' equity	1,019,000	966,000
Total liabilities and equity..............	$1,684,000	$1,678,000

PLANNING THE SOLUTION

● Set up a four-column income statement; enter the 2017 and 2016 amounts in the first two columns and then enter the dollar change in the third column and the percent change from 2016 in the fourth column.

● Set up a four-column balance sheet; enter the 2017 and 2016 year-end amounts in the first two columns and then compute and enter the amount of each item as a percent of total assets.

● Compute the required ratios using the data provided. Use the average of beginning and ending amounts when appropriate (see Exhibit 13.16 for definitions).

SOLUTION

1.

PRECISION COMPANY Comparative Income Statements For Years Ended December 31, 2017 and 2016			Increase (Decrease) in 2017	
	2017	**2016**	**Amount**	**Percent**
Sales..............................	$2,486,000	$2,075,000	$411,000	19.8%
Cost of goods sold...................	1,523,000	1,222,000	301,000	24.6
Gross profit.........................	963,000	853,000	110,000	12.9
Operating expenses				
Advertising expense	145,000	100,000	45,000	45.0
Sales salaries expense	240,000	280,000	(40,000)	(14.3)
Office salaries expense.............	165,000	200,000	(35,000)	(17.5)
Insurance expense	100,000	45,000	55,000	122.2
Supplies expense	26,000	35,000	(9,000)	(25.7)
Depreciation expense..............	85,000	75,000	10,000	13.3
Miscellaneous expenses............	17,000	15,000	2,000	13.3
Total operating expenses	778,000	750,000	28,000	3.7
Operating income	185,000	103,000	82,000	79.6
Interest expense	44,000	46,000	(2,000)	(4.3)
Income before taxes	141,000	57,000	84,000	147.4
Income taxes	47,000	19,000	28,000	147.4
Net income........................	$ 94,000	$ 38,000	$ 56,000	147.4
Earnings per share..................	$ 0.99	$ 0.40	$ 0.59	147.5

2.

PRECISION COMPANY Common-Size Comparative Balance Sheets December 31, 2017 and 2016	December 31		Common-Size Percents	
	2017	**2016**	**2017***	**2016***
Assets				
Current assets				
Cash	$ 79,000	$ 42,000	4.7%	2.5%
Short-term investments..............	65,000	96,000	3.9	5.7
Accounts receivable, net............	120,000	100,000	7.1	6.0
Merchandise inventory	250,000	265,000	14.8	15.8
Total current assets.................	514,000	503,000	30.5	30.0
Plant assets				
Store equipment, net...............	400,000	350,000	23.8	20.9
Office equipment, net	45,000	50,000	2.7	3.0
Buildings, net......................	625,000	675,000	37.1	40.2
Land	100,000	100,000	5.9	6.0
Total plant assets...................	1,170,000	1,175,000	69.5	70.0
Total assets........................	$1,684,000	$1,678,000	100.0	100.0
Liabilities				
Current liabilities				
Accounts payable	$ 164,000	$ 190,000	9.7%	11.3%
Short-term notes payable	75,000	90,000	4.5	5.4
Taxes payable	26,000	12,000	1.5	0.7
Total current liabilities...............	265,000	292,000	15.7	17.4
Long-term liabilities				
Notes payable (secured by				
mortgage on buildings).............	400,000	420,000	23.8	25.0
Total liabilities......................	665,000	712,000	39.5	42.4
Stockholders' Equity				
Common stock, $5 par value..........	475,000	475,000	28.2	28.3
Retained earnings	544,000	491,000	32.3	29.3
Total stockholders' equity	1,019,000	966,000	60.5	57.6
Total liabilities and equity	$1,684,000	$1,678,000	100.0	100.0

* Columns do not always exactly add to 100 due to rounding.

3. Ratios for 2017:

a. Current ratio: $514,000/$265,000 = 1.9:1 (liquidity and efficiency)

b. Acid-test ratio: ($79,000 + $65,000 + $120,000)/$265,000 = 1.0:1 (liquidity and efficiency)

c. Average receivables: ($120,000 + $100,000)/2 = $110,000

Accounts receivable turnover: $2,486,000/$110,000 = 22.6 times (liquidity and efficiency)

d. Days' sales uncollected: ($120,000/$2,486,000) × 365 = 17.6 days (liquidity and efficiency)

e. Average inventory: ($250,000 + $265,000)/2 = $257,500

Inventory turnover: $1,523,000/$257,500 = 5.9 times (liquidity and efficiency)

f. Debt ratio: $665,000/$1,684,000 = 39.5% (solvency)

g. Debt-to-equity ratio: $665,000/$1,019,000 = 0.65 (solvency)

h. Times interest earned: $185,000/$44,000 = 4.2 times (solvency)

i. Profit margin ratio: $94,000/$2,486,000 = 3.8% (profitability)

j. Average total assets: ($1,684,000 + $1,678,000)/2 = $1,681,000

Total asset turnover: $2,486,000/$1,681,000 = 1.48 times (liquidity and efficiency)

k. Return on total assets: $94,000/$1,681,000 = 5.6% or 3.8% × 1.48 = 5.6% (profitability)

l. Average total common equity: ($1,019,000 + $966,000)/2 = $992,500

Return on common stockholders' equity: $94,000/$992,500 = 9.5% (profitability)

APPENDIX

Sustainable Income

13A

A2

Explain the form and assess the content of a complete income statement.

When a company's revenue and expense transactions are from normal, continuing operations, a simple income statement is usually adequate. When a company's activities include income-related events not part of its normal, continuing operations, it must disclose information to help users understand these events and predict future performance. To meet these objectives, companies separate the income statement into continuing operations, discontinued segments, comprehensive income, and earnings per share. For illustration, Exhibit 13A.1 shows

EXHIBIT 13A.1

Income Statement (all-inclusive) for a Corporation

ComUS Income Statement For Year Ended December 31, 2016		
Net sales		$ 8,478,000
Operating expenses		
Cost of goods sold	$5,950,000	
Depreciation expense	35,000	
Other selling, general, and administrative expenses........................	515,000	
Interest expense..	20,000	
① Total operating expenses..........................		(6,520,000)
Other unusual and/or infrequent gains (losses)		
Loss on plant relocation...............................		(45,000)
Gain on sale of surplus land		72,000
Income from continuing operations before taxes..........................		1,985,000
Income taxes expense		(595,500)
Income from continuing operations.....................		1,389,500
Discontinued segment		
② Income from operating Division A (net of $180,000 taxes)	420,000	
Loss on disposal of Division A (net of $66,000 tax benefit).....................	(154,000)	266,000
Net income		1,655,500
Earnings per common share (200,000 outstanding shares)		
③ Income from continuing operations		$ 6.95
Discontinued operations		1.33
Net income (basic earnings per share).....................................		$ 8.28

such an income statement for ComUS. These separate distinctions help us measure *sustainable income,* which is the income level most likely to continue into the future. Sustainable income is commonly used in PE ratios and other market-based measures of performance.

① **Continuing Operations**   The first major section (①) shows the revenues, expenses, and income from continuing operations. Users especially rely on this information to predict future operations and view this section as the most important.

Gains and losses that are neither unusual nor infrequent are reported as part of continuing operations. Gains and losses that are either unusual and/or infrequent are reported as part of continuing operations *but after* the normal revenues and expenses. Items typically considered unusual and/or infrequent include (1) expropriation (taking away) of property by a foreign government, (2) condemning of property by a domestic government body, (3) prohibition against using an asset by a newly enacted law, (4) losses and gains from an unusual and infrequent calamity ("act of God"), and (5) financial effects of labor strikes. (At one time, the FASB identified *extraordinary items*; that is no longer the case.)

② **Discontinued Segments**   A **business segment** is a part of a company's operations that serves a particular line of business or class of customers. A segment has assets, liabilities, and financial results of operations that can be distinguished from those of other parts of the company. A company's gain or loss from selling or closing down a segment is separately reported. Section ② of Exhibit 13A.1 reports both (1) income from operating the discontinued segment for the current period prior to its disposal and (2) the loss from disposing of the segment's net assets. The income tax effects of each are reported separately from the income taxes expense in section ①.

■ **Decision** Maker

Small Business Owner   You own an orange grove near Jacksonville, Florida. A bad frost destroys about one-half of your oranges. You are currently preparing an income statement for a bank loan. Where on the income statement do you report the loss of oranges? ■   *Answer:* The frost loss is likely unusual, meaning it is reported in the nonrecurring section of continuing operations. Managers would highlight this loss apart from ongoing, normal results so that the bank views it separately from normal operations.

③ **Earnings per Share**   The final section ③ of the income statement in Exhibit 13A.1 reports earnings per share for each of the two subcategories of income (continuing operations and discontinued segments) when they both exist.

Changes in Accounting Principles   The *consistency concept* directs a company to apply the same accounting principles across periods. Yet a company can change from one acceptable accounting principle (such as FIFO, LIFO, or weighted-average) to another as long as the change improves the usefulness of information in its financial statements. A footnote would describe the accounting change and why it is an improvement.

Point: Changes in principles are sometimes required when new accounting standards are issued.

Changes in accounting principles require retrospective application to prior periods' financial statements. *Retrospective application* involves applying a different accounting principle to prior periods as if that principle had always been used. Retrospective application enhances the consistency of financial information between periods, which improves the usefulness of information, especially with comparative analyses. Accounting standards also require that *a change in depreciation, amortization, or depletion method for long-term operating assets is accounted for as a change in accounting estimate*—that is, prospectively over current and future periods. This reflects the notion that an entity should change its depreciation, amortization, or depletion method only with changes in estimated asset benefits, the pattern of benefit usage, or information about those benefits.

Summary

C1 **Explain the purpose and identify the building blocks of analysis.** The purpose of financial statement analysis is to help users make better business decisions. Internal users want information to improve company efficiency and effectiveness. External users want information to make better and more informed decisions in pursuing their goals. The common goals of all users are to evaluate a company's (1) past and current performance, (2) current financial position, and (3) future performance and risk. Financial statement analysis focuses on four "building blocks" of analysis: (1) liquidity and efficiency—ability to meet short-term obligations and efficiently generate revenues; (2) solvency—ability to generate future revenues and meet long-term obligations; (3) profitability—ability to provide financial rewards sufficient to attract and retain financing; and (4) market prospects—ability to generate positive market expectations.

C2 **Describe standards for comparisons in analysis.** Standards for comparisons include (1) intracompany—prior performance and relations between financial items for the company under analysis; (2) competitor—one or more direct competitors of the company; (3) industry—industry statistics; and (4) guidelines (rules of thumb)—general standards developed from past experiences and personal judgments.

A1 **Summarize and report results of analysis.** A financial statement analysis report is often organized around the building blocks of analysis. A good report separates interpretations and conclusions of analysis from the information underlying them. An analysis report often consists of six sections: (1) executive summary, (2) analysis overview, (3) evidential matter, (4) assumptions, (5) key factors, and (6) inferences.

A2ᴬ **Explain the form and assess the content of a complete income statement.** An income statement has three sections: (1) continuing operations, (2) discontinued segments—provided any exist, and (3) earnings per share.

P1 **Explain and apply methods of horizontal analysis.** Horizontal analysis is a tool to evaluate changes in data across time. Two important tools of horizontal analysis are comparative statements and trend analysis. Comparative

statements show amounts for two or more successive periods, often with changes disclosed in both absolute and percent terms. Trend analysis is used to reveal important changes occurring from one period to the next.

P2 **Describe and apply methods of vertical analysis.** Vertical analysis is a tool to evaluate each financial statement item or group of items in terms of a base amount. Two tools of vertical analysis are common-size statements and graphical analyses. Each item in common-size statements is expressed as a percent of a base amount. For the balance sheet, the base amount is usually total assets, and for the income statement, it is usually sales.

P3 **Define and apply ratio analysis.** Ratio analysis provides clues to and symptoms of underlying conditions. Ratios, properly interpreted, identify areas requiring further investigation. A ratio expresses a relation between two quantities such as a percent, rate, or proportion. Ratios can be organized into the building blocks of analysis: (1) liquidity and efficiency, (2) solvency, (3) profitability, and (4) market prospects.

Key Terms

Business segment	Financial statement analysis	Ratio analysis
Common-size financial statement	General-purpose financial statements	Solvency
Comparative financial statement	Horizontal analysis	Vertical analysis
Efficiency	Liquidity	Working capital
Equity ratio	Market prospects	
Financial reporting	Profitability	

Multiple Choice Quiz

1. A company's sales in 2016 were $300,000 and in 2017 were $351,000. Using 2016 as the base year, the sales trend percent for 2017 is:

  a. 17%.   **c.** 100%.   **e.** 48%.

  b. 85%.   **d.** 117%.

Use the following information for questions 2 through 5.

ELLA COMPANY
Balance Sheet
December 31, 2017

Assets

Cash	$ 86,000
Accounts receivable	76,000
Merchandise inventory	122,000
Prepaid insurance	12,000
Long-term investments	98,000
Plant assets, net	436,000
Total assets	$830,000

Liabilities and Equity

Current liabilities	$124,000
Long-term liabilities	90,000
Common stock	300,000
Retained earnings	316,000
Total liabilities and equity	$830,000

2. What is Ella Company's current ratio?

  a. 0.69

  b. 1.31

  c. 3.88

  d. 6.69

  e. 2.39

3. What is Ella Company's acid-test ratio?

  a. 2.39

  b. 0.69

  c. 1.31

  d. 6.69

  e. 3.88

4. What is Ella Company's debt ratio?

  a. 25.78%

  b. 100.00%

  c. 74.22%

  d. 137.78%

  e. 34.74%

5. What is Ella Company's equity ratio?

  a. 25.78%

  b. 100.00%

  c. 34.74%

  d. 74.22%

  e. 137.78%

ANSWERS TO MULTIPLE CHOICE QUIZ

1. d; ($351,000/$300,000) × 100 = 117%
2. e; ($86,000 + $76,000 + $122,000 + $12,000)/$124,000 = 2.39
3. c; ($86,000 + $76,000)/$124,000 = 1.31
4. a; ($124,000 + $90,000)/$830,000 = 25.78%
5. d; ($300,000 + $316,000)/$830,000 = 74.22%

[A] *Superscript letter A denotes assignments based on Appendix 13A.*

🔲 Icon denotes assignments that involve decision making.

Discussion Questions

1. Explain the difference between financial reporting and financial statements.
2. What is the difference between comparative financial statements and common-size comparative statements?
3. Which items are usually assigned a 100% value on (a) a common-size balance sheet and (b) a common-size income statement?
4. 🔲 What three factors would influence your evaluation as to whether a company's current ratio is good or bad?
5. 🔲 Suggest several reasons why a 2:1 current ratio might not be adequate for a particular company.
6. 🔲 Why is working capital given special attention in the process of analyzing balance sheets?
7. 🔲 What does the number of days' sales uncollected indicate?
8. 🔲 What does a relatively high accounts receivable turnover indicate about a company's short-term liquidity?
9. 🔲 Why is a company's capital structure, as measured by debt and equity ratios, important to financial statement analysts?
10. 🔲 How does inventory turnover provide information about a company's short-term liquidity?
11. 🔲 What ratios would you compute to evaluate management performance?
12. 🔲 Why would a company's return on total assets be different from its return on common stockholders' equity?
13. Where on the income statement does a company report an unusual gain not expected to occur more often than once every two years or so?
14. Refer to **Apple**'s financial statements in Appendix A. Compute its profit margin for the years ended September 26, 2015, and September 27, 2014. **APPLE**
15. Refer to **Google**'s financial statements in Appendix A to compute its equity ratio as of December 31, 2015, and December 31, 2014. **GOOGLE**
16. Refer to **Samsung**'s financial statements in Appendix A. Compute its debt ratio as of December 31, 2015, and December 31, 2014. **Samsung**
17. Use **Samsung**'s financial statements in Appendix A to compute its return on total assets for fiscal year ended December 31, 2015. **Samsung**

🔲 **connect**

QUICK STUDY

QS 13-1
Financial reporting
C1

Which of the following items *a* through *i* are part of financial reporting but are *not* included as part of general-purpose financial statements?

____ **a.** Income statement
____ **b.** Balance sheet
____ **c.** Prospectus
____ **d.** Financial statement notes
____ **e.** Company news releases
____ **f.** Statement of cash flows
____ **g.** Stock price information and analysis
____ **h.** Statement of shareholders' equity
____ **i.** Management discussion and analysis of financial performance

QS 13-2
Standard of comparison
C2

Identify which standard of comparison, (a) intracompany, (b) competitor, (c) industry, or (d) guidelines, is best described by each of the following.

____ **1.** Is often viewed as the best standard of comparison.
____ **2.** Rules of thumb developed from past experiences.
____ **3.** Provides analysis based on a company's prior performance.
____ **4.** Compares a company against industry statistics.

Compute the annual dollar changes and percent changes for each of the following accounts.

	2017	2016
Short-term investments	$374,634	$234,000
Accounts receivable..............	97,364	101,000
Notes payable..................	0	88,000

QS 13-3
Horizontal analysis
P1

Use the following information for Tide Corporation to determine the 2016 and 2017 trend percents for net sales using 2016 as the base year.

$ thousands	2017	2016
Net sales........................	$801,810	$453,000
Cost of goods sold	392,887	134,088

QS 13-4
Trend percents
P1

Refer to the information in QS 13-4. Use that information for Tide Corporation to determine the 2016 and 2017 common-size percents for cost of goods sold using net sales as the base.

QS 13-5
Common-size analysis   P2

For each ratio listed, identify whether the change in ratio value from 2016 to 2017 is usually regarded as favorable or unfavorable.

QS 13-6
Ratio interpretation
P3

Ratio	2017	2016	Ratio	2017	2016
_____ 1. Profit margin......	9%	8%	_____ 5. Accounts receivable turnover.......	5.5	6.7
_____ 2. Debt ratio	47%	42%	_____ 6. Basic earnings per share	$1.25	$1.10
_____ 3. Gross margin	34%	46%	_____ 7. Inventory turnover...............	3.6	3.4
_____ 4. Acid-test ratio.....	1.00	1.15	_____ 8. Dividend yield	2.0%	1.2%

The following information is available for Morgan Company and Parker Company, similar firms operating in the same industry. Write a half-page report comparing Morgan and Parker using the available information. Your discussion should include their ability to meet current obligations and to use current assets efficiently.

QS 13-7
Analysis of short-term financial condition
A1

	A	B	C	D	E	F	G	H
1		Morgan				Parker		
2		2017	2016	2015		2017	2016	2015
3	Current ratio	1.7	1.6	2.1		3.2	2.7	1.9
4	Acid-test ratio	1.0	1.1	1.2		2.8	2.5	1.6
5	Accounts receivable turnover	30.5	25.2	29.2		16.4	15.2	16.0
6	Merchandise inventory turnover	24.2	21.9	17.1		14.5	13.0	12.6
7	Working capital	$70,000	$58,000	$52,000		$131,000	$103,000	$78,000

Team Project: Assume that the two companies apply for a one-year loan from the team. Identify additional information the companies must provide before the team can make a loan decision.

A review of the notes payable files discovers that three years ago the company reported the entire $1,000 cash payment (consisting of $800 principal and $200 interest) toward an installment note payable as interest expense. This mistake had a material effect on the amount of income in that year. How should the correction be reported in the current-year financial statements?

QS 13-8^A
Error adjustments
A2

Answer each of the following related to international accounting and analysis.

a. Identify a limitation to using ratio analysis when examining companies reporting under different accounting systems such as IFRS versus U.S. GAAP.

b. Identify an advantage to using horizontal and vertical analyses when examining companies reporting under different currencies.

QS 13-9
International ratio analysis
C2

EXERCISES

Exercise 13-1

Building blocks of analysis

C1

Match the ratio to the building block of financial statement analysis to which it best relates.

A. Liquidity and efficiency   **B.** Solvency   **C.** Profitability   **D.** Market prospects

_____ **1.** Equity ratio
_____ **2.** Return on total assets
_____ **3.** Dividend yield
_____ **4.** Book value per common share
_____ **5.** Days' sales in inventory

_____ **6.** Accounts receivable turnover
_____ **7.** Debt-to-equity ratio
_____ **8.** Times interest earned
_____ **9.** Gross margin ratio
_____ **10.** Acid-test ratio

Exercise 13-2

Identifying financial ratios

C2

Identify which of the following six metrics *a* through *f* best completes questions 1 through 3 below.

a. Days' sales uncollected
b. Accounts receivable turnover
c. Working capital

d. Return on total assets
e. Total asset turnover
f. Profit margin

1. Which two ratios are key components in measuring a company's operating efficiency? _____ _____ Which ratio summarizes these two components? _____

2. What measure reflects the difference between current assets and current liabilities? _____

3. Which two short-term liquidity ratios measure how frequently a company collects its accounts? _____ _____

Exercise 13-3

Computation and analysis of trend percents

P1

Compute trend percents for the following accounts, using 2013 as the base year (round the percents to whole numbers). State whether the situation as revealed by the trends appears to be favorable or unfavorable for each account.

	2017	2016	2015	2014	2013
Sales	$282,880	$270,800	$252,600	$234,560	$150,000
Cost of goods sold	128,200	122,080	115,280	106,440	67,000
Accounts receivable.	18,100	17,300	16,400	15,200	9,000

Exercise 13-4

Common-size percent computation and interpretation

P2

Express the following comparative income statements in common-size percents and assess whether or not this company's situation has improved in the most recent year (round the percents to one decimal).

GOMEZ CORPORATION Comparative Income Statements For Years Ended December 31, 2017 and 2016		
	2017	2016
Sales	$740,000	$625,000
Cost of goods sold	560,300	290,800
Gross profit.	179,700	334,200
Operating expenses.	128,200	218,500
Net income	$ 51,500	$115,700

Exercise 13-5

Determination of income effects from common-size and trend percents

P1   P2

Common-size and trend percents for Rustynail Company's sales, cost of goods sold, and expenses follow. Determine whether net income increased, decreased, or remained unchanged in this three-year period.

	Common-Size Percents			Trend Percents		
	2017	2016	2015	2017	2016	2015
Sales.	100.0%	100.0%	100.0%	105.4%	104.2%	100.0%
Cost of goods sold.	63.4	61.9	59.1	113.1	109.1	100.0
Total expenses.	15.3	14.8	15.1	106.8	102.1	100.0

Simon Company's year-end balance sheets follow. Express the balance sheets in common-size percents. Round amounts to the nearest one-tenth of a percent. Analyze and comment on the results.

Exercise 13-6
Common-size percents

P2

At December 31	2017	2016	2015
Assets			
Cash	$ 31,800	$ 35,625	$ 37,800
Accounts receivable, net	89,500	62,500	50,200
Merchandise inventory........................	112,500	82,500	54,000
Prepaid expenses............................	10,700	9,375	5,000
Plant assets, net	278,500	255,000	230,500
Total assets	$523,000	$445,000	$377,500
Liabilities and Equity			
Accounts payable............................	$129,900	$ 75,250	$ 51,250
Long-term notes payable secured by			
mortgages on plant assets	98,500	101,500	83,500
Common stock, $10 par value..................	163,500	163,500	163,500
Retained earnings	131,100	104,750	79,250
Total liabilities and equity.....................	$523,000	$445,000	$377,500

Refer to Simon Company's balance sheets in Exercise 13-6. Analyze its year-end short-term liquidity position at the end of 2017, 2016, and 2015 by computing (1) the current ratio and (2) the acid-test ratio. Comment on the ratio results. (Round ratio amounts to two decimals.)

Exercise 13-7
Liquidity analysis

P3

Refer to the Simon Company information in Exercise 13-6. The company's income statements for the years ended December 31, 2017 and 2016, follow. Assume that all sales are on credit and then compute: (1) days' sales uncollected, (2) accounts receivable turnover, (3) inventory turnover, and (4) days' sales in inventory. Comment on the changes in the ratios from 2016 to 2017. (Round amounts to one decimal.)

Exercise 13-8
Liquidity analysis and interpretation

P3

For Year Ended December 31	2017		2016	
Sales		$673,500		$532,000
Cost of goods sold	$411,225		$345,500	
Other operating expenses............	209,550		134,980	
Interest expense....................	12,100		13,300	
Income taxes......................	9,525		8,845	
Total costs and expenses............		642,400		502,625
Net income		$ 31,100		$ 29,375
Earnings per share		$ 1.90		$ 1.80

Refer to the Simon Company information in Exercises 13-6 and 13-8. Compare the company's long-term risk and capital structure positions at the end of 2017 and 2016 by computing these ratios: (1) debt and equity ratios—percent rounded to one decimal, (2) debt-to-equity ratio—rounded to two decimals, and (3) times interest earned—rounded to one decimal. Comment on these ratio results.

Exercise 13-9
Risk and capital structure analysis

P3

Refer to Simon Company's financial information in Exercises 13-6 and 13-8. Evaluate the company's efficiency and profitability by computing the following for 2017 and 2016: (1) profit margin ratio—percent rounded to one decimal, (2) total asset turnover—rounded to one decimal, and (3) return on total assets—percent rounded to one decimal. Comment on these ratio results.

Exercise 13-10
Efficiency and profitability analysis

P3

Exercise 13-11

Profitability analysis

P3

Refer to Simon Company's financial information in Exercises 13-6 and 13-8. Additional information about the company follows. To help evaluate the company's profitability, compute and interpret the following ratios for 2017 and 2016: (1) return on common stockholders' equity—percent rounded to one decimal, (2) price-earnings ratio on December 31—rounded to one decimal, and (3) dividend yield—percent rounded to one decimal.

Common stock market price, December 31, 2017	$30.00
Common stock market price, December 31, 2016	28.00
Annual cash dividends per share in 2017.	0.29
Annual cash dividends per share in 2016.	0.24

Exercise 13-12

Analysis of efficiency and financial leverage

A1

Roak Company and Clay Company are similar firms that operate in the same industry. Clay began operations in 2015 and Roak in 2012. In 2017, both companies pay 7% interest on their debt to creditors. The following additional information is available.

	Roak Company			Clay Company		
	2017	**2016**	**2015**	**2017**	**2016**	**2015**
Total asset turnover	3.1	2.8	3.0	1.7	1.5	1.1
Return on total assets	9.0%	9.6%	8.8%	5.9%	5.6%	5.3%
Profit margin ratio	2.4%	2.5%	2.3%	2.8%	3.0%	2.9%
Sales	$410,000	$380,000	$396,000	$210,000	$170,000	$110,000

Write a half-page report comparing Roak and Clay using the available information. Your analysis should include their ability to use assets efficiently to produce profits. Also comment on their success in employing financial leverage in 2017.

Exercise 13-13ᴬ

Income statement categories

A2

In 2017, Randa Merchandising, Inc., sold its interest in a chain of wholesale outlets, taking the company completely out of the wholesaling business. The company still operates its retail outlets. A listing of the major sections of an income statement follows:

A. Net sales less operating expense section

B. Other unusual and/or infrequent gains (losses)

C. Taxes reported on income (loss) from continuing operations

D. Income (loss) from operating a discontinued segment, or gain (loss) from its disposal

Indicate where each of the following income-related items for this company appears on its 2017 income statement by writing the letter of the appropriate section in the blank beside each item.

Section	Item	Debit	Credit
_____	1. Net sales.		$2,900,000
_____	2. Gain on state's condemnation of company property		230,000
_____	3. Cost of goods sold	$1,480,000	
_____	4. Income taxes expense	217,000	
_____	5. Depreciation expense	232,000	
_____	6. Gain on sale of wholesale business segment, net of tax.		775,000
_____	7. Loss from operating wholesale business segment, net of tax.	444,000	
_____	8. Loss of assets from meteor strike	640,000	

Exercise 13-14ᴬ

Income statement presentation   A2

Use the financial data for Randa Merchandising, Inc., in Exercise 13-13 to prepare its income statement for calendar-year 2017. (Ignore the earnings per share section.)

Nintendo Company, Ltd., reports the following financial information as of, or for the year ended, March 31, 2015. Nintendo reports its financial statements in both Japanese yen and U.S. dollars as shown (amounts in millions).

Exercise 13-15
Ratio analysis under different currencies

P3

Current assets...............	¥1,097,597	$ 9,110
Total assets.................	1,352,944	11,229
Current liabilities............	144,232	1,197
Net sales...................	549,780	4,562
Net income	41,843	347

1. Compute Nintendo's current ratio, net profit margin, and sales-to-total-assets ratio using the financial information reported in (*a*) yen and (*b*) dollars. Round amounts to two decimals.
2. What can we conclude from a review of the results for part 1?

≡ connect

Selected comparative financial statements of Haroun Company follow.

PROBLEM SET A

Problem 13-1A
Calculation and analysis of trend percents

A1   P1

HAROUN COMPANY Comparative Income Statements For Years Ended December 31, 2017–2011							
$ thousands	**2017**	**2016**	**2015**	**2014**	**2013**	**2012**	**2011**
Sales	$1,694	$1,496	$1,370	$1,264	$1,186	$1,110	$928
Cost of goods sold	1,246	1,032	902	802	752	710	586
Gross profit.................	448	464	468	462	434	400	342
Operating expenses...........	330	256	234	170	146	144	118
Net income	$ 118	$ 208	$ 234	$ 292	$ 288	$ 256	$224

HAROUN COMPANY Comparative Balance Sheets December 31, 2017–2011							
$ thousands	**2017**	**2016**	**2015**	**2014**	**2013**	**2012**	**2011**
Assets							
Cash	$ 58	$ 78	$ 82	$ 84	$ 88	$ 86	$ 89
Accounts receivable, net	490	514	466	360	318	302	216
Merchandise inventory...........	1,838	1,364	1,204	1,032	936	810	615
Other current assets.............	36	32	14	34	28	28	9
Long-term investments	0	0	0	146	146	146	146
Plant assets, net................	2,020	2,014	1,752	944	978	860	725
Total assets....................	$4,442	$4,002	$3,518	$2,600	$2,494	$2,232	$1,800
Liabilities and Equity							
Current liabilities................	$1,220	$1,042	$ 718	$ 614	$ 546	$ 522	$ 282
Long-term liabilities	1,294	1,140	1,112	570	580	620	400
Common stock	1,000	1,000	1,000	850	850	650	650
Other paid-in capital..............	250	250	250	170	170	150	150
Retained earnings	678	570	438	396	348	290	318
Total liabilities and equity...........	$4,442	$4,002	$3,518	$2,600	$2,494	$2,232	$1,800

Required

1. Compute trend percents for all components of both statements using 2011 as the base year. (Round percents to one decimal.)

Check (1) 2017, Total assets trend, 246.8%

Analysis Component

2. Analyze and comment on the financial statements and trend percents from part 1.

Problem 13-2A
Ratios, common-size
statements, and trend
percents

P1   P2   P3

Selected comparative financial statements of Korbin Company follow.

KORBIN COMPANY Comparative Income Statements For Years Ended December 31, 2017, 2016, and 2015			
	2017	**2016**	**2015**
Sales	$555,000	$340,000	$278,000
Cost of goods sold	283,500	212,500	153,900
Gross profit	271,500	127,500	124,100
Selling expenses.	102,900	46,920	50,800
Administrative expenses	50,668	29,920	22,800
Total expenses	153,568	76,840	73,600
Income before taxes.	117,932	50,660	50,500
Income taxes.	40,800	10,370	15,670
Net income	$ 77,132	$ 40,290	$ 34,830

KORBIN COMPANY Comparative Balance Sheets December 31, 2017, 2016, and 2015			
	2017	**2016**	**2015**
Assets			
Current assets.	$ 52,390	$ 37,924	$ 51,748
Long-term investments	0	500	3,950
Plant assets, net	100,000	96,000	60,000
Total assets	$152,390	$134,424	$115,698
Liabilities and Equity			
Current liabilities.	$ 22,800	$ 19,960	$ 20,300
Common stock	72,000	72,000	60,000
Other paid-in capital.	9,000	9,000	6,000
Retained earnings	48,590	33,464	29,398
Total liabilities and equity.	$152,390	$134,424	$115,698

Required

1. Compute each year's current ratio. (Round ratio amounts to one decimal.)

2. Express the income statement data in common-size percents. (Round percents to two decimals.)

Check (3) 2017, Total
assets trend, 131.71%

3. Express the balance sheet data in trend percents with 2015 as the base year. (Round percents to two decimals.)

Analysis Component

4. Comment on any significant relations revealed by the ratios and percents computed.

Problem 13-3A
Transactions, working
capital, and liquidity ratios

P3

Plum Corporation began the month of May with $700,000 of current assets, a current ratio of 2.50:1, and an acid-test ratio of 1.10:1. During the month, it completed the following transactions (the company uses a perpetual inventory system).

May 2 Purchased $50,000 of merchandise inventory on credit.
     8 Sold merchandise inventory that cost $55,000 for $110,000 cash.
    10 Collected $20,000 cash on an account receivable.
    15 Paid $22,000 cash to settle an account payable.
    17 Wrote off a $5,000 bad debt against the Allowance for Doubtful Accounts account.
    22 Declared a $1 per share cash dividend on its 50,000 shares of outstanding common stock.
    26 Paid the dividend declared on May 22.
    27 Borrowed $100,000 cash by giving the bank a 30-day, 10% note.
    28 Borrowed $80,000 cash by signing a long-term secured note.
    29 Used the $180,000 cash proceeds from the notes to buy new machinery.

Check May 22: Current ratio,
2.19; Acid-test ratio, 1.11

       May 29: Current
ratio, 1.80; Working capital,
$325,000

Required

Prepare a table, *similar to the following,* showing Plum's (1) current ratio, (2) acid-test ratio, and (3) working capital after each transaction. Round ratios to two decimals.

	A	B	C	D	E	F	G
1		Current	Quick	Current	Current	Acid-Test	Working
2	Transaction	Assets	Assets	Liabilities	Ratio	Ratio	Capital
3	Beginning	$700,000	—	—	2.50	1.10	—

Selected year-end financial statements of Cabot Corporation follow. (All sales were on credit; selected balance sheet amounts at December 31, 2016, were inventory, $48,900; total assets, $189,400; common stock, $90,000; and retained earnings, $22,748.)

Problem 13-4A
Calculation of financial statement ratios

P3

CABOT CORPORATION Income Statement For Year Ended December 31, 2017	
Sales	$448,600
Cost of goods sold	297,250
Gross profit	151,350
Operating expenses	98,600
Interest expense	4,100
Income before taxes	48,650
Income taxes	19,598
Net income	$ 29,052

CABOT CORPORATION Balance Sheet December 31, 2017			
Assets		**Liabilities and Equity**	
Cash	$ 10,000	Accounts payable	$ 17,500
Short-term investments	8,400	Accrued wages payable	3,200
Accounts receivable, net	29,200	Income taxes payable	3,300
Notes receivable (trade)*	4,500	Long-term note payable, secured	
Merchandise inventory	32,150	by mortgage on plant assets	63,400
Prepaid expenses	2,650	Common stock	90,000
Plant assets, net	153,300	Retained earnings	62,800
Total assets	$240,200	Total liabilities and equity	$240,200

* These are short-term notes receivable arising from customer (trade) sales.

Required

Compute the following: (1) current ratio, (2) acid-test ratio, (3) days' sales uncollected, (4) inventory turnover, (5) days' sales in inventory, (6) debt-to-equity ratio, (7) times interest earned, (8) profit margin ratio, (9) total asset turnover, (10) return on total assets, and (11) return on common stockholders' equity. Round to one decimal place; for part 6, round to two decimals.

Check   Acid-test ratio, 2.2 to 1; Inventory turnover, 7.3

Summary information from the financial statements of two companies competing in the same industry follows.

Problem 13-5A
Comparative ratio analysis

A1   P3

	Barco Company	Kyan Company		Barco Company	Kyan Company
Data from the current year-end balance sheets			**Data from the current year's income statement**		
Assets			Sales	$770,000	$880,200
Cash	$ 19,500	$ 34,000	Cost of goods sold	585,100	632,500
Accounts receivable, net	37,400	57,400	Interest expense	7,900	13,000
Current notes receivable (trade)	9,100	7,200	Income tax expense	14,800	24,300
Merchandise inventory	84,440	132,500	Net income	162,200	210,400
Prepaid expenses	5,000	6,950	Basic earnings per share	4.51	5.11
Plant assets, net	290,000	304,400	Cash dividends per share	3.81	3.93
Total assets	$445,440	$542,450			
			Beginning-of-year balance sheet data		
Liabilities and Equity			Accounts receivable, net	$ 29,800	$ 54,200
Current liabilities	$ 61,340	$ 93,300	Current notes receivable (trade)	0	0
Long-term notes payable	80,800	101,000	Merchandise inventory	55,600	107,400
Common stock, $5 par value	180,000	206,000	Total assets	398,000	382,500
Retained earnings	123,300	142,150	Common stock, $5 par value	180,000	206,000
Total liabilities and equity	$445,440	$542,450	Retained earnings	98,300	93,600

Required

1. For both companies compute the (*a*) current ratio, (*b*) acid-test ratio, (*c*) accounts (including notes) receivable turnover, (*d*) inventory turnover, (*e*) days' sales in inventory, and (*f*) days' sales uncollected. Identify the company you consider to be the better short-term credit risk and explain why. Round to one decimal place.

2. For both companies compute the (*a*) profit margin ratio, (*b*) total asset turnover, (*c*) return on total assets, and (*d*) return on common stockholders' equity. Assuming that each company's stock can be purchased at $75 per share, compute their (*e*) price-earnings ratios and (*f*) dividend yields. Round to one decimal place. Identify which company's stock you would recommend as the better investment and explain why.

Problem 13-6A^A

Income statement computations and format

A2

Selected account balances from the adjusted trial balance for Olinda Corporation as of its calendar year-end December 31, 2017, follow.

	Debit	Credit
a. Interest revenue.		$ 14,000
b. Depreciation expense—Equipment.	$ 34,000	
c. Loss on sale of equipment.	25,850	
d. Accounts payable.		44,000
e. Other operating expenses.	106,400	
f. Accumulated depreciation—Equipment		71,600
g. Gain from settlement of lawsuit		44,000
h. Accumulated depreciation—Buildings		174,500
i. Loss from operating a discontinued segment (pretax).	18,250	
j. Gain on insurance recovery of tornado damage		20,000
k. Net sales.		998,000
l. Depreciation expense—Buildings.	52,000	
m. Correction of overstatement of prior year's sales (pretax)	16,000	
n. Gain on sale of discontinued segment's assets (pretax)		34,000
o. Loss from settlement of lawsuit.	23,250	
p. Income taxes expense.	?	
q. Cost of goods sold	482,500	

Required

Answer each of the following questions by providing supporting computations.

1. Assume that the company's income tax rate is 30% for all items. Identify the tax effects and after-tax amounts of the three items labeled pretax.

2. Compute the amount of income from continuing operations before income taxes. What is the amount of the income taxes expense? What is the amount of income from continuing operations?

3. What is the total amount of after-tax income (loss) associated with the discontinued segment?

4. What is the amount of net income for the year?

PROBLEM SET B

Selected comparative financial statements of Tripoly Company follow.

Problem 13-1B

Calculation and analysis of trend percents

A1   P1

$ thousands	TRIPOLY COMPANY Comparative Income Statements For Years Ended December 31, 2017–2011						
	2017	**2016**	**2015**	**2014**	**2013**	**2012**	**2011**
Sales	$560	$610	$630	$680	$740	$770	$860
Cost of goods sold	276	290	294	314	340	350	380
Gross profit	284	320	336	366	400	420	480
Operating expenses.	84	104	112	126	140	144	150
Net income	$200	$216	$224	$240	$260	$276	$330

TRIPOLY COMPANY							
Comparative Balance Sheets							
December 31, 2017–2011							
$ thousands	2017	2016	2015	2014	2013	2012	2011
Assets							
Cash	$ 44	$ 46	$ 52	$ 54	$ 60	$ 62	$ 68
Accounts receivable, net	130	136	140	144	150	154	160
Merchandise inventory..............	166	172	178	180	186	190	208
Other current assets...............	34	34	36	38	38	40	40
Long-term investments	36	30	26	110	110	110	110
Plant assets, net	510	514	520	412	420	428	454
Total assets......................	$920	$932	$952	$938	$964	$984	$1,040
Liabilities and Equity							
Current liabilities...................	$148	$156	$186	$190	$210	$260	$ 280
Long-term liabilities	92	120	142	148	194	214	260
Common stock	160	160	160	160	160	160	160
Other paid-in capital................	70	70	70	70	70	70	70
Retained earnings	450	426	394	370	330	280	270
Total liabilities and equity...........	$920	$932	$952	$938	$964	$984	$1,040

Required

1. Compute trend percents for all components of both statements using 2011 as the base year. (Round percents to one decimal.)

Check (1) 2017, Total assets trend, 88.5%

Analysis Component

2. Analyze and comment on the financial statements and trend percents from part 1.

Selected comparative financial statement information of Bluegrass Corporation follows.

Problem 13-2B
Ratios, common-size statements, and trend percents

P1 P2 P3

BLUEGRASS CORPORATION			
Comparative Balance Sheets			
December 31, 2017, 2016, and 2015			
	2017	2016	2015
Assets			
Current assets.................	$ 54,860	$ 32,660	$ 36,300
Long-term investments	0	1,700	10,600
Plant assets, net	112,810	113,660	79,000
Total assets..................	$167,670	$148,020	$125,900
Liabilities and Equity			
Current liabilities..............	$ 22,370	$ 19,180	$ 16,500
Common stock	46,500	46,500	37,000
Other paid-in capital...........	13,850	13,850	11,300
Retained earnings	84,950	68,490	61,100
Total liabilities and equity........	$167,670	$148,020	$125,900

BLUEGRASS CORPORATION			
Comparative Income Statements			
For Years Ended December 31, 2017, 2016, and 2015			
	2017	2016	2015
Sales	$198,800	$166,000	$143,800
Cost of goods sold	108,890	86,175	66,200
Gross profit	89,910	79,825	77,600
Selling expenses.............	22,680	19,790	18,000
Administrative expenses	16,760	14,610	15,700
Total expenses	39,440	34,400	33,700
Income before taxes.........	50,470	45,425	43,900
Income taxes................	6,050	5,910	5,300
Net income	$ 44,420	$ 39,515	$ 38,600

Required

1. Compute each year's current ratio. (Round ratio amounts to one decimal.)
2. Express the income statement data in common-size percents. (Round percents to two decimals.)
3. Express the balance sheet data in trend percents with 2015 as the base year. (Round percents to two decimals.)

Check (3) 2017, Total assets trend, 133.18%

Analysis Component

4. Comment on any significant relations revealed by the ratios and percents computed.

Problem 13-3B
Transactions, working
capital, and liquidity
ratios **P3**

Check   June 3:
Current ratio, 2.88;
Acid-test ratio, 2.40

*June 30: Working
capital, $(10,000); Current
ratio, 0.97*

Koto Corporation began the month of June with $300,000 of current assets, a current ratio of 2.5:1, and an acid-test ratio of 1.4:1. During the month, it completed the following transactions (the company uses a perpetual inventory system).

June 1   Sold merchandise inventory that cost $75,000 for $120,000 cash.
       3   Collected $88,000 cash on an account receivable.
       5   Purchased $150,000 of merchandise inventory on credit.
       7   Borrowed $100,000 cash by giving the bank a 60-day, 10% note.
      10   Borrowed $120,000 cash by signing a long-term secured note.
      12   Purchased machinery for $275,000 cash.
      15   Declared a $1 per share cash dividend on its 80,000 shares of outstanding common stock.
      19   Wrote off a $5,000 bad debt against the Allowance for Doubtful Accounts account.
      22   Paid $12,000 cash to settle an account payable.
      30   Paid the dividend declared on June 15.

Required

Prepare a table, similar to the following, showing the company's (1) current ratio, (2) acid-test ratio, and (3) working capital after each transaction. Round ratios to two decimals.

	A	B	C	D	E	F	G
1							
2	Transaction	Current Assets	Quick Assets	Current Liabilities	Current Ratio	Acid-Test Ratio	Working Capital
3	Beginning	$300,000	—	—	2.50	1.40	—

Problem 13-4B
Calculation of financial
statement ratios

P3

Selected year-end financial statements of Overton Corporation follow. (All sales were on credit; selected balance sheet amounts at December 31, 2016, were inventory, $17,400; total assets, $94,900; common stock, $35,500; and retained earnings, $18,800.)

OVERTON CORPORATION
Income Statement
For Year Ended December 31, 2017

Sales	$315,500
Cost of goods sold	236,100
Gross profit	79,400
Operating expenses	49,200
Interest expense	2,200
Income before taxes	28,000
Income taxes	4,200
Net income	$ 23,800

OVERTON CORPORATION
Balance Sheet
December 31, 2017

Assets		Liabilities and Equity	
Cash	$ 6,100	Accounts payable	$ 11,500
Short-term investments	6,900	Accrued wages payable	3,300
Accounts receivable, net	12,100	Income taxes payable	2,600
Notes receivable (trade)*	3,000	Long-term note payable, secured	
Merchandise inventory	13,500	by mortgage on plant assets	30,000
Prepaid expenses	2,000	Common stock, $5 par value	35,000
Plant assets, net	73,900	Retained earnings	35,100
Total assets	$117,500	Total liabilities and equity	$117,500

* These are short-term notes receivable arising from customer (trade) sales.

Required

Check   Acid-test ratio, 1.6
to 1; Inventory turnover, 15.3

Compute the following: (1) current ratio, (2) acid-test ratio, (3) days' sales uncollected, (4) inventory turnover, (5) days' sales in inventory, (6) debt-to-equity ratio, (7) times interest earned, (8) profit margin ratio, (9) total asset turnover, (10) return on total assets, and (11) return on common stockholders' equity. Round to one decimal place; for part 6, round to two decimals.

Problem 13-5B
Comparative ratio
analysis   **A1**   **P3**

Summary information from the financial statements of two companies competing in the same industry follows.

	Fargo Company	Ball Company		Fargo Company	Ball Company
Data from the current year-end balance sheets			**Data from the current year's income statement**		
Assets			Sales	$393,600	$667,500
Cash	$ 20,000	$ 36,500	Cost of goods sold	290,600	480,000
Accounts receivable, net	77,100	70,500	Interest expense....................	5,900	12,300
Current notes receivable (trade)	11,600	9,000	Income tax expense	5,700	12,300
Merchandise inventory................	86,800	82,000	Net income	33,850	61,700
Prepaid expenses....................	9,700	10,100	Basic earnings per share	1.27	2.19
Plant assets, net	176,900	252,300			
Total assets........................	$382,100	$460,400			
			Beginning-of-year balance sheet data		
Liabilities and Equity			Accounts receivable, net	$ 72,200	$ 73,300
Current liabilities.....................	$ 90,500	$ 97,000	Current notes receivable (trade)	0	0
Long-term notes payable..............	93,000	93,300	Merchandise inventory...............	105,100	80,500
Common stock, $5 par value...........	133,000	141,000	Total assets	383,400	443,000
Retained earnings	65,600	129,100	Common stock, $5 par value	133,000	141,000
Total liabilities and equity.............	$382,100	$460,400	Retained earnings...................	49,100	109,700

Required

1. For both companies compute the (*a*) current ratio, (*b*) acid-test ratio, (*c*) accounts (including notes) receivable turnover, (*d*) inventory turnover, (*e*) days' sales in inventory, and (*f*) days' sales uncollected. Identify the company you consider to be the better short-term credit risk and explain why. Round to one decimal place.

2. For both companies compute the (*a*) profit margin ratio, (*b*) total asset turnover, (*c*) return on total assets, and (*d*) return on common stockholders' equity. Assuming that each company paid cash dividends of $1.50 per share and each company's stock can be purchased at $25 per share, compute their (*e*) price-earnings ratios and (*f*) dividend yields. Round to one decimal place; for part b, round to two decimals. Identify which company's stock you would recommend as the better investment and explain why.

Check (1) Fargo: Accounts receivable turnover, 4.9; Inventory turnover, 3.0

(2) Ball: Profit margin, 9.2%; PE, 11.4

Selected account balances from the adjusted trial balance for Harbor Corp. as of its calendar year-end December 31, 2017, follow.

Problem 13-6B[A]
Income statement computations and format

A2

	Debit	Credit
a. Accumulated depreciation—Buildings		$ 400,000
b. Interest revenue...		20,000
c. Net sales...		2,640,000
d. Income taxes expense...	$?	
e. Loss on hurricane damage	48,000	
f. Accumulated depreciation—Equipment....................................		220,000
g. Other operating expenses..	328,000	
h. Depreciation expense—Equipment	100,000	
i. Loss from settlement of lawsuit	36,000	
j. Gain from settlement of lawsuit		68,000
k. Loss on sale of equipment..	24,000	
l. Loss from operating a discontinued segment (pretax)	120,000	
m. Depreciation expense—Buildings...	156,000	
n. Correction of overstatement of prior year's expense (pretax)		48,000
o. Cost of goods sold...	1,040,000	
p. Loss on sale of discontinued segment's assets (pretax)	180,000	
q. Accounts payable..		132,000

Required

Answer each of the following questions by providing supporting computations.

1. Assume that the company's income tax rate is 25% for all items. Identify the tax effects and after-tax amounts of the three items labeled pretax.

2. What is the amount of income from continuing operations before income taxes? What is the amount of income taxes expense? What is the amount of income from continuing operations?

Check   (3) $(225,000)

3. What is the total amount of after-tax income (loss) associated with the discontinued segment?

(4) $522,000

4. What is the amount of net income for the year?

SERIAL PROBLEM
Business Solutions

P3

© Alexander Image/Shutterstock RF

(This serial problem began in Chapter 1 and continues through most of the book. If previous chapter segments were not completed, the serial problem can begin at this point.)

SP 13   Use the following selected data from **Business Solutions**'s income statement for the three months ended March 31, 2018, and from its March 31, 2018, balance sheet to complete the requirements below: computer services revenue, $25,307; net sales (of goods), $18,693; total sales and revenue, $44,000; cost of goods sold, $14,052; net income, $18,833; quick assets, $90,924; current assets, $95,568; total assets, $120,268; current liabilities, $875; total liabilities, $875; and total equity, $119,393.

Required

1. Compute the gross margin ratio (both with and without services revenue) and net profit margin ratio (round the percent to one decimal).

2. Compute the current ratio and acid-test ratio (round to one decimal).

3. Compute the debt ratio and equity ratio (round the percent to one decimal).

4. What percent of its assets are current? What percent are long term? (Round the percents to one decimal.)

Beyond the Numbers

REPORTING IN ACTION

A1   P1   P2

APPLE

BTN 13-1   Refer to **Apple**'s financial statements in Appendix A to answer the following.

1. Using fiscal 2013 as the base year, compute trend percents for fiscal years 2013, 2014, and 2015 for net sales, cost of sales, operating income, other income (expense) net, provision for income taxes, and net income. (Round percents to one decimal.)

2. Compute common-size percents for fiscal years 2014 and 2015 for the following categories of assets: (*a*) total current assets; (*b*) property, plant and equipment, net; and (*c*) goodwill plus acquired intangible assets, net. (Round percents to one decimal.)

3. Comment on any notable changes across the years for the income statement trends computed in part 1 and the balance sheet percents computed in part 2.

Fast Forward

4. Access Apple's financial statements for fiscal years ending after September 26, 2015, from its website (**Apple.com**) or the SEC database (**SEC.gov**). Update your work for parts 1, 2, and 3 using the new information accessed.

COMPARATIVE ANALYSIS

C2   P2

APPLE

GOOGLE

BTN 13-2   Key figures for **Apple** and **Google** follow.

$ millions	Apple	Google
Cash and equivalents..............	$ 21,120	$ 16,549
Accounts receivable, net	16,849	11,556
Inventories	2,349	0
Retained earnings	92,284	90,892
Cost of sales	140,089	28,164
Revenues	233,715	74,989
Total assets.....................	290,479	147,461

Required

1. Compute common-size percents for each of the companies using the data provided. (Round percents to one decimal.)
2. Which company retains a higher portion of cumulative net income in the company?
3. Which company has a higher gross margin ratio on sales?
4. Which company holds a higher percent of its total assets as inventory?

BTN 13-3   As Beacon Company controller, you are responsible for informing the board of directors about its financial activities. At the board meeting, you present the following information.

	2017	2016	2015
Sales trend percent	147.0%	135.0%	100.0%
Selling expenses to sales.	10.1%	14.0%	15.6%
Sales to plant assets ratio	3.8 to 1	3.6 to 1	3.3 to 1
Current ratio	2.9 to 1	2.7 to 1	2.4 to 1
Acid-test ratio	1.1 to 1	1.4 to 1	1.5 to 1
Inventory turnover	7.8 times	9.0 times	10.2 times
Accounts receivable turnover	7.0 times	7.7 times	8.5 times
Total asset turnover	2.9 times	2.9 times	3.3 times
Return on total assets.	10.4%	11.0%	13.2%
Return on stockholders' equity	10.7%	11.5%	14.1%
Profit margin ratio.	3.6%	3.8%	4.0%

After the meeting, the company's CEO holds a press conference with analysts in which she mentions the following ratios.

	2017	2016	2015
Sales trend percent	147.0%	135.0%	100.0%
Selling expenses to sales.	10.1%	14.0%	15.6%
Sales to plant assets ratio	3.8 to 1	3.6 to 1	3.3 to 1
Current ratio	2.9 to 1	2.7 to 1	2.4 to 1

Required

1. Why do you think the CEO decided to report 4 ratios instead of the 11 prepared?
2. Comment on the possible consequences of the CEO's reporting of the ratios selected.

BTN 13-4   Each team is to select a different industry, and each team member is to select a different company in that industry and acquire its financial statements. Use those statements to analyze the company, including at least one ratio from each of the four building blocks of analysis. When necessary, use the financial press to determine the market price of its stock. Communicate with teammates via a meeting, e-mail, or telephone to discuss how different companies compare to each other and to industry norms. The team is to prepare a single one-page memorandum reporting on its analysis and the conclusions reached.

BTN 13-5   Access the February 26, 2016, filing of the December 31, 2015, 10-K report of **The Hershey Company** (ticker: HSY) at **SEC.gov** and complete the following requirements.

Required

Compute or identify the following profitability ratios of Hershey for its years ending December 31, 2015, *and* December 31, 2014. Interpret its profitability using the results obtained for these two years.

1. Profit margin ratio (round the percent to one decimal).
2. Gross profit ratio (round the percent to one decimal).

Continued on next page . . .

3. Return on total assets (round the percent to one decimal). (Total assets at year-end 2013 were $5,349,724 in thousands.)

4. Return on common stockholders' equity (round the percent to one decimal). (Total shareholders' equity at year-end 2013 was $1,616,052 in thousands.)

5. Basic net income per common share (round to the nearest cent).

TEAMWORK IN ACTION

P1 P2 P3

BTN 13-6   A team approach to learning financial statement analysis is often useful.

Required

1. Each team should write a description of horizontal and vertical analysis that all team members agree with and understand. Illustrate each description with an example.

2. *Each* member of the team is to select *one* of the following categories of ratio analysis. Explain what the ratios in that category measure. Choose one ratio from the category selected, present its formula, and explain what it measures.

Hint: Pairing within teams may be necessary for part 2. Use as an in-class activity or as an assignment. Consider presentations to the entire class using team rotation with slides.

    a. Liquidity and efficiency   **c.** Profitability

    b. Solvency   **d.** Market prospects

3. Each team member is to present his or her notes from part 2 to teammates. Team members are to confirm or correct other teammates' presentations.

ENTREPRENEURIAL DECISION

A1 P1 P2 P3

BTN 13-7   Assume that Carla Harris of **Morgan Stanley** (**MorganStanley.com**) has impressed you with the company's success and its commitment to ethical behavior. You learn of a staff opening at Morgan Stanley and decide to apply for it. Your resume is successfully screened from the thousands received and you advance to the interview process. You learn that the interview consists of analyzing the following financial facts and answering analysis questions below. (The data are taken from a small merchandiser in outdoor recreational equipment.)

	2017	2016	2015
Sales trend percents	137.0%	125.0%	100.0%
Selling expenses to sales	9.8%	13.7%	15.3%
Sales to plant assets ratio	3.5 to 1	3.3 to 1	3.0 to 1
Current ratio	2.6 to 1	2.4 to 1	2.1 to 1
Acid-test ratio	0.8 to 1	1.1 to 1	1.2 to 1
Merchandise inventory turnover	7.5 times	8.7 times	9.9 times
Accounts receivable turnover	6.7 times	7.4 times	8.2 times
Total asset turnover	2.6 times	2.6 times	3.0 times
Return on total assets	8.8%	9.4%	11.1%
Return on equity	9.75%	11.50%	12.25%
Profit margin ratio	3.3%	3.5%	3.7%

Required

Use these data to answer each of the following questions with explanations.

1. Is it becoming easier for the company to meet its current liabilities on time and to take advantage of any available cash discounts? Explain.

2. Is the company collecting its accounts receivable more rapidly? Explain.

3. Is the company's investment in accounts receivable decreasing? Explain.

4. Is the company's investment in plant assets increasing? Explain.

5. Is the owner's investment becoming more profitable? Explain.

6. Did the dollar amount of selling expenses decrease during the three-year period? Explain.

HITTING THE ROAD

C1 P3

BTN 13-8   You are to devise an investment strategy to enable you to accumulate $1,000,000 by age 65. Start by making some assumptions about your salary. Next compute the percent of your salary that you will be able to save each year. If you will receive any lump-sum monies, include those amounts in your calculations. Historically, stocks have delivered average annual returns of around 10%. Given this history, you should probably not assume that you will earn above 10% on the money you invest. It is not necessary to specify exactly what types of assets you will buy for your investments; just assume a rate you expect to earn. Use the future value tables in Appendix B to calculate how your savings will grow. Experiment a bit with your figures to see how much less you have to save if you start at, for example, age 25 versus age 35 or 40. (For this assignment, do not include inflation in your calculations.)

BTN 13-9 Samsung (Samsung.com), a leading manufacturer of consumer electronic products, along with **Apple** and **Google**, are competitors in the global marketplace. Key figures for Samsung follow (in KRW millions).

GLOBAL DECISION

A1

Samsung

APPLE

GOOGLE

Cash and equivalents...............	₩ 22,636,744	Cost of sales	₩123,482,118
Accounts receivable, net	28,520,689	Revenues	200,653,482
Inventories	18,811,794	Total assets......................	242,179,521
Retained earnings	185,132,014		

Required

1. Compute common-size percents for Samsung using the data provided. (Round percents to one decimal.)

2. Compare the results with Apple and Google from BTN 13-2.

GLOBAL VIEW

The analysis and interpretation of financial statements are, of course, impacted by the accounting system in effect. This section discusses similarities and differences for analysis of financial statements when prepared under U.S. GAAP vis-à-vis IFRS.

Horizontal and Vertical Analyses   Horizontal and vertical analyses help eliminate many differences between U.S. GAAP and IFRS when analyzing and interpreting financial statements. Financial numbers are converted to percentages that are, in the best-case scenario, consistently applied across and within periods. This enables users to effectively compare companies across reporting regimes. However, when fundamental differences in reporting regimes impact financial statements, such as with certain recognition rule differences, the user must exercise caution when drawing conclusions. Some users will reformulate one set of numbers to be more consistent with the other system to enable comparative analysis. This reformulation process is covered in advanced courses. The important point is that horizontal and vertical analyses help strip away differences between the reporting regimes, but several key differences sometimes remain and require adjustment of the numbers.

Ratio Analysis   Ratio analysis of financial statement numbers has many of the advantages and disadvantages of horizontal and vertical analyses discussed above. Importantly, ratio analysis is useful for business decisions, with some possible changes in interpretation depending on what is and what is not included in accounting measures across U.S. GAAP and IFRS. Still, we must take care in drawing inferences from a comparison of ratios across reporting regimes because what a number measures can differ across regimes. **Piaggio**, which manufactures two-, three-, and four-wheel vehicles and is Europe's leading manufacturer of motorcycles and scooters, offers the following example of its own ratio analysis applied to its financing objectives: "The object of capital management . . . , [and] consistent with others in the industry, the Company monitors capital on the basis of a total liabilities to equity ratio. This ratio is calculated as total liabilities divided by equity."

 Global View Assignments

Discussion Questions 16 & 17

Quick Study 13-9

Exercise 13-15

BTN 13-9

appendix A

Financial Statement Information

This appendix includes financial information for (1) **Apple**, (2) **Google**, and (3) **Samsung**. Apple states that it designs, manufactures, and markets mobile communication and media devices, personal computers, and portable digital music players, and sells a variety of related software, services, peripherals, networking solutions, and third-party digital content and applications; it competes with both Google and Samsung in the United States and globally. The information in this appendix is taken from their annual 10-K reports (or annual report for Samsung) filed with the SEC or other regulatory agency. An **annual report** is a summary of a company's financial results for the year along with its current financial condition and future plans. This report is directed to external users of financial information, but it also affects the actions and decisions of internal users.

A company often uses an annual report to showcase itself and its products. Many annual reports include photos, diagrams, and illustrations related to the company. The primary objective of annual reports, however, is the financial section, which communicates much information about a company, with most data drawn from the accounting information system. The layout of an annual report's financial section is fairly established and typically includes the following:

- Letter to Shareholders
- Financial History and Highlights
- Management Discussion and Analysis
- Management's Report on Financial Statements and on Internal Controls
- Report of Independent Accountants (Auditor's Report) and on Internal Controls
- Financial Statements
- Notes to Financial Statements
- List of Directors and Officers

This appendix provides the financial statements for Apple (plus selected notes), Google, and Samsung. The appendix is organized as follows:

- **Apple A-2** through **A-9**
- **Google A-10** through **A-13**
- **Samsung A-14** through **A-17**

Many assignments at the end of each chapter refer to information in this appendix. We encourage readers to spend time with these assignments; they are especially useful in showing the relevance and diversity of financial accounting and reporting.

APPLE
GOOGLE
Samsung

Special note: The SEC maintains the EDGAR (**E**lectronic **D**ata **G**athering, **A**nalysis, and **R**etrieval) database at **SEC.gov** for U.S. filers. The **Form 10-K** is the annual report form for most companies. It provides electronically accessible information. The **Form 10-KSB** is the annual report form filed by small businesses. It requires slightly less information than the Form 10-K. One of these forms must be filed within 90 days after the company's fiscal year-end. (Forms 10-K405, 10-KT, 10-KT405, and 10-KSB405 are slight variations of the usual form due to certain regulations or rules.)

APPLE

Apple Inc.
CONSOLIDATED BALANCE SHEETS
(In millions, except number of shares which are reflected in thousands and par value)

	September 26, 2015	September 27, 2014
ASSETS		
Current assets		
Cash and cash equivalents	$ 21,120	$ 13,844
Short-term marketable securities	20,481	11,233
Accounts receivable, less allowances of $82 and $86, respectively	16,849	17,460
Inventories	2,349	2,111
Deferred tax assets	5,546	4,318
Vendor non-trade receivables	13,494	9,759
Other current assets	9,539	9,806
Total current assets	89,378	68,531
Long-term marketable securities	164,065	130,162
Property, plant and equipment, net	22,471	20,624
Goodwill	5,116	4,616
Acquired intangible assets, net	3,893	4,142
Other assets	5,556	3,764
Total assets	$ 290,479	$ 231,839
LIABILITIES AND SHAREHOLDERS' EQUITY		
Current liabilities		
Accounts payable	$ 35,490	$ 30,196
Accrued expenses	25,181	18,453
Deferred revenue	8,940	8,491
Commercial paper	8,499	6,308
Current portion of long-term debt	2,500	0
Total current liabilities	80,610	63,448
Deferred revenue – non-current	3,624	3,031
Long-term debt	53,463	28,987
Other non-current liabilities	33,427	24,826
Total liabilities	171,124	120,292
Commitments and contingencies		
Shareholders' equity		
Common stock and additional paid-in capital, $0.00001 par value: 12,600,000 shares authorized; 5,578,753 and 5,866,161 shares issued and outstanding, respectively	27,416	23,313
Retained earnings	92,284	87,152
Accumulated other comprehensive income	(345)	1,082
Total shareholders' equity	119,355	111,547
Total liabilities and shareholders' equity	$ 290,479	$ 231,839

See accompanying Notes to Consolidated Financial Statements.

Apple Inc.
CONSOLIDATED STATEMENTS OF OPERATIONS
(In millions, except number of shares which are reflected in thousands and per share amounts)

Years ended	September 26, 2015	September 27, 2014	September 28, 2013
Net sales	$ 233,715	$ 182,795	$ 170,910
Cost of sales	140,089	112,258	106,606
Gross margin	93,626	70,537	64,304
Operating expenses			
Research and development	8,067	6,041	4,475
Selling, general and administrative	14,329	11,993	10,830
Total operating expenses	22,396	18,034	15,305
Operating income	71,230	52,503	48,999
Other income, net	1,285	980	1,156
Income before provision for income taxes	72,515	53,483	50,155
Provision for income taxes	19,121	13,973	13,118
Net income	$ 53,394	$ 39,510	$ 37,037
Earnings per share:			
Basic	$ 9.28	$ 6.49	$ 5.72
Diluted	$ 9.22	$ 6.45	$ 5.68
Shares used in computing earnings per share:			
Basic	5,753,421	6,085,572	6,477,320
Diluted	5,793,069	6,122,663	6,521,634
Cash dividends declared per common share	$ 1.98	$ 1.82	$ 1.64

See accompanying Notes to Consolidated Financial Statements.

Apple Inc.
CONSOLIDATED STATEMENTS OF COMPREHENSIVE INCOME
(In millions)

Years ended	September 26, 2015	September 27, 2014	September 28, 2013
Net income	$ 53,394	$ 39,510	$ 37,037
Other comprehensive income (loss):			
Change in foreign currency translation, net of tax effects of $201, $50 and $35, respectively	(411)	(137)	(112)
Change in unrealized gains/losses on derivative instruments:			
Change in fair value of derivatives, net of tax benefit (expense) of $(441), $(297) and $(351), respectively	2,905	1,390	522
Adjustment for net losses (gains) realized and included in net income, net of tax expense (benefit) of $630, $(36) and $255, respectively	(3,497)	149	(458)
Total change in unrecognized gains/losses on derivative instruments, net of tax	(592)	1,539	64
Change in unrealized gains/losses on marketable securities:			
Change in fair value of marketable securities, net of tax benefit (expense) of $264, $(153) and $458, respectively	(483)	285	(791)
Adjustment for net (gains) losses realized and included in net income, net of tax expense (benefit) of $(32), $71 and $82, respectively	59	(134)	(131)
Total change in unrealized gains/losses on marketable securities, net of tax	(424)	151	(922)
Total other comprehensive income (loss)	(1,427)	1,553	(970)
Total comprehensive income	$ 51,967	$ 41,063	$ 36,067

See accompanying Notes to Consolidated Financial Statements.

Apple Inc.
CONSOLIDATED STATEMENTS OF SHAREHOLDERS' EQUITY
(In millions, except number of shares which are reflected in thousands)

	Common Stock and Additional Paid-In Capital		Retained Earnings	Accumulated Other Comprehensive Income (Loss)	Total Shareholders' Equity
	Shares	Amount			
Balances as of September 29, 2012	6,574,458	$ 16,422	$ 101,289	$ 499	$ 118,210
Net income	0	0	37,037	0	37,037
Other comprehensive income (loss)	0	0	0	(970)	(970)
Dividends and dividend equivalents declared	0	0	(10,676)	0	(10,676)
Repurchase of common stock	(328,837)	0	(22,950)	0	(22,950)
Share-based compensation	0	2,253	0	0	2,253
Common stock issued, net of shares withheld for employee taxes	48,873	(143)	(444)	0	(587)
Tax benefit from equity awards, including transfer pricing adjustments	0	1,232	0	0	1,232
Balances as of September 28, 2013	6,294,494	19,764	104,256	(471)	123,549
Net income	0	0	39,510	0	39,510
Other comprehensive income (loss)	0	0	0	1,553	1,553
Dividends and dividend equivalents declared	0	0	(11,215)	0	(11,215)
Repurchase of common stock	(488,677)	0	(45,000)	0	(45,000)
Share-based compensation	0	2,863	0	0	2,863
Common stock issued, net of shares withheld for employee taxes	60,344	(49)	(399)	0	(448)
Tax benefit from equity awards, including transfer pricing adjustments	0	735	0	0	735
Balances as of September 27, 2014	5,866,161	23,313	87,152	1,082	111,547
Net income	0	0	53,394	0	53,394
Other comprehensive income (loss)	0	0	0	(1,427)	(1,427)
Dividends and dividend equivalents declared	0	0	(11,627)	0	(11,627)
Repurchase of common stock	(325,032)	0	(36,026)	0	(36,026)
Share-based compensation	0	3,586	0	0	3,586
Common stock issued, net of shares withheld for employee taxes	37,624	(231)	(609)	0	(840)
Tax benefit from equity awards, including transfer pricing adjustments	0	748	0	0	748
Balances as of September 26, 2015	5,578,753	$ 27,416	$ 92,284	$ (345)	$ 119,355

See accompanying Notes to Consolidated Financial Statements.

APPLE

Apple Inc.
CONSOLIDATED STATEMENTS OF CASH FLOWS
(In millions)

Years ended	September 26, 2015	September 27, 2014	September 28, 2013
Cash and cash equivalents, beginning of the year	$ 13,844	$ 14,259	$ 10,746
Operating activities:			
Net income	53,394	39,510	37,037
Adjustments to reconcile net income to cash generated by operating activities:			
Depreciation and amortization	11,257	7,946	6,757
Share-based compensation expense	3,586	2,863	2,253
Deferred income tax expense	1,382	2,347	1,141
Changes in operating assets and liabilities:			
Accounts receivable, net	611	(4,232)	(2,172)
Inventories	(238)	(76)	(973)
Vendor non-trade receivables	(3,735)	(2,220)	223
Other current and non-current assets	(179)	167	1,080
Accounts payable	5,400	5,938	2,340
Deferred revenue	1,042	1,460	1,459
Other current and non-current liabilities	8,746	6,010	4,521
Cash generated by operating activities	81,266	59,713	53,666
Investing activities:			
Purchases of marketable securities	(166,402)	(217,128)	(148,489)
Proceeds from maturities of marketable securities	14,538	18,810	20,317
Proceeds from sales of marketable securities	107,447	189,301	104,130
Payments made in connection with business acquisitions, net	(343)	(3,765)	(496)
Payments for acquisition of property, plant and equipment	(11,247)	(9,571)	(8,165)
Payments for acquisition of intangible assets	(241)	(242)	(911)
Other	(26)	16	(160)
Cash used in investing activities	(56,274)	(22,579)	(33,774)
Financing activities:			
Proceeds from issuance of common stock	543	730	530
Excess tax benefits from equity awards	749	739	701
Taxes paid related to net share settlement of equity awards	(1,499)	(1,158)	(1,082)
Dividends and dividend equivalents paid	(11,561)	(11,126)	(10,564)
Repurchase of common stock	(35,253)	(45,000)	(22,860)
Proceeds from issuance of term debt, net	27,114	11,960	16,896
Change in commercial paper, net	2,191	6,306	0
Cash used in financing activities	(17,716)	(37,549)	(16,379)
Increase (decrease) in cash and cash equivalents	7,276	(415)	3,513
Cash and cash equivalents, end of the year	$ 21,120	$ 13,844	$ 14,259
Supplemental cash flow disclosure:			
Cash paid for income taxes, net	$ 13,252	$ 10,026	$ 9,128
Cash paid for interest	$ 514	$ 339	$ 0

See accompanying Notes to Consolidated Financial Statements.

APPLE

APPLE INC.
SELECTED NOTES TO CONSOLIDATED FINANCIAL STATEMENTS

Basis of Presentation and Preparation

The Company's fiscal year is the 52 or 53-week period that ends on the last Saturday of September. The Company's fiscal years 2015, 2014 and 2013 ended on September 26, 2015, September 27, 2014 and September 28, 2013, respectively. An additional week is included in the first fiscal quarter approximately every six years to realign fiscal quarters with calendar quarters. Fiscal years 2015, 2014 and 2013 each spanned 52 weeks. Unless otherwise stated, references to particular years, quarters, months and periods refer to the Company's fiscal years ended in September and the associated quarters, months and periods of those fiscal years.

Revenue Recognition

Net sales consist primarily of revenue from the sale of hardware, software, digital content and applications, accessories, and service and support contracts. The Company recognizes revenue when persuasive evidence of an arrangement exists, delivery has occurred, the sales price is fixed or determinable and collection is probable. Product is considered delivered to the customer once it has been shipped and title, risk of loss and rewards of ownership have been transferred. For most of the Company's product sales, these criteria are met at the time the product is shipped. For online sales to individuals, for some sales to education customers in the U.S., and for certain other sales, the Company defers revenue until the customer receives the product because the Company retains a portion of the risk of loss on these sales during transit. For payment terms in excess of the Company's standard payment terms, revenue is recognized as payments become due unless the Company has positive evidence that the sales price is fixed or determinable, such as a successful history of collection, without concession, on comparable arrangements. The Company recognizes revenue from the sale of hardware products, software bundled with hardware that is essential to the functionality of the hardware and third-party digital content sold on the iTunes Store in accordance with general revenue recognition accounting guidance. The Company recognizes revenue in accordance with industry specific software accounting guidance for the following types of sales transactions: (i) standalone sales of software products, (ii) sales of software upgrades and (iii) sales of software bundled with hardware not essential to the functionality of the hardware.

For the sale of most third-party products, the Company recognizes revenue based on the gross amount billed to customers because the Company establishes its own pricing for such products, retains related inventory risk for physical products, is the primary obligor to the customer and assumes the credit risk for amounts billed to its customers. For third-party applications sold through the App Store and Mac App Store and certain digital content sold through the iTunes Store, the Company does not determine the selling price of the products and is not the primary obligor to the customer. Therefore, the Company accounts for such sales on a net basis by recognizing in net sales only the commission it retains from each sale. The portion of the gross amount billed to customers that is remitted by the Company to third-party app developers and certain digital content owners is not reflected in the Company's Consolidated Statements of Operations.

The Company records deferred revenue when it receives payments in advance of the delivery of products or the performance of services. This includes amounts that have been deferred for unspecified and specified software upgrade rights and non-software services that are attached to hardware and software products. The Company sells gift cards redeemable at its retail and online stores, and also sells gift cards redeemable on iTunes Store, App Store, Mac App Store and iBooks Store for the purchase of digital content and software. The Company records deferred revenue upon the sale of the card, which is relieved upon redemption of the card by the customer. Revenue from AppleCare service and support contracts is deferred and recognized over the service coverage periods. AppleCare service and support contracts typically include extended phone support, repair services, web-based support resources and diagnostic tools offered under the Company's standard limited warranty.

The Company records reductions to revenue for estimated commitments related to price protection and other customer incentive programs. For transactions involving price protection, the Company recognizes revenue net of the estimated amount to be refunded. For the Company's other customer incentive programs, the estimated cost of these programs is recognized at the later of the date at which the Company has sold the product or the date at which the program is offered. The Company also records reductions to revenue for expected future product returns based on the Company's historical experience. Revenue is recorded net of taxes collected from customers that are remitted to governmental authorities, with the collected taxes recorded as current liabilities until remitted to the relevant government authority.

Shipping Costs

Amounts billed to customers related to shipping and handling are classified as revenue, and the Company's shipping and handling costs are classified as cost of sales.

Warranty Costs

The Company generally provides for the estimated cost of hardware and software warranties at the time the related revenue is recognized. The Company assesses the adequacy of its accrued warranty liabilities and adjusts the amounts as necessary based on actual experience and changes in future estimates.

Apple Inc. Notes—continued

Software Development Costs

Research and development ("R&D") costs are expensed as incurred. Development costs of computer software to be sold, leased, or otherwise marketed are subject to capitalization beginning when a product's technological feasibility has been established and ending when a product is available for general release to customers. In most instances, the Company's products are released soon after technological feasibility has been established and as a result software development costs were expensed as incurred.

Advertising Costs

Advertising costs are expensed as incurred and included in selling, general and administrative expenses. Advertising expense was $1.8 billion, $1.2 billion and $1.1 billion for 2015, 2014 and 2013, respectively.

Other Income and Expense

$ millions	2015	2014	2013
Interest and dividend income	$2,921	$1,795	$1,616
Interest expense	(733)	(384)	(136)
Other expense, net	(903)	(431)	(324)
Total other income (expense), net	$1,285	$ 980	$1,156

Earnings Per Share

Basic earnings per share is computed by dividing income available to common shareholders by the weighted-average number of shares of common stock outstanding during the period. Diluted earnings per share is computed by dividing income available to common shareholders by the weighted-average number of shares of common stock outstanding during the period increased to include the number of additional shares of common stock that would have been outstanding if the potentially dilutive securities had been issued.

Cash Equivalents and Marketable Securities

All highly liquid investments with maturities of three months or less at the date of purchase are classified as cash equivalents. The Company's marketable debt and equity securities have been classified and accounted for as available-for-sale. Management determines the appropriate classification of its investments at the time of purchase and reevaluates the classifications at each balance sheet date. The Company classifies its marketable debt securities as either short-term or long-term based on each instrument's underlying contractual maturity date. Marketable debt securities with maturities of 12 months or less are classified as short-term and marketable debt securities with maturities greater than 12 months are classified as long-term. Marketable equity securities, including mutual funds, are classified as either short-term or long-term based on the nature of each security and its availability for use in current operations. The Company's marketable debt and equity securities are carried at fair value, with unrealized gains and losses, net of taxes, reported as a component of accumulated other comprehensive income ("AOCI") in shareholders' equity, with the exception of unrealized losses believed to be other-than-temporary which are reported in earnings in the current period. The cost of securities sold is based upon the specific identification method.

Accounts Receivable (Trade Receivables)

The Company has considerable trade receivables outstanding with its third-party cellular network carriers, wholesalers, retailers, value-added resellers, small and mid-sized businesses, and education, enterprise and government customers.

As of September 26, 2015, the Company had one customer that represented 10% or more of total trade receivables, which accounted for 12%. The Company's cellular network carriers accounted for 71% and 72% of trade receivables as of September 26, 2015 and September 27, 2014, respectively.

Allowance for Doubtful Accounts

The Company records its allowance for doubtful accounts based upon its assessment of various factors, including historical experience, age of the accounts receivable balances, credit quality of the Company's customers, current economic conditions and other factors that may affect the customers' ability to pay.

Inventories

Inventories are stated at the lower of cost, computed using the first-in, first-out method and net realizable value. Any adjustments to reduce the cost of inventories to their net realizable value are recognized in earnings in the current period. As of September 26, 2015 and September 27, 2014, the Company's inventories consist primarily of finished goods.

Property, Plant and Equipment

Property, plant and equipment are stated at cost. Depreciation is computed by use of the straight-line method over the estimated useful lives of the assets, which for buildings is the lesser of 30 years or the remaining life of the underlying building; between one to five years for machinery and equipment, including product tooling and manufacturing process equipment; and the shorter of lease terms or ten years for leasehold improvements. The Company capitalizes eligible costs to acquire or develop internal-use software that are incurred subsequent to the preliminary project stage. Capitalized costs related to internal-use software are amortized using the straight-line method over the estimated useful lives of the assets, which range from three to five years. Depreciation and amortization expense on property and equipment was

APPLE

Apple Inc. Notes—continued

$9.2 billion, $6.9 billion and $5.8 billion during 2015, 2014 and 2013, respectively.

Property, Plant and Equipment, Net

$ millions	2015	2014
Land and buildings	$ 6,956	$ 4,863
Machinery, equipment and internal-use software	37,038	29,639
Leasehold improvements	5,263	4,513
Gross property, plant and equipment	49,257	39,015
Accumulated depreciation and amortization	(26,786)	(18,391)
Total property, plant and equipment, net	$ 22,471	$ 20,624

Long-Lived Assets Including Goodwill and Other Acquired Intangible Assets

The Company reviews property, plant and equipment, inventory component prepayments and certain identifiable intangibles, excluding goodwill, for impairment. Long-lived assets are reviewed for impairment whenever events or changes in circumstances indicate the carrying amount of an asset may not be recoverable. Recoverability of these assets is measured by comparison of their carrying amounts to future undiscounted cash flows the assets are expected to generate. If property, plant and equipment, inventory component prepayments and certain identifiable intangibles are considered to be impaired, the impairment to be recognized equals the amount by which the carrying value of the assets exceeds its fair value.

The Company does not amortize goodwill and intangible assets with indefinite useful lives, rather such assets are required to be tested for impairment at least annually or sooner whenever events or changes in circumstances indicate that the assets may be impaired. The Company performs its goodwill and intangible asset impairment tests in the fourth quarter of each year. The Company did not recognize any impairment charges related to goodwill or indefinite lived intangible assets during 2015, 2014 and 2013. The Company established reporting units based on its current reporting structure. For purposes of testing goodwill for impairment, goodwill has been allocated to these reporting units to the extent it relates to each reporting unit. In 2015 and 2014, the Company's goodwill was primarily allocated to the Americas and Europe reporting units.

The Company amortizes its intangible assets with definite useful lives over their estimated useful lives and reviews these assets for impairment. The Company typically amortizes its acquired intangible assets with definite useful lives over periods from three to seven years.

Goodwill and Other Intangible Assets

On July 31, 2014, the Company completed the acquisitions of Beats Music, LLC, which offers a subscription streaming music service, and Beats Electronics, LLC, which makes Beats® headphones, speakers and audio software (collectively, "Beats"). The total purchase price consideration for these acquisitions was $2.6 billion, which

consisted primarily of cash, of which $2.2 billion was allocated to goodwill, $636 million to acquired intangible assets and $258 million to net liabilities assumed. The Company also completed various other business acquisitions during 2014 for an aggregate cash consideration, net of cash acquired, of $957 million, of which $828 million was allocated to goodwill, $257 million to acquired intangible assets and $128 million to net liabilities assumed. The Company's acquired intangible assets with definite useful lives primarily consist of patents and licenses and are amortized over periods typically from three to seven years. The following table summarizes the components of gross and net intangible asset balances as of September 26, 2015:

$ millions	2015		
	Gross Carrying Amount	Accumulated Amortization	Net Carrying Amount
Definite-lived and amortizable acquired intangible assets	$ 8,125	$ (4,332)	$ 3,793
Indefinite-lived and non-amortizable acquired intangible assets	100	0	100
Total acquired intangible assets	$ 8,225	$ (4,332)	$ 3,893

Fair Value Measurements

The Company applies fair value accounting for all financial assets and liabilities and non-financial assets and liabilities that are recognized or disclosed at fair value in the financial statements on a recurring basis. The Company defines fair value as the price that would be received from selling an asset or paid to transfer a liability in an orderly transaction between market participants at the measurement date. When determining the fair value measurements for assets and liabilities, which are required to be recorded at fair value, the Company considers the principal or most advantageous market in which the Company would transact and the market-based risk measurements or assumptions that market participants would use in pricing the asset or liability, such as risks inherent in valuation techniques, transfer restrictions and credit risk. Fair value is estimated by applying the following hierarchy, which prioritizes the inputs used to measure fair value into three levels and bases the categorization within the hierarchy upon the lowest level of input that is available and significant to the fair value measurement:

Level 1—Quoted prices in active markets for identical assets or liabilities.

Level 2—Observable inputs other than quoted prices in active markets for identical assets and liabilities, quoted prices for identical or similar assets or liabilities in inactive markets, or other inputs that are observable or can be corroborated by observable market data for substantially the full term of the assets or liabilities.

Apple Inc. Notes—continued

Level 3—Inputs that are generally unobservable and typically reflect management's estimate of assumptions that market participants would use in pricing the asset or liability.

The Company's valuation techniques used to measure the fair value of money market funds and certain marketable equity securities were derived from quoted prices in active markets for identical assets or liabilities. The valuation techniques used to measure the fair value of the Company's debt instruments and all other financial instruments, all of which have counterparties with high credit ratings, were valued based on quoted market prices or model driven valuations using significant inputs derived from or corroborated by observable market data.

In accordance with the fair value accounting requirements, companies may choose to measure eligible financial instruments and certain other items at fair value. The Company has not elected the fair value option for any eligible financial instruments.

Accrued Warranty and Indemnification

The following table shows changes in the Company's accrued warranties and related costs for 2015 and 2014 (in millions):

	2015	2014
Beginning accrued warranty and related costs	$ 4,159	$ 2,967
Cost of warranty claims	(4,401)	(3,760)
Accruals for product warranty	5,022	4,952
Ending accrued warranty and related costs	$ 4,780	$ 4,159

Long-Term Debt

As of September 26, 2015, the Company had outstanding floating- and fixed-rate notes with varying maturities for an aggregate principal amount of $55.7 billion (collectively the "Notes"). The Notes are senior unsecured obligations, and interest is payable in arrears. The Company recognized $722 million, $381 million and $136 million of interest expense on its term debt for 2015, 2014 and 2013, respectively. As of September 26, 2015 and September 27, 2014, the fair value of the Company's Notes, based on Level 2 inputs, was $54.9 billion and $28.5 billion, respectively.

Dividends

The Company declared and paid cash dividends per share during the periods presented as follows:

	2015		2014	
	Dividends Per Share	Amount (in millions)	Dividends Per Share	Amount (in millions)
Fourth quarter	$ 0.52	$ 2,950	$ 0.47	$ 2,807
Third quarter	0.52	2,997	0.47	2,830
Second quarter	0.47	2,734	0.44	2,655
First quarter	0.47	2,750	0.44	2,739
Total cash dividends declared and paid	$ 1.98	$ 11,431	$ 1.82	$ 11,031

Segment Information and Geographic Data

Net sales by product for 2015, 2014 and 2013 are as follows (in millions):

Net Sales by Product	2015	2014	2013
iPhone	$155,041	$101,991	$ 91,279
iPad	23,227	30,283	31,980
Mac	25,471	24,079	21,483
Services	19,909	18,063	16,051
Other Products	10,067	8,379	10,117
Total net sales	$233,715	$182,795	$170,910

The following table shows information by reportable operating segment for 2015, 2014 and 2013 (in millions):

	2015	2014	2013
Americas:			
Net sales	$93,864	$80,095	$77,093
Operating income	$31,186	$26,158	$24,829
Europe:			
Net sales	$50,337	$44,285	$40,980
Operating income	$16,527	$14,434	$12,767
Greater China:			
Net sales	$58,715	$31,853	$27,016
Operating income	$23,002	$11,039	$ 8,499
Japan:			
Net sales	$15,706	$15,314	$13,782
Operating income	$ 7,617	$ 6,904	$ 6,668
Rest of Asia Pacific:			
Net sales	$15,093	$11,248	$12,039
Operating income	$ 5,518	$ 3,674	$ 3,762

APPLE

Google Inc.
CONSOLIDATED BALANCE SHEETS
(In millions, except share and par value amounts which are reflected in thousands, and par value per share amounts)

As of December 31	2014	2015
Assets		
Current assets		
Cash and cash equivalents	$ 18,347	$ 16,549
Marketable securities	46,048	56,517
Total cash, cash equivalents, and marketable securities (including securities loaned of $4,058 and $4,531)	64,395	73,066
Accounts receivable, net of allowance of $225 and $296	9,383	11,556
Receivable under reverse repurchase agreements	875	450
Income taxes receivable, net	591	1,903
Prepaid revenue share, expenses and other assets	3,412	3,139
Total current assets	78,656	90,114
Prepaid revenue share, expenses and other assets, non-current	3,187	3,181
Non-marketable investments	3,079	5,183
Deferred income taxes	176	251
Property and equipment, net	23,883	29,016
Intangible assets, net	4,607	3,847
Goodwill	15,599	15,869
Total assets	$ 129,187	$ 147,461
Liabilities and Stockholders' Equity		
Current liabilities		
Accounts payable	$ 1,715	$ 1,931
Short-term debt	2,009	3,225
Accrued compensation and benefits	3,069	3,539
Accrued expenses and other current liabilities	4,408	4,768
Accrued revenue share	1,952	2,329
Securities lending payable	2,778	2,428
Deferred revenue	752	788
Income taxes payable, net	96	302
Total current liabilities	16,779	19,310
Long-term debt	3,228	1,995
Deferred revenue, non-current	104	151
Income taxes payable, non-current	3,340	3,663
Deferred income taxes	758	189
Other long-term liabilities	1,118	1,822
Commitments and contingencies (Note 11)		
Stockholders' equity:		
Convertible preferred stock, $0.001 par value per share; 100,000 shares authorized, no shares issued and outstanding; 0.5 shares authorized, no shares issued and outstanding	0	0
Class A and Class B common stock, and Class C capital stock and additional paid-in capital, $0.001 par value per share: 15,000,000 shares authorized (Class A 9,000,000, Class B 3,000,000, Class C 3,000,000); 680,172 (Class A 286,560, Class B 53,213, Class C 340,399), and par value of $680 (Class A $287, Class B $53, Class C $340); and 1.5 shares authorized (Class A 0.5, Class B 0.5, Class C 0.5); 0.3 (Class A 0.1, Class B 0.1, Class C 0.1), and par value of $0, shares issued and outstanding	28,767	31,313
Accumulated other comprehensive income (loss)	27	(1,874)
Retained earnings	75,066	90,892
Total stockholders' equity	103,860	120,331
Total liabilities and stockholders' equity	$ 129,187	$ 147,461

See accompanying notes.

Google Inc.
CONSOLIDATED STATEMENTS OF INCOME
(In millions)

Year Ended December 31	2013	2014	2015
Revenues	$ 55,519	$ 66,001	$ 74,989
Costs and expenses			
Cost of revenues	21,993	25,691	28,164
Research and development	7,137	9,832	12,282
Sales and marketing	6,554	8,131	9,047
General and administrative	4,432	5,851	6,136
Total costs and expenses	40,116	49,505	55,629
Income from operations	15,403	16,496	19,360
Other income (expense), net	496	763	291
Income from continuing operations before income taxes	15,899	17,259	19,651
Provision for income taxes	2,739	3,639	3,303
Net income from continuing operations	$ 13,160	$ 13,620	$ 16,348
Net income (loss) from discontinued operations	(427)	516	0
Net income	$ 12,733	$ 14,136	$ 16,348
Less: Adjustment Payment to Class C capital stockholders	0	0	522
Net income available to all stockholders	$ 12,733	$ 14,136	$ 15,826

See accompanying notes.

Google Inc.
CONSOLIDATED STATEMENTS OF COMPREHENSIVE INCOME
(In millions)

Year Ended December 31	2013	2014	2015
Net income	$ 12,733	$ 14,136	$ 16,348
Other comprehensive income (loss):			
Change in foreign currency translation adjustment	89	(996)	(1,067)
Available-for-sale investments:			
Change in net unrealized gains (losses)	(392)	505	(715)
Less: reclassification adjustment for net (gains) losses included in net income	(162)	(134)	208
Net change (net of tax effect of $212, $60, and $29)	(554)	371	(507)
Cash flow hedges:			
Change in net unrealized gains	112	651	676
Less: reclassification adjustment for net gains included in net income	(60)	(124)	(1,003)
Net change (net of tax effect of $30, $196, and $115)	52	527	(327)
Other comprehensive loss	(413)	(98)	(1,901)
Comprehensive income	$ 12,320	$ 14,038	$ 14,447

See accompanying notes.

Google Inc.
CONSOLIDATED STATEMENTS OF STOCKHOLDERS' EQUITY
(In millions, except share amounts which are reflected in thousands)

	Class A and Class B Common Stock, Class C Capital Stock and Additional Paid-In Capital		Accumulated Other Comprehensive Income (Loss)	Retained Earnings	Total Stockholders' Equity
	Shares	Amount			
Balance as of December 31, 2012	659,958	$ 22,835	$ 538	$ 48,197	$ 71,570
Common stock issued	11,706	1,174	0	0	1,174
Stock-based compensation expense		3,343	0	0	3,343
Stock-based compensation tax benefits		449	0	0	449
Tax withholding related to vesting of restricted stock units		(1,879)	0	0	(1,879)
Net income		0	0	12,733	12,733
Other comprehensive loss		0	(413)	0	(413)
Balance as of December 31, 2013	671,664	25,922	125	60,930	86,977
Common and capital stock issued	8,508	465	0	0	465
Stock-based compensation expense		4,279	0	0	4,279
Stock-based compensation tax benefits		625	0	0	625
Tax withholding related to vesting of restricted stock units		(2,524)	0	0	(2,524)
Net income		0	0	14,136	14,136
Other comprehensive loss		0	(98)	0	(98)
Balance as of December 31, 2014	680,172	28,767	27	75,066	103,860
Common and capital stock issued	6,659	331	0	0	331
Stock-based compensation expense		5,151	0	0	5,151
Stock-based compensation tax benefits		815	0	0	815
Tax withholding related to vesting of restricted stock units		(1,954)	0	0	(1,954)
Alphabet share exchange	(687,684)	0	0	0	0
Capital transactions with Alphabet		(2,272)	0	0	(2,272)
Adjustment Payment to Class C capital stockholders	853	475	0	(522)	(47)
Net income		0	0	16,348	16,348
Other comprehensive loss		0	(1,901)	0	(1,901)
Balance as of December 31, 2015	0	$ 31,313	$ (1,874)	$ 90,892	$ 120,331

See accompanying notes.

GOOGLE

Google Inc.
CONSOLIDATED STATEMENTS OF CASH FLOWS
(In millions)

Year Ended December 31	2013	2014	2015
Operating activities			
Net income	$ 12,733	$ 14,136	$ 16,348
Adjustments:			
Depreciation and impairment of property and equipment	2,781	3,523	4,132
Amortization and impairment of intangible assets	1,158	1,456	931
Stock-based compensation expense	3,343	4,279	5,203
Excess tax benefits from stock-based award activities	(481)	(648)	(548)
Deferred income taxes	(437)	(104)	(179)
Gain on divestiture of business	(700)	(740)	0
(Gain) loss on marketable and non-marketable investments, net	(166)	(390)	334
Other	272	192	212
Changes in assets and liabilities, net of effects of acquisitions:			
Accounts receivable	(1,307)	(1,641)	(2,094)
Income taxes, net	588	591	(179)
Prepaid revenue share, expenses and other assets	(930)	459	(318)
Accounts payable	605	436	203
Accrued expenses and other liabilities	713	757	1,597
Accrued revenue share	254	245	339
Deferred revenue	233	(175)	43
Net cash provided by operating activities	18,659	22,376	26,024
Investing activities			
Purchases of property and equipment	(7,358)	(10,959)	(9,915)
Purchases of marketable securities	(45,444)	(56,310)	(74,368)
Maturities and sales of marketable securities	38,314	51,315	62,905
Purchases of non-marketable investments	(569)	(1,227)	(2,172)
Cash collateral related to securities lending	(299)	1,403	(350)
Investments in reverse repurchase agreements	600	(775)	425
Proceeds from divestiture of business	2,525	386	0
Acquisitions, net of cash acquired, and purchases of intangibles and other assets	(1,448)	(4,888)	(236)
Net cash used in investing activities	(13,679)	(21,055)	(23,711)
Financing activities			
Net payments related to stock-based award activities	(781)	(2,069)	(1,612)
Excess tax benefits from stock-based award activities	481	648	548
Adjustment Payment to Class C capital stockholders	0	0	(47)
Capital transactions with Alphabet	0	0	(2,543)
Proceeds from issuance of debt, net of costs	10,768	11,625	13,705
Repayments of debt	(11,325)	(11,643)	(13,728)
Net cash used in financing activities	(857)	(1,439)	(3,677)
Effect of exchange rate changes on cash and cash equivalents	(3)	(433)	(434)
Net increase (decrease) in cash and cash equivalents	4,120	(551)	(1,798)
Cash and cash equivalents at beginning of period	14,778	18,898	18,347
Cash and cash equivalents at end of period	$ 18,898	$ 18,347	$ 16,549
Supplemental disclosures of cash flow information			
Cash paid for taxes	$ 1,932	$ 2,819	$ 3,338
Cash paid for interest	72	86	96

See accompanying notes.

Samsung Electronics Co., Ltd. and Subsidiaries
CONSOLIDATED STATEMENTS OF FINANCIAL POSITION

(In millions of Korean won)	December 31, 2015	December 31, 2014
	KRW	KRW
Assets		
Current assets		
Cash and cash equivalents	22,636,744	16,840,766
Short-term financial instruments	44,228,800	41,689,776
Short-term available-for-sale financial assets	4,627,530	3,286,798
Trade receivables	25,168,026	24,694,610
Non-trade receivables	3,352,663	3,539,875
Advances	1,706,003	1,989,470
Prepaid expenses	3,170,632	3,346,593
Inventories	18,811,794	17,317,504
Other current assets	1,035,460	1,795,143
Assets held-for-sale	77,073	645,491
Total current assets	124,814,725	115,146,026
Non-current assets		
Long-term available-for-sale financial assets	8,332,480	12,667,509
Investment in associates and joint ventures	5,276,348	5,232,461
Property, plant and equipment	86,477,110	80,872,950
Intangible assets	5,396,311	4,785,473
Long-term prepaid expenses	4,294,401	4,857,126
Deferred income tax assets	5,589,108	4,526,595
Other non-current assets	1,999,038	2,334,818
Total assets	242,179,521	230,422,958
Liabilities and Equity		
Current liabilities		
Trade and other payables	6,187,291	7,914,704
Short-term borrowings	11,155,425	8,029,299
Other payables	8,864,378	10,318,407
Advances received	1,343,432	1,427,230
Withholdings	992,733	1,161,635
Accrued expenses	11,628,739	12,876,777
Income tax payable	3,401,625	2,161,109
Current portion of long-term liabilities	221,548	1,778,667
Provisions	6,420,603	5,991,510
Other current liabilities	287,135	326,259
Liabilities held-for-sale	—	28,316
Total current liabilities	50,502,909	52,013,913
Non-current liabilities		
Debentures	1,230,448	1,355,882
Long-term borrowings	266,542	101,671
Long-term other payables	3,041,687	2,562,271
Net defined benefit liabilities	358,820	201,342
Deferred income tax liabilities	5,154,792	4,097,811
Provisions	522,378	499,290
Other non-current liabilities	2,042,140	1,502,590
Total liabilities	63,119,716	62,334,770
Equity attributable to owners of the parent		
Preferred stock	119,467	119,467
Common stock	778,047	778,047
Share premium	4,403,893	4,403,893
Retained earnings	185,132,014	169,529,604
Other components of equity	(17,580,451)	(12,729,387)
Accumulated other comprehensive income attributable to assets held-for-sale	23,797	80,101
	172,876,767	162,181,725
Non-controlling interests	6,183,038	5,906,463
Total equity	179,059,805	168,088,188
Total liabilities and equity	242,179,521	230,422,958

The accompanying notes are an integral part of these consolidated financial statements.

Samsung Electronics Co., Ltd. and Subsidiaries
CONSOLIDATED STATEMENTS OF INCOME

For the year ended December 31	2015	2014
(In millions of Korean won)	KRW	KRW
Revenue	200,653,482	206,205,987
Cost of sales	123,482,118	128,278,800
Gross profit	77,171,364	77,927,187
Selling and administrative expenses	50,757,922	52,902,116
Operating profit	26,413,442	25,025,071
Other non-operating income	1,685,947	3,801,357
Other non-operating expense	3,723,434	2,259,737
Share of profit of associates and joint ventures	1,101,932	342,516
Financial income	10,514,879	8,259,829
Financial expense	10,031,771	7,294,002
Profit before income tax	25,960,995	27,875,034
Income tax expense	6,900,851	4,480,676
Profit for the year	19,060,144	23,394,358
Profit attributable to owners of the parent	18,694,628	23,082,499
Profit attributable to non-controlling interests	365,516	311,859
Earnings per share for profit attributable to owners of the parent		
—Basic	126,305	153,105
—Diluted	126,303	153,096

Samsung Electronics Co., Ltd. and Subsidiaries
CONSOLIDATED STATEMENTS OF COMPREHENSIVE INCOME

For the year ended December 31	2015	2014
(In millions of Korean won)	KRW	KRW
Profit for the year	19,060,144	23,394,358
Other comprehensive loss		
Items not to be reclassified to profit or loss subsequently:		
Remeasurement of net defined benefit liabilities, net of tax	263,978	(710,318)
Items to be reclassified to profit or loss subsequently:		
Changes in value of available-for-sale financial assets, net of tax	(414,961)	(232,105)
Share of other comprehensive income (loss) of associates and joint ventures, net of tax	(41,261)	(128,932)
Foreign currency translation, net of tax	268,315	(922,059)
Other comprehensive income (loss) for the year, net of tax	76,071	(1,993,414)
Total comprehensive income for the year	19,136,215	21,400,944
Comprehensive income attributable to:		
Owners of the parent	18,804,189	20,990,732
Non-controlling interests	332,026	410,212

The accompanying notes are an integral part of these consolidated financial statements.

SAMSUNG

Samsung Electronics Co., Ltd. and Subsidiaries
CONSOLIDATED STATEMENTS OF CHANGES IN EQUITY

(In millions of Korean won)	Preferred stock	Common stock	Share premium	Retained earnings	Other components of equity	Accumulated other comprehensive income attributable to assets held-for-sale	Equity attributable to owners of the parent	Non-controlling interests	Total
Balance as at January 1, 2014	119,467	778,047	4,403,893	148,600,282	(9,459,073)	—	144,442,616	5,573,394	150,016,010
Profit for the year	—	—	—	23,082,499	—	—	23,082,499	311,859	23,394,358
Changes in value of available-for-sale financial assets, net of tax	—	—	—	—	(314,069)	—	(314,069)	81,964	(232,105)
Share of other comprehensive income (loss) of associates and joint ventures, net of tax	—	—	—	—	(128,495)	—	(128,495)	(437)	(128,932)
Foreign currency translation, net of tax	—	—	—	—	(954,999)	—	(954,999)	32,940	(922,059)
Remeasurement of net defined benefit liabilities, net of tax	—	—	—	—	(694,204)	—	(694,204)	(16,114)	(710,318)
Classified as held-for-sale	—	—	—	—	(80,101)	80,101	—	—	—
Total comprehensive income (loss)	—	—	—	23,082,499	(2,171,868)	80,101	20,990,732	410,212	21,400,944
Dividends	—	—	—	(2,157,011)	—	—	(2,157,011)	(74,216)	(2,231,227)
Capital transaction under common control	—	—	—	—	(158)	—	(158)	244	86
Changes in consolidated entities	—	—	—	—	—	—	—	569	569
Acquisition of treasury stock	—	—	—	—	(1,125,322)	—	(1,125,322)	—	(1,125,322)
Disposal of treasury stock	—	—	—	—	32,764	—	32,764	—	32,764
Stock option activities	—	—	—	—	(9,436)	—	(9,436)	—	(9,436)
Others	—	—	—	3,834	3,706	—	7,540	(3,740)	3,800
Total transactions with owners	—	—	—	(2,153,177)	(1,098,446)	—	(3,251,623)	(77,143)	(3,328,766)
Balance as at December 31, 2014	119,467	778,047	4,403,893	169,529,604	(12,729,387)	80,101	162,181,725	5,906,463	168,088,188
Profit for the year	—	—	—	18,694,628	—	—	18,694,628	365,516	19,060,144
Changes in value of available-for-sale financial assets, net of tax	—	—	—	—	(348,068)	(24,750)	(372,818)	(42,143)	(414,961)
Share of other comprehensive income (loss) of associates and joint ventures, net of tax	—	—	—	—	12,686	(54,118)	(41,432)	171	(41,261)
Foreign currency translation, net of tax	—	—	—	—	266,061	(1,233)	264,828	3,487	268,315
Remeasurement of net defined benefit liabilities, net of tax	—	—	—	—	258,983	—	258,983	4,995	263,978
Classified as held-for-sale	—	—	—	—	(23,797)	23,797	—	—	—
Total comprehensive income (loss)	—	—	—	18,694,628	165,865	(56,304)	18,804,189	332,026	19,136,215
Dividends	—	—	—	(3,073,481)	—	—	(3,073,481)	(54,603)	(3,128,084)
Capital transaction under common control	—	—	—	—	(5,314)	—	(5,314)	423	(4,891)
Changes in consolidated entities	—	—	—	—	—	—	—	(152)	(152)
Acquisition of treasury stock	—	—	—	—	(5,015,112)	—	(5,015,112)	—	(5,015,112)
Disposal of treasury stock	—	—	—	—	3,406	—	3,406	—	3,406
Stock option activities	—	—	—	—	(806)	—	(806)	—	(806)
Others	—	—	—	(18,737)	897	—	(17,840)	(1,119)	(18,959)
Total transactions with owners	—	—	—	(3,092,218)	(5,016,929)	—	(8,109,147)	(55,451)	(8,164,598)
Balance as at December 31, 2015	119,467	778,047	4,403,893	185,132,014	(17,580,451)	23,797	172,876,767	6,183,038	179,059,805

The accompanying notes are an integral part of these consolidated financial statements.

SAMSUNG

Samsung Electronics Co., Ltd. and Subsidiaries
CONSOLIDATED STATEMENTS OF CASH FLOWS

For the year ended December 31	2015	2014
(In millions of Korean won)	KRW	KRW
Cash flows from operating activities		
Profit for the period	19,060,144	23,394,358
Adjustments	29,610,971	22,323,765
Changes in assets and liabilities arising from operating activities	(4,682,032)	(3,837,136)
Cash generated from operations	43,989,083	41,880,987
Interest received	2,151,741	1,555,373
Interest paid	(748,256)	(463,740)
Dividend received	266,369	1,495,658
Income tax paid	(5,597,176)	(7,492,889)
Net cash generated from operating activities	**40,061,761**	**36,975,389**
Cash flows from investing activities		
Net increase in short-term financial instruments	(5,762,783)	(1,110,842)
Proceeds from disposal of short-term available-for-sale financial assets	2,143,384	1,954,158
Acquisition of short-term available-for-sale financial assets	(509,349)	(2,667,610)
Proceeds from disposal of long-term financial instruments	3,999,710	94,089
Acquisition of long-term financial instruments	(132,733)	(3,248,374)
Proceeds from disposal of long-term available-for-sale financial assets	200,502	202,904
Acquisition of long-term available-for-sale financial assets	(232,530)	(6,212,102)
Proceeds from disposal of associates and joint ventures	278,009	2,014,430
Acquisition of associates and joint ventures	(137,917)	(719,800)
Disposal of property, plant and equipment	357,154	385,610
Purchases of property, plant and equipment	(25,880,222)	(22,042,943)
Disposal of intangible assets	1,083	31,731
Purchases of intangible assets	(1,501,881)	(1,324,307)
Cash outflows from business combinations	(411,445)	(176,625)
Others	421,231	13,273
Net cash used in investing activities	**(27,167,787)**	**(32,806,408)**
Cash flows from financing activities		
Net increase in short-term borrowings	3,202,416	1,833,419
Acquisition of treasury stock	(5,015,112)	(1,125,322)
Disposal of treasury stock	3,034	27,582
Proceeds from long-term borrowings and debentures	192,474	1,740,573
Repayment of long-term borrowings and debentures	(1,801,465)	(3,299,595)
Payment of dividends	(3,129,544)	(2,233,905)
Net increase in non-controlling interests	(25,312)	139
Net cash generated(used) in financing activities	**(6,573,509)**	**(3,057,109)**
Effect of exchange rate changes on cash and cash equivalents	(524,487)	(555,886)
Net increase(decrease) in cash and cash equivalents	**5,795,978**	**555,986**
Cash and cash equivalents		
Beginning of the period	16,840,766	16,284,780
End of the period	22,636,744	16,840,766

The accompanying notes are an integral part of these consolidated financial statements.

SAMSUNG

B appendix

Time Value of Money

Appendix Preview

PRESENT AND FUTURE VALUE CONCEPTS

C1 Time is money

Concept of interest

VALUE OF A SINGLE AMOUNT

P1 Present value of a single amount

P2 Future value of a single amount

NTK B-1, B-2

VALUE OF AN ANNUITY

P3 Present value of an annuity

P4 Future value of an annuity

NTK B-3, B-4

Learning Objectives

CONCEPTUAL

C1 Describe the earning of interest and the concepts of present and future values.

PROCEDURAL

P1 Apply present value concepts to a single amount by using interest tables.

P2 Apply future value concepts to a single amount by using interest tables.

P3 Apply present value concepts to an annuity by using interest tables.

P4 Apply future value concepts to an annuity by using interest tables.

PRESENT AND FUTURE VALUE CONCEPTS

The old saying "Time is money" means that as time passes, the values of assets and liabilities change. This change is due to *interest,* which is a borrower's payment to the owner of an asset for its use. The most common example of interest is a savings account. Cash in the account earns interest paid by the financial institution. An example of a liability is a car loan. As we carry the balance of the loan, we accumulate interest costs on it. We must ultimately repay this loan with interest.

Present and future value computations enable us to measure or estimate the interest component of holding assets or liabilities over time. The present value computation is used to compute the value of future-day assets *today.* The future value computation is used to compute the value of present-day assets *at a future date.* The first section focuses on the present value of a single amount. The second section focuses on the future value of a single amount. Then both the present and future values of a series of amounts (called an *annuity*) are defined and explained.

C1_____

Describe the earning of interest and the concepts of present and future values.

■ **Decision** Insight ▬▬▬▬▬▬▬▬▬▬▬▬▬▬▬▬▬▬▬▬▬▬▬▬▬▬▬▬▬▬▬ ♟

What's Five Million Worth?   A maintenance worker duped out of a $5 million scratch-off ticket got his winnings seven years later. Robert Miles bought the ticket in 2006 at a convenience store where the owner and his two sons convinced Miles the ticket was worth $5,000 and paid him $4,000 for it. The brothers waited until 2012 to claim the jackpot, prompting an investigation, which uncovered the fraud. The $5 million will be paid to Miles as a $250,000 annuity from 2014 to 2033 or as a lump-sum payment of $3,210,000, which is about $2,124,378 after taxes. ■

PRESENT VALUE OF A SINGLE AMOUNT

Graph of PV of a Single Amount   We graphically express the present value, called *p,* of a single future amount, called *f,* that is received or paid at a future date in Exhibit B.1.

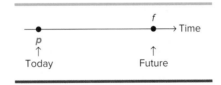

EXHIBIT B.1

Present Value of a Single Amount Diagram

Formula of PV of a Single Amount   The formula to compute the present value of a single amount is shown in Exhibit B.2, where p = present value (PV); f = future value (FV); i = rate of interest per period; and n = number of periods. (Interest is also called the *discount,* and an interest rate is also called the *discount rate.*)

$$p = \frac{f}{(1 + i)^n}$$

P1_____

Apply present value concepts to a single amount by using interest tables.

EXHIBIT B.2

Present Value of a Single Amount Formula

Illustration of PV of a Single Amount for One Period   To illustrate present value concepts, assume that we need $220 one period from today. We want to know how much we must invest now, for one period, at an interest rate of 10% to provide for this $220. For this illustration, the *p,* or present value, is the unknown amount—the specifics are shown graphically as follows:

Conceptually, we know *p* must be less than $220. This is clear from the answer to: Would we rather have $220 today or $220 at some future date? If we had $220 today, we could invest it and see it grow to something more than $220 in the future. Therefore, we would prefer the $220 today. This means that if we were promised $220 in the future, we would take less than $220 today. But how much less? To answer that question, we compute an estimate of the present value of the $220 to be received one period from now using the formula in Exhibit B.2 as follows:

$$p = \frac{f}{(1+i)^n} = \frac{\$220}{(1+0.10)^1} = \$200$$

We interpret this result to say that given an interest rate of 10%, we are indifferent between $200 today or $220 at the end of one period.

Illustration of PV of a Single Amount for Multiple Periods

We can use this formula to compute the present value for *any number of periods*. To illustrate, consider a payment of $242 at the end of two periods at 10% interest. The present value of this $242 to be received two periods from now is computed as follows:

$$p = \frac{f}{(1+i)^n} = \frac{\$242}{(1+0.10)^2} = \$200$$

Together, these results tell us we are indifferent between $200 today, or $220 one period from today, or $242 two periods from today given a 10% interest rate per period.

The number of periods (n) in the present value formula does not have to be expressed in years. Any period of time such as a day, a month, a quarter, or a year can be used. Whatever period is used, the interest rate (i) must be compounded for the same period. This means that if a situation expresses n in months and i equals 12% per year, then i is transformed into interest earned per month (or 1%). In this case, interest is said to be *compounded monthly*. For example, the present value of $1 when n is 12 months and i is 12% compounded monthly follows:

$$p = \frac{1}{(1+0.01)^{12}} = \$0.8874$$

Point: Excel for PV.

	A	B
1	Future value	$242
2	Periods	2
3	Period int. rate	10%
4	Present value	

=PV(B3,B2,0,−B1) = $200

I will pay your allowance at the end of the month. Do you want to wait or receive its present value today?

Using Present Value Table to Compute PV of a Single Amount

A present value table helps us with present value computations. It gives us present values (factors) for a variety of both interest rates (i) and periods (n). Each present value in a present value table assumes that the future value (f) equals 1. When the future value (f) is different from 1, we simply multiply the present value (p) from the table by that future value to give us the estimate. The formula used to construct a table of present values for a single future amount of 1 is shown in Exhibit B.3.

EXHIBIT B.3

Present Value of 1 Formula

$$p = \frac{1}{(1+i)^n}$$

This formula is identical to that in Exhibit B.2 except that f equals 1. Table B.1 at the end of this appendix is such a present value table. It is often called a **present value of 1 table**. A present value table has three factors: p, i, and n. Knowing two of these three factors allows us to compute the third. (A fourth is f, but as already explained, we need only multiply the 1 used in the formula by f.) To illustrate the use of a present value table, consider three cases.

Case 1 **Solve for p when knowing i and n.** To show how we use a present value table, let's look again at how we estimate the present value of $220 (the f value) at the end of one period ($n = 1$) where the interest rate (i) is 10%. To solve this case, we go to the present value table (Table B.1) and look in the row for one period and in the column for 10% interest. Here we find a present value (p) of 0.9091 based on a future value of 1. This means, for instance, that $1 to be received one period from today at 10% interest is worth $0.9091 today. Because the future value in this case is not $1 but $220, we multiply the 0.9091 by $220 to get an answer of $200.

Case 2 **Solve for n when knowing p and i.** To illustrate, assume a $100,000 future value ($f$) that is worth $13,000 today ($p$) using an interest rate of 12% (i) but where n is unknown. In particular, we want to know how many periods (n) there are between the present value and the future value. To put this in context, it would fit a situation in which we want to retire with $100,000 but currently have only $13,000 that is earning a 12% return and we are unable to save additional money. How long will it be before we can retire? To answer this, we go to Table B.1 and look in the 12% interest column. Here we find a column of present values (p) based on a future value of 1. To use the present value table for this solution, we must divide $13,000 ($p$) by $100,000 ($f$), which equals 0.1300. This is necessary because *a present value table defines* f *equal to 1, and* p *as a fraction of 1.* We look for a value nearest to 0.1300 (p), which we find in the row for 18 periods (n). This means that the present value of $100,000 at the end of 18 periods at 12% interest is $13,000; alternatively stated, we must work 18 more years.

Case 3 **Solve for *i* when knowing *p* and *n*.** In this case, we have, say, a $120,000 future value ($f$) worth $60,000 today ($p$) when there are nine periods (n) between the present and future values, but the interest rate is unknown. As an example, suppose we want to retire with $120,000 in nine years, but we have only $60,000 and we are unable to save additional money. What interest rate must we earn to retire with $120,000 in nine years? To answer this, we go to the present value table (Table B.1) and look in the row for nine periods. To use the present value table, we must divide $60,000 ($p$) by $120,000 ($f$), which equals 0.5000. Recall that this step is necessary because a present value table defines f equal to 1 and p as a fraction of 1. We look for a value in the row for nine periods that is nearest to 0.5000 (p), which we find in the column for 8% interest (i). This means that the present value of $120,000 at the end of nine periods at 8% interest is $60,000 or, in our example, we must earn 8% annual interest to retire in nine years.

A company is considering an investment expected to yield $70,000 after six years. If this company demands an 8% return, how much is it willing to pay for this investment today?

NEED-TO-KNOW B-1

Present Value of
a Single Amount

Solution

Today's value = $70,000 × 0.6302 = $44,114 (using PV factor from Table B.1, $i = 8\%$, $n = 6$)

P1

FUTURE VALUE OF A SINGLE AMOUNT

Formula of FV of a Single Amount   We must modify the formula for the present value of a single amount to obtain the formula for the future value of a single amount. In particular, we multiply both sides of the equation in Exhibit B.2 by $(1 + i)^n$ to get the result shown in Exhibit B.4.

$$f = p \times (1 + i)^n$$

Illustration of FV of a Single Amount for One Period   The future value (f) is defined in terms of p, i, and n. We can use this formula to determine that $200 ($p$) invested for one ($n$) period at an interest rate of 10% (i) yields a future value of $220 as follows:

$$f = p \times (1 + i)^n$$
$$= \$200 \times (1 + 0.10)^1$$
$$= \$220$$

Illustration of FV of a Single Amount for Multiple Periods   This formula can be used to compute the future value of an amount for *any number of periods* into the future. To illustrate, assume that $200 is invested for three periods at 10%. The future value of this $200 is $266.20, computed as follows:

$$f = p \times (1 + i)^n$$
$$= \$200 \times (1 + 0.10)^3$$
$$= \$200 \times 1.3310$$
$$= \$266.20$$

P2

Apply future value concepts to a single amount by using interest tables.

EXHIBIT B.4

Future Value of a Single Amount Formula

Point: The FV factor in Table B.2 when $n = 3$ and $i = 10\%$ is 1.3310.

Point: Excel for FV.

	A	B
1	Present value	$200
2	Periods	3
3	Period int. rate	10%
4	Future value	

=FV(B3,B2,0,−B1) = $266.20

Using Future Value Table to Compute FV of a Single Amount   A future value table makes it easier for us to compute future values (f) for many different combinations of interest rates (i) and time periods (n). Each future value in a future value table assumes the present value (p) is 1. If the future amount is something other than 1, we multiply our answer by that amount. The formula used to construct a table of future values (factors) for a single amount of 1 is in Exhibit B.5.

EXHIBIT B.5

Future Value of 1 Formula

$$f = (1 + i)^n$$

Table B.2 at the end of this appendix shows a table of future values for a current amount of 1. This type of table is called a **future value of 1 table**.

There are some important relations between Tables B.1 and B.2. In Table B.2, for the row where $n = 0$, the future value is 1 for each interest rate. This is so because no interest is earned when time does not pass. We also see that Tables B.1 and B.2 report the same information but in a different manner. In particular, one table is simply the *reciprocal* of the other. To illustrate this inverse relation, let's say we invest $100 for a period of five years at 12% per year. How much do we expect to have after five years? We can answer this question using Table B.2 by finding the future value (f) of 1, for five periods from now, compounded at 12%. From that table we find $f = 1.7623$. If we start with $100, the amount it accumulates to after five years is $176.23 ($100 × 1.7623). We can alternatively use Table B.1. Here we find that the present value (p) of 1, discounted five periods at 12%, is 0.5674. Recall the inverse relation between present value and future value. This means that $p = 1/f$ (or equivalently, $f = 1/p$). We can compute the future value of $100 invested for five periods at 12% as follows: $f = $100 × (1/0.5674) = $176.24 (which equals the $176.23 just computed, except for a 1 cent rounding difference).

A future value table has three factors: f, i, and n. Knowing two of these three factors allows us to compute the third. To illustrate, consider three possible cases.

Point:
1/PV factor = FV factor.
1/FV factor = PV factor.

Point: The FV factor when $n = 2$ and $i = 10\%$, is 1.2100. Its reciprocal, 0.8264, is the PV factor when $n = 2$ and $i = 10\%$.

Case 1   Solve for f when knowing i and n. Our preceding example fits this case. We found that $100 invested for five periods at 12% interest accumulates to $176.24.

Case 2   Solve for n when knowing f and i. In this case, we have, say, $2,000 ($p$) and we want to know how many periods (n) it will take to accumulate to $3,000 ($f$) at 7% interest ($i$). To answer this, we go to the future value table (Table B.2) and look in the 7% interest column. Here we find a column of future values (f) based on a present value of 1. To use a future value table, we must divide $3,000 ($f$) by $2,000 ($p$), which equals 1.500. This is necessary because *a future value table defines* p *equal to 1, and* f *as a multiple of 1*. We look for a value nearest to 1.50 (f), which we find in the row for six periods (n). This means that $2,000 invested for six periods at 7% interest accumulates to $3,000.

Case 3   Solve for i when knowing f and n. In this case, we have, say, $2,001 ($p$), and in nine years ($n$) we want to have $4,000 ($f$). What rate of interest must we earn to accomplish this? To answer that, we go to Table B.2 and search in the row for nine periods. To use a future value table, we must divide $4,000 ($f$) by $2,001 ($p$), which equals 1.9990. Recall that this is necessary because a future value table defines p equal to 1 and f as a multiple of 1. We look for a value nearest to 1.9990 (f), which we find in the column for 8% interest (i). This means that $2,001 invested for nine periods at 8% interest accumulates to $4,000.

NEED-TO-KNOW B-2

Future Value of a Single Amount

P2

Assume that you win a $150,000 cash sweepstakes today. You decide to deposit this cash in an account earning 8% annual interest, and you plan to quit your job when the account equals $555,000. How many years will it be before you can quit working?

Solution

Future value factor = $555,000/$150,000 = 3.7000

Searching for 3.7 in the 8% column of Table B.2 shows you cannot quit working for <u>17 years</u> if your deposit earns 8% interest.

PRESENT VALUE OF AN ANNUITY

Graph of PV of an Annuity   An *annuity* is a series of equal payments occurring at equal intervals. One example is a series of three annual payments of $100 each. An *ordinary annuity* is defined as equal end-of-period payments at equal intervals. An ordinary annuity of $100 for three periods and its present value (*p*) are illustrated in Exhibit B.6.

P3

Apply present value concepts to an annuity by using interest tables.

EXHIBIT B.6

Present Value of an Ordinary Annuity Diagram

```
                    $100           $100           $100
        ●───────────●──────────────●──────────────●──────→ Time
        p           ↑              ↑              ↑
        ↑
       Today    Future (n = 1)  Future (n = 2)  Future (n = 3)
```

Formula and Illustration of PV of an Annuity   One way to compute the present value of an ordinary annuity is to find the present value of each payment using our present value formula from Exhibit B.3. We then add each of the three present values. To illustrate, let's look at three $100 payments at the end of each of the next three periods with an interest rate of 15%. Our present value computations are

$$p = \frac{\$100}{(1 + 0.15)^1} + \frac{\$100}{(1 + 0.15)^2} + \frac{\$100}{(1 + 0.15)^3} = \$228.32$$

Using Present Value Table to Compute PV of an Annuity   This computation is identical to computing the present value of each payment (from Table B.1) and taking their sum or, alternatively, adding the values from Table B.1 for each of the three payments and multiplying their sum by the $100 annuity payment.

A more direct way is to use a present value of annuity table. Table B.3 at the end of this appendix is one such table. This table is called a **present value of an annuity of 1 table**. If we look at Table B.3 where *n* = 3 and *i* = 15%, we see the present value is 2.2832. This means that the present value of an annuity of 1 for three periods, with a 15% interest rate, equals 2.2832.

A present value of an annuity formula is used to construct Table B.3. It can also be constructed by adding the amounts in a present value of 1 table. To illustrate, we use Tables B.1 and B.3 to confirm this relation for the prior example.

From Table B.1		From Table B.3	
i = 15%, *n* = 1	0.8696		
i = 15%, *n* = 2	0.7561		
i = 15%, *n* = 3	0.6575		
Total.	2.2832	*i* = 15%, *n* = 3	2.2832

Point: Excel for PV annuity.

	A	B
1	Payment	$100
2	Periods	3
3	Period int. rate	15%
4	Present value	

=−PV(B3,B2,B1) = $228.32

We can also use business calculators or spreadsheet programs to find the present value of an annuity.

Decision Insight

Count Your Blessings   "I don't have good luck—I'm blessed," proclaimed Andrew "Jack" Whittaker, a sewage treatment contractor, after winning the largest ever undivided jackpot in a U.S. lottery. Whittaker had to choose between $315 million in 30 annual installments or $170 million in one lump sum ($112 million after-tax). ■

A company is considering an investment that would produce payments of $10,000 every six months for three years. The first payment would be received in six months. If this company requires an 8% annual return, what is the maximum amount it is willing to pay for this investment today?

NEED-TO-KNOW B-3

Present Value of an Annuity

P3

Solution

Maximum paid = $10,000 × 5.2421 = $52,421 (using PV of annuity factor from Table B.3, *i* = 4%, *n* = 6)

FUTURE VALUE OF AN ANNUITY

P4

Apply future value concepts to an annuity by using interest tables.

Graph of FV of an Annuity   The future value of an *ordinary annuity* is the accumulated value of each annuity payment with interest as of the date of the final payment. To illustrate, let's consider the earlier annuity of three annual payments of $100. Exhibit B.7 shows the point in time for the future value (f). The first payment is made two periods prior to the point when future value is determined, and the final payment occurs on the future value date.

EXHIBIT B.7

Future Value of an Ordinary Annuity Diagram

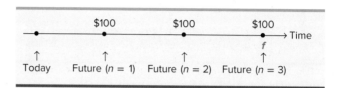

Point: An ordinary annuity is a series of equal cash flows, with the payment at the *end* of each period.

Formula and Illustration of FV of an Annuity   One way to compute the future value of an annuity is to use the formula to find the future value of *each* payment and add them. If we assume an interest rate of 15%, our calculation is

$$f = \$100 \times (1 + 0.15)^2 + \$100 \times (1 + 0.15)^1 + \$100 \times (1 + 0.15)^0 = \$347.25$$

This is identical to using Table B.2 and summing the future values of each payment, or adding the future values of the three payments of 1 and multiplying the sum by $100.

Using Future Value Table to Compute FV of an Annuity   A more direct way is to use a table showing future values of annuities. Such a table is called a **future value of an annuity of 1 table**. Table B.4 at the end of this appendix is one such table. Note that in Table B.4 when $n = 1$, the future values equal 1 ($f = 1$) for all rates of interest. This is because such an annuity consists of only one payment and the future value is determined on the date of that payment—no time passes between the payment and its future value. The future value of an annuity formula is used to construct Table B.4. We can also construct it by adding the amounts from a future value of 1 table. To illustrate, we use Tables B.2 and B.4 to confirm this relation for the prior example:

Point: Excel for FV annuity.

	A	B
1	Payment	$100
2	Periods	3
3	Period int. rate	15%
4	Future value	

=−FV(B3,B2,B1) = $347.25

From Table B.2		From Table B.4	
$i = 15\%, n = 0$	1.0000		
$i = 15\%, n = 1$	1.1500		
$i = 15\%, n = 2$	1.3225		
Total..................	3.4725	$i = 15\%, n = 3$..........	3.4725

Note that the future value in Table B.2 is 1.0000 when $n = 0$, but the future value in Table B.4 is 1.0000 when $n = 1$. Is this a contradiction? No. When $n = 0$ in Table B.2, the future value is determined on the date when a single payment occurs. This means that no interest is earned because no time has passed, and the future value equals the payment. Table B.4 describes annuities with equal payments occurring at the end of each period. When $n = 1$, the annuity has one payment, and its future value equals 1 on the date of its final and only payment. Again, no time passes between the payment and its future value date.

NEED-TO-KNOW **B-4**

Future Value of an Annuity

P4

A company invests $45,000 per year for five years at 12% annual interest. Compute the value of this annuity investment at the end of five years.

Solution

Future value = $45,000 × 6.3528 = $285,876 (using FV of annuity factor from Table B.4, $i = 12\%, n = 5$)

Summary

C1 **Describe the earning of interest and the concepts of present and future values.** Interest is payment by a borrower to the owner of an asset for its use. Present and future value computations are a way for us to estimate the interest component of holding assets or liabilities over a period of time.

P1 **Apply present value concepts to a single amount by using interest tables.** The present value of a single amount received at a future date is the amount that can be invested now at the specified interest rate to yield that future value.

P2 **Apply future value concepts to a single amount by using interest tables.** The future value of a single amount

invested at a specified rate of interest is the amount that would accumulate by the future date.

P3 **Apply present value concepts to an annuity by using interest tables.** The present value of an annuity is the amount that can be invested now at the specified interest rate to yield that series of equal periodic payments.

P4 **Apply future value concepts to an annuity by using interest tables.** The future value of an annuity invested at a specific rate of interest is the amount that would accumulate by the date of the final payment.

connect

Assume that you must estimate what the future value will be two years from today using the *future value of 1 table* (Table B.2). Which interest rate column *and* number-of-periods row do you use when working with the following rates?

1. 8% annual rate, compounded quarterly

2. 12% annual rate, compounded annually

3. 6% annual rate, compounded semiannually

4. 12% annual rate, compounded monthly (the answer for number-of-periods in part 4 is not shown in Table B.2)

QUICK STUDY

QS B-1
Identifying interest rates in tables
C1

Ken Francis is offered the possibility of investing $2,745 today; in return, he would receive $10,000 after 15 years. What is the annual rate of interest for this investment? (Use Table B.1.)

QS B-2
Interest rate on an investment P1

Megan Brink is offered the possibility of investing $6,651 today at 6% interest per year in a desire to accumulate $10,000. How many years must Brink wait to accumulate $10,000? (Use Table B.1.)

QS B-3
Number of periods of an investment P1

Flaherty is considering an investment that, if paid for immediately, is expected to return $140,000 five years from now. If Flaherty demands a 9% return, how much is she willing to pay for this investment?

QS B-4
Present value of an amount P1

CII, Inc., invests $630,000 in a project expected to earn a 12% annual rate of return. The earnings will be reinvested in the project each year until the entire investment is liquidated 10 years later. What will the cash proceeds be when the project is liquidated?

QS B-5
Future value of an amount P2

Beene Distributing is considering a project that will return $150,000 annually at the end of each year for the next six years. If Beene demands an annual return of 7% and pays for the project immediately, how much is it willing to pay for the project?

QS B-6
Present value of an annuity P3

Claire Fitch is planning to begin an individual retirement program in which she will invest $1,500 at the end of each year. Fitch plans to retire after making 30 annual investments in the program earning a return of 10%. What is the value of the program on the date of the last payment (30 years from the present)?

QS B-7
Future value of an annuity P4

EXERCISES

Exercise B-1
Present value of an
amount P1

Mike Derr Company expects to earn 10% per year on an investment that will pay $606,773 six years from now. Use Table B.1 to compute the present value of this investment. (Round the amount to the nearest dollar.)

Exercise B-2
Present value of an
amount P1

On January 1, 2016, a company agrees to pay $20,000 in three years. If the annual interest rate is 10%, determine how much cash the company can borrow with this agreement.

Exercise B-3
Number of periods of an
investment P2

Tom Thompson expects to invest $10,000 at 12% and, at the end of a certain period, receive $96,463. How many years will it be before Thompson receives the payment? (Use Table B.2.)

Exercise B-4
Interest rate on an
investment P2

Bill Padley expects to invest $10,000 for 25 years, after which he wants to receive $108,347. What rate of interest must Padley earn? (Use Table B.2.)

Exercise B-5
Future value of an
amount P2

Mark Welsch deposits $7,200 in an account that earns interest at an annual rate of 8%, compounded quarterly. The $7,200 plus earned interest must remain in the account 10 years before it can be withdrawn. How much money will be in the account at the end of 10 years?

Exercise B-6
Future value of an
amount P2

Catten, Inc., invests $163,170 today earning 7% per year for nine years. Use Table B.2 to compute the future value of the investment nine years from now. (Round the amount to the nearest dollar.)

Exercise B-7
Interest rate on an
investment P3

Jones expects an immediate investment of $57,466 to return $10,000 annually for eight years, with the first payment to be received one year from now. What rate of interest must Jones earn? (Use Table B.3.)

Exercise B-8
Number of periods of an
investment P3

Keith Riggins expects an investment of $82,014 to return $10,000 annually for several years. If Riggins earns a return of 10%, how many annual payments will he receive? (Use Table B.3.)

Exercise B-9
Present value of an
annuity P3

Dave Krug finances a new automobile by paying $6,500 cash and agreeing to make 40 monthly payments of $500 each, the first payment to be made one month after the purchase. The loan bears interest at an annual rate of 12%. What is the cost of the automobile?

Exercise B-10
Present values of annuities

P3

C&H Ski Club recently borrowed money and agreed to pay it back with a series of six annual payments of $5,000 each. C&H subsequently borrows more money and agrees to pay it back with a series of four annual payments of $7,500 each. The annual interest rate for both loans is 6%.

1. Use Table B.1 to find the present value of these two separate annuities. (Round amounts to the nearest dollar.)
2. Use Table B.3 to find the present value of these two separate annuities. (Round amounts to the nearest dollar.)

Exercise B-11
Present value with
semiannual compounding

C1   P3

Otto Co. borrows money on April 30, 2016, by promising to make four payments of $13,000 each on November 1, 2016; May 1, 2017; November 1, 2017; and May 1, 2018.

1. How much money is Otto able to borrow if the interest rate is 8%, compounded semiannually?
2. How much money is Otto able to borrow if the interest rate is 12%, compounded semiannually?
3. How much money is Otto able to borrow if the interest rate is 16%, compounded semiannually?

Exercise B-12
Present value of bonds

P1   P3

Spiller Corp. plans to issue 10%, 15-year, $500,000 par value bonds payable that pay interest semiannually on June 30 and December 31. The bonds are dated December 31, 2016, and are issued on that date. If the market rate of interest for the bonds is 8% on the date of issue, what will be the total cash proceeds from the bond issue?

Compute the amount that can be borrowed under each of the following circumstances:

1. A promise to repay $90,000 seven years from now at an interest rate of 6%.
2. An agreement made on February 1, 2016, to make three separate payments of $20,000 on February 1 of 2017, 2018, and 2019. The annual interest rate is 10%.

Exercise B-13
Present value of an amount and of an annuity P1 P3

Algoe expects to invest $1,000 annually for 40 years to yield an accumulated value of $154,762 on the date of the last investment. For this to occur, what rate of interest must Algoe earn? (Use Table B.4.)

Exercise B-14
Interest rate on an investment P4

Steffi Derr expects to invest $10,000 annually that will earn 8%. How many annual investments must Derr make to accumulate $303,243 on the date of the last investment? (Use Table B.4.)

Exercise B-15
Number of periods of an investment P4

Kelly Malone plans to have $50 withheld from her monthly paycheck and deposited in a savings account that earns 12% annually, compounded monthly. If Malone continues with her plan for two and one-half years, how much will be accumulated in the account on the date of the last deposit?

Exercise B-16
Future value of an annuity P4

Starr Company decides to establish a fund that it will use 10 years from now to replace an aging production facility. The company will make a $100,000 initial contribution to the fund and plans to make quarterly contributions of $50,000 beginning in three months. The fund earns 12%, compounded quarterly. What will be the value of the fund 10 years from now?

Exercise B-17
Future value of an amount plus an annuity

P2 P4

a. How much would you have to deposit today if you wanted to have $60,000 in four years? Annual interest rate is 9%.
b. Assume that you are saving up for a trip around the world when you graduate in two years. If you can earn 8% on your investments, how much would you have to deposit today to have $15,000 when you graduate?
c. Would you rather have $463 now or $1,000 ten years from now? Assume that you can earn 9% on your investments.
d. Assume that a college parking sticker today costs $90. If the cost of parking is increasing at the rate of 5% per year, how much will the college parking sticker cost in eight years?
e. Assume that the average price of a new home is $158,500. If the cost of a new home is increasing at a rate of 10% per year, how much will a new home cost in eight years?
f. An investment will pay you $10,000 in 10 years *and* it will also pay you $400 at the end of *each* of the next 10 years (years 1 thru 10). If the annual interest rate is 6%, how much would you be willing to pay today for this type of investment?
g. A college student is reported in the newspaper as having won $10,000,000 in the Kansas State Lottery. However, as is often the custom with lotteries, she does *not* actually receive the entire $10 million now. Instead she will receive $500,000 at the end of the year for *each* of the next 20 years. If the annual interest rate is 6%, what is the present value (today's amount) that she won? (Ignore taxes.)

Exercise B-18
Practical applications of the time value of money

P1 P2 P3 P4

For each of the following situations, identify (1) the case as either (a) a present or a future value and (b) a single amount or an annuity, (2) the table you would use in your computations (but do not solve the problem), and (3) the interest rate and time periods you would use.

a. You need to accumulate $10,000 for a trip you wish to take in four years. You are able to earn 8% compounded semiannually on your savings. You plan to make only one deposit and let the money accumulate for four years. How would you determine the amount of the one-time deposit?
b. Assume the same facts as in part (a) except that you will make semiannual deposits to your savings account.
c. You want to retire after working 40 years with savings in excess of $1,000,000. You expect to save $4,000 a year for 40 years and earn an annual rate of interest of 8%. Will you be able to retire with more than $1,000,000 in 40 years? Explain.
d. A sweepstakes agency names you a grand prize winner. You can take $225,000 immediately or elect to receive annual installments of $30,000 for 20 years. You can earn 10% annually on any investments you make. Which prize do you choose to receive?

Exercise B-19
Using present and future value tables

C1 P1 P2 P3 P4

TABLE B.1*

Present Value of 1

$$p = 1/(1+i)^n$$

Periods	1%	2%	3%	4%	5%	6%	7%	8%	9%	10%	12%	15%
1	0.9901	0.9804	0.9709	0.9615	0.9524	0.9434	0.9346	0.9259	0.9174	0.9091	0.8929	0.8696
2	0.9803	0.9612	0.9426	0.9246	0.9070	0.8900	0.8734	0.8573	0.8417	0.8264	0.7972	0.7561
3	0.9706	0.9423	0.9151	0.8890	0.8638	0.8396	0.8163	0.7938	0.7722	0.7513	0.7118	0.6575
4	0.9610	0.9238	0.8885	0.8548	0.8227	0.7921	0.7629	0.7350	0.7084	0.6830	0.6355	0.5718
5	0.9515	0.9057	0.8626	0.8219	0.7835	0.7473	0.7130	0.6806	0.6499	0.6209	0.5674	0.4972
6	0.9420	0.8880	0.8375	0.7903	0.7462	0.7050	0.6663	0.6302	0.5963	0.5645	0.5066	0.4323
7	0.9327	0.8706	0.8131	0.7599	0.7107	0.6651	0.6227	0.5835	0.5470	0.5132	0.4523	0.3759
8	0.9235	0.8535	0.7894	0.7307	0.6768	0.6274	0.5820	0.5403	0.5019	0.4665	0.4039	0.3269
9	0.9143	0.8368	0.7664	0.7026	0.6446	0.5919	0.5439	0.5002	0.4604	0.4241	0.3606	0.2843
10	0.9053	0.8203	0.7441	0.6756	0.6139	0.5584	0.5083	0.4632	0.4224	0.3855	0.3220	0.2472
11	0.8963	0.8043	0.7224	0.6496	0.5847	0.5268	0.4751	0.4289	0.3875	0.3505	0.2875	0.2149
12	0.8874	0.7885	0.7014	0.6246	0.5568	0.4970	0.4440	0.3971	0.3555	0.3186	0.2567	0.1869
13	0.8787	0.7730	0.6810	0.6006	0.5303	0.4688	0.4150	0.3677	0.3262	0.2897	0.2292	0.1625
14	0.8700	0.7579	0.6611	0.5775	0.5051	0.4423	0.3878	0.3405	0.2992	0.2633	0.2046	0.1413
15	0.8613	0.7430	0.6419	0.5553	0.4810	0.4173	0.3624	0.3152	0.2745	0.2394	0.1827	0.1229
16	0.8528	0.7284	0.6232	0.5339	0.4581	0.3936	0.3387	0.2919	0.2519	0.2176	0.1631	0.1069
17	0.8444	0.7142	0.6050	0.5134	0.4363	0.3714	0.3166	0.2703	0.2311	0.1978	0.1456	0.0929
18	0.8360	0.7002	0.5874	0.4936	0.4155	0.3503	0.2959	0.2502	0.2120	0.1799	0.1300	0.0808
19	0.8277	0.6864	0.5703	0.4746	0.3957	0.3305	0.2765	0.2317	0.1945	0.1635	0.1161	0.0703
20	0.8195	0.6730	0.5537	0.4564	0.3769	0.3118	0.2584	0.2145	0.1784	0.1486	0.1037	0.0611
25	0.7798	0.6095	0.4776	0.3751	0.2953	0.2330	0.1842	0.1460	0.1160	0.0923	0.0588	0.0304
30	0.7419	0.5521	0.4120	0.3083	0.2314	0.1741	0.1314	0.0994	0.0754	0.0573	0.0334	0.0151
35	0.7059	0.5000	0.3554	0.2534	0.1813	0.1301	0.0937	0.0676	0.0490	0.0356	0.0189	0.0075
40	0.6717	0.4529	0.3066	0.2083	0.1420	0.0972	0.0668	0.0460	0.0318	0.0221	0.0107	0.0037

* Used to compute the present value of a known future amount. For example: How much would you need to invest today at 10% compounded semiannually to accumulate $5,000 in 6 years from today? Using the factors of $n = 12$ and $i = 5\%$ (12 semiannual periods and a semiannual rate of 5%), the factor is 0.5568. You would need to invest $2,784 today ($5,000 × 0.5568).

TABLE B.2†

Future Value of 1

$$f = (1+i)^n$$

Periods	1%	2%	3%	4%	5%	6%	7%	8%	9%	10%	12%	15%
0	1.0000	1.0000	1.0000	1.0000	1.0000	1.0000	1.0000	1.0000	1.0000	1.0000	1.0000	1.0000
1	1.0100	1.0200	1.0300	1.0400	1.0500	1.0600	1.0700	1.0800	1.0900	1.1000	1.1200	1.1500
2	1.0201	1.0404	1.0609	1.0816	1.1025	1.1236	1.1449	1.1664	1.1881	1.2100	1.2544	1.3225
3	1.0303	1.0612	1.0927	1.1249	1.1576	1.1910	1.2250	1.2597	1.2950	1.3310	1.4049	1.5209
4	1.0406	1.0824	1.1255	1.1699	1.2155	1.2625	1.3108	1.3605	1.4116	1.4641	1.5735	1.7490
5	1.0510	1.1041	1.1593	1.2167	1.2763	1.3382	1.4026	1.4693	1.5386	1.6105	1.7623	2.0114
6	1.0615	1.1262	1.1941	1.2653	1.3401	1.4185	1.5007	1.5869	1.6771	1.7716	1.9738	2.3131
7	1.0721	1.1487	1.2299	1.3159	1.4071	1.5036	1.6058	1.7138	1.8280	1.9487	2.2107	2.6600
8	1.0829	1.1717	1.2668	1.3686	1.4775	1.5938	1.7182	1.8509	1.9926	2.1436	2.4760	3.0590
9	1.0937	1.1951	1.3048	1.4233	1.5513	1.6895	1.8385	1.9990	2.1719	2.3579	2.7731	3.5179
10	1.1046	1.2190	1.3439	1.4802	1.6289	1.7908	1.9672	2.1589	2.3674	2.5937	3.1058	4.0456
11	1.1157	1.2434	1.3842	1.5395	1.7103	1.8983	2.1049	2.3316	2.5804	2.8531	3.4785	4.6524
12	1.1268	1.2682	1.4258	1.6010	1.7959	2.0122	2.2522	2.5182	2.8127	3.1384	3.8960	5.3503
13	1.1381	1.2936	1.4685	1.6651	1.8856	2.1329	2.4098	2.7196	3.0658	3.4523	4.3635	6.1528
14	1.1495	1.3195	1.5126	1.7317	1.9799	2.2609	2.5785	2.9372	3.3417	3.7975	4.8871	7.0757
15	1.1610	1.3459	1.5580	1.8009	2.0789	2.3966	2.7590	3.1722	3.6425	4.1772	5.4736	8.1371
16	1.1726	1.3728	1.6047	1.8730	2.1829	2.5404	2.9522	3.4259	3.9703	4.5950	6.1304	9.3576
17	1.1843	1.4002	1.6528	1.9479	2.2920	2.6928	3.1588	3.7000	4.3276	5.0545	6.8660	10.7613
18	1.1961	1.4282	1.7024	2.0258	2.4066	2.8543	3.3799	3.9960	4.7171	5.5599	7.6900	12.3755
19	1.2081	1.4568	1.7535	2.1068	2.5270	3.0256	3.6165	4.3157	5.1417	6.1159	8.6128	14.2318
20	1.2202	1.4859	1.8061	2.1911	2.6533	3.2071	3.8697	4.6610	5.6044	6.7275	9.6463	16.3665
25	1.2824	1.6406	2.0938	2.6658	3.3864	4.2919	5.4274	6.8485	8.6231	10.8347	17.0001	32.9190
30	1.3478	1.8114	2.4273	3.2434	4.3219	5.7435	7.6123	10.0627	13.2677	17.4494	29.9599	66.2118
35	1.4166	1.9999	2.8139	3.9461	5.5160	7.6861	10.6766	14.7853	20.4140	28.1024	52.7996	133.1755
40	1.4889	2.2080	3.2620	4.8010	7.0400	10.2857	14.9745	21.7245	31.4094	45.2593	93.0510	267.8635

† Used to compute the future value of a known present amount. For example: What is the accumulated value of $3,000 invested today at 8% compounded quarterly for 5 years? Using the factors of $n = 20$ and $i = 2\%$ (20 quarterly periods and a quarterly interest rate of 2%), the factor is 1.4859. The accumulated value is $4,457.70 ($3,000 × 1.4859).

$$p = \left[1 - \frac{1}{(1+i)^n}\right]/i$$

TABLE B.3‡

Present Value of an Annuity of 1

Periods						Rate						
	1%	**2%**	**3%**	**4%**	**5%**	**6%**	**7%**	**8%**	**9%**	**10%**	**12%**	**15%**
1	0.9901	0.9804	0.9709	0.9615	0.9524	0.9434	0.9346	0.9259	0.9174	0.9091	0.8929	0.8696
2	1.9704	1.9416	1.9135	1.8861	1.8594	1.8334	1.8080	1.7833	1.7591	1.7355	1.6901	1.6257
3	2.9410	2.8839	2.8286	2.7751	2.7232	2.6730	2.6243	2.5771	2.5313	2.4869	2.4018	2.2832
4	3.9020	3.8077	3.7171	3.6299	3.5460	3.4651	3.3872	3.3121	3.2397	3.1699	3.0373	2.8550
5	4.8534	4.7135	4.5797	4.4518	4.3295	4.2124	4.1002	3.9927	3.8897	3.7908	3.6048	3.3522
6	5.7955	5.6014	5.4172	5.2421	5.0757	4.9173	4.7665	4.6229	4.4859	4.3553	4.1114	3.7845
7	6.7282	6.4720	6.2303	6.0021	5.7864	5.5824	5.3893	5.2064	5.0330	4.8684	4.5638	4.1604
8	7.6517	7.3255	7.0197	6.7327	6.4632	6.2098	5.9713	5.7466	5.5348	5.3349	4.9676	4.4873
9	8.5660	8.1622	7.7861	7.4353	7.1078	6.8017	6.5152	6.2469	5.9952	5.7590	5.3282	4.7716
10	9.4713	8.9826	8.5302	8.1109	7.7217	7.3601	7.0236	6.7101	6.4177	6.1446	5.6502	5.0188
11	10.3676	9.7868	9.2526	8.7605	8.3064	7.8869	7.4987	7.1390	6.8052	6.4951	5.9377	5.2337
12	11.2551	10.5753	9.9540	9.3851	8.8633	8.3838	7.9427	7.5361	7.1607	6.8137	6.1944	5.4206
13	12.1337	11.3484	10.6350	9.9856	9.3936	8.8527	8.3577	7.9038	7.4869	7.1034	6.4235	5.5831
14	13.0037	12.1062	11.2961	10.5631	9.8986	9.2950	8.7455	8.2442	7.7862	7.3667	6.6282	5.7245
15	13.8651	12.8493	11.9379	11.1184	10.3797	9.7122	9.1079	8.5595	8.0607	7.6061	6.8109	5.8474
16	14.7179	13.5777	12.5611	11.6523	10.8378	10.1059	9.4466	8.8514	8.3126	7.8237	6.9740	5.9542
17	15.5623	14.2919	13.1661	12.1657	11.2741	10.4773	9.7632	9.1216	8.5436	8.0216	7.1196	6.0472
18	16.3983	14.9920	13.7535	12.6593	11.6896	10.8276	10.0591	9.3719	8.7556	8.2014	7.2497	6.1280
19	17.2260	15.6785	14.3238	13.1339	12.0853	11.1581	10.3356	9.6036	8.9501	8.3649	7.3658	6.1982
20	18.0456	16.3514	14.8775	13.5903	12.4622	11.4699	10.5940	9.8181	9.1285	8.5136	7.4694	6.2593
25	22.0232	19.5235	17.4131	15.6221	14.0939	12.7834	11.6536	10.6748	9.8226	9.0770	7.8431	6.4641
30	25.8077	22.3965	19.6004	17.2920	15.3725	13.7648	12.4090	11.2578	10.2737	9.4269	8.0552	6.5660
35	29.4086	24.9986	21.4872	18.6646	16.3742	14.4982	12.9477	11.6546	10.5668	9.6442	8.1755	6.6166
40	32.8347	27.3555	23.1148	19.7928	17.1591	15.0463	13.3317	11.9246	10.7574	9.7791	8.2438	6.6418

‡ Used to calculate the present value of a series of equal payments made at the end of each period. For example: What is the present value of $2,000 per year for 10 years assuming an annual interest rate of 9%. For ($n = 10$, $i = 9\%$), the PV factor is 6.4177. $2,000 per year for 10 years is the equivalent of $12,835 today ($2,000 × 6.4177).

TABLE B.4§

Future Value of an Annuity of 1

$$f = [(1+i)^n - 1]/i$$

Periods						Rate						
	1%	**2%**	**3%**	**4%**	**5%**	**6%**	**7%**	**8%**	**9%**	**10%**	**12%**	**15%**
1	1.0000	1.0000	1.0000	1.0000	1.0000	1.0000	1.0000	1.0000	1.0000	1.0000	1.0000	1.0000
2	2.0100	2.0200	2.0300	2.0400	2.0500	2.0600	2.0700	2.0800	2.0900	2.1000	2.1200	2.1500
3	3.0301	3.0604	3.0909	3.1216	3.1525	3.1836	3.2149	3.2464	3.2781	3.3100	3.3744	3.4725
4	4.0604	4.1216	4.1836	4.2465	4.3101	4.3746	4.4399	4.5061	4.5731	4.6410	4.7793	4.9934
5	5.1010	5.2040	5.3091	5.4163	5.5256	5.6371	5.7507	5.8666	5.9847	6.1051	6.3528	6.7424
6	6.1520	6.3081	6.4684	6.6330	6.8019	6.9753	7.1533	7.3359	7.5233	7.7156	8.1152	8.7537
7	7.2135	7.4343	7.6625	7.8983	8.1420	8.3938	8.6540	8.9228	9.2004	9.4872	10.0890	11.0668
8	8.2857	8.5830	8.8923	9.2142	9.5491	9.8975	10.2598	10.6366	11.0285	11.4359	12.2997	13.7268
9	9.3685	9.7546	10.1591	10.5828	11.0266	11.4913	11.9780	12.4876	13.0210	13.5795	14.7757	16.7858
10	10.4622	10.9497	11.4639	12.0061	12.5779	13.1808	13.8164	14.4866	15.1929	15.9374	17.5487	20.3037
11	11.5668	12.1687	12.8078	13.4864	14.2068	14.9716	15.7836	16.6455	17.5603	18.5312	20.6546	24.3493
12	12.6825	13.4121	14.1920	15.0258	15.9171	16.8699	17.8885	18.9771	20.1407	21.3843	24.1331	29.0017
13	13.8093	14.6803	15.6178	16.6268	17.7130	18.8821	20.1406	21.4953	22.9534	24.5227	28.0291	34.3519
14	14.9474	15.9739	17.0863	18.2919	19.5986	21.0151	22.5505	24.2149	26.0192	27.9750	32.3926	40.5047
15	16.0969	17.2934	18.5989	20.0236	21.5786	23.2760	25.1290	27.1521	29.3609	31.7725	37.2797	47.5804
16	17.2579	18.6393	20.1569	21.8245	23.6575	25.6725	27.8881	30.3243	33.0034	35.9497	42.7533	55.7175
17	18.4304	20.0121	21.7616	23.6975	25.8404	28.2129	30.8402	33.7502	36.9737	40.5447	48.8837	65.0751
18	19.6147	21.4123	23.4144	25.6454	28.1324	30.9057	33.9990	37.4502	41.3013	45.5992	55.7497	75.8364
19	20.8109	22.8406	25.1169	27.6712	30.5390	33.7600	37.3790	41.4463	46.0185	51.1591	63.4397	88.2118
20	22.0190	24.2974	26.8704	29.7781	33.0660	36.7856	40.9955	45.7620	51.1601	57.2750	72.0524	102.4436
25	28.2432	32.0303	36.4593	41.6459	47.7271	54.8645	63.2490	73.1059	84.7009	98.3471	133.3339	212.7930
30	34.7849	40.5681	47.5754	56.0849	66.4388	79.0582	94.4608	113.2832	136.3075	164.4940	241.3327	434.7451
35	41.6603	49.9945	60.4621	73.6522	90.3203	111.4348	138.2369	172.3168	215.7108	271.0244	431.6635	881.1702
40	48.8864	60.4020	75.4013	95.0255	120.7998	154.7620	199.6351	259.0565	337.8824	442.5926	767.0914	1,779.0903

§ Used to calculate the future value of a series of equal payments made at the end of each period. For example: What is the future value of $4,000 per year for 6 years assuming an annual interest rate of 8%. For ($n = 6$, $i = 8\%$), the FV factor is 7.3359. $4,000 per year for 6 years accumulates to $29,343.60 ($4,000 × 7.3359).

Index

Chart of Accounts

Following is a typical chart of accounts, which is used in several assignments. Each company has its own unique set of accounts and numbering system.
*An asterisk denotes a contra account.

Assets

Current Assets

101 Cash
102 Petty cash
103 Cash equivalents
104 Short-term investments
105 Fair value adjustment, _____ securities (S-T)
106 Accounts receivable
107 Allowance for doubtful accounts*
108 Allowance for sales discounts*
109 Interest receivable
110 Rent receivable
111 Notes receivable
112 Legal fees receivable
119 Merchandise inventory (or Inventory)
120 _____ inventory
121 Inventory returns estimated
124 Office supplies
125 Store supplies
126 _____ supplies
128 Prepaid insurance
129 Prepaid interest
131 Prepaid rent
132 Raw materials inventory
133 Work in process inventory, _____
134 Work in process inventory, _____
135 Finished goods inventory

Long-Term Investments

141 Long-term investments
142 Fair value adjustment, _____ securities (L-T)
144 Investment in _____
145 Bond sinking fund

Plant Assets

151 Automobiles
152 Accumulated depreciation—Automobiles*
153 Trucks
154 Accumulated depreciation—Trucks*
155 Boats
156 Accumulated depreciation—Boats*
157 Professional library
158 Accumulated depreciation—Professional library*
159 Law library
160 Accumulated depreciation—Law library*
161 Furniture
162 Accumulated depreciation—Furniture*
163 Office equipment

164 Accumulated depreciation—Office equipment*
165 Store equipment
166 Accumulated depreciation—Store equipment*
167 _____ equipment
168 Accumulated depreciation—_____ equipment*
169 Machinery
170 Accumulated depreciation—Machinery*
173 Building _____
174 Accumulated depreciation—Building _____ *
175 Building _____
176 Accumulated depreciation—Building _____ *
179 Land improvements _____
180 Accumulated depreciation—Land improvements _____ *
181 Land improvements _____
182 Accumulated depreciation—Land improvements _____ *
183 Land

Natural Resources

185 Mineral deposit
186 Accumulated depletion—Mineral deposit*

Intangible Assets

191 Patents
192 Leasehold
193 Franchise
194 Copyrights
195 Leasehold improvements
196 Licenses
197 Accumulated amortization—_____*
199 Goodwill

Liabilities

Current Liabilities

201 Accounts payable
202 Insurance payable
203 Interest payable
204 Legal fees payable
207 Office salaries payable
208 Rent payable
209 Salaries payable
210 Wages payable
211 Accrued payroll payable
212 Factory wages payable
214 Estimated warranty liability
215 Income taxes payable

216 Common dividend payable
217 Preferred dividend payable
218 State unemployment taxes payable
219 Employee federal income taxes payable
221 Employee medical insurance payable
222 Employee retirement program payable
223 Employee union dues payable
224 Federal unemployment taxes payable
225 FICA taxes payable
226 Estimated vacation pay liability
227 Sales refund payable

Unearned Revenues

230 Unearned consulting fees
231 Unearned legal fees
232 Unearned property management fees
233 Unearned _____ fees
234 Unearned _____ fees
235 Unearned janitorial revenue
236 Unearned _____ revenue
238 Unearned rent

Notes Payable

240 Short-term notes payable
241 Discount on short-term notes payable*
245 Notes payable
251 Long-term notes payable
252 Discount on long-term notes payable*

Long-Term Liabilities

253 Long-term lease liability
255 Bonds payable
256 Discount on bonds payable*
257 Premium on bonds payable
258 Deferred income tax liability

Equity

Owner's Equity

301 _____, Capital
302 _____, Withdrawals
303 _____, Capital
304 _____, Withdrawals
305 _____, Capital
306 _____, Withdrawals

Paid-In Capital

307 Common stock, $ _____ par value
308 Common stock, no-par value
309 Common stock, $ _____ stated value
310 Common stock dividend distributable
311 Paid-in capital in excess of par value, Common stock

312 Paid-in capital in excess of stated value, No-par common stock
313 Paid-in capital from retirement of common stock
314 Paid-in capital, Treasury stock
315 Preferred stock
316 Paid-in capital in excess of par value, Preferred stock

Retained Earnings

318 Retained earnings
319 Cash dividends (or Dividends)
320 Stock dividends

Other Equity Accounts

321 Treasury stock, Common*
322 Unrealized gain—Equity
323 Unrealized loss—Equity

Revenues

401 _____ fees earned
402 _____ fees earned
403 _____ revenues
404 Revenues
405 Commissions earned
406 Rent revenue (or Rent earned)
407 Dividends revenue (or Dividends earned)
408 Earnings from investment in _____
409 Interest revenue (or Interest earned)
410 Sinking fund earnings
413 Sales
414 Sales returns and allowances*
415 Sales discounts*

Cost of Sales

Cost of Goods Sold

502 Cost of goods sold
505 Purchases
506 Purchases returns and allowances*
507 Purchases discounts*
508 Transportation-in

Manufacturing

520 Raw materials purchases
521 Freight-in on raw materials
530 Direct labor
540 Factory overhead
541 Indirect materials
542 Indirect labor
543 Factory insurance expired
544 Factory supervision
545 Factory supplies used
546 Factory utilities
547 Miscellaneous production costs
548 Property taxes on factory building
549 Property taxes on factory equipment
550 Rent on factory building
551 Repairs, factory equipment
552 Small tools written off
560 Depreciation of factory equipment
561 Depreciation of factory building

Standard Cost Variances

580 Direct material quantity variance
581 Direct material price variance
582 Direct labor quantity variance
583 Direct labor price variance
584 Factory overhead volume variance
585 Factory overhead controllable variance

Expenses

Amortization, Depletion, and Depreciation

601 Amortization expense—_____
602 Amortization expense—_____
603 Depletion expense—_____
604 Depreciation expense—Boats
605 Depreciation expense—Automobiles
606 Depreciation expense—Building _____
607 Depreciation expense—Building _____
608 Depreciation expense—Land improvements _____
609 Depreciation expense—Land improvements _____
610 Depreciation expense—Law library
611 Depreciation expense—Trucks
612 Depreciation expense—_____ equipment
613 Depreciation expense—_____ equipment
614 Depreciation expense—_____
615 Depreciation expense—_____

Employee-Related Expenses

620 Office salaries expense
621 Sales salaries expense
622 Salaries expense
623 _____ wages expense
624 Employees' benefits expense
625 Payroll taxes expense

Financial Expenses

630 Cash over and short
631 Discounts lost
632 Factoring fee expense
633 Interest expense

Insurance Expenses

635 Insurance expense—Delivery equipment
636 Insurance expense—Office equipment
637 Insurance expense—_____

Rental Expenses

640 Rent expense
641 Rent expense—Office space
642 Rent expense—Selling space
643 Press rental expense
644 Truck rental expense
645 _____ rental expense

Supplies Expenses

650 Office supplies expense
651 Store supplies expense
652 _____ supplies expense
653 _____ supplies expense

Miscellaneous Expenses

655 Advertising expense
656 Bad debts expense
657 Blueprinting expense
658 Boat expense
659 Collection expense
661 Concessions expense
662 Credit card expense
663 Delivery expense
664 Dumping expense
667 Equipment expense
668 Food and drinks expense
671 Gas and oil expense
672 General and administrative expense
673 Janitorial expense
674 Legal fees expense
676 Mileage expense
677 Miscellaneous expenses
678 Mower and tools expense
679 Operating expense
680 Organization expense
681 Permits expense
682 Postage expense
683 Property taxes expense
684 Repairs expense—_____
685 Repairs expense—_____
687 Selling expense
688 Telephone expense
689 Travel and entertainment expense
690 Utilities expense
691 Warranty expense
692 _____ expense
695 Income taxes expense

Gains and Losses

701 Gain on retirement of bonds
702 Gain on sale of machinery
703 Gain on sale of investments
704 Gain on sale of trucks
705 Gain on _____
706 Foreign exchange gain or loss
801 Loss on disposal of machinery
802 Loss on exchange of equipment
803 Loss on exchange of _____
804 Loss on sale of notes
805 Loss on retirement of bonds
806 Loss on sale of investments
807 Loss on sale of machinery
808 Loss on _____
809 Unrealized gain—Income
810 Unrealized loss—Income
811 Impairment gain
812 Impairment loss

Clearing Accounts

901 Income summary
902 Manufacturing summary

BRIEF REVIEW: MANAGERIAL ANALYSES AND REPORTS

① Cost Types

Variable costs: Total cost changes in proportion to volume of activity.
Fixed costs: Total cost does not change in proportion to volume of activity.
Mixed costs: Cost consists of both a variable and a fixed element.

② Product Costs

Direct materials: Raw materials costs directly linked to finished product.
Direct labor: Employee costs directly linked to finished product.
Overhead: Production costs indirectly linked to finished product.

③ Costing Systems

Job order costing: Costs assigned to each unique unit or batch of units.
Process costing: Costs assigned to similar products that are mass-produced in a continuous manner.

④ Costing Ratios

Contribution margin ratio = (Net sales − Variable costs)/Net sales
Predetermined overhead rate = Estimated overhead costs/Estimated activity base
Break-even point in units = Total fixed costs/Contribution margin per unit

⑤ Planning and Control Metrics

Cost variance = Actual cost − Standard (budgeted) cost
Sales (revenue) variance = Actual sales − Standard (budgeted) sales

⑥ Capital Budgeting

Payback period = Time expected to recover investment cost
Accounting rate of return = Expected annual net income/Average annual investment
Net present value (NPV) = Present value of future cash flows − Investment cost
NPV rule: 1. Compute net present value (NPV in $)
        2. If NPV > 0, then accept project; If NPV < 0, then reject project
Internal rate   1. Compute internal rate of return (IRR in %)
of return rule: 2. If IRR > hurdle rate, accept project; If IRR < hurdle rate, reject project

⑦ Costing Terminology

Relevant range: Organization's normal range of operating activity.
Direct cost: Cost incurred for the benefit of one cost object.
Indirect cost: Cost incurred for the benefit of more than one cost object.
Product cost: Cost that is necessary and integral to finished products.
Period cost: Cost identified more with a time period than with finished products.
Overhead cost: Cost not separately or directly traceable to a cost object.
Relevant cost: Cost that is pertinent to a decision.
Opportunity cost: Benefit lost by choosing an action from two or more alternatives.
Sunk cost: Cost already incurred that cannot be avoided or changed.
Standard cost: Cost computed using standard price and standard quantity.
Budget: Formal statement of an organization's future plans.
Break-even point: Sales level at which an organization earns zero profit.
Incremental cost: Cost incurred only if the organization undertakes a certain action.
Transfer price: Price on transactions between divisions within a company.

⑧ Standard Cost Variances

| Total materials variance | = | Materials price variance | + | Materials quantity variance |

| Total labor variance | = | Labor (rate) variance | + | Labor efficiency (quantity) variance |

| Total overhead variance | = | Overhead controllable variance | + | Overhead volume variance |

Overhead controllable variance = Actual total overhead − Budgeted total overhead

Overhead volume variance = Budgeted fixed overhead − Applied fixed overhead

Variable overhead variance = Variable overhead spending variance + Variable overhead efficiency variance

Fixed overhead variance = Fixed overhead spending variance + Fixed overhead volume variance

⎫ = Total overhead variance

Materials price variance	= [AQ × AP] − [AQ × SP]
Materials quantity variance	= [AQ × SP] − [SQ × SP]
Labor (rate) variance	= [AH × AR] − [AH × SR]
Labor efficiency (quantity) variance	= [AH × SR] − [SH × SR]

Variable overhead spending variance = [AH × AVR] − [AH × SVR]
Variable overhead efficiency variance = [AH × SVR] − [SH × SVR]
Fixed overhead spending variance = Actual fixed overhead − Budgeted fixed overhead

where AQ is Actual Quantity of materials; AP is Actual Price of materials; AH is Actual Hours of labor; AR is Actual Rate of wages; AVR is Actual Variable Rate of overhead; SQ is Standard Quantity of materials; SP is Standard Price of materials; SH is Standard Hours of labor; SR is Standard Rate of wages; SVR is Standard Variable Rate of overhead.

⑨ Sales Variances

| Sales price variance | = [AS × AP] − [AS × BP] |
| Sales volume variance | = [AS × BP] − [BS × BP] |

where AS = Actual Sales units; AP = Actual sales Price; BP = Budgeted sales Price; BS = Budgeted Sales units (fixed budget).

Schedule of Cost of Goods Manufactured
For *period* Ended *date*

Direct materials		
Raw materials inventory, Beginning	$	#
Raw materials purchases		#
Raw materials available for use		#
Less raw materials inventory, Ending		(#)
Direct materials used		#
Direct labor		#
Overhead costs		
Total overhead costs		#
Total manufacturing costs		#
Add work in process inventory, Beginning		#
Total cost of work in process		#
Less work in process inventory, Ending		(#)
Cost of goods manufactured	$	#

Contribution Margin Income Statement
For *period* Ended *date*

Net sales (revenues)	$	#
Total variable costs		#
Contribution margin		#
Total fixed costs		#
Net income (pretax)	$	#

Flexible Budget
For *period* Ended *date*

	Flexible Budget		Flexible Budget for Unit Sales of #
	Variable Amount per Unit	Fixed Cost	
Sales (revenues)	$ #		$ #
Variable costs			
Examples: Direct materials, Direct labor,			
Other variable costs	#		#
Total variable costs	#		#
Contribution margin	$ #		#
Fixed costs			
Examples: Depreciation, Manager		$ #	#
salaries, Administrative salaries		#	#
Total fixed costs		$ #	#
Income from operations			$ #

Budget Performance Report*
For *period* Ended *date*

	Budget	Actual Performance	Variances†
Sales: In units	#	#	
In dollars	$ #	$ #	$ # F or U
Cost of sales			
Direct costs	#	#	# F or U
Indirect costs	#	#	# F or U
Selling expenses			
Examples: Commissions	#	#	# F or U
Shipping expenses	#	#	# F or U
General and administrative expenses			
Examples: Administrative salaries	#	#	# F or U
Total expenses	$ #	$ #	$ # F or U
Income from operations	$ #	$ #	$ # F or U

* Applies to both flexible and fixed budgets. † F = Favorable variance; U = Unfavorable variance.

Master Budget Sequence

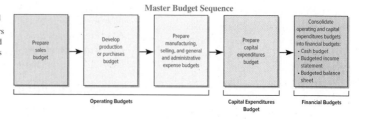

Prepare sales budget → Develop production or purchases budget → Prepare manufacturing, selling, and general and administrative expense budgets → Prepare capital expenditures budget → Consolidate operating and capital expenditures budgets into financial budgets: • Cash budget • Budgeted income statement • Budgeted balance sheet

Operating Budgets   Capital Expenditures Budget   Financial Budgets